澳门基金会
※
北京外国语大学
中国海外汉学研究中心
※
大象出版社

合作项目

卫三畏文集
Selected Works of
Samuel Wells Williams

中国总论

（卷II）（上）

The Middle Kingdom

［美］
卫三畏 著
Samuel Wells Williams

大象出版社

中國總論

THE MIDDLE KINGDOM

A SURVEY OF THE GEOGRAPHY, GOVERNMENT, LITERATURE, SOCIAL LIFE, ARTS, AND HISTORY

OF

THE CHINESE EMPIRE

AND

ITS INHABITANTS

BY

S. WELLS WILLIAMS, LL.D.

PROFESSOR OF THE CHINESE LANGUAGE AND LITERATURE AT YALE COLLEGE; AUTHOR OF TONIC AND SYLLABIC DICTIONARIES OF THE CHINESE LANGUAGE

REVISED EDITION, WITH ILLUSTRATIONS AND A NEW MAP OF THE EMPIRE

VOLUME II.

PARAGON BOOK REPRINT CORP.
NEW YORK
1966

Library of Congress Catalog Card Number

66-16895

An unaltered and unabridged
reprint of the revised edition
published by Charles Scribner's
Sons in 1895

Reprinted by
Paragon Book Reprint Corp.
14 East 38th Street, New York, N. Y. 10016

Printed in the United States of America

主编序言

陶德民　张西平　吴志良

2008年8月8日，在北京奥运会开幕的当天，新落成的美国驻华使馆举行了剪彩仪式。美国国务院历史文献办公室为此发行了纪念图册，题为《共同走过的日子——美中交往两百年》，其中把1833年抵达广州的卫三畏(Samuel Wells Williams, 1812-1884)称扬为美国"来华传教第一人"，虽然他并非是第一个来到中国的美国传教士。图册对卫三畏在促进美中两国人民的相互了解方面所作的贡献作了这样的概括和评价："传教士成为介绍中国社会与文化的重要信息来源，因为他们与大部分来华经商的外国人不一样，这些传教士学习了中文。例如，美国传教士卫三畏就会说流利的广东话和日语。他曾参与编辑英文期刊《中国丛报》，供西方传教士及时了解中国的最新动态，方便在美国的读者了解中国人的生活。卫三畏还编辑出版了《汉英拼音字典》(即《汉英韵府》——序者)和分为上下两卷的历史巨著《中国总论》。时至今日，他依然被公认为对19世纪的中国生活认识得最为精透的观察家。"

图册中也提到"蒲安臣于1862年成为第一个常驻北京的美国代表，在促进中国的国际关系上扮演了更为积极的角色。蒲安臣迅速结识了一批清政府的主要改革派官员，其中就包括咸丰皇帝的弟弟，设立了中国第一个外务部(应为总理各国事务衙门-序者)的恭亲王奕䜣"，以及他1867年辞去驻华公使后作为清朝使节率团访问欧美，与当时的美国国务卿签订《蒲安臣条约》一事。"该条约扩展了中美两国的往来领域。条约规定，两国人民享有在彼此国家游历、居住的互惠权，并可入对方官学；中国领事在美国口岸享有完全的外交权利；鼓励华工移民美国；美国政府支持中国的领土主权。"其实，蒲安臣的卓有成效的外交活动及其维护正义的外交主张，与当时担任使馆秘书兼翻译的卫三畏的鼎力相助是分不开的。卫三畏的儿子卫斐列后来倾注极大热忱为蒲安臣撰写传记，其重要原因之一也在于此。

今天，当我们出版这部文集以纪念卫三畏诞辰200周年，并重新探讨其经历和成就之际，有必要思考这样一个问题，即卫三畏一生所体现的诸多志趣和倾向之中，什么是值得我们加以特别关注的呢？虽然这是一个"仁者见仁，智者见智"的问题，多数人恐怕都不会对以下见解持有异议，即卫三畏在对华态度上所发生的"从教化到对话"的某种转变可以说是他留给后世的最重要的精神遗产之一。而这恰恰可以从耶鲁大学校园里留存至今的两件文物上得到印证。

第一件文物是该校公共大食堂(Commons Dining Hall)墙上的卫三畏肖像画,它其实是设在纽约的美国圣经协会所藏同一油画的一个复本。如所周知,卫三畏的在华生涯大抵分为两个阶段,作为传教士的前22年(1833-1855)和作为外交官的后20年(1856-1876)。在前22年的最后一段时间里,他还作为首席翻译官随同佩里将军的舰队两次远征日本,在改变日本锁国政策的外交谈判过程中发挥了重要作用。佩里将军对其语言天赋和交涉手腕的赏识,无疑是卫三畏转而步入为期20年的外交生涯的一个契机。1877年辞职回国后不久,他受聘为耶鲁大学的中国语言文学讲座教授。1881年春被遴选为美国圣经协会会长后,他便提出希望有才华的画家制作自己的肖像画,并将其献给圣经协会。结果,由耶鲁大学艺术学院的韦约翰教授制作的油画所呈现的是这样一个形象:等身大的卫三畏站立在放有纸、笔和一个中国式花瓶的桌子边上,目视前方,手持1858年《中美天津条约》的文本。

很显然,这样的构图反映了卫三畏本人的意思:他一直把基督教传教自由的条款得以列入1858年《中美天津条约》看作自己毕生的最大成就。这是因为当时负责谈判的美国公使列卫廉对是否要在条约中加入该条款并不经意,只是在卫三畏的坚持之下才获得了最后的成功。此一事实,不仅可见于耶鲁大学斯德龄纪念图书馆附属档案馆所藏卫三畏的亲笔日记,也可以由当时协助他进行谈判工作的丁韪良牧师后来所写的《花甲忆记》得到证实:"那份现在成为条约荣耀之处的条款是卫三畏博士提出的。"在预定签约的6月18日即"决定命运的那天早上,卫三畏博士告诉我他一夜未眠,一直在考虑这份宽容条款。现在他想到了一种新的形式,可能会被对方接受。他写了下来,我建议我们应当马上坐轿子直接奔赴中方官邸解决这个问题。……中方代表接见了我们,他们当中的负责人稍作修改,就接受了卫三畏博士的措辞。"(详见陶德民《从卫三畏档案看1858年中美之间的基督教弛禁交涉——写在〈基督教传教士传记丛书〉问世之际》)。1876年夏天,美国国务院接受卫三畏的辞呈,在正式解职通知中对他赞扬有加:"您对中国人的性格与习惯的熟悉,对该民族及其政府愿望与需求的了解,对汉语的精通,以及您对基督教与文明进步事业的贡献,都使您有充分的理由自豪。您无与伦比的中文字典与有关中国的诸多著作已为您赢得科学与文学领域内相应的崇高地位。更为重要的是,宗教界不会忘记,尤其多亏了您,我们与中国订立的条约中才得以加入自由传教这一条。"而卫三畏则在复信中坦承,这一嘉许是"最最让他感动与满意的"(见卫斐列著,顾钧、江莉译《卫三畏生平及书信——一位美国来华传教士的心路历程》)。顺便提到,在1858年6月19日,亦即《中美天津条约》签订的第二天,美国驻日总领事哈里斯便与德川幕府的代表签订了《美日修好通商条约》。卫三畏闻讯后,又不失时机地向美国的新教诸团体提出派遣牧师赴日传教的建议,并得到了切实的响应。所以,对美国基督教会的东亚传教事业来说,卫三畏确实是一位有功之臣。

那么,卫三畏是基于一种什么样的信念而企图以基督教义来教化东亚的所谓异教徒的呢?试举一个例子。1853年7月16日,在佩里将军初访日本,成功向日方递交美国总统国书一周之后,卫三畏曾从停泊在江户湾的军舰上给他在土耳其传教的弟弟W. F. 威廉斯写了一封长信,其中指出:"佩里告诉日本官员,他将在次年率领一支更大的舰队以求得到他们对所提要求的回答，即所有前来访问或遇难流落日本海岸的美国人应得到善待，美国汽船在一个日本港口得到煤炭以及有关物资的补给。这些是我们花费巨大开支和派出强大舰队到日本水域的表面上的理由，而真正的理由是为了提高我们民族的名誉和得到称扬我们自己的材料。在这些理由的背后并通过这些理由，存有上帝的目的，即将福音传达给所有国家，并将神旨和责任送达这个至今为止只是在拙劣地模仿耶稣之真的民族。我十分确信，东亚各民族的锁国政策决非根据上帝的善意安排，其政府必须在恐怖和强制之下将之改变，尔后其人民或可自由。朝鲜人、中国人、琉球人和日本人必须承认这唯一活着的和真实的上帝，他们的锁国之墙必将为我们所拆除，而我们西方的太平洋沿岸城市正开始派出船队前往大洋的彼岸。”从卫三畏对佩里访日使命的解读来看，他固然赞成打开东亚各国的大门，但更重视把上帝的福音传入各国人们的心扉，期盼由此引发一系列的变革。因为他认定上帝所代表的真善美的品格和力量是美国等基督教国家所拥有的绝对优势和无比强势的源泉。（详见陶德民《十九世纪中叶美国对日人权外交的启示——写在日本开国150周年之际》）

然而，卫三畏在以后长期驻节北京的岁月里，逐步加深了对中国的悠久历史和深厚文化传统的了解，使他在对华态度上开始发生“从教化到对话”的某种转变。而这一点可以耶鲁校园里的另一件艺术杰作来作为象征，那就是在卫三畏于1884年2月16日去世两周之后，在举行其丧礼的巴特尔教堂（Battell Chapel）东北角中心位置安装的一块非常别致的彩色纪念玻璃。玻璃的中央写有《论语》中的七个汉字：“敏则有功，公则说。”（意思大体为，勤勉能积成事功，公道则众人心悦诚服）。玻璃的下方用英文记载了卫三畏的名字、生卒年份以及他一生所扮演的角色与身份，即“传教士、学者、外交官、耶鲁学院中文教授”。这块玻璃由纽约的路易斯·第法尼公司（Louis C. Tiffany & Co.）负责制作，其别出心裁的设计显然是出于卫三畏生前的授意。

卫三畏选用孔子的话作为自己一生的概括，可谓恰如其分。勤勉能积成事功的道理，可以从他孜孜不倦编纂而成的《中国丛报》、《中国总论》以及《汉英韵府》等多种刊物和名著得到了解。公道则众人心悦诚服的道理，则充分体现在了他辞职回国之际所受到的各界朋友的赞扬。他在信中告诉他的妻子，“临行前威妥玛于周六、西华于周一为我举办了两次特别宴会，我见到了北京的所有名流，并受到了他们的盛赞。然后，似乎是为了区别于外交聚会，丁韪良、艾约瑟、怀定先后请我吃饭。我告诉过你，我在丁韪良家见到了所有的传教士，那真是一次令人难忘的聚会”。“接连不断的登门送别者中有三四位是总理衙门的官员，京城中最位高权重的大官也来为我送行。除了亲王之外，我都是在办公室里会见他们，彼此依依惜别。九位官员每人赠我一柄折扇作为纪念，这充分显示了中国人的友善”。不仅北京的新教传教士们发给他一封送别信以示友谊与敬意，上海的同仁也发给他一封相似的信，恰如其分地总结了他在中国的生活：“您长期担任美国使馆秘书、翻译，九次代理公使的职务，这些工作给了您许多重要的机遇，使您得以把知识、经验用于为中国人造福、为您自己的国家谋利，尤其是为基督教在中国的传播效力。对您工作中表现出的高度责任感，我们不胜钦佩。”对这些热情洋溢的赞美之辞，卫三畏则表示自己的所作所为只不过是在执行上帝的旨意，“我在传教过程中与同伴们相处融洽、身体健康、工作愉快，为此我要虔诚地赞美造物主”。

在某种意义上说，卫三畏选用孔子的话来概括自己的一生，也显示了他对中国文化传统的敬重之意。而这种敬重之意，可以由1879年他为反对加州的排华风潮而撰写的《中国移民》中的一节得到佐证："当加州的法庭想用立法来反对中国人时，它将中国人等同于印第安人的简单态度是颇为古怪的。生理学家查尔斯·匹克林将中国人和印第安人归为蒙古的成员，但加州的最高法院却认为'印第安族包括汉族和蒙古族'。这样在概念错误的同时，它还支持了一种错误的观点。它把现存最古老国度的臣民和一个从未超越部落关系的种族相提并论；把这样一个民族——它的文学早于《诗篇》和《出埃及记》，并且是用一种如果法官本人肯于学习就不会叫作印第安语的语言写就，而它的读者超过了其他任何民族的作品——与最高的写作成就仅是一些图画和牛皮上的符号的人群混为一谈；把勤奋、谨慎、技艺、学识、发明等所有品质和全部保障人类生命和财产安全的物品等同于猎人和游牧民族的本能和习惯。它诋毁了一个教会我们如何制作瓷器、丝绸、火药，给予我们指南针，展示给我们茶叶的用处，启迪我们采用考试选拔官员的制度的民族；把它和一个轻视劳动，没有艺术、学校、贸易的种族归为同类，后者的一部分现在还混迹于加州人中间，满足于以挖草根过活。"虽然卫三畏在赞扬中国人的同时，也表达了他对印第安人的歧视态度，他的观点还是得到当时耶鲁学院全体教授的同情，他们纷纷签名支持他起草的请愿书，呼吁海斯总统否决1879年的反移民法，其中包含这样的警告：如果我们的政府首先改变条约的规定，中国政府也可以根据国际法取消治外法权，致使美国在华公民失去领事的保护。此外，1878年中国北方发生大饥荒时，身处太平洋彼岸的卫三畏利用他对美国在华传教士和商社的影响，不遗余力地推动救灾。他还试图劝说国会归还1859年中方赔款余额的一部分来帮助缓解灾区的困境。而早在1860年，他就曾建议国务院用这笔赔款余额在中国建立一所美中学院，以培养中方的翻译、通商和外交人才。这个建议得到了新上任的总统林肯的同意，只因为当时的国会未予批准而搁浅。卫三畏这个未能实现的建议完全可以称之为后来退回庚款吸引中国学生留美的先驱性方案。

卫三畏还对亲眼目睹的中国同时代的缓慢而确凿的变化做了一定的正面评价。1883年7月，即辞世的半年多之前，卫三畏在儿子的帮助下终于完成了《中国总论》这一巨著的修订工作，在增补版的序言中他写下了如下字句："我在1833年到达广州时，和另外两位美国人作为'番鬼'向行商经官正式报告，在他的监护之下才得以生存。1874年，我作为美国驻北京公使馆秘书，跟随艾忭敏公使觐见同治皇帝，美国使节站在与'天子'完全平等的地位呈上国书。由于一生之中的这两次遭遇，并念念不忘在思想和道德上的重大进步是使一个孤傲的政府从强加于人的姿态改而听从他人所必需的，毫不足怪的是，我确信汉人的子孙有着伟大的未来，不过，唯有纯正基督教的发展才是能使这一成长过程中的各个冲突因素免于互相摧残的充分条件。无论如何，这个国家已经度过被动时期，这是肯定无疑的。中国不可能再安于懒散隔绝—像过去那样，以过于自负的态度俯视其他国家，就像面对她所无需劳神的星星一样。"

如果说，17世纪的礼仪之争最后是以天主教士在康熙禁令之下被逐出中国告终的，那么，这场可谓19世纪的礼仪之争则是以"天朝上国"在第二次鸦片战争之后所做出的巨大让步来结局的，包括废除以夷相称、公使驻京、平身觐见皇帝而不必行三跪九叩之礼。卫三畏的字里行间所透露的，既有在礼仪上争得与最古老“中央王国”之“天子”平等地位的自豪，又有从其所信奉的上帝的立场针砭这个王国“懒散隔绝”和“过于自负”的高傲。联系到上述1853年他给在土耳其传教的弟弟W. F. 威廉斯的长信，可见这时的卫三畏虽然在其对华态度上开始了“从教化到对话”的转变，但并未把“异教徒”放在完全对等的位置上，特别是在道德和精神的层面上。在这个意义上说，自以为占据着道德精神的制高点，只有基督教可以拯救中国的卫三畏也难免“过于自负”的诟病。这就是笔者在前文中提到其转变时，始终不忘加上“某种”一词来予以限定的缘故。

尽管如此，卫三畏在序言中宣称，修订版“坚持初版序言中所述的观点——为中国人民及其文明洗刷掉古怪的、模糊不清的可笑印象”。卫三畏相信，在传教“事业取得成功的基础上，中国作为一个民族，在道义和政治两方面，将会得到拯救。这一成功有可能和人民的需要同步前进。他们将会变得适应于自己着手处理问题，并且和外国文明以多种活动形式结合起来。不久，将会引进铁路、电报和制造业，随之而来的是中国人民中成百万地受到启发，无论在宗教、政治和家庭生活的每一方面”。这种力图呈现中国文明及民族的美好品质和衷心期待中国在对外交往中日益开放进步的善意态度，自然是应该予以充分肯定的。

从卫三畏的例子不难联想到，身处所谓“轴心文明”（主要以几大世界性宗教作为标识）的人们往往患有“老子天下第一”的自恋症，而以“居高临下”的态度傲视其他人，难以免俗和根治。反观我们自己，历代国人的“华夷之辨”又何尝不是如此？而时至今日，仍不乏“宅兹中国”的自尊和输出“天下体系”的自负。但也不必悲观，因为这个五彩缤纷的世界本来就是由形形色色、各有偏好的人们构成的。他们之间有相辅相成的关系，也有相反相成的因素。虽然各派宗教和文化的代表自以为有“替上帝传教”或“替天行道”的使命，谁都无法垄断真理和剥夺他人的信仰，也不能指望按照自己的面貌来彻底改造他人。其出于宗教或政治动机的种种努力的后果，客观上会推动各国和各民族之间的交往和融合，并推动人类文明的进步和升华，则是毫无疑义的。从这一点来看，卫三畏一生的变化过程所显示的方向对我们建构今日地球村的和平共处规则还是不乏启迪作用的，那就是要逐渐学会把“老子化胡”的心态改为“相敬如宾”的心理，对异民族、异文化和异文明采取更加宽容、尊重和善于调适的态度，以便用文明对话来取代文明对抗，从而把亨廷顿认为不可避免的“文明冲突”消弭于萌芽状态和无形之间。

CONTENTS OF VOLUME II.

CHAPTER XV.

CHAPTER XVI.

PAGE

CHAPTER XXIII.

CHAPTER XXIV.

PAGE

LIST OF ILLUSTRATIONS IN VOLUME II.

MAP OF THE CHINESE EMPIRE.

(In pocket at end of this volume.)

THE MIDDLE KINGDOM.

CHAPTER XV

INDUSTRIAL ARTS OF THE CHINESE.

The superiority of the Chinese over their immediate neighbors in the enjoyments of life and in the degree of security for which individuals can look under the protection of law have their bases chiefly in the industry of the people. Agriculture holds the first place among the branches of labor, and the honors paid to it by the annual ploughing ceremony are given from a deep sense of its importance to the public welfare; not alone to provide a regular supply of food and labor for the population, but also to meet the wants of government by moderate taxes, and long experience of the greater ease of governing an agricultural than a mercantile or warlike community. Notwithstanding the encouragement given to tillage, many tracts of land still lie waste, some of it the most fertile in the country; partly because the people have not the skill and capital to drain and render it productive, partly because they have not sufficient prospect of remuneration to encourage them to make the necessary outlay, and sometimes from the outrages of local banditti making it unsafe to live in secluded districts.

Landed property is held in clans or families as much as possible, and is not entailed, nor are overgrown estates frequent. The land is all held directly from the crown, no allodial property being acknowledged; if mesne lords existed in feudal times they are now unknown. The conditions of common tenure are the payment of an annual tax, the fee for alienation, with a money composition for personal service to the government, a charge generally incorporated into the direct tax as a kind of scutage. The proprietors of land record their names in the district and take out a *hung ki*, or 'red deed,' which secures them in possession as long as the ground tax is paid. This sum varies according to the fertility, location, and use of the land, from $1.50 per acre for the best, down to twenty or thirty cents for unproductive or hilly fields. As the exactions for alienation or sale of lands are high, amounting to as much as one-third of the sale price sometimes, the people accept white deeds from each other as proofs of ownership and responsibility for taxes. As many as twenty or thirty such deeds of sale occasionally accompany the original *hung ki*, without which they are suspicious if not valueless. In order to keep the knowledge of the alienations of land in government offices, so that the taxes can be assured, it is customary to furnish a *ki-wei*, or 'deed-end,' containing a note of the terms of sale and amount of tax liable on the property. There is no other proof of ownership required; and the simplicity and efficiency of this mode of transfer offer a striking contrast to the cumbrous rules enforced in western kingdoms. Revised codes of land laws are issued by the provincial authorities when necessary, as was done in 1846 at Canton.[1]

The paternal estate and houses thereon descend to the eldest son, but his brothers can remain upon it with their families, and devise their portion *in perpetuo* to their children, or an amicable composition can be made; daughters never inherit, nor can an adopted son of another clan succeed. A mortgagee must enter into possession of the property and make himself responsible for the payment of the taxes; unless explicitly stated, the land can be redeemed any time within thirty years on payment of the original sum. Sections XC. to C. of the Code contain the laws relating to this subject, some of which bear a resemblance to those established among the Hebrews, and intended to secure a similar result of retaining the land in the same clan or tribe.

---

[1] T. T. Meadows in *N. C. Br. R. A. S. Transactions*, Hongkong, 1848, Vol. I

The enclosure of recent alluvial deposits cannot be made without the cognizance of the authorities, but the terms are not onerous; for waste hillsides and poor spots ample time is allowed for a return of the capital expended in reclaiming them before assessment is made.

The Chinese are rather gardeners than farmers, if regard be had to the small size of their grounds. They are ignorant, too, of many of those operations whereby soils naturally unfruitful are made fertile and the natural fertility sustained at the cheapest rate by proper manuring and rotation of crops; but they make up for the disadvantages of poor implements by hard work. Their agricultural utensils are few and simple, and are probably now made similar to those used centuries ago. The broad hoe is used in soft land more than any other tool; the weight of its large wooden blade, which is edged with iron, adds impetus to the blow. Spades, rakes, and mattocks are employed in kitchen gardening, and the plough and harrow in rice cultivation. The plough is made of wood, except the iron-edged share, which lies flat and penetrates the soil about five inches. The whole implement is so simple and rude that one would think the inventor of it was a laborer, who, tired of the toil of spading, called the ox to his aid and tied his shovel to a rail;—fastening the animal at one end and guiding the other, he was so pleased with the relief that he never thought of improving it much further than to sharpen the spade to a coulter and bend the rail to a beam and handle. The harrow is a heavy stick armed with a single row of stout wooden teeth, and furnished with a framework to guide it; or a triangular machine, with rows of iron teeth, on which the driver rides to sink it in the ooze.

The buffalo is used in rice cultivation, and the ox and ass in dry ploughing; horses, mules, cows, and goats likewise render service to the farmer in various ways, and are often yoked in most ludicrous combinations. The team which Nieuhoff depicts of a man driving his wife and his ass yoked to the same plough is too bad for China often to present, though it has been so frequently repeated and used to point a comparison that one almost expects on landing to see half the women in the harness. It may be doubted, however, if this country can vie with some portions of Germany and Holland in the matter of mongrel teams employed on farms.

The arrangements of farriers' shops in China are very similar to those of European countries, saving that the tools are of the simplest character. The manner of trussing up the poor beast

Manner of Shoeing Horses.

which is to be shod would seem, however, an unnecessary exercise of caution in the case of a majority of the over-worked horses and mules. The animal is fastened to a frame and lifted almost entirely off the ground, while a rope twisted about his nose and tightened at will with a turn-stick controls the least attempt at unruliness. Iron shoes are employed in the north; in the south, where horses are little used, they are usually left unshod, though the fore feet are often covered with leather shoes which fit the hoof.

An early rain is necessary to the preparation of rice-fields, except where water can be turned upon them. The grain is first soaked, and when it begins to swell is sown very thickly in a small plat containing liquid manure. When about six inches high the shoots are planted into the fields, which, from being an unsightly marsh, are in a few days transformed to fields clothed with living green. Holding the seedlings in one hand, the laborer wades through the mud, at every step sticking into it five or six sprouts, which take root without further care; six men can transplant two acres a day, one or two of whom are engaged in supplying the others with shoots. The amount of grain required to sow a Chinese *mao* in this way is thirty-seven and one-half catties, or three hundred and thirty pounds—about two and one-half bushels to an English acre. The produce is on an average tenfold. Rent of land is usually paid according to the amount of the crop, the landlord paying the taxes and the tenant stocking the farm; leases are for three, four, or seven years; the terms vary according to the position and goodness of the soil.[1]

Grain is not sown broadcast, and this facilitates hoeing and weeding the fields as they require. Two crops are planted, one of which ripens after the other; maize and pulse, millet and sesamum, or sorghum and squash are thus grown together. The plough is an efficient tool in soft soil, but a wide hoe, the blade set almost at a right angle, is the common implement in the north. Barrow describes a drill-plough in common use in the north which remarkably economizes time and seed. "It consisted of two parallel poles of wood shod at the lower extremity

[1] The amount of tribute rice sent to Peking from

Kiangsu Province is		......696,000 tons of	640 catties,	or		974,400	peculs
Chehkiang	"	445,000	"	"	"	633,000	"
Kiangsí	"	80,000	"	"	"	112,000	"
Hupeh	"	50,000	"	"	"	70,000	"
						1,789,400	"
Of this the Chinese Company carried in 1875 to Tientsin..						626,900	"
Went by junks						1,162,500	"

with iron to open the furrows; these poles were placed upon wheels; a small hopper was attached to each pole to drop the seeds into the furrow, which were covered with earth by a transverse piece of wood fixed behind, that just swept the face of the ground."[1]

The extent to which terrace cultivation has been described as common is a good instance of the way in which erroneous impressions concerning China obtain currency from accounts not exactly incorrect, perhaps, but made to convey wrong notions by the mode of their description. The hills are terraced chiefly for rice cultivation or to retain soil which would otherwise be washed away; and this restricts their gradation, generally speaking, to the southern and eastern provinces. Most of the hills in Kwangtung and Fuhkien are unfit for the plough except near their bases, while in the north it is unnecessary to go to great expense in terracing for a crop of cotton, wheat, or millet. Much labor has been expended in terracing, and many hillsides otherwise useless are thus rendered productive; but this does not mean that every hill is cut into plats, nor that the entire face of the country is one vast garden. Terracing was probably a more important feature of agriculture in Palestine in former days than it is in China. The natural terraces of the loess districts, and their extraordinary convenience as well as fertility, have already been noticed in a former chapter. These, it should however be remembered, do not occur south of the Yangtsz' River.

The ingenuity of the farmer is well exhibited in the various modes he employs to insure a supply of water for his rice. In some places pools are made in level fields as reservoirs of rain, from which the water is lifted as occasion requires by well-sweeps. It is also expeditiously raised by two men holding a pail between them by ropes, and with a swinging motion rapidly dipping the water out of the tank into little furrows. A favorite plan is to use a natural brooklet and conduct it from one plat to another till it has irrigated the whole hillside. It is where such water privileges offer that the terrace cultivation is best

---

[1] *Travels in China*, London, 1804.

developed, especially in the neighborhood of large cities, where the demand for provisions promises the cultivator a sure reward for his labor. The appearance of the slopes thus graduated into small ledges is beautiful; each plat is divided by a bank serving the triple purpose of fence, path, and dyke, and near which the rills glide with refreshing lapse, turning whithersoever the master willeth. This primitive method of upland irrigation is carried out far more perfectly in China than in Switzerland, where it is better known to the generality of travellers. Water is not often wasted upon grass meadows in the former country. The food these marshy plats furnish to insects, mollusks, snakes, and birds is surprising to one who examines them for the first time. Wheels of various sorts are also contrived to assist in this labor, some worked by cattle, some by human toil, and others carried round by the stream whose waters they elevate. The last are very common on the banks of the rivers Siang, Kan, Min, and their affluents, wherever the banks are convenient for this purpose. High wheels of bamboo, firmly fixed on an axle in the bank, or on pillars driven into the bed, and furnished with buckets, pursue their stately round, and pour their earnings of two hundred and fifty or three hundred tons a day into troughs fixed at an elevation of twenty or thirty feet above the stream. The box-trough, containing an axle to be turned by two men treading the pedals, is rather a more clumsy contrivance, used for slight elevations; the chain of paddles runs around two axles and in the trough as closely as possible, and raises the water ten or twelve feet in an equable current.

Few carts or wagons are used with animals in the southern and eastern provinces where boats are at all available, human strength supplying the means of transportation; the implements of husbandry and the grain taken from the fields both being carried on the back of the laborer. It is not an uncommon sight about Canton to see a ploughman, when he has done his work, turn his buffalo loose and shoulder his plough, harrow, and hoe, with the harness, and carry them all home. It is when one crosses the Yangtsz' on his way north that pack animals are met transporting goods and food in great droves; here, too, people on carts and wheelbarrows fill the roads. On the Great

Plain a sail is raised on the latter when a fair wind will help the man to trundle it over a level way.

The Chinese manure the plant rather than the ground, both in the seed and growing grain. The preparation of manure from night soil, by mixing it with earth and drying it into cakes, furnishes employment to multitudes who transport at all hours their noisome loads through the narrow city streets. Tanks

Pedler's Barrow.

are dug by the wayside, pails are placed in the streets and retiring stalls opened among the dwellings, whose contents are carried away in boats and buckets; but it is a small compensation for this constant pollution of the sweet breath of heaven to know that the avails are to be by and by brought to market. Science may yet ascertain how the benefits of this necessary work can be obtained without its disgusting exposure among the Chinese. Besides this principal ingredient of manure vats, other substances are diligently collected, as hair from the barber's shop, exploded fire-crackers and sweepings from the streets, lime and plaster from kitchens and old buildings, soot, bones, fish and animal remains, the mud from the bottom of canals and tanks, and dung of every kind. In Kiangsu a small leaf clover (*Medicago sativa*) is grown through the winter upon ridges raised in the rice-fields, and the plants pulled up in the spring and scattered over the fields to be ploughed and harrowed into the wet soil with the stubble, their decomposition furnishing large quantities of ammonia to the seedlings. Vegetable rubbish is also collected and covered with turf, and then slowly burned; the residue is a rich black earth, which is laid upon the seeds themselves when planted. The refuse left after expressing the oil from ground-nuts, beans, vegetable tallow, tea, and cabbage seeds, etc., is mixed with earth and made into cakes, to be sold to farmers. The bean-cake made in Liautung thus aids the cotton and sugar planter in Swatow with a rich compost.

The ripe grain is cut with bill-hooks and sickles, or pulled up by the roots; scythes, mowing-machines, and cradles are unknown where human arms are so plenty. Rice-straw is made into brooms and besoms; the rice is thrashed out against the side of a tub having a curtain on one side, or bound into sheaves and carried away to be stacked. The thrashing-floors about Canton are made of a mixture of sand and lime, well pounded upon an inclined surface enclosed by a curb; a little cement added in the last coat makes it impervious to the rain; with proper care it lasts many years, and is used by all the villagers for thrashing rice, peas, mustard, turnips, and other seeds, either with unshod oxen or flails. Where frost and snow come the ground requires to be repaired every season; and each farmer usually has his own.

The cultivation of food plants forms so large a proportion of those demanding the attention of the Chinese, that excepting hemp, indigo, cotton, silk, and tea, those raised for manufacture are quite unimportant. The great cotton region is the basin of the Yangtsz' kiang, where the white and yellow varieties grow side by side. The manure used is mud taken from the canals and spread with ashes over the ploughed fields, in which seeds are sown about the 20th of April. The seeds are planted, after sprouting, five or six in a hole, being rubbed with ashes as they are put in, and weeded out if necessary. After the winter crops have been gathered cotton-fields are easily made ready for the shoots, which, while growing, are carefully tended, thinned, hoed, and weeded, until the flowers begin to appear about August. As the pods begin to ripen and burst the cultivator collects them before they fall, to clean the cotton of seeds and husks. The weather is carefully watched, for a dry summer or a wet autumn are alike unpropitious, and as the pods are ripening from August to October, it is not uncommon for the crop to be partially lost. The seeds are separated by a wheel turning two rollers, and the cotton sold by each farmer to merchants in the towns. Some he keeps for weaving at home; spinning-wheels and looms being common articles of furniture in the houses of the peasantry. Cotton is cultivated in every province, and most of it is used where it grows. Around Peking the plant is hardly a foot high; the bolls are cleaned for wadding to a great extent, while the woody stalks supply fuel to the poor. Minute directions are given in Sü's *Encyclopædia of Agriculture* respecting the cultivation of this plant, whose total crop clothes the millions of the Empire without depending on any other land.[1]

Hemp is largely cultivated north of the Mei ling, and also grows in Fuhkien; grass-cloth made from the *Dolichos bulbosus* is used for summer dresses. There are four plants which produce a fibre made into cloth known under this name, viz.: the *Cannabis sativa*, or common hemp, at Canton; the *Bœhmeria nivea*, a species of nettle; the *Sida tiliæfolia*, or abutilon hemp, in Chihlí; and the *Hibíscus cannabinus*. The coloring matter used for dyeing blue is derived from two plants, the *Polygonum tinctorium* at the south, and the *tien tsing* (*Isatis indigotica*), cultivated at Shanghai and Chusan. The mulberry is raised as a shade and fruit tree in the northern provinces, where it forms a beautiful plant fifty feet high; elsewhere the consumption of the leaves renders its culture an important branch of labor in

[1] Fortune's *Wanderings*, Chap. XIV.; *Chinese Repository*, Vol. XVIII., pp. 449–469.

the silk-producing provinces. Some growers allow it to attain its natural height, others cut it down to increase the branches and the produce of leaves. In Chehkiang it is cut in January and deprived of its useless branches, leaving only the outer ones, which are trimmed into two or three points in order to force the plant to extend itself. The trees are set out in rows twelve feet or more apart, each tree being half that distance from its neighbor and opposite the intervals in the parallel rows; the interspaces are occupied with legumes or greens. The trees are propagated by seed and by suckers, but soon losing their vigor from being constantly stripped of leaves, are then rooted up and replaced by fresh nurslings.

Sugar is only a southern and southeastern crop. The name *ché*, by which it is known, is an original character, which favors the opinion that the plant is indigenous in China, and the same argument is applicable to wheat, hemp, mulberry, tea, and some of the common fruits, as the plum, pear, and orange. The canes are pressed in machines, and the juice boiled to sugar or boiled and hawked about the streets for consumption by the people. The sugar-mill consists merely of two upright cylinders, between which the cane is introduced as they turn, and the juice received into reservoirs; it is then boiled down and sent to the refiners to undergo the necessary processes to fit it for market; much is lost by this slovenly manufacture.

Many plants are cultivated for their oil, used in the arts or in cooking. The seeds of two or three species of *Eleococea* belonging to the Euphorbiaceous family, and the *Curcas purgans*, are gathered, and by pressure furnish an oil to mix with lacker and paints, or to smear boats as a preservative against teredoes and other insects. It is deleterious when taken into the system, but does not appear to injure those who use or express it. The tallow-tree (*Stillingia sebifera*) grows over the eastern provinces; it is a beautiful tree, resembling the aspen in its shape and foliage, and would form a valuable addition to the list of shade-trees in any country. Mr. Denny, the United States Consul at Shanghai, has recently sent a quantity of these seeds to California, where efforts are being made to grow them. The tree has been introduced into India for its timber. The seeds grow in clusters like ivy berries, and are collected in November; when ripe the capsule divides, and falling off discovers two or three kernels covered with the pure, hard white tallow. When the tallow is to be prepared, these are picked from the stalks and put into an open wooden cylinder with a perforated bottom, in which they are well steamed over boiling water. In ten or fifteen minutes the tallow covering the seeds becomes soft, and they are thrown into a stone mortar and gently beaten with mallets to detach it. The whole is then sifted on a hot sieve, by which the tallow is separated from the kernels, though containing the brown skin which envelops the latter and presenting a dirty appearance. The tallow in this state is enclosed in a straw cylinder, or laid upon layers of straw held together by iron hoops, and subjected to pressure in a rude press, from which it runs clear in a semifluid state and soon hardens into cakes. The candles made from it become soft in hot weather, and are sometimes coated by dipping them in colored wax.[1] From one hundred and thirty-three pounds of nuts is obtained some forty or fifty pounds of tallow.

The departments of floriculture and arboriculture have received great attention, but the efforts of their promoters are directed to producing something curious or bizarre, rather than improving the quality of their fruits or enlarging the number of their flowers. A common mode of multiplying specimens is to slit the stem and insert half of it in damp earth tied around the stalk until it has rooted, and then cutting off the whole. Dwarfing trees or forcing them to grow in grotesque shapes employs much time and patience. The juniper, cypress, pine, elm, bamboo, peach, plum, and flowering-almond are selected for this purpose; the former is trained into the shapes of deer or other animals, pagodas, etc., with extraordinary fidelity, the eyes, tongue, or other parts being added to complete the resemblance. The principle of the operation depends upon retarding the circulation of the sap by stinting the supply of water, confining the roots, and bending the branches into the desired form when young and pliable, afterwards retaining them in

[1] Fortune's *Wanderings*, p. 78.

their forced position in pots, and clipping off all the vigorous shoots, until, as is the case of the cramped feet of women, nature gives up the contest and yields to art. These, like the similar exhibitions in sculpture and painting, indicate the uncultivated taste of the people, who admire the fantastic and monstrous more than the natural. Some of the clumps placed in large earthen vases, consisting of bamboos, flowers, and dwarf trees growing closely together upon a piece of rock-work, and overshadowing the water in the vase, in which gold-fish swim through the crevices of the stone, are beautiful specimens of Chinese art. Without understanding the principles of an aquarium, the people have succeeded in combining animal and vegetable life in these elegant ornaments of their houses.

The annual ceremony of ploughing is of very ancient origin. At Peking it consists in ploughing the sacred field in the Temple of Agriculture with a highly ornamented plough kept for the purpose, the Emperor holding it while turning over three furrows, the princes five, and the high ministers nine. These furrows were, however, so short that the monarchs of the present dynasty altered the ancient rule, ploughing four furrows and returning again over the ground. The ceremony finished, the Emperor and his ministers repair to the terrace adjoining the plat, and remain till it has all been ploughed. The crop of wheat is used in idolatrous services. The rank of the actors renders the ceremony more imposing at Peking, but the people of the capital only know that such a performance takes place, as they are not admitted inside of the enclosure when it is observed by the Emperor and his suite. This ceremony is also required of all high officers throughout the Empire, and is attended with more or less parade in April.

In the provinces its celebration varies, and as there are two festivals coming near together connected with agriculture, one or the other of them is apt to predominate. The annual ploughing ritual is one, and the *lih chun*, or 'First day of spring,' is the other and prior in date. The prefect of every city and his subordinates on that day repair to the appointed spot outside of the walls, accompanied by music and a great procession of the citizens, carrying through the streets a paper image of the buffalo or ox, which, with the idol image worshipped at the same time, are at some places taken into his *yamun*. Here the whole is placed on an altar, and the officials present walk around and whip the effigy with rods before it is set on fire and scrambled for by the people present. Besides the paper ox, a clay one is also made and taken beyond the eastern gate, sometimes accompanied by or holding hundreds of little images inside; after the ceremonies are over it is broken up, and the pieces and small images are carried off by the crowd to scatter the powder on their own fields, in the hope of thereby insuring a good crop.

In Ningpo the principal features of the ceremony consist of a solemn worship by all the local officers of a clay image of a buffalo and an idol of a cow-herd. The prefect then ploughs a small piece of ground, and he and his associates disperse till the morrow, when they come together in another temple at dawn. Here a series of prostrations and recitals of prayers are performed by the "fathers of the people" in their presence, some of whom have no respect for the worship, while others, perhaps, evince deep reverence. As soon as it is over the clay ox is brought out, and a procession consisting of all the officers pass around it repeatedly, striking the body at a given signal, and concluding the ceremony by a heavy blow on the head. The crowd then rush in and tear the effigy to pieces, each one carrying off a portion to strew on his fields.[1]

The various modes of catching and rearing fish exhibit the contrivance and skill of the Chinese quite as much as their agricultural operations. Some persons reckon that at least one-tenth of the population in the prefecture of Kwangchau derive their food from the water, and necessity leads them to invent and try many ingenious ways of securing the finny tribes.

---

[1] Père Cibot in *Mém. conc. les Chinois*, Tome III., p. 499. *Penal Code*, pp. 94–106, 526. *Chinese Repository*, Vol. II., p. 350; Vol. III., pp. 121, 231; Vol. V., p. 485. *La Chine Ouverte*, p. 346. *Foreign Missionary Chronicle*, Vol. XIII., p. 296. Gray's *China*, Vol. II., pp. 115–117. Doolittle's *Social Life*, Vol. II., pp. 18–23. *Revue de l'Orient*, Tome V. (1844), p. 297. Baron d'Hervey Saint-Denys, *Recherches sur l'Agriculture et l'Horticulture des Chinois*, Paris, 1850. *Journal N. C. Br. R. A. Soc.*, No. IV., pp. 209 ff.

Nets woven of hempen thread are boiled in a solution of gambier to preserve them from rotting. The smacks which swarm along the coast go out in pairs, partly that the crews may afford mutual relief and protection, but chiefly to join in dragging the net. In the shallows of rivers rows of heavy posts are driven down and nets secured to them, which are examined and changed at every tide. Those who attend these nets, more-

Group and Residence of Fishermen near Canton.

over, attach scoops or drag-nets to their boats, so loaded that they will sink and gather the sole, ray, and other fish feeding near the bottom. Lifting-nets, twenty feet square, are suspended from poles elevated and depressed by a hawser worked by a windlass on shore; the nets are baited with the whites of eggs spread on the meshes.

The fishermen along the coast form an industrious, though rather turbulent community, by no means confining their enterprises to their professed business when piracy, dakoity, or marauding on shore hold out greater prospects of gain. When their boats become unseaworthy they are still considered landworthy, and are transformed into houses by setting them bodily upon a stone foundation above the reach of the tide, or breaking them up to construct rude huts.

Cormorants are trained in great numbers to capture fish in the rivers and lakes; they will disperse at a given signal and return with their prey, but not often without the precaution of a neck-ring. A single boatman can easily oversee twelve or fifteen of these birds, and although hundreds may be out upon the

The Fishing Cormorant.

water each one knows its own master. If one seize a fish too heavy for him alone, another comes to his assistance, and the two carry it aboard; but such cases are very rare compared with others where the weak or young bird is unceremoniously robbed of its capture. When several hundreds of them fish together the scene becomes animated and noisy in the extreme. The birds themselves are fed on bean-curd and eels or fish. They lay eggs when three years old, which are often hatched under barnyard hens, and the chickens fed with eel's blood and hash. They do not fish during the summer months. The price of a pair varies from five to eight dollars.

Mussels are caught in cylindrical basket-traps attached to a single rope and drifted with the tide near the bottom. Similar traps for catching land-crabs are laid along the edges of rice-fields, baited with dried fish. When the receding tide leaves the river banks dry the boat people get overboard and wade in the mud, or push themselves along on a board with one foot, in search of such things as harbor in the ooze.

In moonlight nights low, narrow shallops, provided with a wide white board fastened to the wale and floating upon the water, are anchored in still water; as the moon shines on the board the deceived fish leap out upon it or into the boat; twenty or thirty of these decoy boats can be seen near Macao engaged in this fishery on moonlight evenings. Sometimes a boat furnished with a treadle goes up and down near the shores striking boards against its bottom and sides; the startled fish are caught in the net dragging astern. The crews of many small boats combine to drive the fish into their nets by splashing and striking the water, or into a pool on the margin of the river at high tide, in which they are easily retained by wattles, and scooped out when the water has fallen. Divers clap sticks together under water to drive their prey into the nets set for them, or catch them with their toes when, terrified at the noise, they hide in the mud. Neither fly-fishing nor angling with hook and line is much practised; its tedium and small returns would be poor amends to a Chinese for the elegance of the tackle or the science displayed in adapting the fly to the fish's taste.

By these and other contrivances the Chinese capture the finny tribes, and it is no surprise to hear that China contains as many millions of people as there are days in the year when one sees upon what a large proportion of them feed and how they live. Their expenditure of human labor appears enormous to those who are accustomed to the manufactories and engines of western lands, but perhaps nothing would cause so much distress in China as the premature and inconsiderate introduction of labor-saving machines. Population is so close upon the means of production, not seldom overpassing them, that those who would be thrown out of employment would, owing to their ignorance as to the best resources and want of means to do anything by themselves, suffer and cause incalculable distress before relief and labor could be furnished them. There are, for instance, six or seven yards near Canton where logs are sawed by hand, but all of them together hardly turn out as many feet of boards as one water-wheel turning three or four saws would do. Yet the two hundred men employed in these yards would perhaps be half-starved if turned off in their present condition, even if they did not destroy their competitor; though there is every reason for believing that improvements will be introduced as soon as those who see their superiority are assured they can be made profitable.

The mechanical arts and implements of the Chinese partake of the same simplicity which has been remarked in their agricultural,—as if the faculty of invention or the notion of altering a thing had died with the discoverer, and he had had the best guarantee for the patent of his contrivance in the deprivation of all desire in his successors to alter it. This servility of imitation marks them in many things, but in machinery and metallurgy is chiefly owing to ignorance of the real nature of the materials they use, a knowledge which has only recently become familiar to ourselves. In the absence of superior models, it produces a degree of apathy to all improvement which strangely contrasts with their general industry and literary tastes. Simplicity of design pervades all operations, and when a machine directs in the best known manner the power of the hand which wields it, or aids in executing tiresome operations, its purpose is considered to be fully answered, for it was intended to assist and not to supplant human labor. Yet with all their simplicity some of them are both effectual and ingenious, and not a few are made to answer two or three ends. For example, the bellows, an oblong box divided into two compartments, and worked by a piston and two valves in the upper, which forces the wind into the lower part and out of the nozzle, is used by the travelling tinker as a seat when at work and a chest for his tools when his work is done; though it does not, indeed, serve all these purposes with efficiency.

In the arts of metallurgy the Chinese have attained only to mediocrity, and on the whole do not equal the Japanese. To this deficiency may perhaps be ascribed their little progress in some other branches which could not be executed without tools of peculiar size or nicety. Mines of iron, lead, copper, and zinc are worked, though the modes employed in digging the ore, preparing and smelting it, and purifying the metals have not yet been fully examined. Gold is used sparingly for ornaments, but is consumed in vast quantities for gilding; gold thread is commonly imported, and the ingots are known only as bullion. Mr. Gordon found the people in the country parts of Fuhkien quite ignorant of its value, for he could only pass doubloons for a dollar apiece, the natives having never seen them before.

The Chinese workmanship in chased, repoussé, and carved work of gold and silver—baskets, card-cases, teapots, combs, etc.—is almost unequalled. Their jewelry, too, admirably exhibits the delicate filigree work which agrees so well with their genius. Flower-baskets with chased flowers and figures of various sorts enamelled on the outside of the open work of wire, and set with precious stones, may perhaps be regarded as the masterpiece of native art in the working of metals.

Steel is everywhere manufactured in a rude way, but the foreign importation is gradually supplying a better article. The quality of this metal made is best shown by the carvings in the hardest stones for ornaments, which have never been exceeded elsewhere. Iron is cast into thin plates and various machines of considerable size, but the largest pieces they make, viz., bells and cannon, are small compared with the shafts and steam-hammers turned out abroad. Wrought iron is chiefly worked up into nails, screws, hinges, and small articles needed in daily life, though its quality is remarkably good. The *peh tung*, argentan or 'white copper' of the Chinese, is an alloy of copper 40.4, zinc 25.4, nickel 31.6, and iron 2.6, and occasionally a little silver; these proportions are nearly the same as German-silver. "When in a state of ore, it is said to be powdered, mixed with charcoal dust, and placed in jars over a slow fire, the metal rising in the form of vapor in a distilling apparatus, and afterward condensed in water."[1] When new, this alloy ap-

[1] Davis' *Chinese*, Vol. II., p. 235. *Penny Cyclopædia*, Art. COPPER. Natalis Rondot, *Commerce de la Chine*, 1849, p. 142.

pears as lustrous as silver, and is manufactured into incense-jars, flower-stands for temple service, boxes, a vast variety of fancy articles, and a few household utensils not intended to be used near the fire. Puzzling specimens of work are made of it, such as teapots enclosed in chinaware and ornamented with a handle and a spout of stone, and having characters on the sides. The white copper varies a good deal in its appearance and malleability, owing probably to mixtures added after distillation.

Copper is less used than iron for culinary vessels, but will probably increase as rapid importation diminishes the cost, for iron rusts quickly in the southern parts. The manufactures of gongs, cymbals and trumpets, lamps, brass-leaf for working into the *kin hwa*, or tinsel-flowers used in worship, and the copper coin of the country, consume probably four-fifths of all the copper used. The gong is employed on all occasions, and its piercing clamor can be heard at any time of day and night, especially if one lives near the water. It is an alloy of twenty parts of tin with eighty of copper, and is made by melting one hundred catties of *hung tung*, or 'red copper,' with twenty-five catties of tin. The alloy is run into thin plates, and the gongs are made by long and expert hammering until the requisite sonorousness is obtained.

Bells and tripods are frequently cast of a large size. The bells at Peking (mentioned in Volume I., p. 79) are peculiarly rich in quality of tone; they are almost invariably made without tongues, being sounded with a mallet. The tripods for receiving the ashes of papers consumed in worship also bear inscriptions of a religious character; the priests of temples containing them take great pride in showing their ancient bells, tripods, and other like rarities. The pieces of bronze formerly produced under the patronage of the Emperor Kienlung, as incense tripods, lions, astronomical instruments, and the infinite variety of ornaments, probably represent their highest attainments in this branch of metallurgy for beauty and excellence. The metallic mirrors, once the only reflectors the Chinese manufactured, are now nearly superseded by glass; the alloy is like that of gongs with a little silver added. These mirrors have long been remarkable for a singular property which some of them possess of reflecting the raised characters or device on the back when held in the sun; this is caused by their outline being traced upon the polished surface in very shallow lines, the whole plate being afterward rubbed until the lines are equally bright with the other parts, and only rendered visible by the strongest sunlight.[1] Besides the metallic articles already mentioned, the ornamental and antique bronze and copper figures, noticeable for their curious forms and fine polishing and tracery, afford the best specimens of Chinese art in imitating the human figure. They are mostly statuettes, representing men, gods, birds, monsters, etc., in grotesque shapes and attitudes; some of them are beautifully ornamented with delicate scrolls and flowers in niello work of silver or gold wire inserted into grooves cut in the metal.

The manufacture of glass is carried on chiefly at Canton, and its increasing use for windows, tumblers, lamps, mirrors, and other articles of household furniture, shows that the Chinese are quite ready to adopt such things from foreign countries as they find to be advantageous. The importation of broken glass for remelting has entirely ceased, but flints are carried from England for the use of glass-blowers. The furnaces are small, and from the ignorance, on the part of the workmen, of the constituents of good glass, their products are not uniform. Foreign window-glass is now brought so cheaply that the native inferior article, which distorts objects seen through it, is disappearing; colored articles and chandeliers are still made. The most finished articles which the Chinese have yet produced are ground shades for Argand lamps. Beautiful ornaments are made of the *liao-li*, the old native name for a vitreous composition like strass, between glass and porcelain. Ear-rings, wristlets, snuff-bottles, jars, cups, etc., are made of it, plain, colored, and variegated, in vast variety. Some of these articles exhibit different tints in layers, each layer being ground away where it is not wanted, as in cameo carving; blue, red, and yel-

[1] Other and perhaps more correct explanations of this peculiarity have been given.

low are the prevailing colors. The art of producing it has been known longer than glass-making, but was invented later than that of porcelain.

The cutting and setting of hard and precious stones is carried on to some extent. Spectacles are cut and ground in lathes from crystal, smoky quartz, and a variety of rose quartz resembling the cairngorm-stone, which the Chinese call *cha-tsing*, or 'tea-stone,' from its color. Their spectacles are not always true, and the wearer is obliged to have them ground away until his eyes are suited. The pebble is cut in a lathe, by a wire-saw working in its own dust, into a round shape with plane edges. When worn, the rim rests upon the cheek-bones; the frame has a hinge between the glasses, and the machine is sometimes kept on the ears by loops or weights. Foreign-shaped spectacles are supplanting these primitive optics, but the prejudice is still in favor of crystal. The cutting of diamonds is sometimes attempted, but it is not a favorite gem among the Chinese. Diamonds and corundums are both employed to drill holes in clamping and mending broken glass and porcelain; tumblers, jars, etc., are joined so securely in this way without cement as to hold fluids. Both these gems are used to cut glass, but another mode, not uncommon, is to grease the place to be fractured, and slowly follow the line along by a lighted joss-stick until it breaks.

Sir John Davis condensed all the important information known half a century ago concerning the materials and manufacture of porcelain in his valuable work, but great advance has since been made in a better understanding of this branch of Chinese industry. The word *porcelain* is derived from *porcellana*, which was given to the ware by the Portuguese under the belief that it was made from the fusion of egg-shells and fish's glue and scales to resemble the nacre of sea-shells (Cypræa) or porcellana. This instance of off-hand nomenclature is like that of the Chinese calling caoutchouc *elephant's skin* from its appearance.

M. Julien's translation of the *King-teh chin Tau Luh* (Paris, 1856) furnishes the native accounts of the porcelain manufactures at Kingteh chin, in Kiangsí, and adds so much from other sources that his work is a veritable classic in its special branch. He places the invention of porcelain between B.C. 185 and A.D. 85, and opening the first kiln, at Sinping (not far from the present centre of Honan province), under the reign of Changtí of the Eastern Han dynasty. From this the manufacture gradually extended as raw materials were found in other localities, especially in Fauliang, on the eastern shores of the Poyang Lake, where the best ware is still made. A second preface to this work, written by M. Salvétat, of the manufactory at Sèvres, gives the details of the introduction of the art into Europe about 1722, and the subsequent improvement to the time when European wares far exceeded the Chinese or Japanese for beauty. During the dreadful ravages of the Taiping rebellion the manufactories at Kingteh were all stopped.

A very brief epitome of M. Salvétat's paper will indicate the ingredients of porcelain and their manipulation: Two substances enter into all kinds of this ware; one a strong, infusible material which endures great heat, and the other, fusible at a low temperature, which communicates its transparency to the other as they together pass through the furnace. The first of these is called *kaolin*, from the name of a range of hills east of Kingteh chin, known as *Kao Ling* or 'High Ridge,' a word that has been adopted in Europe as a term for all varieties of the argillaceous or feldspathic components of porcelain. The other is known as *peh-tun tsz'*, a Chinese term properly applied to the bricks of prepared silex, called *tun*, but now generally adopted to denote the fusible element. The discovery near Taochau fu of both of these in great purity led to the establishment of the kilns there in A.D. 583; and Chinese artists discriminate many varieties of each. It is apparently only since A.D. 1000, or thereabouts, that these kilns have produced the choice pieces now so highly prized.

The kaolin comes from decomposed granite, and is reduced by trituration and several washings to an impalpable powder; this last precipitate is put on cloths, one above another, and dried under slight pressure to a uniform paste ready for the furnace. The cakes of *peh-tun-tsz'* are prepared in a similar manner; other workmen mix the clay and the quartz—the bones and the flesh, as they are aptly called by the Chinese—in such proportions as the ware requires. In general, Chinese porcelain is more silicious than European, containing 70 parts of silex, 22 of alumine, 6 of potash and soda, with traces of lime, manganese, magnesia, and iron. Sèvres ware has 58 silex, 34½ alumine, 3 alkali, and 4½ lime; as the feldspar decreases the beauty of the ware diminishes, but its durability and usefulness increase.

To make ready the paste for the furnace, the bricks of both ingredients are trodden in a large basin by buffaloes or men till they are well mixed into a watery mass, which is then worked and kneaded again on slate slabs in small pieces till it is delivered into the hands of workmen to be fashioned on lathes and frames into the desired forms and sizes. These craftsmen work with very simple machinery, as is apparent from the rude drawings of their operations. M. Salvétat gives high praise to their skill in producing large jars without the aid of the machinery used in Europe, and indicates the great use they make of their feet in these operations—a feature of all Asiatic artisans which attracts the traveller's notice wherever he goes. Some of their procedures are inferior and ruder than the Japanese potters exhibit, but space does not allow them to be described in this sketch.

The glazing on Chinese ware contains silex mixed with lime and the ashes of burnt ferns, in such proportions as are found suitable for the different varieties. During the mixing of these ingredients the ashes are mostly eliminated, and the glazing really consists of quartz flexed by carbonate of lime. The liquid glaze is applied to the biscuit by dipping, by aspersion, and by washing, according to the nature of the ware; sometimes it is blown through a tube in a dewy shower oft repeated.

When ready for the furnace, the pieces are carried to workmen specially skilled in properly firing them, where the different sizes are placed in ovens particularly fitted to bake each kind. Large jars require a separate oven so as to adapt the fire to their size and thickness, continuing it at a uniform blast for several days. Cups and small pieces are baked one on top of another in smaller ovens, some of which are open and others closed. Coal and wood are both used for fuel. The pieces are taken from the furnaces when successfully baked, to be decorated and colored in all the various hues and pictures which have made Chinese porcelain so much sought after. Some of their ground colors of red, yellow, and green have not been equalled elsewhere; a careful analysis indicates the presence of the oxides of copper, cobalt, iron, lead, antimony, and manganese. Some of the rarest and most beautiful tints seem to have been the result of happy experiment, the knowledge of which died with its manufacture. It is not often that the Chinese artist adorns his plaque or jar with mythological or religious characters, preferring to let his fancy run riot in grotesque combinations of natural scenes, amid which, however, the unerring instinct or the accumulated experience of many successive generations seldom permit him to wander from a truly artistic conception. The amount of labor devoted to some minute treasure of porcelain decoration is little short of fabulous. Mr. Matthew Arnold's picture of the "cunning workman" who

> Pricks with vermilion some clear porcelain vase,
> An emperor's gift—at early morn he paints,
> And all day long, and when night comes, the lamp
> Lights up his studious forehead and thin hands,

could probably be seen scores of times in the humbler quarters of great cities in China.

Their ignorance of analytical chemistry compels them to follow a rule of thumb in the composition of their colors; but generally they use oxide of copper for green and bluish greens, gold for reds, oxide of cobalt for blues, of antimony for yellows, and of arsenic and tin for whites. The preparation and application of these materials admit of less scope and beauty than are found on the finest European ware, and their result is more like enamelling than painting. M. Salvétat admits that the Chinese potter has excelled in producing craquele ware, and certain hues, as sea-green, deep rosedon reds, and brilliant blues, which have not been equalled in Europe.

One elegant mode of ornament peculiar to them is seen in the *tao-ming tsz'-kí*, *lit.*, 'clear, bright porcelain,' called eyelet-hole ware or grains of rice, made in the reign Kienlung. The paste is cut through by a kind of stamp which takes out enough to form the figure, in which the glaze is inserted before the piece is finally joined and ready for the kiln. When fired the glaze becomes transparent; different patterns are frequently painted on the two surfaces, in which advantage is taken of the eyelet-holes to adapt them to two sets of figures. An instance of mechanical skill is occasionally seen in their articulated vases, in which one jar is baked inside of another, the outer one being perforated so as to show off the object within; the baking of such pieces must be very difficult and uncertain.

The ware sold at Canton for foreign use is painted in that city to suit the caprice of purchasers, and during the present century has become identified abroad with Chinese art, while it is really a combination of two or three styles. Its peculiarity consists in covering the dish with medallions and vignettes in bright colors, containing figures of heroes, arms, birds, etc., or scenes on a colored or white ground. Such ware is not commonly used by the Chinese, but its manufacture is unhappily beginning to affect their national taste. This style is quite different from the well-known blue willow pattern which has long been regarded as the *real Celestial ware.* This color does mark the common pottery and stoneware used all over the Empire by the poor, but the pattern is not so common.

It is not possible to enter here into all the niceties of this subject, which is now attracting great attention, and has been examined by Jacquemart, Prime, Young, and many others. Further researches into native and foreign books and collections will bring out new facts, legends, and specimens, while we may look for rare old pieces, as has been the case with the discovery of the small perfume bottles in Egypt, as soon as full liberty is given over all Asia to seek and dig.

Besides table furniture, porcelain statuettes and idols are common, and vases often bring extravagant prices, owing to some quality of fineness, coloring, antiquity, or shape, which native connoisseurs can only appreciate. The god of porcelain himself is usually made of this material. D'Entrecolles, in his account of the manufacture of the ware, says that this deity owes his divinity to his self-immolation in one of the furnaces in utter despair at being able to accomplish the Emperor's orders for the production of some vases of peculiar fineness; the pieces which came out of the furnace after the wretch was burned pleased his Majesty so much that he deified him. Cheap stoneware is made at Shauking, in Kwangtung, and many other places, some of it very pure and white.

The exportation of porcelain has formed a very ancient branch of commerce westward, and it is not strange that specimens should occasionally be met with even at a great distance from China. The discovery of Chinese bottles in Egypt and Asia Minor, containing quotations from Chinese poets, shows that intercourse existed between the extremes of Asia in the tenth or eleventh centuries. Rosellini seems to have been the earliest to notice these relics of an ancient trade, during his researches in Egypt in 1828, when he obtained two or three. In a letter written in reply to one from Sir J. F. Davis, he states that he found one of these little bottles in a "petit panier tissu de feuilles de palmier," with other objects of Egyptian manufacture, in a tomb, whose date he places between B.C. 1800 and 1100. His words are, "Ayant penétré dans un de ces trois tombeaux j'y ai trouvé," etc., which is as explicit as possible. He also adds, that many fragments of similar bottles had been offered to him by the peasants, which he had looked upon as quite modern till this discovery showed that they were real antiques.

Since then, several more have been picked up; Dr. Abbott's Egyptian collection in New York contains seventeen, all of which came from Egypt, but none, besides Rosellini's, out of a tomb directly into the hands of an Egyptologist. Layard and Cesnola bought similar bottles in Cyprus and Arban. However, one well-authenticated fact, like that of Rosellini's discovery, gives some evidence of a similar ancient origin to others precisely like it in shape, coloring, and inscriptions, for the trade between Arabia and Egypt to China has long since ceased; but as fifty years have passed without another bottle occurring in any of the numerous tombs opened by careful and competent persons, one is inclined to think that Rosellini's tomb may have been twice used to bury mummies in, or that he mistook its age.

The inscriptions and style of writing of five different kinds have been engraved, and Sir Walter H. Medhurst gives a translation of each, tracing the lines to their original authors. One of them is from Wang Wai (A.D. 702–745), and reads, *Ming yueh sung chung chao*, 'The bright moon shines amidst the firs.' A second reads, *Chih tsai tsz' shan chung*, 'Only in the midst of these mountains,' and it dates A.D. 831–837. A third is contracted from a line by Wei Ying-wuh (A.D. 702–795), being part of a stanza of eight lines, as follows: *Hwo kai yiu yih nien*, 'The flowers open, and lo, another year!' A fourth dates from A.D. 1068–1085, and is from the famous poet Su Tung-po: *Hăng hwa hung shih lí*, 'The apricot flowers bloom for miles around;' this is abridged from a distich in pentameter as follows:

> One mass of color, the apricot flowers bloom for miles around;
> The successful graduate urges on his steed as if flying.

Sir John Davis ascribes this inscription to a Chinese song written prior to the Christian era, but gives no proof of so early a date, and he is probably in error. The fifth inscription is of the same date as the last; it forms part of a quatrain by Chao Yung, and reads, *Liao teh shao jin chí*, 'Which few, I ween, can comprehend.' In Prime's work on pottery he has given fac-similes of five bottles whose inscriptions are the same as those explained by Medhurst; his No. 142 and No. 146 is the second in this list; his No. 143 is the first; his 144 is the third; and his 145 is the fifth and is different in shape from the others. The characters on the one found at Arban by Layard are written in a very cursive style.[1]

The age and origin of these bottles has excited much inquiry, but the weight of evidence points to their having been taken to Egypt and Arabia by the Arabs who traded at Canton and Hangchau down to the end of the Sung dynasty in 1278. They were, as Wilkinson suggests in his *Ancient Egyptians*, probably used by the purchasers to hold *kohl* to paint the eyes and

[1] Davis' *Sketches*, Vol. II., pp. 72–84. Medhurst's *China*, p. 135. Julien's *Histoire de la Porcelain Chinoise*, pp. xi–xxii. Prime's *Pottery and Porcelain*, p. 232. *N. C. Br. R. A. S. Transactions*, 1852, pp. 34–40; 1854, p. 93.

eyelids of women; their original use was probably to hold peppermint and other oils, bandoline and tooth-powders, though snuff is now generally carried in them, as glass bottles contain the essences and oils seen in shops. The uniformity in size, shape, coloring, and decoration in these bottles indicates that the trade was rather confined to one port in China, for at present a vast variety in all these particulars would be seen, as I ascertained some years ago at Canton when unsuccessfully looking in the shops for some having inscriptions like those discovered in Egypt. Mr. Fortune found one having the same inscription as No. 2, and Sir Harry Parkes came across three others, but their rarity now proves the change; and these were probably real antiques. The latter found two other inscriptions on similar bottles in China, whose authors lived A.D. 584 and later; and argues against their high antiquity from the metre having been introduced in later times. The strongest proof of their modern origin is the material and the date of the style of writing, neither of which could have been prior to the Han dynasty if Chinese records are worth anything; such simple lines as these five could indeed have been handed down and adopted by later poets from lost authors, but this possibility weighs nothing against the others. The more antiquarian researches extend in Asia, however, the more shall we find that the books and inscriptions now extant do not contain the earliest dates of inventions and travels.

The cheap pottery of the Chinese resembles the Egyptian ware in color and brittleness, but is less porous when unglazed. Tea-kettles, pans, plates, teapots, and articles of household use, bathing-tubs, immense jars, comparable to hogsheads, for holding water, fancy images, statuettes, figurines, toys, flower-pots, and a thousand other articles are everywhere burned from clay and sold at extremely low prices. The jars are used in shops to contain liquids, powders, etc.; in gardens to keep fish, collect rain, and receive manure and offal; and in boats and houses for the same purposes that barrels, pails, and pans are put to elsewhere. Water will boil sooner and a dish of vegetables be cooked more expeditiously in one of these earthen pots than in metal; the caloric seems to permeate the clay almost as soon as it is over the fire. Drum-shaped stools and garden seats, vitruvian ornaments for balustrades, fanciful flower-pots in the shape of buffaloes, representing the animal feeding under the shade of a tree growing out of its body, fishes, dragons, phœnixes, and other objects for decorating the ridges and for gargoyles are manufactured of this ware. Flat figures of the human form are set into frames to represent groups of persons, or elegantly shaped characters are arranged into sentences, both of them to put on the walls of rooms, making altogether a great variety of purposes to which this material is applied.

The lacquered-ware peculiar to China and Japan owes its lustre to the prepared sap of a kind of sumach (*Rhus vernicifera*) cultivated in both countries for this purpose. Wood oils are obtained from other plants, such as the *Curcas*, *Augia*, *Elcococcus*, and *Rhus semi-alatus*, and the different qualities of lacquered-ware are owing to the use of these inferior ingredients. The real varnish-tree is described by De Guignes as resembling the ash in its foliage and bark; it is about fifteen feet in height, and when seven years old furnishes the sap, which is carefully collected in the summer nights from incisions cut in the trunk. It comes to market in tubs holding the cakes, and those who collect it are careful to cover their faces and hands from contact with this irritating juice as they prepare it for market. A good yield of a thousand trees in one night would be twenty pounds avoirdupois weight of sap. The best sort is tawny rather than white in its inspissated state, and is kept well protected from the air by tarred paper. The body of lacquered-ware is usually seasoned pine, well smoothed, and the grooves covered with hempen lint or paper. A sizing of pig's gall, often mixed with very fine sand, makes a priming. The prepared lacquer is composed of the sap dissolved in spring-water, adding ground-nut oil, pig's gall, and rice vinegar in the sunshine with broad flat brushes till it is thoroughly mixed.

The principal object in preparing the wood is to cover it with a priming that will receive the lacquer and remain impervious to changes in temperature. This preparation varies a good deal according to the quality of the ware; it is laid on evenly, coat after coat, allowing each to dry before the next is spread.

The last coating is rubbed with pumice or the finest sandstone, finishing this priming with a smooth piece of slate. When ready the piece is taken into a close room having paper lattices and shut out from any air, where it receives a coating of clear lacquer. It is then put into a dark room to dry. The operation is repeated ten or fifteen times for the best kinds. Some workmen are so sensitive to the liquid lacquer that they cannot safely do this part of the manufacture; others go through all the processes without annoyance. Coloring matter to give the lacquer a brown hue, or to make an imitation of *venturina* (or *aventurine*, a brownish glass spangled throughout with copper filings) by mixing gold leaf, is added during these operations.

The gilding is performed by another set of workmen in a large workshop. The figures of the design are drawn on thick paper, which is then pricked all over to allow the powdered chalk to fall on the table and form the outline. Another workman completes the picture by cutting the lines with a burin or needle, and filling them with vermilion mixed in lacquer, as thick as needed. This afterward is covered by means of a hair-pencil with gold in leaf, or in powder laid on with a dossil; the gold is often mixed with fine lampblack. The proper lacquer is seldom used otherwise than in making this ware. The Chinese term for *tsih* includes this and all kinds of oils and paints, so that some confusion arises in describing their materials.[1] A beautiful fabric of lacquered-ware is made by inlaying the nacre of fresh and salt-water shells in a rough mosaic of flowers, animals, etc., into the composition, and then varnishing it. Another highly prized kind is made by covering the wood with a coating of fine powdered cinnabar and varnish three or four lines in thickness, and then carving figures upon it in relief. The great labor necessary to produce this ware renders it expensive, and it is not now produced.

The oils obtained from the nuts of other trees by simple pressure and by refining them afterward are quite numerous.

---

[1] N. Rondot, *Commerce de la Chine*, p. 120; *Journal Asiatique*, IV. Series, Tome XI., 1848, pp. 34–65; *Chinese Commercial Guide*, 5th Ed., p. 124.

The details of their manufacture and application may yet furnish many new hints and processes to western arts. The oil of the Eleococcus, after pressing (according to De Guignes), is boiled with Spanish white in the proportion of one ounce to half a pound of oil; as it begins to thicken it is taken off and poured into close vessels. It dissolves in turpentine and is used as a varnish, either clear or mixed with different colors; it defends woodwork from injury for a long time, and forms a good painter's oil. Boiled with iron rust it forms a reddish brown varnish. In order to prevent its penetrating into the wood when used clear, and to increase the lustre, a priming of lime and hog's blood simmered together into a paste is previously laid on.

The manufacture of silk is original among the Chinese, as well as those of porcelain and lacquered-ware, and in none of these have foreigners yet succeeded in fully equalling the native products. The notices of the cultivation of the mulberry and the rearing of silk-worms found in Chinese works have been industriously collected and published by M. Julien by order of the French government—another instance of the intelligent care of this nation to aid one of its great industries. The introduction by M. Beauvais indicates certain points worthy of the notice of cultivators; it has been remarked that the hints thus obtained from Julien's translation have been of more value to the people employed in silk culture in France than all that has been paid by the government for the promotion of Chinese literature from their first outlay in the last century.

The earliest notice in the *Shu King* of silk culture occurs in the *Yu Kung*. It is said the mulberry grounds were made fit for silk-worms, when speaking of the draining of Yen Chau (parts of Shantung and Chihlí), as if it was an usual culture; other references to silk in the same book show it to have been a well-known fabric at that date (B.C. 2204). The allusion, therefore, in the *Book of Odes* to silks of many sorts also strengthen the notice in the *Wei Kí*, which says:

> Síling shí, the Empress of Hwangtí, began to rear silk-worms:
> At this period Hwangtí invented the art of making clothing.

This legend carries the art back to B.C. 2600, or perhaps five centuries after the Deluge. Síling is said to have been her birthplace, and Lui Tsu her right name; she was deified and is still worshipped as the goddess of silk under the name of Yuenfí. In this act, as De Guignes observes, the Chinese resemble other ancient nations in ascribing the invention of spinning to women, and deifying them; thus the Egyptian Isis, the Lydian Arachne, and the Grecian Athene also handled the distaff. A temple called the *Sien-tsan Tao* exists in the palace grounds dedicated to Yuenfí, wherein she is worshipped annually in April by the Empress. The altar, grounds, sacrifices, ritual, and buildings are all in imitation of those in the Temple of Agriculture, of which they are a counterpart. The *Book of Rites* contains a notice of the festival held in honor of weaving, which corresponds to that of ploughing by the Emperor. "In the last month of spring the young Empress purified herself and offered a sacrifice to the goddess of silk-worms. She went into the eastern fields and collected mulberry leaves. She forbade noble dames and the ladies of statesmen adorning themselves, and excused her attendants from their sewing and embroidery, in order that they might give all their care to the rearing of silk-worms." The present enclosure was put up by Yungching in 1742, but its buildings are now much dilapidated.

The attention of the Chinese government to this important branch of industry has been unremitted, and at this day it supplies perhaps one-half of all the garments worn by the people. In the paraphrase to the fourth maxim of the *Shing Yu*, it is remarked: "In ancient times emperors ploughed the lands and empresses cultivated the mulberry. Though the most honorable, they did not disdain to toil and labor, as examples to the whole Empire, in order to induce all the people to seek these essential supports." One-half of the *Illustrations of Agriculture and Weaving* are devoted to delineating the various processes attending this manufacture; and Julien quotes more than twenty works and authors on this subject. Among other uses to which this material is put, may be remembered, in the second chapter of this work, the burning of many thousand pieces of plain, coarse silk as part of the offerings to the gods at Peking, and in the annual sacrifices before the tablets of Confucius.[1]

While the worms are growing, care is taken to keep them undisturbed by either noise or bright light; they are often changed from one hurdle to another that they may have roomy and cleanly places; the utmost attention is paid to their condition and feeding, and noting the right time for preparing them for spinning cocoons. Three days are required for this, and in six it is time to stifle the larvæ and reel the silk from the cocoons; but this being usually done by other workmen, those who rear the worms enclose the cocoons in a jar buried in the ground and lined with mats and leaves, interlaying them with salt, which kills the pupæ but keeps the silk supple, strong, and lustrous; preserved in this manner, they can be transported to any distance, or the reeling of the silk can be delayed until convenient. Another mode of destroying the cocoons is to spread them on trays and expose them by twos to the steam of boiling water, putting the upper in the place of the lower one according to the degree of heat they are in, taking care that the chrysalides are killed and the silk not injured. After exposure to steam the silk can be reeled off immediately, but if placed in the jars they must be put into warm water to dissolve the glue before the floss can be unwound.

The commission sent from France to China in 1844 to make inquiries into its industries consisted of skilled men, and their reports embody a great amount of details nowhere else to be found. The digested catalogue of the exhibits of M. Hedde at St. Etienne in 1848 contains four hundred and fifty-three articles relating to silk and mulberry alone. The amount of silk goods exported has never regained its value previous to 1854, in consequence of the destruction of skilled workmen and manufactories during the Tai-ping rebellion, and raw silk still forms the bulk of the export. The finest silk comes from Chehkiang province, and is known as *tsatli*, *tay-saam*, and *yuenhwa* in com-

[1] Julien, *Culturer des Muriers*, 1837; Pauthier, *Chine Moderne*, p. 21; Hedde, *Catalogue des Produits Sérigènes*, 1848, pp. 106–287; *Chinese Repository*, Vol. XVIII., pp. 303–314; *Commercial Guide*, 5th Ed., p. 136; Mailla, *Histoire de la Chine*, Tome I., p. 24; Biot, *Tcheou-li*, passim, 1851.

merce; the centre of the culture is at Hü-chau, a prefecture in the northwest of that province. The mulberry grows everywhere, and none of the provinces are without some silk, but Kwangtung, Sz'chuen, and Chehkiang furnish the best and most.

Great attention is paid in Shantung, Sz'chuen, and Kweichau to collecting wild silk from the cocoons of worms which feed on the ailantus, oak, and xanthoxylum. The insect is the *Attacus cynthia*, and its food the tender leaves of the ailantus and *Quercus mongholica* in Shantung, where great quantities of durable silk is woven. It is not so lustrous as that produced by the bombyx-worm, which feeds on the mulberry leaf, and comparatively little is exported. The proportion of manufactured silks sent abroad is less now than it was fifty years ago, but the home consumption is so enormous that an annual export to the value of nearly ninety millions of dollars has little effect on the prices. In 1854 the price of the best raw silk was about $330 a bale, and the export over fifty-one thousand bales; in 1860, the same sort was $550, and the export nearly eighty thousand bales; this increase in price was owing chiefly to disease in the trees in Europe, though the ravages of war in both Chehkiang and Kwangtung had destroyed much property in this branch.

The loom in China is worked by two hands, one of whom sits on the top of the frame, where he pulls the treadles and assists in changing the various parts of the machine. The workmen imitate almost any pattern, excelling particularly in crapes, and flowered satins and damasks for official dresses. The common people wear pongee and senshaw, which they frequently dye in gambier to a dust or black color; these fabrics constitute most durable garments. Many of the delicate silk tissues known in Europe are not manufactured by the Chinese, most of their fabrics being heavy. The *lo*, or law, is a beautiful article like grenadine and seldom sent abroad; it is used for summer robes, musquito curtains, festoons, and other purposes. The English words *satin*, *senshaw*, and *silk* are probably derived from the Chinese terms *sz'-twan*, *sien-sha*, and *sz'*, intermediately through other languages.

The skill of the Chinese in embroidery is well known, and the demand for such work to adorn the dresses of officers and ladies of every rank, for ornamenting purses, shoes, caps, fans, and other appendages of the dress of both sexes, and in working shawls, table covers, etc., for exportation, furnishes employment to myriads of men and women. The frame is placed on pivots and the pattern marked out upon the plain surface. There are many styles, with thread, braid, or floss, and an infinite variety in the quality, pattern, and beauty of the work; it is the art of Chinese women, and every young lady is expected to know how to do it. On fire screens the design appears the same on both sides, the ends of the threads being neatly concealed. This mode of embroidery seems also to have been known among the Hebrews, from the expression in Deborah's song (Judges v. 30), "Of divers colors of needle-work on both sides," which Sisera's mother vainly looked for him to bring home as spoil for her. Books are prepared for embroiderers containing patterns for their imitation or combination. The silk used is of the finest kind and color, gold and silver thread being introduced to impart a lustre to the figures on caps, purses, and shoes. Tassels and twisted cords for sedans or lanterns, knobs or buttons worn on the winter caps, and elegant fan and pipe-cases, purses or fobs, constitute only a few of the products of their needles. Spangles are made from brass leaves by cutting out a small ring by means of a double-edged stamp, which at one drive detaches from the sheet a wheel-shaped circle; these are flattened by a single stroke of the hammer upon an anvil, leaving a minute hole in the centre. Another way of making them is to bend a copper wire into a circle and flatten it. Their own needles are very slender, and are rapidly giving way to the foreign article; in sewing the tailor holds it between the forefinger and thumb, pressing against the thimble on the thumb as he pushes it into the cloth.

Our ascertaining the date of the introduction of cotton as a textile plant into China depends very much on the meaning of certain words rendered *cotton* by some annotators in the *Shu King*. The weight of proof is, however, strongly adverse to this view; but a historical notice dated about A.D. 500 plainly refers to cotton robes; in A.D. 670 it was called by a foreign name *kih-pei*, a contracted form of the Sanscrit name *karpasi*. The present name of *mien-hwa*, or 'cotton flower,' was naturally given to it from the resemblance of its seed envelope to the silky covering of the seeds of the *muh-mien shu*, or tree cotton (*Bombax*), common in Southern China. It was, however, one thing to admire cotton cloth brought as tribute, and quite another to introduce cotton-growing into China, which does not seem to have been attempted until the Sung dynasty. Early in the eleventh century the plant was brought over and cultivated in the northwestern provinces by persons from Khoten, where it was grown. If this tardy adoption seems difficult to explain, the still slower introduction of silk-growing (in A.D. 550) into Asia Minor from China, twelve centuries after her fabrics had been seen there, is more surprising. The opposition to cotton cultivation on the part of silk and hemp growers was so persistent that the plant had not fairly won its way into favor until the Yuen dynasty; and this was owing to a public-spirited woman, Lady Hwang, who distributed seeds throughout Kiangnan, now the great cotton region.

The durable cotton cloth made in the central provinces, called *nankeen* by foreigners, because Nanking is famous for its manufacture, is the chief produce of Chinese looms. It is now seldom sent out of the country, and the natives are even taking to the foreign fabric in its stead. Cotton seed in that part of China is sown early in June, about eighty pounds to an acre; in a good year the produce is about two thousand pounds, diminishing to one-half in poor seasons. It is manured with liquid bean-cake, often hoed, and the bolls gathered in October, usually by each family in its own plot. The seeds are separated by passing the pods between an iron and wooden roller on a frame, which presses out the seeds and does not break them. The cleaned cotton is then bowed ready for spinning, and the cloth is woven in simple looms by the people who are to wear it after it is dyed blue. The looms used in weaving cotton vary from twelve to sixteen inches in width; they are simple in their construction; no figures are woven in cotton fabrics, nor have the Chinese learned to print them as chintz or calico.

Whether the varied articles from the west now brought into close competition with this primitive Chinese manufacture will finally captivate the consumer's choice, and neutralize its production, depends chiefly on what can be substituted therefor. At present, such is the extent of the native crop that prices would not probably advance ten per cent. if the whole foreign importation of raw and manufactured cotton should suddenly stop. The only attempt to estimate the product has been in Kiangnan, at

The Cobbler and his Movable Workshop.

twenty-eight thousand five hundred tons, a figure below rather than above the truth.[1]

Leather is used to protect the felt soles of shoes and make saddles, bridles, quivers, harness, etc., but the entire consumption is small, and the leather extremely poor. Buffalo and horse-hides are tanned for sole leather, and calf-skin for upper leather to supply shoes for foreigners at the ports. Alum, saltpetre, gambier, and urine are the tanning materials employed, and the rapid manner in which the process is completed renders the leather both porous and tender.

Cobblers go about the streets plying their trade, provided

[1] *Journal N. C. Br. R. A. S.* (1859); *Chinese Repository*, XVIII., pp. 449–469; N. Rondot, *Commerce de la Chine*, 1849, p. 72; Fortune, *Wanderings*, Chap. XIV. (1847); Grosier, *Histoire de la Chine*, Tome III., pp. 193–204.

with a few bits of nankeen, silk, and yellowish sole leather with which to patch their customers' shoes. It is no small convenience to a man, as he passes along the street, to give his old shoe to a cobbler and his ragged jacket to a seamstress, while he calls the barber to shave him as he waits for them; and such a trio at work for a man is not an uncommon sight.

The chief woollen fabrics produced are felts of different qualities and rugs or carpets woven from coarse camel's-hair yarn. Tanned sheep-skins furnish the laboring poor in the northern provinces with clothing, and elsewhere felt supplies them with material for shoes, hats, and carpets. The fulling process is not very thoroughly done, and the fabric soon disintegrates unless protected by matting or cotton. The consumption of the good qualities for hats is large among out-door workmen, who prefer the doubled kind made in the shape of a hollow cycloid, so that it can be turned inside out. Camel's-hair rugs supply a durable and cheap covering for the brick divans and tiled floors in the colder districts, but the thick soles of Chinese shoes obviate the need of additional protection to the feet. Some of these rugs are fine specimens of art in their arrangement of patterns and figures in colored woollen yarns, though far inferior to the Persian. Pretty rugs are also made of dog, deer, and fox-skins sewed together in a kind of mosaic. Knitting and ornamental works in wool are unknown, since the far more elegant and durable embroidery in silk takes the place of these as fancy work among dames of high and low degree.

The subject of tea culture and the preparation of its leaf have engaged the attention of writers among the Chinese and Japanese; while its effects on the human system as a beverage have been discussed most carefully by eminent western chemists and pathologists. Its virtue in restoring the energies of the body and furnishing a drink of the gentlest and most salubrious nature has been fully tested in its native land for many centuries, and is rapidly becoming known the world over. The following are some of the leading facts relating to the plant and the preparation and nature of the leaf, derived from personal observation in the country or from the writings of competent observers.

Tea does not grow in the northern provinces of China and Japan; its range lies between the twenty-third and thirty-fifth degrees of latitude, and reaching in longitude from Yedo to Assam. No accounts have come to us of the tea shrub being cultivated for its infusion till A.D. 350. The people in different parts of China gave different names to the successive pickings of the leaves, which have now become disused. Our word *tea* is derived from the common sound of the character for the plant at the city of Amoy, where it is *tay;* at Canton and Peking it is *cha*, at Shanghai *dzo*, at Fuhchau *ta*. The Russians and Portuguese have retained the word *cha*, the Spanish is *te* or *tay*, and the Italians have both *te* and *cha*. Tea is so nearly akin to the various species of camellia that the Chinese have only one name for all. The principal difference to the common observer is in the thin leaf of the tea and the leathery glabrous leaf of the beautiful Camellia Japonica. When allowed to grow they both become high trees. The tea flower is small, single, and white, has no smell, and soon falls; its petals are less erect than the camellia. The seeds are three small nuts, like filberts in color, enclosed in a triangular shell which splits open when ripe, with valves between the seeds. Its taste is oily and bitter. Two species of camellia are cultivated for their oily seeds, the oil being known as tea-oil among the natives; it is used for lamps and cooking. There is probably only one species of the tea plant, and all the varieties have resulted from culture; but the *Thea viridis* is most cultivated. The nuts are ripe in October. They are put in a mixture of sand and earth, dampened to keep them fresh till spring; they generate heat and spoil if not thus separated. In March they are sown in a nursery, and the thrifty shoots transplanted the next year in rows about four feet apart. Leaves are collected when the plant is three years old, and this process is continued annually to a greater or less extent, according to the demand and strength, until the whole bush becomes so weak and diseased that it is pulled up for firewood to give place to a new shoot. On the average this is about the eighth year. The plants seldom exceed three feet; most of them are half that height, straggling and full of twigs, often covered with lichens, but well hoed and clean around their roots.

All tea plantations are merely patches of the shrubs cared for by small farmers, who cultivate the plants and sell the leaves to middle-men, or more often pick the crop themselves if they can afford to do so. The great plantation or farm, with its landlord and the needy laborer, each class trying to get as much as possible out of the other, are unknown in China; the farmer has not there learned to employ skill, machinery, and capital all for his own advantage, but each farmstead is worked by the family, who rather emulate each other in the reputation of their tea. Tea is cultivated on the slopes or bases of hills, where the drainage is quick and the moisture unfailing. This is of more consequence than the ingredients of the soil, but plants so continually depauperated and stripped require rich manure to supply their waste. In Japan the tea shrubs are sometimes grown as a hedge around a garden lot, but such plants are not stripped in this way. In gathering the earliest leaves, the pickers are careful to leave enough foliage at the end of the twigs; and the spring rains are depended on to stimulate the second and full crop of leaves. When these are scant or fail, the tea harvest diminishes, and the regularity of the rains is so essential to a profitable cultivation that it will be one of the causes of failure where everything else in soil, climate, manuring, and manufacture may be favorable.

The first gathering is the most carefully done, for it goes to make the best sorts of black and green tea; and as the greatest part of the leaves are still undeveloped, the price must necessarily be very much higher. Such tea has a whitish down, like that on young birch leaves, and is called *pecoe*, or 'white hair,' and is most of it sent to England and Russia. In the last century, the green tea known as Young Hyson was made of these half-opened leaves picked in April and named from two words meaning 'rains before.' The second gathering varies somewhat according to the latitude—May 15th to June, when the foliage is fullest. This season is looked forward to by women and children in the tea districts as their working time; they run in crowds to the middle-men, who have bargained for the leaves on the plants, or apply to farmers who have not hands. The average produce is from sixteen to twenty-two ounces of green leaves for the healthiest plants, down to ten and eight ounces. The tea when cured is about one-fifth of its first weight, and one thousand square yards will contain about three hundred and fifty plants, each two feet across. They strip the twigs in the most summary manner, and fill their baskets with healthy leaves as they pick out the sticks and yellow leaves, for they are paid in this manner. Fifteen pounds is a good day's work, and six to eight cents is a day's wages. The time for picking lasts only ten or twelve days. There are curing houses, where families who grow and pick their own leaves bring them for sale at the market rate. The sorting employs many hands, for it is an important point in connection with the purity of the various descriptions, and much care is taken by dealers, in maintaining the quality of their lots, to have them cured carefully as well as sorted properly.

The management of this great branch of industry exhibits some of the best features of Chinese country life. It is only over a portion of each farm that the plant is grown, and its cultivation requires but little attention compared with rice and vegetables. The most delicate kinds are looked after and cured by priests in their secluded temples among the hills; these often have many acolytes who aid in preparing small lots to be sold at a high price.

When the leaves are brought in to the curers they are thinly spread on shallow trays to dry off all moisture by two or three hours' exposure. Meanwhile the roasting pans are heating, and when properly warmed some handfuls of leaves are thrown on them, and rapidly moved and shaken up for four or five minutes. The leaves make a slight crackling noise, become moist and flaccid as the juice is expelled, and give off even a sensible vapor. The whole is then poured out upon the rolling table, where each workman takes up a handful and makes it into a manageable ball, which he rolls back and forth on the rattan table to get rid of the sap and moisture as the leaves are twisted. This operation chafes the hands even with great precaution. The balls are opened and shaken out and then passed on to other workmen, who go through the same operation till they reach the headman, who examines the leaves to see if they have become curled. When properly done, and cooled, they are returned to the iron pans, under which a low charcoal fire is burning in the brickwork which supports them, and there kept in motion by the hand. If they need another rolling on the table it is now given them; an hour or more is spent in this manipu-

Mode of Firing Tea.

lation, when they are dried to a dull green color, and can be put away for sifting and sorting. This color becomes brighter after the exposure in sifting the cured leaves through sieves of various sizes; they are also winnowed to separate the dust, and afterward sorted into the various descriptions of green tea. Finally, the finer kinds are again fired three or four times, and the coarse kinds, as Twankay, Hyson, and Hyson Skin, once. The others furnish the Young Hyson, Gunpowder, Imperial, etc. Tea cured in this way is called *luh cha*, or 'green tea,' by the Chinese, while the other, or black tea, is termed *hung cha*, or 'red tea,' each name being taken from the tint of the infusion.

After the fresh leaves are allowed to lie exposed to the air on the bamboo trays over night or several hours, they are thrown into the air and tossed about and patted till they become soft; a heap is made of these wilted leaves and left to lie for an hour or more, when they have become moist and dark in color. They are then thrown on the hot pans for five minutes and rolled on the rattan table, previous to exposure out-of-doors for three or four hours on sieves, during which time they are turned over and opened out. After this they get a second roasting and rolling to give them their final curl. When the charcoal fire is ready, a basket shaped something like an hour-glass is placed endwise over it, having a sieve in the middle on which the leaves are thinly spread. When dried five minutes in this way they undergo another rolling, and are then thrown into a heap, until all the lot has passed over the fire. When this firing is finished, the leaves are opened out and are again thinly spread on the sieve in the basket for a few minutes, which finishes the drying and rolling for most of the heap, and makes the leaves a uniform black. They are now replaced in the basket in greater mass, and pushed against its sides by the hands in order to allow the heat to come up through the sieve and the vapor to escape; a basket over all retains the heat, but the contents are turned over until perfectly dry and the leaves become uniformly dark.

It will be seen from this that green tea retains far more of the peculiar oil and sap in the leaves than the black, which undergo a partial fermentation and emit a sensibly warm vapor as they lie in heaps after the first roasting. They thus become oxidized by longer contact in a warm moist state with the atmosphere, and a delicate analysis will detect a greater amount of oxidized insoluble extract in an infusion of black than green tea. The same difference has been observed in drying medicinal plants, as hemlock, belladonna, etc., for the apothecary's shop.

Green teas are mostly produced in the region south of the Yangtsz' River and west of Ningpo among the hills as one goes toward the Poyang Lake in Chehkiang and Nganhwui. The black tea comes from Fuhkien in the southeast and Hupeh and Hunan in the central region; Kwangtung and Sz'chuen provinces produce black, green, and brick teas. While the leaves of each species of the shrub can be cured into either green or black tea, the workmen in one district are able, by practice, to produce one kind in a superior style and quality; those in another region will do better with another kind. Soil, too, has a great influence, as it has in grape culture, in modifying the produce. Though the natives distinguish only these three kinds, their varieties are far too numerous to remember, and the names are mostly unknown in commerce.

Of black teas, the great mass is called *Congou*, or the 'well-worked,' a name which took the place of the *Bohea* of one hundred and fifty years ago, and is now itself giving way to the term English Breakfast tea. The finest sorts are either named from the place of their growth, or more frequently have fancy appellations in allusion to their color or form. Orange Pekoe is named "superior perfume;" pure Pekoe is "Lau-tsz' eyebrows;" "carnation hair," "red plum blossom," "lotus kernel," "sparrow's tongue," "dragon's pellet," "dragon's whiskers," "autumn dew," "pearl flower," or *Chu-lan*, are other names; *Souchong* and *Powchong* refer to the modes of packing.

In the trade, teas are more commonly classified by their locality than their names, as it is found that well-marked differences in the style of the produce continue year after year, all equally well-cured tea. These arise from diversities in soil, climate, age, and manufacturing, and furnish materials for still further multiplying the sorts by skilfully mixing them. Thus in black teas we have Hunan and Hupeh from two provinces, just as Georgia uplands and Sea Island indicate two sorts of cotton; Ningyong, Kai-sau, Ho-hau, Sing-chune-kí, etc., and many others, which are unknown out of China, are all names of places. One gentleman has given a list of localities, each furnishing its quota and peculiar product, amounting in all to forty-five for black and nine for green. The area of these regions is about four hundred and seventy thousand square miles.

It will have been seen already that the color of green tea, as well as its quality, depends very much on rapid and expert drying. When this kind is intended for home consumption soon after it is made, the color is of little consequence; but when the hue influences the sale, then it is not to be overlooked by the manufacturer or the broker. The first tea brought to Europe was from Fuhkien and all black; but as the trade extended probably some of the delicate Hyson sorts were now and then seen at Canton, and their appearance in England and Holland appreciated as more and more was sent. It was found, however, to be very difficult to maintain a uniform tint. If cured too slightly, the leaf was liable to fermentation during the voyage; if cured too much, it was unmarketable, which for the manufacturer was worse yet. Chinese ingenuity was equal to the call. Though no patent office was at hand to register the date when coloring green tea commenced, it is probably more than one hundred years since. The three hundred and forty-two chests and half chests which were so summarily opened on board the Dartmouth, the Eleanor, and the Beaver, when their contents were thrown overboard in Boston harbor, on December 16, 1773, furnishes probably no index of the consumption of tea in New England at that time. It was all called Bohea by John Adams, who speaks of three cargoes, as if the vessels had nothing else of note in their holds.

Dr. Holmes, in his ballad on the Boston Tea Party at its centennial celebration, says in the last verse:

> The waters in the rebel bay
>   Have kept the tea-leaf savor—
> Our old North Enders in their spray
>   Still taste a Hyson flavor;
> And Freedom's teacup still o'erflows
>   With ever fresh libations,
> To cheat of slumber all her foes
>   And cheer the wakening nations.

It has been noticed that emigrants to Australia, who had seldom tasted green tea before leaving England, usually prefer it in their new homes, as new settlers do in this country. The prevailing notion that green tea is cured on copper arose, no doubt, from the conclusion that real verdigris was the only source of a verdigris color, and the astringent taste confirmed the wrong idea. A more difficult question to answer is the inquiry, Why is it still believed?

The operation of giving green tea its color is a simple one. A quantity of Prussian blue is pulverized to a very fine powder, and kept ready at the last roasting. Pure gypsum is burned in the charcoal fire till it is soft and fit for easily triturating. Four parts are then thoroughly mixed with three parts of Prussian blue, making a light blue powder. About five minutes before finally taking off the dried leaves this powder is sprinkled on them, and instantly the whole panful of two or three pounds is turned over by the workman's hands till a uniform color is obtained. His hands come out quite blue, but the compound gives the green leaves a brighter green hue. The quantity is not great, say about half a pound in a hundred of tea; and as gypsum is not a dangerous or irritating substance, being constantly eaten by the Chinese, the other ingredient remains in an almost infinitesimal degree. If foreigners preferred yellow teas no doubt they could be favored, for the Chinese are much perplexed to account for this strange predilection, as they never drink this colored or faced tea. Turmeric root has been detected, too, in a very few analyses, but probably these were lots that needed to be refined at Canton to cover up mildew or supply a demand. The reasons for not drinking this tea are, however, owing more to the nature than the color of the leaf. The kinds of green tea are fewer than the black, and the regions producing it are less in area. Gunpowder and Imperial are foreign-made terms; the teas are known as *siau chu* and *ta chu* by native dealers. The first is rolled to resemble shot or coarse gunpowder; the other is named "sore crab's eyes," "sesamum seeds," and "pearls." Hyson is a corruption of *yu-tsien*, 'before the rains,' and of *Hí-chun*, meaning 'flourishing spring.' The last is alleged to be the name of a maiden who suggested to her father as long ago as 1700, or thereabouts, a better mode of sorting tea, and his business increased so much as his fine Hyson became known that he gave it her name. Members of this same family are still engaged in making this same tea, and the chop, known as the *Lí Yih-hing*, or 'Li's Extra Perfume,' is now in market, and has maintained its reputation for nearly two hundred years. Oolong is obtained in Fuhkien—a black tea with a green tea flavor, named Black Dragon from a story that Su was struck with the fragrance of the leaf from a plant where a black snake was found coiled. The great mart for green tea is Twankay, in Chehkiang province.

A *chop* is a well-known term in the tea trade; it is derived from the Chinese word *chop*, or 'stamp', such as an official uses, and in the tea trade denotes a certain number of packages from the same place, and all of the same quality. In the course of years the uniform excellence of a certain chop, like that of a certain vineyard, gives it a marketable value. A lawsuit arose in 1873 between two American houses at Canton in regard to the right to a certain chop of tea, among two brokers, each of whom claimed to sell the genuine lot. Such chops range from fifty to one thousand two hundred chests, averaging six hundred. English tea-tasters have learned that an admixture of scented teas in common sorts of Congou adds much to the flavor and sale. This is not often done for native-drank tea, and is chiefly practised at Canton. The flowers used are roses, Olea fragrans, tuberose, orange, jasmine, gardenia, and azalea. The stems, calyx, and other parts are carefully sorted out, so that only the petals remain. When the tea is ready for packing, dry and warm, the fresh flowers are mixed with it (forty pounds to one hundred pounds for the orange), and left thus in a mass for twenty-four hours; it is then sifted and winnowed in a fanning mill till the petals are separated. If the odor is insufficient, the operation may be repeated with the jasmine or orange. The proportion of jasmine is a little more than orange; of the azalea, nearly half and half. The length of time required to obtain the proper smell from these flowers differs, and among them all tea scented with the azalea is said to keep its perfume the longest.

The mode of scenting tea differs somewhat according to the flower itself, for the small blossom of the Olea cannot be separated by sifting as rose or jasmine leaves can. Tea thus perfumed is sent to England as Orange Pekoe and Scented Caper. It is mixed with fine teas; and there is much to commend in thus increasing the aroma and taste of this healthy beverage. The Scented Caper comes in the form of round pellets, which are made of black tea softened by sprinkling water on it until it is pliable; it is then tied in canvas bags and rolled with the feet by treading on it for a good while till most of the quantity takes this form; as soon as perfumed it is packed for shipment. When rolled and dried, such tea needs only a facing to make it into Imperial and Gunpowder among the green teas.

The Chinese have been charged with adulterating their tea by mixing in other leaves with the true tea-leaf, and adding other ingredients far worse than rose, jujube, and fern leaves, and the cases which have been proved of *lie-tea* being sent off have been applied to the entire export. The stimulus for some of this adulteration has come from the foreigner, who desires to get good pure tea at half its cost of manufacture. The foregoing details will plainly show that an article which has to go through so many hands before its infusion is poured out of the teapot on the other side of the world, and where the only machinery used is a fanning mill and a roasting pan, cannot be furnished at much under twenty-five cents a pound for the common sorts. The villanous mixture known at Shanghai as *ma-lu cha*, or 'race-course tea,' was the answer on the part of the native manufacturer to the demand for cheap tea, until the consumers in Great Britain protested at the deception put on them, and its importation was prohibited. Which of the parties was most blameworthy may be left for them to settle, but in our own papers, of course, most of the blame rested on the tempted party. It is not to be inferred, however, that all cheap tea is adulterated. The process of manufacture leaves a large percentage of broken material, which can be worked into passable tea; the produce of many regions has not the flavor of the finest sorts, and, as it is with wines, will not bear so much cost in curing. The tea brokers know this, and things equalize themselves. The dust, the leaf ribs, and the siftings are all consumed by the poor natives, who mix other leaves, too, with the real leaf. Tea can perhaps bear comparison with any other great staple of food in this respect; and when we can fairly estimate the consumption of tea sent out of China and Japan at more than three hundred millions of pounds, it must be conceded that it is a very pure article—not as much, probably, as even five per cent. of false leaf.

One mode of using tea known among Tibetans and Mongols remains to be noticed. The rich province of Sz'chuen, in the western part of China, furnishes an abundance of good tea; much of which is exported to Russia by way of Sí-ngan fu and Kansuh, to supply the inhabitants of Siberia. This brick tea is cured by pressing the damp leaves into the form of a brick or tile, varying in size and weight, eight to twelve inches long and one thick; in this form it is far more easily carried than in the leaf. In Tibet, as we have seen, it appears more as a soup than an infusion. The brick tea is composed of coarse leaves, or of stalks moistened by steaming over boiling water, and then pressed till dry and hard. When used, a piece is broken off and simmered with milk and butter and water, with a touch of vinegar or pepper. The dish is not inviting at first, but Abbé Huc endorses its refreshing qualities in restoring the failing energies. The pressing and drying is assisted by sprinkling the mass with rice-water as it is forced into the moulds. The Chinese mix other leaves with real tea to eke it out, in districts where it is not commonly grown, but they do not regard this as adulteration. Willow leaves are common in such mixtures. Large caravans cross the plateau laden with brick tea.

Packing tea is mostly done in the interior, where it is cured. The large dry leaves frequently found inside are usually furnished by a peculiar species of bamboo; the lead is made into thin sheets by pouring the melted metal on to a large square brick, covered with several thicknesses of paper, and letting another brick drop down instantly on it. In order to test the honesty of the packing, the foreign merchant often walks over the three hundred to six hundred chests which make a chop, and selects any four or five he may choose for examination. If they stand the inspection the whole is taken on their guaranty, and are then weighed, papered, labelled, and mottoed ready for shipping. In all these matters the Chinese are very expert. It is impossible to calculate the number of persons to whom the tea trade furnishes employment; nor could machinery well come into use to displace human labor.

The introduction of tea among western nations was slow at first. Marco Polo has no notice of its use. The Dutch brought it to Europe in 1591 according to some accounts; but a sample or two did not make a trade, and there would have been reference to it if it had been used. In 1660 Samuel Pepys writes, September 28th: "I did send for a cup of tea (a China drink), of which I had never drank before." Nearly seven years after he says: "Home, and there find my wife making of tea, a drink which Mr. Pellin, the pothicary, tells her is good for her cold and defluxions." In 1670 the importation into England was 79 pounds; in 1685 it was 12,070 pounds; most of it came from Batavia and sold for a long time between £10 and £5 a pound weight. In 1657 Mr. Garney opened a shop in London to sell the infusion, and paid an excise of 8d. per gallon; the present duty is 2s. 1d. per pound, or 4½ pounds to each person in a year, nearly all of which, as it is in Europe and elsewhere, is black tea. In 1725 only 375,000 pounds were consumed in Great Britain. The actual quantity now in the United Kingdom is 126,000,000 pounds, besides much on the way. The importation into the United States is worth $18,000,000 to $19,000,000, say 60,000,000 pounds. Russia takes more good tea than any other nation and pays more for it, because the former overland trade to Siberia could not afford to transport poor tea. The export from Assam is now 20,000,000 pounds, but those sorts are too strong for the public taste when used alone, and are consumed in mixtures. Tea is a native of Assam, but its discovery only dates from 1836 or thereabouts. It is cultivated in Java and Brazil, but there is not much to encourage the manufacturer in any country where coffee supplies a similar beverage, and the price of labor makes it equal to the imported article.

The remarkable work on agriculture of Paul Sü, a convert to Christianity in 1620, contains a brief account and directions for cultivating tea. In concluding the chapter he urges the greater use of tea as against spirits. "Tea is of a cooling nature, and if drunk too freely will produce exhaustion and lassitude. Country people before drinking it add ginger and salt to counteract this cooling property. It is an exceedingly useful plant; cultivate it and the benefit will be widely spread; drink it and the animal spirits will be lively and clear. The chief rulers, lords, and great men esteem it; the lower people, the poor and beggarly, will not be destitute of it; all use it daily and like it."

The chemical analyses which have made known to us the components of the four or five substances used as warm beverages, viz., tea, coffee, maté, cocoa, guarana, and kola, indicate three constituents found in them, to which, no doubt, their virtues are owing.

A volatile oil is observed when tea is distilled with water; about one pound comes from one hundred pounds of dried tea, possessing its peculiar aroma and flavor to a high degree. Much of it is pressed from the leaves when rolled and cured, but little as still remains, its effects upon the human system are noticeable and sometimes powerful. Tea-tasters who continually taste the quality of the various lots submitted by sample for their approval, do so by breathing upon a handful of leaves and instantly covering the nose, so as to get this volatile aroma as one important test. They also examine the infusion in several different ways, by its taste, color, and strength. Long practice in this business is alleged to have deleterious influence upon their nervous systems. The other beverages we drink, as well as tea, derive their peculiar and esteemed flavor and aroma from chemical substances produced in them during the process of drying and roasting; at least nothing of them can be perceived in their natural state. Another substance in tea regarded as the chief inducement and reward in its effect on the system is the peculiar principle called theine. If a few finely powdered leaves are placed on a watch-glass, covered with a paper cap and placed on a hot plate, a white vapor slowly rises and condenses in the cap in the form of colorless crystals. They exist in different proportions in the different kinds of tea, from one and one-half to five or six per cent. in green tea. Theine has no smell and a slightly bitter taste, and does not therefore attract us to drink the infusion; but the chemists tell us that it contains nearly thirty per cent. of nitrogen. The salts in other beverages, as coffee and cocoa, likewise contain much nitrogen, and all tend to repair the waste going on in the human system, reduce the amount of solid food necessary, diminish too the wear and tear of the body and consequent lassitude of the mind, and maintain the vigor of both upon a smaller amount of food. Tea does this more pleasantly, perhaps, than any of the others; but it does more than they do for old people in supplementing the impaired powers of digestion, and helping them to maintain their flesh and uphold the system in health longer than they otherwise would. It is no wonder, therefore, that tea has become one of the necessaries of life; and the sexagenarian invalid, too poor to buy a bit of meat for her meal, takes her pot of tea with what she has, and knows that she feels lighter, happier, and better fitted for her toil, and enjoys life more than if she had no tea. Unconsciously she echoes what the Chinese said centuries ago, "Drink it, and the animal spirits will be lively and clear."

The third substance (which is contained in tea more than in the other beverages mentioned) forms also an important ingredient in betel-nut and gambier, so extensively chewed in Southern Asia, viz., tannin or tannic acid. This gives the astringent taste to tea-leaves and their infusion, and is found to amount to seventeen per cent. in well-dried black tea, and much more than that in green tea, especially the Japan leaf. The effects of tannin are not clearly ascertained as apart from the oil and the theine, but Johnston considers them as conducing to the exhilarating, satisfying, and narcotic action of the beverage.

A remaining ingredient worthy of notice in tea, in common with other food-plants, is gluten. This forms one-fourth of the weight of the leaves, but in order to derive the greatest good from it which proper methods of cooking might bring out, we must contrive a mode of eating the leaves. The nutritious property of the gluten accounts for the general use of brick tea throughout the Asiatic plateau. Huc says he drank the dish in default of something better, for he was unaccustomed to it, but his cameleers would often take twenty to forty cups a day.

If the sanitary effects of tea upon the system are so great and wholesome, its influence since its general introduction among occidentals cannot be overlooked. The domestic, quiet life and habits of the Chinese owe much of their strength to the constant use of this beverage, for the weak infusion which they sip allows them to spend all the time they choose at the tea-table. If they were in the habit of sipping even their weak whiskey in the same way, misery, poverty, quarrels, and sickness would take the place of thrift, quiet, and industry. The general temperance seen among them is owing to the tea much more than any other cause. It has, moreover, won its way with us, till in the present generation the associations that cluster around the tea-table form an integral part of the social life among English-speaking peoples. One of the most likely means to restrict the use of spirits among them is to substitute the use of warm beverages of all kinds by those whose system has not become vitiated. Tea is one of the greatest benefits to the Chinese, Japanese, and Mongols, and its universal use, for at least fifteen centuries, throughout their territories has proven its satisfaction as a nervine, a stimulant, and a beverage. If one passing through the streets of Peking, Canton, or Ohosaka, and seeing the good-natured hilarity of the groups of laborers and loiterers around the *cha-kwan* and the *cha-ya* of those cities, doubts the value of tea as a harmonizer and satisfier of human wants and passions, it must be taken as a proof of his own unsatisfied cravings.

It is a necessary of life to all classes of natives, and that its use is not injurious is abundantly evident from its general acceptance and increasing adoption; the prejudice against the beverage out of China may be attributed chiefly to the use of strong green tea, which is no doubt prejudicial. If those who have given it up on this account will adopt a weaker infusion of black tea, general experience is proof that it will do them no harm, and they may be sure that they will not be so likely to be deceived by a colored article. Neither the Chinese nor Japanese use milk or sugar in their tea, and the peculiar taste and aroma of the infusion is much better perceived without those additions. Tea, when clear, cannot be drunk so strong without tasting an unpleasant bitterness, which these diluents partly hide.[1]

Among other vegetable productions whose preparation affords employment are cassia and camphor. The cassia tree (*Cinnamomum cassia*) grows commonly in Kwangsí, Yunnan, and further south; the leading mart for all the varieties of this spice in China is Ping-nan, in the former of these provinces. The kind known as *kwei-pí*, or 'skinny cassia,' affords the principal part of that spice used at the west. The bark is stripped from the twigs by running a knife along the branch and gradually loosening it; after it is taken off it lies a day in the sun, when the epidermis is easily scraped off, and it is dried into the quilled shape in which it comes to market. The immature flowers of this and two other species of Cinnamomum are also collected and dried under the name of *cassia buds*, and often packed with the bark; they require little or no other preparation than simple drying. The leaves and bark of the tree are also distilled, and furnish oil of cassia, a powerful and pleasant oil employed by perfumers and cooks. Few genera of plants are more useful to man than those included under the old name of Laurus, to which these fragrant spices of cassia and cinnamon belong; their wood, bark, buds, seeds, flowers, leaves, and oil are all used by the Chinese in carpentry, medicine, perfumery, and cookery. The confusion arising from using the term *cassia* for the spice instead of confining it to the medicine (*Cassia senna*) has been a constant source of error.

The camphor tree (*Camphora officinarum*) is another species of Laurus, found along the southern maritime regions and Formosa, and affords both timber and gum for exportation and domestic use. The tree itself is large, and furnishes excellent planks, beams, and boards. The gum is procured from the branches, roots, leaves, and chips by soaking them in water until the liquid becomes saturated; a gentle heat is then applied to this solution, and the sublimed camphor received in inverted cones made of rice-straw, from which it is detached in impure

---

[1] Fortune's *Tea Districts* (1852); *Chinese Repository*, Vol. VIII., pp. 132–164, Vol. XVIII., pp. 13–18; Davis' *Chinese*, Vol. II., pp. 336–449; *Chinese Commercial Guide* (1863), pp. 141–148; Ball's *Tea Culture and Manufacture.*

grains, resembling unrefined sugar in color. Grosier describes another mode of getting it by taking out the coagulum inspissated from the solution into an iron dish and covering with powdered earth; two or three layers are thus placed in the dish, when a cover is luted on, and by a slow heat the camphor sublimes into it in a cake. It comes to market in a crude state, and is refined after reaching Europe. The preparation of the gum, sawing the timber for trunks, articles of furniture, and vessels in whole or in part, occupies great numbers of carpenters, shipwrights, and boat-builders. The increasing demand for the gum and boards has caused the rapid destruction of so many trees in Formosa that there is some ground for fear lest they ere long be all cut off.

Many of the common manipulations of Chinese workmen afford good examples of their ingenious modes of attaining the same end which is elsewhere reached by complex machinery. For instance, the baker places his fire on a large iron plate worked by a crane, and swings it over a shallow pan embedded in masonry, in which the cakes and pastry are laid and soon baked. The price of fuel compels its economical use wherever it is employed; in the forge, the kitchen, the kiln, or the dwelling, no waste of wood or coal is seen. As an instance in point, the mode of burning shells to lime affords a good example. A low wall encloses a space ten or twelve feet across, in the middle of which a hole communicates underneath the wall through a passage to the pit, where the fire is urged by a fan turned by the feet. The wood is loosely laid over the bottom of the area, and the fire kindled at the orifice in the centre and fanned into a blaze as the shells are rapidly thrown in until the wall is filled up; in twelve hours the shells are calcined. Toward evening scores of villagers collect around the burning pile, bringing their kettles of rice or vegetables to cook. The good-humor manifested by these groups of old and young is a pleasing instance of the sociability and equality witnessed among the lower classes of Chinese. The lime is taken out next morning and sifted for the mason.

Handicraftsmen of every name are content with coarse-looking tools compared with those turned out at Sheffield, but the work produced by some of them is far from contemptible. The bench of a carpenter is a low, narrow, inclined form, like a drawing-knife frame, upon which he sits to plane, groove, and work his boards, using his feet and toes to steady them. His augurs, bits, and gimlets are worked with a bow, but most of the edge-tools employed by him and the blacksmith, though similar in shape, are less convenient than our own. They are sharpened with hones or grindstones, and also with a cold steel like a spoke-shave, with which the edge is scraped thin. The aptitude of Chinese workmen has often been noticed, and

Travelling Blacksmith and Equipment.

among them all the travelling blacksmith takes the palm for his compendious establishment. "I saw a blacksmith a few days since," writes one observer, "mending a pan, the arrangement of whose tools was singularly compact. His fire was held in an iron basin not unlike a coal-scuttle in shape, in the back corner of which the mouthpiece of the bellows entered. The anvil was a small square mass of iron, not very unlike our own, placed on a block, and a partition basket close by held the charcoal and tools, with the old iron and other rubbish he carried. The water to temper his iron was in an earthen pot, which just at this time was most usefully employed in boiling his dinner over the forge fire After he had done the job he took off his dinner, threw the water on the fire, picked out the coals and put them back into the basket, threw away the ashes, set the anvil astride of the bellows, and laying the fire-pan on the basket, slung the bellows on one end of his pole and the basket on the other, and walked off."[1] The mode of mending holes in cast-iron pans here noticed is a peculiar operation. The smith first files the lips of the hole clean, and after heating the dish firmly

Itinerant Dish-mender.

places it on a tile covered with wet felt. He then pours the liquid iron, fused in a crucible by the assistance of a flux, upon the hole, and immediately patters it down with a dossil of felt until it covers the edges of the pan above and below, and is then, while cooling, hammered until firmly fixed in its place.

Another ingenious and effectual method of mending porcelain and all manner of crockery ware is performed by itinerant workmen, who travel about with their workshop on their

---

[1] *Chinese Repository*, Vol. X., p. 473.

shoulders, as seen in the cut. By means of minute copper clamps, even the most delicate article of China-ware may be repaired and made to answer the purpose of a new piece; since no cement is used in this style of mending, it has the additional advantage of standing immersion in water.

The great number of craftsmen who ply their vocations in the street, as well as the more numerous class of hucksters who supply food as they go from house to house, furnish much to amuse and interest. Each of them has a peculiar call. The barber twangs a sort of tweezers like a long tuning-fork, the peddler twirls a hand-drum with clappers strung on each side, the refuse-buyer strikes a little gong, the fruiterer claps two bamboo sticks, and the fortune-teller tinkles a gong-bell; these, with the varied calls and cries of beggars, cadgers, chapmen, etc., fill the streets with a concert of strange sounds.

The delicate carving of Chinese workmen has often been described; many specimens of it are annually sent abroad. Few products of their skill are more remarkable than the balls containing ten or twelve separate spheres one within another. The manner of cutting them is ingenious. A piece of ivory or wood is first made perfectly globular, and then several conical holes are bored into it in such a manner that their apices all meet at the centre, which becomes hollow as the holes are bored into it. The sides of each having been marked with lines to indicate the number of globes to be cut out, the workman inserts a chisel or burin with a semicircular blade, bent so that the edge cuts the ivory, as the shaft is worked on the pivot, at the same depth in each hole. By successively cutting a little on the inside of each conical hole, the incisures meet, and a sphericle is at last detached, which is now turned over and its faces one after another brought opposite the largest hole, and firmly secured by wedges in the other apertures, while its surfaces are smoothed and carved. When the central sphere is done, a similar tool, somewhat larger, is again introduced into the holes, and another sphere detached and smoothed in the same way, and then another, until the whole is completed, each being polished and carved before the next outer one is commenced. It takes three or four months to complete a ball with fifteen inner globes, the price of which ranges from twenty to thirty dollars, according to the delicacy of the carving. Some writers have asserted that these curious toys were made of semispheres nicely luted together, and they have been boiled in oil for hours in order to separate them and solve the mystery of their construction.

Fans and card-cases are carved of wood, ivory, and mother-of-pearl in alto-relievo, with an elaborateness which shows the great skill and patience of the workman, and at the same time his crude conception of drawing, the figures, houses, trees, and other objects being grouped in violation of all propriety and perspective. Beautiful ornaments are made by carving roots of plants, branches, gnarled knots, etc., into fantastic groups of birds or animals, the artist taking advantage of the natural form of his material in the arrangement of his figures. Models of pagodas, boats, and houses are entirely constructed of ivory, even to representing the ornamental roofs, the men working at the oar, and women looking from the balconies. Baskets of elegant shape are woven from ivory splinths; and the shopmen at Canton exhibit a variety of seals, paper-knives, chessmen, counters, combs, etc., exceeding in finish and delicacy the same kind of work found anywhere else in the world. The most elaborate coat of arms, or complicated cypher, will also be imitated by these skilful carvers. The national taste prefers this style of carving on plane surfaces; it is seen on the walls of houses and granite slabs of fences, the woodwork of boats and shops, and on articles of furniture. Most of it is pretty, but the disproportion and cramped position of the figures detract from its beauty when judged by strict rules of western art.

The manufacture of enamels and cloisonné wares has lately received a great stimulus from their foreign demand. A copper vase is formed of the desired shape by hammering and soldering, on whose clean surface the figures to be enamelled are etched to show where the strips of copper are to be soldered before their interspaces are enamelled. This solder is made of borax and silver, and melts at a higher temperature than the enamel, which is reduced to a paste and filled into each cell of the pattern by brushes and styles, until the whole design is gone over. The various colored *liao*, or ingredients, are prepared in cakes by artists who keep their composition secret, but all the substances occur in China. The quality of the ware depends on the skill in mixing these cakes and fusing the colors in a charcoal fire, into which the piece is placed; imperfections and holes are covered and filled up when it is cooled, and the piece is again and again exposed to the fire. After the third ordeal it is ground smooth and polished on a lathe, and the brass work gilt. The specimens now made show very fine work, but their coloring hardly equals those of Kienlung's reign or still earlier in the Ming dynasty. Much inferior work has also been palmed off for that of the golden period of this art.

Fancy Carved Work.

The manufacture of mats for sails of junks and boats, floors, bedding, etc., employs thousands. A sail containing nearly four hundred square feet can be obtained for ten dollars. The rolls are largely exported, and still more extensively used in the country for covering packages for shipment. A stouter kind made of bamboo splinths serves as a material for huts, and fulfils many other purposes that are elsewhere attained by boards or canvas. Rattans are largely worked into mats, chairs, baskets, and other articles of domestic service. Several branches of manufacture have entirely grown up, or been much encouraged by the foreign trade, among which the preparation of vermilion, beating gold-leaf, cutting pearl buttons, dyeing and trimming pith-paper for artificial flowers, weaving and painting fancy window-blinds, and the preparation of sweetmeats are the principal.

The beautiful vermilion exported from Canton is prepared by triturating one part of quicksilver with two of sulphur until they form a blackish powder, which is put into a crucible having an iron lid closely luted down. When the fire acts on the mixture the lid is cooled to effect the sublimation; the deposit on the top is cinnabar and that on the sides is vermilion, according to the Chinese; all of them are powdered, levigated, decanted, and dried on tiles for use in painting and pharmacy, coloring candles and paper, and making red ink. The excellence of Chinese vermilion depends on the thoroughness of the grinding.[1]

It has often been said that the Chinese are so averse to change and improvement that they will obstinately adhere to their own modes, but, though slow to alter well-tried methods, such is not the case. Three new manufactures have been introduced during the present century, viz., that of glass, bronze-work, and Prussian blue. A Chinese sailor brought home the manufacture of the latter, which he had learned thoroughly in London, and the people now supply themselves. Works in bronze and brass have of late been set up, and watches and clocks are both extensively manufactured, with the exception of the springs. Fire-engines in imitation of foreign hand-engines are gradually coming into use. Brass cannon were made during the war with England in imitation of pieces taken from a wreck, and the frames of one or two vessels to be worked with wheels by men at a crank, in imitation of steamers, were found on the stocks at Ningpo when the English took the place. Since then the establishment of government arsenals at Fuhchau, Shanghai, Nanking, and Tientsin has stimulated and suggested as well as taught the people many applications of machinery. Yet until they can see their way clear to be remunerated for their outlay, it is unwise to urge or start doubtful experiments. This was shown at Canton ten years ago when a native company was formed to spin cotton yarn by steam machinery, and when the apparatus was all ready for work the cotton growers were quite unwilling to trust their raw cotton out of their hands. Moreover, it should be observed that few have taken the trouble to

---

[1] Compare an article by Julien in the *Nouv. Journ. Asiatique*, Tome V., 1830, pp. 208 ff.

explain or show them the improvements they are supposed to be so disinclined to adopt. Ploughs have been given the farmers near Shanghai, but they would not use them, which, however, may have been as much owing to the want of a proper harness, or a little instruction regarding their use, as to a dislike to take a new article.

The general aspect of Chinese society, in an industrial point of view, is one of its most pleasing features. The great body of the people are obliged to engage in manual labor in order to subsist, yet only a trifling proportion of them can be called beggars, while still fewer possess such a degree of wealth that they can live on its income. Property is safe enough to afford assurance to honest toil that it shall generally reap the reward of its labors, but if that toil prosper beyond the usual limits, the avarice of officials and the envy of neighbors easily find a multitude of contrivances to harass and impoverish the fortunate man, and the laws are not executed with such strictness as to deter them. The mechanical arts supply their wants, but having no better models before them, nor any scientific acquaintance with elementary principles and powers applicable to a great number of purposes, these arts have remained stationary. The abundance of labor must be employed, and its cheapness obviates the necessity of finding substitutes in machinery. The adoption of even a few things from abroad might involve so many changes, that even those intelligent natives who saw their advantages would hesitate in view of the momentous contingencies of a failure. The conflict between capital and labor in its various phases and struggles is becoming more and more marked the world over as civilization advances, and the Chinese polity is destined to endure its greatest strain in adjusting their forces among its industrious millions.

Imitation is a remarkable trait in the Chinese mind, though invention is not altogether wanting; the former leads the people to rest content with what they can get along with, even at some expense of time and waste of labor, where, too, an exhibition of ingenuity and science would perhaps be accompanied with suspicion, expense, or hindrances from both neighbors and rulers. The existence of the germ of arts and discoveries, whose development would have brought with them so many advantages and pointed to still further discoveries, leads one to inquire the reason why they were not carried out. Setting aside the view, which may properly be taken, that the wonderful discoveries now made in the arts by Europeans form part of God's great plan for the redemption of the race, the want of mutual confidence, insecurity of property, and debasing effects of heathenism upon the intellect will explain much of the apathy shown toward improvement. Invention among them has rather lacked encouragement than ceased to exist:—more than that, it has been checked by a suspicious, despotic sway, while no stimulus of necessity has existed to counterbalance and urge it forward, and has been stunted by the mode and materials of education. It was not till religious liberty and discussion arose in Europe that the inhabitants began to improve in science and arts as well as morals and good government; and when the ennobling and expanding principles of an enlarged civilization find their way into Chinese society and mind, it may reasonably be expected that rapid advances will be made in the comforts of this life, as well as in adopting the principles and exhibiting the conduct which prove a fitness for the enjoyments of the next.

CHAPTER XVI.

SCIENCE AMONG THE CHINESE.

THAT enlargement of the mind which results from the collection and investigation of facts, or from extensive reading of books on whose statements reliance can be placed, and which leads to the cultivation of knowledge for its own sake, has no existence in China. Sir John Davis justly observes that the Chinese "set no value on abstract science, apart from some obvious and immediate end of utility;" and he properly compares the actual state of the sciences among them with their condition in Europe previous to the adoption of the inductive mode of investigation. Even their few theories in explanation of the mysteries of nature are devoid of all fancy to make amends for want of fact and experiment, so that in reading them we are neither amused by their imagination nor instructed by their research. Perhaps the rapid advances made by Europeans, during the two past centuries, in the investigation of nature in all her departments and powers, has made us somewhat impatient of such a parade of nonsense as Chinese books exhibit. In addition to the general inferiority of Chinese mind to European in genius and imagination, it has moreover been hampered by a language the most tedious and meagre of all tongues, and wearied with a literature abounding in tiresome repetitions and unsatisfactory theories. Under these conditions, science, whether mathematical, physical, or natural, has made few advances during the last few centuries, and is now awaiting a new impulse from abroad in all its departments.

Murray's *China* (Vol. III., Chap. IV.) contains a fair account of the attainments of the Chinese in mathematics and astronomy. The notation of the Chinese is based on the decimal principle, but as their figures are not changed in value by position, it is difficult to write out clearly the several steps in solving a problem. Experiments have shown that it is easy enough to perform them with Chinese figures used in our way, omitting the characters for 100, 1,000, and 10,000 (*peh*, *tsien*, and *wan*); but it will be long before the change will become general, even if it be desirable. Arithmetical calculations are performed with the assistance of an abacus, called a *swanpan*, or 'counting board,' which is simply a shallow case divided longitudinally by a bar and crossed by several wires; on one side of this bar the wires bear five balls, on the other two. The five balls stand for units, the two balls being each worth five units. When the balls on any wire are taken for units, those next to the right stand for tens, the third for hundreds, and so on; while those on the left denote tenths, hundredths, etc. Simple calculations are done on this machine with accuracy and rapidity, but as it is only a convenient index for the progress and result of a calculation performed in the head, if an error be made the whole must be performed again, since the result only appears when the sum is finished. There are three sorts of figures, partly answering to the English, Roman, and Arabic forms—as *Seven*, VII., and 7—the most common of which are given on page 619 of Vol. I.; the complicated form is used for security in drafts and bills, and the abbreviated in common operations, accounts, etc., and in setting down large amounts in a more compact form than can be done by the other characters. This mode of notation is employed by the Japanese and Cochinchinese, and possesses some advantages over the method of using letters practised by the Greeks and Romans, as well as over the counters once employed in England, but falls far behind the Arabic system now in general use in the west.

Treatises on arithmetic are common, in which the simple rules are explained and illustrated by examples and questions. One of the best is the *Swan-fah Tung Tsung*, or 'General Comprehensive Arithmetic,' in five volumes, octavo, the author of which, Ching Yu-sz', lived in the Ming dynasty. The *Tsu-wei-shan Fang Sho Hioh*, or 'Mathematics of the Lagerstræmia Hill Institution,' in thirty-eight books, octavo, 1828, contains a complete course of mathematical instruction in geometry, trigonometry, mensuration, etc., together with a table of natural sines and tangents, and one of logarithmic sines, tangents, secants, etc., for every degree and minute. Both these compilations derive most of their value from the mathematical writings of the Roman Catholic missionaries; it is stated in the latter work that "the western scholar, John Napier, made logarithms."

The study of arithmetic has attracted attention among the Chinese from very early times, and the notices found in historical works indicate some treatises even extant in the Han dynasty, followed by a great number of general and particular works down to the Sung dynasty. One author of the Tang dynasty, in his problems on solid mensuration, offered one thousand taels of silver to whoever found a single word of error in the book. The Hindu processes in algebra were known to Chinese mathematicians, and are still studied, though all intellectual intercourse between the countries has long ceased. Down to the end of the Ming dynasty, these branches made slow progress. Since foreigners have begun to apply western science, the development has been rapid. Mr. Wylie has given, in his *Notes on Chinese Literature* (pp. 86–104), a digested account of the most valuable native works on astronomy and mathematics. One very comprehensive work on them is the *Thesaurus of Mathematics and Chronology*, published by imperial order about 1750.

The knowledge of mathematics, even among learned men, is very small, and the common people study it only as far as their business requires; the cumbersome notation and the little aid such studies give in the examinations doubtless discourage men from pursuing what they seem to have no taste for as a people.[1] A curious fact regarding the existence of six errors in these tables, discovered by Babbage to have been perpetuated in most of the European logarithmic tables since the publication of the *Trigonometria Artificialis* of Vlacq in 1633, proves the source whence the Chinese derived them, and their imitative fidelity in copying them. Chinese authors readily acknowledge the

[1] See *Notes and Queries on C. and J.*, Vol. I., p. 166, and Vol. III., p. 153.

superiority of western mathematicians, and generally ascribe their advances in the exact sciences to them.

The attainments made by the ancient Chinese in astronomy are not easily understood from their scanty records, for the mere notice of an eclipse is a very different thing from its calculation or description. They have been examined recently with renewed interest and care in view of the discoveries at Nineveh, which have furnished so many reliable notices in Western Asia of early days, and may lend some rays of light to illustrate the history and condition of Eastern Asia when more fully studied. The *Book of Records* contains some notices of instructions given by Yao to his astronomers Hí and Ho to ascertain the solstices and equinoxes, to employ intercalary months, and to fix the four seasons, in order that the husbandman might know when to commit his seed to the ground. If the time of the deluge be reckoned, according to Hales, at B.C. 3155, there will be an interval of about eight centuries to the days of Yao, B.C. 2357; this would be ample time for the observation that the primitive sacred year of three hundred and sixty days in Noah's time was wrong; also that the lunar year of about three hundred and fifty-four days was quite as incorrect, and required additional correction, which this ancient monarch is said to have made by an intercalation of seven lunar months in nineteen years. It is remarkable, too, that the time given as the date of the commencement of the astronomical observations sent to Aristotle from Babylon by command of Alexander should be B.C. 2233, or only a few years after the death of Yao; at that time the five additional days to complete the solar year were intercalated by the Chaldeans, and celebrated as days of festivity. Dr. Hales, who mentions this, says that many ancient nations, and also the Mexicans, had the same custom, but there are no traces of any particular observance of them by the Chinese, who, indeed, could not notice them in a lunar year.

The intercalation made by Yao has continued with little variation to this day. The Romish missionaries rectified the calendar during the reign of Kanghí, and have continued its preparation since that time. The adoption of the Julian solar year of three hundred and sixty-five and one-fourth days at this remote period is far from certain, though the fact of its existence among nations in the west is mentioned by the commentator upon the *Book of Records*, who flourished A.D. 1200. The attention the Chinese paid to the lunar year, and the very small difference their seven intercalations left between the true harmonizing of the lunar and solar years (only 1h. 27m. 32s.), would not derange the calculations to a degree to attract their notice. The period of the adoption of the cycle of sixty years, called *luh-shih hwa kiah-tsz'*, cannot be ascertained even with any close approach to probability. Though negative evidence is always the poorest basis on which to found a theory in any branch of knowledge, it still bears great influence in early Chinese history and science, and in no department more than astronomy. This sexagenary cycle, the Chinese assert, was contrived nearly three centuries before the time of Yao (B.C. 2637), and seems to have been perfectly arbitrary, for no explanation now exists of the reasons which induced its inventor, Hwangtí, or his minister, Nao the Great, to select this number. The years have each of them a separate name, formed by taking ten characters, called *shih kan*, or 'ten stems,' and joining to them twelve other characters, called the *shih-'rh chí*, or 'twelve branches,' five times repeated.

These two sets of horary characters are also applied to minutes and seconds, hours, days, and months, signs of the zodiac, points of the compass, etc. By giving the twelve branches the names of as many animals and apportioning the ten stems in couplets among the five elements, they are also made to play an important part in divination and astrology. The present year (1882) is the eighteenth year of the seventy-sixth cycle, or the four thousand five hundred and eighteenth since its institution; but no trace of a serial numbering of the sexagenary periods has yet been found in Chinese writings. The application of the characters to hours and days dates from about B.C. 1752, according to the *Shu King*, perhaps even before they were combined in a cyclic arrangement. This sexagenary division existed in India in early times, too, and is still followed there, where it is named the Cycle of Jupiter, "because the length of its years is measured by the passage of that planet, by its mean motion, through one sign of the zodiac." Rev. E. Burgess, in his translation of the *Surya Siddhanta*, says that the length of Jupiter's years is reckoned in that book at 361d. 0h. 38m., and adds: "It was doubtless on account of the near coincidence of this period with the true solar year that it was adopted as a measure of time; but it has not been satisfactorily ascertained, as far as we are aware, where the cycle originated, or what is its age, or why it was made to consist of sixty years, including five whole revolutions of the planet." It is not improbable, therefore, that the cycle, the two sets of characters, the twenty-four solar terms, with the twelve and twenty-eight lunar mansions or zodiacal asterisms, all of which play such an important part in Chinese astrology and astronomy, will be found to have been derived from the Chaldeans, and not from the Hindus, as has been confidently asserted. Though confessedly ancient in both India and China, their adoption was slow in its growth, while some striking similarities indicate a common origin, and so remote that its genesis is all a mystery.

The year is lunar, but its commencement is regulated by the sun. New Year falls on the first new moon after the sun enters Aquarius, which makes it come not before January 21st nor after February 19th. Besides the division into lunar months, the year is apportioned into twenty-four *tsieh*, or 'terms,' of about fifteen days each, depending upon the position of the sun; these are continued on from year to year, irrespective of the intercalations, the first one commencing about February 6th, when the sun is 15° in Aquarius. Their names have reference to the season of the year and obvious changes in nature at the time they come round, as *rain-water*, *vernal-equinox*, *spiked-grain*, *little-heat*, etc.

The Chinese divide the zodiac (*hwang tao*, or 'yellow road') into twenty-eight *siu* or *kung*, 'constellations' or 'lunar mansions,' but instead of an equable allotment, the signs occupy from 1° up to 31°; the Hindus arrange them nearly in spaces of 13° each. Their names and corresponding animals, with the principal stars answering to each asterism, are given in the table.

	Chin siu.	Corresponding Animal.	Constellation.		Chin siu.	Corresponding Animal.	Constellation.
1	*Kioh.*	Earth Dragon.	Spica, ζ Virgo.	15	*Kwei.*	Wolf.	Mirac.
2	*Kang.*	Sky Dragon.	ι κ λ μ Virgo.	16	*Leu.*	Dog.	αβ Aries.
3	*Ti.*	Badger.	α β γ δ Libra.	17	*Wei.*	Pheasant.	Musca.
4	*Fang.*	Hare.	β δ Scorpio.	18	*Mao.*	Cock.	Pleiades.
5	*Sin.*	Fox.	Antares.	19	*Pih.*	Raven.	Hyades.
6	*Wei.*	Tiger.	ε μ Scorpio.	20	*Tsui.*	Monkey.	λ Orion.
7	*Ki.*	Leopard.	γ δ Sagittarius.	21	*Tsan.*	Ape.	Rigel, Orion.
8	*Teu.*	Griffon.	ξ λ Sagittarius.	22	*Tsing.*	Tapir.	Gemini.
9	*Niu.*	Ox.	α β Sagittarius.	23	*Kwei.*	Sheep.	γ δ θ Cancer.
10	*Nü.*	Bat.	ε μ γ Aquarius.	24	*Liu.*	Muntjak.	δ ε ζ Hydra.
11	*Hü.*	Rat.	β Aquarius.	25	*Sing.*	Horse.	Alphard.
12	*Wei.*	Swallow.	α Aquarius & ε Pegasus.	26	*Chang.*	Deer.	κ λ μ Hydra.
				27	*Yih.*	Snake.	α Crater.
13	*Shih.*	Boar.	Markab.	28	*Chăn.*	Worm.	γ ε Corvus.
14	*Pih.*	Porcupine.	Algenib.				

Instead of being equally divided in the four seasons, they are apportioned very empirically. Those numbered 7 to 14 belong to Aquarius and the north, and measure 98¼°; those from 1 to 7 belong to Scorpio and the east, and measure 75°; those from 15 to 21 belong to Taurus and the west, and measure 80°; and the last 7 belong to Leo and the south, and measure 112°. All these things show very crude knowledge of the heavenly bodies.

The zodiac is further divided into twelve signs or palaces, varying from 25° to 38° in length, named after the twelve branches or animals representing them, commencing with Aquarius or the rat, followed by the ox, tiger, hare, dragon, snake, horse, sheep, monkey, cock, dog, and bear. These animals also occur among the twenty-eight asterisms, but they are used to denote the twelve branches in all astrological calculations, and not often referred to the zodiac. They are in constant use among the nations of Eastern Asia, so that the common people of Mongolia, Siam, and Japan are really more conversant with them, through their application to times of various length, than they are with the technical characters. The Hindus and Arabians, on the other hand, do not associate these or any other animals with the twelve signs, hours, and months, nor with the twenty-eight mansions; and this fact tends to show that the Chinese obtained them from a more ancient source. The name of one of the twenty-eight lunar mansions is given to every day in the year in perpetual rotation, consequently the same day of our week in every fourth week has the same character applied to it. The days are numbered from the first to the last day of the month, and the months from one to twelve through the year, except the intercalary month, called *jun yueh;* and there is also a trine division of the month into decades.[1]

The astronomical ideas of the common Chinese are vague and inaccurate. The knowledge contained in their own scientific books has not been taught, and they still believe the earth to be a plain surface, measuring each way about one thousand five hundred miles; around it the sun, moon, and stars revolve, the first at a distance of four thousand miles. This figure comes so near the earth's radius that it is reasonable to infer, with Chalmers, that it was calculated from the different elevation of the sun in different latitudes. The distance of the heavens from the earth was ascertained by one observer to be 81,394 *li*, and by another subsequent to him to be 216,781½ *li*, or about 73,000 miles; all of which indicates the lack of careful observation. The constellation of the *Peh Tao*, or Dipper, plays an important part in popular astronomy; the common saying is: 'When the handle of the *Northern Peck* points east at nightfall, it is spring over the land; when it points south, it is summer; and when west or north, it is respectively autumn and winter.' The Dipper has become a kind of natural clock from this circumstance, and as its handle always points to the bright stars in Scorpio, these two constellations are among the most familiar. These popular notions must not, however, be taken as a test of what was known in early times; it is quite as just to their scientific attainments in this branch to give them credit (as Wylie does) for having known more than has come down to our days; as to deny belief in the little that remains, because it presents some insoluble difficulties, as Chalmers is disposed to do.

---

[1] *Chinese Repository*, Vol. IX., pp. 573–584. De Guignes' *Voyages*, Vol. II., p. 414. *Chinese Chrestomathy*. Legge's *Shoo King*, passim. Chalmers, *On the Astronomy of the Ancient Chinese*. *Journal of the Am. Oriental Society*, Vol. VI., Art. III., and Vol. VIII., Arts. I. and VII. Whitney's *Oriental and Linguistic Studies*, Art. XII. *North China Br. R. A. S. Journal*, Nos. III. and IV.

Astronomy has been studied by the Chinese for astrological and state purposes, and their recorded observations of eclipses, comets, etc., have no small value to European astronomers and chronologists. Mailla has collected the notices of 460 solar eclipses, extending from B.C. 2159 to A.D. 1699, and Wylie furnishes a careful list of 925 solar and 574 lunar eclipses, extracted from Chinese works, observed between 2150 and A.D. 1785. Comets have been carefully noted whenever their brilliancy has enabled them to be seen, for they are regarded as portents by the people, and their course among the stars somewhat determines their influence. A list of 373 comets mentioned in Chinese records has been published by John Williams,[1] mostly extracted from Ma Twan-lin's *Antiquarian Researches*, and the *Shi Ki*. They extend from B.C. 611 to A.D. 1621; the general value of these records is estimated by the learned author as entitling them to credence. The curious and intimate connection between geomancy, horoscopy, and astrology, which the Chinese suppose exists, has a powerful influence in maintaining their errors, because of its bearing on every man's luck. Even with all the aid they have derived from Europeans, the Chinese seem to be unable to advance in the science of astronomy, when left to themselves, and to cling to their superstitions against every evidence. Some clouds having on one occasion covered the sky, so that an eclipse could not be seen, the courtiers joyfully repaired to the Emperor to felicitate him, that Heaven, touched by his virtues, had spared him the pain of witnessing the "eating of the sun." A native writer on astronomy, called Tsinglai, who published several works under the patronage of Yuen Yuen, the liberal-minded governor of Kwangtung in 1820, even at that late day, "makes the heavens to consist of ten concentric hollow spheres or envelopes: the first contains the moon's orbit; the second that of Mercury; those of Venus, the Sun, Mars, Jupiter, Saturn, and the twenty-eight constellations, follow; the ninth envelops and binds together the eight interior ones, and revolves daily; while the tenth is the abode of the

---

[1] *Observations of Comets, from* B.C. 611 *to* A.D. 1640. *Extracted from the Chinese Annals.* London, 1871.

Celestial Sovereign, the Great Ruler, with all the gods and sages, where they enjoy eternal tranquillity." He further says, "there are two north and two south poles, those of the equator and those of the ecliptic. The poles of the ecliptic regulate the varied machinery of the heavenly revolutions, and turn round unceasingly. The poles of the equator are the pivots of the primitive celestial body, and remain permanently unmoved. What are called the two poles, therefore, are really not stars, but two immovable points in the north and in the south."[1] The author of this astute cosmogony studied under Europeans, and published these remarks as the fruit of his researches.

The action and reaction of the elements furnish a satisfactory explanation to Chinese philosophers of the changes going on in the visible universe, for no possible contingency can arise which they are not prepared to solve by their analysis of the evolution of its powers. Through their speculations by this curious system they have been led away from carefully recording facts and processes, and have gone on, like a squirrel in a cage, making no progress toward the real knowledge of the elements they treat of. The following table contains the leading elementary correspondences which they use, but a full explanation would be out of place here.

This fanciful system is more or less received by their most intelligent men; and forms a sort of abracadabra in the hands of geomancers and fortune-tellers, by which, with a show of great learning, they impose on the people. The sun, moon, and planets influence sublunary events, especially the life and death of human beings, and changes in their color menace approaching calamities. Alterations in the appearance of the sun announce misfortunes to the state or its head, as revolts, famines, or the death of the Emperor; when the moon waxes red, or turns pale, men should be in awe at the unlucky times thus foreomened.

The sun is symbolized by the figure of a raven in a circle, and the moon by a rabbit on his hind legs pounding rice in a mortar, or by a three-legged toad. The last refers to the

---

[1] *Chinese Chrestomathy*, p. 397.

POWERS AND FUNCTIONS OF ELEMENTARY NATURE—PRINCIPLES WHICH ACT AND REACT ON EACH OTHER IN PRODUCING ALL THINGS.

Five *Hing*, or Elemental Powers.	Qualities of the Five *Hing* given in the *Shu King*.	Five Tastes produced by the Five *Hing*.	Five Points of Compass.	Dualities of the Ten Stems influenced by the Five *Hing*.	Activities of the Five *Hing*.	Five Corresponding Planets.	Five Colors.	Five Viscera.	Five Musical Notes.	Five Early Emperors.	Four Seasons.	Four Quarters of Lunar Zodiac.
水 Water.	Imbuing and Descending.	Salt.	North.	Jin-kwei.	Strengthening.	Mercury.	Black.	Kidneys.	Yu.	Chuen-hüh, B.C. 2513.	Winter.	Sable Warrior.
火 Fire.	Blazing and Ascending.	Bitter.	South.	Ping-ting.	Penetrating.	Mars.	Carnation.	Heart.	Wei.	Yentí, (Shinnung) B.C. 2737.	Summer.	Vermilion Sparrow.
木 Wood.	Bending, Straightening.	Sour.	East.	Kiah-yih.	Nourishing.	Jupiter.	Azure.	Liver.	Kioh.	Tai-hao, (Fuh-hi) B.C. 2852.	Spring.	Azure Dragon.
金 Metal.	Obeying, Resisting.	Acid.	West.	Käng-sin.	Destroying.	Venus.	White.	Lungs.	Shang.	Shao-hao, B.C. 2597.	Autumn.	White Tiger.
土 Earth.	Sowing, Reaping.	Sweet.	Centre.	Wu-ki.	Harmonizing.	Saturn.	Yellow.	Stomach.	Kung.	Hwangtí, B.C. 2697.		

legend of an ancient beauty, Chang-ngo, who drank the liquor of immortality and straightway ascended to the moon, where she was transformed into a toad, still to be traced in its face. It is a special object of worship in autumn, and moon-cakes dedicated to it are sold at this season. All the stars are ranged into constellations, and an emperor is installed over them, who resides at the north pole; five monarchs, also, live in the five stars in Leo, where is a palace, called *Wu Tí tso*, or 'Throne of the Five Emperors.' In this celestial government there is also an heir-apparent, empresses, sons and daughters, tribunals, and the constellations receive the names of men, animals, and other terrestrial objects. The Dipper is worshipped as the residence of the fates, where the duration of life, and other events relating to mankind, are measured and meted out. Doolittle's *Social Life* contains other popular notions connected with the stars, showing the ignorance still existing, and the fears excited by unusual phenomena among the heavenly bodies. Both heaven and the sun are worshipped by the government in appropriate temples on the west and east sides of Peking. The rainbow is the product of the impure vapors ascending from the earth meeting those descending from the sun.

If their knowledge of astronomy can be criticised as being anything but an exact science, the Chinese should not be denied credit for a certain amount of beauty in what may be called the romantic side of this study. In the myths and legends which have clustered about and doubtless in many cases perverted their observations of the stars, there are the sources of fêtes and subjects for pictorial illustration without number. One of these stories, forming the motive of a bowl decoration given upon the opposite page, is the fable of Aquila (*niu*) and Vega, known in Chinese and Japanese mythology as the Herdsman and Weaver-girl. The latter, the daughter of the sun-god, was so continually busied with her loom that her father became worried at her close habits and thought that by marrying her to a neighbor, who herded cattle on the banks of the Silver Stream of Heaven (the Milky Way), she might awake to a brighter manner of living.

"No sooner did the maiden become wife than her habits

and character utterly changed for the worse. She became not only very merry and lively, but quite forsook loom and needle, giving up her nights and days to play and idleness; no silly lover could have been more foolish than she. The sun-king, in great wrath at all this, concluded that the husband was the cause of it and determined to separate the couple. So he ordered him to remove to the other side of the river of stars, and told him that hereafter they should meet only once a year, on the seventh night of the seventh month. To make a bridge over the flood of stars, the sun-king called myriads of magpies, which thereupon flew together, and, making a bridge, supported the poor lover on their wings and backs as if it were a roadway of solid land. So bidding his weeping wife farewell, the lover-husband sorrowfully crossed the River of Heaven, and all the magpies instantly flew away. But the two were separated, the one to lead his ox, the other to ply her shuttle during the long hours of the day with diligent toil, and the sun-king again rejoiced in his daughter's industry.

"At last the time for their reunion drew near, and only one fear possessed the loving wife. What if it should rain? For the River of Heaven is always full to the brim, and one extra drop causes a flood which sweeps away even the bird bridge. But not a drop fell; all the heavens were clear. The magpies flew joyfully in myriads, making a way for the tiny feet of the little lady. Trembling with joy, and with heart fluttering more than the bridge of wings, she crossed the River of Heaven and was in the arms of her husband. This she did every year. The husband staid on his side of the river, and the wife came to him on the magpie bridge, save on the sad occasion when it rained. So every year the people hope for clear weather, and the happy festival is celebrated alike by old and young." [1]

These two constellations are worshipped principally by women, that they may gain cunning in the arts of needlework and making of fancy flowers. Watermelons, fruits, vegetables, cakes, etc., are placed with incense in the reception-room, and

---

[1] Somewhat abridged from Mr. W. E. Griffis' *Japanese Fairy World*, a book which has given us the cream of a great variety of stories from Eastern wonder-lore.

before these offerings are performed the kneelings and knockings in the usual way.

The entire day is divided into twelve two-hour periods called *shin*, commencing at eleven o'clock, P.M.; each hour is further subdivided into *kih*, or eighths, equal to fifteen of our minutes, and receives the same characters. There are various means employed to measure time, but the people are rapidly learning to reckon its progress by watches and clocks, and follow our divisions in preference to their own. A common substitute for watches are *time-sticks*, long round pieces of a composition of clay and sawdust, well mixed and wound in a spiral manner; the lapse of time is indicated by its equable slow combustion from one hour mark to another, until the whole is consumed, which in the longest is not less than a week. Dials are in common use, and frequently attached to the mariner's compass, by making the string which retains the cover in its place cast a shadow on the face of it. This lesson in dialing, Davis supposes they learned from the Jesuits. Clepsydras of various forms were anciently employed, some of which, from their description, were so disproportionately elegant and costly for such a clumsy mode of noting time, that their beauty more than their use was perhaps the principal object in preparing them.

The almanac holds an important place, its preparation having been early taken under the special care of the government, which looks upon a present of this important publication as one of the highest favors which it can confer on tributary vassals or friendly nations. It is annually prepared at Peking, under the direction of a bureau attached to the Board of Rites, and, by making it a penal offence to issue a counterfeit or pirated edition the governmental astrologers have monopolized the management of the superstitions of the people in regard to the fortunate or unlucky conjunctions of each day and hour. Besides the cabalistic part of it, the ephemeris also contains tables of the rising of the sun according to the latitudes of the principal places, times of the new and full moon, the beginning and length of the twenty-four terms, eclipses, application of the horary characters, conjunction of the planets, etc. Two or three editions are published for the convenience of the people, the prices of which vary from three to ten cents a copy. No one ventures to be without an almanac, lest he be liable to the greatest misfortunes, and run the imminent hazard of undertaking important events on black-balled days. The Europeans who were employed for many years in compiling the calendar were not allowed to interfere in the astrological part; it is to the discredit of the Chinese to aid thus in perpetuating folly and ignorance among the people, when they know that the whole system is false and absurd. Such governments as that of China, however, deem it necessary to uphold ancient superstitions, if they can thereby influence their security, or strengthen the reverence due them.

If their astronomical notions are vague, their geographical knowledge is ridiculous. The maps of their own territories are tolerably good, being originally drawn from actual surveys by nine of the Jesuits, between the years 1708–1718, and since that time have been filled up and changed to conform to the alterations and divisions. Their full surveys were engraved on copper at Paris, by order of Louis XIV., on sheets, measuring in all over a hundred square feet, and have formed the basis of all subsequent maps. The Chinese do not teach geography in their schools, even of their own empire. The common people have no knowledge, therefore, of the form and divisions of the globe, and the size and position of the kingdoms of the earth. Their common maps delineate them very erroneously, not even excepting their own possessions in Mongolia and Ílí—scattering islands, kingdoms, and continents, as they have heard of their existence, at haphazard in various corners beyond the frontiers. The two Americas and Africa are entirely omitted on most of them, and England, Holland, Portugal, Goa, Luçonia, Bokhara, Germany, France, and India, are arranged along the western side, from north to south, in a series of islands and headlands. The southern and eastern sides are similarly garnished by islands, as Japan, Lewchew, Formosa, Siam, Birmah, Java, the Sulu Islands, and others, while Russia occupies the whole of the northern frontier of their Middle Kingdom.

The geographical works of Tsinglai are not quite so erroneous as his astronomical, but the uneducated people, notwithstanding his efforts to teach them better, still generally suppose the earth to be an immense extended stationary plain. Their notions of its inhabitants are equally whimsical, and would grace the pages of Sir John Mandeville. In some parts of its surface they imagine the inhabitants to be all dwarfs, who tie themselves together in bunches for fear of being carried away by the eagles; in others they are all women, who conceive by looking at their shadows; and in a third kingdom, all the people have holes in their breasts, through which they thrust a pole, when carrying one another from place to place. Charts for the guidance of the navigator, or instruments to aid him in determining his position at sea, the Chinese are nearly or quite destitute of; they have retrograded rather than advanced in navigation, judging from the accounts of Fa-hian, Ibn Batuta, and other travellers, when their vessels frequented the ports in the Persian Gulf and on the Malabar coast, and carried on a large trade with the Archipelago. Itineraries are published, containing the distances between places on the principal thoroughfares throughout the provinces, and also lists of the ports, harbors, and islands on the coast, but nothing like sailing directions accompany the latter, nor do maps of the routes illustrate the former. Such knowledge as they have on these points is hidden away in their libraries, as the Latin and Greek classics were in European convents and castles a thousand years ago.

In the various branches of mensuration and formulæ used to describe the dimensions and weight of bodies, they have reached only a practical mediocrity. With a partial knowledge of trigonometry, and no instruments for ascertaining the heights of objects or their distances from the observer, still their lands are well measured, and the area of lots in towns and cities accurately ascertained. The *chih* or foot is the integer of length, but its standard value cannot be easily ascertained. In the *Chinese Commercial Guide*, p. 285, is a table of eighty-four observations on this point, taken at different times and places in China, whose extremes differ more than six inches. It is fixed by the Board of Works at 13⅛ in. English, but tradesmen at Canton employ foot measures varying from 14.625 to 14.81 in.; according to the tariff, it is reckoned at 14.1 in. English, and the *chang* of ten *chih* at $3\frac{1}{12}$ yds. During the past thirty years, the tariff weights and measures have gradually obtained acceptance as the standards, and this will probably result in securing uniformity in course of time. The *chih* is subdivided into ten *tsun* or puntos, and each *tsun* into ten *făn*. The *lí* is used for distances, and is usually reckoned at 1,825.55 ft. English, which gives 2.89 *lí* to an English mile; this is based on the estimate of 200 *lí* to a degree, but there were only 180 *lí* to a degree before Europeans came, which increases its length to 2,028.39 ft. or 2.6 *lí* to a mile, which is nearer the common estimate. The French missionaries divided the degree into 250 *lí* (each being then exactly 1,460.44 ft. English, or one-tenth of a French astronomical league), and also into sixty minutes and sixty seconds, to make it correspond to western notation; this measure has not been adopted in common use. The present rulers have established post-houses very generally, at intervals of ten *lí*, or about a league. The land measures are the *mao* and *king;* the former measures 6,000 square *chih*, or 808.6 square yards, and a hundred of them make a *king*. Taxes are collected, land is leased, and crops are estimated by the *mao* and its decimal parts; but examination has shown that the actual area of a *mao* grows less as one goes north; in Canton, it is about 4.76 *mao* to an acre, and at Peking it is six, and even smaller.

The weights and measures of the Chinese are twenty-four in all, and vary in their value even more than those of long measure. The common weights are called *tael*, *catty*, and *pecul* by foreigners; their values are respectively $1\frac{1}{3}$ oz. av., $1\frac{1}{3}$ lb. av., and $133\frac{1}{3}$ lbs. av., and thus roughly correspond to the English ounce, pound, and hundredweight. The Chinese deal in many articles by weight which among western nations are sold according to their quality—such as wood, silk, oil, whiskey, cloth, grain, poultry, etc.—so that it has been humorously observed that the Chinese sell everything by weight, except eggs and children. Their common measures correspond nearly to our gill, half-pint, pint, and peck, and are used to retail rice, beans, etc. The smaller ones are not very accurately constructed from bamboo-joints, but the peck measure, or *tao*, shaped like the frustum of a pyramid, must be officially examined and sealed before it can be used; at Canton it contains 6½ catties weight, or about 1.13 gallon. The decimals of the tael, called *mace*, *candareen*, and *cash* (*tsien*, *făn*, and *lí*), are employed in reckoning bullion, pearls, gems, drugs, etc.; ten cash making one candareen, ten candareens one mace, etc. The proportions between the Chinese and American moneys and weights is such that so many taels per pecul, or candareens per catty, is the same as so many dollars per hundredweight, or cents per pound.[1]

The monetary system is arranged on the principle of weight, and the divisions have the same names, *tael*, *mace*, *candareen*, and *cash*. The only native coin is a copper piece called *tsien*, because it originally weighed a mace; it is thin and circular, rather more than an inch in diameter, with a square hole in the middle for the convenience of stringing. The obverse bears the word *pao*, or 'current,' and the name of the province in Manchu, on each side of the square hole; the reverse has four words, *Taukwang*, *tung*, *pao*, *i.e.*, 'money current [during the reign of] Taukwang.' Mints for casting cash are established in each provincial capital under the direction of the Board of Revenue. The coin should consist of an alloy of copper, 50; zinc, 41½; lead, 6½; and tin, 2; or of equal parts of copper and zinc; but it has been so debased by iron and reduced in size during the last fifty years that it does not pay to counterfeit it. Each piece should weigh 58 grains troy, or 3.78 grammes, but most of those now in circulation are under 30 grains, and the rate of exchange varies in different parts of tho land from 900 to 1,800 for a silver dollar.

The workmen in the mint are required to remain within the building except when leave of absence is obtained, but in spite of all the efforts of government, private coinage is issued to a great amount, and sometimes with the connivance of the mint-master. Neither silver nor gold has ever been coined to any extent in China. In seeking for the cause of this difference from all other Asiatic nations, it seems to lie in the commercial freedom which has done so much to elevate them. The gov-

---

[1] *Chinese Repository*, Vol. X., p. 650; *Chinese Chrestomathy; Chinese Commercial Guide*, Fifth Ed., pp. 265–288; Rondot, *Commerce de la Chine*, 1819.

ernment on the one hand is not strong enough to restrain counterfeiters, and not honest enough, on the other hand, to issue pieces of uniform standard for a series of years till it has obtained the confidence of its subjects. It will not receive base metal for taxes, and cannot force merchants to accept adulterated coins. As its foreign relations extend it will no doubt be obliged to issue a better national currency in the three metals. Attempts have been made to introduce a silver piece of the size of a tael, and specimens were made at Shanghai in 1856. A large coinage of native dollars was attempted in Fuhkien and Formosa, about 1835, to pay the troops on that island. One of them indicated that the piece was "pure silver for current use from the Chang-chau Commissariat; [weight] seven *mace* two *candareens*." The other was of the same weight and purity (417.4 grains troy), and besides the inscription in Chinese on the obverse, and in Manchu on the reverse, it had an effigy of the god of Longevity on the head and a tripod on the tail, to authenticate its official origin. These pieces were either melted or counterfeited to such an extent on their appearance, that they soon disappeared.

Foreign dollars are imported in great quantities from Mexico and San Francisco, and form the medium of trade at the open ports. They are often stamped by the person who pays them out, which soon destroys them as a coin, and they are then melted and refined to be cast into ingots of bullion, called *shoes of sycee*, from *sí-sz'* or 'fine floss'; these weigh from five mace to fifty taels, the larger pieces being stamped with the district magistrate's title and the date, to verify them. They are from ninety-seven to ninety-nine per cent. pure silver, but small ingots of ten or fifteen taels weight are less pure than the large *shoes*, as they are called from their shape. Gold bullion is cast into bars like cakes of India-ink in shape, weighing about ten taels, or hammered into thick leaves which can be examined but not separated by driving a punch through a pile of a hundred or more—a precaution against cheating. Large quantities are sent abroad in this shape.

Taxes and duties are paid in sycee of ninety-eight per cent. fineness, and licensed bankers are connected with the revenue department to whom the proceeds are paid, and who are allowed a small percentage for refining and becoming responsible for its purity. Dollars and ingots are counterfeited, and all classes have them inspected by *shroffs*, who, by practice, are able to decide by the sight alone upon the degree of alloy in a piece of silver, though usually they employ touchstone needles to assist them, different degrees of fineness imparting a different color to the needle. Books are prepared as aids to the detection of counterfeit dollars; in these the process of manufacture is carefully described; some of the pieces are marvels of skill in forgery.

Chartered banking companies are unknown, for a government warrant or charter would carry no weight with it, but private bankers are found in all large towns. Paper money was issued in immense quantities under the Mongol dynasty, and its convenience is highly praised by Marco Polo, who looked upon its emission by the Grand Khan as the highest secret of alchemy. Polo's ideas of this operation would please the "greenbackers" in the United States. He says, when describing Kublai's purchases: "So he buys such a quantity of those precious things every year that his treasure is endless, while all the while the money he pays away costs him nothing at all. If any of those pieces of paper are spoilt the owner carries them to the mint, and by paying three per cent. on the value he gets new pieces in exchange." The total issues of this highest secret of alchemy during Kublai's reign of thirty-four years are reckoned by Pauthier, the *Yuen Annals*, at equal to $624,135,500. The Khan's successors, however, overdid the manufacture, and when the people found out that they had nothing but paper to show for all the valuables they had parted with to the Mongols, it added strength to the rebellion of Hung-wu (A.D. 1359), which ended in their expulsion nine years afterward. The new dynasty was, nevertheless, obliged to issue its notes at first, but the mercantile instincts of the people soon asserted their power, and as industry revived they were superseded about 1455. The Manchus did not issue any Governmental paper till 1858, during the Tai-ping rebellion, and its circulation was limited to the capital from the first; seeing that even then it was known to have no basis of credit or funds.

A bank can be opened by any person or company, subject to certain laws and payments to Government, on reporting its organization. The number of these offices of deposit and emission is large in proportion to the business of a town, but their capital averages only two or three thousand taels; the number in Tientsin is stated at three hundred, at Peking it is less than four hundred, of which scores in each are mere branches. The check on over-issue of notes lies in the control exercised by the clearing-house of every city, where the standing of each bank is known by its operations. The circulation of the notes is limited in some cases to the street or neighborhood wherein the establishment is situated; often the payee has a claim on the payer of a bill for a full day if it be found to be counterfeit or worthless—a custom which involves a good deal of scribbling on the back of the bill to certify the names. Proportionally few counterfeit notes are met with, owing more to the limited range of the bills, making it easy to ask the bank, which recognizes its own paper by the check-tallies, of which the register contains two or three halves printed across the check-book. When silver is presented for exchange, the bills are usually, in Peking, filled up and dated as the customer wishes while he waits for them. Their face value ranges from one to a hundred *tiao*, or strings of cash, but their worth depends on the exchange between silver and cash, and as this fluctuates daily, the bills soon find their way home. These notes are unknown in the southern provinces, where dollars have long circulated; but their convenience is so great that people are willing to run slight risks on this account. Hongkong bills circulate on the mainland to very remote districts.

Banks issue circular letters of credit to travel through the Empire, and the system of remittance by drafts is as complete as in Europe; the rates charged are high, however, and vast sums of silver are constantly on the move. The habit of pawning goods is very general, and carries its disastrous results among all classes. There are three kinds of pawnshops, and the laws regulating them are strict and equitable; the chief evil arising from their number is the facility they give to thieves. Pawn tickets are exposed for sale in the streets, and form a curious branch of traffic. These establishments are generally very extensive, and the vast amount of goods stored in them, especially garments and jewelry, shows their universal patronage. One pawnbroker's warehouse at Tinghai was used by the English forces as a hospital, and accommodated between two and three hundred patients. The insecurity of commercial operations involves, of course, a high rate of interest, sometimes up to three per cent. a month, lowering according to circumstances to twelve or ten per cent. per annum. The legal pawnshops (*tang pu*) are allowed three years to redeem, and give three years' notice of dissolution. The restrictions on selling pawned articles works injuriously to the shops, in consequence of rapid depreciation or risks to the articles. If a fire occurs on the premises the pawner claims the full amount of his pledge; only one-half is paid if it communicates from a neighbor's house.[1]

One characteristic feature of Chinese society cannot be omitted in this connection, namely, its tendency to associate. It is a fertile principle applied to every branch of life, but especially conspicuous in all industrial operations. The people crystallize into associations; in the town and in the country, in buying and in selling, in studies, in fights, and in politics, everybody must co-operate with somebody else—women as well as men. To belong to one or more *hwui*, and be identified with its fortunes, and enlisted in its struggles, seems to be the stimulus to activity, resulting from the democratic element in the Chinese polity, to which we are to refer the continuity as well as many singular features of the national character. In trade capitalists associate to found great banks, to sell favorite medicines, or engross leading staples; little farmers club together to buy an ox, pedlers to get the custom of a street, porters to monopolize the loads in a ward, or chair-bearers to furnish all the sedans for a town. Beggars are allotted to one or

---

[1] Ed. Biot in *Journal Asiatique*, 1837, Tome III., p. 422, and Tome IV., pp. 97, 209; *Chinese Commercial Guide*, 1863, pp. 264–275; *N. C. As. Journal*, No. VI., pp. 52–71; Yule's *Marco Polo*, 1871, Vol. I., p. 378–385; Pauthier *Le Livre de M. Polo*, Cap. XCV., p. 319; Vissering *On Chinese Currency*, 1877; *Chinese Repository*, Vol. XX., p. 289; Doolittle's *Social Life*, Vol. II., pp. 138–247; *Notes and Queries on C. and J.*, Vol. II., p. 108.

two streets by their *hwui*, and driven off another's beat if they encroach. Each guild of carpenters, silkmen, masons, or even of physicians and teachers, works to advance its own interests, keep its own members in order, and defend itself against its opponents. Villagers form themselves into organizations against the wiles of powerful clans; and unscrupulous officials are met and balked by popular unions when they least expect it. Women and mothers get up a company to procure a trousseau, to buy an article of dress or furniture, to pay for a son's wedding. Associations are limited to a year, to a month, to a decade, according to their design. These various forms of co-operation teach the people to know each other, while they also furnish agencies for unscrupulous men to oppress and crush out their enemies, gratify their revenge, and intimidate enterprise. Nevertheless, until the people learn higher principles of morality, these habits of combining themselves bring more benefits to the whole body than evils, at the same time quickening the vitality of the mass, without which it would die out in brigandage and despair.[1]

The theory of war has received more attention among the Chinese than its practice, and their reputation as an unwarlike people is as ancient and general among their neighbors as that of their seclusion and ingenuity. The Mongols and Manchus, Huns and Tartars, all despised the effeminate braggadocio of Chinese troops, and easily overcame them in war, but were themselves in turn conquered in times of peace. Minute directions are given in books with regard to the drilling of troops, which are seldom reduced to practice. The puerile nature of the examinations which candidates for promotion in the army pass through, proves the remains of the ancient hand-to-hand encounter, and evinces the low standard still entertained of what an officer should be. Personal courage and brawn are highly esteemed, and the prowess of ancient heroes in the battle-field is lauded in songs, and embellished in novels.

The arms of the Chinese still consist of bows and arrows.

---

[1] For an account of the money *hwui* and details of their system, see M. Eug. Simon, Les Petites Sociétés d'Argent en Chine, *N. C. Br. R. As. Soc. Journal*, No. V., Art. I. (1868).

spears, matchlocks, swords, and cannon of various sizes and lengths. The bow is used more for show in the military examinations, than for service in battle. Rattan shields, painted with tigers' heads, are used on board the revenue cutters to turn the thrust of spears, and on ceremonial occasions, when the companies are paraded in full uniforms and equipments. The uniform of the different regiments of the *luh-ying* or 'native army,' consists of a jacket of brown, yellow, or blue, bordered with a wide edging of another color; the trowsers are usually blue. The cuirass is made of quilted and doubled cotton cloth, and covered with iron plates or brass knobs connected by copper bands; the helmet is iron or polished steel, sometimes inlaid, weighing two and one-fourth pounds, and has neck and ear lappets to protect those parts. The back of the jacket bears the word *yung*, 'courage,' and on the breast is painted the service to which the corps is attached, whether to the governor, commandant, or Emperor. The exhibition of courage among Chinese troops is not, however, always deferred to the time when they run away, spite of the disparaging reputation they have obtained in this respect from their British conquerors—who have, nevertheless, on more than one occasion, been led to admire the cool pluck of the same men when led by competent officers.

The matchlock is of wrought iron and plain bore; it has a longer barrel than a musket, so long that a rest is sometimes attached to the stock for greater ease in firing; the match is a cord of hemp or coir, and the pan must be uncovered with the hand before it can be fired, which necessarily interferes with, and almosts prevents its use in wet or windy weather. The cannon are cast, and although not of very uniform calibre from the mode of manufacture, are serviceable for salutes. The ginjal is a kind of swivel from six to fourteen feet long, resting on a tripod; being less liable to burst than the cannon, it is the most effective gun the Chinese possess.

Gunpowder was probably known to the Chinese in the latter part of the Han dynasty (A.D. 250), but its application in firearms at that time is not so plain. The exploits of Kung-ming in that period owe their interest to his use of gunpowder in modes like the Greek fire of the Byzantines, though the animated narratives of Lo Kwan-chung (A.D. 1300) in his *History of the Three States*, are not reliable history in this particular. Grosier (Vol. VII., pp. 176–200) has adduced the evidences proving the use of powder at or before the Christian era. The inferences that Europe obtained it from India rather than China have, however, a good deal of weight. Early Arab historians refer to it as Chinese snow and Chinese salt—a fact which only shows its eastern origin—while the Chinese compound term of *hwo-yioh*, or 'fire drug,' rather indicates a foreign source than otherwise.

Mr. W. F. Mayers has searched out and collated a considerable mass of evidence from Chinese sources bearing upon the introduction of explosives in native warfare and ordinary life. The conclusions of this writer point both to a foreign origin of gunpowder in China, and a much later use of the compound among their warriors than has generally been supposed. Coming, probably, from India or Central Asia about the fifth century A.D. the invention, he says, "perhaps found its way into China in connection with the manufacture of fireworks for purposes of diversion; and supplanting at some unascertained period the practice of producing a crepitating noise by burning bamboos as a charm against evil spirits." No evidence exists of the use of gunpowder as an agent of warfare until the middle of the twelfth century, nor did a knowledge of its propulsive effects come to the Chinese until the reign of Yungloh, in the fifteenth century—a thousand years after its first employment in fire-crackers.[1]

Fire-arms of large size were introduced toward the end of the Ming dynasty by foreign instructors; ginjals and matchlocks were known four centuries earlier in all the eastern and central regions of Asia, but none of those people could forge or cast large artillery, owing to their imperfect machinery. The gunpowder is badly mixed and triturated, though the proportions are nearly the same as our own. The native arms are now

[1] *North China Br. Royal Asiatic Soc. Journal*, 1870, No. VI., Art. V. Compare *Notes and Queries on C. and J.*

rapidly giving place to foreign in the imperial army, and the establishment of four or five arsenals under the management of competent instructors, where implements of warfare of every kind are manufactured, will, ere long, make an entire change in Chinese weapons and tactics. Some of their brass guns were of enormous size and great strength, but were of little use for practical warfare, owing to the bad carriages and rude means of working them.

The uniforms of Chinese troops are not even calculated to give them a fine appearance when drawn up for parade, and no one, looking at them, can believe that men dressed in loose jackets and trousers, with heavy shoes and bamboo caps, could be trained to cope with western soldiers. Fans or umbrellas are often made use of on parade to assuage the heat or protect from the rain, while the chief object of these reviews is to salute and knock head before some high officer. In order to repress insurrection, the government has been frequently compelled to buy off turbulent leaders with office and rewards, and thus disorganize and scatter the enemy it could not vanquish.

But however ridiculous the army and navy of the Chinese were half a century ago, in the isolation and ignorance which then held them, it cannot be alleged of what has been attempted within twenty years, and the promise of what may be done in as many more. The following *résumé* of the qualities of the Chinese soldier, from experience with Col. Gordon's "Ever Victorious Force" during the Tai-ping insurrection will be *à propos* of this subject to which this work cannot devote further space. "The old notion is pretty well got rid of, that they are at all a cowardly people when properly paid and efficiently led; while the regularity and order of their habits, which dispose them to peace in ordinary times, give place to a daring bordering upon recklessness in time of war. Their intelligence and capacity for remembering facts make them well fitted for use in modern warfare, as do also the coolness and calmness of their disposition. Physically they are on the average not so strong as Europeans, but considerably more so than most of the other races of the East; and on a cheap diet of rice, vegetables, salt fish, and pork, they can go through a vast amount of fatigue, whether in a temperate climate or a tropical one, where Europeans are ill-fitted for exertion. Their wants are few; they have no caste prejudices, and hardly any appetite for intoxicating liquors. Being of a lymphatic or lymphatic-bilious temperament, they enjoy a remarkable immunity from inflammatory disease, and the tubercular diathesis is little known amongst them."[1]

Their progress in real civilization is not to be fairly measured by their attainments in war, although it has been said that the two best general criteria of civilization among any people are superior skill in destroying their fellow men, and the degree of respect they pay to women. China falls far behind her place among the nations if judged by these tests alone, and in reality owes her present advance in numbers, industry, and wealth mainly to her peaceful character and policy. She would have probably presented a spectacle similar to the disunited hordes of Central Asia, had her people been actuated by a warlike spirit, for when divided into fifty or more feudal states, as was the case in the days of Confucius, she made no progress in the arts of life. The Manchu Emperors have endeavored to conquer their neighbors, the Birmans and Coreans, but in both cases had to be satisfied with the outward homage of a *kotow*, and a few articles of tribute, when a formal embassy presented itself in Peking. The Siamese, Cochinchinese, Coreans, Tibetans, Lewchewans, and some of the tribes of Turkestan, are nominally vassals of the Son of Heaven, and their names remain on the roll of feifs. The first two have ceased to *tsin kung*, or send tribute, since about 1860; and the Lewchewans are not likely to revisit their old quarters at Peking in any capacity; while the others derive advantage from the facilities of traffic which they are unwilling to give up.

The precepts of Confucius taught the rulers of China to conquer their neighbors by showing the excellence of a good government, for then their enemies would come and voluntarily range themselves under their sway; and although the kindness

---

[1] Andrew Wilson, *The "Ever Victorious Army." A History of the Chinese Campaign under Lieut.-Col. Gordon.* London, 1868, p. 269.

of the rulers of China to those fully in their power is as hypocritical as their rule is unjust, those nations who pay them this homage do it voluntarily, and experience no interference in their internal affairs. The maxims of Confucian polity, aided by the temper of the people, have had some effect, in the lapse of years, upon the nature of this quasi feudality. The weaker nations looked up to China, since they could look no higher, and their advances in just government, industry, and arts, is not a little owing to their political intercourse during past centuries. The Chinese Empire is a notable example of the admirable results of a peaceful policy ; and the sincere desire of every well-wisher of his race doubtless is that this mighty mass of human beings may be Christianized and elevated from their present ignorance and weakness by a like peaceful infusion of the true principles of good order and liberty.

Many treatises upon the art and practice of war exist, one of which, called the *Soldier's Manual*,[1] in eighteen chapters, contains some good directions. The first chapter treats of the mode of marching, necessity of having plans of the country through which the army is to pass, and cautions the troops against harassing the people unnecessarily—not a useless admonition, for a body of Chinese soldiers is too often like a swarm of locusts upon the land. The second chapter teaches the mode of building bridges, the need there is of cautious explorations in marching, and of sending out scouts ; this subject is also continued in the next section, and directions given about castrametation, placing sentries, and keeping the troops on the alert, as well as under strict discipline in camp. The rest of the book is chiefly devoted to directions for the management of an actual battle, sending out spies beforehand, choosing positions, and bringing the various parts of the army into action at the best time. The hope of reward is held out to induce the soldier to be brave, and the threats of punishment and death if he desert or turn his back in time of battle.

The utility of music in encouraging the soldiers and exciting them to the charge is fully appreciated, but to our notions it

---

[1] *Chinese Repository*, Vol. XI., p. 487.

no more deserves the name of music than the collection of half-drilled louts in petticoats does that of an army, when compared with a European force. Still, its antiquity, if nothing else, renders it a subject of great interest to the musical student, while its power over the people seems to be none the less because it is unscientific. However small their attainments in the theory and practice of music, no nation gives to this art a higher place. It was regarded by Confucius as an essential part in the government of a state, harmonizing and softening the relations between the different ranks of society, and causing them all to move on in consentaneous accord. It is remarked of the sage himself that having heard a tune in one of his ramblings, he did not know the taste of food for three weeks after—but, with all deference to the feelings of so distinguished a man, we cannot help thinking his food might have been quite as palatable without music, if it was no better then than it is at the present day. The Chinese never had anything like the musical contests among the Greeks, and their efforts have been directed to develop instrumental rather than vocal music.

The names and characters used for notes in vocal music are here given, though their real tone cannot be accurately represented by our staff. The second octave is denoted by affixing the sign *jin*, 'a man,' to the simple notes, or as shown in the second *ché*, by a peculiar hooked bottom.

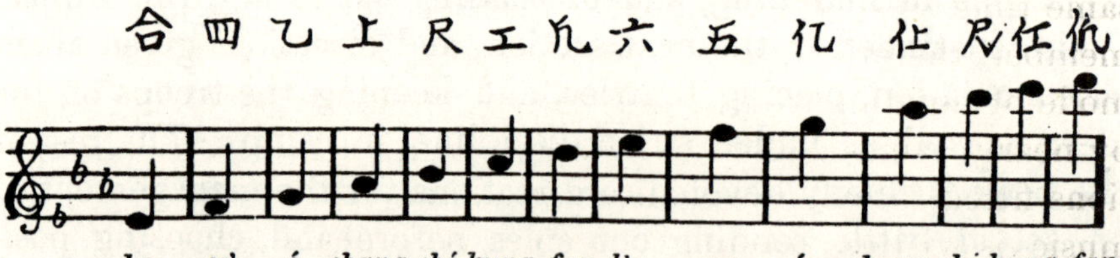

If the first note in this scale be taken as the tonic, then they form a diatonic octave, with a supernumerary note, which is an octave above the second one *sz'*, the first one, *ho*, being an octave below *liu*, the eighth. But the semitones *í* and *fan* are very little used, and it loses in some degree its diatonic character. No chromatic scale exists among them, at least none of their instruments are made to express flat and sharp notes.

Barrow says that the Chinese learned this mode of writing music from Pereira, a Roman Catholic missionary, in 1670, but its existence in Japan and Corea invalidates this statement.

There are two kinds of music, known as the Southern and Northern, which differ in their character, and are readily recognized by the people. The octave in the former seems to have had only six notes, and the songs of the Miaotsz' and rural people in that portion of China are referable to such a gamut, while the eight-tone scale generally prevails in all theatres and more cultivated circles. Further examination by competent observers who can jot down on such a gamut the airs they hear in various regions of China, is necessary to ascertain these interesting points, which now seem to carry us back to remote antiquity, and have been noticed in other countries than China.

In writing instrumental music, marks, meaning to *push*, *fillip*, *hook*, etc., are added to denote the mode of playing the string; the two are united into very complicated combinations. For instance, in writing a tune for the lute or *kin*, "each note is a cluster of characters; one denotes the string, another the stud, a third informs you in what manner the fingers of the right hand are to be used, a fourth does the same in reference to the left, a fifth tells the performer in what way he must slide the hand before or after the appropriate sound has been given, and a sixth says, perhaps, that two notes are to be struck at the same time." These complex notes are difficult to learn and remember, therefore the Chinese usually play by the ear. This mode of notation, in addition to its complexity, must be varied by nearly every kind of instrument, inasmuch as the combinations fitted for one instrument are inapplicable to another; but music is written for only a few instruments, such as the lute and the guitar.

These notes, when simply written without directions combined with them as described above, indicate only their pitch in a certain scale, and do not denote either the length or the absolute pitch; they are written perpendicularly, and various marks of direction are given on the side of the column regarding the proportionate length of time in which certain notes are to be played, others to be trilled or repeated once, twice, or more times, and when the performer is to pause. Beats occur at regular intervals in some of the written tunes; all music is in common time and no triple measures are used, yet time is pretty well observed in orchestras. Of harmony and counterpoint they know nothing; the swell, diminish, flat, sharp, appogiatura, tie, and other marks which assist in giving expression to our written music, are for the most part unknown, nor are tunes set to any key. The neatness and adaptation of the European notation is better appreciated after studying the clumsy, imperfect mode which is here briefly described.[1]

No description can convey a true idea of Chinese vocal music, and few persons are able to imitate it when they have heard it. De Guignes says, "It is possible to sing a Chinese song, but I think it would be very difficult to give it the proper tone without having heard it by a native, and I rather believe that no one can perfectly imitate their notes." They seem, in some cases, to issue from the larynx and nose, the tongue, teeth, and lips having little to do with them, the modulation being made mostly with the muscles of the bronchia; at other times, the enunciation of the words requires a little more use of the lips and teeth. Singing is generally on a falsetto key; and this feature prevails throughout. Whether in the theatre or in the street, about the house or holding the guitar or lute, both men and women sing in this artificial tone somewhere between a squeal and a scream, and which no western musical instrument is able to imitate. Its character is plaintive and soft, not full or exhibiting much compass, though when two or three females sing together in recitative, not destitute of sweetness. Bass and tenor are not sung by men, nor a second treble by females, and the two performers are seldom heard together among the thousands of street musicians who get a precarious living by their skill in this line, as they accompany the guitar or rebeck. The chanting in Buddhist services resembles the Ambrosian and early Gregorian tones, and is accompanied only by striking a block

[1] Compare Dr. Jenkins in the *Journal N. C. Br. R. A. S.*, Vol. V., 1868, pp. 30 ff., and Rev. E. W. Syle in *ib.* Vol. II., 1859, p. 176; Père Amiot in *Mém. conc. les Chinois*, Vol. VI., pp. 1 ff.; *Notes and Queries on C. and J.*, Vol. IV., Arts. 2 and 3. Perny *Dict.*, app. No. XIV., p. 443.

and marking the time; the tenor voices of boys make a strong contrast to the gruff bass voices of the men in this service; some of the latter will carry their part as low as an octave below C or D in the bass, sounding most sepulchrally, like a trombone.

Three of the tunes inserted in Barrow's *Travels* are here quoted as specimens of Chinese airs The first is the most popular, the second, common at Shanghai, is called *Luh pan*, or 'Six Boards,' it has a strain at the beginning and end additional to the usual form.

MOH-LÍ HWA; OR, THE JASMINE FLOWER.

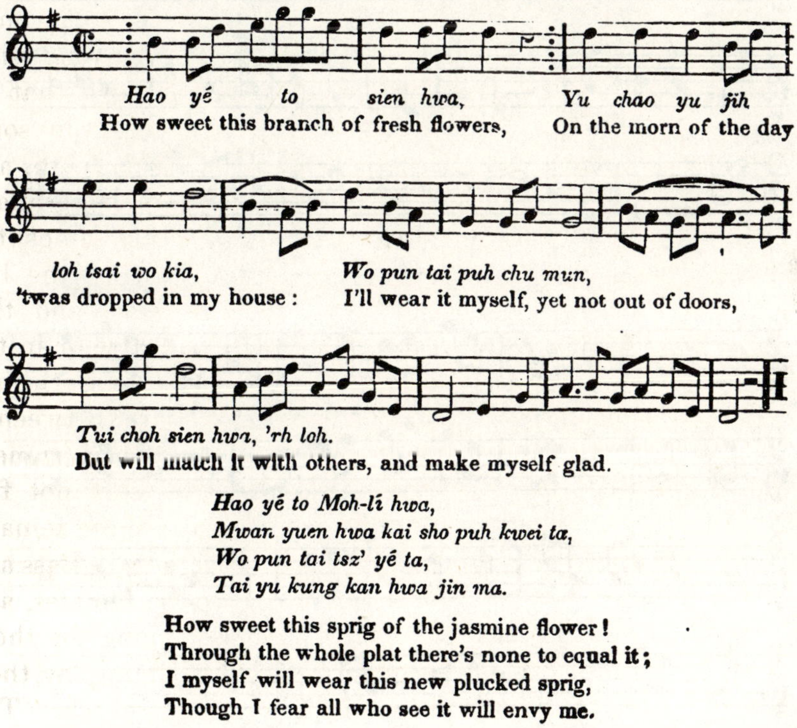

Hao yé to Moh-lí hwa,
Mwan yuen hwa kai sho puh kwei ta,
Wo pun tai tsz' yé ta,
Tai yu kung kan hwa jin ma.

How sweet this sprig of the jasmine flower!
Through the whole plat there's none to equal it;
I myself will wear this new plucked sprig,
Though I fear all who see it will envy me.

LUH PAN; OR, THE SIX BOARDS.

The literature on the art of music is large. One treatise on beating drums scientifically dates from about the year 860 A.D., and contains a list of about one hundred and twenty-nine symphonies, many of which are of Indian origin. Among the seventy-two instruments briefly described in the *Chinese Chrestomathy*, there are seventeen kinds of drums, from the large ones suspended in temples to assist in worship to others of lesser size and diverse shape used in war, in theatres, and in bands. Gongs, cymbals, tambourines, and musical vases are also described in considerable variety; the last consisting of a curious arrangement of twelve cups, more or less filled with water, and struck with rods. The Chinese are fond of the tinkling of small pieces of sonorous glass, caused by the wind striking them against each other as they are suspended from a frame or lamp. The simple succession of sounds arising from striking upon a harmonicon, jingling these glasses together, or touching different sized cymbals suspended in a frame, is a favorite species of music.

The stringed instruments to be played by thrumming are not as numerous as those of percussion, but they display more science. Nothing resembling the harp or Apollo's lyre has been observed among them. The *kin*, or 'scholar's lute,' is considered as the most finished, and has received more attention than any other orchestral implement; to excel in playing it is regarded as a scholarly accomplishment. A work entitled *The Lute-Player's Easy Lessons*, in two volumes, contains explanations of one hundred and nine terms and is illustrated by twenty-nine pictures of the position of the hands to aid in a full understanding of the twenty-three sets of tunes given in the second volume. This lute, it may be added, is of very ancient origin and derives its name from the word *kin*, 'to prohibit,' "because it restrains and checks evil passions and corrects the human heart." It is a board about four feet in length and eighteen inches wide, convex above and flat beneath, where are two holes opening into hollows. There are seven strings of silk, which pass over a bridge near the wide end through the board, and are tightened by nuts beneath; they are secured on two pegs at the smaller end. The sounding-board is divided by thirteen studs, "so placed that the length of the strings is divided first into two equal parts, then into three, etc., up to eight, with the omission of the seventh. The seven strings inclose the compass of a ninth or two-fifths, the middle one being treated like A upon the violin, viz., as a middle string, and each of the outer ones is tuned a fifth from it. This interval is treated like our octave in the violin, for the compass of the *kin* is made up of fifths. Each of the outer strings is tuned a fourth from the alternate string within the system, so that there is a major tone, an interval tone less than a minor third, and a major tone in the fifth. The Chinese leave the interval entire, and skip the half tone, while we divide it into two unequal parts. It will therefore readily appear that the mood or character of the music of the *kin* must be very different from that of western instruments, so that none of them can exactly do justice to the Chinese airs. One of the peculiarities in performing on the lute is sliding the left hand fingers along the string, and the trilling and other evolutions they are made to execute."

There are other instruments similar to the *kin*, one with thirty, and another with thirteen strings, played with plectrums. The number of instruments resembling the guitar, lute, cithern, spinet, etc., is considerable, some with silken, others with wire strings, but none of catgut. The balloon-shaped guitar, or *pípa*, has four strings arranged and secured like those of a violin; it is about three feet long, and the unvarnished upper table has twelve frets to guide the performer. The strings are tuned at the intervals of a fourth, a major tone, and a fourth, so that the outer strings are octaves to each other; but the player generally avoids the semitones. The *pípa* frequently accompanies the songs of strolling musicians and ballad singers. The *san hien*, or 'three-stringed guitar,' resembles a rebeck in its contour, but the neck and head is three feet long, and the body is cylindrical and hollow, usually covered with snake's skin, upon which the bridge is set. The strings are tuned as fourths to each other, and in this respect it seems to be the counterpart of the Grecian mercurian; their sound is low and dull, and the instrument is sometimes played in company with the *pípa*. Another kind of guitar, called *yueh kin*, or 'full moon guitar,' has a large round belly and short neck, resembling the theorbo or arch lute of Europe, but with only four strings, while that had ten or more. These four strings stand in pairs that are unisons with each other, having an interval of a fifth interposed between the pairs. The sound is smarter than that from the *pípa* or *kin*, and it is used in lively tunes, the strings being struck briskly with the nail or a plectrum. Similar in its construction to the *san hien* is the rebeck, or two-stringed fiddle, the rude appearance of which corresponds to the thin grating sounds which issue from it. This instrument is merely a bamboo stick thrust into a cylinder of the same material, and having two strings fastened at one end of the stick on pegs, and passing over a bridge on the cylinder to the other end; they are tuned at intervals of a fifth. The bow passes between the two strings, and as they are near each other, much of the skill required to play it is exhibited in wielding the bow so as not to make discord by scraping it against the wrong string while trying to produce a given sound. Europeans wonder how the Chinese can be delighted with the harsh gratings of this wretched machine, but none of their musical instruments are more popular, and the skill they exhibit in playing it deserves a better reward in the melody of the notes. A modification of it, called *tí kin*, or 'crowing lute,' is made by employing a cocoanut for the belly; its sounds are, if anything, more dissonant.

The *yang kin* is a kind of dulcimer, consisting of a greater or less number of brass wires of different lengths, tuned at proper intervals, and fastened upon a sounding-board; it is played with light hammers, and forms a rudimentary piano-forte, but the sounds are very attenuated. The *săng* is in like manner the embryo of the organ; it is a hollow conical-shaped box, which corresponds to a wind-chest, having a mouthpiece on one side, and communicating with thirteen reeds of different lengths inserted in the top; some of the tubes are provided with valves, part of them opening upward and part downward, so that some of them sound when the breath fills the wind-box, and others are only heard when it is sucked out and the air rushes down the tubes to refill it. The tubes stand in groups of four, four, three, two, around the top, and those having ventiges are placed so that the performer can open or close them at pleasure as he holds it. By covering the first set of holes and gently breathing in the mouthpiece, a sweet concert of sounds is produced, augmented to the octave and twelfth as the force of the breath is increased. By stopping certain groups, other notes, shriller and louder, are emitted; and any single tube can be sounded by inhaling the wind from the wind-box and stopping the other holes. It is a simple thing and no doubt among the most ancient of musical instruments, but it possesses no scope nor means of varying the tone of the tubes. Mr. Lay thinks it to be identical in principle and form with the organ invented by Jubal; the Chinese regard it more as a curious instrument than one possessing claims to admiration or attention.

Their wind instruments are numerous, but most of them are remarkable rather for clamor than sweetness or compass. The *hwang tih*, or flute, is about twice the length of our fife, and made of a bamboo tube neatly prepared and pierced with ten holes, two of which are placed near the end and unused, and one midway between the embouchure and the six equidistant ones for the fingers. This additional hole is covered with a thin film; the mouth-hole is bored about one-third of the way from the top. There are no keys, and the performers generally blow upon the embouchure so violently that the sounds are shrill and harsh, but when several of them play together the concert is more agreeable. The congener of the flute is the *shu tih*, or clarinet, which takes the lead in all musical performances, as it does in western bands. It has seven effective holes, one of which is stopped by the thumb, but no keys; the bell is of copper and sits loose upon the end, and the copper mouthpiece is ornamented with rings, and blown through a reed. The tones produced by it are shrill and deafening, and none of their instruments better characterize Chinese musical taste. A smaller one, of a sweeter tone, like a flageolet, is sometimes fitted with a singular shaped reed, so that it can be played upon by the nose. Street musicians sometimes endeavor to transform themselves into a travelling orchestra. One of these peripatetic Orpheuses will fit a flageolet to his nose, sling a small drum under one shoulder, and suspend a framework of four small cymbals upon the breast; the man, thus accoutred, aided by a couple of monkeys running after him, or sitting on his head and shoulders, goes from street to street singing a plaintive ditty, and accompanying his voice with his instruments, and drawing a crowd with his monkeys.

The horn resembles a trombone in principle, for the shaft is retractible within the cylindrical copper bell, and can be lengthened at pleasure. The sound is very grave, and in processions its hollow booming forms a great contrast to the shrill clarinets and cymbals. Another kind of horn, less grave, is made of a crooked stem expanding into a small bell at the end; the shaft is of two parts, one drawing into the other, so that the depth of tone can be modified. A long straight horn, resembling the funeral pipe of the Jews, is sometimes heard on funeral occasions, but this and the clarion, trumpet, and other kinds of pipes of ancient and modern make are not common.

The *lo*, or gong, is the type of Chinese music: a crashing harangue of rapid blows upon this sonorous plate, with a rattling accompaniment on small drums, and a crackling symphony of shrill notes from the clarinet and cymbal, constitute the chief features of their musical performances. The Emperor Kanghí endeavored to introduce foreign tunes and instruments among his courtiers, and the natives at Macao have heard good music from the Portuguese bands and choirs in that city from childhood, but not an instrument or a tune has been adopted by them. It seems to be a rule in Chinese music that the gong should only vary in rapidity of strokes, while the alternations of time into agreeable intervals are left to the drums. "This want of perception as to what is pleasing in rhythmical succession of sounds," Lay well observes, "is connected with another fact—the total absence of metrical effect in national poetry. The verses contain a particular number of words and set pauses in each line, but there is nothing like an interchange of long and short sounds. Among the Greeks the fall of the smith's hammer, the stroke of the oar, and the tread of the soldier in armor suggested some poetic measure, and their music exhibits a world of curious metres. But nothing of the sort can be heard in China, amid all the sounds and noises that salute the ear in a noisy country." It is probable that the impracticable, monosyllabic nature of the language has contributed to this result; though the genius and temperament of the people are the chief reasons.

A Chinese orchestra or band, when in full note, strikes upon the ear of a European as a collection of the most discordant sounds, and he immediately thinks of Hogarth's picture of the

Enraged Musician, as the best likeness of its dissonance. It seems, when hearing them, as if each performer had his own tune, and was trying to distinguish himself above his competitors by his zeal and force; but on listening carefully he will observe, amid the clangor, that they keep good time, one taking the octave, and the different instruments striking in with some regard to parts, only, however, to confound the confusion still more because they are not tuned on the same key. Bands and orchestras are employed on occasions of marriages and funerals, theatrical exhibitions, religious or civic processions, and reception of officers, but not to a very great extent in temples or ancestral worship; no nation makes more use of such music as they have than the Chinese. The people have an ear for music, and young men form clubs to learn and practise on various instruments and fit themselves for playing at weddings or birthday festivals. In respect to adopting foreign harmonies, which youths soon learn to appreciate when taught in mission schools, there is likely to be no competition, owing to the great differences between them.[1]

From this account of Chinese music, it may be readily inferred that it is not of such a character as to start the hearers off in a lively dance. A sort of mummer or posture-making is practised by persons attached to theatrical companies, and pantomimic art seems to have been understood in ancient times, but the exhibitions of it were probably as jejune as the caperings of puppets. As acrobats the Chinese are equal to any nation, and companies have performed in many western capitals within a few years past. Some of their performances are highly exciting, as throwing sharp cleavers at a man fastened to a post, till he cannot stir without cutting himself against their blades, is a common exhibition. To go through the tragedy of trying, con-

---

[1] *Chinese as They Are*, Chap. VIII. *Chinese Repository*, Vol. VIII., pp. 30–54. *Chinese Chrestomathy*, pp. 356–365. *Journal N. C. Br. R. A. Soc.*, No. II., 1859, p. 176; No. V., 1868, p. 30. *Journal of the Asiatic Soc. of Japan*, 1877, Vol. V., pp. 170–179. *German Asiatic Soc. of Japan*, 1876. Grosier, *Description générale de la Chine*, Tome VI., p. 258. Doolittle, *Social Life*, Vol. II., p. 216. Barrow's *Travels*, pp. 313–323. *Mémoires conc. les Chinois*, Tomes I., III., VI., etc.; for ancient musical knowledge, the last still furnishes the best analysis yet made.

demning, and killing a boy by stabbing him in the belly is not so common; the imitation of the gasping chest and pallid death hue are wonderfully natural. Ventriloquism, writing answers to questions asked of the spirits by means of rods moving over a dusted table, and other black art or magical tricks have long been known. In dancing and other forms of graceful motion they are entirely wanting, and one would almost as soon think of associating music and medicine as that Chinese music should be accompanied by quadrilles and cotillons, or that men with shoes like pattens could lead off women with feet like hoofs through the turns and mazes of a waltz or fandango.

Their deficiencies in music will not lead us to expect much from them in painting or sculpture, for all flow so much from the same general perception of the beautiful in sound, form, and color, that where one is deficient all are likely to be unappreciated. This want in Chinese mind (for we are hardly at liberty to call it a defect) is, to a greater or less degree, observable in all the races of Eastern Asia, none of whom exhibit a high appreciation of the beautiful or sublime in nature or art, or have produced much which proves that their true principles were ever understood. Painting is rather behind sculpture, but neither can be said to have advanced beyond rude imitations of nature.

Even the best painters have no proper idea of perspective or of blending light and shade, but the objects are exhibited as much as possible on a flat surface, as if the painter drew his picture from a balloon, and looked at the country with a vertical sun shining above him. As might be inferred from their deficiencies in linear drawing and landscapes, they eminently fail in delineating the human figure in its right proportions, position, and expressions, and of grouping the persons introduced into a piece in natural attitudes. The study of the human figure in all its proportions has not been attended to by painters any more than its anatomy has by surgeons. Shadows upon portraits are considered a great defect, and in order to avoid them a front view is usually taken. Landscapes are also painted without shading, the remote objects being as minutely depicted as those in the foreground, and the point of view in pieces of any size is changed for the nearer and remote parts. There is no vanishing point to their pictures, as might be inferred from their ignorance of perspective and the true elements of art.

Outline drawing is a favorite style of the art, and the wealthy adorn their houses with rough sketches in ink of figures and landscapes; but the humblest of such compositions as are common in the galleries and studios of western countries have never been produced by Chinese artists. Some of their

Representation of a Man Dreaming.

representations of abstract ideas are at least singular to us, and, like many other things brought from their country, attract notice from their oddity.

Their coloring is executed with great skill and accuracy—too much, indeed, in many cases, so that the painting loses something of the effect it would otherwise have from the scrupulous minuteness of the detail, though it looks well in paintings of flowers, animals, costumes, ornaments, and other single objects where this filling up is necessary to a true idea of the original. The tints of the human countenance are no better done, however, than its lineaments, and the lifeless opacity suggests the idea that the artist was not called in until his patron was about to be entombed from the sight of his sorrowing family. The paintings obtained at Canton may, some of them, seem to disprove these opinions of the mediocrity attained by the artists in that country, but the productions of the copyists in that city are not the proper criteria of native uneducated art. Some of them have had so much practice in copying foreign productions that it has begun to correct their own notions of designing. These constitute, however, a very small proportion of the whole, and have had no effect on national taste. The designs to be seen on plates and bowls are, although not the best, fairer specimens of art than the pieces sometimes procured at Canton. The beautiful fidelity with which engravings are copied at Canton is well seen in the paintings on ivory, especially miniatures and figures, some of which fully equal similar productions made elsewhere.[1]

As samples of Chinese illustrative art, the two adjoining wood-cuts may be considered as quite up to the average of their fairest achievements. The story of the first in brief is as follows: In the district of Tsung-ngan lived a crafty plebeian, who, envying the good fortune of all about him, became especially covetous of the burial ground of his district magistrate Chu. Hoping to gain a surreptitious benefit from the felicitous luck of the plat, he secretly buriod his own tombstone there, and at the end of several years brought suit for its recovery. Unable to comprehend the affair, Chu repaired to the burial spot, where indeed the geomancy of the grave was found to be entirely in accord with the rules, but upon removing the earth the stone of his enemy's remote ancestry was disclosed. The suit was in consequence declared against him, Chu removed his residence to the black tea country, and his envious neighbor entered in triumph upon possession of the graveyard.

Not so readily, however, did the powers above condone this iniquity. One night there arose a tempest of unheard-of vio-

[1] Compare Owen Jones, *Grammar of Ornament*, Chap. XIV., and *Examples of Chinese Ornament* (London, 1867). *Gazette des Beaux-Arts* for October and November, 1873, and January, 1874.

The Vengeance of Heaven upon the False Grave.

lence, when the thunder and lightning were indescribable, the hideous roar and flash of which terrified the country far and near, boding no good to its wretched inhabitants. The following morning the grave was discovered in ruins, stone and epitaph uprooted, even the corpse and coffin missing. The vengeance of Heaven had repaired the injustice of man.

The illustration which depicts the tempest personified in its full terror shows us the *Lui Kung*, or God of Thunder, almost the only Chinese mythological deity who is drawn with wings. The cock's head and claws, the hammer and chisel, representing the splitting peal attending a flash, the circlet of fire encompassing a number of drums to typify the reverberating thunder and the ravages of the irresistible lightning, present a grotesque ensemble which is quite unique even among the *bizarrerie* of oriental figures; the somewhat juvenile attempts of the artist to sketch the destruction and rifling of the grave are much less notable.

Concerning the subject of the second illustration (taken, with the other, from the *Sacred Edict* of Kanghi), we are told that one Yuen, having conceived a violent hatred against an acquaintance, set out one morning, knife in hand, with the purpose of killing him. A venerable man sitting in a convent saw him pass, and was amazed to observe several scores of spirits closely following him, some of whom clutched his weapon, while others seemed endeavoring to delay his progress. "About the space of a meal-time" the patriarch noticed Yuen's return, accompanied this time by more than a hundred spirits wearing golden caps and bearing banners raised on high. Yuen himself appeared with so happy a face, in place of his gloomy countenance of the early morning, that the old man sadly concluded that his enemy must be dead and his revenge gratified. "When you passed this way at daybreak," he asked, "where were you going, and how do you return so soon?" "It was owing to my quarrel with Miu," said Yuen, "that made me wish to kill him. But in passing this convent door better thoughts came to me as I pondered upon the stress his wife and children would come to, and of his aged mother, none of whom had done me wrong. I determined then not to kill him, and return thus promptly

A would-be Assassin followed by Spirits.

from my evil purpose." It hardly needed the sage's commendations to increase the reformed murderer's inner contentment, imparted by the train of ghostly helpers; he continued on his way rejoicing. The reader may notice a pictorial idea as well as a moral not unlike those of more western countries.

The symbolism of the Chinese has not attracted the notice of foreign writers as much as it deserves. It meets us everywhere—on plates and crockery, on carpets, rugs, vases, wall pictures, shop signs, and visiting cards. Certain animals stand for well-understood characters in the language, and convey their sense to the native without any confusion. Owing to the similarity of sound, *fuh* denotes *bat* and *happiness*, and *luh* stands for *deer* and *official emolument*. The character *shao*, meaning 'longevity,' is represented in many ways—an old man leaning on his staff; a pine tree cut into the form of the character; a tortoise, which is among the longest-lived reptiles; a stork, supposed to be a bird which attains a great age, and a fabulous peach which is a thousand years ripening. A dragon and a phœnix, or *fung-whang*, are emblems of a newly wedded pair, and various modes of combination are adopted to represent marriage relations.

A rug will sometimes tell a story very neatly to the eye. In the centre is the *swastica*, or 'hammer of Thor,' which denotes *all*, and symbolizes all happiness that humanity desires. On the right is the *luh*, or 'deer,' which denotes honor and success in study, carrying the *yü-i*, or Buddhist sceptre, in its mouth, meaning success in literary labors. On the left is pictured a goose, indicating domestic felicity, and two bats complete the rug, with its good wishes.

In the plate represented in the picture the central figure is clad in the ancient costume of officials bearing the insignia or baton of a minister of State. The old man, with his gourd and peach, indicates an extreme and happy old age; and the figure with the basket corresponds to the cornucopia of western emblems. The five *bats* symbolize the *wu fuh*, or 'five happinesses,' which all mankind desires—riches, longevity, sound body, love of virtue, and a peaceful end.

The visiting card and note paper often indicate in their

adornments a good wish and a motto which does credit to the taste and heart of the designer. A most graceful and not uncommon way of wishing a guest good luck is to depict some happy emblem or a sentence of the language with a fortunate meaning on the bottom of his tea-cup. The characters "May your happiness know no bounds" frequently occur in this posi-

Symbols of Happiness and Old Age. (From a plaque.)

tion, and the oft-recurring five bats or three peaches can be employed with like signification. The mandarin duck is a well-understood emblem for conjugal affection; again, a cock and hen standing on an artificial rock-work symbolize the pleasures of a country life. Sometimes the eight symbols peculiar to the Buddhist sect, or the *pah sien* ('eight genii') indicative of their protection, are seen in the border of a plaque amid a device of running arabesques. The favorite dragon, in an infinite diversity of shapes, adorns the finer qualities of cups, plates, bowls, and vases, to represent imperial grandeur, but common people are not wont to use such patterns.

The brilliant paintings on pith-paper, or *rice-paper*, as it is commonly but incorrectly called, deserve special mention for their singular delicacy and spirit. This substance, whose velvety surface contrasts so admirably with bright colors, is a delicate vegetable film, consisting of long hexagonal cells, whose length is parallel to the surface of the film, and which are filled with air when the film is in its usual state; the peculiar softness which so well adapts it for receiving colors is owing to this structure. It is obtained from the pith of a species of Fatsia, a plant allied to the Aralia, growing in Formosa and Yunnan, in marshy districts. It is cultivated to some extent, but mostly gathered by cutting the branches of the wild plants, which resemble the elder. This pith forms a large item in the internal trade of China, and is worked up into toys as well as cut into sheets. The fragments are used to stuff pillows or fill up the soles of shoes, or wherever a light, dry material is needed. The largest and best sheets (ten by fifteen inches) are selected for the painters at Hongkong and Canton, where many hundreds of workmen are employed in making them. Under the direction of foreign ladies at Amoy and elsewhere, most accurate imitations of flowers and bouquets are now made by natives out of pith-paper. The pieces are cut nearly a foot long, and the pith is forced out by driving a stick into one end; it is then wet and put into bamboos, where it swells and dries straight. If too short to furnish the required breadth, several bits are pressed together until they adhere and make one long straight piece. The paring knife resembles a butcher's cleaver, a thin and sharp blade, which is touched up on a block of iron-wood at the last moment. The pith is pared on a square tile, having its ends guarded by a thin strip of brass, on which the knife rests. The pith is rolled over against its edge with the left hand; the right firmly holds it, slowly moving it leftward, as the workman pulls and rolls the pith in the same direction, as far as the tile allows. The pared sheet runs under the knife, and the paring goes on until only a centre three or four lines thick is left; and this remnant the thrifty workmen use or sell for an aperient. The paring resembles the operation of cutting out corks, and produces a smooth sheet about four feet long, the first half foot being too much grooved to be of use. The fresh sheets are pressed in a pile, smoothed by ironing and their fractures mended with mica. Most of the paper is trimmed into square sheets for the makers of artificial flowers, and sold in Formosa at about eight cents for five hundred sheets. An India-ink outline is first transferred by dampening and pressing it upon the paper, when the ink strikes off sufficiently to enable the workman to fill up the sketch; one outline will serve for limning several copies, and in large establishments the separate colors are laid on by different workmen. The manufacture of these paintings at Canton employs between two and three thousand hands.

Another tissue sometimes used by the Chinese for painting, more remarkable for its singularity than elegance, is the reticulated nerve-work of leaves, the parenchyma of the leaf having been removed by maceration, and the membrane filled with isinglass. The appearance of a painting on this transparent substance is pretty, but the colors do not retain their brilliancy. The Chinese admire paintings on glass, and some of the moonlight scenes or thunderstorms are good specimens of their art. The clouds and dark parts are done with India-ink, and a dark shade well befitting the subject is imparted to the whole scene by underlaying it with a piece of blackish paper. Portraits and other subjects are also done on glass, but the indifferent execution is rendered still more conspicuous by the transparency of the ground; the Hindus purchase large quantities of such glass pictures of their gods and goddesses. Looking-glasses are also painted on the back with singular effect by removing the quicksilver with a steel point according to a design previously sketched, and then painting the denuded portion.

Statuary is confined chiefly to molding idols out of clay or cutting them from wood, and carving animals to adorn balustrades and temples. Idols are generally made in a sitting posture and dressed, the face and hands being the only parts of the body seen, so that no opportunity is afforded for imitating the muscles and contour of the figure. The hideous monsters which guard the entrance of temples often exhibit more artistic skill than the unmeaning images enshrined within, and some even display much knowledge of character and proportion. Among their best performances in statuettes are the accurate baked and painted models of different classes of people; Canton and Tientsin artists excel in this branch.

Animals are sculptured in granite and cast in bronze, showing great skill and patience in the detail work; deformity in the model has resulted in the production of such animals, indeed, as were probably never beheld in any world. Images of lions, tigers, tortoises, elephants, rams, and other animals ornament bridges, temples, and tombs. The elephants in the long avenue of warriors, horses, lions, etc., leading up to the tomb of the Emperor Hungwu at Nanking are the only tolerable representations of their originals; the gigantic images guarding the tomb of Yungloh, his son, at Changping, near Peking, are noticeable for size alone. The united effect of the elaborate carving and grotesque ornaments seen upon the roofs, woodwork, and pillars of buildings is not devoid of beauty, though in their details there is a great violation of the true principles of art, just as the expression of a face may please which still has not a handsome feature in it. Short columns of stone or wood, surmounted by a lion, and a dragon twining around the shaft, the whole cut out of one block; or a lion sejant with half a dozen cubs crawling over his body, are among the ornaments of temples and graves which show the taste of the people.

The Chinese have a sense of the ridiculous, and exhibit it both in their sculpture and drawing in many ways. Lampoons, pasquinades, and caricatures are common, nor is any person below the dragon's throne spared by their pens or pencils, though they prefer subjects not likely to involve the authors—as in the one here selected from the many elicited during the war of 1840.

By far the best specimens of sculpture are their imitations of fruits, flowers, animals, etc., cut out of many kinds of stone, from gnarled roots of bamboo, wood, and other materials; but in these we admire the unwearied patience and cunning of the workmen in making grotesque combinations and figures out of apparently intractable materials, and do not seek for any indications of a pure taste or embodiment of an exalted conception. Inscriptions of a religious or geomantic character are often cut upon the faces of rocks, as was the case in India and Arabia,[1] and the picturesque characters of the language make a pretty appearance in such situations.

The small advances made in architecture have already been noticed in Chapter XIII.—a deficiency exhibited in the Huns and other nations of the Mongolian stock long after they had

Caricature of an English Foraging Party.

settled in Europe and Western Asia; nor was it until their amalgamation with the imaginative nations of Southern Europe had changed their original character that grand performances in architecture appeared among the latter. If the Chinese had a model of the Parthenon or the Pantheon in their own country, belike they would measurably imitate it in every part, but they would erect dozens in the same fashion. Perhaps an infusion of elegance and taste would have been imparted to them if the people had had frequent intercourse with more im-

[1] Compare Job XXX., 24.

aginative nations, but when there were no models of this superior kind to follow there was no likelihood of their originating them. In lighter edifices, as pavilions, rest-houses, kiosks, and arbors, there is, however, a degree of taste and adaptation that is unusual in other buildings, and quite in keeping with their fondness for tinsel and gilding rather than solidity and grandeur. On this point Lay's remark on the characteristics of the Attic, Egyptian, Gothic, and Chinese styles is apposite. "If we would see beauty, size, and proportion in all their excellence, we should look for it among the models of Greece; if we desire something that was wild and stupendous, we should find it in Egypt; if grandeur with a never-sated minuteness of decoration please us, we need look no further than to a cathedral; and lastly, if the romantic and the old-fashioned attract our fancy, the Chinese can point us to an exhaustless store in the recesses of their vast Empire. A lack of science and of conception is seen in all their buildings, but fancy seems to have had free license to gambol at pleasure; and what the architect wanted in developing a scheme he made up in a redundancy of imagination."

The Chinese have made but little progress in investigating the principles and forces of mechanics, but have practically understood most of the common powers in the various applications of which they are capable. The lever, wheel and axle, wedge and pinion, are all known in some form or other, but the modification of the wedge in the screw is not frequent. The sheave-blocks on board their vessels have only one pulley, but they understand the advantages of the windlass, and have adopted the capstain in working vessels, driving piles, raising timber, etc. They have long understood the mode of raising weights by a hooked pulley running on a rope, attached at each end to a cylinder of unequal diameters; by this contrivance, as the rope wound around the larger diameter it ran off the smaller one, raising the weight to the amount of the difference between the circumference of the two cylinders at a very small expense of strength. The graduations of the weighing-beam indicate their acquaintance with the relations between the balance and the weight on the long and short arm of the lever, and this mode of weighing is preferred for gold, pearls, and other valuable things. The overshot water-wheel is used to turn stones for grinding wheat and set in motion pestles to hull rice and press oil from seeds, and the undershot power for raising water. There is a great expenditure of human strength in most of their contrivances; in many, indeed, the object seems to have been rather to give a direction to this strength than to abridge it. For instance, they put a number of slings under a heavy stone and carry it off bodily on poles, in preference to making a low car to roll it away at half the expense of human power.

In other departments of science the attainments of the people are few and imperfect. Chemistry and metallurgy are unknown as sciences, but many operations in them are performed with a considerable degree of success. Sir J. Davis gives the detail of some experiments in oxidizing quicksilver and preparation of mercurial medicines which were performed by a native in the presence and at the request of Dr. Pearson at Canton, and "afforded a curious proof of similar results obtained by the most different and distant nations possessing very unequal scientific attainments, and bore no unfavorable testimony to Chinese shrewdness and ingenuity in the existing state of their knowledge."[1] The same opinion might be safely predicated of their metallurgic manipulations; the character of the work is the only index of the efficacy of the process. In bronzes they take a high place, and the delicacy of their niello work in gold and silver, upon wood as well as metal, cannot be surpassed.

This compendious review of the science of the Chinese can be brought to a close by a brief account of their theory and practice of medicine and surgery. Although they are almost as superstitious as the Hindus or North American Indians, they do not depend upon incantations and charms for relief in case of sickness, but resort to the prescriptions of the physician as the most reasonable and likely way to recover; mixed up, indeed, with many strange practices to assist the efficacy of the doses. These vary in every part of the Empire, and show the power of ignorance to perpetuate and strengthen the strangest supersti-

[1] *The Chinese*, Vol. II., pp. 266–270, 286.

tions where health and life are involved. Doolittle has collected many instances, and the experience of medical missionaries is uniform in this matter.

The dissection of the human body is never attempted, though some notions of its internal structure are taught in medical works, which are published in many forms. Mr. Wylie notices fifty-nine treatises of a medical and physiological character in his *Notes on Chinese Literature*. They contain references to a far greater number of authors, some of whom flourished in the earliest days of China, and many of whose writings exhibit good sense and sound advice amid the strangest theories. Dr. Harland has described the Chinese ideas of the organization of the body and the functions of the chief viscera in a lucid manner, and the diagram shown on p. 120 presents the popular opinions on this subject, for whatever foreigners may have imparted to them has not yet become generally known.

The Chinese seem to have no idea of the distinction between venous and arterial blood, nor between muscles and nerves, applying the word *kin* to both tendons and nerves. According to these physiologists, the brain (A) is the abode of the *yin* principle in its perfection, and at its base (B), where there is a reservoir of the marrow, communicates through the spine with the whole body. The larynx (C) goes through the lungs directly to the heart, expanding a little in its course, while the pharynx (D) passes over them to the stomach. The lungs (*a, a, a, a, a, a*) are white, and placed in the thorax; they consist of six lobes or leaves suspended from the spine, four on one side and two on the other; sound proceeds from holes in them, and they rule the various parts of the body. The centre of the thorax (or pit of the stomach) is the seat of the breath; joy and delight emanate from it, and it cannot be injured without danger. The heart (*b*) lies underneath the lungs, and is the prince of the body; thoughts proceed from it. The pericardium (*c*) comes from and envelops the heart and extends to the kidneys. There are three tubes communicating from the heart to the spleen, liver, and kidneys, but no clear ideas are held as to their office. Like the pharynx, they pass through the diaphragm, which is itself connected with the spine, ribs, and bowels. The

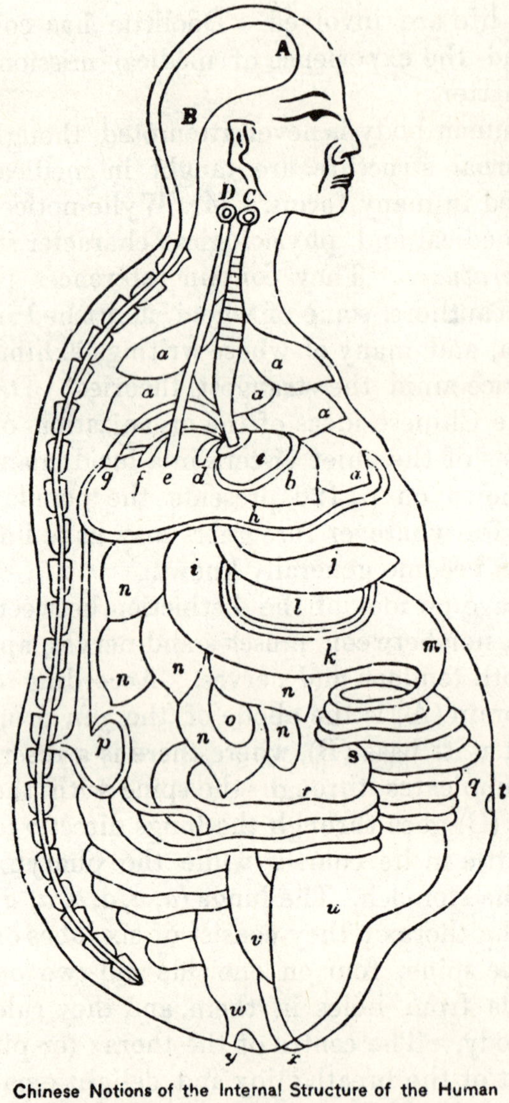

Chinese Notions of the Internal Structure of the Human Body.

A,B—The brain. *C*—Larynx. *D*—Pharynx. *a,a,a,a,a*—Lungs. *b*—Heart. *c*—Pericardium. *d*—Bond of connection with the spleen. *e*—The œsophagus. *f*—Bond of connection with the liver. *g*—Bond of connection with the kidneys. *h*—The diaphragm. *i*—Cardiac extremity. *j*—The spleen. *k*—The stomach. *l*—Omentum. *m*—The pylorus. *n,n,n,n,n,n*—The liver. *o*—The gall-bladder. *p*—The kidneys. *q*—The small intestines. *r*—The large intestines. *s*—Caput coli. *t*—The navel. *u*—The bladder. *v*—The "gate of life," sometimes placed in the right kidney. *w*—The rectum. *x, y*—The urinal and fœcal passages.

liver (*n, n, n, n, n, n*) is on the right side and has seven lobes; the soul resides in it, and schemes emanate from it; the gall-bladder (*o*) is below and projects upward into it, and when the person is angry it ascends; courage dwells in it; hence the Chinese sometimes procure the gall-bladder of animals, as tigers and bears, and even of men, especially notorious bandits executed for their crimes, and eat the bile contained in them, under the idea that it will impart courage. The spleen (*j*) lies between the stomach and diaphragm and assists in digestion, and the food passes from it into the stomach (*k*), and hence through the pylorus (*m*) into the large intestines. The omentum (*l*) overlies the stomach, but its office is unknown, and the mesentery and pancreas are entirely omitted.

The small intestines (*q*) are connected with the heart, and the urine passes through them into the bladder, separating from the food or fæces at the caput coli (*s*), where they divide from the larger intestines. The large intestines (*r*) are connected with the lungs and lie in the loins, having sixteen convolutions. The kidneys (*p*) are attached to the spinal marrow, and resemble an egg in shape, and the subtle generative fluid is eliminated by them above to the brain and below to the spermatic cord and sacral extremity; the testes, called *wai shin*, or 'outside kidneys,' communicate with them. The right kidney, or the passage from it (*v*), is called the "gate of life," and sends forth the subtle fluid to the spermatic vessels. The bladder (*u*) lies below the kidneys, and receives the urine from the small intestines at the iliac valve.

The osteology of the frame is briefly despatched: the pelvis, skull, forearm, and leg are considered as single bones, the processes of the joints being quite dispensed with, and the whole considered merely as a kind of internal framework, on and in which the necessary fleshy parts are upheld, but with which they have not much more connection by muscles and ligaments than the post has with the pile of mud it upholds. The *Tai-i Yuen*, or Medical College at Peking, contains a copper model of a man, about six feet high, on which are given the names of the pulses in different places; it is pierced with many small holes. In A.D. 1027 the Emperor had two anatomical figures made to illustrate the art of acupuncture, which is still practised. The irrigation of the body with blood is rather complicated, and authors vary greatly as to the manner in which it is accomplished. Some pictures represent tubes issuing from the fingers and toes, and running up the limbs into the trunk, where they are lost, or reach the heart, lungs, or some other organ as well as they can, wandering over most parts of the body in their course.

Theories are furnished in great variety to account for the nourishment of the body and the functions of the viscera, and upon their harmonious connection with each other and the five metals, colors, tastes, and planets is founded the well-being of the system; with all they hold an intimate relation, and their actions are alike built on the all-pervading functions of the *yin* and *yang*—those universal solvents in Chinese philosophy. The pulse is very carefully studied, and its condition regarded as the index of every condition of the body, even to determining the sex of an unborn infant; great parade is usually made by every practitioner in examining this important symptom.

Dr. Harland has made a table showing the sympathy supposed to exist between the different points of the pulses and the internal organs.[1] In each wrist the pulses are named *Inch*, *Bar*, and *Cubit* (the first being nearest the hand); a change in degree of pressure doubles the range of viscera thus indexed:

LEFT WRIST.

Inch,	when	lightly pressed,	indicates	the state	of the	small intestines.
"	"	heavily	"	"	"	"	heart.
Bar,	"	lightly	"	"	"	"	gall-bladder.
"	"	heavily	"	"	"	"	liver.
Cubit,	"	lightly	"	"	"	"	urinary bladder.
"	"	heavily	"	"	"	"	kidneys.

RIGHT WRIST.

Inch,	when	lightly pressed,	indicates	the state	of the	large intestines.
"	"	heavily	"	"	"	"	lungs.
Bar,	"	lightly	"	"	"	"	stomach.
"	"	heavily	"	"	"	"	spleen.
Cubit,	"	lightly	"	"	"	"	*san tseaou.*
"	"	heavily	"	"	"	"	*ming măn.*

The two latter meaning respectively 'Three Passages' and 'Gate of Life,' being purely imaginary organs, are difficult to describe.

A diseased state of an organ is supposed to be owing to a disagreement of the *yin* and *yang*, the presence of bad humors, or the more powerful agency of evil spirits, and until these agencies are corrected medicines cannot exercise their full efficacy. The surface of the body receives the closest attention, for there is not a square inch without its appropriate name. Plasters and lotions are applied to these places according to the diagnosis of the disease, predicated on the dual theory; and the strolling quacks and regular practitioners both administer the rationale and the dose together—considering, probably, that the medicine would lose half its efficacy upon the organs it was intended to affect if it was not mixed with faith to operate upon the sentient principle lodged there.

[1] *Transactions of the China Br. of Royal Asiatic Society*, Hongkong, Part I., 1847, p. 43.

The practice of the Chinese is far in advance of their theory, and some of their treatises on dietetics and medical practice contain good advice, the result of experience. Dr. W. Lockhart has translated a native treatise on midwifery, in which the author, confining himself principally to the best modes of treatment in all the stages of parturition, and dwelling briefly on the reasons of things, has greatly improved upon the physiologists. This branch of the profession is almost entirely in the hands of women. Surgical operations are chiefly confined to removing a tooth, puncturing sores and tumors with needles, or trying to reduce dislocations and reunite fractures by pressure or bandaging. Sometimes they successfully execute more difficult cases, as the amputation of a finger, operation for a harelip, and insertion of false teeth. In one case of dentistry four incisor teeth made of ivory were strung upon a piece of catgut and secured in their place by tying the string to the eye-teeth; they were renewed quarterly, and served their purpose tolerably well. The practice of acupuncture has some good results among the bad ones.[1] That of applying cauteries and caustics of various degrees of power is more general, and sometimes entails shocking distress upon the patient. Cases have presented themselves at the hospitals, where small sores, by the application of escharotics, have extended until a large part of the tissue, and even important organs, have been destroyed, the charlatan amusing his suffering patient by promises of ultimate cure. The moxa, or burning the flowers of the amaranthus upon the skin, is attended with less injury.

Turning in of the eyelashes is a common ailment, and native practitioners attempt to cure it by everting the lid and fastening it in its place by two slips of bamboo tightly bound on, or by a pair of tweezers, until the loose fold on the edge sloughs off; the eye is, however, more frequently disfigured by this clumsy process than is the trouble remedied. Poultices made of many strange or disgusting substances are applied to injured parts.

[1] Compare Rémusat (*Nouveaux Mélanges Asiatiques*, Tome I., pp. 358–380), who says that the first notion of acupuncture as practised in China was brought into Europe by one Ten-Rhyne, a Dutch surgeon, at the end of the seventeenth century.

Dr. Parker mentions the case of a man who, having injured the iris by a fall, was ordered by his native physician to cut a chicken in halves, laying one portion on the eye as a cataplasm and eating the other as an internal cure. Venesection is rarely attempted, but leeches and cupping are employed to remove the blood from a particular spot. Blood-letting is disapproved in fevers, "for," says the Chinese reasoner, "a fever is like a pot boiling; it is requisite to reduce the fire and not diminish the liquid in the vessel if we wish to cure the patient."

Many of the operations in cases of fracture present a strange mixture of folly and sense, proceeding from their ideas of the internal structure of the human body conflicting with those which common sense and experience teach. Père Ripa's description of the treatment he underwent to prevent the ill effects of a fall will serve as an illustration. Having been thrown from his horse and left fainting in the street, he was carried into a house, where a surgeon soon visited him. "He made me sit up in bed, placing near me a large basin filled with water, in which he put a thick piece of ice to reduce it to a freezing point. Then stripping me to the waist, he made me stretch my neck over the basin, while he continued for a good while to pour the water on my neck with a cup. The pain caused by this operation upon those nerves which take their rise from the pia mater was so great and insufferable that it seemed to me unequalled, but he said it would stanch the blood and restore me to my senses, which was actually the case, for in a short time my sight became clear and my mind resumed its powers. He next bound my head with a band drawn tight by two men who held the ends, while he struck the intermediate parts vigorously with a piece of wood, which shook my head violently, and gave me dreadful pain. This, he said, was to set the brain, which he supposed had been displaced, and it is true that after the second operation my head felt more free. A third operation was now performed, during which he made me, still stripped to the waist, walk in the open air supported by two persons; and while thus walking he unexpectedly threw a basin of freezing cold water over my breast. As this caused me to draw my breath with great vehemence, and as my chest had been injured by the fall, it may easily be imagined what were my sufferings under this infliction; but I was consoled by the information that if any rib had been dislocated, this sudden and hard breathing would restore it to its natural position. The next proceeding was not less painful and extravagant. The operator made me sit on the ground, and, assisted by two men, held a cloth upon my mouth and nose till I was almost suffocated. 'This,' said the Chinese Esculapius, 'by causing a violent heaving of the chest, will force back any rib that may have been dislocated.' The wound in my head not being deep, he healed it by stuffing it with burnt cotton. He then ordered that I should continue to walk much, supported by two persons; that I should not sit long, nor be allowed to sleep till ten o'clock at night, at which time I should eat a little thin rice soup. He assured me that these walks in the open air while fasting would prevent the blood from settling upon the chest, where it might corrupt. These remedies, though barbarous and excruciating, cured me so completely that in seven days I was able to resume my journey."[1]

The active daily practice of a popular Chinese doctor may be very well illustrated from Dr. Hobson's description of one Ta wang siensăng, or 'Dr. Rhubarb,' a medical practitioner in Canton. This man, after prescribing for the sick at his office until the hour of ten in the morning, would commence his rounds "in the sedan chair carried in great haste by three or four men. Those patients were visited first who had their names and residences first placed in the entry book, and as the streets were narrow and crowded, to avoid trouble in finding the house, a copy of the doctor's sign-board would be posted up outside the patient's door, so that the chairmen should be able at once to recognize the house without delay."

The doctor being ushered into the hall, or principal room, is met with bows and salutations by the father or elder brother of the family. Tea and pipes are offered in due form, and he is requested to feel his patient's pulse; if a male, he sits opposite

[1] Père Ripa, *Memoirs and Residence at Peking*, translated by F. Prandi, London, 1844, p. 67.

to him; if a female, a screen of bamboo intervenes, which is only removed in case it is requisite to see the tongue. The right hand is placed upon a book to steady it, and the doctor, with much gravity and a learned look, places his three fingers upon the pulsating vessel, pressing it alternately with each finger on the inner and outer side, and then making with three fingers a steady pressure for several minutes, not with watch in hand, to note the frequency of its beats, but with a thoughtful and calculating mind, to diagnose the disease and prognosticate its issue. The fingers being removed the patient immediately stretches out the other hand, which is felt in the same manner. Perhaps certain questions are asked of the father or mother concerning the sick person, but these are usually few, as it is presumed the pulse reveals everything needful to know. Ink and paper are produced and a prescription is written out, which consists of numerous ingredients, but there are one or two of only prime importance—the rest are servants or adjuvants. They are all taken from the vegetable kingdom, and are mostly simples of little efficacy. The prescription is taken to a druggist to be dispensed; the prescriber seldom makes up the medicine himself, and as large doses are popular (a *quid pro quo*), so the decoction made from the whole amounts to pints or even quarts, which are swallowed in large portions with the greatest ease; powders, boluses, pills, and electuaries are also used. If the patient is an officer of the government or a wealthy person, the nature of the disease, prognosis, and treatment are written down for the inspection of the family; for this the doctor's fee is a dollar. But generally speaking, both the doctor and the patient's friends are quite satisfied with a verbal communication; and if the man has a gift for speaking and has brass enough to use it to his advantage (both of which are seldom wanting in time-serving men), he will describe with a learned, self-satisfied air the ailment of the patient, and the number of days it will take to cure him. The fee is wrapped up in red paper, and called "golden thanks," varying in amount from fifteen to seventy cents or more, according to the means of the patient; the chair-bearers being paid extra. The doctor returns to make another visit if invited, but not otherwise. It is more common, if the patient is not at once benefited by the prescription, to call in another, then a third, then a fourth, and even more, until tired of physicians (for the Chinese patience is soon exhausted, and their faith by no means strong in all their doctors' asseverations) they have, as a last resort, application made to one of the genii, or a god possessing wonderful healing powers. The result is that the patient dies or lives, not according to the treatment received, for that must be generally inefficacious, but according as his natural strength is equal to surmount the difficulties by which he is surrounded.[1]

Dr. Hobson has given an analysis of 442 medicinal agents enumerated in one of the popular dispensatories; of the whole number, 314 are vegetable, 50 mineral, and 78 animal. The author gives the name of each one, the organ it affects, its properties, and lastly the mode of its exhibition. Medicines are arranged under six heads—tonics, astringents, resolvents, purgatives, alteratives of poisonous humors, and of the blood. Among the agents employed are many strange and repulsive substances, as snake-skins, fossil bones, rhinoceros or hart's horn shavings, silk-worm and human secretions, asbestos, moths, oyster-shells, etc. Calomel, vermilion, red precipitate, minium, arsenic, plumbago, and sulphate of copper are among the metallic medicines used by physicians; Dr. Henderson enumerates thirty-three distinct mineral medicines. The number of apothecary shops in towns indicates the great consumption of medicine; their arrangement is like the druggist shops in the west, though instead of huge glass jars at the windows filled with bright colored liquids, and long rows of vials and decanters in glass cases, three or four branching deer's horns are suspended from the walls, and lines of white and black gallipots cover the shelves. Hartshorn is reduced to a dust by filing, for exhibition in consumption. Many roots, as rhubarb, gentian, etc., are prepared by paring them into thin laminæ; others are powdered in a mortar with a pestle, or triturated in a narrow iron trough in which a close-fitting wheel is worked. The use of acids

[1] Dr. James Henderson in *Journal of the N. C. Br. of Royal Asiatic Society*, 1864, No. I., p. 54.

and reagents is unknown, for they imply more knowledge of chemistry than the Chinese possess. Vegetable substances, as camphor, myrrh, ginseng, rhubarb, gentian, and a great variety of roots, leaves, seeds, and barks, are generally taken as pills or decoctions. Many valuable recipes will probably be discovered in their books as soon as the terms used are accurately ascertained, and a better acquaintance with the botany and mineralogy enables the foreign student to test them intelligently.

The people sometimes cast lots as to which one of a dozen doctors they shall employ, and then scrupulously follow his directions, whatever they may be, as a departure therefrom would vitiate the sortilege. Sometimes an invalid will go to a doctor and ask for how much he will cure him, and how soon the cure can be performed. He states the diagnosis of his case, the pulse is examined, and every other symptom investigated, when the bargain is struck and a portion of the price paid. The patient then receives the suitable medicines, in quantity and variety better fitted for a horse than a man, for the doctor reasons that out of a great number it is more likely that some will prove efficacious, and the more he gets paid for the more he ought to administer. A decoction of a kettleful of simples is drunk down by the sick man, and he gives up both working and eating; if, however, at the expiration of the time specified he is not cured, he scolds his physician for an ignorant charlatan who cheats him out of his money, and seeks another, with whom he makes a similar bargain, and probably with similar results. Sagacious observance of cause and effect, symptoms and pains, gradually give a shrewd physician great power over his ignorant patients, and some of them become both rich and influential; a skilful physician is termed the "nation's hand."

A regular system of fees exists among the profession, but the remuneration is as often left to the generosity of the patient. New medicines, pills, powders, and salves are advertised and puffed by flaunting placards on the walls of the streets, some of them most disgustingly obscene; but the Chinese do not puff new nostrums by publishing a long list of recommendations from patients. The various ways devised by persons to dispose of their medicines exhibit much ingenuity. Sometimes a man, having spread a mat at the side of the street, and marshalled his gallipots and salves, will commence a harangue upon the goodness and efficacy of his preparations in loud and eloquent tones, until he has collected a crowd of hearers, some of whom he manages to persuade will be the better for taking some of his potions. He will exhibit their efficacy by first pounding his naked breast with a brick till it is livid, and then immediately healing the contusion by a lotion, having previously fortified the inner parts with a remedy; or he will cut open his flesh and heal the wound in a few moments by a wonderful elixir, which he alone can sell. Others, more learned or more professional, erect a pavilion or awning, fluttering with signs and streamers, and quietly seat themselves under it to wait for customers; or content themselves with a flag perched on a pole setting forth the potency of their pills. Dentists make a necklace of the rotten teeth they have obtained from the jaws of their customers, and perambulate the streets with these trophies of their skill hanging around their necks like a rosary. In general, however, the Chinese enjoy good health, and when ill from colds or fevers, lie abed and suspend working and eating, which in most cases allows nature to work her own cure, whatever doses they may take. They are perhaps as long-lived as most nations, though sanatory statistics are wanting to enable us to form any indisputable conclusions on this head.

The classes of diseases which most prevail in China are ophthalmic, cutaneous, and digestive; intermittent fevers are also common. The great disproportion of affections of the eye has often attracted observation. Dr. Lockhart ascribes it partly to the inflammation which often comes on at the commencement of winter, and which is allowed to run its course, leaving the organ in an unhealthy condition and very obnoxious to other diseases. This inflammation is beyond the skill of the native practitioners, and sometimes destroys the sight in a few days. Another fruitful source of disease is the practice of the barbers of turning the lids over and clearing their surfaces of the mucus which may be lodged there. He adds: "If the person's eyes be examined after this process, they will be found to be very red and irritated, and in process of time chronic conjunctivitis supervenes, which being considered proof of insufficient cleansing, the practice is persisted in, and the inner surface of the lid becomes covered with granulations. In other cases it becomes indurated like thin parchment, and the tarsal cartilages contract and induce entropium." Dense opacity of the cornea itself is frequently caused by this *barberous* practice, or constant pain and weeping ensues, both of which materially injure the sight, if the patient does not lose it. The practice of cleansing the ears in a similar way frequently results in their serious injury, and sometimes destruction. When the ill effects of such treatment of these delicate organs must be plain to every observing person in his own case, it is strange that he should still allow the operation to be repeated.

The physicians in charge of the missionary hospitals successfully established at so many cities in Eastern China have attended more to tumors, dislocations, wounds, and surgical cases, ophthalmic and cutaneous diseases, than to common clinical ailments. The hospitals here spoken of are little more than dispensaries, with a room or two for extreme or peculiarly interesting cases; there is little visiting the natives at their own houses.

Asthma, even in boys, is common at Amoy, and consumption at Canton and Chusan. Intermittent fevers prevail more or less wherever the cultivation of rice is carried on near villages and towns. Elephantiasis is known between Shanghai and Canton, but in the southern provinces leprosy seems to exist as its equivalent. This loathsome disease is regarded by the Chinese as incurable and contagious. Lazar-houses are provided for the residence of the infected, but as the allowance of poor patients is insufficient for their support, they go from street to street soliciting alms, to the great annoyance of every one. As soon as it appears in an individual, he is immediately separated from his family and driven forth an outcast, to herd with others similarly affected, and get his living from precarious charity. The institution of lazarettoes is praiseworthy, but they fail of affording relief on account of the mismanagement and peculation of those who have their supervision; and those who cannot get in are obliged to live in a village set apart for them north of the city. Lepers can intermarry among themselves, but on account of poverty and other causes they do not often do so, and the hardships of their lot soon end their days. This disease will probably exist among the Chinese until houses are built more above the ground, better ventilation of cities and improvement in diet are adopted, when it will disappear as it has in Southern Europe.

Diseases of an inflammatory nature are not so fatal or rapid among the Chinese as Europeans, nor do consumptions carry off so large a proportion of the inhabitants as in the United States. Dyspepsia has been frequently treated; it is ascribed by Dr. Hepburn to the abundant use of salt provisions, pickled vegetables, and fish, irregularity in eating, opium smoking, and immoderate use of tea; though it may be questioned whether the two last reasons are more general and powerful at Amoy than Canton, where dyspepsia is comparatively rare. The surgeons at the latter place have successfully treated hundreds of cases of stone, losing less than fifteen per cent. of all. Some of the patients were under ten years, and a few of the calculi weighed nearly half a pound. This malady is almost unknown in Northern China. The diseases which result from intemperate and licentious habits are not as violent in their effects as in countries where a greater use of animal food and higher living render the system more susceptible to the noxious consequences of the virus.

The existence of tumors and unnatural growths in great abundance and variety is satisfactorily accounted for by the inability of the native practitioners to remove them. Those which had a healthy growth increased until a morbid action supervened, and consequently sometimes grew to an enormous size. A peasant named Hu Lu went to England in 1831 to have an abdominal tumor extirpated weighing about seventy pounds; he died under the operation. No patients bear operations with more fortitude than the Chinese, and, owing to their lymphatic temperament, they are followed with less inflammation than is usual in European practice. Goitre is very common in the mountainous regions of the northern provinces; Dr. Gillan estimated that nearly one-sixth of the inhabitants met in the villages on the high land between Peking and Jeh ho were afflicted with this deformity, which, however, is said not to be so considered by the villagers themselves.

The Asiatic cholera has been a great scourge in China, but does not often become an epidemic anywhere, though sporadic cases constantly occur. It raged at Ningpo in May, 1820, and an intelligent native doctor informed Mr. Milne[1] that it was computed that ten thousand persons were carried off by it in the city and department of Ningpo during the summers of 1820-23. In 1842 it prevailed at Amoy and Changchau and their vicinity; more than a hundred deaths daily occurred at the former place for six or seven weeks. It raged violently at Hangchau in Chehkiang during the years 1821 and 1822, persons dropping down dead in the streets, or dying within an hour or two after the attack; many myriads were computed to have fallen victims, and the native doctors, finding their remedies useless, gave up all treatment. It carried off multitudes in Shantung and Kiangsu during the same years, and was as fitful in its progress in China as in Europe, going from one city to another, passing by towns apparently as obnoxious as those visited. The plague is said to have existed in Southern China about the beginning of the sixteenth century, but it has not been heard of lately.

Small-pox is a terrible scath, and although the practice and utility of vaccination have been known for fifty years past at Canton, its adoption is still limited even in that city. It was introduced in 1820 by Dr. Pearson, of the East India Company's establishment, and native assistants were fully instructed by him in the practice. Vaccination has now extended over all the Eighteen Provinces, and the government has given its sanction and assistance; it is chiefly owing to the heedlessness of the people in not availing themselves of it in time that it has done no more to lessen the ravages of the disease. Where children were gratuitously vaccinated it was found almost impossible to induce parents to bring them; and when the chil-

---

[1] *Chinese Repository*, Vol. XII., p. 487.

dren had been vaccinated it was increasingly difficult to get them to return to allow the physician to see the result of the operation. Inoculation has long been practised by inserting a pledget in the nostrils containing the virus; this mode is occasionally adopted in vaccination. The slovenly habits of the people, as well as insufficient protection and unwholesome food, give rise to many diseases of the skin, some of them incurable.

The science of medicine attracted very early attention, and there are numerous treatises on its various branches. But the search for the liquor of immortality and the philosopher's stone, with careful observations on the pulse as the leading tests of diseases, have led them astray from accurate diagnosis age after age. The common classification of diseases is under nine heads, viz., those which affect the pulse violently or feebly, those arising from cold, female and cutaneous diseases, those needing acupuncture, and diseases of the eyes, the mouth and its parts, and the bones. A professor of each of these classes is attached to the imperial family, who is taken from the Medical College at Peking; but he has no greater advantages there than he could get in his own reading and practice. No museums of morbid or comparative anatomy exist in the country, nor are there any lectures or dissections; and the routine which old custom has sanctioned will go on until modern practice, now rapidly taking its place, wins its way. Section CCXCVII. of the code orders that "whenever an unskilful practitioner, in administering medicine or using the puncturing needle, proceeds contrary to the established forms, and thereby causes the death of a patient, the magistrate shall call in other practitioners to examine the medicine or the wound, and if it appear that the injury done was unintentional, the practitioner shall then be treated according to the statute for accidental homicides, and shall not be any longer allowed to practise medicine. But if designedly he depart from the established forms, and deceives in his attempt to cure the malady in order to obtain property, then, according to its amount, he shall be treated as a thief; and if death ensue from his malpractice, then, for having thus used medicine with intent to kill, he shall be beheaded."[1] This statute is seldom carried into execution, however, and the doctors are allowed to kill and cure, *secundum artem*, as their patients give them the opportunity.

Natural history, in its various branches of geology, botany, zoölogy, etc., has received some attention, because the objects which come under it could not escape the notice of all the writers in Chinese literature. As sciences, however, none of them have an existence, and they are studied chiefly for their assistance in furnishing articles for the materia medica of the native physician. To these persons nothing comes amiss, and, like the ingredients of the bubbling, bubbling caldron of Macbeth's witches, the stranger it is the more potent they think a dose will be; in this particular they now act very much as the faculty did in England two centuries ago. It is to be regretted that their investigation should have taken such a direction, but the man of commanding influence has not yet arisen to direct their researches into nature and divert them from the marvellous and theoretical. On the whole, it may be said that in all departments of learning the Chinese are unscientific; and that while they have collected a great variety of facts, invented many arts, and brought a few to a high degree of excellence, they have never pursued a single subject in a way calculated to lead them to a right understanding of it, or reached a proper classification of the information they possessed relating to it.

---

[1] *Chinese Chrestomathy*, Chap. XVI., pp. 497–532. *Asiatic Soc. Transactions*, Hongkong, Art. III., 1847; No. III., 1852, Art. III. *Jour. N. C. Br. R. A. Soc.*, No. I., 1864, and No. VI., 1869. W. Lockhart, *Medical Missionary in China*, 1861. *Chinese Repository*, *passim*. Porter Smith's *Contributions to Chinese Materia Medica*, Shanghai, 1871. Flückiger & Hanbury, *Pharmacographia*, London, 1874. *China Review*, Vol. I., p. 176; Vol. III., p. 224. J. Dudgeon, *The Diseases of China*, Glasgow, 1877; *id.* in the *Chinese Recorder*, Vols. II., III., and IV., *passim*.

CHAPTER XVII.

HISTORY AND CHRONOLOGY OF CHINA.

THE history of the Chinese people has excited less attention among western scholars than it deserves, though in some respects no nation offers more claims to have its chronicles carefully and fairly examined. The belief is generally entertained that their pretensions to antiquity are extravagant and ridiculous, and incompatible with the Mosaic chronology; that they not only make the world to have existed myriads of years, but reckon the succession of their monarchs far beyond the creation, and ascribe to them a longevity that carries its own confutation on its face. In consequence of this opinion, some have denied the credibility of native historians altogether, and the whole subject of the settlement and early progress of this ancient race has been considered beyond the reach, and almost unworthy the attempt, of sober investigation. This erroneous and hasty conclusion is gradually giving way to a careful inquiry into those histories which show that the early records of the sons of Han contain much which is worthy of credence, and much more that is highly probable. A wide field is here opened for the researches of a Gibbon or a Niebuhr; for as long as we are destitute of a good history of China and its connections with other Asiatic nations, we shall not only be unable to form a correct opinion respecting the people, but shall lack many important data for a full illustration of the early history of the human race. It is easy to laud the early records of the Chinese to the skies, as French writers have done; and it is quite as easy to cry them down as worthless—manufactured in after-ages to please the variety of their writers. The reputation both people and records have received is owing, in some measure, to this undue laudation and depreciation, as well as to the intrinsic merits and defects of their histories. These, however, still mostly remain in their originals, and will require the united labors of many scholars to be fully brought to light and made a part of the world's library.

The enormous difficulties arising from the extent and tedious minuteness of native historians, coupled with the scarcity of translators competent or willing to undertake the labor of even such a *résumé* of these works as will satisfy rational curiosity, are now being slowly overcome, both by Chinese and foreign students. These researches, it is to be earnestly hoped, will be rewarded by promoting a juster estimate in the minds of both classes of their relative positions among the nations of the earth.

China, like other countries, has her mythological history, and it should be separated from the more recent and received, as her own historians regard it, as the fabrication of subsequent times. She also has her ancient history, whose earliest dates and events blend confusedly with the mythological, but gradually grow more credible and distinct as they come down the stream of time to the beginning of modern history. The early accounts of every nation whose founding was anterior to the practice of making and preserving authentic records must necessarily be obscure and doubtful. What is applicable to the Chinese has been true of other ancient people: "national vanity and a love of the marvellous have influenced them all, and furnished materials for many tales, as soon as the spirit of investigation has supplanted that appetite for wonders which marks the infancy of nations as well as of individuals." The ignorance of the "art preservative of all arts" will greatly explain the subsequent record of the wonderful, without supposing that the infancy of nations partook of the same traits of weakness and credulity as that of individuals. There is neither space nor time in this work to give the details concerning the history and succession of dynasties that have swayed the Middle Kingdom, for to one not specially engaged in their examination their recital is proverbially dry; the array of uncouth names destitute of lasting interest, and the absence of the charm of association with western nations render them uninviting to the general reader. Some account of the leading events and changes is all that is necessary to explain what has been elsewhere incidentally referred to.[1]

Chinese historians have endeavored to explain the creation and origin of the world around them; but, ignorant of the sublime fact that there is one Creator who upholds his works by the word of his power, they have invented various modes to account for it, and wearied themselves in theorizing and disputing with each other. One of them, Yangtsz', remarks, in view of these conflicting suppositions: "Who knows the affairs of remote antiquity, since no authentic records have come down to us? He who examines these stories will find it difficult to believe them, and careful scrutiny will convince him that they are without foundation. In the primeval ages no historical records were kept. Why then, since the ancient books that described those times were burnt by Tsin, should we misrepresent those remote ages, and satisfy ourselves with vague fables? However, as everything except heaven and earth must have a cause, it is clear that they have always existed, and that cause produced all sorts of men and beings, and endowed them with their various qualities. But it must have been man who in the beginning produced all things on earth, and who may therefore be viewed as the lord, and from whom rulers derive their dignities."

This extract is not a bad example of Chinese writers and historians; a mixture of sense and nonsense, partially laying the foundation of a just argument, and ending with a tremendous non-sequitur, apparently satisfactory to themselves, but showing pretty conclusively how little pains they take to gather facts and discuss their bearings. Some of these writers imagine that the world owes its existence to the retroactive agency of the dual powers *yin* and *yang*, which first formed the outline of the universe, and were themselves influenced by

---

[1] Among the works which will repay perusal on this topic are Mailla's *Histoire de la Chine* and Pauthier's *Chine*, in French, and Du Halde's *History*, translated into English; besides the briefer compilations of Murray, Grosier, Gutzlaff, Davis, and more recently of Boulger and Richthofen, Band I.

their own creations. One of the most sensible of their authors says:

> Heaven was formless, an utter chaos; the whole mass was nothing but confusion. Order was first produced in the pure ether, and out of it the universe came forth; the universe produced air, and air the milky-way. When the pure male principle *yang* had been diluted, it formed the heavens; the heavy and thick parts coagulated, and formed the earth. The refined particles united very soon, but the union of the thick and heavy went on slowly; therefore the heavens came into existence first, and the earth afterward. From the subtle essence of heaven and earth, the dual principles *yin* and *yang* were formed; from their joint operation came the four seasons, and these putting forth their energies gave birth to all the products of the earth. The warm effluence of the *yang* being condensed, produced fire; and the finest parts of fire formed the sun. The cold exhalations of the *yin* being likewise condensed, produced water; and the finest parts of the watery substance formed the moon. By the seminal influence of the sun and moon, came the stars. Thus heaven was adorned with the sun, moon, and stars; the earth also received rain, rivers, and dust.[1]

But this acute explanation, like the notions of Hesiod among the Greeks, was too subtle for the common people; they also wanted to personify and deify these powers and operations, but lacking the imaginative genius and fine taste of the Greeks, their divine personages are outrageous and their ideal beings shapeless monsters. No creator is known or imagined who, like Brahm, lives in space, ineffable, formless; but the first being, Pwanku, had the herculean task to mould the chaos which produced him and chisel out the earth that was to contain him. One legend is that "the dual powers were fixed when the primeval chaos separated. Chaos is bubbling turbid water, which enclosed and mingled with the dual powers, like a chick *in ovo*, but when their offspring Pwanku appeared their distinctiveness and operations were apparent. *Pwan* means a 'basin,' referring to the shell of the egg; *ku* means 'solid,' 'to secure,' intending to show how the first man Pwanku was hatched from the chaos by the dual powers, and then settled and exhibited the arrangement of the causes which produced him."

The Rationalists have penetrated furthest into the Dædalian

---

[1] *Chinese Repository*, Vol. III., p. 55.

mystery of this cosmogony,[1] and they go on to show what Pwanku did and how he did it. They picture him holding a chisel and mallet in his hands, splitting and fashioning vast

Pwanku Chiselling Out the Universe.

masses of granite floating confusedly in space. Behind the openings his powerful hand has made are seen the sun, moon, and stars, monuments of his stupendous labors; at his right

[1] For the Buddhist notions of cosmography and creation, see **Rémusat**, *Mélanges Posthumes*, pp. 65–131.

hand, inseparable companions of his toils, but whose generation is left in obscurity, stand the dragon, the phœnix, and the tortoise, and sometimes the unicorn, divine types and progenitors with himself of the animal creation. His efforts were continued eighteen thousand years, and by small degrees he and his work increased; the heavens rose, the earth spread out and thickened, and Pwanku grew in stature, six feet every day, till, his labors done, he died for the benefit of his handiwork. His head became mountains, his breath wind and clouds, and his voice thunder; his limbs were changed into the four poles, his veins into rivers, his sinews into the undulations of the earth's surface, and his flesh into fields; his beard, like Berenice's hair, was turned into stars, his skin and hair into herbs and trees, and his teeth, bones, and marrow into metals, rocks, and precious stones; his dropping sweat increased to rain, and lastly (*nascitur ridiculus mus*) the insects which stuck to his body were transformed into people!

Such was Pwanku, and these were his works. But these grotesque myths afford none of the pleasing images and personifications of Greek fable or Egyptian symbols; they fatigue without entertaining, and only illustrate the childish imagination of their authors. Pwanku was succeeded by three rulers of monstrous forms called the Celestial, Terrestrial, and Human sovereigns, impersonations of a trinity of powers, whose traces and influences run through Chinese philosophy, religion, and politics; their acts and characters are detailed with the utmost gravity, and more than Methusalean longevity allowed them to complete their plans. Their reigns continued eighteen thousand years (more or less according to the author quoted), during which time good government commenced, men learned to eat and drink, the sexes united, sleep was invented, and other improvements adopted. One would think, if the subjects of these wonderful beings were as long-lived, great perfection might have been attained in these and other useful arts; but the mysterious tortoise, companion of Pwanku, on whose carapace was written, in tadpole-headed characters, the history of the anterior world, did not survive, and their record has not come down. After them flourished two other monarchs, one of them called

Yu-chau, which means 'having a nest,' and the other Sui-jin, or 'match-man.' Whether the former invented nests for the abodes of his subjects, such as the Indians on the Orinoco have, is not stated; but the latter brought down fire from heaven for them to cook with, and became a second, or rather the first, Prometheus.

These fancies are gathered from a popular summary of knowledge, called the *Coral Forest of Ancient Matters*, and from the opening chapters of *History Made Easy*. A higher style of philosophizing is found in Chu Hí's disquisition, from which an extract has been given in Chapter XII. Another on Cosmogony will show that he comes no nearer to the great fact of creation than ancient western writers.

In the beginning heaven and earth were just the light and dark air. This one air revolved, grinding round and round. When it ground quickly much sediment was compressed, which, having no means of exit, coagulated and formed the earth in the centre. The subtle portion of the air then became heaven and the sun, moon, and stars, which unceasingly revolve on the outside. The earth is in the centre and motionless; it is not below the centre.

Heaven revolving without ceasing, day and night also revolve, and hence the earth is exactly in the centre. If heaven should stand still for one moment, then the earth must fall down; but heaven revolves quickly, and hence much sediment is coagulated in the centre. The earth is the sediment of the air; and hence it is said, the light, pure air became heaven, the heavy, muddy air became earth. . . .

At the beginning of heaven and earth, before chaos was divided, I think there were only two things—fire and water; and the sediment of the water formed the earth. When one ascends a height and looks down, the crowd of hills resemble the waves of the sea in appearance: the water just flowed like this. I know not at what period it coagulated. At first it was very soft, but afterward it coagulated and became hard. One asked whether it resembled sand thrown up by the tide? He replied, Just so; the coarsest sediment of the water became earth, and the purest portion of the fire became wind, thunder, lightning, sun, and stars. . . .

Before chaos was divided, the *yin-yang*, or light-dark air, was mixed up and dark, and when it divided the centre formed an enormous and most brilliant opening, and the two *i* or principles were established. Shao Kang-tsieh considers one hundred and twenty-nine thousand six hundred years to be a *yuen*, or kalpa; then, before this period of one hundred and twenty-nine thousand six hundred years there was another opening and spreading out of the world; and before that again, there was another like the present; so that motion and rest, light and darkness, have no beginning. As little things shadow forth great things, this may be illustrated by the revolutions of day and night. . . .

Kang-tsieh says, Heaven rests upon form, and earth reclines upon air. The reason why he repeats this frequently, and does not deviate from the idea, is lest people should seek some other place beyond heaven and earth. There is nothing outside heaven and earth, and hence their form has limits, while their air has no limit. Because the air is extremely condensed, therefore it can support the earth; if it were not so the earth would fall down.[1]

A third belief respecting the position of the earth in the centre of the universe derives great strength in the opinion of intelligent natives from these speculations of Chu Hí. His theory considers the world to be a plane surface, straight, square, and large, measuring each way about 1,500 miles (5,600 *lí*), and bounded on the four sides by the four seas. The sun is estimated to be about 4,000 miles from the earth. Another calculation made it 81,394 *lí*, and a third 216,781½ *lí*.

One thing is observable in these fictions, characteristic of the Chinese at the present day: there is no hierarchy of gods brought in to rule and inhabit the world they made, no conclave on Mt. Olympus, nor judgment of the mortal soul by Osiris; no transfer of human love and hate, passions and hopes, to the powers above; all here is ascribed to disembodied agencies or principles, and their works are represented as moving on in quiet order. There is no religion, no imagination; all is impassible, passionless, uninteresting. It may, perhaps, be considered of itself as sensible as the Greek or Egyptian mythology, if one looks for *sense* in such figments; but it has not, as in the latter countries, been explained in sublime poetry, shadowed forth in gorgeous ritual and magnificent festivals, represented in exquisite sculptures, nor preserved in faultless, imposing fanes and temples, filled with ideal creations. For this reason it appears more in its true colors, and, when compared with theirs, "loses discountenanced and like folly shows"—at least to us, who can examine both and compare them with the truth.

Their pure mythological history ends with the appearance of Fuh-hí, and their chronology has nothing to do with the long periods antecedent, varying from forty-five to five hundred

[1] Canon McClatchie's *Confucian Cosmogony*, pp. 53–59.

thousand years. These periods are, however, a mere twinkling compared with the kulpas of the Hindus, whose highest era, called the Unspeakably Inexpressible, requires four million four hundred and fifty-six thousand four hundred and forty-eight cyphers following a unit to represent it. If the epoch of Fuh-hí could be ascertained with any probability by comparison with the history of other nations, or with existing remains, it would tend not a little to settle some disputed chronological points in other countries; but the isolation of the Chinese throughout their whole existence makes it nearly impossible to weave in the events of their history with those of other nations, by comparing and verifying them with biblical, Egyptian, or Persian annals. Perhaps further investigations in the vast regions of Eastern and Central Asia may bring to light corroborative testimony as striking and unexpected as the explorations in Mosul, Persepolis, and Thebes.

The accession of Fuh-hí is placed in the Chinese annals B.C. 2852,[1] and with him commences the period known among them as the "highest antiquity." The weight of evidence which the later chronological examinations of Hales and Jackson have brought to bear against the common period of four thousand and four years prior to the Advent, is such as to cast great doubt over its authenticity, and lead to the adoption of a longer period in order to afford time for many occurrences, which otherwise would be crowded into too narrow a space. Chinese chronology, if it be allowed the least credit, strongly corroborates the results of Dr. Hales' researches, and particularly so in the date of Fuh-hí's accession. This is not the place to discuss the respective claims of the two eras, but by reckoning, as he does, the creation to be five thousand four hundred and eleven years, and the deluge three thousand one hundred and fifty-five years, before the Advent, we bring the commencement of ancient Chinese history three hundred and three years subsequent to the deluge, forty-seven before the death of Noah, and about three centuries before the confusion of tongues. If we suppose that the ante-

[1] Or 3322, according to Dr. Legge, whose date has been used elsewhere in this work, and has probably quite as much authority as the one above.

diluvians possessed a knowledge of the geography of the world, and that Noah, regarding himself as the monarch of the whole, divided it among his descendants before his death, there is nothing improbable in the further supposition that the progenitors of the black-haired race, and others of the house and lineage of Shem, found their way from the valley of the Euphrates across the defiles and steppes of Central Asia, to the fertile plains of China before the end of the third diluvian century. Whether the surface of the world was the same after the cataclysm as before does not affect this point; there was ample time for the multiplication of the species with the blessing promised by God, sufficient to form colonies, if there was time enough to increase to such a multitude as conspired to build the tower of Babel.

The views of Dr. Legge, that the present Chinese descend from settlers who came through Central Asia along the Tarim Valley and across the Desert into Kansuh, about B.C. 2200, and settled around the elbow of the Yellow River, under the leadership of Yao, Shun, Yu, and others, are very reasonable. These settlers found the land at that time occupied with tribes, whom they partly merged with themselves or drove into mountain recesses in Kweichau, where some of their descendants perhaps still remain. These earlier tribes may have furnished the names and reigns prior to Yao, and the later Chinese annalists incorporated them into their own histories, taking everything in early times as of course belonging to the *lí min*, or 'black-haired race.' The lapse of a millennium between the Deluge and Yao allows plenty of time for several successive emigrations from Western and Central Asia into the inviting plains of China, which, through the want of a written language or the destruction of records, have come down to us in misty, doubtful legends.

Fuh-hí and his seven successors are stated to have reigned seven hundred and forty-seven years, averaging ninety-three each. Those who follow Usher consider these monarchs to be Chinese travesties of the eight antediluvian patriarchs; and Marquis d'Urban has gone so far as to write what he calls the *Antediluvian History of China*, collecting all the notices history affords of their acts. The common chronology brings the deluge about thirteen years after the accession of Yao and the death of Shun (the last of the eight), B.C. 2205, or twenty-five years after the confusion of tongues. According to Hales, the last epoch is one hundred and twelve years before the call of Abraham, and these eight Chinese monarchs are therefore contemporaries of the patriarchs who lived between Shem and Abraham, commencing with Salah and ending with Nahor. The duration of their reigns, moreover, is such as would bear the same proportion to ages of five hundred years, which their contemporaries lived, as the present average of twenty and twenty-five years does to a life of sixty. The Assyrian tablets, deciphered by George Smith, contain a reference to the twenty-eighth century B.C., as the founding of that monarchy; which is a notice of more value as a chronological epoch than anything in Chinese annals, indeed, and may help to countenance a date that had before been regarded as mythological.

Supposing that the descendants of Shem, Ham, and Japheth, knowing from their fathers and grandfather, that the void world was before them, began to colonize almost as soon as they began to form families, three centuries would not be too long a time for some of them to settle in China, perhaps offsetting from Elam and Asshur, and other descendants of Shem in Persia. The capital of Fuh-hí slightly indicates, it may be thought, their route through Central Asia across the Desert to Kiayü kwan in Kansuh, and then down the Yellow River to the Great Plain near Kaifung. But these suppositions are only by the way, as is also the suggestion that teaching of fishing and grazing, the regulation of times and seasons, cultivation of music, and establishment of government, etc., compare well enough with the duties that might reasonably be supposed to belong to the founder of a colony and his successors, and subsequently ascribed to them as their own inventions. The long period allotted to human life at that date would allow these arts and sciences to take root and their memory to remain in popular legends until subsequent historians incorporated them into their writings. The Chinese annalists fill up the reigns of these chiefs, down to the time of Yao, with a series of inventions and improvements in the arts of life and good government, sufficient to bring society to that degree of comfort and order they suppose consonant with the character of the monarchs. The earliest records of the Chinese correspond much too closely with their present character to receive full belief; but they present an appearance of probability and naturalness not possessed by the early annals of Greece. No one contends for their credibility as history, but they are better than the Arabian Nights.

The commencement of the sexagenary cycle[1] in the sixty-first year of Hwangti's reign (or B.C. 2637), five hundred and eighteen years after the deluge, eighty-two years after the death of Arphaxad, and about that time before the confusion of tongues, is worthy of notice. The use of the ten horary characters applied to days in order to denote their chronological sequence dates from the reign of Yu in the twentieth century B.C., and there are other passages in the *Shu King* showing similar application. Sz'ma Tsien's history now contains the first attempt to arrange the years in cycles of sixty; but he cannot fairly be claimed as the inventor of this system. He might almost as well be regarded as the inventor of his whole *annals*, for all the materials out of which he compiled them have now perished except the canonical books. The mention of the individual Nao the Great, who invented it, and the odd date of its adoption in the middle of a reign, do not weaken the alleged date of its origin in the minds of those who are inclined to take a statement of this kind on its own basis.

Three reigns, averaging eighty years' duration, intervened between that of Hwangtí and Yao, whose occupants were elected by the people, much as were Shemgar, Jephthah, and other judges in Israel, and probably exercised a similar sway. The reigns and characters of Yao and Shun have been immortalized by Confucius and Mencius; whatever was their real history, those sages showed great sagacity in going back to those remote times for models and fixing upon a period neither fabulous nor certain, one which prevented alike the cavils of scepticism and the appearance of complete fabrication.

---

[1] *Journal Asiatique*, Avril, 1836, p. 394.

A tremendous deluge occurred during the reign of Yao, B.C. 2293, caused, it is said, by the overflowing of the rivers in the north of China. Those who place the Noachic deluge B.C. 2348 regard this as only a different version of that event; Klaproth, who favors the Septuagint chronology, says that it is nearly synchronous with the deluge of Xisuthrus, B.C. 2297, a name derived, as is reasonably inferred by George Smith, from the Assyrian name Hasisadra, the ancient hero who survived the deluge. The record of this catastrophe in the *Shu King* is hardly applicable to an overwhelming flood: "The Emperor said, Oh! chief of the four mountains, destructive in their overthrow are the waters of the inundation. In their vast extent they embrace the mountains and overtop the hills, threatening the heavens with their floods, so that the inferior people groan and murmur. Is there a capable man to whom I can assign the correction of this calamity?"[1] They presented Kwăn as a proper man, but he showed his inefficiency in laboring nine years without success to drain off the waters. Yao was then advised to employ Shun, who called in Yu, a son of Kwăn, to his aid, and the floods were assuaged by deepening the beds of the rivers and opening new channels. These slight notices hardly comport with a flood like the Noachic deluge, and are with much greater probability referred to an overflow or a change in the bed of the Yellow River from its present course into the Gulf of Pechele through Chihlí northeast, to its recent one along the lowlands of Kiangsu. The weight of topographical evidence, combined with the strong chronological argument, the discussions in council said to have taken place regarding the disaster, and the time which elapsed before the region was drained, all pre-suppose and indicate a partial inundation, and strengthen the assumption that no traces of the Deluge exist in the histories of the Chinese. In our view of the chronology of the Bible, as compared with the Chinese, it requires a far greater constraint upon these records to bring them to refer to that event, than to suppose they allude to a local disaster not beyond the power of remedy.

---

[1] Legge's *Shu King*, p. 24, Hongkong, 1867.

The series of chieftains down to the accession of Yu may here be recapitulated. The entirely fabulous period ends with Sui-jin, and legendary history commences with Fuh-hí, who with four of his successors (Nos. 2, 3, 7, and 8) are commonly known as the Five Sovereigns. Their names and reigns are as follows:

	Names.	Years reigned.	Began B.C.	Other Events.
1	Fuh-hí..........	115	2852	The Deluge, B.C. 3155.
2	Shinnung	140	2737	Death of Noah, B.C. 2805.
3	Hwangtí	100	2697	
4	Shauhau	84	2597	Death of Arphaxad, 2715.
5	Chwenhüh	78	2513	Death of Shem, 2555.
6	Kuh	78	2435	Rise of Egyptian monarchy, 2450.
7	Yao	102	2357	Rise of Babylonian " 2300.
8	Shun	50	2255	Abraham's birth, 2153.

The records in the *Shu King* of Yao, Shun, and Yu the Great (B.C. 2205) are longer than those of any other persons who lived prior to Abraham. The chronicle represents the merits of Yu to have been first exhibited in reducing the waters and dividing the country into nine regions, and as he had assisted Shun in his government during his lifetime, he was unanimously called to the vacant dignity, and became the founder of the Hia dynasty. Allowing that the records of these times and people are brief and disjointed, and many things in them impossible to reconcile, still they are superior to the absurd tales describing the formation of some other ancient States, and should not be ridiculed as trivial or rejected as fabulous. The great advances made in settling obscure points in early history, by the success in deciphering records brought to light in Western Asia, lead to more respect for what we possess in Eastern Asia, rather than to reject the fragmentary records remaining. No one regards them as trustworthy, like the clay tablets exhumed at Nineveh, but if Abraham found the Egyptians to be living under a regular government not one hundred and fifty years after this, and Damascus, Babylon, Erech, and other cities were then old, no one need be unwilling to give the Chinese a line of monarchs, and a population quite sufficient to have deepened the channel of a river or raised dikes to restrain it. The glorious reigns and spotless characters of these three sovereigns are looked upon by the Chinese with much the same feelings of veneration that the Jews regard their three patriarchs; and to have had, or to have imagined, such progenitors and heroes is, to say the least, as much to their credit as the Achilles, Ulysses, and Romulus of the Greeks and Romans. A curious analogy can also be traced between the scheming Ulysses, warlike Romulus, and methodical Yao, and the subsequent character of the three great nations they represent.

Chinese historians supply many details regarding the conduct of Yu and Kieh Kwei, the first and last princes of the house of Hia, all the credible particulars of which are taken from the *Book of Records* and the *Bamboo Annals*. Dr. Legge candidly weighs the arguments in respect to the eclipse mentioned in the *Yuh Ching*, and gives his opinion as to its authenticity, even if it cannot yet be certainly referred to the year B.C. 2154. One such authentic notice lends strength to the reception of many vague statements, which are more likely to be the relics of fuller documents long since lost than the fabrications of later writers, such as were the Decretals of Isidore in the Middle Ages. In giving a full translation of the *Bamboo Books* in the prolegomena of the *Shu King*, Dr. Legge has shown one of the sources of ancient Chinese history outside of that work. There were many other works accessible to Sz'ma Tsien, nearly four centuries before they were discovered (A.D. 279), when he wrote his *Annals*. Pan Ku gives a list of the various books recovered after the death of Tsin Chí Hwangtí, amounting in all to thirteen thousand two hundred and nineteen volumes or chapters contained in six hundred and twenty different works. Well does Pauthier speak of the inestimable value which a similar catalogue of the extant literature of Greece and Rome at that epoch (B.C. 100) would now be.

One of the alleged records of the reign of Yu is an inscription traced on the rocks of Kau-lau shan, one of the peaks of Mount Hăng in Hunan, relating to the inundation. It contains seventy-seven characters only, and Amiot, who regarded it as genuine, has given its sense as follows:

The venerable Emperor said, Oh! aid and councillor! Who will help me in administering my affairs? The great and little islets (the inhabited places), even to their summits, the abodes of the beasts and birds, and all beings are widely inundated. Advise, send back the waters, and raise the dikes. For a long time, I have quite forgotten my family; I repose on the top of the mountain Yoh-lu. By prudence and my labors, I have moved the spirits; I know not the hours, but repose myself only in my incessant labors. The mountains Hwa, Yoh, Tai, and Hăng, have been the beginning and end of my enterprise; when my labors were completed, I offered a thanksgiving sacrifice at the solstice. My affliction has ceased; the confusion in nature has disappeared; the deep currents coming from the south flow into the sea; clothes can now be made, food can be prepared, all kingdoms will be at peace, and we can give ourselves to continual joy.[1]

Since Amiot's time, however, further opportunities have offered for more thorough inquiry into this relic by foreigners, and the results of their researches throw much doubt upon its authenticity, though they do not altogether destroy it. In the Introduction to the *Shu King*, Dr. Legge discusses the value of this tablet among other early records of that reign, and comes to the conclusion that it is a fabrication of the Han dynasty, if not later. The poet Han Yu (A.D. 800) gave it wide notoriety by his verses about its location and nature; but when he was there he could not find it on the peak, and cited only a Taoist priest as having seen it. More than three centuries afterward Chu Hí was equally unsuccessful, and his opinion that it was made by the priests of that sect has had much weight with his countrymen. It was not till one Ho Chi went to Mount Hăng, about A.D. 1210, and took a copy of the inscription from the stone then in a Taoist temple, that it was actually seen; and not till about 1510, that Chang Kí-wăn, another antiquary of Hunan province, published his copy in the form now generally accepted. In 1666 one Mao Tsăng-kien again found the tablet on the summit of Kau-lau, but reached it with much difficulty by the help of ladders and hooks, and found it so broken that the inscription could not be made out. A reduced *fac-simile* of Mao's copy is given by

---

[1] Pauthier, *La Chine*, p. 53; J. Hager's *Inscription of Yu*, Paris, 1802; Legge's *Shu King*, pp. 67–74; *Transactions of the N. C. Br. R. A. Soc.*, No. V., 1869, pp. 78–84; *Journal Asiatique*, 1867, Tome X., pp. 197–337.

Dr. Legge, whose translation differs from Amiot's in some particulars.

I received *the words of* the Emperor, saying, "Ah! Associate helper, aiding noble! The islands and islets may now be ascended, *that were* doors for the birds and beasts. *You* devoted your person to the great overflowings, and with the daybreak you rose up. Long were *you* abroad, forgetting your family; *you* lodged at the mountain's foot as in a hall; *your* wisdom schemed; *your* body was broken; *your* heart was all in a tremble. *You* went and sought to produce order and settlement. At Hwa, Yoh, Tai, and Hăng, by adopting the principle of dividing *the waters*, *your* undertakings were completed. With the remains of a taper, *you* offered your pure sacrifice. There were entanglement and obstruction, being swamped, and removals. The southern river flows on its course; for ever is the provision of food made sure; the myriad States enjoy repose; the beasts and birds are for ever fled away."

The characters in which this tablet is written are of an ancient tadpole form, and so difficult to read that grave doubts exist as to their proper meaning—and even as to which of two or three forms is the correct one. Since the copy of Mao was taken, the Manchu scholar Kwan-wăn, when Governor-General of Liang Hu in 1868, erected a stone tablet at Wu-chang, in the Pavilion of the Yellow Stork, upon the eminence overlooking the Yangtsz'. This he regarded as a true copy of the authentic *Yu Pai*, or 'Tablet of Yu.' A *fac-simile* of this tablet, and of another rubbing from a stone now existing at the foot of Mount Hăng (which is alleged to be an exact reproduction of the original on its top), was published by W. H. Medhurst in the *N. C. Asiatic Society Journal* for 1869. A comparison of these three will give the reader an idea of the difficulties and doubts attending the settlement of the credibility of this inscription. A living native writer quoted by Mr. Medhurst says that the earliest notice of the tablet is by Tsin Yung of the Tăng dynasty, about A.D. 700, from which he infers that the people of the time of Tăng must have seen the rock and its inscription. He regards the latter as consisting of fairy characters, utterly unreadable, and therefore all attempts to decipher them as valueless and misleading.

Amid so many conflicting opinions among native scholars, the verdict of foreigners may safely await further discoveries, and the day when competent observers can examine these localities and tablets for themselves. Without exaggerating the importance and credibility of the *Shu King* and other ancient Chinese records, they can be received as the writings of a very remote period; and while their claims to trustworthiness would be fortified if more intimations had been given of the manner in which they were kept during the long period antecedent to the era of Confucius, they still deserve a more respectful consideration than some modern writers are disposed to allow them. For instance, Davis remarks: "Yu is described as nine cubits in height, and it is stated that the skies rained gold in those days, which certainly (as Dr. Morrison observes) lessens the credit of the history of this period." Now, without laying too much stress upon the record, or the objections against it, this height is but little more than that of Og of Bashan, even if we adopt the present length of the cubit fourteen and one-tenth inches, English; and if *kin*, here called *gold*, be translated *metal* (which it can just as well be), it may be a notice of a meteoric shower of extraordinary duration. Let these venerable writings be investigated in a candid, cautious manner, weighing their internal evidence, and comparing their notices of those remote periods as much as they can be with those of other nations, and they will illustrate ancient history and customs in no slight degree. Mr. Murray has given a synopsis from Mailla of what is recorded of the Hia dynasty, which will fairly exhibit the matter of Chinese history. It is here introduced somewhat abridged, with dates inserted.

The accession of Yu (B.C. 2205) forms a remarkable era in Chinese history. The throne, which hitherto had been more or less elective, became from this period hereditary in the eldest son, with only those occasional and violent interruptions to which every despotic government is liable. The national annals, too, assume a more regular and authentic shape, the reigns of the sovereigns being at the same time reduced to a probable duration.

Yu justly acquired a lasting veneration, but it was chiefly by his labors under his two predecessors. When he himself ascended the throne, age had already overtaken him; still the lustre of his government was supported by able councillors, till it closed with his life at the end of seven years. Many of the grandees wished, according to former practice, to raise to the throne Pí-yih, his first minister, and a person of distinguished merit; but regard for the father, in this case, was strengthened by the excellent qualities of his son

Kí, or Tí Kí (*i.e.*, the Emperor Kí), and even Pí-yih insisted that the prince should be preferred (2197). His reign of nine years was only disturbed by the rebellion of a turbulent subject, and he was succeeded (2188) by his son, Tai Kang. But this youth was devoted to pleasure; music, wine, and hunting entirely engrossed his attention. The Chinese, after enduring him for twenty-nine years, dethroned him (2159), and his brother, Chung Kang, was nominated to succeed, and held the reins of government for thirteen years with a vigorous hand. He was followed by his son, Siang (2146), who, destitute of the energy his situation required, gave himself up to the advice of his minister Yeh, and was by him, in connection with his accomplice, Hantsu, declared incapable of reigning. The usurper ruled for seven years, when he was killed; and the rightful monarch collected his adherents and gave battle to Hantsu and the son of Yeh in the endeavor to regain his throne. Siang was completely defeated, and lost both his crown and life; the victors immediately marched to the capital, and made so general a massacre of the family that they believed the name and race of Yu to be for ever extinguished.

The Empress Min, however, managed to escape, and fled to a remote city, where she brought forth a son, called Shau Kang; and the better to conceal his origin, she employed him as a shepherd boy to tend flocks. Reports of the existence of such a youth, and his occupation, at length reached the ears of Hantsu, who sent orders to bring him, dead or alive. The royal widow then placed her son as under-cook in the household of a neighboring governor, where the lad soon distinguished himself by a spirit and temper so superior to this humble station, that the master's suspicions were roused, and obliged him to disclose his name and birth. The officer, being devotedly attached to the house of Yu, not only kept the secret, but watched for an opportunity to reinstate him, and meanwhile gave him a small government in a secluded situation, which he prudently administered. Yet he was more than thirty years old before the governor, by engaging other chiefs in his interest, could assemble such a force as might justify the attempt to make head against the usurper. The latter hastily assembled his troops and led them to the attack, but was defeated and taken prisoner by the young prince Chu himself; and Shau Kang, with his mother, returned with acclamations to the capital. His reign is reckoned to have been sixty-one years' duration in the chronology of the time, which includes the usurpation of forty years of Hantsu.

The country was ably governed by Shau Kang, and also by his son, Chu (2057), who ruled for seventeen years; but the succeeding sovereigns, in many instances, abandoned themselves to indolence and pleasure, and brought the kingly name into contempt. From Hwai to Kieh Kwei, a space of two hundred and twenty-two years, between B.C. 2040 and 1818, few records remain of the nine sovereigns, whose bare names succeed each other in the annals. At length the throne was occupied by Kieh Kwei (1818), a prince who is represented as having, in connexion with his consort, Mei-hí, practised every kind of violence and extortion, in order to accumulate treasure, which they spent in unbridled voluptuousness. They formed a large pond of wine, deep enough to float a boat, at which three thousand men drank at once. It was surrounded, too, by pyramids of delicate viands, which no one, however, was allowed to taste, till he had first intoxicated himself out of the lake. The drunken quarrels which ensued were their favorite amusement. In the interior of the palace the vilest orgies were celebrated, and the venerable ministers, who attempted to remonstrate against these excesses, were either put to death or exiled. The people were at once indignant and grieved at such crimes, which threatened the downfall of the dynasty; and the discarded statesmen put themselves under the direction of the wise Í Yin, and advised Chingtang, the ablest of their number, and a descendant of Hwangtí, to assume the reins of government, assuring him of their support. He with reluctance yielded to their solicitations, and assembling a force marched against Kieh Kwei, who came out to meet him at the head of a numerous army, but fled from the contest on seeing the defection of his troops, and ended his days in despicable obscurity, after occupying the throne fifty-two years.[1]

Chinese annals are generally occupied in this way; the Emperor and his ministers fill the whole field of historic vision; little is recorded of the condition, habits, arts, or occupations of the people, who are merely considered as attendants of the monarch, which is, in truth, a feature of the ancient records of nearly all countries and people. Monarchs controlled the chronicles of their reigns, and their own vanity, as well as their ideas of government and authority led them to represent the people as a mere background to their own stately dignity and acts.

The Shang dynasty began B.C. 1766, or about one hundred and twenty years before the Exodus, and maintained an unequal sway over the feudal States composing the Empire for a period of six hundred and forty-four years. Its first monarch, Chingtang, or Tang the Successful, is described as having paid religious worship to Shangtí, under which name, perhaps, the true God was intended. On account of a severe drought of seven years' duration, this monarch is reported to have prayed, saying, "I the child Lí presume to use a dark colored victim, and announce to thee, O Shang-tien Hao ('High Heaven's Ruler'). Now there is a great drought, and it is right I should be held responsible for it. I do not know but that I have offended the powers above and below." With regard to his own conduct, he blamed himself in six particulars, and his words were not ended when the rain descended copiously.

The fragmentary records of this dynasty contained in the *Shu King* are not so valuable to the student who wishes merely

---

[1] Hugh Murray, *China*, Vol. I., pp. 51–55 (edition of 1843).

to learn the succession of monarchs in those days, as to one who inquires what were the principles on which they ruled, what were the polity, the religion, the jurisdiction, and the checks of the Chinese government in those remote times. The regular records of those days will never be recovered, but the preservation of the last two parts of the *Shu King* indicates their existence by fair inference, and encourages those who try to reconstruct the early annals of China to give full value even to slight fragments. But these parts have been of great service to the people since they were written, in teaching them by precept and example on what the prosperity of a State was founded, and how their rulers could bring it to ruin. In these respects there are no ancient works outside of the Bible with which they can at all be compared. The later system of examination has given them an unparalleled influence in molding the national character of the Chinese. Of the eleven chapters now remaining all are occupied more or less with the relative duties of the prince and rulers, enforcing on each that the welfare of all was bound up with their faithfulness. One quotation will give an idea of their instructions. "Order your affairs by righteousness, order your heart by propriety, so shall you transmit a grand example to posterity. I have heard the saying, He who finds instructors for himself comes to the supreme dominion; he who says that others are not equal to himself comes to ruin. He who likes to ask becomes enlarged; he who uses *only* himself becomes small. Oh! he who would take care for his end must be attentive to his beginning. There is establishment for the observers of propriety, and overthrow for the blinded and wantonly indifferent. To revere and honor the way of Heaven is the way ever to preserve the favoring regard of Heaven."[1]

The chronicles of the Shang dynasty, as gathered from the *Bamboo Books* and other later records, resemble those of the Hia in being little more than a mere succession of the names of the sovereigns, interspersed here and there with notices of some remarkable events in the natural and political world. Luxurious and despised princes alternate with vigorous and warlike ones

[1] Part IV., Book II., Chap. IV., 8–9.

who commanded respect, and the condition of the State measurably corresponds with the character of the monarchs, the feudal barons sometimes increasing in power and territory by encroaching on their neighbors, and then suffering a reduction from some new State. The names of twenty-eight princes are given, the accounts of whose reigns are indeed fuller than those of the dukes of Edom in Genesis, but their slight notices would be more interesting if the same confidence could be reposed in them.

The bad sovereigns occupy more room in these *fasti* than the good ones, the palm of wickedness being given to Chau-sin, with whom the dynasty ended. The wars which broke out during this dynasty were numerous, but other events also find a place, though hardly anything which throws light on society or civilization. Droughts, famines, and other calamities were frequent and attended by dreadful omens and fearful sights; this fancied correlation between natural casualties and political convulsions is a feature running through Chinese history, and grows out of the peculiar position of the monarch as the vicegerent of heaven. The people seem to have looked for control and protection more to their local masters than to their lord paramount, ranging themselves under their separate banners as they were bidden. The *History Made Easy* speaks of the twenty-fifth monarch, Wu-yih (B.C. 1198), as the most wicked of them all. "Having made his images of clay in the shape of human beings, dignified them with the name of gods, overcome them at gambling, and set them aside in disgrace, he then, in order to complete his folly, made leathern bags and filled them with blood, and sent them up into the air, exclaiming, when his arrows hit them and the blood poured down, 'I have shot heaven,' meaning, I have killed the gods."

The names of Chau-sin and Tan-kí are coupled with those of Kieh and Mí-hí of the Hia dynasty, all of them synonymous in the Chinese annals for the acme of cruelty and licentiousness —as are those of Nero and Messalina in Roman history. Chau-sin is said one winter's morning to have seen a few women walking barelegged on the banks of a stream collecting shellfish, and ordered their legs to be cut off, that he might see the marrow of persons who could resist cold so fearlessly. The heart of one of his reprovers was also brought him, in order to see wherein it differed from that of cowardly ministers. The last *Book of Shang* contains the vain remonstrance of another of them, who tells his sovereign that his dynasty is in the condition of one crossing a large stream who can find neither ford nor bank. Many acts of this nature alienated the hearts of the people, until Wăn wang, the leader of a State in the northwest of China, united the principal men against his misrule; but dying, bequeathed his crown and power to his son, Wu wang. He gradually gathered his forces and met Chau-sin at the head of a great army at Muh, near the junction of the rivers Kí and Wei, north of the Yellow River in Honan, where the defeat of the tyrant was complete. Feeling the contempt he was held in, and the hopeless struggle before him, he fled to his palace and burned himself with all his treasures, like another Sardanapalus, though his immolation (in B.C. 1122) preceded the Assyrian's by five centuries.

Wu wang, the martial king, the founder of the Chau dynasty, his father, Wăn wang, and his brother, Duke Chau, are among the most distinguished men of antiquity for their erudition, integrity, patriotism, and inventions. Wăn wang, Prince of Chau, was prime minister to Tai-ting, the grandfather of Chau-sin, but was imprisoned for his fidelity. His son obtained his liberation, and the sayings and acts of both occupy about twenty books in Part V. of the *Shu King*. Duke Chau survived his brother to become the director and support of his nephew; his counsels, occupying a large part of the history, are full of wisdom and equity. Book X. contains his warning advice about drunkenness, which has been remarkably influential among his countrymen ever since. No period of ancient Chinese history is more celebrated than that of the founding of this dynasty, chiefly because of the high character of its leading men, who were regarded by Confucius as the impersonations of everything wise and noble. Wu wang is represented as having invoked the assistance of Shangtí in his designs, and, when he was successful, returned thanks and offered prayers and sacrifices. He removed the capital from the province of Honan to the present

Sí-ngan, in Shensí, where it remained for a long period. This prince committed a great political blunder in dividing the Empire into petty states, thus destroying the ancient pure monarchy, and leaving himself only a small portion of territory and power, which were quite insufficient, in the hands of a weak prince, to maintain either the state or authority due the ruling sovereign. The number of States at one time was one hundred and twenty-five, at another forty-one, and, in the time of Confucius, about six hundred years after the establishment of the dynasty, fifty-two, some of them large kingdoms. From about B.C. 700 the imperial name and power lost the allegiance and respect of the feudal princes, and gradually became contemptible. Its nominal sway extended over the country lying north of the Yangtsz' kiang, the regions on the south being occupied by tribes of whom no intelligible record has been preserved.

The duration of the three dynasties, the Hia, Shang, and Chau, comprises a long and obscure period in the history of the world, extending from B.C. 2205 to 249, from the time when Terah dwelt in Charran, and the sixteenth dynasty of Theban kings ruled in Egypt, down to the reigns of Antiochus Soter and Ptolemy Philadelphus and the translation of the Septuagint.

I.—The Hia dynasty, founded by Yu the Great, existed four hundred and thirty-nine years, down to B.C. 1766, under seventeen monarchs, the records of whose reigns are very brief. Among contemporary events of importance are the call of Abraham, in the year B.C. 2093, Jacob's flight to Mesopotamia in 1916, Joseph's elevation in Egypt in 1885, and his father's arrival in 1863.

II.—The Shang dynasty began with Tang the Successful, and continued six hundred and forty-four years, under twenty-eight sovereigns, down to B.C. 1122. This period was characterized by wars among rival princes, and the power of the sovereign depended chiefly upon his personal character. The principal contemporary events were the Exodus of the Israelites in 1648, their settlement in Palestine in 1608, judgeship of Othniel, 1564; of Deborah, 1406; of Gideon, 1359; of Samson, 1202; and death of Samuel in 1122.

III.—The Chau dynasty began with Wu wang, and continued for eight hundred and seventy-three years, under thirty-five monarchs, down to B.C. 249, the longest of any recorded in history. The sway of many of these was little more than nominal, and the feudal States increased or diminished, according to the vigor of the monarch or the ambition of the princes. In B.C. 770 the capital was removed from Kao, near the River Wei in Shensí, to Lohyang, in the western part of Honan; this divides the house into the Western and Eastern Chau. The contemporary events of these eight centuries are too numerous to particularize. The accession of Saul in 1110; of David, 1070; of Rehoboam, 990; taking of Troy, 1084; of Samaria, 719; of Jerusalem, 586; death of Nebuchadnezzar, 561; accession of Cyrus and return of the Jews, 551; battle of Marathon, 490; accession of Alexander, 235; etc. The conquest of Egypt by Alexander in 322 brought the thirty-first and last dynasty of her native kings to an end, the first of which had begun under Menes about B.C. 2715, or twenty-two years after the supposed accession of Shinnung.

The absence of any great remains of human labor or art previous to the Great Wall, like the Pyramids, the Temple of Solomon, or the ruins and mounds in Syria, has led many to doubt the credibility of these early Chinese records. They ascribe them to the invention of the historians of the Han dynasty, working up the scattered relics of their ancient books into a readable narrative, and therefore try to bring every statement to a critical test for which there are few facts. The analogies between the records in the *Shu King* and the Aryan myths are skilfully explained by Mr. Kingsmill by reference to the meanings of the names of persons and places and titles, and a connection shown which has the merit at least of ingenuity and beauty. Almost the only actual known relic of these three dynasties is the series of ten stone drums (*shih ku*) now in the Confucian temple at Peking. They were discovered about A.D. 600, in the environs of the ancient capital of the Chau dynasty, and have been kept in Peking since the year 1126. They are irregularly shaped pillars, from eighteen to thirty-five inches high and about twenty-eight inches across; the inscriptions are much worn, but enough remains to show that they commemorate a great hunt of Süen wang (B.C. 827) in the region where they were found.[1]

Among the feudal States under the house of Chau, that of Tsin, on the northwest, had long been the most powerful, occupying nearly a fifth of the country, and its inhabitants forming a tenth of the whole population. One of the princes, called Chausiang wang, carried his encroachments into the acknowledged imperial possessions, and compelled its master, Tungchau kiun, the last monarch, to humble himself at his feet. Although, in fact, master of the whole Empire, he did not take the title, but left it to his son, Chwangsiang wang, who exterminated the blood royal and ended the Chau dynasty, yet lived only three years in possession of the supreme power.

The son carried on his father's successes until he had reduced all the petty States to his sway. He then took the name of Chí Hwangtí ('Emperor First') of the Tsin dynasty, and set himself to regulate his conquests and establish his authority by securing to his subjects a better government than had been experienced during the feudal times. He divided the country into thirty-six provinces, over which he placed governors, and went throughout them all to see that no injustice was practised.

This monarch, who has been called the Napoleon of China, was one of those extraordinary men who turn the course of events and give an impress to subsequent ages; Klaproth gives him a high character as a prince of energy and skill, but native historians detest his name and acts. It is recorded that at his new capital, Hienyang, on the banks of the Hwai, he constructed a palace exactly like those of all the kings who had submitted to him, and ordered that all the precious furniture of each and those persons who had inhabited them should be transported to it, and everything rearranged. The whole occupied an immense space, and the various parts communicated with each other by a magnificent colonnade and gallery. He made progresses through his dominions with a splendor hitherto unknown, accompanied by officials and troops from all parts, thus making

---

[1] *Journal of the N. C. Branch of R. A. Society*, Vols. VII., p. 137; VIII., pp. 23, 133. In the last paper, by Dr. Bushell, translations and fac-similes of the inscriptions are given, with many historical notices.

the people interested in each other and consenting to his sway. He also built public edifices, opened roads and canals to facilitate intercourse and trade between the various provinces, and repressed the incursions of the Huns, driving them into the wilds of Mongolia. In order to keep them out effectually, he conceived the idea of extending and uniting the short walls which the princes of some of the Northern States had erected on their frontier into one grand wall, stretching across the Empire from the sea to the Desert. This gigantic undertaking was completed in ten years (B.C. 204), at a vast expense in men and material, and not until the family of its builder had been destroyed. This mode of protecting the country, when once well begun, probably commended itself to the nation. It is impossible, indeed, to imagine otherwise how it could have been done, for the people were required to supply a quota of men from each place, feed and clothe them while at work, and continue this expense until their portion was built. No monarch could have maintained an army which could force his subjects against their will to do such a work or carry it on to completion after his death. It is one of the incidental proofs of a great population that so many laborers were found. However ineffectual it was to preserve his frontiers, it has made his name celebrated throughout the world, and his dynasty *Tsin* has given its name to China for all ages and nations.[1]

The vanity of the new monarch led him to endeavor to destroy all records written anterior to his own reign, that he might be by posterity regarded as the first Emperor of the Chinese race. Orders were issued that every book should be burned, and especially the writings of Confucius and Mencius, explanatory of the *Shu King* upon the feudal States of Chau, whose remembrance he wished to blot out. This strange command was executed to such an extent that many of the Chinese literati believe that not a perfect copy of the classical works escaped destruction, and the texts were only recovered by rewriting them from the memories of old scholars, a mode of reproduction

[1] Pauthier, *La Chine*, pp. 30, 221 ; *Mém. conc. les Chinois*, Tome III., p. 183.

that does not appear so singular to a Chinese as it does to us. If the same literary tragedy should be re-enacted to-day, thousands of persons might easily be found in China who could rewrite from memory the text and commentary of their nine classical works. "Nevertheless," as Klaproth remarks, "they were not in fact all lost; for in a country where writing is so common it was almost impossible that all the copies of works universally respected should be destroyed, especially at a time when the material on which they were written was very durable, being engraved with a stylet on bamboo tablets, or traced upon them with dark-colored varnish." The destruction was no doubt as nearly complete as possible, and not only were many works entirely destroyed, but a shade of doubt thereby thrown over the accuracy of others, and the records of the ancient dynasties rendered suspicious as well as incomplete. Not only were books sought after to be destroyed, but nearly five hundred literati were buried alive, in order that no one might remain to reproach, in their writings, the Emperor First with having committed so barbarous and insane an act.

The dynasty of Tsin, set up in such cruelty and blood, did not long survive the death of its founder; his son was unable to maintain his rule over the half-subdued feudal chieftains, and after a nominal reign of seven years he was overcome by Liu Pang, a soldier of fortune, who, having been employed by one of the chiefs as commander of his forces, used them to support his own authority when he had taken possession of the capital. Under the name of Kautsu he became the founder of the Han dynasty, and his accession is regarded as the commencement of modern Chinese history. The number and character of its heroes and literati are superior to most other periods, and to this day the term *Han-tsz'*, or 'Sons of Han,' is one of the favorite names by which the Chinese call themselves.

The first fourteen princes of this dynasty reigned in Shensí, but Kwangwu removed the capital from Chang-an to Lohyang, as was done in the Chau dynasty seven centuries before, the old one being ruined. During the reign of Ping í (or the 'Emperor Peace') the Prince of Peace, our Lord Jesus Christ, was born in Judea, a remarkable coincidence which has often attracted notice. During the reign of Ming tí, A.D. 65, a deputation was sent to India to obtain the sacred books and authorized teachers of Buddhism, which the Emperor intended to publicly introduce into China. This faith had already widely spread among his subjects, but henceforth it became the popular belief of the Chinese and extended eastward into Japan. This monarch and his successor, Chang tí, penetrated with their armies as far westward as the Caspian Sea, dividing and overcoming the various tribes on the confines of the Desert and at the foot of the Tien shan, and extending the limits of the monarchy in that direction farther than they are at present. The Chinese sway was maintained with varied success until toward the third century, and seems to have had a mollifying effect upon the nomads of those regions. In these distant expeditions the Chinese heard of the Romans, of whom their authors speak in the highest terms: "Everything precious and admirable in all other countries," say they, "comes from this land. Gold and silver money is coined there; ten of silver are worth one of gold. Their merchants trade by sea with Persia and India, and gain ten for one in their traffic. They are simple and upright, and never have two prices for their goods; grain is sold among them very cheap, and large sums are embarked in trade. Whenever ambassadors come to the frontiers they are provided with carriages to travel to the capital, and after their arrival a certain number of pieces of gold are furnished them for their expenses." This description, so characteristic of the shop-keeping Chinese, may be compared to many accounts given of the Chinese themselves by western authors.

Continuing the *résumé* of dynasties in order—

IV.—The TSIN dynasty is computed to end with Chwangsiang by the authors of the *History Made Easy*, and to have existed only three years, from B.C. 249 to 246.

V.—The AFTER TSIN dynasty is sometimes joined to the preceding, but Chí Hwangtí regarded himself as the first monarch, and began a new house, which, however, lasted only forty-four years, from B.C. 246 to 202. The commotions in the farthest East during this period were not less destructive of life than the wars in Europe between the Carthaginians and Romans, and the Syrians, Greeks, and Egyptians.

VI., VII. The Han and Eastern Han dynasties.—Liu Pang took the title of Han for his dynasty, after the name of his principality, and his family swayed the Middle Kingdom from B.C. 202 to A.D. 221, under twenty-six monarchs. The Han dynasty was the formative period of Chinese polity and institutions, and an instructive parallel can be drawn between the character and acts of the Emperors who reigned four hundred years in China, and the numerous consuls, dictators, and emperors who governed the Roman Empire for the same period from the time of Scipio Africanus to Heliogabalus. The founder of the Han is honored for having begun the system of competitive examinations for office, and his successors, Wăn tí, Wu tí, and Kwang-wu, developed literature, commerce, arts, and good government to a degree unknown before anywhere in Asia. In the West the Romans became the great world power, and the advent of Christ and establishment of His church within its borders only, render this period the turning epoch of progress among mankind.

The period between the overthrow of the Han dynasty, A.D. 190, and the establishment of the Eastern Tsin, A.D. 317, is one of the most interesting in Chinese history, from the variety of characters which the troubles of the times developed. The distractions of this period are described in the *History of the Three States*, but this entertaining work cannot be regarded as much better than a historical novel. It has, however, like Scott's stories, impressed the events and actors of those days upon the popular mind more than any history in the language.

VIII.—The After Han dynasty began A.D. 211, and continued forty-four years, under two princes, to A.D. 265. The country was divided into three principalities, called Wei, Wu, and Shuh. The first, under the son of Tsao Tsao, ruled the whole northern country at Lohyang, and was the most powerful of them for about forty years. The second, under Siun Kien, occupied the eastern provinces, from Shantung and the Yellow River down to the mountains of Fuhkien, holding his court at Nanking. The third, under Liu Pí, is regarded as the legitimate dynasty from his affinity with the Han; he had his capital at Chingtu fu, in Sz'chuen.

IX.—The Tsin dynasty was founded by Sz'ma Chao, a general in the employ of Hau of the last house, who seated himself on the throne of his master A.D. 265, the year of the latter's death. His son, Sz'ma Yen, took his place and extended his power over the whole Empire by 280. The inroads of the Huns and internal commotions were fast reducing the people to barbarism. Four Emperors of this house held their sway at Lohyang during fifty-two years, till A.D. 317. The Huns maintained their sway in Shensí until A.D. 352, under the designations of the Han and Chau dynasties. It is related of Liu Tsung, one of this barbaric race, that he built a great palace at Chang-an, where he gathered a myriad of the first subjects of his kingdom and lived in luxury and magnificence quite unknown before in China. Among his attendants was a body-guard of elegantly dressed women, many of whom were good musicians, which accompanied him on his progresses.

X.—The Eastern Tsin is the same house as the last, but Yuen tí having moved his capital in 317 from Lohyang to Nanking, his successors are distinguished as the Eastern Tsin. Eleven princes reigned during a period of one hundred and three years, down to A.D. 420. Buddhism was the chief religion at this time, and the doctrines of Confucius were highly esteemed; "children of concubines, priests, old women, and nurses administered the government," says the indignant annalist. At this period twelve independent and opposing kings struggled for the ascendency in China, and held their ephemeral courts in the north and west. It was at this time that Constantine moved the capital of the Roman Empire in 328, and the nations of northern Europe under Attila invaded Italy in 410.

XI.—The Sung, or Northern Sung dynasty, as it is often called to distinguish it from the XXIId dynasty (A.D. 970), is the first of the four dynasties known as the *Nan-peh Chao*, or 'South-north dynasties,' which preceded the Sui. It was founded by Liu Yu, who commanded the armies of Tsin, and gradually subdued all the opposing States. Displeased at the weakness of his master, Ngan tí, he caused him to be strangled, and placed his brother, Kung tí, upon the throne, who, fearing a like fate, abdicated the empty crown, and Liu Yu became monarch under the name of Kautsu, A.D. 420. Eight princes held the throne till A.D. 479, many of them monsters of cruelty, and soon cut off, when Siau Tau-ching, Duke of Tsí, the prime minister, recompensed them as their ancestor had those of Tsin.

XII. Tsí dynasty.—The new monarch took the name of Kau tí, or 'High Emperor,' but enjoyed his dignity only four years. Four princes succeeded him at Nanking, the last of whom, Ho tí, was besieged in his capital by a faithless minister, assisted by the prince of Liang, who overthrew the dynasty A.D. 502, after a duration of twenty-three years.

XIII. Liang dynasty.—The first Emperor, Wu tí, reigned forty-eight years, and reduced most of his opponents; his dominions are described as being mostly south of the Yangtsz' River, the Wei ruling the regions north of it. Wu tí did much to restore literature and the study of Confucius; envoys from India and Persia also came to his court, and his just sway allowed the land to recruit. In his latter days he was so great a devotee of Buddhism that he retired to a monastery, like Charles V., but being persuaded to resume his crown, employed his time in teaching those doctrines to his assembled courtiers. Three successors occupied the throne, the last of whom, King tí, was killed A.D. 557, after surrendering himself, by the general of the troops, who then seized the crown.

XIV. Chin dynasty.—Three brothers reigned most of the time this house held its sway. During this period and that of the three preceding families, the Hunnish kingdom of Wei ruled the northern parts of China from A.D. 386 to 534, under eleven monarchs, when it was violently separated into the Eastern and Western Wei, and a third one called Chau, which ere long destroyed the last Wei at Chang-an and occupied northwest China. It is probable that the intercourse between China and other parts of Asia was more extensive and complete during the Wei dynasty than at any other period. Its sovereigns had preserved peaceful relations with their ancestral seats, and with the tribes beyond Lake Baikal and the Obi River to the North Sea. Trade seems to have flourished throughout the regions lying between the Caspian Sea and Corea, and the records of this period present accounts of the State in this vast tract to be found nowhere else. One of these works referred to by Rémusat is the report of officers sent by Tai-wu during his reign to travel through his dominions (424–451) and give full accounts of them.

One of the sovereigns of Chau, Wu tí (A.D. 561–572), had given his daughter in marriage to Yang Kien, the Prince of Sui, one of his ministers, who, gradually extending his influence, took possession of the throne of his master Tsing tí in 580. In a few years he restored order to a distracted land by bringing the several States under his sway and reuniting all China under his hand A.D. 589, after it had been divided nearly four centuries.

XV. SUI dynasty.—The founder of this house has left an enduring name in Chinese annals by a survey of his dominions and division of them into interdependent *chau*, *kiun*, and *hien*, with corresponding officers, an arrangement which has ever since existed. He patronized letters and commerce, and tried to introduce the system of caste from India. After a vigorous reign of twenty-four years he was killed by his son Yang tí, who carried on his father's plans, and during the fourteen years of his reign extended the frontiers through the Tarim Valley and down to the Southern Ocean. His murder by one of his generals was the signal for several ambitious men to rise, but the Prince of Tang aided the son to rule for a year or two till he was removed, thus bringing the Sui dynasty to an end after thirty-nine years, but not before its two sovereigns had taught their subjects the benefits of an undivided sway.

XVI. TANG dynasty.—This celebrated line of princes began its sway in peace, and during the two hundred and eighty-seven years (618 to 908) they held the throne China was probably the most civilized country on earth; the darkest days of the West, when Europe was wrapped in the ignorance and degradation of the Middle Ages, formed the brightest era of the East. They exercised a humanizing effect on all the surrounding countries, and led their inhabitants to see the benefits and understand the management of a government where the laws were above the officers. The people along the southern coast were completely civilized and incorporated into the Chinese race, and mark the change by always calling themselves *Tang Jin*, or Men of Tang.' An interesting work on the trade and condition of China at this time is the *Akhbar-al-Syn oual-Hind*, or 'Observations on China and India,' by two Arab travellers to those lands in the years 851 and 878, compiled by Abu Zaid and translated by Reinaud in 1845.[1] Lí Shí-min, the son of Lí Yuen the founder of this dynasty, may be regarded as the most accomplished monarch in the Chinese annals—famed alike for his wisdom and nobleness, his conquests and good government, his temperance, cultivated tastes, and patronage of literary men. While still Prince of Tang he contributed greatly to his father's elevation and to the extension of his sway over the regions of Central Asia. When the house of Tang was fully acknowledged, and the eleven rival States which had started up on the close of the house of Sui had been overcome, the capital was removed from Lohyang back to Chang-an, and everything done to compose the disordered country and reunite the distracted State under a regular and vigorous administration. Feeling himself unequal to all the cares of his great office, Lí Yuen, known as Kau-tsu Shin Yao tí (lit. 'High Progenitor, the Divine Yao Emperor'), resigned the yellow in favor of his son, who took the style of *Ching kwan* ('Pure Observer') for his reign, though his posthumous title is Tai-tsung Wăn-wu tí ('Our Exalted Ancestor, the Literary-Martial Emperor'), A.D. 627, and still further extended his victorious arms. One of his first acts was to establish schools and institute a system of literary examinations; he ordered a complete and accurate edition of all the classics to be published under the supervision of the most learned men in the Empire, and honored the memory of Confucius with special ceremonies of respect. Extraordinary pains were taken to prepare and preserve the historical records of former days and draw up full annals of the recent dynasties; these still await the examination of western scholars.

He constructed a code of laws for the direction of his high officers in their judicial functions, and made progresses through

[1] *Chinese Repository*, Vol. I., p. 6; Reinaud, *Relations des Voyages*, 2 Vols., Paris, 1845. Yule, *Cathay and the Way Thither*, Introd., p. cii.

his dominions to inspect the condition of the people. During his reign the limits of the Empire were extended over all the Turkish tribes lying west of Kansuh and south of the Tien shan as far as the Caspian Sea, which were placed under four satrapies or residences, those of Kuché, Pisha or Khoten, Harashar, and Kashgar, as their names are at present. West of the last many smaller tribes submitted and rendered a partial subjection to the Emperor, who arranged them into sixteen governments under the management of a governor-general over their own chieftains. His frontiers reached from the borders of Persia, the Caspian Sea, and the Altai of the Kirghís steppe, along those mountains to the north side of Gobi eastward to the Inner Hing-an. Sogdiana and part of Khorassan, and the regions around the Hindu-kush, also obeyed him. The rulers of Nipal and Magadha or Bahar in India sent their salutations by their ambassadors, and the Greek Emperor Theodosius sent an envoy to Sí-ngan in 643 carrying presents of rubies and emeralds, as did also the Persians. The Nestorian missionaries also presented themselves at court. Tai-tsung received them with respect, and heard them rehearse the leading tenets of their doctrine; he ordered a temple to be erected at his capital, and had some of their sacred books translated for his examination, though there is no evidence now remaining that any portion of the Bible was done into Chinese at this time.

Near the close of his life Tai-tsung undertook an expedition against Corea, but the conquest of that country was completed by his son after his death. A sentiment has been preserved at this time of his life which he uttered to his sons while sailing on the River Wei: "See, my children, the waves which float our fragile bark are able to submerge it in an instant; know assuredly that the people are like the waves, and the Emperor like this fragile bark." During his reign his life was attempted several times, once by his own son, but he was preserved from these attacks, and died after a reign of twenty-three years, deeply lamented by a grateful people. The Chinese accounts state that the foreign envoys resident at his court cut off their hair, some of them disfigured their faces, bled themselves, and sprinkled the blood around the bier in testimony of their grief.

Whatever may have been the truth in this respect, many proofs exist of the distinguished character of this monarch, and that the high reputation he enjoyed during his lifetime was a just tribute to his excellences. He will favorably compare with Akbar, Marcus Aurelius, and Kanghí, or with Charlemagne and Harun Al Raschid, who came to their thrones in the next century.

Tai-tsung was succeeded by his son Kau-tsung, whose indolent imbecility appeared the more despicable after his father's vigor, but his reign fills a large place in Chinese history, from the extraordinary career of his Empress, Wu Tsih-tien, or Wu hao ('Empress Wu') as she is called, who by her blandishments obtained entire control over him. The character of this woman has, no doubt, suffered much from the bad reputation native historians have given her, but enough can be gathered from their accounts to show that with all her cruelty she understood how to maintain the authority of the crown, repress foreign invasions, quell domestic sedition, and provide for the wants of the people. Introduced to the harem of Tai-tsung at the age of fourteen, she was sent at his death to the retreat where all his women were condemned for the rest of their days to honorable imprisonment. While a member of the palace Kau-tsung had been charmed with her appearance, and, having seen her at one of the state ceremonies connected with the ancestral worship, brought her back to the palace. His queen, Wang-shí, also favored his attentions in order to draw them off from another rival, but Wu Tsih-tien soon obtaining entire sway over the monarch, united both women against her; she managed to fill the principal offices with her friends, and by a series of manœuvres supplanted each in turn and became Empress. One means she took to excite suspicion against Wang-shí was, on occasion of the birth of her first child, after the Empress had visited it and before Kau-tsung came in to see his offspring, to strangle it and charge the crime upon her Majesty, which led to her trial, degradation, and imprisonment, and ere long to her death.

As soon as she became Empress (in 655), Wu began gradually to assume more and more authority, until, long before the Emperor's death in 684, she engrossed the whole management of affairs, and at his demise openly assumed the reins of government, which she wielded for twenty-one years with no weak hand. Her generals extended the limits of the Empire, and her officers carried into effect her orders to alleviate the miseries of the people. Her cruelty vented itself in the murder of all who opposed her will, even to her own sons and relatives; and her pride was rather exhibited than gratified by her assuming the titles of Queen of Heaven, Holy and Divine Ruler, Holy Mother, and Divine Sovereign. When she was disabled by age her son, Chung-sung, supported by some of the first men of the land, asserted his claim to the throne, and by a palace conspiracy succeeded in removing her to her own apartments, where she died aged eighty-one years. Her character has been blackened in native histories and popular tales, and her conduct held up as an additional evidence of the evil of allowing women to meddle with governments.[1]

A race of twenty monarchs swayed the sceptre of the house of Tang, but after the demise of the Empress Wu Tsih-tien none of them equalled Tai-tsung, and the Tang dynasty at last succumbed to ambitious ministers lording over its imbecile sovereigns. In the reign of Hiuen-tsung, about the year 722, the population of the Fifteen Provinces is said to have been 52,884,818. The last three or four Emperors exhibited the usual marks of a declining house—eunuchs or favorites promoted by them swayed the realm and dissipated its resources. At last, Lí Tsüen-chung, a general of Chau-tsung, whom he had aided in quelling the eunuchs in 904, rose against his master, destroyed him, and compelled his son, Chau-siuen tí, to abdicate, A.D. 907.

XVII. After Liang dynasty.—The destruction of the famous dynasty loosened the bonds of all government, and nine separate kings struggled for its provinces, some of whom, as Apkí over the Kítan in the north-east, succeeded in founding kingdoms. The Prince of Liang, the new Emperor, was unable to extend his sway beyond the provinces of Honan and Shantung. After

---

[1] *Chinese Repository*, Vol. III., p. 543; *Canton Miscellany*, No. 4, 1831, pp. 246 ff.

a short reign of six years he was killed by his brother, Liang Chu-tien, who, on his part, fell under the attack of a Turkish general, and ended this dynasty, A.D. 923, after a duration of sixteen years.

XVIII. AFTER TANG dynasty.—The conqueror called himself Chwang-tsung, and his dynasty Tang, as if in continuation of that line of princes, but this mode of securing popularity was unsuccessful. Like Pertinax, Aurelian, and others of the Roman emperors, he was killed by his troops, who chose a successor, and his grandson, unable to resist his enemies, burned himself in his palace, A.D. 936, thus ending the weak dynasty after thirteen years of struggle.

XIX. AFTER TSIN dynasty.—The Kítan or Tartars of Liautung, who had assisted in the overthrow of the last dynasty, compelled the new monarch to subsidize them at his accession, A.D. 936, by ceding to them sixteen cities in Chihlí, and promising an annual tribute of three hundred thousand pieces of silk. This disgraceful submission has ever since stigmatized Tien-fuh ('Heavenly Happiness') in the eyes of native historians. His nephew who succeeded him is known as Chuh tí (the 'Carried-away Emperor'), and was removed in 947 by those who put him on the throne, thus ending the meanest house which ever swayed the black-haired people.

XX. AFTER HAN dynasty.—The Tartars now endeavored to subdue the whole country, but were repulsed by Liu Chí-yuen, a loyal general who assumed the yellow in 947, and called his dynasty after the renowned house of Han; he and his son held sway four years, till A.D. 951, and then were cut off.

XXI. AFTER CHAU dynasty.—Ko Wei, the successful aspirant to the throne, maintained his seat, but died in three years, leaving his power to an adopted son, Shí-tsung, whose vigorous rule consolidated his still unsettled sway. His early death and the youth of his son decided his generals to bestow the sceptre upon the lately appointed tutor to the monarch, which closed the After Chau dynasty A.D. 960, after a brief duration of nine years. He was honored with a title, and, like Richard Cromwell, allowed to live in quiet till his death in 973, a fact creditable to the new monarch. These short-lived houses between A.D. 907-

960 are known in Chinese history as the *Wu tai*, or 'Five Dynasties.' While they struggled for supremacy in the valley of the Yellow River, the regions south and west were portioned among seven houses, who ruled them in a good degree of security. Fuhkien was held by the King of Min, and Kiangnan by the King of Wu; the regions of Sz'chuen, Nganhwui, and Kansuh were held by generals of note in the service of Tang; another general held Kwangtung at Canton through two or three reigns; and another exercised sway at Kingchau on the Yangtsz' River. It is needless to mention them all. During this period Europe was distracted by the wars of the Normans and Saracens, and learning there was at a low ebb.

XXII.—Sung dynasty began A.D. 970, and maintained its power over the whole Empire for one hundred and fifty-seven years, till A.D. 1127. The mode in which its founder, Chau Kwang-yun, was made head of the State, reminds one of the way in which the Prætorian guards sometimes elevated their chiefs to the throne of the Cæsars. After the military leaders had decided upon their future sovereign they sent messengers to announce to him his new honor, who found him drunk, and "before he had time to reply the yellow robe was already thrown over his person." At the close of his reign of seventeen years the provinces had mostly submitted to his power at Kaifung, but the two Tartar kingdoms of Liau and Hia remained independent. This return to a centralized government proves the unity of the Chinese people at this time in their own limits, as well as their inability to induce their neighbors to adopt the same system of government. The successors of Tai-tsu of Sung had a constant struggle for existence with their adversaries on the north and west, the Liau and Hia, whose recent taste of power under the last two dynasties had shown them their opportunity. On the return of prosperity under his brother's reign of twenty-two years, the former institutions and political divisions were restored throughout the southern half of the Empire; good government was secured, aided by able generals and loyal ministers, and the rebels everywhere quelled. Chin-tsung was the third sovereign, and his reign of forty-one years is the brightest portion of the house of Sung. The kings of Hia in Kansuh acknowledged themselves to be his tributaries, but he bought a cowardly peace with the Liau on the north-east. During his reign and that of his son, Tin-tsung, a violent controversy arose among the literati and officials as to the best mode of conducting the government. Some of them, as Sz'ma Kwang the historian, contended for the maintenance of the old principles of the sages. Others, of whom Wang Ngan-shí was the distinguished leader, advocated reform and change to the entire overthrow of existing institutions. For the first time in the history of China, two political parties peacefully struggled for supremacy, each content to depend on argument and truth for the victory. The contest soon grew too bitter, however, and the accession of a new monarch, Shin-tsung, enabled Wang to dispossess his opponents and manage State affairs as he pleased. After a trial of eight or ten years the voice of the nation restored the conservatives to power, and the radicals were banished beyond the frontier. A discussion like this, involving all the cherished ideas of the Chinese, brought out deep and acute inquiry into the nature and uses of things generally, and the writers of this dynasty, at the head of whom was Chu Hí, made a lasting impression on the national mind.

The two sons of Shin-tsung were unable to oppose the northern hordes of Liau and Hia, except by setting a third aspirant against both. These were the Niu-chih or Kin,[1] the ancestors of the present Manchus, who carried away Hwui-tsung as a captive in 1125, and his son too the next year, pillaging Lohyang and possessing themselves of the region north of the Yellow River. This closed the Northern Sung. The Kin established themselves at Peking in 1118, whence they were driven in 1235 by Genghis Khan, and fled back to the ancestral haunts on the Songari and Liau Rivers.

XXIII.—Southern Sung dynasty forms part of the preceding, for Kao-tsung, the brother of the last and ninth monarch of the weakened house of Northern Sung, seeing his capital in ruins, fled to Nanking, and soon after to the beautiful city of Hangchau on the eastern coast at the mouth of the Tsientang River.

[1] Two graves of the Kin monarchs exist on a hill west of Fangshan hien, fifty miles south-west of Peking; they were repaired by Kanghí. Dr. Bushell visited them in 1870.

Nanking was pillaged by the Kin, but Hangchau was too far for them. It gradually grew in size and strength, and became a famous capital. Kao-tsung resigned in 1162, after a reign of thirty-six years, and survived his abdication twenty-four years. The next Emperor was Hiao-tsung, who also resigned the yellow to Kwang-tsung, his son, and he again yielded it to his son Ning-tsung. This last, in his distress, called the rising Mongols into his service in 1228 to help against the Kin. The distance from the northern frontier, where the Mongols were flushed with their successes over the Tangouth of Hia at Ninghia in 1226, was too far for them to aid Ning-tsung at this time. He was, however, relieved from danger to himself, and the Mongols deferred their intentions for a few years. From this date for about fifty years the Sung grew weaker and weaker under the next five sovereigns, until the last scion, Tí Ping, was drowned with some of his courtiers, one of whom, clasping him in his arms, jumped from the vessel, and ended their life, dignity, and dynasty together. It had lasted one hundred and fifty-two years under nine monarchs, who showed less ability than those of Northern Sung, and were all much inferior as a whole to the house of Tang. Their patronage of letters and the arts of peace was unaccompanied by the vigor of their predecessors, for they were unwilling to leave the capital and risk all at the head of their troops. It is the genius and philosophy of its scholars that has made the Sung one of the great dynasties of the Middle Kingdom.

XXIV.—The Yuen dynasty was the first foreign sway to which the Sons of Han had submitted; their resistance to the army, which gradually overran the country, was weakened, however, by treachery and desultory tactics until the national spirit was frittered away. During the interval between the capture of Peking by Genghis and the final extinction of the Sung dynasty, the whole population had become somewhat accustomed to Mongol rule. Having no organized government of their own, these khans were content to allow the Chinese the full exercise of their own laws, if peace and taxation were duly upheld. Kublai had had ample opportunity to learn the character of his new subjects, and after the death of Mangu khan in 1260 and his own establishment at Peking in 1264, he in fifteen years brought his vast dominions under a methodical sway and developed their resources more than ever. Though failing in his attempt to conquer Japan, he enlarged elsewhere his vanishing frontiers during his life till they could neither be defined nor governed. His patronage of merit and scholarship proves the good results of his tutelage in China, while the short-lived glory of his administration in other hands chiefly proved what good material he had to work with in China in comparison with his own race.[1] He was a vigorous and magnificent prince, and had, moreover, the advantage of having his acts and splendor related by Marco Polo—a chronicler worthy of his subject. The Grand Canal, which was deepened and lengthened during his reign, is a lasting token of his sagacity and enlightened policy. An interesting monument of this dynasty, erected in 1345, is the gateway in the Kü-yung kwan (pass) of the Great Wall north of Peking. Upon the interior of this arch is cut a Buddhist charm in six different kinds of character—Mongolian, Chinese, Oigour, antique Devanagari, Niu-chih, and Tibetan.[2]

After the Grand Khan's death the Mongols retained their power under the reign of Ching-tsung, or Timur khan, a grandson of Kublai, and Wu-tsung, or Genesek khan,[3] a nephew of the former, but their successors met with opposition, or were destroyed by treachery. The offices were also filled with Mongols, without any regard to the former mode of conferring rank according to literary qualifications, and the native Chinese began to be thoroughly dissatisfied with a sway in which they had no part. The last and eleventh, named Ching-tsung, or Tohan-Timur, came to the throne at the age of thirteen, and gave himself up to pleasure, his eunuchs and ministers dividing the possessions and offices of the Chinese among themselves and their adherents. This conduct aroused his subjects, and Chu Yuen-chang, a plebeian by birth, and formerly a priest, raised the standard of

[1] See Rémusat, *Nouveaux Mélanges*, Tomes I., p. 427; II., pp. 64, 88, and 89–97, for a series of notices concerning the Mongol generals and history.

[2] Compare Wylie in the *R. A. Soc. Jour.*, Vol. V. (N.S.), p. 14; Fergusson, *Hist. Ind. and East. Architecture*, p. 708; Yule's *Polo*, I., pp. 28, 409.

[3] This should be Kaishau-kulluk khan, called *Kai-sang* in Chinese. Rémusat, *Nouveaux Mélanges*, Tome II., pp. 1–4.

GATEWAY OF THE YUEN DYNASTY, KŪ-YUNG KWAN, GREAT WALL.

revolt, and finally expelled the Mongols, A.D. 1368, after a duration of eighty-nine years.[1]

Like most of the preceding dynasties, the new one established itself on the misrule, luxury, and weakness of its predecessors; the people submitted to a vigorous rule, as one which exhibited the true exposition of the decrees of Heaven, and upheld its laws and the harmony of the universe; while a weak sovereign plainly evinced his usurpation of the "divine utensil" and unfitness for the post by the disorders, famines, piracies, and insurrections which afflicted the mismanaged State, and which were all taken by ambitious leaders as evidences of a change in the choice of Heaven, and reasons for their carrying out the new selection which had fallen on them. Amid all the revolutions in China, none have been founded on principle; they were mere mutations of masters, attended with more or less destruction of life, and no better appreciation of the rights of the subject or the powers of the rulers. Nor without some knowledge of the high obligations man owes his Maker and himself is it easy to see whence the sustaining motive of free religious and political institutions can be derived.

XXV. The MING, *i.e.*, 'BRIGHT dynasty.'—The character of Hungwu, as Chu Yuen-chang called his reign on his accession, has been well drawn by Rémusat, who accords him a high rank for the vigor and talents manifested in overcoming his enemies and cementing his power. He established his capital at Nanking, or the 'Southern Capital,' and after a reign of thirty years transmitted the sceptre to his grandson, Kienwăn, a youth of sixteen. Yungloh, his son, dissatisfied with this arrangement, overcame his nephew and seized the crown after five years, and moved the capital back to Peking in 1403. This prince is distinguished for the code of laws framed under his auspices, which has, with some modifications and additions, ever since remained as the basis of the administration. During the reign of Kiahtsing the Portuguese came to China, and in that of Wanleih, about 1580, the Jesuits gained an entrance into the

[1] One of the causes of their easy overthrow is stated to have been the enormous robbery of the people by the lavish issue of paper money, which at last became worthless.

country. In his time, too, the Niu-chih, or Kin, whom Genghis had driven away in 1235, again became numerous and troublesome, and took possession of the northern frontiers. The first chieftain of the Manchus who attained celebrity was Tienming, who in 1618 published a manifesto of his designs against the house of Ming, in which he announced to Heaven the seven things he was bound to revenge. These consisted of petty oppressions upon persons passing the frontiers, assisting his enemies, violating the oath and treaty of peace entered into between the two rulers, and killing his envoys. The fierce nomad had already assumed the title of Emperor, and "vowed to celebrate the funeral of his father with the slaughter of two hundred thousand Chinese." Tienming overran the north-eastern parts of China, and committed unsparing cruelties upon the people of Liautung, but died in 1627, before he had satisfied his revenge, leaving it and his army to his son Tientsung.

The Chinese army fought bravely, though unsuccessfully, against the warlike Manchus, whose chief not only strove to subdue, but endeavored, by promises and largesses, to win the troops from their allegiance. The apparently audacious attempt of this small force to subdue the Chinese was assisted by numerous bodies of rebels, who, like wasps, sprung up in various parts of the country, the leaders of each asserting his claims to the throne, and all of them rendering their common country an easier prey to the invader. One of them, called Lí Tsz'-ching, attacked Peking, and the last Emperor Hwai-tsung, feeling that he had little to hope for after the loss of his capital, and had already estranged the affections of his subjects by his ill conduct, first stabbed his daughter and then hung himself, in 1643, and ended the house of Ming, after two hundred and seventy-six years. The usurper received the submission of most of the eastern provinces, but the Chinese general, Wu San-kwei, in command of the army on the north, refused to acknowledge him, and, making peace with the Manchus, invoked the aid of Tsung-teh in asserting the cause of the rightful claimant to the throne. This was willingly agreed to, and the united army marched to Peking and speedily entered the capital, which the rebel chief had left a heap of ruins when he took away his booty. The

Manchus now declared themselves the rulers of the Empire, but their chief dying, his son Shunchí, who at the age of six succeeded his father in 1644, is regarded as the first Emperor; his uncle, Aina-wang, ruled and reorganized the administration in his name.

XXVI. The Tsing,[1] *i.e.*, 'Pure dynasty.'—During the eighteen years he sat upon the throne Shunchí and his officers subdued most of the northern and central provinces, but the maritime regions of the south held out against the invaders, and one of the leaders, by means of his fleets, carried devastation along the whole coast. The spirit of resistance was in some parts crushed, and in others exasperated by an order for all Chinese to adopt as a sign of submission the Tartar mode of shaving the front of the head and braiding the hair in a long queue. Those who gave this order, as Davis remarks, must have felt themselves very strong before venturing so far upon the spirit of the conquered, and imposing an outward universal badge of surrender upon all classes of the people. "Many are the changes which may be made in despotic countries, without the notice or even the knowledge of the larger portion of the community; but an entire alteration in the national costume affects every individual equally, from the highest to the lowest, and is perhaps of all others the most open and degrading mark of conquest." This order was resisted by many, who chose to lose their heads rather than part with their hair, but the mandate was gradually enforced, and has now for about two centuries been one of the distinguishing marks of a Chinese, though to this day the natives of Fuhkien near the seaboard wear a kerchief around their head to conceal it. The inhabitants of this province and of Kwangtung held out the longest against the invaders, and a vivid account of their capture of Canton, November 26, 1650, where the adherents of the late dynasty had intrenched themselves, has been left us by Martini, an eye-witness. Some time after its subjugation a brave man, Ching Chí-lung, harassed them by his fleet; and his son, Ching

[1] For the origin of the Manchus see Klaproth, *Mémoires sur l'Asie*, Tome I., p. 441.

Ching-kung, or Koxinga, molested the coast to such a degree that the Emperor Kanghí, in 1665, ordered all the people to retire three leagues inland, in order to prevent this heroic man from reaching them. This command was generally obeyed, and affords an instance of the singular mixture of power and weakness seen in many parts of Chinese legislation; for it might be supposed that a government which could compel its maritime subjects to leave their houses and towns and go into the country at great loss, might have easily armed and equipped a fleet to have defended those towns and homes. Koxinga, finding himself unable to make any serious impression upon the stability of the new government, went to Formosa, drove the Dutch out of Zealandia, and made himself master of the island.[1]

Shunchí died in 1661 and was succeeded by his son Kanghi,[2] who was eight years old at his accession, and remained under guardians till he was fourteen, when he assumed the reins of government, and swayed the power vested in his hands with a prudence, vigor, and success that have rendered him more celebrated than almost any other Asiatic monarch. It was in 1661 that Louis XIV. had assumed the sovereignty of France at about the same age, and for fifty-four years the reigns of these two monarchs ran parallel. During Kanghi's unusually long reign of sixty-one years (the longest in Chinese annals, except Taimao of the Shang dynasty, B.C. 1637–1562), he extended his dominions to the borders of Kokand and Badakshan on the west, and to the confines of Tibet on the south-west, simplifying the administration and consolidating his power in every part of his vast dominions. To his regulations, perhaps, are mainly owing the unity and peace which the Empire has exhibited for more than a century, and which has produced the impression abroad of the unchangeableness of Chinese institutions and character. This may be ascribed, chiefly, to his indefatigable applica-

[1] Compare the interesting translation from a Chinese record of the capture of Fort Zealandia, by H. E. Hobson, *Journal of N. C. Br. R. A. Society*, No. XI., Art. I., 1876.

[2] Rémusat, *Nouveaux Mélanges*, Tome II., pp. 21–44; Bouvet, *Life of Kanghí*; Gutzlaff, *Life of Kanghí*.

tion to all affairs of State, to his judgment and penetration in the choice of officers, his economy in regard to himself and liberal magnificence in everything that tended to the good of his dominions, and his sincere desire to promote the happiness of his people by a steady and vigorous execution of the laws and a continual watchfulness over the conduct of his high officers. These qualities have perhaps been unduly extolled by his foreign friends and biographers, the Romish missionaries, and if their expressions are taken in their strictest sense, as we understand them, they do elevate him too high. He is to be compared not with Alfred or William III. of England, Louis IX. or Henry IV. of France, and other European kings, but with other Chinese and Asiatic princes, few of whom equal him. The principal events of his long reign are the conquest of the Eleuths, and subjugation of several tribes lying on the north and south of the Tien shan; an embassy across the Russian Possessions in 1713 to the khan of the Tourgouth Tartars, preparatory to their return to the Chinese territory; the settlement of the northern frontier between himself and the czar, of which Gerbillon has given a full account; the survey of the Empire by the Romish missionaries; and the publication of a great thesaurus of the language. In many things he showed himself liberal toward foreigners, and the country was thrown open to their commerce for many years.

His son Yungching succeeded in 1722, and is regarded by many natives as superior to his father. He endeavored to suppress Christianity and restore the ancient usages, which had somewhat fallen into desuetude during his father's sway, and generally seems to have held the sceptre to the benefit of his subjects. Yungching is regarded as an usurper, and is said to have changed the figure four to fourteen on the billet of nomination, himself being the fourteenth son, and the fourth being absent in Mongolia, where he was soon after arrested and imprisoned, and subsequently died in a palace near Peking; whether he was put to death or not is uncertain. Kienlung succeeded Yungching in 1736, and proved himself no unworthy descendant of his grandfather Kanghí; like him he had the singular fortune to reign sixty years, and for most of that period in peace.[1] Some local insurrections disturbed the general tranquillity, principally among the aborigines in Formosa and Kweichau, and in an unprovoked attack upon Birmah his armies sustained a signal defeat and were obliged to retreat. The incursions of the Nipalese into Tibet induced the Dalai Lama to apply to him for assistance, and in doing so he contrived to establish a guardianship over the whole country, and place bodies of troops in all the important positions, so that in effect he annexed that vast region to his Empire, but continued the lamas in the internal administration.

During his long reign Kienlung exhausted the resources of his Empire by building useless edifices and keeping up large armies. He received embassies from the Russians, Dutch, and English, by which the character of the Chinese and the nature of their country became better known to western nations. These embassies greatly strengthened the impression on the side of the Chinese of their superiority to all other nations, for they looked upon them as acknowledgments on the part of the governments who sent them of their allegiance to the court of Peking. The presents were regarded as tribute, the ambassadors as deputies from their masters to acknowledge the supremacy of the Emperor, and the requests they made for trade as rather another form of receiving presents in return than a mutual arrangement for a trade equally beneficial to both. Kienlung abdicated the throne in favor of his fifth son and retired with the title of *Supreme Emperor*, while his son, Kiaking, had that of Emperor.

The character of this prince was dissolute and superstitious, and his reign of twenty-five years was much disturbed by secret combinations against the government and by insurrections[2] and

---

[1] His character and enthusiasm for literary pursuits merit, on the whole, the lines inscribed by the Roman Catholic missionaries beneath his portrait in the *Mémoires conc. les Chinois*:

> Occupé sans relâche à touts les soins divers
> D'un gouvernement qu'on admire,
> Le plus grand potentat qui soit dans l'univers
> Et le meilleur lettré qui soit dans son Empire.

[2] Among the most serious of these was the revolt of the Peh lien kiao. *Lettres Édifiantes*, Tome III., pp. 291–298, 353, 379, etc. In 1789 the ladrones infested the southern coasts. *Ib.*, Tome II., p. 492.

pirates in and about the Empire. A conspiracy against him broke out in the palace in 1813, where he was for a time in some danger, but was rescued by the courage of his guard and family; one of his sons, Mien-ning, was designated as his successor for his bravery on this occasion. A fleet of about six hundred piratical junks, under Ching Yih and Chang Pau, infested the coasts of Kwangtung for several years, and were at last put down in 1810 by the provincial government taking advantage of internal dissensions between the leaders. The principal scene of the exploits of this fleet was the estuary of the Pearl River, whose numerous harbors and channels afforded shelter and escape to their vessels when pursued by the imperialists, while the towns upon the islands were plundered and the inhabitants killed if they resisted. The internal government of this audacious band was ascertained by two Englishmen, Mr. Turner and Mr. Glasspoole, who at different times fell into their hands and were obliged to accompany them in their marauding expeditions. To so great a height did they proceed that the governor of Canton went to Macao to reside, and entered into some arrangements with the Portuguese for assistance in suppressing them. The piratical fleet was attacked and blockaded for ten days by the combined forces, but without much damage; there was little prospect of overcoming them had not rivalry between the two leaders gone so far as to result in a severe engagement and loss on both sides. The conquered pirate soon after made his peace with the government, and the victor shortly afterward followed the same course. The story of those disturbed times to this day affords a frequent subject for the tales of old people in that region, and the same waters are still infested by the "foam of the sea," as the Chinese term these freebooters.

The reign of Kiaking ended in 1820; by the Emperor's will his second son was appointed to succeed him, and took the style Taukwang. He exhibited more energy and justice than his father, and his efforts purified the administration by the personal supervision taken of their leading members. His reign was marked by many local insurrections and disasters in one quarter or another of his vast dominions. A rebellion in Turkestan in 1828 was attended with great cruelty and treachery on the part of the Chinese, and its leader, Jehangír, was murdered, in violation of the most solemn promises. An insurrection in Formosa and a rising among the mountaineers of Kwangtung, in 1830–32, were put down more by money than by force, but as peace is both the end and evidence of good government in China, the authorities are not very particular how it is brought about.

The rapid increase of opium-smoking among his people led to many efforts to restrain this vice by prohibitions, penalties, executions, and other means, but all in vain. The Emperor's earnestness was stimulated by the death of his three eldest sons from its use, and the falling off of the revenue by smuggling the pernicious drug. In 1837–38 the collective opinion of the highest officials was taken after hearing their arguments for legalizing its importation; it was resolved to seize the dealers in it. The acts of Commissioner Lin resulted in the war with Great Britain and the opening of China to an extended intercourse with other nations. Defeated in his honest efforts to protect his people against their bane, the Emperor still fulfilled his treaty obligations, and died in 1850, just as the Tai-ping rebellion broke out.

His fourth son succeeded him under the style of Hienfung, but without his father's earnestness or vigor when the State required the highest qualities in its leader. The devastations of the rebels laid waste the southern half of the Empire, and their approach to Peking in 1853 was paralyzed by floods and want of supplies more than by the imperial troops. A second war with Great Britain, in 1858–60, completely broke down the seclusion of China, and at its conclusion an inglorious reign of eleven years ended at Jeh-ho in August, 1860. His only son succeeded to the throne at the age of five years, under the style of Tungchí; the government being under the control of two Empress-regents and Prince Kung, his uncle. During his reign of twelve years the vigor of the new authorities succeeded in completely quelling the Tai-ping rebellion, destroying the Mohammedan rising in Yunnan and Kansuh, and opening up diplomatic intercourse with the Treaty Powers. Just as the

Emperor began to exercise his authority, he died in January, 1875, without issue. The vacant "utensil" has been filled by the appointment of his cousin, a boy of four years, whose reign was styled Kwangsü. Affairs continue to be conducted by the same regency as before, now still more conversant with the new relations opening up with other lands. The real Empress-dowager, or *Tung Kung*, died April 18, 1881.

So far as can be judged from the imperfect data of native historians of former days, compared with the observations of foreigners at present, there is little doubt that this enormous population has been better governed by the Manchus than under the princes of the Ming dynasty; there has been more vigor in the administration of government and less palace favoritism and intrigue in the appointment of officers, more security of life and property from the exactions of local authorities, bands of robbers, or processes of law; in a word, the Manchu sway has well developed the industry and resources of the country, of which the population, loyalty, and content of the people are the best evidences.

The sovereigns of the Ming and Tsing dynasties, being more frequently mentioned in history than those of former princes, are here given, with the length of their reigns. For convenience of reference a table of the dynasties is appended, taken from the author's *Syllabic Dictionary of the Chinese Language*. In this list, compiled from a Chinese work (the *Digest of the Reigns of Emperors and Kings*), the Tsin and After Tsin dynasties are joined in one (No. 4), making a total of twenty-six dynasties.[1]

The whole number of acknowledged sovereigns in the twenty-six dynasties, according to the received Chinese chronology, from Yu the Great to Kwangsü, is 238, or 246 commencing with Fuh-hí; by including the names of some ursurpers and moribund claimants, the first number is increased to 250. From Yu the Great to the accession of Kwangsü (B.C. 2205 to A.D. 1875) is 4,080 years, which gives to each dynasty a duration of 157

[1] Compare the Chinese Chronological Tables by W. F. Mayers in *N. C. Br. R. A. S. Journal*, No. IV., Art. VIII., 1867.

Kwoh Hiao, or Reigning Title.	Miao Hiao, or Temple Title.	Began to Reign.	Length of Reign.	Contemporary Monarchs.
1. Hungwu....	Taitsu........	1368	30	Tamerlane, Richard II., Robert II.
2. Kienwan....	Kienwan tí	1398	5	Manuel-Paleologus, Henry IV, of Eng.
3. Yungloh	Taitsung.......	1403	22	James I., Henry V., Martin V.
4. Hunghí.....	Jintsung.......	1425	1	} Amurath II., Henry VI., Charles VII.
5. Siuentih	Siuentsung.....	1426	10	} Albert II., Cosmo de Medicis.
6. Chingtung ..	Yingtsung	1436	21	James II., Fred. III. of Aus., Nich. V.
7. Kingtai	Kingtí	1457	8	Mahomet II., Edward IV., Sixtus IV.
8. Chinghwa...	Hientsung	1465	23	James III., Ferd. and Isabella, Louis XI.
9. Hungchí....	Hiautsung	1488	18	Bajazet II., James IV., Henry VII.
10. Chingtih	Wutsung.......	1506	16	James V., Henry VIII., Charles V.
11. Kiahtsing...	Shítsung.......	1522	45	Solyman II., Mary, Philip II., Henry II.
12. Lungking ...	Muhtsung......	1567	6	Selim II., Elizabeth, Gregory III.
13. Wanleih	Shintsung......	1573	47	James I., Henry IV., Louis XIII.
14. Taichang ...	Kwangtsung ...	1620	1	Othman II., Philip IV., Gregory XV.
15. Tienkí......	Hitsung	1621	7	Amurath IV., Charles I., Urban VIII.
16. Tsungching.	Hwaitsung.....	1628	16	Innocent X., Frederick the Great.
1. Shunchí[1] ...	Chang hwangtí.	1644	18	Mahomet IV., Cromwell, Louis XIV.
2. Kanghí	Jin hwangtí ...	1662	61	Charles II., Clement IX., Sobieskv.
3. Yungching..	Hien hwangtí..	1723	13	Mahomet V., George II., Louis XV.
4. Kienlung ...	Shun hwangtí..	1736	60	Osman III., George III., Clement XIV
5. Kiaking	Jui hwangtí....	1796	25	Selim III., Napoleon, Fred. Wm. II.
6. Taukwang ..	Ching hwangtí .	1821	30	Mahmoud, George IV., Louis XVIII.
7. Hienfung ...	Hien hwangtí ..	1851	11	Mahmoud, Victoria, Louis XVIII.
8. Tungchí	....	1862	12	Napoleon III., Alexander II.
9. Kwangsü[2] ..	....	1875		

Dynasty.	Number of Sovereigns.	Began.	Ended.	Duration.
1. Hia	Seventeen, averaging 26 years to each monarch's reign	B.C. 2205	B.C. 1766	439
2. Shang	Twenty-eight, averaging 23 years...........	1766	1122	644
3. Chau	Thirty four, averaging 25½ years	1122	255	867
4. Tsin........	Two, one reigning 37 years, the second 3 years.	255	206	40
5. Han........	Fourteen, averaging 16½ years	206	A.D. 25	231
6. East Han ...	Twelve, averaging 16½ years...............	A.D. 25	221	196
7. After Han..	Two, one reigning 2, the other 41 years......	221	264	43
8. Tsin........	Four, averaging 14¼ years	265	322	57
9. East Tsin ..	Eleven, averaging about 9½ years	323	419	106
10. Sung	Eight, averaging 7¼ years	420	478	58
11. Tsí.......	Five, averaging 4⅗ years	479	502	23
12. Liang.......	Four, one 48 years, and three together 7 years.	502	556	54
13 Chin	Five, averaging about 6½ years	557	589	32
14. Sui	Three, one reigning 16, another 12, and another 2 years	589	619	30
15. Tang	Twenty, averaging 14⅛ years	620	907	287
16. After Liang.	Two, one 8 and one 7 years	907	923	16
17. After Tang .	Four, averaging 3¼ years..................	923	936	13
18. After Tsin..	Two, one 7 and one 3 years	936	946	10
19. After Han..	Two, one 3 years, another 1 year	947	951	4
20. After Chau .	Three, averaging 3 years..................	951	960	9
21. Sung	Nine, averaging 18½ years.................	960	1127	167
22. South Sung.	Nine, averaging 17 years	1127	1280	153
23. Yuen.......	Nine, averaging 9⅜ years	1280	1368	88
24. Ming	Sixteen, averaging 17 years	1368	1644	276
25. Tsing	Eight up to 1875, averaging nearly 30 years ..	1644		

[1] Shunchí and the four following monarchs are named in Manchu, Chidzueldimbukhé, Elkhe taifin, Khowaligasoun tob, Abkai wekhiyekhe, and Saichunga fengchen, respectively.

[2] Kwangsü was born August 14, 1871.

years, and to each monarch an average of 17 1/7 years. From Wu wang's accession to Kwangsü is 2,997 years, giving an average of 125 years to a dynasty and 15 1/2 to each sovereign. From the days of Menes in Egypt, B.C. 2719 to 331, Manetho reckons 31 dynasties and 378 kings, which is about 77 years to each family and 6 1/3 to each reign. In England the 34 sovereigns from William I. to Victoria (A.D. 1066 to 1837) averaged 22 2/3 years each; in Israel, the 23 kings from Saul to Zedekiah averaged 22 years during a monarchy of 507 years.

CHAPTER XVIII.

RELIGION OF THE CHINESE.

As results must have their proportionate causes, one wishes to know what are the reasons for the remarkable duration of the Chinese people. Why have not their institutions fallen into decrepitude, and this race given place to others during the forty centuries it claims to have existed? Is it owing to the geographical isolation of the land, which has prevented other nations easily reaching it? Or have the language and literature unified and upheld the people whom they have taught? Or, lastly, is it a religious belief and the power of a ruling class working together which has brought about the security and freedom now seen in this thrifty, industrious, and practical people? Probably all these causes have conduced to this end, and our present object is to outline what seems to have been their mode of operation.

The position of their country has tended to separate them from other Asiatic races, even from very early times. It compelled them to work out their own institutions without any hints or modifying interference from abroad. They seem, in fact, to have had no neighbors of any importance until about the Christian era, up to which time they occupied chiefly the basin of the Yellow River, or the nine northern provinces as the Empire is now divided. Till about B.C. 220 feudal States covered this region, and their quarrels only ended by their subjection to Tsin Chí Hwangtí, or the 'Emperor First,' whose strong hand molded the people as he led them to value security and yield to just laws. He thus prepared the way for the Emperors Wăn tí (B.C. 179–156) and Wu tí (B.C. 140–86), of the Han dynasty, to consolidate, during their long reigns of twenty-nine and fifty-four years, their schemes of good government.

The four northern provinces all lie on the south-eastern slope of the vast plateau of Central Asia, the ascent to which is confined to a few passes, leading up five or six thousand feet through mountain defiles to the sterile, bleak plains of Gobi. This desolate region has always given subsistence to wandering nomads, and enough to enable traders to cross its grassy wastes. When their numbers increased they burst their borders in periodical raids, ravaging and weakening those whom they were too few to conquer and too ignorant to govern. The Chinese were too unwarlike to keep these tribes in subjection for long, and never themselves colonized the region, though the attempt to ward off its perpetual menace to their safety, by building the Great Wall to bar out their enemies, proves how they had learned to dread them. Yet this desert waste has proved a better defense for China against armies coming from the basin of the Tarim River than the lofty mountains on its west did to ancient Persia and modern Russia. It was easier and more inviting for the Scythians, Huns, Mongols, and Turks successively to push their arms westward, and China thereby remained intact, even when driven within her own borders.

The western frontiers, between the Kiayü Pass in Kansuh, at the extreme end of the Great Wall, leading across the country south to the island of Hainan, are too wild and rough to be densely inhabited or easily crossed, so that the Chinese have always been unmolested in that direction. To invade the eastern sides, now so exposed, the ancients had no fleets powerful enough to attack the Middle Kingdom; and it is only within the present century that armies carried by steam have threatened her seaboard.

The Chinese have, therefore, been shut out by their natural defenses from both the assaults and the trade of the dwellers in India, Tibet, and Central Asia, to that degree which would have materially modified their civilization. The external influences which have molded them have been wholly religious, acting through the persistent labors of Buddhist missionaries from India. These zealous men came and went in a ceaseless stream for ten centuries, joining the caravans entering the northwestern marts and ships trading at southern ports.

In addition to this geographical isolation, the language of the Chinese has tended still more to separate them intellectually from their fellow-men. It is not strange, indeed, that a symbolic form of writing should have arisen among them, for the Egyptians and Mexicans exhibit other fashions of ideographic writing, as well as its caprices and the difficulty of extending it. But its long-continued use by the Chinese is hardly less remarkable than the proof it gives of their independence of other people in mental and political relations. Outside nations did not care to study Chinese books through such a medium, and its possessors had, without intending it, shut themselves out of easy interchange of thought. This shows that they could not have had much acquaintance in early times with any alphabetic writing like Sanscrit or Assyrian, for it is almost certain that, in that case, they would soon have begun to alter their ideographs into syllables and letters as the Egyptians did; while the manifest advantages of the phonetic over the symbolic principle would have gradually insured its triumph. In that case, however, the rivalries of feudal States would have resulted, as in Europe, in the formation of different languages, and perhaps prevented the growth of a great Chinese race. In Japan and Corea the struggle between symbols and sounds has long existed, and two written languages, the Chinese and a derived demotic, are now used side by side in each of those kingdoms.

This isolation has had its disadvantageous effects on the people thus cut off from their fellows, but the results now seen could not otherwise have been attained. Their literary tendencies could never have attained the strength of an institution if they had been surrounded by more intelligent nations; nor would they have filled the land to such a degree if they had been forced to constantly defend themselves, or had imbibed the lust of conquest. Either of these conditions would probably have brought their own national life to a premature close.

Isolation, however, is merely a potential factor in this question. It does not by itself account for that life nor furnish the reasons for its uniformity and endurance. These must be sought for in the moral and social teachings of their sages and great rulers, who have been leaders and counsellors, and in the character of the political institutions which have grown out of those teachings. A comparison of their national characteristics with those of other ancient and modern people shows four striking contrasts and deductions. The Chinese may be regarded as the only pagan nation which has maintained democratic habits under a purely despotic theory of government. This government has respected the rights of its subjects by placing them under the protection of law, with its sanctions and tribunals, and making the sovereign amenable in the popular mind for the continuance of his sway to the approval of a higher Power able to punish him. Lastly, it has prevented the domination of all feudal, hereditary, and priestly classes and interests by making the tenure of officers of government below the throne chiefly depend on their literary attainments. Not a trace of Judaistic, Assyrian, or Persian customs or dogmas appears in Chinese books in such definite form as to suggest a western origin. All is the indigenous outcome of native ideas and habits.

The real religious belief and practices of a heathen people are hard to describe intelligibly to those who have not lived among them. Men naturally exercise much freedom of thought in such matters, and feel the authority of their fellow-men over their minds irksome to bear; and though it is comparatively easy to depict their religious ceremonies and festivals, their real belief —that which constitutes their religion, their trust in danger and guide in doubt, their support in sorrow and hope for future reward—is not quickly examined nor easily described. The want of a well understood and acknowledged standard of doctrine, and the degree of latitude each one allows himself in his observance of rites or belief in dogmas, tends to confuse the inquirer; while his own diverse views, his imperfect knowledge, and misapprehension of the effect which this tenet or that ceremony has upon the heart of the worshipper, contribute still further to embarrass the subject. This, at least, is the case with the Chinese, and notwithstanding what has been written upon their religion, no one has very satisfactorily elucidated the true nature of their belief and the intent of their ritual. The reason is owing partly to the indefinite ideas of the people themselves upon the character of their ceremonies, and their consequent inability to give a clear notion of them; partly also to the variety of observances found in distant parts of the country, and the discordant opinions entertained by those belonging to the same sect; so that what is seen in one district is sometimes utterly unknown in the next province, and the opinions of one man are laughed at by another.

Before proceeding with the present outline two negative features of Chinese religion deserve to be noticed, which distinguish it from the faith of most other heathen nations. These are the absence of human sacrifices and the non-deification of vice. The prevalence of human offerings in almost all ages of the world, and among nations of different degrees of civilization, not only widely separated in respect of situation and power, but flourishing in ages remote from each other, and having little or no mutual influence, has often been noticed. Human sacrifices are offered to this day in some parts of Asia, Africa, and Polynesia, which the extension of Christian instruction and power has, it is to be hoped, greatly reduced and almost accomplished the extinction of; but no clear record of the sacrificial immolation of man by his fellow, "offering the fruit of his body for the sin of his soul," has been found in Chinese annals in such a shape as to carry the conviction that it formed part of the belief or practice of the people—although the Scythian custom of burying the servants and horses of a deceased prince or chieftain with him was perhaps observed before the days of Confucius, and may have been occasionally done since his time. This feature, negative though it be, stands in strong contrast with the appalling destruction of human life for religious reasons, still existing among the tribes of Western and Central Africa, and recorded as having been sanctioned among Aztecs and Egyptians, Hindus and Carthaginians, and other ancient nations, not excepting Syrians and Jews, Greeks and Romans.

The other, and still more remarkable trait of Chinese idolatry, is that there is no deification of sensuality, which, in the name of religion, could shield and countenance those licentious rites and orgies that enervated the minds of worshippers and polluted their hearts in so many other pagan countries. No Aphrodite or Lakshmi occurs in the list of Chinese goddesses; no weeping for Thammuz, no exposure in the temple of Mylitta or obscene rites of the Durga-puja, have ever been required or sanctioned by Chinese priests; no nautch girls as in Indian temples, or courtesans as at Corinth, are kept in their sacred buildings. Their speculations upon the dual powers of the *yin* and *yang* have never degenerated into the vile worship of the *linga* and *yoni* of the Hindus, or of Amun-kem, as pictured on the ruins of Thebes. Although they are a licentious people in word and deed, the Chinese have not endeavored to lead the votaries of pleasure, falsely so called, further down the road of ruin, by making its path lie through a temple and trying to sanctify its acts by putting them under the protection of a goddess. Nor does their mythology teem with disgusting relations of the amours of their deities; on the contrary, like the Romanists, they exalt and deify chastity and seclusion as a means of bringing the soul and body nearer to the highest excellence. Vice is, in a great degree, kept out of sight, as well as out of religion, and it may be safely said that no such significant sign as has been uncovered at Pompeii, with the inscription *Hic habitat felicitas*, was ever exhibited in a Chinese city.

To these traits of Chinese character may be added the preservative features of their regard for parents and superiors and their general peaceful industry. If there be any connection between the former of these virtues and the promise attached to the fifth commandment, "That thy days may be long in the land which the Lord thy God giveth thee," then the long duration of the Chinese people and Empire is a stupendous monument of the good effects of even a partial obedience to the law of God, by those who only had it inscribed on their hearts and not written in their hands.

The last point in the Chinese polity which has had great influence in preserving it is the religious beliefs recognized by the people and rulers. There are three sects (*san kiao*), which are usually called Confucianism, Buddhism, and Taoism, or Rationalism; the first is a foreign term, and vaguely denotes the belief of the literati generally, including the State religion. These three sects do not interfere with each other, however, and a man may worship at a Buddhist shrine or join in a Taoist festival while he accepts all the tenets of Confucius and worships him on State occasions; much as a lawyer in England may attend a Quaker meeting or the Governor of a State in America may be a Methodist minister. In China there is no generic term for religion in its usual sense. The word *kiao*, which means 'to teach,' or 'doctrines taught,' is applied to all sects and associations having a creed or ritual; the ancestral worship is never called a *kiao*, for everybody observes that at home just as much as he obeys his parents; it is a duty, not a sect.

No religious system has been found among the Chinese which taught the doctrine of atonement by the shedding of blood; an argument in favor of their antiquity. The State religion of China has had a remarkable history and antiquity, and, though modified somewhat during successive dynasties, has retained its main features during the past three thousand years. The simplicity and purity of this worship have attracted the notice of many foreigners, who have disagreed on various points as to its nature and origin. Their discussions have brought out sundry most interesting details respecting it; and whoever has visited the great Altar and Temple of Heaven at Peking, where the Emperor and his courtiers worship, must have been impressed with its simple grandeur. What was the precise idea connected with the words *tien*, 'heaven,' and *hwang tien*, 'imperial heaven,' as they were used in ancient times, is a very difficult point to determine; the worship rendered to them was probably of a mixed sort, the material heavens being taken as the most sublime manifestation of the power of their Maker, whose character was then less obscured and unknown than in after times, when it degenerated to Sabianism.

These discussions are not material to the present subject, and it is only needful to indicate the main results. The prime idea in this worship is that the Emperor is *Tien-tsz'*, or 'Son of Heaven,' the coördinate with Heaven and Earth, from whom he directly derives his right and power to rule on earth among mankind, the One Man who is their vicegerent and the third of the trinity (*san tsai*) of Heaven, Earth, and Man. With these ideas of his exalted position, he claims the homage of all his fellow-men. He cannot properly devolve on any other mortal his functions of their high priest to offer the oblations on the altars of Heaven and Earth at Peking at the two solstices. He is not, therefore, a despot by mere power, as other rulers are, but is so in the ordinance of nature, and the basis of his authority is divine. He is accountable personally to his two superordinate powers for its record and result. If the people suffer from pestilence or famine he is at fault, and must atone by prayer, sacrifice, and reformation as a disobedient son. One defect in all human governments—a sense of responsibility on the part of rulers to the God who ordains the powers that be—has thus been partly met and supplied in China. It has really been a check, too, on their tyranny and extortion; for the very books which contain this State ritual intimate the amenability of the sovereign to the Powers who appointed him to rule, and hint that the people will rise to vindicate themselves. The officials, too, all springing from the people, and knowing their feelings, hesitate to provoke a wrath which has swept away thousands of their number.

The objects of State worship are chiefly things, although persons are also included. There are three grades of sacrifices, the *great*, *medium*, and *inferior*, the last collectively called *kiun sz'*, or 'the crowd of sacrifices.' The objects to which the great sacrifices are offered are only four, viz.: *tien*, the heavens or sky, called the imperial concave expanse; *tí*, the earth, likewise dignified with the appellation imperial; *tai miao*, or the great temple of ancestors, wherein the tablets of deceased monarchs of this dynasty are placed; and, lastly, the *shié tsih*, or gods of the land and grain, the special patrons of each dynasty. The tablets representing these four great objects are placed on an equality by the present monarchs, which is strong presumptive proof that by *tien* is now meant the material heavens.

The medium sacrifices are offered to nine objects: The sun, or "great light," the moon, or "night light," the manes of the emperors and kings of former dynasties, Confucius, the ancient patrons of agriculture and silk, the gods of heaven, earth, and the cyclic year. The first six have separate temples erected for their worship in Peking. The inferior herd of sacrifices are offered to the ancient patron of the healing art and the innumerable spirits of deceased philanthropists, eminent statesmen, martyrs to virtue, etc.; clouds, rain, wind, and thunder; the five celebrated mountains, four seas, and four rivers; famous hills, great watercourses, flags, triviæ, gods of cannon, gates, queen goddess of earth, the north pole, and many other things. The State religion has been so far corrupted from its ancient simplicity, as given in the *Shu King* and *Lí Kí*, as to include gods terrestrial and stellar, ghosts infernal, flags, and cannon, as well as idols and tablets, the effigies and mementoes of deified persons.

The personages who assist the Emperor in his worship of the four superior objects, and perform most of the ceremonies, belong to the Imperial Clan and the Board of Rites; but while they go through with the ceremony, he, as pontifex maximus, refuses to pay the same homage that he demands of all who approach him, and puts off these superior Powers with three kneelings and nine profound bows. When he is ill, or in his minority, these services are all forborne, for they cannot properly be done by a substitute. When he worships Heaven he wears robes of a blue color, in allusion to the sky; and when he worships earth he puts on yellow to represent the clay of this earthly clod; so, likewise, he wears red for the sun and pale white for the moon. The princes, nobles, and officers who assist are clad in their usual court dresses, but no priests or women are admitted. The worship of Yuenfí, the goddess of silk, is alone, as we have seen, conducted by the Empress and her court. The temple of the sun is east, and that of the moon west of the city, and at the equinoxes a regulus, or prince of the Imperial Clan, is commissioned to perform the requisite ceremonies and offer the appointed sacrifices.

The winter solstice is the great day of this State worship. The Emperor goes from his palace the evening before, drawn by an elephant in his state car and escorted by about two thousand grandees, princes, musicians, and attendants, down to the Temple of Heaven. The cortége passes out by the southern road, reaching the Ching Yang Gate, opened only for his Majesty's use, and through it goes on two miles to the *Tien Tan*. He first repairs to the *Chai Kung*, or 'Palace of Fasting,' where he prepares himself by lonely meditation for his duty; "for the idea is that if there be not pious thoughts in his mind the spirits of the unseen will not come to the sacrifice." To assist him he looks at a copper statue, arrayed like a Taoist priest, whose mouth is covered by three fingers, denoting silence, while the other hand bears a tablet inscribed with 'Fast three days.' When the worship commences, and all the officiating attendants are in their places, the animals are killed, and as the odor of their burning flesh ascends to convey the sacrifice to the gods, the Emperor begins the rite, and is directed at every step by the masters of ceremonies. The worship to Heaven is at midnight, and the numerous poles around the great altar, and the fires in the furnaces shedding their glare over the marble terraces and richly dressed assembly, render this solemnity most striking.[1]

The hierophants in this worship of nature, so lauded by some infidels, are required to prepare themselves for the occasion by fasting, ablutions, change of garments, separation from their wives and pleasurable scenes, and from the dead; "for sickness and death defile, while banqueting dissipates the mind and unfits it for holding communion with the gods." The sacrifices consist of calves, hares, deer, sheep, or pigs, and the offerings of silks, grain, jade, etc. No garlands are placed on the victim when its life is taken, nor is the blood sprinkled on any particular spot or article. "The idea is that of a banquet; and when a sacrifice is performed to the supreme spirit of Heaven, the honor paid is believed by the Chinese to be increased by inviting other guests. The Emperors invite their ancestors to sit at the banquet with *Shangtí*. A father is to be honored as heaven, and a mother as earth. In no way could more perfect reverence be shown than in placing a father's tablet on the altar with that of Shangtí." To these remarks of Dr. Edkins explanatory of this union of the objects worshipped, it may be added that the Emperors regard their predecessors of every dynasty as still invested with power in Hades, and therefore invoke their blessing and presence by sacrifice and prayers.

---

[1] Compare the frontispiece of Volume I.; also *ibid.*, p. 76.

The statutes annex penalties of fines or blows in various degrees of punishment in case of informality or neglect, but "in these penalties there is not the least allusion to any displeasure of the things or beings worshipped; there is nothing to be feared but man's wrath—nothing but a forfeiture or a fine." Heavier chastisement, however, awaits any of the common people or the unauthorized who should presume to state their wants to high Heaven or worship these objects of imperial adoration; strangulation or banishment, according to the demerits of the case, would be their retribution. The *ignobile vulgus* may worship stocks and stones in almost any form they please, but death awaits them if they attempt to join the Son of Heaven, the Vicegerent of Heaven and Earth, in his adorations to the supposed sources of his power.[1]

In his capacity of Vicegerent, High Priest, and Mediator between his subjects and the higher Powers, there are many points of similarity between the assumptions of the Emperor and of the Pope at Rome. The idea the Chinese have of heaven seems to be pantheistic, and in worshipping heaven, earth, and terrestrial gods they mean to include and propitiate all superior powers. If, as seems probable, the original idea of *Shangtí*, as it can be imperfectly gleaned from early records, was that of a supreme Intelligence, it has since been lost. Of this worship, the effects in China upon the nation have been both positive and negative. One of the negative influences has been to dwarf the State hierarchy to a complete nullity—to prevent the growth of a class which could or did use the power of the monarchy to strengthen its own hold upon the people as their religious advisers, and on the government as a necessary aid to its efficiency.

The High Priests of China love power and adulation too well to share this worship with their subjects, and in engrossing it entirely they have escaped the political evils of a powerful hierarchy and the people the combined oppressions of a church

[1] *Chinese Repository*, Vol. III., pp. 49–53. Dr. J. Edkins, *Religions of China*, Chap. II.; this chapter, on Imperial Worship, gives a good account of these ceremonies. Legge's *Notions of the Chinese concerning God and Spirits*, pp. 23–36, 41–43, for the forms of prayer used.

and State. We have seen that the popular rights which are so plainly taught in the classics have been inculcated and perpetuated by the common school education; we shall soon see, moreover, that the ancestral worship could not admit the interference of priest, altar, or sacrifice outside of the door-posts. Yet it is probable that all combined would have been too weak to resist the seductive influence of a hierarchy in some form, if it had not been that the Emperor himself would yield his own unapproachable grandeur to no man. Being everything in his own person, it is too much to expect that he is going to vacate or reduce his prerogative, surrender his right to make or degrade gods of every kind for his subjects to worship, weaken his own prestige, or mortify the pride of his fellow-worshippers, the high ministers of State. The chains of caste woven in India, the fetters of the Inquisition forged in Spain, the silly rites practised by the augurs in old Rome, or the horrid cruelties and vile worship once seen in Egypt and Syria—in each case done under the sanction of the State—have all been wanting along the Yellow River, and spread none of their evils to hamper the rule of law in China.

This State religion is, therefore, a splendid and wonderful pageant; but it can no more be called the religion of the Chinese than the teachings of Socrates could be termed the faith of the Greeks. It is, however, intimately connected with the *Ju kiao*, or 'Sect of the Learned,' commonly called Confucianists by foreigners, because all its members and priests are learned men who venerate the classical writings. It is somewhat inappropriate to designate the *Ju kiao* a religious sect, or regard it otherwise than as a comprehensive term for those who adopt the writings of Confucius and Chu Hí and their disciples. The word *ju* denotes one of the literati, and was first adopted A.D. 1150, as an appellation for those who followed the speculations of Chu Hí regarding the *tai kih*, or 'Great Extreme.' This author's comments on the classics and his metaphysical writings have had greater influence on his countrymen than those of any other person except Confucius and Mencius; whose works, indeed, are received according to his explanations.

The remarks of Confucius upon religious subjects were very

few; he never taught the duty of man to any higher power than the head of the State or family, though he supposed himself commissioned by heaven to restore the doctrine and usages of the ancient kings. He admitted that he did not understand much about the gods; that they were beyond and above the comprehension of man; and that the obligations of man lay rather in doing his duty to his relatives and society than in worshipping spirits unknown. "Not knowing even life," said he, "how can we know death?" and when his disciples asked him in his last illness whom he would sacrifice to, he said he had already worshipped. Chu Hí resolved the few and obscure references to Shangtí in the *Shu King* into pure materialism; making nature to begin with the *tai kih*, called *premier principe matériel* by the French, which operating upon itself resolved itself into the dual powers, the *yin* and *yang*.

Sir John Davis compares this production of the *yin* and *yang* to the masculo-feminine principle in the development of the mundane egg in the Egyptian cosmogony, and quotes an extract showing that the idea was entertained among the Hindus, and that the androgyn of Plato was only another form of this myth. The Chinese have also the notion of an egg, and that the *tai kih* was evolved from it, or acted like the process of hatching going on in it, though it may be that with them the introduction of the egg is more for the sake of illustration than as the form of the cause. Some of Chu Hí's philosophical notions have already been quoted in Volume I.[1] His system of materialism captivates his countrymen, for it is far more thoroughly worked out than any other, and allows scope for the vagaries of every individual who thinks he understands and can apply it to explain whatever phenomena come in his way. Heat and cold, light and darkness, fire and water, mind and matter, every agent, power, and substance, known or supposed, are regarded as endued with these principles, which thus form a simple solution for every question. The infinite changes in the universe, the multiform actions and reactions in nature, and all the varied consequences seen and

---

[1] Pp. 683 ff. Canon McClatchie has made a careful translation of Chapter XLIX. of his works, giving his views on cosmogony.

unseen are alike easily explained by this form of cause and effect, this ingenious theory of evolution. With regard to the existence of gods and spirits, Chu Hí affirmed that sufficient knowledge was not possessed to say positively that they existed, and he saw no difficulty in omitting the subject altogether—a species of agnosticism or indifferentism, therefore, which has become the creed of nearly the entire body of educated men in the Empire. His system is also silent respecting the immortality of the soul, as well as future rewards and punishments. Virtue is rewarded and vice is punished in the individual or in his posterity on earth; but of a separate state of existence he or his disciples do not speak.

In thus disposing of the existence of superior powers, the philosophers do not shut out all intelligent agencies, but have instituted a class of sages or pure-minded men of exalted intellects and simple hearts, who have been raised up from time to time by Heaven, Shangtí, or some other power, as instructors and examples to mankind, and who therefore deserve the reverence of their fellows. The office of these *shing jin*, 'perfect men' or saints, is to expound the will of heaven and earth; they did not so much speak their own thoughts as illustrate and settle the principles on which the world should be governed; they were men intuitively wise without instruction, while common people must learn to be wise. Of all the saints in the calendar of the *Ju kiao* Confucius is the chief; with him are reckoned the early kings, Yao and Shun, with King Wăn and his two sons King Wu and Duke Chau; but China has produced no one since the "most holy teacher of ancient times" whom his proud disciples are willing to regard his equal—Mencius being only a "number two saint." The deceased Emperors of the reigning dynasty are canonized as its efficient and divine patrons, but a new line of monarchs would serve them as they did their predecessors, by reducing them to mere spirits. The demonolatry of the learned has gradually become so incorporated with popular superstitions that there is now little practical distinction; every one is willing to worship whatever can promise relief or afford assistance. A student of the classical works naturally adopts their views on these points, without supposing that they militate against worshipping his ancestors, joining the villagers in adoring the goddess of Mercy or any other Buddhistic idol, or calling in a Rationalist to write a charm. He also, on coming into office, expects to perform all the ex-officio religious ceremonies required of him, and add the worship of the Emperor to the rest.

Every magistrate is officially required to perform various idolatrous ceremonies at the temples. The objects of worship are numerous, including many others besides those forming the "herd of inferior sacrifices," and new deities are frequently made by the Emperor, on the same principle that new saints are canonized by the Pope. The worship of certain hills and rivers, and of spirits supposed to preside over particular cities and districts, has prevailed among the Chinese from ancient times, long before the rise of Rationalism or introduction of Buddhism, and is no doubt the origin of this official worship. In every city the *Ching-hwang miao*, *i.e.*, 'City and Moat Temple,' contains the tutelar divinity of the city called *Ching-hwang*, with other gods, and here on the solstices, equinoxes, new and full moons, etc., officers repair to sacrifice to it and to the gods of the land and grain. Over the door of the one in Canton is written, "Right and wrong, truth and falsehood are blended on earth, but all are most clearly distinguished in heaven." Capt. Loch thus describes the Ching-hwang miao at Shanghai, as it stood in 1842:

In the centre of a serpentine sheet of water there is a rocky island, and on it a large temple of two stories, fitted up for the accommodation of the wealthy public. Pillars of carved wood support the roof, fretted groups of uncouth figures fill up the narrow spaces, while movable lattices screen the occupants from the warmth of the noonday sun. Nothing can surpass the beauty and truth to nature of the most minutely carved flowers and insects prodigally scattered over every screen and cornice. This is the central and largest temple. A number of other light aerial-looking structures of the same form are perched upon the corners of artificial rocky precipices and upon odd little islands. Light and fanciful wooden bridges connect most of these islands, and are thrown across the arms of the serpentine water, so that each sequestered spot can be visited in turn. At a certain passage of the sun the main temple is shaded in front by a rocky eminence, the large masses of which are connected with great art and propriety of taste, but in shape and adjustment most studiously grotesque. Trees and flowers and tufts of grass are planted where art must have been taxed to the utmost to procure them a lodgment. In another part of the garden there is a miniature wood of dwarf trees, with a dell and waterfall; the leaves, fruit, and blossoms of the trees are proportionate to their size. Tortuous pathways lead to the top of the artificial mountain, each turn formed with studied art to surprise and charm by offering at every point fresh views and objects. Flowers and creepers sprout out from crevices, trees hang over the jutting crags, small pavilions are seen from almost every vista, while grottoes and rocky recesses, shady bowers and labyrinths, are placed to entrap the unwary, each with an appropriate motto, one inviting the wanderer to repose, another offering a secluded retreat to the philosopher.[1]

Official Chinese records enumerate 1,560 temples dedicated to Confucius attached to the examination halls, the offerings presented in which are all eaten or used by the worshippers; there are, it is said, 62,606 pigs, rabbits, sheep, and deer, and 27,000 pieces of silk, annually offered upon their altars.[2] The municipal temple is not the only one where officers worship, but, like the common people, they bow before whatever they think can aid them in their business or estates. It has already been stated that the duty of Chinese officers extends to the securing of genial seasons by their good administration, and consequently if bad harvests ensue or epidemics rage the fault and removal of the calamity belong to them. The expedients they resort to are both ludicrous and melancholy. In 1835 the prefect of Canton, on occasion of a distressing drought of eight months, issued the following invitation, which would have better befitted a chieftain of the Sechuanas:

Pan, acting prefect of Kwangchau, issues this inviting summons. Since for a long time there has been no rain, and the prospects of drought continue, and supplications are unanswered, my heart is scorched with grief. In the whole province of Kwangtung, are there no extraordinary persons who can force the dragon to send rain? Be it known to you, all ye soldiers and people, that if there be any one, whether of this or any other province, priest or such like, who can by any craft or arts bring down abundance of rain, I respectfully request him to ascend the altar [of the dragon], and sincerely and reverently pray. And after the rain has fallen, I will liberally reward him with money and tablets to make known his merits.

This invitation called forth a Buddhist priest as a "rain maker," and the prefect erected an altar for him before his own office, upon which the man, armed with cymbal and wand, for three

[1] *Events in China*, p. 47. London, 1843.

[2] During the Han dynasty (A.D. 59) wine was drunk and sacrifices made to Confucius in the study halls. The victim offered was a dog. Biot, *Essai sur l'Instruction en Chine*, p. 168.

days vainly repeated his incantations from morning to night, exposed bareheaded to the hot sun, the butt of the jeering crowd. The prefect himself was lampooned by the people for his folly, the following quatrain being pasted under a copy of his invitation:

> Kwangchau's great protector, the magnate Pan,
> Always acting without regard to reason;
> Now prays for rain, and getting no reply,
> Forthwith seeks for aid to force the dragon.

The unsuccessful efforts of the priest did not render the calamity less grievous, and their urgent necessities led the people to resort to every expedient to force their gods to send rain. The authorities forbade the slaughter of animals, or in other words a fast was proclaimed, to keep the hot winds out of the city, the southern gate was shut, and all classes flocked to the temples. It was estimated that on one day twenty thousand persons went to a celebrated shrine of the goddess of Mercy, among whom were the Governor and Prefect and their suites, who all left their sedans and walked with the multitude. The Governor, as a last expedient, the day before rain came, intimated his intention of liberating all prisoners not charged with capital offences. As soon as the rain fell the people presented thank-offerings, and the southern gate of the city was opened, accompanied by an odd ceremony of burning off the tail of a live sow while the animal was held in a basket.

The officers and literati, though acknowledging the folly of these observances, and even ridiculing the worship of senseless blocks, still join in it. As an example of this: In 1867 a severe drought near Peking called forth a suggestion from a censor that if a white tiger were sacrificed by the Emperor to the dragon the rain would be liberated; for "it was his powerful enemies which kept the rain-god from acting." Wănsiang was deputed to perform the rite; rain came not many days later. The officer laughed, indeed, at the fancy, yet could not disenthrall himself from some degree of belief in its efficacy. Devotees sometimes become irritated against their gods, and resort to summary means to force them to hear their petitions.

It is said that the Governor in Canton, having repeatedly ascended in a time of drought to the temple of the god of Rain, dressed in his burdensome robes, through the heat of a tropical sun, on one of his visits said: "The god supposes I am lying when I beseech his aid; for how can he know, seated in his cool niche in the temple, that the ground is parched and the sky hot?" Whereupon he ordered his attendants to put a rope around his neck and haul his godship out of doors, that he might see and feel the state of the weather for himself. After his excellency had become cooled in the temple the idol was reinstated in its shrine, and the good effects of this treatment were deemed to be fully proved by the copious showers which soon after fell. The Emperor himself on such occasions resorts to unusual sacrifices, and sends his relatives and courtiers almost daily to various temples to pray and burn incense. Imperial patronage of the popular superstitions is sought after by the officers in one way and another to please the people, but it does not involve much outlay of funds.[1] One common mode is to solicit his Majesty for an inscription to be placed over the doorway of a temple, or memorialize him to confer a higher title upon the god. On occasion of a victory over the rebels in Kwangtung in 1822, the shrine of a neighboring deity, supposed to have assisted in obtaining it, received a new title commemorative of the event, and a temple was built for him at the expense of government.

The combined effect of the State religion and classical writings, notwithstanding their atheism and coldness, has had some effect in keeping the people out of the swinish ditch of pollution. It is one of their prime tenets that human nature is originally virtuous, and becomes corrupt entirely by bad precept and example. This is taught children from their earliest years, and officers refer repeatedly to it in their exhortations to obedience; its necessary results of happiness, if carried out, are illustrated by trite comparisons drawn from common life and general ex-

---

[1] Klaproth cites (among many) an instance of the manner in which favorable auguries are regarded and made use of by officials. *Mémoires sur l'Asie*, Tome I., p. 459.

perience. The Chinese seldom refer to the vengeance of the gods or future punishment as motives for reform, but to the well-being of individuals and good order of society in this world. Examples of this type of human perfection, fully developed, are constantly set before the people in Confucius and the ancient kings he delineates. The classical tenets require duties that carry their own arguments in their obedience, as well as afford matter of thought, while the standard books of Buddhists and Rationalists, where they do not reiterate the same obligations, are mostly filled with unprofitable speculations or solemn nonsense. Consequently the priests of those sects had only the superstitious fear of the people to work upon where reason was at fault, and so could not take the whole man captive; for his reason accorded with the teaching of the classics as far as they went, and only took up with divination and supplication of higher powers where their instructions ceased. The government, therefore, being composed chiefly of such people, educated to venerate pure reason, could not be induced to take the initiatory step of patronizing a religion of such an uncertain character, and confessedly inferior in its moral sanctions to what they already possessed. The current has, more or less, always set this way, and the two other sects have been tolerated when they did not interfere with government. It is too true that the instructions of Confucius and his school are imperfect and erroneous when measured by the standard of revelation. and the people can never emerge from selfish atheism and silly superstition as long as they have nothing better; but the vagaries of the Buddhists neither satisfy the reason nor reprove vice, nor does their celibate idleness benefit society. If the former be bad, the latter is worse.

The sect of the Rationalists, or *Tao kia*, is derived from Lautsz', or Lau-kiun. According to the legends he was born B.C. 604, in Ku, a hamlet in the kingdom of Tsu, supposed to lie in Luh-yeh hien, in the province of Honan. His birth was fifty-four years before Confucius. The story is that he had white hair and eyebrows at his birth, and was carried in the womb eighty years, whence he was called Lau-tsz', the 'old boy,' and Lau-kiun, the 'venerable prince.' Nothing reliable about his early life has come down to us, but, as was the case with Hesiod, his disciples have enveloped his actions and character in a nimbus of wonders. M. Julien has given a translation of their history, dated about A.D. 350, in his version of the *Tao Teh King*. Pauthier says he was appointed librarian by the Emperor, and diligently applied himself to the study of the ancient books, becoming acquainted with all the rites and histories of former times. During his life he is reported to have journeyed westward, but the extent and duration of his travel are not recorded, and even its occurrence is reasonably doubted. De Guignes says he went to Ta Tsin, a country under the rule of the Romans, but he forgets that the Romans had not then even conquered Italy; some suppose Ta Tsin to be Judea. His only extant work, the *Tao Teh King*, or 'Canons of Reason and Virtue,'[1] was written in Ling-pao, in Honan, before his travels, but whether the teachings contained in it are entirely his own or were derived from hints imported from India or Persia cannot be decided. It contains only five thousand three hundred and twenty characters, divided into eighty-one short chapters; the text of one edition is said to have been found in a tomb A.D. 574. It has been translated by Julien, Chalmers, and von Strauss. A parallel has been suggested between the sects of the Rationalists of China, the Zoroastrians of Persia, Essenes of Judea, Gnostics of the primitive church, and the eremites of the Thebaid, but a common source for their similarity—the desire of their members, after the sect had become recognized, to live without labor on the credulity of their fellowmen—explains most of the likeness, without supposing that their tenets were derived from each other.

The teachings of Lau-tsz' are not unlike those of Zeno; both recommend retirement and contemplation as the most effectual means of purifying the spiritual part of our nature, annihilating the passions, and finally returning to the bosom of *Tao*. His teachings on the highest subjects of human thought have furnished his countrymen ample materials for the most diverse

[1] Perhaps this may be rendered as the *Logos* of Plato, as near as any dogma can be compared to it.

views on these same themes according to their various fancies. In his striving after the infinite he can only describe *Tao* by what it is not and delineate *Teh* as an ideal virtue which no man can attain to. In Chapter XXI. they are thus blended: "The visible forms of the highest *Teh* only proceed from *Tao;* and *Tao* is a thing impalpable, indefinite. How indefinite! How impalpable! And [yet] therein are forms indefinite, impalpable! and [yet] therein are things (or entities). Profound and indistinct too, and [yet] therein are essences. These essences are profoundly real, and therein faith is found. From of old till now its name has never passed away. It gives issue to all existences at their beginnings. How [then] can I know the manner of the beginning of all existences? I know it by this [*Tao*]."

Such teachings are susceptible of almost any explanation, and Julien's extracts from the commentaries give one some idea of their diversity, though probably much well worth reading still lies buried in their pages. The names of sixty-four commentators are known, of whom three were reigning emperors; and their explanations have given their countrymen very doubtful guidance through this mystic book. To those who can compare its aspirations and dogmas with the speculations of Greek and Roman writers, the teachings of the Zendavesta, and the declarations of the Bible, the work of Lau-tsz' becomes of immense interest. His countrymen, however, to whom these great writers were all unknown, have looked upon this system of philosophy rather as the reveries of a wise man than the instructions of a practical thinker.

In Chapter I. he tries to define *tao*. It is reaching after the unknown. "The *tao* which can be expressed is not the eternal *tao;* the name which can be named is not the eternal name. The Nameless [being] is before heaven and earth; when named it is the mother of all things. Therefore, to be constantly passionless is to be able to see its spiritual essence; and to be constantly passionate is to see the forms (or limits) [of *tao*]. These two conditions are alike but have different names; they can both be called a mystery. The more it is examined into the more mysterious it is seen to be. It is the gate of all spiritual things." By the phrases "constantly passionless" and "constantly passionate" are denoted *non-existence* and *existence*, according to the commentators.

In Chapter LXV. there is a similar striving to describe *teh.* "In olden times those who practised *tao* did not do so to enlighten the people, but rather to render them simple-minded. When the people have too much worldly wisdom it makes them hard to govern. He who encourages this worldly wisdom in the government of a State is its misfortune; as he who governs without it is its blessing. To know aright these two things is to have a model State; and the constant exhibition of this ideal is what I call sublime *teh.* This sublime virtue [*teh*] is profound, is incommensurable, is opposed to time-serving plans. If followed it will bring about a state of general accord."

In Chapter XX. the lonely cynic seems to utter his sad cry at the little progress of his teachings. "All men are full of ambitious desires, like those greedy for the stalled ox, or the high delights of spring time. I alone am calm; my affections have not yet germinated; I am as a new-born babe which has not yet smiled on its mother. I am forlorn as one who has no home. All others have and to spare, I alone am like one who has lost all. In mind I am like a fool; I am all in a maze. Common people are bright enough; I am enveloped in darkness. Common people are sagacious enough; I am in gloom and confusion. I toss about as if on the sea; I float to and fro as if I was never to rest. Others have something they can do; I alone am good for nothing, and just like a lout. I am entirely solitary, differing from other men in that I glory in my Mother who nurses [all beings]."

The main object kept in view throughout this work is the inculcation of personal virtue, and Lau-tsz' founds his argument for its practice in the fitness of things, as he tries to prove by referring all the manifestations and laws of mind and matter to the unknown factor *tao.* In Chapter IV. he attempts to embody his struggling thoughts in these few words describing *tao:* "*Tao* is a void; still if one uses it, it seems to be inexhaustible. How profound it is! It seems like the patriarch of all things.

It softens sharp things, loosens tangled things, harmonizes brilliant things, and assimilates itself to worldly things of the dust. How tranquil it is! It seems to endure perpetually. I know not whose son it is. It seems so have existed before *Tí* [or Shangtí]."

Such utterances as these carry neither comfort nor repentance to the sorrowing, sinful heart of man; he cannot go to such an abnegation for guidance or relief in his troubles, and therefore the maxims of Lau-tsz' have fallen on callous hearts. Another extract, Chapter XLIX., is, however, more practical; it is not the only one which furnishes instruction of the highest character. "The perfect man [*shing jin*] has no immutable sentiments of his own, [for] he makes the mind of mankind his own. He who is good, I would meet with goodness; and he who is not good, I would still also meet with goodness; [for] *teh* is goodness. He who is sincere I would meet with sincerity; and he who is insincere, I would still also meet with sincerity; [for] *teh* is sincerity. The perfect man dwells in the world calm and reserved, his soul preserving the same regard for all mankind. The people all turn their eyes and ears toward him, and he regards them alike as his children."

In order to better understand these aphorisms, they need to be read with the help of the various commentaries; these furnish us with a better estimate of their value than any other guides. Foreign writers necessarily judge such a work by their own higher standard; as does M. Pauthier when he remarks upon the last extract: "La sagesse humaine ne peut être jamais exprimé des paroles plus saintes et plus profondes." He compares Lau-tsz' to his own countryman Rousseau—and these two had a good deal in common in their sad reflections upon the evils of the times. In another place the French author goes even farther, and regards the vague expressions in Chapter XLII., which show their derivation from the *Yih King*—viz.: "Tao produced one, one produced two, two produced three, and three produced all things"—as the Asiatic form of the doctrine and procession of the Holy Trinity and the biblical idea of the reunion of good men with their Maker!

One more extract from the *Tao-teh King* will fill the space at command; but sententious apothegms like these in Chapter XXXIII. are scattered throughout the book: "He who knows men is wise; [while] he who knows himself is perspicacious. He who conquers men is strong; [while] he who conquers himself is mighty. He who knows when he has enough is rich. He who acts energetically has a fixed purpose in view. He who does not miss his nature endures; [while] he who deceases and still is not extinct has immortality"—referring, as the commentators agree, to the life of the soul after it leaves the body.

Such a work can hardly be accurately translated into a European language; a perusal of all the translations enables one to appreciate this point. Some translators have missed the point of Lau-tsz's teachings by not attending to the parallelisms running through them, where one limb of the couplet illustrates and defines the other. In conclusion, it is still true that the absence of clear exposition on the duties of men in their marital, parental, and fraternal relations; the want of all instruction upon their obligations and rights as members of the family, the village, and the State; and lastly, his silence upon the voice of conscience and the effects of sin upon the soul of man, show that Lau-tsz' was more an ascetic than a philanthropist, more of a metaphysician than a humanitarian.

Mr. Samuel Johnson has indicated the high position this ancient relic holds in his examination of its tenets. "Nothing like this book exists in Chinese literature; nothing, so far as yet known, so lofty, so vital, so restful at the roots of strength; in structure as wonderful as in spirit; the fixed syllabic characters, formed for visible and definite meaning, here compacted into terse aphorisms of a mystical and universal wisdom, so subtly translated out of their ordinary spheres to meet a demand for spiritual expression that it is confessedly almost impossible to render them with certainty into another tongue. . . . It is a book of wonderful ethical and spiritual simplicity, and deals neither in speculative cosmogony nor in popular superstitions. It is not the speculations of an old philosopher, as Chalmers calls it. It is in practical earnest, and speaks from the heart and to the heart. Its religion resembles that of Fenelon or

Thomas à Kempis, combined with a perceptive rationalism of which they were not masters."[1]

The historian Sz'ma Tsien relates an interview which Confucius had with Lau-tsz' when, at the age of thirty-four (B.C. 517), he visited the capital to study the ritual of State worship, at which time the latter would be eighty-seven years old. Dr. Legge gives an account of this meeting, which it is to be wished could be better known, for the account is not very certain. The legendary history amplifies it largely, but in no extravagant style, and quite consonant to their different characters. Sz'ma Tsien makes the elder lecture the younger philosopher in the following style: "Those whom you talk about are dead, and their bones mouldered to dust; only their words remain. When the superior man gets his time, he mounts aloft; but when the time is against him, he moves as if his feet were entangled. I have heard that a good merchant, though he has rich treasures deeply stored, appears as if he were poor; and that the superior man whose virtue is complete is yet to outward seeming stupid. Put away your proud air and many desires, your insinuating habit and wild will. They are of no advantage to you. This is all which I have to tell you." To the reply of Confucius, that he had sought to get *tao* for twenty years, and had sought in vain, Lau-tsz' rejoined in a strain worthy of Diogenes, which Chwang-tsz' thus reports: "If tao could be offered to men, there is no one who would not willingly offer it to his prince; if it could be presented to men, everybody would like to present it to his parents; if it could be announced to men, each man would gladly announce it to his brothers; if it could be handed down to men, who would not wish to transmit it to his chil-

---

[1] Johnson, *Oriental Religions: China*, pp. 862–865. Pauthier, *La Chine*, pp. 110–120. Chalmers, *Speculations of the Old Philosopher*. Julien, *La Livre de la Voie et de la Vertu*, Paris, 1859; this last is the most scholarly work on this classic which has yet appeared. R. von Reinhold, *Der Weg zur Tugend*, Leipzig, 1870. Victor von Strauss, *Laò-Tsì's Taò Tè King, Aus dem Chinesischen ins Deutsche übersetzt*, Leipzig, 1870. See also Doolittle's *Vocabulary*, Vol. II., Part III. T. Watters, *Lao-Tzû, A Study in Chinese Philosophy*, Hongkong, 1870. Dr. Edkins in *Transactions of N. C. Br. R. A. S.* for 1855, Art. IV. F. H. Balfour, *Chuang Tsze's Divine Classic of Nan-hua*, Shanghai, 1881.

dren? Why then can you not obtain it? This is the reason. You are incapable of giving it an asylum in your heart."[1]

Such speculative teachings and waiting till the times were good were not adapted to entertain or benefit, and Confucius understood his countrymen and his own duty much better than Lau-tsz', in doing all he could by precept and practice to show them the excellence of what he believed to be right. The divergence of these two great men sprung from the differences in human minds in all climes and ages. The teachings of the *Tao-teh King*, however, are no more responsible for the subsequent organization and vagaries of the sect of Taoists down to the present time than the New Testament is for the legends of monkery or the absurdities of mystics. M. Bazin has endeavored to show that in China there has been, from early times, a progression from magic to mythology, from mythology to philosophy; and when philosophy began to crystallize into parties and take on an organized discipline of sects, during and after the Han dynasty down to the Tang, they took up the old native mythology against the newly arrived Buddhists, and imitated them by adopting Lau-tsz' as their god and his book as the foundation of their tenets. Previous to this period he was one among the philosophers of the Flowery Land; in time he has been taken as the founder of a system of religion. If the Gnostics had deified Lucretius and taken his poem as their text-book the cases would have been similar.

The earliest writers on Taoism are Chwang-tsz' and Lih-tsz' in the fourth century, who have been amplified by their followers. It is, as Wylie well observes, difficult to educe a well-ordered system out of the motley chaos of modern Taoism, where the pursuit of immortality, the conquest of the passions, a search after the philosopher's stone, the use of amulets, and the observance of fasts and sacrifices before gods, are mixed with the profound speculations of recluses upon abstruse questions of theology and philosophy. Some of the later writers of the Taoists discourse upon Reason in a way that would please Brownson and befit the pages of the *Dial*. The teachings of

[1] Legge, *Chinese Classics*, I. Proleg., p. 65. Julien, *Tao-te King*, Int., p. xxvii.

the ancient and modern transcendentalists are alike destitute of common sense and unproductive of good to their fellow-men. Dr. Medhurst quotes one of the Chinese Rationalists, who praises reason in a marvellous rhapsody:

> What is there superior to heaven, and from which heaven and earth sprang? Nay, what is there superior to space and which moves in space? The great Tao is the parent of space, and space is the parent of heaven and earth, and heaven and earth produced men and things. . . . The venerable prince (Reason) arose prior to the great original, standing at the commencement of the mighty wonderful, and floating in the ocean of deep obscurity. He is spontaneous and self-existing, produced before the beginning of emptiness, commencing prior to uncaused existences, pervading all heaven and earth, whose beginning and end no years can circumscribe.

The sectarians suppose their founder was merely an impersonation of this power, and that he whom they call "the venerable prince, the origin of primary matter, the root of heaven and earth, the occupier of infinite space, the commencement of all things, farther back than the utmost stretch of numbers can reach," created the universe. They notice three incarnations of him during the present epoch, one during the Shang dynasty, B.C. 1407, one at the time of Confucius, and a third about A.D. 623, when a man of Shansi reported having seen an old man who called himself Lau-kiun. Only the priests of this sect are regarded as its members; they live in temples and small communities with their families, cultivating the ground attached to the establishment, and thus perpetuate their body; many lead a wandering life, and derive a precarious livelihood from the sale of charms and medical nostrums. They shave the sides of the head and coil the rest of the hair in a tuft upon the crown, thrusting a pin through it, and are readily recognized by their slate-colored robes. They study astrology and profess to have dealings with spirits, their books containing a great variety of stories of priests who have done wonderful acts by their help. The *Pastimes of the Study*, already noticed, is one of these books, and Davis introduces a pleasant story of Chwang and his wife from another work.[1] They long endeavored to find a beverage

[1] *The Chinese*, Vol. II., pp. 113–128. Wylie, *Notes on Chinese Literature*, p. 173. Giles, *Strange Stories from a Chinese Studio*, 1880.

which would insure immortality, and during the Tang dynasty the Emperor and highest officers were carried away with their delusions. The title of 'Heavenly Doctors' was conferred on them, and a superb temple erected to Lau-tsz' in Chang-an, containing his statue; examinations were ordered in A.D. 674, to be held in the *Tao-teh King*, and some of the priests reached the highest honors in the State. Since that time they have degenerated, and are now looked upon as ignorant cheats and designing jugglers, who are quite as willing to use their magical powers to injure their enemies as to help those who seek their aid.

In some places the votaries of Tao, on the third day of the third month, go barefoot over ignited charcoal; and on the anniversary of the birthday of the High Emperor of the Sombre Heavens, "they assemble together before the temple of this imaginary being, and having made a great fire, about fifteen or twenty feet in diameter, go over it barefoot, preceded by the priests, and bearing the gods in their arms. The previous ceremonies consist in chanting prayers, ringing bells, sprinkling holy water, blowing horns, and brandishing swords in and over the flames in order to subdue the demon, after which they dart through the devouring element. They firmly assert that if they possess a sincere mind they will not be injured by the fire, but both priests and people get miserably burnt on these occasions.[1] Yet such is the delusion, and the idea the people entertain of the benefit of these services, that they willingly contribute large sums to provide the sacrifices and pay the performers."[2]

This ceremony is practised in Fuhkien and at Batavia, but is not very general, for the Chinese are the antipodes of the Hindus in their endurance and relish for sufferings and austerities in the hope of obtaining future happiness. The Rationalists worship a great variety of idols, among which *Yuh-hwang Shangtí* is one of the highest; their pantheon also includes genii, devils, inferior spirits, and numberless other objects of

---

[1] Compare Escayrac de Lauture, *Mémoire sur la Chine*, *Religion*, pp. 87, 102. Yule's *Marco Polo*, Vol. I., p. 286. Also Bode's *Bokhara*, p. 271, for a similar practice among the Moslems.

[2] Medhurst's *China, its State and Prospects*, p. 168.

worship. The *Siu Shin Kí*, or 'Records of Researches concerning the Gods,' contains an account of the birth of the deity whose anniversary is celebrated as above described.

There was once a childless emperor called Tsingtih ('Pure Virtue'), who summoned a large company of Tao priests to perform their rites in his behalf, and continued their worship half a year. The Empress Pao Yueh-kwang ('Gemmeous Moonlight') on a night dreamed that she saw the great and eminent Lau-kiun, together with a large number of superior deities, riding in parti-colored carriages with vast resplendent banners and shaded by bright variegated umbrellas. Here was the great founder Lau-kiun sitting in a dragon carriage, and holding in his arms a young infant, whose body was entirely covered with pores, from which unbounded splendors issued, illuminating the hall of the palace with every precious color. Banners and canopies preceded Lau-kiun as he came floating along. Then was the heart of the Empress elated with joy, and reverently kneeling before him, said: "At present our monarch has no male descendants, and I wishfully beseech you for this child that he may become the sovereign of our hearts and altars. Prostrate I look up to your merciful kindness, earnestly imploring thee to commiserate and grant my request." He at once answered, "It is my special desire to present the boy to you;" whereupon she thankfully received him, and immediately returned from the pursuit of the dream, and found herself advanced a year in pregnancy. When the birth took place a resplendent light poured forth from the child's body, which filled the whole country with brilliant glare. His entire countenance was super-eminently beautiful, so that none became weary in beholding him. When in childhood he possessed the clearest intelligence and compassion, and taking the possessions of the country and the funds of the treasury, he distributed them to the poor and afflicted, the widowers and widows, orphans and childless, the houseless and sick, halt, deaf, blind, and lame.

Not long after this the demise of his father took place, and he succeeded to the government; but reflecting on the instability of life, he resigned his throne and its cares to his ministers, and repaired to the hills of Puming, where he gave himself up to meditation, and being perfected in merit ascended to heaven to enjoy eternal life. He however descended to earth again eight hundred times, and became the companion of the common people to instruct them in his doctrines. After that he made eight hundred more journeys, engaging in medical practice and successfully curing the people; and then another similar series, in which he exercised universal benevolence in hades and earth, expounded all abstract doctrines, elucidated the spiritual literature, magnanimously promulged the renovating ethics, gave glory to the widely spread merits of the gods, assisted the nation, and saved the people. During another eight hundred descents he exhibited patient suffering; though men took his life, yet he parted with his flesh and blood. After this he became the first of the verified golden genii, and was denominated the pure and immaculate one, self-existing, of highest intelligence.[1]

---

[1] *Chinese Repository*, Vol. X., p. 306.

These figments are evidently a reproduction of the vagaries of Hindu theosophists, and not the teachings of Lau-tsz', but they amuse his followers, to whom his own abstruse utterances are quite unintelligible. The learned Confucianists laugh at their fables, but are still so much the prey of fears as to be often duped by them, and follow even when sure of being deceived.

The organization of the Rationalists is a regular hierarchy. It is under the supervision of the government, which holds the chiefs responsible for the general conduct and teachings of the members. The head resides at Lung-hu Shan in Kiangsí, where is a large establishment, resorted to by many votaries, and gathering in a large revenue from their offerings. When he dies a piece of iron is cast into a well near by, and when it floats the name of his successor is found to be written on it. By their extravagant professions and pretences the priests of this sect maintain their influence over a laity as ignorant and credulous as themselves; their power to delude will only wane with the progress of truth and Christianity. The full history of the authors, divinities, vagaries, and varied fortunes of the Rationalists has yet to be written; when this is done it will illustrate the question King David asked six centuries before Lau-tsz' lived: Who will show us any good? And when his followers are able to say, Lord, lift thou up the light of thy countenance upon us, they will know why he failed to find *La Voie et la Vertu.*[1]

The most popular religious sect is that of the followers of Fuh, Fo, Făt, Hwut, or Fuh-tu, as it is called in different dialects in imitation of the Hindu word *Bodh*, or Truth;[2] this name is sometimes confounded with that of Fuh-hí, one of the early rulers in Chinese history. Their tenets had been promulged in Central Asia for centuries, and were known in Western China, but during the long period of disorders previous to the Han dy-

---

[1] Douglas, *Taouism*, London, 1879: this is by far the most readable account of it. Edkins, *Journal of Shanghai Scien. and Lit. Soc.*, No. III., 1859, pp. 309–314. Mayers, *No. Ch. Br. Roy. As. Soc.*, Vol. VI., 1870, pp. 31–44. Bazin, *Recherches sur l'origine, l'histoire, et la constitution des ordres religieux dans l'empire Chinois*, Paris, 1856, p. 70. Johnson, *Oriental Religions: China*, Part V., pp. 859–904. Nevius, *China and the Chinese*, Chap. IX., New York, 1869. Dr. W. A. P. Martin, *The Chinese*, p. 97, etc.

[2] Hardy enumerates fifty-six modes of writing the name. *Manual*, p. 354.

nasty they found little favor. In A.D. 65 the Emperor Ming tí sent an embassy to India, in consequence—as the Chinese historians say—of having dreamed that he saw the image of a foreign god. The embassy returned in A.D. 67, bringing with it some teachers of the faith to Lohyang. One cannot tell whether it was sent at first at the suggestion of the Rationalists, to seek for a wise man said to have appeared there, or whether, according to others, it arose from the remarkable expression of Confucius, already quoted, "The people of the west have sages [or a sage]." It may have been that this mission was excited by some indistinct tidings of the advent and death of Christ, though there is no trace of such a rumor having reached the land of Sinim. At that epoch they might have heard of or met the Apostles in their first tours through the Roman Empire and Syria.

The incidents in the life of Buddha have been enveloped in so much legendary narrative by his followers in India that the Chinese have placed his birth much too early—B.C. 1027—while the true date is B.C. 623 according to the best authorities; but when his actual mortal life is regarded as one in a series of incarnations, no surprise need be felt at these discrepancies. He was the son of Suddhodana, king of Kapilavastu, a city and country near Nipal, subject to the king of Magadha, now a part of Bahar. His mother, Maya, or Maha-maya déva, died ten days after his birth, which, according to the legends, was accomplished without pain and accompanied by amazing wonders. His name was Siddharta, or the 'Establisher,' until he became a Buddha, *i.e.*, him by whom truth is known. The name Gotama, or Samona-Godam, is a patronymic better known in Siam than China, where another family or clan name, Sakya-muni, is more common. At the age of fifteen he was made heir-apparent; at seventeen he was married to Yashodara, a Brahmin maiden of the Sakya clan, and his son Rahula was born the next year. At twenty-five he determined to become a recluse, and left his prospects and his father's court for an abode in the forest beyond Kapilavastu, in solitary spots "trying various methods to attain mental satisfaction, but in vain." After five years of this ascetic life "he came to the perception of the true condition and wants of mankind," and began his ministry of forty-nine years. He was now a *Buddha*, which is described as "entering into a state of reverie, emitting a bright light and reflecting on the four modes of truth."

He began his preaching at Benares by discourses on the four truths, which was termed the revolving of the wheel of the law. He formed his first disciples into a community, to whom he gave their rules, and when the number increased to fifty-six he sent them over the land to give instruction in the *four miseries*, and carry out the system by which all his disciples were taught they could attain final happiness in nirvana. This system, which exists in full strength to this day, is founded on monastic vows for the individual, living in spiritual communities for the disciples, voluntary poverty and universal preaching. Sakya-muni infused such energy into his followers that in a few years India was covered with their communities; and he developed rules for instruction, employment, punishment, and promotion, which have served ever since. His own life, after his visit to his father in the year 586, when thirty-seven years old, was passed mostly in delivering the *sutras*, or laws, thirty-five discourses in all; these are reverenced by all Buddhists, and copies are held to have moral and hygienic effects on those who do so, and bring good luck to the family and the State. As Sakya-muni lived long enough to see and correct the dangers of his system, at his death, in the year 543, he was able to confer much of his authority on his two chief disciples, Ananda and Kashiapa, and thus hand down the organization to posterity.

The few facts here stated respecting this remarkable man are selected from Hardy's *Manual of Buddhism*, where is given a good digest of the Hindu writers respecting their sage. One thing impresses the reader of this work as a peculiarity of Sakya-muni's teaching, and standing in strong contrast to the Brahminic system that followed it: it is the manner in which he has weakened and almost destroyed the power of the unseen world and of spiritual beings as agencies of restraint upon the heart of man, and of assistance in seeking after good. By his system of good works and self-denials, his followers are brought into such close relationship with the whole creation of invisible beings, into whose presence and fellowship they can enter by their own efforts and mediation, that the moral sanctions of a Supreme Ruler and God over all are neutralized, and the sense of sin in the human conscience done away with. Its removal is put under the control of the soul, and the degree of happiness and power attained in the future world depends on the individual—so many prayers, alms, austerities, and obediences result in so much honor, power, and enjoyment in the coming infinite. The past infinite is also made part of the conscious present, and moral fate worked like physical attraction, innumerable causes producing retributive results for rewards or for punishments. In such a theology, salvation by faith is rendered impossible, and sacrifice for sin by way of atonement useless. In this feature the ancient worship of China and the teachings of Confucius rise superior to Buddhism, and leave the soul of man more open to moral law.

The personal life and character of Buddha presents a wonderful exhibition of virtues, and one is not disposed to weigh the testimony of their reality as drawn out in Hardy's *Manual* so carefully as to neutralize the effect; but the glowing picture of his good actions for his fellow-men given in the fervid lines of Arnold's *Light of Asia*, takes one quite into the realm of fable, engendering the wish that the Confucian Analects and their matter-of-fact details could have been imitated by the disciples of Siddharta. In regard to both these great teachers, Confucius and Buddha, however, one may gladly adopt Dean Stanley's remark, "that it is difficult for those who believe the permanent elements of the Jewish and Christian religion to be universal and divine, not to hail these corresponding forms of truth or goodness elsewhere, or to recognize that the mere appearance of such saintlike or godlike characters in other parts of the earth, if not preparing the way for a greater manifestation, illustrates that manifestation by showing how mighty has been the witness borne to it even under circumstances of such discouragement, and even with effects inadequate to their grandeur."

Buddhist priests are more numerous in China than the Tao sz', and they obtained influence more rapidly over the people. Their demonolatry allows the incorporation of the deities and spirits of other religions, and goes even further, in permitting the priests to worship the gods of other pantheons, so that they could adapt themselves to the popular superstitions of the countries they went to, and ingraft all the foreign divinities into their calendar they saw fit. The Emperors at various times have, moreover, shown great devotion to their ceremonies and doctrines, and have built costly temples, and supported more priests than ever Jezebel did; but the teachings of Confucius and Mencius were too well understood among the people to be uprooted or overridden. The complete separation of the State religion from the worship of the common people accounts for the remarkable freedom of belief on religious topics. Mohammedanism and Buddhism, Taoist ceremonies and Lama temples, are all tolerated in a certain way, but none of them have in the least interfered with the State religion and the autocracy of the monarch as the Son of Heaven. They are, as every one knows, all essentially idolatrous, and the coming struggle between these various manifestations of error and the revealed truths and requirements of the Bible has only begun to cast its shadow over the land. The more subtile conflict, too, between the preaching of the Cross and faith alone in its sacrifice for salvation, and reliance on good works, and priestly interference in every form, has not yet begun at all.

The power of Buddhism in China has been owing chiefly to its ability and offer to supply the lack of certainty in the popular notions respecting a future state, and the nature of the gods who govern man and creation. Confucius uttered no speculations about those unseen things, and ancestral worship confined itself to a belief in the presence of the loved ones, who were ready to accept the homage of their children. That longing of the soul to know something of the life beyond the grave was measurably supplied by the teachings of Sakya-muni and his disciples, and, as was the case with Confucius, was illustrated and enforced by the earnest, virtuous life of their founder. Though the sect did not receive the imperial sanction till about A.D. 65, these teachings must have gradually grown familiar during the previous age. The conflict of opinions which ere long arose between the definite practical maxims of the Confucian moralists, and the vague speculations, well-defined good works and hopeful though unproved promises of future well-being, set forth by the Hindu missionaries, has continued ever since. It is an instructive chapter in human experience, and affords another illustration of the impossibility of man's answering Job's great question, "But how shall man be just with God?" The early sages opened no outlook into the blank future, offered no hopes of life, love, happiness, or reunion of the friends gone before, and their disciples necessarily fell back into helpless fatalism. Buddhism said, Keep my ten commandments, live a life of celibacy and contemplation, pray, fast, and give alms, and according to your works you will become pure, and be rewarded in the serene nirvana to which all life tends. But the Buddhist priesthood had no system of schools to teach their peculiar tenets, and, as there is only one set of books taught in the common schools, the elevating precepts of the sages brought forth their proper fruit in the tender mind. Poverty, idleness, and vows made by parents in the day of adversity to dedicate a son or a daughter to the life-long service of Buddha, still supply that priesthood with most of its members. The majority are unable to understand their own theological literature, and far more is known about its peculiar tenets in Europe than among the mass of the Chinese. The Confucianist, in his pride of office and learning, may ridicule their mummeries, but in his hour of weakness, pain, and death he turns to them for help, for he has nowhere else to go. Both are ignorant of the life and light revealed in the gospels, and cry out, "Who will show us any good?"

If the mythology of Buddhism was trivial and jejune, as we judge it after comparing it with the beautiful imagery and art of Greece and Egypt, it brought in nothing that was licentious in its rites or cruel in its sacrifices. Coming from India, where worship of the gods involved the prostitution of women, the adoration of the lingam, and the sacrifice of human beings, Buddhism was remarkably free from all revolting features. If it had nothing to offer the Chinese higher in morals or more exalted or true in its conception of the universe or its Maker, it did not sanction impurity or murder, or elevate such atrocities above the reach of law by making them sacred to the gods.

This last outrage of the Prince of Darkness on the soul of man, so common in Western Asia, has never been known or accepted to any great extent in the Middle Kingdom.

But, while it is true that Buddhism gave them a system of precepts and observances that set before them just laws and high motives for right actions, and proportionate rewards for the good works it enjoined, it could not furnish the highest standards, sanctions, and inducements for holy living. On becoming a part of the people, the Buddhists soon entered into their religious life as acknowledged teachers. They adapted their own tenets to the national mythology, took its gods and gave it theirs, acted as mediators and interpreters between men and gods, the living and the dead, and shaped popular belief on all these mysteries. The well-organized hierarchy numbered its members by myriads, and yet history records no successful attempts on its part to usurp political power, or place the priest above the laws. This tendency was always checked by the literati, who really had in the classics a higher standard of ethical philosophy than the Buddhists, and would not be driven from their position by imperial orders, nor coaxed by specious arguments to yield their ground. Constant discussions on these points have served to keep alive a spirit of inquiry and rivalry, and preserve both from stagnation. Though Buddhism, in its vagaries and will-worship, gave them nothing better than husks, put hypocrisy in place of devotion, taught its own dogmas instead of truth, and left its devotees with no sense of sin against any law, yet its salutary influence on the national life of China cannot be denied.

The worship of ancestors and of good and bad spirits supposed to pervade and rule this world was perfectly compatible with the reception of Buddhism; thus its priests gradually became the high priests of the popular superstition, and have since remained so. They first ingratiated themselves by making their services useful in the indigenous ritual, and were afterwards looked upon as necessary for its execution. They propagated their doctrines principally by books and tracts, rather than by collecting schools or disciples in their temples; the quiet, indolent life they led, apparently absorbed in books and worship, and yet not altogether estranged from the world, likewise held out charms to some people. China is full of temples, in most of which Buddhist priests are found, but it is not quite the true inference to suppose that all the buildings were erected or the priests hired, because the people wish to do reverence to Buddha. It is impossible to state the proportion in which Buddhist temples are found; there are one hundred and twenty-four in Canton alone, containing idols of every name and attribute, in most of which they live and act as the assistants of whoever comes to worship.

The tenets of Buddhism require a renunciation of the world and the observance of austerities to overcome evil passions and fit its disciples for future happiness.[1] A vow of celibacy is taken, the priests dwelling together for mutual assistance in attaining perfection by worship of Buddha and calling upon his name. They shave the entire head as a token of purity, but not the whole body, as the ancient Egyptian priests did; they profess to eat no animal food, wear no skin or woollen garments, and get their living by begging, by the alms of worshippers, and the cultivation of the grounds of the temple. Much of their support is derived from the sale of incense sticks, gilt paper, and candles, and from fees for services at funerals. In the great monasteries, like the Hai-chwang sz' at Canton, the priests perform the whole service; but in other temples they contrive to gain a livelihood, and many of those better situated derive a large portion of their income from entertaining strangers of wealth and distinction. The sale of charms, the profits of theatrical exhibitions, the fees paid by neighborhoods for feeding hungry ghosts on All-Souls' day, and other incidental services performed for the living or the dead, also furnish resources. Their largest monasteries contain extensive libraries, and a portion of the fraternity are well acquainted with letters, though most of them are ignorant even of their own books. Their moral character, as a class, is on a par with their countrymen, and many of them are respectable, intelligent, and sober-minded persons, who seem

[1] Rémusat terms these tenets not inaptly "a mixture of pantheism, rationalism, and idolatry." In Hardy (*Manual*, p. 212) we find that the *Wá-ling sz'* to five hundred Lo-hán is to honor five hundred rahats. In India this number seems to stand for *all*.

to be sincerely desirous of making themselves better, if possible, by their religious observances.

The liturgy is in Sanscrit transliterated in Chinese characters, with which priest and people are alike unacquainted, nor are there now any bilingual glossaries or dictionaries to explain the words. Dr. Milne, speaking of the use of unknown tongues in liturgies, remarks: "There is something to be said in favor of those Christians who believe in the magic powers of foreign words, and who think a prayer either more acceptable to the Deity, or more suited to common edification, because the people do not generally understand it. They are not singular in this belief. Some of the Jews had the same opinion; the followers of Buddha and Mohammed all cherish the same sentiment. From the chair of his holiness at Rome, and eastward through all Asia to the mountain retreats of the Yama-bus in Japan, this opinion is espoused. The bloody Druids of ancient Europe, the gymnosophists of India, the Mohammedan hatib, the Buddhists of China, the talapoins of Siam, and the bonzes of Japan, the Romish clergy, the vartabeds of the Armenian church, and the priests of the Abyssinian and Greek communions, all entertain the notion that the mysteries of religion will be the more revered the less they are understood, and the devotions of the people (performed by proxy) the more welcome in heaven for being dressed in the garb of a foreign tongue. Thus the synagogue and mosque, the pagan temple and Christian church, seem all to agree in ascribing marvellous efficacy to the sounds of an unknown language; and, as they have Jews and Mohammedans, Abyssinians and pagans, on their side, those Christians who plead for the use of an unknown tongue in the services of religion have certainly the majority. That Scripture, reason, and common sense should happen to be on the other side is indeed a misfortune for them, but there is no help for it."[1]

The following canon for exterminating misfortune is extracted from the Buddhist liturgy, but it is as unintelligible to the Chinese as it will be to the English reader. While repeating it

---

[1] *Encyclopædia Britannica*, Art. BUDDHISM. *Indochinese Gleaner*, Vol. III., p. 141. *Chinese Repository*, Vol. IX., p. 640. Yule's *Marco Polo*, Vol. II., p 260, and passim.

the priest strikes upon a sounding board called *muh yü*, or 'wooden fish,' shaped somewhat like a skull, in order to mark the time of his monotonous chant:

Nan-mo O-mí-to po-yé, to-ta-kia to-yé, to-tí-yé-ta O-mí-lí-to po-kwăn, O-mí-lí-to, sieh-tan-po-kwăn, O-mí-lí-to, kwăn-kia-ian-tí O-mí-lí-to, kwăn-kia-lan-tí; kia-mí-ní kia-kia-na, chih-to-kia-lí po-po-ho.

Similar invocations, with the name *O-mí-to*[1] *Fuh* (Amida Buddha), are repeated thousands and myriads of times to attain perfection, affording a good illustration of the propriety of our Saviour's direction, "When ye pray, use not vain repetitions as the heathen do; for they think they shall be heard for their much speaking." A plate in one Buddhistic work contains five thousand and forty-eight open dots, arranged in the shape of a pear; each dot to be filled up when the name of Buddha has been repeated a hundred or a thousand times, and then the paper to be burned to pass into the other world to the credit of the devotee. The Buddhists have a system of merits and demerits, of which Sir John Davis remarks that "this method of *keeping a score* with heaven is as foolish and dangerous a system of morality as that of penances and indulgences in the Romish church." In this Buddhist scale of actions, to repair a road, make a bridge, or dig a well, ranks as ten; to cure a disease, or give enough ground for a grave, as thirty; to set on foot some useful scheme ranks still higher. On the other hand, to reprove another unjustly counts as three on the debtor side; to level a tomb, as fifty; to dig up a corpse, as one hundred; to cut off a man's male heirs, as two hundred, and so on. This notion of keeping accounts with heaven prevails among all classes of the Chinese, and the score is usually settled about the end of the year by fasting and doing charitable acts, such as making a piece of road, repairing a temple, or distributing food, to prove their repentance and benefit the world. Festival days are chosen by devout people to distribute alms to the poor, and on such occasions troops of beggars cluster about their doors, holding clap-dishes in their outstretched hands, while the donor stands

---

[1] *O-mi-to* is derived from *amirta*, or 'deathless.' Hardy, *Manual*, p. 355.

behind the half-opened door dealing out rice to the clamorous crowd which he dares not trust inside.

Considering how few restraints this religion imposes on the evil propensities of the human heart, and how easily it provides for the expiation of crimes, it is surprising that it has not had as great success among the Chinese as among the Tibetans, Birmese, and Siamese. The thorough education in the reasonable teachings of the classics, and the want of filial duty shown by celibates to their parents in leaving them to take care of themselves, have had their effects in maintaining the purer but heartless moralities of the Confucianists. The priests have always had the better judgment of the people against them, and being shut out by their profession from entering into society as companions or equals, and regarded as servants to be sent for when their services were wanted, they can neither get nor maintain that influence over their countrymen which would enable them to form a party or a powerful sect. One of the officers in the reign of Chingtih of the Ming dynasty, Wang Yang-ning, who addressed a remonstrance to his sovereign against sending an embassy to India to fetch thence Buddhist books and priests, relies for his chief argument on a comparison between the precepts and tendency of that faith and the higher doctrines of the classics, proving to his own satisfaction that the latter contained all the good there was in the former, without its nonsense and evil. The opposition to Buddhism on the part of the literati has been in fact a controversy between common sense (imperfectly enlightened indeed) and superstitious fear; the first inclines the person to look at the subject with reference to the principles and practical results of the system, as exhibited in the writings and lives of its followers, while, not having themselves anything to look forward to beyond the grave, they are still led to entertain some of its dogmas, because there may be something in them after all, and they have themselves nothing better. The result is, as Dr. Morrison has observed, "Buddhism in China is decried by the learned, laughed at by the profligate, yet followed by all."

The paraphrase and commentary on the seventh of Kanghí's maxims against strange religions present a singular anomaly;

for while the Emperor Yungching in the paraphrase decries Buddhism and Rationalism, and exalts the "orthodox doctrine," as he terms the teachings of the classics, he was himself a daily worshipper of Buddhist idols served by the lamas. He inveighs against selling poor children to the priests in no measured terms, and shows the inutility and folly of repeating the books or reciting the unintelligible charms written by the priests, where the person never thought of performing what was good. He speaks against the promiscuous assemblage of men and women at the temples, which leads to unseemly acts, and joins in with another of his own class, who remarked, in reference to a festival, that "most of the worshippers are women, who like these worshipping days, because it gives them an opportunity to see and be seen in their fine clothes; and most of the men who go there, go to amuse themselves and look at the women." "The sum of the whole is, these dissolute priests of Buddha are lazy; they will neither labor in the fields nor traffic in the markets, and being without food and clothing, they set to work and invent means of deceiving people." But though this upholder of the good old way well exhibits the follies of these idolatrous sects, he has nothing better to present his countrymen than "the two living divinities placed in the family," nothing to lead their thoughts beyond this world. His best advice and consolation for their troubled and wearied souls is, "Seek not for happiness beyond your own sphere; perform not an action beyond the bounds of reason; attend solely to your own duty; then you will receive the protection of the gods." [1]

The instructions of Sakya-muni himself have now become so interwoven in the additions, ritualism, and errors of his followers during the ages since he died, that he is charged with many things which he probably never taught. Unlike the founders of Islamism and Zoroastrianism, his personal influence and identity have been lost amid the fables which have enveloped his acts, and the diversities of worship and doctrine baffle all explanation. When the patriarchs and missionaries of the sect

---

[1] Milne's *Sacred Edict*, pp. 133–143. *Chinese Repository*, Vol. I., p. 207; Vol. II., p. 265.

began to increase in Central Asia and China after the embassy of Ming tí, they were obliged to defend, explain, and develop their tenets against the Chinese literati, and also commend them to the observance of the people. In the former region their conquests were complete, and the Mongols still hold to the Buddhist faith as completely as the European nations did to popery until the Reformation. The history of Chinese Buddhism down to the present day has not yet been fully examined, but much has been done within the past few years by Julien, Beal, Edkins, Watters, Neumann, Kœppen, and others to make it known. Translations from Chinese Buddhistic travellers and moralists have brought out many obscure opinions and unexpected events in this branch of religious thought and missionary work, during a period of the world's history hitherto quite unknown to Europeans.[1]

The mutual forbearance exhibited by the different sects in China is owing a good deal to apathy, for where there is nothing to reach there is little to stimulate to effort. The government tolerates no denomination suspected of interfering with its own influence, and as none of the sects have any State patronage, none of them hold any power to wield for persecution, and the people soon tire of petty annoyances and unavailing invectives. The Buddhist priesthood is perpetuated mostly by the children given by parents who have vowed to do so in their distress, and by others purchased for serving in large monasteries. Persons occasionally enter late in life, weary with the vexations of the world; Mr. Milne was acquainted with one who had two sons when he took the vows upon him, but gave himself no care as to what had become of them. The only education which most of the acolytes receive consists in memorizing the prayers in the liturgy and reading the canonical works. A few fraternities have tutors from whom they receive instruction.

Nunneries also exist, most of them under the patronage of

---

[1] See Alabaster's *Wheel of the Law*, pp. 228–241, for a well-digested Life of Buddha, from the Siamese. Beal's *Romantic History of Buddha*, and *Catena of Buddhist Scriptures*. Edkins, *Chinese Buddhism*, Chaps. I to VI., gives a good *résumé* of the early progress of the faith. G. Bühler, *Three New Edicts of Asoka*, London (Trübner).

the Holy Mother, Queen of Heaven. The priests advocate their establishment as a good means of working upon the feelings of the more susceptible part of society, to whom they themselves cannot get admittance. The succession among the "sisters" is kept up by purchase and by self-consecration; the feet of children bought young are not bandaged. The novice is not admitted to full orders till she is sixteen, though previous to this she adopts the garb of the sisterhood; the only difference consists in the front part of the head being shaved and the hair plaited in a queue, while nuns shave the whole. It is not easy to distinguish monks from nuns as they walk the streets, for both have natural feet, wear clumsy shoes, long stockings drawn over full trousers, short jackets, and bald pates. Like her sister in Romish countries, the Chinese nun, when her head has been shaved—the opposite of taking the veil, though the hair of both is sacrificed—is required to live a life of devotion and mortification, eat vegetables, care nothing for the world, and think only of her eternal canonization, keeping herself busy with the service of the temple. "Daily exercises are to be conducted by her; the furniture of the small sanctuary that forms a part of the convent must be looked after and kept clean and orderly; those women or men who come to worship at the altars, and seek guidance and comfort, must be cared for and assisted. When there is leisure the sick and the poor are to be visited; and all who have placed themselves under her special direction and spiritual instruction have a strong claim upon her regard. That she may live the life of seclusion and self-denial, she must vow perpetual virginity. The thought of marriage should never enter her head, and the society of men must be shunned. On her death she will be swallowed up in nihility!" In Fuhchau the nunneries were all summarily abolished nearly fifty years ago by an officer who learned the dissolute lives of their inmates. They have not since been reopened for their residence, though this official provided husbands for most of their nuns. Such a proceeding would have been impossible in almost any other country, and shows the functions of Chinese officials for the welfare of society.

Most of them are taught to read the classics as well as their own liturgies, and a few of the sisterhood are said to be well read in the lore of the country. Each nun has her own disciples among the laity, and cultivates and extends her acquaintances as much as she can, inasmuch as upon them her support principally depends. Each of her patrons, whether male or female, receives a new name from her, as she herself also did when her head was shaven. Contributors' names are written or engraved in conspicuous places in the building; casual fees or donations go to the general expenses. Each nun also receives ten cents when public masses are recited for those who have engaged them. Their moral character is uniformly represented as dissolute, but while despised for their profligacy they are dreaded for the supposed power they can exert by means of their connection with spirits. The number of nunneries in the department of Ningpo is stated to be thirty, and the sisterhood in them all to amount to upward of three hundred persons.[1]

The numerous points of similarity between the rites of the Buddhists and those of the Romish church early attracted attention. Abbé Huc enumerates many of them: "The cross, the mitre, the dalmatica, the cope which the lamas wear on their journeys, or when performing some ceremony out of the temple; the service with double choirs, the psalmody, the exorcisms, the censer suspended from five chains, which you can open or close at pleasure; the benedictions given by extending the right hand over the heads of the faithful; the rosary, ecclesiastical celibacy, spiritual retirement, worship of the saints; the fasts, processions, litanies, and holy water—all these are analogies between ourselves and the Buddhists." In addition to these, the institution of nuns, worship of relics, masses for the dead, and burning of candles and incense, with ringing of bells during worship, are prominent usages common to both. Their priests alike teach a purgatory from which the soul can be released by their prayers; they also conduct service in a dead language, and pretend to miracles. Lastly, the doctrine of the perpetual virginity of Maya, the mother of Sakya-muni, is an article taught

[1] *Chinese Repository*, Vol. XIII., pp. 93–98. Doolittle's *Social Life*, I., p. 253. Milne's *Life in China*, pp. 134–146. Gray's *China*, I., pp. 105, 131–135.

by the Mongol Buddhists, who also practise a form of infant baptism, in which the lama dips the child three times under the water as he pronounces its name and gives it a blessing.

These numerous and striking resemblances led the Roman Catholic missionaries to conclude that some of them had been derived from the papal or Syrian priests who entered China before Kublai khan. M. Huc brings forward his hypothesis that Tsong Kaba, the teacher of the Buddhist reformer in Mongolia about that time, had adopted them from some of the Europeans who taught him the Christian doctrines.[1] Others refer them to St. Thomas, but Prémare ascribes them to the devil, who had thus imitated holy mother church in order to scandalize and oppose its rites. But as Davis observes, "To those who admit that most of the Romish ceremonies are borrowed directly from paganism, there is less difficulty in accounting for the resemblance." On this point it will be impossible to reach certainty. There have probably been some things borrowed by each from the other at various ages, without either knowing from whence they came or what were their tendencies. Fergusson shows the great probability that the monastic system, celibacy, and ascetic good works were adopted in the Eastern church from India; but the want of reliable records on either side hitherto has left much to inference and conjecture.

The worship is similar and equally imposing. One eye-witness describes the scene he saw in a Buddhist temple: "There stood fourteen priests, seven on each side of the altar, erect, motionless, with clasped hands and downcast eyes, their shaven heads and flowing gray robes adding to their solemn appearance. The low and measured tones of the slowly moving chant they

[1] Huc's *Travels in Tartary*, II., p. 50. Hardy's *Manual*, p. 142. *Missionary Recorder*, III., pp. 142, 181. Eitel, *Lectures on Buddhism*, and *Handbook for the Student of Chinese Buddhism*, Hongkong, 1870. James Fergusson, *Hist. Indian and Eastern Architecture*, Introduction. Rémusat, *Mélanges Posthumes*, p. 44. Klaproth in *Journal Asiatique*, Tome VII. (1831), p. 190; also Tome XI. (IVe Sér.), 1848, p. 535. Prof. E. E. Salisbury in *Journal Am. Or. Soc.*, Vol. I., No. II., 1844. *Jour. of the R. As. Soc.*, passim. Yule's *Marco Polo*, Vol. I., p. 406; also *Cathay and the Way Thither*, II., p. 551. W. Wordsworth, *The Church of Thibet and the Historical Analogies of Buddhism and Christianity*, London, 1877.

were singing might have awakened solemn emotions, too, and called away the thoughts from worldly objects. Three priests kept time with the music, one beating an immense drum, another a large iron vessel, and a third a wooden ball. After chanting, they kneeled upon low stools and bowed before the colossal image of Buddha, at the same time striking their heads upon the ground. Then rising and facing each other, they began slowly chanting some sentences, and rapidly increasing the music and their utterance until both were at the climax of rapidity, they diminished in the same way until they had returned to the original measure. In the meantime, some of the number could not restrain their curiosity, and, even while chanting and counting their beads, left their places to ask for books. The whole service forcibly reminded me of scenes in Romish chapels; the shaven heads of the priests, their long robes, mock solemnity, frequent prostrations, chantings, beads—yea, and their idol, too, all suggested their types, or their antitypes, in the apostate church."[1]

The expulsion of Buddhism from India, after its triumphs in the reign of Asoka, King of Majadha, was so complete that it henceforth divided into the northern and southern schools, the first taking Sanscrit and the other Pali as its sacred language. In the course of time the divergencies became fixed, and thus, without any actual schism, the Buddhists of Ceylon and Ultra Ganges have come to differ from those of Central Asia and China. The form of Buddhism prevailing among the Mongols and Tibetans differs more in its state and power than in its doctrines; it is called Shamanism, or *Hwang kiao* ('Yellow Sect') in Chinese, from the color of the priestly robes—a *Shaman* being one who has overcome all his passions; it is a Hindu word. The Dalai-Lama at H'lassa, in the great monastery of the Putala, is the pope of the religion, the abode of deity.[2] Mongolia swarms with lamas, and the government at Peking aids in sup-

---

[1] *Foreign Missionary Chronicle*, Vol. XIV., p. 300.

[2] For his origin see Klaproth, *Mémoires sur l'Asie*, Tome II., p. 90. Also Ré musat, *Mélanges Posthumes*, pp. 1–64, for some observations on this faith in a review of De Guignes' *Huns*. E. Schlagintweit, *Buddhism in Tibet*, with folio atlas of plates, Leipzig, 1863. J. Summers in *The Phœnix*, I., 1870, pp. 9–11.

porting them in order to maintain its sway more easily over the tribes, though the Manchus have endeavored to supplant the civil authority of the Dalai-Lama and banchin-erdeni, by partially aiding and gradually subdividing their power. The ritual of the Shamans, in which the leading tenets taught by the lamas are exhibited, contains their ten principal precepts, or decalogue, viz.: 1. Do not kill. 2. Do not steal. 3. Do not commit fornication. 4. Speak not falsely. 5. Drink no wine nor eat flesh. 6. Look not on gay silks or necklaces, use no perfumed ointment, and paint not the body. 7. Neither sing nor dance, and do no sleight of hand tricks or gymnastic acts, and go not to see or hear them. 8. Sit not on a high large couch. 9. Do not eat out of time. 10. Do not grasp hold of living images, gold, silver, money, or any valuable thing.[1] The book contains also twenty-four sections of directions as to the conduct to be observed in various places, and before different persons. When using the sacred books the devotee must consider himself to be in the presence of Buddha, and he is forbidden to study books of divination, physiognomy, medicine, drawing lots, astronomy, geography, alchemy, charms, magic, or poetry. No wonder the priests are ignorant when almost every source of instruction is thus debarred them. The number of temples scattered over Mongolia and Tibet and the proportion of priests are far greater than in China, and the literature is not less enormous for bulk than are the contents of the volumes tedious and uninstructive.[2] A good device for a religion of formality to economize time and accommodate ignorance is adopted by the lamas, which is to write the prayers on a piece of paper and fasten them to a wheel carried round by the wind or twirled by the hand; chests are also set up in temples having prayers engraved on the outside

[1] *Annales de la Foi*, Tome IX., p. 460.

[2] "The dreariest literature, perhaps," says Professor Whitney, "that was ever painfully scored down, and patiently studied, and religiously preserved" (*Oriental and Linguistic Studies*, Second Series, p. 98). For foreign bibliographies of Buddhism the reader may be referred to *L'Histoire de Çakya-Mouni*, par Foucaux (ad fin.), and Otto Kistner, *Buddha and his Doctrines: A Bibliographical Essay*, London, 1869. See also Trübner's *Record* for 1869, p. 513.

in large letters, and the prayer is repeated as often as the wind or the hand revolves the wheel or chest.

The Buddhist temples present much uniformity in their arrangement, and some of the monastic establishments are among the finest buildings in China. No cave temples are known, but caves have been turned into temples in many places, and miserable places they are for worship. On entering a Buddhist temple, one sees four colossal statues of the Four Great Kings who are supposed to govern the continents on each side of Mount Sumeru and guard or reward the devotees who honor their Lord; they have black, blue, red, and white faces, and usually hold a sword, guitar, umbrella, and snake in their hands. Opposite the door is a shrine containing an image of Maitreya Buddha, or the Merciful One, a very fat, jolly personage, who is to have an avatar three thousand years hence; images of Kwantí, the God of War, and of Wei-to, a general under the Four Kings, clad in armor, are often seen near the shrine. Going behind a screen, the next great hall contains a high gilded image of Sakya-muni sitting on a lotus flower, with smaller statues of Ananda and Kashiapa on his sides; their shrine often has standing images of attendants. In this hall are other images or pictures of the Eighteen Arhans, deified missionaries who propagated their faith early in China. In the rear of these is represented some form of Kwanyin, the Goddess of Mercy, the popular idol of the sects. In large temples the five hundred Arhans, placed on as many seats, each having some distinguishing attribute, fill a large hall. Besides these occur the disciples of Buddha listening to his teachings, the horrible punishments of hell, and various honored deities, sages, or local gods, so that few temples are alike in all respects. In all of them are guest-chambers of various sizes, refectories, study rooms, and cloisters, according to the wants and resources of the fraternity.

The hold of the Buddhist priesthood upon the mass of Chinese consists far more in the position they occupy in relation to the rites performed in honor of the dead than in their tenets. This brings us to the consideration of the real religion of the Chinese, that in which more than anything else they trust, and to which they look for consolation and reward—the worship of deceased ancestors. The doctrines of Confucius and the ceremonial of the State religion, exhibit the speculative, intellectual dogmas of the educated literati and thinkers, who have early been taught the high ideal of the Princely Man set forth by their sages. The tenets of Lau-tsz' and the sorcery and incantations of his followers show the mystic and marvellous part of the popular belief. Buddhism takes hold of the common life of man, offers relief in times of distress, escape from a future hell at a cheap rate, and employment in a round of prayers, study, or work, ending in the nirvana. But the heart of the nation reposes more upon the rites offered at the family shrine to the two "living divinities" who preside in the hall of ancestors than to all the rest. This sort of family worship has been popular in other countries, but in no part of the world has it reached the consequence it has received in Eastern Asia; every natural feeling serves, indeed, to strengthen its simple cultus.

In the *Shí King*, whose existence, as we have already pointed out, is coeval with Samuel or earlier, are many references to this worship, and to certain rites connected with its royal observance. At some festivals the dead were personated by a younger relative, who was supposed to be taken possession of by their spirits, and thereby became their visible image. He was placed on high, and the sacrificer, on appearing in the temple, asked him to be seated at his ease, and urged him to eat, thereby to prepare himself to receive the homage given to the dead. When he had done so he gave the response in their name; the defied spirits returned to heaven, and their personator came down from his seat. In one ode the response of the ancestors through their personator is thus given:

> What said the message from your sires?
> "Vessels and gifts are clean;
> And all your friends, assisting you,
> Behave with reverent mien.
>
> "Most reverently you did your part,
> And reverent by your side
> Your son appeared. On you henceforth
> Shall ceaseless blessings bide.

"What shall the ceaseless blessings be?
That in your palace high,
For myriad years you dwell in peace,
Rich in posterity." [1]

The teachings of this ancient book intimate that the protecting favor of the departed could be lost by the vile, cruel, or unjust conduct of their descendants—thus connecting ancestral worship and reward with personal character. Another ode sums up this idea in the expression, "The mysterious empyrean is able to strengthen anything; do not disgrace your imperial ancestors, and it will save your posterity." Many stories occur in the native literature exemplifying this idea by actual experiences of blessing and cursing, all flowing from the observance or neglect of the required duties.

The great sages Confucius and Mencius, with the earlier rulers, King Wăn and Duke Chau, and their millions of followers, have all upheld these sentiments, and those teachings and examples are still as powerful as ever. In every household, a shrine, a tablet, an oratory, or a domestic temple, according to the position of the family, contains the simple legend of the two ancestral names written on a slip of paper or carved on a board. Incense is burned before it, daily or on the new and full moons; and in April the people everywhere gather at the family graves to sweep them, and worship the departed around a festive sacrifice. To the children it has all the pleasant associations of our Christmas or Thanksgiving; and all the elder members of the family who can do so come together around the tomb or in the ancestral hall at the annual rite. Parents and children meet and bow before the tablet, and in their simple cheer contract no associations with temples or idols, monasteries or priests, processions, or flags and music. It is the family, and a stranger intermeddleth not with it; he has his own tablet to look to, and can get no good by worshipping before that bearing the names of another family.

As the children grow up the worship of the ancestors, whom they never saw, is exchanged for that of nearer ones who bore and nurtured, clothed, taught, and cheered them in helpless

[1] Legge's *She King*, p. 309, London, 1876.

childhood and hopeful youth, and the whole is thus rendered more personal, vivid, and endearing. There is nothing revolting or cruel connected with it, but everything is orderly, kind, and simple, calculated to strengthen the family relationship, cement the affection between brothers and sisters, and uphold habits of filial reverence and obedience. Though the strongest motive for this worship arises out of the belief that success in worldly affairs depends on the support given to parental spirits in hades, who will resent continued neglect by withholding their blessing, yet, in the course of ages, it has influenced Chinese character, in promoting industry and cultivating habits of domestic care and thrift, beyond all estimation.

It has, moreover, done much to preserve that feature of the government which grows out of the oversight of heaven as manifested to the people through their Emperor, the Son of Heaven, whom they regard as its vicegerent. The parental authority is also itself honored by that peculiar position of the monarch, and the child grows up with the habit of yielding to its injunctions, for to him the family tablet is a reality, the abode of a personal Being who exerts an influence over him that cannot be evaded, and is far more to him as an individual than any of the popular gods. Those gods are to be feared and their wrath deprecated, but the "illustrious ones who have completed their probation" represent love, care, and interest to the worshippers if they do not fail in their duties.

Another indirect result has been to define and elevate the position of the wife and mother. All the laws which could be framed for the protection of women would lack their force if she were not honored in the household. As there can be only one "illustrious consort" (*hien pi*) named on the tablet, there is of course only one wife (*tsi*) acknowledged in the family. There are concubines (*tsieh*), whose legal rights are defined and secured, and who form an integral part of the family; but they are not admitted into the ancestral hall, and their children are reckoned with the others as Dan and Asher were in Jacob's household. Polygamous families in China form a small proportion of the whole; and this acknowledged parity of the mother with the father, in the most sacred position she can be placed, has done much to maintain the purity and right influence of woman amid all the degradations, pollutions, and moral weakness of heathenism. It is one of the most powerful supports of good order. It may even be confidently stated that woman's legal, social, and domestic position is as high in China as it has ever been outside of Christian culture, and as safe as it can be without the restraints of Christianity. Another benefit to the people, that of early marriages, derives much of its prevalence and obligation from the fear that, if neglected, there may be no heirs left to carry on the worship at the family tomb.

The three leading results here noticed, viz., the prevention of a priestly caste, the confirmation of parental authority in its own sphere, and the elevation of the woman and wife to a parity with the man and husband, do much to explain the perpetuity of Chinese institutions. The fact that filial piety in this system has overpassed the limit set by God in his Word, and that deceased parents are worshipped as gods by their children, is both true and sad. That the worship rendered to their ancestors by the Chinese is idolatrous cannot be doubted; and it forms one of the subtlest phases of idolatry—essentially evil with the guise of goodness—ever established among men.

The prevalence of infanticide and the indifference with which the crime is regarded may seem to militate against this view of Chinese social character, and throw discredit on the degree of respect and reverence paid to parents; for how, some will ask, can a man thus worship and venerate parents who once imbrued their hands in his sister's blood? Such anomalies may be found in the distorted minds and depraved hearts educated under the superstitions of heathenism in every country, and the Chinese are no exception. It is exceedingly difficult, however, to ascertain the extent of infanticide in China, and all the reasons which prompt to the horrid act. Investigations have been made about Canton, and evidence obtained to show that it is comparatively rare, and strongly discountenanced by public opinion; though by no means unknown, nor punished by law when done. Similar investigations at Amoy have disclosed a fearful extent of murders of this nature; yet while the latter are believed, the assertions of the former are regarded as evasions of the truth from the fear of being reproached for it or a sense of shame. The whole nation has been branded as systematic murderers of their children from the practice of the inhabitants of a portion of two provinces, who are generally regarded by their countrymen as among the most violent and poorest fraction of the whole. Sir John Barrow heard that the carts went about the streets of Peking daily to pick up dead and dying infants thrown out by their unnatural parents, but he does not mention ever having seen a single corpse in all his walks or rides about the capital. It has now been ascertained that this cart contains so many dead bodies of both sexes, that the inference by Dr. Dudgeon that not one in a hundred was killed seems to be sustained. The bodies of children are not as often seen in the lanes and creeks of Canton as those of adults, and the former are as likely to have died natural deaths as the latter.

In Fuhkien province, especially in the departments of Tsiuen-chau and Changchau, infanticide prevails to a greater extent than in any other part of the Empire yet examined. Mr. Abeel extended his inquiries to forty different towns and villages lying in the first, and found that the percentage was between seventy and eighty down to ten, giving an average of about forty per cent. of all girls born in those places as being murdered. In Changchau, out of seventeen towns, the proportion lies between one-fourth and three-tenths in some places, occasionally rising to one-third, and in others sinking to one-fifth, making an average of one-fourth put to death. In other departments of the province the practice is confessed, but the proportion thought by intelligent natives to be less, since there is less poverty and fewer people than formerly. The examination was conducted in as fair a manner as possible, and persons of all classes were questioned as to the number of children they had killed themselves, or knew had been killed by their relatives or neighbors. One of eight brothers told him that only three girls were left among all their children, sixteen having been killed. On one occasion he visited a small village on Amoy Island, called Bo-au, where the whole population turned out to see him and Dr. Cumming, the latter of whom had recently cut out a large tumor from a fellow villager. He says:

From the number of women in the crowd which turned out to greet us, we were pretty well persuaded that they were under as little restraint as the men from indulging their curiosity ; and upon inquiry, found it to be so. We were conducted to a small temple, when I had the opportunity of conversing with many who came around us. On a second visit, while addressing them, one man held up a child, and publicly acknowledged that he had killed five of the helpless beings, having preserved but two. I thought he was jesting, but as no surprise or dissent was expressed by his neighbors, and as there was an air of simplicity and regret in the individual, there was no reason to doubt its truth. After repeating his confession he added with affecting simplicity, "It was before I heard you speak on this subject; I did not know it was wrong; I would not do so now." Wishing to obtain the testimony of the assembled villagers, I put the question publicly, "What number of female infants in this village are destroyed at birth ?" The reply was, "More than one-half." As there was no discussion among them, which is not the case when they differ in opinion, and as we were fully convinced from our own observation of the numerical inequality of the sexes, the proportion of deaths they gave did not strike us as extravagant.

The reasons assigned for committing the unnatural deed are various. Poverty is the leading cause ; the alternative being, as the parents think, a life of infamy or slavery, since if they cannot rear their offspring themselves they must sell them. The fact of the great numbers of men who emigrate to the Archipelago from the coast districts has no doubt also had its effect in inducing parents to destroy daughters for whom they had little expectation of finding husbands if they did rear them. Many who are able to support their daughters prefer to destroy them rather than incur the expenses of their marriage, but the investigation showed that the crime was rather less among the educated than the ignorant, and that they had done something to dissuade their poor neighbors from putting their girls to death. In the adjoining departments of Chauchau and Kiaying in Kwangtung, the people admit the practice, and, as their circumstances are similar, it is probable that it is not much less than around Amoy Dr. Dudgeon, of Peking, has had very favorable opportunities for prosecuting inquiries in that region, and has shown that the stories formerly credited are wrong, and that most of the children thus disposed of are born of nuns. Inquiries instituted at Hankow by Dr. F. P. Smith, of the hospital, showed a wide prevalence of the crime among the poor and rural population, for which he ascribes several reasons; the proportion of the sexes is ten men to seven women.

While one of the worst features of the crime is the little degree of detestation everywhere expressed at it, yet the actual proportion is an important inquiry, and this, taking the whole nation, has been much exaggerated, chiefly from applying such facts and estimates as the preceding to the whole country. The governor of Canton once issued a dissuasive exhortation on this subject to the people, telling them that if they destroyed all their daughters they would soon have no mothers. Until investigations have been made elsewhere, it is not fair to charge all the Chinese with the atrocities of a small portion, nor to disbelieve the affirmations of the inhabitants of Canton, Ningpo, and Shanghai, and elsewhere, that they do not usually put their daughters to death, until we have overwhelming testimony that they deny and conceal what they are ashamed to confess.[1]

Comparing their lamentable practice with those of other and European nations, we find, according to Hume, that "the exposure of new-born infants was an allowed practice in almost all the States of Greece and Rome; even among the polite and civilized Athenians, the abandoning of one's child to hunger or wild beasts was regarded without blame or censure. This practice was very common; and it is not spoken of by any author of those times with the horror it deserves, or scarcely even with disapprobation. Plutarch, the humane, good-natured Plutarch, mentions it as a merit in Attalus, king of Pergamus, that he murdered, or, if you will, exposed all his own children, in order to leave his crown to the son of his brother Eumenes. It was Solon, the most celebrated of the sages of Greece, that gave parents permission by law to kill their children." Aristotle

[1] *Chinese Repository*, Vol. XVII., p. 11, for a native essay against it; Vol. XVI., p. 513; Vol. XII., pp. 540–548; Vol. XI., p. 508; Vol. VII., p. 54. Bishop Smith's *China*, p. 443. *Report of Peking Hospital*, 1865. Dr. F. P. Smith's *Five Annual Reports of Hankow Hospital*, 1870, pp. 45–52. Doolittle, *Social Life*, II., pp. 203–209. *Notes and Queries on C. and J.*, Vol. III., pp. 156, 172. *L'infanticide et l'Oeuvre de la Ste.-Enfance en Chine*, par Père G. Palatre, Changhai. *Autographie de la Mission Catholique à l'orphelinat de Tousè-wè*, 1878. M. E. Martin, *Étude Médico-Légale sur l'Infanticide et l'Avortement dans l'Empire Chinois*, Paris, 1872.

thought it should be encouraged by the magistrates, and Plato maintained the same inhuman doctrine. It was complained of as a great singularity that the laws of Thebes forbade the practice. In all the provinces, and especially in Italy, the crime was daily perpetrated.[1]

The ceremonies attendant upon the decease of a person vary in different parts of the country, though they are not necessarily elaborate or expensive anywhere, and all the important ones can be performed by the poorest mourner. The inhabitants of Fuhkien put a piece of silver in the mouth of the dying person, and carefully cover his nose and ears. Scarcely is he dead when they make a hole in the roof to facilitate the exit of the spirits proceeding from his body, of which they imagine each person possesses seven animal senses which die with him, and three souls, one of which enters elysium and receives judgment, another abides with the tablet, and a third dwells in the tomb. In some places, as a man approaches his last hour, the relatives come into the room to array him in his best garments and carry him into the main hall to breathe his life away while dressed in the costume with which he is to appear in Hades. The popular ideas regarding their fate vary so much that it is difficult to describe the national faith in this respect; transmigration is more or less believed in, but the detail of the changes the good or evil spirit undergoes before it is absorbed in Buddha varies almost according to the fancy of the worshipper. Those who are sent to hell pass through every form of suffering inflicted upon them by hideous monsters, and are at last released to wander about as houseless demons to torment mankind, or vex themselves in the bodies of animals and reptiles.

When the priests come the corpse is laid out upon the floor in the principal room, and a tablet set up by its side; a table is near, on which are placed meats, lamps, and incense. While the priests are reciting prayers to deliver the soul from purgatory and hell, they occasionally call on all present to weep and lament, and on these occasions the females of the household are particularly clamorous in their grief, alternately uttering the

[1] McIlvaine, *Evidences of Christianity*, p. 291.

most doleful accents, and then tittering with some of the new-comers. Papers having figures on them and Peter's pence in the form of paper money are burned; white lanterns, instead of the common red ones, and a slip of paper containing the name, titles, age, etc., of the dead are hung at the door; a mat porch is put up for the musicians and the priests.[1] The soul, having crossed the bridge leading out of hell with the aid of the priests, gets a letter of recommendation from them to be admitted into the western heavens.

Previous to burial a lucky place for interment, if the family have moved away from its paternal sepulchre, must be found. The body is coffined soon after death, arrayed in the most splendid habiliments the family can afford; a fan is put in one hand and a prayer on a piece of paper in the other. The form of a Chinese coffin resembles the trunk of a tree; the boards are three or four inches thick and rounded on top (from whence a coffin is called "longevity boards"), making a very substantial case. When the corpse is put in it is laid in a bed of lime or cotton, or covered with quicklime, and the edges of the lid are closed with mortar in the groove so that no smell escapes; the coffin is varnished if it is to remain in the house before burial. The Chinese often expend large sums in the purchase and preparation of a coffin during their lifetime; the cheapest are from five to ten dollars, and upward to five hundred and even two thousand dollars, according to the materials and ornamenting.

Bodies are sometimes kept in or about the house for many years and incense burned morning and evening. They are placed either on trestles near the doorway and protected by a covering in the principal hall, or in the ancestral chamber, where they remain until the fortunes of the family improve so as to enable them to bury the remains, or a lucky place is found, or until opportunity and means allow the survivors to lay them in their patrimonial sepulchre.

The lineal relatives of the deceased are informed of his death,

[1] Ball says that money is put into the mouth of the dead by rich people to buy favor and passage into heaven; others affirm that the money is to make the spirit ready of speech. The phrase "no silver to hit the mouth" has reference to this custom.

and as many as can do so repair to the house to condole with and assist the family. The eldest son or the nearest descendant repairs to an adjoining river or well with a bowl in his hand, and accompanied by two relatives, to "buy water" with money which he carries and throws into it. Upon the way to the well it is customary to carry lanterns—even at noon—and to make a great wailing: with the water thus obtained he washes the corpse before it is dressed. After the body is laid in the coffin and before interment the sons of the deceased among the poor are frequently sent around to the relatives and friends of the family to solicit subscriptions to buy a grave, hire mourners, or provide a suitable sacrifice, and it is considered a good act to assist in such cases; perhaps fear of the ill-will of the displeased spirit prompts to the charity. The coffin is sometimes seized or attached by creditors to compel the relatives to collect a sum to release it, and instances of filial sons are mentioned who have sold themselves into temporary or perpetual slavery in order to raise money to bury their parents. In other cases a defaulting tenant will retain a coffin in the house to forestall an ejectment for the back rent. On the day of burial an offering of cooked provisions is laid out near the coffin. The chief mourners, clothed in coarse white sackcloth, then approach and kneel before it, knocking their heads upon the ground and going through with the full kotow; two persons dressed in mourning hand them incense-sticks, which are placed in jars. After the male mourners have made their parting prostrations the females perform the same ceremonies, and then such friends and relations as are present; during these observances a band of music plays. The funeral procession is formed of all these persons—the band, the tablets, priests, etc. In Peking, where religious processions are prohibited, great display is made in funerals according to the means and rank of the deceased. The coffin is borne on an unwieldy bier carried by sixty-four men or more and covered by a richly embroidered catafalque, attended by musicians, mourners, priests, etc. Sometimes the carts are covered with white cloth and the mules wear white harness.

Burial-places are selected by geomancers, and their location has important results on the prosperity of the living. The supposed connection between these two things has influenced the science, religion, and customs of the Chinese from very early days, and under the name of *fung-shui*, or 'wind and water' rules, still contains most of their science and explains most of their superstitions. As true science extends this travestie of natural philosophy will fade away and form a subject of fascination among the people as it now does a source of terror. Every strange event is interpreted by *fung-shui*, and its professors employ the doctrines of Buddhists and Taoists to enforce their dicta, as they do their little knowledge of astronomy, medicine, and natural science to explain them. The whole has gradually grown into a system of geomancy, involving, however, their cosmogony, natural philosophy, spiritualism, and biology so far as they have these sciences. It was in the twelfth century that it became systematized, and its influence has spread ever since. Were it only a picturesque kaleidoscope of facts and fancies it would be a harmless pastime; but it now enters into every act of life, since the human soul and body, whether in this world or the next, are regarded as constantly influenced by their actions, their relatives, and their locations. Thus the choice of a burial-place is supposed to affect the past, present, and future, and the *fung-shui siensăng*, or 'wind and water doctors,' know therein how to benefit their customers and themselves.

Regarding all nature as a living organism and each person surrounded by invisible beings, the Chinese try to propitiate these essences through their departed relatives. They consider them as restrained by their animal nature to the tomb where their bodies lie, while the spiritual nature seeks to hover about its old scenes and children. If a tomb is placed so that the spirit dwelling therein is comfortable, the inference is that the deceased will grant those who supply its wants all that the spirit world can grant. A tomb located where no star on high or dragon below, no breath of nature or malign configuration of hills, can disturb the repose of the dead, must therefore be lucky, and worth great effort to secure.

The principles of geomancy depend much on two supposed currents running through the earth, known as the dragon and the tiger; a propitious site has these on its left and right. A skilful observer can detect and describe them, with the help of the compass, direction of the watercourses, shapes of the male and female ground, and their proportions, color of the soil, and the permutations of the elements. The common people know nothing of the basis on which this conclusion is founded, but give their money as their faith in the priest or charlatan increases.[1]

At the south, uncultivated hills are selected because they are dry and the white ants will not attack the coffin; and a hill-side in view of water, a copse, or a ravine near a hill-top, are all lucky spots. At the north, where ants are unknown, the dead are buried in fields; but nowhere collected in graveyards in cities or temples. The form of the grave is sometimes a simple tumulus with a tombstone at the head; in the southern provinces oftener in the shape of the Greek letter Ω, or that of a huge arm-chair. The back of the supposed chair is the place for the tombstone, while the body is interred in the seat, the sides of which are built around with masonry and approach each other in front. A tomb is occasionally built of stone in a substantial manner, and carved pillars are placed at the corners, the whole often costing thousands of dollars. The case of one necromancer is recorded, who, after having selected a grave for a family, was attacked with ophthalmia, and in revenge for their giving him poisonous food which he supposed had caused the malady, hired men to remove a large mass of rock near the grave, whereby its efficacy was completely spoiled. The position is thought to be the better if it command a good view. Some of the graves occupy many hundred square feet, the corners being defined by low stones bearing two characters, importing whose *chih*, or 'house,' it is. The shapes of graves vary more at the north; some are conical mounds planted with shrubs or flowers, others made of mason-work shaped like little houses, others mere square tombs or earthly tumuli; not a few coffins are simply left upon the ground. It is seldom the Chinese hew graves out of

[1] Compare Dr. Edkins in the *Chinese Recorder*, Vol. IV., 1871-72. *Feng-shui; or the Rudiments of Natural Science in China*, by Ernest J. Eitel, London, 1873. The *Cornhill Magazine* for March, 1874. *Notes and Queries on C. and J.*, Vol. II., p. 69.

the rock or dig large vaults; their care is to make a showy grave, and at the same time a convenient one for performing the prescribed rites. The mausolea of emperors and grandees occupy vast enclosures laid out as parks and adorned with ornamental buildings to which lead avenues of stone guardians.[1] The tomb of Yungloh (A.D. 1403–1425) is reached through a *dromos* of gigantic statues nearly a mile long—two pairs each of lions, unicorns, elephants, camels, and horses, one erect, the other couchant, and six pairs of civil and military officers; each figure is a monolith. The origin of this custom can be traced back nearly to the tenth century, but was probably known in the Tang dynasty. Officials are allowed to erect a few statues to become their guardians.[2]

When the day of interment arrives, which is usually the nearest lucky day to the third seventh after death, the friends assemble at the house. A band of musicians accompanies the procession, in which is also carried the ancestral tablet of the deceased in a separate sedan, accompanied sometimes by a sacrifice and the red tablets of the offices held by the family. The mourners are dressed entirely in white, or wear a white fillet around the head; the sons of the deceased must put on the expression and habiliments of woe, and the eldest one is at times supported along the street to the grave in all the eloquence and attitude of grief, although it may have been years since his father went to "wander among the genii." The women and children of the family follow, and at intervals cry and wail. A man goes ahead and scatters paper money to purchase the good-will of such stray spirits as are prowling about. Different figures and banners are carried according to the means and rank of the family, which, with the friends and crowd attracted by the show, sometimes swell the train to a great length. The grave is deep, and lime is freely mixed with the earth thrown

---

[1] In the Yih chin the custodian reported in the *Peking Gazette* of January 3, 1871, that there were 92,690 trees, mostly fir, pine, elm, etc. The people in charge of such grounds are used to girdling the timber, in order afterward to get the dead trees as firewood for themselves.

[2] Mayers in *North China Br. Royal Asiatic Society Journal*, No. XII., 1878. Doolittle, *Social Life*, II., p. 337.

in; a body is never put into an old grave while anything remains of the former occupant; crackers are fired, libations poured out, prayers recited, and finally paper models of houses, clothes, horses, money, and everything he can possibly want in the land of shadows (which Davis calls a *wise economy*) are burned. The tablet and sacrifice are then carried back; the family feast on the latter or distribute it among the poor around the door, while the former is placed in the ancestral hall. The married daughters of the dead are not considered part of the family, and wear no mourning; nor are they invited to their father's funeral.

The period of mourning for a father is nominally three years, but actually reduced to twenty-seven months; the persons required to observe this are enumerated in the Code, and Sections CLXXIX.–CLXXXI. contain the penalties for concealing the death of a parent, or misrepresenting it, and of omitting the proper formalities. Burning the corpse, or casting it into the water, unfeelingly exposing it in the house longer than a year, and making the funeral ceremony and feast an occasion of merrymaking and indecorous meeting of males and females, are also prohibited. For thirty days after the demise the nearest kindred must not shave their heads nor change their dress, but rather exhibit a slovenly, slipshod appearance, as if grief had taken away both appetite and decorum. In the southern districts half-mourning is blue, usually exhibited in a pair of blue shoes and a blue silken cord woven in the queue, instead of a red one; grass shoes neatly made are now and then worn. In the northern provinces white is the only mourning color seen. The visiting cards also indicate that the time of mourning has not passed. The expenses incurred by the rich are great, and the priests receive large sums for masses, ten thousand dollars being often spent. In the north still greater expenses are incurred in buying a piece of land for a burial plot and its glebe. Here they erect a lodge, where the keeper of the grave lives, cultivating the land and keeping the tomb in order.[1]

When the Empress dies officers put on mourning, take the

[1] *Chinese Repository*, Vol. IV., p. 352; Vol. II., p. 499.

buttons and fringes from their caps, stamp their seals with blue ink, and go through a prescribed set of ceremonies; they must not shave their heads for a hundred days, nor the people for a month. Full details of the ceremonies ordered on the occasion of the decease of the Empress, or "interior assistant, who for thirteen years had held the situation of earth to heaven," were published in 1833, in both Manchu and Chinese. When the Emperor dies all his subjects let their hair grow for a hundred days, marriages are postponed, theatres and sports disallowed, and a ceremonial gloom and dishabille pervades the Empire. On the morning after the death of the Emperor Tungchí, January 12, 1875, the streets of Peking presented a surprising contrast to their usual gaiety in the removal of everything red. In early times human beings were immolated at the obsequies of rulers, and voluntary deaths of their attendants and women are occasionally mentioned. De Guignes says that the Emperor Shunchí ordered thirty persons to be immolated at the funeral of his consort; but Kanghí, his son, forbade four women from sacrificing themselves on the death of his Empress.[1]

The hall of ancestors is found in the house of almost every member of the family, but always in that of the eldest son. In rich families it is a separate building; in others a room set apart for the purpose, and in many a mere shelf or shrine. The tablet, or *shin chu*, is a board about twelve inches long and three wide, placed upright in a block. The inscriptions on two are like the following: "The tablet of Hwang Yung-fuh (late Ching-teh), the head of the family, who finished his probation with honor during the Imperial Tsing dynasty, reaching a sub-magistracy." His wife's reads: "The tablet of Madame, originally of the noble family Chin, who would have received the title of lady, and in the Imperial Tsing dynasty became his illustrious consort." A receptacle is often cut in the back, containing pieces of paper bearing the names of the higher ancestors, or other members of the family. Incense and papers are daily burned before them, accompanied by a bow or act of homage, forming

[1] *N. C. Br. R. As. Soc. Journal*, No. II., 1865, pp. 173 ff. De Guignes' *Voyages*, Tome II., p. 304. *Mémoires conc. les Chinois*, Tome VI., pp. 346 ff *Chinese and Japanese Repository* for May, 1864.

in fact a sort of family prayer. The tablets are ranged in chronological order, those of the same generation being placed in a line. When the hall is large, and the family rich, no pains are spared to adorn it with banners and insignia of wealth and rank, and on festival days it serves as a convenient place for friends to meet, or for any extraordinary family occasion. A person residing near Macao spent about one thousand five hun-

Ancestral Hall and Mode of Worshipping the Tablets.

dred dollars in the erection of a hall, and on the dedication day the female members of his family assembled with his sons and descendants to assist in the ceremonies. The portraits of the deceased are also suspended in the hall, but effigies or images are not now made.

In the wood-cut adjoining, the tablets are arranged on the

same level, and the sacrifice laid on the altar before them; the character *shao*, 'longevity,' is drawn on the wall behind. During the ceremonies fire-crackers are let off and papers burned; after it the feast is spread.

In the first part of April, one hundred and six days after the winter solstice, during the term called *tsing-ming*, a general worship of ancestors is observed. In Kwangtung this is commonly called *pai shan*, or 'worshipping on the hills,' but the general term is *siu făn tí*, or 'sweeping the tombs.' The whole population, men, women, and children, repair to their family tombs, carrying a tray containing the sacrifice, libations for offering, and candles, paper, and incense for burning, and there go through a variety of ceremonies and prayers. The grave is at this season repaired and swept, and at the close of the service three pieces of turf are placed at the back and front of the grave to retain long strips of red and white paper; this indicates that the accustomed rites have been performed, and these fugitive testimonials remain fluttering in the wind long enough to announce it to all the friends as well as enemies of the family; for when a grave has been neglected three years it is sometimes dug over and the land resold. The enormous amount of litigation connected with sepulchral boundaries, transfer of grave glebes or sale of the ancient plats, injury, robbery, and repairs of tombs, all indicate the high importance of this kind of property.

"Such are the harmless, if not meritorious, forms of respect for the dead," says Davis, "which the Jesuits wisely tolerated in their converts, knowing the consequences of outraging their most cherished prejudices; but the crowds of ignorant monks who flocked to the breach which those scientific and able men had opened, jealous, perhaps, of their success, brought this as a charge against them until the point became one of serious controversy and reference to the Pope. His Holiness espoused the bigoted and unwiser part, which led to the expulsion of the monks of all varieties." And elsewhere he says the worship paid to ancestors is "not exactly idolatrous, for they sacrifice to the invisible spirit and not to any representation of it in the figure of an idol." This distinction is much the same as that alleged by the Greek church, which disallows images but permits gold and silver pictures having the face and hands only painted, for Sir John Davis, himself being a Protestant, probably admits that worship paid to any other object besides the true God is idolatry; and that the Chinese do truly worship their ancestors is evident from a prayer, such as the following, offered at the tombs:

Taukwang, 12th year, 3d moon, 1st day. I, Lin Kwang, the second son of the third generation, presume to come before the grave of my ancestor, Lin Kung. Revolving years have brought again the season of spring. Cherishing sentiments of veneration, I look up and sweep your tomb. Prostrate I pray that you will come and be present, and that you will grant to your posterity that they may be prosperous and illustrious. At this season of genial showers and gentle breezes I desire to recompense the root of my existence and exert myself sincerely. Always grant your safe protection. My trust is in your divine spirit. Reverently I present the five-fold sacrifice of a pig, a fowl, a duck, a goose, and a fish; also an offering of five plates of fruit, with libations of spirituous liquors, earnestly entreating that you will come and view them. With the most attentive respect this annunciation is presented on high.

It is not easy to perceive, perhaps, why the Pope and the Dominicans were so much opposed to the worship of ancestral penates among the Chinese when they performed much the same services themselves before the images of Mary, Joseph, Cecilia, Ignatius, and hundreds of other deified mortals; but it is somewhat surprising that a Protestant should describe this worship as consisting of "harmless, if not meritorious, forms of respect for the dead." Mr. Fortune, too, thinks "a considerable portion of this worship springs from a higher and purer source than a mere matter of form, and that when the Chinese periodically visit the tombs of their fathers to worship and pay respect to their memory, they indulge in the pleasing reflection that when they themselves are no more their graves will not be neglected or forgotten." This feeling does actuate them, but there can be no dispute, one would think, about its idolatrous character. The Chinese who have embraced the doctrines of the New Testament, and who may be supposed qualified to judge of their own acts and feelings, regard the rites as superstitious and sinful. It is a form of worship, indeed, which presents fewer revolting features than most systems of false religion—consisting merely of pouring out libations and burning paper and candles at the grave, and then a family meeting at a social feast, with a few simple prostrations and petitions. No bacchanalian companies of men and women run riot over the hills, as in the Eleusinian mysteries, nor are obscene rites practised in the house; all is pleasant, decorous, and harmonious. The junior members of the family come from a distance, sometimes two or three hundred miles, to observe it, and the family meeting on this occasion is looked forward to by all with much the same feelings that Christmas is in Old England or Thanksgiving in New England. Brothers and sisters, cousins and other relatives join in the worship and feast, and it is this pleasant reunion of dear ones, perhaps the most favorable to the cementing of family affection to be found in heathen society, which constitutes much of its power and will present such an obstacle to the reception of the Gospel and removal of the "two divinities" from the house.

The funeral ceremonies here described are performed by sons for their parents, especially for the father; but there are few or no ceremonies and little expense for infants, unmarried children, concubines, or slaves. These are coffined and buried without parade in the family sepulchre; the poor sometimes tie them up in mats and boards and lay them in the fields to shock the eyes and noses of all who pass. The municipal authorities of Canton issued orders to the people in 1832 to bring such bodies as had no place of burial to the potter's field, where they would be interred at public expense; societies, moreover, exist in all the large cities whose object is to bury poor people. In some parts the body is wrapped in cloth or coffined and laid in graveyards on the surface of the ground. When one dies far away from home the coffin is often lodged in *larariums*, or public depositories maintained by societies, where they remain many years. Few acts during the war of 1841 irritated the people about Canton against the English more than forcing open the coffins found in these mausolea and mutilating the corpses. One building contained hundreds of coffins from which, when opened, a pungent aromatic smell was perceptible, while the features of the corpses presented a dried appearance. One traveller tells a story of his guide, when he was conducting him over the hills in Hupeh, ordering him to conceal his blue eyes by putting on green spectacles as they were approaching some houses, and describes his surprise at finding them all filled with coffins arranged in an orderly manner. Graves are not enclosed; cattle pasture among them and paths lead over and through them.

Tombstones are usually made of granite and their inscriptions soon become defaced. Epitaphs are short, giving the name of the dynasty, his place of birth, number of his generation in the family, and his temple name. Laudatory expressions are rare, and quotations from the classics or stanzas of poetry to convey a sentiment entirely unknown. The corpses of officers who die at their stations are carried to their paternal tombs, sometimes at public expense. The Emperor, in some instances, orders the funeral rites of distinguished statesmen to be defrayed. This was done during the war with England in the cases of Commissioner Yukien and General Hailing, who burned himself at Chinkiang fu.[1]

Besides these funeral rites and religious ceremonies to their departed ancestors the Chinese have an almost infinite variety of superstitious practices, most of which are of a deprecatory character, growing out of their belief in demons and genii who trouble or help people. It may be said that most of their religious acts performed in temples are intended to avert misfortune rather than supplicate blessings. In order to ward off malignant influences amulets are worn and charms hung up, such as money-swords made of coins of different monarchs strung together in the form of a dagger; leaves of the sweet-flag (*Acorus*) and Artemisia tied in a bundle, or a sprig of peach-blossoms; the first is placed near beds, the latter over the lintel, to drive away demons. A man also collects a cash or two from each of his friends and gets a lock made which he hangs to his son's neck in order to lock him to life and make the subscribers surety for

[1] *Chinese Repository*, Vol. XVIII., pp. 363–384. Doolittle, *Social Life*, II., pp. 45–48. M. T. Yates, *Ancestral Worship*, *Missionary Conference* (of 1867), p. 367. Johnson, *Oriental Religions: China*, pp. 693–708. Gray's *China*, I., pp. 320–328. *China Review*, Vol. IV., p. 296. P. D. de Thiersant, *La Piété Filiale en Chine*, Paris, 1877. E. Faber in the *Chinese Recorder*, Vol. IX., pp. 329, 401.

his safety; adult females also wear a neck lock for the same purpose. Charms are common. One bears the inscription, "May you get the three *manys* and the nine *likes;*" another, "To obtain long eyebrowed longevity." The three *manys* are many years of happiness and life and many sons. Old brass mirrors to cure mad people are hung up by the rich in their halls, and figures or representations of the unicorn, of gourds,

Buddhist Priests.

tigers' claws, or the eight diagrams, are worn to insure good fortune or ward off sickness, fire, or fright. Stones or pieces of metal with short sentences cut upon them are almost always found suspended or tied about the persons of children and women, which are supposed to have great efficacy in preventing evil. The rich pay large sums for rare objects to promote this end.

In addition to their employment in the worship and burial of the dead and cultivation of glebe lands (some of which are very extensive[1]), priests resort to many expedients to increase their incomes, few of which have the improvement of their countrymen as a ruling motive. Some go around the streets collecting printed or written paper in baskets, to burn them lest the venerable names of Confucius or Buddha be defiled; others obtain a few pennies by writing inscriptions and charms on doors; and many in rural places get a good living off the lands owned by their temples. The priests of both sects are under the control of officials recognized by and amenable to the authorities, so that the vicious and unprincipled among them are soon restrained.

The Buddhists issue small books, called *Girdle Classics*, containing prayers addressed to the deity under whose protection the person has placed himself. Spells are made in great variety, some of them to be worn or pasted up in the house, while others are written on leaves, paper, or cloth, and burned, and their ashes thrown into a liquid for the patient or child to drink. These spells are sold by Rationalists, and consist of characters, like *fuh* ('happiness') or *shao* ('longevity'), fancifully combined. The god of doors, of the North Pole, Pwanku, the heavenly astronomer, the god of thunder and lightning, or typhoons, the god of medicine, demigods and genii of almost every name and power, are all invoked, and some of them by all persons. In shops the word *shin* is put up in a shrine and incense placed before it, all objects of fear and worship being included under this general term. The threshold is peculiarly sacred, and incense-sticks are lighted morning and evening at its side.[2]

The Chinese dread wandering and hungry ghosts of wicked men, and the priests are hired to celebrate a mass called *ta tsiao*, to appease these disturbers of human happiness, which, in its general purport, corresponds to All Souls' Day, and from its splendor and the general interest taken in its success is very popular. The streets at Canton are covered with awnings, and

---

[1] *Lettres Edifiantes*, Tome III., p. 33.

[2] *Lettres Edifiantes*, Tome IV., p. 310—where other ceremonies of the Taoists to ward off pestilence, are described.

festoons of cheap silk, of brilliant colors, are hung across and along the streets. Chandeliers of glass are suspended at short intervals, alternating with small trays, on which paper figures in various attitudes, intended to illustrate some well-known scene in history, amuse the spectators. At night the glare of a thousand lamps shining through myriads of lustres lights up the whole scene in a gorgeous manner. The priests erect a staging somewhere in the vicinity, for the rehearsal of prayers to *Yen wang* (Yama or Pluto), and display tables covered with eatables for the hungry ghosts to feed on. Their acolytes mark the time when the half-starved ghosts, who have no children or friends to care for them, rush in and shoulder the viands, which they carry off for their year's supply. Bands of music chime in from time to time, to refresh these hungry spirits with the dulcet tones they once heard ; for the Chinese, judging their gods by themselves, provide what is pleasing to those who pay for the entertainment, as well as to those who are supposed to be benefited by it. After the services are performed the crowd carry off what is left, but when this is permitted the priests sometimes cheat them with merely a cover of food on the tops of the baskets, the bottoms being filled with shavings.

Another festival in August is connected with this, called *shau i*, or 'burning clothes,' at which pieces of paper folded in the form of garments are burned for the use of the suffering ghosts, with a large quantity of what may be properly called *fiat money*, paper ingots which become valuable chiefly when they are burned. Paper houses with proper furniture, and puppets to represent household servants, are likewise made. Medhurst adds that "writings are drawn up and signed in the presence of witnesses to certify the conveyance of the property, stipulating that on its arrival in hades it shall be duly made over to the individuals specified in the bond ; the houses, servants, clothes, money and all are then burned with the bond, the worshippers feeling confident that their friends obtain the benefit of what they have sent them." Thus "they make a covenant with the grave, and with hell they are at agreement." This festival, like all others, is attended with feasting and music. In order still further to provide for childless ghosts, their ancestral tablets are collected in temples and placed together in a room set apart for the purpose, called *wu sz' tan*, or 'orbate temple,' and a man hired to attend and burn incense before them. The sensations which arise on going into a room of this sort, and seeing one or two hundred small wooden tablets standing in regular array, and knowing that each one, or each pair, is like the silent tombstone of an extinct family, are such as no hall full of staring idols can ever inspire. The tablets look old, discolored, and broken, covered with dust and black with smoke, so that the gilded characters are obscured, and one cannot behold them long in their silence and forgetfulness without almost feeling as if spirits still hovered around them. All these ghosts are supposed to be propitiated by the sacrifices on All Souls' Day.

The patronage given to idolatry and superstition is constant and general among all classes, and thousands of persons get their livelihood by shrewdly availing themselves of the fears of their countrymen. The peepul, *pu-tí* (*Ficus religiosa*) at the south and the Sophora at the north, with perhaps other aged trees, are worshipped for long life.[1] Special efforts are made from time to time to build or repair a temple or pagoda, in order to insure or recall prosperity to a place, and large sums are subscribed by the devout. A case occurred in 1843, which illustrates this spirit. One of the English officers brought an image of *Wa-kwang*, the god of fire, from Chinkiang fu, which he presented as a curiosity to a lady in Macao. It remained in her house several months, and on the breaking up of the establishment, previous to a return to India, it was exposed for sale at auction with the furniture. A large crowd collected, and the attention of the Chinese was attracted to this image, which they examined carefully to see if it had the genuine marks of its ordination upon it; for no image is supposed to be properly an object of worship until the spirit has been inaugurated into it by the prescribed ceremonies. Having satisfied themselves, the idol was purchased for thirty dollars by two or three zealous

---

[1] Compare C. F. Koeppen, *Die Religion des Buddha*, Berlin, 1857, who describes the peepul (Bôdhi) tree—the "symbol of the spread and growth of the Buddhist church"—in India. E. Bernouf, *Introduction à l'histoire du Buddhisme Indien*, Paris, 1844. *Notes and Queries on C. and J.*, Vol. III., p. 100.

persons, and carried off in triumph to a shop and respectfully installed in a room cleared for the purpose. A public meeting was shortly after called, and resolutions passed to improve the propitious opportunity to obtain and preserve the protecting power of so potent a deity, by erecting a pavilion where he would have a respectable lodgment and receive due worship. A subscription was thereupon started, some of its advocates putting down fifty and others thirty dollars, until about one thousand two hundred dollars were raised, with which a small lot was purchased on the island west of Macao, and a pavilion or temple erected where *Wa-kwang* was enshrined with pompous parade amid theatrical exhibitions, and a man hired to keep him and his domicile in good order.

No people are more enslaved by fear of the unknown than the Chinese, and none resort more frequently to sortilege to ascertain whether an enterprise will be successful or a proposed remedy avail to cure. This desire actuates all classes, and thousands and myriads of persons take advantage of it to their own profit. The tables of fortune-tellers and the shops of geomancers are met at street corners, and a strong inducement to repair to the temples is to cast lots as to the success of the prayers offered. One way of divining is to hold a bamboo root cut in halves, resembling in size and color a common potato, and let it drop as the petition is put up. Sometimes the worshipper drops it many times, in order to see if a majority of trials will not be favorable, and when disappointed the first time not unfrequently tries again, if mayhap he can force the gods to be more propitious. The devotee may determine himself what position of the blocks shall be deemed auspicious, but usually one face up and one down is regarded as promising. The countenances of worshippers as they leave the shrines, some beaming with hope and resolution to succeed, and others, notwithstanding their repeated knockings and divinings, going away with vexation and gloom written on their faces at the obduracy of the gods and sadness of their prospects, offer a study not less melancholy than instructive. "Such is the weakness of mortals: they dread, even after mature reflection, to undertake a project, and then enter blindly upon it at a chance after consulting chance itself as blind."

The fortune-tellers also consult fate by means of bamboo slips bearing certain characters, as the sixty-four diagrams, titles of poetical responses, or lists of names, etc. The applicant comes up to the table and states his desire; he wishes to know whether it will be fair weather, which of a dozen doctors shall be selected to cure his child, what sex an unborn infant will be, where his stolen property is, or any other matter. Selecting a slip, the diviner dissects the character into its component parts, or in some other way, and writes the parts upon a board lying before him, joining to them the time, the names of the person, five planets, colors, viscera, and other heterogeneous things, and from them all, putting on a most cabalistic, sapient look, educes a sentence which contains the required answer.

Consulting a Fortune-teller.

The man receives it as confidently as if he had entered the sybil's cave and heard her voice, pays his fee, and goes away. Others, less shrewd, refer to books in which the required answer is contained in a sort of equivocal delphian distich. The Chinese method of sortilege is not far different from that practised by the ancient Romans. "The lots preserved at Preneste were slips of oak with ancient characters engraved on them. They were shaken up together by a boy, and one of them was drawn for the person who consulted the oracle. They remind us of the Runic staves. Similar divining lots were found in other places."[1]

[1] Niebuhr, *History of Rome*, Vol. I., p. 246. See, further, Doolittle's *Social Life*, Vol. II., Chap. IV. Gray's *China*, Chap. XII. Prof. Douglas, *China*, Chap. XV.

The purchase of a building lot, and especially the selection of a grave, involve much expense, sortilege, and inquiry. When a succession of misfortunes comes upon a family, they will sometimes disinter all their relatives and bury them in a new place to remove the ill luck. Before a house is built a written prayer is tied to a pole stuck in the ground, petitioning for good luck, that no evil spirits may arise from beneath; when the ridge-pole is laid another prayer is pasted on and charms hung to it to insure the building against fire; and lastly, when the house is done it is dedicated to some patron, and petitions offered for its safety. Prayers are sometimes offered according to forms, at others the suppliant himself speaks. Two middle-aged women, attended by a maid-servant, were once found opposite Canton in the fields among the graves. They had placed a small paper shrine upon a tomb near the pathway, and one of them was kneeling before it, her lips moving in prayer; there was nothing in the shrine, but over it was written the most common petition known in China, "Ask and ye shall receive."

Answers are looked for in various ways. A man was once met at dusk repairing a lonely grave before which candles were burning and plates of rice and cups of spirits arranged. He knelt, and knocking his head began to repeat some words in a half audible manner, when he was asked if the spirits of his ancestors heard his supplications. At the instant a slight puff of air blew the candles, when he replied, "Yes; see, they have come; don't interrupt me." Contingent vows are often made, and useful acts performed in case the answer be favorable. A sick man in Macao once made a vow that if he recovered he would repave a bad piece of road—which he actually performed, aided a little by his neighbors; but it was deemed eminently unlucky that a toper who was somewhat flustered, passing soon after, should, fall into the public well. Persons sometimes insult the gods, spit at them or whip them, or even break the ancestral tablets, in their vexation at having been deluded into foolish deeds or misled by divination. Legends are told of the vengeance which has followed such impiety, as well as the rewards attending a different course; and the *Kanying*

Pien, or Book of Rewards and Punishments,' has strengthened these sentiments by its stories of the results of human acts.

The worship of street divinities is not altogether municipal; some of the shrines in Canton are resorted to so much by women as to obstruct the path. The unsocial character of heathenism is observable at such places and in temples; however great the crowd may be, each one worships by himself as much as if no one else were present. Altars are erected in fields, on which a smooth stone is placed, where offerings are presented and libations poured out to secure a good crop. Few farmers omit all worship in the spring to the gods of the land and grain; and some go further and present a thanksgiving after harvest. Temples are open night and day, and in towns are the resort of crowds of idle fellows. Worshippers go on with their devotions amid all the hubbub, strike the drum and bell to arouse the god, burn paper prayers, and knock their heads upon the ground to implore his blessing, and then retire.

The Chinese collectively spend enormous sums in their idolatry, though they are more economical of time and money than the Hindus. Rich families give much for the services of priests, papers, candles, etc., at the interment of their friends, but when a large sacrifice is provided none goes to the priests, who are prohibited meat. The aggregate outlay to the whole people is very large, made up of repairs of temples, purchasing idols, petty costs, such as incense-sticks, candles, paper, etc., charms and larger sacrifices prepared from time to time. The sum cannot of course be ascertained, but if the daily expenditure of each person be estimated at one-third of a cent, or four cash, the total will exceed four hundred millions of dollars per annum, and this estimate is more likely to be under than over the mark, owing to the universality and constancy of the daily service.

This brief sketch of Chinese religious character will be incomplete without some notice of the benevolent institutions found among them. Good acts are required as proofs of sincerity; the classics teach benevolence, and the religious books of the Buddhists inculcate compassion to the poor and relief of the sick. Private alms of rice or clothes are frequently given, and the modes of collecting the poor-tax are very direct and economical, bringing the householders into some intercourse with the beggars in their neighborhoods, but offering no rewards to tramps and idlers. A retreat for poor aged and infirm or blind people is situated near the east side of Canton, the expenses of which are stated at about seven thousand dollars, but the number of persons relieved is not mentioned. The peculation and bad faith of the managers vitiate many of these institutions, and indispose the charitable to patronize them. Lazarettos are established in all large towns in Southern China, where a large entrance fee will secure a comfortable living for these outcasts to the end of their days; the prevalence of the disease leads everybody to aid the measures taken to restrict its ravages. A full account of the report issued by the directors of a long-established foundling hospital in Shanghai is given in the *Chinese Repository* (Vol. XIV.), and shows the methodical character of the people, and that no priests are joined in its management. In the report full credit is given to the benefactors, and an appeal made for funds to carry it on, as it is nearly out of supplies. Various modes of raising money are proposed, and arguments are brought forward to induce people to give, all in the same manner as is common with charitable institutions in western lands, as its closing paragraph shows:

> If, for the extension of kindness to our fellow creatures, and to those poor and destitute who have no father and mother, all the good and benevolent would daily give one cash ($\frac{1}{1100}$ of a dollar), it would be sufficient for the maintenance of the foundlings one day. Let no one consider a small good unmeritorious, nor a small subscription as of no avail. Either you may induce others to subscribe by the vernal breeze from your mouth, or you may nourish the blade of benevolence in the field of happiness, or cherish the already sprouting bud. Thus by taking advantage of opportunities as they present themselves, and using your endeavors to accomplish your object, you may immeasurably benefit and extend the institution.

The deaths are reported as being nearly one-half of the admissions, and the number of inmates about one hundred and thirty in all. The details of the receipts and expenditures are given at the end of the report in a business-like manner. The annual disbursement was about one thousand five hundred and fifty dollars, and the receipts from all sources more than that, so that a balance of five thousand dollars is reported on hand, four-fifths of which was derived from interest on subscriptions invested and on wares from pawnbrokers.

Similar establishments are found in all large towns, some of them partly supported by the government. That in Canton was founded in 1698, and contains accommodations for three hundred children, whose annual support was reckoned at three thousand five hundred dollars in 1833, at which date the money was filched from foreigners by a tax on their ships. These hospitals seem to be of modern origin, less than two centuries old, and may have been imitated from or suggested by the Roman Catholics. Candida, a distinguished convert about 1710, did much to establish them and show the excellence of the religion she professed. Mr. Milne, who visited one at Ningpo, says, after entering the court: "A number of coarse-looking women were peeping through the lattice at us, with squallababies at their breasts and squalid boys and girls at their heels; these women are the nurses, and these children are the foundlings, each woman having two or three to look after. But I have rarely beheld such a collection of filthy, unwashen, ragged brats. There are at present between sixty and seventy children, the boys on one side, the girls on the other. Boys remain here till the age of fourteen, when they are hired out or adopted; girls stay till sixteen, when they are betrothed as wives or taken as concubines or servants. It is supported by the rental of lands and houses, and by an annual tax of thirty-six stone or *shih* (about five hundred pounds) of rice from each district in the department."

In large towns other voluntary societies are found, having for their object the relief of suffering, which ought to be mentioned, as the Chinese have not been fairly credited with what they do in this line. Humane societies for restoring life to persons rescued from the water, and providing coffins if they are dead, exist along the riverine towns. Associations to give decent interment to the poor in a public potter's field are found in large cities, where gratuitous vaccination is often given to all who apply. Soup-kitchens are constantly opened as cold weather comes on, and houses prepared for vagrants and outcasts who have been suddenly reduced. Societies for the relief of indigent and virtuous widows are of long standing, and a kind of savings bank for the purpose of aiding a man to get married or to bury his parent exists among the people.[1]

Charity is a virtue which thrives poorly in the selfish soil of heathenism, but even badly managed establishments like these are praiseworthy, and promise something better when higher teachings shall have been engrafted into the public mind. The government is obliged to expend large sums almost every year for relieving the necessities of the starving and the distressed, and strong calls are made on the rich to give to these objects. During the great famine in 1877–78 in the north-eastern provinces, the common habits of industry, thrift, and order were united with these practices of voluntary benevolence among the people, and aided greatly in enabling those who distributed food and money to reach the greatest number possible with the means. The sufferers had already learned that violence and robbery would only increase their miseries and hasten their end.

The general condition of religion among the Chinese is effete; and the stately formalities of imperial worship, the doctrines of Confucius, the ceremonies of the Buddhists, the sorceries of the Rationalists, alike fail to comfort and instruct. But the fear of evil spirits and the worship of ancestors, the two beliefs which hold all ranks and abilities in their thrall, are still strong; and the principal sway the two sects exert is owing to the connection of their priests with the ceremonies of burial. Each has exerted its greatest possible power over the people, but all have failed to impart present happiness or assure future joy to their votaries. Confucianism is cold and unsatisfactory to the affectionate, the anguished, or the inquiring mind, and the transcendentalism of Rationalism or the vagaries of Bud-

[1] *Chinese Repository*, Vol. XIV., pp. 177–195. Lockhart, *Medical Missionary in China*, Chapter II., London, 1861.

dhism are a little worse. All classes are the prey of unfounded fears and superstitions, and dwell in a mist of ignorance and error which the light of true religion and knowledge alone can dissipate.

Besides the two leading idolatrous sects, there are also many combinations existing among the people, partly religious and partly political, one of which, the *Pih-lien kiao*, or the Triad Society, has already been mentioned in Chapter VIII. The *Wăn kiang*, or 'Incense-burning sect,' is also denounced in the *Sacred Commands*, but has not been mentioned in late times. The Triad Society is comparatively peaceful throughout China Proper in overt acts, the members of the auxiliary societies contenting themselves with keeping alive the spirit of resistance to the Manchus, getting new members, and countenancing one another in their opposition ; but in Siam, Singapore, Malacca, and the Archipelago, it has become a powerful body, and great cruelties are committed on those who refuse to join. The members are admitted with formalities bearing strong resemblance to those of the Freemasons, and the professed objects of the society are the same. The novice swears before an idol to maintain inviolate secrecy, and stands under naked swords while taking the oath, which is then read to him ; he afterward cuts off a cock's head, the usual form of swearing among all Chinese, intimating that a like fate awaits him if treacherous. There are countersigns known among the members, consisting of grips and motions of the fingers. Such is the secrecy of their operations in China, however, that very little is known of their numbers, internal organization, or character ; the dislike of their machinations is the best security against their ultimate success. Local delusions, caused by some sharp-witted fellow, now and then arise in one part and another of the country, but they are speedily put down or dissipate of themselves. There has transpired not an item of news concerning any of these seditious organizations since the suppression of the Tai-ping rebellion in 1868. None of them are allowed to erect temples or make a public exhibition or procession, and exhortations are from time to time issued by the magistrates against them ; while the penalties annexed to the statute against all illegal associations give the rulers great power to crush whatever they may deem suspicious or treasonable.[1]

The introduction of Islamism into China was so gradual that it is not easy to state the date or manner. The trade between China and ports lying on the Arabian Sea early attracted its adherents (called *Hwui-hwui kiao*) to the Middle Kingdom, and as long ago as the Tang dynasty its missionaries came to the seaports, especially of Canton and Hangchau. They likewise formed a large portion of the caravans which went to and fro through Central Asia, and seem to have been received without resistance, if not with favor, until they grew by natural increase to be a large and an integral part of the population. Mosques were built, schools taught, pilgrimages made, books printed, and converts allowed to exercise their rites without serious hindrance almost from the first. The two great features of the faith—the existence of one only true God and the wickedness of idolatry—have not been kept hidden; but, though promulgated, they have not been accepted outside of the sect and have not made the least impression upon the State religion.

The reasons for this are not far to seek. The rigid rule that the Koran must not be translated has kept this book out of reach of the literati, and the faithful could not even appeal to it in support of their belief, for not one in thousands knew how to read it. The Chinese naturally neither could nor would learn Arabic, and there was no sword hanging over them, as was the case in Persia, to force them into Moslem ranks. The simplicity of the State religion and ancestral worship gave very little handle to iconoclasts to declaim against polytheism and idolatry. The prohibition of pork to all true believers seemed a senseless injunction among a frugal people which depended largely on swine for meat and had never felt any the worse, bodily or mentally, from its use. The inhibition of wine, moreover, was needless among so temperate a race as the Chinese. Those who liked to keep Fridays or other days as fasts, practise circumcision as a symbol of faith, and worship in a temple with-

[1] Compare the *Chinese Repository*, Vol. XVIII., p. 281.

out images, could do so if they chose; but they must obey the laws of the land and honor the Emperor as good subjects. They have done so, and, generally speaking, have never been molested on account of their beliefs. Their chief strength lies in the northern part. The recent struggle in the north-western provinces, which cost so many lives, began almost wholly at the instigation of Turk or Tartar sectaries, and was a simple trial of strength as to who should rule. While cities and towns in Kansuh occupied by them were destroyed (in 1860–73), the two hundred thousand Moslems in Peking remained perfectly quiet and were unmolested by the authorities.

Some hold office, and pass through the examinations to obtain it, most of them being military men. In their mosques they exhibit a tablet with the customary ascription of reverence to the Emperor, but place the Prophet's name behind. They have no images or other tablets in the mosques, but suspend scrolls referring to the tenets of the faith. The Plain Pagoda in Canton was built during the Tang dynasty and called 'Remember-the-Holy Temple;' it is one hundred and sixty-five cubits high; it was built by foreigners, who used to go to the top during the fifth and sixth moons at dawn and pray to a golden weathercock there, crying out in a loud voice. These notices are taken from the native *Topography*, where also is reference to the tomb of a maternal uncle of Mohammed buried north of the city. The mosques throughout China are similar in their arrangement and resemble temples in many respects, the large arches and inscriptions in Arabic on the walls forming the chief peculiarities. Arabic is studied under great difficulties by the mollahs, and few of the faithful can read or speak it, contenting themselves with observing its ritual relating to circumcision, abstinence from pork, and idolatry. So far as can be seen, their worship of the true God under the name of *Chu*, or Lord, has not had the least influence on the polytheism of the nation or in elevating the tone of morals. A well-digested summary of their tenets has been published at Canton by an unknown author under the title of *True Comments on the Correct Doctrine*, in two volumes, pp. 240, 1801. No restrictions have been laid on this sect by the government during the present dynasty; the struggle which continued during the last twenty years between them was simply a question of dominion, not of religion.

Mr. Milne visited the mosque in Ningpo and made the acquaintance of the mollah. "He is a man about forty-five years of age, of a remarkably benign and intelligent countenance and gentlemanly bearing. His native place is Shantung, but his ancestors came from Medina. He readily reads the Arabic scriptures and talks that language fluently, but can neither read nor write Chinese, which is somewhat surprising considering he can talk it well, was born in China, and is a minister of religion among the Chinese. His supporters number between twenty and thirty families, and one or two of his adherents are officers. He took me into the place of worship which adjoins his apartments. A flight of steps leads into a room, covered with a plain roof, on either side of which lay a mass of dusty furniture and agricultural implements; the pillars are ornamented with sentences out of the Koran. Facing you is an ornamented pair of small doors hung upon the wall, within which the sacred seat is supposed to lie, and on one side is a convenient bookcase containing their scriptures. He showed me his usual officiating dress—a white robe with a painted turban—but he never wears this costume except at service, appearing in the Chinese habit at other times. They have a weekly day of rest, which falls on our Thursday. On asking if I might be permitted to attend any of their services, he replied that if their adherents had business on that day they did not trouble themselves to attend. The stronghold of his religion is in Hangchau fu, where are several mosques, but the low state of Mohammedanism seemed to dampen his spirits. Happening to see near the entrance a tablet similar to that found in every other temple, with the inscription, 'The Emperor, ever-living, may he live forever!' I asked him how he could allow such a blasphemous monument to stand in a spot which he regarded as consecrated to the worship of Aloha, as he styles the true God. He protested he did not and never could worship it, and pointed to the low place given it as evidence of this, and added that it was only for the sake of expediency it was allowed lodgment in the building, for if they were ever charged with disloyalty by the enemies of their faith they could appeal to it! His reigning desire was to make a pilgrimage to Mecca, and he inquired particularly respecting the price of a passage."[1]

Since the introduction of steamers great numbers of pilgrims visit Mecca, who cannot fail to extend the knowledge of western lands as they return among their people. The Mohammedan inhabitants of Turkestan and Ílí are distinguished into three classes by the color and shape of their turbans; one has red and another white sugar-loaf, the third the common Arab turban. The number throughout the region north of the Yangtsz' River cannot be stated, but it probably exceeds ten millions. In some places they form a third of the population; a missionary in Sz'chuen reckons eighty thousand living in one of its cities.[2]

The existence of Jews in China has long been known, but the information possessed relative to their past number, condition, and residences is very imperfect. They were once numbered by thousands, and are supposed by Mr. Finn to have belonged to the restoration from Chaldea, as they had portions of Malachi and Zechariah, adopted the era of Seleucus, and had many rabbinical customs. They probably entered China through the north-western route, and there is no good reason for rejecting their own date, during the Han dynasty. Within the last three centuries all have lived in Kaifung, the capital of Honan, wherever they may have lived in earlier days. Marco Polo just mentions their existence at Cambaluc, as do John of Montecorvino and Marignolli about the same time, and Ibn Batuta at an earlier date. In the Chinese annals of the Mongol dynasty the Jews are first referred to in 1329, and again in 1354, when they were invited to Peking in the decline of its power to join the army of the Imperialists. They are styled *Shu-hwuh*, or Jehudi, and must have been numerous enough

---

[1] Compare Milne's *Life in China*, p. 96, London, 1857.

[2] *Chinese Repository*, Vols. XIII., p. 32; XX., pp. 77–84; II., p. 256. De Guignes, *Voyages à Peking*, Tome II., p. 68. Gray, *China*, I., pp. 137–142. Edkins, *Religions in China*, Chap. XV. *Annales de la Foi*, II., p. 245. Reinaud, *Relation des Voyages à la Chine*.

to make them worth noticing with Mohammedans, and their help in men and means implored; but no hint is given of their places of abode. Further research into Chinese histories may disclose other notices of their existence.

The Jews were early known by the term of *Tiao-kin kiao*, or the 'sect which pulls out the sinew.' De Guignes says they are also called *Lan-mao Hwui-tsz'*, or 'Mohammedans with Blue Caps,' because they wore a blue cap in the synagogue; but this latter must be a local name. The first description of this colony was written by the Jesuit Gozani, about the year 1700, and shows that the *Tsing-chin sz'*, or 'Pure and True Temple,' was then a large establishment consisting of four separate courts, various buildings enclosed for residence, worship, and work. The *Li-pai sz'*, or Synagogue, measured about sixty by forty feet, having a portico with a double row of four columns before it. In the centre of the room, between the rows of pillars, is the throne of Moses, a magnificent and elevated chair with an embroidered cushion, upon which they place the book of the law while it is read.

This account of Gozani remained as the latest information until Bishop Smith sent two native Christians from Shanghai to Kaifung to learn the present condition of the Jews. They were ignorant of Hebrew, but had been instructed how to copy the letters, and did their work very creditably, bringing away with them some portions of the Old Testament written on vellum-like paper of an old date. The synagogue had suffered during the great inundation of 1849, and the colony of two hundred individuals was found in abject poverty, ignorance, and dejection. Not one of them knew a word of Hebrew, and many of their buildings had been sold for the materials to support their lives.

In February, 1866, Rev. W. A. P. Martin, President of the Tung-wăn Kwan at Peking, visited Kaifung, and learned that during the interval of fifteen years they had become still more impoverished. Having learned from the mollah of a mosque where they lived, he "passed through streets crowded with curious spectators to an open square, in the centre of which there stood a solitary stone. On one side was an inscription commemorating the erection of the synagogue in A.D. 1183, and on the other of its rebuilding in 1488. . . . 'Are there among you any of the family of Israel?' I inquired. 'I am one,' responded a young man, whose face corroborated his assertion; and then another and another stepped forth, until I saw before me representatives of six of the seven families into which the colony is divided. There, on that melancholy spot where the very foundations of the synagogue had been torn from the ground, and there no longer remained one stone upon another, they confessed, with shame and grief, that their holy and beautiful house had been demolished by their own hands. It had long been, they said, in a ruinous condition; they had no money to make repairs. They had lost all knowledge of the sacred tongue; the traditions of the fathers were no longer handed down, and their ritual worship had ceased to be observed. They had at last yielded to the pressure of necessity, and disposed of the timbers and stones of the venerable edifice to obtain relief for their bodily wants."

They estimated their number at between three hundred and four hundred persons, all of them poor, and, now that the centre of attraction had disappeared, likely to become dispersed and lost. The entrance tablet in gilt characters, stating that the building was "Israel's Possession," had been placed in a mosque, and some of the colony had entered its worship.

Since that date one of their own race, now Bishop Schereschewsky, of Shanghai, has also visited them, but the literati of the city refused to allow him to remain among them. A company of the colony came up to Peking about twelve years ago, but, finding that no money was to be obtained for their support, ere long went back. It is probable that in a few years their unity will be so destroyed in the removal of their synagogue that they will be quite mingled with their countrymen. One or two are now Buddhist priests, others are literary graduates, and all of them are ignorant of their peculiar rites and festivals. Like the Mohammedans, they have never translated their sacred books into Chinese; but during their long existence in China they have remained indeed, as Dr. Martin says, like "a rock rent from the sides of Mount Zion by some great national catastrophe, and projected into the central Plain of China, which has stood there while the centuries rolled by, sublime in its antiquity and solitude."[1]

---

[1] *Chinese Repository*, Vol. XX., pp. 436–466. Yule's *Marco Polo*, 1871, Vol. I., p. 309. *Cathay*, pp. 225, 341, 497. James Finn, *Jews in China*, 1843. Bp. Smith, *Mission of Inquiry to Jews at Kai-fung*, 1851. Dr. Martin, *The Chinese*, N. Y., 1881. *Journal of Royal Geog. Soc.*, London, Vol. XXVII., p. 297. *Versuch einer Geschichte der Juden in Sina, nebst P. J. Kögler's Beschreibung ihrer heiligen Bücher*, herausg. von C. G. von Murr, Halle, 1806. Milne, *Life in China*, p. 403.

CHAPTER XIX.

CHRISTIAN MISSIONS AMONG THE CHINESE.

THE earliest recorded attempt to impart the knowledge of the true God to the Chinese ascribes it to the Nestorian church in the seventh century; though the voice of tradition, and detached notices in ecclesiastical writers of the Eastern Empire collated by Fabricius, lead to the belief that not many years elapsed after the times of the apostles before the sound of the gospel was heard in China and Chin-India. If the tradition contained in the breviary used among the Malabar Christians, that by Saint Thomas himself the Chinese were converted to the truth, be not received, Mosheim well remarks that "we may believe that at an early period the Christian religion extended to the Chinese, Seres, and Tartars. There are various arguments collected from learned men to show that the Christian faith was carried to China, if not by the apostle Thomas, by the first teachers of Christianity." Arnobius, A.D. 300, speaks of the Christian deeds done in India, and among the Seres, Persians, and Medes. The Nestorian monks who brought the eggs of the silk-worm to Constantinople (A.D. 551) had resided long in China, where it is reasonable to suppose they were not the first nor the only ones who went thither to preach the gospel. The extent of their success must be left to conjecture, but "if such beams have travelled down to us through the darkness of so many ages, it is reasonable to believe they emanated from a brighter source."

The time of the arrival of the Nestorians in China cannot be specified certainly, but there are grounds for placing it as early as A.D. 505. Ebedjesus Sobiensis remarks that "the Catholicos Salibazacha created the metropolitan sees of Sina and Samarcand, though some say they were constituted by Achæus and Silas." Silas was patriarch of the Nestorians from A.D. 505 to 520; and Achæus was archbishop at Seleucia in 415. The metropolitan bishop of Sina is also mentioned in a list of those subject to this patriarch, published by Amro, and it is placed in the list after that of India, according to the priority of foundation.

The only record yet found in China itself of the labors of the Nestorians is the celebrated monument which was discovered at Sí-ngan fu in Shensí, in 1625; and though the discussion re-

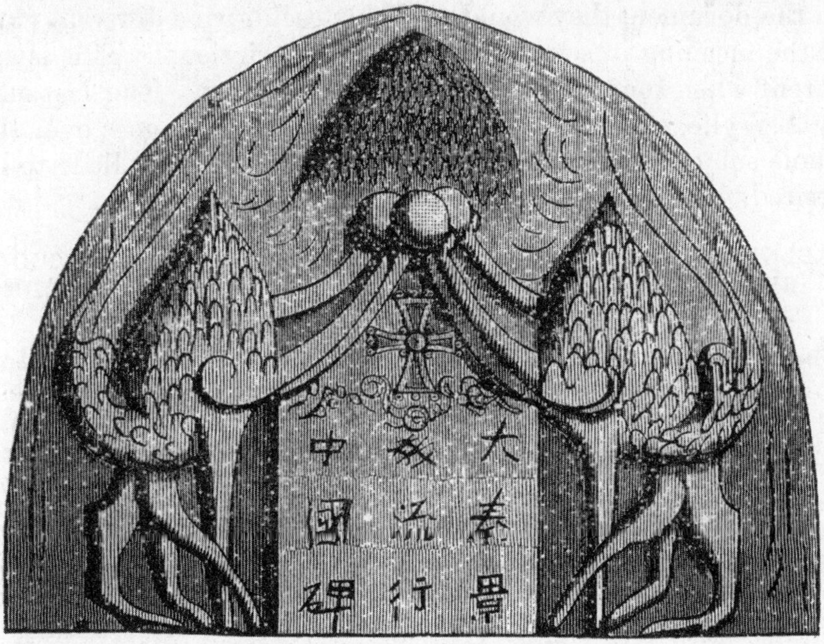

Head of Nestorian Tablet at Si-ngan.

garding its authenticity has been rather warm between the Jesuits and their opponents, the weight of evidence, both internal and external, leaves no doubt regarding its verity. It has been found quite recently to be in good preservation, and rubbings taken from it are nearly perfect. The Syriac characters composing the signatures of Olopun and his associates have made it an object of much interest to the natives; these, as well as the singular cross on its top (seen in the illustration), have doubtless contributed to its preservation. It was set up in 1859 by a

Chinese who had so much regard for it as to rebuild it in the brick wall where it had once stood outside of the city. The stone seems to be a coarse marble.

It has been often translated since the first attempt by Boime, published with the original by Kircher in Holland. In 1845 Dr. E. C. Bridgman published Kircher's Latin translation with the French version of Dalquié, and another of his own, which brought it more into notice. The style is very terse, and the exact meaning not easily perceived even by learned natives. As Dr. Bridgman says, " Were a hundred Chinese students employed on the document they would probably each give a different view of the meaning in some parts of the inscription." This is apparent when four or five of them are compared. The last one, by A. Wylie, of the London Mission at Shanghai, goes over the whole subject with a fullness and care which leaves little to be desired.[1]

TABLET EULOGIZING THE PROPAGATION OF THE ILLUSTRIOUS RELIGION IN CHINA, WITH A PREFACE; COMPOSED BY KING-TSING, A PRIEST OF THE SYRIAN CHURCH.

Behold the unchangeably true and invisible, who existed through all eternity without origin; the far-seeing perfect intelligence, whose mysterious existence is everlasting; operating on primordial substance he created the universe, being more excellent than all holy intelligences, inasmuch as he is the source of all that is honorable. This is our eternal true lord God, triune and mysterious in substance. He appointed the cross as the means for determining the four cardinal points, he moved the original spirit, and produced the two principles of nature; the sombre void was changed, and heaven and earth were opened out; the sun and moon revolved, and day and night commenced; having perfected all inferior objects, he then made the first man; upon him he bestowed an excellent disposition, giving him in charge the government of all created beings; man, acting out the original principles of his nature, was pure and unostentatious; his unsullied and expansive mind was free from the least inordinate desire; until Satan introduced the seeds of falsehood, to deteriorate his purity of principle; the opening thus commenced in his virtue

---

[1] Visdelou in *Bibliotheque Oriental*, Vol. IV. Kircher's *China Illustrata*, Part I., Antwerp, 1667. *Chinese Repository*, XIV., pp. 201–229. Huc, *Christianity in China*, I., pp. 49–58. Wylie, *North China Herald*, 1855, reprinted in *Journal of Am Oriental Soc.*, Vol. V., p. 277. Archimandrite Palladius published a Russian version. Williamson, *Journeys in North China*, I., p. 382. *Le Catholicisme en Chine au VIIIe Siècle de notre ère avec une nouvelle traduction de l'inscription de Sy-nganfou*, par P. D. de Thiersant, Paris, 1877.

gradually enlarged, and by this crevice in his nature was obscured and rendered vicious; hence three hundred and sixty-five sects followed each other in continuous track, inventing every species of doctrinal complexity; while some pointed to material objects as the source of their faith, others reduced all to vacancy, even to the annihilation of the two primeval principles; some sought to call down blessings by prayers and supplications, while others by an assumption of excellence held themselves up as superior to their fellows; their intellects and thoughts continually wavering, their minds and affections incessantly on the move, they never obtained their vast desires, but being exhausted and distressed they revolved in their own heated atmosphere; till by an accumulation of obscurity they lost their path, and after long groping in darkness they were unable to return. Thereupon, our Trinity being divided in nature, the illustrious and honorable Messiah, veiling his true dignity, appeared in the world as a man; angelic powers promulgated the glad tidings, a virgin gave birth to the Holy One in Syria; a bright star announced the felicitous event, and Persians [1] observing the splendor came to present tribute; the ancient dispensation, as declared by the twenty-four holy men,[2] was then fulfilled, and he laid down great principles for the government of families and kingdoms; he established the new religion of the silent operation of the pure spirit of the Triune; he rendered virtue subservient to direct faith; he fixed the extent of the eight boundaries,[3] thus completing the truth and freeing it from dross; he opened the gate of the three constant principles,[4] introducing life and destroying death; he suspended the bright sun to invade the chambers of darkness, and the falsehoods of the devil were thereupon defeated; he set in motion the vessel of mercy by which to ascend to the bright mansions, whereupon rational beings were then released; having thus completed the manifestation of his power, in clear day he ascended to his true station. Twenty-seven sacred books [5] have been left, which disseminate intelligence by unfolding the original transforming principles. By the rule for admission, it is the custom to apply the water of baptism, to wash away all superficial show and to cleanse and purify the neophytes. As a seal, they hold the cross, whose influence is reflected in every direction, uniting all without distinction. As they strike the wood, the fame of their benevolence is diffused abroad; worshipping toward the east, they hasten on the way to life and glory; they pre-

---

[1] *Po-sz'*, 'Persians.' This name was well known to the Chinese at that time, being the designation of an extensive sect then located in the Empire, and the name of a nation with which they had held commercial and political intercourse for several centuries. The statement here is in admirable harmony with the general tradition of the early church, that the Magi or wise men mentioned in Matthew's gospel were no other than philosophers of the Parsee sect.

[2] The "holy men" denote the writers of the books of the Old Testament.

[3] The "eight boundaries" are inexplicable; some refer them to the beatitudes.

[4] The "three constant principles" may perhaps mean faith, hope, and charity.

[5] Exactly the number we have in the New Testament.

serve the beard to symbolize their outward actions, they shave the crown to indicate the absence of inward affections; they do not keep slaves, but put noble and mean all on an equality; they do not amass wealth, but cast all their property into the common stock; they fast, in order to perfect themselves by self-inspection; they submit to restraints, in order to strengthen themselves by silent watchfulness; seven times a day they have worship and praise, for the benefit of the living and the dead; once in seven days they sacrifice, to cleanse the heart and return to purity.

It is difficult to find a name to express the excellence of the true and unchangeable doctrine; but as its meritorious operations are manifestly displayed, by accommodation it is named the Illustrious Religion. Now without holy men, principles cannot become expanded; without principles, holy men cannot become magnified; but with holy men and right principles, united as the two parts of a signet, the world becomes civilized and enlightened.

In the time of the accomplished Emperor Taitsung, the illustrious and magnificent founder of the dynasty, among the enlightened and holy men who arrived was the Most-virtuous Olopun, from the country of Syria. Observing the azure clouds, he bore the true sacred books; beholding the direction of the winds, he braved difficulties and dangers. In the year A.D. 635 he arrived at Chang-an; the Emperor sent his Prime Minister, Duke Fang Hiuen-ling; who, carrying the official staff to the west border, conducted his guest into the interior; the sacred books were translated in the imperial library, the sovereign investigated the subject in his private apartments; when becoming deeply impressed with the rectitude and truth of the religion, he gave special orders for its dissemination. In the seventh month of the year A.D. 638 the following imperial proclamation was issued:

"Right principles have no invariable name, holy men have no invariable station; instruction is established in accordance with the locality, with the object of benefiting the people at large. The Greatly-virtuous Olopun, of the kingdom of Syria, has brought his sacred books and images from that distant part, and has presented them at our chief capital. Having examined the principles of this religion, we find them to be purely excellent and natural; investigating its originating source, we find it has taken its rise from the establishment of important truths; its ritual is free from perplexing expressions, its principles will survive when the framework is forgot; it is beneficial to all creatures; it is advantageous to mankind. Let it be published throughout the Empire, and let the proper authority build a Syrian church in the capital in the Í-ning Way, which shall be governed by twenty-one priests. When the virtue of the Chau dynasty declined, the rider on the azure ox ascended to the west; the principles of the great Tang becoming resplendent, the Illustrious breezes have come to fan the East."

Orders were then issued to the authorities to have a true portrait of the Emperor taken; when it was transferred to the wall of the church, the dazzling splendor of the celestial visage irradiated the Illustrious portals. The sacred traces emitted a felicitous influence, and shed a perpetual splendor over the holy precincts. According to the Illustrated Memoir of the Western Regions, and the historical books of the Han and Wei dynasties, the kingdom of Syria reaches south to the Coral Sea; on the north it joins the Gem Mountains; on the west it extends toward the borders of the immortals and the flowery forests; on the east it lies open to the violent winds and tideless waters. The country produces fire-proof cloth, life-restoring incense, bright moon-pearls, and night-lustre gems. Brigands and robbers are unknown, but the people enjoy happiness and peace. None but Illustrious laws prevail; none but the virtuous are raised to sovereign power. The land is broad and ample, and its literary productions are perspicuous and clear.

The Emperor Kautsung respectfully succeeded his ancestor, and was still more beneficent toward the institution of truth. In every province he caused Illustrious churches to be erected, and ratified the honor conferred upon Olopun, making him the great conservator of doctrine for the preservation of the State. While this doctrine pervaded every channel, the State became enriched and tranquillity abounded. Every city was full of churches, and the royal family enjoyed lustre and happiness. In the year A.D. 699 the Buddhists, gaining power, raised their voices in the eastern metropolis;[1] in the year A.D. 713, some low fellows excited ridicule and spread slanders in the western capital. At that time there was the chief priest Lo-han, the Greatly-virtuous Kie-leih, and others of noble estate from the golden regions, lofty-minded priests, having abandoned all worldly interests; who unitedly maintained the grand principles and preserved them entire to the end.

The high-principled Emperor Hiuentsung caused the Prince of Ning and others, five princes in all, personally to visit the felicitous edifice; he established the place of worship; he restored the consecrated timbers which had been temporarily thrown down; and re-erected the sacred stones which for a time had been desecrated.

In 742 orders were given to the great general Kau Lih-sz', to send the five sacred portraits and have them placed in the church, and a gift of a hundred pieces of silk accompanied these pictures of intelligence. Although the dragon's beard was then remote, their bows and swords were still within reach; while the solar horns sent forth their rays, and celestial visages seemed close at hand.[2]

In 744 the priest Kih-ho, in the kingdom of Syria, looking toward the star (of China), was attracted by its transforming influen e, and observing the sun (*i.e.*, Emperor), came to pay court to the most honorable. The Emperor commanded the priest Lo-han, the priest Pu-lun, and others, seven in all, together with the Greatly-virtuous Kih-ho, to perform a service of merit in the Hing-king palace. Thereupon the Emperor composed mottoes for the sides of the church, and the tablets were graced with the royal inscriptions; the accumulated gems emitted their effulgence, while their sparkling brightness vied with the ruby clouds; the transcripts of intelligence suspended in the

[1] "Eastern metropolis" is *Tung Chau*, literally 'Eastern Chau.' The Empire was at this time under the government of the Empress Wu Tsih-tien, who had removed her residence from Chang-an to Lohyang in Honan.

[2] These personages are the first five Emperors of the Tang dynasty, Hiuentsung's predecessors. Their portraits were so admirably painted that they seemed to be present, their arms could almost be handled, and their foreheads, or "horns of the sun," radiated their intelligence.

void shot forth their rays as reflected by the sun; the bountiful gifts exceeded the height of the southern hills; the bedewing favors were deep as the eastern sea. Nothing is beyond the range of right principle, and what is permissible may be identified; nothing is beyond the power of the holy man, and that which is practicable may be related.

The accomplished and enlightened Emperor Suhtsung rebuilt the Illustrious churches in Ling-wu and four other places; great benefits were conferred, and felicity began to increase; great munificence was displayed, and the imperial State became established.

The accomplished and military Emperor Taitsung magnified the sacred succession, and honored the latent principle of nature; always, on the incarnation-day, he bestowed celestial incense, and ordered the performance of a service of merit; he distributed of the imperial viands, in order to shed a glory on the Illustrious Congregation. Heaven is munificent in the dissemination of blessings, whereby the benefits of life are extended; the holy man embodies the original principle of virtue, whence he is able to counteract noxious influences.

Our sacred and sage-like, accomplished and military Emperor Kienchung appointed the eight branches of government, according to which he advanced or degraded the intelligent and dull; he opened up the nine categories, by means of which he renovated the illustrious decrees; his transforming influence pervaded the most abstruse principles, while openness of heart distinguished his devotions. Thus, by correct and enlarged purity of principle, and undeviating consistency in sympathy with others; by extended commiseration rescuing multitudes from misery, while disseminating blessings on all around, the cultivation of our doctrine gained a grand basis, and by gradual advances its influence was diffused. If the winds and rains are seasonable, the world will be at rest; men will be guided by principle, inferior objects will be pure; the living will be at ease, and the dead will rejoice; the thoughts will produce their appropriate response, the affections will be free, and the eyes will be sincere; such is the laudable condition which we of the Illustrious Religion are laboring to attain.

Our great benefactor, the Imperially-conferred-purple-gown priest,[1] Î-sz', titular Great Statesman of the Banqueting-house, Associated Secondary Military Commissioner for the Northern Region, and Examination-palace Overseer, was naturally mild and graciously disposed; his mind susceptible of sound doctrine, he was diligent in the performance; from the distant city of Râjagriha,[2] he came to visit China; his principles more lofty than those of the

---

[1] It was no rare occurrence for priests to occupy civil and military offices in the State during the Tang and preceding dynasties. Of the three titles here given, the first is merely an indication of rank, by which the bearer is entitled to a certain emolument from the State; the second is his title as an officer actively engaged in the imperial service; and the third is an honorary title, which gives to the possessor a certain status in the capital, without any duties or emolument connected therewith.

[2] *Wang-shih*, literally 'Royal residence,' which is also the translation of the Sanskrit word Râjagriha, is the name of a city on the banks of the Ganges,

three dynasties, his practice was perfect in every department; at first he applied himself to duties pertaining to the palace, eventually his name was inscribed on the military roll. When the Duke Koh Tsz'-í, Secondary Minister of State and Prince of Făn-yang, at first conducted the military in the northern region, the Emperor Suhtsung made him (Í-sz') his attendant on his travels; although he was a private chamberlain, he assumed no distinction on the march; he was as claws and teeth to the duke, and in rousing the military he was as ears and eyes; he distributed the wealth conferred upon him, not accumulating treasure for his private use; he made offerings of the jewelry which had been given by imperial favor, he spread out a golden carpet for devotion; now he repaired the old churches, anon he increased the number of religious establishments; he honored and decorated the various edifices, till they resembled the plumage of the pheasant in its flight; moreover, practising the discipline of the Illustrious Religion, he distributed his riches in deeds of benevolence; every year he assembled those in the sacred office from four churches, and respectfully engaged them for fifty days in purification and preparation; the naked came and were clothed; the sick were attended to and restored; the dead were buried in reposo; even among the most pure and self-denying of the Buddhists, such excellence was never heard of; the white-clad members of the Illustrious Congregation, now considering these men, have desired to engrave a broad tablet, in order to set forth a eulogy of their magnanimous deeds.

ODE.

The true Lord is without origin,
Profound, invisible, and unchangeable;
With power and capacity to perfect and transform,
He raised up the earth and established the heavens.

Divided in nature, he entered the world,
To save and to help without bounds;
The sun arose, and darkness was dispelled,
All bearing witness to his true original.

The glorious and resplendent, accomplished Emperor,
Whose principles embraced those of preceding monarchs,
Taking advantage of the occasion, suppressed turbulence;
Heaven was spread out and the earth was enlarged.

When the pure, bright Illustrious Religion
Was introduced to our Tang dynasty,
The Scriptures were translated, and churches built,
And the vessel set in motion for the living and the dead;
Every kind of blessing was then obtained,
And all the kingdoms enjoyed a state of peace.

---

which occurs in several Buddhist works. As this was one of the most important of the Buddhist cities in India, it is natural to suppose that Í-sz' was a Buddhist priest.

When Kautsung succeeded to his ancestral estate,
He rebuilt the edifices of purity;
Palaces of concord, large and light,
Covered the length and breadth of the land.

The true doctrine was clearly announced,
Overseers of the church were appointed in due form;
The people enjoyed happiness and peace,
While all creatures were exempt from calamity and distress.

When Hiuentsung commenced his sacred career,
He applied himself to the cultivation of truth and rectitude;
His imperial tablets shot forth their effulgence,
And the celestial writings mutually reflected their splendors.

The imperial domain was rich and luxuriant,
While the whole land rendered exalted homage;
Every business was flourishing throughout,
And the people all enjoyed prosperity.

Then came Suhtsung, who commenced anew,
And celestial dignity marked the imperial movements;
Sacred as the moon's unsullied expanse,
While felicity was wafted like nocturnal gales.

Happiness reverted to the imperial household,
The autumnal influences were long removed;
Ebullitions were allayed, and risings suppressed,
And thus our dynasty was firmly built up.

Taitsung the filial and just
Combined in virtue with heaven and earth;
By his liberal bequests the living were satisfied,
And property formed the channel of imparting succor.

By fragrant mementoes he rewarded the meritorious,
With benevolence he dispensed his donations;
The solar concave appeared in dignity,
And the lunar retreat was decorated to extreme.

When Kienchung succeeded to the throne,
He began by the cultivation of intelligent virtue;
His military vigilance extended to the four seas,
And his accomplished purity influenced all lands.

His light penetrated the secresies of men,
And to him the diversities of objects were seen as in a mirror;
He shed a vivifying influence through the whole realm of nature,
And all outer nations took him for example.

The true doctrine how expansive!
Its responses are minute;
How difficult to name it!
To elucidate the three in one.

The sovereign has the power to act!
While the ministers record;
We raise this noble monument!
To the praise of great felicity.

This was erected in the 2d year of Kienchung, of the Tang dynasty (A.D. 781), on the 7th day of 1st month, being Sunday.

Written by Lu Siu-yen, Secretary to Council, formerly Military Superintendent for Taichau; while the Bishop Ning-shu had the charge of the congregations of the Illustrious in the East.

The two lines of Syriac, of which the following is a transcript, are in the Estrangelo character, and run down the right and left sides of the Chinese respectively:

Adam Kasiso Vicur-apiskupo va Papasi de Zinstan.
Beyumi aba dabahotha Mar Hana Jesua katholika patriarchis.

Kircher translates this as follows:

"Adam, Deacon, Vicar-episcopal and Pope of China.
In the time of the Father of Fathers, the Lord John Joshua, the Universal Patriarch."

The transcript of the Syriac at the foot of the stone is given here on the authority of Kircher:

Besanath alf utisaain vtarten diavanoiè. Mor Jibuzad Kasiso Vcurapiskupo de Cumdan medinah malcutho bar nihh napso Milis Kasiso dmen Balehh medintho Tahhurstan Akim Lucho hono Papa dictabon beh medabarnutho dpharukan Vcaruzuthon dabhain daluat malche dizinio.

"In the year of the Greeks one thousand and ninety-two, the Lord Jazedbuzid, Priest and Vicar-episcopal of Cumdan the royal city, son of the enlightened Mailas, Priest of Balach a city of Turkestan, set up this tablet, whereon is inscribed the Dispensation of our Redeemer, and the preaching of the apostolic missionaries to the King of China."

After this, in Chinese characters, is "The Priest Lingpau." Then follows:

Adam meschamschŏno Bar Jidbuzad Curapiskupo.
Mar Sargis Kasiso, Vcurapiskupo.
Sabar Jesua Kasiso.
Gabriel Kasiso Varcodiakun, Vrisch medintho de Cumdan vdasrag.

"Adam the Deacon, son of Jazedbuzid, Vicar-episcopal.
The Lord Sergius, Priest and Vicar-episcopal.
Sabar Jesus, Priest.
Gabriel, Priest, Archdeacon, and Ecclesiarch of Cumdan and Sarag."

The following subscription is appended in Chinese:

"Assistant Examiner: the High Statesman of the Sacred rites, the Imperially-conferred-purple-gown Chief Presbyter and Priest Yí-lí."

On the left hand edge are the Syriac names of sixty-seven priests, and sixty-one are given in Chinese.

This truly oriental writing is the most ancient Christian inscription yet found in Asia, and shows plainly that Christianity had made great progress among the Chinese. Kircher and Le Comte claimed it as a record of the success of the Romish church in China, but no one now doubts that it commemorates the exertions of the Nestorians.

Timothy, a patriarch, sent Subchal-Jesus in 780, who labored in Tartary and China for many years, and lost his life on his return, when his place was supplied by Davidis, who was consecrated metropolitan. In the year 845 an edict of Wu-tsung commanded the priests that belonged to the sect that came from Ta Tsin, amounting to no less than three thousand persons, to retire to private life. The two Arabian travellers in the ninth century report that many Christians perished in the siege of Canfu. Marco Polo's frequent allusions lead us to conclude that the Nestorians were both numerous and respected.

He mentions the existence of a church at Hangchau, and two at Chinkiang, built by the prefect Marsarchis, who was himself a member of that church, and alludes to their residence in most of the towns and countries of Central Asia.

The existence of a Christian prince called Prester John, in Central Asia, is spoken of by Marco Polo and Montecorvino. The exact position of his dominions, and the extent of his influence in favor of that faith, have been examined by Col. Yule and

M. Pauthier in their editions of the Venetian, and the glamour which once surrounded him has been found to have arisen mostly from hearsay reports, and from confounding different persons under one name. When the conquests of Genghis khan and his descendants threw all Asia into commotion, this Prester John, ruler of the Kara Kitai Tartars in northern China, fell before him, A.D. 1203. The Nestorians suffered much, but maintained a precarious footing in China during the time of the Yuen dynasty, having been cut off from all help and intercourse with the mother church since the rise of the Moslems. They had ceased long before this period to maintain the purity of the faith, however, and had apparently done nothing to teach and diffuse the Bible, which the tablet intimates was in part or in whole translated by Olopun, under the Emperor's auspices.

At the present time no works composed by their priests, or remains of any churches belonging to them or buildings erected by them, are known to exist in the Empire, though perhaps some books may yet be found. The buildings erected by the Nestorians for churches and dwellings were, of course, no better built than other Chinese edifices, and would not long remain when deserted; while, to account still further for the absence of books, the Buddhists and other opposers may have sought out and destroyed such as existed, which even if carefully kept would not last many generations. The notices of the tablet in Chinese authors, which Mr. Wylie has brought together, prove that those writers had confounded the *King kiao* with Zoroastrianism and Manicheism, and such a confusion is not surprising. The records of futurity alone will disclose to us the names and labors of the devoted disciples and teachers of true Christianity in the Nestorian church, who lived and died for the gospel among the Chinese.[1]

The efforts of the Roman Catholics in China have been great, but not greater than the importance of the field demanded.

---

[1] Yule's *Marco Polo*, Vol. I., p. 275, passim. *N. C. As. Soc. Journal*, Arch. Palladius' notes on it, Vol. X., pp. 20–23. Huc, *Christianity in China*, Chap. II. Pauthier's *Marco Polo*, Chaps. XLVIII.–L. Yule, *Cathay and the Way Thither*, Vol. I., pp. 174–183.

They have met with varied success, and their prudence in the choice of measures and zeal in the work of evangelizing have reflected the highest credit upon them, and would probably, if their object had simply been that of preaching the gospel, have gradually made the entire mass of the population acquainted with the leading doctrines of Christianity. The history of their missions is voluminous, and the principles on which they have been conducted can be learned from their own writings, especially the *Lettres Édifiantes*, the *Annales de la Foi*, and in the elaborate works of Huc and Marshall in later times. The present sketch need embrace only the principal points, for which we shall depend chiefly upon those writers who have already examined these sources.

The first epoch of their missions in China is the thirteenth century. Subsequent to the mission of John of Plano Carpini to Kuyuk khan in 1246-47, there were several envoys sent by one party to the other whose intercourse resulted in nothing permanent. The first attempt which can be called a settled mission was that of John of Montecorvino, from Nicholas IV., in 1288. Corvino arrived in India in 1291, and after preaching there a twelvemonth, during which time he baptized a hundred persons, he joined a caravan going to Cathay and was kindly received by Kublai khan. The Nestorians opposed his progress, and for eleven years he carried on the work alone, but not till the latter part of this period with much success. He built a church at Cambaluc, "which had a steeple and belfry with three bells that were rung every hour to summon the new converts to prayer." He baptized nearly six thousand persons during that time, "and bought one hundred and fifty children, whom he instructed in Greek and Latin and composed for them several devotional books." [1]

Clement V., hearing of Corvino's success, appointed him archbishop in 1307 and sent him seven suffragan bishops as assistants. Two letters of his are extant in which he gives a pleasing account of his efforts to preach the gospel, but of the

[1] *Chinese Repository*, Vol. III., p. 112; Vol. XIII., passim. Lowrie, *Land of Sinim.*

subsequent success of the endeavors made by him and his coadjutors to propagate the faith there are only imperfect records. Corvino was ordered to have the mysteries of the Bible represented by pictures in all his churches, for the purpose of captivating the eyes of the barbarians. He died in 1328, when about eighty years of age, "after having converted more than thirty thousand infidels." One of the accounts relates that at his funeral "all the inhabitants of Cambaluc, without distinction, mourned for the man of God, and both Christians and pagans were present at the funeral ceremony, the latter rending their garments in token of grief, . . . and the place of his burial became a pilgrimage to which the inhabitants of Cambaluc resorted with pious eagerness." It is not easy to estimate the real value of the labors of this priest and his successors, nor to decide how much better they were than those of the Nestorians in making known the Cross of Christ among the Mongols. The short record preserved of Corvino speaks well of his character and favorably of the toleration granted by the Mongols to his efforts to instruct them. It is affecting to hear him say, "It is now twelve years since I have heard any news from the West. I am become old and grayheaded, but it is rather through labors and tribulations than through age, for I am only fifty-eight years old. I have learned the Tartar language and literature, into which I have translated the whole New Testament and the Psalms of David, and have caused them to be transcribed with the utmost care. I write and read and preach openly and freely the testimony of the law of Christ."

The Pope sent Nicholas to succeed Montecorvino at Peking, and a company of twenty-six Franciscans with him, but no authentic record of their arrival there has been preserved. In 1336 the last Mongol Emperor, Shuntí, whose reign was then called Chĭyuen, sent André, a Frank, as his ambassador to the Pope, to whom was also addressed a letter from the Alain Christians asking for a bishop to take Corvino's place, Nicholas not having then reached his see. Benedict XII. sent four nuncios, one of whom, John of Florence, returned to Europe in 1353, after residing and travelling in China twelve years, bringing friendly letters from the Emperor Shuntí. At this period there was another bishopric among the Mongols at Ílí, or Kuldja, and a letter from Pascal, a Spanish friar, dated from that city in 1338, has been preserved. It would seem that during the sway of the Mongol princes these missionaries carried on their work chiefly among their tribes. It is, if such was the case, less surprising, therefore, that we hear nothing of them and their converts after the Chinese troops had expelled Kublai's weak descendants from the country in 1368, since they would naturally follow them into Central Asia. After the final establishment of the Ming dynasty almost nothing is known concerning either them or the Nestorians, and it is probable that during the wanderings of the defeated Mongols the adherents of both sects gradually lapsed into ignorance and thence easily into Mohammedanism and Buddhism. There is no reasonable doubt, however, that during the three centuries ending with the accession of Hungwu, the greater part of Central Asia and Northern China was the scene of many flourishing Christian communities.

The second period in the history of Romish missions in China includes a space of one hundred and fifty years, extending from the time when Matteo Ricci first established himself at Shauking in 1582 to the death of the Emperor Yungching in 1736. Before Ricci entered the country there had been some efforts made to revive the long-deferred work among the Chinese, but the Portuguese and Spanish merchants were opposed to the extension of a faith which their flagiticus conduct so outrageously belied. The Chinese government was still more strongly opposed to the residence of the foreign missionaries. Francis Xavier started from Goa in 1552 in company with an ambassador to China, but the embassy was hindered by the Governor of Malacca, who detained Pereyra and his ship, and Xavier was obliged to go alone. He died, however, at Shangchuen, Sançian, or St. John's, an island about thirty miles south-west of Macao, disappointed in his expectations and thwarted in his plans by the untoward opposition of his countrymen. Other attempts were made to accomplish this design, but it was reserved for the Jesuits to carry it into effect. Valignani, the Superior of their missions in the East, selected Michael Ruggiero, or Roger, for this enterprise. He arrived at Macao in 1580 and commenced the study of the language. Soon after he was joined by Matthew Ricci, and after a series of efforts and disappointments they succeeded, in 1582, in obtaining lodgment at Shauking, then the residence of the Governor of Kwangtung. He granted them permission to build a house there, as they had told him that "they had at last ascertained with their own eyes that the Celestial Empire was even superior to its brilliant renown. They therefore desired to end their days in it, and wished to obtain a little land to construct a house and a church where they might pass their time in prayer and study, in solitude and meditation, which they could not do at Macao on account of the tumult and bustle which the perpetual activity of commerce occasioned." A beginning like this indicated the policy which has marked the progress of their work during the three centuries now passed. Nothing is said of making known Christ and him crucified as the great theme of their preaching. Huc tells us, too, that they took down the picture of the Virgin, because "the report had been spread that the strangers worshipped a woman," and replaced it by an image of the Saviour; and in this also they set the example, which successive ages have strengthened, of upholding the native idolatry. In their intercourse with the people of all classes they won good opinions by their courtesy, presents, and scientific attainments, and Huc sums up their principles in his approving remark, "they thought justly that the philosopher would make more impression than the priest upon minds so sceptic and so imbued with literary conceit." The appointed means given by the Founder of Christianity for its propagation are never mentioned as their guide and authority, and the building corresponds to the foundations laid.

In 1594 Valignani advised Ricci and his associates to exchange their garb of Buddhist priests for the more respected dress of the literati; and soon after he set out from Shauchau, in the north of Kwangtung, for Nanchang, the capital of Kiangsí, and thence made his way to Nanking, still a place of great importance, although not the capital of the Empire. He was directed to depart, and returned to Nanchang, where he was permitted to lay the foundation of a religious institution and establish his associates. He then left again for Nanking, but finding many obstacles proceeded to Suchau, the capital of Kiangnan, and there, too, established a school. The times becoming favorable, he appeared a third time at Nanking, in 1598, where he was received with amity, frankness, and good breeding, and his lectures on the exact sciences listened to with rapture. The progress of the mission had been so considerable that Valignani had appointed Ricci its Superior-General, which gave him power to regulate its internal concerns, for which he was well fitted.

An officer whom he had known in Shauchau, and who had been appointed President of the Board of Civil Office, was induced to take him to Peking on his return there from a mission to Hainan; but opposition arising this friend, Kwang, advised him to return with him to Nanking, as the officials at the capital were much disappointed to find that he knew nothing about making silver and gold, which was wanted to pay for the expedition to Japan. After Kwang's departure he and his colleague, Cataneo, found themselves nearly penniless, and he decided to return south, although it was winter. He reached Suchau in a very weak condition, but, having recovered, went to Nanking in 1599, where the high provincial authorities visited and aided him, heard his discourses on astronomy, and enabled him to get a house.

Everything progressed favorably, and Cataneo had returned from Macao with funds and presents. Ricci availed himself of a timely proposal from a eunuch to go with him to Peking, and started in a junk with his presents. The eunuch, however, wished to keep the latter, and by misrepresentations contrived to detain Ricci and his companion, Pantoja, at Tientsin for six months, at the end of which the villany was exposed, and the foreigners invited to court by imperial orders. They reached Peking January 4, 1601, twenty-one years after Ricci landed in Macao. The pleasing manners and extensive acquirements of Ricci, joined to a distribution of presents, gained him the favor of men in authority. He soon numbered some of them among his adherents, among whom Sü, baptized Paul, was one of his earliest and most efficient co-operators, and assisted him in translating Euclid.

The Emperor Wanleih received him with kindness, and allowed him and Pantoja to be accommodated at the place where foreign envoys usually remained; he subsequently permitted them to hire a house, and assigned them a stipend. In the meantime other Jesuits joined him at Peking, and were also settled in all the intermediate stations, where they carried on the work of their missions under his direction with success and favor. Paul Sü and his widowed daughter, who took the baptismal name of Candida, proved efficient supporters of the new faith. The new religion encountered many obstacles, and the officers who saw its progress felt the necessity of checking its growth before it got strength to set at naught the commands of government. Much excitement arose in 1605 between the Portuguese and the officials at Canton in consequence of a rumor of the former going to attack the city; and it was carried to such a height that the latter seized a convert named Martinez and punished him so severely that he died. A decree in 1617 ordered the missionaries to depart from court to Canton, there to embark for Europe, but, like many others of the same import subsequently issued, it received just as much obedience as they thought expedient to give it—and properly too; for if they were not disturbers of the peace or seditious, they ought not to be sent out of the country. This edict hindered their work only partially, and such was their diligence that by the year 1636 they had published no fewer than three hundred and forty treatises, some of them religious, but mostly on natural philosophy and mathematics. Ricci formulated a set of rules for their guidance, in which he allowed the converts to practise the rites of ancestral worship, because he considered them purely civil in their nature. The matter subsequently became a bone of contention between the Jesuits and Franciscans.

The talented founder of these missions died in 1610, at the age of fifty-eight, and for skill, perseverance, learning, and tact, his name deservedly stands highest among their missionaries. His withholding the Bible from the Chinese, and substitution of image worship, ritualism, and priestly ordinances for the pure truths of the gospel, have been maintained by his successors, for they are essential features of the church which sent them forth. He has been extolled by the Jesuits as a man possessed of every virtue. Another writer of the same church gives him the following character: "Ricci was active, skilful, full of schemes, and endowed with all the talents necessary to render him agreeable to the great or to gain the favor of princes; but at the same time so little versed in matters of faith that, as the Bishop of Conon said, it was sufficient to read his work on the true religion to be satisfied that he was ignorant of the first principles of theology. Being more a politician than a theologian, he discovered the secret of remaining peacefully in China. The kings found in him a man full of complaisance; the pagans a minister who accommodated himself to their superstitions; the mandarins a polite courtier skilled in all the trickery of courts; and the devil a faithful servant, who, far from destroying, established his reign among the heathen, and even extended it to the Christians. He preached in China the religion of Christ according to his own fancy; that is to say, he disfigured it by a faithful mixture of pagan superstitions, adopting the sacrifices offered to Confucius and ancestors, and teaching the Christians to assist and cooperate at the worship of idols, provided they only addressed their devotions to a cross covered with flowers, or secretly attached to one of the candles which were lighted in the temples of the false gods."[1] His work was described by Trigault in 1616, when full materials were accessible, so that his actions and motives are known more fully than many who have come after him.

After his death his place was filled by Longobardi, whose experience, learning, and judgment well fitted him for the post. The efforts of many enemies caused a reaction in 1616, and an edict was issued ordering all missionaries to leave the country; but they were sheltered by their converts, especially through the exertions of Sü, who in 1622 obtained the reversal of the edict of expulsion, and thereby caused the persecution

---

[1] *Anecdotes de la Chine*, Tome I., Pref. vi, vii. Huc, *Christianity in China*, Vol. II., Chaps. II. to V. Rémusat, *Nouveaux Mélanges*, Tome II., p. 207.

to cease.[1] The talents and learning of Schaal, a German Jesuit, who was recommended by Sü to the Emperor's regard in 1628, soon placed him at the head of all his brethren and ranked him among the most distinguished men in the Empire. The Dominicans and Franciscans also flocked to the land which had thus been opened by the Jesuits, but they were not welcomed by those who wished to build up their own power. After the death of Wanleih, in 1620, and those converts within the palace who had favored the cause, new influences against it arose, and during the short reign of his young grandson, Tienhí, troubles increased. Amid the breaking up of the Ming dynasty and the establishment of the present family on the throne (1630–1660), the missions suffered much, their spiritual guides retired to places of safety from the molestations of soldiers and banditti, and converts were necessarily left without instruction. The missionaries in the north sided with the Manchus, and Schaal became a favorite with the new monarch and his advisers, by whom he was appointed to reform the calendar. He succeeded in showing the incompetency of the persons who had the supervision of it, and after its revision was appointed president of the *Kin Tien Kien*, an astronomical board established for this object, and invested with the insignia and emoluments of a grandee of the first class. He employed his influence and means in securing the admission of other missionaries, and to build two churches in the capital and repair many of those which had fallen to decay in the provinces.

The exertions of the native converts did much to advance the cause of religion, and the baptismal names of Leon, Michel, etc., have been preserved among these early confessors; but none are more famous than Sü and his daughter, Candida. He gave his influence in its favor and his property to assist in building churches, while his revision of their writings made them acceptable to fastidious scholars. His daughter also spent her life in good works. According to Du Halde, she exhibited the sincerity of her profession by building thirty-nine churches

---

[1] Sü's *Apology* is given in full in the *Chinese Repository*, Vol. XIX., p. 118.

in different provinces, and printing one hundred and thirty Christian books for the instruction of her countrymen. Having heard that the pagans in several of the provinces were accustomed to abandon their children as soon as born, she established a foundling hospital; and seeing many blind people telling idle stories in the streets for the sake of gain, she got them instructed and sent forth to relate the different events of the gospel history. A few years before her death the Emperor conferred on her the title of *sho jin*, or 'virtuous woman,' and sent her a magnificent habit and head-dress adorned with pearls, which it is said she gradually sold, expending the proceeds in benevolent works. She received the last sacrament with a lively faith of being united to that God whom she had so zealously loved and served. She and her father have since been deified by the people, and are worshipped now at Shanghai for their good deeds. The large mission establishment at Sikawé (properly *Sü Kia-wei*, or the 'Sü Family Hamlet'), situated near that city, under the care of the Roman Catholics, now covers the same ground once owned by this eminent man. Candida's example was emulated by another lady of high connections, named Agatha, who was zealous in carrying on the same works. We can but hope that although the worship of these converts was mixed with much error, and Mary, Ignatius, and others received their homage as well as Christ, their faith was genuine and their works done by an actuating spirit of humble love.[1]

The Romish missionaries had friends among the high families in the land during the first hundred years of their labors, besides converts of both sexes. Few missions in pagan countries have been more favored with zealous converts, or their missionaries more aided and countenanced by rich and noble supporters, than the early papal missions to China. Le Comte speaks of the high favor enjoyed by all the laborers in this work through the reputation and influence of Schaal at court. One of those who obtained celebrity was Faber, whose efforts in Shensí were attended with great success, and who wrought many

---

[1] Medhurst's *China*, p. 188. Du Halde's *China*, Vol. II., p. 8.

miracles during his ministry in that province. Among others he mentions that "the town of Hang ching was at a certain time overrun with a prodigious multitude of locusts, which ate up all the leaves of the trees and gnawed the grass to the very roots. The inhabitants, after exhausting all the resources of their own superstitions and charms, applied to Faber, who promised to deliver them from the plague provided they would become Christians. When they consented he marched in ceremony into the highways in his stole and surplice, and sprinkled up and down the holy water, accompanying this action with the prayers of the church, but especially with a lively faith. God heard the voice of his servant, and the next day all the insects disappeared. But the people refused to perform their promise, and the plague grew worse than before. With much contrition they came to the father, confessing their fault and entreating his renewed interposition; again he sprinkled the holy water, and the insects a second time disappeared. Then the whole borough was converted, and many years afterward was reckoned one of the devoutest missions in China. His biographer mentions that Faber was carried over rivers through the air; he foretold his own death, and did several other such wonders; but the greatest miracle of all was his life, which he spent in the continual exercise of all the apostolical virtues and a tender devotion to the mother of God."

The increase of churches and converts in the northern provinces was rapid during the reign of Shunchí, but the southern parts of the Empire not being completely subdued, the claimant to the throne of Ming was favored by the missionaries there, and his troops led on by two Christian Chinese officers, called Thomas Kiu and Luke Chin. His mother, wife, and son were baptized with the names of Helena, Maria, and Constantine, and the former wrote a letter to Pope Alexander VII., expressing her attachment to the cause of Christianity, and wishing to put the country through him under the protection of God. He kindly answered her, but the expectations of the Romanists were disappointed by the death of Tunglieh, the Emperor.

During the reign of Shunchí Schaal and his coadjutors stood high at Peking, and missions prospered in the provinces; but on the Emperor's death the administration fell into the hands of four regents, and as they were known to be opposed to the new sect, a memorial was sent to court setting forth the evils likely to arise if it was not repressed. It should be mentioned that several monks of the Dominican and Franciscan orders, especially of Fuhkien province, where Capellas, a Spaniard, had been martyred in 1648, had resumed the labors of Archbishop John of Montecorvino at Peking, more than thirty years before this date. "Their presence had been resisted by the Jesuits [so ran the memorial], and the strifes between these orders about the meaning and worship of *tien* and *shangtí* (words used for the Supreme Being) revealed the important secret that the principles of the new doctrine were made to subserve the purposes of those who were aspiring to influence. It was remembered also that while the Catholics continued in Japan, nothing but intrigue, schism, and civil war was heard of, calamities that might sooner or later befal China if the criminal eagerness of the missionaries in enlisting people of all classes was not checked. The members of the different orders wore distinctive badges of medals, rosaries, crosses, etc., and were always ready to obey the calls of their chiefs, who could have no scruple to lead them on to action the moment a probability of success in subverting the existing political order and the ancient worship of China should offer." The regents took the memorial into consideration, and in 1665 the tribunals under their direction decreed that "Schaal and his associates merited the punishment of seducers, who announce to the people a false and pernicious doctrine."

Notwithstanding the honorable position Schaal held as tutor of the young Emperor Kanghí, he was proscribed and degraded with several high officers who had been baptized. Some of them perished, Schaal himself dying of grief and suffering August 16th of the same year, at the age of seventy-eight, having been thirty-seven years in imperial employ, under five monarchs. Verbiest and others were imprisoned, one of whom died; and twenty-one Jesuits, with some of other sects, were sent out of the country. Magaillans says he himself was "loaden for four whole months together with nine chains, three about his neck, his arms, and his legs; he was also condemned to have forty lashes, and to be banished out of Tartary as long as he lived. But a great earthquake that happened at that time at Peking delivered both him and the rest of his companions."[1] Their relief, however, was probably owing more to the favor of Kanghí on taking the reins of government in 1671 than to the earthquake; he soon released Verbiest to appoint him astronomer, and allowed the missionaries to return to their stations, though he forbade his subjects embracing Christianity. This favorable change is partly ascribed, too, to the errors Verbiest pointed out in the calendar, which showed an utter ignorance of the commonest principles of astronomy on the part of those who prepared it. An intercalary month had been erroneously introduced, and the unfortunate astronomers were made to exchange places with the imprisoned missionaries, while their intercalary month was discarded and the year shortened, to the astonishment of the common people. It may reasonably be doubted whether the priest acted with sagacity and prudence in thus exasperating those in high places by this public ridicule of their incompetency. Verbiest also prepared an astronomical work entitled "The Perpetual Astronomy of the Emperor Kanghí," which he graciously received and conferred the title of *tajin*, or 'magnate,' on him, and ennobled all his kindred. "He had no relatives in China, but as the Jesuits called each other brother, they did not hesitate to use the same title. The greatest part of the religious caused it to be inscribed on the doors of their houses."

The favor of the Emperor continued, and the missionaries requited his kindness with many signal services, besides those of a literary and astronomical nature, among which was casting cannon for his army. In 1636 Schaal had made a number for Tsungching, and Verbiest, his successor, cast several hundreds in all for the Emperor Kanghí. On one occasion, in 1680, the pieces, three hundred and twenty of all sizes, were to be tested in the presence of the court; but before doing so Verbiest "had an altar prepared on which he placed a cross. Then, clothed in his surplice and stole, he worshipped the true God, prostrating himself nine times, and striking the earth nine times with his forehead, in

[1] Magaillans' *China*, p. 147. *Chinese Repository*, Vol. I., p. 434.

the Chinese manner of expressing adoration; and after that he read the prayers of the church and sprinkled the cannon with holy water, having bestowed on each of them the name of a female saint, which he had himself drawn on the breech."[1] Some of the high officers were still opposed to the toleration of foreign priests, and the Governor of Chehkiang undertook to carry into effect the laws against their admission into the country and their proselyting labors; but Verbiest, on informing the Emperor of their character as excellent mathematicians and scholars, obtained their liberation. No foreigner has ever enjoyed so great favor and confidence from the rulers of China as this able priest. He seems indeed to have deserved this for his diligence, knowledge, and purity of conduct in devoting all his energies and opportunities to their good. His residence of thirty years at Peking (1658-1688) was passed under the eyes of suspicious observers; but his modesty in the end won their confidence as his writings and devotions called forth their approval.

During all this time—or at least since the other sects came to assist in the work—there had been constant disputes, as has already been intimated, between the disciples of Loyola, Dominic, and Francis, excited probably by rivalry, but ostensibly relating to the rites paid to deceased ancestors and to Confucius. Ricci had drawn up rules for the regulation of the Jesuits, in which he considered these customs to be merely civil and secular, and such as might be tolerated in their converts. Morales, a Spanish Dominican, however, opposed this view, declaring them to be idolatrous and sinful, and they were condemned as such by the Propaganda, which sentence was confirmed by Innocent X. in 1645. This decree of the see at Rome gave the Jesuits some annoyance, and they set themselves at work to procure its revision. Martinez was sent to Rome as their principal agent in this, and by many explanations and testimonials proved to the satisfaction of the tribunal of inquisitors their civil nature, and Alexander VII., in 1656, approved this opinion. There were thus two infallible decrees nearly opposed to each other, for Alexander took care not to directly contradict the bull of Inno-

[1] Huc, *Christianity in China*, Vol. III., p. 81.

cent, and worded his decision so that both claimed it. When all the missionaries were imprisoned or sent to Canton, a good opportunity offered for mutual consultation and decision upon these and other points. Twenty-three priests met in the Jesuit seminary at Canton in 1665, and drew up forty-two articles to serve hereafter for rules of conduct, all of which were unanimously adopted. The one relating to the ceremonies was as follows:

In respect to the customs by which the Chinese worship Confucius and the deceased, the answer of the congregation of the universal Inquisition, sanctioned in 1656 by his Holiness Alexander VII., shall be invariably followed; for it is founded upon the most probable opinion, without any evident proof to the contrary; and this probability being admitted, the door of salvation must not be shut against innumerable Chinese, who would abandon our Christian religion were they forbidden to attend to those things that they may lawfully and without injury to their faith attend to, and forced to give up what cannot be abandoned without serious consequences.

One member of this meeting, the Dominican Navarette, soon expressed his dissent, and the dispute was renewed as virulently as ever. The opponents of the Jesuits complained that they taught their converts that there was but little difference generally between Christianity and their own belief, and allowed them to retain their old superstitions; they were charged, moreover, with luxury and ambition, and neglecting the duties of their ministry that they might meddle in the affairs of State. These allegations were rebutted by the Jesuits, though it appears from Mosheim that some of them partially acknowledged their truth. In 1693 Maigrot, a bishop and apostolic vicar living in China, issued a mandate on his own authority diametrically opposed to the decision of the Inquisition and the Pope, in which he declared that *tien* signified nothing more than the material heavens, and that the Chinese customs and rites were idolatrous. In 1699 the Jesuits brought the matter before the Emperor in the following memorial:

We, your faithful subjects, although originally from distant countries, respectfully supplicate your Majesty to give us clear instructions on the following points. The scholars of Europe have understood that the Chinese practise certain ceremonies in honor of Confucius, that they offer sacrifices to heaven, and that they observe peculiar rites toward their ancestors; but persuaded that these ceremonies, sacrifices, and rites are founded in reason, though ignorant of their true intention, earnestly desire us to inform them. We have always supposed that Confucius was honored in China as a legislator, and that it was in this character alone, and with this view solely, that the ceremonies established in his honor were practised. We believe that the ancestral rites are only observed in order to exhibit the love felt for them, and to hallow the remembrance of the good received from them during their life. We believe that the sacrifices offered to heaven are not tendered to the visible heavens which are seen above us, but to the Supreme Master, Author, and Preserver of heaven and earth, and of all they contain. Such are the interpretation and the sense which we have always given to these Chinese ceremonies; but as strangers cannot be considered competent to pronounce on these important points with the same certainty as the Chinese themselves, we presume to request your Majesty not to refuse to give us the explanations which we desire concerning them. We wait for them with respect and submission.[1]

The Emperor's reply in 1700 to this petition, and another one presented to him, was sent to the Pope; in it he declared that "*tien* means the true God, and that the customs of China are political." The enemies of the Jesuits say that they "confirmed the sentiments expressed in the imperial rescript by the oaths which they exacted from a multitude of Chinese, among whom were many from the lowest classes, not only entirely ignorant of the meaning of many characters in their own language, but even of Christian doctrine." The strongest efforts were made by both parties to influence the decision of the Pope, but the Jesuits failed. In 1704 a decree of Clement XI. confirmed the decision of Bishop Maigrot. It had been reached after careful and candid examination, and was substantially as follows: "As the true God cannot conveniently be named in the Chinese language with European words, we must employ the words *Tien Chu*, *i.e.*, 'Lord of Heaven,' in use for a long time in China, and approved by both missionaries and their converts. We must, on the contrary, absolutely reject the appellation of *Tien* (Heaven) and *Shangtí* (August Emperor); and for this reason it must on no account be permitted that tablets shall be suspended in churches with the inscription *King Tien* (Adore Heaven)." The court of the Vatican had already dispatched a legate *à latere* and apostolic visitor to China in the person of

[1] *Life of Saint-Martin*, p. 292.

Tournon, who was consecrated Patriarch of Antioch in order to give him a title of sufficient dignity in the distant regions to which he was bound.

The legate landed at Macao in April, 1705, and was received with a show of honor by the governor and bishop. He arrived at Peking in December, but the Jesuits had already prejudiced the Emperor against him, and at an audience accorded to him in June, 1706, the former brought forward the subject to learn the legate's views. After some delay, however, the patriarch issued the Pope's mandate, which was contrary to the monarch's decision. Kanghí was not the man who would transfer to a pope the right of legislating over his own subjects, and in December, 1706, he decreed that he would countenance those missionaries who preached the doctrines of Ricci, but persecute those who followed the opinion of Maigrot. Examiners were appointed for ascertaining their sentiments, but Tournon, who had been banished to Macao, forbade the missionaries, under pain of excommunication, holding any discussion on these points with the examiners. The Bishop of Macao confined the legate in a private house, and when he used his ecclesiastical authority and powers against his enemies, stuck up a monitory on the very door of his residence, exhorting him to revoke his censures within three days under pain of excommunication, and exhibit proofs of his legation to his diocesan. This was re-echoed from Tournon by a still severer sentence against the bishop. Three new missionaries reached Macao at this juncture in January, 1710, and one of them, Père Ripa, gives an account of a nocturnal visit they paid the legate in his prison after eluding the vigilance of his guards. Ripa remarks that about forty missionaries of different religious orders were confined with Tournon, who had lately been made a cardinal, but he himself and his companions were left at liberty. His eminence sent a remonstrance to the Governor of Canton against his imprisonment, and also a memorial to the Emperor stating that six missionaries had arrived from Europe, three of whom were acquainted with mathematics, music, and painting. Ripa, who was to be the painter, says that he knew only the rudiments of the art, and records his dissatisfaction at this change in his vocation, but soon resigned himself to obedience. Tournon died in his confinement in July of the same year.

The proceedings of Tournon were mainly confirmed by the Pope, and in 1715 he dispatched Mezzabarba, another legate, by way of Lisbon, who was favorably received at Peking. He "was instructed to express the Pope's sincere gratitude to Kanghí for his magnanimous kindness toward the missionaries, to beg leave to remain in China as their head or as superior of the whole mission, and to obtain from Kanghí his consent that the Christians in China might submit to the decision of his Holiness concerning the rites." The Emperor evaded all reference to the rites, and the legate, soon perceiving that his Majesty would not surrender any part of his inherent authority, solicited and obtained permission at his last audience to return to Europe, which he did March 3, 1721. The first fifteen years of the eighteenth century was the period of the greatest prosperity to the Romish missions in China. It is stated that in the governor-generalship of Kiangnan and Kiangsí alone there were one hundred churches and a hundred thousand converts. The survey of the Empire was carried on by the Emperor's command from 1708 to 1718, under the direction of ten Jesuits, of whom Regis, Bouvet, and Jartoux were the most prominent.[1] It was a great work for that day, and considering the instruments they had, the vast area they traversed, and the imperfect education of their assistants, its accuracy and completeness form the best index of the ability of the surveyors.

The disputes between the various orders of missionaries and the resistance of some converts to the Emperor's commands respecting the ancestral rites, together with the representations of his own officers upon the tendency of the new religion to undermine his own authority, gradually opened his eyes to the true character of the propagandists. In 1718 he forbade any missionary remaining in the country without permission from himself, given only after their promise to follow the rules of Ricci. Yet no European missionary could repair to China

[1] An additional re-survey was made and presented to the Emperor Kienlung in 1761 by Benoit and Allerstein.

without subscribing a formula in which he promised fully and entirely to obey the orders of Clement XI. upon these ceremonies, and observe those injunctions without any tergiversation. Kanghí was made acquainted with all these matters and took his measures, gradually restraining the missionaries in their work and keeping them about him at court, while he allowed persecuting measures to be carried on in the provinces. The work of Ripa affords evidence of this plan, and it was characteristic of Chinese policy.

After the death of Kanghí in 1723 the designs of the government under his son Yungching were still more evident. In 1724 an order was promulgated in which every effort to propagate the *Tien Chu kiao*, or 'Religion of the Lord of Heaven,' as it was then and has ever since been called, was strictly prohibited. All missionaries not required at Peking for scientific purposes were ordered to leave the country, by which more than three hundred thousand converts were deprived of teachers. Many of the missionaries secreted themselves, and the converts exhibited the greatest fidelity in adhering to them even at the risk of death. When the missionaries reached Canton, where they were allowed to remain, they devised measures to return to their flocks, and frequently succeeded. The influence of those remaining at Peking was exerted to regain their former toleration, but with partial success. Their enemies in the provinces harassed the converts in order to extort money, and found plenty of assistants who knew the names and condition of all the leading adherents of the proscribed faith, and aided in compelling them to violate their consciences or lose their property.

The edict of Yungching forms an epoch in the Romish missions in China. Since that time they have experienced various degrees of quiet and storm, but on the whole decreasing in number and influence until the new era inaugurated by the treaties of 1858. The troubles in France and Europe toward the latter part of the eighteenth century withdrew the attention of the supporters of missions from those in China, while in the country itself the maintenance of the laws against the propagation of Christianity, and an occasional seizure of priests and converts by a zealous officer, caused a still further diminution. The edicts of Kienlung, soon after his accession in 1736, showed that no countenance was to be expected from court; the rulers were thoroughly dissatisfied with the foreigners, and ready to take almost any measures to relieve the country of them. Perhaps their personal conduct had something to do with this course of procedure, for Ripa, who cannot be accused of partiality, says, when speaking of the number of converts, that "if our European missionaries in China would conduct themselves with less ostentation, and accommodate their manners to persons of all ranks and conditions, the number of converts would be immensely increased. Their garments are made of the richest materials; they go nowhere on foot, but always in sedans, on horseback, or in boats, and with numerous attendants following them. With a few honorable exceptions, all the missionaries live in this manner; and thus, as they never mix with the people, they make but few converts. The diffusion of our holy religion in these parts has been almost entirely owing to the catechists who are in their service, to other Christians, or to the distribution of Christian books in the Chinese language. Thus there is scarcely a single missionary who can boast of having made a convert by his own preaching, for they merely baptize those who have been already converted by others."[1] But this missionary himself afterward assigns a much better reason for their not preaching, when he adds that, up to his time in 1714, "none of the missionaries had been able to surmount the language so as to make himself understood by the people at large." This remark must, however, be taken with some explanations. There had been about five hundred missionaries sent from Europe between 1580 and 1724, which was less than an annual average of four individuals during a century and a half.

When the intentions of the new Emperor were known, there would not long be wanting occasions to harass the Christians. In 1747 a persecution extended over all the provinces, and Bishop Sanz and five Dominican priests in Fuhkien lost their lives. All the foreign priests who could be found elsewhere were

---

[1] *Residence at Peking*, p. 43.

sent away—a mark of leniency the more striking when it was supposed by the Chinese that some of them had already once returned from banishment. The missions in Sz'chuen and Shansi suffered most, but through the zeal of their pastors maintained themselves better than elsewhere; their bishops, Muliener, and after him Pottier, contrived to remain in the country most of the time between 1712 and 1792. The missions in Yunnan and Kweichau were not so flourishing as that in Sz'chuen. In this province M. Gleyo was apprehended in 1767, and endured much suffering for the faith he came to preach; he remained in prison ten years, when he was liberated through the efforts of a Jesuit in the employ of government. For several years after this the order enjoyed comparative quiet, but in 1784 greater efforts than ever were made to discover and apprehend all foreign priests and their abettors, owing to the detection of four Europeans in Hukwang while they were going to their mission. M. de la Tour, the procureur of the mission at Canton, through whose instrumentality they were sent through the country, was apprehended and carried to Peking; and the hong merchant who had been his security was glad to purchase his own safety by the sacrifice of one hundred and twenty thousand taels of silver.

Didier Saint-Martin, who was then in Sz'chuen, gives a long account of his own capture, trial, and imprisonment, and many particulars of the sufferings of his fellow missionaries. Eighteen Europeans were taken away from the missions by it, but none of them were actually executed; twelve were sentenced to perpetual imprisonment, six having died, but for some reason the Emperor revoked the decree soon after it was made, and gave them all the choice to enter his service or leave the country; nine of the twelve preferred to depart, the other three joining the priests at the capital. This search was so close that few of the foreigners escaped. Pottier was not taken, though he was obliged at one time to conceal himself for a month in a small house, and in so confined a place that he hardly dared either to cough or to spit for fear of being discovered. Saint-Martin and Dufresse retired to Manila, where they were received with great honors, and were enabled to return after a time to Sz'chuen. The former died in 1801 in peace, but Dufresse was beheaded in 1814;[1] in 1816 M. Triora was strangled in Hupeh, and M. Clet three years after; in the interval, Schoeffler, Bounard, and Diaz perished, and Chapdelaine in 1856. But no data are available to show the number of native priests and converts who suffered death, torture, imprisonment, and banishment in these storms. The records of constancy and cheerful fortitude exhibited under tortures and cruel mockings, given in the writings of the time, show their faith in Christ. The details are summarized in Marshall's work, and probably the number may reasonably be estimated by hundreds.

The period which elapsed after the promulgation of the edicts of 1767 up to 1820 contains less to interest the reader than since the last date. At that time restored quiet in Europe urged a resumption of the work; and the *Annales de la Foi* henceforth continue the narratives of the missions, formerly recorded in the *Lettres Édifiantes*, with the approval of the directors and bishops. It is not easy at any period to learn their condition and number, for only vague estimates of hundreds of churches, hundreds of thousands of converts, scores of missionaries, schools, catechists, priests, and stations, comprise the data given in the flourishing days of Verbiest and Parennin. Perhaps many of the early statistics have perished, yet it has never been easy to obtain accurate data, and often they have been withheld from public knowledge. There is no responsibility or reckoning required from the managers of the missions by the body of the church as to what is done with the funds, as among Protestant missions. In 1820 an estimate gives 6 bishops, 2 coadjutors, 23 foreign missionaries, 80 native priests, and 215,000 converts. In 1839 a table in the *Annales* gives for that year, 8 bishops, 57 foreigners, 114 native priests, and 303,000 converts. In 1846 the record shows 12 bishops, 7 or 8 coadjutors, 80 foreign missionaries, 90 natives, and 400,000 converts; 54 boys' and 114 girls' schools are put down for Sz'chuen. In 1866 they report 20 bishops,

---

[1] *Annales de la Foi*, Tome I., pp. 25, 53, 68. Dufresse was afterward canonized.

233 foreign missionaries, 237 native priests, 12 colleges, 331 students in seven of them, and 363,000 converts; these figures include only those in the Eighteen Provinces. In 1870 the tables show 254 foreigners, bishops and missionaries, 138 native priests in nine provinces, and 404,530 converts.

Lastly, from the Hong Kong *Catholic Register* we learn that the statistics in 1881 were: Bishops, 41; European priests, 664; native priests, 559; converts *in toto*, 1,092,818; colleges, 34; convents, 34. The paper which publishes this summary, "from a most reliable source," gives no information as to where the missions or colleges are located, or what numbers are found in the different provinces. It is, moreover, somewhat difficult to learn what constitutes a college, or whether the grade in these institutions is uniform throughout the land. In addition to the education imparted at home, a number of Chinese are yearly sent to Rome to be educated at the College of the Propaganda. The total number of converts includes all the members of the various families who give an outward adherence to the rites of the church. In the persecutions which these adherents have endured at various times, some have left the faith, but a large number of the descendants of these early converts have remained faithful, generation after generation, to the religion which their ancestors had embraced under more favorable auspices. Hence this estimate represents the number now adhering to them, many of them being the descendants of early converts; and this number of followers has become so numerous largely by natural increase. We have no information as to the number of converts year by year. In one village of South China, where there are some Roman Catholics resident, it has been noted that the increase is almost entirely by natural generation. The girls of Catholic families are only permitted co-religionists. The men marry heathen wives on the promise that they will become Romanists. One man and his wife of this village first became converts. The number of adherents now here is over one hundred, all descendants of this first pair; and this increase is entirely by natural descent and by marriage.

With the increased openings since the treaties of 1858 the regulation of the missions has devolved on different societies, which have apportioned their laborers in the provinces. The Lazarists have Chihlí, Kiangsí, and Chehkiang; the Franciscans, Shantung, Shansí, Shensí, and Hukwang; the Jesuits, Kíangnan and eastern Chihlí; the Dominicans, Fuhkien; the Gallic church, all the western and south-western regions, with Manchuria; one society in Milan has charge of Honan, and another in Belgium labors in Mongolia. The successful efforts of M. Lagrené, the French envoy to China in 1844, to obtain formal recognition of the Christian religion and protection to its professors from their own rulers, entitle him to the thanks of every well-wisher of missions. The intention of the Chinese authorities in tolerating such efforts was to limit them to the newly opened ports, where alone churches could be erected, for the missionaries are disallowed free entrance into the country. This partial permission of 1844 prepared the way for the toleration articles in the treaties of 1858, when the four Powers present at Tientsin obtained a more explicit acknowledgment from the Emperor of the rights of Christian laborers and professors among the Chinese. Those articles have been in force during the past twenty years, and have proved a safeguard and a warrant for the faith of Christ and its adherents even beyond the hopes of those who first proposed them.

The exclusive labors of the Roman Catholics among the Chinese comprise a period of about two hundred and fifty years from the date of Ricci's reception at Peking. The various works written by them during this period contained not only the details of their labors, but nearly everything that was then known relating to the Chinese. The essays, translations, histories, travels, etc., of Visdelou, Mailla, Trigault, Semido, Amiot, Le Comte, and scores of others, still remain to inform those who seek to learn their acts.[1] Every reader must honor the men who thus suffered and labored, prospered and died, in the prosecution of their work. It is worthy of consideration, as to the self-supporting character of this work, that their constant experience has shown that, however numerous and zealous the converts, the presence of European pastors and overseers is

[1] Rémusat, *Nouveaux Mélanges*, pp. 207 ff.

indispensable to their spiritual prosperity.[1] Whether this is owing to the character of the Chinese mind, or to the little Christian instruction and principle these converts really have, cannot in most cases be easily decided. It can hardly be expected that pagans should perceive much difference immediately between their old worship and the ceremonies of the new faith in the presence of pictures, images, and crosses, before which they were taught to prostrate themselves. The native priests and catechists were not instructed to maintain the authority of the law and word of God above all human teachings in this respect, for the second commandment had been early expunged from the Decalogue, and thus the command of God made void, which prohibits man to make, to serve, or to bow down to such things. It may be this defect in their religious training which keeps these native priests in tutelage under the foreigners, and prevents the maintenance of self-supporting, indigenous churches under their oversight.

In former days the entrance of missionaries into the interior of China was attended with considerable hazard, delay, and uncertainty, arising from the weakness or ignorance of those guides to whose care they were entrusted, and the risks they ran if detected. This has now all passed away, and access to all parts of the Empire is even more free than it was in the days of the Emperor Kanghí. In those early times the development of missionary work was not as well understood as it is now after long experience, and less attention was paid to education and self-support. Those points were not appreciated even in Europe, and we should not look for stronger growth in the branches of the tree than in its trunk. Within the last twenty years, not only have the theological schools of the Romish missions increased so that eighteen were open in 1859, but with the introduction of the Sisters of Charity many thousands of young children are taught needlework, reading, and various handicrafts to prepare them for useful lives. These schools and orphanages exert a widespread and lasting influence. The baptism of children and adults has ever been a very

---

[1] *Lettres Édifiantes*, Tome IV., p. 77.

important work with the Roman Catholic missionaries, and especially (if its frequent mention is an evidence) the baptism of *moribunds*, or dying children of heathens. The agents in this work are usually elderly women, says Verolles, "who have experience in the treatment of infantile diseases. Furnished with innocent pills and a bottle of holy water whose virtues they extol, they introduce themselves into the houses where there are sick infants, and discover whether they are in danger of death; in this case they inform the parents, and tell them that before administering other remedies they must wash their hands with the purifying waters of their bottle. The parents, not suspecting this *pieuse ruse*, readily consent, and by these innocent frauds we procure in our mission the baptism of seven or eight thousand infants every year." Another missionary, Dufresse, one of the most distinguished of late years, says: "The women who baptize the infants of heathen parents announce themselves as consecrated to the healing of infants, and to give remedies gratis, that they may satisfy the vow of their father who has commanded this as an act of charity." The number of baptized children thus saved from perdition is carefully detailed in the annual reports, and calculations are made by the missionaries for the consideration of their patrons in France and elsewhere as to the expense incurred for this branch of labor, and the cost of each soul thus saved; and appeals for aid in sending out these female baptists are based upon the tabular reports. It may, however, be a question, even with a candid Romanist who believes that unbaptized infants perish eternally, whether baptism performed by women and unconsecrated laymen is valid; and still more so, whether it is ritual when done by stealth and under false pretences. The number thus annually baptized in all the missions cannot be placed much under fifty thousand, and some years it exceeds a hundred thousand. No attention seems to be given to the child in ordinary cases if it happen to live after this surreptitious baptism.

The degree of instruction given to the converts is trifling, partly owing to the great extent of a single diocese and partly to imperfect knowledge of the language on the part of missionaries. The vexations constantly experienced urge them to be cautious; and truly if a missionary believes that baptism, confirmation, confession, and absolution, are all the evidences of faith that are required in a convert to entitle him to salvation, it cannot be supposed he will deem it necessary to give them long-continued instruction. The causes which usually bring the converts into trouble with their countrymen or the officials were thus described many years ago by the Bishop of Caradre in Sz'chuen; they are still partly applicable.

First. Christians are frequently confounded with the members of the Triad Society, or of the White Lily sect, both by their enemies and by persons belonging to those associations.

Second. The Christians refuse to contribute to the erection or repair of temples, or subscribe to idolatrous feasts and superstitious rites; though, according to the *Annales*, they sometimes defray the charges of the theatrical exhibitions which follow, in order to avoid the malice of their adversaries.

Third. "Espousals are almost indissoluble in China, and whenever the Christians refuse to ratify them by proceeding to a marriage already commenced, they are regarded as lawbreakers and treated as such."[1] This is the most common source of trouble, especially when the parents of the girl have become converts since the betrothment, and the other party is anxious to fulfil the contract. These engagements are sometimes broken in a sufficiently unscrupulous manner, and nothing draws so much odium upon Christians as their refusal to adhere to these contracts. On one occasion this bishop assisted in breaking up such an engagment, when the parents, on the death of a sister of the girl, asserted that the deceased was the one who had been betrothed. He adds: "I think the faith of the parents and the purity of their motives will readily excuse them before God for the sin of lying." On other occasions the missionaries endeavor to dissolve these engagements by exhorting the believing party to take vows of celibacy.

Fourth. All communication with Europeans being interdicted, the magistrates seek diligently for every evidence of their exist-

---

[1] *Lettres Édifiantes*, Tome III., p. 37, where there appear two or three cases of this and Saint-Martin's reasoning on the point.

ence in the country, by searching for the objects used in worship, as crosses, breviaries, etc.

Fifth. The little respect the converts have for their ancestors is always an offence in the eyes of the pagans, and leads to recrimination and vexatious annoyances.

Sixth. As the converts are obliged to take down the ancestral tablets in order to put up those of their own religion, they are seldom forgiven in this change, and occasion is taken therefrom to persecute.

Seventh. The indiscreet zeal of the neophytes leading them to break the idols or insult the objects of public worship is one of the most common causes of persecution.

Eighth. The disputes between the missionaries themselves, regarding the ceremonies, have frequently excited troubles.

In addition to these causes, some of which are now removed, there are others which have grown up since the toleration granted to Christianity by the treaties, and which may develop still more. They are discussed in the minute drawn up by the Chinese government in 1871, after the Tientsin riot, in which eight rules for their regulation are proposed. The grievances refer to the seclusion of children in orphanages; to the presence of women in religious assemblies; to missionaries interfering in legal cases so as to screen criminals, and their interchanging passports; to the neophytes rescuing criminals from justice; to the missionaries affecting the style of native officials; and, lastly, to their demand for land alleged to have once belonged to them, whatever may have been its ownership meanwhile. This has since ceased, and the others have been somewhat restrained.

Christians sometimes refuse to have their deceased friends buried with the idolatrous ceremonies required by their relatives, upon which the latter occasionally carry the matter before the officers, or resort to petty annoyances. In order to keep up the spirit of devotion among the neophytes, crucifixes, reliquaries, and other articles were given them, and "God wrought several miracles among them to authorize the practice." These articles, in the estimation of both priest and people, probably have no little influence over the demons which vex and harass the pagans, but which never trouble Christians. Saint-Martin, writing to his father from the capital of Sz'chuen in 1774, says: "The most sensible proof for the pagans, and one always in force, is the power the Christians have over demons.[1] It is astonishing how these poor infidels are tormented, and they can find remedy only in the prayers of Christians, by whose help they are delivered and then converted. Seven or eight leagues from this spot is a house which has been infested with demons for a month; they maltreat all who come near them, and have set the dwelling on fire at different times. They have had recourse to all kinds of superstitious ceremonies, calling in the native priests, but all to no effect; and the master of the family where I am staying has now gone to assist them. He is a man of lively faith, and has already performed many miraculous cures."[2]

It is interesting to compare with this the account of Friar Odoric, "How the friars deal with devils in Tartary." In his *Travels* we read that "God Almighty hath bestowed such grace upon the Minor friars that in Great Tartary they think it a mere nothing to expel devils from the possessed, no more, indeed, than to drive a dog out of the house. For there be many in those parts possessed of the devil, both men and women, and these they bind and bring to our friars from as far as ten days' journey off. The friars bid the demons depart forth instantly from the bodies of the possessed, in the name of Jesus Christ, and they do depart immediately in obedience to this command. Then those who have been delivered from the demon straightway cause themselves to be baptized; and the friars take their idols, which are made of felt, and carry them to the fire, while all the people of the country round assemble to see their neighbor's gods burnt. The friars accordingly cast the idols into the fire, but they leap out again. And so the friars take holy water and sprinkle it upon the fire, and that straightway drives away the demon from the fire; so the friars again casting the idols into the fire, they are consumed.

[1] *Lettres Édifiantes*, Tomes I., pp. 39 and 151, passim, and IV., p. 27.
[2] *Life of Didier Saint-Martin*, p. 35.

And then the devil in the air raises a shout, saying: 'See then! see then! how I am expelled from my dwelling place!' And in this way our friars baptize great numbers in that country."[1]

When persons educated in a country like France allow their converts to entertain such ideas, even if they do not favor them

Roman Catholic Altar near Shanghai.

themselves, and countenance their endeavors to exorcise the possessed, we cannot look for a very high degree of knowledge or piety. If they are brought out of pagan darkness, it is but little if any better than into light hardly bright enough to enable them even to distinguish trees from men.

The points of similarity between Buddhism and Romanism have already been noticed, and the converts from one to the

[1] Yule, *Cathay and the Way Thither*, Vol. I., p. 155.

other see but little more change than they do when going from Buddhism to the metaphysical speculations of the learned *ju kiao.* If Romish priests have allowed their converts to worship before pagan images, provided a cross is put into the candles, it would not be difficult for the latter to put the names of their departed parents behind the "tablets of religion," and worship them together. Similar to such a permission is the combination of the cross and dragon carved on a Romish altar near Shanghai, given on the preceding page, and at which both pagans and Christians could alike worship.

Agnuses, crosses, etc., are easily substituted for coins and charms, and it does not surely require much faith to believe the former as effectual as the latter. The neophyte takes away the tablet in his house or shop having *shin*, 'æon' or 'spirit,' written on it,[1] and puts up another, on which is written *shin, chin chu, tsao tien ti jin-wuh*, or 'God, true Lord, Creator of heaven, earth, man, and all things,' and burns the same incense before this as before that. Chinese demigods are changed for foreign saints, with this difference, that now they worship they know not what, while before they knew something of the name and character of the ancient hero from popular accounts and historical legends. They cease, indeed, to venerate the queen of Heaven, holy mother Ma tsupu, but what advance in true religion has been made by falling down before the Queen of Heaven, holy mother Mary? The people call the Buddhist idols and the Romish images by the same name, and apply much the same terms to their ceremonies. Such converts can easily be numbered by thousands; and it is a wonder, indeed, when one considers the nature of the case, that the whole population of China have not long since become "devout confessors" of this faith. Conversions depend, in such cases, on almost every other kind of influence than that of the Holy Spirit blessing his own word in an intelligent mind and a quickened conscience. The missionaries write that "being forced in three or four months after their arrival to preach

---

[1] Converts in Sz'chuen sometimes steal the idols from the roadside. *Lettres Édifiantes*, Tome I., p. 219.

when they do not know the language sufficiently either to be understood or to understand themselves, they have seen their auditors immediately embrace Christianity."

We pass no decision upon these converts, except what is given or drawn from the writings of their teachers. Human nature is everywhere the same in its great lineaments, and the effect of living godly lives in Christ Jesus will everywhere excite opposition, calumny, persecution, and death, according to the liberty granted the enemies of the truth. There may have been true converts among the adherents to Romanism; but what salutary effects has this large body of Christians wrought in the vast population of China during the three hundred years since Ricci established himself at Nanking? None, absolutely none, that attract attention. The letters of some of the missionaries written to their friends breathe a spirit of pious ardor and true Christian principle worthy of all imitation. Among the best letters contained in the *Annales* is one from Dufresse to his pupils then at Penang. It is a long epistle, and contains nothing (with one exception) which the most scrupulous Protestant would not approve. The same may be said of most of the letters contained in the same collection written in prison by Gagelin, a missionary who was strangled in Annam in 1833. It is hardly possible to doubt, when reading the letters of these two men, both of whom were martyred for the faith they preached, that they sincerely loved and trusted in the Saviour they proclaimed. Many of their converts also exhibit the greatest constancy in their profession, preferring to suffer persecution, torture, imprisonment, banishment, and death rather than to deny their faith, though every inducement of prevarication and mental reservation was held out to them by the magistrates in order to avoid the necessity of proceeding to extreme measures. If undergoing the loss of all things is an evidence of piety, many of them have abundantly proved their title to this virtue. But until there shall be a complete separation from idolatry and superstition; until the confessional shall be abolished, and the worship of the Virgin, wearing crosses and rosaries, and reliance on ceremonies and penances be stopped; until the entire Scriptures and Decalogue be taught to the converts; until, in short, the essential doctrine of justification by faith alone be substituted for the many forms of justification by works, the mass of converts to Romanism in China can hardly be considered as much better than baptized pagans.[1]

Turn we now to a brief survey of the efforts of Protestants among the Chinese, and the results which have attended their labors. Hardly forty years have passed since the treaty of Nanking opened the five ports to their direct work in the Empire, and the results thus far necessarily partake of the incompleteness of new enterprises. The radical distinction between their modes of operation and those of their predecessors is indicated in the names 'Religion of Heaven's Lord' and 'Religion of Jesus;' the Romanists depend much on their teachings and ceremonies to convert men, the Protestants on the preaching of the word of God and a blessing on its vital truths.

The first Protestant missionary to China was Rev. Robert Morrison, of Morpeth, England, who was sent out by the London Missionary Society. He arrived at Canton, by way of New York, in September, 1807, and lived there for a year, in a quiet manner, in the factory of Messrs. Milner and Bull, of New York. He early made the acquaintance of Sir George T. Staunton, one of his firmest friends, and already well versed in Chinese studies; Mr. Robarts, the chief of the British factory, advised him to avow his intention to the Chinese of translating the Scriptures into their language, on the ground that it was a divine book which Christians highly esteemed and which the Chinese should have the opportunity of examining. In consequence of difficulties connected with the trade, he was obliged to leave Canton in 1808 with all British subjects and repair to Macao, where he deemed it prudent to maintain a careful retirement in

[1] An exhaustive collection of the titles of every work of importance upon Catholic missions in China, as well as a *résumé* of their periodical publications, may be found in M. Cordier's *Dictionnaire bibliographique des ouvrages Chinois*, Tome I., pp. 330–578, and following these pages are the works concerning Protestant missions, pp. 578–633. Compare also Thos. Marshall, *Christian Missions: their Agents and their Results*, London, 1863, and Chr. H. Kalkar, *Geschichte der christlichen Mission unter den Heiden*, Gütersloh, 1879–80.

order not to attract undue notice from the Portuguese priests. His associate, Dr. Milne, observed, with reference to these traits in his character, that "the patience that refuses to be conquered, the diligence that never tires, the caution that always trembles, and the studious habit that spontaneously seeks retirement were best adapted for the first Protestant missionary to China."

He married Miss Mary Morton in 1809, and accepted the appointment of translator under the East India Company, in whose service he continued until 1834. His position was now a well-understood one, and his official connexion obtained for him all necessary security so that he could prosecute his work with diligence and confidence. He no doubt did wisely in the circumstances in which he was placed, for his dictionary could hardly have been printed, or his translation of the Scriptures and other works been so successfully carried on, without the countenance and assistance of that powerful body. The entire New Testament was published in 1814, about half of it having been translated by Morrison and the remainder revised from a manuscript which had been deposited in 1739 in the British Museum.

Rev. W. Milne arrived in July, 1813, as his associate, and resided in Canton, leaving his wife at Macao. In 1814 he sailed for the Indian Archipelago, provided with about seventeen thousand copies of Testaments and tracts for distribution among the Chinese there. He stopped at Banca on his route, and then proceeded to Java, where he was received by Sir Stamford Raffles, a man far in advance of the times in his support and patronage of missions. Milne was enabled to travel over the island and distribute such books as he had. From Java he went to Malacca, then a Dutch settlement, afterward returning to Canton, where he remained undisturbed, though a severe persecution, in which Dufresse lost his life, was waging against the Christians throughout the Empire. Milne, finding it difficult to prosecute his labors in China (for the East India Company would not countenance him), embarked for Malacca in 1815, accompanied by a teacher and workmen for printing Chinese books; here he resided till his death in 1822.

The leading objects in sending Morrison to Canton, namely, the translation of the Bible and preparation of a dictionary, occupied the greater portion of his time. He soon commenced a Sabbath service with his domestics and acquaintances in his own apartments, which he never relinquished, though it did not expand into a regular public congregation during his lifetime. He considered this as one of the most important parts of his work, and was much encouraged when in 1814 one of his audience, Tsai A-ko, made a profession of his faith and was baptized. He was the first convert, and it is reasonably to be hoped, judging from his after-life, that he sincerely believed to salvation.

The compilation of the dictionary progressed so well that in 1814 a few members of the Company's establishment, among whom Mr. Elphinstone and Sir George Staunton were prominent, interested themselves in getting it printed. The Court of Directors responded to the application on the most liberal scale, sending out as printer P. P. Thoms, together with a printing office. The first volume was issued in 1817, and the whole was completed in six quarto volumes, containing four thousand five hundred and ninety-five pages, in 1823, at an expense of about twelve thousand pounds sterling. It consisted of three parts, viz., characters arranged according to their radicals, according to their pronunciation, and an English and Chinese part. This work contributed much to the advancement of a knowledge of Chinese literature, and its aid in missions has been manifold greater. The plan was rather too comprehensive for one man to fill up, and also involved much repetition; a reprint of the second part was issued in a smaller volume, in 1854, without material addition.

While the dictionary was going through the press, the translation of the Old Testament was progressing by the joint labors of Morrison and Milne, and in November, 1818, the entire Bible was published. Another version, by Dr. Marshman at Serampore, was completed and printed with movable types in 1822. A second edition of the Baptist version was never struck off, and comparatively few copies have ever been circulated among the Chinese. Both these versions are such that a sincere inquirer after the truth cannot fail to comprehend the meaning, though both are open to criticisms and contain mistakes incident to first translations. They are now numbered among superseded versions like those of Wiclif and Tyndal, the Italic and Ulfilas in other languages, but will ever be regarded with gratitude.[1]

During the years he was thus engaged Morrison published a tract on Redemption, a translation of the Assembly's Catechism, church of England liturgy, a synopsis of Old Testament history, a hymn book, and a Tour of the World; altogether, nearly thirty thousand copies were printed and distributed. He prepared a Chinese grammar on the model of a common English grammar, which was printed at Serampore in 1815; also a volume of miscellaneous information on the chronology, festivals, geography, and other subjects relating to China, under the title of *View of China for Philological Purposes*. The list of his writings comprises thirty-one titles, of which nineteen are in English; each work bears witness to his learning and piety.

In 1821 Mrs. Morrison died, and about eight months after he visited Malacca and Singapore, where he was much delighted by what he saw. The Anglo-Chinese College was then under the care of Collie, and this visit from its founder encouraged both principal and students. In 1824 he returned to England and was honorably received by his Majesty George IV., and obtained the approbation of all who took an interest in the promotion of religion and learning. He published a volume of sermons and a miscellany called *Horæ Sinicæ* while in England; and having formed a second matrimonial connection, left his native land again in May, 1826, under different circumstances from the first time. During his absence the mission at Canton was left in charge of the first native preacher, Liang Kung-fah, or Liang A-fah, whom Morrison had ordained as an evangelist. This worthy man carried on his useful labors in preaching and writing until his death in 1855 at that city, from whence, in 1834, he had been forced to flee for his life. He takes a deservedly high position at the head of the native Protestant Christian min-

---

[1] Medhurst's *China*, p. 217. *Chinese Repository*, Vol. IV., p. 249. *Life of Morrison*, by his widow, passim, 2 Vols., London, 1839. Wylie in *Chinese Recorder*, Vol. I., pp. 121, 145. *Lives of the Leaders of our Church Universal*, p. 819, Phila., 1879.

istry among the Chinese in respect to time, and his writings have been highly successful and beneficial.

During the years which elapsed between the return and death of Morrison, he was principally occupied by his duties as translator to the Company and in literary labors. His *Memoirs* furnish all the particulars of their contents, as well as the details of his useful and uneventful life. His last years were cheered by the arrival of five fellow-laborers from the United States, the first who had come to his assistance since Milne left him in 1814. On the dissolution of the East India Company's establishment, in April, 1834, he was appointed interpreter to the King's Commission, but his death took place August 1, 1834, at the age of fifty-two, even then much worn out with his unaided labors of twenty-seven years.

Perhaps no two persons were ever less alike than the founders of the Romish and Protestant missions to China, but no plans of operations could be more dissimilar than those adopted by Ricci and Morrison. We have already sketched the life-work of the former, obtained from friendly sources. When Morrison was sent out the directors of the London Missionary Society thus expressed their views of his labors: "We trust that no objection will be made to your continuing in Canton till you have accomplished your great object of acquiring the language; when this is done, you may probably soon afterward begin to turn this attainment into a direction which may be of extensive use to the world; perhaps you may have the honor of forming a Chinese dictionary, more comprehensive and correct than any preceding one, or the still greater honor of translating the sacred Scriptures into a language spoken by a third part of the human race." The enterprise thus committed to the hands of a single individual was only part of a system which neither the projectors nor their collaborator supposed would end there. They knew that the great work of evangelizing and elevating a mass of mind like that using the Chinese language required large preparatory labors, of which those here mentioned were among the most important. China was a sealed country when Morrison landed on its shores, and he could not have forced his way into it if he had tried, with any prospect of ultimate success, even by adopting the same plans which Ricci did. It is doubtful if he could have lived there at all had it not been for the protection of the East India Company. After all his toil, and faith, and prayer, he only saw three or four converts, no churches, schools, or congregations publicly assembled; but his last letter breathes the same desires as when he first went out: "I wait patiently the events to be developed in the course of Divine Providence. The Lord reigneth. If the kingdom of God our Saviour prosper in China, all will be well; other matters are comparatively of small importance." He died just as the day of change and progress was dawning in Eastern Asia, but his life was very far from being a failure in its results or influence. The principles of these two missionaries have been followed out by their successors, and we are quite willing to let their results be the test of their foundation upon the Chief Corner Stone.

Protestant missions among the Chinese emigrants in Malacca, Penang, Singapore, Rhio, Borneo, and Batavia have never taken much hold upon them, and they are at present all suspended or abandoned. The first named was established in 1815 by Milne, and was conducted longest and with the most efficiency, though the labors at the other points have been carried on with zeal and a degree of success. The comparatively small results which have attended all these missions may be ascribed to two or three reasons, besides the fewness of the laborers. The Chinese residing in these settlements consist chiefly of emigrants who have fled or left their native countries, in all cases without their families, some to avoid the injustice or oppression of their rulers, but more to gain a livelihood they cannot find so well at home. Consequently they lead a roving life; few of them marry or settle down to become valuable citizens, and fewer still are sufficiently educated to relish or care for instruction or books. These communities are much troubled by branches of the Triad Society, and the restless habits of the Malays are congenial to most of the emigrants who enter among them. The Chinese, coming as they do from different parts of their own land, speak different dialects, and soon learn the Malay language as a lingua franca: their children also learn it still more thoroughly from their mothers, notwithstanding the education their fathers give them in Chinese. The want of fixedness in the Chinese population therefore partly accounts for the little permanent impression made on it in these settlements by missionary efforts.

It was at Malacca that the Anglo-Chinese College was established in 1818 by Dr. Morrison, assisted by other friends of religion. Its objects were to afford Europeans the means of acquiring the Chinese language and enable Chinese to become acquainted with the religion and science of the West. It was productive of good up to the time of its removal to Hongkong in 1844. About seventy persons were baptized while the mission remained at Malacca, and about fifty students finished their education, part of whom were sincere Christians and all of them respectable members of society. Three or four of the converts have become preachers. There is little hesitation, however, in saying that the name and array of a college were too far in advance of the people among whom it was situated. The efforts made in it would probably have been more profitably expended in establishing common schools among the people, in which Christianity and knowledge went hand in hand. It is far better among an ignorant pagan people that a hundred persons should know one thing than that one man should know a hundred; the widest diffusion of the first elements of religion and science is most desirable. The mission was not, however, large enough at any one time for its members to superintend many common schools. Among the books issued besides Bibles and tracts were a periodical called the *Indo-Chinese Gleaner*, edited by Dr. Milne; a translation of the Four Books, by Mr. Collie; an edition of Prémare's *Notitia Linguæ Sinicæ;* a life of Milne, and a volume of sermons by Morrison. The number of volumes printed in Chinese was about half a million.

The mission at Georgetown, in the island of Penang, like that at Malacca, was established in 1819 by the London Missionary Society, and continued till 1843, at which time it was suspended. The mission at Singapore was commenced in 1819 by Mr. Milton; the colonial government granted a lot, and a chapel and other buildings were erected in the course of a few years. Messrs. Smith and Tomlin came to the settlement in 1827, but did not remain long. Gutzlaff came over from the Dutch settlement at Rhio, but did not remain long enough to effect anything; nor did Abeel, who came from China in 1831 and left soon after for Siam. The German missionary at this station, Thomsen, when about to leave in 1834, sold his printing apparatus to the mission newly established there under the American Board by Tracy. The prospects in China appearing unpromising at this time, it was designed by the directors of the American society to establish a well-regulated school for both Chinese and Malays, which was by degrees to become a seminary, and as many primary schools as there were means to support; besides the usual labors in preaching and visiting, a type foundry and printing office for manufacturing books in Chinese, Malay, Bugis, and Siamese were also contemplated. In December, 1834, Tracy was joined by the Rev. P. Parker, M.D., who opened a hospital in the Chinese part of the town for the gratuitous relief of the sick; in 1835 Wolfe arrived from England, and two years afterward Rev. Messrs. Dickinson, Hope, and Travelli, and North from the United States, to take charge of the schools and printing office. The school established by the American mission was carried on until 1844, when the mission was removed to China and the Malay portion of it given up.

The English mission, after the death of Wolfe in 1837, was under the care of Messrs. Dyer and Stronach, the former of whom had removed there from Penang and Malacca. Dyer had been for many years engaged in preparing steel punches for a font of movable Chinese type, and his patient labors had already overcome the principal difficulties in the way when the work was arrested by his death in 1843. He had, however, finished matrices for so many characters of two fonts that the enterprise needed only to be carried on by a practised mechanic to assure its success. This was afterward done by Messrs. Cole and Gamble of the American Presbyterian Board. In their superior styles and the different sizes now in use we must not forget Dyer's initiatory steps. This gentleman labored nearly seventeen years with a consecration of energy and singleness of purpose seldom exceeded, and won the affectionate respect of the natives wherever he lived. The mission was continued until 1845, when the printing office was removed to Hongkong, and nearly all proselyting efforts in the colony by British Christians suspended. This point of influence has peculiar claims on them as a radiating centre for the various nations and tribes which trade in Singapore.

The mission to the Chinese in Java was commenced by Slater in 1819 and reinforced in 1822 by Medhurst, who continued in charge of it, with some interruptions, until 1843, when he removed to Shanghai. The Dutch churches have carried on evangelizing work in all their colonies, aided and guided somewhat by the government officials, but have done almost nothing for the Chinese, except as they have been addressed in Malay. Such labors in the Dutch colonies have been left to them, and foreign societies have now withdrawn from the Archipelago in a great measure. The efforts of the American missionaries were confined to Borneo and Singapore up to 1844, when they all removed to China. The suspicious and restrictive bearing of the Dutch authorities toward such efforts had its influence in making this change.

A summary of labors at the stations was given by Medhurst in 1837, who refers in it almost exclusively to the English missionaries, as the Americans had at that time only recently commenced operations. "Protestant missionaries, considering themselves excluded from the interior of the Empire of China, and finding a host of emigrants in the various countries in the Malayan Archipelago, aimed first to enlighten these, with the hope that if properly instructed and influenced they would, on their return to their native land, carry with them the gospel they had learned and spread it among their countrymen. With this view they established themselves in the various colonies around China, studied the language, set up schools and seminaries, wrote and printed books, conversed extensively with the people, and tried to collect congregations to whom they might preach the word of life. Since the commencement of their missions they have translated the Holy Scriptures and printed two thousand complete Bibles in two sizes, ten thousand Testaments and thirty thousand separate books, and upward of half a million of tracts in Chinese; besides four thousand Testaments and one hundred and fifty thousand tracts in the languages of the archipelago, making about twenty millions of printed pages. About ten thousand children have passed through the mission schools, nearly one hundred persons have been baptized, and several native preachers raised up, one of whom has proclaimed the gospel to his countrymen and endured persecution for Jesus' sake."

Since this was written the number of pages printed and circulated has more than doubled, the number of scholars taught has increased many thousands, and preaching proportionably extended; while a few more have professed the gospel by baptism and a generally consistent life. All these missions, so far as the Chinese are concerned, are now suspended, and, unless the Dutch resume them, are not likely to be soon revived. The greater openings in China itself, and the small number of qualified men ready to enter them, invited all the laborers away from the outskirts and colonies to the borders, and into the mother country itself. The idea entertained, that the colonists would react upon their countrymen at home, proved illusive; for the converts, when they returned to dwell among their heathen countrymen, were lost in the crowd, and though they may not have adopted or sanctioned their old heathen customs, were too few to work in concert and too ignorant and unskilled to carry on such labors.[1]

When Robert Morrison died at Canton in 1834, the prospect of the extension of evangelistic work among the people was nearly as dark as when he landed; in China itself during that time only three assistants had come to his help, for there were few encouragements for them to stay. Bridgman, the first missionary from the American churches to China, in company with D. Abeel, seaman's chaplain at Whampoa, arrived in February, 1830. Abeel remained nearly a year, when he went to Singapore, and subsequently to Siam. They were received in Canton

[1] Besides the regular publications of the societies engaged in this branch of missions which give authentic details, see the memoirs of Abeel, Dyer, Milne, and Morrison, Tomlin's *Missionary Letters*, and Abeel's *Residence in China* and the neighboring countries.

by the house of Olyphant & Co., in whose establishment one or both were maintained during the first three years, and whose partners remained the friends and supporters of all efforts for the evangelization of the Chinese till its close, fifty years afterward. Bridgman took four or five boys as scholars, but his limited accommodations prevented the enlargement of the school, and in 1834 it was disbanded by the departure of its pupils, whose friends feared to be involved in trouble.

During the summer of 1833 Liang A-fah distributed a large number of books in and about Canton, a work which well suited his inclinations. Many copies of the Scriptures and his own tracts had reached the students assembled at the literary examinations, when the officers interfered to prevent him. In 1834 the authorities ordered a search for those natives who had "traitorously" assisted Lord Napier in publishing an appeal to the Chinese, and Liang A-fah and his assistants were immediately suspected. Two of the latter were seized, one of whom was beaten with forty blows upon his face for refusing to divulge; the other made a full disclosure, and the police next day repaired to his shop and seized three printers, with four hundred volumes and blocks; the men were subsequently released by paying about eight hundred dollars. Liang A-fah fled, and a body of police arrived at his native village to arrest him, but not finding him or his family they seized three of his kindred and sealed up his house. He finally made his way to Macao and sailed to Singapore.

Few books were distributed after this at Canton until ten years later, but numerous copies were circulated along the coast as far north as Tientsin, accompanied with such explanations as could be given. The first and most interesting of these voyages was made by Gutzlaff, on board a junk proceeding from Bangkok to Tientsin, June 9, 1831, in which the sociable character of the Chinese and their readiness to receive and entertain foreigners when they could do so without fear of their rulers was plainly seen.[1] After his arrival at Macao, December 13th,

[1] For an account of a trip much like it, see *Annales de la Foi*, Tome VII., p. 356.

he was engaged by the enlightened chief of the English factory, Charles Marjoribanks, as interpreter to accompany Lindsay in the ship Lord Amherst, on an experimental commercial voyage which occupied about seven months (February 26 to September 5, 1832), and presented further opportunities for learning the feelings of the Chinese officers regarding foreign intercourse. Many religious and scientific books were distributed, among which was one giving a general account of the English nation that was eagerly received by all classes. Within a few weeks after his return Gutzlaff started a third time, October 20th, in the Sylph, an opium vessel in the employ of a leading English firm at Canton, and went as far as Manchuria while the winds were favorable. She returned to Macao April 29, 1833, visiting many places on the downward trip. The interest aroused in England and America among political, commercial, and religious people, fifty years ago, by the reports of these three voyages can now hardly be appreciated. They opened the prospect of new relations with one-half of mankind, and the other half who had long felt debarred from entering upon their rightful fields in all these diversified interests prepared for great efforts.

Great Britain took the lead in breaking down the barriers, and the religious world urged on the work of missions. Contributions were sent to Gutzlaff from England and America, encouraging him to proceed, and grants were made to aid in printing Bibles and tracts. In 1835 he gave up his connection with the opium trade and took the office of interpreter to the English consular authorities on a salary of eight hundred pounds sterling, which he retained till his death, August 9, 1851, aged forty-eight. He was a man of great industry and knowledge of Chinese, and carried on a missionary organization at Hongkong by means of native Christians for several years. His publications in the Chinese, Japanese, Dutch, German, English, Siamese, Cochinchinese, and Latin languages number eighty-five in all; they are now seldom seen.

In 1835 Medhurst visited China, and, assisted by the house of Olyphant & Co., embarked in the brig Huron, accompanied by the American missionary Stevens and furnished with a supply of books. During the three months of the voyage, they "went through various parts of four provinces and many villages, giving away about eighteen thousand volumes, of which six thousand were portions of the Scriptures, among a cheerful and willing people, without meeting with the least aggression or injury; having been always received by the people with a cheerful smile, and most generally by the officers with politeness and respect." Medhurst's ability to speak the Amoy dialect introduced him to the people in the junks at all the ports on the coast. Years after this voyage the Methodist missionaries at Fuhchau found that some of the books given away on Haitan Island had been read and remembered, and thus prepared the people there for listening to further preaching.

The most expensive enterprise for this object was set on foot in 1836, and few efforts to advance the cause of religion among the Chinese have been planned on a scale of greater liberality. The brig Himmaleh was purchased in New York by the firm of Talbot, Olyphant & Co., principally for the purpose of aiding missionaries in circulating religious books on the coasts of China and the neighboring countries, and arrived in August, 1836. Gutzlaff, who was then engaged as interpreter to the English authorities, declined going in her, because in that case he must resign his commission, and there was no other missionary in China acquainted with the dialects spoken on the coast. The brig remained unemployed, therefore, until December, when she was dispatched on a cruise among the islands of the archipelago under the direction of Mr. Stevens, accompanied by G. T. Lay, agent of the British and Foreign Bible Society, recently arrived. This decision of Gutzlaff, who had again and again urged such a measure, and had himself ceased his voyages on the coast because of his implied connection thereby with the opium trade, was quite unexpected. The death of Mr. Stevens at Singapore, in January, threw the chief responsibility and direction of the undertaking upon Capt. Frazer, who seems to have been poorly qualified for any other than the maritime part. Rev. Messrs. Dickinson and Wolfe went in Stevens' place, but as none of these gentlemen understood the Malayan language, less direct intercourse was had with the people at the places where they stopped than was anticipated. The Himmaleh reached China in July, 1837, and as there was no one qualified to go in her, she returned to the United States. An account of the voyage was written by Lay and published in New York, in connection with that of the ship Morrison to Japan in August, 1837, by C. W. King, of the firm of Olyphant & Co., under whose direction the trip of the latter was taken for the purpose of restoring seven shipwrecked Japanese to their native land. Gutzlaff accompanied this vessel as interpreter, for three of the men were under the orders of the English superintendent; the expedition failed in its object, and all the men were brought back. Probably fifty thousand books in all were scattered on the coast in these and other voyages, and more than double that number about Canton, Macao, and their vicinity.

This promiscuous distribution of books has been criticised by some as injudicious and little calculated to advance the objects of a Christian mission. The funds expended in printing and circulating books, it was said by these critics, who have never undertaken aught themselves, could have been much better employed in establishing schools. To scatter books broadcast among a people whose ability to read them was not ascertained, and under circumstances which prevented any explanation of the design in giving them or inquiries as to the effects produced, was not, at first view, a very wise or promising course. But it must be remembered that prior to the treaty of Nanking this was the only means of approaching the people of the country. The Emperor forbade foreigners residing in his borders except at Canton, and Protestant missionaries did not believe that it was the best means of recommending their teachings to come before his subjects as persistent violators of his laws; God's providence would open the way when the laborers were ready. No one supposed that the desire to receive books was an index of the ability of the people to understand them or love of the doctrines contained in them. If the plan offered a reasonable probability of effecting some good, it certainly could do almost no harm, for the respect for printed books assured us that they would not be wantonly destroyed, but rather, in most cases, carefully preserved. The business of tract distribution and colportage may, however, be carried too far in advance of other parts of missionary work. It is much easier to write, print, and give away religious treatises, than it is to sit down with the people and explain the leading truths of the Bible; but the two go well together among those who can read, and in no nation is it more desirable that they should be combined. If the books be given away without explanation, the people do not understand the object and feel too little interest in them to take the trouble to find out; if the preacher deliver an intelligible discourse, his audience will probably remember its general purport, but they will be likely to read the book with more attention and understand the sermon better when the two are combined; the voice explains the book and the book recalls the ideas and teachings of the preacher.

It is not surprising that the fate of these books cannot be traced, for that is true of such labors in other lands. On the one hand, they have been seen on the counters of shops cut in two for wrapping up medicines and fruit—which the shopman would not do with the worst of his own books; on the other, a copy of a gospel containing remarks was found on board the admiral's junk at Tinghai, when that town was taken by the English in 1840. They certainly have not all been lost or contemptuously destroyed, though perhaps most have been like seed sown by the wayside. In missions, as in other things, it is impossible to predict the result of several courses of action before trying them; and if it was believed that many of those who receive books can read them, there was a strong inducement to press this branch of labor, when, too, it was the only one which could be brought to bear upon large portions of the people.

In 1832 the *Chinese Repository* was commenced by Bridgman and encouraged by Morrison, who, with his son, continued to furnish valuable papers and translations as long as they lived. Its object was to diffuse correct information concerning China, while it formed a convenient repertory of the essays, travels, translations, and papers of contributors. It was issued monthly for twenty years under the editorship of Messrs. Bridgman and Williams, and contains a history of foreign intercourse and missions during its existence. The *Chinese Recorder* has since chronicled the latter cause and the *China Review* taken the literary branch.

In 1834 Dr. Parker joined the mission at Canton, and opened a hospital, in October, 1835, for the gratuitous relief of such diseases among the Chinese as his time and means would allow, devoting his attention chiefly to ophthalmic cases and surgical operations. This branch of Christian benevolence was already not unknown in China. Morrison in 1820 had, in connection with Dr. Livingstone, commenced dispensing medicines at Macao, while T. R. Colledge, also of the East India Company, opened a dispensary at his own expense, in 1827, and finding the number of patients rapidly increasing, he rented two small houses at Macao, where in four years more than four thousand patients were cured or relieved. The benevolent design was encouraged by the foreign community, and about six thousand five hundred dollars were contributed, so that it was, after the first year, no other expense to the founder than giving his time and strength. It was unavoidably closed in 1832, and a philanthropic Swede, Sir Andrew Ljungstedt, prepared a short account of its operations, and inserted several letters written to Dr. Colledge, one of which is here quoted:

To knock head and thank the great English doctor. Venerable gentleman: May your groves of almond trees be abundant, and the orange trees make the water of your well fragrant. As heretofore, may you be made known to the world as illustrious and brilliant, and as a most profound and skilful doctor. I last year arrived in Macao blind in both eyes; I have to thank you, venerable sir, for having by your excellent methods cured me perfectly. Your goodness is as lofty as a hill, your virtue deep as the sea; therefore all my family will express their gratitude for your new-creating goodness. Now I am desirous of returning home. Your profound kindness it is impossible for me to requite; I feel extremely ashamed of myself for it. I am grateful for your favors, and shall think of them without ceasing. Moreover, I am certain that since you have been a benefactor to the world and your good government is spread abroad, heaven must surely grant you a long life, and you will enjoy every happiness. I return to my mean province. Your illustrious name, venerable sir, will extend to all time; during a thousand ages it will not decay. I return thanks for your great kindness. Impotent are my words to sound your fame and to express my thanks. I wish you everlasting tranquillity.

Presented to the great English doctor and noble gentleman in the 11th year of Taukwang, by Ho Shuh, of the district of Chau-ngan, in the department of Changchau in Fuhkien, who knocks head and presents thanks.

Another patient, in true Chinese style, returned thanks for the aid he had received in a poetical effusion:

This I address to the English physician: condescend, sir, to look upon it. Diseased in my eyes, I had almost lost my sight, when happily, sir, I met with you. You gave me medicine; you applied the knife; and, as when the clouds are swept away, now again I behold the azure heavens. My joys know no bounds. As a faint token of my feelings, I have composed a stanza in heptameter, which, with a few trifling presents, I beg you will be pleased to accept. Then happy, happy shall I be!

He lavishes his blessings, but seeks for no return;
Such medicine, such physician, since Tsin were never known:
The medicine—how many kinds most excellent has he!
The surgeon's knife—it pierced the eye, and spring once more I see.
If Tung has not been born again to bless the present age,
Then sure 'tis Sü reanimate again upon the stage.
Whenever called away from far, to see your native land,
A living monument I'll wait upon the ocean's strand.

When Dr. Parker's scheme was made known to Howqua, the hong merchant, he readily fell in with it and let his building for the purpose, and after the first year gave it rent free till its destruction in 1856. It was opened for the admission of patients November 4, 1835. The peculiar circumstances under which this enterprise was started imposed some caution on its superintendent, and the hong merchants themselves seem to have had a lurking suspicion that so purely a benevolent object, involving so much expense of time, labor, and money, must have some latent object which it behooved them to watch. A linguist's clerk was often in attendance, partly for this purpose, for three or four years, and made himself very useful. The patients, who numbered about a hundred daily, were often restless, and hindered their own relief by not patiently awaiting their turn; but the habits of order in which they are trained made even such a company amenable to rules. The surgical operations attracted much notice, and successful cures were spoken of abroad and served to advertise and recommend the institution to the higher ranks of native society. It is difficult at this date to fully appreciate the extraordinary ignorance and prejudice respecting foreigners which the Chinese then entertained, and which could be best removed by some such form of benevolence. On the other hand, the repeated instances of kind feeling between friends and relatives exhibited among the patients, tender solicitude of parents for the relief of children, and the fortitude shown in bearing the severest operations, or faith in taking unknown medicines from the foreigners' hands, all tended to elevate the character of the Chinese in the opinion of every beholder, as their unfeigned gratitude for restored health increased his esteem.

The reports of this hospital in Sin-tau-lan Street gave the requisite information as to its operations, and means were taken to place the whole system upon a surer footing by forming a society in China. Suggestions for this object were circulated in October, 1836, signed by Messrs. Colledge, Parker, and Bridgman, in which the motives for such a step and the good effects likely to result from it were thus explained:

We cannot close these suggestions without adverting to one idea, though this is not the place to enlarge upon it. It is affecting to contemplate this Empire, embracing three hundred and sixty millions of souls, where almost all the light of true science is unknown, where Christianity has *scarcely* shed one genial ray, and where the theories concerning matter and mind, creation and providence, are wofully destitute of truth; it is deeply affecting to see the multitudes who are here suffering under maladies from which the hand of charity is able to relieve them. Now we know, indeed, that it is the glorious gospel of the blessed God only that can set free the human mind, and that it is only when enlightened in the true knowledge of God that man is rendered capable of rising to his true intellectual elevation; but while we take care to give this truth the high place which it ought ever to hold, we should beware of depreciating other truth. In the vast conflict which is to revolutionize the intellectual and moral world, we may not underrate the value of any weapon. As a means, then, to waken the dormant mind of China, may we not place a high value upon medical truth, and seek its introduction with good hope of its becoming the handmaid of religious truth? If an inquiry after truth upon any subject is elicited, is there not a great point gained? And that inquiry after medical truth may be provoked, there is good reason to expect; for, exclusive as China is in all her systems, she cannot exclude disease nor shut her people up from the desire of relief. Does not, then, the finger of Providence point clearly to one way that we should take with the people of China, directing us to seek the introduction of the remedies for sin itself by the same door through which we convey those which are designed to mitigate or remove its evils? Although medical truths cannot restore the sick and afflicted to the favor of God, yet perchance the spirit of inquiry about it once awakened will not sleep till it inquires about the source of truth; and he who comes with the blessings of health may prove an angel of mercy to point to the Lamb of God. At any rate, this seems the only open door; let us enter it. A faith that worketh not may wait for other doors. None can deny that *this* is a way of charity that worketh no ill, and our duty to walk in it seems plain and imperative.[1]

This paper was favorably received, and in February, 1838, a public meeting was convened at Canton for the purpose of forming a society, "the object of which shall be to encourage gentlemen of the medical profession to come and practise gratuitously among the Chinese by affording the usual aid of hospitals, medicines, and attendants; but that the support or remuneration of such medical gentlemen be not at present within its contemplation." Some other rules were laid down, but the principle here stated has been since adhered to in all the similar establishments opened in other places. It has served, moreover, to retain them under the oversight and their resident physicians in the employ of missionary societies. No directions were given by the framers of the first society concerning the mode of imparting religious instruction, distributing tracts, or doing missionary work as they had opportunity. The signers of the original paper of suggestions also issued an address, further setting forth their views and expectations:

To restore health, to ease pain, or in any way to diminish the sum of human misery, forms an object worthy of the philanthropist. But in the prosecution of our views we look forward to far higher results than the mere relief of human suffering. We hope that our endeavors will tend to break down the walls of prejudice and long-cherished nationality of feeling, and to teach the Chinese that those whom they affect to despise are both able and willing to become their benefactors. They shut the door against the teachers of the gospel; they find our books often written in idioms which they cannot readily understand; and they have laid such restrictions upon commerce that it does not awaken among them that love of science, that spirit of invention, and that love of thought which it uniformly excites and fosters whenever it is allowed to take its own course without limit or interference. In the way of doing them good our opportunities are few; but among these that of practis-

[1] *Chinese Repository*, Vol. V., p. 372; Vol. VII., pp. 33–40. Lockhart's *Medical Missionary in China*, 1861, p. 134.

ing medicine and surgery stands pre-eminent. Favorable results have hitherto followed it, and will still continue to do so. It is a department of benevolence peculiarly adapted to China. . . .

In the department of benevolence to which our attention is now turned, purity and disinterestedness of motive are more clearly evinced than in any other. They appear unmasked; they attract the gaze and excite the admiration and gratitude of thousands. *Heal the sick* is our motto, constituting alike the injunction under which we act and the object at which we aim; and which, with the blessing of God, we hope to accomplish by means of scientific practice in the exercise of an unbought and untiring kindness. We have called ours a missionary society because we trust it will advance the cause of missions, and because we want men to fill our institutions who to requisite skill and experience add the self-denial and high moral qualities which are looked for in a missionary.

The undertaking so auspiciously begun at Canton, in 1835, has been carried on ever since, and was the pattern of many similar hospitals at the stations afterward occupied. The greatest part of the funds needed for carrying them on has been contributed in China itself by foreigners, who certainly would not have done so had they not felt that it was a wise and useful charity, and known something of the way their funds were employed. The hospital at Canton has exceeded even the hopes of its founders, and its many buildings and wards attest the liberality of the community which presented them to the society. The native rulers, gentry, and merchants are now well acquainted with the institution, and contribute to carry it on. During the forty-five years of its existence it has been conducted by Drs. Parker and Kerr nearly all the time, who have relieved about seven hundred and fifty thousand patients entered on the books; the outlay has been over one hundred and twenty-five thousand dollars. Several dispensaries in the country have also been carried on with the society's grants in aid. A separate hospital was conducted in Canton from 1846 to 1856 by B. Hobson, F.R.C.S., who has left an enduring record of his labors in eighteen medical works in Chinese, many of them illustrated. J. G. Kerr, M.D., has also issued several small treatises, and the publications of this kind in Chinese suitable for the people, issued by them and other missionary physicians, already number nearly fifty.

In these details of the inception of the plan of combining

medical labors with the work of Christian missions in China, it will be seen how the confined position of foreigners at Canton proved to be an incentive and an aid to its prosecution for some years—long enough to show its place and fitness. On the cessation of hostilities between China and Great Britain in 1842, other fields were opened, where its benefits were even more strongly shown. The war had left the people amazed and irritated at what they deemed to be a causeless and unjust attack by superior power. This was the case at Amoy, where no foreigners had lived until the British army took possession in August, 1841. In February, 1842, Revs. D. Abeel and W. J. Boone went there and made the acquaintance of the people on Kulang su, who were much pleased to meet with those who could converse with them and answer their inquiries. Dr. Cumming was able, by their assistance, as soon as he opened his dispensary, to inform the people of his designs; and the missionaries, on their part, preached the gospel to the patients, distributing in addition suitable books. The people were so ready to accept the proffered relief that it was soon impossible for one man to do more than wait upon the blind, lame, diseased, and injured who thronged his doors. A few months more equally proved that while the physician was attending to the patients in one room, the preacher could not ask for a better audience than those who were waiting in the adjoining one. An invitation to attend more formal services on the Sabbath was soon accepted by a few, whose curiosity led them to come and hear more of foreigners and their teachings. The reputation of the hospital was seen when taking short excursions in the vicinity, for persons who had been relieved constantly came forward to express their heartfelt thanks. Thus suspicion gave way to gratitude, enemies were converted to friends, and those who had enjoyed no opportunity of learning the character of foreigners, and had been taught to regard them as barbarians and demons, were disabused of their error. The favorable impression thus made at Amoy, forty years ago, has never been suspended, and numerous native churches have been gathered in all that region. Just the same union of preaching and practice was begun at Shanghai by Dr. W.

Lockhart after the capture of that city in 1844, and has been continued to this time. Ningpo and Fuhchau received similar benefits soon after; these and many others have received aid from foreigners residing in the Empire. Several thousand dollars were sent from Great Britain and the United States to further the object, and one society was formed in Edinburgh in 1856 to develop this branch of missionary work.

The proposition in the original scheme of educating Chinese youth as physicians and surgeons has not been carried out to a great extent. The practising missionary has hardly the time to do his students justice, and unless they show great aptitude for operations, the assistants get weary of the routine of attending to the patients and go away. Dr. Lockhart speaks of his own disappointments in this respect. Dr. Parker had only one pupil, Kwan A-to, who took up the profession among his countrymen. Dr. Wong A-fun received a complete medical education in Edinburgh, and rendered efficient help for many years in the hospital at Canton till his death. The college at Peking has now a chair of anatomy and physiology, which will aid in introducing better practice. Dr. Kerr gives some other reasons for the small number of skilled physicians educated in the missionary hospitals, yet some of his pupils had obtained lucrative practice. Others had imposed themselves in remote places on the people as such, who had only been employed as students a few months—a gratifying index of progress. It is not likely, however, that the Chinese generally will immediately discard their own mode of practice and adopt another from their countrymen so far as to support them in their new system. They have not enough knowledge of medicine to appreciate the difference between science and charlatanism; and a native physician himself might reasonably have fears of the legal or personal results of an unsuccessful or doubtful surgical case among his ignorant patients, so far as often to prevent him trying it.

The successive annual reports issued from the various missionary hospitals in China furnish the amplest information concerning their management, and numerous particulars respecting the people who resort to them. At the Missionary Conference in Shanghai (1877) Drs. Kerr and Gould presented papers relating to this branch of labor in all its various aspects. The latter discussed the advantages of hospital versus itinerary practice; the modes of bringing the patients under religious instruction; how to limit their number so as to not wear out the physician; oversight of assistants and education of pupils; how far this gratuitous relief should be extended; what was the best mode of getting a fee from those natives who were able to pay something; and, finally, the reasons for not uniting the ministerial functions with the medical. These various points show clearly how the experience of past years had manifested the wisdom and foresight of those who originated the work, and the manner it has developed in connection with other branches. If kept as an auxiliary agency, there seems to be no reason for reducing the efforts now made by foreign societies until native physicians and surgeons are able to take up this work, just as native preachers are to oversee their own churches.

Another benevolent society, whose name and object was the Diffusion of Useful Knowledge in China, was established in December, 1834. The designs of the association were "by all means in its power to prepare and publish, in a cheap form, plain and easy treatises in the Chinese language, on such branches of useful knowledge as are suited to the existing state and condition of the Chinese Empire." It published six or eight works and a magazine during the few years of its existence, and their number would have been larger if there had been more persons capable of writing treatises. Since then this kind of mission work has been taken up by various agencies better fitted to develop its several departments, and, excepting newspapers, the preparation of suitable histories, geographies, and scientific books has been done by Protestant missionaries. The Chinese government has directed its employés in the arsenal schools to translate such works as will furnish the scholars with good elementary books.

Their usefulness as aids and precursors of the introduction of the gospel is very great. Among a less intelligent population they are not so important until the people get a taste for knowledge in schools; but where the conceit of false learning and pride of literary attainments cause such a contempt for all other than their own books, as is the case in Chinese society, entertaining narratives and notices of other people and lands, got up in an attractive form, tend to disabuse them of these ideas (the offspring of arrogant ignorance rather than deliberate rejection) and incite them to learn and read more. The influence of newspapers and other periodical literature will be very great among the Chinese when they begin to think for themselves on the great truths and principles which are now being introduced among them. They have already begun to discuss political topics, and the great advantage of movable types over the old blocks tends to hasten the adoption of foreign modes of printing. It may, by some, be considered as not the business of a missionary to edit a newspaper; but those who are acquainted with the debased inertness of heathen minds know that any means which will convey truth and arouse the people tends to advance religion. The influence of the *Dnyanodya* in Bombay, and other kindred publications in various places in India, is great and good; hundreds of the people read them and then talk about the subjects treated in them, who would neither attend religious meetings, look at the Scriptures, nor have a tract in their possession. The same will be the case in China, and it is not irrelevant to the work of a missionary to adopt such a mode of imparting truths, if it be the most likely way of reaching the prejudiced, proud, and ignorant people around him. When the native religious community has begun to take form, this mode of instruction and disputation will be left to its most intelligent members.

In January, 1835, the foreign community in China established a third association, which originated entirely with a few of its leading members. Soon after the death of Dr. Morrison, a paper was circulated containing suggestions for the formation of an association to be called the Morrison Education Society, intended both as a testimonial of the worth and labors of that excellent man, more enduring than marble or brass, and a means of continuing his efforts for the good of China. A provisional committee was formed from among the subscribers to this paper, consisting of Sir G. B. Robinson, Bart., Messrs. W. Jardine, D.

W. C. Olyphant, Lancelot Dent, J. R. Morrison, and Rev. E. C. Bridgman; five thousand nine hundred and seventy-seven dollars were immediately subscribed, and about one thousand five hundred volumes of books presented to its library. This liberal spirit for the welfare of the people among whom they sojourned reflected the highest credit on the gentlemen interested in it, as well as upon the whole foreign community, inasmuch as, with only four or five exceptions, none of them were united to the country by other than temporary business relations.

The main objects of the Morrison Education Society were "the establishment and improvement of schools in which Chinese youth shall be taught to read and write the English language in connection with their own, by which means shall be brought within their reach all the instruction requisite for their becoming wise, industrious, sober, and virtuous members of society, fitted in their respective stations of life to discharge well the duties which they owe to themselves, their kindred, their country, and their God." The means of accomplishing this end by gathering a library, employing competent teachers, and encouraging native schools were all pointed out in this programme of labors, whose comprehensiveness was equalled only by its philanthropy. Applications were made for teachers both in England and America; from the former, an answer was received that there was no likelihood of obtaining one; a person was selected in the latter, the Rev. S. R. Brown, who with his wife arrived at Macao in February, 1839. In the interval between the formation of the Society and the time when its operations assumed a definite shape in its own schools, something was done in collecting information concerning native education and in supporting a few boys, or assisting Mrs. Gutzlaff's school at Macao. The Society's school was opened at Macao in November, 1839, with six scholars; four years afterward it removed to Morrison Hill in Hongkong, into the commodious quarters erected by its president, Lancelot Dent, on a site granted by the colonial government for the purpose. In 1845 Brown had thirty pupils, who filled all the room there was in the house. He stated in his report of that year, as a gratifying evidence of confidence on their part, that no parent had asked to have his child leave during the year. "When the school was commenced," observes Mr. Brown, "few offered their sons as pupils, and even they, as some of them have since told me, did it with a good deal of apprehension as to the consequences. 'We could not understand,' says one who first brought a boy to the school, 'why a foreigner should wish to feed and instruct our children for nothing. We thought there must be some sinister motive at the bottom of it. Perhaps it was to entice them away from their parents and country, and transport them by and by to some foreign land.' At all events, it was a mystery. 'But now,' said the same father to me a few weeks ago, 'I understand it. I have had my three sons in your school steadily since they entered it, and no harm has happened to them. The eldest has been qualified for service as an interpreter. The other two have learned nothing bad. The religion you have taught them, and of which I was so much afraid, has made them better. I myself believe its truth, though the customs of my country forbid my embracing it. I have no longer any fear; you labor for others' good, not your own. I understand it now.'"

This suspicion was not surprising, considering the common estimate of foreigners among the people, and indicates that it was high time to attempt something worthy of the Christianity which they professed. The school was conducted as it would have been if removed to a town in New England; and when its pupils left they were fitted for taking a high rank in their own country. Their attachment to their teacher was great. One instance is taken from the fourth report: "Last spring the father of one in the older class came to the house and told his son that he could not let him remain here any longer but that he must put him out to service and make him earn something. His father is a poor miserable man, besotted by the use of opium, and has sold his two daughter into slavery to raise money. The boy ran away to his instructor and told him what his father had said, adding, 'I cannot go.' Willing to ascertain the sincerity of the boy and the strength of his attachment to his friends, his teacher coolly replied, 'Perhaps it will be well for you to go, for probably you could be a table-boy in some gentleman's house and so get two dollars a month, which is two more than you get here, where only your food is given you.' The little fellow looked at him steadily while he made these remarks, as if amazed at the strange language he used, and when he had done, turned hastily about and burst into tears, exclaiming, 'I cannot go; if I go away from this school I shall be lost.' He did not leave, for his father did not wish to force him away."

Another case shows the confidence of a parent on the occasion of the death of one of the pupils, his only child: "He heard of his son's illness too late to arrive before he died, and when he came it was to bury his remains. He was naturally overwhelmed with grief at the affliction that had come upon him, and his apprehensions of the effect of the tidings upon the boy's mother were gloomy enough. After the funeral was over, I conversed with him. To my surprise he made not the least complaint as to what had been done for the sick lad, either in the way of medical treatment or otherwise, but expressed many thanks for the kind and assiduous attentions that had been bestowed upon him. He said he had entertained great hope of his son's future usefulness, and in order to promote it had placed him here at school. But now his family would end in himself. I showed him some specimens of his son's drawing, an amusement of which he was particularly fond. The tears gushed faster as his eyes rested on these evidences of his son's skill. 'Do not show them to me,' said he; 'it is too much. I cannot speak now. I know you have done well to my son. I pity *you*, for all your labor is lost.' I assured him I did not think so. He had been a very diligent and obedient learner, and had won the esteem of his teachers and companions. He had been taught concerning the true God and the way of salvation, and it might have done him everlasting good. As the old man was leaving me, he turned and asked if, in case he should adopt another boy, I would receive him as a pupil, to which I replied in the affirmative."

An assistant teacher, Wm. A. Macy, joined Mr. Brown in 1846; the latter returned to America in 1847, and the school was closed in 1849, owing chiefly to the departure of its early patrons from China and the opening of new ports of trade, scattering the foreign community so that funds could not be obtained. Mission societies began to enlarge their work at these ports and occupy the same department of education as the Morrison School. It, however, did a good work in its education of half a score of men who now fill high places in their country's service, or occupy posts of usefulness most honorably to themselves. The boy mentioned in a previous paragraph afterward went through a medical course at Edinburgh, became a practising surgeon and physician at Canton, and died there in 1878, honored by foreigners and natives during a life of usefulness and benevolence. In that year Mr. Brown visited China for his health, and was received by this Dr. Wong and others of his old pupils with marks of regard honorable and gratifying to both; they fitted up a house there for him, presented him with a beautiful piece of silver plate, and paid his passage up to Peking and back to Shanghai.

The efforts of Protestants for the evangelization of China were largely of a preparatory nature until the year 1842. Most of the laborers were stationed out of China, and those in the Empire itself were unable to pursue their designs without many embarrassments. Mrs. Gutzlaff experienced many obstacles in her endeavors to collect a school at Macao, partly from the fears of the parents and the harassing inquiries of the police, the latter of which naturally increased the former; partly again from the short period the parents were willing to allow their children to remain. The Portuguese clergy and government of Macao have done nothing themselves to impede Protestant missionaries in their labors in the colony since 1833, when the governor ordered the Albion press, belonging to Dr. Morrison's son, to be stopped, on account of his publishing a religious newspaper called the *Miscellanea Sinicæ;* and this he was encouraged to do from knowing that the East India Company was opposed to its continuance. The governor intimated to one of the American missionaries in 1839 that no tracts must be distributed or public congregations gathered in the colony, but no objection would be made to audiences collected in his own house for instruction. No obstacle was put in the way of printing, and the press that was interdicted in 1833 was carried back to Macao in 1835, after the dissolution of the East

India Company, under the direction of the American mission. Several aids in the study of the Chinese language were issued from it during the nine years it was there under the author's charge.

The city of Canton was long in China one of the most unpromising fields for missionary labors, not alone when it was the only one in the Empire, but until recently. This was owing to several causes. The pursuits of foreigners were limited to trade. Their residence was confined to an area of a few acres held by the guild of hong merchants allowed to trade with them, and all intercourse was carried on in the jargon known as *Pigeon-English.* They were systematically degraded by the native rulers in the eyes of the people, who knew no other appellation for the strangers than *fan-kwei*, or 'foreign devil.' The opium war of 1839–42 had aroused the worst passions of the Cantonese, and their conceit had been increased by the unsuccessful attempts to take the city in 1841 and 1847 by the English forces. Since 1858 the citizens have been accessible to other influences, and learned that their isolation and ignorance brought calamity on themselves.

When Morrison died, Dr. Bridgman and the writer of these pages were the only fellow-laborers belonging to any missionary society then in China; the Christian church formed in 1835 contained only three members. It was indeed a day of small things, but from henceforth grew more and more bright. The contrast even in twelve years is thus described in Dr. Hobson's report of his hospital; the extract shows the little freedom then enjoyed in comparison with what it now is, nearly forty years after:

The average attendance of Chinese has been over a hundred, and none have been more respectful and cordial in their attention than those in whom aneurism has been cured or sight restored, from whom the tumor has been extirpated or the stone extracted. These services must be witnessed to understand fully their interest. Deep emotions have been awakened when contrasting the restrictions of the first years of Protestant missions in China with the present freedom. Then, not permitted to avow our missionary character and object lest it might eject us from the country; nor could a Chinese receive a Christian book but at the peril of his safety, or embrace that religion without hazarding his life. Now he may receive and practise the doctrines of Christ, and transgress no law of the Empire. Our interest may be more easily conceived than expressed as we have declared the truths of the gospel, or when looking upon the evangelist Liang A-fah, and thought of him fleeing for his life and long banished from his native land, and now returned to declare boldly the truths of the gospel in the city from which he had fled. Well did he call upon his audience to worship and give thanks to the God of heaven and earth for what he had done for them. With happy effect he dwelt upon the Saviour's life and example, and pointing to the paintings suspended on the walls of the room, informed his auditors that these were performed by his blessing and in conformity to his precepts and example. Portions of the Scriptures and religious tracts are given to all the hearers on the Sabbath, and likewise to all the patients during the week, so that thousands of volumes have been sent forth from the hospital to scores of villages and to distant provinces.

Before the capture of the city the people had become quite friendly to all missionary labors, through the ameliorating influences of the hospitals. While the city was beleaguered by the insurgents in 1855, the wounded soldiers were attended to by Dr. Hobson, who sometimes had his house full. After Canton was occupied by the allies in 1858 there was an enlargement of mission work in the city and environs, which has been growing in depth and extent till the changes draw the attention of the most casual observer. Foreigners are now seldom addressed as *fan-kwei*, and their excursions into the country and along the streams are made in safety. The Germans have established stations in many places between Canton and Hongkong, and easterly along the river up to Kia-ying, where the people are more turbulent than around the city or toward the west.

The occupation of Hongkong in 1841 induced the American Baptists to make it a station immediately, and Messrs. Roberts and Shuck began the mission work, followed by the London Mission two years after, when Dr. Legge removed there from Malacca. The Roman Catholic missionaries also moved over from Macao at the earliest date. The colonial authorities in time began a system of common schools for all their subjects, so that mission schools have been less necessary since that date, but are still opened to some extent. The benevolent labors by German, British, and American missionaries in Hongkong and its vicinity have been zealously carried on in harmony, and there are fully fifty separate stations on the mainland northerly from the island which are worked from this colony. The number in the whole province of Kwangtung amounts to more than seventy-five, all of them efficiently established since 1858.

The mission at Amoy was commenced in 1842 by Messrs. Abeel and Boone under the most favorable auspices. The English expedition took that city in August, 1841, and on leaving it stationed a small naval and military force on the island of Kulang su. The people of Amoy and its environs cared perhaps little for the merits of the war then raging, but they knew that they had suffered much from it, and no interpreters were available to carry on communication between the two parties. Both these gentlemen could converse in the local dialect, and were soon applied to by many desirous of learning something of the foreigners or who had business with them. The Chinese authorities were also pleased to obtain the aid of competent interpreters, and the good opinion of these dignitaries exercised considerable influence in inducing the people to attend upon the ministrations of the missionaries. Both officers and private gentlemen invited them to their residences, where they had opportunity to answer their reasonable inquiries concerning foreign lands and customs, and convey an outline of the Christian faith. One of these officers was Seu Ki-yu, afterward governor of the province and author of the *Ying Hwan Chí Lioh*, in which he mentions Abeel's name and speaks of his indebtedness to him in preparing that work. The number of books given away was not great, but part of every day was spent in talking with the people; when the hospital was opened by Dr. Cumming, greater facilities were afforded for intercourse. The irritation caused by what the people naturally looked upon as an unprovóked outrage was gradually allayed. There had been no long education of intercommunication between natives and foreigners in Amoy as at Canton. The work so pleasantly begun in 1842 in Kulang su has extended over most parts of the province of Fuhkien, and westward into the prefecture of Chauchau in Kwangtung. There are more converts, native pastors, and schools in this province than any other in China.

Its capital was never visited by a foreign enemy, nor did it suffer from the Tai-ping rebels, so that the gentry of Fuhchau have never been scattered nor their influence broken, like those of many other provincial centres. The mission work was commenced there in 1847 by Rev. Stephen Johnson, from Bangkok, who was soon joined by other American and English colleagues. He speaks of the great prejudices against all foreigners among the citizens in consequence of the evil effects of opium-smoking, which destroyed the people who would not cease to buy it. An experience of thirty years has not altogether removed this dislike, which even lately found an opportunity to exhibit itself in removing the Church Missionary Society's mission from the Wu-shih Hill, where it had rented buildings for that period and "injured the good luck of the city." These prejudices will gradually give way with a new generation of scholars and merchants, and we can afford to be patient with them when we reflect on their slow progress in other things.

The American Board, American Methodist, and Church Missionary Societies have each extended their stations beyond the city into the country almost to the borders of Chehkiang and Kiangsí, occupying in all nearly two hundred localities with their assistants. Besides these agencies, the China Inland mission has occupied three cities on the eastern coast and about sixteen other stations. The whole number of places in the province of Fuhkien where Protestants have opened their work in one form and another is now over two hundred and fifty, under seven separate societies. In most of these towns the good will of the people has remained with them when their objects have been fully understood; and the contrasts of destroying their chapels or book-shops, as at Kien-ning, have been found to be mixed up with other causes. Since the year 1863 the island of Formosa has been occupied by two or three British societies, and the work of their missionaries in the chief towns has been greatly prospered. Dr. Maxwell has carried on his hospital at Taiwan with eminent success as a means of winning the good opinion of suspicious natives and aborigines and inclining them to listen to the gospel. Native churches have been gathered in various parts remote from the coast, and thirty-five stations are now worked by the two British societies which have taken up this field. This progress has not been without opposition, for two of the converts were martyred a few years ago by their countrymen.

The first missionary efforts north of Canton of a permanent nature were made in 1840 by Dr. Lockhart, in the establishment of a hospital at Tinghai in Chusan. They were resumed by Milne in 1842, and while the island was under the control of British troops. Gutzlaff occupied the office of Chinese magistrate of Tinghai in 1842, and endeavored to hold meetings. Milne left Ningpo in June, 1843, and came to Hongkong overland dressed in a native costume. After his departure, some time elapsed before his place was supplied. The journal of his residence in that city indicated a great willingness on the part of people of all ranks to cultivate intercourse with such foreigners as could converse with them. Drs. Macgowan and McCarty went there in 1843 and 1844 to open a hospital, and were followed by Messrs. Lowrie, Culbertson, Loomis, and Cole, the latter in charge of a printing office of English and Chinese type and a type foundry. Religious services are held at the hospitals in that city, and Dr. Macgowan says: "Each patient is exhorted to renounce all idolatry and wickedness and to embrace the religion of the Saviour. They are admitted by tens into the prescribing room, and before being dismissed are addressed by the physician and the native Christian assistant on the subject of religion. Tracts are given to all who are able to read." The more such labors are carried on the better will the prospect of peace and a profitable intercourse between China and western nations become; the more the people learn of the science and resources, the character and designs, and partake of the religion and benevolence of western nations, the less chance will there be of collisions, and the more each party will respect the other. The fear is, however, that the disruptive and disorganizing influences will preponderate over the peaceful, and precipitate new outbreaks before these influences obtain much hold upon the Chinese.

The occupation of Ningpo in 1841 by the British troops, and their excursions into the country, had the effect of preparing the people of Chehkiang province to listen to foreigners. The mission work begun at Ningpo by three or four societies in 1842–48 has been carried on with marked success and completeness in its agencies. The various missions have taken different parts of the province for their particular fields, and by means of chapels, hospitals, schools, printing offices, itinerating and preaching excursions, and the sale of religious books, have made known the truth. A large part of the province was ravaged by the Tai-ping rebels, and after their dispersion in 1867 Hangchau and Shauking were occupied. These two cities were well nigh destroyed, but their inhabitants are learning that no force or governmental influence accompanies the preaching of the doctrines of Jesus. This idea has considerable strength among all the Chinese, and no disclaimer or explanations have much effect at first. The people of Chehkiang province have less energy and individuality than their countrymen in the southern provinces, but they have received the faith in simplicity, maintaining its ordinances and bearing its expenses in many cases without foreign aid. In the seventy stations now occupied by six societies from England and America, the advance is seen to be great since the capture of Ningpo and Tinghai forty years ago, even by the confession of those who still hold aloof. The good reputation of the missionaries was shown in the amicable settlement of an irritating question in Hangchau city in 1874. It arose from the occupation of the hillside by the Americans, who had bought the spot when it was bare of houses and erected their own dwellings. These were deemed to be detrimental to its prosperity, and a riot arose which was quelled by the authorities. A proposal was then made by the gentry to remove them by getting another site in the lower city, and this harmonized all parties while establishing a good precedent for future observance.

The great city of Shanghai was almost unknown to foreign nations until the treaty of Nanking opened it to their trade in 1842. Its inhabitants suffered greatly at its capture, but the growing commerce ere long brought prosperity. As soon as arrangements could be made the London Mission moved its hospital from Chusan Island to Shanghai (in 1844), and Dr. Lockhart immediately commenced his work. His rooms were thronged, and it is stated that ten thousand nine hundred and seventy-eight patients were attended to between May, 1844, and June, 1845. The knowledge of this charity spread over the province of Kiangsu, and removed much of the ill-will and ignorance of the people toward foreigners. One effect in the city was to incite the inhabitants to open a dispensary during four summer months, for the gratuitous relief of the sick. It was called *Shí Í Kung-kiuh*, or 'Public Establishment for Dispensing Healing.' "It was attended by eight or nine native practitioners, who saw the patients once in five days; this attendance was gratuitous on the part of some of them, and was paid for in the case of others. The medicines are supplied from the different apothecary shops, one furnishing all that is wanted during one day, which is paid for by subscriptions to the dispensary. The patients vary from three hundred to five hundred. The reason given for the recent establishment of this dispensary for relieving the sick is that it has been done by a foreigner who came to reside at the place, and therefore some of the wealthy natives wished to show their benevolence in the same way." Such a spirit speaks well for the inhabitants of Shanghai, for nothing like competition in doing good has ever been started elsewhere, nor even a public acknowledgment made of the benefits conferred by the hospitals.

During the voyage along the coast of China made by Messrs. Medhurst and Stevens, in 1835, they visited Shanghai; and an abstract of Medhurst's interview with the officers on that occasion is taken from his journal. He had already been invited by them to enter a temple hard by the landing-place, to the end that they might learn the object of the visit, and was conversing with them.

The party was now joined by another officer named Chin, a hearty, rough-looking man, with a keen eye and a voluble tongue. He immediately took the lead in the conversation, and asked whether we had not been in Shantung and had communication with some great officers there? He inquired after Messrs. Lindsay and Gutzlaff, and wished to know whither we intended to proceed. I told him these gentlemen were well; but we could hardly tell where we should go, quoting a Chinese proverb, "We know not to day what will take place to-morrow." But, I continued, as your native conjurors are reckoned very clever, they may perhaps be able to tell you. "I am conjuror enough for that," said Chin; "but what is your profession?" I told him that I was a teacher of religion. . . . After a little time a great noise was heard outside, and the arrival of the chief magistrate of the city was announced, when several officers came in and requested me to go and see his worship. He appeared to be a middle-aged man, but assumed a stern aspect as I entered, though I paid him the usual compliments and took my seat in a chair placed opposite. This disconcerted him much, and as soon as he could recover himself from the surprise at seeing a barbarian seated in his presence, he ordered me to come near and stand before him, while all the officers called out, "Rise! Rise!" I arose accordingly, and asked whether I could not be allowed to sit at the conference, and as he refused, I bowed and left the room. I was soon followed by Chin and Wang, who tried every effort to persuade me to return; this, however, I steadfastly refused to do unless I could be allowed to sit, as others of my countrymen had done in like circumstances. . . .

Having been joined by Mr. Stevens (who had been distributing books among the crowd without), we proceeded to converse more familiarly and to deliver out books to the officers and their attendants, as well as to some strangers that were present, till they were all gone. A list of such provisions as were wanted had been given to Wang, whom we requested to purchase them for us, and we would pay for them. By this time the articles were brought in, which they offered to give us as a present, and seeing that there was no other way of settling the question, we resolved to accept of the articles and send them something in return. The rain having moderated, we arose to take a walk and proceeded toward the boat, where the sailors were busy eating their dinner. Wishing to enter the city we turned off in that direction, but were stopped by the officers and their attendants, and reluctantly returned to the temple. After another hour's conversation, and partaking of refreshments with the officers, they departed. On the steps near the boat we observed a basket nearly full of straw, and on the top about half a dozen books torn in pieces and about to be burnt. On inquiry, they told us that these were a few that had been torn in the scuffle, and in order to prevent their being trodden under foot they were about to burn them. Recollecting, however, that Chin had told his servant to do something with the books he had received, it now occurred to us that he had directed them to be burned in our presence. On the torch being applied, therefore, we took the presents which were lying by and threw them on the fire, which put it out. The policeman, taking off the articles, applied the torch again, while we repeated the former operation; to show them that if they despised our presents, we also disregarded theirs. Finally the basket was thrown into the river and we left, much displeased at this insulting conduct.[1]

This extract might be thought to refer to an event which took place in the days of Ricci instead of one within the memory of the living. The progress and changes since it occurred in that city typify what has been going on throughout the

[1] *China: Its State and Prospects*, pp. 371–377. *Chinese Repository*, Vol. IV., pp. 330, 331.

whole land. Medhurst came back to Shanghai to live, within nine years after this incident, and when his failing health compelled his retirement in 1856, he closed an honorable service of thirty-nine years in the mission field. His dictionaries, translations, and writings in Chinese and English (ninety-three in all) indicate his industry; and through them he, being dead, yet speaketh to the Chinese upon his favorite themes of redemption. The work which he began was reinforced by colleagues from Great Britain and America until the whole population was reached, and towns lying south of the Yangtsz' River were all visited. After the rebellion was quelled in 1867 other cities were occupied, until about forty-five localities in all parts of Kiangsu are now held as preaching stations. People are returning to their deserted homes, and lands that lay fallow for years are retilled; thither foreign and native preachers and colportors bring the living word without hindrance.[1]

The consequences of the introduction of the gospel into China are likely to be the same that they have been elsewhere, in stirring up private and public antagonism to what is so opposed to the depravity of the human heart. There are some grounds for hoping that there will not be much systematic opposition from the imperial government when once the chiefs of the nation learn the popular sentiments and will. The principal reasons for this are found in the character of the people, who are not cruel or disposed to take life for opinions when those opinions are held by numbers of respectable and intelligent men. The fact that the officers of government all spring from the body of the people, and that these dignitaries are neither governed nor influenced by any State hierarchy—by any body of priestly men, who, feeling that the progress of the new faith will cause the loss of their influence and position, are determined to use the power of the State to put it down—leads us to hope that such officers as may adopt the new faith will not, on account of their profession, be banished or disgraced. Such was the case with Sü, who assisted and countenanced Ricci.

---

[1] In this connection the work of Dr. Lockhart (*Medical Missionary in China*, London, 1861) may profitably be read for the details and results of mission labors in Shanghai.

The general character of the Chinese is irreligious, and they care much more for money and power than they do for religious ceremonies of any kind; they would never lose a battle as the Egyptians did because the Persians placed cats between the armies. There are no ceremonies which they consider so binding as to be willing to fight for them, and persecute others for omitting, except those pertaining to ancestral worship;—these are of so domestic a nature that thousands of converts might discard them before much would be known or done by the people in relation to the matter. The conscientious Christian magistrate would be somewhat obnoxious to his master, and liable to be removed for refusing to perform his functions at the *ching-hwang miao* before the tutelar gods of the Empire. These and other reasons, growing out of the character of the people and the nature of their political and religious institutions, lead to the hope that the leaven of truth will permeate the mass of society and renovate, purify, and strengthen it without weakening, disorganizing, or destroying the government. There are, also, some causes to fear that such will not be the case, arising from the ignorance of the people of the proper results of Christian doctrines; from a dread of the government respecting its own stability from foreign aggression; from the evil consequences of the use of opium, and the drainage of the precious metals; and from the disturbing effects of the intercourse with unscrupulous foreigners and irritated natives often leading to riots and the interference of government authorities.

The toleration of the Christian religion had been allowed throughout the Empire by imperial edicts issued in the reign of Shunchí and his son; and often and often discountenanced and persecuted after those dates. The governmental policy had been long settled to disallow its profession by its subjects or the residence of the Roman Catholic missionaries in its borders. In 1844 the French envoy, M. de Lagrené, brought their disabilities to the notice of Kíying, who memorialized the throne and received the following rescript, which reversed the bloody decrees of 1722 and later years. For his efforts in this matter he deserves the thanks and remembrance of every friend of Christianity and the Chinese.

Kíying, imperial commissioner, minister of State, and governor-general of Kwangtung and Kwangsí, respectfully addresses the throne by memorial.

On examination it appears that the religion of the Lord of Heaven is that professed by all the nations of the West; that its main object is to encourage the good and suppress the wicked; that since its introduction to China during the Ming dynasty it has never been interdicted; that subsequently, when Chinese, practising this religion, often made it a covert for wickedness, even to the seducing of wives and daughters, and to the deceitful extraction of the pupils from the eyes of the sick,[1] government made investigation and inflicted punishment, as is on record; and that in the reign of Kiaking special clauses were first laid down for the punishment of the guilty. The prohibition, therefore, was directed against evil-doing under the covert of religion, and not against the religion professed by the western foreign nations.

Now the request of the French ambassador, Lagrené, that those Chinese who, doing well, practise this religion, be exempt from criminality, seems feasible. It is right therefore to make the request, and earnestly to crave celestial favor to grant that, henceforth, all natives and foreigners without distinction, who learn and practise the religion of the Lord of Heaven, and do not excite trouble by improper conduct, be exempted from criminality. If there be any who seduce wives and daughters, or deceitfully take the pupils from the eyes of the sick, walking in their former paths, or are otherwise guilty of criminal acts, let them be dealt with according to the old laws. As to those of the French and other foreign nations who practise the religion, let them only be permitted to build churches at the five ports opened for commercial intercourse. They must not presume to enter the country to propagate religion. Should any act in opposition, turn their backs upon the treaties, and rashly overstep the boundaries, the local officers will at once seize and deliver them to their respective consuls for restraint and correction. Capital punishment is not to be rashly inflicted, in order that the exercise of gentleness may be displayed. Thus, peradventure, the good and the profligate will not be blended, while the equity of mild laws will be exhibited.

This request, that well-doers practising the religion may be exempt from criminality, I (the commissioner), in accordance with reason and bounden duty, respectfully lay before the throne, earnestly praying the august Emperor graciously to grant that it may be carried into effect. A respectful memorial.

Taukwang, 24th year, 11th month, 19th day (December 28, 1844), was received the vermilion reply: "Let it be according to the counsel [of Kíying]." This is from the Emperor.[2]

---

[1] This is thus explained by a Chinese: "It is a custom with the priests who teach this religion, when a man is about to die, to take a handful of cotton, having concealed within it a sharp needle, and then, while rubbing the individual's eyes with the cotton, to introduce the needle into the eye and puncture the pupil with it; the humors of the pupil saturate the cotton and are afterward used as a medicine." This foolish idea has its origin in the extreme unction administered by Catholic priests to the dying. See, moreover, the *Lettres Édifiantes*, Tome IV., p. 44.

[2] *Chinese Repository*, Vol. XIV., p. 195.

This rescript granted toleration to the Christians already in the country, known only by the term *Tien Chu kiao*, or 'Religion of the Lord of Heaven,' and referring only to those persons who profess Catholicism. Subsequently the French minister was asked to state whether, in making this request of the Chinese officers, he intended to include Christians of all sects, as there had been some doubts on that point. He therefore brought the subject again before Kíying, who issued an explanatory notice, without making a second appeal to his sovereign. It is not necessary to quote the entire reply, which granted as complete toleration to all Christian sects as its writer was able to do from his knowledge of their differences. The term *Yésu kiao*, since adopted for Protestants, was not then current. After quoting the purport of M. de Lagrené's communication, Kíying thus sums up his conclusions:

Now I find that, in the first place, when the regulations for free trade were agreed upon, there was an article allowing the erection of churches at the five ports. This same privilege was to extend to all nations; there were to be no distinctions. Subsequently the commissioner Lagrené requested that the Chinese who, acting well, practised this religion, should equally be held blameless. Accordingly, I made a representation of the case to the throne, by memorial, and received the imperial consent thereto. After this, however, local magistrates having made improper seizures, taking and destroying crosses, pictures, and images, further deliberations were held, and it was agreed that these [crosses, etc.] might be reverenced. Originally I did not know that there were, among the nations, these differences in their religious practices. Now with regard to the religion of the Lord of Heaven—no matter whether the crosses, pictures, and images be reverenced or be not reverenced—all who, acting well, practise it, ought to be held blameless. All the great western nations being placed on an equal footing, only let them by acting well practise their religion, and China will in no way prohibit or impede their so doing. Whether their customs be alike or unlike, certainly it is right that there should be no distinction and no obstruction.—December 22, 1845.

The sentence in this document which speaks of local magistrates making improper seizures probably refers to something which had occurred in the country. At Shanghai the intendant of circuit issued a proclamation in November, 1845, based upon the Emperor's rescript, in which he defines the *Tien Chu kiao* "to consist in periodically assembling for unitedly worshipping the Lord of Heaven, in respecting and venerating the cross, with pictures and images, as well as in reading aloud the works of the said religion; these are customs of the said religion in question, and practices not in accordance with these cannot be considered as the religion of the Lord of Heaven." The various associations and sects found throughout China are all included under the vague name of *kiao*, or 'doctrine;' they are an annoyance to the government and well disposed people, and are referred to and excepted against in this proclamation. In a decree received by Kíying at Canton, February 20, 1846, relating to the restoration of the houses belonging to Romanists, the views of the Chinese government respecting the foreign missionaries were further made known.

On a former occasion Kíying and others laid before Us a memorial, requesting immunity from punishment for those who doing well profess the religion of Heaven's Lord: and that those who erect churches, assemble together for worship, venerate the cross and pictures and images, read and explain sacred books, be not prohibited from so doing. This was granted. The religion of the Lord of Heaven, instructing and guiding men in well-doing, differs widely from the heterodox and illicit sects; and the toleration thereof has already been allowed. That which has been requested on a subsequent occasion, it is right in like manner to grant.

Let all the ancient houses throughout the provinces, which were built in the reign of Kanghí, and have been preserved to the present time, and which, on personal examination by proper authorities, are clearly found to be their *bona fide* possessions, be restored to the professors of this religion in their respective places, excepting only those churches which have been converted into temples and dwelling-houses for the people.

If, after the promulgation of this decree throughout the provinces, the local officers irregularly prosecute and seize any of the professors of the religion of the Lord of Heaven, who are not bandits, upon all such the just penalties of the law shall be meted out.

If any, under a profession of this religion, do evil, or congregate people from distant towns, seducing and binding them together; or if any other sect or bandits, borrowing the name of the religion of the Lord of Heaven, create disturbances, transgress the laws, or excite rebellion, they shall be punished according to their respective crimes, each being dealt with as the existing statutes of the Empire direct.

Also, in order to make apparent the proper distinctions, foreigners of every nation are, in accordance with existing regulations, prohibited from going into the country to propagate religion.

For these purposes this decree is given. Cause it to be made known. From the Emperor.[1]

[1] *Chinese Repository*, Vol. XV., p. 155, where the original is given.

The directors of Protestant missions did not think it right to violate the last paragraph in this rescript, and confined their efforts to the open ports, where their agents had much preliminary work to do. This went on quietly, and on the whole peaceably, as the inhabitants found that the missionaries were their friends. Chapels, schools, hospitals, printing offices, and dwellings were erected at all the ports, so that by the year 1858 about one hundred Protestants were carrying them on. The number of converts was few, and there was not much result to show in tabular lists. It was a time of seed-sowing.

In 1849 the adherents of Hung Siu-tsuen began to make trouble in the west of Kwangtung, and to be called the *Shangti hwui*; and the Peking authorities were unable to distinguish them from Protestants, who had thus rendered the name for God in the version of the Bible used by these misguided men. Their rapid successes against the imperial troops soon roused the utmost energies of the government to suppress them and retake Nanking. In 1856 a more dangerous struggle was precipitated by the impolitic action of Yeh Ming-chin, the governor-general at Canton, in respect to the Arrow, a smuggling lorcha carrying the British flag, which ended in a declaration of war against China. When hostilities ceased in 1858 by signing treaties of peace at Tientsin with envoys of the four nations there assembled, it was deemed to be a favorable time to introduce some definite stipulations respecting the toleration of Christianity in China. The rescripts of the Emperor Taukwang in 1844 had never carried any real weight among rulers or people, nor had the Romanists ever been able to re-possess their old churches and other real estate taken from them. The largest part had long been occupied or destroyed.

Any opposition to such a proposal was not likely to be very persistent on the part of the Chinese plenipotentiaries in face of the force at the call of those who had just captured the forts at Taku and held the city of Tientsin under their guns. The four nations, Great Britain, France, the United States, and Russia, were, as representatives of Christendom, in the providence of God brought face to face with China, the representative of paganism. They came to demand an arrangement of commercial, diplomatic, civil, and ex-territorial rights, and the introduction of religious privileges did not enter into their plans. The war on the part of the two first-named powers had no reference to religion, and their two colleagues would doubtless have omitted the articles on toleration if the Chinese had held out on those alone. At this singular and most unexpected correlation of moral and physical forces among the nations of the world, involving the greater part of its inhabitants, the freedom of the rising church of Christ in China was quietly secured by the four following articles of toleration inserted in the treaties signed in June, 1858. They are here given in the order of their dates:

Russian. ART. VIII.—The Chinese government having recognized the fact that the Christian doctrine promotes the establishment of order and peace among men, promises not to persecute its Christian subjects for the exercise of the duties of their religion; they shall enjoy the protection of all those who profess other creeds tolerated in the Empire. The Chinese government, considering the Christian missionaries as worthy men who do not seek worldly advantages, will permit them to propagate Christianity among its subjects, and will not hinder them from moving about in the interior of the Empire. A certain number of missionaries setting out from the open ports, or cities, shall be provided with passports signed by Russian authorities.

American. ART. XXIX.—The principles of the Christian religion, as professed by the Protestant and Roman Catholic churches, are recognized as teaching men to do good, and to do to others as they would have others do to them. Hereafter, those who quietly profess and teach these doctrines shall not be harassed or persecuted on account of their faith. Any person, whether citizen of the United States or Chinese convert, who according to these tenets peaceably teaches and practises the principles of Christianity, shall in no case be interfered with or molested.

British. ART. VIII.—The Christian religion, as professed by Protestants or Roman Catholics, inculcates the practice of virtue, and teaches man to do as he would be done by. Persons teaching it or professing it, therefore, shall alike be entitled to the protection of the Chinese authorities; nor shall any such, peaceably pursuing their calling, and not offending against the laws, be persecuted or interfered with.

French. Art. XIII.—La religion Chrétienne, ayant pour objet essentiel, de porter les hommes à la vertu, les membres de toutes communions Chrétiennes jouiront d'une entière sécurité pour leurs personnes, leurs propriétés, et le libre exercice de leurs pratiques religieuses; et une protection efficace sera donnée aux missionnaires qui se rendront pacifiquement dans l'intérieur du pays, munis des passeports réguliers dont il est parlé dans l'Article VIII. Aucune entrave ne sera apportée par les autorités de l'Empire Chinois au droit qui est reconnu à tout individu en Chine d'embrasser, s'il le veut, le Christianisme et d'en suivre les pratiques, sans être passible d'aucune peine infligée pour ce fait. Tout ce qui a été précédemment écrit, proclamé, ou publié en Chine par ordre du gouvernement contre le culte Chrétien, est complètement abrogé, et reste sans valeur dans toutes les provinces de l'Empire.

An article similar to these in its general import has been inserted in nearly all the treaties subsequently signed with the Chinese. They contain as much freedom of faith and practice by converts as could be desired by any reasonable man; but many missionaries were disappointed that their provisions were violated or disregarded by native officials. These sanguine persons often forgot that forbearance and time were both needed to bring the people and their rulers up to an appreciation of the new liberties and obligations contained in the treaties, and that their ignorance would be best and thoroughly removed by the living evidences of the purity and power of Christianity among its converts. These have already begun to show their faith by their works.

The only additional action of the Chinese government in this direction that needs to be noticed is Article VI., agreed upon with the French envoy and contained in the convention signed at Peking in October, 1860, in relation to the restoration of property once owned by the Romanists. The translation is as follows:

Art. VI.—It shall be promulgated throughout the length

and breadth of the land, in the terms of the imperial edict of February 20, 1846, that it is permitted to all people in all parts of China to propagate and practise the teachings of the Lord of Heaven, to meet together for preaching the doctrines, to build churches and to worship; further, all such as indiscriminately arrest [Christians] shall be duly punished, and such churches, schools, cemeteries, lands, and buildings as were owned on former occasions by persecuted Christians shall be paid for, and the money handed to the French representative at Peking for transmission to the Christians in the locality concerned. *It is in addition permitted to French missionaries to rent and purchase land in all the provinces, and to erect buildings thereon at pleasure.*[1]

In carrying out the details of this article, so much injustice and violence were exhibited by native Romanists, supported by the missionaries in claiming lands alleged to have belonged to them as far back as the days of Ricci and in the Ming dynasty, and forcing their owners and occupants to yield them without any or sufficient compensation, that riots and hatreds arose in many parts of China. Temples, houses, and shops which had been in the legal possession of natives for one or two centuries were claimed under this stipulation, and they forcibly resisted the surrender. The discontent became so great that the French minister at last issued a notice, about 1872, that no more claims of this kind would be received from the missionaries, and further complaints ceased. The imbroglio was heightened by the murder of two or three missionaries in Kweichau and Sz'chuen during the previous years, and the escape of the guilty parties into other provinces.

The feelings of all the Romish missionaries at the removal of the many disabilities under which they had long lived and bravely suffered were expressed by the Bishop of Shantung in

[1] This sentence in italics is not contained in the French text of the convention; but as that language is made, in Art. III of the Treaty of Tientsin, the *only* authoritative text, the surreptitious insertion of this important stipulation in the Chinese text makes it void. The procedure was unworthy of a great nation like France, whose army environed Peking when the convention was signed.

an encyclical letter to his people, in which he exhorts them to "maintain and diligently learn the holy religion. . . . Let them also pray that the holy religion may be greatly promoted, remembering that the kind consideration of the Emperor toward our holy religion springs entirely from the favor of the Lord of Heaven. After the reception of this order, let thanks be offered up to God for his mercies in the churches, for three Lord's days in succession. While the faithful rejoice in this extraordinary favor, let Ave Marias be recited to display grateful feelings."

The subject of the thorough revision of the Chinese Bible had long occupied the thoughts of those best acquainted with the need of such a work; and when the English missionaries met at Hongkong in 1843, a general conference of all Protestant missionaries was called to take measures for the preparation of so desirable a work. The version of Morrison and Milne was acknowledged by themselves to be imperfect, and the former had begun some corrections in it before his death. Messrs. Medhurst, Gutzlaff, Bridgman, and J. R. Morrison had united their labors in revising the New Testament, and published it in 1836.

The greatest harmony existed at this meeting, and the books of the New Testament were distributed among the missionaries at the several stations without regard to denomination. Some discussion arose as to the best word for *baptism*, for all agreed that it could not well be transliterated. The question was referred to a committee, which, finding itself unable to agree upon a term, recommended that in the proposed version this word should be left for each party to adopt which it liked. The term *sí lí*, which had been in use to denote this rite since the days of Ricci, by Romanists of all opinions, had been taken by Morrison and Medhurst, and by those associated with them. Marshman preferred another word, *tsan*, which was so unusual that it would almost always require explanation; and in fact could only be fully explained by the ceremony itself. Some of the American Baptist missionaries have taken Marshman's term, and others have proposed a third one, *yuh*. Their joint action with their brethren in regard to a common version was afterward repudiated by the societies in the United States, which directed them to prepare separate translations.

The question of the proper word for God in Chinese was also referred to a committee at this meeting in Hongkong, which reported its inability to agree; and this point, like the word for baptism, was therefore left to the decisions of the respective missions, after the version itself was finished. The delegates on the projected translation were chosen by the body of missionaries at each station, and met at Shanghai in June, 1847. They consisted of Rev. Messrs. Medhurst, J. Stronach, and Milne from the London Missionary Society, and Rev. Messrs. Bridgman, Boone, Shuck, Lowrie, and Culbertson from American societies; of the last five, Culbertson took Lowrie's place after his death, and Bp. Boone was never able to take an active share in the work. The New Testament was finished July 25, 1850, and was published soon after with different terms for God and Spirit.

The Old Testament was translated by the three first named in 1853; while another, more adapted to common readers, was completed in 1862 by Messrs. Bridgman and Culbertson. Gutzlaff also issued two or three revisions by himself. In 1865 a committee was formed in Peking for the purpose of making a version of the SS. in the Mandarin dialect, especially that prevalent in the northern provinces. It was done by Rev. Messrs. Blodget, Edkins, Burdon, and Schereschewsky; the New Testament was completed by them jointly in 1872, and the Old Testament in 1874 by the last named alone. It made the sixth complete translation of the Bible into Chinese during this century. Other translations have been made into the five southern patois of several books of the Bible—and at Ningpo and Amoy they are issued in the Romanized letters, and not in the Chinese character. These last, of course, are unintelligible to all natives not taught in mission schools.

The influence and labors of female missionaries in China is, from the constitution of society in that country, likely to be the only, or principal means of reaching their sex for a long time to come, and it is desirable, therefore, that they should engage in the work by learning the language and making the acquaintance of the families around them. No nation can be elevated, or Christian institutions placed upon a permanent basis, until females are taught their rightful place as the companions of men, and can teach their children the duties they owe to their God, themselves, and their country. Female schools are the necessary complement of boys', and a heathen wife soon carries a man back to idolatry if he is only intellectually convinced of the truths of Christianity. The comparatively high estimation the Chinese place upon female education is an encouragement to multiply girls' schools. The formation of mission boards in western lands, conducted entirely by women, has made these schools and medical work among women in China both practical and necessary. No large mission is now regarded as complete without one or more women to carry on such parts of the work as belong to them; and this is true of the Romish missions as well as Protéstants.

The advance in the work of evangelization since the opening of the Empire in 1842 by the Treaty of Nanking has been in the highest degree encouraging. It was soon ascertained that the hatred and contempt of foreigners which were supposed to dwell in the minds of all Chinese, needed only to be met with kindness and patient teachings to give place to respect and confidence. The sufferings from the war with England, and the evils resulting from the smuggling and use of opium among the people, had embittered the minds of dwellers along the coast; but as most of this was local, the enlargement of mission work did much to remove the ignorance which nursed the dislike. The free relief of disease and pain in the hospitals aided greatly to improve intercourse, so that at this day the natives in and around the open ports have become entirely changed in their feelings.

This outline of Protestant mission work in China may be closed by a notice of the conference held at Shanghai in May, 1877, at which one hundred and twenty-six men and women, connected with twenty different bodies, assembled to discuss their common work in its various departments. The report of their proceedings gives fuller statistics of the work then going on than is to be found elsewhere, and the twenty-seven papers read and discussed in the three-days' sessions contain the ripened views of competent thinkers upon the most serious questions connected with the welfare of China. The following table has been taken from this report, and exhibits a remarkable development in education and preaching, considering that most of the stations have been opened since 1860.

STATISTICS OF PROTESTANT MISSIONS TO CHINA FOR THE YEAR 1877.

Branches of Mission Work.	American Missions.	British Missions.	Continental Missions.	Total.
Stations where missionaries reside	41	43	8	92
Out-stations	215	290	27	532
Organized churches	150	156	12	318
(*a*) Wholly self-supporting	11	7	....	18
(*b*) Partially self-supporting	115	149	....	264
Communicants, { males	3,117	4,504	687	8,308
Communicants, { females	2,183	2,440	584	5,207
Pupils in 31 boys' boarding-schools	347	154	146	647
" 177 boys' day-schools	1,255	1,470	265	2,991
" 39 girls' boarding-schools	464	206	124	794
" 82 girls' day-schools	957	335	15	1,307
" 21 theological schools	94	120	22	236
" 115 Sunday-schools	2,110	495	....	2,605
Pastors and preachers ordained	42	28	3	73
Assistant preachers	212	273	34	519
Colportors	28	46	3	77
Bible women	62	28	2	92
Church buildings for worship	113	118	15	246
Chapels and preaching places	183	249	25	457
In-patients, { in 18 hospitals, 1876 }	1,390	3,905	....	5,295
Out-patients, { in 18 hospitals, 1876 }	47,635	41,170	....	88,805
Patients treated in 24 dispensaries, 1876	25,107	16,174	....	41,281
Medical students	19	13	1	33
Contributions of native Christians, 1876	$4,482	$5,089	....	$9,571

The total number of men who have joined the Protestant missions to the Chinese up to 1876, as nearly as can be ascertained, has been 484. Of these 41 were laymen, chiefly physicians, and no women or natives are included. Twelve American societies had sent out 212 ordained missionaries, and the same number of British societies had sent 196; all the agents of the 8 or 10 continental societies amounted to 35. The number in 1847 was 112 of all nations; in 1858, this figure had increased to 214; and a table made out in 1877 by the Shanghai Conference gives 473 as the total number of persons then engaged in active missionary work in China, including 15 not employed by any of the 25 societies enumerated. Of these 210 belonged to 10 American, 242 to 13 British, and 26 to 2 German societies; 172 of the whole number being wives of missionaries, and 63 unmarried females.

No one acquainted with the practical evangelical work in China needs to be told that these statistics give no idea of the character and attainments of the fourteen thousand converts which have joined native churches, or the extent and thoroughness of the education given the five thousand seven hundred children counted in. Those who look for more than the merest beginnings of faith and culture in the minds of natives just brought out of the ignorance, sottishness, and impurity of heathenism into the brightness of Christianity, or those who harshly criticise these results of mission work, will do well to examine for themselves more fully the limitations and nature of all its branches.

No mention is made in these items of the amount of printing done at mission presses, for those particulars are scattered over hundreds of reports issued during the last score or two years. The presses formerly conducted by Williams, Wylie, and Cole at Canton, Shanghai, and Hongkong during an aggregate of nearly forty years, have been superseded by more and larger establishments; moreover, the facilities for transporting books render their issues more available at the remotest parts of the country. The manufacture of Chinese and Japanese types by the Presbyterian Mission press and foundry furnishes native workmen with the means of printing newspapers and books, which otherwise could never have been done (so as to become self-supporting) by means of blocks. At this establishment over thirty millions of pages are annually sent forth, and this amount is more than doubled by all the other mission presses. The effects of this literature upon the native mind, which these agencies are scattering wider every year, will be apparent in the near future.

The worth and labors of many men comprised in this number of missionaries have long been known to the Christian public. Milne and Collie ardently longed and labored diligently for the coming and extension of the kingdom of Christ in China, though not allowed to live in its borders. Few men in the missionary corps have exceeded Edwin Stevens in sound judgment and steady pursuit of a well-formed purpose, which in his case was to aid in perfecting the version of the Bible. He was employed nearly three years as seamen's chaplain at Whampoa before entering the service among the Chinese, and his labors in that department were highly acceptable to those who frequented the port.

The warm-hearted, humble piety and singleness of purpose of Samuel Dyer were also well known to every one engaged with him. His long and assiduous labors to complete a fount of Chinese metallic type, amid many obstacles and hindrances, were prompted by the hope that, when once finished, books could be printed with more elegance, cheapness, and rapidity than in any other way. He lived to see it brought into partial use, and to satisfy himself concerning the feasibility of this plan. If the impulses of private friendship and the esteem generally entertained for David Abeel should prompt a notice of his character and labors, it would soon extend to many pages; they have been well worthy the fuller notice which is given in his memoir. Among other biographies may be mentioned those of Walter M. Lowrie, William C. Burns, D. Sandeman, J. Henderson, Samuel Dyer, E. C. Bridgman, and W. Aitcheson, which will furnish information upon the details of their labors. Female missionaries have also done much, and will do more, in this work, which requires minds and labors in large variety. Mrs. Mary Morrison, Mrs. Sarah Boone, Mrs. Theodosia Dean, Mrs. Lucy Ball, Mrs. Henrietta Shuck, Mrs. Doty, and Mrs. Pohlman, all died in China before 1846—the first of scores of honorable women who have since thus ended their lives.

Before closing this brief sketch of Christian missions among the Chinese, it may be well to mention some of the peculiar facilities and difficulties which attend the work. The business of transforming heathen society and reconstructing it on Christian principles is a great and protracted undertaking, and is to be commenced in all communities by working on individuals. The opposition of the unregenerate heart can be overcome only by the transforming influences of the Spirit, but the intellect must be enlightened, and the moral sense instructed by a system of means, before the truths of the Bible can be intelligently received or rejected. This opposition is not peculiar to China, but it will probably assume a more polemic and argumentative cast there than in some other countries. The proud literati are not disposed to abase Confucius below the Saviour, but rather inclined to despise the reiteration of his name and atonement as a seesaw about "one Jesus who was dead, whom we affirm to be alive." Medhurst notices a tract written against him by a Chinese, in which it is argued that "it was monstrous in barbarians to attempt to improve the inhabitants of the Celestial Empire when they were so miserably deficient themselves. Thus, introducing among the Chinese a poisonous drug, for their own benefit to the injury of others, they were deficient in benevolence; sending their fleets and armies to rob other nations of their possessions, they could make no pretentions to rectitude; allowing men and women to mix in society and walk arm in arm through the streets, they showed that they had not the least sense of propriety; and in rejecting the doctrines of the ancient kings they were far from displaying wisdom; indeed, truth was the only good quality to which they could lay the least claim. Deficient, therefore, in four out of the five cardinal virtues, how could they expect to renovate others? Then, while foreigners lavished money in circulating books for the renovation of the age, they made no scruple of trampling printed paper under foot, by which they showed their disrespect for the inventors of letters. Further, these would-be exhorters of the world were themselves deficient in filial piety, forgetting their parents as soon as dead, putting them off with deal coffins only an inch thick, and never so much as once sacrificing to their manes, or burning the smallest trifle of gilt paper for their support in the future world. Lastly, they allowed the rich and noble to enter office without passing through any literary examinations, and did not throw open the road to advancement to the poorest and meanest in the land. From all these, it appeared that foreigners were inferior to Chinese, and therefore most unfit to instruct them."

To these arguments, which commend themselves to a Chinese with a force that can hardly be understood by a foreigner, they often add the intemperate, immoral lives and reckless cupidity of professed Christians who visit their shores, and ask what good it will do them to change their long-tried precepts for the new-fangled teachings of the Bible? The pride of learning is a great obstacle to the reception of the humiliating truths of the Gospel everywhere, but perhaps especially in China, where letters are so highly honored and patronized. The language is another difficulty in the way of the diffusion of the Gospel, both on the part of the native and the missionary. The mode of education among the Chinese is admirably fitted for the ends they propose, viz., of forming the mind to implicit belief and reverence for the precepts of Confucius, and obedience to the government which makes those precepts the outlines of its actions, but it rather weakens the intellect for independent thought on other subjects. The language itself, as we have had opportunity to observe, is an unwieldy vehicle for imparting new truths, either by writing or speaking, chiefly because of the additional burden every new character or term imposes upon the memory. The immense number, who read and speak this language, reconciles one, however, to extra labor and patience to become familiar with its forms of speech, and ascertain the best modes of conveying truth.

When the five ports were opened in 1845 to practical missionary work among the two or three millions of people living in and around them, it was soon found that they were tolerably well-disposed to foreigners when they understood what was said to them. Fifteen years of constant labor changed the ignorance and suspicion with which they regarded the first missionaries, into respectful regard if not acceptance of their message. At the end of this period, the capture of Peking and the ratification of the treaties of Tientsin completed the opening of China to such labors as far as diplomatic agency could go. Congregations are now collected, and truth explained to them with a good degree of acceptance every Sabbath, and all that is wanted to get more congregations is more preachers; long before missionary labors are accomplished in all the ports, the whole land will afford every choice of climate and position. Facilities for learning the language are constantly increasing. Dictionaries, vocabularies, phrase books, grammars, and chrestomathies in all the dialects will soon be prepared; and the list now is not small. They have all, with few exceptions, been made and printed by Protestant missionaries.

Churches have increased since the first one was formed in Canton in 1835, and some of them are served by native evangelists, two of whom, Liang A-fah and Tsin Shen, of the London Mission, deserve mention as among the first of their countrymen who became educated, earnest preachers of the gospel. The future is full of promise, and the efforts of the church with regard to China will not cease until every son and daughter of the race of Han has been taught the truths of the Bible, and has had them fairly propounded for reception or rejection. They will progress until all the cities, towns, villages, and hamlets of that vast Empire have the teacher and professor of religion living in them; until their children are educated, their civil liberties understood, and political rights guaranteed; their poor cared for, their literature purified, their condition bettered in this world by the full revelation of another made known to them. The work of missions will go on until the government is modified, and religious and civil liberty granted to all, and China takes her rank among the Christian nations of the earth, reciprocating all the courtesies due from people professing the same faith.

CHAPTER XX.

COMMERCE OF THE CHINESE.

It is probable that the applications made in remote times to the rulers of China for liberty to trade with their subjects, partook in their opinion very much of the nature of an acknowledgment of their power; the presents accompanying the request were termed *kung*, and regarded as tribute, while the traders themselves also looked upon the intercourse in somewhat the same light. The chapter of the *Book of Records*, called the "Tribute of Yu," is one of the most ancient documents in existence relating to the products of a country, and indicates a trade in them of no small extent. Silk, lacquer, furs, grass-cloth, salt, gems, gold, silver, and other metals, ivory and manufactured goods are enumerated; they are mostly identified with articles still produced, as Legge has shown in his translation. The records of the origin and early course of this trade are lost to a great extent, but the Chinese annals furnish proof of similar traffic for two thousand years after the days of Yu. It had the effect of extending the influence of Chinese institutions among less civilized neighbors, and of making foreign commerce a means of benefit to all parties. The restrictions and charges upon all trade were of small amount at this early period; as it extended, the cupidity of local officers led them to burden it with numerous illegal fees, which gradually reduced its value, and finally, in some instances, drove it away altogether.

The materials in Chinese literature for investigating this subject after the period of the Han dynasty are abundant, and they will reward the careful analysis of foreign scholars. Marco Polo, the two Arab travellers in A.D. 850 and 878, and Ibn Batuta, in 1330, have each contributed their narratives, hinting therein more than they could carefully investigate of the wide range and value of the Chinese foreign commerce. During the Ming dynasty this trade fell off, owing to the impoverishment of the land by the Mongols; but when (about 1600) the stimulus of European ships along the coast began to develop and reward native manufactures, foreign nations and merchants appreciated the fact that it was more profitable to trade with China than attack her.

The principal items of export and import have not materially changed during the last century; the splendid fabrics of Chinese looms, their tea, lacquered ware, and products of their kilns, being still bartered for the cottons, metals, furs, and woollens of the west. Such articles as possess peculiar interest, and have not been already described, together with a few notices respecting the present extent and mode of conducting the trade, will suffice to explain its general features.[1] The history of the culture and trade in tea by Samuel Ball of Canton in 1835, may yet be considered as an authority upon the subject. The growth in the use of tea is instructive, too, rising from an importation of about eighty pounds into England in 1670, till it had so well vindicated its virtues and enlarged its use among that people, that in 1880 one hundred and eighty million pounds were required to supply them; and more than that was exported elsewhere from China.

The first item which attracts attention in the table of trade with China is opium, whose growth and momentous consequences require a detailed account. The use of opium as a medicine has not long been known to Chinese doctors, though, from the way the poppy is mentioned in the *Herbal*, there is reason to suppose it to be indigenous. The drug is called *apien*, in imitation of the word *opium*, while the plant is called *afuyung*, a transliteration of the Arabic name *Afyun*, from which country it was brought about the ninth century. It has many

[1] **Ample materials are now provided in the full reports of the Custom's service and the Exhibition Catalogues of Vienna, Paris, Philadelphia, etc.; the reports of Rondot, Hedde, and other members of the French Legation in 1844 are still valuable.**

names, as *great smoke*, *black commodity*, *black earth*, *foreign medicine;* the last is the term used in the tariff. The compiler of the *Herbal*, who wrote two centuries ago, speaks of the plant and its inspissated juice, saying that both were formerly but little known; he then concisely describes the mode of collecting it, which leads to the inference that it was then used in medicine. None was imported coastwise for scores of years after that date, but the poppy is now grown in every province and in Manchuria, and no real restraint is anywhere put on its cultivation. The juice is collected and prepared by the people for their own consumption in much the same manner as in India; as long ago as 1830 we find one official observing in respect to the cultivation, which was extending, that it was "not only bringing injury on the good, but greatly retarding the work of the husbandmen."

The mode of raising the poppy in the Patna district in India is thus described: The ryot or cultivator having selected a piece of ground, always preferring (*cæteris paribus*) that which is nearest his house, fences it in. He then, by repeated ploughings and manuring, makes it rich and fine, and removes all the weeds and grass. Next, he divides the field into two or more beds by small dikes of mould, running lengthwise and crosswise according to the slope and nature of the ground, and again into smaller squares by other dikes leading from the principal ones. A tank is dug about ten feet deep at one end of the field, from which by a leathern bucket, water is raised into one of the principal dikes and carried to every part as required; this irrigation is necessary because the cultivation is carried on in the dry weather. The seed is sown in November, and the juice collected in February and March, during a period, usually, of about six weeks; weeding and watering commence as soon as the plants spring up, and are continued till the poppies come to maturity. Cuts are then made in the capsule with a *nusktur* or notched iron instrument made of three or four sharp lancet-like plates; this is done at sunrise, and the exudation is scraped off next morning by a scoop or *sittuha*, and deposited in the dish hanging at the ryot's side. He takes it home and after draining it dry in a large shallow dish, turns it over and over in the air for a month till the mass is equally dried, and it is fit to carry to the godown. Here it is thrown into a great tank, and kneaded to a uniform consistence; when ready it is rolled into balls according to the size of a brass bowl; these balls are covered with a coating of poppy petals, and stored in a drying-house till ready for packing. The quality of the article depends very much upon the care taken in the drying and covering with *liwa* or opium paste when the ball is prepared.

The cultivator must deliver a certain quantity at the stipulated price to the collector, the amount being fixed by a survey of the field when in bloom; he receives about one dollar and sixty-five cents for a seer (one pound thirteen ounces) of the poppy juice, which must be of a certain consistence. The ryot has, in most cases, already received the advance money, and if he sell this crude opium to any other than the collector, or if he fail to deliver the estimated quantity, and there is reason for supposing he has embezzled it, he is liable to punishment. In all parts of India, the cultivation of the poppy, the preparation of the drug, and the traffic in it until it is sold at auction for exportation, are under a strict monopoly. Should an individual undertake the cultivation without having entered into engagements with the government to deliver the produce at the fixed rate, his property would be immediately attached, and he compelled either to destroy the poppies, or give security for the faithful delivery of the product. The cultivation of the plant is compulsory, for if the ryot refuse the advance for the year's crop, the simple plan of throwing the rupees into his house is adopted; should he attempt to abscond, the agents seize him, tie the advance up in his clothes, and push him into his house. There being then no remedy, he applies himself as he may to the fulfilment of his contract. The chief opium district is on the Ganges valley, occupying the best land in Benares and Behar, to the extent of about a thousand square miles. The northern and central parts of India are now covered with poppies, while other plants used for food or clothing have nearly been driven out. In Turkey, Persia, India, and China many myriads of acres and millions of people are employed in the cultivation of poppies.[1] The growth has extended so much in Persia that opium has lately come from thence to China.

The preparation of the opium is superintended by official examiners, and is a business of some difficulty, from the many substances put into the juice to adulterate or increase its weight. Wetting it so that the mass shall be more fluid than it naturally is, mixing sand, soft clayey mud, sugar, coarse molasses, cow-dung, pounded poppy-seeds, and the juice of stramony, quinces, and other plants, are all resorted to, though with the almost certain result of detection and loss. When the juice has been dried properly, to about seventy per cent. spissitude, it appears coppery brown in the mass, and when spread thin on a white plate, shows considerable translucency, with a gallstone yellow color and a slightly granular texture. When cut with a knife it exhibits sharp edges without drawing out into threads; and is tremulous like strawberry-jam, to which it has been aptly compared. It has considerable adhesiveness, a handful of it not dropping from the inverted hand for some seconds.

All the opium grown is brought to Calcutta and stored in government warehouses, until it is exposed for sale at auction, at an upset price, graduated according to the market price in China. It is supposed not to cost much more than seven hundred rupees a chest, and is sold at as high an advance as it will bear. Great care is taken to suit the taste of the Chinese; on one occasion, the East India Company refunded part of the price on a lot which had been differently prepared, to try whether that people would prefer it. There are several sorts of opium: Turkey and Persian, which sell cheapest, and reach China from Aden; Patna and Benares which are sold at Calcutta; and Malwa, which is cultivated out of British jurisdiction. In order to equalize its competition, an export duty was until 1842 put on each chest of one hundred and twenty-five rupees, which has been increased to six hundred rupees. The drug is rolled in balls, and then packed in strong boxes, weighing from one hundred and sixteen pounds for

[1] *Chinese Repository*, Vol V., p. 472.

Patna, to one hundred and thirty-four pounds or one hundred and forty pounds for Malwa. Malwa opium is grown and prepared by natives, and is often extensively adulterated; between four hundred and five hundred cakes are in a chest, and the cultivator there receives double the wages of the ryot in Bengal.

Opium chests are made of mango wood in Patna and Benares and consist of two parts, in each of which there are twenty partitions; the balls are carefully rolled in dry poppy leaves. The chest is covered with hides or gunny bags, and the seams closed so as to render it as impervious to the air as possible. After the drug is sold at auction, there is no further tax on it. The revenue from this monopoly has become so great and important, that its continuance is described by a leading editor in India as a matter of life and death to the Government. In 1840, the income was somewhat over two millions sterling; it has since steadily increased, till in 1872 it amounted to £7,657,000; the average annual sum between the years 1869 to 1876 was £6,524,000, and it has been over five millions ever since the peace of Tientsin. The purity and flavor of the drug has been carefully maintained by competent scientists, and by this date the prejudice in its favor has become so strong among the Chinese, as to induce them to pay an enormous premium for the Indian article over any native product.

The use of opium among the Chinese two centuries ago must have been very little, or the writings of Romish missionaries, from 1580 down to the beginning of the nineteenth century, would certainly have contained some account of it. It was not till the year 1767 that the importation reached a thousand chests, and continued at that rate for some years, most of the trade being in the hands of the Portuguese. The East India Company made a small adventure in 1773; and seven years after, a dépôt of two small vessels was established by the English in Lark's Bay, south of Macao; the price was then about $550 a chest. In 1781 the company freighted a vessel to Canton, but were obliged to sell the lot of 1,600 chests at $200 a chest, to Sinqua, one of the hong-merchants, who, not being able to dispose of it to advantage, reshipped it to the Archipelago. The price in

1791 was about $370 a chest, and was imported under the head of medicine at a duty of about seven dollars a hundredweight, including charges. The authorities at Canton began to complain of the two ships in Lark's Bay in 1793, and their owners being much annoyed by the pirates and revenue boats, and inconvenienced by the distance from Canton, loaded the opium on board a single vessel, and brought her to Whampoa, where she lay unmolested for more than a year. She was then loaded and sent out of the river, and the drug introduced in another ship; this practice continued until 1820, when the governor-general and collector of customs issued an edict, forbidding any vessel to enter the port in which opium was stored, and making the pilots and hong-merchants responsible for its being on board. The Portuguese were also forbidden to introduce it into Macao, and every officer in the Chinese custom-house there was likewise made responsible for preventing it, under the heaviest penalties. "Be careful," says his excellency in conclusion, "and do not view this document as mere matter of form, and so tread within the net of the law, for you will find your escape as impracticable as it is for a man to bite his own navel."

The importation had been prohibited by the Emperor Kia-king in 1800, under heavy penalties, on account of its use wasting the time and destroying the property of the people of the Inner Land, and exchanging their silver and commodities for the "vile dirt" of foreign countries. The supercargoes of the Company therefore recommended the Directors to prohibit its shipment to China from England and India, but this could not be done; and they contented themselves by forbidding their own ships bringing it to China. The hong-merchants were required to give bonds, in 1809, that no ship which discharged her cargo at Whampoa had opium on board; but they contrived to evade the restriction. The traffic was carried on at Whampoa and Macao by the connivance of local officers, some of whom watched the delivery of every chest and received a fee; while their superiors, remote from the scene of smuggling, pocketed an annual bribe for overlooking the violation of the imperial orders.

The system of bribery and condoning malpractices, so common

in China, is well illustrated by a case which occurred in connection with this business. In September, 1821, a Chinese inhabitant of Macao, who had been the medium of receiving from the Portuguese, and paying to the Chinese officers the several bribes annually given for the introduction of opium, was arrested by government for hiring banditti to assault one of his personal opponents. Having got the man in their power, quicksilver was poured into his ears, to injure his head without killing him; they also forced him to drink a horrible potion of scalding tea mixed with the short hairs shaved from his head. The vile wretch who originated this cruel idea and paid the perpetrators of it, was a pettifogging notary, who brought gain to the officials by intimidating the people, until he was the pest and terror of the neighborhood. An official enemy at last laid his character and doings before the governor, who had him seized and thrown into prison, when he turned his wrath on his former employers, and confessed that he held the place of bribe-collector, and that all the authorities received so much per chest, even up to the admiral of the station. The governor, though doubtless aware of these practices, was now obliged to notice them ; but instead of punishing those who were directly guilty, he accused the senior hong-merchant, a rich man, nicknamed the "timid young lady," and charged him with neglecting his suretyship in not pointing out every foreign ship which contained opium. It was in vain for him to plead that he had never dealt in opium, nor had any connection with those who did deal in it; nor could he search the ships to ascertain what was in them, or control the authorities who encouraged and protected the smuggling of opium: notwithstanding all his pleas, the governor was determined to hold him responsible. He was accordingly disgraced, and a paper, combining admonition, with exhortation and entreaty, was addressed by his excellency to the foreigners, Portuguese, English, and Americans. The gods, he said, would conduct the fair dealers in safety over the ocean, but over the contraband smugglers of a pernicious poison, the terrors of the royal law on earth, and the wrath of the infernal gods in hades were suspended. The Americans brought opium, he observed, "because they had no king to rule them." The opium ships thus being driven from Whampoa, and the Portuguese unwilling or afraid to admit it into Macao unless at a high duty, the merchants established a floating dépôt of receiving-ships at Lintin, an island between Macao and the Bogue. In summer, the ships moved to Kumsing moon, Kapshui moon, Hongkong, and other anchorages off the river, to be more secure against the tyfoons; remaining near Lintin during the north-east monsoon, until 1839.[1]

The mode of introducing opium into the country, when the prohibitions against its use were upheld by the moral approval of the best portion of the native society, has hardly any interest now, except as a matter of history. It is a sad exhibition of power, habit, skill, and money all combining to weaken and overpower the feeble, desultory resistance of a pagan and ignorant people against the progress of what they knew was destroying them. The finality of such a struggle could hardly be doubted, and when the tariff of 1858 allowed opium to enter by the payment of a duty, the already enfeebled moral resistance seemed to die out with the extinction of the smuggling trade in opium, now raised to a licensed commerce. The rise and course of the trade up to that year can be learned from the volumes of the *Chinese Repository* and newspapers issued in China.

The utensils used in preparing the opium for smoking, consist chiefly of three hemispherical brass pans, two bamboo filters, two portable furnaces, earthen pots, ladles, straining-cloths, and sprinklers. The ball being cut in two, the interior is taken out, and the opium adhering to or contained in the leafy covering is previously simmered three several times, each time using a pint of spring water, and straining it into an earthen pot; some cold water is poured over the dregs after the third boiling, and from half a cake (weighing at first about twenty-eight pounds, and with which this process is supposed to be conducted), there will be about five pints of liquid. The interior of the cake is then boiled with this liquid for about an hour, until the whole is reduced to a paste, which is spread out with a spatula in two pans, and exposed to the fire for two or three minutes at

[1] *Chinese Repository*, Vol. V., pp. 546–553.

a time, till the water is driven off; during this operation it is often broken up and re-spread, and at the last drying cut across with a knife. It is all then spread out in one cake, and covered with six pints of water, being allowed to remain several hours or over night for digestion. When sufficiently soaked, a rag filter is placed on the edge of the pan, and the whole of the valuable part drips slowly through the rag into a basket lined with coarse bamboo paper, from which it falls into the other brass pan, about as much liquid going through as there was water poured over the cake. The dregs are again soaked and immediately filtered till found to be nearly tasteless; this weaker part usually makes about six pints of liquid.

The first six pints are then briskly boiled, being sprinkled with cold water to allay the heat so as not to boil over, and removing the scum by a feather into a separate vessel. After boiling twenty minutes, five pints of the weak liquid are poured in and boiled with it, until the whole is evaporated to about three pints, when it is strained through paper into another pan, and the remaining pint thrown into the pan just emptied, to wash away any portion that may remain in it, and also boiled a little while, when it is also strained into the three pints. The whole is then placed over a slow fire in the small furnace, and boiled down to a proper consistency for smoking; while it is evaporating a ring forms around the edge, and the pan is taken off the fire at intervals to prolong the process, the mass being the while rapidly stirred with sticks, and fanned until it becomes like thick treacle, when it is taken out and put into small pots for smoking. The boxes in which it is retailed are made of buffalo's horn, of such a size as easily to be carried about the person. The dregs containing the vegetable residuum, together with the scum and washings of the pans, are lastly strained and boiled with water, producing about six pints of thin, brownish liquid, which is evaporated to a proper consistence for selling to the poor. The process of seething the crude opium is exceedingly unpleasant to those unaccustomed to it, from the overpowering narcotic fumes which arise, and this odor marks every shop where it is prepared and every person who smokes it. The loss in weight by this mode of preparation is about one-half. The Malays prepare it in much the same manner. The custom in Penang is to reduce the dry cake made on the first evaporation to a powder, and when it is digested and again strained and evaporated, reducing it to a consistence resembling shoemaker's wax.

The opium pipe consists of a tube of heavy wood furnished at the head with a cup which serves to collect the residuum or ashes left after combustion; this cup is usually a small cavity in the end of the pipe, and serves to elevate the bowl to a level with the lamp. The bowl of the pipe is made of earthenware, of an ellipsoid shape, and sets down upon the hole, itself having a small rimmed orifice on the flat side. The opium-smoker always lies down, and the impossible picture given by Davis of a "Mandarin smoking an opium-pipe," dressed in his official robes and sitting up at a table, becomes still more singular if the author ever saw a smoker at his pipe. Lying along the couch, he holds the pipe, aptly called *yen tsiang*, *i.e.*, 'smoking-pistol,' so near the lamp that the bowl can be brought close up to the flame. A pellet of the size of a pea being taken on the end of a spoon-headed needle, is put upon the hole of the bowl and set on fire at the lamp, and inhaled at one whiff so that none of the smoke shall be lost. Old smokers will retain the breath a long time, filling the lungs and exhaling the fumes through the nose. The taste of the half-fluid extract is sweetish and oily, somewhat like rich cream, but the smell of the burning drug is rather sickening. When the pipe has burned out, the smoker lies listless for a moment while the fumes are dissipating, and then repeats the process until he has spent all his purchase, or taken his prescribed dose. When the smoking commences, the man becomes loquacious, and breaks out into boisterous, silly merriment, which gradually changes to a vacant paleness and shrinking of the features, as the quantity increases and the narcotic acts. A deep sleep supervenes from half an hour to three or four hours' duration, during which the pulse becomes slower, softer, and smaller than before the debauch. No refreshment is felt from this sleep, when the person has become a victim to the habit, but a universal sinking of the powers of the body and mind is experienced, and complete recklessness of all consequences, if only the craving for more can be appeased.

A novice is content with one or two whiffs, which produce vertigo, nausea, and headache, though practice enables him to gradually increase the quantity; "temperate smokers," warned by the sad example of the numerous victims around them, endeavor to keep within bounds, and walk as near the precipice as they can without falling over into hopeless ruin. In order to do this, they limit themselves to a certain quantity daily, and take it at, or soon after meals, so that the stomach may not be so much weakened. A "temperate smoker" (though this term is like that of a *temperate* robber, who only takes shillings from his employer's till, or a *temperate* blood-letter, who only takes a spoonful daily from his veins) can seldom exceed a mace weight, or about as much of prepared opium as will balance a pistareen or a franc piece; this quantity will fill twelve pipes. Two mace weight taken daily is considered an immoderate dose, which few can bear for any length of time; and those who are afraid of the effects of the drug upon themselves endeavor not to exceed a mace. Some persons, who have strong constitutions and stronger resolution, continue the use of the drug within these limits for many years without disastrous effects upon their health and spirits though most of even these moderate smokers are so much the slaves to the habit that they feel too wretched, nerveless, and imbecile to go on with their business without the stimulus.

The testimony regarding the evil effects of the use of this pernicious drug, which deserves better to be called an "article of destruction" than an "article of luxury," are so unanimous that few can be found to stand up strongly in its favor. Dr. Smith, a physician in charge of the hospital at Penang, says: "The baneful effects of this habit on the human constitution are particularly displayed by stupor, forgetfulness, general deterioration of all the mental faculties, emaciation, debility, sallow complexion, lividness of lips and eyelids, languor and lack-lustre of eye, and appetite either destroyed or depraved, sweetmeats or sugar being the articles that are most relished." These symptoms appear when the habit has weakened the physical powers, but the unhappy man soon begins to feel the power of the drug in a general languor and sinking, which disables him, mentally more than bodily, from carrying on his ordinary pursuits. A dose of opium does not produce the intoxication of ardent spirits, and so far as the peace of the community and his family are concerned, the smoker is less troublesome than the drunkard; the former never throws the chairs and tables about the room, or drives his wife out of doors in his furious rage; he never goes reeling through the streets or takes lodgings in the gutter; but contrariwise, he is quiet or pleasant, and fretful only when the effects of the pipe are gone. It is in the insupportable languor throughout the whole frame, the gnawing at the stomach, pulling at the shoulders, and failing of the spirits that the tremendous power of this vice lies, compelling the "victimized" slave "to seek it yet again." There has not yet been opportunity to make those minute investigations respecting the extent opium is used among the Chinese, what classes of people use it, their daily dose, the proportion of reprobate smokers, and many other points which have been narrowly examined into in regard to the use of alcohol; so that it is impossible to decide the question as to which of the two is the more dreadful habit. These statistics have, heretofore, been impossible to obtain in China, and it will be very difficult to obtain them, even when a person who may have the leisure and abilities shall undertake the task.

Various means have been tried by benevolent natives to dissuade their countrymen from using it, such as distributing tracts showing its ruinous effects, compounding medicines for the smoker to take to aid him in breaking off the habit, and denouncing the smoking-shops to government. A painter at Canton made a series of admonitory pictures, showing the several steps in the downward course of the opium-smoker, until beggary and death ended the scene; one of them, showing the young debauchee at his revels, is here introduced.

A Chinese scholar thus sums up the bad effects of opium, which, he says, is taken at first to raise the animal spirits and prevent lassitude: "It exhausts the animal spirits, impedes the regular performance of business, wastes the flesh and blood, dissipates every kind of property, renders the person ill-favored, promotes obscenity, discloses secrets, violates the laws, attacks the vitals, and destroys life." Under each of these heads he lucidly shows the mode of the process, or gives examples to uphold his assertions: "In comparison with arsenic, I pronounce it tenfold the greater poison; one swallows arsenic because he has lost his reputation, and is so involved that he cannot extricate himself. Thus driven to desperation, he takes

Manner of Smoking Opium.

the dose and is destroyed at once; but those who smoke the drug are injured in many ways. It may be compared to raising the wick of a lamp, which, while it increases the blaze, hastens the exhaustion of the oil and the extinction of the light. Hence, the youth who smoke will shorten their own days and cut off all hopes of posterity, leaving their parents and wives without any one on whom to depend. From the robust who smoke the flesh is gradually consumed and worn away, and the skin hangs like a bag. Their faces become cadaverous and black, and their bones naked as billets of wood. The habitual smokers doze for days over their pipes, without appetite; when the desire for opium comes on, they cannot resist its impulse. Mucus flows from their nostrils and tears from their eyes; their very bodies are rotten and putrid. From careless observers the sight of such objects is enough to excite loud peals of laughter. The poor smoker, who has pawned every article in his possession, still remains idle; and when the periodical thirst comes on, will even pawn his wives and sell his daughters. In the province of Nganhwui I once saw a man named Chin, who, being childless, purchased a concubine and got her with child; afterward, when his money was expended and other means all failed him, being unable to resist the desire for the pipe, he sold her in her pregnancy for several tens of dollars. This money being expended, he went and hung himself. Alas, how painful was his end!"[1]

The thirst and burning sensation in the throat which the wretched sufferer feels, only to be removed by a repetition of the dose, proves one of the strongest links in the chain which drags him to his ruin. At this stage of the habit his case is almost hopeless; if the pipe be delayed too long, vertigo, complete prostration, and discharge of water from the eyes ensue; if entirely withheld, coldness and aching pains are felt over the body, an obstinate diarrhœa supervenes, and death closes the scene. The disastrous effects of the drug are somewhat delayed or modified by the quantity of nourishing food the person can procure, and consequently it is among the poor who can least afford the pipe, and still less the injury done to their energies, that the destruction of life is the greatest. The evils suffered and crimes committed by the desperate victims of the opium pipe are dreadful and multiplied. Theft, arson, murder, and suicide are perpetrated in order to obtain it or escape its effects. Some try to break off the fatal habit by taking a tincture of the opium dirt in spirits, gradually diminishing its strength until it is left off entirely; others mix opium with tobacco and smoke the compound in a less and less proportion, until tobacco alone remains. The general belief is that the vice can be overcome without

---

[1] *Chinese Repository*, Vol. VII., p. 108.

fatal results, if the person firmly resolve to forsake it and keep away from sight and smell of the pipe, laboring as much as his strength will allow in the open air until he recovers his spirits and no longer feels a longing for it. Few, very few, however, emancipate themselves from the tyrannous habit which enslaves them; they are able to resist its insidious effects until the habit has become strong, and the resolution to break it off is generally delayed until their chains are forged and deliverance felt to be hopeless.

Swallowing opium is commonly resorted to as a means of suicide; the papers published in China constantly report cases where physicians have tried to save the patient by injections of atrophine before life is gone, and the number of these applications painfully show how lightly the Chinese esteem life. A comparison is sometimes drawn between the opium-smoker and drunkard, and the former averred to be less injured by the habit; but the balance is struck between two terrible evils, both of which end in the loss of health, property, mind, influence, and life. Opium imparts no benefit to the smoker, impairs his bodily vigor, beclouds his mind, and unfits him for his station in society; he is miserable without it, and at last dies by what he lives upon.

The import having been legalized in 1858, under the pressure of war, it was useless for the imperial government longer to prevent the cultivation of the poppy, and the growth has rapidly extended throughout the provinces. Since all the opium brought to China reaches it through Hongkong, and the consumption upon that island must be comparatively insignificant, the table on the following page, taken from the Chinese Customs Reports, will convey a very fair idea of the amount and value of the import during the past six years.

Although it is difficult to make a general statement regarding an import of such varying quantity and value, the average total may be safely enough put at between twelve and thirteen million pounds, the approximate value of which is something over sixty million dollars, per annum. The prices range from $540 to $580 per pecul for Benares, $740 for Malwa, $560 for Patna, $540 for Persian, and nearly $1,500 for the prepared drug. The imports of Persian and Turkish, though steadily increasing, amount as yet to hardly one-fiftieth of the total. But the merest guesses can be made at the production of native opium.

TOTAL IMPORT OF OPIUM AT HONGKONG.

Year.	Quantity.	Value.
	Peculs.	*Hk. Tls.*[1]
1876............	96,985	36,491,288
1877............	94,200	32,303,963
1878............	94,899	37,470,465
1879............	107,970	41,479,892
1880............	96,839	42,823,721
1881............	89,688	38,115,154

The British consul at Canton reported in 1877 "on good authority" that the out-turn came to 32,000 peculs, while in the Customs Special Report on Opium of 1881 the estimates of the several commissioners vary from 12,000 (Mr. McKean, of Canton) to 265,000 peculs (Mr. Drew, of Ningpo). In this report only seven out of the nineteen trade ports present any figures upon this head.[2]

This *résumé* of facts connected with the growth and condition of this trade are enough, probably, for the present purpose. "Opium is the only article of all her imports that China cannot

[1] The *Haikwan tael* is equivalent to \$1.36½ in American gold. The *pecul* weighs 133⅓ pounds avoirdupois.

[2] Compare *Returns of Trade at the Treaty Ports* for 1881, and *Opium* (Special, Series II., No. 4), published by the Im. Mar. Customs at Shanghai. *Portfolio Chinensis*, by J. Lewis Shuck, Macao, 1840. Rev. A. S. Thelwall, *The Iniquities of the Opium Trade with China*, London, 1839. *L'Opium en Chine, Étude statistique et morale*, par le Dr. E. Martin, Paris, 1871. Alonzo Calkins, *Opium and the Opium Appetite*, Philadelphia, 1871. F. S. Turner, *British Opium Policy and its Results to India and China*, London, 1876. Dr. D. J. Macgowan in *Transactions of the N. C. Br. R. A. S.*, Part IV., Art. II. Fernand Papillon, *Revue des Deux Mondes*, 1er Mai, 1873. Dr. H. H. Kane, *Opium Smoking*, New York, 1882. *The Friend of China*, published at London bi-monthly; and publications of the Anglo-Oriental Society for the Suppression of the Opium Trade.

do without now," said a British minister once in a sorrowing mood, as he acknowledged its evils; but there are many other commodities, and a survey of the native and foreign commerce will exhibit the extent and variety of the resources of the Empire. The Chinese trade with foreign ports in native vessels is at present nearly extinct, in consequence of the increase of foreign shipping and advantages of insurance enabling the native trader to send and receive commodities with less risk and more speed than by junks. The facilities and security of commerce in a country are among the best indices of its government being administered, on the whole, in a tolerably just manner, and on those principles which give the mechanic, farmer, and merchant a good prospect of reaping the fruits of their industry. This security is afforded in China to a considerable degree—far more than in Western Asia—and is one of the most satisfactory proofs, amid all the extortions and depravity seen in their courts and in society at large, that the people, generally speaking, enjoy the rewards of industry. Tranquillity may often be owing to the strong arm of power, but trade, manufactures, voyages, and large commercial enterprises must remunerate those who undertake them, or they cease. The Chinese are eminently a trading people; their merchants are acute, methodical, sagacious, and enterprising, not over-scrupulous as to their mercantile honesty in small transactions, but in large dealings exhibiting that regard for character in the fulfilment of their obligations which extensive commercial engagements usually produce. The roguery and injustice which an officer of government may commit without disgrace would blast a merchant's reputation, and he undertakes the largest transactions with confidence, being guaranteed in his engagements by a combination of mercantile security and responsibility, which is more effectual than legal sanctions. These are like the rings and guilds, the corporations, patents, co-operative societies, etc., which are found in Europe and America, and enter into all branches of industry.

The coasting trade is disproportionately small compared with the inland commerce; large junks cross the seas, but smaller ones proceed cautiously along the coast from one headland to another, and sail chiefly by day. Their cargoes consist of rice, stockfish, vegetables, timber, poles, coal, stones, and other bulky articles. Between the unopened ports the native trade still employs thousands of small craft, whose crews know no other homes; but the progress of steam and sailing ships has gradually turned the coasting trade into foreign bottoms.

The foreign ports now visited by Chinese junks are Singapore, Labuan, Borneo, Bangkok and elsewhere in Siam, Manila, Corea, and Japan. The cargoes carried to these places comprise coarse crockery, fruits, cottons, cheap silks, and metallic articles of great variety. European goods are not brought to any great amount by junks, but the variety of articles of food or domestic use and raw materials for manufactures, known under the general denomination of *Straits produce*, is large. Rice is the chief import from Bangkok and Manila; rattans, pepper, and betel-nut from Singapore and Borneo; biche-de-mer from the Sulu Sea. Of the amount of capital embarked in this commerce, the number of vessels, the mode in which it is carried on, and the degree of risk attending it, little is known. It is gradually decreasing, and all the valuable portions are already transferred to foreign bottoms.

The natural facilities for inland navigation in China are, as the first chapters of this work have pointed out, unusually great, and have been, moreover, improved by art for travel and transportation. It will be a hazardous experiment for the peace of the country to hastily supplant the swarms of boats on its rivers and canals by shallow-draught steamers and launches, and throw most of their poor and ignorant crews out of employment. The sugar, oil, and rice of the southern provinces, the tea, silk, cotton, and crockery of the eastern, the furs, grain, and medicines of the northern, and the metals and minerals of the western, are constantly going to and fro and demand myriads of boats; add thereto the immense number of governmental boats required for the transportation of salt and the taxes paid in kind, the passage-boats plying in great numbers between contiguous towns, the pleasure and official barges and revenue cutters, and lastly, the far greater number used for family residences, and the total of the inland shipping, it will be seen, must be enormous. It is, however, impossible to state the amount in any satisfactory manner, or give an idea of the proportion between the different kinds of boats. The transit duties levied on the produce carried in these vessels partake of the nature of an excise duty, and afford a very considerable revenue to the government, the greatest so, probably, next to the land tax. It was estimated that the additional charges for transit duty and transportation on only those teas brought to Canton overland for exportation amounted to about a million of dollars. Whenever a boat loaded with produce passes the custom-house, the supercargo presents his manifest, stating his name and residence, the name of the boat and its crew, and the description of the cargo, and when the charges are paid proceeds on his voyage. The tariff on goods at these places is light, but their number in a journey of any length, and the liability to unforeseen detention and exaction by the tidewaiters, greatly increase the expense and delay.

Since the treaties of 1842 and 1858, the Chinese and British authorities have been in constant dispute about the right and mode of levying transit dues on foreign and native produce going through the country—a dispute which involves and disturbs the whole revenue system of the country.

The mode of conducting the foreign trade with China now presents few of those peculiarities which formerly distinguished it, for the monopoly of the hong merchants and of the East India Company both being abolished, native and foreign traders are free to choose with whom they will deal. The introduction of regular printed permits, clearances, and other customs blanks to facilitate trade, followed the treaty of 1842, and their acceptance has now extended to every port. The employment of foreigners to conduct the details of the trade in connection with native officers and clerks has worked easily, and its extension to all commerce is gradually perfecting.

The articles of trade are likely to increase in variety and amount, and a brief account of the principal ones, taken from the *Chinese Commercial Guide*, may be interesting to those unacquainted with the character of this commerce. The foreign export and import trade divides itself into two branches, that between India and the Archipelago and China, and that beyond the Isthmus of Suez; the former comprises the greatest variety, but its total value is much less. *Alum* of an inferior quality is sent to India to use in dyeing, making glass, and purifying water. *Aniseed stars*, seeds of many sorts of *amomum*, *cubebs*, and *turmeric* are all sought after for their aromatic properties. The first is the small five-rayed pod of the *Illicium anisatum*; the pods and seeds are both prized for their aromatic qualities, and a volatile oil, used in perfumery and medicine in Europe, is obtained from them; the Asiatics employ them in cooking. *Cubebs*, the produce of a vine (*Cubeba officinalis*), are externally distinguished from black pepper chiefly by their lighter color, and a short process where the seed is attached to the stalk. The taste is warm or pungent and slightly bitter, with a pleasant aromatic smell; the Chinese article goes to India, the consumption of Europe being supplied from Java. Turmeric is the root of the *Curcuma longa*, and is used over the Archipelago and India for its coloring and aromatic properties, and for food. The roots are uneven and knotty, of a yellowish-saffron color; the smell resembles ginger, with a bitterish taste; and the two are usually combined in the composition of curry-powders. Its color is too fugacious for a dye, no mordant having yet been found to set it.

Cassia and *cassia oil* are sent abroad in amounts far exceeding the whole of the preceding; *cassia buds* also form an article of commerce. Cassia oil is used for confectionery and perfumery, and the demand is usually much greater than the supply. *Arsenic* is exported to India for medicinal purposes, and the native sulphuret or orpiment is sometimes shipped under the Hindustani name of *hartall*, as a yellow coloring drug. Wrist and ankle rings, known by the Hindu name of *bangles*, are exported largely, with false pearls, coral, and beads; the Chinese imitate jade and chalcedony in their manufacture, in which the Hindus do not succeed so well. The universal use and brittle nature of these ornaments render their consumption enormous in Eastern Asia. *Brass foil*, or *tinsel*, is made into the *kin hwa*, or 'golden flowers,' which are placed before shrines and adorn the rooms of houses, imitating bouquets and tableaux with cunning art; it is also used for coatings of toys. *Bones* and *horns* are manufactured into buttons, opium-boxes, hair-pins, etc., some of which go abroad. Many kinds of useful and fancy articles are made from bamboo and rattan, and their export forms an item of some importance. Chairs, baskets, canes and umbrella handles, fishing-rods, furniture, and similar articles are still made in vast variety. The same may be said of the great assortment of articles comprised under the head of *curiosities*, as vases, pots, jars, cups, images, boxes, plates, screens, statuettes, etc., made of copper, iron, bronze, porcelain, stone, wood, clay, or lacquered-ware. During the last twenty years the native shops have been nearly cleared of the choicer specimens of Chinese art and skill in these various departments.

Capoor cutchery, corrupted from the Hindu name *kafúr-kuchri*, or camphor root, is the aromatic root of the *Hedychium*, and also of the *Kæmpferia;* it goes to Bombay for perfumery, plasters, and other medicinal ends, as well as preserving clothes from insects. It is about half an inch in diameter, and cut up when brought to market; it has a pungent, bitterish taste. *Galangal* is another aromatic root exported for perfumery and medicine. The name is probably a corruption of *Kao-liang*, or *Ko-long*, meaning 'mild ginger,' from Kauchau, in the southwest of Kwangtung, where the best is found. It is the dried root of the *Alpinia officinarum* (Hance) and other species, and thousands of peculs reach Europe and America, where it is used as a cordial and tonic. There are two or three sorts; the smaller is a reddish-colored root, light and firm in texture, with an acrid, peppery taste.

The larger is from a different plant (*Kæmpferia galanga*), and inferior in every respect. Both are used as spicery, and the powder is mixed in tea among the Tartars, and to flavor a liquor called *nastoika* drank in Russia. All the plants whose roots have the aromatic sharp taste of ginger are prized by the Chinese. *China-root* is a commercial name applied to two different products, for which the native name *fuh-ling* rather misleads. One is the root of *Smilax China*, a vine-like dodder in appearance; it is a knotty and jointed brown tuber, white and starchy when cut, and sweetish. The other is a curious fungus (*Pachyma*) produced by fir roots apparently as it is found under that tree. The article is whitish and reddish when cut, bitterish and sharp to the taste, and eaten hot as a stomachic in rice-cakes where it is cheap. It is similar to the Indian bread, or *tuck-ahoo*, of the Carolinas.

The exportation of *porcelain* and *chinaware*, which was so great last century, diminished as European skill produced finer sorts at cheaper rates, and ceased altogether about twenty-five years ago, when the Tai-ping rebellion dispersed the workmen in Kingteh chin. Since the peace, those kilns have resumed work, and the demand for their finest pieces has arisen once more from western lands, so that China bids fair to regain her original reputation. She still supplies most parts of Asia with coarse stoneware and crockery for domestic use. *Glue* of a tolerably good quality, made from ox-hides, supplies the Chinese and furnishes an article for export to India. *Isinglass*, or fish-glue, is made from the sounds and noses of sturgeons and other sorts of fish, as the bynni carp, or *Polynemus;* it is used in sizing silk and in cookery, as well as in manufacturing of india-ink, water-colors, and false pearls.

A kind of parasol, made of oiled paper, or silk called *kittysol* (*i.e.*, *quitté sol*), is exported to India; the article is durable, considering its material, and its cheapness induces a large consumption. *Tobacco*, one of the most widely cultivated plants in China (for men, women, and children smoke), is also sent to the Indian Islands in considerable quantity, for use among the natives. Ware made from ivory, tortoise-shell, mother-o'-pearl, and gold and silver constitutes altogether a considerable item in the trade, for the beautiful carving of the Chinese always commands a market. The workmen easily imitate new patterns for boxes, combs, and buttons of mother-o'-pearl or tortoise-shell, while the cheapness and beauty with which silver table furniture is made cause a large demand. *Lacquered-ware* is not so much sent abroad now as formerly, the foreign imitations of the trays and tables having nearly superseded the demand for the Chinese ware. *Marble slabs* of a clouded blue limestone are wrought out in Kwangtung province for floors, and some go abroad; square tiles are used everywhere for pavements, roofing, brick stoves, and drains. In the southern provinces they are well burned and make serviceable floors.

澳门基金会
※
北京外国语大学
中国海外汉学研究中心
※
大象出版社

合作项目

卫三畏文集
Selected Works of Samuel Wells Williams

中国总论

（卷 I）（上）

The Middle Kingdom

［美］
卫三畏 著
Samuel Wells Williams

大象出版社

图书在版编目(CIP)数据

中国总论(全四册)/(美)卫三畏著.—影印本.—郑州:大象出版社,2013.3
ISBN 978-7-5347-7425-6

Ⅰ.①中… Ⅱ.①卫… Ⅲ.①社会生活—史料—中国—清后期—英文 Ⅳ.①K252.06

中国版本图书馆 CIP 数据核字(2012)第 320486 号

卫三畏文集

中国总论

出 版 人 王刘纯
责任编辑 李光洁
监　　制 杨吉哲

出版发行 大象出版社(郑州市开元路 16 号 邮政编码 450044)
发行科 0371-63863551 总编室 0371-63863572
网　　址 www.daxiang.cn
印　　刷 河南省瑞光印务股份有限公司
经　　销 各地新华书店经销
开　　本 787×1092 1/16
印　　张 106.25
版　　次 2013 年 3 月第 1 版 2013 年 3 月第 1 次印刷
定　　价 810.00 元(全四册)

印厂地址 郑州市二环支路 35 号
邮政编码 450012 电话 (0371)63956290

論總國中

THE MIDDLE KINGDOM

A SURVEY OF THE GEOGRAPHY, GOVERNMENT, LITERATURE, SOCIAL LIFE, ARTS, AND HISTORY

OF

THE CHINESE EMPIRE

AND

ITS INHABITANTS

BY

S. WELLS WILLIAMS, LL.D.

PROFESSOR OF THE CHINESE LANGUAGE AND LITERATURE AT YALE COLLEGE, AUTHOR OF TONIC AND SYLLABIC DICTIONARIES OF THE CHINESE LANGUAGE

REVISED EDITION, WITH ILLUSTRATIONS AND A NEW MAP OF THE EMPIRE

VOLUME I.

PARAGON BOOK REPRINT CORP.
NEW YORK
1966

Library of Congress Catalog Card Number

66-16895

An unaltered and unabridged
reprint of the revised edition
published by Charles Scribner's
Sons in 1895

Reprinted by
Paragon Book Reprint Corp.
14 East 38th Street, New York, N. Y. 10016

Printed in the United States of America

To

GIDEON NYE, Jr.,

OF CANTON, CHINA,

A

TESTIMONIAL OF THE

Respect and Friendship

OF THE AUTHOR.

主编序言

陶德民　张西平　吴志良

2008年8月8日,在北京奥运会开幕的当天,新落成的美国驻华使馆举行了剪彩仪式。美国国务院历史文献办公室为此发行了纪念图册,题为《共同走过的日子——美中交往两百年》,其中把1833年抵达广州的卫三畏(Samuel Wells Williams, 1812-1884)称扬为美国"来华传教第一人",虽然他并非是第一个来到中国的美国传教士。图册对卫三畏在促进美中两国人民的相互了解方面所作的贡献作了这样的概括和评价:"传教士成为介绍中国社会与文化的重要信息来源,因为他们与大部分来华经商的外国人不一样,这些传教士学习了中文。例如,美国传教士卫三畏就会说流利的广东话和日语。他曾参与编辑英文期刊《中国丛报》,供西方传教士及时了解中国的最新动态,方便在美国的读者了解中国人的生活。卫三畏还编辑出版了《汉英拼音字典》(即《汉英韵府》——序者)和分为上下两卷的历史巨著《中国总论》。时至今日,他依然被公认为对19世纪的中国生活认识得最为精透的观察家。"

图册中也提到"蒲安臣于1862年成为第一个常驻北京的美国代表,在促进中国的国际关系上扮演了更为积极的角色。蒲安臣迅速结识了一批清政府的主要改革派官员,其中就包括咸丰皇帝的弟弟,设立了中国第一个外务部(应为总理各国事务衙门-序者)的恭亲王奕訢",以及他1867年辞去驻华公使后作为清朝使节率团访问欧美,与当时的美国国务卿签订《蒲安臣条约》一事。"该条约扩展了中美两国的往来领域。条约规定,两国人民享有在彼此国家游历、居住的互惠权,并可入对方官学;中国领事在美国口岸享有完全的外交权利;鼓励华工移民美国;美国政府支持中国的领土主权。"其实,蒲安臣的卓有成效的外交活动及其维护正义的外交主张,与当时担任使馆秘书兼翻译的卫三畏的鼎力相助是分不开的。卫三畏的儿子卫斐列后来倾注极大热忱为蒲安臣撰写传记,其重要原因之一也在于此。

今天,当我们出版这部文集以纪念卫三畏诞辰200周年,并重新探讨其经历和成就之际,有必要思考这样一个问题,即卫三畏一生所体现的诸多志趣和倾向之中,什么是值得我们加以特别关注的呢?虽然这是一个"仁者见仁,智者见智"的问题,多数人恐怕都不会对以下见解持有异议,即卫三畏在对华态度上所发生的"从教化到对话"的某种转变可以说是他留给后世的最重要的精神遗产之一。而这恰恰可以从耶鲁大学校园里留存至今的两件文物上得到印证。

第一件文物是该校公共大食堂(Commons Dining Hall)墙上的卫三畏肖像画，它其实是设在纽约的美国圣经协会所藏同一油画的一个复本。如所周知，卫三畏的在华生涯大抵分为两个阶段，作为传教士的前22年(1833–1855)和作为外交官的后20年(1856–1876)。在前22年的最后一段时间里，他还作为首席翻译官随同佩里将军的舰队两次远征日本，在改变日本锁国政策的外交谈判过程中发挥了重要作用。佩里将军对其语言天赋和交涉手腕的赏识，无疑是卫三畏转而步入为期20年的外交生涯的一个契机。1877年辞职回国后不久，他受聘为耶鲁大学的中国语言文学讲座教授。1881年春被遴选为美国圣经协会会长后，他便提出希望有才华的画家制作自己的肖像画，并将其献给圣经协会。结果，由耶鲁大学艺术学院的韦约翰教授制作的油画所呈现的是这样一个形象：等身大的卫三畏站立在放有纸、笔和一个中国式花瓶的桌子边上，目视前方，手持1858年《中美天津条约》的文本。

很显然，这样的构图反映了卫三畏本人的意思：他一直把基督教传教自由的条款得以列入1858年《中美天津条约》看作自己毕生的最大成就。这是因为当时负责谈判的美国公使列卫廉对是否要在条约中加入该条款并不经意，只是在卫三畏的坚持之下才获得了最后的成功。此一事实，不仅可见于耶鲁大学斯德龄纪念图书馆附属档案馆所藏卫三畏的亲笔日记，也可以由当时协助他进行谈判工作的丁韪良牧师后来所写的《花甲忆记》得到证实："那份现在成为条约荣耀之处的条款是卫三畏博士提出的。"在预定签约的6月18日即"决定命运的那天早上，卫三畏博士告诉我他一夜未眠，一直在考虑这份宽容条款。现在他想到了一种新的形式，可能会被对方接受。他写了下来，我建议我们应当马上坐轿子直接奔赴中方官邸解决这个问题。……中方代表接见了我们，他们当中的负责人稍作修改，就接受了卫三畏博士的措辞。"(详见陶德民《从卫三畏档案看1858年中美之间的基督教弛禁交涉——写在〈基督教传教士传记丛书〉问世之际》)。1876年夏天，美国国务院接受卫三畏的辞呈，在正式解职通知中对他赞扬有加："您对中国人的性格与习惯的熟悉，对该民族及其政府愿望与需求的了解，对汉语的精通，以及您对基督教与文明进步事业的贡献，都使您有充分的理由自豪。您无与伦比的中文字典与有关中国的诸多著作已为您赢得科学与文学领域内相应的崇高地位。更为重要的是，宗教界不会忘记，尤其多亏了您，我们与中国订立的条约中才得以加入自由传教这一条。"而卫三畏则在复信中坦承，这一嘉许是"最最让他感动与满意的"(见卫斐列著，顾钧、江莉译《卫三畏生平及书信——一位美国来华传教士的心路历程》)。顺便提到，在1858年6月19日，亦即《中美天津条约》签订的第二天，美国驻日总领事哈里斯便与德川幕府的代表签订了《美日修好通商条约》。卫三畏闻讯后，又不失时机地向美国的新教诸团体提出派遣牧师赴日传教的建议，并得到了切实的响应。所以，对美国基督教会的东亚传教事业来说，卫三畏确实是一位有功之臣。

那么，卫三畏是基于一种什么样的信念而企图以基督教义来教化东亚的所谓异教徒的呢？试举一个例子。1853年7月16日，在佩里将军初访日本，成功向日方递交美国总统国书一周之后，卫三畏曾从停泊在江户湾的军舰上给他在土耳其传教的弟弟W. F. 威廉斯写了一封长信，其中指出："佩里告诉日本官员，他将在次年率领一支更大的舰队以求得到他们对所提要求的回答，即所有前来访问或遇难流落日本海岸的美国人应得到善待，美国汽船在一个日本港口得到煤炭以及有关物资的补给。这些是我们花费巨大开支和派出强大舰队到日本水域的表面上的理由，而真正的理由是为了提高我们民族的名誉和得到称扬我们自己的材料。在这些理由的背后并通过这些理由，存有上帝的目的，即将福音传达给所有国家，并将神旨和责任送达这个至今为止只是在拙劣地模仿耶稣之真的民族。我十分确信，东亚各民族的锁国政策决非根据上帝的善意安排，其政府必须在恐怖和强制之下将之改变，尔后其人民或可自由。朝鲜人、中国人、琉球人和日本人必须承认这唯一活着的和真实的上帝，他们的锁国之墙必将为我们所拆除，而我们西方的太平洋沿岸城市正开始派出船队前往大洋的彼岸。”从卫三畏对佩里访日使命的解读来看，他固然赞成打开东亚各国的大门，但更重视把上帝的福音传入各国人们的心扉，期盼由此引发一系列的变革。因为他认定上帝所代表的真善美的品格和力量是美国等基督教国家所拥有的绝对优势和无比强势的源泉。（详见陶德民《十九世纪中叶美国对日人权外交的启示——写在日本开国150周年之际》）

然而，卫三畏在以后长期驻节北京的岁月里，逐步加深了对中国的悠久历史和深厚文化传统的了解，使他在对华态度上开始发生“从教化到对话”的某种转变。而这一点可以耶鲁校园里的另一件艺术杰作来作为象征，那就是在卫三畏于1884年2月16日去世两周之后，在举行其丧礼的巴特尔教堂（Battell Chapel）东北角中心位置安装的一块非常别致的彩色纪念玻璃。玻璃的中央写有《论语》中的七个汉字：“敏则有功，公则说。”（意思大体为，勤勉能积成事功，公道则众人心悦诚服）。玻璃的下方用英文记载了卫三畏的名字、生卒年份以及他一生所扮演的角色与身份，即“传教士、学者、外交官、耶鲁学院中文教授”。这块玻璃由纽约的路易斯·第法尼公司（Louis C. Tiffany & Co.）负责制作，其别出心裁的设计显然是出于卫三畏生前的授意。

卫三畏选用孔子的话作为自己一生的概括，可谓恰如其分。勤勉能积成事功的道理，可以从他孜孜不倦编纂而成的《中国丛报》、《中国总论》以及《汉英韵府》等多种刊物和名著得到了解。公道则众人心悦诚服的道理，则充分体现在了他辞职回国之际所受到的各界朋友的赞扬。他在信中告诉他的妻子，“临行前威妥玛于周六、西华于周一为我举办了两次特别宴会，我见到了北京的所有名流，并受到了他们的盛赞。然后，似乎是为了区别于外交聚会，丁韪良、艾约瑟、怀定先后请我吃饭。我告诉过你，我在丁韪良家见到了所有的传教士，那真是一次令人难忘的聚会”。“接连不断的登门送别者中有三四位是总理衙门的官员，京城中最位高权重的大官也来为我送行。除了亲王之外，我都是在办公室里会见他们，彼此依依惜别。九位官员每人赠我一柄折扇作为纪念，这充分显示了中国人的友善”。不仅北京的新教传教士们发给他一封送别信以示友谊与敬意，上海的同仁也发给他一封相似的信，恰如其分地总结了他在中国的生活：“您长期担任美国使馆秘书、翻译，九次代理公使的职务，这些工作给了您许多重要的机遇，使您得以把知识、经验用于为中国人造福、为您自己的国家谋利，尤其是为基督教在中国的传播效力。对您工作中表现出的高度责任感，我们不胜钦佩。”对这些热情洋溢的赞美之辞，卫三畏则表示自己的所作所为只不过是在执行上帝的旨意，“我在传教过程中与同伴们相处融洽、身体健康、工作愉快，为此我要虔诚地赞美造物主”。

在某种意义上说，卫三畏选用孔子的话来概括自己的一生，也显示了他对中国文化传统的敬重之意。而这种敬重之意，可以由1879年他为反对加州的排华风潮而撰写的《中国移民》中的一节得到佐证："当加州的法庭想用立法来反对中国人时，它将中国人等同于印第安人的简单态度是颇为古怪的。生理学家查尔斯·匹克林将中国人和印第安人归为蒙古的成员，但加州的最高法院却认为'印第安族包括汉族和蒙古族'。这样在概念错误的同时，它还支持了一种错误的观点。它把现存最古老国度的臣民和一个从未超越部落关系的种族相提并论；把这样一个民族——它的文学早于《诗篇》和《出埃及记》，并且是用一种如果法官本人肯于学习就不会叫作印第安语的语言写就，而它的读者超过了其他任何民族的作品——与最高的写作成就仅是一些图画和牛皮上的符号的人群混为一谈；把勤奋、谨慎、技艺、学识、发明等所有品质和全部保障人类生命和财产安全的物品等同于猎人和游牧民族的本能和习惯。它诋毁了一个教会我们如何制作瓷器、丝绸、火药，给予我们指南针，展示给我们茶叶的用处，启迪我们采用考试选拔官员的制度的民族；把它和一个轻视劳动，没有艺术、学校、贸易的种族归为同类，后者的一部分现在还混迹于加州人中间，满足于以挖草根过活。"虽然卫三畏在赞扬中国人的同时，也表达了他对印第安人的歧视态度，他的观点还是得到当时耶鲁学院全体教授的同情，他们纷纷签名支持他起草的请愿书，呼吁海斯总统否决1879年的反移民法，其中包含这样的警告：如果我们的政府首先改变条约的规定，中国政府也可以根据国际法取消治外法权，致使美国在华公民失去领事的保护。此外，1878年中国北方发生大饥荒时，身处太平洋彼岸的卫三畏利用他对美国在华传教士和商社的影响，不遗余力地推动救灾。他还试图劝说国会归还1859年中方赔款余额的一部分来帮助缓解灾区的困境。而早在1860年，他就曾建议国务院用这笔赔款余额在中国建立一所美中学院，以培养中方的翻译、通商和外交人才。这个建议得到了新上任的总统林肯的同意，只因为当时的国会未予批准而搁浅。卫三畏这个未能实现的建议完全可以称之为后来退回庚款吸引中国学生留美的先驱性方案。

卫三畏还对亲眼目睹的中国同时代的缓慢而确凿的变化做了一定的正面评价。1883年7月，即辞世的半年多之前，卫三畏在儿子的帮助下终于完成了《中国总论》这一巨著的修订工作，在增补版的序言中他写下了如下字句："我在1833年到达广州时，和另外两位美国人作为'番鬼'向行商经官正式报告，在他的监护之下才得以生存。1874年，我作为美国驻北京公使馆秘书，跟随艾忭敏公使觐见同治皇帝，美国使节站在与'天子'完全平等的地位呈上国书。由于一生之中的这两次遭遇，并念念不忘在思想和道德上的重大进步是使一个孤傲的政府从强加于人的姿态改而听从他人所必需的，毫不足怪的是，我确信汉人的子孙有着伟大的未来，不过，唯有纯正基督教的发展才是能使这一成长过程中的各个冲突因素免于互相摧残的充分条件。无论如何，这个国家已经度过被动时期，这是肯定无疑的。中国不可能再安于懒散隔绝—像过去那样，以过于自负的态度俯视其他国家，就像面对她所无需劳神的星星一样。"

如果说，17世纪的礼仪之争最后是以天主教士在康熙禁令之下被逐出中国告终的，那么，这场可谓19世纪的礼仪之争则是以"天朝上国"在第二次鸦片战争之后所做出的巨大让步来结局的，包括废除以夷相称、公使驻京、平身觐见皇帝而不必行三跪九叩之礼。卫三畏的字里行间所透露的,既有在礼仪上争得与最古老“中央王国”之“天子”平等地位的自豪,又有从其所信奉的上帝的立场针砭这个王国“懒散隔绝”和“过于自负”的高傲。联系到上述1853年他给在土耳其传教的弟弟W. F. 威廉斯的长信,可见这时的卫三畏虽然在其对华态度上开始了“从教化到对话”的转变,但并未把“异教徒”放在完全对等的位置上,特别是在道德和精神的层面上。在这个意义上说,自以为占据着道德精神的制高点,只有基督教可以拯救中国的卫三畏也难免“过于自负”的诟病。这就是笔者在前文中提到其转变时,始终不忘加上“某种”一词来予以限定的缘故。

尽管如此,卫三畏在序言中宣称,修订版“坚持初版序言中所述的观点——为中国人民及其文明洗刷掉古怪的、模糊不清的可笑印象”。卫三畏相信,在传教“事业取得成功的基础上,中国作为一个民族,在道义和政治两方面,将会得到拯救。这一成功有可能和人民的需要同步前进。他们将会变得适应于自己着手处理问题,并且和外国文明以多种活动形式结合起来。不久,将会引进铁路、电报和制造业,随之而来的是中国人民中成百万地受到启发,无论在宗教、政治和家庭生活的每一方面”。这种力图呈现中国文明及民族的美好品质和衷心期待中国在对外交往中日益开放进步的善意态度,自然是应该予以充分肯定的。

从卫三畏的例子不难联想到,身处所谓“轴心文明”(主要以几大世界性宗教作为标识)的人们往往患有“老子天下第一”的自恋症,而以“居高临下”的态度傲视其他人,难以免俗和根治。反观我们自己,历代国人的“华夷之辨”又何尝不是如此?而时至今日,仍不乏“宅兹中国”的自尊和输出“天下体系”的自负。但也不必悲观,因为这个五彩缤纷的世界本来就是由形形色色、各有偏好的人们构成的。他们之间有相辅相成的关系,也有相反相成的因素。虽然各派宗教和文化的代表自以为有“替上帝传教”或“替天行道”的使命,谁都无法垄断真理和剥夺他人的信仰,也不能指望按照自己的面貌来彻底改造他人。其出于宗教或政治动机的种种努力的后果,客观上会推动各国和各民族之间的交往和融合,并推动人类文明的进步和升华,则是毫无疑义的。从这一点来看,卫三畏一生的变化过程所显示的方向对我们建构今日地球村的和平共处规则还是不乏启迪作用的,那就是要逐渐学会把“老子化胡”的心态改为“相敬如宾”的心理,对异民族、异文化和异文明采取更加宽容、尊重和善于调适的态度,以便用文明对话来取代文明对抗,从而把亨廷顿认为不可避免的“文明冲突”消弭于萌芽状态和无形之间。

PREFACE.

During the thirty-five years which have elapsed since the first edition of this work was issued, a greater advance has probably been made in the political and intellectual development of China than within any previous century of her history. While neither the social habits nor principles of government have so far altered as to necessitate a complete rewriting of these pages, it will be found, nevertheless, that the present volumes treat of a reformed and in many respects modern nation. Under the new régime the central administration has radically increased its authority among the provincial rulers, and more than ever in former years has managed to maintain control over their pretentions. The Empire has, moreover, established its foreign relations on a well-understood basis by accredited envoys; this will soon affect the mass of the people by the greater facilities of trade, the presence of travellers, diffusion of education, and other agencies which are awaking the people from their lethargy. Already the influences which will gradually transform the face of society are mightily operating.

The changes which have been made in the book comprise such alterations and additions as were necessary to describe the country under its new aspects. In the constant desire to preserve a convenient size, every doubtful or superfluous sentence has been erased, while the new matter incorporated has increased the bulk of the present edition about one-third. The arrangement of chapters is the same. The first four, treating of the geography, combine as many and accurate details of recent explorers or residents as the proportions of this section will permit. The extra-provincial regions are described from the researches of Russian, English, and Indian travellers of the last twenty years. It is a waste, mountainous territory for the most part and can never support a large population. Great pains have been taken by the cartographer, Jacob Wells, to consult the most authentic charts in the construction of the map of the Empire. By collating and reducing to scale the surveys and route charts of reliable travellers throughout the colonies, he has produced in all respects as accurate a map of Central Asia as is at this date possible. The Eighteen Provinces are in the main the same as in my former map.

The chapter on the census remains for the most part without alteration, for until there has been a methodical inspection of the Empire, important questions concerning its population must be held in abeyance. It is worth noticing how generally the estimates in this chapter—or much larger figures—have since its first publication been accepted for the population of China. Foreign students of natural history in China have, by their researches in every department, furnished material for more extensive and precise descriptions under this subject than could possibly have been gathered twoscore years ago. The sixth chapter has, therefore, been almost wholly rewritten, and embraces as complete a summary of this wide field as space would allow or the general reader tolerate. The specialist will, however, speedily recognize the fact that this rapid glance serves rather to indicate how immense and imperfectly explored is this subject than to describe whatever is known.

That portion of the first volume treating of the laws and their administration does not admit of more than a few minor changes. However good their theory of jurisprudence, the people have many things to bear from the injustice of their rulers, but more from their own vices. The *Peking Gazette* is now regularly translated in the Shanghai papers, and gives a *coup d'œil* of the administration of the highest value.

The chapters on the languages and literature are considerably improved. The translations and text-books which the diligence of foreign scholars has recently furnished could be only partially enumerated, though here, as elsewhere in the work, references in the foot-notes are intended to direct the more interested student to the bibliography of the subject, and present him with the materials for an exhaustive study. The native literature is extensive, and all branches have contributed somewhat to form the résumé which is contained in this section, giving a preponderance to the Confucian classics. The four succeeding chapters contain notices of the arts, industries, domestic life, and science of the Chinese—a necessarily rapid survey, since these features of Chinese life are already well understood by foreigners. Nothing, however, that is either original or peculiar has been omitted in the endeavor to portray their social and economic characteristics. The emigration of many thousands of the people of Kwangtung within the last thirty years has made that province a representative among foreign nations of the others; it may be added that its inhabitants are well fitted, by their enterprise, thrift, and maritime habits, to become types of the whole.

The history and chronology are made fuller by the addition of several facts and tables;[1] but the field of research in this direction has as yet scarcely been defined, and few certain dates have been determined prior to the Confucian era.

---

[1] An alphabetical arrangement of all the tables scattered throughout the work may be found under this word in the Index.

The entire continent of Asia must be thoroughly investigated in its geography, antiquities, and literature in order to throw light on the eastern portion. The history of China offers an interesting topic for a scholar who would devote his life to its elucidation from the mass of native literature.

The two chapters on the religions, and what has been done within the past half century to promote Christian missions, are somewhat enlarged and brought down to the present time. The study of modern scholars in the examination of Chinese religious beliefs has enabled them to make comparisons with other systems of Asiatics, as well as discuss the native creeds with more certainty.

The chapter on the commerce of China has an importance commensurate with its growing amount. Within the past ten years the opium trade has been attacked in its moral and commercial bearings between China, India, and England. There are grounds for hope that the British Government will free itself from any connection with it, which will be a triumph of justice and Christianity. The remainder of Volume II. describes events in the intercourse of China with the outer world, including a brief account of the Tai-ping Rebellion, which proximately grew out of foreign ideas. No connected or satisfactory narrative of the events which have forced one of the greatest nations of the world into her proper position, so far as I am aware, has as yet been prepared. A succinct recital of one of the most extraordinary developments of modern times should not be without interest to all.

The work of condensing the vast increase of reliable information upon China into these two volumes has been attended with considerable labor. Future writers will, I am convinced, after the manner of Richthofen, Yule, Legge, and others, confine themselves to single or cognate subjects rather than attempt such a comprehensive synopsis as is here presented. The number of illustrations in this edition is nearly doubled, the added ones being selected with particular reference to the subject-matter. I have availed myself of whatever sources of information I could command, due acknowledgment of which is made in the foot-notes, and ample references in the Index.

The revision of this book has been the slow though constant occupation of several years. When at last I had completed the revised copy and made arrangements as to its publication, in March, 1882, my health failed, and under a partial paralysis I was rendered incapable of further labor. My son, Frederick Wells Williams, who had already looked over the copy, now assumed entire charge of the publication. I had the more confidence that he would perform the duties of editor, for he had already a general acquaintance with China and the books which are the best authority. The work has been well done, the last three chapters particularly having been improved under his careful revision and especial study of the recent political history of China. The Index is his work, and throughout the book I am indebted to his careful supervision, especially on the chapters treating of geography and literature. By the opening of this year I had so far recovered as to be able to superintend the printing and look over the proofs of the second volume.

My experiences in the forty-three years of my life in China were coeval with the changes which gradually culminated in the opening of the country. Among the most important of these may be mentioned the cessation of the East India Company in 1834, the war with England in 1841–42, the removal of the monopoly of the hong merchants, the opening of five ports to trade, the untoward attack on the city of Canton which grew out of the lorcha Arrow, the operations in the vicinity of Peking, the establishment of foreign legations in that city, and finally, in 1873, the peaceful settlement of the *kotow*, which rendered possible the approach of foreign ministers to the Emperor's presence. Those who trace the hand of God in history will gather from such rapid and great changes in this Empire the foreshadowing of the fulfilment of his purposes; for while these political events were in progress the Bible was circulating, and the preaching and educational labors of missionaries were silently and with little opposition accomplishing their leavening work among the people.

On my arrival at Canton in 1833 I was officially reported, with two other Americans, to the hong merchant Kingqua as *fan-kwai*, or 'foreign devils,' who had come to live under his tutelage. In 1874, as Secretary of the American Embassy at Peking, I accompanied the Hon. B. P. Avery to the presence of the Emperor Tungchí, when the Minister of the United States presented his letters of credence on a footing of perfect equality with the 'Son of Heaven.' With two such experiences in a lifetime, and mindful of the immense intellectual and moral development which is needed to bring an independent government from the position of forcing one of them to that of yielding the other, it is not strange that I am assured of a great future for the sons of Han; but the progress of pure Christianity will be the only adequate means to save the conflicting elements involved in such a growth from destroying each other. Whatever is in store for them, it is certain that the country has passed its period of passivity. There is no more for China the repose of indolence and seclusion—when she looked down on the nations in her overweening pride like the stars with which she could have no concern.

In this revision the same object has been kept in view that is stated in the Preface to the first edition—to divest the Chinese people and civilization of that peculiar and indefinable impression of ridicule which has been so generally given them by foreign authors. I have endeavored to show the better traits of their national character, and that they have had up to this time no opportunity of learning many things with which they are now rapidly becoming acquainted. The time is speedily passing away when the people of the Flowery Land can fairly be classed among uncivilized nations. The stimulus which in this labor of my earlier and later years has been ever present to my mind is the hope that the cause of missions may be promoted. In the success of this cause lies the salvation of China as a people, both in its moral and political aspects. This success bids fair to keep pace with the needs of the people. They will become fitted for taking up the work themselves and joining in the multiform operations of foreign civilizations. Soon railroads, telegraphs, and manufactures will be introduced, and these must be followed by whatsoever may conduce to enlightening the millions of the people of China in every department of religious, political, and domestic life.

The descent of the Holy Spirit is promised in the latter times, and the preparatory work for that descent has been accomplishing in a vastly greater ratio than ever before, and with increased facilities toward its final completion. The promise of that Spirit will fulfil the prophecy of Isaiah, delivered before the era of Confucius, and God's people will come from the land of Sinim and join in the anthem of praise with every tribe under the sun.

S. W. W.

NEW HAVEN, July, 1883.

CONTENTS OF VOLUME I.

CHAPTER I.

CHAPTER II.

CHAPTER IV.

CHAPTER V.

PAGE

CHAPTER VIII.

CHAPTER XIII.

CHAPTER XIV.

LIST OF ILLUSTRATIONS IN VOLUME I.

NOTE RESPECTING THE SYSTEM OF PRONUNCIATION ADOPTED IN THIS WORK.

In this the values of the vowels are as follows:

1. *a* as the italicized letters in f*a*ther, f*a*r (never like *a* in hat); e.g., *chang, hang*—sounded almost as if written *chahng, hahng*, not flat as in the English words *sang, bang, man*, etc.
2. *ă* like the short *u* in b*u*t, or as any of the italicized vowels in *A*meric*a*n, s*u*mmer, m*o*ther; the German *ö* approaches this sound, while Wade writes it *ê*; e.g., *păn, tăng*, to be pronounced as *pun, tongue.*
3. *e* as in m*e*n, d*ea*d, s*ai*d; as *teh, shen, yen.*
4. *é*, the French *é*, as in th*ey*, n*eigh*, pr*ay*; as *ché, yé*, pronounced *chay, yay.*
5. *i* as in p*i*n, f*i*n*i*sh; as *sing, lin, Chihlí.*
6. *í* as in mach*i*ne, bel*ie*ve, f*ee*l, m*e*; as *lí, Kíshen, Kanghí.*
7. *o* as in l*o*ng, l*aw*n; never like n*o*, cr*ow*; as *to, soh, po.*
8. *u* as in r*u*le, t*oo*, f*oo*l; as *Turk, Belur, ku, sung*, pronounced *Toork, Beloor, koo, soong.* This sound is heard less full in *fuh, tsun*, and a few other words; this and the next may be considered as equivalent to the two *u*-sounds found in German.
9. *ü* nearly as in l'*u*ne (French), or *u*nion, rh*eu*m; as *hü, tsü.*
10. *ai* as in *ai*sle, h*igh*, or longer than *i* in pine; as *Shanghai, Hainan.* The combination *ei* is more slender than *ai*, though the difference is slight; e.g., *Kwei-chau.*
11. *au* and *ao* as in r*ou*nd, *ou*r, h*ow*; as *Fuhchau, Macao, Taukwang.*
12. *éu* as in the colloquial phrase *say 'em*; e.g., *chéung.* This diphthong is heard in the Canton dialect.

13. *ia* as in *y*ard ; e.g., *hia, kiang ;* not to be sounded as if written *high-a, kigh-ang,* but like *heä, keäng.*
14. *iau* is made by joining Nos. 5 and 11 ; *hiau, Liautung.*
15. *ie* as in s*ie*rra (Spanish), R*ie*nzi ; e.g., *hien, kien.*
16. *iu* as in p*ew*, p*u*re, lengthened to a diphthong ; *kiu, siun.*
17. *iue* is made by adding a short *e* to the preceding ; *kiuen, hiuen.*
18. *ui* as in L*oui*siana, s*ui*cide ; e.g., *sui, chui.*

The consonants are sounded generally as they are in the English alphabet. *Ch* as in *ch*urch ; *hw* as in *wh*en ; *j* soft, as *s* in pleasure ; *kw* as in aw*kw*ard ; *ng*, as an initial, as in si*nging*, leaving off the first two letters ; *sz'* and *tsz'* are to be sounded full with one breathing, but none of the English vowels are heard in it ; the sound stops at the *z* ; Dr. Morrison wrote these sounds *tsze* and *sze*, while Sir Thomas Wade, whose system bids fair to become the most widely employed, turns them into *ssŭ* and *tzŭ*. The *hs* of the latter, made by omitting the first vowel of *hissing*, is written simply as *h* by the author. *Urh*, or *'rh*, is pronounced as the three last letters of *purr*.

All these, except No. 12, are heard in the court dialect, which has now become the most common mode of writing the names of places and persons in China. Though foreign authors have employed different letters, they have all intended to write the same sound ; thus *chan, shan,* and *xan*, are only different ways of writing 門 ; and *tsse, tsze, tsz', ʒh, tzŭ,* and *tzu*, of 字. Such is not the case, however, with such names as *Macao, Hongkong, Amoy, Whampoa,* and others along the coast, which are sounded according to the local patois, and not the court pronunciation—*Ma-ngau, Hiangkiang, Hiamun, Hwangpu,* etc. Many of the discrepancies seen in the works of travellers and writers are owing to the fact that each is prone to follow his own fancy in transliterating foreign names ; uniformity is almost unattainable in this matter. Even, too, in what is called the court dialect there is a great diversity among educated Chinese, owing to the traditional way all learn the sounds of the characters. In this work, and on the map, the sounds are written uniformly according to the pronunciation given in Morrison's Dictionary, but not according to his orthography. Almost every writer upon the Chinese language seems disposed to propose a new system, and the result is a great confusion in writing the same name; for example, *eull, olr, ul, ulh, lh, urh, 'rh, í, e, lur, nge, ngí, je, jí,* are different ways of writing the sounds given to a single character. Amid these discrepancies, both among the Chinese themselves and those who endeavor to catch their pronunciation, it is almost impossible to settle upon one mode of writing the names of places. That which seems to offer the easiest pronunciation has been adopted in this work. It may, perhaps, be regarded as an unimportant matter, so long as the place is known, but to one living abroad, and unacquainted with the language, the discrepancy is a source of great confusion. He is unable to decide, for instance, whether *Tung-ngan, Tungon hien, Tang-oune,* and *Tungao,* refer to the same place or not.

In writing Chinese proper names, authors differ greatly as to the style of placing them; thus, Fuhchaufu, Fuh-chau-fu, Fuh Chau Fu, Fuh-Chau fu, etc., are all seen. Analogy affords little guide here, for New York, Philadelphia, and Cambridge are severally unlike in the principle of writing them: the first, being really formed of an adjective and a noun, is not in this case united to the latter, as it is in Newport, Newtown, etc.; the second is like the generality of Chinese towns, and while it is now written as one word, it would be written as two if the name were translated—as 'Brotherly Love;' but the third, *Cambridge,* despite its derivation, is never written in two words, and many Chinese names are like this in origin. Thus applying these rules, properly enough, to Chinese places, they have been written here as single words, *Suchau, Peking, Hongkong;* a hyphen has been inserted in some places only to avoid mispronunciation, as *Hiau-í, Sí-ngan,* etc. It is hardly supposed that this system will alter such names as are commonly written otherwise, nor, indeed, that it will be adhered to with absolute consistency in the following pages; but the principle of the arrangement is perhaps the simplest possible. The additions *fu, chau, ting,* and *hien,* being classifying terms, should form a separate word. In conclusion, it may be stated that this system could only be carried out approximately as regards the proper names in the colonies and outside of the Empire.

THE

MIDDLE KINGDOM.

CHAPTER I.

GENERAL DIVISIONS AND FEATURES OF THE EMPIRE.

The possessions of the ruling dynasty of China,—that portion of the Asiatic continent which is usually called by geographers the Chinese Empire,—form one of the most extensive dominions ever swayed by a single power in any age, or any part of the world. Comprising within its limits every variety of soil and climate, and watered by large rivers, which serve not only to irrigate and drain it, but, by means of their size and the course of their tributaries, affording unusual facilities for intercommunication, it produces within its own borders everything necessary for the comfort, support, and delight of its occupants, who have depended very slightly upon the assistance of other climes and nations for satisfying their own wants. Its civilization has been developed under its own institutions; its government has been modelled without knowledge or reference to that of any other kingdom; its literature has borrowed nothing from the genius or research of the scholars of other lands; its language is unique in its symbols, its structure, and its antiquity; its inhabitants are remarkable for their industry, peacefulness, numbers, and peculiar habits. The examination of such a people, and so extensive a country, can hardly fail of being both instructive and entertaining, and if rightly pursued, lead to a stronger conviction of the need of the precepts and sanctions of the Bible to the highest development of every nation in its personal, social, and political relations in this world, as well as to individual happiness in another. It is to be hoped, too, that at this date in the world's history, there are many more than formerly, who desire to learn the condition and wants of others, not entirely for their own amusement and congratulation at their superior knowledge and advantages, but also to promote the well-being of their fellow-men, and impart liberally of the gifts they themselves enjoy. Those who desire to do this, will find that few families of mankind are more worthy of their greatest efforts than those comprised within the limits of the Chinese Empire; while none stand in more need of the purifying, ennobling, and invigorating principles of our holy religion to develop and enforce their own theories of social improvement.

The origin of the name *China* has not yet been fully settled. The people themselves have now no such name for their country, nor is there good evidence that they ever did apply it to the whole land. The occurrence in the *Laws of Manu* and in the *Mahâbhárata* of the name *China*, applied to a land or people with whom the Hindus had intercourse in the twelfth century B.C., and who were probably the Chinese, throws the origin far back into the remotest times, where probability must take the place of evidence. The most credible account ascribes its origin to the family of Tsin, whose chief first obtained complete sway, about B.C. 250, over all the other feudal principalities in the land, and whose exploits rendered him famous in India, Persia, and other Asiatic states. His sept had, however, long been renowned in Chinese history, and previous to this conquest had made itself widely known, not only in China, but in other countries. The kingdom lay in the northwestern parts of the empire, near the Yellow River, and according to Visdelou, who has examined the subject, the family was illustrious by its nobility and power. "Its founder was Tayé, son of the emperor Chuen-hü. It existed in great splendor for more than a thousand years, and was only inferior to the royal dignity. Feitsz', a prince of this family, had the superintendence of the stud of the emperor Hiao, B.C. 909, and as a mark of favor his majesty conferred on him the sovereignty of the city of Tsinchau in *mesne tenure*, with the title of sub-tributary king. One hundred and twenty-two years afterwards, B.C. 770, Siangkwan, *petit roi* of Tsinchau (having by his bravery revenged the insults offered to the emperor Ping by the Tartars, who slew his father Yu), was created king in full tenure, and without limitation or exception. The same monarch, abandoning Sí-ngan (then called Hao-king, the capital of his empire) to transport his seat to Lohyang, Siangkwan was able to make himself master of the large province of Shensí, which had composed the proper kingdom of the emperor. The king of Tsin thus became very powerful, but though his fortune changed, he did not alter his title, retaining always that of the city of Tsinchau, which had been the foundation of his elevation. The kingdom of Tsin soon became celebrated, and being the place of the first arrival by land of people from western countries, it seems probable that those who saw no more of China than the realm of Tsin, extended this name to all the rest, and called the whole empire Tsin or Chin." [1]

This extract refers to periods long before the dethronement of the house of Chau by princes of Tsin; the position of this latter principality, contiguous to the desert, and holding the passes leading from the valley of the Tarim across the desert eastward to China, renders the supposition of the learned Jesuit highly probable. The possession of the old imperial capital would strengthen this idea in the minds of the traders resorting to China from the West; and when the same family did obtain paramount sway over the whole empire, and its head render himself celebrated by his conquests, and by building the Great Wall, the name Tsin was still more widely diffused, and regarded as the name of the country. The Malays and Arabians, whose vessels were early found between Aden and Canton, knew it as China, and probably introduced the name into Europe before 1500. The Hindus contracted it into *Machin*, from *Maha-china*, *i.e.*, 'Great China;' and the first of

[1] D'Herbelot, *Bibliothèque Orientale*, quarto edition, 1779, Tome IV., p. 8. Yule, *Cathay and the Way Thither*, Vol. I., pp. xxxiv., lxviii. Edkins, *Chinese Buddhism*, p. 93.

these was sometimes confounded with *Manji*, a term used for the tribes in Yunnan. Thus it appears that these and other nations of Asia have known the country or its people by no other terms than *Jin*, *Chin*, *Sin*, *Sinæ*, or *Tzinistæ*. The Persian name *Cathay*, and its Russian form of *Kitai*, is of modern origin; it is altered from *Ki-tah*, the race which ruled northern China in the tenth century, and is quite unknown to the people it designates. The Latin word *Seres* is derived from the Chinese word *sz'* (silk), and doubtless first came into use to denote the people during the Han dynasty.

The Chinese have many names to designate themselves and the land they inhabit. One of the most ancient is *Tien Hia*, meaning 'Beneath the Sky,' and denoting the World; another, almost as ancient, is *Sz' Hai*, *i.e.*, '[all within] the Four Seas,' while a third is *Chung Kwoh*, or 'Middle Kingdom.' This dates from the establishment of the Chau dynasty, about B.C. 1150, when the imperial family so called its own special state in Honan because it was surrounded by all the others. The name was retained as the empire grew, and thus has strengthened the popular belief that it is really situated in the centre of the earth; *Chung Kwoh jin*, or 'men of the Middle Kingdom,' denotes the Chinese. All these names indicate the vanity and ignorance of the people respecting their geographical position and their rank among the nations; they have not been alone in this foible, for the Egyptians, Greeks and Romans all had terms for their possessions which intimated their own ideas of their superiority; while, too, the area of none of those monarchies, in their widest extent, equalled that of China Proper. The family of Tsin also established the custom, since continued, of calling the country by the name of the dynasty then reigning; but, while the brief duration of that house of forty-four years was not long enough to give it much currency among the people, succeeding dynasties, by their talents and prowess, imparted their own as permanent appellations to the people and country. The terms *Han-jin* and *Han-tsz'* (*i.e.*, men of Han or sons of Han) are now in use by the people to denote themselves; the last also means a "brave man." *Tang-jin*, or 'Men of Tang,' is quite as frequently heard in the southern provinces, where the phrase *Tang Shan*, or 'Hills of Tang,' denotes the whole country. The Buddhists of India called the land *Chin-tan*, or the 'Dawn,' and this appellation has been used in Chinese writings of that sect.

The present dynasty calls the empire *Ta Tsing Kwoh*, or 'Great Pure Kingdom;' but the people themselves have refused the corresponding term of *Tsing-jin*, or 'Men of Tsing.' The empire is also sometimes termed *Tsing Chau*, *i.e.*, '[land of the] Pure Dynasty,' by metonymy for the family that rules it. The term now frequently heard in western countries—the Celestial Empire—is derived from *Tien Chau*, *i.e.*, 'Heavenly Dynasty,' meaning the kingdom which the dynasty appointed by heaven rules over; but the term *Celestials*, for the people of that kingdom, is entirely of foreign manufacture, and their language could with difficulty be made to express such a patronymic. The phrase *Lí Min*, or 'Black-haired Race,' is a common appellation; the expressions *Hwa Yen*, the 'Flowery Language,' and *Chung Hwa Kwoh*, the 'Middle Flowery Kingdom,' are also frequently used for the written language of the country, because the Chinese consider themselves to be among the most polished and civilized of all nations—which is the sense of *hwa* in these phrases. The phrase *Nui Ti*, or 'Inner Land,' is often employed to distinguish it from countries beyond their borders, regarded as the desolate and barbarous regions of the earth. *Hwa Hia* (the Glorious Hia) is an ancient term for China, the Hia dynasty being the first of the series; *Tung Tu*, or "Land of the East," is a name used in Mohammedan writings alone.

The present ruling dynasty has extended the limits of the empire far beyond what they were under the Ming princes, and nearly to their extent in the reign of Kublai, A.D. 1290. In 1840, its borders were well defined, reaching from Sagalien I. on the north-east, in lat. 48° 10′ N. and long. 144° 50′ E., to Hainan I. in the China Sea, on the south, in lat. 18° 10′ N., and westward to the Belur-tag, in long. 74° E., inclosing a continuous area, estimated, after the most careful valuation by McCulloch, at 5,300,000 square miles. The longest line which could be drawn in this vast region, from the south-western part of Ílí, bordering on Kokand, north-easterly to the sea of Okhotsk, is 3,350 miles; its greatest breadth is 2,100 miles, from the Outer Hing-an or Stanovoi Mountains to the peninsula of Luichau in Kwangtung:—the first measuring 71 degrees of longitude, and the last over 34 of latitude.

Since that year the process of disintegration has been going on, and the cession of Hongkong to the British has been followed by greater partitions to Russia, which have altogether reduced it more than half a million of square miles on the north-east and west. Its limits on the western frontiers are still somewhat undefined. The greatest breadth is from Albazin on the Amur, nearly south to Hainan, 2,150 miles; and the longest line which can be drawn in it runs from Sartokh in Tibet, north-east to the junction of the Usuri River with the Amur.

The form of the empire approaches a rectangle. It is bounded on the east and south-east by various arms and portions of the Pacific Ocean, beginning at the frontier of Corea, and called on European maps the gulfs of Liautung and Pechele, the Yellow Sea, channel of Formosa, China Sea, and Gulf of Tonquin. Cochinchina and Burmah border on the provinces of Kwangtung, Kwangsí, and Yunnan, in the south-west; but most of the region near that frontier is inhabited by half-independent tribes of Laos, Kakyens, Singphos, and others. The southern ranges of the Himalaya separate Assam, Butan, Sikkim, Nípal and states in India from Tibet, whose western border is bounded by the nominally dependent country of Ladak, or if that be excluded, by the Kara-korum Mountains. The kingdoms or states of Cashmere, Badakshan, Kokand, and the Kirghís steppe, lie upon the western frontiers of Little Tibet, Ladak, and Ílí, as far north as the Russian border; the high range of the Belur-tag or Tsung-ling separates the former countries from the Chinese territory in this quarter. Russia is conterminous with China from the Kirghís steppe along the Altai chain and Kenteh range to the junction of the Argun and the Amur, from whence the latter river and its tributary, the Usuri, form the dividing line to the border of Corea, a total stretch of 5,300 miles. The circuit of the whole empire is 14,000 miles, or considerably over half the circumference of the globe. These measurements, it must be remembered, are of the roughest character. The coast line from the mouth of the river Yaluh in Corea to that of the Annam in Cochinchina is not far from 4,400 miles. This immense country comprises about one-third of the continent, and nearly one-tenth of the habitable part of the globe; and, next to Russia, is the largest empire which has existed on the earth.

It will, perhaps, contribute to a better comprehension of the area of the Chinese Empire to compare it with some other countries. Russia is nearly 6,500 miles in its greatest length, about 1,500 in its average breadth, and measures 8,369,144[1] square miles, or one-seventh of the land on the globe. The United States of America extends about 3,000 miles from Monterey on the Pacific in a north-easterly direction to Maine, and about 1,700 from Lake of the Woods to Florida. The area of this territory is now estimated at 2,936,166 square miles, with a coast line of 5,120 miles. The area of the British Empire is not far from 7,647,000 square miles, but the boundaries of some of the colonies in Hindostan and South Africa are not definitely laid down; the superficies of the two colonies of Australia and New Zealand is nearly equal to that of all the other possessions of the British crown.

The Chinese themselves divide the empire into three principal parts, rather by the different form of government in each, than by any geographical arrangement.

I. The *Eighteen Provinces*, including, with trivial additions, the country conquered by the Manchus in 1664.

II. *Manchuria*, or the native country of the Manchus, lying north of the Gulf of Liautung as far as the Amur and west of the Usuri River.

III. *Colonial Possessions*, including Mongolia, Îlí (comprising Sungaria and Eastern Turkestan), Koko-nor, and Tibet.

The first of these divisions alone is that to which other nations have given the name of China, and is the only part which is entirely settled by the Chinese. It lies on the eastern

[1] Or 21,759,974 sq. km.—*Gotha Almanach.*

slope of the high table-land of Central Asia, in the south-eastern angle of the continent; and for beauty of scenery, fertility of soil, salubrity of climate, magnificent and navigable rivers, and variety and abundance of its productions, will compare with any portion of the globe. The native name for this portion, as distinguished from the rest, is *Shih-pah Săng* or the 'Eighteen Provinces,' but the people themselves usually mean this part alone by the term *Chung Kwoh.* The area of the Eighteen Provinces is estimated by McCulloch at 1,348,870 square miles, but if the full area of the provinces of Kansuh and Chihlí be included, this figure is not large enough; the usual computation is 1,297,999 square miles; Malte Brun reckons it at 1,482,091 square miles; but the entire dimensions of the Eighteen Provinces, as the Chinese define them, cannot be much under 2,000,000 square miles, the excess lying in the extension of the two provinces mentioned above. This part, consequently, is rather more than two-fifths of the area of the whole empire.

The old limits are, however, more natural, and being better known may still be retained. They give nearly a square form to the provinces, the length from north to south being 1,474 miles, and the breadth 1,355 miles; but the diagonal line from the north-east corner to Yunnan is 1,669 miles, and that from Amoy to the north-western part of Kansuh is 1,557 miles. China Proper, therefore, measures about seven times the size of France, and fifteen times that of the United Kingdom; it is nearly half as large as all Europe, which is 3,650,000 square miles. Its area is, however, nearer that of all the States of the American Union lying east of the Mississippi River, with Texas, Arkansas, Missouri and Iowa added; these all cover 1,355,309 square miles. The position of the two countries facing the western borders of great oceans is another point of likeness, which involves considerable similarity in climate; there is moreover a further resemblance between the size of the provinces in China and those of the newer States.

Before proceeding to define the three great basins into which China may be divided, it will give a better idea of the whole subject to speak of the mountain ranges which lie within and near or along the limits of the country. The latter in themselves form almost an entire wall inclosing and defining the old empire; the principal exceptions being the western boundaries of Yunnan, the border between Íli and the Kirghís steppe, and the trans-Amur region.

Commencing at the north-eastern corner of the basin of the Amur above its mouth, near lat. 56° N., are the first summits of the Altai range, which during its long course of 2,000 miles takes several names; this range forms the northern limit of the table-land of Central Asia. At its eastern part, the range is called Stanovoi by the Russians, and *Wai Hing-an* by the Chinese; the first name is applied as far west as the confluence of the Songari with the Amur, beyond which, north-west as far as lake Baikal, the Russians call it the Daourian Mountains. The distance from the lake to the ocean is about 600 miles, and all within Russian limits. Beyond lake Baikal, westward, the chain is called the Altai, *i.e.*, Golden Mountains, and sometimes *Kin shan*, having a similar meaning. Near the head-waters of the river Selenga this range separates into two nearly parallel systems running east and west. The southern one, which lies mostly in Mongolia, is called the Tangnu, and rises to a much higher elevation than the northern spur. The Tangnu Mountains continue under that name on the Chinese maps in a south-westerly direction, but this chain properly joins the Tien shan, or Celestial Mountains, in the province of Cobdo, and continues until it again unites with the Altai further west, near the junction of the Kirghís steppe with China and Russia. The length of the whole chain is not far from 2,500 miles, and except near the Tshulyshman River, does not, so far as is known, rise to the snow line, save in detached peaks. The average elevation is supposed to be in the neighborhood of 7,000 feet; most of it lies between latitudes 47° and 52° N., largely covered with forests and susceptible of cultivation.

The next chain is the Belur-tag, Tartash ling, in Chinese *Tsung ling*, Onion Mountains, or better, Blue Mountains, so called from their distant hue.[1] This range lies in the south-west of Son-

[1] Klaproth (*Mémoires sur l'Asie*, Tome II., p. 295) observes that the name is derived from the abundance of onions found upon these mountains. M. Abel-Rémusat prefers to attribute it to the "bluish tint of onions."

garia, separating that territory from Badakshan; it commences about lat. 50° N., nearly at right angles with the Tien shan, and extends south, rising to a great height, though little is known of it. It may be considered as the connecting link between the Tien shan and the Kwănlun; or rather, both this and the latter may be considered as proceeding from a mountain knot, detached from the Hindu-kush, in the south-western part of Turkestan called Pushtikhur, the Belur-tag coming from its northern side, while the Kwănlun issues from its eastern side, and extends across the middle of the table-land to Koko-nor, there diverging into two branches. This mountain knot lies between latitudes 36° and 37° N., and longitudes 70° and 74° E. The Himalaya range proceeds from it south-easterly, along the southern frontier of Tibet, till it breaks up near the head-waters of the Yangtsz', Salween, and other rivers between Tibet, Burmah, and Yunnan, thus nearly completing the inland frontier of the empire. A small spur from the Yun ling, in the west of Yunnan, in the country of the Singphos and borders of Assam, may also be regarded as forming part of the boundary line. The *Chang-peh shan* lies between the head-waters of the Yaluh and Tounen rivers, along the Corean frontier, forming a spur of the lower range of the Sihota or *Sih-hih-teh* Mountains, east of the Usuri.

Within the confines of the empire are four large chains, some of the peaks in their course rising to stupendous elevations, but the ridges generally falling below the snow line. The first is the Tien shan or Celestial Mountains, called Tengkiri by the Mongols, and sometimes erroneously Alak Mountains. This chain begins at the northern extremity of the Belur-tag in lat. 40° N., or more properly comes in from the west, and extends from west to east between longitudes 76° and 90° E., and generally along the 22° of north latitude, dividing Íli into the Northern and Southern Circuits. Its western portion is called Muz-tag; the Muz-daban, about long. 79° E., between Kuldja and Aksu, is where the road from north to south runs across, leading over a high glacier above the snow line. East of this occurs a mass of peaks among the highest in Central Asia, called Bogdo-ula; and at the eastern end, near Ur umtsi, as it declines to the desert, are traces of volcanic action seen in solfataras and spaces covered with ashes, but no active volcanoes are now known. The doubtful volcano of Pí shan, between the glacier and the Bogdo-ula, is the only one reported in continental China. The Tien shan end abruptly at their eastern point, where the ridge meets the desert, not far from the meridian of Barkul in Kansuh, though Humboldt considers the hills in Mongolia a continuation of the range eastward, as far as the Nui Hing-an. The space between the Altai and Tien shan is very much broken up by mountainous spurs, which may be considered as connecting links of them both, though no regular chain exists. The western prolongation of the Tien shan, under the name of the Muz-tag, extends from the high pass only as far as the junction of the Belur-tag, beyond which, and out of the Chinese Empire, it continues nearly west, south of the river Sihon toward Kodjend, under the names of Ak-tag and Asferah-tag; this part is covered with perpetual snow.

Nearly parallel with the Tien shan in part of its course is the Nan shan, Kwănlun or Koulkun range of mountains, also called *Tien Chu* or 'Celestial Pillar' by Chinese geographers. The Kwănlun starts from the Pushtikhur knot in lat. 36° N., and runs along easterly in nearly that parallel through the whole breadth of the table-land, dividing Tibet from the desert of Gobi in part of its course. About the middle of its extent, not far from long. 90° E., it divides into several ranges, which decline to the south-east through Koko-nor and Sz'chuen, under the names of the Bayan-kara, the Burkhan-buddha, the Shuga and the Tangla Mountains,—each more or less parallel in their general south-east course till they merge with the Yun ling (*i.e.*, Cloudy Mountains), about lat. 33° N. Another group bends northerly, beyond the sources of the Yellow River, and under the names of Altyn-tag, Nan shan, Ín shan, and Ala shan, passes through Kansuh and Shensí to join the Nui Hing-an, not far from the great bend of the Yellow River. Some portion of the country between the extremities of these two ranges is less elevated, but no plains occur, though the parts north of Kansuh, where the Great Wall runs, are rugged and unfertile. The large tract between the basins of the Tarim River and that of the Yaru-tsang..ı, including the Kwănlun range, is mostly occupied by the desert of Gobi, and is now one of the least known parts of the globe. The mineral treasures of the Kwănlun are probably great, judging from the many precious stones ascribed to it; this desolate region is the favorite arena for the monsters, fairies, genii, and other beings of Chinese legendary lore, and is the Olympus where the Buddhist and Taoist divinities hold their mystic sway, strange voices are heard, and marvels accomplished.[1]

From near the head-waters of the Yellow River, the four ridges run south-easterly, and converge hard by the confines of Burmah and Yunnan, within an area about one hundred miles in breadth. The Yun ling range constitutes the western frontier of Sz'chuen, and going south-east into Yunnan, thence turns eastward, under the names of Nan ling, Mei ling, Wu-í shan, and other local terms, passing through Kweichau, Hunan, and dividing Kwangtung and Fuhkien from Kiangsí and Chehkiang, bends northeast till it reaches the sea opposite Chusan. One or two spurs branch off north from this range through Hunan and Kiangsí, as far as the Yangtsz', but they are all of moderate elevation, covered with forests, and susceptible of cultivation. The descent from the Siueh ling or Bayan-kara Mountains, and the western part of the Yun ling, to the Pacific, is very gradual. The Chinese give a list of fifty peaks lying in the provinces which are covered with snow for the whole or part of the year, and describe glaciers on several of them.

Another less extensive ridge branches off nearly due east from the Bayan-kara Mountains in Koko-nor, and forms a moderately high range of mountains between the Yellow River and Yangtsz' kiang as far as long. 112° E., on the western borders of Nganhwui; this range is called Ko-tsing shan, and Peh ling (*i.e.*, Northern Mountains), on European maps. These two chains, viz., the Yun ling—with its continuation of the Mei ling—and the Peh ling, with their numerous offsets, render the whole of the western part of China very uneven.

[1] Compare Rémusat, *Histoire de la Ville de Khotan*, p. 65, ff.

On the east of Mongolia, and commencing near the bend of the Yellow River, or rather forming a continuation of the range in Shansí, is the Nui Hing-an ling or Sialkoi, called also Soyorti range, which runs north-east on the west side of the basin of the Amur, till it reaches the Wai Hing-an, in lat. 56° N. The sides of the ridge toward the desert are nearly naked, but the eastern acclivities are well wooded and fertile. On the confines of Corea a spur strikes off westward through Shingking, called Kolmin-shanguin alin by the Manchus, and Chang-peh shan (*i.e.*, Long White Mountains) by the Chinese. Between the Sialkoi and Sihota are two smaller ridges defining the basin of the Nonni River on the east and west. Little is known of the elevation of these chains except that they are low in comparison with the great western ranges, and under the snow line.

The fourth system of mountains is the Himalaya, which bounds Tibet on the south, while the Kwănlun and Burkhan Buddha range defines it on the north. A small range runs through it from west to east, connected with the Himalaya by a high table-land, which surrounds the lakes Manasa-rowa and Ravan-hrad, and near or in which are the sources of the Indus, Ganges, and Yaru-tsangbu. This range is called Gang-dis-ri and Zang, and also Kailasa in Dr. Buchanan's map, and its eastern end is separated from the Yun ling by the narrow valley of the Yangtsz', which here flows from north to south. The country north of the Gang-dis-ri is divided into two portions by a spur which extends in a north-west direction as far as the Kwănlun,[1] called the Kara-korum Mountains. On the western side of this range lies Ladak, drained by one of the largest branches of the Indus, and although included in the imperial domains on Chinese maps, has long been separated from imperial cognizance. The Kara-korum Mountains may therefore be taken as composing part of the boundary of the empire; Chinese geographers regard them as forming a continuation of the Tsung ling.

---

[1] One among many native names given to the Kwănlun, or Koulkun Mountains, is *Tien chu*, 天柱 'Heaven's Pillar,' which corresponds precisely with the *Atlas* of China.

This hasty sketch of the mountain chains in and around China needs to be further illustrated by Pumpelly's outlines of their general course and elevation in what he suitably terms the *Sinian System*, applied "to that extensive northeast-southwest system of upheaval which is traceable through nearly all Eastern Asia, and to which this portion of the continent owes its most salient features." He has developed this system in the *Researches in China, Mongolia and Japan*, issued by the Smithsonian Institution in 1866. The mountains of China correspond in many respects to the Appalachian system in America, and its revolution probably terminated soon after the deposition of the Chinese coal measures. Mr. Pumpelly describes the principal anticlinal axes of elevation in China Proper, beginning with the Barrier Range, extending through the northern part of Chihlí and Shansí, where it trends W.S.W., prolonging across the Yellow River at Pao-teh, and hence S.W. through Shansí and Kansuh, coinciding with the watershed between the bend of that river, which traverses it through an immense gorge.

The next axis east begins at the Tushih Gate, and goes S.W. to the Nankau Pass, both of them in the Great Wall, and thence across Shansí to the elbow of the Yellow River, and onward to Western Sz'chuen, forming the watershed within the bend of the Yangtsz'. In the regions between these two axes are found coal deposits. A central axis succeeds this in Shansí, crossing the Yangtsz' near Íchang, and passing on S.W. through Kweichau to the Nan ling; going N.E., it runs through Honan and subsides as it gets over the Yellow River, till in Shantung and the Regent's Sword it rises higher and higher as it stretches on to the Chang-peh shan in Manchuria, and the ridge between the Songari and Usuri rivers. Between the last two ranges lie the great coal, iron, and salt deposits in the provinces, and each side of the central axis huge troughs and basins occur, such as the valley of the Yangtsz' in Yunnan, the Great Plain in Nganhwui and Chihlí, the Gulf of Pechele, and the basins of the Liao and Songari rivers.

The coast axis of elevation is indicated by ranges of granitic mountains between Kiangsí and Kiangsu on the north, and Chehkiang and Fuhkien on the south, extending S.W. through

Kwangtung into the Yun ling, and N.E. into the Chusan Archipelago, thence across to Corea and the Sihota Mountains east of the Usuri River. An outlying granitic range, reaching from Hongkong north-easterly to Wănchau, and S.W. to Hainan Island, marks a fifth axis of elevation.

Crossing these anticlinal axes are three ranges, coming into China Proper from the west in such a manner as to prove highly beneficial to its structure. The northern is apparently a continuation of the Bayan-kara Mountains in a S.E. direction into Kansuh, and south of the river Wei into Honan, under the name of the Hiung shan or 'Bear Mountains.' The centre is an offset from this, going across the north of Hupeh. The southern appears to be a prolongation of the Himalaya into Yunnan and Kwangsí, making the watershed between the Yangtsz' and Pearl river basins.

Between the Tien shan and the Kwănlun range on the south-west, and reaching to the Sialkoi on the north-east, in an oblique direction, lies the great desert of Gobi or Sha-moh, both words signifying a *waterless plain*, or *sandy floats*.[1] The entire length of this waste is more than 1,800 miles, but if its limits are extended to the Belur-tag and the Sialkoi, at its western and eastern extremity, it will reach 2,200 miles; the average breadth is between 350 and 400 miles, subject, however, to great variations. The area within the mountain ranges which define it is over a million square miles, and few of the streams occurring in it find their way to the ocean. The whole of this tract is not a barren desert, though no part of it can lay claim to more than comparative fertility; and the great altitude of most portions seems to be as much the cause of its sterility as the nature of the soil. Some portions have relapsed into a waste because of the destruction of the inhabitants.

The western portion of Gobi, lying east of the Tsung ling and north of the Kwănlun, between long. 76° and 94° E., and in lat. 36° and 41° N., is about 1,000 miles in length, and between 300 and 400 wide. Along the southern side of the

---

[1] Another interpretation makes Gobi (Kopi) to apply to the stony, while Sha-moh denotes the sandy tracks of this desert, in which case the name would more correctly read, "Great Desert of Gobi *and* Sha-moh."

Tien shan extends a strip of arable land from 50 to 80 miles in width, producing grain, pasturage, cotton, and other things, and in which lie nearly all the Mohammedan cities and forts of the *Nan Lu*. The Tarim and its branches flow eastward into Lob-nor, through the best part of this tract, from 76° to 89° E.; and along the banks of the Khoten River a road runs from Yarkand to that city, and thence to H'lassa. Here the desert is comparatively narrow. This part is called *Han hai*, or 'Mirage Sea,' by the Chinese, and is sometimes known as the desert of Lob-nor. The remainder of this region is an almost unmitigated waste, and north of Koko-nor assumes its most terrific appearance, being covered with dazzling stones, and rendered insufferably hot by the reflection of the sun's rays from these and numerous movable mountains of sand. Nor in winter is the climate milder or more endurable. "The icy winds of Siberia, the almost constantly unclouded sky, the bare saline soil, and its great altitude above the sea, combine to make the Gobi, or desert of Mongolia, one of the coldest countries in the whole of Asia." [1]

The sandhills—*kuzupchi*, as the Mongols call them—appear north of the Ala shan and along the Yellow River, and when the wind sets them in motion they gradually travel before it, and form a great danger to travellers who try to cross them. One Chinese author says, "There is neither water, herb, man, nor smoke;—if there is no smoke, there is absolutely nothing." The limits of the actual desert are not easily defined, for near the base of the mountain ranges, streams and vegetation are usually found.

Near the meridian of Hami, long. 94° E., the desert is narrowed to about 150 miles. The road from Kiayü kwan to Hami runs across this narrow part, and travellers find water at various places in their route. It divides Gobi into two parts—the desert of Lob-nor and the Great Gobi—the former being about 4,500 feet elevation, and the latter or eastern not higher than 4,000 feet. The borders of Kansuh now extend across this tract to the foot of the Tien shan.

---

[1] Col. Prejevalsky, *Travels in Mongolia*, etc. Vol. II., p. 22. London, 1876.

The eastern part, or Great Gobi, stretches from the eastern declivity of the Tien shan, in long. 94° to 120° E., and about lat. 40° N., as far as the Inner Hing-an. Its width between the Altai and the Ín shan range varies from 500 to 700 miles. Through the middle of this tract extends the depressed valley properly called Sha-moh, from 150 to 200 miles across, and whose lowest depression is from 2,600 to 2,000 feet above the sea. Sand almost covers the surface of this valley, generally level, but sometimes rising into low hills. The road from Urga to Kalgan, crossing this tract, is watered during certain seasons of the year, and clothed with grass. It is 660 miles, and forty-seven posts are placed along the route. The crow, lark, and sand-grouse are abundant on this road, the first being a real pest, from its pilfering habits. Such vegetation as occurs is scanty and stunted, affording indifferent pasture, and the water in the small streams and lakes is brackish and unpotable. North and south of the Sha-moh the surface is gravelly and sometimes rocky, the vegetation more vigorous, and in many places affords good pasturages for the herds of the Kalkas tribes. In those portions bordering on or included in Chihlí province, among the Tsakhars, agricultural labors are repaid, and millet, oats, and barley are produced, though not to a great extent. Trees are met with on the water-courses, but not to form forests. This region is called *tsau-ti*, or Grassland, and maintains large herds of sheep and cattle. It extends more or less northward towards Siberia. The Etsina is the largest inland stream in this division of Gobi, but on its north-eastern borders are some large tributaries of the Amur. On the south of the Sialkoi range the desert-lands reach nearly to the Chang-peh shan, about five degrees beyond those mountains. The general features of this portion of the earth's surface are less forbidding than Sahara, but more so than the steppes of Siberia or the pampas of Buenos Ayres. The whole of Gobi is regarded by Pumpelly as having formed a portion of a great ocean, which, in comparatively recent geological times, extended south to the Caspian and Black Seas, and between the Ural and Inner Hing an Mountains, and was drained off by an upheaval whose traces and effects can be detected in many parts. "It appears to me," he adds, "that the ancient physical geography of this region, and the effects of its elevation, present one of the most important fields of exploration." It will no doubt soon be more fully explored. Baron Richthofen describes Central Asia as properly a shallow trough, 1,800 miles long and about 400 miles wide, whose bottom is about 1,800 feet above the ocean; its ancient shore-line extended between the Kwănlun and Tien shan ranges on the west, from 5,000 to 10,000 feet high, and gradually falling to 3,600 feet in its eastern shore. This is the *Han-hai;* eastward is *Sha-moh*, and outside of both these wildernesses are the peripheral regions, where the waters flow to the ocean, carrying their silt, the erosions from the mountains. Inside of the shore-line nothing reaches the oceans, and these results of degradation are washed or blown into the valleys, and the country is buried in its own dust.[1]

The *rivers* of China are her glory, and no country can compare with her for natural facilities of inland navigation. The people themselves consider that portion of geography relating to their rivers as the most interesting, and give it the greatest attention. The four largest rivers in the empire are the Yellow River, the Yangtsz', the Amur, and the Tarim; the Yaru-tsangbu also runs more than a thousand miles within its borders.

The *Hwang ho*, or 'Yellow River,' rises in the plain of Odontala, called in Chinese *Sing-suh hai*, or 'Starry Sea,' from the numerous springs or lakelets found there between the Shuga and Bayan-kara Mountains, in lat. 35⅛°, and about long. 96° E., and not a hundred miles from the Yangtsz'. The Chinese popularly believe that the Yellow River runs underground from Lob-nor to Sing-suh hai. In this region are two lakes—the Dzaring and Oling, which are its fountains; and its course is very crooked after it leaves them. It turns first south 30 miles, then east 160, then nearly west about 120, winding through gorges of the Kwănlun; the river then flows north-east and east to Lanchau in Kansuh, having gone about 700 miles in its devious line. From Lanchau it turns northward along the

[1] Von Richthofen, *China. Ergebnisse eigener Reisen, Band I. Berlin*, 1877.

Great Wall for 430 miles, till deflected eastward by the Ín shan, on the edge of the plateau, and incloses the country of the Ortous Mongols within this great bend. A spur of the Peh ling forces it south, about long. 110° E., between Shansí and Shensí, for some 500 miles, till it enters the Great Plain, having run 1,130 miles from Lanchau. Through this loess region it becomes tinged with the soil which imparts both color and name to it. At the northern bend it separates in several small lakes and branches, and during this part of its course, for more than 500 miles, receives not a single stream of any size, while it is still so rapid, in descending from the plateau, as to demand much care when crossing it by boats. At the south-western corner of Shansí this river meets its largest tributary, the Wei, which comes in from the westward after a course of 400 miles, and is more available as a navigable stream than any other of the affluents. The area of the whole basin is less than that of the Yangtsz', and may be estimated at about 475,000 square miles; though the source of this stream is only 1,290 miles in a direct line from its mouth, its numerous windings prolong its course to nearly double that distance.

The great differences of level in winter and summer have always made this river nearly useless, except as a drain; while the effect of the long-continued deposit of silt along its lower level course has finally choked the mouth altogether. This remarkable result has been hastened, no doubt, by the dikes built along the banks to the east of Kaifung, which thus forced the floods to fill up the channel, and pushed the waters back over 500 miles to Honan-fu. Here the land is low, and the refluent waters gradually worked their way through marshes and creeks into the river Wei on the north bank, and thus found a north-east channel into the Canal and the Ta-tsing River, till they reached the Gulf of Pechele. A small part of these floods have perhaps gone south into the head-waters of the river Hwai, and thence into Hung-tsih Lake; but that lake has shrivelled, like its great feeder, and all its waters flow into the Yangtsz'. The history of the Yellow River furnishes a conclusive argument against diking a river's banks to restrain its floods. It has now reverted to the channel it occupied about fourteen centuries ago.[1]

Far more tranquil and useful is its rival, the Yangtsz' kiang, called also simply *Kiang* or *Ta kiang*, the 'River,' or 'Great River.' It is often erroneously named on western maps, Kyang Ku, which merely means 'mouth of the river.' The sources of the Kiang are in the Tangla Mountains and the Kwănlun range, and are placed on native maps in three streams flowing from the southern side of the Bayan-kara. This has been partly confirmed by Col. Prejevalsky. In January, 1873, he reached the Murui-ussu (Tortuous River) in lat. 35°, long. 94°, at its junction with the Napchitai, the northern of the three branches, and found it 750 feet wide at that season. In spring, the river's bed there is filled up a mile wide. Its course thence is south-east, receiving three other streams, all of which may be considered as its head-waters. All their channels are over ten thousand feet above the sea, but the ranges near them are under the snow-line. There is no authentic account of its course from this union till it joins the Yalung kiang in Sz'chuen, a distance of nearly 1,300 miles; but Chinese maps indicate a south-easterly direction through the gorges of the Yun ling, till it bursts out from the mountains in lat. 26° N., where it turns north-east. During much of this distance it bears the name of the Po-lai-tsz'. The Yalung River rises very near the Yellow River, and runs parallel with the Kiang in a valley further east, flowing upwards of 600 miles before they join. Great rafts of timber are floated down both these streams, for sale at the towns further east, but no large boats are seen on them before they leave the mountains. The town of Batang, in Sz'chuen, on the road from H'lassa, is the first large place on the river. The main trunk is called Kin-sha kiang (*i.e.*, Golden-sand River), until it receives the Yalung in the southern part of Sz'chuen, which the Chinese there regard as the principal stream of the two. Beyond the junction, the united river is called Ta kiang as far as Wuchang, in Hupeh, beyond which

[1] Report by Dr. W. A. P. Martin in *Journal of N. C. Branch of R. A. Society*, Vol. III., pp. 33–38; 1866. Same journal, Vol. IV., pp. 80–86; 1867; Notes by Ney Elias. Pumpelly's *Researches*, 1866, chap. v., pp. 41–51.

the people know it also as the Chang kiang, or 'Long River.' They do not often call it Yangtsz', which is properly applied only to the reach from Nanking out to sea, which lay within the old region of Yangchau. This name has been erroneously written in Chinese, and thence translated 'Son of the Ocean.' The French often call it the *Fleuve Bleu*, but the Chinese have no such name. Its general course from Wuchang is easterly, receiving various tributaries on both shores, until it discharges its waters at Tsungming Island, by two mouths, in lat. 32° N., more than 1,850 miles from its mouth in a direct line, but flowing nearly 3,000 miles in all its windings.[1]

One of the largest and most useful of its tributaries in its lower course is the Kan kiang in Kiangsí, which empties through the Poyang lake, and continues the transverse communication from north to south, connecting with the Grand Canal. The Tungting lake receives the Siang and Yuen, which drain the northern sides of the Nan ling in Hunan; and west of them is the Kungtan or Wu, which comes in with its surplus waters from Kweichau. These are on the south; the Han in Hupeh, and the Kialing, Min, and Loh in Sz'chuen, are the main affluents on the north, contributing the drainage south of the Peh ling. The Grand Canal comes in opposite Chinkiang, and from thence the deep channel, able to carry the largest men-of-war on its bosom, finds its way to the Pacific. No two rivers can be more unlike in their general features than these two mighty streams. While the Yellow River is unsteady, the Yangtsz' is uniform and deep in its lower course, and available for rafts from Batang in the western confines of Sz'chuen, and for boats from beyond Tungchuen in Yunnan, more than 1,700 miles from its mouth. Its great body and depth afford ample room for ocean steam-ships 200 miles, as far as Nanking, where in some places no bottom could be found at twenty fathoms, while the banks are not so low as to be often injured by the freshets, even when the flood is over thirty feet.

---

[1] See the account of Père Laribe's voyage on this river in 1843, *Annales de la Propagation de la Foi*, Tome XVII., pp. 207, 286, ff. *Five Months on the Yang-tsze*, by Capt. Thos. W. Blakiston; London, 1862. Pumpelly's *Researches*, chap. ii., pp. 4–10. Capt. Gill, *The River of Golden Sand.*

At Pingshan above Süchau in Sz'chuen, 1,550 miles from its mouth, Blakiston reckons the river to be 1,500 feet above tide-water, which gives an average fall of 12 inches to a geographical mile; the inclination is increased to 19 inches in some portions, and it is this force which carries the silt of this stream out to sea, but which is wanting in the Yellow River. The fall of the Yangtsz' is nearly double that of the Nile and Amazon, and half that of the Mississippi. The amount of water discharged is estimated at 500,000 cubic feet a second at Íchang, about 700 miles up, and it may reasonably be concluded that at Tsungming it discharges in times of flood a million cubic feet per second. Barrow calculated the discharge of the Yellow River in 1798 to be 11,616 cubic feet per second, when the current ran seven miles an hour. No river in the world exceeds the Yangtsz' for arrangement of subsidiary streams, which render the whole basin accessible as far as the Yalung. When a ship-canal has been dug around the gorges and rapids between Íchang and Kwei, steam-vessels can ascend nearly two thousand miles. The area of its basin is estimated at 548,000 square miles; and from its central course, and the number of provinces through which it passes, it has been termed the Girdle of China; while for its size, perennial and ample supply of water, and accessibility for navigation, it ranks with the great rivers of the world.[1]

Besides these two notable rivers, numerous others empty into the ocean along the coast from Hainan to the Amur, three of which drain large tracts of country, and afford access to many populous cities and districts. The third basin is that south of the Nan ling to the ocean; it is drained chiefly by the Chu kiang, and its form is much less regular than those of the Yellow River and Yangtsz'. The Chu kiang or Pearl River, like most of the rivers in China, has many names during its course, and is formed by three principal branches, respectively called East, North, and West rivers, according to the quarter from whence they come. The last is by far the largest, and all

---

[1] Staunton's *Embassy*, Vol. III., p. 233. Blakiston's *Yang-tsze*, p. 294, etc. *Chinese Repository*, Vol. II., p. 316.

of them are navigable most of their length. They disembogue together at Canton, and drain a region of not much less than 130,000 square miles, being all the country east of the Yun ling and south of the Nan ling ranges. The rivers in Yunnan, for the most part, empty into the Salween, Saigon, Meikon, and other streams in Cochinchina. The Min, which flows by Fuhchau, the Tsih, upon which Ningpo lies, the Tsientang, leading up to Hangchau, and the Pei ho, or White River, emptying into the Gulf of Pechele, are the most considerable among these lesser outlets in the provinces; while the Liau ho and Yahluh kiang, discharging into the Gulf of Liautung, are the only two that deserve mention in Southern Manchuria. The difference between the number of river-mouths cutting the Chinese coast and that of the United States is very striking, resulting from the different direction of the mountain chains in the interior.

The *lakes* of China are comparatively few and small; all those in the provinces of any size lie within the Plain, and are connected with the two great rivers. The largest is the Tungting in Hunan, about 220 miles in circumference, through which the waters of the Siang and Yuen rivers flow, and fill its channels and beds according to the season; it is now the silted-up bed of a former inland sea in Hupeh, lying on both sides of the Yangtsz', and through which countless lakes, creeks, and canals form a navigable network between that river and the Han. The lake receives the silt as the tributaries flow on through it, and discharge themselves along the deep outlet near Yohchau; this depression altogether is about 200 miles long and 80 broad. About 320 miles eastward lies the Poyang Lake in Kiangsí, which also discharges the surplus waters of the Kan into the Yangtsz'. It is nearly 90 miles long, and about 20 in breadth, inclosing within its bosom many beautiful and populous islets. The scenery around this lake is highly picturesque, and its trade and fisheries are more important than those of the Tungting. The Yangtsz' receives the waters of several other lakes as it approaches the ocean, the largest of which are the Ta hu or 'Great Lake' near Suchau, and the Tsau hu, lying on the northern bank, between Nganking and Nanking; both these lakes join the river by navigable streams.

and thé former is connected with the ocean by more than one channel.

The only considerable lake connected with the Yellow River is the Hungtsih in Kiangsu, situated near the junction of that river and the Grand Canal, into which it discharges the drainings of the Hwai River; it is more remarkable for the fleets of boats upon it than for scenery in the vicinity. The larger part of the country between the mouths of the two rivers is so marshy and full of lakes, as to suggest the idea that the whole was once an enormous estuary where their waters joined, or else that their deposits have filled up a huge lake which once occupied this tract, leaving only a number of lesser sheets. Besides these, there are small lakes in Chihlí and Shantung; also the *Tien*, the *Sien*, and the *Tali*, of moderate extent, in Yunnan; all of them support an aquatic population upon the fish taken from their waters.

The largest lake in Manchuria is the Hinkai-nor in Kirin, near the source of the Usuri; the two lakes Hurun and Puyur, or Pir, in the basin of the Nonni River, give their name to Hurun-pir, the western district of Tsitsihar; but of the extent and productions of these sheets of water little is known.

The regions lying north and south of Gobi contain many salt lakes, none of them individually comparing with the Aral Sea, but collectively covering a much larger extent, and most of them receiving the waters of the streams which drain their own isolated basins. The peculiarities of these little known parts, especially the depression on each side of the Tien shan, are such as to render them among the most interesting fields for geographical and geological research in the world. The largest one in Turkestan is Lob-nor, stated to be a great marsh overgrown with tall reeds and having a length of 75 miles and width of 15 miles.[1] Bostang-nor, said to connect with this lake, is placed on Chinese maps some 30 miles north of it. North of the Tien shan the lakes are larger and more numerous; the Dzaisang, Kisil-bash and Issik-kul are the most important. All these lakes are salt.

---

[1] Prejevalsky, *From Kulja Across the Tien shan to Lob-nor*, p. 99.

The whole region of Koko-nor is a country of lakes. The Oling and Dzaring are among the sources of the Yellow River; and the *Tsing hai*, or Azure Sea, better known as Koko-nor, gives its name to the province. The Tengkiri-nor in Tibet lies to the north of H'lassa, and is the largest sheet of water within the frontiers of the empire. In its neighborhood are numerous small lakes extending northward into Koko-nor. The Palti or Yamorouk is shaped like a ring, an island in its centre occupying nearly the whole surface. Ulterior Tibet possesses many lakes on both sides of the Gang-dis-ri range; the Yik and Paha, near Gobi, are the largest, being only two of a long row of them south of the Kwănlun range.

The Eighteen Provinces are bounded on the north-east by the colony of Shingking, from which they are separated by the line of a former palisade marking the boundary from the town of Shan-hai kwan to the Hwang ho. Following this stream to its sources in the Ĭn shan, the boundary then crosses these mountains and pursues a west and south-west course, through the territories of roving Mongol tribes, until it finds the Yellow River at the settlement of Hokiuh in Shensí. West of this the Great Wall divides the provinces of Shensí and Kansuh from the Mongolian deserts as far as the Kiayü Pass, beyond which lies the desert of Gobi, called *Peh hai* (North Sea) and *Hah hai* (Black Sea). On the east are the Gulf of Pechele and the Yellow Sea or *Hwang hai*, also called *Tung hai* (Eastern Sea) as far south as the Channel of Formosa. This channel and the China Sea lie on the south-east and south, as far as the Gulf of Tongking and the confines of Annam. Kwangsí and Yunnan border on Annam and Siam on their south sides, while Burmah marks the western frontier, but nearly the whole south-west and western frontiers beyond Yunnan and Sz'chuen are possessed by small tribes of uncivilized people, over whom neither the Chinese nor Burmese have much real control. Koko-nor bounds Sz'chuen and Kansuh on their western and south-western sides.

The coast of China, from Hainan to the mouth of the Yangtsz', is bordered with multitudes of islands and rocky islets; from that point northward to Liautung, the shores are low, and, except in Shantung, the coast is rendered dangerous by shoals.

South of the Pei ho, along to the end of Shantung Promontory, the coast is bolder, increasing in height after passing the Miautau Islands, though neither side of the promontory presents any point of remarkable elevation; Cape Macartney, at the eastern end, is a conspicuous bluff when approaching it from sea. From this cape to the mouth of the Tsientang River, near Chapu, a distance of about 400 miles, the coast is low, especially between the mouths of the Yangtsz' and Yellow rivers, and has but few good harbors. Quicksands in the regions near these rivers and the Bay of Hangchau render the navigation dangerous to native junks. From Kitto Point, near Ningpo, down to Hongkong, the shores assume a bolder aspect, and numerous small bays and coves occur among the islands, affording safe refuge for vessels. The aspect along this part is uninviting in the extreme, consisting principally of a succession of yellowish cliffs and naked headlands, giving little promise of the highly cultivated country beyond them. This bleak appearance is caused by the rains washing the decomposed soil off the surface; the rock being granite in a state of partial and progressive disintegration, the loose soil is easily carried down into the intervals. Another reason for its treeless surface is owing to the practice of annually cutting the coarse grass for fuel, and after the crop is gathered setting the stubble on fire, in order to manure the ground for the coming year; the fire and thinness of the soil together effectually prevent any large growth of trees or shrubbery upon the hills.

The estuary of the Pearl River from the Bocca Tigris down to the Grand Ladrones, a distance of 70 miles, and from Hongkong westerly to the Island of Tungku, about 100 miles, is interspersed with islands. The strait which separates Hainan from the Peninsula of Luichau has been supposed to be the place called by Arabian travellers in the ninth century the Gates of China, but that channel was probably near the Chusan Archipelago. That group of fertile islands is regarded as the broken termination of the continental range of mountains running through Chehkiang.

The Island of Formosa, or Taiwan, connects the islands of Japan and Lewchew with Luçonia. Between Formosa and the coast lie the Pescadores or Panghu Islands, a group much less in extent and number than the Chusan Islands. The Chinese have itineraries of all the places, headlands, islands, etc., along the entire coast, but they do not afford much information respecting the names of positions.[1]

The first objects that invite attention in the general aspect of China Proper are the Great Plain in the north-east, and the three longitudinal basins into which the country is divided by mountain chains running east and west.[2] The three great rivers which drain these basins flow through them very irregularly, but by means of their main trunks and the tributaries, water communication is easily kept up, not only from west to east along the great courses, but also across the country. These natural facilities for inland navigation have been greatly improved by the people, but they still, in most cases, await the introduction of steam to assist them in stemming the rapid currents of some of their rivers, and bringing distant places into more frequent communication.

The whole surface of China may be conveniently divided into the mountainous and hilly country and the Great Plain. The mountainous country comprehends more than half of the whole, lying west of the meridian of 112° or 114° (nearly that of Canton), quite to the borders of Tibet. The hilly portion is that south of the Yangtsz' kiang and east of this meridian, comprising the provinces of Fuhkien, Kiangsí, Kwangtung, and sections of Hunan and Hupeh. The Great Plain lies in the north-east, and forms the richest part of the empire.

This Plain extends in length 700 miles from the Great Wall and Barrier Range north of Peking to the confluence of Poyang Lake with the Yangtsz' in Kiangsí, lat. 30° N. The latter river is considered as its southern boundary as far down

---

[1] *Chinese Repository*, Vol. V., p. 337; Vol. X., pp. 351, 371. Williams' *Chinese Commercial Guide*, fifth edition, second part, 1863.

[2] Rémusat (*Nouveaux Mélanges*, Tome I., p. 9) adds a fourth basin, that of the Sagalien. The latter, however, scarcely deserves the name, having so many interrupting cross-chains.

as Nganking in Nganhwui, whence to the sea it is formed by a line drawn nearly east through Hangchau. The western boundary may be marked by a line drawn from Kingchau in Hupeh (lat. 30° 36′), nearly north to Hwaiking, on the Yellow River, and thence due north to the Great Wall, 50 miles north-west of Peking. The breadth varies. North of lat. 35°, where it partly extends to the Yellow Sea, and partly borders on the western side of Shantung, thence across to the Bear Mountains and Shansí, its measure is between 150 and 250 miles; stating the average at 200 miles, this portion has an area of 70,000 square miles. Between 34° and 35° the Plain enlarges, and in the parallel of the Yellow River has a breadth of some 300 miles from east to west; while further south, along the course of the Yangtsz', it reaches nearly 400 miles inland. Estimating the mean breadth of this portion at 400 miles, there are 140,000 square miles, which, with the northern part, make an area of about 210,000 square miles—a surface seven times as large as that of Lombardy, and about the same area as the plain of Bengal drained by the Ganges. The northern portion in Chihlí up to the edge of the Plateau is mostly a deposit of the yellow loess and alluvial on the river bottoms; that lying near the coast in Kiangsu is low and swampy, covered by lakes and intersected by water-courses. This portion is extremely fertile, and furnishes large quantities of silk, tea, cotton, grain, and tobacco. The most interesting feature of this Plain is the enormous population it supports, which is, according to the census of 1812, not less than 177 millions of human beings, if the whole number of inhabitants contained in the six provinces lying wholly or partly in it be included; making it by far the most densely settled of any part of the world of the same size, and amounting to nearly two-thirds of the whole population of Europe.[1]

The public works of China are probably unequalled in any land or by any people, for the amount of human labor bestowed upon them; the natural aspect of the country has been

---

[1] *Penny Cyclopædia*, Vol. VII., p. 74. McCulloch's *Geographical Dictionary*, Vol. I., p. 596.

materially changed by them, and it has been remarked that the Great Wall is the only artificial structure which would arrest attention in a hasty survey of the surface of the globe. But their usefulness, or the science exhibited in their construction, is far inferior to their extent. The Great Wall, called *Wan-lí Chang Ching* (*i.e.*, Myriad-mile Wall), was built by Tsin Chí-hwangtí, in order to protect his dominions from the incursions of the northern tribes. Some portions of it were already in existence, and he formed the plan of joining and extending them along the whole northern frontier to guard it. It was finished B.C. 204, having been ten years in building, seven of which were done after the Emperor's death. This gigantic work was probably a popular one in the main, and still remains as its own chief evidence of the energy, industry, and perseverance of its builders, as well as their unwisdom and waste. Its construction probably cost less than the usual sums spent by European States for their standing armies. It commences at Shanhai wei or Shanhai kwan (lat. 40°, long. 119° 50′), a coast town of some importance as on the boundary between Chihlí and Shingking, and a place of considerable trade. Lord Jocelyn describes the wall, when observed from the ships, as "scaling the precipices and topping the craggy hills of the country, which have along this coast a most desolate appearance."

It runs along the shore for several miles, and terminates on the beach near a long reef. Its course from this point is west, a little northerly, along the old frontiers of the province of Chihlí, and then in Shansí, till it strikes the Yellow River, in lat. 39½° and long. 111½°. This is the best built part, and contains the most important gates, where garrisons and trading marts are established. Within the province of Chihlí there are two walls, inclosing a good part of the basin of the Sang-kan ho west of Peking; the inner one was built by an emperor of the Ming dynasty. From the point where it strikes the Yellow River, near Pau-teh, it forms the northern boundary of Shensí, till it touches that stream again in lat. 37°, inclosing the country of the Ortous Mongols. Its direction from this point is north-west along the northern frontier of Kansuh to its termination near Kiayü kwan, through which the road passes leading to Hami.

From near the eastern extremity of the Wall in the province of Chihlí, extending in a north-easterly direction, there was once a wooden stockade or palisade, forming the boundary between Liautung and Kirin, which has been often taken from its representation on maps as a continuation of the Great Wall. It was erected by the Manchus, but has long since become decayed and disused.

The entire length of the Great Wall between its extremities is 22½ degrees of latitude, or 1,255 miles in a straight line; but its turnings and doublings increase it to fully 1,500 miles. It would stretch from Philadelphia to Topeka, or from Portugal to Naples, on nearly the same latitude. The construction of this gigantic work is somewhat adapted to the nature of the country it traverses, and the material was taken or made on the spot where it was used. In the western part of its course, it is in some places merely a mud or gravel wall, and in others earth cased with brick.

The eastern part is generally composed of earth and pebbles faced with large bricks, weighing from 40 to 60 lbs. each, supported on a coping of stone. The whole is about 25 feet thick at the base, and 15 feet at the top, and varying from 15 to 30 feet high; the top is protected with bricks, and defended by a slight parapet, the thinness of which has been taken as proof that cannon were unknown at the time it was erected. There are brick towers at different intervals, some of them more than 40 feet high, but not built upon the Wall. These are independent structures, usually about 40 feet square at the base, diminishing to 30 at the top; at particular spots the towers are of two stories.

The impression left upon the mind of a foreigner, on seeing this monument of human toil and unremunerative outlay, is respect for a people that could in any manner build it. Standing on the peak at *Ku-peh Kau* (Old North Gate), one sees the cloud-capped towers extending away over the declivities in single files both east and west, until dwarfed by miles and miles of skyward perspective as they dwindle into minute piles, yet stand with solemn stillness where they were stationed twenty centuries ago, as though condemned to wait the march of time till their builders returned. The crumbling dike at their feet may be followed, winding, leaping across gorges, defiles, and steeps, now buried in some chasm, now scaling the cliffs and slopes, in very exuberance of power and wantonness, as it vanishes in a thin, shadowy line, at the horizon. Once seen, the Great Wall of China can never be forgotten.

At present this remarkable structure is simply a geographical boundary, and except at the Gates nothing is done to keep it in repair. Beyond the Yellow River to its western extremity, the Great Wall, according to Gerbillon, is mostly a mound of earth or gravel, about fifteen feet in height, with only occasional towers of brick, or gateways made of stone. At Kalgan portions of it are made of porphyry and other stones piled up in a pyramidal form between the brick towers, difficult to cross but easy enough to pull down. The appearance of this rampart at Ku-peh kau is more imposing; the entire extent of the main and cross walls in sight from one of the towers there is over twenty miles. In one place it runs over a peak 5,225 feet high, where it is so steep as to make one wonder as much at the labor of erecting it on such a cliff as on the folly of supposing it could be of any use there as a defence. The wall is most visited at Nan-kau (South Gate), in the Ku-yung Pass, a remarkable Thermopylæ fifteen miles in length, which leads from the Plain at Peking up to the first terrace above it, and at one time was guarded by five additional walls and gates, now all in ruins. From this spot, the wall reaches across Shansí, and was built at a later period.

The other great public work is the Grand Canal, or *Chah ho* (*i.e.*, river of Flood-gates), called also *Yun ho* or 'Transit River,' an enterprise which reflects far more credit upon the monarchs who devised and executed it, than does the Great Wall, and if the time in which it was dug, and the character of the princes who planned it, be considered, few works can be mentioned in the history of any country more admirable and useful. When it was in order, before the inflow of the Yellow River failed, by means of its connection with its feeders, an uninterrupted water communication across the country from Peking to Canton existed, and goods and passengers passed from the capital to nearly every large town in the basins of the two great rivers. The canal was designed by Kublai to reach from his own capital as far as Hangchau, the former capital of the Sung dynasty, and cannot be better described than in Marco Polo's language: "You must understand that the Emperor has caused a water communication to be made from this city [Kwa-chau] to Cambaluc, in the shape of a wide and deep channel dug between stream and stream, between lake and lake, forming as it were a great river on which large vessels can ply."[1] The northern end is a channel fourteen miles long, from Tung-chau up to Peking, which, passing under the city walls, finishes its course of some 600 miles at the palace wall, close by the British Legation; here it is called *Yu ho*, or 'Imperial River,' but all boats now unlade at the eastern gate. An abridged account of Davis's observations[2] will afford a good idea of its construction and appearance.

"Early on the 23d September, we entered the canal through two stone piers and between very high banks. The mounds of earth in the immediate vicinity were evidently for the purpose of effecting repairs, which, to judge from the vestiges of inundation on either side, could not be infrequent. The canal joins the Yu ho, which we had just quitted, on its eastern bank, as that river flows towards the Pei ho. One of the most striking features of the canal is the comparative clearness of its waters, when contrasted with that of the two rivers on which we had hitherto travelled; a circumstance reasonably attributable to the depositions occasioned by the greater stillness of its contents. The course of the canal at this point was evidently in the bed of a natural river, as might be perceived from its winding course, and the irregularity and inartificial appearance of its banks. The stone abutments and flood-gates are for the purpose of regulating its waters, which at present were in excess and flowing out of it. As we proceeded on the canal, the stone flood-gates or sluices occurred

[1] Yule's *Marco Polo*, Vol. II., p. 136. [2] *Sketches of China*, Vol. I., p. 245.

at the rate of three or four a day, sometimes oftener, according as the inequalities in the surface of the country rendered them necessary. . . . .

"As we advanced, the canal in some parts became narrower, and the banks had rather more of an artificial appearance than where we first entered it, being occasionally pretty high; but still the winding course led to the inference, that as yet the canal was for the most part only a natural river, modified and regulated by sluices and embankments. The distance between the stone piers in some of the flood-gates was apparently so narrow as only just to admit the passage of our largest boats. The contrivance for arresting the course of the water through them was extremely simple; stout boards, with ropes fastened to each end, were let down edgewise over each other through grooves in the stone piers. A number of soldiers and workmen always attended at the sluices, and the danger to the boats was diminished by coils of rope being hung down at the sides to break the force of blows. The slowness of our progress, which for the last week averaged only twenty miles a day, gave us abundant leisure to observe the country. . . . .

"We now began to make better progress on the canal than we had hitherto done. The stream, though against us, was not strong, except near the sluices, where it was confined. In the afternoon we stopped at Kai-ho chin (*i.e.*, River-opening mart), so called, perhaps, because the canal was commenced near here. On the 28th we arrived at the influx of the Yun ho, where the stream turned in our favor, and flowed to the southward, being the highest point of the canal, and a place of some note. The Yun ho flows into the canal on its eastern side nearly at right angles, and a part of its waters flow north and part south, while a strong facing of stone on the western bank sustains the force of the influx. At this point is the temple of the Dragon King, or genius of the watery element, who is supposed to have the canal in his special keeping. This enterprise of leading in this river seems to have been the work of Sung Lí, who lived under Hungwu, the first emperor of the Ming dynasty, about 1375. In his time, a part of the canal in Shantung became so impassable that the coasting passage by sea began to be most used. This was the very thing the canal had been intended to prevent; Sung accordingly adopted the plan of an old man named Píying, to concentrate the waters of the Yun ho and neighboring streams, and bring them down upon the canal as they are at present. History states that Sung employed 300,000 men to carry the plan into operation, and that the work was completed in seven months. On both sides of us, nearly level with the canal, were extensive swamps with a shallow covering of water, planted with the Nelumbium; they were occasionally separated by narrow banks, along which the trackers walked, and the width of the canal sometimes did not exceed twenty-five yards. On reaching the part which skirts the Tu-shan Lake, the left bank was entirely submerged, and the canal confounded with the lake. All within sight was swamp, coldness, and desolation—in fact, a vast inland sea, as many of the large boats at a distance were hull down. The swamps on the following day were kept out of sight by some decent villages on the high banks, which from perpetual accumulation assumed in some places the aspect of hills.

"A part of our journey on the first of October lay along a portion of the canal where the banks, particularly to the right, were elaborately and thoroughly faced with stone; a precaution which seemed to imply a greater than ordinary danger from inundations. In fact, the lakes, or rather floods, seemed to extend at present nearly to the feet of the mountains which lay at a distance on our left. We were now approaching that part of China which is exposed to the disastrous overflowings of the Yellow River, a perpetual source of wasteful expenditure to the government, and of peril and calamity to the people; it well deserves the name of China's Sorrow. We observed the repairs of the banks diligently proceeding under the superintendence of the proper officer. For this purpose they use the natural soil in combination with the thick stalks of the gigantic millet."

The canal reaches the Yellow River about 70 miles from its mouth; but before leaving the lakes in the southern part of Shantung, it used to run nearly parallel with that stream for more than a hundred miles, and between it and the New Salt River during a good part of this distance. It is hard to understand how, by natural causes, so powerful a river, as it is described to be by the historians of both the British embassies less than one hundred years ago, should have become so completely choked up. The difference of level near Kaifung is found to be so very little that the siltage there has been enough to turn the current into the river Wei and elsewhere. When Amherst's embassy passed, the boats struck right across the stream, and gained the opposite bank, about three-fourths of a mile distant, in less than an hour. They drifted about two miles down, and then slowly brought up against the current to the spot where the canal entered. This opening was a sluice nearly a hundred yards across, and through it the waters rushed into the river like a mill-race; the banks were constructed of earth, strengthened with sorghum stalks, and strongly bound with cordage. Sir John Davis remarks, with the instinct of a tradesman, as he commends the perseverance and industry which had overcome these obstacles, that if the science of a Brunel could be allowed to operate on the Yellow River and Grand Canal, "a benefit might be conferred on the Chinese that would more than compensate for all the evil that we have inflicted with our opium and our guns." The boats were dragged through and up the sluice close to the bank by ropes communicating with large windlasses worked on the bank, which safely, though slowly, brought them into still water.

The distance between the Yellow and Yangtsz' rivers is about ninety miles, and the canal here is carried largely upon a raised work of earth, kept together by retaining walls of stone, and not less that twenty feet above the surrounding country in some parts. This sheet of water is about two hundred feet wide, and its current nearly three miles an hour. South of the Hwang ho several large towns stand near the levees, below their level, whose safety wholly depends upon the care taken of the banks of the canal. Hwai-ngan and Pauying lie thus under and near them, in such a position as to cause an involuntary shudder at the thought of the destruction which would take place if they should give way. The level descends from these towns to the Yangtsz', and at Yangchau the canal is much below the houses on its sides. It also connects with every stream or lake whose waters can be led into it. There are two or three inlets into the Yangtsz' where the canal reaches the northern bank, but Chinkiang, on the southern shore, is regarded as the principal defence and post of its crossing. The canal leaves the river east of that city, proceeds south-east to Suchau, and thence southerly on the eastern side of lake Tai, with which it communicates, to Hangchau in Chehkiang. This portion is by far the most interesting and picturesque of the whole line, owing to its rich and populous cities, the fertility and high cultivation of the banks, and the lively aspect imparted by the multitude of boats. Though Kublai has had the credit of this useful work, it existed in parts of its course long before his day. The reach between the two great rivers was opened in the Han dynasty, and repaired by the wise founder of the Sui dynasty (A.D. 600). The princes of the Tang dynasty kept it open, and when the Sung emperors lived at Hangchau they made the extension up to Chinkiang the great highway which it is to this day. The work from Peking to the Yellow River was opened by the Mongols about 1289, in which they merely joined the rivers and lakes to each other as they now exist. The Ming and Tsing emperors have done all they could to keep it open throughout, and lately an attempt has been made to reopen the passage from Hungtsih Lake north into the old bed, so that boats can reach Tientsin from Kwachau. Its entire length is about 650 miles, or not quite twice that of the Erie Canal, but it varies in its breadth and depth more than any important canal either of America or Europe.

As a work of art, compared with canals now existing in western countries, the Transit River does not rank high; but even at this day there is no work of the kind in Asia which can compare with it, and there was none in the world equal to it when first put in full operation. It passes through alluvial soil in every part of its course, and the chief labor was expended in constructing embankments, and not in digging a deep channel. The junction of the Yun ho, about lat. 36° N., was probably taken as the summit level. From this point northward the trench was dug through to Lintsing to join the Yu ho, and embankments thrown up from the same place southward to the Yellow River, the whole being a line of two hundred miles. In some places the bed is cut down thirty, forty, and even seventy feet, but it encountered no material obstacle. The sluices which keep the necessary level are of rude construction, and thick planks, sliding in grooves hewn in stone buttresses, form the only locks. Still, the objects intended are all fully gained, and the simplicity of the means certainly does not derogate from the merit and execution of the plan.[1]

There are some other inferior canals in the empire. Kienlung constructed a waste-weir for carrying off the surplus waters of the Yellow River of about a hundred miles in length, by cutting a canal from Ífung hien in Honan, to one of the principal affluents of lake Hungtsih. It also answered as a drain for the marshy land in that part, and has probably recently served to convey the floods from the main stream into the lake. In the vicinity of Canton and Suchau are many channels cut through the plains, which serve both for irrigation and navigation, but they are not worthy the name of canals. Similar conveniences are more or less frequently met with in all parts of the provinces, notably those on the Plain and low coast-lands.

The public roads, in a country so well provided with navigable streams, are of minor consequence, but these media of travel are not neglected. "I have travelled near 600 leagues by land in China," observes De Guignes, "and have found many good roads, most of them wide and planted with trees. They are not usually paved, and consequently in rainy weather are either channelled by the water or covered with mud, and in dry weather so dusty that travellers are obliged to wear spectacles to protect their eyes. In Kwangtung transportation is performed almost wholly by water, the only roads being across the lines of navigation. The pass across the Mei ling is paved or filled up with stones; at Kih-ngan, in Kiangsí, are paved roads in good condition, but beyond the Yangtsz', in Nganhwui, they were

---

[1] Klaproth, *Mémoires*, Tome III., p. 312 *sqq.* De Guignes' *Voyages à Peking*, Tome II., p. 195. Davis's *Sketches*, Vol. I., *passim.*

almost impracticable, but became better as we proceeded northward, and in many places had trees on both sides. Beyond the Hwang ho they were broader, and we saw crowds of travellers, carts, mules, and horses. In Shantung and Chihlí they were generally broad and shady, and very dusty. This is, no doubt, disagreeable, but we went smoothly over these places, while in the villages and towns we were miserably jolted on the pavements. I hope, for the sake of those who may come after me, that the Chinese will not pave their roads before they improve their carriages. Some of the thoroughfares leading to Peking are paved with thick slabs of stone. One feature of the roads through the northern provinces which attracts attention is the great number that lie below the level of the country. It is caused by the wind sweeping along them, and carrying over

A Road-Cut in the Loess.

the fields the dust made and raised by the carts. As soon as the pools left by the rains dry enough to let the carts pass, the earth is reduced to powder; as the winds sweep through the passage and clear it out, the process in a few years cuts a defile through the loam often fifteen feet deep, which impedes travel by its narrow gauge, hindering the carts as they meet. The banks are protected by revetment walls or turf, if necessary. Those near Hangchau, and the great road leading from Chehkiang into Kiangsí, are all in good condition. Generally speaking, however, as is the case with most things in China, the roads are not well repaired, and large holes are frequently allowed to remain unfilled in the path, to the great danger of those who travel by night."[1]

Mountain passes have been cut for facilitating the transit of goods and people over the high ranges in many parts of the empire. The great road leading from Peking south-west through Shansí and Shensí, and thence to Sz'chuen, is carried across the Peh ling and the valley of the river Hwai by a mountain road, "which, for the difficulties it presents and the art and labor with which they have been overcome, does not appear to be inferior to the road over the Simplon."[2] At one place on this route, called Lí-nai, a passage has been cut through the rock, and steps hewn on both sides of the mountain from its base to the summit. The passage across the peak being only wide enough for one codan, the guards are perched in little houses placed on poles over the pass. This road was in ancient times the path to the metropolis, and these immense excavations were made from time to time by different monarchs. The pass over the Mei ling, at Nan-ngan, is a work of later date, and so are most of the other roads across this range in Fuhkien and Kwangtung.

The general aspect of the country is perhaps as much modi-

---

[1] *Voyages à Peking*, Vol. II., p. 214. Compare the letter of a Jesuit missionary (*Annales de la Foi*, Tome VII., p. 377), who describes houses of rest on the wayside. These singular road-gullies of the loess region have been very thoroughly examined by Baron von Richthofen, from whose work the cut above is taken.

[2] *Penny Cyclopædia*, Vol. XXVII., p. 656.

fied by labor of man in China as in England, but the appearance of a landscape in the two kingdoms is unlike. Whenever water is available, streams are led upon the rice fields, and this kind of cultivation allows few or no trees to grow in the plats. Such fields are divided by raised banks, which serve for pathways across the marshy enclosure, and assist in confining the water when let in upon the growing crop. The bounds of other fields are denoted by stones or other landmarks, and the entire absence of walls, fences, or hedgerows, makes a cultivated plain appear like a vast garden.

The greatest sameness exists in all the cities. A wall encloses all towns above a *sz'* or township, and the suburbs are not unfrequently larger than their enceinte. The streets in large towns south of the Hwang ho are paved, and the sewers run under the cross slabs. What filth is not in them is generally in the street, as these drains easily become choked. The roadways are not usually over ten feet wide, but the low houses on each side make them appear less like alleys than would be the case in western cities. Villages have a pleasant appearance at a distance, usually embowered among trees, between which the whitewashed houses look prettily; but on entering them one is disappointed at their irregularity, dirtiness, and generally decayed look. The gardens and best houses are mostly walled in from sight, while the precincts of temples are the resort of idlers, beggars, and children, with a proportion of pigs and dogs.

Elegance or ornament, orderly arrangement and grandeur of design, cleanliness, or comfort, as these terms are applied in Europe, are almost unknown in Chinese houses, cities, or gardens. Commanding or agreeable situations are chosen for temples and monasteries, which are not only the abode of priests but serve for inns, theatres, and other purposes. The terrace cultivation sometimes renders the acclivities of hills beautiful in the highest degree, but it does not often impart a distinguishing feature to the landscape. A lofty solitary pagoda, an extensive temple shaded by trees in the opening of a vale, a commemorative *pai-lau*, or boats moving in every direction through narrow creeks or on broad streams, are some of the peculiar lineaments of Chinese scenery. No imposing mansions with beautiful grounds are found on the skirts of a town, for the people huddle together in hamlets and villages for mutual aid and security. No tapering spires pointing out the rural church, nor towers, pillars, domes, or steeples in the cities, indicating buildings of public utility, rise upon the low level of dun-tiled roofs. No meadows or pastures, containing herds and flocks, are visible from the hill-tops in China; nor are coaches or railroad cars observed hurrying across its landscapes. Steamers have just begun to course through some of its rivers, and disturb, by their whistles and wheels, the drowsy silence of past ages and the slow progress of unwieldy junks—the other changes have yet to come.

The condition and characteristics of the various families of man inhabiting this great empire, render its study far more interesting than anything relating to its physical geography or public works. The Chinese forms the leading family, but the Miaotsz', the Li-mu, the Kakyens, and other aborigines in the southern provinces, the Manchus, the Mongols, and various Tartar tribes, the Tibetans, and certain wild races in Kirin and Formosa, must not be overlooked. The sons of Han are indeed a remarkable race, whether regard be had to their antiquity, their numbers, their government, or their literature, and on these accounts deserve the study and respect of every intelligent student of mankind; while their unwearied industry, their general peaceableness and good humor, and their attainments in domestic order and mechanical arts, commend them to the notice of every one who sees in these points of character an earnest of their future position amid the great family of civilized nations when once they shall have attained the same.

The physical traits of the Chinese may be described as being between the light and agile Hindu, and the muscular, fleshy European. Their form is well built and symmetrical; their color is a brunette or sickly white, rather approaching to a yellowish than to a florid tint, but this yellow hue has been much exaggerated; in the south they are swarthy but not black, never becoming as dark even as the Portuguese, whose fifth or sixth ancestors dwelt near the Tagus. The shades of complexion differ much according to the latitude and degree of exposure to the weather, especially in the females. The hair of the head is lank, black, coarse, and glossy; beard always black, thin, and deficient; scanty or no whiskers; and very little hair on the body. Eyes invariably black, and apparently oblique, owing to the slight degree in which the inner angles of the eyelids open, the internal canthi being more acute than in western races, and not allowing the whole iris to be seen; this peculiarity in the eye distinguishes the eastern races of Asia from all other families of man. There is a marked difference between the features of the mixed race living south of the Mei ling, and the inhabitants of the Great Plain and in Shansí or further west; the latter are the finer appearing. The hair and eyes being always black, a European with blue eyes and light hair appears strange to them; one reason given by the people of Canton for calling foreigners *fan kwei*, or 'foreign devils,' is, that they have sunken blue eyes, and red hair like demons.

The cheek-bones are high, and the outline of the face remark ably round. The nose is rather small, much depressed, nearly even with the face at the root, and wide at the extremity; there is, however, considerable difference in this respect, but no aquiline noses are seen. Lips thicker than among Europeans, but not at all approaching those of the negro. The hands are small, and the lower limbs better proportioned than among any other Asiatics. The height of those living north of the Yangtsz' is about the same as that of Europeans. A thousand men taken as they come in the streets of Canton, will hardly equal in stature and weight the same number in Rome or New Orleans, while they would, perhaps, exceed these, if gathered in Peking; their muscular powers, however, would probably be less in either Chinese city than in those of Europe or America.

In size, the women are smaller than European females; and in the eyes of those accustomed to the European style of beauty, the Chinese women possess little; the broad upper face, low nose, and linear eyes, being quite the contrary of handsome. Nevertheless, the Chinese face is not destitute of beauty, and when animated with good humor and an expressive eye, and lighted by the glow of youth and health, the features lose much of their repulsiveness. Nor do they fade so soon and look as ugly and withered when old as some travellers say, but are in respect to bearing children and keeping their vigor, more like Europeans than the Hindus or Persians.

The mountainous regions in Yunnan, Kwangsí, and Kweichau, give lodgement to many clans of the Miaotsz' or "children of the soil," as the words may be rendered. It is singular that any of these people should have maintained their independence so long, when so large a portion of them have partially submitted to Chinese rule. Those who will not are called *săng Miaotsz'*, *i.e.*, wild or 'unsubdued,' while the others are termed *shuh* or 'subdued.' They present so many physical points of difference as to lead one to infer that they are a more ancient race than the Chinese around them, and the aborigines of Southern China. They are rather smaller in size and stature, have shorter necks, and their features are somewhat more angular. They are divided into many tribes, and have been described by Chinese travellers, who have illustrated their habits by paintings and sketches, from which a good idea can be obtained of their condition. Dr. Bridgman has translated such an account, written by a Chinese native traveller, in which he sketches the manners of eighty-two clans, especially those customs relating to worship and marriage, showing how little they have learned from their rulers or improved from the savage state. An examination of their languages shows that those of the Miaotsz' proper have strong affinities with the Siamese and Annamese, and those known as *Lolo* exhibit a decided likeness to the Burmese. The former of these are mentioned in Chinese history during 4,000 years; the latter about A.D. 250, when a Shan nation came under Chinese influence in Yunnan, and was the object of a warlike expedition. The same race still remain on the Upper Irrawadi and in Assam as Shans and Khamti, and in the basins of the Meinam and Mei-lung, all of them akin to the Tibetans and Burmese. They form together an interesting relic of the ancient peoples of the land, and further inquiries will doubtless develop something of their history and origin.[1]

[1] *Chinese Repository*, Vol. XIV., p. 105. *Shanghai Journal*, No. III., 1859. *Journal of Indian Archipelago*, 1852. *Missionary Recorder*, Vol. III., pp. 33, 62, 149, etc. T. T. Cooper, *Travels of a Pioneer of Commerce*, passim.

An aboriginal race—the *Li-mu*—exists in the centre of Hainan, an offset from the Miaotsz', judging by the little that is known of their language. The natives of Formosa seem to have more affinity with their neighbors in Luzon and southward than with the Chinese.

The Mongol and Manchu races have been considered as springing from the same stock, but during centuries of separation under different circumstances they have altered much. The Mongols are essentially a nomadic race, while the Manchus are an agricultural or a hunting people, according to the part of their country they inhabit. The Manchus are of a lighter complexion and somewhat larger than the Chinese, have the same conformation of the eyelids, but rather more beard, while their countenances indicate greater intellectual capacity. They seem to partake of both the Mongol and Chinese character, possessing more determination and largeness of plan than the latter, with much of the rudeness and haughtiness of the former. They have fair, if not florid, complexions, straight noses, and, in a few cases, brown hair and heavy beards. They are more allied to the Chinese, and when they ruled the northern provinces as the Kin dynasty, amalgamated with them. They may be regarded as the most improvable race in Central Asia, if not on the continent; and the skill with which they have governed the Chinese empire, and adopted a civilization higher than their own, gives promise of still further advances when they become familiar with the civilization of Christian lands.

Under the term Mongols or Moguls a great number of tribes occupying the steppes of Central Asia are comprised. They extend from the borders of the Khirgís steppe and Kokand eastward to the Sialkoi Mountains, and it is particularly to this race that the name *Tartars* or *Tatars* is applicable. No such word is now known among the people, except as an ignominious epithet, by the Chinese, who usually write it with two characters—*tah-tsz'*—meaning 'trodden-down people.' Klaproth confines the appellation of *Tartars* to the Mongols, Kalmucks, Kalkas, Eleuths, and Buriats, while the Kirghís, Usbecks, Cossacks, and Turks are of Kurdish and *Turkoman* origin.

The Mongol tribes generally are a stout, squat, swarthy, ill-favored race of men, having high and broad shoulders, short, broad noses, pointed and prominent chins, long teeth distant from each other, eyes black, elliptical, and unsteady, thick, short necks, extremities bony and nervous, muscular thighs, but short legs, with a stature nearly or quite equal to the European. They have a written language, but their literature is limited and mostly religious. The same language is spoken by all the tribes, with slight variations and only a small admixture of foreign words. Most of the accounts of their origin, their wars, and their habits, were written by foreigners living or travelling among them; but they themselves, as McCulloch remarks, know as little of these things as rats or marmots do of their descent. Yet it is not so easy to find the typical Mongol among the medley of nationalities in their towns. A crowd in a town like Yarkand exhibits all the varieties of the human race. The gaunt, almost beardless Manchu, with sunken eyes, high cheekbones, and projecting jowl, contrasts with the smooth face, pinky yellow, oblique eye, flat cheeks, and rounded jowl of the Chinese. The bearded, sallow Toork, the angular, rosy Kirghís, the coarse, hard Dungani, and thick-lipped, square-faced Eleuth, all show poorly with the tall, handsome Cashmerian, the swarthy Badakshi, and robust, intelligent Uzbek. The fate of the vast swarms of this race which have descended from the table-land of Central Asia and overrun, in different ages, the plains of India, China, Syria, Egypt, and Eastern Europe, and the rise and fall of the gigantic empire they themselves erected under Genghis in the eleventh and twelfth centuries, are among the most remarkable episodes in the world's history. They have always maintained the same character in their native wilds, their conquests have been exterminations rather than subjugations, their history a record of continual quarrels between clans.

The last of the five races is the Tibetan, who partake of the physical characteristics of the Mongols and Hindus. They are short, squat, and broad-shouldered in body, with angular faces, wide, high cheek-bones, small black eyes, and scant beard. They are mild in disposition, have a stronger religious feeling than the Chinese, and have never left their own highlands either for emigration or conquest. Their civilization is fully equal to that of the Siamese and Burmese, and life and property are more secure with them than among their turbulent neighbors in Butan, Lahore, or Cabul.

It will be seen from this short survey that a full account of the geography, government, manners, literature, and civilization of so large a part of the world and its inhabitants requires the combined labors of many observers, all of them well acquainted with the languages and institutions of the people whom they describe. No one will look, therefore, for more than a brief outline of these subjects in the present work, minute enough, however, to enable readers to form a fair opinion of the people. It is the *industry* of the Chinese which has given them their high place among the nations of the earth. Not only has the indigenous vegetation been superseded wherever culture would remunerate toil, but lofty hills have been tilled and terraced almost to their tops, cities have been built upon them, and extensive ranges of wall erected along their summits. They practise all the industrial arts whose objects are to feed, clothe, educate or adorn mankind, and maintain the largest population ever united under one system of rule. Ten centuries ago they were the most civilized nation on earth, and the incredulity manifested in Europe, five hundred years ago, at the recitals of Marco Polo regarding their condition, is the counterpart of the sentiments now expressed by the Chinese when they hear of the power and grandeur of western nations.

Isolated by natural boundaries from other peoples, their civilization, developed under peculiar influences, must be compared to, rather than judged of, by European. A people from whom some of the most distinguishing inventions of modern Europe came (such as the compass, porcelain, gunpowder, and printing), and were known and practised many centuries earlier; who probably amount to more than three hundred millions, united in one system of manners, letters, and polity; whose cities and capitals rival in numbers the greatest metropoles of any age; who have not only covered the earth, but the waters, with towns and streets—such a nation must occupy a conspicuous place in the history of mankind, and the study of their character and condition commend itself to every well-wisher of his race.

It has been too much the custom of writers to overlook the influence of the Bible upon modern civilization; but when a comparison is to be drawn between European and Asiatic civilization, this element forces itself upon the attention as the main cause of the superiority of the former. It is not the civilization of luxury or of letters, of arts or of priestcraft; it is not the spirit of war, the passion for money, nor its exhibitions in trade and the application of machinery, that render a nation permanently great and prosperous. "Christianity is the summary of all civilization," says Chenevix; "it contains every argument which could be urged in its support, and every precept which explains its nature. Former systems of religion were in conformity with luxury, but this alone seems to have been conceived for the region of civilization. It has flourished in Europe, while it has decayed in Asia, and the most civilized nations are the most purely Christian." Christianity is essentially the religion of the people, and when it is covered over with forms and contracted into a priesthood, its vitality goes out; this is one reason why it has declined in Asia. The attainments of the Chinese in the arts of life are perhaps as great as they can be without this spring of action, without any other motives to industry, obedience, and morality, than the commands or demands of the present life.

A survey of the world and its various races in successive ages leads one to infer that God has some plan of national character, and that one nation exhibits the development of one trait, while another race gives prominence to another, and subordinates the first. Thus the Egyptian people were eminently a priestly race, devoted to science and occult lore; the Greeks developed the imaginative powers, excelling in the fine arts; the Romans were warlike, and the embodiment of force and law; the Babylonians and Persians magnificent, like the head of gold in Daniel's vision; the Arabs predacious, volatile, and imaginative; the Turks stolid, bigoted, and impassible; the Hindus are contemplative, religious, and metaphysical; the Chinese industrious, peaceful, literary, atheistic, and self-contained.[1] The same religion, and constant intercommunication among European nations, has assimilated them more than these other races ever could have become; but every one knows the national peculiarities of the Spaniards, Italians, French, English, etc., and how they are maintained, notwithstanding the motives to imitation and coalescence. The comparison of national character and civilization, with the view of ascertaining such a plan, is a subject worthy the profound study of any scholar, and one which would offer new views of the human race. The Chinese would be found to have attained, it is believed, a higher position in general security of life and property, and in the arts of domestic life and comfort among the mass, and a greater degree of general literary intelligence, than any other heathen or Mohammedan nation that ever existed—or indeed than some now calling themselves Christian, as Abyssinia. They have, however, probably done all they can do, reached as high a point as they can without the Gospel; and its introduction, with its attendant influences, will erelong change their political and social system. The rise and progress of this revolution among so mighty a mass of human beings will form one of the most interesting parts of the history of the world during the nineteenth century, and solve the problem whether it be possible to elevate a race without the intermediate steps of disorganization and reconstruction.

---

[1] For observations on the Chinese as compared with other nations, see Schlegel's *Philosophy of History*, p. 118, Bohn's edition.

CHAPTER II.

GEOGRAPHICAL DESCRIPTION OF THE EASTERN PROVINCES.

The provinces of China Proper are politically subdivided in a scientific manner, but in the regions beyond them, these divisions are considerably modified. Manchuria is regarded as belonging to the reigning family, somewhat as Hanover once pertained to the kings of England, and its scanty population is ruled by a simple military organization, the higher officials being appointed by his majesty himself. The khans of the Mongols in Mongolia and Ili, the Mohammedan begs in Turkestan, and the lamas in Tibet, are assisted in their rule by Chinese residents and generals who direct and uphold the government.

The geography of foreign countries has not been studied by the Chinese; and so few educated men have travelled even into the islands of the Indian Archipelago, or the kingdoms of Siam, Corea, or Burmah, that the people have had no opportunity to become acquainted with the countries lying on their borders, much less with those in remoter parts, whose names, even, they hardly know. A few native works exist on foreign geography, among which four may be here noticed. "1. *Researches in the East and West*, 6 vols. 8vo. It was written about two centuries ago; the first volume contains some rude charts intended to show the situation and form of foreign countries. 2. *Notices of the Seas*, 1 vol. Its author, Yang Ping-nan, obtained his information from a townsman, who, being wrecked at sea, was picked up by a foreign ship, and travelled abroad for fourteen years; on his return to China he became blind, and was engaged as an interpreter in Macao. 3. *Notices of Things heard and seen in Foreign Countries*, 2 vols. 12mo; written about a century ago, containing among other things a chart of the whole

Chinese coast. 4. *The Memoranda of Foreign Tribes*, 4 vols. 8vo, published in the reign of Kienlung."[1] A more methodical work is that of Lí Tsing-lai, called '*Plates Illustrative of the Heavens*,' being an astronomical and geographical work, much of whose contents were obtained from Europeans residing in the country. But even if the Chinese had better treatises on these subjects, the information contained in them would be of little use until it was taught in their schools. The high officers in the government begin now to see the importance of a better acquaintance with general geography. Commissioner Lin, in 1841, published a partial translation of Murray's *Cyclopædia of Geography*, in 20 volumes; Gov. Seu Ki-yu, in 1850, issued a compend of geographical notices with maps, and many others, more accurate and extensive, are now extant.

However scarce their geographical works upon foreign countries may be, those delineating the topography of their own are hardly equalled in number and minuteness in any language: every district and town of importance in the empire, as well as every department and province, has a local geography of its own. It may be said that the topographical and statistical works form, after the ethical, the most valuable portion of Chinese literature. It would not be difficult to collect a library of 10,000 volumes of such treatises alone; the topography of the city of Suchau, and of the province of Chehkiang, are each in 40 vols., while the *Kwangtung Tung Chí*, an 'Historical and Statistical Account of Kwangtung,' is in 182 volumes. None of these works, however, would bear to be translated entire, such is the amount of legendary and unimportant matter contained in them; but they contain many data not to be overlooked by one who undertakes to write a geography of China.

The *Climate* of the Eighteen Provinces has been represented in meteorological tables sufficiently well to ascertain its general salubrity. Pestilences do not frequently visit the land, nor, as in Southern India, is it deluged with rain during one monsoon, and parched with drought during the other. The average temperature of the whole empire is lower than that of any other

[1] Bridgman's *Chinese Chrestomathy*, p. 420. Macao, 1841.

country on the same latitude, and the coast is subject to the same extremes as that of the Atlantic States in America. The isothermal line of 70° F. as the average for the year, which passes south of Canton, runs by Cairo and New Orleans, eight degrees north of it; the line of 60° F. average passes from Shanghai to Marseilles, Raleigh, St. Louis, and north of San Francisco; and the line of 50° F. average goes near Peking, thence on to Vienna, Dublin, Philadelphia, and Puget's Sound, in lat. 52°. These various lines show that while Shanghai and Peking have temperatures similar to Raleigh and Philadelphia, nearly on their own parallels, Canton is the coldest place on the globe in its latitude, and the only place within the tropics where snow falls near the sea-shore. One result of this projection of the temperate zone into the tropical is seen in the greater vigor and size of the people of the three southern provinces over any races on the same parallel elsewhere; and the productions are not so strictly tropical. The isothermal lines for the year, as given above, are not so irregular as those for winter. The line of 60° F. runs by the south of Formosa and Hongkong, to Cairo and St. Augustine, a range of nine degrees; but the winter line of 40° F. passes from Shanghai to Constantinople, Milan, Dublin, and Raleigh, ending at Puget's Sound, a range of twenty degrees. A third line of 32° for winter passes through Shantung to N. Tibet and the Black Sea, Norway, New York, and Sitka—a range of twenty-five degrees.

Peking (lat. 39° 55′ N.) exhibits a fair average of the climate in that part of the Plain. The extremes range from 104° to zero F., but the mean annual temperature is 52.3° F., or more than 9° lower than Naples; the mean winter range is 12° below freezing, or about 18° lower than that of Paris (lat. 48° 50′), and 15° lower than Copenhagen. The rainfall seldom reaches sixteen inches in a year, most of it coming in July and August; the little snow that descends remains only two or three days on the ground, and is blown away rather than melted; no one associates white with winter, but snow is earnestly prayed for as a purifier of the air against diphtheria and fevers. The winds from the Plateau cause the barometer and thermometer to fall, but the sky is clear. In the spring, as the heat increases, the winds raise the dust and sand over the country; some of these sand-storms extend even to Shanghai, carrying millions of tons of soil from its original place. The dryness of the region has apparently increased during the last century, and constant droughts destroy the trees, which by their absence increase the desiccation now going on. Frost closes the rivers for three months, and ice is cheap. After the second crops fully start in August, the autumns become mild, and till the 10th of December are calm and genial.[1]

The climate of the Plain is generally good, but near the rivers and marshy grounds along the Grand Canal, agues and bowel complaints prevail. A resident speaks of the temperature of Nanking and the region around it: "This vast Plain being only a marsh half drained, the moisture is excessive, giving rise to many strange diseases, all of them serious, and not unfrequently mortal. The climate affects the natives from other provinces, and Europeans. I have not known one of the latter who was not sick for six months or a year after his arrival. Every one who comes here must prepare himself for a tertian or quotidian. For myself, after suffering two months from a malignant fever, I had ten attacks of a malady the Chinese here call the *sand*, from the skin being covered with little blackish pimples, resembling grains of dust. It is prompt and violent in its progress, and corrupts the blood so rapidly that in a few minutes it stagnates and coagulates in the veins. The best remedy the people have is to cicatrize the least fleshy parts of the body with a copper cash. The first attack I experienced rendered all my limbs insensible in two minutes, and I expected to die before I could receive extreme unction. After recovering a little, great lassitude succeeded."[2] The monsoons form an important element in the seaside climate as far north as latitude 31°. The dry and wet seasons correspond to the north-east and south-west monsoons, assuaging the heats of summer by their cooling showers, and making the winters

[1] Compare an article in the *China Review* for September–October, 1881, by H. Fritsche: *The Amount of Rain and Snow in Peking.*

[2] *Annales de la Foi,* Tome XVI., p. 293.

bracing and healthy. Above the Formosa Channel they are less regular in the summer than in winter.

The inhabitants of Shanghai suffer from rapid changes in the autumn and spring months, and pulmonary and rheumatic complaints are common. The maximum of heat is 100° F., and the minimum 24°, but ice is not common, nor does snow remain long on the ground. The average temperature of the summer is from 80° to 93° by day, and from 60° to 75° by night; the thermometer in winter ranges from 45° to 60° by day, and from 36° to 45° by night.

Owing in some degree to the hills, the extremes are rather greater at Ningpo than Shanghai. The thermometer ranges from 24° to 107° during the twelvemonth, and changes of 20° in the course of two hours are not unusual, rendering it the most unhealthy station along the coast. There is a hot and cold season of three months each at this place. The cold is very piercing when the north-east winds set in, and fires are needed, but natives content themselves with additional clothing. The large brick beds (*kang*) common in Chihlí are not often seen. Ice forms in pools, and is gathered to preserve fish. Snow frequently falls, but does not remain long. Occasionally it covers the hills in Chehkiang for several weeks to the depth of six inches. Fuhchau and Canton lie at the base of hills, within a hundred miles of the sea-coast, and their climates exhibit greater extremes than Amoy and Hongkong. Frost and ice are common every winter at each of the former, and fires are therefore pleasant in the house. The extremes at Fuhchau are from 38° to 95°, with an average of 56° during December and 82° for August. Along this whole coast the most refreshing monsoon makes the summers very agreeable. The climate of Amoy is delightful, but its insular position renders a residence somewhat less agreeable than on the main. Here the thermometer ranges from 40° to 96° during the year, without the rapid changes of Ningpo. The heat continues longer, though assuaged by breezes from the sea.

Meteorology at Canton and its vicinity has been carefully studied; on the whole, its climate, and especially that of Macao, may be considered more salubrious than in most other places situated between the tropics. The thermometer at Canton in July and August stands on an average at 80° to 88°, and in January and February at 50° to 60°. The highest recorded observation in 1831 was 94°, in July; and the lowest, 29° in January. Ice sometimes forms in shallow vessels a line or two in thickness, but no use is made of it. A fall of snow nearly two inches deep occurred there in February, 1835, which remained on the ground three hours. Having never seen any before, the citizens hardly knew what was its proper name, some calling it *falling cotton*, and every one endeavoring to preserve a little for a febrifuge. Another similar fall occurred in the winter of 1861. Fogs are common during February and March, and the heat sometimes renders them very disagreeable, it being necessary to keep up a little fire to dry the house. Most of the rain falls in May and June, but there is nothing like the rainy season at Calcutta and Manilla in July, August, and September. The regular monsoon comes from the south-west, with frequent showers to allay the heat. In the succeeding months, northerly winds commence, but from October to January the temperature is agreeable, the sky clear, and the air invigorating. Few large cities are more healthy than Canton; no epidemics nor malaria prevail, notwithstanding the fact that much of the town is built upon piles.

The climate of Macao and Hongkong has not so great a range as Canton, from their proximity to the sea. Few cities in Asia are more salutiferous than Macao, though it has been remarked that few of the natives there attain a great age. The maximum is 90°, with an average summer heat of 84°. The minimum is 50°, and average winter weather 68°, with almost uninterrupted sunshine. Fogs are not often seen here, but on the river they prevail, being frequent at Whampoa. North-easterly gales are common in the spring and autumn, and have a noticeable periodicity of three days. The vegetation does not change its general aspect during the winter, the trees cease to grow, and the grass becomes brownish; but the stimulus of the warm moisture in March soon makes a sensible difference in the appearance of the landscape, and bright green leaves rapidly replace the old. The reputed insalubrity of Hongkong, in early days, was owing to other causes than climate, and when it became a well-built and well-drained town, its unwholesomeness disappeared. The rain-fall is greater than in Macao, owing to the attraction of the high peaks. During the rainy weather the walls of houses become damp, and if newly plastered, drip with moisture.

The Chinese consider the provinces of Kwangtung, Kwangsí, and Yunnan to be the most unhealthy of the eighteen, and for this reason employ them as places of banishment for criminals from the north-eastern districts. The central portions of the country are on some accounts the most bracing, not so liable to sudden changes as the coast, nor so cold as the western and northern districts. Sz'chuen and Kweichau are cooler than Fuhkien and Chehkiang, owing to the mountains in and upon their borders.

The marked contrast between the Chinese and American coasts in regard to rain is doubtless owing, in a great degree, to the outlying islands from Formosa to Sagalien on the former, whose high mountains arrest the clouds in their progress inland. The *Kuro-siwo*, being outside of them, allows a far greater mass of cold water between it and the shore on the Chinese, than is the case on the Atlantic coast, and renders it the colder of the two by nearly eight degrees of latitude, if isothermal lines alone are regarded. This mass of cold water, having less evaporation, deprives the maritime provinces of rain in diminishing supply as one goes north along the skirts of the Plain, until the Chang-peh shan are reached. The rains which fall in the western provinces and the slopes of the Bayan kara Mountains, coming up from the Indian Ocean during the south-west monsoon, fall in decreasing quantities as the clouds are driven north-east across the basins of the Yangtsz' and Yellow rivers. In the western part of Kansuh the humidity covers the mountains with more vegetation than further east, toward the ocean. Snow falls as late as June, and frosts occur in every month of the year. The enormous elevation of the western side of China near Tibet, the absence of an expanse of water like the great lakes, and the bareness of the mountains north of the Mei ling, account for much of this difference between the United States and China; but more extended data are needed for accurate deductions.

The fall of rain at Canton is 70 inches annually, which is the mean of sixteen years' observation. Ninety inches was registered during one of these years. Nearly one-half of the whole falls during May, June, and September. The average at Shanghai for four years was 36 inches. No observations are recorded for the valley of the Yangtsz'. Near the edge of the Plateau the rainfall averages 16 inches in the province of Chihlí, and rather more in Shansí and Shantung, where moisture is attracted by the mountains. More than three-fourths of the rain falls during the ten weeks ending August 31st. Snow seldom remains on the level over a fortnight.

The increased temperature on the southern coast during the months of June and July operates, with other causes, to produce violent storms along the seaboard, called *tyfoons*, a word derived from the Chinese *ta-fung*, or 'great wind.' These destructive tornadoes occur from Hainan to Chusan, between July and October, gradually progressing northward as the season advances, and diminishing in fury in the higher latitudes. They annually occasion great losses to the native and foreign shipping in Chinese waters, more than half the sailing ships lost on that coast having suffered in them. Happily, their fury is oftenest spent at sea, but when they occur inland, the loss of life is fearful. In August, 1862, and September 21, 1874, the deaths reported in two such storms near Canton, Hongkong, and their vicinity, were upward of 30,000 each. In the latter instance the American steamer Alaska, of 3,500 tons, was lifted from her anchorage and quietly put down in five feet of water near the shore, from whence she was safely floated some months afterward.

Tyfoons exhaust their force within a narrow track, which, in such cases as have been registered, lies in no uniform direction, other than from south to north, at a greater or less angle, along the coast. The principal phenomena indicating their approach are the direction of the wind, which commences to blow in soft zephyrs from the north, without, however, assuaging the heat or disturbing the stifling calm, and the falling barometer. The glass usually begins to fall several hours before the storm commences, and the rarefaction of the air is further shown by the heavy swell rolling in upon the beach, though the sea remains unruffled. The wind increases as it veers to the north-east, and from that point to south-east blows with the greatest force in fitful gusts. The rain falls heaviest toward the close of the gale, when the glass begins to rise. The barometer not unfrequently falls below 28 *in.* Capt. Krusenstern in 1804 records his surprise at seeing the mercury sink out of sight.

The Chinese have erected temples in Hainan to the Tyfoon Mother, a goddess whom they supplicate for protection against these hurricanes. They say "that a few days before a tyfoon comes on, a slight noise is heard at intervals, whirling round and then stopping, sometimes impetuous and sometimes slow. This is a 'tyfoon brewing.' Then fiery clouds collect in thick masses; the thunder sounds deep and heavy. Rainbows appear, now forming an unbroken curve and again separating, and the ends of the bow dip into the sea. The sea sends back a bellowing sound, and boils with angry surges; the loose rocks dash against each other, and detached sea-weed covers the water; there is a thick, murky atmosphere; the water-fowl fly about affrighted; the trees and leaves bend to the south—the tyfoon has commenced. When to it is superadded a violent rain and a frightful surf, the force of the tempest is let loose, and away fly the houses up to the hills, and the ships and boats are removed to the dry land; horses and cattle are turned heels over head, trees are torn up by the roots, and the sea boils up twenty or thirty feet, inundating the fields and destroying vegetation. This is called *tieh kü*, or an *iron whirlwind*."[1] Those remarkable gusts which annually occur in the Atlantic States, called *tornadoes*, defined as local storms affecting a thread of surface a few miles long, are unknown in China. The healthy climate of China has had much to do with the civilization of its inhabitants. No similar area in the world exceeds it for general salubrity.

The Chinese are the only people who have, by means of a

---

[1] *Chinese Repository*, Vol. VIII., p. 230; Vol. IV., p. 197. See also Fritsche's paper in *Journal of N. C. Branch Royal Asiatic Society*, No. XII., 1878, pp. 127–335; also Appendix II. in No. X., containing observations taken at Zi-ka-wei.

term added to the name of a place, endeavored to designate its relative rank. Three of the words used for this purpose, viz., *fu*, *chau*, and *hien*, have been translated as 'first,' 'second,' and 'third' rank; but this gradation is not quite correct, for the terms do not apply to the city or town alone, but to the portions of country of which it is the capital. The nature of these and other terms, and the divisions intended by them, are thus explained:

"The Eighteen Provinces are divided into *fu*, *ting*, *chau*, and *hien*. A *fu* is a large portion or department of a province, under the general control of one civil officer immediately subordinate to the heads of the provincial government. A *ting* is a division of a province smaller than a *fu*, and either like it governed by an officer immediately subject to the heads of the provincial government, or else forming a subordinate part of a *fu*. In the former case it is called *chih-lí*, *i.e.* under the 'direct rule' of the provincial government; in the latter case it is simply called *ting*. A *chau* is a division similar to a *ting*, and like it either independent of any other division, or forming part of a *fu*. The difference between the two consists in the government of a *ting* resembling that of a *fu* more nearly than that of a *chau* does: that of the *chau* is less expensive. The *ting* and *chau* of the class to which the term *chih-lí* is attached, may be denominated in common with the *fu*, *departments* or *prefectures*; and the term *chih-lí* may be rendered by the word *independent*. The subordinate *ting* and *chau* may both be called *districts*. A *hien*, which is also a *district*, is a small division or subordinate part of a department, whether of a *fu*, or of an independent *chau* or *ting*.

"Each *fu*, *ting*, *chau*, and *hien*, possesses at least one walled town, the seat of its government, which bears the same name as the department or district to which it pertains. Thus Hiangshan is the chief town of the district Hiangshan hien; and Shauking, that of the department Shauking fu. By European writers, the chief towns of the *fu* or departments have been called cities of the first order; those of the *chau*, cities of the second order; and those of the *hien*, cities of the third order. The division called *ting*, being rarely met with, has been left out of the arrangement—an arrangement not recognized in China. It must be observed that the chief town of a *fu* is always also the chief town of a *hien* district; and sometimes, when of considerable size and importance, it and the country around are divided into two *hien* districts, both of which have the seat of their government within the same walls: but this is not the case with the *ting* and *chau* departments. A district is not always subdivided; instances may occur of a whole district possessing but one important town. But as there are often large and even walled towns not included in the number of chief or of district towns, consequently not the seat of a regular *chau* or *hien* magistracy, a subdivision of a district is therefore frequently rendered necessary; and for the better government of such towns and the towns surrounding them, magistrates are appointed to them, secondary to the magistrates of the departments or the districts in which they are comprised. Thus Fuhshan is a very large commercial town or mart called a *chin*, situated in the district of Nanhai, of the department of Kwangchau, about twelve miles distant from Canton. The chief officer of the department has therefore an assistant residing there, and the town is partly under his government and partly under that of the Nanhai magistrate, within whose district it is included, but who resides at Canton. There are several of these *chin* in the provinces, as Kingteh in Kiangsí, Siangtan in Hunan, etc.; they are not inclosed by walls. Macao affords another instance: being a place of some importance, both from its size and as the residence of foreigners, an assistant to the Hiangshan hien magistrate is placed over it, and it is also under the control of an assistant to the chief magistrate of the *fu*. Of these assistant magistrates, there are two ranks secondary to the chief magistrate of a *fu*, two secondary to the magistrate of a *chau*, and two also secondary to the magistrate of a *hien*. The places under the rule of these assistant magistrates are called by various names, most frequently *chin* and *so*, and sometimes also *chai* and *wei*. These names do not appear to have reference to any particular form of municipal government existing in them; but the *chai* and the *wei* are often military posts; and sometimes a place is, with respect to its civil government, the chief city of a *fu*, while with respect to its military position it is called *wei*. There are other towns of still smaller importance; these are under the government of inferior magistrates who are called *siun kien*: a division of country under such a magistrate is called a *sz'*, which is best represented by the term township or *commune*. The town of Whampoa and country around it form one such division, called Kiautang sz', belonging to the district of Pwanyu, in the department of Kwangchau.

"In the mountainous districts of Kwangsí, Yunnan, Kweichau, and Sz'chuen, and in some other places, there are districts called *tu sz'*. Among these, the same distinctions of *fu*, *chau*, and *hien* exist, together with the minor division *sz'*. The magistrates of these departments and districts are hereditary in their succession, being the only hereditary local officers acknowledged by the supreme government.

"There is a larger division than any of the above, but as it does not prevail universally, it was not mentioned in the first instance. It is called *tau*, a *course* or *circuit*, and comprises two or more departments of a province, whether *fu*, or independent *ting* or *chau*. These circuits are subject to the government of officers called *tau-tai* or intendants of circuit, who often combine with political and judicial powers a military authority and various duties relating to the territory or to the revenue."[1]

The eighteen provinces received their present boundaries and divisions in the reign of Kienlung; and the little advance which has been made abroad in the geography of China is shown by the fact, that although these divisions were established a hundred years ago, the old demarkations, existing at

[1] *Chinese Repository*, Vol. IV., p. 54.

the time of the survey in 1710, are still found in many modern European geographies and maps. The following table shows their present divisions and government. The three columns under the head of *Departments* contain the *fu*, *chihlí ting*, and *chihlí chau*, all of which are properly prefectures; the three columns under the head of *Districts* contain the *ting*, *chau*, and *hien*.

The province of CHIHLÍ is the most important of the whole. On foreign maps it is sometimes written Pechele (*i.e.*, North Chihlí), a name formerly given it in order to distinguish it from Kiangnan, or *Nan-chihlí*, in which the seat of government was once located. This name is descriptive, rather than technical, and means 'Direct rule,' denoting that from this province the supreme power which governs the empire proceeds; any province, in which the Emperor and court should be fixed, would therefore be termed *Chihlí*, and its chief city *King*, 'capital,' or *King-tu* or *King-sz'*, 'court of the capital.' The surface of this province lying south of the Great Wall is level, excepting a few ridges of hills in the west and north, while the eastern parts, and those south to the Gulf, are among the flattest portions of the Great Plain.

It is bounded on the north-east by Liautung, where for a short distance the Great Wall is the frontier line; on the east by the Gulf of Pechele; on the south-east and south by Shantung; on the south-west by Honan; on the west by Shansí; and north by Inner Mongolia, where the river Liau forms the boundary. The extensive region beyond the Wall, occupied mostly by the Tsakhar Mongols, is now included within the jurisdiction, and placed under the administration of officers residing at one of the garrisoned gates of the Great Wall; the area of this part is about half that of the whole province. The chief department in the province, that of Shuntien, being both large and important, as containing the metropolis, is divided into four *lu* or circuits, each under the rule of a sub-prefect, who is subordinate to the prefect living at Peking.

Peking[1] (*i.e.*, Northern Capital) is situated upon a sandy

[1] This word should not be written Pekin; it is pronounced *Pei-ching* by the citizens, and by most of the people north of the Great River.

PROVINCES.	AREA IN ENGLISH SQ. MLS.	DEPARTMENTS.			DISTRICTS.			CAPITAL.	GOVERNMENT.
		Fu.	Ting.	Chau.	Ting.	Chau.	Hien.		
NORTHERN PROVINCES.									
Chihli	58,949	11	..	6	3	17	124	Pauting fu.	Ruled by a governor-general or *tsungtuh*.
Shantung	65,104	10	..	2	..	9	96	Tsínan fu.	Each separately ruled by a lieutenant-governor or *fuyuen*.
Shansí	55,268	9	..	10	3	6	85	Taiyuen fu.	
Honan	65,104	9	..	4	..	6	97	Kaifung fu.	
EASTERN PROVINCES.									
Kiangsu	92,961	8	1	3	2	3	62	Kiangning fu.	Each under a lieutenant-governor, subordinate to one governor-general, called *Liang Kiang tsungtuh*.
Nganhwui		8	..	5	..	4	50	Nganking fu.	
Kiangsí	72,176	13	..	1	2	1	75	Nanchang fu.	
Chehkiang	39,150	11	..	..	1	1	76	Hangchau fu.	Each under a lieutenant-governor, subordinate to a governor-general, called *Min Cheh tsungtuh*.
Fuhkien	53,480	10	..	2	3	..	62	Fuhchau fu.	
CENTRAL PROVINCES.									
Hupeh	144,770	10	..	1	..	7	60	Wuchang fu.	Each under a lieutenant-governor, subordinate to a governor-general, called *Liang Hu tsungtuh*.
Hunan		9	[illegible]	4	..	3	64	Changsha fu.	
SOUTHERN PROVINCES.									
Kwangtung	79,456	9	2	4	3	7	79	Kwangchau fu, or Canton.	Two lieutenant-governors, subordinate to a governor-general, called *Liang Kwang tsungtuh*.
Kwangsí	78,250	11	..	1	3	16	47	Kweilin fu.	
Yunnan	107,969	14	3	4	5	27	39	Yunnan fu.	Two lieutenant-governors, subordinate to a governor-general, called *Yun Kwei tsungtuh*.
Kweichau	64,554	12	3	1	5	13	34	Kweiyang fu.	
WESTERN PROVINCES.									
Shensí	154,008	7	..	5	5	5	73	Síngan fu.	Under a governor-general, called *Shen Kan tsungtuh*, and one lieutenant-governor over Shensí.
Kansuh		9	..	6	7	7	51	Lanchau fu.	
Sz'chuen	166,800	12	6	8	9	11	111	Chingtu fu.	Ruled by a governor-general.

plain, about twelve miles south-west of the Pei ho, and more than a hundred miles west-north-west of its mouth, in lat. 39° 54′ 36″ N., and long. 116° 27′ E., or nearly on the parallel of Samarkand, Naples, and Philadelphia. It is a city worthy of note on many accounts. Its ancient history as the capital of the *Yen Kwoh* (the 'Land of Swallows') during the feudal times, and its later position as the metropolis of the empire for many centuries, give it historical importance; while its imperial buildings, its broad avenues with their imposing gates and towers, its regular arrangement, extent, populousness, and diversity of costume and equipage, combine to render it to a traveller the most interesting and unique city in Asia. It is now ruinous and poor, but the remains of its former grandeur under Kienlung's prosperous reign indicate the justness of the comparisons made by the Catholic writers with western cities one hundred and eighty years ago. The entire circuit of the walls and suburbs is reckoned by Hyacinthe at twenty-five miles, and its area at twenty-seven square miles, but more accurate measurements of the walls alone give forty-one *li*, or 14.25 miles (or 23.55 kilometres) for the Manchu city, including the cross-wall, and twenty-eight *li*, or ten miles, for the Chinese city on its south; not counting the cross-wall, the circuit measures almost twenty-one miles. The suburbs near the thirteen outer gates altogether form a small proportion to the whole; the area within them is nearly twenty-six square miles. Those residents who have had the best opportunities estimate the entire population at a million or somewhat less; no census returns are available to prove this figure, nor can it be stated what is the proportion of Manchus, Mongols, and Chinese, except that the latter outnumber all others. Du Halde reckoned it to be about three millions, and Klaproth one million three hundred thousand; and each was probably true at some period, for the number has diminished with the poverty of the Government.

Peking is regarded by the Chinese as one of their ancient cities, but it was not made the capital of the whole empire until Kublai established his court at this spot in 1264. The Ming emperors who succeeded the Mongols held their court

THE AN-TING GATE, WALL OF PEKING.

at Nanking until Yungloh transferred the seat of government to Peking in 1411, where it has since remained. Under the Mongols, the city was called *Khan-baligh* (*i.e.*, city of the Khan), changed into Cambalu in the accounts of those times; on Chinese maps it is usually called *King-sz'*.

Peking has, during its history, existed under many different names; after each disaster her walls have been changed and her houses rebuilt, so that to-day she stands, like the capitals of the ancient Roman and Byzantine empires, upon the débris of centuries of buildings. The most important renovations have been those by the Liao dynasty, in 937 A.D., who entirely rebuilt the city, and by the Kin rulers in 1151.

It was at first surrounded by a single wall pierced by nine gates, whence it is sometimes called the City of Nine Gates. The southern suburbs were inclosed by Kiatsing in 1543, and the city now consists of two portions, the northern or inner city (*Nui ching*), containing about fifteen square miles, where are the palace, government buildings, and barracks for troops; and the southern or Outer city (*Wai ching*), where the Chinese live. The wall of the Manchu city averages fifty feet high, forty wide at top, and about sixty at bottom, most of the slope being on the inner face. That around the Outer city is no more than thirty in height, twenty-five thick at bottom, and about fifteen at top. The terre-plein throughout is paved with bricks weighing sixty pounds each; a crenellated parapet runs around the entire town, intended only for archers or musketeers, as no port-holes for cannon exist. It is undoubtedly the finest wall surrounding any city now extant. Near the gates, of which there are sixteen in all, the walls are faced with stone, but in other places with these large bricks, laid in a concrete of lime and clay, which in process of time becomes almost as durable as stone. The intermediate space between facings is filled up with the earth taken from the ditch which surrounds the city. Square buttresses occur at intervals of sixty yards on the outer face, each projecting fifty feet, and every sixth one being twice the size of the others; their tops furnish room for the troops posted there to resist side attacks. Each gate is surmounted with a brick tower of many stories, over a hundred feet high, built in galleries with port-holes, and giving a very imposing appearance to the city as one approaches it from the wide plain. The gates of the Manchu city have a double entrance formed by joining their supporting bastions with a circular wall in which are side entrances, thus making an enceinte of several acres, in which the yellow-tiled temple to the tutelary God of War is conspicuous. The arches of all the gates are built solidly of granite; the massive doors are closed and barred every night soon after dark.

At the sides of the gates, and also between them, are esplanades for mounting to the top; this is shut to the common people, and the guards are not allowed to bring their women upon the wall, which would be deemed an affront to Kwantí. The moat around the city is fed from the Tunghwui River, which also supplies all the other canals leading across or through the city. The approach to Peking from Tung chau is by an elevated stone road, but nothing of the buildings inside the walls is seen; and were it not for the lofty towers over the gates, it would more resemble an encampment inclosed by a massive wall than a large metropolis. No spires or towers of churches, no pillars or monuments, no domes or minarets, nor even many dwellings of superior elevation, break the dull uniformity of this or any Chinese city. In Peking, the different colored yellow or green tiles on official buildings,[1] mixed with the brown roofs of common houses, impart a variety to the scene, but the chief objects to relieve the monotony are the large clumps of trees, and the flag-staffs in pairs near the temples. The view from the walls impresses one with the grand ideas of the founders of the city; and the palaces in the Forbidden City, towering above everything else, worthily exhibit their notions of what was befitting the sovereigns of the Middle Kingdom. The Bell and Clock Towers, the Prospect Hill, the dagobas, pagodas, and gate towers, and lastly the Temple of

[1] "You would think them all made of, or at least covered with, pure gold enamelled in azure and green, so that the spectacle is at once majestic and charming." Magaillans, *Nouvelle Description de la Chine*, p. 353.

Heaven, are all likewise visible from this point, and render the scene picturesque and peculiar.[1]

The plan of the city here given is reduced from a large Chinese map, but is not very exact. The northern portion occupies for the most part the same area as the Cambaluc of Marco Polo, which, however, extended about two miles north, where the remains of the old north wall of the Mongols still exist. On their expulsion Hungwu erected the present northern wall, and his son Yungloh rebuilt the other three sides in 1419 on a rather larger scale; but the arrangement of the streets and gates is due to the Great Khan. When taken possession of by the Manchus in 1644, they found a magnificent city ready for them, uninjured and strong, which they apportioned among their officers and bannermen; but necessity soon obliged these men, less frugal and thrifty than the natives, to sell them, and content themselves with humbler abodes; consequently, the greater part of the northern city is now tenanted by Chinese. The innermost inclosure in the *Nui Ching* contains the palace and its surrounding buildings; the second is occupied by barracks and public offices, and by many private residences; the outer one, for the most part, consists of dwelling-houses, with shops in the large avenues. The inner inclosure measures 6.3 *li*, or 2.23 miles, in circuit, and is called *Tsz' Kin Ching*, or 'Carnation Prohibited City;' the wall is less solid and high than the city wall; it is covered with bright yellow tiles, guarded by numerous stations of bannermen and gendarmerie, and surrounded by a deep, wide moat. Two gates, the *Tung-hwa* and *Si-hwa*, on the east and west, afford access to the interior of this habitation of the Emperor, as well as the space and rooms appertaining, which furnish lodgment to the guard defending the approach to the Dragon's Throne; a tower at each corner, and one over each gateway, also give accommodation to other troops. The interior of this inclosure is divided

---

[1] See also *L'Univers Pittoresque, Chine Moderne*, par MM. Pauthier et Bazin, Paris, 1853, for a good map of Peking, with careful descriptions. Yule's *Marco Polo*, passim. De Guigues, *Voyages*, Tome I. Williamson, *Journeys in North China*, Vol. II. Dr. Rennie, *Peking and the Pekingese*. *Tour du Monde* for 1864, Tome II.

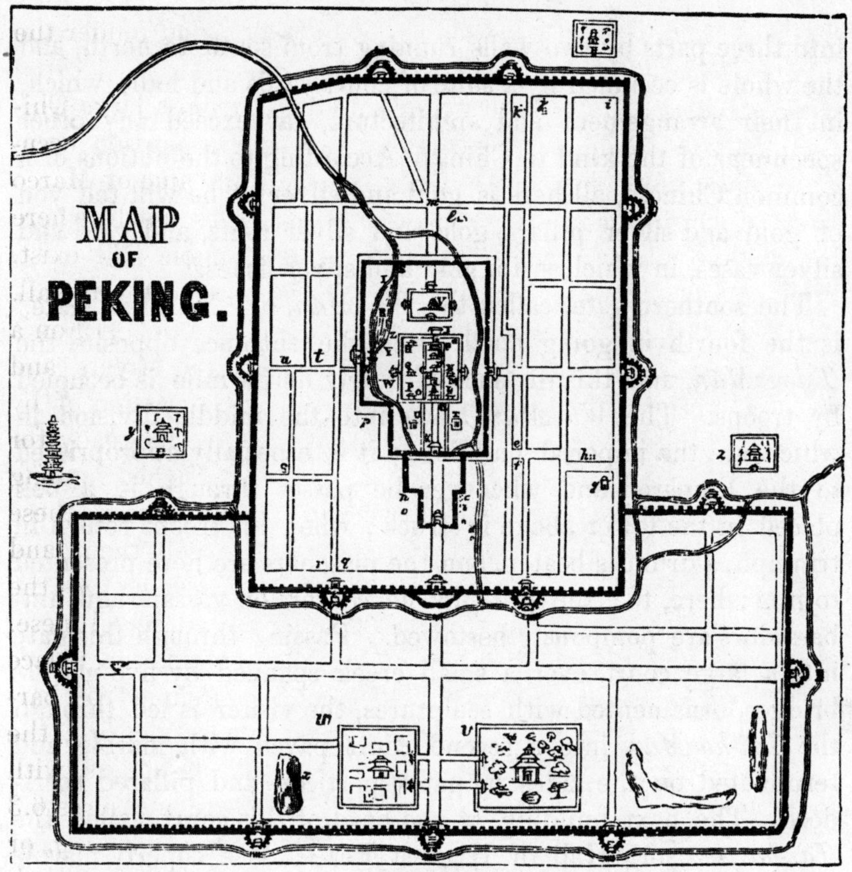

REFERENCES.

A. The Meridian Gate.
B. Gate of Extensive Peace.
C. Hall of Perfect Peace.
D. Hall of Secure Peace.
E. Palace of Heaven—the Emperor's.
F. Palace of Earth's Repose—the Empress'.
G. Gate to Earth's Repose, leads to a Garden.
H. Ching-hwang miao.
I. Temple of Great Happiness.
J. Northern gate of Forbidden City.
K. Nui Koh, or Privy Council Chamber, lies within the wall.
K. Gate of Heavenly Rest.
L. Hall of Intense Mental Exercises.
M. Library, or Hall of Literary Abyss.
N. Imperial Ancestral Hall.
O. Hall of National Portraits.
P. Printing Office.
Q. Court of Controllers of Imperial Clan.
R. Marble Isle; a marble bridge leads to it.
S Five Dragon Pavilion.
T. Great Ancestral Temple.
U. Altar to the Gods of Land and Grain.
V. Artificial Mountain. The Russian school lies just north of the Eastern gate near N.
W. A summer-house.
X. Military Examination Hall.
Y. Plantain Garden, or Conservatory.
Z. A Pavilion.

a. Medical College.
b. Astronomical Board.
c. Five of the Six Boards. The Hanlin Yuen lies just above them.
d. House of the Russian Mission.
e. Colonial Office.
f. Temple for Imperial worship.
g. Imperial Observatory, partly on the wall.
h. Hall of Literary Examination.
i. Russian Church of the Assumption.
j. Temple of Eternal Peace of the lamas.
k. Kwoh Tsz' Kien, a Manchu College.
l. Temple of the God of the North Star.
m. High Watch-tower and Police Office.
n. Board of Punishments.
o. Censorate.
p. Mohammedan Mosque.
q. Portuguese Church.
r. Elephant's Inclosure.
s. Principal Ching-hwang miau.
t. Temple of Deceased Emperors of all ages.
u. Obelisk covering a scab of Buddha.
v. Altar to Heaven.—Altar to Earth is on the north of the city.
w. Altar to Agriculture.
x. Black Dragon Pool, and Temple of God of Rain.
y. Altar to the Moon.
z. Altar to the Sun.

into three parts by two walls running from south to north, and the whole is occupied by a suite of court-yards and halls, which, in their arrangement and architecture, far exceed any other specimens of the kind in China. According to the notions of a common Chinese, all here is gold and silver; "he will tell you of gold and silver pillars, gold and silver roofs, and gold and silver vases, in which swim gold and silver fishes."

The southern gate, called the *Wu Măn*, or 'Meridian Gate,' is the fourth in going north from the entrance opposite the *Tsien Măn*, and this distance of nearly half a mile is occupied by troops. The *Wu Măn* leads into the middle division, in which are the imperial buildings; it is especially appropriated to the Emperor, and whenever he passes through it, a bell placed in the tower above is struck; when his troops return in triumph, a drum is beaten, and the prisoners are here presented to him; here, too, the presents he confers on vassals and ambassadors are pompously bestowed. Passing through this gate into a large court, over a small creek spanned by five marble bridges, ornamented with sculptures, the visitor is led through the *Tai-ho Măn* into a second court paved with marble, and terminated on the sides by gates, porticos, and pillared corridors. The next building, at the head of this court, called the *Tai-ho tien*, or 'Hall of Highest Peace,' is a superb marble structure, one hundred and ten feet high, standing on a terrace that raises it twenty feet above the ground; five flights of stairs, decorated with balustrades and sculptures, lead up to it, and five doors open through it into the next court-yard. It is a great hall of seventy-two pillars, measuring about two hundred feet by ninety broad, with a throne in the midst. Here the Emperor holds his levees on New Year's Day, his birthdays, and other state occasions; a cortége of about fifty household courtiers stand near him, while those of noble and inferior dignity and rank stand in the court below in regular grades, and, when called upon, fall prostrate as they all make the fixed obeisances. It was in this hall that Titsingh and Van Braam were banqueted by Kienlung, January 20, 1795, of which interesting ceremony the Dutch embassador gives an account, and since which event no European has entered the building. The three *Tien* in this inclosure are the audience halls, and the side buildings contain stores and treasures under the charge of the Household Board, with minor bureaus.

Beyond it are two halls; the first, the *Chung-ho tien*, or 'Hall of Central Peace,' having a circular roof, that rests on columns arranged nearly four-square. Here the Emperor comes to examine the written prayers provided to be offered at the state worship. The second is the *Pao-ho tien*, or 'Hall of Secure Peace,' elevated on a high marble terrace, and containing nine rows of pillars. The highest degrees for literary merit are here conferred triennially by the Emperor upon one hundred and fifty or more scholars; here, also, he banquets his foreign guests and other distinguished persons the day before New Year's Day. After ascending a stairway, and passing the *Kien Tsing Măn*, the visitor reaches the *Kien Tsing Kung*, or 'Palace of Heavenly Purity,' into which no one can enter without special license. In it is the council-chamber, where the Emperor usually sits at morning audience up to eight o'clock, to transact business with his ministers, and see those appointed to office. The building is the most important as it is described to be the loftiest and most magnificent of all the palaces. In the court before it is a small tower of gilt copper, adorned with a great number of figures, and on each side are large incense vases, the uses of which are no doubt religious. It was in this palace that Kanghí celebrated a singular and unique festival, in 1722, for all the men in the empire over sixty years of age, that being the sixtieth year of his reign. His grandson Kienlung, in 1785, in the fiftieth year of his reign, repeated the ceremony, on which occasion the number of guests was about three thousand.[1] Beyond it stands the 'Palace of Earth's Repose,' where 'Heaven's consort' rules her miniature court in the imperial harem; there are numerous buildings of lesser size in this part of the inclosure, and adjoining the northern wall of the Forbidden City is the imperial Flower Garden, designed for the use of its inmates. The gardens are adorned with elegant pavilions, temples, and

---

[1] *Chinese Repository*, Vol. IX., p. 259.

groves, and interspersed with canals, fountains, pools, and flower-beds. Two groves rising from the bosoms of small lakes, and another crowning the summit of an artificial mountain, add to the beauty of the scene, and afford the inmates of the palace an agreeable variety.

In the eastern division of the Prohibited City are the offices of the Cabinet, where its members hold their sessions, and the treasury of the palace. North of it lies the 'Hall of Intense Thought,' where sacrifices are presented to Confucius and other sages. Not far from this hall stands the *Wăn-yuen koh*, or the Library, the catalogue of whose contents is published from time to time, forming an admirable synopsis of Chinese literature. At the northern end of the eastern division are numerous palaces and buildings occupied by princes of the blood, and those connected with them; and in this quarter is placed the *Fung Sien tien*, a small temple where the Emperor comes to 'bless his ancestors.' Here the Emperor and his family perform their devotions before the tablets of their departed progenitors; whenever he leaves or returns to his palace, the first day of a season, and on other occasions, the monarch goes through his devotions in this hall.

The western division contains a great variety of edifices devoted to public and private purposes, among which may be mentioned the hall of distinguished sovereigns, statesmen, and literati, the printing-office, the Court of Controllers for the regulation of the receipts and disbursements of the court, and the *Ching-hwang Miao*, or 'Guardian Temple' of the city. The number of people residing within the Prohibited City cannot be stated, but probably is not large; most of them are Manchus.

The second inclosure, which surrounds the imperial palaces, is called *Hwang Ching*, or 'Imperial City,' and is an oblong rectangle about six miles in circuit, encompassed by a wall twenty feet high, and having a gate in each face. From the southern gate, called the *Tien-an Măn*, or 'Heavenly Rest,' a broad avenue leads up to the *Kin Ching;* and before it, outside of the wall, is an extensive space walled in, and having one entrance on the south, called the gate of Great Purity, which no one is allowed to enter except on foot, unless by special permission. On the right of the avenue within the wall is a gateway leading to the *Tai Miao*, or 'Great Temple' of the imperial ancestors, a large collection of buildings inclosed by a wall 3,000 feet in circuit. It is the most honored of religious structures next to the Temple of Heaven, and contains tablets to princes and meritorious officers. Here offerings are presented before the tablets of deceased emperors and empresses, and worship performed at the end of the year by the members of the imperial family and clan to their departed forefathers. Across the avenue from this temple is a gateway leading to the *Shié-Tsih tan*, or altar of the gods of Land and Grain. These were originally *Kau-lung*, a Minister of Works, B.C. 2500, and *Hau-tsih*, a remote ancestor of Chau Kung; here the Emperor sacrifices in spring and autumn. This altar consists of two stories, each five feet high, the upper one being fifty-eight feet square; no other altar of the kind is found in the empire, and it would be tantamount to high treason to erect one and worship upon it. The north, east, south, and west altar are respectively black, green, red, and white, and the top yellow; the ceremonies connected with the worship held here are among the most ancient practised among the Chinese.

On the north of the palace, separated by a moat, and surrounded by a wall more than a mile in circuit, is the *King Shan*, or 'Prospect Hill,' an artificial mound, nearly one hundred and fifty feet high, and having five summits, crowned with as many temples; many of these show the neglect in which public edifices soon fall. Trees of various kinds border its base, and line the paths leading to the tops. Its height allows the spectator to overlook the whole city, while, too, it is itself a conspicuous object from every direction. The earth and stone in it were taken from the ditches and pools dug in and around the city, and near its base are many tanks of picturesque shape and appearance; so that altogether it forms a great ornament to the city. Another name for it is *Mei Shan*, or 'Coal Hill,' from a tradition that a quantity of coal was placed there, as a supply in case of siege. The western part of this inclosure is chiefly occupied by the *Si Yuen*, or 'Western Park,' in and around which are found some of the most beautiful objects and spots in the metropolis. An artificial lake, more than a mile long, and averaging a furlong in breadth, occupies the centre; it is supplied from the Western Hills, and its waters are adorned with the splendid lotus. A marble bridge of nine arches crosses it, and its banks are shaded by groves of trees, under which are well-paved walks. On its south-eastern side is a large summer-house, consisting of several edifices partly in or over the water, and inclosing a number of gardens and walks, in and around which are artificial hills of rock-work beautifully alternating or supporting groves of trees and parterres of flowers.

On the western side is the hall for examining military candidates, where his majesty in person sees them exhibit their prowess in equestrian archery. At the north end of the lake is a bridge leading to an islet, which presents the aspect of a hill of gentle ascent covered with groves, temples, and summer-houses, and surmounted with a tower, from which an extensive view can be enjoyed. On the north of the bridge is a hill on an island called *Kiung-hwa tan*, capped by a white dagoba. Near by is an altar forty feet in circuit, and four feet high, inclosed by a wall, and a temple dedicated to Yuenfí, the reputed discoverer of the silk-worm, where the Empress annually offers sacrifices to her; in the vicinity a plantation of mulberry trees and a cocoonery are maintained. Near the temple of 'Great Happiness,' not far distant from the preceding, on the northern borders of the lake, is a gilded copper statue of *Maitreya*, or the coming Buddha, sixty feet high, with a hundred arms; the temple is one of the greatest ornaments of the Park. Across the lake on its western bank, and entered through the first gate on the south side of the street, is the *Tsz'-kwang Koh*, where foreign ministers are received by the Emperor; the inclosure is kept with great care, and numerous halls and temples are seen amidst groves of firs. The object kept in view in the arrangement of these gardens and grounds has been to make them an epitome of nature, and then furnish every part with commodious buildings. But however elegant the palaces and grounds may have appeared when new, it is to be feared that his majesty has no higher ideas of cleanliness and order than his subjects, and that the various public and private edifices and gardens in these two inclosures are despoiled of half their beauty by dirt and neglect. The number of the palaces in them both is estimated to be over two hundred, "each of which," says Attinet, in vague terms, "is sufficiently large to accommodate the greatest of European noblemen, with all his retinue."

Along the avenue leading south from the Imperial City to the division wall, are found the principal government offices. Five of the Six Boards have their bureaus on the east side, the Board of Punishments with its subordinate departments being situated with its courts on the west side; immediately south of this is the Censorate. The office attached to the Board of Rites, for the preparation of the Calendar, commonly called the Astronomical Board, stands directly east of this; and the Medical College has its hall not far off. The *Hanlin Yuen*, or National Academy, and the *Li-fan Yuen*, or Colonial Office, are also near the south-eastern corner of the Imperial City. Opposite to the Colonial Office is the *Tang Tsz'*, where the remote ancestors of the reigning family are worshipped by his majesty together with the princes of his family; when they come in procession to this temple in their state dresses, the Emperor, as high-priest of the family, performs the highest religious ceremony before his deified ancestors, viz., three kneelings and nine knockings. After he has completed his devotions, the attendant grandees go through the same ceremonies. The temple itself is pleasantly situated in the midst of a grove of fir and other trees, and the large inclosure around it is prettily laid out.

In the south-eastern part of the city, built partly upon the wall, is the Observatory, which was placed under the superintendence of the Romish missionaries by Kanghí, but is now confided to the care of Chinese astronomers. The instruments are arranged on a terrace higher than the city wall, and are beautiful pieces of bronze art, though now antiquated and useless for practical observations. Nearly opposite to the Observatory stands the Hall for Literary Examinations, where the candidates of the province assemble to write their essays. In the north-eastern corner of the city is the Russian Mission and

Astronomical Office, inclosed in a large compound; near it live the converts. About half a mile west is the *Yung-ho Kung*, or 'Lamasary of Eternal Peace,' wherein about 1,500 Mongol and Tibetan priests study the dogmas of Buddhism, or spend their days in idleness, under the control of a *Gegen* or living Buddha. Their course of study comprises instruction in metaphysics, ascetic duties, astrology, and medicine; their daily ritual is performed in several courts, and the rehearsal of prayers and chants by so many men strikes the hearer as very impressive. The rear building contains a wooden image, 70 feet in height, of Maitreya, the coming Buddha; the whole establishment exhibits in its buildings, pictures, images, cells, and internal arrangements for study, living, and worship, one of the most complete in the empire. Several smaller lamasaries occur in other parts of the city.

Directly west of the *Yung-ho Kung*, and presenting the greatest contrast to its life and activity, lies the Confucian Temple, where embowered in a grove of ancient cypresses stands the imposing *Wăn Miao*, or 'Literary Temple,' in which the Example and Teacher of all Ages and ten of his great disciples are worshipped. The hall is 84 feet in front, and the lofty roof is supported on wooden pillars over 40 feet high, covering the single room in which their tablets are placed in separate niches, he in the high seat of honor. All is simple, quiet, and cheerless; the scene here presents an impressive instance of merited honors paid to the moral teachers of the people. Opposite and across the court are ten granite stones shaped like drums, which are believed to have been made about the eighth century B.C., and contain stanzas recording King Süen's hunting expeditions. In another court are many stone tablets containing the lists of *Tsin-sz'* graduates since the Mongol dynasty, many thousands of names with places of residence. Contiguous to this temple is the *Pih-yung Kung*, or 'Classic Hall,' where the Emperor meets the graduates and literati. It is a beautiful specimen of Chinese architectural taste. Near it are 300 stone tablets on which the authorized texts of the classics are engraved.[1]

---

[1] Dr. Martin, *The Chinese* (New York, 1881), p. 85.

North of the Imperial City lies the extensive *yamun* of the *Ti-tuh*, who has the police and garrison of the city under his control, and exercises great authority in its civil administration. The Drum and Bell Towers stand north of the *Ti-ngan Măn* in the street leading to the city wall, each of them over a hundred feet high, and forming conspicuous objects; the drum and bell are sounded at night watches, and can be heard throughout the city; a clepsydra is still maintained to mark time—a good

Portal of Confucian Temple, Peking.

instance of Chinese conservatism, for clocks are now in general use, and correct the errors of the clepsydra itself.

Outside of the south-western angle of the Imperial City stands the Mohammedan mosque, and a large number of Turks whose ancestors were brought from Turkestan about a century ago live in its vicinity; this quarter is consequently the chief resort of Moslems who come to the capital. South-west of the mosque, near the cross-wall, stands the *Nan Tang*, or old Por tuguese church, and just west of the Forbidden City, inside of the *Hwang Ching*, is the *Peh Tang*, or Cathedral; both are imposing edifices, and near them are large schools and seminaries for the education of children and neophytes. There are religious edifices in the Chinese metropolis appropriated to many forms of religion, viz., the Greek, Latin, and Protestant churches, Islamism, Buddhism in its two principal forms, Rationalism, ancestral worship, state worship, and temples dedicated to Confucius and other deified mortals, besides a great number in which the popular idols of the country are adored. One of the most worthy of notice is the *Ti-Wang Miao*, lying on the avenue leading to the west gate, a large collection of halls wherein all the tablets of former monarchs of China from remote ages are worshipped. The rule for admission into this Walhalla is to accept all save the vicious and oppressive, those who were assassinated and those who lost their kingdoms. This memorial temple was opened in 1522; the Manchus have even admitted some of the Tartar rulers of the Kin and Liao dynasties, raising the total number of tablets to nearly three hundred. It is an impressive sight, these simple tablets of men who once ruled the Middle Kingdom, standing here side by side, worshipped by their successors that their spirits may bless the state. This selection of the good sovereigns alone recalls to mind the custom in ancient Jerusalem of allowing wicked princes no place in the sepulchres of the kings. Distinguished statesmen of all ages, called by the Chinese *kwoh chu*, or 'pillars of state,' are associated with their masters in this temple, as not unworthy to receive equal honors.

A little west of this remarkable temple is the *Peh-ta sz'*, or 'White Pagoda Temple,' so called from a costly dagoba near it erected about A.D. 1100, renovated by Kublai in the thirteenth century, and rebuilt in 1819. Its most conspicuous feature is the great copper umbrella on the top. When finished, the dagoba was described as covered with jasper, and the projecting parts of the roof with ornaments of exquisite workmanship tastefully arranged. Around this edifice, which contains twenty beads or relics of Buddha, two thousand clay pagodas and five books of charms, are also one hundred and eight small pillars on which lamps are burned. The portion of the city lying south of the cross-wall is inhabited mostly by Chinese, and contains hundreds of *hwui-kwan*, or club-houses, erected by the gentry of cities and districts in all parts of the empire to accommodate their citizens resorting to the capital. Its streets are narrow and the whole aspect of its buildings and markets indicates the life and industry of the people. Hundreds of inns accommodate travellers who find no lodging-places in the *Nui Ching*, and storehouses, theatres, granaries and markets attract or supply their customers from all parts. There is more dissipation and freedom from etiquette here, and the Chinese officials feel freer from their Manchu colleagues.

Three miles south of the Palace, in the Chinese City, is situated the *Tien Tan*, or 'Altar to Heaven,' so placed because it was anciently customary to perform sacrifices to Heaven in the outskirts of the Emperor's residence city. The compound is inclosed by more than three miles of wall, within which is planted a thick grove of locust (*Sophora*), pine and fir trees, interspaced with stretches of grass. Within a second wall, which surrounds the sacred buildings, rises a copse of splendid and thickly growing cypress trees, reminding one of the solemn shade in the vicinity of famous temples in Ancient Greece, or of those celebrated shrines described in Western Asia. The great South Altar, the most important of Chinese religious structures, is a beautiful triple circular terrace of white marble, whose base is 210, middle stage 150, and top 90 feet in width, each terrace encompassed by a richly carved balustrade. A curious symbolism of the number three and its multiples may be noticed in the measurements of this pile. The uppermost terrace, whose height above the ground is about eighteen feet, is paved with marble slabs, forming nine concentric circles—the inner of nine stones inclosing a central piece, and around this each receding layer consisting of a successive multiple of nine until the square of nine (a favorite number of Chinese philosophy) is reached in the outermost row. It is upon the single round stone in the centre of the upper plateau that the Emperor kneels when worshipping Heaven and his ancestors at the winter solstice.

Four flights of nine steps each lead from this elevation to the next lower stage, where are placed tablets to the spirits of the sun, the moon, the stars, and the Year God. On the ground at the end of the four stairways stand vessels of bronze in which are placed the bundles of cloth and sundry animals constituting part of the sacrificial offerings. But of vastly greater importance than these in the matter of burnt-offering is the great furnace, nine feet high, faced with green porcelain, and ascended on three of its sides by porcelain staircases. In this receptacle, erected some hundred feet to the south-east of the altar, is consumed a burnt-offering of a bullock—entire and without blemish—at the yearly ceremony. The slaughter-house of the sacrificial bullock stands east of the North Altar, at the end of an elaborate winding passage, or cloister of 72 compartments, each 10 feet in length.

Separated from the Altar to Heaven by a low wall, is a smaller though more conspicuous construction called *Ki-kuh Tan*, or 'Altar of Prayer for Grain.' Its proportions and arrangement are somewhat similar to those of the South Altar, but upon its upper terrace rises a magnificent triple-roofed, circular building known to foreigners as the 'Temple of Heaven.' This elaborate house of worship, whose surmounting gilded ball rests 100 feet above the platform, was originally roofed with blue, yellow and green tiles, but by Kienlung these colors were changed to blue. When, added to these brilliant hues, we consider the richly carved and painted eaves, the windows shaded by venetians of blue-glass rods strung together, and the rare symmetry of its proportions, it is no exaggeration to call this temple the most remarkable edifice in the capital—or indeed in the empire. The native name is *Ki-kien Tien*, or 'Temple of Prayer for the Year.' In the interior, the large shrines of carved wood for the tablets correspond to the movable blue wooden huts which on days of sacrifice are put up on the Southern Altar. Here, upon some day following the first of spring (Feb. 6), the Emperor offers his supplications to Heaven for a blessing upon the year. In times of drought, prayer for rain is also made at this altar, the Emperor being obliged to proceed on foot, as a repentant suppliant, to the 'Hall of Peni-

MONUMENT, OR TOPE, OF A LAMA. HWANG SZ', PEKING.

tent Fasting,' a distance of three miles. A green furnace for burnt-offerings lies to the south-east of this, as of the North Altar; while in the open park not far from the two and seventy cloisters are seven great stones, said to have fallen from heaven and to secure good luck to the country.

Across the avenue upon which is situated this great inclosure of the *Tien Tan*, is the *Sien Nung Tan*, or 'Altar dedicated to Shinnung,' the supposed inventor of agriculture. These precincts are about two miles in circumference, and contain four separate altars: to the gods of the heavens, of the earth, of the planet Jupiter, and to Shinnung. The worship here is performed at the vernal equinox, at which time the ceremony of ploughing a part of the inclosed park is performed by the Emperor, assisted by various officials and members of the Board of Rites. The district magistrates and prefect also plough their plats; but no one touches the imperial portion save the monarch himself. The first two altars are rectangular; that to the gods of heaven, on the east, is 50 feet long and 4½ feet high: four marble tablets on it contain the names of the gods of the clouds, rain, wind, and thunder. That to the gods of earth is 100 feet long by 60 wide; here the five marble tablets contain the names of celebrated mountains, seas, and lakes in China. Sacrifices are offered to these divinities at various times, and, with the prayers presented, are burned in the furnaces, thus to come before them in the unseen world; the idea which runs through them partakes of the nature of homage, not of atonement.

Nearly one-half of the Chinese City is empty of dwellings, much of the open land being cultivated; a large pond for rearing gold-fish near the *Tien Tan* is an attractive place. West of this city wall is an old and conspicuous dagoba in the *Tienning sz'*, nearly 200 feet high, and a landmark for the city gate. This part of Peking was much the best built when the Liao and Kin dynasties occupied it. West of the main city is the Temple of the Moon, and on the east side, directly opposite, stands the Temple to the Sun; the *Ti Tan*, or 'Altar to Earth,' is on the north over against the Altar to Heaven, just described. At all these the Emperor performs religious rites during the twelve months.

The inclosure of the Altar to Earth is smaller, and everything connected with the sacrifices is on an inferior scale to those conducted in the Altar to Heaven. The main altar has two terraces, each 6 feet high, and respectively 106 feet and 60 feet square; the tablet to Imperial Earth is placed on the upper with those to the Imperial Ancestors, and all are adored at the summer solstice. The bullock for sacrifice is afterwards buried and not burned. Adjoining the terraced altar on the south is a small tank for water.

About two miles from the *Ti Tan*, in a northerly direction, passing through one of the ruined gates of the Peking of Marco Polo's time on the way, is found the *Ta-chung sz'*, or 'Bell Temple,' in which is hung the great bell of Peking. It was cast about 1406, in the reign of Yungloh, and was covered over in 1578 by a small temple. It is 14 feet high, including the umbones, 34 feet in circumference at the rim, and 9 inches thick; the weight is 120,000 lbs. av.; it is struck by a heavy beam swung on the outside. The Emperor cast five bells in all, but this one alone was hung. It is covered with myriads of Chinese characters, both inside and out, consisting of extracts from the *Fah-hwa King* and *Ling-yen King*, two Buddhist classics. In some respects this may be called the most remarkable work of art now in China; it is the largest suspended bell in the world. A square hole in the top prevents its fracture under the heaviest ringing.[1]

A short distance outside the northern gate, *Tah-shing Măn*, is an open ground for military reviews, and near it a Buddhist temple of some note, called *Hwang sz'*, containing in its enceinte a remarkable monument erected by Kienlung. In 1779 the Teshu Lama started for Peking with an escort of 1,500 men; he was met by the Emperor near the city of Si-ning in Kansuh, conducted to Peking with great honor, and lodged in this temple for several months. He died here of small-pox, November 12, 1780, and this cenotaph of white marble was erected to his

[1] Compare Kircher, *China Illustrata*, where an engraving of it may be seen. A bell near Mandalay, mentioned by Dr. Anderson, is 12 feet high, 16 feet across the lips, and weighs 90 tons—evidently a heavier monster than this in Peking. (*Mandalay to Momien*, p. 18.)

memory; the body was inclosed in a gold coffin and sent to the Dalai Lama at Lhassa in 1781. The plinth of this beautiful work contains scenes in the prelate's life carved on the panels, one of which represents a lion rubbing his eyes with his paw as the tears fall for grief at the Lama's death.

The Summer Palace at *Yuen-ming Yuen* lies about seven miles from the north-west corner of Peking, and its entire circuit is reckoned to contain twelve square miles. The country in this direction rises into gentle hills, and advantage has been taken of the original surface in the arrangement of the different parts of the ground, so that the whole presents a great variety of hill and dale, woodlands and lawns, interspered with pools, lakes, caverns, and islets joined by bridges and walks, their banks thrown up or diversified like the free hand of nature. Some parts are tilled, groves or tangled thickets occur here and there, and places are purposely left wild to contrast the better with the cultivated precincts of a palace, or to form a rural pathway to a retired temple or arbor. Here were formerly no less than thirty distinct places of residence for various palace officials, around which were houses occupied by eunuchs and servants, each constituting a little village.

But all was swept away by the British and French troops in 1860, and their ruins still remain to irritate the officials and people of Peking against all foreigners. Near the Summer Palace is the great cantonment of Hai-tien, where the Manchu garrison is stationed to defend the capital, and whose troops did their best in the vain effort to stay the attack in 1860. As a contrast to the proceedings connected with this approach of the British, an extract from Sir John Davis's *Chinese* (chap. x.) will furnish an index of the changed condition of things.

"It was at a place called Hai-tien, in the immediate vicinity of these gardens, that the strange scene occurred which terminated in the dismissal of the embassy of 1816. On his arrival there, about daylight in the morning, with the commissioners and a few other gentlemen, the ambassador was drawn to one of the Emperor's temporary residences by an invitation from Duke Ho, as he was called, the imperial relative charged with the conduct of the negotiations. After passing through an open court, where were assembled a vast number of grandees in their dresses of ceremony, they were shown into a wretched room, and soon encompassed by a well-dressed crowd, among whom were princes of the blood by dozens, wearing yellow girdles. With a childish and unmannerly curiosity, consistent enough with the idle and disorderly life which many of them are said to lead, they examined the persons and dress of the gentlemen without ceremony; while these, tired with their sleepless journey, and disgusted at the behavior of the celestials, turned their backs upon them, and laid themselves down to rest. Duke Ho soon appeared, and surprised the ambassador by urging him to proceed directly to an audience of the Emperor, who was waiting for him. His lordship in vain remonstrated that to-morrow had been fixed for the first audience, and that tired and dusty as they all were at present, it would be worthy neither of the Emperor nor of himself to wait on his majesty in a manner so unprepared. He urged, too, that he was unwell, and required immediate rest. Duke Ho became more and more pressing, and at length forgot himself so far as to grasp the ambassador's arm violently, and one of the others stepped up at the same time. His lordship immediately shook them off, and the gentlemen crowded about him; while the highest indignation was expressed at such treatment, and a determined resolution to proceed to no audience this morning. The ambassador at length retired, with the appearance of satisfaction on the part of Duke Ho, that the audience should take place to-morrow. There is every reason, however, to suppose that this person had been largely bribed by the heads of the Canton local government to frustrate the views of the embassy, and prevent an audience of the Emperor. The mission, at least, was on its way back in the afternoon of the same day."

The principal part of the provisions required for the supply of this immense city comes from the southern provinces, and from flocks reared beyond the wall. It has no important manufactures, horn lanterns, wall papers, stone snuff-bottles, and pipe mouth-pieces, being the principal. Trade in silks, foreign fabrics, and food is limited to supplying the local demand, inasmuch as a heavy octroi duty at the gates restrains all enterprise. No foreign merchants are allowed to carry on business here. The government of Peking differs from that of other cities in the empire, the affairs of the department being separated from it, and administered by officers residing in the four circuits into which it is divided. "A minister of one of the Boards is appointed superintendent of the city, and subordinate to him is a *fuyin*, or mayor. Their duties consist in having charge of the metropolitan domain, for the purpose of extending good government to its four divisions. They have under them two district magistrates, each of whom rules half the city; none of these officers are subordinate to the provincial governor, but carry affairs which they cannot determine to the Emperor. They preside or assist at many of the festivals observed in the capital, superintend the military police, and hold the courts which take cognizance of the offences committed there."[1]

The thoroughfares leading across Peking, from one gate to the other, are broad, unpaved avenues, more than a hundred feet wide, which appear still wider owing to the lowness of the buildings; the centre is about two feet higher than the sides. The cross-streets in the main city are generally at right angles with them, not over forty feet wide, and for the most part occupied with dwellings. The inhabitants of the avenues are required to keep them well sprinkled in summer; but in rainy weather they are almost impassable from the mud and deep puddles, the level surface of the ground, and obstructed, neglected drains, preventing rapid drainage. The crowds which throng these avenues, some engaged in various callings, along the sides or in the middle of the way, and others busily passing and repassing, together with the gay appearance of the signboards, and an air of business in the shops, render the great streets of the Chinese metropolis very bustling, and to a foreigner a most interesting scene. Shop-fronts can be entirely opened when necessary; they are constructed of panels or shutters fitting into grooves, and secured to a row of strong posts which set into mortises. At night, when the shop is

---

[1] *Chinese Repository*, Vol. IV., p. 181.

closed, nothing of it is seen from without; but in the daytime, when the goods are exposed, the scene becomes more animated.

The sign-boards are often broad planks, fixed in stone bases on each side of the shop-front, and reaching to the eaves, or above them; the characters are large and of different colors, and in order to attract more notice, the signs are often hung with various colored flags, bearing inscriptions setting forth the excellence of the goods. The shops in the outer city are frequently constructed in this manner, others are made more compact for warmth in winter, but as a whole they are not brilliant in their fittings. Their signs are, when possible, images of the articles sold and always have a red pennon attached; the finer shop-fronts are covered with gold-leaf, brilliant when new, but shabby enough when faded, as it soon does. The appearance of the main streets exhibits therefore a curious mixture of decay and renovation, which is not lessened by the dilapidated temples and governmental buildings everywhere seen, all indicating the impoverished state of the exchequer. In many parts of the city are placed *pai-lau*, or honorary gateways, erected to mark the approach to the palace, and worthy, by their size and ornamental entablatures, to adorn the avenues and impress the traveller, if they were kept in good condition.

The police of the city is connected with the Bannermen, and is, on the whole, efficient and successful in preserving the peace. During the night the thoroughfares are quiet; they are lighted a little by lanterns hanging before the houses, but generally are dark and cheerless. In the metropolis, as in all Chinese cities, the air is constantly polluted by the stench arising from private vessels and public reservoirs for urine and every kind of offal, which is all carefully collected by scavengers. By this means, although the streets are kept clean, they are never sweet; but habit renders the people almost insensible to this as well as other nuisances. Carts, mules, donkeys and horses are to be hired in all the thoroughfares. The Manchu women ride astride; their number in the streets, both riding and walking, imparts a pleasant feature to the crowd, which is not seen in cities further south. The extraordinary length and elaborateness of marriage and funeral processions daily passing through the avenues, adds a pretty feature to them, which other cities with narrow streets cannot emulate.

The environs beyond the suburbs are occupied with mausolea, temples, private mansions, hamlets, and cultivated fields, in or near which are trees, so that the city, viewed from a distance, appears as if situated in a thick forest. Many interesting points for the antiquarian and scientist are to be found in and around this old city, which annually attracts more and more the attention of other nations. Its population has decreased regularly since the death of Kienlung in 1797, and is now probably rather less than one million, including the immediate suburbs. The climate is healthy, but subject to extremes from zero to 104°; the dryness during ten months of the year is, moreover, extremely irritating. The poor, who resort thither from other parts, form a needy and troublesome ingredient of the population, sometimes rising in large mobs and pillaging the granaries to supply themselves with food, but more commonly perishing in great numbers from cold and hunger. Its peace is always an object of considerable solicitude with the imperial government, not only as it may involve the personal safety of the Emperor, but still more from the disquieting effect it may have upon the administration of the empire. The possession of this capital by an invading force is more nearly equivalent to the control of the country than might be the case in most European kingdoms, but not as much as it might be in Siam, Burmah, or Japan. The good influences which may be exerted upon the nation from the metropolis are likewise correspondingly great, while the purification of this source of contamination, and the liberalizing of this centre of power, now well begun in various ways, will confer a vast benefit upon the Chinese people.[1]

Chihlí contains several other large cities, among which Pau-

---

[1] Compare the *Annales de la Foi*, Tome X., p. 100, for interesting details concerning the Romish missionaries in Peking. Also Pauthier's *Chine Moderne*, pp. 8–36 (Paris, 1852), containing an excellent map. Bretschneider's *Archeological and Historical Researches on Peking*, etc., published in the *Chinese Recorder*, Vol. VI. (1875, passim). *Mémoires concernant l'Histoire, les Sciences, les Arts, les Moeurs, les Usages, etc., des Chinois, par les Missionnaires de Pekin;* 16 vols., Paris, 1797–1814. N. B. Dennys, *Notes for Tourists in the North of China;* Hongkong, 1866.

ting, the former residence of the governor-general, and Tientsin, are the most important. The former lies about eighty miles south-west of the capital, on the Yungting River and the great road leading to Shansí. The whole department is described as a thoroughly cultivated, populous region; it is well watered, and possesses two or three small lakes.

Tientsin is the largest port on the coast above Shanghai. Owing, however, to the shallowness of the gulf and the bar at the mouth of the Pei ho, over which at neap tide only three or four feet of water flow, the port is rendered inaccessible to large foreign vessels. Its size and importance were formerly chiefly owing to its being the terminus of the Grand Canal, where the produce and taxes for the use of the capital were brought. Mr. Gutzlaff, who visited Tientsin in 1831, described it as a bustling place, comparing the stirring life and crowds on the water and shores outside of the walls of the city with those of Liverpool. The enormous fleet of grain junks carrying rice to the capital is supplemented by a still greater number of vessels which take the food up to Tung chau. Formerly the coast trade increased the shipping at Tientsin to thousands of junks, including all which lined the river for about sixty miles. This native trade has diminished since 1861, inasmuch as steamers are gradually ousting the native vessels, no one caring to risk insurance on freight in junks. The country is not very fertile between the city and the sea, owing to the soda and nitre in the soil; but scanty crops are brought forth, and these only after much labor; one is a species of grass (*Phragmites*) much used in making floor-mats. Sometimes the rains cause the Pei ho and its affluents to break over their banks, at which periods their waters deposit fertilizing matter over large areas.

The approach to Tientsin from the eastward indicates its importance, and the change from the sparsely populated country lying along the banks of the Pei ho, to the dense crowds on shore and the fleets of boats, adds greatly to the vivacity of its aspect. "If fine buildings and striking localities are required to give interest to a scene," remarks Mr. Ellis, "this has no claims; but, on the other hand, if the gradual crowding of junks till they become innumerable, a vast population, buildings, though not elegant, yet regular and peculiar, careful and successful cultivation, can supply these deficiencies, the entrance to Tientsin will not be without attractions to the traveller."[1] The stacks of salt along the river arrest the attention of the voyager; the immense quantity of this article collected at this city is only a small portion of the amount consumed in the interior. Tientsin will gradually increase in wealth, and now perhaps contains half a million of inhabitants. Its position renders it one of the most important cities in the empire, and the key of the capital.

Near the embouchure of the river is Ta-ku, with its forts and garrison, a small town noticeable as the spot where the first interview between the Chinese and English plenipotentiaries was held, in August, 1840; and for three engagements between the British and Chinese forces in 1858, 1859, and 1860. The general aspect of the province is flat and cheerless, the soil near the coast unproductive, but, as a whole, rich and well cultivated, though the harvests are jeopardized by frequent droughts.

The port of Peking is Tung chau on the Pei ho, twelve miles from the east gate, and joined to it by an elevated stone causeway. All boats here unload their passengers and freight, which are transported in carts, wheelbarrows, or on mules and donkeys. The city of Tung chau presents a dilapidated appearance amidst all its business and trade, and its population depends on the transit of goods for their chief support. The streets are paved, the largest of them having raised footpaths on their sides. The houses indicate a prosperous community. A single pagoda towers nearly 200 feet above them, and forms a waymark for miles across the country. Tung chau is only 100 feet above the sea, from which it is distant 120 miles in a direct line; consequently, its liability to floods is a serious drawback to its permanent prosperity.

Another city of note is Siuenhwa fu, finely situated between the branches of the Great Wall. Timkowski remarks, "the crenated wall which surrounds it is thirty feet high, and puts one in mind of that of the Kremlin, and resembles those of

[1] *Journal of Lord Amherst's Embassy to China*, 2d ed., p. 22. London, 1840

several towns in Russia; it consists of two thin parallel brick walls, the intermediate space being filled with clay and sand. The wall is flanked with towers. We passed through three gates to enter the city: the first is covered with iron nails; at the second is the guard-house; we thence proceeded along a broad street, bordered with shops of hardware; we went through several large and small streets, which are broad and clean; but, considering its extent, the city is thinly peopled."[1]

The department of Chahar, or Tsakhar, lies beyond the Great Wall, north and west of the province, a mountainous and thinly settled country, chiefly inhabited by Mongol shepherds who keep the flocks and herds of the Emperor.[2]

In the north-east of their grounds lies the thriving town of Dolon-nor (*i.e.*, Seven Lakes), or Lama-miao, of about 20,000 Chinese, founded by Kanghí. The Buddhist temples and manufactories of bells, idols, praying machines, and other religious articles found here, give it its name, and attract the Mongols, whose women array themselves in the jewelry made here. It is in latitude 42° 16′ N., about ten miles from the Shangtu River, a large branch of the river Liao, on a sandy plain, and is approached by a road winding among several lakes. North-west of Dolon-nor are the ruins of the ancient Mongolian capital of Shangtu, rendered more famous among English reading people by Coleridge's exquisite poem—

> In Xanadu did Kubla Khan
> A stately pleasure-dome decree:
> Where Alph, the sacred river, ran
> Through caverns measureless to man
> Down to a sunless sea.
> So twice five miles of fertile ground
> With walls and towers were girdled round—

than by Marco Polo's relation, which moved the poet to pen the lines. It was planned as Mukden now is, an outer and inner wall inclosing separate peoples, and its tumuli will probably furnish many tablets and relics of the Mongol emperors, when

---

[1] *Travels of the Russian Mission through Mongolia to China*, Vol. I., p. 293. London, 1827.

[2] Williamson, *Journeys in North China*, Vol. II., p. 90.

carefully dug over. It was too far from Peking for the Manchu monarchs to rebuild, and the Ming emperors had no power there. It was visited in 1872 by Messrs. Grosvenor and Bushell of the British Legation; Dr. Bushell's description corroborates Polo's account and Gerbillon's later notices of its size.[1]

There are several lakes, the largest of which, the Peh hu, in the south-western part, connects with the Pei ho through the river Hü-to. The various branches of the five rivers, whose united waters disembogue at Ta-ku, afford a precarious water communication through the southern half of Chihlí. Their head-waters rise in Shansí and beyond the Great Wall, bringing down much silt, which their lower currents only partially take out into the gulf; this sediment soon destroys the usefulness of the channels by raising them dangerously near the level of the banks. The utilization of their streams is a difficult problem in civil engineering, not only here but throughout the Great Plain.

Near the banks of the Lan ho, a large stream flowing south from the eastern slopes of the Chahar Hills, past Yungping fu into the gulf, and about one hundred and seventy-four miles north of Ta-ku, lies Chingpeh, or Jeh-ho, the Emperor's country palace. The approach to it is through a pass cut out of the rock, and resembles that leading to Damascus. The imperial grounds are embraced by a high range of hills forming a grand amphitheatre, which at this point is extremely fine. This descent to the city presents new and captivating views at every turn of the road. The hunting grounds are inclosed by a high wall stretching twenty miles over the hills, and stocked with deer, elks, and other game. The Buddhist temples form the chief attraction to a visitor. The largest one is square and castellated, eleven stories high, and about two hundred feet on each of its sides; the stories are painted red, yellow and green alternating. There are several similar but smaller structures below this one, and on each of the first two or three series is a row of small chinaware pagodas of a blue color; their tiles are

[1] *Journal of the Roy. Geog. Soc.*, 1874. Yule's *Marco Polo*, Vol. I., pp. 263-268. *Cathay and the Way Thither*, Vol. I., p. 134. Gerbillon, *Mémoires concernant les Chinois* (Astley's ed.), Vol. IV., pp. 701–716. *Journal Asiatique*, Ser. II., Tome XI., p. 345. Huc, *Tartary, etc.*, Vol. I., p 34, 2d ed., London

likewise blue. In the bright sunlight the effect of these brilliant bands is very good, and the general neatness adds to the pleasing result of the gay coloring. Nearly a thousand lamas live about these shrines. The town of Jeh-ho (*i.e.*, Hot River) consists mostly of one street coiling around the hills near the palace; its inhabitants are of a higher grade than usual in Chinese cities, the greater part being connected with the government. The road through Ku-peh kau in the Great Wall from Peking to Jeh-ho is one of the best in the province, and the journey presents a variety of charming scenery; its chief interest to foreigners is connected with the visit there of Lord Macartney, in 1793.[1] This fertile prefecture is rapidly settling by Chinese, whose numbers are now not far from two millions.

The principal productions of Chihlí are millet and wheat, sorghum, maize, oats, and many kinds of pulse and fruits, among which are pears, dried and fresh dates (*Rhamnus*), apples and grapes; all these are exported. Coal, both bituminous and anthracite, exists in great abundance; one mode of using hard coal is to mix its dust with powdered clay and work them into balls and cakes for cooking and fuel. The province also furnishes good marble, granite, lime, and iron, some kinds of precious stones, and clay for bricks and pottery.

The province of SHANTUNG (*i.e.*, East of the Hills) has a long coast-line, its maritime border being more than half its whole circuit. It lies south of the Gulf of Pechele, south-east of Chihlí, north of Kiangsu, and borders on Honan, where the Yellow River divides the two. Most of its area is level, the hilly part is the peninsula portion, where the highest points rise too high to admit of cultivation. The Grand Canal enters the province on its course from Tientsin at Lintsing chau in the north-west, passing in a south-easterly direction to the old Yellow River, and adds greatly to its importance. The shores of the promontory are generally bold, and full of indentations, presenting several excellent harbors; no important river disembogues within the province, and on each side of the peninsula

---

[1] Sir G. L. Staunton, *Account of an Embassy from the King of Great Britain to the Emperor of China.* 2 vols. Lond., 1796.

the waters are shallow. Chifu, in the prefecture of Tăngchau, has the best harbor, and its trade will gradually draw toward it a large population. The hills along the shore have a remarkably uniform, conical shape, resembling the bonnets worn by officers. The hilly regions are arranged in a series of chains running across the promontory, the longest and highest of which runs with the general trend of the coast in Tai-ngan fu, some peaks reaching over five thousand feet, but most of them being under three thousand feet high. Their intervales are highly cultivated. The soil is generally productive, except near the shores of the gulf, where it is nitrous. Two crops are annually produced here as elsewhere in Northern China. The willow, aspen, ailantus, locust (*Sophora*), oak, mulberry, and conifera, are common trees; silk-worms fed on oak leaves furnish silk.

This province is one of the most celebrated in Chinese history, partly from its having been the scene of many remarkable events in the early history of the people up to B.C. 200, but more particularly from its containing the birthplaces of Confucius and Mencius, whose fame has gone over the earth. The inhabitants of the province are proud of their nativity on this score, much as the woman of Samaria was because Jacob's cattle had drunk water at the well of Sychar.

The high mountain called Tai shan, or 'Great mount,' is situated near Tai-ngan fu in this province. This peak is mentioned in the *Shu King* as that where Shun sacrificed to Heaven (B.C. 2254); it is accordingly celebrated for its historical as well as religious associations. It towers high above all other peaks in the range, as if keeping solitary watch over the country roundabout, and is the great rendezvous of devotees; every sect has there its temples and idols, scattered up and down its sides, in which priests chant their prayers, and practise a thousand superstitions to attract pilgrims to their shrines. During the spring, the roads leading to the Tai shan are obstructed with long caravans of people coming to accomplish their vows, to supplicate the deities for health or riches, or to solicit the joys of heaven in exchange for the woes of earth. A French missionary mentions having met with pilgrims going to it, one party of whom consisted of old dames, who had with infinite fatigue and discomfort come from the south of Honan, about three hundred miles, to "remind their god of the long abstinence from flesh and fish they had observed during the course of their lives, and solicit, as a recompense, a happy transmigration for their souls." The youngest of this party was 78, and the oldest 90 years.[1] Another traveller says that the pilgrims resort there during the spring, when there are fairs to attract them; high and low, official and commoner, men and women, old and young, all sorts gather to worship and traffic. A great temple lies outside the town, whose grounds furnish a large and secure area for the tents where the devotees amuse themselves, after they have finished their devotions. The road to the summit is about five miles, well paved and furnished with rest-houses, tea-stalls, and stairways for the convenience of the pilgrims, and shaded with cypresses. It is beset with beggars, men and women with all kinds of sores and diseases, crippled and injured, besieging travellers with cries and self-imposed sufferings, frequently lying across the path so as to be stepped upon. A vast number of them live on alms thus collected, and have scooped themselves holes in the side of the way, where they live; their numbers indicate the great crowds whose offerings support such a wretched throng on the hill.

The capital of the province is Tsínan, a well-built city of about 100,000 inhabitants It was an important town in ancient times as the capital of Tsí, one of the influential feudal States, from B.C. 1100 to its conquest by Chí Hwangtí about 230; the present town lies not far east of the Ta-tsing ho, or new Yellow River, and is accessible by small steamers from sea. It has hills around it, and is protected by three lines of defence, composed of mud, granite, and brick. Three copious springs near the western gate furnish pure water, which is tepid and so abundant as to fill the city moat and form a lake for the solace of the citizens whether in boats upon its bosom or from temples around its shores. Its manufactures are strong fabrics of wild silk, and ornaments of *liu-lí*, a vitreous substance like strass, of

[1] *Annales de la Foi*, 1844, Tome XVI., p. 421.

which snuff-bottles, bangles, cups, etc., are made in great variety, to resemble serpentine, jade, ice, and other things. East of Tsí-nan is the prefect city of Tsing chau, once the provincial capital, and the centre of a populous and fertile region. Tsíning chau is an opulent and flourishing place, judging from the gilded and carved shops, temples, and public offices in the suburbs, which stretch along the eastern banks of the Canal; just beyond the town, the Canal is only a little raised above the level of the extensive marshes on each side, and further south the swamps increase rapidly: when Amherst's embassy passed, the whole country, as far as the eye could reach, displayed the effects of a most extensive recent inundation. Davis adds, "The waters were on a level with those of the Canal, and there was no need of dams, which were themselves nearly under water, and sluices for discharging the superfluous water were occasionally observed. Clumps of large trees, cottages, and towers, were to be seen on all sides, half under water, and deserted by the inhabitants; the number of the latter led to the inference that they were provided as places of refuge in case of inundation, which must be here very frequent. Wretched villages occurred frequently on the right-hand bank, along which the tracking path was in some places so completely undermined as to give way at every step, obliging them to lay down hurdles of reeds to afford a passage." [1]

Lin-tsing chau, on the Yu ho, at its junction with the Canal, lies in the midst of a beautiful country, full of gardens and cultivated grounds, interspersed with buildings. This place is the dépôt for produce brought on the Canal, and a rendezvous for large fleets of boats and barges. Near it is a pagoda in good repair, about 150 feet high, the basement of which is built of granite, and the other stories of glazed bricks.

The towns and villages of Shantung have been much visited during the past few years, and their inhabitants have become better acquainted with foreigners, with whom increased intercourse has developed its good and bad results. The productions of this fertile province comprise every kind of grain and vege-

---

[1] *Sketches of China*, Vol. I., p. 257.

table found in Northern China, and its trade by sea and along the Canal opens many outlets for enterprising capital. Among its mineral productions are gold, copper, asbestos, galena, antimony, silver, sulphur, fine agates, and saltpetre; the first occurs in the beds of streams. All these yield in real importance, however, to the coal and iron, which are abundant, and have been worked for ages. Its manufactures supply the common clothing and utensils of its people; silk fabrics, straw braid woven from a kind of wheat, glass, cheap earthenware, and rugs of every pattern.

Mr. Stevens, an American missionary who visited Wei-hai wei and Chifu in 1837, gives a description of the people, which is still applicable to most parts of the province: "These poor people know nothing, from youth to old age, but the same monotonous round of toil for a subsistence, and never see, never hear anything of the world around them. Improvements in the useful arts and sciences, and an increase of the conveniences of life, are never known among them. In the place where their fathers lived and died, do they live, and toil, and die, to be succeeded by another generation in the same manner. Few of the comforts of life can be found among them; their houses consisted in general of granite and thatched roofs, but neither table, chair, nor floor, nor any article of furniture could be seen in the houses of the poorest. Every man had his pipe, and tea was in most dwellings. They were industriously engaged, some in ploughing, others in reaping, some carrying out manure, and others bringing home produce; numbers were collected on the thrashing-floors, winnowing, sifting and packing wheat, rice, millet, peas, and in drying maize, all with the greatest diligence. Here, too, were their teams for ploughing, yoked together in all possible ludicrous combinatious; sometimes a cow and an ass; or a cow, an ox and an ass; or a cow and two asses; or four asses; and all yoked abreast. All the women had small feet, and wore a pale and sallow aspect, and their miserable, squalid appearance excited an indelible feeling of compassion for their helpless lot. They were not always shy, but were generally ill-clad and ugly, apparently laboring in the fields like the men. But on several occasions, young ladies clothed in gay silks and satins, riding astride upon bags on donkeys, were seen. No prospect of melioration for either men or women appears but in the liberalizing and happy influences of Christianity."[1]

The province of SHANSÍ (*i.e.*, West of the Hills) lies between Chihlí and Shensí, and north of Honan; the Yellow River bounds it on the west and partly on the south, and the Great Wall forms most of the northern frontier. It measures 55,268 square miles, nearly the same as England and Wales, or the State of Illinois. This province is the original seat of the Chinese people; and many of the places mentioned and the scenes recorded in their ancient annals occurred within its borders. Its rugged surface presents a striking contrast to the level tracts in Chihlí and Shantung. The southern portion of Shansí, including the region down to the Yellow River, in all an area of 30,000 square miles, presents a geological formation of great simplicity from Hwai king as far north as Ping ting. The plain around the first-named city is bounded on the north by a steep, castellated range of hills which varies from 1,000 to 1,500 feet in height; it has few roads or streams crossing it. On reaching the top, an undulating table-land stretches northward, varying from 2,500 to 3,000 feet above the Plain, consisting of coal formation, above the limestone of the lower steep hills. About forty miles from those hills, there is a second rise like the first, up which the road takes one to another plateau, nearly 6,000 feet above the sea. This plateau is built up of later rocks, sandstones, shales, and conglomerates of green, red, yellow, lilac, and brown colors, and is deeply eroded by branches of the Tsin River, which finally flow into the Yellow River. This plateau has its north-west border in the Wu ling pass, beyond which begins the descent to the basin of the Făn River. That basin is traversed near its eastern side by the Hoh shan nearly to Taiyuen; its peaks rise to 8,000 feet in some places; the rocks are granite and divide the coal measures, anthracite lying on its eastern side and bituminous on the west, as far as the Yellow

[1] *Chinese Repository*, Vol. IV., pp. 308–335. W. H. Medhurst's *China*, chaps. xv.–xix.

River, and north as far as Ta-tung. On top of both plateaus is spread the loess deposit, varying in depth from ten to five hundred feet, and deeply gullied by water-courses in every direction, which expose coal and iron mines.

On the eastern side of Shansí the rocks are made up of ancient formations or deposits of the Silurian age, presenting a series of peaks, passes and ranges that render travel very difficult down to the Plain. By these outlying ranges the province is isolated from Chihlí, as no useful water communication exists. This coal and iron formation is probably the largest in the world, and when railroads open it up to easy access it can be readily worked along the water-courses. The northern part of the province is drained through the rivers ending at Tientsin. This elevated region cannot be artificially irrigated, and when the rainfall is too small or too late, the people suffer from famine. The northern and southern prefectures exhibit great diversity in their animal, mineral, and vegetable productions. Some of the favorite imperial hunting-grounds are in the north; from the coal, iron, cinnabar, copper, marble, lapis-lazuli, jasper, salt, and other minerals which it affords, the inhabitants gain much of their wealth. The principal grains are wheat and millet, a large variety of vegetables and fruits, such as persimmons, pears, dates and grapes. The rivers are not large, and almost every one of them is a tributary of the Yellow River. The Făn ho, about 300 miles long, is the most important, and empties into it near the south-western corner of the province, after draining the central section. East of this stream, as far as the headwaters of those rivers flowing into Chihlí, extends an undulating table-land, having a general altitude of 3,000 feet above the Plain. South of it runs the river Kiang, also an affluent of the Yellow River, and near this, in Kiai chau, is a remarkable deposit of salt in a shallow lake (18 miles long and 3 broad), which is surrounded by a high wall. The salt is evaporated in the sun under government direction, the product bringing in a large revenue; the adjacent town of Lung-tsüen, containing 80,000 inhabitants, is devoted to the business. Salt has been obtained from this region for two thousand years; the water in some of the springs is only brackish, and used in culinary operations. There are two smaller lakes nearer the Yellow River.

The iron obtained in the lower plateau, in the south-east near Tsih chau, is from clay iron-ore and spathic ore with hematite, which occurs in limestone strata at the bottom of the coal formations. It is extracted in a rude manner, but the produce is equal to any iron in the world, while its price is only about two cents a pound. The working and transportation of coal and iron employ myriads of people, though they are miserably paid. The province barely supplies its own cotton, but woollen garments and sheepskins are produced to make up the demand for clothing.

Taiyuen fu, the capital, lies on the northern border of a fertile plain, 3,000 feet above the sea level; this plain extends about 2,000 square miles, and owes its existence to the gradual filling up of a lake there, the waters having cut their way out, and left the river Făn to drain the surplus. Across the Ho shan range lies another basin of equal fertility and mineral wealth, in Ping-ting chau, where coal, iron, clay and stone exist in unlimited quantities. In the northern part of this province the Buddhist temples at Wu-tai shan in Tai chau draw vast crowds of votaries to their shrines. The hills in which they are built rise prominently above the range, and each celebrated locality is memorialized by its own particular divinity, and the buildings where he is worshipped. The presence of a living Buddha, or *Gegen*, here attracts thousands of Mongols from the north to adore him; their toilsome journey adding to the worth of the visit. Most of the lamas are from the north and west. The region north of this seems to be gradually losing its fertility, owing to the sand which is drifted by north winds from the Ortous steppes; and as all the hills are bare of trees, the whole of Shansí seems destined to increasing poverty and barrenness. Its inhabitants are shrewd, enterprising traders as well as frugal agriculturists; many of the bankers in the Empire are from its cities.

The great roads from Peking to the south-west and west pass through all the chief towns of this province, and when new probably equalled in engineering and construction anything of the kind ever built by the Romans. The stones with which they are paved average 15 inches in thickness. Few regions can exceed in natural difficulties some of the passes over the loess-covered tracts of this province, where the road must wind

View over the Loess-clefts from the Han-sing ling Pass, Shansi. From Richthofen.

through miles of narrow cuts in the light and tenacious soil, to emerge before a landscape such as that seen in the illustration.[1]

The province of HONAN (*i.e.*, South of the River) comprises some of the most fertile parts of the Plain, and, on account of its abundance and central position, early received the name of

---

[1] Richthofen, *China.* Band I. S. 68. Rev. Arthur Smith, *Glimpses of Travel in the Middle Kingdom.* Shanghai, 1875.

Chung Hwa Tí, or the 'Middle Flowery Land,' afterwards enlarged into *Chung Kwoh*, or 'Middle Kingdom.' Its form is an irregular triangle, and its size nearly the same as Shantung; it has Shansí and Chihlí on the north, Nganhwui on the south-east, Hupeh on the south and south-west, and Shensí on the west, bordering also on Shantung and Kiangsu. This area is divided into three basins, that of the Yellow River in the north, of the Hwai River on the south, and the Han River on the south-west; the last two are separated by a marked range of mountains, the Fuh-niu shan, which is regarded as the eastern terminus of the Kwănlun Mountains; it is about 300 miles long, and its eastern end is near Jü-ning fu. This range maintains an elevation of 4,000 to 6,000 feet, and is crossed at Nanchau, where a remarkable natural pass about 30 miles long, rising to 1,200 or 1,500 feet, affords the needed facilities for trade and travel between the central and northern provinces. The Peh and Tan rivers drain its southern slopes into the Han, and the eastern sides are abundantly watered by the numerous branches of the Hwai River as they flow into Hungtsih Lake. The northern portion of Honan along the Yellow River is level, fertile and populous, forming one of the richest portions of the province.

For its climate, productions, literary reputation, historical associations, and variety of scenery, this province takes a prominent rank. The earliest records of the Black-haired race refer to this region, and the struggles for dominion among feudal and imperial armies occurred in its plains. Its present difficulty of access from the coast will ere long be overcome by railroads, when its capabilities may be further developed, and the cotton, hemp, iron, tutenag, silk and coal be increased for exportation. The people at present consume their own food and manufactures, and only require a good demand to increase the quality and amounts and exchange them for other things. The three prefectures north of the Yellow River are low-lying; through these the waters of that river have recently found their way into the River Wei and thence to the Gulf of Pechele, at Măng-tsin or east of it; the gradual rise of the bed renders their levels nearly the same, while it makes the main stream so broad and shallow that it is of little use for navigation. These plains are traversed by wheelbarrows and carts, whose drivers and trundlers form a vast body of stalwart men constantly going about in their employment from one city to another.

Kaifung fu, or Pien-liang, the capital, is situated about a league from the southern bank of the Yellow River, whose bed is here elevated above the adjacent country. It was the metropolis from A.D. 960 to 1129, and has often suffered from attacks of armies as well as from inundations. The dikes are mostly on the northern shore, and exhibit the industry and unavailing efforts of the people for scores of leagues. During the period of the Manchu conquest Kaifung was defended by a loyal general, who, seeing no other resource against the invaders, broke down the embankments to drown them, by which manœuvre upwards of 300,000 of the inhabitants perished. The city was rebuilt, but it has not attained to its ancient splendor, if credit can be given to the *Statistics of Kaifung*, in which work it is described as having been six leagues in circuit in the twelfth century, approached by five roads, and containing numerous palaces, gardens, and government houses. The valley of the River Loh lies between the Yellow River and the Fuh-niu Mountains, a fertile, populous region wherein many of the remarkable events of Chinese history were enacted. Loh-yang, near Honan, was the metropolis at three different intervals, and probably further researches here will bring to light many ancient relics; rock-cut temples and old inscriptions, with graceful bas-reliefs, near the natural gate of Lung-măn, where the road crosses Sung shan, have already been seen. Owing to the direction of the roads leading through this region from the south and east, and the passes for travel towards the north-west, it will form a very important centre of trade in the future of Central Asia and western China.

The province of KIANGSU is named from the first syllable of the capital, Kiangning, joined to Su, part of the name of the richest city, Suchau. It lies along the sea-coast, in a north-westerly direction, having Shantung on the north, Nganhwui on the west, and Chehkiang on the south. The area is about 45,000 square miles, equalling Pennsylvania or a little less than

England by itself. It consists, with little interruption, of level tracts interspersed with lakes and marshes, through which flow their two noble rivers, which as they are the source of the extraordinary fertility of this region, so also render it obnoxious to freshes, or cover the low portions with irreclaimable morasses. The region of Kiangnan is where the beauty and riches of China are most amply displayed; "and whether we consider," remarks Gutzlaff, speaking of this and the adjoining province, "their agricultural resources, their great manufactures, their various productions, their excellent situation on the banks of these two large streams, their many canals and tributary rivers, these two provinces doubtless constitute the best territory of China." The staple productions are grain, cotton, tea, silk, and rice, and most kinds of manufactures are here carried to the greatest perfection. The people have an exceptional reputation for intelligence and wit, and although the province has long ceased to possess a court, its cities still present a gayer aspect, and are adorned with better structures than any others in the empire. This province was the scene of the dreadful ravages of the Tai-ping rebellion, and large districts are still desolate, while their cities lie waste.

Probably no other country of equal extent is better watered than Kiangsu. The Great River, the Grand Canal, many smaller streams and canals, and a succession of lakes along the line of the canal, afford easy communication through every part. The sea-coast has not been surveyed north of the Yangtsz', where it is unapproachable in large vessels; dykes have been constructed in some portions to prevent the in-flow of the ocean. The largest lake is the Hungtsih, about two hundred miles in circumference. South of it lies Kauyu Lake, and on the eastern side of the canal opposite is Pauying Lake, both of them broad sheets of water. Numerous small lakes lie around them. Tai hu, or 'Great Lake,' lies partly in Kiangsu and partly in Chehkiang, and is the largest in the province. Its borders are skirted by romantic scenery, while its bosom is broken by numerous islets, affording convenient resort to the fishermen who get their subsistence from its waters.

Kiangning fu (better known abroad as Nanking), the capital

of the province, is situated on the south shore of the Yangtsz', 194 miles from Shanghai. It was the metropolis from A.D. 317 to 582, and again for 35 years during the Ming dynasty (1368-1403). This city is the natural location of an imperial court, accessible by land and water from all quarters, and susceptible of sure defence. When the Tai-pings were expelled in 1865, the city was nearly destroyed, and has since that date only slowly revived. When Hungwu made it his capital, he strengthened the wall around it, inclosing a great area, 35 miles in circuit, which was never fully covered with buildings, and at present has a most ruinous appearance. Davis remarks the striking resemblance between Rome and Nanking, the area within the walls of both being partially inhabited, and ruins of buildings lying here and there among the cultivated fields, the melancholy remains of departed glory. Both of them, however, have now brighter prospects for the future.

The part occupied by the Manchus is separated by a cross wall from the Chinese town. The great extent of the wall renders the defence of the city difficult, besides which it is overlooked from the hills on the east, from one of which, the Chung shan, a wide view of the surrounding country can be obtained. On this eastern face are three gates; the land near the two toward the river is marshy, and the gates are approached on stone causeys. A deep canal runs up from the river directly under the walls on the west, serving to strengthen the approaches on that side. Nanking is laid out in four rather wide and parallel avenues intersected by others of less width; and though not so broad as those of Peking, are on the whole clean, well-paved, and bordered with handsomely furnished shops.

The only remarkable monuments of royalty which remain are several guardian statues situated not far from the walls. These statues form an avenue leading up to the sepulchre where the Emperor Hungwu was buried about 1398. They consist of gigantic figures like warriors cased in armor, standing on either side of the road, across which at intervals large stone tablets are extended, supported by great blocks of stone instead of pillars Situated at some distance are a number of rude colossal figures of horses, elephants, and other animals, all intended to represent the guardians of the mighty dead.[1]

Nothing made Nanking more celebrated abroad than the Porcelain Tower, called *Pao-ngăn tah*, or the 'Recompensing Favor Monastery,' which stood pre-eminent above all other similar buildings in China for its completeness and elegance, the material of which it was built, and the quantity of gilding with which its interior was embellished. It was erected by Yungloh to recompense the great favor of her majesty the Empress, and occupied 19 years (1411–1430) in its construction. It was maintained in good condition by the government, and three stories which had been thrown down by lightning in 1801 were rebuilt. The Tai-pings blew it up and carried off the bricks in 1856, fearing lest its geomantic influences should work against the success of their cause. As to its dimensions: Its form was octagonal, divided into nine equal stories, the circumference of the lower story being 120 feet, decreasing gradually to the top. Its base rested upon a solid foundation of brick-work ten feet high, up which a flight of twelve steps led into the tower, whence a spiral staircase of 190 steps carried the visitor to the summit, 261 feet from the ground. The outer face was covered with slabs of glazed porcelain of various colors, principally green, red, yellow, and white, the body of the edifice being brick. At every story was a projecting roof, covered with green tiles; from each corner and from the top of these roofs were suspended bells, numbering 150 in all.

This beautiful structure was visited in 1852 by Dr. Charles Taylor, an American missionary, who has left a full account of his observations.[2] It was to have been raised to an altitude of 329 feet and of thirteen stories, but only nine were built; careful measurement gave 261 feet as its height, $8\frac{1}{2}$ feet its thickness at top, and 12 feet at the base, where it was 96 feet 10 inches

---

[1] The curious reader can consult the article by Mayer, in Vol. XII. of the *North China Branch Royal Asiatic Society's Journal*, 1878, for the meaning of these various objects.

[2] *Five Years in China*, Nashville, Tenn., 1860. See also *Voyages of the Nemesis*, pp. 450–452, for further details of this city in 1842; the *Chinese Repository*, Vols. I., p. 257, and XIII., p. 261, contain more details on the Pagoda

in diameter. The facing was of bricks made of fine porcelain clay; the prevailing color was green, owing to the predominance of the tiles on the numerous stories. The woodwork supporting these successive roofs was strong, curiously carved and richly painted. The many-colored tiles and bricks were highly glazed, giving the building a gay and beautiful appearance, that was greatly heightened when seen in the reflected sunlight. When new it had 140 lamps, most of them hanging outside; and a native writer says "that when lighted they illumine the 33 heavens, and detect the good and evil among men, as well as forever ward off human miseries." The destruction of a building like this, from mere fanciful ideas, goes far to explain the absence of all old or great edifices in China.

Nanking has extensive manufactories of fine satin and crape, Nankeen cotton cloth, paper and ink of fine quality, and beautiful artificial flowers of pith paper. In distant parts of the empire, any article which is superior to the common run of workmanship, is said to be from Nanking, though the speaker means only that it was made in that region. It is renowned, too, for its scholars and literary character, and in this particular stands among the first places of learning in the country. It is the residence of the governor-general of three provinces, and consequently the centre of a large concourse of officials, educated men, and students seeking for promotion; these, with its large libraries and bookstores, all indicating and assisting litorary pursuits, combine to give it this distinguished position. In the monastery on Golden Island, near Chinkiang, a library was found by the English officers, but there was no haste in examining its contents, as they intended to have carried off the whole collection, had not peace prevented.

The city of Suchau now exceeds Nanking in size and riches. It is situated on islands lying in the Ta hu, and from this sheet of water many streams and canals connect the city with most parts of the department. The walls are about ten miles in circumference; outside of them are four suburbs, one of which is said to extend ten miles, besides which there is an immense floating population. The whole space includes many canals and pools connected with the Grand Canal and the lake, and presented in 1859 a scene of activity, industry, and riches which could not be surpassed elsewhere in China. The population probably then exceeded a million, including the suburbs. It lies north-west of Shanghai, the way passing through a continual range of villages and cities; the environs are highly cultivated, producing cotton, silk, rice, wheat, fruits, and vegetables. It was captured in 1860 by the rebels, and when retaken in 1865 was nearly reduced to a heap of ruins. It is, however, rapidly reviving, as the loss of life was comparatively small.

The Chinese regard this as one of their richest and most beautiful cities, and have a saying, "that to be happy on earth, one must be born in Suchau, live in Canton, and die in Liauchau, for in the first are the handsomest people, in the second the most costly luxuries, and in the third the best coffins." It has a high reputation for its buildings, the elegance of its tombs, the picturesque scenery of its waters and gardens, the politeness and intelligence of its inhabitants, and the beauty of its women. Its manufactures of silk, linen, cotton, and works in iron, ivory, wood, horn, glass, lackered-ware, paper, and other articles, are the chief sources of its wealth and prosperity; the kinds of silk goods produced here surpass in variety and richness those woven in any other place. Vessels can proceed up to the city by several channels from the Yangtsz' kiang, but junks of large burden anchor at Shanghai, or Sungkiang; the whole country is so intersected by natural and artificial watercourses, that the people have hardly any need for roads and carts, but get about in barrows and sedans. Small steamers find their way to every large village at high tide.

Chinkiang, situated at the junction of the Grand Canal with the Yangtsz' kiang, was captured by the British in July, 1842, at a great loss of life to its defenders; the Manchu general Hailing, finding the city taken, seated himself in his office, and set fire to the house, making it his funeral pyre. Its position renders it the key of the country, in respect to the transport of produce, taxes and provisions for Peking, inasmuch as when the river and canal are both blockaded, the supplies for the north and south are to a great extent intercepted. In times of peace the scenes at the junction afford a good exhibition of the industry and trade of the people. Barrow describes, in 1794, "the multitude of ships of war, of burden and of pleasure, some gliding down the stream, others sailing against it; some moving by oars, and others lying at anchor; the banks on either side covered with towns and houses as far as the eye could reach; as presenting a prospect more varied and cheerful than any that had hitherto occurred. Nor was the canal, on the opposite side, less lively. For two whole days we were continually passing among fleets of vessels of different construction and dimensions."[1]

The country in the vicinity is well cultivated, moderately hilly, and presents a characteristic view of Chinese life and action. "On the south-east, the hills broke into an undulating country clothed with verdure, and firs bordering upon small lakes. Beyond, stretched the vast river we had just ascended. In the other direction, the land in the foreground continued a low and swampy flat, leaving it difficult at a little distance to determine which of the serpentine channels was the main branch; there were innumerable sheets of water, separated by narrow mounds, so that the whole resembled a vast lake, intersected by causeways. Willows grew along their sides, and dwellings were erected on small patches somewhat higher than the common surface."[2] This whole country was the scene of dreadful fighting for many years. Between the Imperialists and Tai-pings the city was totally destroyed, so that in 1861 hardly a house was left. It is now regaining its natural trade and prosperity.

Near the mouth of the Grand Canal is Kin shan, or Golden Island,[3] a beautiful spot, covered with temples and monastic establishments. A pagoda crowns the summit, and there are many pavilions and halls, of various sizes and degrees of elegance, on its sides and at the base, many of them showing their imperial ownership by the yellow or green tiling. Since the river has been open to traffic, and the devastations of the Tai-pings have ceased, the priests have returned in small num-

---

[1] *Travels in China.* [2] Capt. G. G. Loch, *Events in China*, p. 74.
[3] Mentioned by Marco Polo. Yule's edition, Vol. II., p. 137.

bers to their abodes, but the whole settlement is a poor mockery of its early splendor. A similar one, rather larger, is found at Siung shan, or Silver Island, below Chinkiang; it is, however, on a less extensive scale, though in a beautiful situation. Priests are the only occupants; temples and palaces the principal buildings, surrounded by gardens and bowers. Massive granite terraces, decorated with huge stone monsters, are reached from the water by broad flights of steps; fine temples, placed to be seen, and yet shaded by trees, open pavilions, and secluded summer-houses, give it a delightful air of retreat and comfort, which a nearer inspection sadly disappoints.

The banks of the Yangtsz' during the 250 miles of its course through this province, are uniformly low, and no towns of importance occur close to them, as they would be exposed to the floods. The vast body of water, with its freight of millions of tons of silt goes on its way in a quiet equable current into the Yellow Sea. The dense population of the prefectures on the south bank, contrasted with the sparseness of the region between the Canal and seashore on the north side, indicate the comparative barrenness of the latter, and the difficulty of cultivating marshy lands so nearly level with the sea.

The largest seaport in Kiangsu is Shanghai (*i.e.*, Approaching the Sea), now become one of the leading emporia in Asia. It lies on the north shore of the Wusung River, about fourteen miles from its mouth, in lat. 31° 10′ N., and long. 121° 30′ E., at the junction of the Hwang-pu with it, and by means of both streams communicates with Suchau, Sungkiang, and other large cities on the Grand Canal; while by the Yangtsz' it receives produce from Yunnan and Sz'chuen. In these respects its position resembles that of New Orleans.

The town of Wusung is at the mouth of that river, here about a mile wide; and two miles beyond lies the district town of Paushan. The wall of Shanghai is three miles in circuit, through which six gates open into extensive suburbs; around the ramparts flows a ditch twenty feet wide. The city stands in a wide plain of extraordinary fertility, intersected by numerous streamlets, and affording ample means of navigation and communication; its population is estimated to be at present over 500,-

000, but the data for this figure are rather imperfect. Since it was opened to foreign commerce in 1843, the growth of the town has been rapid in every element of prosperity, though subject to great vicissitudes by reason of the rebellion which devastated the adjoining country. Its capture by the insurgents in 1851, and their expulsion in February, 1853, with the destruction of the eastern and southern suburbs in 1860, have been its chief disasters since that date. The native trade has gradually passed from the unwieldy and unsafe junks which used to throng the Hwang-pu east of the city, into steamers and foreign craft, and is now confined, so far as the vessels are concerned, to the inland and coast traffic in coarse, cheap articles.

Shanghai city itself is a dirty place, and poorly built. The houses are mostly made of bluish square brick, imperfectly burned; and the walls are constructed in a cellular manner by placing bricks on their edges, and covering them with stucco. The streets are about eight feet wide, paved with stone slabs, and in the daytime crowded with people. Silk and embroidery, cotton, and cotton goods, porcelain, ready-made clothes, beautiful skins and furs, bamboo pipes of every size, bamboo ornaments, pictures, bronzes, specimens of old porcelain, and other curiosities, to which the Chinese attach great value, attract the stranger's notice. Articles of food form the most extensive trade of all; and it is sometimes a difficult matter to get through the streets, owing to the immense quantities of fish, pork, fruit, and vegetables, which crowd the stands in front of the shops. Dining-rooms, tea-houses, and bakers' shops, are met with at every step, from the poor man who carries around his kitchen or bakehouse, altogether hardly worth a dollar, to the most extensive tavern or tea-house, crowded with customers. For a few cash, a Chinese can dine upon rice, fish, vegetables, and tea; nor does it matter much to him, whether his table is set in the streets or on the ground, in a house or on a deck, he makes himself merry with his chopsticks, and eats what is before him.[1] The buildings composing the Ching-hwang miao, and the grounds attached to this establishment, present a good

[1] Fortune's *Wanderings in China*, p. 120.

instance of Chinese style and taste in architecture. Large warehouses for storing goods, granaries, and temples, are common; but neither these, nor the public buildings, present any distinguishing features peculiar to this city alone.

The contrast between the narrow, noisome and reeking parts of the native city, and the clean, spacious, well-shaded and well-paved streets and large houses of the foreign municipalities, is like that seen in many cities in India. The Chinese are ready enough to enjoy and support the higher style of living, but they are not yet prepared to adopt and maintain similar improvements among themselves. The difficulty of being sure of the co-operation of the rulers in municipal improvements deters intelligent natives from initiating even the commonest sanitary enterprise of their foreign neighbors.

The remaining cities and districts of Kiangsu present nothing worthy of special remark. The Grand Canal runs from north to south, and affords a safe and ample thoroughfare for multitudes of boats in its entire length. Tsing-kiang-pu and Hwai-ngan, near the old Yellow River, receive the traffic from the north and Hungtsih Lake, while Yangchau near the Yangtsz' River, takes that going north. In this part of the channel, constant dyking has resulted in raising the banks; the city of Hwai-ngan, for example, lies below the canal which brings trade to its doors, and may one day be drowned by its benefactor. Salt is manufactured in the districts south of the Yellow River, where the people cultivate but rare patches of arable land.

The island of Tsungming, at the mouth of the Yangtsz', is about sixty miles long, and sixteen wide, containing over nine hundred square miles, and is gradually enlarging by the constant deposits from the river; it is flat, but contains fresh water. It is highly cultivated and populous, though some places on the northern side are so impregnated with salt, and others so marshy, as to be useless for raising food. This island produces a variety of *kaoliang* or sorghum (*Holcus*), which is sweet enough to furnish syrup, and is grown for that purpose in the United States.

The province of NGANHWUI was so named by combining the

first words in its two large cities, Nganking and Hwuichau, and forms the south-western half of Kiangnan; it is both larger and more uneven than Kiangsu, ranges of hills stretching along the southern portions, and between the River Hwai and the Yangtsz'. It lies in the central and southern parts of the Plain, north of Kiangsí, west of Kiangsu and Chehkiang, and between them and Honan and Hupeh. Its productions and manufactures, the surface, cultivation of the country, and character of the people, are very similar to those of Kiangsu, but the cities are less celebrated. The terrible destruction of life in this province during the Tai-ping rule has only been partially remedied by immigration from other provinces; it will require years of peace and industry to restore the prosperous days of Taokwang's reign.

The surface of the country is naturally divided into that portion which lies in the hilly regions around Hwaichau and Ningkwoh connected with the Tsientang River, the central plain of the Yangtsz' with its short affluents, and the northern portion which the River Hwai drains. The southern districts are superior for climate, fertility, and value of their products to most parts of the Empire; and the numerous rivulets which irrigate and open their beautiful valleys to traffic with other districts, render them attractive to settlers. No expense has been spared in erecting and preserving the embankments along the streams, whose waters are thereby placed at the service of the farmers.

The Great River passes through the south from south-west to north-east; several small tributaries flow into it on both banks, one of which connects with Chau hu, or Nest Lake, in Luchau fu, the principal sheet of water in the province. The largest section is drained by the River Hwai and its branches, which flow into Hungtsih Lake; most of these are navigable quite across to Honan. The productions comprise every kind of grain, vegetables, and fruit known in the Plain; most of the green tea districts lie in the south-eastern parts, particularly in the Sunglo range of hills in Hwuichau prefecture. Silk, cotton, and hemp are also extensively raised; but excepting iron, few metals are brought to market.

The provincial capital, Nganking or Anking, lies close to the northern shore of the Kiang. Davis describes the streets as very narrow, and the shops as unattractive; the courts and gateways of many good dwelling-houses presented themselves as he passed along the streets. "The palace of the governor we first took for a temple, but were soon undeceived by the inscriptions on the huge lanterns at the gateway. These official residences seldom display any magnificence. The pride of a Chinese officer of rank consists in his power and station, and as the display of mere wealth attracts little respect, it is neglected more than in any country of the world. The best shops that we saw were for the sale of horn lanterns and porcelain. They possess the art of softening horn by the application of a very high degree of moist heat, and extending it into thin laminæ of any shape. These lamps are about as transparent as ground-glass, and, when ornamented with silken hangings, have an elegant appearance." During the fifty years since his visit, this large city has been the sport of prosperous and adverse fortunes, and is now slowly recovering from its demolition during the Tai-ping rebellion. It is situated on rising ground near the base of a range of hills far in the north, the watershed of two basins.

The banks of the river, between Nanking and Nganking, a distance of 300 miles, are well cultivated, and contain towns and villages at short intervals. The climate, the scenery, the bustle on the river near the towns, and the general aspect of peaceful thrift along this reach, makes it on ordinary occasions one of the bright scenes in China. Wuhu hien, about sixty miles above Nanking, lies near the mouth of the Hwangchi, a stream connecting it with the back country, and making it the mart for much of that trade. It was next in importance to Chinkiang, but its sufferings between the rebels and imperialists nearly destroyed it. The revival in population and trade has been encouraging, and its former importance is sure to revive.

Hwuichau (or in Cantonese, Fychow) is celebrated, among other things, for its excellent ink and lackered-ware. Fung-yang (*i.e.*, the Rising Phœnix), a town lying north-west of Nanking, on the River Hwai, was intended, by Hungwu, the founder of the Ming dynasty, to have been the capital of the Empire instead of Nanking, and was thus named in anticipation of its future splendor.

The province of KIANGSÍ (*i.e.*, West of the River) lies south of Nganhwui and Hupeh, between Chehkiang and Fuhkien on the east, and Hunan on the west, reaching from the Yangtsz' to the Mei ling on the south. Its form is oblong, and its entire area is made up of the beautiful basin of the Kan kiang, including all the affluents and their minor valleys. The hilly portions form part of the remarkable series of mountainous ridges, which cover all south-eastern and southern China, an area of about 300,000 square miles, extending from Ningpo south-westerly to Annam. It is made up of ranges of short and moderate hills, cut up by a complicated net of water-courses, many of which present a succession of narrow defiles and gentle valleys with bottom lands from five to twelve miles wide. That part of this region in Kiangsí has an irregular watershed on the east, separating it from the Min basin, and a more definite divide on the west from Hunan and its higher mountains. The province entire is a little larger than all New England, or twice the size of Portugal, but, in population, vastly exceeds those countries. The surface of the land is rugged, and the character of the inhabitants partakes in some respects of the roughness of their native hills. It is well watered and drained by the River Kan and its tributaries, most of which rise within the province; the main trunk empties into Poyang Lake by numerous mouths, whose silt has gradually made the country around it swampy. For many miles on its eastern and southern banks extends an almost uninhabitable marsh, presenting a dreary appearance. The soil, generally, is productive, and large quantities of rice, wheat, silk, cotton, indigo, tea, and sugar, are grown and exported. It shares, in some degree, the manufactures of the neighboring provinces, especially in Nankeen cloth, vast quantities of which are woven here, but excels them all in the quality and amount of its porcelain. The mountains produce camphor, varnish, oak, banian, fir, pine, and other trees; those on the west are well wooded, but much of the timber has been carried away during the late rebellion, and left the hill-sides bare and profitless.

Nanchang, the provincial capital, lies near the southern shore of the Poyang Lake; the city walls are six miles in circuit, and accessible by water from all sides. The character of its population is not favorable among their countrymen, and owing to the difficulty of reaching it from the Yangtsz', it escaped the ruin and rapine which befel Kiukiang. Small steamers can come up to its jetties, but as the tea and porcelain are shipped on the south-east side of the lake, Nanchang is not likely to become a large mart; few of the cities above it can ever be reached by steamers. Barrow estimated that there were, independent of innumerable small craft, 100,000 tons of shipping lying before the place. The banks of the Kan kiang, near the lake, are flat, and not highly cultivated, but the scenery becomes more varied and agreeable the further one ascends the stream; towns and villages constantly come in sight, and the cultivation, though not universal, is more extended. Among other sights on this river are the bamboo water-wheels, which are so built on the steep banksides, that the buckets lift their freight 20 or 25 feet, and pour it out in a ceaseless stream over the fields. The flumes thrown out into the stream to turn a stronger current on the wheel, often seriously interfere with navigation. Many pagodas are seen on either bank of this water-course, some of them undoubtedly extremely old. As the voyager ascends the river, several large cities are passed, as Linkiang, Kih-ngan, Kanchau, and Nan-ngan (all capitals of departments), besides numerous towns and villages; so that if the extent of this river and the area of the valley it drains be considered, it will probably bear comparison with that of any valley in the world for populousness, amount and variety of productions, and diligence of cultivation.

Beyond Kihngan are the Shihpah tan, or 'Eighteen Rapids,' which are torrents formed by ledges of rocks running across the river, but not of such height or roughness as to seriously obstruct the navigation except at low water. The shores in their vicinage are exceedingly beautiful. The transparency of the stream, the bold rocks fringed with wood, and the varied forms of the mountains, call to mind those delightful streams that are discharged from the lakes and north counties of England. The hilly banks are in many places covered with the Camellia oleifera, whose white blossoms give them the appearance of snow, when the plant is in flower. Kanchau is the town where large boats are obliged to stop; but Nan-ngan is at the head of navigation, about three hundred miles from the lake, where all goods for the south are debarked to be carried across the Mei ling, or 'Plum Pass.'

Within the department of Jauchau in Fauliang hien, east of Poyang Lake, are the celebrated porcelain manufactories of Kingteh chin, named after an Emperor of the Sung dynasty, in whose reign, A.D. 1004, they were established. This mart still supplies all the fine porcelain used in the country, but was almost wholly destroyed during the rebellion, the kilns broken up, and the workmen dispersed to join the rebels or die from want. The million of workmen said to have been employed there thirty years ago are now only gradually resuming their operations, and slowly regaining their prosperity. The approach to the spot is announced by the smoke, and at night it appears like a town on fire, or a vast furnace emitting flames from numerous vents, there being, it is said, five hundred kilns constantly burning. Kingteh chin stands on the river Chang in a plain flanked by high mountains, about forty miles north-east from Jauchau, through which its ware is distributed over the empire.

Genius in China, as elsewhere, renders a place illustrious, and few spots are more celebrated than the vale of the White Deer in the Lü hills, near Nankang, on the west side of Lake Poyang, where Chu Hí, the great commentator of Confucius, lived and taught, in the twelfth century. It is a secluded valley about seven miles from the city, situated in a nook by the side of a rivulet. The unpretending buildings are comprised in a number of different courts, evidently intended for use rather than show. In one of the halls, the White Deer is represented, and near by a tree is pointed out, said to have been planted by the philosopher's own hand. This spot is a place of pilgrimage to Chinese literati at the present day, for his writings are prized by them next to their classics. The beauty and sublimity of this region are lauded by Davis, and its praises are frequent themes for poetical celebration among native scholars.[1]

The maritime province of CHEHKIANG, the smallest of the eighteen, lies estward of Kiangsi and Nganhwui, and between Kiangsu and Fuhkein north and south, and derives its name from the river Cheh or 'Crooked,' which runs across its southern part. Its area is 39,000 square miles, or nearly the same as Ohio; it lies south-east of the plain at the end of the Nan shan, and for fertility, numerous water-courses, rich and populous cities, variety of productions, and excellence of manufactures, is not at all inferior to the larger provinces. Baron Richthofen's letter to the Shanghai Chamber of Commerce, July 25, 1871, contains a good account of its topography. The whole province produces cotton, silk, tea, rice, ground nuts, wheat, indigo, vegetable tallow (*stillingia*), and pulse, in abundance. It possesses within its limits every requisite for the food and clothing of its inhabitants, while the excellence of its manufactures insures it in exchange a supply of the luxuries of other regions.

The rivers in Chehkiang rise in the province; and, as might be inferred from the position of the hills, their course is generally short and the currents rapid. Fourteen principal streams are enumerated, of which the Tsientang is the most important. The main branch of this river rises in the southern districts in two head-waters, which join at Küchau fu and run thence into Hangchau Bay. The bore which comes up into this river fifteen miles, as far as Hangchau, is the only one along the coast. As its wall of water approaches the city, the junks and boats prepare by turning their bows to meet it, and usually rise over its crest, 6 or 10 feet at times, without mishap. The basin of the Tsientang River measures nearly half of the province; by means of rafts and boats the people transport themselves and their produce for about 300 miles to its head-waters. The valley of Lanki is the largest of the bottom lands, 140 miles long and 5 to 15 wide, and passes north through a gorge 70 miles in length into the lower valley, where it receives

[1] Davis's *Sketches*, Vol. II., p. 55.

the Sin-ngan River from the west in Nganhwui, and thus communicates with Hwuichau at times of high water. It is just fitted for the rafting navigation of the region, and by means of its tortuous channels each one of the 29 districts in its entire basin can be reached by water.

The forest and fruit trees of Chehkiang comprise almost every valuable species known in the eastern provinces. The larch, elcococcus, camphor, tallow, fir, mulberry, varnish, and others, are common, and prove sources of wealth in their timber and products. The climate is most salubrious; the grains, vegetables, animals, and fishes, furnish food; while its beautiful manufactures of silk are unrivalled in the world, and have found their way to all lands. Hemp, lackered- and bamboo-wares, tea, crockery, paper, ink, and other articles, are also exported.

The inhabitants emulate those in the neighboring regions for wealth, learning, and refinements, with the exception of the hilly districts in the south bordering on Kiangsí and Fuhkien. The dwellers of these upland valleys are shut out by position and inclination, so that they form a singularly clannish race. Their dialects are peculiar and very limited in range, and each group of villagers suspects and shuns the others. They are sometimes rather turbulent, and in some parts the cultivation of the mountain lands is interdicted, and a line of military posts extends around them in the three provinces, in order to prevent the people from settling in their limits; though the interdiction does not forbid cutting the timber growing there.[1]

Hangchau, the capital of the province, lies in the northern part, less than a mile from the Tsientang. The velocity of this stream indicates a rapid descent of the country towards the ocean, but it discharges very little silt; the tide rises six or seven feet opposite the city, and nearly thirty at the mouth.

Only a moiety of the inhabitants reside within the walls of the city, the suburbs and the waters around them supporting a large population. A portion of the space in the north-western part is walled off for the accommodation of the Manchu garri-

---

[1] See *Chinese Repository*, Vol. IV., p. 488; *Journal of N. C. Br. R. A. Society*, Vol. VI., pp. 123–128; and *Chinese Recorder*, Vol. I., 1869, pp. 241-248. These people are relics of tribes of Miaotsz'.

son, which consists of 7,000 troops. The governor-general of Chehkiang and Fuhkien has an official house here, as well, also, as the governor of the province, but since the increased importance of Fuhchau, he seldom resides in this city; these, with their courts and troops, in addition to the great trade passing through, render it one of the richest and most important cities in the empire. The position is the most picturesque of any of the numerous localities selected by the Chinese for their capital. It lies in full view of the ocean, and from the hill-top in the centre a wide view of the plains south and east is obtained. The charming lake, Si Hu, and the numerous houses on its shores, with the varied scenery of the hills, copses, glades, and river banks, all highly cultivated, within a radius of ten miles, fully bear out the praises of the Chinese as to its singular beauty. Marco Polo lavishes all his admiration upon its size, riches, manufactures, and government, from which it is to be inferred that it suffered little in the Mongolian conquest. He visited the place when governor of Yangchau in 1286, and enthusiastically describes it as "beyond dispute the finest and the noblest in the world."[1] The Chinese have a proverb—*Shang yu tien tang: Hia yu Su Hang*—the purport of which is that Hangchau and Suchau are fully equal to paradise; but the comparison of the Venetian traveller gives one a poorer idea of the European cities of his day, than it does of the magnificence of the Chinese, to those who have seen them. The streets are well-paved, ornamented with numerous honorary tablets erected to the memory of distinguished individuals, and agreeably interrupting the passage through them. The long main street extending along the Grand Canal into and through the city, thence out by the Tsientang, was, before its ruthless demolition by the Tai-pings in 1863, probably one of the finest streets in the whole Empire. The shops and warehouses, in point of size and stock of goods contained in them, might vie with the best in London. In population, luxury, wealth, and influence this city rivals Suchau, and for excellence of manufactures probably exceeds the latter place. Were Hangchau easily reached by

---

[1] Yule's *Marco Polo*, Vol. II., p. 145.

sea, and had it ample harbors, it would engross the trade of the eastern coast; but furious tides (running sometimes 11½ knots an hour); the bore jeoparding passage-boats and other small crafts; sand banks and quicksands;—these present insuperable difficulties to the commerce by the ocean.

This city was the metropolis of the country during the nine latter princes of the Sung dynasty (1129 to 1280), when the northern parts were under dominion of the tribe of Kin Tartars. One cause of celebrity is found in the beauty of its environs, especially those near the Si Hu, or West Lake, an irregular sheet of water about 12 miles in circuit. Barrow observes that "the natural and artificial beauties of this lake far exceeded anything we had hitherto had an opportunity of seeing in China. The mountains surrounding it were lofty, and broken into a variety of forms that were highly picturesque; and the valleys were richly clothed with trees of different kinds, among which three species were remarkably striking, not only by their intrinsic beauty, but also by the contrast they formed with themselves and the rest of the trees of the forest. These were the camphor and tallow trees, and the arbor vitæ. The bright, shining green foliage of the first, mingled with the purple leaves of the second, and over-topped by the stately tree of life, of the deepest green, produced a pleasing effect to the eye; and the landscape was rendered still more interesting to the mind by the very singular and diversified appearance of several thousand repositories of the dead upon the sloping sides of the inferior hills. Here, as well as elsewhere, the sombre and upright cypress was destined to be the melancholy companion of the tombs.

"Higher still, among the woods, avenues had been opened to admit of rows of small blue houses, exposed on white colonnades, which, on examination, were also found to be mansions of the dead. Naked coffins, of extraordinary thickness, were everywhere lying on the surface of the ground. The margins of the lake were studded with light aerial buildings, among which one of more solidity and greater extent than the rest was said to belong to the emperor. The grounds were inclosed with brick walls, and mostly planted with vegetables and fruit trees;

but in some there appeared to be collections of such shrubs and flowers as are most esteemed in the country." [1]

Staunton speaks of the lake as a beautiful sheet of water, perfectly pellucid, full of fish, in most places shallow, and ornamented with a great number of light and fanciful stone bridges, thrown across the arms of the lake as it runs up into the hills. A stone tower on the summit of a projecting headland attracted attention, from its presenting a different architecture from that usually seen in Chinese buildings. This tower, called the *Lui Fung tah*, *lit.* 'Tower of the Thunder Peak' (not Thundering Wind, as Staunton renders it), from the hill being at first owned by Mr. Lui, was built about A.D. 950, and is to-day a solid structure, though much ruined. It has now four stories, and is about 120 feet high; something like a regular order is still discernible in the moldering cornices. The legend of the White Snake is associated with this structure, and people constantly carry away pieces of its bricks as charms.

An interesting corroboration of this account is given by Polo, who says, "Inside the city there is a lake which has a compass of some 30 miles; and all around it are erected beautiful palaces and mansions, of the richest and most exquisite structure that you can imagine, belonging to the nobles of the city. There are also on its shores many abbeys and churches of the idolaters. In the middle of the lake are two islands, on each of which stands a rich, beautiful and spacious edifice, furnished in such a style as to seem fit for the palace of an emperor. And when any one of the citizens desired to hold a marriage feast, or to give any other entertainment, it used to be done at one of these palaces." [2]

The splendor and size of the numerous Buddhist temples in and around Hangchau attracted travellers to the city more even than did its position; these shrines have, however, all been destroyed, and their thousands of priests driven away; the Taipings left no building untouched. The Yoh Miao stands near the north-west corner of the Si Hu, and contains the tombs of the patriot general Yoh Fi of the Sung dynasty (A.D. 1125), and his son, who were unjustly executed as traitors. Two conical

---

[1] *Travels in China*, p. 522. [2] Yule's *Marco Polo*, Vol. II., p. 146.

mounds mark their resting places, and separated by a wall, but inside the inclosure are four iron statues cast in a kneeling posture and loaded with chains,—on his right Tsin Kwei and his wife, on the left a judge and general, who subserved Tsin Kwei's hatred of Yoh Fi by their flagitious conduct. All four are here doing homage and penance to this just man whom they killed, and by the obloquy they receive serve as a warning to other traitors. In a temple, called *Ting-tsz' sz'*, not far from the city, the party of the Dutch embassy were well lodged, and attended by three hundred priests. The establishment was in good repair, and besides two guardian monsters more than thirty feet high, near the entrance, contained five hundred images of the Buddhist Arhans, with miniature pagodas of bronze, of beautiful workmanship.

Hangchau is better known abroad for manufactures of silk than for any other fabrics, but its position at the termination of the Canal may perhaps give its name to many articles which are not actually made there, for Huchau is now a greater dépôt for raw and woven silks. In the northern suburbs lies an irregular basin, forming the southern extremity of the Canal; but between the river and the basin there is no communication, so that all goods brought hither must be landed. The city contains, among other public buildings, a mosque, bearing an inscription in Arabic, stating that it is a "temple for Mussulmen, when travelling, who wish to consult the Koran."[1] It is higher than the adjacent buildings, and adorned with a cupola, pierced with holes at short intervals. It was spared in 1863, as not being an idolatrous temple. There are also several others in the city, it being a stronghold of Islamism in China. Water communication exists between Hangchau and Yüyau, south-east through Shauhing, and thence to Ningpo, by means of which goods find their way to and from the capital. A good road also runs between the two former cities; indeed, elsewhere in the province the thoroughfares are very creditable; they are laid with broad slabs of granite and limestone, and lead over plains and hills in numberless directions.

---

[1] De Guignes, *Voyages à Peking*, Vol. II., pp. 65–77.

Ningpo fu ('Peaceful Wave city') is the next important city in Chehkiang, in consequence of its foreign relations. It is admirably situated for trade and influence, at the junction of three streams, in lat. 29° 55′ N., and long. 121° 22′ E.; the united river flows on to the ocean, eleven and a half miles distant, under the name of the Tatsieh. Opposite the city itself, there are but two streams, but the southern branch again subdivides a few miles south-west of Ningpo. Its population has been variously estimated from one-fourth to one-third of a million, and even more, including the suburban and floating inhabitants. This place was called *King-yuen* by the Sung, and received its present name from the Mongols. It was captured in 1862 by the insurgents, who were deterred from destroying it by the presence of foreign men-of-war; the prosperity of the mart has since increased. When foreigners first resorted to China for trade, Ningpo soon became a centre of silk and other kinds of commodities; the Portuguese settled there, calling it *Liampo*, which is the same name. It is, moreover, an ancient city, and its Annals afford full information upon every point interesting to a Chinese antiquarian, though a foreigner soon tires of the many insignificant details mixed up with a few valuable statements.[1]

"The plain in which Ningpo lies is a magnificent amphitheatre, stretching away from twelve to eighteen miles on one side to the base of the distant hills, and on the other to the verge of the ocean. As the eye travels along, it catches many a pleasing object. Turn landward, it will see canals and water-courses, fields and snug farm-houses, smiling cottages, family residences, hamlets and villages, family tombs, monasteries and temples. Turn in the opposite direction, and you perceive a plain country descending toward the ocean; but the river alive with all kinds of boats, and the banks studded with ice-houses, most of all attract the attention. From without the city, and while still

---

[1] Compare R. M. Martin's *China* (Vol. II., p. 304), who gives considerable miscellaneous information about the open ports, previous to 1846; also Dennys' *Treaty Ports of China*, 1867, pp. 326–349; Richthofen's *Letters*, No. 5, 1871; Yule's *Marco Polo*, Vol. II., p. 181; *Missionary Recorder*, 1869, pp. 156, 177.

upon the ramparts, look within its walls, you will be no less gratified. Here there is nothing European, little to remind you of what you have seen in the west. The single-storied and the double-storied houses, the heavy prison-like family mansions, the family vaults and graveyards, the glittering roofs of the temples, the dilapidated official residences, the deserted literary and examination halls, and the prominent sombre Tower of Ningpo, are entirely Chinese. The attention is also arrested for a moment or two by ditches, canals, and reservoirs of water, with their wooden bridges and stone arches."[1] Two serious drawbacks to a residence here are the stifling heat of summer and the bad quality of the water.

The circumference of the walls is nearly five miles; they are about twenty-five feet high, fifteen feet wide at the top, and twenty-two at the base, built solidly, though somewhat dilapidated, and overgrown with grass. A deep moat partly surrounds them; commencing at the North gate, it runs on the west, south, and south-east side as far as Bridge gate, a distance of nearly three miles, and is in some places forty yards wide. Its constant use as a thoroughfare for boats insures its repair and proper depth; the other faces of the city are defended by the river. There are six gates, and two sally-ports near the south and west approaches intended for the passage of the boats that ply on the city canals.

On the east is Bridge gate, within which, and near the walls, the English factory was once situated. This opening leads out to the floating bridge; the latter structure is two hundred yards long and five broad, made of planks firmly lashed, and laid upon sixteen lighters closely linked and chained together, but which can be opened. A busy market is held on the bridge, and the visitor following the lively crowd finds his way to an extensive suburb on the opposite side. Ferry boats ply across both streams in vast numbers, adding greatly to the vivacity of the scene. The custom-house is situated beyond the bridge, and this eastern suburb contains several buildings of a religious

---

[1] Milne, in *Chinese Repository*, Vol. XIII., p. 22, and in his *Life in China*, part second. London, 1857.

and public character, lumber-yards, dock-yards, and rows of ice-houses, inviting the notice of the traveller. The environs beyond the north gate are not so thickly settled as those across the rivers; the well cultivated fields, divided and irrigated by numerous water-courses, with scattered hamlets, beguile the visitor in his rambles, and lead him onward.

There are numerous temples and monasteries, and a large variety of assembly-halls, governmental offices, and educational establishments, but none of these edifices are remarkable in an architectural point of view. The assembly-halls or club-houses are numerous, and in their internal arrangements form a curious feature of native society. It is the practice among residents or merchants from other provinces, to subscribe and erect on the spot where they are engaged in business, a temple, dedicated to the patron deity of their native province, in which a few priests are supported, and plays acted in its honor. Sometimes the building is put in charge of a layman, called a "master of ceremonies," and the current expenses defrayed by subscription. The club-houses are places of resort for travellers from the several provinces or districts, and answer, moreover, to European coffee-houses, in being points where news from abroad is heard and exchanged.

The streets are well paved, and interrupted here and there by honorary portals of considerable size and solidity, which also give variety to an otherwise dull succession of shops and signboards, or dead walls. Two small lagoons afford space for some aquatic amusements to the citizens. One called Sun Lake is only a thousand yards in circuit; the other, called Moon Lake, is near the West gate, and has three times its perimeter. Both are supplied by sluices passing through the city gates, while many canals are filled from them, which aid in irrigating the suburbs. Some of the pleasantest residences of the city are built on their banks.

Among interesting edifices is the *Tien-fung tah* (*i.e.*, Heaven-conferred pagoda), a hexagonal seven-storied tower upward of 160 feet high, which, according to the *Annals of Ningpo*, was first erected 1100 years ago, though during that period it has been destroyed and rebuilt several times. Upon the authority

TEMPLE OF THE GODDESS MA TSU-PU, NINGPO.

of this work, the tower was constructed before the city itself, and its preservation is considered as connected with the good luck of the place. The visitor mounts to the summit by a flight of narrow stone steps, ascending spirally within the walls.

The most elegant and solid building of the city lies on the water's edge outside the walls, between the East and Bridge gates; it is a temple dedicated to the marine goddess Ma Tsupu, and was founded by Fuhkien men in the 12th century, but the present structure was erected in 1680, and largely endowed. Its ornaments are elaborate and rich, and its appearance on festival days, gay and animated in an unusual degree. The lanterns and scrolls hanging from the ceiling attract attention by the curious devices and beautiful characters written and drawn on them in bright colors, while the walls are concealed by innumerable drawings.

Chinhai, at the mouth of the river, is so situated by nature and fortified by art, that it commands the passage. Its environs were the scene of a severe engagement between the Chinese and English in October, 1841, on which occasion great slaughter was committed upon the imperial troops. The town lies at the foot of a hill on a tongue of land on the northern bank of the river, and is partly sheltered from the sea on the north by a dyke about three miles long, composed of large blocks of hewn granite, and proving an admirable defence in severe weather. The walls are twenty feet high and three miles in circumference, but the suburbs extend along the water, attracted by, and for the convenience of, the shipping. Merchant ships report here when proceeding up the river, along whose banks the scenery is diversified, while the water, as usual in China, presents a lively scene. Numerous ice-houses are seen constructed of thick stone walls twelve feet high, each having a door on one side and an incline on the other for the removal and introduction of the ice, and protected by straw and a heavily thatched roof.

The Chusan archipelago forms a single district of which Tinghai is the capital; it is divided into thirty-four *chwang* or townships, whose officers are responsible to the district magistrate. The southern limit of the group is Quesan or the Kiu shan islands, in lat. 29° 21′ N., and long. 121° 10′ E., consisting of eleven islets, the northernmost of which is False Saddle Island; their total number is over a hundred. Tinghai city lies on the southern side of Chau shan or Boat Island, which gives its name on foreign maps to the whole group. It is twenty miles long, from six to ten wide, and fifty one and a half in circumference. The archipelago seems to be the highest portion of a vast submarine plain, geologically connected with the Nan shan range on the Continent and the mountains in Kiusiu and Nippon; it is a pivot for the changes in weather and temperature observed north and south of this point along the coast.

The general aspect of these islands and the mainland, is the same beautiful alternation of hills and narrow valleys, everywhere fertile and easily irrigated, with peaks, cascades, and woodlands interspersed. In Chusan itself the fertile and well-watered valleys usually reach to the sea, and are furnished with dykes along the beach, which convert them into plains of greater or less extent, through which run canals, used both for irrigation and navigation. Rice and barley, beans, yams, sweet potatoes, etc., are grown; every spot of arable soil being cultivated, and terraces constructed on most of the slopes. The view from the tops of the ridges, looking athwart them, or adown their valleys, or to seaward, is highly picturesque. The prevailing rocks belong to the ancient volcanic class, comprising many varieties, but principally clay-stone, trachyte, and compact and porphyritic felspar. The brief occupation of this island by the British forces in 1841 led to no permanent improvement in the condition of the people, and it has neither trade nor minerals sufficient to attract capital thither. Owing in part, perhaps, to this poverty, Tinghai escaped the ravages of the Tai-pings, and has now recovered from the damage sustained by its first capture.

Puto and a few smaller islands are independent of civil jurisdiction, being ruled by the abbot of the head monastery. This establishment, and that on Golden Island in the Yangtsz' are among the richest and best patronized of all the Buddhist monasteries in China; both of them have been largely favored by emperors at different periods.

Puto is a narrow islet, $3\frac{1}{2}$ miles long, and lies $1\frac{1}{2}$ miles from the eastern point of Chusan. Its surface is covered with sixty monasteries, pavilions, temples, and other religious buildings, besides grottos and sundry monuments of superstition, in which at least 2,000 idle priests chant the praises of their gods. One visitor describes his landing and ascending "a broad and well-beaten pathway which led to the top of one of the hills, at every crag and turn of which we encountered a temple or a grotto, an inscription or an image, with here and there a garden tastefully laid out, and walks lined with aromatic shrubs, which diffused a grateful fragrance through the air. The prospect from these heights was extremely delightful; numerous islands, far and near, bestudded the main, rocks and precipices above and below, here and there a mountain monastery rearing its head, and in the valley the great temple, with its yellow tiles indicative of imperial distinction, basked like a basilisk in the noonday-sun. All the aid that could be collected from nature and from Chinese art, was here concentrated to render the scene enchanting. But to the eye of the Christian philanthropist it presented a melancholy picture of moral and spiritual death. The only thing we heard out of the mouths of the priests was Ometo Fuh; to every observation that was made, re-echoed Ometo Fuh; and the reply to every inquiry was Ometo Fuh. Each priest was furnished with a rosary which he was constantly counting, and as he counted repeated the same senseless, monotonous exclamation. These characters met the eye at every turn of the road, at every corner of the temples, and on every scrap of paper; on the bells, on the gateways, and on the walls, the same words presented themselves; indeed the whole island seemed to be under the spell of this talismanic phrase, and devoted to recording and re-echoing Ometo Fuh."[1] The pristine glory of these temples has become sadly dimmed, many of the buildings present marks of decay, and some of the priesthood are obliged to resort to honest labor in order to gain a living. Deaths in their number are supplied by purchasing youths, who are taught nothing but re-

[1] Medhurst's *China, its State and Prospects*, p. 393.

ligious literature, a fit training to stunt their minds to pursue the dull mummery of singing Ometo Fuh. The two imperial temples present good specimens of Chinese architecture; but they as well as all other things to be seen at Puto are dilapidated and effete.

Temples were erected on this island as early as A.D. 550, and since it became a resort for priests it seems to have enjoyed the patronage of the government. The goddess of Mercy is said to have visited this spot, and her image is the principal object of worship. No females are allowed to live on the island, nor any persons other than the priests, unless in their employ. The revenues are derived from rent of the lands belonging to the temples, from the collection of those priests who go on begging excursions over the Empire, and from the alms of pilgrims who resort to this agreeable locality. It appears like one of the most beautiful spots on the earth when the traveller lands, just such a place as his imagination had pictured as exclusively belonging to the sunny East, and so far as nature and art can combine, it is really so: but here the illusion ends. Idleness and ignorance celibacy and idolatry, vice, dirt, and dilapidation, in the inmate or in their habitations, form a poor back-ground for the well dressed community, and gay, variegated prospect seen when stepping ashore.

A town of considerable importance in this province is Chapu, about fifty miles north-west from Chinhai, across Hangchau Bay, and connected with that city through a luxuriant plain by a well-paved causeway about thirty miles long. Chapu was the port of Hangchau, and when it possessed the entire trade with Japan, boasted of being the largest mart on the seacoast of Chehkiang. The town lies at the bottom of a bay on the western face of some hills forming its eastern point; and at low tide the mud extends a long way from the lowland. The suburbs are situated near a small headland; the walled town stands about half a mile behind. When attacked by the British in May, 1842, the walls were found in poor condition, but the Manchu garrison stationed here upheld their ancient reputation for bravery. This body of troops occupies a separate division of the city, and their cantonment is planned on the model of a camp. The outer defences are numerous, but most of the old fortifications are considerably decayed. The country in the vicinity is highly cultivated, and possesses an unusual number of finely constructed, substantial houses.

South-west from Chapu lies the old town of Canfu (called Kanpu by the Chinese), which was once the port of Hangchau, but now deserted, since the stream on which it is situated has become choked with sand. This place is mentioned in the voyages of two Arabian travellers in the ninth century, as the chief port of China, where all shipping centred. The narrow entrance between Buffalo Island and Kitto Point is probably the Gates of China mentioned by them; and Marco Polo, in 1290, says, "The Ocean Sea comes within 25 miles of the city at a place called Ganfu, where there is a town and an excellent haven, with a vast amount of shipping which is engaged in the traffic to and from India and other foreign parts. . . . And a great river flows from the city of Kinsay to that sea-haven, by which vessels can come up to the city itself."[1] Marsden erroneously supposes Kanpu to be Ningpo. If this was in fact the *only* port allowed to be opened for foreign trade, it shows that, even in the Tang dynasty, the same system of exclusion was maintained that has so recently been broken up; though at that date the Emperors in Shansí had very little authority along the southern coasts. The changes in the Bay of Hangchau have been more potent causes for the loss of trade, and Yule reasonably concludes that the upper part of it is believed to cover now the old site in Polo's time.

The province of FUHKIEN (*i.e.* Happily Established) is bounded on the north by Chehkiang, north-west and west by Kiangsí, south-west by Kwangtung, and east by the channel of Formosa. Its western borders are determined, for the most part, by the watershed of the basins of the rivers Min and Kan; a rugged and fertile region of the Nan shan. The line of seacoast is bold, and bordered with a great number of islands, whose lofty granitic or trappean peaks extend in precipitous,

---

[1] Yule's *Marco Polo*, Vol. II., p. 149. *Cathay and the Way Thither*, p. cxciii. Reinaud, *Relations des Voyages faits par les Arabes dans l'Inde et à la Chine, etc.* (Paris, 1845), Tome I., p. 19.

barren headlands from Namoh as far as the Chusan archipelago. In the general features of its surface, the islands on its coasts, and its position with reference to the ocean, it resembles the region lying east of New Hampshire in the United States; including Formosa, it about equals Missouri in size.

The River Min is formed by the union of three large streams at Yenping fu; it drains all the country lying east of the Wu-í (Bohea) hills, or about three-fourths of the province. It is more than three hundred miles long, and owing to its regular depth, is one of the most useful streams in China; twenty-seven walled towns stand on its banks. The tide rises eighteen or twenty feet at the entrance, and this, with the many islands and reefs, renders the approach difficult. At Min-ngan hien, about fourteen miles from the mouth, the stream is contracted to less than half a mile for about three miles, the water being from twelve to twenty-five fathoms deep; the hills on each side rise from fifteen hundred to two thousand feet. One traveller speaks of the walls of its forts and batteries, in this part, as affording a sort of stairs for the more convenient ascent of the hills on which they are situated. From the top, "the view embraces a beautiful scene; nothing can be more picturesque than the little plats of wheat and barley intermixing their yellow crops on the acclivities with bristling pines and arid rocks, and crowned with garden spots, or surrounded with rice fields and orchards of oranges. The valley of the Min, viewed from the summit of the fortress, is truly a beautiful sight."[1] The scenery on this river, though of a different character, will bear comparison with that of the Hudson for sublimity and beauty; the hills are, however, much higher, and the country less fruitful, on the Min.

Beyond Pagoda Anchorage the passage is too shallow for large vessels, and this obstacle tends to prevent Fuhchau from becoming a place of commerce in keeping with its size and geographical advantages. From the city upwards the river is partially obstructed with rocks and banks, rendering the navigation troublesome as far as Mintsing hien, about thirty miles

[1] Borget, *La Chine Ouverte*, p. 126.

above it, beyond which the strong rapids render the passage to Yenping extremely tedious,—in high water impossible even with trackers. The banks are steep, and the tow-rope is sometimes taken 50 to 70 feet above the water.

Mr. Stevens says of this river, that "bold, high, and romantic hills give a uniform yet ever varying aspect to the country; but it partakes so much of the mountainous character, that it may be truly said that beyond the capital we saw not one plain even of small extent. Every hill was covered with verdure from the base to the summit. The less rugged were laid out in terraces, rising above each other sometimes to the number of thirty or forty. On these the yellow barley and wheat were waving over our heads. Here and there a laborer, with a bundle of grain which he had reaped, was bringing it down on his shoulder to thrash out. Orange, lemon, and mulberry, or other trees, sometimes shaded a narrow strip along the banks, half concealing the cottages of the inhabitants."[1]

Next in size is the Lung kiang, which flows by Changchau, and disembogues near Amoy after a course of two hundred miles. A large number of small islands lie on the coast of Fuhkien, the first of which, on the west, is Namoh or Nan-au, about thirteen miles long. Amoy and Quemoy are the largest islands of a group lying off the estuary of the Lung kiang. Chimmo Bay is north-east of Amoy, and is the entrance of the passage up to Chinchew, or Tsiuenchau fu, the *Zayton*[2] of Marco Polo, and still celebrated for the commercial enterprise of its inhabitants. Before the introduction of steamers into the coasting trade, the harbors and creeks along the provinces of Fuhkien and Kwangtung were infested with numerous fleets of pirates, which used to "sneak about like rats," and prey upon the peaceful traders.

The grain raised in Fuhkien is hardly enough to support its

---

[1] *Chinese Repository*, Vol. IV., p. 92.

[2] Yule's *Marco Polo*, Vol. II., pp. 183–185, etc. A Turkish geography, printed at Constantinople, describes this port under the name of *Zeitoun*. Compare Klaproth, *Mémoires sur l'Asie*, Tome II., p. 208. See further, *Chinese Recorder*, Vol. III., p. 87; Vol. IV., p. 77; Vol. V., p. 327, and Vol. VI., p. 31, sqq.

population, especially on the sea-board, and large quantities of rice are brought from Siam, Formosa, and elsewhere. Black tea, camphor and other woods, sugar, chinaware, and grass-cloth, are the principal exports.

The city of Fuhchau (*i.e.*, Happy City), or Hokchiu, as it is called by the inhabitants, lies in lat. 26° 5′ north, and long. 119° 20′ east, on the northern side of the Min, thirty-four miles from its mouth, and nine from Pagoda Island. The city lies in a plain, surrounded by hills, forming a natural and most magnificent amphitheatre of vast dimensions, whose fertility emulates and adds to its beauty. Suburbs extend from the walls three miles to the banks, and stretch along on both sides the stream. They are connected with each other, and a small islet in the river, by a stone bridge built in the eleventh century. The scenery is bold, and such parts of the surrounding hills as are not cultivated or used for graves, are covered with pines; some of the hills north of the city are three thousand feet high. Opposite Fuhchau the land is lower, and the suburb is built upon an island formed by the division of the main channel, seven miles above the city; the branches reunite at Pagoda Island. This island, and the plain on each side, forms a large basin, about twenty miles long by fifteen wide. The river is crowded with floating habitations, ferry-boats, and trading craft, rendering its surface an animated and noisy scene. The flowers grown in pots on the boats, and those usually worn by the boatwomen in their hair, all assist in imparting a pleasing aspect to the lively sight.

The city walls are about thirty feet high and twelve wide at the top. The gates, seven in number, are overlooked by high towers; smaller guard-houses stand upon the walls at short intervals, in which a few soldiers lodge, and where two or three cannon indicate their object. The city is divided into wards and neighborhoods, each of which is under its own police and headmen, who are responsible for the peace of their respective districts.

From the Wu-shih shan, an eminence on the south of the city, the view is extensive, and presents a great diversity of charming objects. The square battlements of the wall are seen extending in a devious and irregular circuit for more than eight miles, and inclosing most of the buildings, except on the south. On the south-east, a hill rises abruptly more than two hundred feet, its sides built up with interspersed dwellings; and another on the extreme north of the city, surmounted by a watch-tower, closes the prospect in that direction. Two pagodas within, and fantastic looking watch-towers upon the walls, large, regular-built granaries, and a vast number of flag-staffs in pairs indicating temples and offices, contribute to relieve the otherwise dull monotony, which is still further diversified by many large trees. Several lookout houses are placed over the streets, or upon the roofs of buildings, for the accommodation of watchmen, one of which immediately attracts the attention of the visitor, from its height, and its clock-dial with Roman letters. Few vacant spaces occur within the walls of the city, which is everywhere equally well built.

Serpentine canals divide the country round about into plats of greater or less extent, of every form and hue; while they help drain the city and provide channels for boats coming from the river. These parts of the landscape are dotted with hamlets and cottages, or, where the ground is higher, with graves and tombstones. To one seated on this eminence, the confused hum of mingling cries ascending from the town below, —the beating of gongs, crackling of fireworks, reports of guns, vociferous cries of hucksters and coolies, combining with the barking of dogs and other domestic sounds, as well as those from the crows, fish-hawks, and magpies nearer by,—inform him in the liveliest manner that the beautiful panorama he is looking down upon is filled with teeming multitudes in all the tide of life. On the western side of the city is a sheet of water, called Si Hu, or West Lake, with a series of unpretending buildings and temples lying along its margin, a bridge crossing its expanse, and fishing-nets and boats floating upon its bosom. The watch-tower, on the hill in the northern part of the city, is upon the wall, which here runs near a precipice two hundred feet high; it is a most conspicuous object when approaching the place.

The Manchus occupy the eastern side of the city, and number altogether about 8,000 persons; the natives generally are not allowed to enter their precincts. They live under their own officers, in much the same style as the Chinese, and, not having any regular occupation, give no little trouble to the provincial authorities. Though vastly larger than Ningpo, the number of temples and substantial private residences in Fuhchau is much less, and as a whole it is not so well built. The streets are full of abominations, for which the people seem to care very little. Before foreign trade attained importance, paper money used to be issued by native mercantile firms in the city, varying in denomination from forty cents to a thousand dollars, and supplying all the advantages with few of the dangers of bank notes. The blue, red, and black colors, which are blended on these promissory bills, present a gay appearance of signatures and endorsings. The name of the issuing house, and a number of characters traced around the page, in bright blue ink, form the original impression. The date of issue, and some ingeniously wrought cyphers, for the reception of signatures and prevention of forgeries, are of a deep red; while the entry of the sum, and names of the partners and receiver, stand forth in large black characters. On the back are the endorsements of various individuals, through whose hands the bill has passed, in order to facilitate the detection of forgeries, but not rendering the writer at all liable. These bills have now nearly disappeared, and bank bills from Hongkong are gradually coming into use. The streets usually are thronged with craftsmen and hucksters, in the fashion of Chinese towns, where the shopmen, in their desire to attract buyers, seem to imagine, that the more they get in their customers' way, the more likely they are to sell them something. The shops are thrown open so widely, and display such a variety of articles, or expose the workmen so plainly, that the whole street seems to be rather the stalls of a market, or the aisle in a manufactory, than the town-thoroughfare.

The chief civil and military dignitaries of the province reside here, besides the prefect and the magistrates of Min and Haukwan districts. The *Ching-hwang miao* is one of the largest religious edifices in the place, and the temples of the goddess of Mercy, and god of War, the most frequented. The

Kiu Sien shan, or 'Hill of the Nine Genii,' on the southern side of the town, is a pretty object. The city wall runs over it, and on its sides little houses are built upon rocky steps; numerous inscriptions are carved in the face of the rocks. Near the eastern gate, called *Tang măn*, or 'Bath gate,' is a small suburb, where Chinese and Manchus live together, and take care of many hot wells filled from springs near by; the populace resort hither in large crowds to wash and amuse themselves.

The citizens of Fuhchau bear the character of a reserved, proud, rather turbulent people, unlike the polite, affable natives further north. They are better educated, however, and plume themselves on never having been conquered by foreigners. Their dialect is harsh, contrasting strongly with the nasal tones of the patois of Amoy, and the mellifluous sounds heard at Ningpo. There are few manufactures of importance in the city, its commerce and resources depending almost wholly on the trade with the interior by the River Min. Many culprits wearing the cangue are to be seen in the streets, and in passing none of the hilarious merriment which is heard elsewhere greets the ear. There is also a general lack of courtesy between acquaintances meeting in the highway, a circumstance quite unusual in China. Beggars crowd the thoroughfares, showing both the poverty and the callousness of the inhabitants. One half the male population is supposed to be addicted to the opium pipe, and annually expend millions of dollars for this noxious gratification. The population of the city and suburbs is reckoned at rather over than under a million souls, including the boat people; it is, no doubt, one of the chief cities in the Empire in size, trade, and influence.

The island in the river is settled by a trading population, a great part of whom consist of sailors and boatmen. The country women, who bring vegetables and poultry to market, are a robust race, and contrast strikingly with the sickly-looking, little-footed ladies of the city. Fishing-boats are numerous in the river, many of which are furnished with cormorants.[1]

Amoy is the best known port in the province, and 150 years

---

[1] *Chinese Repository*, Vol. XV., pp. 185, 225.

ago was the seat of a large foreign commerce. It lies in the district of Tung-ngan, within the prefecture of Tsiuenchau, in lat. 24° 40′ N., and long. 118° 20′ E., upon the south-western corner of the island of Amoy, at the mouth of the Lung Kiang. The island itself is about forty miles in circumference, and contains scores of large villages besides the city. The scenery within the bay is picturesque, caused partly by the numerous islands which define it, some of them surmounted by pagodas or temples, and partly by the high hills behind the city, and crowds of vessels in the harbor in the foreground.[1] There is an outer and inner city, as one approaches it seaward—or more properly a citadel and a city—divided by a ridge of rocky hills having a fortified wall along the top. A paved road connects the two, which is concealed from the view of the beholder as he comes in from sea, until he has entered the Inner harbor. The entire circuit of the city and suburbs is about eight miles, containing a population of 185,000, while that of the island is estimated at 100,000 more.

The harbor of Amoy is one of the best on the coast; the tide rises and falls from fourteen to sixteen feet. The western side of the harbor is formed by the island of Kulang su, the batteries upon it completely commanding the city. It is about a mile long and two and three-quarters around, and maintains a large rural population, scattered among four or five hamlets. The foreign residences scattered over its hills add measurably to the charm of its aspect when viewed from the harbor. Eastward of Amoy is the island of Quemoy (*i.e.*, Golden harbor), whose low, rice grounds on the south-west shore produce a very different effect as opposed to the high land on Amoy; its population is, moreover, much less.

The country in this part of Fuhkien is thickly settled and highly cultivated. Mr. Abeel, describing a trip toward Tung-ngan, says, "For a few miles up, the hills wore the same rugged, barren aspect which is so common on the southern coast of China, but fertility and cultivation grew upon us as we

[1] The *Boston Missionary Herald* for 1845 (p. 87) contains a notice of the "White Deer Cavern," in the neighborhood.

advanced; the mountains on the east became hills, and these were adorned with fields. The villages were numerous at intervals; many of them were indicated in the distance by large groves of trees, but generally the landscape looked naked. Well-sweeps were scattered over the cultivated hills, affording evidence of the need and the means of irrigation."[1]

In the other direction, toward Changchau, the traveller, beyond Pagoda Island, enters an oval bay ten or twelve miles long, bounded by numerous plains rising in the distance into steep barren mountains, and upon which numerous villages are found; twenty-three were counted at once by Mr. Abeel, and the boatmen said that all could not be seen. Several large towns, and "villages uncounted" are visible in every direction, as one proceeds up the river toward Changchau, thirty-five miles from Amoy. This city is well built, the streets paved with granite, some of them twelve feet wide, and intolerably offensive. A bridge, about eight hundred feet long, spans the river, consisting of beams stretching from one abutment to another, covered with cross pieces. From the hill-top behind a temple at the north-western corner of the city, the prospect is charming.

"Imagine an amphitheatre," says Mr. Lowrie, "thirty miles in length and twenty in breadth, hemmed in on all sides by bare pointed hills, a river running through it, an immense city at our feet, with fields of rice and sugar-cane, noble trees and numerous villages stretching away in every direction. It was grand and beautiful beyond every conception we had ever formed of Chinese scenery. Beneath us lay the city, its shape nearly square, curving a little on the river's banks, closely built, and having an amazing number of very large trees within and around. The guide said that in the last dynasty it had numbered 700,000 inhabitants, and now he thought it contained a million—probably a large allowance. The villages around also attracted our attention. I tried to enumerate them, but after counting thirty-nine of large size distinctly visible in less than half the field before us, I gave over the attempt. It is cer-

---

[1] *Chinese Repository*, Vol. XI., p. 506.

tainly within the mark to say that within the circuit of this immense plain there are at least one hundred villages, some of them small, but many numbering hundreds and even thousands of inhabitants." [1]

Changchau was the last city in the eastern provinces held by the Tai-pings, a small remnant of their forces having come across the country after the loss of Nanking. They were expelled in 1866, after the town had suffered much from the contending forces. Traces of this destruction have not yet entirely disappeared from the vicinity.

Shihma, or Chiohbé, is a place of some trade, extending a mile along the shore, and larger than Haitang hien, a district town between it and Amoy. Large numbers of people dwell in boats on this river, rendering a voyage up its channel somewhat like going through a street, for the noise and bustle.

The city of Chinchew (or Tsiuenchau), north of Amoy, was once the larger of the two. It is described by Marco Polo, who reached it after five days' journey from Fuhchau, meeting with a constant succession of flourishing cities, towns and villages. "At this city is the haven of Zayton, frequented by all the ships from India, . . . and by all the merchants of Manzi, for hither is imported the most astonishing quantity of goods and of precious stones and pearls. . . . For it is one of the two greatest havens in the world for commerce." [2] It was gradually forsaken for Amoy, which was more accessible to junks. From Zayton, Kublai Khan's expedition to Java and Japan sailed, and here the men from Egypt and Arabia traded for silks, sugar, and spices long after the Portuguese reached China.

The department of Hinghwa, situate on the coast between Tsiuenchau and Fuhchau, is exceedingly populous, and its dialect differs distinctly from both of the adjoining prefectures. Its people have a bad reputation, and female infanticide prevails here to a greater degree than elsewhere. At Yenping, on the Min River, the people speak the dialect of Nanking, showing their origin of not many scores of years past; there are

---

[1] *Chinese Repository*, Vol. XII., p. 530; Fortune's *Tea Districts*, chaps. xiv and xv.

[2] Yule's *Marco Polo*, Vol. II., p. 186.

many patois in these hilly parts of Fuhkien, and the province as a whole exhibits probably greater discrepancies in its dialects than any other. Its produce is exported north and west, as well as coastwise, and this intercourse tends to assimilate the speech of the inhabitants with their neighbors. The natural scenery in the ranges near the Bohea Hills in the borders of Kiangsí attracts visitors from afar. Fortune describes the picturesque grouping of steep rocks, lonely temples on jutting ledges and hidden adits, alternating with hamlets, along the banks of the stream which carries the boats and produce away to a market. The rocks and cliffs here have furnished Chinese artists with many subjects for pen and pencil, while the valley in addition to its natural beauty brings forth the best of teas.

The island of Formosa, lying 90 miles west of Amoy, together with the Pescadore group, forms a department called Taiwan. The former is a fertile, well-watered region, possessing a salubrious climate, and meriting in every respect its name *Formosa*—a descriptive term first given by the Portuguese to their settlement at Kilung in 1590, and extended afterward to the entire island. Its total length is about 235 miles, while the width at the centre is not far from 80 miles; the limits of Chinese jurisdiction do not, however, embrace more than the western or level portion, leaving to untamed aborigines the thickly wooded districts beyond the *Muh kan shan*, a lofty range of mountains running north and south and forming the backbone of the island. The western coast presents no good harbors, and vessels lying a long distance off shore are exposed to the double inconvenience of a dangerous anchorage and an inhospitable reception from the natives; the eastern side is still less inviting, owing to its possession by savage tribes. From recent reports it appears, moreover, that the whole coast line is rising with unusual persistence and regularity, and that the streams are being choked up at their mouths.

The aborigines of this island are, in those districts that remain uncontaminated by mixture with Chinese settlers, a remarkably well-built, handsome race, strong, large of eye, bold, and devoted to hunting and ardent spirits (when the latter is procurable), after the manner of wild people the world over;

no written language exists among them, nor do they employ any fixed method of reckoning time. They and the inhabitants of Lewchew and neighboring islands are probably of the same race with the Philippine Tagalas, though some have supposed them to be of Malay or Polynesian origin. Like the North American Indians they are divided into numerous clans, whose mutual feuds are likely to last until one party or another is exterminated; this turbulence restrains them from any united action against the Chinese, whose occupation of the island has always been irksome to the natives. Their social condition is extremely low; though free from the petty vices of thieving and deception, and friendly toward strangers, the principle of blood-requital holds among them with full force, and family revenge is usually the sole object of life among the men. No savage is esteemed who has not beheaded a Chinaman, while the greater the number of heads brought home from a fray, the higher the position of a brave in the community. The women are forced to attend both to house and field, but share the laziness of their masters, insomuch that they never cut from the growing rice or millet more than enough for the day's provision. "Although these people have men's forms," observes a Chinese writer in the peculiar antithetical style common to their literary productions, "they have not men's natures. To govern them is impossible; to exterminate them not to be thought of; and so nothing can be done with them. The only thing left is to establish troops with cannon at all the passes through which they issue on their raids, and so overawe them, by military display, from coming out of their fastnesses. The savage tracks lie only through the dense forests, thick with underbrush, where hiding is easy. When they cut off a head, they boil it to separate the flesh, adorn the skull with various ornaments, and hang it up in their huts as evidence of their valor." In addition to a few native clans who have submitted to the rulers from the mainland and dwell in the border region between the colonists and aborigines proper, a peculiarly situated race, called *Hakkas*, maintains a neutral position between the hill tribes and the Chinese. These people were formerly industrious but persecuted inhabitants of Kwangtung province, who, in order to better their lot, emigrated to Formosa and established close communication with the natives there, making themselves indispensable to them by procuring arms, powder, and manufactured goods, while owing to their industry they were able in time to monopolize the camphor trade. Though retaining the Chinese costume and shaving their heads, they practically ignore Chinese rule, paying tribute and intermarrying with the mountaineers, from whom they have also obtained large tracts of land.

Maize, potatoes, fruits, tobacco, indigo, sugar, rice, and tea, are all grown on this island, the three latter in rapidly increasing quantities for purposes of export. Of natural products salt, coal, sulphur, petroleum, and camphor are of the first importance. The vast coal basins have hardly been opened or even explored, the only mines now worked being those in the northern part, near Kilung. Native methods of mining are, however, the only ones employed thus far, and it is not surprising, considering their extreme simplicity, that they have not been able to extract coal from remote districts, where the natural difficulties encountered are greatest. Hand labor alone is used, and draining a pit unheard of—compelling a speedy abandoning of the mines when pierced to any great depth in the mountain side. The cost of the coal at the mouth of the pit is about 65 cents per ton for the first qualities, which price improved methods might reduce a third. The presence of volcanoes on this island will, nevertheless, present a serious obstacle to the employment of western mining machinery, especially along the coast, where the measures appear to be excessively dislocated and the work of draining is rendered more difficult. Petroleum is abundant in certain tracts of northern Formosa, flowing plentifully from crevices in the hills, and used to some extent for burning and medicinal purposes by the natives, but not exported. The possibilities of a large sulphur trade are much more important. It is brought from solfatarae and geysers at Tah-yu kang, near Kilung, where it is found in a nearly pure state, as well, too, as a great quantity of sulphurous acid which might with profit be used in the sugar refineries on the island. The manufacture of sulphur is, however, forbidden by treaty, though its exportation goes on in small quantities, the contractors taking on themselves all risk of seizure. Camphor, perhaps the greatest source of wealth to Formosa, is obtained here by saturating small sticks of the wood with steam, not by boiling as in Japan. The crystals of camphor condense in a receiver placed above the furnace; during the process of distillation an essential oil is produced, which when chemically treated with nitric acid becomes solid camphor. The trees from which the wood is cut grow in the most inaccessible tracts of the island, and are, according to all descriptions, of immense extent, though chopped down by the natives without discrimination or idea of encouraging a second growth.

Among the most interesting natural phenomena of this district are the so-called volcanoes, whose occasional eruptions have been noticed by many. Mr. Le Gendre, United States Consul at Amoy in 1869, upon a visit to Formosa took occasion to examine more closely into this subject. It appears from his report[1] that a gas is constantly issuing from the earth, and when a hole to the depth of a few inches is made it can be lighted. It is most likely, he continues, that from time to time gas jets break forth at points of the hills where they had not been observed before, rushing through its long grass and forests of huge trees, and the rock oil which as a general thing flows in their vicinity. As they are apt to spontaneously ignite in contact with the atmosphere, they must set fire to these materials and cause a local conflagration, that gives to the many peaks of the chain the appearance of volcanoes.

Previous to the first half of the fifteenth century the Chinese had little knowledge of Formosa, nor was their sway established over any part of it until 1683. It was never really colonized, and became a misgoverned and refractory region from the earliest attempts at subjection. A great emigration is constantly going on from the main, and lands are taken up by capitalists, who not only encourage the people in settling there, but actually purchase large numbers of poor people to occupy these districts. Taiwan fu, the seat of local government, is the

[1] *Commercial Relations between the U. S. and Foreign Nations.* 1869.

largest place on the island; other harbors or places of importance are Ku-sia and Takow, some miles south of Taiwan, the latter, with Tamsui, on the north-west coast, being one of the recently opened ports of trade. Kílung possesses a good harbor and is the entrepôt of goods for the northern end of the island. Since the opening (in 1861) of these three towns to foreign intercourse, and the more careful examination of the neutral territory at the foot of the mountains, the resources, peoples, and condition of this productive isle have become better known.

It may be of interest to refer, before leaving Formosa, to the extraordinary fabulous history of the island by one George Psalmanazar, the *nom de plume* of a remarkable impostor of the commencement of the eighteenth century, who pretended to be a Japanese convert to Christianity from Formosa, and who created a profound sensation in Europe by the publication in Latin of a fictitious notice of that country.[1]

About twenty-five miles west of Formosa, and attached to Taiwan fu, is the district of *Pănghu ting* or Pescadore Islands, consisting of a group of twenty-one inhabited islets, the largest of which, called Pănghu, is eighty-four miles in circumference; none of them rise three hundred feet above the sea. The two largest, called Pănghu and Fisher Islands, are situated near the centre of the cluster, and have an excellent harbor between them. The want of trees, and the absence of sheltered valleys, give these islands a barren appearance. Millet, ground-nuts, pine-apples, sweet potatoes, and vegetables are grown, but for most of their supplies they depend upon Formosa. The population of the group is estimated at 8000, of whom a large part are fishermen. The Dutch seized these islands in 1622, and attempted to fortify them by forced Chinese laborers, but removed to Formosa two years after at the instance of the governor of Fuhkien.

---

[1] "*An Historical and Geographical Description of Formosa, an Island subject to the Emperor of Japan,*" etc. Klaproth (*Mémoires sur l'Asie*, Tome I., p. 321) translates an account of this island from Chinese sources. E. C. Taintor, *The Aborigines of Northern Formosa*—Shanghai, 1874—read before the North China branch of the Royal Asiatic Society. *Chinese Repository*, Vol. II., p. 408, and Vol. V., p. 480.

CHAPTER III.

GEOGRAPHICAL DESCRIPTION OF THE WESTERN PROVINCES.

THE central provinces of Hupeh and Hunan formerly constituted a single one under the name of Hukwang (*i.e.* Broad Lakes), and they are still commonly known by this appellation. HUPEH (*i.e.* North of the Lakes) is the smaller of the two, but contains the most arable land. It is bounded north by Honan, east by Nganhwui and Kiangsí, south by Hunan, and west by Sz'chuen and Shensí. Its area is about 70,000 square miles, or slightly above that of New England.

The Great River flows through the south, where it connects with all the lakes on both its shores, and nearly doubles its volume of water. The Han kiang, or Han shui rises in the southwest of Shensí, between the Fuh-niu shan and Tapa ling, and drains the south of that province and nearly the whole of Hupeh, joining the Yangtsz' at Wuchang. It is very tortuous in its course, flowing about 1,300 miles in all, and is navigable only a portion of the year, during the freshes, as far as Siang-yang, about 300 miles. Boats of small size come down, however, at all times from Sin-pu-wan, near its source in Shensí. The mouth is not over 200 feet broad, but the bed of the river as one ascends soon widens to 400 and 500 feet, and at Sha-yang, 168 miles from Hankow, it is half a mile wide. The area of its whole basin is about the same as the province.

The extraordinary effects of a large body of melted snow poured into a number of streams converging on the slopes of a range of hills, and then centring in a narrow valley, bringing their annual deposit of alluvial and silt are seen along the River Han. The rise of this stream is often fifty feet where it is narrowest, and the shores are high; at Íching the channel varies from 300 to 1,500 feet at different seasons, but the river-bed from 2,000 to 9,000 feet, the water rising 18 feet at the fresh. In these wide places, the river presents the aspect of a broad, winding belt of sand dunes, in which the stream meanders in one or many channels. Navigation, therefore, is difficult and dangerous, since moving sands shift the deep water from place to place, and boats are delayed or run aground. In high water the banks are covered, but the current is then almost as serious an obstacle as the shallows are in winter.

The southeastern part of Hupeh is occupied by an extensive depression filled with a succession of lakes. The length and breadth of this plain are not far from two hundred miles, and it is considered the most fertile part of China, not being subject to overflows like the shores of the Yellow River, while the descent of the land allows its abundance of water to be readily distributed. Every spot is cultivated, and the surplus of productions is easily transported wherever there is a demand. The portions nearest the Yangtsz' are too low for constant cultivation.

The Ax Lake, Millet Lake, Red Horse Lake, and Mienyang Lake, are the largest in the province. The remaining parts of both the Lake provinces are hilly and mountainous; the high range of the Ta-peh shan ('Great White Mountains'), commencing far into Shensí, extends to the west of Hupeh, and separates the basins of the Great River from its tributary, the Han kiang, some of its peaks rising to the snow line. The productions of Hupeh are bread-stuffs, silk, cotton, tea, fish, and timber; its manufactures are paper, wax, and cloth. The climate is temperate and healthy.

The favorable situation of Wuchang, the provincial capital, has drawn to it most of the trade, which has caused in the course of years the settlement of Hanyang and Hankow on the northern bank of the Yangtsz' and River Han. The number of vessels gathered here in former years from the other cities on these two streams was enormous, and gave rise to exaggerated ideas of the value of the trade. The introduction of steamers has destroyed much of this native commerce, and the cities themselves suffered dreadfully by the Tai-pings, from which they are rapidly recovering, and on a surer foundation. The cities lie in lat. 30° 33′ N. and long. 114° 20′ E., 582 geographical miles distant from Shanghai.

Wuchang is the residence of the provincial officers, the Manchu garrison, and a literary population of influence, while the working part depends mostly on Hankow for employment. Its walls are over twelve miles in circuit, inclosing more vacant than occupied surface, whose flatness is relieved by a range of low hills that extend beyond Hanyang on the other side of the river. The narrow streets are noisome from the offal, and in summer are sources of malaria, as the drainage is bad.

When Hankow was opened to foreign trade in 1861, it presented a most ruinous appearance, but the sense of security inspired by the presence of the men and vessels from far lands rapidly drew the scattered citizens and artisans to rebuild the ruins. The foreigners live near the river side, east of Hankow and west of the River Han, where the anchorage is very favorable, and out of the powerful current of the Yangtsz'. The difference in level of the great stream is about forty feet in the year. In the long years of its early and peaceful trade up to 1850, this region had gathered probably more people on a given area than could be found elsewhere in the world; and its repute for riches led foreigners to base great hopes on their share, which have been gradually dissipated. The appearance of the city as it was in 1845 is given by Abbé Huc in a few sentences:

"The night had already closed in when we reached the place where the river is entirely covered with vessels, of every size and form, congregated here from all parts. I hardly think there is another port in the world so frequented as this, which passes, too, as among the most commercial in the empire. We entered one of the open ways, a sort of a street having each side defined by floating shops, and after four hours' toilsome navigation through this difficult labyrinth, arrived at the place of debarkation. For the space of five leagues, one can only see houses along the shore, and an infinitude of beautiful and strange looking vessels in the river, some at anchor and others passing up and down at all hours."[1]

The coup d'œil of these three cities is beautiful, their environs being highly cultivated and interspersed with the mansions of the great; but he adds, "If you draw near, you will find on the margin of the river only a shapeless bank worn away with freshets, and in the streets stalls surmounted with palisades, and workshops undermined by the waters or tumbling to pieces from age. The open spots between these ruins are filled with abominations which diffuse around a suffocating odor. No regulations respecting the location of the dwellings, no sidewalks, no place to avoid the crowd which presses upon one, elbowing and disputing the passage, but all get along pell-mell, in the midst of cattle, hogs, and other domestic animals, each protecting himself as he best can from the filth in his way, which the Chinese collect with care for agricultural uses, and carry along in little open buckets through the crowd."

Above Hankow, the towns on the Yangtsz' lie nearer its banks, as they are not so exposed to the freshets. The largest trading places in this part of Hupeh on the river, are Shasí, opposite Kinchau fu, and Íchang near the borders of Sz'chuen, respectively 293 and 363 miles distance. From the first settlement there is a safe passage by canal across to Shayang, forty miles away on the River Han; the travel thence goes north to Shansí. The other has recently been opened to foreign trade. It is the terminus of navigation for the large vessels used from Shanghai upward, as the rapids commence a few miles beyond, necessitating smaller craft that can be hauled by trackers. These two marts are large centres of trade and travel, and were not made desolate by the Tai-pings, as were all other towns of importance on the lower Yangtsz'.

The portion of the Yangtsz' in this province, between Íchang and the Sz'chuen border, exhibits perhaps some of the most magnificent glimpses of scenery in the world. Breaking

[1] *Annales de la Foi*, 1845, Tome XVII., pp. 287, 290. See also Huc's *Travels in the Chinese Empire*, Harper's Ed., 1855, Vol. II., pp. 142–144. Pumpelly, pp. 224–226; Blakiston's *Yangtsze*, p. 65; *Treaty Ports of China*, 1867. Art. *Hankow*.

through the limestone foundations that dip on either side of the granite core of the rapids, the river first penetrates the Wu shan, Mitan, and Lukan gorges on the one side, then the long defile of Íchang on the other. At various points between and beyond these the stream is broken by more or less formidable rapids. Among these grand ravines the most impressive, though not the longest, is that of Lukan, whose vertical walls rise a thousand feet or more above the narrow river. Nothing can be more striking, observes Blakiston, than suddenly coming upon this huge split in the mountain mass "by which the river escapes as through a funnel."

The eastern portions of Hupeh are rougher than the southern, and were overrun during the rebellion by armed bands, so that their best towns were destroyed. Siangyang fu and Fanching, near the northern borders, are important places in the internal commerce of this region. Its many associations with leading events in Chinese early and feudal history render it an interesting region to native scholars. A large part of the southwestern prefecture of Shingan is hilly, and its mountainous portions are inhabited by a rude, illiterate population, many of whom are partly governed by local rulers.

The province of Hunan is bounded north by Hupeh, east by Kiangsí, south by Kwangtung and Kwangsí, west by Kweichau and Sz'chuen. Its area is reckoned at 84,000 square miles—equal to Great Britain or the State of Kansas. It is drained by four rivers, whose basins comprise nearly the whole province, and define its limits by their terminal watersheds. The largest is the Siang, which, rising in the hills on the south and east in numerous navigable streams, affords facilities for trade in small boats to the borders of Kiangsí and Kwangtung, the traffic concentring at Siangtan; this fertile and populous basin occupies well-nigh half of the province. Through the western part of Hunan runs the Yuen kiang, but the rapids and cascades occur so frequently as to render it far less useful than the Siang. Boats are towed up to the towns in the southwest with great labor, carrying only four or five tons cargo; these are exchanged for mere scows at Hangkia, 200 miles above Changteh, in order to reach Yuenchau. The contrast

'UKAN GORGE, YANGTSZ' RIVER.

between the two rivers as serviceable channels of intercourse is notable. Between these two main rivers runs the Tsz' kiang, navigable for only small batteaux, which must be pulled up so many rapids that the river itself has been called Tan ho, or 'Rapid River;' its basin is narrow and fertile, and the produce is carried to market over the hills both east and west. The fourth river, the Lí shui, empties, like all the others, into the Tungting Lake, and drains the northwestern portion of the province; it is navigable only in its lower course, and is almost useless for travel. These rivers all keep their own channels through the lake, which is rather a cesspool for the overflow of the Yangtsz' during its annual rise than a lake fed by its own springs and affluents. At Siangyin, on the River Siang, the banks are 35 feet above low water, and gradually slope down to its mouth at Yohchau, or near it. The variation of this lake from a large sheet of water at one season to a marsh at another, must of course affect the whole internal trade of the province, inasmuch as the rivers running through it are in a continual condition of flood or low water—either extreme cannot but seriously interfere with steam vessels.

The productions of Hunan do not represent a very high development of its soil or mines. Tea and coal are the main exports; tea-oil, ground-nut and *tung* oils, hemp, tobacco, and rice, with iron, copper, tin, and coarse paper make up the list. The coal-fields of southern Hunan contain deposits equal to those in Pennsylvania; anthracite occurs on the River Lui, and bituminous on the River Siang, both beds reaching over the border into Kwangtung. The timber trade in pine, fir, laurel, and other woods is also important. The population of Hunan was somewhat reduced during the Tai-ping rebellion; its inhabitants have in general a bad reputation among their countrymen for violence and rudeness. The hilly nature of the country tends to segregate them into small communities, which are imperfectly acquainted with each other, because travelling is difficult; nor is the soil fertile enough to support in many districts a considerable increase of population.

The capital of Hunan, Changsha, lies on the River Siang, and is one of the most influential, as it is historically one of the most interesting, cities in the central part of China; the festival of the Dragon Boats originated here. Siangtan, at the confluence of the Lien kí, more than 200 miles above Yohchau, is one of the greatest tea-marts in China. Its population is reckoned to be a million, and it is a centre of trade and banking for the products of this and other regions; it extends for three miles along the west bank, and nearly two miles inland, with thousands of boats lining the shores. Its return to prosperity since the rebellion has been marvellously rapid. The city of Changteh on the Yuen River is the next important town, as it is easily reached from Yohchau on the Yangtsz'; large amounts of rice are grown in the prefecture.

Hunan has a high position for letters, the people are well dressed, healthy, and usually peaceable. The boating population is, however, exceptionally lawless, and forms a difficult class for the local authorities to control. Aboriginal hill-tribes exist in the southwestern districts, which are still more unmanageable, probably through the unjust taxation and oppression of the imperial officers set over them. In addition to these ungovernable elements a large area is occupied by the *Yao-jin*, who have possessed themselves of the elevated territory lying between Yungchau and Kweiyang, in the southern point of the province, and there barricaded the mountain passes so that no one can ascend against their will.

The province of SHENSÍ (*i.e.*, Western Defiles) is bounded north by Inner Mongolia, from which it is divided by the Great Wall, east by Shansí and Honan, southeast by Hupeh, south by Sz'chuen, and west by Kansuh. Its area is not far from 70,000 square miles, which is geologically and politically most distinctly marked by the Tsingling shan, the watershed between the Wei and Han rivers. There is only one good road across it to Hanchung fu near its southern part; another, farther east, goes from Sí-ngan, by a natural pass between it and the Fuh-niu shan, to Shang, on the Tan ho, in the Han basin. This part comprises about one-third of Shensí. The other portion includes the basins of the Wei, Loh and Wu-ting, and some smaller tributaries of the Yellow River, of which the Wei is the most important. This river joins the Yellow at the lowest point of its basin, the Tung-kwan pass, where the larger stream breaks through into the lowlands of Honan, and divides eastern and southern China from the northwestern regions. The whole of this part presents a loess formation, and the beds of the streams are cut deep into it, the roads across them being few. The Wei basin is the most fertile part of the province; the history of the Chinese race has been more connected with its fortunes than with any other portion of their possessions. Its productiveness is shown in the rapid development and peopling of the districts along the banks and affluents.

On the north, the Great Wall separates Shensí from the Ordos Mongols, its western end reaching the Yellow River at Ninghia—the largest and only important city in that region. All the connections with this region are through Shensí and by Kwei-hwa-ching, but the configuration of the ranges of hills prevents direct travel. None of the rivers in this region are serviceable to any great degree for navigation, and but few of them for irrigation; the crops depend on the rainfall. The climate is more equable and mild than in Shansí, and not so wet as in many parts of Kansuh. The harvests of one good year here furnish food for three poor ones. The chief dependence of the people is on wheat, but rice is grown wherever water can be had; sorghum, millet, pulse, maize, barley, ground-nut, and fruits of many sorts fill up the list. Cotton, hemp, tobacco, rapeseed, and poppy are largely cultivated, but the surplus of any crop is not enough in average years to leave much for export. The ruthless civil war recently quenched in the destruction of the Mohammedans in the province has left it quite desolate in many parts, and its restoration to former prosperity and population must be slow.

The travel between Shensí and Sz'chuen is almost wholly confined to the great road reaching from Sí-ngan to Chingtu. It passes along the River Wei to Hienyang hien on the left bank, where the road north into Kansuh diverges, the other continuing west along the river through a populous region to Paokí hien, where it recrosses the Wei. During this portion, the Tai-peh Mountain, about eleven thousand feet high, with its white summit, adds a prominent feature to the scenery. At Paokí, the crossing at the Tsingling shan commences, and occupies seven days of difficult travel through a devious road of 163 miles to Fung hien on the confines of Kansuh. It crosses successive ridges from 6,000 to 9,000 feet high, and is carried along the sides of hills and down the gorges in a manner reflecting much credit on the engineers of the third century A.D. who made it. These mountainous regions are thinly settled all the way down to Paoching, near Hanchung; but upon gaining the River Han, one of the most beautiful and fertile valleys in China is reached. Its western watershed is the Kiu-tiao shan,[1] running southwesterly into Sz'chuen on the west side of the Kialing River.

The city of Sí-ngan is the capital of the northwest of China, and next to Peking in size, population, and importance. It surpasses that city in historical interest and records, and in the long centuries of its existence has upheld its earlier name of *Chang-an*, or 'Continuous Peace.' The approach to it from the east lies across a bluff, whose eastern face is filled with houses cut in the dry earth, and from whose summit the lofty towers and imposing walls are seen across the plain three miles away. These defences were too solid for the Mohammedan rebels, and protected the citizens while even their suburbs were burned. The population occupies the entire enciente, and presents a heterogeneous sprinkling of Tibetans, Mongols and Tartars, of whom many thousand Moslems are still spared because they were loyal. Sí-ngan has been taken and retaken, rebuilt and destroyed, since its establishment in the twelfth century B.C. by the Martial King, but its position has always assured for it the control of trade between the central and western provinces and Central Asia. The city itself is picturesquely situated, and contains some few remains of its ancient importance, while the

[1] Usually known as the Ta-pa ling; but Baron von Richthofen found that the natives of that region "call those mountains the Kiu-tiao shan, that is the 'nine mountain ridges,' designating therewith the fact that the range is made up of a number of parallel ridges. This name should be retained in preference to the other." *Letter on the Provinces of Chihli, Shansí, Shensí*, etc. Shanghai, 1872. See also his *China*, Band II. S. 563–576; Alex. Wylie, *Notes of a Journey from Chingtoo to Hankow*, *Journ. Roy. Geog. Soc.* Vol. XIV., p. 168.

neighborhood promises better returns to the sagacious antiquarian and explorer than any portion of China. The principal record of the Nestorian mission work in China, the famous tablet of A.D. 781, still remains in the yard of a temple. Some miles to the northwest lies the temple Ta-fu-sz', containing a notable colossus of Buddha, the largest in China, said to have been cut by one of the Emperors of the Tang in the ninth century. This statue is in a cave hewn out of the sandstone rock, being cut out of the same material and left in the construction of the grotto. Its height is 56 feet; the proportions of limbs and body of the sitting figure are, on the whole, good, the Buddha being represented with right hand upraised in blessing, and the figure as well as garments richly covered with color and gilt. Before the god stand two smaller colossi of the *Schang-hoa*, Buddha's favorite disciples; their inferior art and workmanship, however, testify to a later origin. The cave is lighted from above, after the manner of the Pantheon, by a single round opening in the vaulting. Sixty feet over the rock temple rises a tile roofing, and upon the hillside without the cavern are a number of minor temples and statues.[1]

Next to this city in importance is Hanchung, near the border of Sz'chuen; it was much injured by the Tai-pings, and is only slowly recovering, like all the towns in that valley which were exposed; none of these rebels crossed the Tsingling Mountains. Yu-lin ('Elm Forest') is an important city on the Great Wall in the north of Shensí, the station of a garrison which overawes the Mongols. Several marts carrying on considerable trade are on or near the Wei and Han Rivers.

Gold mines occur in Shensí, and gold is collected in some of the streams; other metals also are worked. The climate is too cold for rice and silk; wheat, millet, oats, maize, and cotton supply their places; rhubarb, musk, wax, red-lead, coal, and nephrite are exported. The trade of Sí-ngan is chiefly that of bartering the produce of the eastern provinces (reaching it by the great pass of Tung-kwan) and that from Tibet, Kansuh, and Ílí. Wild animals still inhabit the northern parts, and the num-

---

[1] See Kreitner, *Im fernen Osten*, p. 504. Wien, 1881.

ber of horses, sheep, goats, and cattle raised for food and service is large compared with eastern China.

The immense province of KANSUH (*i.e.*, Voluntary Reverence, made by uniting the names of Kanchau fu and Suh chau) belonged at one time to Shensí, and extended no farther west than Kiayü kwan; but since the division by Kienlung, its limits have been stretched across the desert to the confines of Songaria on the northwest, and to the borders of Tibet on the west. It is bounded north and northeast by Gobi and the Dsassaktu khanate, east by Shensí, south by Sz'chuen, southwest by Kokonor and the desert, and northwest by Cobdo and Ílí. Its entire area cannot be much under 400,000 square miles, the greater part of which is a barren waste; it extends across twelve degrees of latitude and twenty-one degrees of longitude, and comprises all the best part of the ancient kingdom of Tangut, which was destroyed by Genghis.

The topography of this vast region is naturally divided into two distinct areas by the Kiayü kwan at the end of the Great Wall; one a fertile, well-watered, populous country, differing *toto cœlo* from the sandy or mountainous wildernesses of the other. The eastern portion is further partitioned into two sections by the ranges of mountains which cross it nearly from south to north in parallel lines, dividing the basins of the Wei and Yellow Rivers near the latter. The passage between them is over the Făn-shui ling, not far from the Tao ho and by the town of Tihtao, leading thence up to Lanchau. This part of the province, watered by the Wei, resembles Shansí in fertility and productions, and its nearness to the elevated ranges of the Bayan-kara induces comparatively abundant rainfall. The streams in the extreme south flow into Sz'chuen, but furnish few facilities for navigation. The affluents of the Yellow River are on the whole less useful for irrigation and navigation, and the four or five which join it near Lanchau vary too much in their supply of water to be depended on.

The peculiar feature of Kansuh is the narrow strip projecting like a wedge into the Tibetan plateau, reaching from Lanchau northwesterly between the Ala shan and Kílien shan to the end of the Great Wall. This strip of territory commands the passage between the basin of the Tarim River and Central Asia and China Proper; its passage nearly controls trade and power throughout the northern provinces. The Ta-tung River flows on the south of the Kílien Mountains, but the travel goes near the Wall, where food and fuel are abundant, a long distance beyond its end—even to the desert. The roads from Sí-ngan to Lanchau pass up the King River to Pingliang and across several ranges, or else go farther up the River Wei to Tsin chau; the distances are between 500 and 600 miles. From Lanchau one road goes along the Yellow River down to Ninghia, a town inhabited chiefly by Mongols. Another leads 90 miles west to Síning, whither the tribes around Koko-nor repair for trade. The most important continues to Suhchau, this being an easier journey, while its trade furnishes employment to denizens of the region, whose crops are taken by travellers on passage; this road is about 500 miles in length. Its great importance from early days is indicated by the erection of the Great Wall, in order to prevent inroads along its sides, and by the fortress of Kiayü, which shuts the door upon enemies.

The climate of Kansuh exhibits a remarkable contrast to that of the eastern provinces. Prejevalsky says it is damp in three of the seasons; clear, cold winds blowing in winter, and alternating with calm, warm weather; out of 92 days up to September 30, he registered 72 rainy days, twelve of them snowy. The highest temperature was 88° F. in July. Snow and hail also fall in May. North of the Ala shan, which divides this moist region from the desert, everything is dry and sandy; their peaks attract the clouds, which sometimes discharge their contents in torrents, and leave the northern slopes dry; a marsh appears over against and only a few miles from a sandy waste.[1]

The country east of the Yellow River is fertile, and produces wheat, oats, barley, millet, and other edible plants. Wild animals are frequent, whose chase affords both food and peltry; large flocks and herds are also maintained by Tartars living within the province. The mountains contain metals and minerals, among which are copper, almagatholite, jade, gold, and

---

[1] Prejevalsky's *Travels in Mongolia*, Vol. II., pp. 256–266.

silver. The capital, Lanchau, lies on the south side of the Yellow River, where it turns northeast; the valley is narrow, and defended on the west by a pass, through which the road goes westward. At Síning fu, about a hundred miles east of Tsing hai, the superintendent of Koko-nor resides; its political importance has largely increased its trade within the last few years. Ninghia fu, in the northeast of the province, is the largest town on the borders of the desert. The destruction of life and all its resources during the recent Mohammedan rebellion, which was crushed out at Suhchau in October, 1873, is not likely to be repeated soon, as the rebels were all destroyed;[1] their Toorkish origin can even now be traced in their features.[2] No reliable description of the towns belonging to Kansuh in the districts around Barkul, since the pacification of the country by the Chinese, has been made.

The province of Sz'CHUEN ('Four Streams') was the largest of the old eighteen before Kansuh was extended across the desert, and is now one of the richest in its productions. It is bounded north by Kansuh and Shensí, east by Hupeh and Hunan, south by Kweichau and Yunnan, west and northwest by Tibet and Koko-nor; its area is 166,800 square miles, or double most of the other provinces, rather exceeding Sweden in superficies, as it falls below California, while it is superior to both in navigable rivers and productions. The emperors at Sí-ngan always depended upon it as the main prop of their power, and in the third century A.D. the After Hans ruled at its capital over the west of China.

Sz'chuen is naturally divided by the four great rivers which run from north to south into the Yangtsz', and thus form parallel basins; as a whole these comprise about half of the entire area, and all of the valuable portion. The western part beyond the Min River belongs to the high table lands of Central Asia, and is little else than a series of mountain ranges, sparsely populated and unfit for cultivation, except in small spaces and

---

[1] *Dip. Cor.*, 1874, p. 251.

[2] That this insurrection was not unprecedented we learn from a notice of a similar Mohammedan revolt here in 1784. *Nouvelles Lettres Edifiantes des Missions de la Chine*, Tome II., p. 23.

bottom lands. The eastern portion is a triangular shaped region surrounded with high mountains composed of Silurian and Devonian formations with intervening deposits, mostly of red clayey sandstone, imparting a peculiar brick color, which has led Baron von Richthofen to call it the Red Basin. The ranges of hills average about 3,500 feet high, but the rivers have cut their channels through the deposits from 1,500 to 2,500 feet deep, making the travel up and down their waters neither rapid nor easy. The towns which define this triangular red basin are Kweichau on the Yangtsz', from which a line running south of the river to Pingshan hien, not far from Süchau at its confluence with the Min, gives the southern border; thence taking a circuit as far west as Yachau fu on the Tsing-í River, and turning northwesterly to Lung-ngan fu, the western side is roughly skirted, while the eastern side returns to Kweichau along the watershed of the River Han. Within this area, life, industry, wealth, prosperity, are all found; outside of it, as a rule, the rivers are unnavigable, the country uncultivable, and the people wild and insubordinate, especially on the south and west.

The four chief rivers in the province, flowing into the Yangtsz', are the Kialing, the Loh, the Min, and the Yalung, the last and westerly being regarded as the main stream of the Great River, which is called the Kin-sha kiang, west of the Min. The Kialing rises in Kansuh, and retains that name along one trunk stream to its mouth, receiving scores of tributaries from the ridges between its basin and the Han, until it develops into one of the most useful watercourses in China, coming perhaps next to the Pearl River in Kwangtung. Chungking, at its embouchure, is the largest depot for trade west of Íchang, and like St. Louis, on the Mississippi, will grow in importance as the country beyond develops. The River Fo Loh (called *Fu-sung* by Blakiston) is the smallest of the four, its headwaters being connected with the Min above Chingtu; the town of Lu chau stands at its mouth; through its upper part it is called Chung kiang. The Min River has its fountains near those of the Kialing in Koko-nor, and like that stream it gathers contributions from the ranges defining and crossing its basin;

as it descends into the plain of Chingtu, its waters divide into a dozen channels below Hwan hien, and after running more than a hundred miles reunite above Mei hien, forming a deep and picturesque river down to Süchau, a thousand miles and more from the source. At its junction, the Min almost doubles the volume of water in summer, when the snows melt. The Yalung River is the only large affluent between the Min and the main trunk; it comes from the Bayan-kara Mountains, between the headwaters of the Yellow and Yangtsz' Rivers, and receives no important tributaries in its long, solitary, and unfructuous course. The Abbé Huc speaks of crossing its rapid channel near Makian-Dsung just before reaching Tatsienlu, the frontier town; it takes three names in its course.

From Chingtu as a centre, many roads radiate to the other large towns in the province, by which travel and trade find free course, and render the connections with other provinces safe and easy. The roads are paved with flagstones wide enough to allow passage for two pack-trains abreast; stairs are made on the inclines, up and down which mules and ponies travel without risk, though most of the goods and passengers are carried by coolies. In order to facilitate travel, footpaths are opened and paved, leading to every hamlet, and wherever the traffic will afford it, bridges of cut stone, iron chains or wire, span the torrent or chasm, according as the exigency requires; towns or hamlets near these structures take pride in keeping them in repair.

The products of this fertile region are varied and abundant. Rice and wheat alternate each other in summer and winter, but the amount of land producing food is barely sufficient for its dense population; pulse, barley, maize, ground-nuts, sorghum, sweet and common potatoes, buckwheat and tobacco, are each raised for home consumption. Sugar, hemp, oils of several kinds, cotton, and fruits complete the list of plants mostly grown for home use. The exports consist of raw and woven silk, of which more is sent abroad than from any province; salt, opium, musk, croton (*tung*) oil, gentian, rhubarb, tea, coal, spelter, copper, iron, and insect wax, are all grown or made for other regions. The peace which Sz'chuen enjoyed while other provinces were ravaged by rebels, has tended to develop all its products, and increase its abundance. The climate of this region favors the cultivation of the hillsides, which are composed of disintegrated sandstones, because the moist and mild winters bring forward the winter crops; snow remains only a few days, if it fall at all, and wheat is cut before May. The summer rains and freshets furnish water for the rice fields by filling the streams on a thousand hills. This climate is a great contrast to the dry regions further north, and it is subject to less extremes of temperature and moisture than Yunnan south of it. When this usual experience is altered by exceptional dry or wet seasons, the people are left without food, and their wants cannot be supplied by the abundance of other provinces, owing to the slowness of transit. Brigandage, rioting, cannibalism, and other violence then add to the misery of the poor, and to the difficulty of government.

Chingtu, the capital, lies on the River Min, in the largest plain in the province, roughly measuring a hundred miles one way, and fifty the other, conspicuous for its riches and populousness. The inhabitants are reckoned to number 3,500,000 souls. This city has been celebrated from the earliest days, but received its present name of the 'Perfect Capital' when Liu Pí made it his residence. Its population approaches a million, and its walls, shops, yamuns, streets, warehouses, and suburbs, all indicate its wealth and political importance. Marco Polo calls it Sindafu, and the province Acbalec Manzi, describing the fine stone bridge, half a mile long, with a roof resting on marble pillars, under which "trade and industry is carried on,"[1] which spans the Kian-suy, *i.e.*, the Yangtsz', as the Min is still often termed. The remarkable cave houses of the old inhabitants still attract the traveller's notice as he journeys up to Chingtu, along its banks.

M. David, who lived at this city several months, declares it to be one of the most beautiful towns in China, placed in the midst of a fertile plain watered by many canals, which form a network of great solidity and usefulness. The number of hon-

[1] Yule's *Marco Polo*, Vol. II., p. 23.

orary gateways in and near it attract the voyager's eye, and their variety, size, inscriptions, and age furnish an interesting field of inquiry. Many statues cut in fine stone are scattered about the city or used to adorn the cemeteries.

The city of Chungking, on the Yangtsz', at the mouth of the Kialing River, 725 miles from Hankow, is the next important city in Sz'chuen, and the centre of a great trade on both rivers. The other marts on the Great River are also at the mouths of its affluents, and from Kwaichau to Süchau and Pingshan hien, a distance of 496 miles, there is easy and safe communication within the province for all kinds of boats; steam vessels will also here find admirable opportunities for their employment.

In the western half of Sz'chuen, the people are scattered over intervales and slopes between the numberless hills and mountains that make this one of the roughest parts of China; they are governed by their own local rulers, under Chinese superintendence. They belong to the Lolos race, and have been inimical and insubordinate to Chinese rule from earliest times, preventing their own progress and destroying all desire on the part of their rulers to benefit them. Yachau fu, Tatsienlu, and Batang are the largest towns west of Chingtu, on the road to Tibet. On the other side of the province, at Fungtu hien, occur the fire-wells, where great supplies of petroleum gas are used to evaporate the salt dug out near by. The many topics of interest in all parts of Sz'chuen, can only be referred to in a brief sketch, for it is of itself a kingdom.[1]

The province of Kwangtung (*i.e.*, Broad East), from its having been for a long time the only one of the eighteen to which foreigners have had access, has almost become synonymous with China, although but little more is really known of it than of the others—except in the vicinage of Canton, and along the course of the Peh kiang, from Nanhiung down to that city. It is bounded north by Kiangsí and Hunan, northeast by Fuh-

[1] *Chinese Repository*, Vol. XIX., pp. 317 and 394. *Annales de la Foi*, Tome III., pp. 369–381, and Tome IV., pp. 409–415. *Letter* by Baron Richthofen *on the Provinces of Chihli*, *Shansi*, *Shensi*, *Sz'chuen*, etc. Shanghai, 1872. Kreitner, *Im fernen Osten*, pp. 780–829.

kien, south by the ocean, and west and northwest by Kwangsí; with an area about the same as that of the United Kingdom. The natural facilities for internal navigation and an extensive coasting trade, are unusually great; for while its long line of coast, nearly a thousand miles in length, affords many excellent harbors, the rivers communicate with the regions on the west, north, and east beyond its borders.

The Nan shan runs along the north, between it and Kiangsí and Hunan, in a northeasterly and southwesterly direction. presenting the same succession of short ridges, with bottom lands and clear streams between them, which are seen in Fuhkien. These ridges take scores of names as they follow one another from Kwangsí to Fuhkien, but no part is so well known as the road, twenty-four miles in length, which crosses the Mei ling (*i.e.* Plum ridge), between Nan-ngan and Nanhiung. The elevation here is about a thousand feet, none of the peaks in this part exceeding two thousand, but rising higher to the west. Their summits are limestone, with granite underlying; granite is also the prevailing rock along the coast. Lí-mu ridge in Hainan has some peaks reaching nearly to the snow-line. The bottoms of the rivers are wide, and their fertility amply repays the husbandman. Fruits, rice, silk, sugar, tobacco, and vegetables, constitute the greater part of the productions. Lead, iron, and coal, are abundant.

The Chu kiang, or Pearl River, which flows past Canton, takes this name only in that short portion of its course; it is however preferable to employ this as a distinctive name, comprehending the whole stream, rather than to confuse the reader by naming the numerous branches. It is formed by the union of three rivers, the West, North, and East, the two first of which unite at Sanshwui, west of the city, while the East River joins them at Whampoa. The Sí kiang, or West River, by far the largest, rises in the eastern part of Yunnan, and receives tributaries throughout the whole of Kwangsí, along the southern acclivities of the Nan shan, and after a course of 500 miles, passes out to sea through numerous mouths, the best known of which is the Bocca Tigris. The Peh kiang, or North River, joins it after a course of 200 miles, and the East River is nearly the same length; these two streams discharge the surplus waters of all the northern parts of Kwangtung. The country drained by the three cannot be much less than 150,000 square miles, and most of their channels are navigable for boats to all the large towns in this and the province of Kwangsí. The Han kiang is the only river of importance in the eastern end of Kwangtung; the large town of Chauchau lies near its mouth. There can hardly be less than three hundred islands scattered along the deeply indented coast line of this province between Namoh Island and Annam, of which nearly one-third belong to the department of Kwangchau.

Canton, or Kwangchau fu (*i.e.* Broad City), the provincial capital, lies on the north bank of the Pearl River, in lat. 23° 7′ 10″ N., and long. 113° 14′ 30″ E., nearly parallel with Havana, Muskat, and Calcutta; its climate is, however, colder than any of those cities. The name *Canton* is a corruption of Kwangtung, derived in English from *Kamtom*, the Portuguese mode of writing it; the citizens themselves usually call it *Kwangtung săng ching*, *i.e.* the provincial capital of Kwangtung or simply *săng ching*. Another name is *Yang-ching*, or the 'City of Rams,' and a third the City of Genii, both derived from ancient legends. It lies at the foot of the White Cloud hills, along the banks of the river, about seventy miles north of Macao in a direct line, and ninety northwest of Hongkong; these distances are greater by the river.

The delta into which the West, North, and East Rivers fall might be called a gulf, if the islands in it did not occupy so much of the area. The whole forms one of the most fertile parts of the province, and one of the most extensive estuaries of any river in the world,—being a rough triangle about a hundred miles long on each side. The bay of Lintin—so called from the islet of that name, where opium and other store ships formerly anchored—is the largest sheet of water, and lies below the principal embouchure of the river, called *Fu Mun*, *i.e.* Bocca Tigris, or Bogue. Few rivers can be more completely protected by nature than this; their defences of walls and guns at this spot, however, have availed the Chinese but little against the skill and power of their enemies. Ships pass through it up to the anchorage at Whampoa, about thirty miles, from whence Canton lies twelve miles nearly due west. The approach to it is indicated by two lofty pagodas within the walls, and the multitude of boats and junks thronging the river, amidst which the most pleasing object to the "far-travelled stranger" is the glimpse he gets through their masts of the foreign houses on Sha-meen, and the flagstaffs bearing their national ensigns.

The part of Canton inclosed by walls is about six miles in circumference; having a partition wall running east and west, which divides it into two unequal parts. The entire circuit, including the suburbs, is nearly ten miles. The population on land and water, so far as the best data enable one to judge, cannot be less than a million of inhabitants. This estimate has been doubted; and certainty upon the subject is not to be attained, for the census affords no aid in determining this point, owing to the fact that it is set down by districts, and Canton lies partly in two districts, Nanhai and Pwanyü, which extend beyond the walls many miles. Davis says, "the whole circuit of the city has been compassed within two hours by persons on foot, and cannot exceed six or seven miles;"—which is true, but he means only that portion contained within the walls; and there are at least as many houses without the walls as within them, besides the boats. The city is constantly increasing, the western suburbs present many new streets entirely built up within the last ten years. The houses stretch along the river from opposite the Fa tí or Flower grounds to French Folly, a distance of four miles, and the banks are everywhere nearly concealed by the boats and rafts.

The situation of Canton is one which would naturally soon attract settlers. The earliest notices of the city date back two centuries before Christ, but traders were doubtless located here prior to that time. It grew in importance as the country became better settled, and in A.D. 700, a regular market was opened, and a collector of customs appointed. When the Manchus overran the country in 1650, this city resisted their utmost efforts to reduce it for the space of eleven months, and was finally carried by treachery. Martini states that a hundred thousand *men* were killed at its sack; and the whole number who lost their lives at the final assault and during the siege was 700,000—if the native accounts are trustworthy.[1] Since then, it has been rebuilt, and has increased in prosperity until it is regarded as the second city in the empire for numbers, and is probably at present the first in wealth.

The foundations of the city walls are of sandstone, their upper part being brick; they are about twenty feet thick, and from twenty-five to forty feet high, having an esplanade on the inside, and pathways leading to the rampart, on three sides. The houses are built near the wall on both sides of it, so that except on the north, one hardly sees it when walking around the city. There are twelve outer gates, four in the partition wall, and two water gates, through which boats pass, into the moat, from east to west. A ditch once encompassed the walls, now dry on the northern side; on the other three, and within the city, it and most of the canals are filled by the tide, which as it runs out does much to cleanse the city from its sewage. The gates are all shut at night, and a guard is stationed near them to preserve order, but the idle soldiers themselves cause at times no little disturbance. Among the names of the gates are *Great-Peace* gate, *Eternal-Rest* gate, *Five-Genii* gate, *Bamboo-Wicket* gate, etc.

The appearance of the city when viewed from the hills on the north is insipid and uninviting, compared with western cities, being an expanse of reddish roofs, often concealed by frames for drying or dyeing clothes, or shaded and relieved by a few large trees, and interspersed with high, red poles used for flagstaffs. Two pagodas shoot up within the walls, far above the watch towers on them, and with the five-storied tower on Kwanyin shan near the northern gate, form the most conspicuous objects in the prospect.

To a spectator at this elevation, the river is a prominent feature in the landscape, as it shines out covered with a great diversity of boats of different colors and sizes, some stationary others moving, and all resounding with the mingled hum of

[1] The French bishop Palafox gives still another account of the capture of Canton; his statement contains, however, one or two glaring errors. Vid. *Histoire de la Conquête de la Chine par les Tartares*, pp. 150 ff.

laborers, sailors, musicians, hucksters, children, and boatwomen, pursuing their several sports and occupations. On a low sandstone ledge, in the channel off the city, once stood the Sea Pearl (*Hai Chu*) Fort, called Dutch Folly by foreigners, the quietude reigning within which contrasted agreeably with the liveliness of the waters around. Beyond, on its southern shore, lie the suburb and island of Honam, and green fields and low hills are seen still farther in the distance; at the western angle of this island the Pearl River divides, at the *Peh-ngo tan* or Macao Passage, the greatest body of water flowing south, and leaving a comparatively narrow channel before the city. The hills on the north rise twelve hundred feet, their acclivities for miles being covered with graves and tombs, the necropolis of this vast city.

The streets are too narrow to be seen from such a spot. Among their names, amounting in all to more than six hundred, are *Dragon* street, *Martial Dragon* street, *Pearl* street, *Golden Flower* street, *New Green Pea* street, *Physic* street, *Spectacle* street, *Old Clothes* street, etc. They are not as dirty as those of some other cities in the empire, and on the whole, considering the habits of the people and surveillance of the government, which prevents almost everything like public spirit, Canton has been a well governed, cleanly city. In these respects it is not now as well kept, perhaps, as it was before the war, nor was it ever comparable to modern cities in the West, nor should it be likened to them: without a corporation to attend to its condition, or having power to levy taxes to defray its unavoidable expenses, it cannot be expected that it should be as wholesome. It is more surprising, rather, that it is no worse than it is. The houses along the waterside are built upon piles and those portions of the city are subject to inundations. On the edge of the stream, the water percolates the soil, and spoils all the wells.

The temples and public buildings of Canton are numerous. There are two pagodas near the west gate of the old city, and one hundred and twenty-four temples, pavilions, halls, and other religious edifices within the circuit of the city. The *Kwang tah* or 'Plain pagoda,' was erected by the Mohammedans (who still reside near it), about ten centuries ago, and is rather a minaret than a pagoda, though quite unlike those structures of

Turkey in its style of architecture; it shoots up in an angular, tapering tower, to the height of one hundred and sixty feet. The other is an octagonal pagoda, of nine stories, one hundred and seventy feet high, first erected more than thirteen hundred years ago. The geomancers say that the whole city is like a junk, these two pagodas are her masts, and the five-storied tower on the northern wall, her stern sheets.

Among the best known monuments to foreigners visiting this city was the monastery of *Chong-show sz'*, 'Temple of Longevity,' founded in 1573, and occupying spacious grounds. "In the first pavilion are three Buddhas; in the second a seven-story, gilt pagoda, in which are 79 images of Buddha. In the third pavilion is an image of Buddha reclining, and in a merry mood. A garden in the rear is an attractive place of resort, and another, on one side of the entrance, has a number of tanks in which gold fish are reared. In the space in front of the temple a fair is held every morning for the sale of jade ornaments and other articles."[1] This temple was destroyed in November, 1881, by a mob who were incensed at the alleged misbehaviour of some of the priests toward the female devotees—an instance of the existence in China of a lively popular sentiment regarding certain matters. Near this compound stands the 'Temple of the Five Hundred Genii,' containing 500 statues of various sizes in honor of Buddha and his disciples.

The *Hai-chwang sz'*, a Buddhist temple at Honam usually known as the Honam Joss-house, is one of the largest in Canton. Its grounds cover about seven acres, surrounded by a wall, and divided into courts, garden-spots, and a burial-ground, where are deposited the ashes of priests after cremation. The buildings consist mostly of cloisters or apartments surrounding a court, within which is a temple, a pavilion, or a hall; these courts are overshadowed by bastard-banian trees, the resort of thousands of birds. The outer gateway leads up a gravelled walk to a high portico guarded by two huge demoniac figures, through which the visitor enters a small inclosure, separated from the largest one by another spacious porch, in which are

---

[1] Dr. Kerr, *Canton Guide*.

four colossal statues. This conducts him to the main temple, a low building one hundred feet square, and surrounded by pillars; it contains three wooden gilded images, in a sitting posture, called *San Pao Fuh*, or the Past, Present, and Future Buddha, each of them about twenty-five feet high, and surrounded by numerous altars and attendant images. Daily prayers are chanted before them by a large chapter of priests, all of whom, dressed in yellow canonicals, go through the liturgy. Beyond this a smaller building contains a marble carving somewhat resembling a pagoda, under which is preserved a relic of Buddha, said to be one of his toe-nails. This court has other shrines, and many rooms for the accommodation of the priests, among which are the printing-office and library, both of them respectable for size, and containing the blocks of books issued by them, and sold to devotees.

There are about one hundred and seventy-five priests connected with the establishment, only a portion of whom can read. Among the buildings are several small temples dedicated to national deities whom the Buddhists have adopted into their mythology. One of the houses adjoining holds the hogs (not *bugs*, as was stated in one work) offered by worshippers who feed them as long as they live.

Two other shrines belonging to the Buddhists, are both of them, like the Honam temple, well endowed. One called *Kwang-hiau sz'*, or 'Temple of Glorious Filial Duty,' contains two hundred priests, who are supported from glebe lands, estimated at three thousand five hundred acres. The number of priests and nuns in Canton is not exactly known, but probably exceeds two thousand, nine-tenths of whom are Buddhists. There are only three temples of the Rationalists, their numbers and influence being far less in this city than those of the Buddhists.

The *Ching-hwang miao* is an important religious institution in every Chinese city, the temple, being a sort of palladium, in which both rulers and people offer their devotions for the welfare of the city. The superintendent of that in Canton pays $4,000 for his situation, which sum, with a large profit, is obtained again in a few years, by the sale of candles, incense, etc., to the worshippers. The temples in China are generally cheerless and gloomy abodes, well enough fitted, however, for the residence of inanimate idols and the performance of unsatisfying ceremonies. The entrance courts are usually occupied by hucksters, beggars, and idlers, who are occasionally driven off to give room for the mat-sheds in which theatrical performances got up by priests are acted. The principal hall, where the idol sits enshrined, is lighted only in front, and the altar, drums, bells, and other furniture of the temple, are little calculated to enliven it; the cells and cloisters are inhabited by men almost as senseless as the idols they serve, miserable beings, whose droning, useless life is too often only a cloak for vice, indolence, and crime, which make the class an opprobrium in the eyes of their countrymen.

Canton is the most influential city in Southern China, and its reputation for riches and luxury is established throughout the central and northern provinces, owing to its formerly engrossing the entire foreign trade up to 1843, for a period of about one hundred years. At that time the residence of the governor-general was at Shao-king fu, west of Canton, and his official guard of 5,000 troops is still quartered there, as the Manchu garrison is deemed enough for the defence of Canton. He and the Hoppo, or collector of customs, once had their yamuns in the New City, but a Romish Cathedral has been built on the site of the former's office since its capture in 1857. The governor, treasurer, Manchu commandant, chancellor, and the lower local magistrates (ten in all), live in the Old City, and with their official retinues compose a large body of underlings. Some of these establishments occupy four or five acres.

The *Kung Yuen* or Examination Hall, lies in the southeastern corner of the Old City, similar in size and arrangement to these edifices in other cities. It is 1,330 feet long, 583 wide, and covers over sixteen acres. The wall surrounding it is entered at the east and west corners of the south end, where door-keepers are stationed to prevent a crowd of idlers. The cells are arranged in two sets on each side of the main passage, which is paved and lined with trees; they are further disposed in rows of 57 and 63 cells each—all reached through one side door. The total is 8,653; each cell is 5 feet 9 inches deep, by 3 feet

8 inches wide; grooves are made in the wall to admit a plank, serving as a table by day and a bed by night. Once within, the students are confined to their several stalls, and the outer gate is sealed. A single roof covers the cells of one range, the ranges being 3 feet 8 inches apart. The northern portion includes about one-third of the whole, and is built over with the halls, courts, lodging-rooms, and guard or eating-houses of the highest examiners, their assistants and copyists, with thousands of waiters, printers, underlings, and soldiers. At the biennial examination the total number of students and others in the Hall reaches nearly twelve thousand men.

There are four prisons in the city, all of them large establishments; all the capital offenders in the province are brought to Canton for trial before the provincial officers, and this regulation makes it necessary to provide spacious accommodations for them. The execution-ground is a small yard near a pottery manufacture between the southern gate and the river side, and unless the ground is newly stained with blood, or cages containing the heads of the criminals are hung around, has nothing about it to attract the attention. Another public building, situated near the governor's palace, is the *Wan-shao kung*, or 'Imperial Presence hall,' where three days before and after his majesty's birthday, the officers and citizens assemble to pay him adoration. The various guilds among the people, and the clubs of scholars and merchants from other provinces, have, each of them, public halls which are usually called *consoo houses* by foreigners, from a corruption of a native term *kung-sz'*, *i.e.*, public hall; but the usual designation is *kwui kwan* or 'Assembly Hall.' Their total number must be quite one hundred and fifty, and some of them are not destitute of elegance.[1]

The former residences of foreigners in the western suburbs were known as *Shih-san Hang*, or 'Thirteen Hongs,'[2] and for

---

[1] *Chinese Repository*, Vol. II., pp. 145, 191, &c.

[2] This word is derived from the Chinese *hong* or *hang*, meaning a row or series, and is applied to warehouses because these consist of a succession of rooms. The foreign factories were built in this manner, and therefore the Chinese called each block a hong; the old security-merchants were dubbed *hong-merchants*, because they lived in such establishments.

nearly two centuries furnished almost the only exhibition to the Chinese people of the *yang jin* or 'ocean-men.' Here the fears and the greed of the rulers, landlords, and traders combined to restrain foreigners of all nations within an area of about fifteen acres, a large part of this space being the Garden or *Respondentia* Walk on the bank of the river. All these houses and out-houses covered a space scarcely as great as the base of the Great Pyramid; its total population, including native and foreign servants, was upwards of a thousand souls. The shops and markets of the Chinese were separated from them only a few feet, and this greatly increased the danger from fire, as may be inferred from the sketch of the street next on the west side. In 1856, the number of hongs was reckoned to be 16, and the local calendar for that year contained 317 names, not including women and children. Besides the 16 hongs, four native streets, bordered with shops for the sale of fancy and silk goods to their foreign customers, ran between the factories. This latter name was given to them from their being the residences of *factors*, for no handicraft was carried on here, nor were many goods stored in them. Fires were not unusual, which demolished portions of them; in 1822 they were completely consumed; another conflagration in 1843 destroyed two hongs and a street of shops; and in 1842, owing to a sudden riot, connected with paying the English indemnity, the British Consulate was set on fire. Finally, as if to inaugurate a new era, they were all simultaneously burned by the local authorities to drive out the British forces, in December, 1856, and every trace of this interesting spot as it existed for so long a time in the annals of foreign intercourse obliterated. Since the return of trade, a new and better site has been formed at Shameen, west of the old spot, by building a solid stone wall and filling in a long, marshy low-tide bank, formerly occupied by boats, to a height of 8 or 10 feet, on which there is room for gardens as well as houses. This is surrounded by water, and thereby secure from fire and mobs to which the old hongs were exposed. Residences are obtainable anywhere in the city by foreigners, and the common sight in the olden times of their standing outside of the *Great Peace Gate* to see the crowd pass in and out while

VIEW OF A STREET IN CANTON.

they themselves could not enter, is no longer seen. A very good map of the enciente was made by an American missionary, Daniel Vrooman, by taking the angles of all the conspicuous buildings therein, with the highest points in the suburbs; he then taught a native to pace the streets between them, compass in hand (noting courses and distances, which he fixed by the principal gates), until a complete plan was filled out. When the city was opened four years afterwards this map was found to need no important corrections.

The trades and manufactories at Canton are mainly connected with the foreign commerce. Many silk fabrics are woven at Fatshan, a large town situated about ten miles west of the city; fire-crackers, paper, mat-sails, cotton cloth, and other articles, are also made there for exportation. The number of persons engaged in weaving cloth in Canton is about 50,000, including embroiderers; nearly 7,000 barbers and 4,200 shoemakers are stated as the number licensed to shave the crowns and shoe the soles of their fellow-citizens.

The opposite suburb of Honam offers pleasant walks for recreation, and the citizens are in the habit of going over the river to saunter in its fields, or in the cool grounds of the great temple; a race-course and many enjoyable rides on horseback also tempt foreigners into the country. A couple of miles up the river are the Fa tí or Flower gardens which once supplied the plants carried out of the country, and are resorted to by pleasure parties; but to one accustomed to the squares, gardens, and esplanades of western cities, these grounds appear mean in the extreme. Foreigners ramble into the country, but rowing upon the river is their favorite recreation. Like Europeans in all parts of the East, they retain their own costume and modes of living, and do not espouse native styles; though if it were not for the shaven crown, it is not unlikely that many of them would adopt the Chinese dress.

The Cantonese enumerate eight remarkable localities, called *pah king*, which they consider worthy the attention of the stranger. The first is the peak of Yuehsiu, just within the walls on the north of the city, and commanding a fine view of the surrounding country. The *Pi-pa Tah*, or Lyre pagoda at

Whampoa, and the 'Eastern Sea Fish-pearl,' a rock in the Pearl River off the city, on which the fort already referred to as the 'Dutch Folly' was formerly situated, are two more; the pavilion of the Five Genii, with the five stone rams, and print of a man's foot in the rock, "always filled with water," near by; the rocks of Yu-shan; the lucky wells of Faukiu in the western suburbs; cascade of Sí-tsiau, forty miles west of the city; and a famous red building in the city, complete the eight "lions."

The foreign shipping all anchored, in the early days, at Whampoa, but this once important anchorage has been nearly deserted since the river steamers began their trips to the outer waters. There are two islands on the south side of the anchorage, called French and Danes' islands, on which foreigners are buried, some of the gravestones marking a century past. The prospect from the summit of the hills hereabouts is picturesque and charming, giving the spectator a high idea of the fertility and industry of the land and its people. The town of Whampoa and its pagoda lie north of the anchorage; between this and Canton is another, called Lob creek pagoda, both of them uninhabited and decaying.

Macao (pronounced *Makow*) is a Portuguese settlement on a small peninsula projecting from the south-eastern end of the large island of Hiangshan. Its Chinese inhabitants have been governed since 1849 by the Portuguese authorities somewhat differently from their own people, but the mixed government has succeeded very well. The circuit of this settlement is about eight miles; its position is beautiful and very agreeable; nearly surrounded with water, and open to the sea breezes, having a good variety of hill and plain even in its little territory, and a large island on the west called *Tui-mien shan* or Lapa Island, on which are pleasant rambles, to be reached by equally pleasant boat excursions, it offers, moreover, one of the healthiest residences in south-eastern Asia. The population is not far from 80,000, of whom more than 7,000 are Portuguese and other foreigners, living under the control of the Portuguese authorities. The Portuguese have refused to pay the former annual ground-rent of 600 taels to the Chinese Government, since the assassination of their governor in 1849, and now control all the inhabitants living within the Barrier wall, most of whom have been born therein. The houses occupied by the foreign population are solidly built of brick or adobie, large, roomy, and open, and from the rising nature of the ground on which they stand, present an imposing appearance to the visitor coming in from the sea.

There are a few notable buildings in the settlement; the most imposing edifice, St. Paul's church, was burned in 1835. Three forts on commanding eminences protect the town, and others outside of the walls defend its waters; the governor takes the oaths of office in the Monte fort; but the government offices are mostly in the Senate house, situated in the middle of the town. Macao was, up to 1843, the only residence for the families of merchants trading at Canton. Of late the authorities are doing much to revive the prosperity of the place, by making it a free port. The Typa anchorage lies between the islands Mackerara and Typa, about three miles off the southern end of the peninsula; all small vessels go into the Inner harbor on the west side of the town. Ships anchoring in the Roads are obliged to lie about three miles off in consequence of shallow water, and large ones cannot come nearer than six or seven miles.[1] Since the ascendancy of Hongkong, this once celebrated port has fallen away in trade and importance, and for many years had an infamous reputation for the protection its rulers afforded the coolie trade.

Eastward from Macao, about forty miles, lies the English colony of Hongkong, an island in lat. 22° 16½′ N., and long. 114° 8½′ E., on the eastern side of the estuary of the Pearl River. The island of Hongkong, or Hiangkiang (*i.e.*, the Fragrant Streams), is nine miles long, eight broad, and twenty-six in circumference, presenting an exceedingly uneven, barren surface, consisting for the most part of ranges of hills, with narrow intervales, and a little level beach land. Victoria Peak is 1,825 feet. Probably not one-twentieth of the surface is availa-

---

[1] *Chinese Repository*, passim. *An Historical Sketch of the Portuguese Settlements in China*. By Sir A. Ljungstedt. Boston, 1836.

ble for agricultural purposes. The island and harbor were first ceded to the Crown of England by the treaty made between Captain Elliot and Kíshen, in January, 1841, and again by the treaty of Nanking, in August, 1842; lastly, by the Convention of Peking, October 24, 1860, the opposite peninsula of Kowlung was added, in order to furnish space for quartering troops and storehouse room for naval and military supplies. The town of Victoria lies on the north side, and extends more than three miles along the shore. The secure and convenient harbor has attracted the settlement here, though the uneven nature of the ground compels the inhabitants to stretch their warehouses and dwellings along the beach.

The architecture of most of the buildings erected in Victoria is superior to anything heretofore seen in China. Its population is now estimated at 130,000, of whom five-sixths are Chinese tradesmen, craftsmen, laborers, and boatmen, few of whom have their families. The government of the colony is vested in a governor, chief-justice, and a legislative council of five, assisted by various subordinate officers and secretaries, the whole forming a cumbrous and expensive machinery, compared with the needs and resources of the colony The Bishop of Victoria has an advisory control over the missions of the establishment in the southern provinces of China, and supervises the schools in the colony, where many youths are trained in English and Chinese literature.

The supplies of the island are chiefly brought from the mainland where an increasing population of Chinese, under the control of the magistrate of Kowlung, find ample demand for all the provisions they can furnish.

Three newspapers are published in English, and two in Chinese. The Seaman's and Military hospitals, the chapels and schools of the London and Church Missionary Society, St. John's Cathedral, Roman Catholic establishment, the government house, the magistracy, jail, the ordnance and engineer departments, Exchange, and the Club house, are among the principal edifices. The amount of money expended in buildings in this colony is enormous, and most of them are substantial stone or brick houses. The view of the city as seen from the harbor is only excelled in beauty by the wider panorama spread out before the spectator on Victoria Peak. During the forty-odd years of its occupation, this colony has slowly advanced in commercial importance, and become an entrepôt for foreign goods designed for native markets in Southern China. Every facility has been given to the Chinese who resort to its shops to carry away their purchases, by making the port free of every impost, and preventing the imperial revenue cutters from interfering with their junks while in sight of the island. The arrangements of this contested point so that the Chinese revenue shall not suffer have not satisfied either party, and as it is in the similar case of Gibraltar, is not likely to soon be settled. Smugglers must run their own risks with the imperial officers. The most valuable article leaving Hongkong is opium, but the greatest portion of its exports pay the duties on entering China at the five open ports in the province of Kwangtung. As the focus of postal lines of passenger steamers, and the port where mercantile vessels come to learn markets, Hongkong exerts a greater influence on the southeast of Asia than her trade and size indicate. The island of Shangchuen or Sançian, where Xavier died, lies southwest of Macao about thirty miles, and is sometimes visited by devout persons from that place to reverence his tomb, which they keep in repair.

The city of Shauchau in the northern part of the province lies at the fork of the river, which compels a change of boats for passengers and goods; it is one of the largest cities after Canton, and a pontoon bridge furnishes the needed facilities for stopping and taxing the boats and goods passing through. Shauking, west of Canton, is another important town, which held out a long time against the Manchus;[1] it was formerly the seat of the provincial authorities, till they removed to Canton in 1630 to keep the foreigners under control. It stretches along six miles of the river bank, a well-built city for China, in a beautiful position. Some of its districts furnish green teas and matting for the Canton market, and this trade has opened the way for a large emigration to foreign countries. Among

---

[1] Palafox, *Conquête de la Chine*, p. 172.

other towns of note is Nanhiung, situated at the head of navigation on the North River, where goods cross the Mei ling. Before the coast was opened to trade, fifty thousand porters obtained a livelihood by transporting packages, passengers, and merchandise to and from this town and Nan-ngan in Kiangsi. It is a thriving place, and the restless habits of these industrious carriers give its population somewhat of a turbulent character. Many of them are women, who usually pair off by themselves and carry as heavy burdens as the men.

Not far from Yangshan hien is a fine cavern, the *Niu Yen* or 'Ox Cave,' on a hillside near the North River. Its entrance is like a grand hall, with pillars 70 feet high and 8 or 10 feet thick. The finest part is exposed to the sun, but many pretty rooms and niches are revealed by torches; echoes resound through their recesses. The stalactites and stalagmites present a vast variety of shapes—some like immense folds of drapery, between which are lamps, thrones and windows of all shapes and sizes, while others hang from the roof in fanciful forms.

The scenery along the river, between Nanhiung and Shauchau, is described as wild, rugged, and barren in the extreme; the summits of the mountains seem to touch each other across the river, and massive fragments fallen from their sides, in and along the river, indicate that the passage is not altogether free from danger. In this mountainous region coal is procured by opening horizontal shafts to the mines. Ellis[1] says, it was brought some distance to the place where he saw it, to be used in the manufacture of green vitriol. Many pagodas are passed in the stretch of 330 miles between Nanhiung and Canton, calculated to attract notice, and assure the native boatmen which swarm on its waters, of the protection of the two elements he has to deal with—wind and water. One of the most conspicuous objects in this part of the river are five rocks, which rise abruptly from the banks, and are fancifully called *Wu-ma-tao*, or 'Five-horses' heads.' The formation of this part of the province consists of compact, dark-colored limestone, overlying

---

[1] *Embassy* (of Lord Amherst) *to China*, Moxon's ed., 1840, p. 98.

sandstone and breccia. Nearly halfway between Shauchau and Canton is a celebrated mountain and cavern temple, dedicated to Kwanyin, the goddess of Mercy, and most charmingly situated amid waterfalls, groves, and fine scenery, near a hill about 1,850 feet high. The cliff has a sheer descent of five hundred feet; the temple is in a fissure a hundred feet above the water, and consists of two stories; the steps leading up to them, the rooms, walls, and cells, are all cut out of the rock. Inscriptions and scrolls hide the naked walls, and a few inane priests inhabit this somewhat gloomy abode. Mr. Barrow draws a proper comparison between these men and the inmates of the Cork Convent in Portugal, or the Franciscan Convent in Madeira, who had likewise "chained themselves to a rock, to be gnawed by the vultures of superstition and fanaticism," but these last have less excuse.

The island of Hainan constitutes a single department, Kiungchau, but its prefect has no power over the central and mountainous parts. In early European travels it is named Aynao, Kainan and Aniam. It is about one hundred and fifty miles long and one hundred broad, being in extent nearly twice the size of Sicily. It is separated from the main by Luichau Strait, sixteen miles wide, whose shoals and reefs render its passage uncertain. The interior of the island is mountainous, and well wooded, and the inhabitants give a partial submission to the Chinese; they are identical in race with the mountaineers in Kweichau. This ridge is called Lí-mu ling; a remarkable peak in the centre of the southern half, *Wu-chi shan* or 'Five-finger Mountain,' probably rises 10,000 feet. The Chinese inhabitants are mostly descendants of emigrants from Fuhkien, and are either trading, agricultural, marine, or piratical in their vocation, as they can make most money. The lands along the coast are fertile, producing areca-nuts, cocoa-nuts, and other tropical fruits, which are not found on the main. Kiungchau fu lies at the mouth of the Lí-mu River, opposite Luichau. The port is Hoihau, nineteen miles distant, but the entrance is too shallow for most vessels, and the trade consequently seeks a better market at Pakhoi, a town which has recently risen to importance as a treaty port on the mainland. All the thirteen district towns are situated on the coast, and within their circuit, on Chinese maps, a line is drawn, inclosing the centre of the island, within which the *Lí min*, or Lí people live, *some* of whom are acknowledged to be independent. They are therefore known as wild and civilized Lí, and are usually in a state of chronic irritation from the harsh treatment of the rulers. It is probable that they originally came from the Malayan Peninsula (as their features, dress, and habits indicate their affinity with those tribes), and have gradually withdrawn themselves into their recesses to avoid oppression. In 1292, the Emperor Kublai gave twenty thousand of them lands free for a time in the eastern parts, but the Ming sovereigns found them all intractable and belligerent. The population of the island is about a million. Its productions are rice, sweet potatoes, sugar, tobacco, fruits, timber, and insect wax.[1]

The province of Kwangsí (*i.e.*, Broad West) extends westward of Kwangtung to the borders of Annam, occupying the region on the southwest of the Nan ling, and has been seldom visited by foreigners, whose journeys have been up the Kwai kiang or 'Cassia River' into Hunan. The banks of the rivers sometimes spread out into plains, more in the eastern parts than elsewhere, on which an abundance of rice is grown. There are mines of gold, silver, and other metals, in this province, most of which are worked under the superintendence of government, but no data are accessible from which to ascertain the produce. Among the commercial productions of Kwangsí, are cassia, cassia-oil, ink-stones, and cabinet-woods; its natural resources supply the principal articles of trade, for there are no manufactures of importance. Many partially subdued tribes are found within the limits of this province, who are ruled by their own hereditary governors, under the supervision of the Chinese authorities; there are twenty-four *chau* districts occupied by these people, the names of whose head-men are given in the Red

[1] E. C. Taintor, *Geographical Sketch of the Island of Hainan*, with map. Canton, 1868. *Journal N. C. Br. R. A. S.*, No. VII., Arts. I., II., and III. *China Review*, Vols. I., p. 124, and II., p. 332. N. B. Dennys, *Report on the newly-opened ports of Kiungchow (Hoihau) in Hainan, and Haiphong in Tonquin*. Hongkong, 1878.

Book, and their position marked in the statistical maps of the empire, but no information is furnished in either, concerning the numbers, language, or occupations, of the inhabitants. Kwangsí is well watered by the West River and its branches, which enable traders to convey timber and surplus produce to Canton, and receive from thence salt and other articles. The mountains on the northwest are occasionally covered with snow; many of the western districts furnish little besides wood for buildings and boats. The basin of the West River is subdivided by ranges of hills into three large valleys, through which flow many tributaries of the leading streams, and as they each usually drop the old name on receiving a new affluent, it is a confusing study to follow them all. On the south the river Yuh rises near Yunnan, and deflects south to Nan-ning near the borders of Kwangtung, joining the central trunk at Sinchau, after a course of five hundred miles. On the north the river Lung and the Hung-shui receive the surplus drainage of the northern districts and of Kweichau, a region where the Miaotsz' have long kept watch and ward over their hilly abodes. The waters are then poured into the central trench a few miles west of Sinchau. This main artery of the province rises in Yunnan and would connect it by batteaux with Canton City if the channel were improved; it is called Sz' ho, and ranks as the largest tributary of the Pearl River.

The capital, Kweilin (*i.e.*, Cassia Forest), lies on the Cassia River, a branch of the West River, in the northeast part of the province; it is a poorly built city, surrounded by canals and branches of the river, destitute of any edifices worthy of notice, and having no great amount of trade. During the Tai-ping rebellion, this and the next town were nearly destroyed between the insurgents and imperialists.

Wuchau fu, on the same river, at its junction with the Lung kiang, or 'Dragon River,' where they unite and form the West River, is the largest trading town in the province. The independent *chau* districts are scattered over the southwest near the frontiers of Annam, and if anything can be inferred from their position, it may be concluded that they were settled by Laos tribes, who had been induced, by the comparative security of life and property within the frontiers, to acknowledge the Chinese sway.[1]

The province of KWEICHAU (*i.e.*, Noble Region) is on the whole the poorest of the eighteen in the character of its inhabitants, amount of its products, and development of its resources. A range of mountains passes from the northeast side in a southwesterly course to Yunnan, forming the watershed between the valleys of the Yangtsz' and Siang Rivers, a rough but fertile region. The western slopes are peopled by Chinese tillers of the soil, a rude and ignorant race, and rather turbulent; the eastern districts are largely in the hands of the Miaotsz', who are considered by the officials and their troops to be lawful objects of oppression and destruction. The climate of the province is regarded as malarious, owing to the quantity of stagnant water and the impurity of that drawn from wells. Its productions consist of rice, wheat, musk, insect wax, tobacco, timber, and cassia, with lead, copper, silver, quicksilver, and iron. The quicksilver mines are in Kai chau, north of the provincial capital, and apparently exceed in extent and richness all other known deposits of this metal; they have been worked for centuries. Cinnabar occurs at various places, about lat. 27°, in a belt extending quite across the province, and terminating near the borders of Yunnan. Two kinds of silk obtained from the worms which feed on the mulberry and oak, furnish material for clothing so cheaply that cotton is imported from other provinces. Horses and other domestic animals are reared in larger quantities than in the eastern provinces.

The largest river is the Wu, which drains the central and northern parts of the province, and empties into the Yangtsz', through the river Kien near Chungking. Other tributaries of that river and West River, also have their sources in this province, and by means of batteaux and rafts are all more or less available for traffic. The natural outlet for the products of Kweichau is the river Yuen in Hunan, whose various branches flow into it from the eastern prefectures, but their unsettled condition prevents regular or successful intercourse.

---

[1] *Chinese Repository*, Vol. XIV., pp. 171 ff.

The capital, Kweiyang, is situated among the mountains; it is the smallest provincial capital of the eighteen, its walls not being more than two miles in circumference. The other chief towns or departments are of inferior note. There are many military stations in the southern prefectures at the foot of the mountains, intended to restrain the unsubdued tribes of Miaotsz' who inhabit them.

Miaotsz' Types.

This name Miaotsz' is used among the Chinese as a general term for all the dwellers upon these mountains, but is not applied to every clan by the people themselves. They consist of eighty-two tribes in all (found scattered over the mountains in Kwangtung, Hunan, and Kwangsí, as well as in Kweichau), speaking several dialects, and differing among themselves in their customs, government, and dress. The Chinese have often described and pictured these people, but the notices are confined to a list of their divisions, and an account of their most striking peculiarities. Their language differs entirely from the Chinese, but too little is known of it to ascertain its analogies to other tongues; its affinities are most likely with the Laos, and those tribes between Burmah, Siam, and China. One clan, inhabiting Lípo hien in the extreme south, is called *Yau-jin*, and although they occasionally come down to Canton to trade, the citizens of that place firmly believe them to be furnished with short tails like monkeys. They carry arms, are inclined to live at peace with the lowlanders, but resist every attempt to penetrate into their fastnesses. The Yau-jin first settled in Kwangsí, and thence passed over into Lien chau about the twelfth century, where they have since maintained their footing. Both sexes wear their hair braided in a tuft on the top of the head—but never shaven and tressed as the Chinese—and dress in loose garments of cotton and linen; earrings are in universal use among them. They live at strife among themselves, which becomes a source of safety to the Chinese, who are willing enough to harass and oppress, but are ill able to resist, these hardy mountaineers. In 1832, they broke out in active hostilities, and destroyed numerous parties of troops sent to subdue them, but were finally induced to return to their retreats by offers of pardon and largesses granted to those who submitted.

A Chinese traveller among the Miautsz' says that some of them live in huts constructed upon the branches of trees, others in mud hovels; and one tribe in cliff houses dug out of the hillsides, sometimes six hundred feet up. Their agriculture is rude, and their garments are obtained by barter from the lowlanders in exchange for metals and grain, or woven by themselves. The religious observances of these tribes are carefully noted, and whatever is connected with marriages and funerals. In one tribe, it is the custom for the father of a new-born child, as soon as its mother has become strong enough to leave her couch, to get into bed himself and there receive the congratulations of his acquaintances, as he exhibits his offspring—a custom which has been found among the Tibetan tribes and elsewhere. Another class has the counterpart of the may-pole and its jocund dance, which, like its corresponding game, is availed of by young men to select their mates.[1]

The province of YUNNAN (*i.e.*, Cloudy South—south of the *Yun ling*, or 'Cloudy Mountains'[2]) is in the southwest of the empire, bounded by north Sz'chuen, east by Kweichau and Kwangsí, south by Annam, Laos, and Siam, and west by Burmah. Its distance from the central authority of the Empire since its partial conquest under the Han dynasty has always made it a weak point, and the uneducated, mixed character of the inhabitants has given an advantage to enterprising leaders to resist Chinese rule. It was recovered from the aborigines by the Tang Emperors, who called it Jung chau, or the region of the Jung tribes, from which the name *Karajang*, *i.e.*, Black Jung, which Marco Polo calls it, is derived; Kublai Khan himself led an army in 1253 thither before he conquered China, and sent the Venetians on a mission there about the year 1278, after his establishment at Peking. A son of the Emperor was his Viceroy over this outlying province at that time. The recent travels of Margary, Baber, and Anderson, of the British service, with Monhot and Garnier of the French, have done much to render this secluded province better known. The central portion is occupied by an extensive plateau, ramifying in various directions and intersected with valley-plains at altitudes of 5,000 to 6,000 feet, in which lie several large lakes and the seven principal cities in the province. These plains are overtopped by the ridges separating them, which, seen from the lower levels, appear, as in Shansí, like horizontal, connected summit-lines. All are built up of red sandstone, like the basin in Sz'chuen, through which rivers, small and large, have furrowed their beds hundreds and thousands of feet, rendering communication almost impossible in certain directions as soon as one leaves the plateau. In the east and northwest, the defiles

[1] *Chinese Repository*, Vol. I., p. 29; Vol. XIV., pp. 105–117; G. T. Lay, *Chinese as They Are*, p. 316; *Journal of N. C. Branch of Royal Asiatic Society*, No. III., 1859, and No. VI., 1869. *Chinese Recorder*, Vols. II., p. 265, and III., pp. 33, 74, 96, 134 and 147. *Peking Gazette* for 1872. *China Review*, Vol. V., p. 92.

[2] Known as *Widiharit* in Pali records. *Chinese Recorder*, Vol. III., pp. 33, 74, sqq.; see also pp. 62, 93, 126, for the record of a visit.

are less troublesome, and in this latter portion of the province are some peaks rising far above the snow line. These are called on Col. Yule's map the *Goolan Sigon* range. The climate is cooler than in Sz'chuen, owing to this elevation, and not very healthy; snow lies for weeks at Yunnan fu, and the summers are charming.

The Yangtsz' enters the province on the northwest for a short distance. The greatest river in it is the Lantsan, which rises in Tibet, and runs for a long distance parallel with and between the Yangtsz' and Nu Rivers till the three break through the mountains not far from each other, and take different courses,—the largest turning to the eastward across China, the Lantsan southeast through Yunnan to the gulf of Siam, under the name of the Meikon or river of Cambodia, and the third, or Salween, westerly through Burmah. The Meikon receives many large tributaries in its course across the province, and its entire length is not less than 1,500 miles. The Lungchuen, a large affluent of the Irrawadi, runs a little west of the Salween. The Meinam rises in Yunnan, and flows south into Siam under the name of the Nanting, and after a course of nearly eight hundred miles, empties into the sea below Bangkok. East of the Lantsan are several important streams, of which three that unite in Annam to form the Sangkoi, are the largest. The general course of these rivers is southeasterly, and their upper waters are separated by mountain ridges, between which the valleys are often reduced to very narrow limits. There are two lakes in the eastern part of the province, south of the capital, called Sien and Tien; the latter is about seventy miles long by twenty wide, and the Sien hu (*i.e.*, 'Fairy Lake') about two-thirds as large. Another sheet of water in the northwest, near Talí fu, communicating with the Yangtsz' kiang, is called Urh hai or Uhr sea, which is more than a hundred miles long, and about twenty in width.

The capital, Yunnan, lies upon the north shore of Lake Tien, and is a town of note, having, moreover, considerable political importance from its trade with other parts of the country through the Yangtsz', and with Burmah. The city was seriously injured in 1834, by an earthquake, which is said to have lasted three entire days, forcing the inhabitants into tents or the open fields, and overthrowing every important building.[1] The traffic between this province and Burmah centres at the fortified post of Tsantah, in the district of Tăngyueh, both of them situated on a branch of the Irrawadi. The principal part of the commodities is transported upon animals from these dépôts to Bhamo, upon the Irrawadi, the largest market-town in this part of Chin-India. The Chinese participate largely in this trade, which consists of raw and manufactured silk to the amount of $400,000 annually, tea, copper, carpets, orpiment, quicksilver, vermilion, drugs, fruits, and other things, carried from their country in exchange for raw cotton to the amount of $1,140,000 annually, ivory, wax, rhinoceros and deer's horns, precious stones, birds' nests, peacocks' feathers, and foreign articles. The entire traffic is probably $2,500,000 annually, and for a few years past has been regularly increasing.

There is considerable intercourse and trade on the southern frontiers with the Lolos, or Laos and Annamese,[2] partly by means of the head-waters of the Meinam and Meikon—which are supposed to communicate with each other by a natural canal—and partly by caravans over the mountains. Yunnan fu was the capital of a Chinese prince about the time of the decadence of the Ming dynasty, who had rendered himself independent in this part of their empire by the overthrow of the rebel Lí, but having linked his fortunes with an imbecile scion of that house, he displeased his officers, and his territories gradually fell under the sway of the conquering Manchus. The southern and western districts of the province are inhabited by half-subdued tribes who are governed by their own rulers, under the nominal sway of the Chinese, and pass and repass across the frontiers in pursuit of trade or occupation.

The extension of British trade from Rangoon toward this part of China, has brought those hill tribes more into notice, and proved in their present low and barbarous condition the accuracy of the ancient description by Marco Polo and the Roman Catholic missionaries. Colonel Yule aptly terms this wide re-

---

[1] *Annales de la Foi*, Tome VIII., p. 87.

[2] Two thousand Chinese families live in Amerapura.

gion an "Ethnological Garden of tribes of various race and in every stage of uncivilization." The unifying influence of the Chinese written language and literary institutions has been neutralized among these races by their tribal dissensions and inaptitude for study of any kind. Anderson gives short vocabularies of the Kakhyen, Shan, Hotha Shan, Le-sau and Poloung languages, all indicating radical differences of origin, the existence of which would keep them from mingling with each other as well as from the Chinese.[1]

The mineral wealth of Yunnan is greater and more varied than that of any other province, certain of the mines having been worked since the Sung dynasty. Coal occurs in many places on the borders of the central plateau; some of it is anthracite of remarkable solidity and uniformity. Salt occurs in hills, not in wells as in Sz'chuen; the brine is sometimes obtained by diving tunnels into the hillsides. Metalliferous ores reach from this province into the three neighboring ones. Copper is the most abundant, and the mines in Ningyuen fu, in the southwestern part of Sz'chuen, have supplied both copper and zinc ores during the troubles in Yunnan. The copper at Hwuilí chau in that prefecture is worked by companies which pay a royalty of two taels a pecul to the government, and furnish the metal to the mine owners for $8 per pecul. The *peh-tung* or argentan ores are mixed with copper, tin, or lead, by the manufacturers according to the uses the alloys are put to. Silver exists in several places in the north, and the exploitation of the mines was successful until within 30 years past; now they cannot be safely or profitably worked, in consequence of political disturbances. Gold is obtained in the sand of some rivers but not to a large extent; lead, iron, tin, and zinc occur in such plenty that they can be exported, but no data are accessible as to the entire product or export.[2]

---

[1] Yule's *Marco Polo*, Vol. II. Anderson, *Mandalay to Momien.*

[2] *Proced. Roy. Geog. Soc.*, Vols. XIII., p. 392, XIV., p. 335, XV., pp. 163 and 343. Col. Yule, *Trade Routes to Western China—The Geographical Magazine*, April, 1875. Richthofen, *Recent Attempts to find a direct Trade-Road to Southwestern China—Shanghai Budget*, March 26, 1874. *Journey of A. R. Margary from Shanghae to Bhamo.* London, 1875. Col. H. Browne in *Blue Books*, Nos. 1, 2, 3, and 4 (1876–77).

CHAPTER IV.

GEOGRAPHICAL DESCRIPTION OF MANCHURIA, MONGOLIA, ILÍ, AND TIBET.

The portions of the Chinese Empire beyond the limits of the Eighteen Provinces, though of far greater extent than China Proper, are comparatively of minor importance. Their vast regions are peopled by different races, whose languages are mutually unintelligible, and whose tribes are held together under the Chinese sway rather by interest and reciprocal hostilities or dislike, than by force. European geographers have vaguely termed all that space lying north of Tibet to Siberia, and east of the Tsung ling to the Pacific, *Chinese Tartary*; while the countries west of the Tsung ling or Belur tag, to the Aral Sea, have been collectively called *Independent Tartary*. Both these names have already become nearly obsolete on good maps of those regions; the more accurate knowledge brought home by recent travellers having ascertained that their inhabitants are neither all Tartars (or Mongols) nor Turks, and further that the native names and divisions are preferable to a single comprehensive one. Such names as Manchuria, Mongolia, Songaria, and Turkestan, derived from the leading tribes dwelling in those countries, are more definite, though these are not permanent, owing to the migratory, changeable habits of the people. From their ignorance of scientific geography, the Chinese have no general designations for extensive countries, long chains of mountains, or devious rivers, but apply many names where, if they were better informed, they would be content with one.

The following table presents a general view of these countries, giving their leading divisions and forms of government.

GENERAL VIEW OF THE COLONIES AND THEIR SUBDIVISIONS.

COLONIES.	PROVINCES.	DIVISIONS.	CAPITALS.	FORMS OF GOVERNMENT.
MANCHURIA.	Shingking	Two fu departments and 15 districts and 13 garrisons	Mukden or Fungtien	Manchuria is ruled by military boards, and generals at the garrisons.
	Kirin	Three ting departments, or 8 garrisoned posts	Kirin ula hotun	Under three generals at the prefectures.
	Tsitsihar	Six commanderies	Tsitsihar hotun	Under six generals.
MONGOLIA	Inner Mongolia	Six corps, subdivided into 24 tribes and 49 standards	No common capital	Each tribe has its own chieftain or general, and is governed by the Lí-fan Yuen in Peking.
	Outer Mongolia	Four khanates, viz.: Tuchétu Sainnoin, Tsetsen, and Dsassaktu	Urga or Kurun	Four khans under the Kutuktu.
	Koko-nor	One residency, having 29 standards	Síning in Kansuh.	Under a Manchu residency.
	Uliasutai	Cobdo, having 11 tribes and 31 standards. Ulianghai tribes under 31 tso-ling	Uliasutai	By an amban over the chieftains.
ÍLÍ	Northern Circuit or Songaria	Ílí	Kuldja	Ruled by a military governor, 2 councillors, and 34 residents in the cities.
		Kur-kara usu	Kur-kara usu	
		Tarbagatai	Sui-tsing ching	Under residents subordinate to the governor.
	Southern Circuit or Eastern Turkestan	Ten cities, viz.: Harashar, Kuché, Sairim, Bai, Ushi, Aksu, Khoten, Kashgar, Yangi Hissar, and Yarkand	Yarkand	Each city under a resident amenable to the governor at Ílí, and native begs.
TIBET	Anterior Tibet	Wei and Kham, divided into eight cantons and 39 feudal townships	H'lassa	Ruled by the Dalai-lama and his hierarchy, overseen by Chinese residents.
	Ulterior Tibet	Tsang and Nari, divided into six cantons	Shigatsé	Ruled by the Teshu-lama, assisted by a resident from Peking.

They cannot be classed, however, in the same manner as the provinces, nor are the divisions and capitals here given to be regarded as definitely settled. Their united area is 3,951,130 square miles, or a little more than all Europe; their separate areas cannot be precisely given. Manchuria contains about 400,000 square miles; Mongolia between 1,300,000 and 1,500,-000 square miles; Ílí about 1,070,000 square miles; and Tibet from 500,000 to 700,000 square miles.

MANCHURIA is so termed from the leading race who dwell there, the *Mandjurs* or *Manchus;* it is a word of foreign origin, the Chinese having no general appellation for the vice-royalty ruled from Mukden. It comprises the eastern portion of the high table land of Central Asia, and lies between latitudes 39° and 52° N., and longitudes 120° to 134° E. These points include the limits in both directions, giving the region a rectangular shape lying in a north-east and south-west direction; roughly speaking, its dimensions are 800 by 500 miles. It is bounded on the south by the Gulf of Pechele, and the highlands of Corea on the north bank of the Yaluh River; on the east by a line running from the Russian town of Possiet northerly to the River Usuri, so as to include Hinka Lake; thence from its headwaters to its junction with the Amur. This river forms the northern frontier; its tributary, the River Argun, together with the large lakes Hurun and Puyur, lie on the west; from the latter lake an artificial line stretching nearly due east for six degrees in lat. 47° strikes the town of Tsitsihar on the River Nonni. The rest of the western border follows the rivers Nonni and Songari to the Palisade. This obsolete boundary commences at Shan-hai kwan on the Gulf of Liatung and runs north-easterly; it nominally separates the Mongols from the Manchus for nearly 300 miles, and really exists only at the passes where the roads are guarded by military.

But a portion of this region has yet been traversed by Europeans, and most of it is a wilderness. The entire population is not stated in the census of 1812, and from the nature of the country and wandering habits of the people, many tribes of whom render no allegiance to the Emperor, it would be impossible to take a regular census. Parts of Manchuria, as here defined, have been known under many names at different periods. *Liautung* ('East of the River Liau') has been applied to the country between that river, Corea, and the Sea of Japan; *Tungking* ('Eastern Capital') referred to the chief town of that region, under the Ming dynasty; and *Kwantung* ('East of the Pass'), denoting the same country, is still a common designation for the whole territory.

Manchuria is now chiefly comprised in the valleys between the Usuri and Nonni Rivers, up to the Amur on the north, while the basin of the Liau on the south embraces the rest. There are three principal mountain chains. Beginning nearly a hundred miles east of Mukden, in lat. 43°, are the Long White Mountains[1] (*Chang-peh shan* of the Chinese, or *Kolmin-shang-uin alin* of the Manchus), which form the watershed between the Songari and Yaluh Rivers and serve for the northern frontier of Corea as far as Russian territory. There it divides and takes the name of Sih-hih-teh, or Sihoti Mountains, for the eastern spur which runs near the ocean, east of the River Usuri; and the name of Hurkar Mountains for the western and lower spurs between that river and the Hurkar. One noted peak, called Mount Chakoran, rising over 10,000 feet, lies south-east of San-săng on the Amur. On the plain, north of Kirin, numerous buttes occur, sometimes isolated, and often in lines fifteen or twenty miles apart; most of them are wooded.

In the western part of Tsitsihar lies the third great range of mountains in Manchuria, called the Sialkoi Mountains, a continuation of the Inner Hing-an range of Mongolia, and separating the Argun and Nonni basins. The Sialkoi range extends over a great part of Mongolia, commencing near the bend of the Yellow River, and reaching in a north-easterly direction, it forms in Manchuria three sides of the extensive valley of the Nonni, ending between the Amur and Songari Rivers at their junction. These regions are more arid than the eastern portions, and the mountains are rather lower; but our information is vague and scanty. As a whole, Manchuria should be called hilly

---

[1] Klaproth (*Mémoires Relatifs à l'Asie*, Tome I., Paris, 1824) has translated from the Manchu a narrative of a visit made in 1677 by one of the grandees of Kanghi's court to a summit in this range. *Chinese Repository*, Vol. XX., p. 296.

rather than mountainous, its intervales alone repaying cultivation.

The country north of the Chang-peh shan as far as the Stanovoi Mountains is drained by one river, viz., the Sagalien, Amur, Kwăntung, or Hehlung kiang (for it is known by all these names), and its affluents; *Sagalien ula* in Manchu and *Hehlung kiang* in Chinese, each mean 'Black' or 'Black Dragon River.' The Amur drains the north-eastern slope of Central Asia by a circuitous course, aided by many large tributaries. Its source is in lat. 50° N. and long. 111° E., in a spur of the Daourian Mountains, called Kenteh, where it is called the Onon. After an east and north-east course of nearly five hundred miles, the Onon is joined in long. 115° E. by the Ingoda, a stream coming from the east of Lake Baikal, where it takes its rise by a peak called Tshokondo, the highest of the Yablonsi Khrebet Mountains. Beyond this junction, under the Russian name of Shilka, it flows about two hundred and sixty miles north-east till it meets the Argun. The Argun rises about three degrees south of the Onon, on the south side of the Kenteh, and under the name of Kerlon runs a solitary north-east course for four hundred and thirty miles to Lake Hurun, Kerlon, or Dalai-nur; the Kalka here comes in from Lake Puyur or Pir, and their waters leave Lake Hurun at Ust-Strelotchnoi (the Arrow's Mouth) under the name of the Argun, flowing north nearly four hundred miles to the union with the Shilka in lat. 53°; from its exit as the Argun and onward to the entrance of the Usuri, it forms the boundary between China and Russia for 1,593 versts, or 1,062 miles.

Beyond this town the united stream takes the name of the Amur (*i.e.*, Great River) or Sagalien of the Manchus, running nearly east about 550 miles beyond Albazin, when its course is south-east till it joins the Songari. Most of the affluents are on the north bank; the main channel grows wider as its size increases, having so many islands and banks as seriously to interfere with navigation. The valley thus watered possesses great natural advantages in soil, climate, and productions, which are now gradually attracting Russian settlers. In lat. 47½° the Songari River (*Sung-hwa kiang* of the Chinese) unites with the

Amur on the right bank, 950 miles from Ust-Strelotchnoi, bringing the drainings of the greater portion of Manchuria, and doubling the main volume of water. The headwaters of this stream issue from the northern slopes of the Chang-peh shan; quickly combined in a single channel, these waters flow past the town of Kirin, scarcely a hundred miles from the mountains, in a river twelve feet deep and 900 wide. Near Petuné the River Nonni joins it from Tsitsihar, and their united stream takes the Chinese name of Kwantung ('Mingled Union'); it is a mile and a half wide here and only three or four feet deep, a sluggish river full of islands. Then going east by north, growing deeper by its affluents, the Hurka, Mayen, Tunni, Hulan, and other smaller ones, it unites with the Amur at at Changchu, a hundred miles west from the Usuri. All accounts agree in giving the Songari the superiority. At Sansing, it is a deep and rapid river, but further down islands and banks interfere with the navigation. The Hurka drains the original country of the Manchus.[1]

The district south-east of the desert, and north of the Great Wall, is drained and fertilized by the Sira-muren, or Liau River, which is nearly valueless for navigation. Its main and western branch divides near the Ín shan Mountains into the Hwang ho and Lahar; the former rises near the Pecha peak, a noted point in those mountains. The Sira-muren runs through a dry region for nearly 400 miles before it turns south, and in a zigzag channel reaches the Gulf of Liautung, a powerful stream carrying its quota of deposit into the ocean; the width at Yingtsz' is 650 feet. The depth is 16 feet on the bar at high tide. The Yaluh kiang, nearly three hundred miles long, runs in a very crooked channel along the northern frontiers of Corea. But little is known about the two lakes, Hurun and Pir, except that their waters are fresh and full of fish; the River Urshun unites them, and several smaller streams run into the latter.

[1] *Voyage Down the Amur*, by Perry McD. Collins, in 1857. New York, 1860, chaps. xxxii.-lx., passim. Ravenstein's *Amur*. *Chinese Repository*, Vol. XIX., p. 289. Rev. A. Williamson, *Journeys in North China*, Vol. II., chaps. x.-xiii.

The larger part of Manchuria is covered by forests, the abode of wild animals, whose capture affords employment, clothing, and food to their hunters. The rivers and coasts abound in fish; among which carp, sturgeon, salmon, pike, and other species, as well as shell-fish, are plenty; the pearl-fishery is sufficiently remunerative to employ many fishermen; the Chinese Government used to take cognizance of their success, and collect a revenue in kind. The argali and jiggetai are found here as well as in Mongolia; bears, wolves, tigers, deer, and numerous fur-bearing animals are hunted for their skins. The troops are required to furnish 2,400 stags annually to the Emperor, who reserves for his own use only the fleshy part of the tail as a delicacy. Larks, pheasants, and crows of various species, with pigeons, thrushes, and grouse, abound. The condor is the largest bird of prey, and for its size and fierceness rivals its congener of the Andes.

The greater half of Shingking and the south of Kirin is cultivated; maize, Setaria wheat, barley, pulse, millet, and buckwheat are the principal crops. Ginseng and rhubarb are collected by troops sent out in detachments under the charge of their proper officers. These sections support, moreover, large herds of various domestic animals. The timber which covers the mountains will prove a source of wealth as soon as a remunerative market stimulates the skill and enterprise of settlers; even now, logs over three feet in diameter find their way up to Peking, brought from the Liau valley.

Manchuria is divided into three provinces, *Shingking*, *Kirin*, and *Tsitsihar*. The province of SHINGKING includes the ancient Liautung, and is bounded north by Mongolia; north-east and east by Kirin; south by the Gulf of Liautung and Corea, from which latter it is separated by the Yaluh River; and west by Chahar in Chihlí. It contains two departments, viz., Fungtien and Kinchau, subdivided into fifteen districts; there are also twelve garrisoned posts at the twelve gates in the Palisade, whose inmates collect a small tax on travellers and goods. Manchuria is under a strictly military government, every male above eighteen being liable for military service, and being, in fact, enrolled under that one of the eight standards to which by birth he belongs. The administration of Shingking is partly civil and partly military; that of Kirin and Tsitsihar is entirely military.

The population of the province has been estimated by T. T. Meadows[1] at twelve millions, consisting of Manchus and Chinese. The coast districts are now mostly occupied and cultivated by emigrants from Shantung, who are pushing the Manchus toward the Amur, or compelling them to leave their hunting and take to farming if they wish to stay where they were born. The conquerors are being civilized and developed by their subjects, losing the use of their own meagre language, and becoming more comfortable as they learn to be industrious. But few aboriginal settlements now remain who still resist these influences. The inhabitants collect near the river, or along the great roads, where food or a market are easiest found.

The capital of Shingking is usually known on the spot as Shin-yang, an older name than the Manchu Mukden, or the Chinese name Fungtien. As the metropolis of Manchuria, it is also known as Shingking (the 'Affluent Capital'), distinguished from the name of the province by the addition of *pun-ching*, or 'head-garrison.' It lies in lat. 41° 50½′ N. and long. 123° 30′ E., on the banks of the Shin, a small branch of the Liau, and is reckoned to be five hundred miles north-east from Peking. The town is surrounded by a low mud wall about ten miles in circuit, at least half a mile distant from the main city wall, whose eight gates have double archways so that the crowd may not interfere in passing; this wall is about three miles around, and its towers and bastions are in good condition. It is 35 or 40 feet high, and 15 feet wide at the top, of brick throughout; a crenulated parapet protects the guard. But for its smaller scale, the walls and buildings here are precisely similar to those at Peking. The streets are wide, clean, and the main business avenues lined with large, well built shops, their counters, windows, and other arrangements indicating a great trade. This capital contains a large proportion of governmental establishments, *yamuns*, and nearly all the officials belong to the ruling race. Main

---

[1] *The Chinese and their Rebellions.* London, 1856.

streets run across the city from gate to gate, with narrow roads or *hu-tung* intersecting them. The palace of the early Manchu sovereigns occupies the centre; while the large warehouses are outside of the inner city. Everywhere marks of prosperity and security indicate an enterprising population, and for its tidy look, industrious and courteous population, Mukden takes high rank among Chinese cities. Its population is estimated to be under 200,000, mostly Chinese. The Manchu monarchs made it the seat of their government in 1631, and the Emperors have since done everything in their power to enlarge and beautify it. The Emperor Kienlung rendered himself celebrated among his subjects, and made the city of Mukden better known abroad, by a poetical eulogy upon the city and province, which was printed in sixty-four different forms of Chinese writing. This curious piece of imperial vanity and literary effort was translated into French by Amyot.

The town of Hingking,[1] sixty miles east of it, is one of the favored places in Shingking, from its being the family residence of the Manchu monarchs, and the burial-ground of their ancestors. It is pleasantly situated in an elevated valley, the tombs being three miles north of it upon a mountain called *Tsz'yun shan.* The circuit of the walls is about three miles. Hingking lies near the Palisade which separates the province from Kirin, and its officers have the rule over the surrounding country, and the entrances into that province. It has now dwindled to a small hamlet, and the guards connected with the tombs comprise most of the inhabitants.

Kinchau, fifteen leagues from Mukden, carries on considerable trade in cattle, pulse, and drugs. Gutzlaff[2] describes the harbor as shallow, and exposed to southern gales; the houses in the town are built of stone, the environs well cultivated and settled by Chinese from Shantung, while natives of Fuhkien conduct the trade. The Manchus lead an idle life, but keep on good terms with the Chinese. When he was there in 1832,

---

[1] Also called *Yenden;* Klaproth, *Mémoires*, Tome I., p. 446. Rémusat informs us that this name formerly included all of Kirin, or that which was placed under it.

[2] *Voyages Along the Coast of China.* New York, 1833.

the authorities had ordered all the females to seclude themselves in order to put a stop to debauchery among the native sailors. Horses and camels are numerous and cheap, but the carriages are clumsy. Kaichau, another port lying on the east side of the gulf, possesses a better harbor, but is not so much frequented.

Since the treaty of 1858 opened the port of Niuchwang or Yingtsz', on the River Liau, to foreign trade, the development of Shingking has rapidly increased. The trade in pulse and bean-cake and oil employs many vessels annually. Opium, silk, and paper are prepared for export through this mart, besides foreign goods. Fung-hwang ting, lying near the Yaluh River, commands all the trade with Corea, which must pass through it. There are many restrictions upon this intercourse by both governments, and the Chinese forbid their subjects passing the frontiers. The trade is conducted at fairs, under the supervision of officers and soldiers; the short time allowed for concluding the bargains, and the great numbers resorting to them, render these bazaars more like the frays of opposing clans than the scenes of peaceable trade. There is a market-town in Corea itself, called Kí-iu wăn, about four leagues from the frontier, where the Chinese "supply the Coreans with dogs, cats, pipes, leather, stags' horns, copper, horses, mules, and asses; and receive in exchange, baskets, kitchen utensils, rice, corn, swine, paper, mats, oxen, furs, and small horses." Merchants are allowed not more than four or five hours in which to conduct this fair, and the Corean officers under whose charge it is placed, drive all strangers back to the frontier as soon as the day closes.[1]

The borders of the sea consist of alluvial soil, efflorescing a nitrous white salt near the beach, but very fertile inland, well cultivated and populous. Beyond, the hill-country is extremely picturesque. Ever-changing views, torrents and fountains, varied and abounding vegetation, flocks of black cattle grazing on the hillsides, goats perched on the overhanging crags, horses, asses, and sheep lower down in the intervales, numerous

---

[1] *Annales de la Foi,* Tome XVIII., 1846, p. 302.

well-built hamlets, everywhere enliven the scene. The department of Kinchau lies along the Gulf of Liautung, between the Palisade and the sea, and contains four small district towns, with forts, around whose garrisons of agricultural troops have collected a few settlers. On the south, toward Chihlí and the Wall, the country is better cultivated.

The climate of Manchuria, as a whole, is healthy and moderate, far removed from the rigor of the plateau on its west, and not so moist as the outlying islands on the east. In summer the ranges are 70° to 90° F., thence down to 10° or 20° below zero. The rivers remain frozen from December nearly to April, and the fall of snow is less than in Eastern America. The seasons are really six weeks of spring, five months of summer, six weeks of autumn and four months of winter; the last is in some respects the enjoyable period, and is used by the farmers to bring produce to market. If the houses were tighter, their inmates would suffer little during the cold season. Huc speaks of hail storms which killed flocks of sheep in Mongolia, near Chahar. Darwin (*Naturalist's Voyage*, 2d ed., 1845, p. 115) corroborates the possibility of his statement by a somewhat similar experience near Buenos Ayres. He here saw many deer and other wild animals killed by "hail as large as small apples and extremely hard." Of the denuded country, near the Liau River, Abbé Huc says: "Although it is uncertain where God placed paradise, we may be sure that he chose some other country than Liautung; for of all savage regions, this takes a distinguished rank for the aridity of the soil and rigor of the climate. On his entrance, the traveller remarks the barren aspect of most of the hills, and the nakedness of the plains, where not a tree nor a thicket, and hardly a slip of a herb is to be seen. The natives are superior to any Europeans I have ever seen for their powers of eating; beef and pork abound on their tables, and I think dogs and horses, too, under some other name; rich people eat rice, the poor are content with boiled millet, or with another grain called *hac-bam*, about thrice the size of millet and tasting like wheat, which I never saw elsewhere. The vine is cultivated, but must be covered from October to April; the grapes are so watery that a hundred litres of juice produce by distillation only forty of poor spirit. The leaves of an oak are used to rear wild silkworms, and this is a considerable branch of industry. The people relish the worms as food after the cocoons have been boiled, drawing them out with a pin, and sucking the whole until nothing but the pellicle is left."[1] Another says, the ground freezes seven feet in Kirin, and about three in Shingking; the thermometer in winter is thirty degrees below zero. The snow is raised into the air by the north-east winds, and becomes so fine that it penetrates the clothes, houses, and enters even the lungs. When travelling, the eyebrows become a mass of ice, the beard a large flake, and the eyelashes are frozen together; the wind cuts and pierces the skin like razors or needles. The earth is frozen during eight months, but vegetation in summer is rapid, and the streams are swollen by the thawing drifts of snow.

The province of KIRIN, or Girin, comprises the country north-east of Shingking, as far as the Amur and Usuri, which bound it on the north and east, while Corea and Shingking lie on the south-east (better separated by the Chang-peh shan than any political confine) and Mongolia on the west. All signs of the line of palisades have disappeared (save at the Passes) in the entire *trajet* between the Songari and Shan-hai kwan. The region is mountainous, except in the link of that river after the Nonni joins it till the Usuri comes in, measuring about one-fourth of the whole. This extensive region is thinly inhabited by Manchus settled in garrisons along the bottoms of the rivers, by Goldies, Mangoons, Ghiliaks, and tribes having affinity with them, who subsist principally by hunting and fishing, and acknowledge their fealty by a tribute of peltry, but who have no officers of government placed over them. Du Halde calls them *K'iching Tatse*, *Yupi Tatse*, and other names, which seem, indeed, to have been their ancient designations. The *Yu-pi Tahtsi*, or 'Fish-skin Tartars,'[2] are said to inhabit the extensive valley of the Usuri, and do not allow the subjects of the Emperor to

[1] *Annales de la Foi*, Tome XVI., p. 359.

[2] The inhabitants of ancient Gedrosia, now Beloochistan, are said to have clothed themselves in fish-skins. Heeren, *Historical Researches among Asiatic Nations*, Vol. I., p. 175.

live among them. In winter they nestle together in kraals like the Bushmen, and subsist upon the products of their summer's fishing, having cut down fuel enough to last them till warm weather. Shut out, as they have been during the past, from all elevating influences, these people are likely to be ere long amalgamated and lost, as well among Russian and other settlers coming in from the north, as amid the Chinese immigrants who occupy their land in the south. The entire population of this province cannot be reckoned, from present information, as high as three millions, the greater part of which live along the Songari valley.

Kirin is divided into three ruling *ting* departments or commanderies, viz., Kirin ula, or the garrison of Kirin, Petuné or Pedné, and Changchun ting. Kirin, the largest of the three, is subdivided into eight garrison districts. The town, called *Chuen Chwang*, or 'Navy Yard,' in Chinese, is finely situated on the Songari, in lat. 43° 45′ N., and long. 127° 25′ E., at the foot of encircling hills, where the river is a thousand feet wide. The streets are narrow and irregular, the shops low and small, and much ground in the city is unoccupied. Two great streets cross each other at right angles, one of them running far into the river on the west supported by piles. The highways are paved with wooden blocks, and adorned with flowers, gold fish, and squares; its population is about 50,000.

The four other important places in Kirin are Petuné, Larin, Altchuku, or A-shi-ho, and Sansing, the latter at the confluent of the Songari and Hurka. Altchuku is the largest, and Petuné next in size, each town having not far from 35,000 inhabitants; Larin is perhaps half as large, and like the others steadily increasing in numbers and importance. Ninguta on the river Hurka has wide regions under its sway where ginseng is gathered; near the stockaded town is a subterranean body of water that furnishes large fish. A great and influential portion of the Chinese population is Moslem, but no Manchus reside in the place. The former control trade and travel in every town.

Petuné, in lat. 45° 20′ N., and long. 125° 10′ E., is inhabited by troops and many persons banished from China for their crimes. Its favorable position renders it a place of considerable trade, and during the summer months it is a busy mart for these thinly peopled regions. It consists of two main streets, with the chief market at their crossing. A large mosque attracts attention. The third commandery of Changchun, west of Kirin and south of Petuné, just beyond the Palisade, is a mere post for overseeing the Manchus and Mongols passing to and fro on the edge of the steppe.

The resources of this wide domain in timber, minerals, metals, cattle and grain have not yet been explored or developed. The hills are wooded to the top, the bottoms bring forth two crops annually, and the rivers take down timber and grain to the Russian settlers. Sorghum, millet, barley, maize, pulse, indigo, and tobacco are the chief crops; and latterly opium, which has rapidly extended, because it pays well. Oil and whiskey are extensively manufactured, packed in wicker baskets lined with paper and transported on wheelbarrows. The wild and domestic animals are numerous. Among the latter the hogs and mules, more than any other kind, furnish food and transportation; while tigers, panthers, and leopards, bears, wolves, and foxes reward the hunters for their pains in killing them.

The province of Tsi-tsi-har, or Hehlung kiang, comprises the northwest of Manchuria, extending four hundred miles from east to west, and about five hundred from north to south. It is bounded north by the Amur, from Shilka to its junction with the Songari; east and southeast by Kirin, from which the Songari partly separates it; southwest by Mongolia, and west by the River Argun, dividing it from Russia. The greatest part of it is occupied by the valley of the Nonni, Noun or Nún; its area of about two hundred thousand square miles is mostly an uninhabited, mountainous wilderness. It is divided into six commanderies, viz.: Tsitsihar, Hulan, Putek, Merguen, Sagalien ula, and Hurun-pir, whose officers have control over the tribes within their limits; of these, Sagalien or Igoon is the chief town in the northeast districts, and is used by the government of Peking as a penal settlement. The town stands on a plain but a rood or so above the river, which sweeps off to the mountains in the distance. Here is posted a large force of officers and men, their extensive barracks indicating the importance attached to the place. The garrison has gradually attracted a population of natives and Chinese from the south, who live by fishing and hunting, as well as farming.

Tsitsihar, the capital of the province, lies on the River Nonni, in lat. 47° 20′ N., and long. 124° E., and is a place of some trade, resorted to by the tribes near the river. Merguen, Hurunpir, and Hulan are situated upon rivers, and accessible when the waters are free from ice. Tsitsihar was built in 1692 by Kanghí to owerawe the neighboring tribes. It is inclosed by a stockade and a ditch. The one-storied houses are constructed of logs, or of brick stuccoed, where timber is dear, and warmed by the brick beds; the tall chimneys outside the main buildings give a peculiar appearance to villages. Pulse, maize, tobacco, millet, and wheat, and latterly poppy are common crops. The valley of the Nonni is cultivated by the Taguri Manchus, among whom six thousand six hundred families of Yakutes settled in 1687, when they emigrated from Siberia. The Korchin Mongols occupy the country south and west of this valley. Some of its streams produce large pearls. The region lying between the Sialkoi Mountains and the River Argun is rough and sterile, presenting few inducements to agriculturalists. Fish abound in all the rivers, and furs are sought in the hills. Pasturage is excellent in the bottoms. Fairs, between the natives and Cossacks, are constantly held at convenient places on the Argun and other rivers. The racial distinction between the Mongols and Manchus is here seen in the agricultural labors of the latter, so opposed to the nomadic habits of the former. This region has, within the last half century, attracted Chinese settlers from Shantung and Chihlí. These colonists are fast filling up the vacant lands along the rivers, dispossessing the Manchus by their thrift and industry, and making the country far more valuable. They will in this way secure its possession to the Peking Government, and bring it, by degrees, under Chinese control, greatly to the benefit of all. In early days the policy of the Manchus, like that of the E. I. Company in India towards British immigration, discountenanced the entrance of Chinese settlers, and in both cases to the disadvantage of the ruling power.

The administration of Manchuria consists of a supreme civil

government at Mukden, and three provincial military ones, though Shingking is under both civil and military. There are five Boards, each under a president, whose duties are analogous to those at Peking. The oversight of the city itself is under a *fuyin* or mayor, superior to the prefect. The three provinces are under as many marshals, whose subordinates rule the commanderies, and these last have garrison officers subject to them, whose rank and power correspond to the size and importance of their districts. These delegate part of their power to "assistant directors," or residents, who are stationed in every town; on the frontier posts, the officers have a higher grade, and report directly to the marshals or their lieutenants. All the officers, both civil and military, are Manchus, and a great portion of them belong to the imperial clan, or are intimately connected with it. By this arrangement, the Manchus are in a measure disconnected with the general government of the provinces, furnished with offices and titles, and induced to recommend themselves for promotion in the Empire by their zeal and fidelity in their distant posts.[1]

MONGOLIA is the first in order of the colonies, by which are meant those parts of the Empire under the control of the *Lí-fan Yuen*, or Foreign Office.[2] According to the statistics of the Empire, it comprises the region lying between lats. 35° and 52° N., and from long. 82° to 123° E.; bounded north by the Russian governments of Trans-Baikalia, Irkutsk, Yeniseisk, Tomsk, and Semipolatinsk; northeast and east by Manchuria; south by the provinces of Chihlí and Shansí, and the Yellow River; southwest by Kansuh; and west by Cobdo and Ílí. These limits are not very strictly marked at all points, but the length from east to west is about seventeen hundred miles, and one thousand in its greatest breadth, inclosing an area of

---

[1] Rev. Alex. Williamson, *Travels in Northern China*. London, 1870. Vol. II., Chaps. I. to XIV.; *Chinese Repository*, Vols. IV., p. 57; XV., p. 454; *Chinese Recorder*, Vol. VII., 1876, "The Rise and Progress of the Manjows," by J. Ross, pp. 155, 235, and 315.

[2] Compare Niebuhr's *History of Rome*, Vol. II., Sect. "Of the Colonies," where can be observed the essential differences between Roman settlements abroad and those of the Chinese; and still greater differences will be found in contrasting these with the offsets of Grecian States.

1,400,000 square miles, supporting an estimated population of two millions. This elevated plain is almost destitute of wood or water, inclosed southward by the mountains of Tibet, and northward by offsets from the Altai range. The central part is occupied by the desert of Gobi, a barren steppe having an average height of 4,000 feet above the sea level, and destitute of all running water. Owing to its elevation, extremely variable climate, and the absence of oases, it may be considered quite as terrible as Sahara, although the sand-waste here is, perhaps, hardly as unmitigated.

The climate of Mongolia is excessively cold for the latitude, arising partly from its elevation and dry atmosphere, and, on the steppes, to the want of shelter from the winds. But this has its compensation in an unclouded sky and the genial rays of the sun, which support and cheer the people to exertion when the thermometer is far below zero. The air has been drained of its moisture by the ridges on every side; day after day the sun's heat reaches the earth with smaller loss than obtains in moister regions in the same latitudes. Otherwise these wastes would support no life at all at such an elevation. In the districts bordering on Chihlí, the people make their houses partly under ground, in order to avoid the inclemency of the season. The soil in and upon the confines of this high land is unfit for agricultural purposes, neither snow nor rain falling in sufficient quantities, except on the acclivities of the mountain ranges; but millet, barley, and wheat might be raised north and south of it. The nomads rejoice in their freedom from tillage, however, and move about with their herds and possessions within the limits marked out by the Chinese for each tribe to occupy.

The space on the north of Gobi to the confines of Russia, about one hundred and fifty miles wide, is warmer than the desert, and supports a greater population than the southern sides. Cattle are numerous on the hilly tracts, but none are found in the desert, where wild animals and birds hold undisputed possession. The thermometer in winter sinks to thirty and forty degrees below zero (Fr.), and sudden and great changes are frequent. No month in the year is free from snow or frost; but on the steppes, the heat in summer is almost intolerable, owing to the radiation from the sandy or stony surface. The snow does not fall very deep, and even in cold weather the cattle find food under it; the flocks and herds are not, however, large.

The principal divisions of Mongolia are four, viz.: 1, Inner Mongolia, lying between the Wall and south of the desert; 2, Outer Mongolia, between the desert and the Altai Mountains, and reaching from the Inner Hing-an to the Tien shan; 3, the country about Koko-nor, between Kansuh, Sz'chuen, and Tibet; and, 4, the dependencies of Uliasutai, lying northwestward of the Kalkas khanates. The whole of this region has been included under the comprehensive name of Tartary, and if the limits of Inner and Outer Mongolia had been the bounds of Tartary, the appellation would have been somewhat appropriate. But when Genghis arose to power, he called his own tribe *Kukai Mongöl*, 'Celestial People,' and designated all the other tribes *Tatars*, that is 'tributaries.'[1] The three tribes of Kalkas, Tsakhars, and Sunnites, now constitute the great body of Mongols under Chinese rule.

INNER MONGOLIA, or *Nui Mungku*, is bounded north by Tsitsihar, the Tsetsen khanate, and Gobi, their frontiers being

---

[1] Abulgasi-Bayadur-chan (*Histoire Genéalogique des Tatars, traduite du Manuscript Tartare*; Leyde: 1726), gives another derivation for these two names. "Alänzä-chan eut deux fils jumeaux l'un appelle Tatar and l'autre Mogull ou pour bien dire Mung'l, entre les quels il partagea ses Estates lorsqu'il se vit sur la fin de sa vie." It is the first prince, he adds, from whom came the name *Tartar*—not from a river called Tata, as some have stated—while of the second: "Le terme Mung'l a esté changé par une corruption generale en Mogull; *Mung veut dire triste ou un homme triste*, et parceque ce prince estoit naturellement d'une humeur fort triste, il porta ce nom dans la verité"—(pp. 27–29). But Visdelon (D'Herbelot, ed. 1778, Tome IV., p. 327) shows more acquaintance with their history in producing proofs that the name *Tatar* was applied in the eighth century by the Chinese to certain tribes living north of the În shan, Ala shan, and River Liau. In the dissensions following upon the ruin of the Tang dynasty, some of them migrated eastwards beyond the Songari, and there in time rallied to subdue the northern provinces, under the name of *Nu-chih*. These are the ancestors of the Manchus. Another fraction went north to the marshy banks of Lakes Hurun and Puyur, where they received the name of *Moungul Tahtsz'*, *i.e.*, Marsh Tatars. This tribe and name it was that the warlike Genghis afterwards made conspicuous. The sound *Mogul* used in India is a dialectal variation.

almost undefinable; east by Kirin and Shingking; south by Chihlí and Shansí; and west by Kansuh. Wherever it runs the Wall is popularly regarded as the boundary between China and Mongolia. The country is divided into six *ming* or *chalkans*, like our corps, and twenty-four *aimaks* [1] (tribes), which are again placed under forty-nine standards or *khochoun*, each of which generally includes about two thousand families, commanded by hereditary princes, or dsassaks. The principal tribes are the Kortchin and Ortous. The large tribe of the Tsakhars, which occupies the region north of the Wall, is governed by a *tutung*, or general, residing at Kalgan, and their pasture grounds are now nominally included in the province of Chihlí. The province of Shansí in like manner includes the lands occupied by the Toumets, who are under the control of a general stationed at Suiyuen, beyond the Yellow River. In the pastures northwest from Kalgan, in the vicinity of Lakes Chazau and Ichí, and reaching more than a hundred miles from the Great Wall, lie the tracts appropriated to raising horses for the "Yellow Banner Corps." Excepting such grazing lands or the vast hunting grounds near Jeh-ho, reserved in like manner by the government, small settlements of Chinese are continually squatting over the plains of Inner Mongolia, from whence they have already succeeded in driving many of the aboriginal Mongol tribes off to the north. Those natives who will not retire are fain to save themselves from starvation or absorption by cultivating the soil after the fashion of their neighbors, the Chinese immigrants. It was, indeed, this influx of settlers which led Kanghí to erect the southern portion of Inner Mongolia into prefectures and districts like China Proper. This alteration of habits among its population seems destined, ere long, to modify the aspect of the country.

Most of the smaller tribes, except the Ortous, live between the western frontiers of Manchuria, and the steppes reaching north to the Sialkoi range, and south to Chahar. These tribes are peculiarly favored by the Manchus, from their having joined them in their conquest of China, and their leading men are

[1] *Abulgasi* (p. 83) furnishes a notice of these *aimaks* and their origin.

often promoted to high stations in the government of the country.

OUTER MONGOLIA, or *Wai Mungku*, is the wild tract lying north of the last as far as Russia. It is bounded north by Russia, east by Tsitsihar, southeast and south by Inner Mongolia, southwest by Barkul in Kansuh, west by Tarbagatai, and northwest by Cobdo and Uliasutai. The desert of Gobi occupies the southern half of the region. It is divided into four *lu*, or circuits, each of which is governed by a khan or prince, claiming direct descent from Genghis, and superintending the internal management of his own khanate. The Tsetsen khanate lies west of Hurun-pir in Tsitsihar, extending from Russia south to Inner Mongolia. West of it, reaching from Siberia across the desert to Inner Mongolia, lies the Tuchétu (or *Tusiétu* of Klaproth[1]) khanate, the most considerable of the four; the road from Kiakhta to Kalgan lies within its borders. West of the last, and bounded south by Gobi and northeast by Uliasutai, lies the region of the Kalkas of Sainnoin; and on its northwest lies the Dsassaktu khanate, south of Uliasutai, and reaching to Barkul and Cobdo on the south and west. All of them are politically under the control of two Manchu residents stationed at Urga, who direct the mutual interests of the Mongols, Chinese, and Russians.

Urga, or Kuren, the capital, is situated in the Tuchétu khanate, in lat. 48° 20′ N., and long. 107½° E., on the Tola River, a branch of the Selenga. It is the largest and most important place in Mongolia, and is divided into *Maimai chin*, the Chinese quarter, and *Bogdo-Kuren*, the Mongol settlement, nearly three miles from the other. Its total population is estimated at 30,000, the Chinese inhabitants of which are forbidden by law to live with their families; of the Mongols here, by far the larger part is composed of lamas. In the estimation of these people Urga stands next to H'lassa in degree of sanctity, being the seat of the third person in the Tibetan patriarchate. According to the Lama doctrine this dignitary—the *Kutuktu*—is the terrestrial impersonation of the Godhead and never dies, but passes,

[1] *Mémoires*, Tome I., p. 2.

after his apparent decease, into the body of some newly born boy, who is sought for afterwards according to the prophetic indications of the Dalai-lama in Tibet. This holy potentate, though of limited education and entirely under the control of the attendant lamas, exercises an unbounded influence over the Kalkas. It is, indeed, by means of him that the Chinese officials control the native races of Mongolia. His wealth, owing to contributions of enthusiastic devotees, is enormous; in and about Urga he owns 150,000 slaves, an abundance of worldly goods, and the most pretentious palace in Mongolia. Outside of its religious buildings, Urga is disgustingly dirty; the filth is thrown into the streets, and the habits of the people are loathsome. Decrepid beggars and starving dogs infest the ways; dead bodies, instead of being interred, are flung to birds and beasts of prey; huts and hovels afford shelter for both rich and poor.[1]

The four khanates constitute one *aimak* or tribe, subdivided into eighty-six standards, each of which is restricted to a certain territory, within which it wanders about at pleasure. There are altogether one hundred and thirty-five standards of the Mongols. The Kalkas chiefly live between the Altai Mountains and Gobi, but do not cultivate the soil to much effect. They are devoted to Buddhism, and the lamas hold most of the power in their hands through the *Kutuktu*. They render an annual tribute to the Emperor of horses, camels, sheep, and other animals or their skins, and receive presents in return of many times its value, so that they are kept in subjection by constant bribing; the least restiveness on their part is visited by a reduction of presents and other penalties. An energetic government, however, is not wanting in addition. The supreme tribunal is at Urga; it is the *yamun*, par excellence, and has both civil and military jurisdiction. The decisions are subject to the revision of the two Chinese residents, and sentences are usually carried into execution after their confirmation. The punishments are horribly severe; but only a decided

[1] Prejevalsky, *Mongolia*, Vol. I.; Pumpelly, *Across America*, pp. 382–385; Michie, *Across Siberia*.

and cruel hand over these wild tribes can keep them from constant strife.

Letters are encouraged among them by the Manchus, but with little success. Many Buddhist books have been translated into Mongolian by order of the Emperors; nor can we wonder at the indifference to literature when this stuff is the aliment provided them. Their tents, or *yurts*, are made of wooden laths fastened together so as to form a coarse lattice-work; the framework consists of several lengths secured with ropes, leaving a door about three feet square. The average size is twelve feet across and ten feet high; its shape is round and the conical roof admits light where it emits smoke. The poles or rafters are looped to the sides, and fastened to a hoop at the top. Upon this framework sheets of heavy felt are secured according to the season. A hearth in the centre holds the fire which heats the kettle hanging over it, and warms the inmates squatted round, who usually place only felt and sheepskins under them. The felt protects from cold, rain, snow, and heat in a wonderful manner. A first-class *yurt* is by no means an uncomfortable dwelling, with its furniture, lining, shrine, and hot kettle in the centre. A carpet for sleeping and sitting on is sometimes seen in *yurts* of the wealthier classes; in these, too, the walls are lined with cotton or silk, and the floors are of wood. The lodges of the rich Kalkas have several apartments, and are elegantly furnished, but destitute of cleanliness, comfort, or airiness. Most of their cloths, utensils, and arms are procured from the Chinese. The Sunnites are fewer than the Kalkas, and roam the wide wastes of Gobi. Both derive some revenue from conducting caravans across their country, but depend for their livelihood chiefly upon the produce of their herds and hunting. Their princes are obliged to reside in Urga, or keep hostages there, in order that the residents may direct and restrain their conduct; but their devotion to the *Kutuktu*, and the easy life they lead, are the strongest inducements to remain.

The trade with Russia formerly all passed through Kiakhta, a town near the frontier, and was carried on by special agents and officials appointed by each nation. The whole business was managed in the interest of the government, and its ramifications furnished employment, position, and support to so many persons as to form a bond of union and guaranty of peace between them and their subjects. Timkowski's journey with the decennial mission to Peking in 1820–21 furnishes one of the best accounts of this trade and intercourse now accessible, and with Klaproth's notes, given in the English translation published in 1827, has long been the chief reliable authority for the divisions and organization of the Mongol tribes. Since the opening of the Suez Canal, through which Russian steamers carry goods to and fro between Odessa and China, the largest portion of the Chinese produce no longer goes to Kiakhta. That which is required for Siberia is sent from Hankow by way of Shańsí, or from Kalgan and Tientsin, under the direction of Russian merchants at those places. Furs, which once formed the richest part of this produce, are gradually diminishing in quality and quantity with the increase of settlers. In 1843 the export of black tea for Russian consumption was only eight millions of pounds, besides the brick tea taken by the Mongols. Cottrell states the total value of the trade, annually, at that period, at a hundred millions of rubles, reckoned then to be equal to $20,830,000, on which the Russians paid, in 1836, about $2,500,000 as import duty. The data respecting this trade of forty years ago are not very accurate, probably; the monopoly was upheld mostly for the benefit of the officials, as private traders found it too much burdened.

Kiakhta is a hamlet of no importance apart from the trade. The frontier here is marked by a row of granite columns; a stockade separates it from Maimai chin. Pumpelly says: "One can hardly imagine a sharper line than is here drawn. On the one side of the stockade wall, the houses, churches, and people are European, on the other, Chinese. With one step the traveller passes really from Asia and Asiatic customs and language, into a refined European society." The goods pay duty at the Russian *douane* in a suburb of fifty houses, near Kiakhta. The Chinese town is also a small place, numbering between twelve and fifteen hundred men (no women being allowed in the settlement) who lived in idleness most of the year. This curious hamlet has two principal streets crossing at right angles, and gates at the four ends, in the wooden wall which surrounds it. These streets are badly paved, while their narrowness barely allows the passage of two camels abreast. The one-storied houses are constructed of wood, roofed with turf or boards, and consist of two small rooms, one used as a shop and the other as a bed-room. The windows in the rear apartment are made of oiled paper or mica, but the door is the only opening in the shop. The dwellings are kept clean, the furniture is of a superior description, and considerable taste and show are seen in displaying the goods. The traders live luxuriously, and attract a great crowd there during the fair in February, when the goods are exchanged. They are under the control of a Manchu, called the *dzarguchi*, who is appointed for three years, and superintends the police of the settlement as well as the commercial proceedings. There are two Buddhist temples here served by lamas, and containing five colossal images sitting cross-legged, and numerous smaller idols.[1]

The western portion of Mongolia, between the meridians of 84° and 96° E., extending from near the western extremity of Kansuh province to the confines of Russia, comprising Uliasutai and its dependencies, Cobdo, and the Kalkas and Tourgouths of the Tangnu Mountains, is less known than any other part of it. The residence of the superintending officer of this province is at Uliasutai (*i.e.*, 'Poplar Grove'), a town lying northwest of the Selenga, in the khanate of Sainnoin, in a well cultivated and pleasant valley.

Cobdo, according to the Chinese maps, lies in the northwest of Mongolia; it is bounded north and west by the government Yeniseisk, northeast by Ulianghai, and southeast by the Dsassaktu khanate, south by Kansuh, and west by Tarbagatai. The part occupied by the Ulianghai or Uriyangkit tribes of the Tangnu Mountains lies northeast of Cobdo, and north of the Sainnoin and Dsassaktu khanates, and separated from Russia by the Altai. These tribes are allied to the Samoyeds, and the rule over them is

---

[1] Cottrell's *Recollections of Siberia*, Chap. IX., p. 314; Timkowski's *Travels*, Vol. I., pp. 4–91, 1821; Pumpelly, *Across America and Asia*, p. 387, 1871; Klaproth, *Mémoires*, Tome I., p. 63; Ritter, *Die Erdkunde von Asien*, Bd. II., pp. 198–226.

administered by twenty-five subordinate military officers, subject to the resident at Uliasutai. This city is said to contain about two thousand houses, is regularly built, and carries on some trade with Urga; it lies on the Iro, a tributary of the Jabkan. Cobdo comprises eleven tribes of Kalkas divided into thirty-one standards, whose princes obey an amban at Cobdo City, himself subordinate to the resident at Uliasutai. The Chinese rule over these tribes is conducted on the same principles as that over the other Mongols, and they all render fealty to the Emperor through the chief resident at Uliasutai, but how much obedience is really paid his orders is not known. The Kalkas submitted to the Emperor in 1688 to avoid extinction in their war with the Eleuths, by whom they had been defeated.

Cobdo contains several lakes, many of which receive rivers without having any outlet. The largest is Upsa-nor, which receives from the east the River Tes, and the Íkí-aral-nor into which the Jabkan runs. The River Irtysh falls into Lake Dzaisang. The existence of so many rivers indicates a more fertile country north of the Altai or Ektag Mountains, but no bounties of nature would avail to induce the inhabitants to adopt settled modes of living and cultivate the soil, if such a clannish state of society exists among them as is described by M. Lévchine to be the case among their neighbors, the Kirghís. The tribes in Cobdo resemble the American Indians in their habits, disputes, and modes of life, more than the eastern Kalkas, who approximate in their migratory character to the Arabs.

The province of Tsing hai, or Koko-nor (called Tsok-gumbam by the Tanguts), is not included in Mongolia by European geographers, nor in the Chinese statistical works is it comprised within its borders; the inhabitants are, however, mostly Mongols, both Buddhist and Moslem, and the government is conducted on the same plan as that over the Kalkas tribes further north. This region is known in the histories of Central Asia under the names of Tangout, Sifan, Turfan, etc. On Chinese maps it is politically called Tsing hai ('Azure Sea'), but in their books is named *Sí Yu* or *Sí Yih*, 'Western Limits.' The borders are now limited on the north by Kansuh, southeast by Sz'chuen, south by Anterior Tibet, and west by the desert, comprising about four degrees of latitude and eleven of longitude.

It includes within its limits several large lakes, which receive rivers into their bosoms, and many of them having no outlets. The Azure Sea is the largest, lying at an altitude of 10,500 feet and overlooked by high mountains, which in winter are covered with snow, and in summer form an emerald frame that deepens the blueness of the water. It is over 200 miles in circuit, and its evaporation is replaced by the inflowing waters of eight large streams; one small islet contains a monastery, whose inmates are freed from their solitude only when the ice makes a bridge, as no boat is known to have floated on its salt water. The wide, moist plains on the east and west furnish pasturage for domestic and wild animals, and constant collisions occur between the tribes resorting there for food. The travels of Abbé Huc and Col. Prejevalsky furnish nearly all that is known concerning the productions and inhabitants of Koko-nor. The country is nominally divided into thirty-four banners, and its Chinese rulers reside at Síning, east of the lake; but they have more to do in defending themselves than in protecting their subjects. The whole country is occupied by the Tanguts of Tibetan origin, who are brigands by profession, and roam over the mountains around the headwaters of the Yangtsz' and Yellow Rivers; by the Mohammedan Dunganis, who have latterly been nearly destroyed in their recent rebellion; and by tribes of Mongols under the various names of Eleuths, Kolos, Kalkas, Surgouths, and Koits. The Chinese maps are filled with names of various tribes, but their statistical accounts are as meagre of information as the maps are deficient in accurate and satisfactory delineations.

The topographical features of this region are still imperfectly known, and its inhospitable climate is rendered more dangerous by man's barbarity. High mountain masses alternate with narrow valleys and a few large depressions containing lakes; the country lying south of the Azure Sea, as far as Burmah, is exceedingly mountainous. West and southwest of the lake extends the plain of Tsaidam, which at a recent geological age has been the bed of a huge lake; it is now covered with morasses, shaking bogs, small rivers, and sheets of water—the most considerable of the latter being Lake Kara, in the extreme western portion. The saline argillaceous soil of this region is not adapted to vegetation. Large animals are scarce, due in part to the plague of insects which compels even the natives to retreat to the mountains with their herds during certain seasons. Its inhabitants are the same as those of Eastern Koko-nor; they are divided into five banners, and number about 1,000 *yurts*, or 5,000 souls.

The Burkhan-buddha range forms the southern boundary of this plain, and the northernmost limit of the lofty plateau of Tibet. Its length from east to west is not far from 130 miles, its eastern extremity being near the Yegrai-ula (the near sources of the Yellow River) and Toso-nor. The range has no lofty peaks, and stretches in an unbroken chain at a height of 15,000 to 16,000 feet; it is terribly barren, but does not attain the line of perpetual snow. The southern range, which separates the headwaters of the Yellow and Yangtsz' Rivers, is called the Bayan-kara Mountains; that northwest of this is called on Chinese maps, Kílien shan and Nan shan, and bounds the desert on the south. On the northern declivities of the Nan shan range are several towns lying on or near the road leading across Central Asia, which leaves the valley of the Yellow River at Lanchau, in Kansuh, and runs N.N.W. over a rough country to Liangchau, a town of some importance situated in a fertile and populous district. From this place it goes northwest to Kanchau, noted for its manufactures of felted cloths which are in demand among the Mongol tribes of Koko-nor, and where large quantities of rhubarb, horses, sheep, and other commodities are procured. Going still northwest, the traveller reaches Suhchau, the last large place before passing the Great Wall, which renders it a mart for provisions and all articles brought from the west in exchange for the manufactures of China. This city was the last stronghold of the Dungani Moslems, and when they were destroyed in 1873 it began to revive out of its ruins. About fifty miles from this town is the pass of Kiayü, beyond which the road to Hami, Urumtsi, and Ilí leads directly across the desert, here about three hundred miles wide. This route has been for ages the line of internal communication between the west of China and the regions lying around and in the basins of the Tarim River and the Caspian.[1] A better idea of the security of traffic and caravans within the Empire, and consequently of the goodness of the Chinese rule, is obtained by comparing the usually safe travel on this route with the hazards, robberies, and poverty formerly met with on the great roads in Bokhara, and the regions south and west of the Belur tag.

The productions of Koko-nor consist of grain and other vegetables raised along the bottoms of the rivers and margins of the lakes; sheep, cattle, horses, camels, and other animals. Alpine hares, wild asses,[2] wild yaks, vultures, lammergeiers, pheasants, antelopes, wolves, mountain sheep, and wild camels are among the denizens of the wilds. The Chinese have settled among the tribes, and Mohammedans of Turkish origin are found in the large towns. There are eight corps between Koko-nor and Uliasutai, comprising all the tribes and banners, and over which are placed as many supreme generals or commanders appointed from Peking. The leading tribes in Koko-nor are Eleuths, Tanguts, and Tourbeths, the former of whom are the remnants of one of the most powerful tribes in Central Asia. Tangout submitted to the Emperor in 1690, and its population since the incorporation has greatly increased. They inhabit the hilly region of Kansuh, Koko-nor, Eastern Tsaidam, and the basin of the Upper Yellow River. They resemble gipsies, being above the average in height, with thick-set features, broad shoulders, hair and whiskers, black, dark eyes, nose straight, lips thick and protruding, face long and never flat, skin tawny. Unlike the Mongols and Chinese they have a strong growth of beard and whiskers which, however, they always shave. They wear no tail, but shave their heads; their dress consists of furs and cloths made into long coats that reach to the knees. Shirts or trowsers are not made use of; their upper legs are generally left bare. Women dress like the men. Their habitations are wooden huts or black cloth tents. The Tangut is cunning,

---

[1] Compare Richthofen, *China*, Band I., 2er Theil.; Yule, *Cathay and the Way Thither*, passim.

[2] The wild ass is called by Prejevalsky the most remarkable animal of these steppes. Compare Yule's *Marco Polo*, Vol. I., p. 220 (2d edition).

stingy, lazy, and shiftless. His sole occupation that of tending cattle (yaks). He is even more zealous a Buddhist than are the Mongols, and extremely superstitious.[1] The trade at Síning is large, but not equal to that between Yunnan and Burmah at Talí and Bhamo; dates, rhubarb, chowries, precious stones, felts, cloths, etc., are among the commodities seen in the bazaar. It lies about a hundred miles from the sea, at an elevation of 7,800 feet, and near it is the famous lamasary of Kumbum, where MM. Huc and Gabet lived in 1845. The town is well situated upon the Síning ho, and though constructed for the most part of wood, presents a fine appearance owing to the number of official buildings therein. The population numbers some 60,000 souls.[2]

The towns lying between the Great Wall and Ílí, though politically belonging to Kansuh, are more connected with the colonies in their form of government than with the Eighteen Provinces. The first town beyond the Kiayü Pass is Yuhmun, distant about ninety miles, and is the residence of officers, who attend to the caravans going to and from the pass. It is represented as lying near the junction of two streams, which flow northerly into the Purunkí. The other district town of Tunhwang lies across a mountainous country, upwards of two hundred miles distant. The city of Ngansí chau has been built to facilitate the communication across the desert to Hami or Kamil, the first town in Songaria, and the dépôt of troops, arms, and munitions of war. "With the town of Hami," says an Austrian visitor in these regions, "the traveller comes upon the southern foot-hills of the Tien shan, and the first traces of Siberian civilization. Magnificent mountain scenery accompanies him on his way toward the west to the Russian line. In the government of Semipolatinsk are the ex-

---

[1] For a notice of the *Ouigours*, who formerly ruled Tangout, consult Klaproth, *Mémoires*, Tome II., p. 301, ff. See also Rémusat, *Nouveaux Mélanges Asiatiques*, Tome II., p. 61, for a notice of the *Ta-ta-tung'o*, who applied their letters to write Mongolian.

[2] *Chinese Repository*, Vol. IX., p. 113; Vol. I., p. 118. *Penny Cyclopædia*, Arts. BAYAN KARA, TANGUT. Kreitner, *Im fernen Osten*, p. 702. Huc, *Travels*, passim.

press mail-wagons which stand ready at his order to carry him at furious speed to the town of the same name, then to the right bank of the River Irtysh, and so to Omsk." [1] This route and that stretching towards the southwest bring an important trade to Hami; the country around it is cultivated by poor Mongols.[2] Barkul, or Chinsí fu, in lat. 43° 40′ N., and long. 93° 30′ E., is the most important place in the department; the district is called Ího hien. A thousand Manchus, and three thousand Chinese, guard the post. The town is situated on the south of Lake Barkul, and its vicinity receives some cultivation. Hami and Turfan each form a *ting* district in the southeast and west of the department. The trade at all these places consists mostly of articles of food and clothing.

Urumtsi, or Tih-hwa chau (the *Bich-balik* of the Ouigours in 1100 [3]), in lat. 43° 45′ N., and long. 89° E., is the westernmost department of Kansuh, divided into three districts, and containing many posts and settlements. In the war with the Eleuths in 1770, the inhabitants around this place were exterminated, and the country afterwards repeopled by upwards of ten thousand troops, with their families, and by exiles; emigrants from Kansuh were also induced to settle there. The Chinese accounts speak of a high mountain near the city, always covered with ice and snow, whose base is wooded, and abounding with pheasants; coal is also obtained in this region. The cold is great, and snow falls as late as July. Many parts produce grain and vegetables. All this department formerly constituted a portion of Songaria. The policy of the Chinese government is to induce the tribes to settle, by placing large bodies of troops with their families at all important points, and sending their exiled criminals to till the soil; the Mongols then find an increasing demand for their cattle and other products, and are induced to become stationary to meet it. So far as is known, this policy had succeeded well in the regions beyond the Wall, and those around Koko-nor; but the rebellion of the Dunganis,

---

[1] Lieut. Kreitner, *Im fernen Osten*.

[2] In Rémusat's *Histoire de la Ville de Khotan* (p. 76) there is an account of a journey made in the 10th century between Kanchan and Khoten.

[3] Rémusat calls it *Pentalope*. *Nouveaux Mélanges*, Tome I., p. 5.

who arose in these outlying regions at the moment when the energies of the Peking government were all directed to suppressing the Tai-ping insurrection, destroyed these improvements, and frustrated, for an indefinite period, the promising development of civilization among the inhabitants.

That part of the Empire called ÍLÍ is a vast region lying on each side of the Tien shan, and including a tract nearly as large as Mongolia, and not much more susceptible of cultivation. Its limits may be stated as extending from lat. 36° to 49° N., and from long. 71° to 96° E., and its entire area, although difficult to estimate from its irregularity, can hardly be less than 900,000 square miles, of which Songaria occupies rather more than one-third. It is divided into two *Lu*, or 'Circuits,' viz., the Tien shan Peh Lu, and Tien shan Nan Lu, or the circuits north and south of the Celestial Mountains. The former is commonly designated Songaria, or Dzungaria, from the Songares or Eleuths, who ruled it till a few scores of years past, and the latter used to be known as Little Bokhara, or Eastern Turkestan.

Ílí is bounded north by the Altai range, separating it from the Kirghís; northeast by the Irtysh River and Outer Mongolia; east and southeast by Urumtsi and Barkul in Kansuh; south by the desert and the Kwănlun range; and west by the Belur-tag, dividing it from Badakshan and Russian territory.[1]

---

[1] The recent treaty between Russia and China (ratified in 1881), marks the boundaries between Ílí and Russian territory in the following sections:

Art. VII. A tract of country in the west of Ílí is ceded to Russia, where those who go over to Russia and are thereby dispossessed of their land in Ílí may settle. The boundary line of Chinese Ílí and Russian territory will stretch from the Pieh-chên-tao [Bedschin-tau] Mountains along the course of the Ho-êrh-kwo-ssŭ [Yehorsos] River, to its junction with the Ílí River, thence across the Ílí River, and south to the east of the village of Kwo-li-cha-tê [Kaldschat] on the Wu-tsung-tau range, and from this point south along the old boundary line fixed by the agreement of Ta-Chêng [Tashkend] in the year 1864.

Art. VIII. The boundary line to the east of the Chi-sang lake, fixed in the year 1864 by the agreement of Ta-Chêng [Tashkend], having proved unsatisfactory, high officers will be specially deputed by both countries jointly to examine and alter it so that a satisfactory result may be attained. That there may be no doubt what part of the Khassak country belongs to China and what to Russia, the boundary will consist of a straight line drawn from the Kwei Tung Mountains across the Hei-i-êrh-te-shih River to the Sa-wu-êrh range, and

In length, the Northern Circuit extends about nine hundred miles, and the width, on an average, is three hundred miles. The Southern Circuit reaches nearly twelve hundred and fifty miles from west to east, and varies from three hundred to five hundred in breadth, as it extends to the Kwănlun range on the south. There is probably most arable land in the Northern Circuit.

Ílí, taken north of the Tarim basin, may be regarded as an inland isthmus, extending southwest from the south of Siberia, off between the Gobi and Caspian deserts, till it reaches the Hindu Kush, leading down to the valley of the Indus. The former of these deserts incloses it on the east and south, the other on the west and northwest, separated from each other by the Belur and Muz-tag ranges, which join with the Tien shan, that divide the isthmus itself into two parts. These deserts united are equal in extent to that of Sahara, but are not as arid and tenantless.

This region has some peculiar features, among which its great elevation, its isolation in respect to its water-courses, and the character of its vegetation, are the most remarkable. Songaria is especially noticeable for the many closed river-basins which occur between the Altai and Tien shan, among the various minor ranges of hills, each of which is entirely isolated, and containing a lake, the receptacle of its drainage. The largest of these singular basins is that of the River Ílí, which runs about three hundred miles westward, from its rise in the Tien shan (lat. 85°) till it falls into Lake Balkash, which also receives some other streams; the superficies of the whole basin is about forty thousand square miles. The other lakes lie northeastward of Balkash; the largest of them are the Dzaisang, which receives the Irtysh, the Kisilbash, into which the Urungu

---

the high officers deputed to settle the boundary will fix the new boundary along such straight line which is within the old boundary.

Art. IX. As to the boundary on the west, between the Province of Fei-ĕrh-kan [Ferghana], which is subject to Russia, and Chinese Kashgar, officials will be deputed by both countries to examine it, and they will fix the boundary line between the territories at present actually under the jurisdiction of either country, and they will erect boundary stones thereon.

flows, and four or five smaller ones between them, lying north of the city of Ílí. Lake Temurtu, or Issik-kul, lies now just beyond the southwestern part of this Circuit, and was until recently contained therein. This sheet of water is deep and never freezes; it is brackish, but full of fish; the dimensions are about one hundred miles long, and thirty-five wide; its superabundant waters flow off through the Chu ho into the Kirghís steppe.

The Ala-tau range defines the lake on the north shore. Says a Russian traveller in describing this region, " It would be difficult to imagine anything more splendid than the view of the Tien shan from this spot. The dark blue surface of the Issik-kul, like sapphire, may well bear comparison with the equally blue surface of Geneva Lake, but its expanse—five times as great—seeming almost unlimited, and the matchless splendor of its background, gives it a grandeur which the Swiss lake does not possess. The unbroken, snowy chain here stretches away for at least 200 miles of the length of the Issik-kul; the sharp outlines of the spurs and dark valleys in the front range are softened by a thin mist, which hangs over the water and heightens the clear, sharp outlines of the white heads of the Tien shan giants, as they rise and glisten on the azure canopy of a central Asian sky. The line of perpetual snow commences at three-fifths of their slope up, but as one looks, their snowless base seems to sink the deeper in the far east, till the waves of the lake seem to wash the snowy crests of Khan-Tengsè." Forty small rivers flow into it, but its size is gradually lessening.[1]

Little is known concerning the topography, the productions, or the civilization of the tribes who inhabit a large part of Songaria, but the efforts of the Chinese government have been systematically directed to developing its agricultural resources, by stationing bodies of troops, who cultivate the soil, there, and by banishing criminals thither, who are obliged to work for and assist the troops. It gives one a higher idea of the rulers of China, themselves wandering nomads originally, when they are seen carrying on such a plan for extending the capabilities of

---

[1] Compare also Schuyler, *Turkistan*, Vol. II., pp. 127 *ff*

these remote parts of their Empire, and teaching, partly by force, partly by bribes, and partly by example, the Mongol tribes under them the advantages of a settled life.

The productions of Songaria are numerous. Wheat, barley, rice and millet, are the chief corn stuffs; tobacco, cotton, melons, and some fruits, are grown; herds of horses, camels, cattle, and sheep, afford means of locomotion and food to the people, while the mountains and lakes supply game and fish. The inhabitants are composed mostly of Eleuths, with a tribe of Tourgouths, and remnants of the Songares, together with Mongols, Manchus, and Chinese troops, settlers and criminals.

TIEN-SHAN PEH LU is divided by the Chinese into three commanderies, *Ílí* on the west, *Tarbagatai* on the north, and *Kurkara usu* on the east, between Ílí and the west end of Kansuh. The government of the North and South Circuits is under the control of Manchu military officers residing at Ílí. This city, called by the Chinese Hwuiyuen ching, and Gouldja (or Kuldja) and Kuren by the natives, lies on the north bank of the Ílí River, in lat. 43° 55′ N., and long. 81½° E.; it contains about fifty thousand inhabitants, and carries on considerable trade with China through the towns in Kansuh. The city was defended by six strong fortresses in its neighborhood, and the solidity of the stone walls enabled it to resist a vigorous assault in the Dungani rebellion. Its circuit is nearly four miles, and two wide avenues cross its contro, dividing it into four equal parts, through each of which run many lanes. Its houses indicate the Turkish origin of its builders in their clay or adobe walls and flat roofs, and this impression is increased by the Jumma mosque of the Taranchis, and the Dungan mosque, outside of the walls. The last has a wonderful minaret built of small-roofed pavilions one over another; both of them affect the Chinese architecture in their roofs, and their walls are faced with diamond-shaped tiles. The Buddhist temple has hardly been rebuilt since the city has returned to Chinese rule. The supply of meats and vegetables is constant, and the variety and quality exceed that of most other towns in the region. The population is gradually increasing with the return of peace and trade, but is still under twenty thousand, of which not one-fifth are Chinese and Manchus: the Taranchis constitute half of the whole, and Dunganis are the next in number. The province is the richest and best cultivated of all this region of Ílí; its coal, metals, and fruits are sources of prosperity, and with its return to Chinese sway under new relations in respect to Russian trade, its future is promising.

The destruction of life was dreadful at the capture of Kuldja and other towns, which were then left a heap of ruins.[1] Schuyler estimates that not more than a hundred thousand people remained in the province, out of a third of a million in 1860. It is stated in Chinese works that when Amursana, the discontented chief of the Songares, applied, in 1775, to Kienlung for assistance against his rival Tawats or Davatsi, and was sent back with a Chinese army, in the engagements which ensued, more than a million of people were destroyed, and the whole country depopulated. At that time, Kuldja was built by Kienlung, and soon became a place of note. Outside of the town are the barracks for the troops, which consist of Eleuths and Mohammedans, as well as Manchus and Chinese. Coal is found in this region, and most of the inland rivers produce abundance of fish, while wild animals and birds are numerous. The resources of the country are, however, insufficient to meet the expenses of the military establishment, and the presents made to the begs, and the deficit is supplied from China.[2]

---

[1] 175,000 perished in Kuldja alone.

[2] The question of the existence of volcanoes in Central Asia, especially on the Kuldja frontier, has always been a matter of doubt and discussion among geologists and Russian explorers. The Governor of Semiretchinsk, General Kolpakofsky, was, in 1881, able to report the discovery of the perpetual fires in the Tien shan range of mountains. The mountain Bai shan was found twelve miles northeast of Kuldja, in a basin surrounded by the massive Ailak mountains; its fires are not volcanic, but proceed from burning coal. On the sides of the mountain there are caves emitting smoke and sulphurous gas. Mr. Schuyler, in his *Turkistan*, mentions that these perpetual fires in the mountains, referred to by Chinese historians, were considered by Severtzoff, a Russian, who explored the region, as being caused by the ignition of the seams of coal, or the carburetted hydrogen gas in the seams. The same author further mentions that Captain Tosnofskey, another Russian explorer, was told of a place in the neighborhood from which steam constantly rose, and that near this crevice there had existed, from ancient times, three pits, where persons afflicted with rheumatism or skin diseases were in the habit of bathing.

Subordinate to the control of the commandant at Kuldja are nine garrisoned places situated in the same valley, at each of which are bodies of Chinese convicts. The two remaining districts of Tarbagatai and Kur-kara usu are small compared with Ílí; the first lies between Cobdo and the Kirghís steppe, and is inhabited mostly by emigrants from the steppes of the latter, who render merely a nominal subjection to the garrisons placed over them, but are easily governed through their tribal rulers. The Tourgouths, who emigrated from Russia in 1772, into China, are located in this district and Cobdo, as well as in the valleys of the Tekes and Kunges rivers. They have become more or less assimilated with other tribes since they were placed here. In the war with the Songares, many of the people fled from the valley of Ílí to this region, and after that country was settled, they submitted to the Emperor, and partly returned to Ílí. The chief town, called Tuguchuk by the Kirghís, and Suitsing ching by the Chinese, is situated not far from the southern base of the Tarbagatai Mountains, and contains about six hundred houses, half of which belong to the garrison. It is one of the nine fortified towns under the control of the commandant at Kuldja, and a place of some trade with the Kirghís. There are two residents stationed here, with high powers to oversee the trade across the frontier, but their duties are inferior in importance to those of the officials at Urga. 2,500 Manchu and Chinese troops remain at this post, and since the conquest of the country in 1772 by Kienlung, its agricultural products have gradually increased under the industry of the Chinese. The tribes dwelling in this distant province are restricted within certain limits, and their obedience secured by presents. The climate of Tarbagatai is changeable, and the cold weather comprises more than half the year. The basin of Lake Ala-kul, or Alaktu-kul, occupies the southwest, and part of the Irtysh and Lake Dzaisang the northeast, so that it is well watered. The trade consists chiefly of domestic animals and cloths.

The town of Kur-kara usu lies on the River Kur, northeast from Kuldja and on the road between it and Urumtsi; it is called Kingsui ching by the Chinese. The number of troops stationed at all these posts is estimated at sixty thousand, and the total population of Songaria under two millions.

The TIEN-SHAN NAN LU, or Southern Circuit of Ílí, the territory of 'the eight Mohammedan cities,' was named *Sin Kiang* ('New Frontier') by Kienlung. It is less fertile than the Northern Circuit, the greatest part of its area consisting of rugged mountains or barren wastes, barely affording subsistence for herds of cattle and goats. The principal boundaries are the Kwănlun Mountains, and the desert, separating it from Tibet on the south; Cashmere lies on the southwest, and Badakshan and Kokand are separated from it on the west and northwest by the Belur-tag, all of them defined and partitioned by the mountain ranges over which the passes 12,000 to 16,000 feet high furnish both defence and travel according to the season.

The greater part of this Circuit is occupied with the basin of the Tarim or Ergu, which flows from the Belur range in four principal branches[1] (called from the towns lying upon their banks the Yarkand, Kashgar, Aksu, and Khoten Rivers), and running eastward, receives several affluents from the north and south, and falls into Lake Lob in long. 89° E., after a course, including windings, of between 1,100 and 1,300 miles. Of the river system from which this stream flows Baron Richthofen says, "the region which gives birth to this river is on a scale of grandeur such as no other river in the world can boast. It is girt round by a wide semicircular collar of mountains of the loftiest and grandest character, often rising in ridges of 18,000 to 20,000 feet in height, while the peaks shoot up to 25,000 and even 28,000 feet. The basin which fills in the horse-shoe shaped space encompassed by these gigantic elevations, though deeply depressed below them, stands at a height above the sea varying from 6,000 feet at the margin to about 2,000 in the middle, and formed the bed of an ancient sea. From its wall-like sides on the south, west, and north, the waters rush headlong down, and though the winds blowing from all directions deposit most of their moisture on the remoter sides of the surrounding

---

[1] Wood, *Journey to the Source of the River Oxus*, p. 356. From the hills that encircle Lake Sir-i-kol rise some of the principal rivers in Asia: the Yarkand, Kashgar, Sirr, Kuner, and Oxus.

ranges, viz., the southern foot of the Himalayas, the west side of the Pamir, and the northern slope of the Tien shan, the streams formed thereby winding through the cloud-capped lofty cradle-land, and breaking through the mountain chains, reach the old ocean bed only partly well watered. The smallest of them disappear in the sand, others flow some distance before expanding into a level salt basin and are there absorbed. Only the largest, whose number the Chinese estimate at sixty, unite with the Tarim, a river 1,150 miles long, and therefore in length between the Rhine and Danube, but far surpassing both in the massiveness of surrounding mountains, just as it exceeds the Danube in the extent of its basin. Its tributaries form along the foot of the mountains a number of fruitful oases, and these by means of artificial irrigation have been converted into flourishing, cultivated states, and have played an important part in the history of these regions."[1] Col. Prejevalsky's explorations in this totally unknown country have brought out a multitude of facts pregnant with interest both for historical and geographical study. Among the most important results of his discoveries is the location of Lob more than a degree to the south of its position on Chinese maps, and a consequent bend of the Tarim from its due eastern course before it reaches its outlet. This lake, consisting of two sheets of water, the Kara-buran and Kara-kurchin (or Chon-kul), lies on the edge of the desert, in an uninhabited region, and surrounded by great swamps, which extend also northwest along the Tarim to its junction with the Kaidu. It is shallow, overgrown with weeds, and is for the most part a morass, the water being fresh, despite the salt marshes in the vicinity. The people living near it speak a language most like that of Khoten; they are Moslems. Lake Lob is elliptical, 90 to 100 versts long and 20 wide, 2,200 feet above the sea. Enormous flocks of birds come from Khoten on the southwest, as they go north, and make Lob-nor their stopping-place. The desert in this region is poor and desolate in the extreme. Its southern side is formed by the Altyn-tag range, a spur of the Kwănlun Mountains that rises about 14,000 feet in a sheer

[1] *Richthofen's Remarks* in Prejevalsky's *Lob-nor*, p. 138. London, 1879.

wall. Wild camels are found in its ravines, whose sight, hearing, and smell are marvellously acute. No other river basins of any size are found within the Circuit, except a large tributary called the Kaidu, which, draining a parallel valley north of Lob-nor, two hundred miles long, runs into a lake nearly as large, called Bostang-nor, from which an outlet on the south continues it into the Tarim, about eighty miles from its mouth. The tributaries of this river are represented as much more serviceable for agricultural purposes than the main trunk is for navigation. The plain through which the Tarim flows is about two hundred miles broad and not far from nine hundred miles long, most of it unfit for cultivation or pasturage. The desert extends considerably west of the two lakes. The climate of this region is exceedingly dry, and its barrenness is owing, apparently, more to the want of moisture than to the nature of the soil. The western parts are colder than those toward Kansuh, the river being passable on ice at Yarkand, in lat. 38°, for three months, while frost is hardly known at Hami, in lat. 43°.

The productions of the valley of the Tarim comprise most of the grains and fruits found in Southern Europe; the sesamum is cultivated for oil instead of the olive. Few trees or shrubs cover the mountain acclivities or plains. All the domestic animals abound, except the hog, which is reared in small numbers by the Chinese. The camel and yak are hunted and raised for food and service, their coats affording both skins and hair for garments. The horse, camel, black cattle, ass, and sheep, are found wild on the edge of the desert, where they find a precarious subsistence. The mountains and marshes contain jackals, tigers, bears, wolves, lynxes, and deer, together with some large species of birds of prey. Gold, copper, and iron are brought from this region, but the amount is not large, and as articles of trade they are less important than the sal-ammoniac, saltpetre, sulphur, and asbestos obtained from the volcanic region in the east of the Celestial Mountains. The best specimens of the *yuh* or nephrite, so highly prized by the Chinese, are obtained in the Southern Circuit.

The present divisions of this Circuit are regulated by the

position of the eight Mohammedan cities. The western departments of Kansuh naturally belong to the same region, and the cities now pertaining to that province are inhabited by entirely similar races, and governed in the same feudal manner, with some advantages in consideration of their early submission to Kienlung. The first town on the road, of note, is Hami; Turfan and Pidshan are less important as trading posts than as garrisons. The eight cities are named in the *Statistics of the Empire* in the following order, beginning at the east: Harashar, Kuché, Ushí (including Sairim and Bai), Aksu, Khoten, Yarkand, Kashgar, and Yingkeshar or Yangi Hissar. The superior officers live at Yarkand, but the Southern Circuit is divided into four minor governments at Harashar, Ushí, Yarkand, and Khoten, each of whose residents reports both to Kuldja and Peking. There is constant restiveness on the part of the subject races, who are all Moslems, arising from their clannish habits and feuds; they have not the elements of substantial progress and national growth, either under their own rulers or Chinese. They have lately thrown off the Peking Government, but they have generally regretted the rapines and waste caused by the strifes and change, and would probably receive the *Kitai* (so they term the Chinese) back again. The latter are not hard masters, and bring trade and wealth the longer they remain. One of the Usbek chiefs under Yakub khan gave the pith of the situation between the two, when he replied to Dr. Bellew's remark that he talked like a Chinese himself, "No, I hate them. But they were not bad rulers. We had everything then; we have nothing now. We never see any signs of the Kitai trade, nor of the wealth they brought here."

Harashar (or Karashar) lies on the Kaidu River, not far from Lake Bagarash or Bostang, about two hundred and ninety miles west of Turfan, in lat. 42° 15′ N., and long. 87° E. It is a large district, and has two towns of some note within the jurisdiction of its officers—namely, Korla and Bukur. Harashar is fortified, and from its being a secure position, and the seat of the chief resident, attracts considerable trade. The embroidery is superior; but the tribes living in the district are more addicted to hunting than disposed to sedentary trades. Korla lies southwest of Harashar on the Kaidu, between lakes Bostang and Lob, and the productions of the town and its vicinity indi cate a fertile soil; the Chinese say the Mohammedans who live here are fond of singing, but have no ideas of ceremony or urbanity. Bukur lies two hundred miles west of Korla and "might be a rich and delicious country," says the Chinese account, "but those idle, vagrant Mohammedans only use their strength in theft and plunder; the women blush at nothing." The town formerly contained upward of ten thousand inhabitants, but Kienlung nearly destroyed it; the district has been since resettled by Hoshoits, Tourbeths, and Turks, and the people carry on some trade in the produce of their herds, skins, copper, and agates.

Kuché, about eighty miles west from Bukur, lat. 41° 37′ N., and long. 83° 20′ E., is a larger and more important city than that of Harashar, for the road which crosses the Tien shan by the pass Muz-daban to Îlí, here joins that coming from Aksu on the west and Hami on the east. It is three miles in circuit, and is defended by ten forts and three hundred troops. The bazaars contain grain, fruits, and vegetables, raised in the vicinity by great labor, for the land requires to be irrigated by hand from wells, pools, and streams. Copper, sulphur, and saltpetre are carried across to Îlí, for use of government as well as traffic, being partly levied from the inhabitants as taxes; linen is manufactured in the town, and sal ammoniac, cinnabar, and quicksilver are procured from the mountains. Kuché is considered the gate of Turkestan, and is the chief town, politically speaking, between Hami and Yarkand. The district and town of Shayar lie south of Kuché, in a marshy valley producing abundance of rice, melons, and fruit; the pears are particularly good. Two small lakes, Baba-kul and Sary-kamysch, lie to the east of this town, and are the only bodies of water between Bostang-nor and Issik-kul. The population is about four thousand, ruled by *begs* subordinate to the general at Kuché.

The valley of the Aksu contains two large towns, Aksu and Ushí or Ush-turfan, besides several posts and villages. Between the former and Kuché, lie the small garrisons and districts of Bai and Sairim. The first contains from four to five hundred families, ruled by their own chiefs. Sairim or Hanlemuh is subordinate to Ushí in some degree, but its productions, climate, and inhabitants are like those of Kuché. "Their manners are simple," remarks a Chinese writer, speaking of the people; "they are neither cowards nor rogues like the other Mohammedans; they are fond of singing, drinking, and dancing, like those of Kuché." Aksu is a large commercial and manufacturing town, containing twenty thousand inhabitants, situated, like Kuché, at the termination of a road leading across the Tien shan to Ílí, and attracting to its market traders from Siberia, Bokhara, and Kokand, as well as along the great road. Its manufactures of cotton, silk, leather, harnesses, crockery, precious stones, and metals are good, and sent abroad in great numbers. The country produces grain, fruits, vegetables, and cattle in perfection, and the people are more civilized than those on the east and north; "they are generous and noble, and both sing and ridicule the oddities and niggardliness of the other Mohammedans." The Chinese garrison consists of three thousand soldiers, and the officers are accountable to those at Ushí.

Ushí lies about 70 miles due west of Aksu, in lat. 41° 15′ N. and long. 79° 40′ E., and is stated to contain ten thousand inhabitants. The Chinese name is Yung-ning ching (*i.e.* 'City of Eternal Tranquillity'). The officers stationed here report to the commandant at Ílí, but they communicate directly with Peking, and receive the Emperor's sanction to their choice of begs, and to the envoys forwarded to the capital with tribute. Copper money is cast here in ingots, somewhat like the ingots of sycee in the provinces. There are six forts attached to Ushí, to keep in order the wandering tribes of the Kirghís, called Pruth Kirghís,[1] which roam over the frontier regions between Ushí and Yarkand. They pay homage to the officers at Ushí, but give no tribute. Those who do pay tribute are taxed a tenth, but the Kirghís on this frontier are usually allowed to roam where they like, provided they keep the peace. This region was nearly depopulated by Kienlung's generals, and at present sup-

---

[1] Called also *Pourouts*. Compare Klaproth (*Mémoires*, Tome III., p. 332), who has a notice of these tribes.

ports a sparse population compared with its fertility and resources.

The government of Kashgar, known, at the time of the Arab conquest, as *Kichik Bukhara*, presents a vast, undulating plain, of which the slope is very gradual toward the east, and of which the general elevation may be reckoned at from three to four thousand feet above the sea. The aspect of its surface is mostly one of unmitigated waste—a vast spread of bare sand and gloomy salts, traversed in all directions by dunes and banks of gravel, with the scantiest vegetation, and all but absence of animal life. Such is the view that meets the eye and joins the horizon everywhere on the plain immediately beyond the river courses and the settlements planted on their banks.[1] The population of this whole district is considerably less than a million and a half. The natural mineral productions here are of great value, and it is a knowledge of this fact which has induced the Chinese to persevere in retaining so expensive and turbulent a frontier province. The gold and jade of Khoten, silver and lead of Cosharab, and copper of Khalistan, have given abundant employment to Chinese settlers; while coal, iron, sulphur, alum, sal ammoniac, and zinc, though worked in unimportant quantities before the insurrection of Yakub khan (Atalik Ghazi), furnished the inhabitants with supplies for domestic use. An important hinderance to building villages in many sections of this territory is the prevalence of sand dunes here. Solitary houses and even whole settlements lying in the path of these moving hills are suddenly overwhelmed and oftentimes totally effaced.

The town of Kashgar is situated at the northwestern angle of the Southern Circuit, on the Kashgar River, a branch of the Tarim, in lat. 39° 25′ N., and long. 76° 5′ E., at the extreme west of the Empire. Several roads meet here. Going in a northwest direction, one leads over the Tien shan to Kokand; a second passes south, through Yarkand and Khoten, to Leh and Cashmere; a third, the great caravan route, from China through

---

[1] H. W. Bellew, *Kashmir and Kashgar. A Narrative of the Journey of the Embassy to Kashgar in* 1873–4, p. 2.

Ushí, may be said to end here; and the fourth and most frequented, leads off northwest over the Tien shan through the Rowat Pass, and along the western banks of Lake Issik-kul to Ílí. Kashgar was the capital of the Oigours for a long time, and its ruler forced his people, as far east as Hami, to accept Islamism about the year 1000. They then came under Genghis' sway, and this city increased its importance, but when Abubahr Miza took Yarkand, he razed Kashgar to the ground. Under Chinese rule it became one of the richest marts in Central Asia, and its future importance is secured by its position. The city is enclosed with high and massive walls, supported by buttress bastions, and protected by a deep ditch on three sides, the river flowing under the fourth. There are but two gates; the area within is about fifty acres. Around it are populous suburbs.

In the middle of the town is a large square, and four bazaars branch from it through to the gates; the garrison is placed without the walls. The manufactures of Kashgar excel those of any other town in the two Circuits, especially in jade, gold, silk, cotton, gold and silver cloths, and carpets. The country around produces fruit and grain in abundance; "the manners of the people have an appearance of elegance and politeness," says the Chinese geographer; "the women dance and sing in family parties; they fear and respect the officers, and have not the wild, uncultivated aspect of those in Ushí." This judgment is in a measure confirmed by Bellew, who credits the people with being singularly free from prejudice against the foreigners, quite indifferent on any score of his nationality or religion, and content so long as he pays his way and does not offend the customs of the natives. Several towns are subordinate to Kashgar, because of its oversight of their rulers, and consumption of their products. Southwest lies Tashbalig, and on the road leading to Yarkand is Yangi Hissar, both of them towns of some importance; the whole distance from Kashgar presents a succession of sandy or saline tracts, alternating with fertile bottoms wherever water runs. Small villages and post houses serve to connect the larger towns, but the soil does not reward the cultivators with much produce.

Yarkand, or Yerkiang, is the political capital of the Southern Circuit, as the highest military officers and strongest force are stationed here. It is situated on the Yarkand River, in lat. 36° 30′ N., and long. 77° 15′ E., in the midst of a sand-girt oasis of great fertility. The environs are abundantly supplied with water by canals. The stone walls are three miles in circumference, but its suburbs are much larger; the houses are built of dried bricks, and the town has a more substantial appearance than others in Ílí. There are many mosques and colleges, which, with the public buildings occupied by the government and troops, add to its consideration. Yarkand is one of the ancient cities of Tartary, and was, in remote times, a royal residence of Turk princes of the Afrasyab dynasty. In modern times it owes its rank as a well-built city chiefly to Abubahr Miza, whose short-lived sway from Aksu to Wakhan left its chief results in the mosques and bazaars erected or enlarged by him. By means of quarrying jade in the Karakash valley, and working the bangles, ear-rings and other articles in the city, thousands of families found employment under Chinese rule.

With the overthrow of that sway and then of Yakub khan in its restoration, all this industry disappeared. In the destruction ensuing on these long struggles for supremacy, one learns the explanation of the barbarism which has succeeded the downfall of mighty empires all over Western Asia. The city has no important manufactures; it enjoys a local reputation for its leather, and boots and shoes made here are esteemed all over the province. Among other articles of trade are horses, silk, and wool, and fabrics made from them; but everything found at Kashgar is sold also at this market. In a Chinese notice of the city, the customs at Yarkand are stated to have yielded over $45,000 annually; the taxes are 35,400 sacks of grain, 57,569 pieces of linen, 15,000 lbs. of copper, besides gold, silk, varnish, and hemp, part of which are carried to Ílí. Jade is obtained from the river in large pieces, yellow, white, black, and reddish, and the articles made from it are carried to China. The Chinese authorities have no objection to the resorting thither of natives of Kokand, Badakshan, and other neighboring states, many of whom settle and marry.

Khoten is situated on the southern side of the desert, and the district embraces all the country south of Aksu and Yarkand, along the northern base of the Kwănlun Mountains, for more than three hundred miles from east to west. The capital is called Ílchí on Chinese maps, and lies in an extensive plain on the Khoten River in lat. 37° N., and long. 80° E. The town of Karakash (meaning 'Black Jade')[1] lies in lat. 37° 10′, long. 80° 13′ 30″, a few miles northwest in the same valley, and is said by traders to be the capital rather than Ílchí; it is located on the road to Yarkand, distant twelve days' journey. On this road the town of Gummí is also placed, whose chief had in his possession a stone supposed to have the power of causing rain. Kirrea lies five days' journey east of Ílchí, near the pass across the mountains into Tibet and Ladak; a gold mine is worked near this place, the produce of which is monopolized by the Chinese. The three towns of Karakash, Ílchí, and Kirrea, are the only places of importance between the valley of the Tarim and Tibet, but none of them have been visited for a long time by Europeans.[2] The population of the town or district is unknown; one notice[3] gives it a very large number, approaching three millions and even more, which at any rate indicates a more fertile soil and genial climate than the regions north and south of it. Dr. Morrison, in his *View of China*, puts it at 44,630 inhabitants; and although the former includes the whole district, and is probably too large, the second seems to be much too small.

Khoten is known, in Chinese books, by the names of *Yu-tien*, *Hwan-na*, *Kieu-tan*, and *Kiu-sa-tan-na*—the last meaning, in Sanscrit, "Breast of the Earth."[4] Its eastern part is marshy, but that the country must have a considerable elevation is manifest from the fact that the river which drains and connects it with the Tarim runs quite across the desert in its course. The country is governed by two high officers and a

---

[1] But Rémusat says that Karakash is a river and no town.

[2] Wood (*Journey to the Oxus*, p. 279) refers to a frontier town by the name of Ecla.

[3] *Penny Cyclopædia*, *Art.* THIAN SHAN NAN LU.

[4] Rémusat, *Histoire de Khotan*, p. 35.

detachment of troops; there are six towns under their jurisdiction, the inhabitants of which are ruled in the same manner as the other Mohammedan cities. The people, however, are said to be mostly of the Buddhist faith, and the Chinese give a good account of their peacefulness and industry. The trade with Leh and H'lassa is carried on by a road crossing the Kwänlun over the Kirrea Pass, beyond which it divides. The productions of Khoten are fine linen and cotton stuffs, jade ornaments, amber, copper, grain, fruits, and vegetables; the former for exportation, the latter for use. It was in this region that Col. Prejevalsky discovered (in 1879) a new variety of wild horse, a specimen of which has been stuffed and exhibited in St. Petersburg. The animal in question, though belonging undoubtedly to the genus *Equus*, presents, in many respects, an intermediate form between the domestic horse and the wild ass.

Rémusat published, in 1820, an account of this country, drawn from Chinese books, in which the principal events in its history are stated, commencing with the Han dynasty, before the Christian era, down to the Manchu conquest. In the early part of its history, Khoten was the resort of many priests from India, and the Buddhist faith was early established there. It was an independent kingdom most of the time, from its earliest mention to the era of Genghis khan, the princes sometimes extending their sway from the Kiayü pass and Koko-nor to the Tsung ling, and then being obliged to contract to the valley now designated as Khoten. After the expulsion of the Mongols from China, Khoten asserted its independence, but afterward fell under the sway of the Songares and Eleuths, and lost many of its inhabitants. The Manchus conquered it in 1770, when the rest of the region between the Tien shan and Kwänlun fell under their sway, but neither have they settled in it to the same extent, nor made thereof a penal settlement, as in other parts of Îlí.[1]

The government of Îlí differs in some respects from that of Mongolia, where religion is partly called in to aid the state. In

---

[1] Concerning the nomenclature of this region compare Rémusat, *Histoire de Khotan*, p. 66. See, moreover, *ib.*, p. 47 ff., the legend of a drove of desert rats assisting the king of this land against the army of his enemies.

the Northern Circuit, the authority is strictly military, exercised by means of residents and generals, with bodies of troops under their control. The supreme command of all Ílí is intrusted by the colonial office to a Manchu *tsiangkiun*, or military governor-general at Kuldja, who has under him two councillors to take cognizance of civil cases, and thirty-four residents scattered about in both Circuits. This governor has also the control of the troops stationed in the three western departments of Kansuh, but has nothing to do with the civil jurisdiction of those towns. The entire number of soldiers under his hand is stated at 60,000, most of whom have families, and add agricultural, mechanical, or other labors to the profession of arms. The councillors are not altogether subordinate to the general, but report to the Colonial Office.

In the Northern Circuit, there is a deputy appointed for every village and town, invested with military powers over the troops and convicts, and civil supervision over the native *píko* or chieftains, who are the real rulers acknowledged by the clans. The character of the inhabitants north of the Tien shan is rendered unlike that of those dwelling in the Southern Circuit, not more by the diversity in their language and nomadic habits, than by the sway religious rites and allegiance have over them. Through this latter motive, the government of Mongolia and the Northern Circuit is rendered far easier and more effectual for the distant court of Peking than it otherwise would be. The appointment of the native chieftains is first announced to the general at Kuldja and the Colonial Office, and they succeed to their post when confirmed, which, as the station is in a measure hereditary, usually follows in course.

The inhabitants of the Southern Circuit are Mohammedans and acknowledge a less willing subjection to the Emperor than those in the Northern, the differences in race, religion, and language being probably the leading reasons. The government of the whole region is divided among the Manchu residents or *ambans* at the eight cities, who are nominally responsible to the general at Ílí, and independent of each other, but there is a gradation in rank and power, the one at Yarkand having the priority. The begs are chosen by the tribes themselves, and exercise authority in all petty cases arising among the people, without the interference of the Chinese. The troops are all Manchu or Chinese, none of the Turks being enrolled in separate bodies, though individuals are employed with safety. There is considerable difference in the rank and influence of the begs, which is upheld and respected by the *ambans*. The allowances and style granted them are regulated in a measure by their feudal importance. The revenue is derived from a monthly capitation tax on each man of about half a dollar, and tithes on the produce; there are no transit duties as in China, but custom-houses are established at the frontier trading towns. The language generally used in the Southern Circuit is the Jaghatai Turki of the Kalmucks; the Usbecks constitute the majority of the people, but Eleuths and Kalmucks are everywhere intermixed. The Tibetans have settled in Khoten, or more probably, remnants still exist there of the former inhabitants.

The history of the vast region constituting the present government of Ílí early attracted the attention of oriental scholars, and few portions of the world have had a more exciting history. After the expulsion of the Mongols from China by Hungwu, A.D. 1366, they found that they, as a tribe, were inferior in power to the western tribes, but it was not till about 1680 that the Eleuths, north of the Tien shan under the Galdan,[1] began to attack the Kalkas, and drive them eastward. The Sunnites, Tsakhars, and Solons, portions of the Eastern Mongols, had already joined the Manchus; and the Kalkas, to avoid extermination, submitted to them also, and besought their assistance against the Eleuths. Kanghí received their allegiance, and tried to settle the difficulties peaceably, but was obliged to send his troops against the Galdan, and drive him from the territory of the Kalkas to the westward of Lob-nor and Barkul. The Emperor was materially aided in this enterprise by the secession from the Eleuths of the Songares, whose khan had taken offence, and drawn his hordes off to the south. The khans of the Kalkas and their vast territory thus

[1] "Galdan, better known by his title of Contaïsch"—Rémusat, *Nouveaux Mélanges*, Tome II., p. 29. See also Schuyler's *Turkistan*, Vol. II., p. 168.

became subject to the Chinese. The Galdan lost all his forces, and expired by poison, in 1697, his power dying with him, and his tribe having already become too weak to resist.

Upon the ruins of his power arose that of Arabdan, the khan of the Songares. He subjugated the Northern Circuit, passed over into Turkestan, Tangout, and Khoten, and gradually reduced to his sway nearly all the elevated region of Central Asia west of Kansuh. He expelled the Tourgouths from their possessions in Cobdo, and compelled them to retreat to the banks of the Volga. Kanghí expelled the Songares from the districts about Koko-nor, but made no impression upon their authority in Songaria. After the death of Arabdan, about 1720, his throne was disputed, and the power weakened by dissensions among his sons, so that it was seized by two usurpers, Amursana and Tawats, who also fell out after their object was gained. Amursana repaired to Peking for assistance, and with the aid of a Chinese army expelled Tawats, and took possession of the throne of Arabdan. But he had no intention of becoming a vassal to Kienlung, and was no sooner reinstated than he resisted him; he defeated two Chinese armies sent against him, but succumbed on the third attack, and fled to Tobolsk, where he died in 1757.

The territory of Arabdan then fell to Kienlung, and he pursued his successes with such cruelty that the Northern Circuit was nearly depopulated, and the Songares and Eleuths became almost extinct as distinct tribes. The banished tribe of Tourgouths was then invited by the Emperor to return from Russian sway to their ancient possessions, which they accepted in 1772; the history of the Chinese embassy to them, and their disastrous journey back to Cobdo over the Kirghís steppe and through the midst of their enemies, is one of the most remarkable instances of nomadic wanderings and unexampled suffering in modern times.[1] Chinese troops, emigrants, exiles, and nomadic tribes and families, were sent and encouraged to come

[1] Compare Rémusat (*Nouveaux Mélanges*, Tome II., p. 102), who has compiled a brief life of their leader Ubusha. De Quincey's essay, *The Flight of a Tartar Tribe.* Ritter, *Asien*, Bd. V. pp. 531–583: *Welthistorischer Einfluss des chinesichen Reichs auf Central- und West-Asien.*

into the vacant territory, so that erelong it began to resume its former importance. In the period which has since elapsed, the Manchus have been enabled to prevent any combination among the clans, and maintain their own authority by a mixed system of coercion and coaxing which they well know how to practise. The agricultural and mineral resources of the country have been developed, many of the nomads induced to attend to agriculture by making their chieftains emulous of each other's prosperity, and by exciting a spirit of traffic among all.

There have been some disturbances from time to time, but no master spirit has arisen who has been able to unite the tribes against the Chinese. In 1825, there was an attempt made from Kokand by Jehangír, grandson of the *kojeh* or prince of Kashgar, to regain possession of Turkestan; the khan of Kokand assisted him with a small army, and such was their dislike of the Chinese, that as soon as Jehangír appeared, the Mohammedans arose and drove the Chinese troops away or put them to death, opening the gates to the invader. He took possession of Yarkand and Kashgar, and advanced to Aksu, where the winter put a stop to the campaign. In the next year, the khan of Kokand, seeing the disposition of the people, thought he would embark himself in the same cause, and made an incursion as far as Aksu and Khoten, reducing more than half the Southern Circuit to himself, but ostensibly in aid of Jehangír. The kojeh, beginning to fear his aid, withdrew; and the khan, having suffered some reverses from the Chinese troops, made his peace on very favorable terms, and returned to his own country. Jehangír went to Khoten from Yarkand, but his conduct there displeasing the people, the Chinese troops, about 60,000 in number, had no difficulty in dispersing his force, and resuming their sway. The adherents of the kojeh fled toward Badakshan, while he himself repaired to Isaac, the newly appointed kojeh of Kashgar, by whom he was delivered up to the Chinese with his family, and all of them most barbarously destroyed.

The kojeh was rewarded with the office of prince of Kashgar, but having been accused of treasonable designs he was ordered to come to Peking for trial; the charges were all disproved, and he returned to Kashgar after several years' residence at the capital of the Empire. The country was gradually reduced by Changling, the general at Ílí, but Kashgar suffered so much by the war and removal of the chief authority to Yarkand, that it has not since regained its importance. During this war, the dislike of the Mohammedans to the Chinese sway was exhibited in the large forces Jehangír brought into the field; and if he had been a popular spirited leader, there is reason for supposing he might have finally wrested these cities from the Chinese. The joy of Taukwang at the successful termination of the expedition and capture of the rebel, was so extravagant as to appear childish; and when Jehangír was executed at Peking, he ordered the sons of two officers who had been reported killed, "to witness his execution, in order to give expansion to the indignation which had accumulated in their breasts; and let the rebel's heart be torn out and given to them to sacrifice it at the tombs of their fathers, and thus console their faithful spirits." Honors were heaped upon Changling at his return to Peking, and rewards and titles showered upon all the troops engaged in the war.

Since this insurrection, the frontiers of Kashgar and Kokand have been passed and repassed by the Pruth Kirghís; in 1830, they excited so much trouble because their trade was restricted, that a large force was called out to restrain them, and many lives were lost before the rising was subdued. The causes of the dispute were then examined, and the trade allowed to go on as before. The oppressions of the residents sometimes goad on the Mohammedans to rise against the Chinese, but the policy of the Emperor is conciliatory, and the complaints of the people are in general listened to. The visits of the begs and princes to Peking with tribute affords them an opportunity to state their grievances, while it also prevents them from caballing among themselves. In 1871 the Russians took possession of nearly the whole of Tien-Shan Peh Lu during an insurrection of the Dunganis against Chinese control. The Tarantchis having attacked a Russian outpost, and Yakub Beg being on suspiciously good terms with the rebels, it was determined to occupy Kuldja—which was effected after a campaign of less than a month, led by Gen. Kolpakofsky. The Chinese government was immediately informed that the place should be restored whenever a sufficient force could be brought there to hold it against attacks, and preserve order. After the final conquest of the Dungan tribes in 1879–80, this territory was returned by the Russians upon conclusion of their last treaty with China, exactly ten years from the date of possession. The old manner of government is now resumed and the country slowly recovering from the frightful devastation of the insurrection. The salaries of the governor-general and his councillors, and the residents, are small, and they are all obliged to resort to illegal means to reimburse their outlays. The highest officer receives about $5,200 annually, and his councillors about $2,000 ; the residents from $2,300 down to $500 and less. These sums do not, probably, constitute one-tenth of the receipts of their situations.[1]

The third great division of the colonial part of the Chinese empire, that of TIBET, is less known than Îlí, though its area is hardly less extensive. It constitutes the most southern of the three great table lands of Central Asia, and is surrounded with high mountains which separate it from all the contiguous regions. The word Tibet or Tubet is unknown among the inhabitants as the name of their country; it is a corruption by the Mongols of *Tu po*,[2] the country of the Tu, a race which overran it in the sixth century; Turner gives another name, *Pue-koachim*, signifying the 'snowy country of the north,' doubtless a local or ancient term. The general appellation by the people is *Pot* or *Bod*, or *Bod yul*—"the land of Bod."[3] It is roughly bounded northeast by Koko-nor; east by Sz'chuen and Yunnan; south by Assam, Butan, Nípal, and Gurhwal; west by Cashmere; and north by the unknown ranges of the Kwănlun Mountains. The southern frontier curves considerably in its course,

---

[1] *Chinese Repository*, Vol. V., pp. 267, 316, 351, etc.; Vol. IX., p. 113. *Penny Cyclopædia*, *Art.* SONGARIA. Boulger, *Russia and England in Central Asia*, 2 Vols., London, 1879. Schuyler, *Turkistan*, 2 vols., N. Y., 1877. Petermann's *Mittheilungen*, Appendices XLII. and XLIII., 1875.

[2] This derivation is explained somewhat differently in Rémusat, *Nouveaux Mélanges*, Tome I., p. 190.

[3] To these Ritter adds the names of Wei, Dzang, Nga-ri, Kham, Bhodi, Peu-u-Tsang, Si-Dzang, Thupho, Tobbat, Töböt, Tübet, Tibet, and Barantola, as all applying to this country. *Asien*, Bd. III., S. 174–183.

but is not less than 1,500 miles from the western extremity of Nípal to the province of Yunnan; the northern border is about 1,300 miles; the western frontiers cannot be accurately defined, and depend more upon the possession of the passes through which trade is carried on than any political separation. Beltistan, Little Tibet, and Ladak, although included in its limits on Chinese maps, have too little subjection or connection with the court of Peking, to be reckoned among its dependencies.

Tibet, in its largest limits, is a table land, the highest plains of which have a mean elevation of 11,510 feet, or about 1,300 feet lower than the plateau of Bolivia, near Lake Titicaca. The snow-line on the north side of the Himalaya is at an altitude of 16,630 feet; on the southern slope it is at 12,982 feet. Several striking analogies may be traced between this country and Peru: the tripartite divisions caused by lofty ranges; their common staples of wool, from alpacas and vicunas in one, and sheep and goats in the other; the abundance of precious metals, and many specific customs. The entire province of Tibet is divided by mountain chains into three distinct parts; its western portion consists of the basin of the Indus, until it breaks through into Cashmere at Makpon-i-Shagaron. It begins near Mount Kailasa, and stretches northwest between the Hindu Kush and Himalaya, comprising the whole of Beltistan and Ladak; the Kara-korum, Mus-tag, or Tsung ling range defines it on the northeast. The second part consists of an extensive desert land, commencing at Mount Kailasa, and having the Tsung ling on the west, the Kwănlun on the north (which separates it from Khoten, and the high watershed of the Yangtsz', Salween, and other rivers), and Lake Tengkiri, on the east; the Himalaya constitutes its southern boundary. This high region, called Katshe or Kor-kache, has not been traversed by intelligent travellers and is one of the few yet unknown regions of the earth, and is nearly uninhabitable, owing to the extreme rigor of its climate.[1]

---

[1] See Rémusat, *Nouveaux Mélanges*, I., p. 190, for notices of tribes anciently inhabiting this district and Bokhara. Compare also Heeren (*Historical Researches*, Vol. I., pp. 180–186), who gives in brief the accounts of Herodotus and Ctesias.

The eastern part, consisting of the basin of the Yaru-tsangbu, contains, in its plains, most of the towns in Tibet, until it reaches the Alpine region which lies between the River Yaru and the Yangtsz', a space extending from long. 95° to 99° E. This district is described as a succession of ridges and gorges, over which the road takes the traveller on narrow and steep paths, crossing the valleys by ropes and bridges enveloped in the clouds. Mount Kailasa, a notable peak lying in the north-eastern part of Nari, is not far from 26,000 feet high. The number of summits covered with perpetual snow exceeds that of any other part of the world of the same extent.

The road from Sz'chuen to H'lassa strikes the Yalung kiang, in the district of Ta tsien lu, and then goes southwesterly to Batang on the Yangtsz' kiang; crossing the river it proceeds up the narrow valley a short distance, and then crosses the mountains northwest to the Lantsan kiang or River Meikon, by a series of pathways leading over the gorges, till it reaches Tsiamdo; from this point the road turns gradually south-west, following the valleys when practicable, till it ends at H'lassa.

The largest river in Tibet is the Erechumbu, or Yaru-tsangbu; *tsangbu* means river, and is often alone used for this whole name. It rises in the Tamchuk range, at the Mariam-la pass in Nari, 60 miles east of Lake Manasarowa, the source of the Sutlej; it flows a little south of east for about seven hundred miles, through the whole of Southern Tibet, between the first and second ranges of the Himalayas, as far as long. 90° E. Its tributaries on the north are numerous, and among them the Nauk-tsangbu and Dzangtsu are the largest. The volume of water which flows through the mountains into Assam by this river, is equal to that by the Indus into Scinde. The disputed question, whether the Yaru-tsangbu joins the Brahmaputra or Irrawadi, has been settled by presumptive evidence in favor of the former, but a distance of about 400 miles is still unexplored;[1] the fall in this part is about 11,000 feet, to where the river Dihong has been traced in Assam. This makes the Brah-

[1] Introduction by Col. Yule, in Gill's *River of Golden Sand.*

maputra the largest and longest river in Southern Asia; its passage into Assam is near 95° E. longitude.

The eastern part of Tibet, beyond this meridian, is traversed by numerous ranges of lofty mountains, having no separate names, the direction of which is from west to east, and from northwest to southeast. From these ranges, lateral branches run out in different directions, containing deep valleys between them. In proportion as the principal chains advance towards the southeast they converge towards one another, and thus the valleys between them gradually become narrower, until at last, on the frontiers of Yunnan and Burmah, they are mere mountain passes, whose entire breadth does not much exceed a hundred miles, having four streams flowing through them. In fact, Tibet incloses the fountain heads of all the large rivers of Southern and Eastern Asia. The names and courses of those in Eastern Tibet are known only imperfectly from Chinese maps, but others have described them after their entrance into the lowlands.

Tibet, especially the central part, is a country of lakes, in this respect resembling Cobdo. The largest, Tengkiri-nor, situated in the midst of stupendous mountains, about one hundred and ten miles northwest of H'lassa, is over a hundred miles long and about thirty wide. The region north of it contains many isolated lakes, most of them salt. Two of the largest, the Bouka and Kara, are represented as connected with the River Nu. Lake Khamba-la, Yamoruk or Yarbrokyu, sometimes called Palti, from a town on its northern shore, is a large lake south of H'lassa, remarkable for its ring shape, the centre being filled by a large island, around which its waters flow in a channel thirty miles or more in width. On the island is a nunnery, called the Palace of the Holy Sow, said to be the finest in the country. In Balti or Little Tibet are many sheets of water, the largest of which, the Yik and Paha, are connected by a river flowing through a marshy country. A long succession of lakes fill one of the basins in Katsche, suggesting the former existence of another Aral Sea. The sacred lakes of Manasarowa and Ravan-hrad (Mapam-dalai and Langga-nor, of the Chinese) form the headwaters of the Sutlej.

The climate of Tibet is characterized by its purity and excessive dryness. The valleys are hot, notwithstanding their proximity to snow-capped mountains; from May to October the sky is clear in the table-lands, and in the valleys the moisture and temperature are favorable to vegetation, the harvest being gathered before the gales and snows set in, after October. The effects of the air resemble or are worse than those of the kamsín in Egypt. The trees wither, and their leaves may be ground to powder between the fingers; planks and beams break, and the inhabitants cover the timbers and wood-work of their houses with coarse cotton, in order to preserve them against the destructive saccidity. The timber neither rots nor is worm-eaten. Mutton, exposed to the open air, becomes so dry that it may be powdered like bread; when once dried it is preserved during years. This flesh-bread is a common food in Tibet. The carcass of the animal, divested of its skin and viscera, is placed where the frosty air will have free access to it, until all the juices of the body dry up, and the whole becomes one stiffened mass. No salt is used, nor does it ever become tainted, and is eaten without any further dressing or cooking; the natives eat it at all periods after it is frozen, and prefer the fresh to that which has been kept some months. The food called *jamba* is prepared by cooking brick tea during several hours, then adding butter and salt, and stirring the mixture until it becomes a thick broth. When eaten the stuff is served in wooden bowls, and a plentiful supply of roasted barley-meal poured in, the whole being kneaded by the hands and devoured in the shape of dough pellets.

The productions of Tibet consist of domestic animals, cattle, horses, pigs; some wild animals, such as the white-breasted argali, orongo-antelope, ata-dzeren, wolf, and steppe-fox; and few plants or forests, presenting a strong contrast with Nípal and Butan, where vegetable life flourishes more luxuriantly. Sheep and goats are reared in immense flocks, for beasts of burden over the passes, and for their flesh, hair, and coats. Chiefest among the animals of this mountain land is the yak.[1] The

[1] Called by Wood *Kash-gow* (*Journey to the Oxus*, p. 319). *Chauri gau*, *sarlyk*, and *sarlac*, are other names.

domesticated variety, or long-haired yak, is the inseparable companion and most trusty servant not only of the Tibetans, but of tribes in Cashmere, Ladak, Tangout, and Mongolia, even as far north as Urga. It is a cross-breed, or mule from the yak bull and native cow, which alone is hardy enough for these elevated regions.[1] These creatures are of the same size as our cattle, strong, sure-footed and possessed of extraordinary endurance; they retain, however, something of their wild nature, even after long domestication, and must be carefully treated,

Domesticated Yak.

especially when being loaded and unloaded. They thrive best in hilly countries, well watered and covered with grass—the two last being indispensable. The hair is black or black and white, seldom entirely white. One sort is without horns, and when crossed with the cow bears sterile males, or females which are fertile for one generation. As to the wild yak of Tibet, a traveller says: "This handsome animal is of extraordinary size and beauty, measuring, when grown, eleven feet in length, exclusive of its bushy tail, which is three feet long; its height at the hump is six feet; girth around the body eleven feet, and its

[1] This cross is mentioned by Marco Polo, *Yule's ed.*, Vol. I., p. 241.

weight ten or eleven hundred weight. The head is adorned with ponderous horns, two feet nine inches long, and one foot four inches in circumference at the root. The body is covered with thick, black hair, which in the old males assumes a chestnut color on the back and upper parts of the sides, and a deep fringe of black hair hangs down from the flanks. The muzzle is partly gray, and the younger males have marks of the same color on the upper part of the body, whilst a narrow, silvery-gray stripe runs down the centre of the back. The hair of young yaks is much softer than that of older ones; they are also distinguishable by their smaller size, and by handsomer horns, with the points turned up. The females are much smaller than the males, and not nearly so striking in appearance; their horns are shorter and lighter, the hump smaller, and the tail and flanks not nearly as hairy."[1] This animal is useful for its milk, flesh, and wool, as well as for agricultural purposes and travel.

There is comparatively little agriculture. The variety of wild animals, birds, and fishes, is very great; among them the musk deer, feline animals, eagles, and wild sheep, are objects of the chase. The brute creation are generally clothed with an abundance of fine hair or wool; even the horses have a shaggier coat than is granted to bears in more genial climes. The Tibetan mastiff is one of the largest and fiercest of its race, almost untamable, and unknown out of its native country. The musk deer is clothed with a thick covering of hair two or three inches long, standing erect over the whole body; the animal resembles a hog in size and form, having, however, slender legs. The Tibetan goat affords the shawl wool, so highly prized for the manufacture of garments.[2]

---

[1] Prejevalsky, *Travels in Mongolia*, etc., Vol. I., p. 187.

[2] B. H. Hodgson, Notice of the Mammals of Tibet, *Journal As. Soc. of Bengal*, Vol. XI., pp. 275 ff.; also *ib.* Vols. XVI., p. 763, XIX., p. 466, and XXVI., No. 3, 1857. Abbé Armand David, Notes sur quelques oiseaux de Thibet, *Nouv. Arch. du Museum*, *Bull.*, V. 1869, p. 33; *ib.* *Bull*, VI., pp. 19 and 33. *Bull*, VIII., 1872, pp. 3–128, IX., pp. 15–48, X., pp. 3–82. *Recherches pour servir à l'histoire naturelle des mammifères comprennant des considérations sur la classification de ces animaux, etc., des études sur la faune de la Chine et du Tibet oriental*, par MM. Milne-Edwards, etc., 2 vols. Paris, 1868–74.

Fruits are common; small peaches, grapes, apples, and nuts, constitute the limited variety. Barley is raised more than any other grain the principal part of agricultural labors being performed by the women. Pulse and wheat are cultivated, but no rice west of H'lassa. Rhubarb, asafœtida, ginger, madder, and safflower are collected or prepared, but most of the medicines come from China and Butan. Turnips, rape, garlic, onions, and melons are raised in small quantities. The mineral productions are exceedingly rich. Gold occurs in mines and placer diggings, and forms a constant article of export; lead, silver, copper, and cinnabar are also dug out of the ground, but iron has not been found to much extent. The great difficulty in the way of the inhabitants availing themselves of their metallic wealth, apart from their ignorance of the best modes of mining, is the want of fuel with which to smelt the ore. Tincal, or crude borax, is gathered on the borders of a small lake in the neighborhood of Tengkiri-nor, where also any quantity of rock salt can be obtained. Precious stones are met with, most of which find their way to China.

The present divisions of Tibet, by the Chinese, are *Tsien Tsang*, or Anterior Tibet, and *Hau Tsang*, or Ulterior Tibet. Anterior Tibet is also called U (Wei) and U-tsang, and includes the central part of Bod-yur where H'lassa is; east of this lies Kham (Kăng) or Khamyul, and northeast toward Koko-nor is Khamsok, *i.e.*, Kham on the River Sok. Near the bend of the Brahmaputra is the district of Kongbo, where rice can be raised; going westward are Takpo, doUs and gTsang on the borders of Nari, ending in a line nearly continuous with the eastern border of Nípal. The Chinese books mention eight cantons in Anterior Tibet, five of them lying east of H'lassa, added to which are thirty-nine feudal townships in Khamsok called *tu-sz'*, all of them chiefly nominal or at present antiquated. Csoma de Körös speaks of several small principalities in Kham, and describes the inhabitants as differing from the rest of the Tibetans in appearance and language; they assimilate probably with the tribes on the Burman and Chinese frontiers. Nari (A-li in Chinese) is divided into Mangyul, Khorsum, and Maryul. The first of these districts lies nearly conterminous with Nípal, and its area is probably about the same, but its cold, dry, and elevated regions, support only a few shepherds; Khorsum and Maryul lie north and northwest in a still more inhospitable clime; the latter adjoins Ladak and Balti and is the reservoir of hundreds of lakes situated from 12,000 to 15,000 feet above the sea. A ridge separates the valley of the Indus from the Sutlej, crossed at the Bogola Pass, 19,220 feet high, and then over the Gugtila Pass, 19,500 feet into Gartok. The people throughout this elevated region are forced to live in tents, wood being almost unknown for building.

H'lassa, the *gyalsa* or capital of Tibet, is situated on the Ki-chu River, about twelve leagues from its junction with the Yaru, in lat. 29° 39′ N., and long. 91° 05′ E.; the name signifies *God's ground*, and it is the largest town in this part of Asia. It is famous for the convents near it, composing the ecclesiastical establishments of the Dalai (or 'Ocean')-lama, whose residence is in the monastery of Pobrang-marbu (*i.e.*, 'Red town') on Mount Putala. The principal building of this establishment is three hundred and sixty-seven feet high, and it contains, as the Chinese expression is, "a myriad of rooms." This city is the head-quarters of Buddhism, and the hierarchy of lamas, who, by means of the Dalai-lama, and his subordinate the Kutuktu, exercise priestly control over wellnigh all Mongolia as well as Tibet. The city lies in a fertile plain nearly 12,000 feet high, about twelve miles wide, and one hundred and twenty-five from north to south, producing harvests of barley and millet, with abundant pasturage and some fruit trees. Mountains and hills encircle it; of these the westernmost is Putala, the river running so near its base that a wall has been built to preserve the buildings from the rise of the waters. The Chinese garrison is quartered about two miles north of this mount, and two large temples, called *H'lassa tso-kang* and *Ramotsie tso-kang*, resplendent with gold and precious stones, stand very near it. The four monasteries, Séra, Brebung, Samyé, and Galdan, constitute as many separate establishments.[1] During the sway of the Songares in

[1] Klaproth, *Description du Tubet*, p. 246.

Ílí, their prince Arabdan made a descent upon H'lassa, and the Lama was killed. Kanghí placed a new one upon the see, in 1720, appointing six leading officers of the old Lama to assist him in the government. Three of these joined in an insurrection, and in the conflicts which succeeded, H'lassa suffered considerably. The population of the town is conjectured to be 24,000; that of the province is reckoned by Csoma at about 650,000.

The town was visited in the year 1811 by Mr. Manning, whose description of its dirty and miserable streets swarming with dogs and beggars, and the meanness of its buildings, corresponds with what Huc and Gabet found in 1846. Mr. Manning remained there nearly five months, and had several interviews with the Dalai-lama; he was much impeded in his observations by a Cantonese *munshí* or teacher, and exposed to danger of illness from insufficient shelter and clothing. His reception by the chief of the Buddhist faith on the 17th of December, was equally remarkable with that by the Teshu-lama of Bogle in 1774, and of Turner in 1783. Mr. Manning was alone and unprotected and had very few presents, but his offering was accepted; it consisted of a piece of fine broadcloth, two brass candlesticks, twenty new dollars, and two vials of lavender water. He rode to the foot of the mountain Putala, and dismounted on the first platform to ascend by a long stairway of four hundred steps, part of them cut in the rock, and the rest ladder steps from story to story in the palace, till he reached a large platform roof off which was the reception hall. Upon entering this he found that the *Tí-mu-fu* or *Gesub Rimboché*, the highest civil functionary in Tibet, was also present, which caused him some confusion: "I did not know how much ceremony to go through with one before I began with the other. I made the due obeisance, touching the ground three times with my head to the Grand Lama, and once to the *Tí-mu-fu.* I presented my gifts, delivering the coins with a handsome silk scarf with my own hands to them both. While I was *kotowing*, the awkward servants let one of the bottles of lavender water fall and break. Having delivered the scarf to the Grand Lama, I took off my hat, and humbly gave him my clean shaven head to lay his hands upon. . . . The Lama's beautiful and interesting face and manner engrossed all my attention. He was about seven years old; had the simple manners of a well educated princely child. His face was, I thought, poetically and affectingly beautiful. He was of a cheerful disposition, his beautiful mouth perpetually unbending into a graceful smile, which illuminated his whole countenance. No doubt my grim beard and spectacles excited his risibility. We had not been seated long before he put questions which we rose to receive and answer. He inquired whether I had met with difficulties on the road; to which I replied that I had had troubles, but now that I had the happiness of being in his presence they were amply compensated. I could see that this answer pleased both him and his people, for they found that I was not a mere rustic, but had some tincture of civility in me."[1]

The capital of Tsang or Ulterior Tibet is Shigatsé, situated 126 miles west of H'lassa, and under its control. The monastery where the Teshu-lama and his court resides is a few miles distant, and constitutes a town of about 4,000 priests, named Teshu-Lumbo. He is styled Panchen Rimboché, and is the incarnation of Amitabha Buddha. His palace is built of dark brick and has a roof of gilded copper; the houses rise one above another and the gilt ornaments on the temples combine to give a princely appearance to the town. The fortress of Shigatsé stands so as to command both places. The plain between this town and H'lassa is a fertile tract, and judging from the number of towns in the valleys of the basin of the Yaru, its productive powers are comparatively great. Ulterior Tibet is divided into six other cantons, besides the territory under the jurisdiction of the chief town, most of their fortified capitals lying westward of Shigatsé.

The degree of skill the Tibetans have attained in manufactures, mechanical arts, and general civilization, is less than that of the Chinese, but superior to the Mongols. They appear to be a mild and humane people, possessing a religious sense

---

[1] *Mission of George Bogle to Tibet and Journey of Thomas Manning to Lhasa.* Edited by C. R. Markham. London, 1876, p. 265.

and enjoying an easy life compared with their southern neighbors. They are well-bred and affable, fond of gossiping and festivities, which soften the heart and cheer the temper. Women are treated with care and are not often compelled to work out of doors. No two people or countries widely separated present a stronger contrast than do the stout, tall, muscular, and florid Butías, upon their fertile fields and wooded hills, with the squat, puny, sluggish, and swarthy Tibetans in their rugged, barren mountains. They distinguish five sorts of people among themselves, the last of whom are the Butías; the others are the inhabitants of Kham, or Anterior Tibet, those in Tsang, the nomads of Kor-kache, and the people of Little Tibet. All of them speak Tibetan with some variations. The Tibetans are clad with woollens and furs to such a degree that they appear to emulate the animals they derive them from in their weight and warmth; and with this clothing is found no small quantity of dirt. The dress of the sexes varies slightly in its shape; yellow and red are the predominant colors. Large bulgar boots of hide are worn by all persons; the remainder of the dress consists of woollen robes and furs like those of the Chinese. The women wear many jewels, and adorn their hair as do the Mongols with pearls, coral, and turquoises. Girls braid their hair in three tresses, married women in two. The head is protected by high velvet caps; the men wear broad-brimmed coverings of various materials.

The two religious sects are distinguished by yellow and red caps; the latter are comparatively few, allow marriage to the lamas, but do not differ materially in their ritual or tenets. There is no country where so large a proportion of the people are devoted to religious service as in Tibet, nor one where the secular part of the inhabitants pays such implicit deference to the clergy. The food of the Tibetans is taken at all hours, mutton, barley, and tea constituting the staple articles. On all visits tea is presented, and the cup replenished as often as it is drained. Spirits and beer, both made from barley, are common beverages. On every visit of ceremony, and whenever a letter is sent from one person to another, it is necessary to connect a silk scarf with it, the size and texture being proportioned to the rank and condition of the parties. The sentence *Om mani padmí hum* is woven upon each end.

The following note by Col. Yule, condensed from Koeppen's *Lamaische Hierarchie und Kirche*, contains the most satisfactory explanation of this puzzling mystic formula: "Om mani padmí hûm!—the primeval six syllables, as the lamas say, among all prayers on earth form that which is most abundantly recited, written, printed, and even spun by machines for the good of the faithful. These syllables form the only prayer known to the ordinary Tibetans and Mongols; they are the first words that the child learns to stammer, and the last gasping utterance of the dying. The wanderer murmurs them on his way, the herdsman beside his cattle, the matron at her household tasks, the monk in all the stages of contemplation (*i.e.*, of *far niente*); they form at once a cry of battle and a shout of victory! They are to be read wherever the Lama church hath spread, upon banners, upon rocks, upon trees, upon walls, upon monuments of stone, upon household utensils, upon strips of paper, upon human skulls and skeletons! They form, according to the idea of the believers, the utmost conception of all religion, of all wisdom, of all revelation, the path of rescue and the gate of salvation! . . . . . . Properly and literally these four words, a single utterance of which is sufficient of itself to purchase an inestimable salvation, signify nothing more than: "O the Jewel in the Lotus! Amen!" In this interpretation, most probably, the *Jewel* stands for the Bodhisatva Avalokiteçvara, so often born from the bud of a lotus flower. According to this the whole formula is simply a salutation to the mighty saint who has taken under his especial charge the conversion of the North, and with him who first employed it the mystic formula meant no more than *Ave Avalokiteçvara!* But this simple explanation of course does not satisfy the Lama schoolmen, who revel in glorifications and multitudinous glossifications of this formula. The six syllables are the heart of hearts, the root of all knowledge, the ladder to re-birth in higher forms of being, the conquerors of the five evils, the flame that burns up sin, the hammer that breaks up torment, and so on. *Om* saves the gods, *ma* the Asuras, *ni* the men, *pad* the animals, *mí* the spectre world of *pretâs*, *hûm* the inhabitants of hell! *Om* is 'the blessing of self-renunciation, *ma* of mercy, *ni* of chastity, etc.' 'Truly monstrous,' says Koeppen, 'is the number of *padmís* which in the great festivals hum and buzz through the air like flies.' In some places each worshipper reports to the highest Lama how many *om manis* he has uttered, and the total number emitted by the congregation is counted by the billion."

Grueber and Dorville describe *Manipe* as an idol, before which *stulta gens insolitis gesticulationibus sacra sua facit, identiden verba haec repetens*:—'O Manipe, mi hum, O Manipe, mi hum; *id est* Manipe, salva nos!'" Rémusat (*Mélanges Posthumes*, Paris, 1843, p. 99) translates this phrase by: "Adoration, O thou precious stone who art in the lotus!" and observes that it illustrates the fundamental dogma of Buddhism, viz.: the production of the material universe by an absolute being; all things which exist are shut up in the breast of the divine substance; the 'precious stone' signifying that *the world is in God*. Mr. Jameson says that the sentence *Om mani padmí hung* is formed of the initial letters of various deities, all of whom are supposed to be implored in the prayer.[1]

In reverential salutations, the cap is removed by the inferior, and the arms hang by the side. The bodies of the dead are placed in an open inclosure, in the same manner as practised by the Parsees, where birds and beasts of prey devour them, or they are dismembered in an exposed place. Lamas are burned, and their ashes collected into urns. As soon as the breath has departed, the body is seated in the same attitude as Buddha is represented, with the legs bent before, and the soles of the feet turned upwards. The right hand rests upon the thigh, the left turns up near the body, the thumb touching the shoulder. In this attitude of contemplation, the corpse is burned.

In Tibet, as in Butan, the custom of polyandry prevails. The choice of a wife lies with the eldest son, who having made known his intentions to his parents sends a matchmaker to pro-

---

[1] Compare, for further discussion of this subject, Timkowski's *Mission to Peking*, London, 1827, Vol. II., p. 349. Wilson's *Abode of Snow*, p. 329.

pose the matter to the parents of the girl. The consent of the parents being obtained, the matchmaker places an ornament of a jewel set in gold, called *sedzia* upon the head of the damsel, and gives her presents of jewels, dresses, cattle, etc., according to the means of the young man. The guests invited on the day of the marriage bring presents of such things as they choose, which augments the dowry. A tent is set up before the bride's house, in which are placed three or four square cushions, and the ground around sprinkled with wheat; the bride is seated on the highest cushion, her parents and friends standing near her according to their rank, and the assembled party there partake of a feast. The bride is then conducted to the house of her lover by the friends present, her person being sprinkled with wheat or barley as she goes along, and there placed by his side, and both of them served with tea and spirits. Soon after, the groom seats himself apart, and every one present gives a scarf, those of superior rank binding them around their necks, equals and inferiors laying them by their sides. The next day, a procession is formed of the relatives of the newly married pair, which visits all the friends, and the marriage is completed. The girl thus becomes the wife of all the brothers, and manages the domestic concerns of their household. The number of her husbands is sometimes indicated by as many points in her cap. This custom is strengthened by the desire, on the part of the family, to keep the property intact among its members; but it does not prevent one of the husbands leaving the roof and marrying another woman, nor is the usage universal. Rémusat speaks of a novel in Tibetan, in which the author admirably portrays the love of his heroine, Triharticha, for her four lovers, and brings their marriage in at the end in the happiest manner.

The dwellings of the poor are built of unhewn stones, rudely piled upon each other without cement, two stories high, and resembling brick-kilns in shape and size; the windows are small, in order not to weaken the structure; the roof is flat, defended by a brushwood parapet, and protected from the molestation of evil spirits by flags, strips of paper tied to strings, or branches of trees. Timber is costly and little used; the floors are of marble or tiles, and the furniture consists of little else than mats and cushions. The temples and convents are more imposing and commodious structures; some of those at H'lassa are among the noblest specimens of architecture in Central Asia.

The mausoleum of the Teshu-lama at Teshu Lumbu resembles a plain square watch-tower surmounted by a double Chinese canopy roof, the eaves of which are hung with bells, on which the breeze plays a ceaseless dirge. The body of the lama reposes in a coffin of gold, and his effigy, also of gold, is placed within the concavity of a large shell upon the top of the pyramidal structure which contains it. The sides of the pyramid are silver plates, and on the steps are deposited the jewels and other costly articles which once appertained to him. An altar in front receives the oblations and incense daily presented before the tomb, and near by is a second statue of the deceased as large as life in the attitude of reading. Scrolls and pennons of silk hang from the ceiling, and the walls are adorned with paintings of priests engaged in prayer. The whole structure is substantially built, and its rich ornaments are placed there not less for security than to do honor to the revered person deposited beneath. The windows are closed with mohair curtains, and a skylight in the upper story serves for lighting the room, and for passing out upon the roof. The roof or parapet is ornamented with cylinders of copper or other materials, which imparts a brilliant appearance to the edifices.

The manufactures of Tibet consist of woollens, cloth, blankets, yarn, goat-hair shawls, musk, paper, metals, and jewelry. Their lapidaries cut every kind of ornament in superior style, and gold and silverware forms a considerable article of trade to China. These and other crafts must necessarily languish, however, from the immense proportion of men who are withdrawn from labor into monasteries, compelling the residue to devote most of their strength to tillage. The most important exports to China consist of gold dust, precious stones, bezoars, asafœtida, musk, woollens, and skins; for which the people receive silks, teas, chinaware, tobacco, musical instruments, and metals. The trade is carried on through Síning fu in Kansuh, and

Batang in Sz'chuen. Tincal, rock-salt, and shawl wool, are additional articles sent to Ladak, Butan, and India.

Music is studied by the priesthood for their ceremonies, and with much better effect than among the Chinese priests. Their amusements consist in archery, dancing, and observance of many festivals connected with the worship of the dead or of the living. Dram-drinking is common, but the people cannot be called a drunken race, nor does the habit of opium eating or smoking, so fatally general in Assam, prevail, inasmuch as the poppy cannot well be cultivated among the mountains.

Education is confined to the priesthood, but the women, who conduct much of the traffic, also learn arithmetic and writing. The language is alphabetical, and reads from left to right; there are two forms of the character, the *uchen* used for books, and the *umin* employed in writing, which do not differ more than the Roman and the running-hand in English. The form of the characters shows their Sanscrit origin, but there are many consonants in the language not found in that tongue, and silent letters are not unfrequent in the written words. There are thirty consonants in the alphabet, distributed into eight classes, with four additional vowel signs; each of them ends in a short *a*, as *ka*, *nga*, *cha*, which can be lengthened by a diacritical mark placed underneath. The syllables are separated from each other by a point; the accented consonant is that which follows the vowel, and the others, whether before or after it, are pronounced as rapidly as possible, and not unfrequently omitted altogether in speaking. The variations in this respect constitute the chief features of the patois found in different parts where Tibetan is spoken. A dictionary and grammar[1] of this language were printed in 1834 in Calcutta by Csoma de Körös, a Hungarian who resided among the priests near Ladak. The literature is almost wholly theological, as far as it has been examined, and such works as are not of this character, have probably been introduced from China. Their divisions of time, numeration, chronology, and weights, have also been adopted

---

[1] *Essay towards a Dictionary, Tibetan and English. A Grammar of the Tibetan Language in English.* Calcutta, 1834.

from that country with a few alterations. An Englishman, Mr. Brian Hodgson, who lived in Nípal from 1820 to 1843, has added more than any one else to our knowledge of the literature of this country. This gentleman procured complete copies of the original documents of the Buddhist canon preserved in Sanscrit in Nípalese monasteries, as well as (by a present from the Dalai-lama) the whole of the existing literary remains of the once flourishing Christian mission at H'lassa. His more important essays on these lands have now been brought together in a single volume.[1]

The history of Tibet has been made partially known to Europe through the Mongol author, Sanang Setsen,[2] but if free access could be had to their annals, it is probable that a methodical history could be extracted, reaching back at least three centuries before Christ. Tibet was ruled by its own princes till the rise of Genghis; the first monarch, who united the various tribes under his sway B. C. 313, was Seger-Sandilutu-Kagan-Tül-Esen,[3] and from the fact that Buddhism was introduced during his reign, it might be inferred that he came from the south. H'lassa was founded by Srongzan-Gambo, or Srong-bdzan sgambouo,[4] about A.D. 630, after which time Tibetan history becomes more authentic, inasmuch as this king introduced the alphabet. The Tang dynasty carried their arms into Tibet from Khoten, but the people threw off their yoke during the decline of that family. Mohammedanism also disturbed the supremacy of the Buddhist faith, and severe persecutions followed about the beginning of the tenth century by an Islam prince Darma, but it was repelled at his death, and has never since made the least impression upon the people. Genghis reduced Tangout, one of the principalities, northeast of Koko-nor, and soon after brought the whole country under his sway; this

---

[1] *Essays on the Language, Literature, and Religion of Nepal and Tibet*, etc. London, 1874.

[2] Rémusat, *Observations sur l'Histoire des Mongols orienteaux de Sanang Setsen*, Paris, l'an 8. *Ssanang Ssetsen*, *Geschichte der Mongolen*, Uebers., von. J. J. Schmidt, Petersb., 1829.

[3] Rémusat relates the story of his origin, *Mélanges Posthumes*, p. 400.

[4] Klaproth, *Description du Tubet*.

Kublai still further settled as a dependency of his empire. The people recovered their independence on the expulsion of the Mongols, and under the Ming dynasty formed several small kingdoms, among which were Ladak and Rodok, both of them still existing.

From a short résumé of letters written from Tibet in 1626, by Romish missionaries living there, it appears that the kingdom of Sopo was the most powerful in the north, and Cogué, U-tsang, and Maryul were three southern principalities. The king of Cogué allowed these missionaries to reside in his territories, and took pleasure in hearing them converse and dispute with the lamas. The Dalai-lama at this time was the king's brother, and possessed subordinate influence in the state, but the priests were numerous and influential. The conquest of Mongolia and Tangout opened the way for Kanghí to enter Tibet, but the intercourse between the Emperor and Dalai-lama was chiefly connected with religion and carrying tribute. An index of the freedom of communication between Tibet and the west is found in the passports issued to the traders visiting H'lassa in 1688. The lamas held the supreme power until towards the end of his reign, when Chinese influence became paramount. The country had already been conquered by the Songar chieftain, so that on his defeat it could offer little resistance. Kanghí appointed six of the highest princes or *gialbo* over the provinces; but soon after his death, in 1727, three of them conspired against Yungching, and were not subdued without considerable resistance. The Emperor then appointed the loyal prince or *gialbo* as governor-general, and he remained in his vice-regal office till his death, about 1750. Kienlung, finding that his son was endeavoring to make himself fully independent, executed him as a rebel, suppressed the office, and appointed two Chinese generals to be associated with the Dalai-lama and his coadjutor, in the administration of the country. The troops were increased and forts erected in all parts of the country to awe the people and facilitate trade.

The present government of Tibet is superintended by two *ta chin*, 'or great ministers,' residing at H'lassa, who act conjointly, while they serve as checks upon each other; they do not hold their office for a long time. They have absolute control over all the troops in the country, and the military are generally confined to the garrisons, and do not cultivate the soil. The collection of revenue, transmission of tribute to Peking, and direction of the persons who carry it, and those who conduct the trade at Batang and Síning fu, are all under their control. The Dalai-lama, and the Teshu-lama are the high religious officers of the country, each of them independent in his own province, but the former holding the highest place in the hierarchy. The Chinese residents confer with each concerning the direction of his own province. All their appointments to office or nobility must be sanctioned by the residents before they are valid, but merely religious officers are not under this surveillance. In the villages, the authority is administered by secular deputy lamas called *deba*, and by commandants called *karpon*, who are sent from the capital. Each *deba* is assisted by a native *vazir* of the place, who, with the chief lama, form the local government, amenable to the supreme magistracy. The western province of Nari is peopled by nomads, who wander over the regions north of Ravan-hrad, and are under the authority of *karpons* sent from H'lassa, without the assistance of lamas. The two high-priests themselves are likewise assisted by councillors. One of these, called Soopoon Choomboo, who held the office of *sadeek* or adviser when Turner visited Teshu-Lumbo, was a Manchu by birth, but had long lived in Tibet.

The nomadic clans of Dam Mongols and other tribes occupying the thirty-nine feudal townships or *tu-sz'* in Anterior Tibet, are governed by the residents without the intervention of the lamas. The disturbances in Ulterior Tibet in 1792, resulting from the irruption of the Nípalese and sack of Teshu-Lumbo, were speedily quelled by the energy of Kienlung's government, and the invaders forced to sue for mercy. The southern frontier was, in consequence of this inroad, strongly fortified by a chain of posts, and the communication with the states between Tibet and India strictly forbidden and watched. It gave the Chinese an opportunity to strengthen their rule and extend their influence north to Khoten and into Ladak. The natural mildness of character of the Tibetans, and similarity of religion renders them much easier under the Chinese yoke, than the Mohammedans.[1]

---

[1] Authorities on Tibet besides those already referred to: *Journal Asiatique*, Tomes IV., p. 281; VIII., p. 117; IX., p. 31; XIV., pp. 177, ff. 277, 406, etc. Du Halde, *Description of China*, Vol. II., pp. 384–388. Capt. Samuel Turner, *Account of an Embassy to the Court of Teshoo Lama in Tibet*, London, 1800. *Histoire de ce qui s'est passé au Royaume du Tibet, en l'année* 1626; trad. de l'Italien. Paris, 1829. P. Kircher, *China Illustrata*. MM. Péron et Billecocq, *Recueil de Voyages du Thibet*, Paris, 1796. *Journal of the Asiatic Society of Bengal*, passim. *Chinese Repository*, Vols. VI., pp. 28, 494, IX., p. 26, and XIII., p. 505. Ritter, *Asien*, Bd. II., 4er Abschnitt, and Bd. III., S. 137–424. Richthofen, *China*, Bd. I., S. 228, 247, 466, 670, 683, etc. C. H. Desgodin, *La mission du Tibet de* 1855 *à* 1870, *comprennant l'exposé des affaires religieuses*, etc. *D'après les lettres de M. l'abbé Desgodins, missionaire apostolique*, Verdun, 1872. Lieut. Kreitner, *Im fernen Osten*, pp. 829 ff., and in *The Popular Science Monthly*, for August, 1882. Emil Schlagintweit, *Tibetan Buddhism, Illustrated by Literary Documents and Objects of Religious Worship*, London, 1863. Abbé Huc, *Travels through Tartary, Tibet and China*, 2 vols.

CHAPTER V.

POPULATION AND STATISTICS.

MUCH of the interest appertaining to the country and people here treated of, in the minds of philanthropic and intelligent men, has arisen from the impression they have received of its vast population. A country twice the size of the Chinese empire would present few attractions to the Christian, the merchant, or the ethnologist, if it were no better inhabited than Sahara, or Arizona: a people might possess most admirable institutions, and a matchless form of government, yet these excellencies would lose their interest, did we hear that it is the republic of San Marino or the kingdom of Muscat, where they are found. The population of few countries in the world has been accurately ascertained, and probably that of China is less satisfactory than any European or American state of the present day. It is far easier to take a census among a people who understand its object, and will honestly assist in its execution, than in a despotic, half-civilized country, where the mass of the inhabitants are afraid of contact or intercourse with their rulers; in most of such states, as Abyssinia, Turkey, Persia, etc., there is either no regular enumeration at all, or merely a general estimate for the purposes of revenue or conscription.

The subject of the population of China has engaged the attention of the monarchs of the present dynasty, and their censuses have been the best sources of information in making up an intelligent opinion upon the matter. Whatever may be our views of the actual population, it is plain that these censuses, with all their discrepancies and inaccuracies, are the only reliable sources of information. The conflicting opinions and conclusions of foreign writers neither give any additional weight to them, nor detract at all from their credibility. As the question stands at present, they can be doubted, but cannot be denied; it is impossible to prove them, while there are many grounds for believing them; the enormous total which they exhibit can be declared to be improbable, but not shown to be impossible.

No one who has been in China can hesitate to acknowledge that there are some strong grounds for giving credit to them, but the total goes so far beyond his calculations, that entire belief must, indeed, be deferred till some new data have been furnished. There are, perhaps, more peculiar encouragements to the increase of population there than in any other country, mostly arising from a salubrious climate, semi-annual crops, unceasing industry, early marriages, and an equable taxation, involving reasonable security of life and property. Turning to other countries of Asia, we soon observe that in Japan and Persia these causes have less influence; in Siam and Burmah they are weak; in Tibet they are almost powerless.

At this point every one must rest, as the result of an examination into the population of the Chinese Empire; though, from the survey of its principal divisions, made in the preceding chapters, its capability of maintaining a dense population needs no additional evidence. The mind, however, is bewildered in some degree by the contemplation of millions upon millions of human beings thus collected under one government; and it almost wishes there might be grounds for disbelieving the enormous total, from the dreadful results that might follow the tyrannical caprice or unrestrained fury of their rulers, or the still more shocking scenes of rapine and the hideous extremities of want which a bad harvest would necessarily cause.

Chinese literature contains many documents describing classes of society comprised in censuses in the various dynasties. The results of those enumerations have been digested by Ma Twan-lin in a judicious and intelligent manner in the chapters treating on population, from which M. Ed. Biot has elaborated many important data.[1] The early records show that the census was designed to contain only the number of taxable people, excluding all persons bound to give personal service, who were under the control of others. Moreover, all officials and slaves, all persons over 60 or 66 years of age, the weak or sick, those needing help, and sometimes such as were newly placed on state lands, were likewise omitted. Deducting these classes, Ma Twan-lin gives one census taken in the ninth century, B.C., as 13,704,923 persons, between the ages of 15 and 65, living within the frontiers north of the Yangtsz' River. This figure would be worth, according to the tables of modern statistics, about 65 per cent. of the entire population, or as representing 21,753,528 inhabitants.

The mighty conqueror, Tsin Chí Hwangtí, changed the personal corvée to scutage, and introduced a kind of poll-tax, by accepting the money from many who could not be forced to do the work required. This practice was followed in the Han dynasty, and in B.C. 194, the poll-tax was legalized, to include all men between 15 and 66, while a lighter impost was levied on those between 7 and 14. During the four centuries of this family's régime, the object and modes of a census were well understood. Ma Twan-lin gives the results of ten taken between A.D. 2 and 155. His details show that it was done simply for revenue, and was omitted in bad years, when drought or freshets destroyed the harvests; they show, too, an increase in the number of slaves, that women were now enumerated, and that girls between 15 and 30 paid a poll-tax. In B.C. 30, the limits of age were placed between 7 and 56. The average of these ten censuses is 63,500,600, the first one being as high as 83,640,000, while the next and lowest, taken fifty-five years afterwards, is only 29,180,000, and the third is 47,396,000. These great variations are explained by the disturbances arising in consequence of the usurpation of Wangmang, A.D. 9–27, and subsequent change of the capital, and the impossibility, during this troubled period, of canvassing all parts of the Empire.

---

[1] This careful digest is contained in the *Journal Asiatique* for 1836 (April and May), and will repay perusal.

The inference from these data, that the real population of the Chinese Empire north of the Nan ling at the time of Christ was at least eighty millions, is as well grounded as almost any fact in its history.[1]

After the downfall of the Han dynasty, a long period of civil war ensued, in which the destruction of life and property was so enormous that the population was reduced to one-sixth of the amount set down in A.D. 230, when disease, epidemics, and earthquakes increased the losses caused by war and the cessation of agriculture, according to Ma Twan-lin; and it is not till A.D. 280, when the Tsin dynasty had subjected all to its sway, that the country began to revive. In that year an enumeration was made which stated the free people between 12 and 66 years in the land at 14,163,863, or 23,180,000 in all. From this period till the Sui dynasty came into power, in 589, China was torn by dissensions and rival monarchs, and the recorded censuses covered only a portion of the land, the figures including even fewer of the people, owing to the great number of serfs or bondmen who had sought safety under the protection of landowners. At this time a new mode of taking the census was ordered, in which the people were classified into those from 1 to 3 years, then 3 to 10, then 10 to 17, and 17 to 60, after which age they were not taxed; the ratio of the land tax was also fixed. A census taken in 606 in this way gives an estimated population of 46,019,956 in all China; the frontiers, at this period, hardly reached to the Nan ling Mountains, and the author's explanation of the manner of carrying on some public works shows that even this sum did not include persons who were liable to be called on for personal service, while all officials, slaves, and beggars were omitted. Troubles arose again from these enforced works, and it was not till the advent to power of the Tang dynasty, in 618, that a regular enumeration was possible.

---

[1] The population of the Roman Empire at the same period is estimated at 85,000,000 by Merivale (Vol. IV., pp. 336–343), but the data are less complete than in China; he reckons the European provinces at 45,000,000, and the Asiatic and African colonies at the remainder, giving 27,000,000 to Asia Minor and Syria. The area of China, at this time, was less than Rome by about one-fourth.

This family reigned 287 years, and Ma Twan-lin gives fifteen returns of the population up to 841. They show great variations, some of them difficult to explain even by omitting or supplying large classes of the inhabitants. The one most carefully taken was in A.D. 754, and gives an estimated total of about seventy millions for the whole Empire, which, though nearly the same as that in the Han dynasty in A.D. 2, extended over a far greater area, even to the whole southern seaboard. In addition to former enumerated classes, many thousands of priests were passed by in this census.

The years of anarchy following the Tang, till A.D. 976, when the Sung dynasty obtained possession, caused their usual effect. Its first census gives only about sixteen millions of taxable population that year, when its authority was not firmly assured; but in 1021 the returns rise to 43,388,380, and thence gradually increase to 100,095,250 in 1102, just before the provinces north of the Yellow River, by far the most fertile and loyal, were lost. The last enumeration, in 1223, while Ma Twan-lin was living, places the returns in the southern provinces at 63,304,000; this was fifty years before Kublai khan conquered the Empire. Our author gives some details concerning the classes included in the census during his own lifetime, which prove to a reasonable mind that the real number of mouths living on the land was, if anything, higher than the estimates. In 1290, the Mongol Emperor published his enumeration, placing the taxable population at 58,834,711, "not counting those who had fled to the mountains and lakes, or who had joined the rebels." This was not long after his ruthless hand had almost depopulated vast regions in the northern provinces, before he could quiet them.

In the continuation of Ma Twan-lin's *Researches*, there are sixteen censuses given for the Ming dynasty between 1381 and 1580; the lowest figure is 46,800,000, in 1506, and the highest, 66,590,000, in 1412, the average for the two centuries being 56,715,360 inhabitants. One of its compilers declares that he cannot reconcile their great discrepancies, and throws doubts on their totals from his inability to learn the mode of enumeration. Three are given for three consecutive years (1402–1404), the difference between the extremes of which amounts to sixteen millions, but they were all taken when Yungloh was fighting Kienwăn, his nephew, at Nanking, and settling himself at Peking as Emperor, during which years large districts could not possibly have been counted.

Before entering upon a careful examination of this question, it will be well to bring together the various estimates taken of the population during the present dynasty. The details given in the table on page 264 have been taken from the best sources, and are as good as the people themselves possess.

Besides these detailed accounts, there have been several aggregates of the whole country given by other native writers than Ma Twan-lin, and some by foreigners, professedly drawn from original sources, but who have not stated their authorities. The most trustworthy, together with those given in the other table, are here placed in chronological order.

	Reign of Monarch.		A.D.	Population.	Authorities.
1.	Hungwu,	13th year,	1381	59,850,000	Continuation of Ma Twan-lin. Ed. Biot, *Journal Asiatique*, 1836.
2.	Yungloh,	9th year,	1412	65,377,000	
3.	Wanleih,	7th year,	1580	60,692,000	
4.	Shunchí,	18th year,	1662	21,068,600	*General Statistics of the Empire;* Medhurst's *China*, p. 53.
5.	Kanghí,	6th year,	1668	25,386,209	
6.	"	49th year,	1710 ?	23,312,200	
7.	"	49th year,	1710 ?	27,241,129	*Yih Tung Chi*, a statistical work; Morrison's *View of China*.
8.	"	50th year,	1711	28,605,716	*General Statistics; Chinese Repository*, Vol. I., p. 359.
9.	Kienlung,	1st year,	1736	125,046,245	*Mémoires sur les Chinois*, Tome VI., p. 277 ff.
10.	"	8th year,	1743	157,343,975	
11.	"	8th year,	1743	149,332,730	
12.	"	8th year,	1743	150,265,475	*Les Missionaires*, De Guignes, Tome III., p. 67.
13.	"	18th year,	1753	103,050,060	*General Statistics; Chinese Repository*, Vol. I., p. 359.
14.	"	25th year,	1760 ?	143,125,225	*Yih Tung Chi*, a statistical work; Morrison's *View of China*.
15.	"	25th year,	1760 ?	203,916,477	*Mémoires sur les Chinois*, Tome VI.
16.	"	26th year,	1761	205,293,053	De Guignes, Tome III., p. 72.
17.	"	27th year,	1762	198,214,553	Allerstein; Grosier; De Guignes, Tome III., p. 67.
18.	"	55th year.	1790	155,249,897	"Z." of Berlin, in *Chinese Repository*, Vol. I., p. 361.
19.	"	57th year,	1792	307,467,200	*General Statistics;* Dr. Morrison, Anglo-Chinese Coll. Report, 1829.
20.	"	57th year,	1792	333,000,000	Statement made to Lord Macartney.
21.	Kiaking,	17th year,	1812	362,467,183	*General Statistics; Chinese Repository*, Vol. I., p. 359.
22.	Tungchí,	8th year,	1868	404,946,514	Vassilivitch.
23.	Kwangsü,	7th year,	1881	380,000,000	*Chinese Custom's Reports.*

Seven of these censuses, viz., the 7th, 8th, 12th, 13th, 17th, 20th, 21st and 23d, are given in detail in the following table.

TABLE OF THE DIFFERENT CENSUSES OF THE EIGHTEEN PROVINCES.

PROVINCES.	Area in English square miles.	Aver. population to a sq. m. in 1812.	Census in 1710, or before.	Census of 1711.	Census of 1753.	Last Census of 1812.	Estimate in 1792, given Macartney.	Census in 1762 by Allerstein.	Census of 1743, from De Guignes.	*Almanac de Gotha*, 1882, taken from Chinese Customs' Reports.	Revenue in taels of $1.33 each.
Chihli	58,949	475	3,260,075	3,274,870	9,374,217	27,990,871	38,000,000	15.222.940	16,702,765	28,000,000	3,942,000
Shantung	65.104	444	....	2,278,595	12.769,872	28,958,764	24,000,000	25,180,734	12,159,680	29.000,000	6,344.000
Shansi	55.268	252	1,792,329	1,727,144	5,162,351	14,004,210	27,000,000	9,768,189	8,969,475	17,056,925	6,313,000
Honan	65,104	420	2,005.088	3,044,150	7,114,346	23,037,171	25,000,000	16,332,507	12,637,280	29,069,771	5,651,008
Kiangsu.........	44.500	850	3,917,707	2,656,465	12,618,967	37,843,501	32,000,000	23,161,409	26,766,365	37,800.000	11,733,000
Nganhwui.......	48,461	705	1,350,131	1,357,829	12,435,361	34.168,059		22,761.030		34,200,000	
Kiangsi	72,176	320	5,528,499	2,172,587	5,055.251	23,046,999	19,000,000	11,006,640	6,681,350	23,000,000	3,744,000
Chehkiang	39,150	671	2,710,649	2,710,312	8,662,808	26,256,784	21,000,000	15,429,690	15,623,990	26,300,000	5,856,000
Fuhkien.........	53,480	276	1,468,145	706,311	4.710,399	14,777,410	15,000,000	8,063,671	7,643,035	14,800,000	2,844,000
Hupeh	70.450	359	469,927	433,948	4,568,860	27,370,098	14,000,000	8,080.603	4,264,850	27,400,000	2,091,000
Hunan	74,320	251	375,782	335,054	4,336,332	18,652,507	18,000,000	8.829,320		20,048,969	1,905,000
Shensi	67,400	153	240,809	2,150,696	3,851,043	10,207,256	18,000,000	7,287,443	14,804,035	10.309,769	3,042,000
Kansuh	86.608	175	311,972	368,525	2,133,222	15,193,125	12,000,000	7,812,014		9,285,377	563.000
Sz'chuen	166.800	128	144,154	3,802,689	1,368,496	21,435,678	27,000,000	2,782.976	15,181,710	55,000,000	2,968,000
Kwangtung......	79,456	241	1,148,918	1,142,747	3,969,248	19,174,030	21,000,000	6,797,597	6,006,600	19,200,000	198,000
Kwangsi	78.250	93	205,995	210,674	1,975,619	7,313,895	10,000.000	3,947,414	1,143,450	8,121.327	794,000
Kweichau	64,554	82	51,089	37,731	1,718,848	5,288,219	9,000,000	3,402,722	255,445	5,679,128	185.000
Yunnan	107,969	51	*2,255.666	145,414	1,003,058	5,561,320	8.000,000	2,078,802	1,189,825	5,823,670	432,000
Shingking.......	......	..	4,194	....	221,742	2,167,286	....	668,852	235,620	....	....
	1,297,999	268	27,241,129	28,605,716	108,050,060	362,447,183	333,000,000	198,214,553	150,265,475	380,000,000	58,097,000

The first three belong to the Ming dynasty, and are taken from a continuation of Ma Twan-lin's *Researches*, whence they were quoted in the *Mirror of History*, without their details. During the Ming dynasty, a portion of the country now called the Eighteen Provinces, was not under the control of Hungwu and his descendants. The wars with the Japanese, and with tribes on the north and west, together with the civil wars and struggles between the Chinese themselves, and with the Nü-chí in Manchuria, must have somewhat decreased the population.

The first census of 1662 (No. 4), is incidentally mentioned by Kienlung in 1791, as having been taken at that time, from his making some observations upon the increase of the population and comparing the early censuses with the one he had recently ordered. This sum of 21,068,600 does not, however, include all the inhabitants of China at that date; for the Manchus commenced their sway in 1644, and did not exercise full authority over all the provinces much before 1700; Canton was taken in 1650, Formosa in 1683.

The census of 1668 (No. 5), shows a little increase over that of 1662, but is likewise confined to the conquered portions; and in those provinces which had been subdued, there were extensive tracts which had been almost depopulated at the conquest. Any one who reads the recitals of Semedo, Martini, Trigautius, and others, concerning the massacres and destruction of life both by the Manchus and by Chinese bandits, between 1630 and 1650, will feel no loss in accounting for the diminution of numbers, down to 1710. But the chief explanation of the decrease from sixty to twenty-seven millions is to be found in the object of taking the census, viz., to levy a poll-tax, and get at the number of men fit for the army—two reasons for most men to avoid the registration.

The census of 1711 (No. 8), is the first one on record which bears the appearance of credibility, when its several parts are compared with each other. The dates of the preceding (Nos. 6 and 7), are rather uncertain; the last was extracted by Dr. Morrison from a book published in 1790, and he thought it was probably taken as early as 1650, though that is unlikely. The other is given by Dr. Medhurst without any explanation, and their great disparity leads us to think that both are dated wrongly. The census of 1711 is much more consistent in itself, though there are some reasons for supposing that neither did it include all the population then in China. The census was still taken for enrolment in the army, and to levy a capitation tax upon all males between the ages of sixteen and sixty. But this tax and registration were evaded and resisted by the indignant Chinese, who had never been chronicled in this fashion by their own princes; the Emperor Kanghí, therefore, abolished the capitation tax. It was not till about this time that the Manchus had subdued and pacified the southern provinces, and it is not improbable that this census, and the survey taken by the Jesuits, were among their acts of sovereignty. Finding the people unwilling to be registered, the poll tax was merged in the land tax, and no census ordered during the reign of Yungching, till Kienlung revived it in order to have some guide in apportioning relief during seasons of distress and scarcity, establishing granaries, and aiding the police in their duties. Many, therefore, who would do all in their power to prevent their names being taken, when they were liable to be taxed or called on to do military service, could have no objection to come forward, when the design of the census was to benefit themselves. It matters very little, however, for what object the census was taken, if there is reason to believe it to have been accurate. It might indeed act as a stimulus to multiply names and figures whom there were no people to represent, as the principle of paying the marshals a percentage on the numbers they reported did in some parts of New York State in 1840.

The three next numbers (9, 10, and 11), are taken from De Guignes, who quotes Amiot, but gives no Chinese authorities. The last is given in full by De Guignes, and both this and that of Allerstein, dated twenty years after, are introduced into the table. There are some discrepancies between these two and the census of 1753, taken from the *General Statistics*, which cannot easily be reconciled. The internal evidence is in favor of the latter, over the census of 1743; it is taken from a new edition of the *Ta Tsing Hwui Tien*, or 'General Statistics of the Empire,' and the increase during the forty-two years which had elapsed since the last census is regular in all the provinces, with the exception of Shantung and Kiangnan. The extraordinary fertility of these provinces would easily induce immigration, while in the war of conquest, their populousness and wealth attracted the armies of the Manchus, and the destruction of life was disproportionably great. The smaller numbers given to the western and southern provinces correspond moreover to the opposition experienced in those regions. On the whole, the census taken in 1753 compares very well with that of 1711, and both of them bear an aspect of verity, which does not belong to the table of 1743 quoted by De Guignes.

From 1711 to 1753, the population doubled itself in about twenty-two years, premising that the whole country was faithfully registered at the first census. For instance, the province of Kweichau, in 1711, presents on the average a mere fraction of a little more than a single person to two square miles; while in 1753 it had increased in the unexampled ratio of three to a square mile, which is doubling its population every seven years; Kwangtung, Kwangsí, and Kansuh (all of them containing to this day, partially subdued tribes), had also multiplied their numbers in nearly the same proportion, owing in great measure, probably, to the more extended census than to the mere increase of population.

The amounts for 1736, three of 1743, and those of 1760, 1761, and 1762 (Nos. 9, 10, 11, 12, 15, 16, and 17), are all extracted from De Guignes, who took them from the *Mémoires sur les Chinois*. The last, that of 1762, is given in detail in the table. The discrepancy of sixty millions between that given by Amiot for 1760, and that by Dr. Morrison for the same year, is owing, there can be little doubt, to foreigners, and not to an error of the Chinese. The work from which Dr. Morrison extracted his estimate for that year was published in 1790, but the census was taken between 1760 and 1765. The same work contains the census of 1711 (No. 8), quoted by him, and there is good cause for believing that Amiot's or Grosier's estimate of 157,343,975 for 1743, is the very same census, he having multiplied the number 28,605,716 by five, supposing them to have been families and not individuals. The three ascribed to the year 1743, are probably all derived from the same native authorities by different individuals.

The three dated in 1760, 1761, and 1762, are harmonious with each other; but if they are taken, those of 1753 and 1760, extracted from the *Yih Tung Chí* by Dr. Morrison, must be rejected, which are far more reasonable, and correspond better with the preceding one of 1711. It may be remarked, that by reckoning five persons to a family in calculating the census of 1753, as Amiot does for 1743, the population would be 189,223,820 instead of 103,050,060, as given in the table. This explains the apparent decrease of fifty millions. All the discrepancies between these various tables and censuses must not be charged upon the Chinese, since it is by no means easy to ascertain their modes of taking the census and their use of terms. In the tables, for example, they employ the phrase *jin-ting*, for a male over 15 years of age, as the integer; this has, then, to be multiplied by some factor of increase to get at the total population; and this last figure must be obtained elsewhere. It must not be overlooked that the object in taking a census being to calculate the probable revenue by enumerating the taxable persons, the margin of error and deficiency depends on the peace of the state at the time, and not chiefly on the estimate of five or more to a household.

The amount for 1736 corresponds sufficiently closely with that for 1743; and reckoning the same number of persons in a family in 1753, that tallies well enough with those for 1760, 1761, and 1762, the whole showing a gradual increase for twenty-five years. But all of them, except that of 1753, are probably rated too high. That for 1762 (No. 17), has been justly considered as one of the most authentic.

The amount given by "Z." of Berlin (No. 18), of 155⅜ millions for 1790 is quoted in the *Chinese Repository*, but the writer states no authorities, was probably never in China, and as it appears at present, is undeserving the least notice. That given by Dr. Morrison for 1792 (No. 19), the year before Lord Macartney's embassy, is quoted from an edition of that date, but probably was really taken in 1765 or thereabouts, but he did not publish it in detail.[1] It is probably much nearer the truth than the amount of 333 millions by the commissioner Chau to the English ambassador. This estimate has had much more respect paid to it as an authentic document than it deserved. The Chinese commissioner would naturally wish to exalt his country in the eyes of its far-travelled visitors, and not having the official returns to refer to, would not be likely to state them less than they were. He gave the population of the provinces in round numbers, perhaps altogether from his own memory, aided by those of his attendant clerks, with the impression that his hearers would never be able to refer to the original native authorities.

The next one quoted (No. 21) is the most satisfactory of all the censuses in Chinese works, and was considered by both the Morrisons and by Dr. Bridgman, editor of the *Chinese Repository*, as "the most accurate that has yet been given of the population."

In questions of this nature, one well authenticated table is worth a score of doubtful origin. It has been shown how apocryphal are many of the statements given in foreign books, but with the census of 1812, the source of error which is chiefly to be guarded against is the average given to a family. This is done by the Chinese themselves on no uniform plan, and it may be the case that the estimate of individuals from the number of families is made in separate towns, from an intimate acquaintance with the particular district, which would be less liable to error than a general average. The number of families given in the census of 1753, is 37,785,552, which is more than one-third of the population.

The four censuses which deserve the most credit, so far as the sources are considered, are those of 1711, 1753, 1792, and 1812 (*i.e.*, Nos. 8, 13, 19, and 21); these, when compared, show the following rate of increase:

From 1711 to 1753, the population increased 74,222,602, which was an annual advance of 1,764,824 inhabitants, or a

[1] Sir G. Staunton, *Embassy to China*, Vol. II., Appendix, p. 615: "Table of the Population and Extent of China proper, within the Great Wall. Taken in round numbers from the Statements of Chow ta-zhin."

little more than six per cent. per annum for forty-two years. This high rate, it must be remembered, does not take into account the more thorough subjugation of the south and west at the later date, when the Manchus could safely enrol large districts, where in 1711 they would have found so much difficulty that they would not have attempted it.

From 1753 to 1792, the increase was 104,636,882, or an annual advance of 2,682,997 inhabitants, or about 2½ per cent. per annum for thirty-nine years. During this period, the country enjoyed almost uninterrupted peace under the vigorous sway of Kienlung, and the unsettled regions of the south and west rapidly filled up.

From 1792 to 1812, the increase was 54,126,679, or an annual advance of 2,706,333—not quite one per cent. per annum —for twenty years. At the same rate of progress the present population would amount to over 450,000,000, and this might have been the case had not the Tai-ping rebellion reduced the numbers. An enumeration (No. 22), was published by the Russian Professor of Chinese Vassilivitch in 1868 as a translation from official documents. Foreigners have had greater opportunities for travel through the country, between the years 1840 to 1880, and have ascertained the enormous depopulation in some places caused by wars, short supplies of food in consequence of scarcity of laborers, famines, or brigandage, each adding its own power of destruction at different places and times. The conclusion will not completely satisfy any inquirer, but the population of the Empire cannot now reasonably be estimated as high as the census of 1812, by at least twenty-five millions. The last in the list of these censuses (No. 23), is added as an example of the efforts of intelligent persons residing in China to come to a definite and independent conclusion on this point from such data as they can obtain. The Imperial Customs' Service has been able to command the best native assistance in their researches, and the table of population given above from the *Gotha Almanac* is the summary of what has been ascertained. The population of extra-provincial China is really unknown at present. Manchuria is put down at twelve millions by one author, and three or four millions, by another, without any official authority for either; and all those vast regions in Ílí and Tibet may easily be set down at from twelve to fifteen millions. To sum up, one must confess that if the Chinese censuses are worth but little, compared with those taken in European states, they are better than the guesses of foreigners who have never been in the country, or who have travelled only partially in it.

The Chinese are doubtless one of the most conceited nations on the earth, but with all their vanity, they have never bethought themselves of rating their population twenty-five or thirty per cent. higher than they suppose it to be, for the purpose of exalting themselves in the eyes of foreigners or in their own. Except in one case none of the estimates were presented to, or intended to be known by foreigners. The distances in *li* between places given in Chinese itineraries correspond very well with the real distances; the number of districts, towns, and villages in the departments and provinces, as stated in their local and general topographical works, agree with the actual examination, so far as it can be made: why should their censuses be charged with gross error, when, however much we may doubt them, we cannot disprove them, and the weight of evidence derived from actual observation rather confirms them than otherwise; and while their account of towns, villages, distances, etc., are unhesitatingly adopted until better can be obtained? Some discrepancies in the various tables are ascribable to foreigners, and some of the censuses are incomplete, or the year cannot be precisely fixed, both of which vitiate the deductions made from them as to the rate of increase. Some reasons for believing that the highest population ascribed to the Chinese Empire is not greater than the country can support, will first be stated, and the objections against receiving the censuses then considered.[1]

---

[1] This interesting subject can then be left with the reader, who will find further remarks in Medhurst's *China*, De Guignes' *Voyages à Peking*, The Missionaries, in Tomes VI. and VIII. of *Mémoires*, Ed. Biot, in *Journal Asiatique* for 1836. *The Numerical Relations of the Population of China during the* 4,000 *Years of its Historical Existence; or the Rise and Fall of the Chinese Population*, by T. Sacharoff. Translated into English by the Rev. W. Lobscheid, Hongkong, 1862. *Notes and Queries on China and Japan*, Vol. II., pp. 88, 103, and 117.

The area of the Eighteen Provinces is rather imperfectly given at 1,348,870 square miles, and the average population, therefore, for the whole, in 1812, was 268 persons on every square mile; that of the nine eastern provinces in and near the Great Plain, comprising 502,192 square miles, or two-fifths of the whole, is 458 persons, and the nine southern and western provinces, constituting the other three-fifths, is 154 to a square mile. The surface and fertility of the country in these two portions differ so greatly, as to lead one to look for results like these. The areas of some European states and their population, are added to assist in making a comparison with China, and coming to a clearer idea about their relative density.

States.	Area.	Population.	Average to sq. m.	Census of
France	204,092	36,905,788	182	December, 1876.
Germany	212,091	45,194,172	213	December, 1880.
Great Britain	121,608	35,246,562	289	April, 1881.
Italy	114,296	28,437,091	249	December, 1879.
Holland	20,497	4,060,580	198	December, 1880.
Spain	190,625	16,053,961	84	December, 1877.
Japan	160,474	34,338,479	213	1877.
Bengal	156,200	68,750,747	440	1881.

All these are regarded as well settled countries, but England and Bengal are the only ones which exceed that of China, taken as a whole, while none of them come up to the average of the eastern provinces. All of them, China included, fall far short, however, of the average population on a square mile of the kingdoms of Judah and Israel, in the reigns of Abijah and Jeroboam, if the 1,200,000 men brought into the field by them can be taken as a ratio of the whole number of inhabitants; or if the accounts given by Josephus of the density in his day are trustworthy. In estimating the capabilities of these European countries to support a dense population, allowances must be made for roads, pasture-lands, and parks of noblemen, all of which afford little or no food.

In England and Wales, there are nearly twenty-nine millions of acres under cultivation, seventeen millions of which are pasture-lands, and only ten millions devoted to grain and vegetables; the other two millions consist of fallow-ground, hop-beds, etc. One author estimates that in England 42 acres in a hundred, and in Ireland 64, are pastures—a little more than half of the whole. There are, then, on the average about two acres of land for the support of each individual, or rather less than this, if the land required for the food of horses be subtracted. It has been calculated that eight men can be fed on the same amount of land that one horse requires; and that four acres of pasture-land will furnish no more food for man than one of ploughed land. The introduction of railroads has superseded the use of horses to such an extent that it is estimated there are only 200,000 horses now in England, instead of a million in 1830. If, therefore, one-half the land appropriated to pasture should be devoted to grain, and no more horses and dogs raised than a million of acres could support, England and Wales could easily maintain a population of more than four hundred to a square mile, supposing them to be willing to live on what the land and water can furnish.

The Irish consume a greater proportion of vegetables than the English, even since the improvement by emigration after 1851; many of these live a beggarly life upon half an acre, and even less, and seldom taste animal food. The quantity of land under cultivation in Belgium is about fifteen-seventeenths of the whole, which gives an average of about two acres to each person, or the same as in England. In these two countries, the people consume more meat than in Ireland, and the amount of land occupied for pasturage is in nearly equal proportions in Belgium and England. In France, the average of cultivated land is $1\frac{2}{3}$ acre; in Holland, $1\frac{4}{5}$ acre to each person.

If the same proportion between the arable and uncultivated land exists in China as in England, namely one-fourth, there are about six hundred and fifty millions of acres under cultivation in China; and we are not left altogether to conjecture, for by a report made to Kienlung in 1745, it appears that the area of the land under cultivation was 595,598,221 acres; a subsequent calculation places it at 640,579,381 acres, which is almost the same proportion as in England. Estimating it at six hundred and fifty millions—for it has since increased rather than diminished—it gives one acre and four-fifths to every person, which is by no means a small supply for the Chinese, considering that there are no cultivated pastures or meadows.

In comparing the population of different countries, the manner of living and the articles of food in use, form such important elements of the calculation, in ascertaining whether the country be overstocked or not, that a mere tabular view of the number of persons on a square mile is an imperfect criterion of the amount of inhabitants the land would maintain if they consumed the same food, and lived in the same manner in all of them. Living as the Chinese, Hindus, Japanese, and other Asiatics do, chiefly upon vegetables, the country can hardly be said to maintain more than one-half or one-third as many people on a square mile as it might do, if their energies were developed to the same extent with those of the English or Belgians. The population of these eastern regions has been repressed by the combined influences of ignorance, insecurity of life and property, religious prejudices, vice, and wars, so that the land has never maintained as many inhabitants as one would have otherwise reasonably expected therefrom.

Nearly all the cultivated soil in China is employed in raising food for man. Woollen garments and leather are little used, while cotton and mulberry cultivation take up only a small proportion of the soil. There is not, so far as is known, a single acre of land sown with grass-seed, and therefore almost no human labor is devoted to raising food for animals, which will not also serve to sustain man. Horses are seldom used for pomp or war, for travelling or carrying burdens, but mules, camels, asses, and goats are employed for transportation and other purposes north of the Yangtsz' River. Horses are fed on cooked rice, bran, sorghum seed, pulse, oats, and grass cut along the banks of streams, or on hillsides. In the southern and eastern provinces, all animals are rare, the transport of goods and passengers being done by boats or by men. The natives make no use of butter, cheese, or milk, and the few cattle employed in agriculture easily gather a living on the waste ground around the villages. In the south, the buffalo is applied more than the ox to plough the rice fields, and the habits of this animal make it cheaper to keep him in good condition, while he can also do more work. The winter stock is grass cut upon the hills, straw, bean stalks, and vegetables. No wool being wanted for making cloth, flocks of sheep and goats are seldom seen—it may almost be said are unknown in the east and south.

No animal is reared cheaper than the hog; hatching and raising ducks affords employment to thousands of people; hundreds of these fowl gather their own food along the river shore, being easily attended by a single keeper. Geese and poultry are also cheaply reared. In fishing, which is carried on to an enormous extent, no pasture-grounds, no manuring, no barns, are needed, nor are taxes paid by the cultivator and consumer.

While the people get their animal food in these ways, its preparation takes away the least possible amount of cultivated soil. The space occupied for roads and pleasure-grounds is insignificant, but there is perhaps an amount appropriated for burial places quite equal to the area used for those purposes in European countries; it is, however, less valuable land, and much of it would be useless for culture, even if otherwise unoccupied. Graves are dug on hills, in ravines and copses, and wherever they will be retired and dry; or if in the ancestral field, they do not hinder the crop growing close around them. Moreover, it is very common to preserve the coffin in temples and cemeteries until it is decayed, partly in order to save the expense of a grave, and partly to worship the remains, or preserve them until gathered to their fathers, in their distant native places. They are often placed in the corners of the fields, or under precipices where they remain till dust returns to dust, and bones and wood both moulder away. These and other customs limit the consumption of land for graves much more than would be supposed, when one sees, as at Macao, almost as much space taken up by the dead for a grave as by the living for a hut. The necropolis of Canton occupies the hills north of the city, of which not one-fiftieth part could ever have been used for agriculture, but where cattle are allowed to graze, as much as if there were no tombs.

Under its genial and equable climate, more than three-fourths of the area of China Proper produces two crops annually. In Kwangtung, Kwangsí, and Fuhkien, two crops of rice are taken year after year from the low lands; while in the loess regions of the northwest, a three-fold return from the grain fields is annually looked for, if the rain-fall is not withheld. In the winter season, in the neighborhood of towns, a third crop of sweet potatoes, cabbages, turnips, or some other vegetable is grown. De Guignes estimates the returns of a rice crop at ten for one, which, with the vegetables, will give full twenty-five fold from an acre in a year; few parts, however, yield this increase. Little or no land lies fallow, for constant manuring and turning of the soil prevents the necessity of repose. The diligence exhibited in collecting and applying manure is well known, and if all this industry result in the production of two crops instead of one, it really doubles the area under cultivation, when its superficies are compared with those of other countries. If the amount of land which produces two crops be estimated at one-fourth of the whole (and it is perhaps as near one-third), the area of arable land in the provinces may be considered as representing a total of 812 millions of acres, or $2\frac{3}{4}$ acres to an individual. The land is not, however, cut up into such small farms as to prevent its being managed as well as the people know how to stock and cultivate it; manual labor is the chief dependence of the farmer, fewer cattle, carts, ploughs, and machines being employed than in other countries. In rice fields no animals are used after the wet land has received the shoots, transplanting, weeding, and reaping being done by men.

In no other country besides Japan is so much food derived from the water. Not only are the coasts, estuaries, rivers, and lakes, covered with fishing-boats of various sizes, which are provided with everything fitted for the capture of whatever lives in the waters, but the spawn of fish is collected and reared. Rice fields are often converted into pools in the winter season, and stocked with fish; and the tanks dug for irrigation usually contain fish. By all these means, an immense supply of food is obtained at a cheap rate, which is eaten fresh or preserved with or without salt, and sent over the Empire, at a cost which places it within the reach of all above beggary. Other articles of food, both animal and vegetable, such as dogs, game, worms, spring greens, tripang, leaves, etc., do indeed compose part of their meals, but it is comparatively an inconsiderable fraction, and need not enter into the calculation. Enough has been stated to show that the land is abundantly able to support the population ascribed to it, even with all the drawbacks known to exist; and that, taking the highest estimate to be true, and considering the mode of living, the average population on a square mile in China is less than in several European countries.

The political and social causes which tend to multiply the inhabitants are numerous and powerful. The failure of male posterity to continue the succession of the family, and worship at the tombs of parents, is considered by all classes as one of the most afflictive misfortunes of life; the laws allow unlimited facilities of adoption, and secure the rights of those taken into the family in this way. The custom of betrothing children, and the obligation society imposes upon the youth when arrived at maturity, to fulfil the contracts entered into by their parents, acts favorably to the establishment of families and the nurture of children, and restricts polygamy. Parents desire children for a support in old age, as there is no legal or benevolent provision for aged poverty, and public opinion stigmatizes the man who allows his aged or infirm parents to suffer when he can help them. The law requires the owners of domestic slaves to provide husbands for their females, and prohibits the involuntary or forcible separation of husband and wife, or parents and children, when the latter are of tender age. All these causes and influences tend to increase population, and equalize the consumption and use of property more, perhaps, than in any other land.

The custom of families remaining together tends to the same result. The local importance of a large family in the country is weakened by its male members removing to town, or emigrating; consequently, the patriarch of three or four generations endeavors to retain his sons and grandsons around him, their houses joining his, and they and their families forming a social, united company. Such cases as those mentioned in the

Sacred Commands are of course rare, where nine generations of the family of Chang Kung-í inhabited one house, or of Chin, at whose table seven hundred mouths were daily fed,[1] but it is the tendency of society. This remark does not indicate that great landed proprietors exist, whose hereditary estates are secured by entail to the great injury of the state, as in Great Britain, for the farms are generally small and cultivated by the owner or on the metayer system. Families are supported on a more economical plan, the claims of kindred are better enforced, the land is cultivated with more care, and the local importance of the family perpetuated. This is, however, a very different system from that advocated by Fourier in France, or Greeley in America, for these little communities are placed under one natural head, whose authority is acknowledged and upheld, and his indignation feared. Workmen of the same profession form unions, each person contributing a certain sum on the promise of assistance when sick or disabled, and this custom prevents and alleviates a vast amount of poverty.

The obstacles put in the way of emigrating beyond sea, both in law and prejudice, operate to deter respectable persons from leaving their native land. Necessity has made the law a dead letter, and thousands annually leave their homes. No better evidence of the dense population can be offered to those acquainted with Chinese feelings and character, than the extent of emigration. "What stronger proof," observes Medhurst, "of the dense population of China could be afforded than the fact, that emigration is going on in spite of restrictions and disabilities, from a country where learning and civilization reign, and where all the dearest interests and prejudices of the emigrants are found, to lands like Burmah, Siam, Cambodia, Tibet, Manchuria, and the Indian Archipelago, where comparative ignorance and barbarity prevail, and where the extremes of a tropical or frozen region are to be exchanged for a mild and temperate climate? Added to this consideration, that not a single female is permitted or ventures to leave the country, when consequently, all the tender attachments that

[1] *Sacred Edict*, pp. 51, 60.

bind heart to heart must be burst asunder, and, perhaps, forever."[1]

Moreover, if they return with wealth enough to live upon, they are liable to the vexatious extortions of needy relatives, sharpers, and police, who have a handle for their fleecing whip in the law against leaving the country;[2] although this clause has been neutralized by subsequent acts, and is not in force, the power of public opinion is against going. A case occurred in 1832, at Canton, where the son of a Chinese living in Calcutta, who had been sent home by his parent with his mother, to perform the usual ceremonies in the ancestral hall, was seized by his uncle as he was about to be married, on the pretext that his father had unequally divided the paternal inheritance; he was obliged to pay a thousand dollars to free himself. Soon after his marriage, a few sharpers laid hold of him and bore him away in a sedan, as he was walking near his house, but his cries attracted the police, who carried them all to the magistrates, where he was liberated—after being obliged to fee his deliverers.[3] Another case occurred in Macao in 1838. A man had been living several years in Singapore as a merchant, and when he settled in Macao still kept up an interest in the trade with that place. Accounts of his great wealth became rumored abroad, and he was seriously annoyed by relatives. One night, a number of thieves, dressed like police-runners, came to his house to search for opium, and their boisterous manner terrified him to such a degree, that in order to escape them he jumped from the terrace upon the hard gravelled court-yard, and broke his leg, of which he shortly afterward died. A third case is mentioned, where the returned emigrants, consisting of a man and his wife, who was a Malay, and two children, were rescued from extortion, when before the magistrate, by the kindness of his wife and mother, who wished to see the foreign woman.[4] Such instances are now unknown,

---

1 *China: Its State and Prospects*, p. 42.

2 *Ta Tsing Leu Lee; being the Fundamental Laws, etc., of the Penal Code of China*, by Sir G. T. Staunton, Bart, London, 1810. Section CCXXV.

3 *Chinese Repository*, Vol. I., p. 332.

4 *Ibid.*, Vol. VII., p. 503; Vol. II., p. 161.

owing to the increase of emigration; they were, indeed, never numerically great, on account of the small number of those who came back.

The anxiety of the government to provide stores of food for times of scarcity, shows rather its fear of the disastrous results following a short crop—such as the gathering of clamorous crowds of starving poor, the increase of bandits and disorganization of society—than any peculiar care of the rulers, or that these storehouses really supply deficiencies. The evil consequences resulting from an overgrown population are experienced in one or another part of the provinces almost every year; and drought, inundations, locusts, mildew, or other natural causes, often give rise to insurrections and disturbances. There can be no doubt, however, that, without adding a single acre to the area of arable land, these evils would be materially alleviated, if the intercommunication of traders and their goods, between distant parts of the country, were more frequent, speedy, and safe; but this is not likely to be the case until both rulers and ruled make greater advances in just government, science, obedience, and regard for each other's right.

It would be a satisfaction if foreigners could verify any part of the census. But this is, at present, impossible. They cannot examine the records in the office of the Board of Revenue, nor can they ascertain the population in a given district from the archives in the hands of the local authorities, or the mode of taking it. Neither can they go through a village or town to count the number of houses and their inhabitants, and calculate from actual examination of a few parts what the whole would be. Wherever foreigners have journeyed, there has appeared much the same succession of waste land, hilly regions, cultivated plains, and wooded heights, as in other countries, with an abundance of people, but not more than the land could support, if properly tilled.

The people are grouped into hamlets and villages, under the control of village elders and officers. In the district of Nanhai, which forms the western part of the city of Canton, and the surrounding country for more than a hundred square miles, there are one hundred and eighty *hiang* or villages; the population of each *hiang* varies from two hundred and upwards to one hundred thousand, but ordinarily ranges between three hundred and thirty-five hundred. If each of the eighty-eight districts in the province of Kwangtung contains the same number of *hiang*, there will be, including the district towns, 15,928 villages, towns, and cities in all, with an average population of twelve hundred inhabitants to each. From the top of the hills on Dane's Island, at Whampoa, thirty-six towns and villages can be counted, of which Canton is one; and four of these contain from twelve to fifteen hundred houses. The whole district of Hiangshan, in which Macao lies, is also well covered with villages, though their exact number is not known. The island of Amoy contains more than fourscore villages and towns, and this island forms only a part of the district of Tung-ngan. The banks of the river leading from Amoy up to Changchau fu, are likewise well peopled. The environs of Ningpo and Shanghai are closely settled, though that is no more than one always expects near large cities, where the demand for food in the city itself causes the vicinity to be well peopled and tilled. In a notice of an irruption of the sea in 1819, along the coast of Shantung, it was reported that a hundred and forty villages were laid under water.

Marco Polo describes the mode followed in the days of Kublai khan: " It is the custom for every burgess of the city, and in fact for every description of person in it, to write over his door his own name, the name of his wife, and those of his children, his slaves, and all the inmates of his house, and also the number of animals that he keeps. And if any one dies in the house, then the name of that person is erased, and if a child is born its name is added. So in this way the sovereign is able to know exactly the population of the city. And this is the practice throughout all Manzi and Cathay."[1] This custom was observed long before the Mongol conquest, and is followed at present; so that it is perhaps easier to take a census in China than in most European countries.

The law upon this subject is contained in Secs. LXXV. and

[1] Yule's *Marco Polo*, Vol. II., p. 152.

LXXVI. of the statutes. It enacts various penalties for not registering the members of a family, and its provisions all go to show that the people are desirous rather of evading the census than of exaggerating it. When a family has omitted to make any entry, the head of it is liable to be punished with one hundred blows if he is a freeholder, and with eighty if he is not. If the master of a family has among his household another distinct family whom he omits to register, the punishment is the same as in the last clause, with a modification, according as the unregistered persons and family are relatives or strangers. Persons in government employ omitting to register their families, are less severely punished. A master of family failing to register all the males in his household who are liable to public service, shall be punished with from sixty to one hundred blows, according to the demerits of the offence; this clause was in effect repealed, when the land tax was substituted for the capitation tax. Omissions, from neglect or inadvertency to register all the individuals and families in a village or town, on the part of the headmen or government clerks, are punishable with different degrees of severity. All persons whatsoever are to be registered according to their accustomed occupations or professions, whether civil or military, whether couriers, artisans, physicians, astrologers, laborers, musicians, or of any other denomination whatever; and subterfuges in representing one's self as belonging to a profession not liable to public service, are visited as usual with the bamboo; persons falsely describing themselves as belonging to the army, in order to evade public service, are banished as well as beaten. From these clauses it is seen that the Manchus have extended the enumeration to classes which were exempted in the Han, Tang, and other dynasties, and thus come nearer to the actual population.

"In the Chinese government," observes Dr. Morrison, "there appears great regularity and system. Every district has its appropriate officers, every street its constable, and every ten houses their tything man. Thus they have all the requisite means of ascertaining the population with considerable accu-

---

[1] *Penal Code*, p. 79, Staunton's translation.

racy. Every family is required to have a board always hanging up in the house, and ready for the inspection of authorized officers, on which the names of all persons, men, women, and children, in the house are inscribed. This board is called *mun-pai* or 'door-tablet,' because when there are women and children within, the officers are expected to take the account from the board at the door. Were all the inmates of a family faithfully inserted, the amount of the population would, of course, be ascertained with great accuracy. But it is said that names are sometimes omitted through neglect or design; others think that the account of persons given in is generally correct." The door-tablets are sometimes pasted on the door, thus serving as a kind of door-plate; in these cases correctness of enumeration is readily secured, for the neighbors are likely to know if the record is below the truth, and the householder is not likely to exaggerate the taxable inmates under his roof. I have read these *mun-pai* on the doors of a long row of houses; they were printed blanks filled in, and then pasted outside for the *pao-kiah* or tithing man to examine. Both Dr. Morrison and his son, than whom no one has had better opportunities to know the true state of the case, or been more desirous of dealing fairly with the Chinese, regarded the censuses given in the *General Statistics* as more trustworthy than any other documents available.

In conclusion, it may be asked, are the results of the enumeration of the people, as contained in the statistical works published by the government, to be rejected or doubted, therefore, because the Chinese officers do not wish to ascertain the exact population; or because they are not capable of doing it; or, lastly, because they wish to impose upon foreign powers by an arithmetical array of millions they do not possess? The question seems to hang upon this trilemma. It is acknowledged that they falsify or garble statements in a manner calculated to throw doubt upon everything they write, as in the reports of victories and battles sent to the Emperor, in the memorials upon the opium trade, in their descriptions of natural objects in books of medicine, and in many other things. But the question is as applicable to China as to France: is the estimated population of France in 1801 to be called in question, because the *Moniteur* gave false accounts of Napoleon's battles in 1813? It would be a strange combination of conceit and folly, for a ministry composed of men able to carry on all the details of a complicated government like that of China, to systematically exaggerate the population, and then proceed, for more than a century, with taxation, disbursements, and official appointments, founded upon these censuses. Somebody at least must know them to be worthless, and the proof that they were so, must, one would think, ere long be apparent. The provinces and departments have been divided and subdivided since the Jesuits made their survey, because they were becoming too densely settled for the same officers to rule over them.

Still less will any one assert that the Chinese are not capable of taking as accurate a census as they are of measuring distances, or laying out districts and townships. Errors may be found in the former as well as in the latter, and doubtless are so; for it is not contended that the four censuses of 1711, 1753, 1792, and 1812 are as accurate as those now taken in England, France, or the United States, but that they are the best data extant, and that if they are rejected we leave tolerable evidence and take up with that which is doubtful and suppositive. The censuses taken in China since the Christian era are, on the whole, more satisfactory than those of all other nations put together up to the Reformation, and further careful research will no doubt increase our respect for them.

Ere long we may be able to traverse a census in its details of record and deduction, and thus satisfy a reasonable curiosity, especially as to the last reported total after the carnage of the rebellion. On the other hand, it may be stated that in the last census, the entire population of Manchuria, Koko-nor, Īlí, and Mongolia, is estimated at only 2,167,286 persons, and nearly all the inhabitants of those vast regions are subject to the Emperor. The population of Tibet is not included in any census, its people not being taxable. It is doubtful if an enumeration of any part of the extra provincial territory has ever been taken, inasmuch as the Mongol tribes, and still less the Usbeck or other Moslem races, are unused to such a thing, and would not be numbered. Yet, the Chinese cannot be charged with exaggeration, when good judges, as Klaproth and others, reckon the whole at between six and seven millions; and Khoten alone, one author states, has three and a half millions. No writer of importance estimates the inhabitants of these regions as high as thirty millions—as does R. Mont. Martin—which would be more than ten to a square mile, excluding Gobi; while Siberia (though not so well peopled) has only 3,611,300 persons on an area of 2,649,600 square miles, or $1\frac{1}{8}$ to each square mile.

The reasons just given why the Chinese desire posterity are not all those which have favored national increase. The uninterrupted peace which the country enjoyed between the years 1700 and 1850 operated to greatly develop its resources. Every encouragement has been given to all classes to multiply and fill the land. Polygamy, slavery, and prostitution, three social evils which check increase, have been circumscribed in their effects. Early betrothment and poverty do much to prevent the first; female slaves can be and are usually married; while public prostitution is reduced by a separation of the sexes and early marriages. No fears of overpassing the supply of food restrain the people from rearing families, though the Emperor Kienlung issued a proclamation in 1793, calling upon all ranks of his subjects to economize the gifts of heaven, lest, erelong, the people exceed the means of subsistence.

It is difficult to see what this or that reason or objection has to do with the subject, except where the laws of population are set at defiance, which is not the case in China. Food and work, peace and security, climate and fertile soil, not universities or steamboats, are the encouragements needed for the multiplication of mankind; though they do not have that effect in all countries (as in Mexico and Brazil), it is no reason why they should not in others. There are grounds for believing that not more than two-thirds of the whole population of China were included in the census of 1711, but that allowance cannot be made for Ireland in 1785; and consequently, her annual percentage of increase, up to 1841, would then be greater than China, during the forty-two years ending with 1753. McCulloch quotes De Guignes approvingly, but the Frenchman takes the rough estimate of 333,000,000 given to Macartney, which is less trustworthy than that of 307,467,200, and compares it with Grosier's of 157,343,975, which is certainly wrong through his misinterpretation. De Guignes proceeds from the data in his possession in 1802 (which were less than those now available), and from his own observations in travelling through the country in 1796, to show the improbability of the estimated population. But the observations made in journeys, taken as were those of the English and Dutch embassies, though they passed through some of the best provinces, cannot be regarded as good evidence against official statistics.

Would any one suppose, in travelling from Boston to Chatham, and then from Albany to Buffalo, along the railroad, that Massachusetts contained, in 1870, exactly double the population on a square mile of New York? So, in going from Peking to Canton, the judgment which six intelligent travellers might form of the population of China could easily be found to differ by one-half. De Guignes says, after comparing China with Holland and France, "All these reasons clearly demonstrate that the population of China does not exceed that of other countries;" and such is in truth the case, if the kind of food, number of crops, and materials of dress be taken into account. His remarks on the population and productiveness of the country are, like his whole work, replete with good sense and candor; but some of his deductions would have been different, had he been in possession of all the data since obtained.[1] The discrepancies between the different censuses have been usually considered a strong internal evidence against them, and they should receive due consideration. The really difficult point is to fix the percentage that must be allowed for the classes not included as taxable, and the power of the government to enumerate those who wished to avoid a census and the subsequent taxation.

After all these reasons for receiving the total of 1812 as the best one, there are, on the other hand, two principal objections against taking the Chinese census as altogether trustworthy. The first is the enormous averages of 850, 705, and 671 inhab-

[1] *Voyages à Peking*, Tome III., pp. 55–86.

itants on a square mile, severally apportioned to Kiangsu, Nganhwui, and Chehkiang, or, what is perhaps a fairer calculation, of 458 persons to the nine eastern provinces. Whatever amount of circumstantial evidence may be brought forward in confirmation of the census as a whole, and explanation of the mode of taking it, a more positive proof seems to be necessary before giving implicit credence to this result. Such a population on such an extensive area is marvellous, notwithstanding the fertility of the soil, facilities of navigation, and salubrity of the climate of these regions, although acknowledged to be almost unequalled. While we admit the full force of all that has been urged in support of the census, and are willing to take it as the best document on the subject extant, it is desirable to have proofs derived from personal observation, and to defer the settlement of this question until better opportunities are afforded. So high an average is, indeed, not without example. Captain Wilkes ascertained, in 1840, that one of the islands of the Fiji group supported a population of over a thousand on a square mile. On Lord North's Island, in the Pelew group, the crew of the American whaler Mentor ascertained there were four hundred inhabitants living on half a square mile. These, and many other islands in that genial clime, contain a population far exceeding that of any large country, and each separate community is obliged to depend wholly on its own labor. They cannot, however, be cited as altogether parallel cases, though if it be true, as Barrow says, "that an acre of cotton will clothe two or three hundred persons," not much more land need be occupied with cotton or mulberry plants, for clothing in China, than in the South Sea Islands.

The second objection against receiving the result of the census is, that we are not well informed as to the mode of enumerating the people by families, and the manner of taking the account, when the patriarch of two or three generations lives in a hamlet, with all his children and domestics around him. Two of the provisions in Sec. XXV. of the *Code*, seem to be designed for some such state of society; and the liability to underrate the males fit for public service, when a capitation tax was ordered, and to overrate the inmates of such a house, when the head of it might suppose he would thereby receive increased aid from government when calamity overtook him, are equally apparent. The door-tablet is also liable to mistake, and in shops and workhouses, where the clerks and workmen live and sleep on the premises, it is not known what kind of report of families the assessors make. On these important points our present information is imperfect, while the evident liability to serious error in the ultimate results makes one hesitate. The Chinese may have taken a census satisfactory for their purposes, showing the number of families, and the average in each; but the point of this objection is, that we do not know how the families are enumerated, and therefore are at fault in reckoning the individuals. The average of persons in a household is set down at five by the Chinese, and in England, in 1831, it was 4.7, but it is probably less than that in a thickly settled country, if every married couple and their children be taken as a family, whether living by themselves, or grouped in patriarchal hamlets.

No one doubts that the population is enormous, constituting by far the greatest assemblage of human beings using one speech ever congregated under one monarch. To the merchants and manufacturers of the West, the determination of this question is of some importance, and through them to their governments. The political economist and philologist, the naturalist and geographer, have also greater or less degrees of interest in the contemplation of such a people, inhabiting so beautiful and fertile a country. But the Christian philanthropist turns to the consideration of this subject with the liveliest solicitude; for if the weight of evidence is in favor of the highest estimate, he feels his responsibility increase to a painful degree. The danger to this people is furthermore greatly enhanced by the opium traffic—a trade which, as if the Rivers Phlegethon and Lethe were united in it, carries fire and destruction wherever it flows, and leaves a deadly forgetfulness wherever it has passed. Let these facts appeal to all calling themselves Christians, to send the antidote to this baleful drug, and diffuse a knowledge of the principles of the Gospel among them, thereby placing life as well as death before them.

If the population of the Empire is not easily ascertained, a satisfactory account of the public revenue and expenditures is still more difficult to obtain; it possesses far less interest, of course, in itself, and in such a country as China is subject to many variations. The market value of the grain, silk, and other products in which a large proportion of the taxes are paid, varies from year to year; and although this does not materially affect the government which receives these articles, it complicates the subject very much when attempting to ascertain the real taxation. Statistics on these subjects are only of recent date in Europe, and should not yet be looked for in China, drawn up with much regard to truth. The central government requires each province to support itself, and furnish a certain surplusage for the maintenance of the Emperor and his court; but it is well known that his Majesty is continually embarrassed for the want of funds, and that the provinces do not all supply enough revenue to meet their own outlays.

The amounts given by various authors as the revenue of China at different times, are so discordant, that a single glance shows that they were obtained from partial or incomplete returns, or else refer only to the surplusage sent to the capital. De Guignes remarks very truly, that the Chinese are so fully persuaded of the riches, power, and resources of their country, that a foreigner is likely to receive different accounts from every native he asks; but there appears to be no good reason why the government should falsify or abridge their fiscal accounts. In 1587, Trigault, one of the French missionaries, stated the revenue at only tls. 20,000,000. In 1655, Nieuhoff reckoned it at tls. 108,000,000. About twelve years after, Magalhaens gave the treasures of the Emperor at $20,423,962; and Le Comte, about the same time, placed the revenue at $22,000,000, and both of them estimated the receipts from rice, silk, etc., at $30,000,000, making the whole revenue previous to Kanghi's death, in 1721, between fifty and seventy millions of dollars. Barrow reckoned the receipts from all sources in 1796 at tls. 198,000,000, derived from a rough estimate given by the commissioner who accompanied the embassy. Sir George Staunton places the total sum at $330,000,000; of which $60,000,000 only were transmitted to Peking. Medhurst, drawing his information from original sources, thus states the principal items of the receipts:

Land taxes in money,	sent to Peking,	Tls.	31,745,966	valued at	$42,327,954
Land taxes in grain,	sent to Peking,	Shih	4,230,957	"	12,692,871
Custom and transit duties,	sent to Peking,	Tls.	1,480,997	"	1,974,662
Land taxes in money,	kept in provinces	Tls.	28,705,125	"	38,273,500
Grain,	kept in provinces	Shih	31,596,569	"	105,689,707
					$200,958.694

The *shih* of rice is estimated at $3, but this does not include the cost of transportation to the capital.[1] At $200,000,000, the tax received by government from each person on an average is about sixty cents; Barrow estimates the capitation at about ninety cents. The account of the revenue in taels from each province given in the table of population on page 264, is extracted from the *Red Book* for 1840;[2] the account of the revenue in rice, as stated in the official documents for that year, is 4,114,000 shih, or about five hundred and fifty millions of pounds, calling each *shih* a pecul. The manner in which the various items of the revenue are divided is thus stated for Kwangtung, in the *Red Book* for 1842:

	Taels.
Land tax in money	1,264,304
Pawnbrokers' taxes	5,990
Taxes at the frontier and on transportation	719,307
Retained	339,143
Miscellaneous sources	59,530
Salt department (gabel)	47,510
Revenue from customs at Canton	43,750
Other stations in the province	53,670
	2,533,204

This is evidently only the sum sent to the capital from this province, ostensibly as the revenue, and which the provincial treasury must collect. The real receipts from this province or any other cannot well be ascertained by foreigners; it is, however, known, that in former years, the collector of customs at Canton was obliged to remit annually from eight hundred thousand to one million three hundred thousand taels, and

[1] The *shih*, says Medhurst, is a measure of grain containing 3,460 English cubic inches. *China: Its State and Prospects*, p. 68. London, 1838.

[2] *Annales de la Foi*, Tome XVI., p. 440.

the gross receipts of his office were not far from three millions of taels.[1] This was then the richest collectorate in the Empire; but since the foreign trade at the open ports has been placed under foreign supervision, the resources of the Empire have been better reported. A recent analysis of the sources of revenue in the Eighteen Provinces has been furnished by the customs service; it places them under different headings from the preceding list, though the total does not materially differ. Out of this whole amount the sum derived from the trade in foreign shipping goes most directly to the central exchequer.

	Taels.
Land tax in money	18,000,000
Li-kin or internal excise on goods	20,000,000
Import and export duties collected by foreigners	12,000,000
Import and export duties on native commerce	3,000,000
Salt gabel	5,000,000
Sales of offices and degrees	7,000,000
Sundries	1,400,000
Amount paid in silver	66,400,000
Land tax paid in produce	13,100,000
	79,500,000

De Guignes has examined the subject of the revenue with his usual caution, and bases his calculations on a proclamation of Kienlung in 1777, in which it was stated that the total income in bullion at that period was tls. 27,967,000.

	Taels.
Income in money as above	27,967,000
Equal revenue in kind from grain	27,967,000
Tax on the second crop in the southern provinces	21,800,000
Gabel, coal, transit duties, etc	6,479,400
Customs at Canton	800,000
Revenue from silk, porcelain, varnish, and other manufactures	7,000,000
Adding house and shop taxes, licenses, tonnage duties, etc	4,000,000
Total revenue	89,713,400

The difference of about eighty millions of dollars between this amount and that given by Medhurst, will not surprise one who has looked into this perplexing matter. All these calculations are based on approximations, which, although easily made

[1] *Chinese Commercial Guide*, 2d edition, 1842, p. 143.

up, cannot be verified to our satisfaction; but all agree in placing the total amount of revenue below that of any European government in proportion to the population. In 1823, a paper was published by a graduate upon the fiscal condition of the country, in which he gave a careful analysis of the receipts and disbursements. P. P. Thoms translated it in detail, and summarized the former under three heads of taxes reckoned at tls. 33,327,056, rice sent to Peking 6,346,438, and supplies to army 7,227,360—in all tls. 46,900,854. Out of the first sum tls. 24,507,933 went to civilians and the army, leaving tls. 5,819,-123 for the Peking government, and tls. 3,000,000 for the Yellow River repairs and Yuen-ming Palace. The resources of the Empire this writer foots up at tls. 74,461,633, or just one-half of what Medhurst gives. The extraordinary sources of revenue which are resorted to in time of war or bad harvests, are sale of office and honors, temporary increase of duties, and demands for contributions from wealthy merchants and landholders. The first is the most fruitful source, and may be regarded rather as a permanent than a temporary expediency employed to make up deficiencies. The mines of gold and silver, pearl fisheries in Manchuria and elsewhere, precious stones brought from Ílí and Khoten, and other localities, furnish several millions.

The expenditures, almost every year, exceed the revenue, but how the deficit is supplied does not clearly appear; it has been sometimes drawn from the rich by force, at other times made good by paltering with the currency, as in 1852–55, and again by reducing rations and salaries. In 1832, the Emperor said the excess of disbursements was tls. 28,000,000;[1] and, in 1836, the defalcation was still greater, and offices and titles to the amount of tls. 10,000,000 were put up for sale to supply it. This deficiency has become more and more alarming since the drain of specie annually sent abroad in payment for opium has been increased by military exactions for suppressing the rebellion up to 1867. At that date the Empire began to recuperate. The principal items of the expenditure are thus stated by De Guignes:

---

[1] *Chinese Repository*, Vol. I., p. 159.

	Taels.
Salary of civil and military officers, a tithe of the impost on lands.	7,773,500
Pay of 600,000 infantry, three taels per month, half in money and half in rations	21,600,000
Pay of 242,000 cavalry, at four taels per month	11,616,000
Mounting the cavalry, twenty taels each	4,840,000
Uniforms for both arms of the service, four taels	3,368,000
Arms and ammunition	842,000
Navy, revenue cutters, etc.	13,500,000
Canals and transportation of revenue	4,000,000
Forts, artillery, and munitions of war	3,800,000
	71,339,500

This, according to his calculation, shows a surplus of nearly twenty millions of taels every year. But the outlays for quelling insurrections and transporting troops, deficiency from bad harvests, defalcation of officers, payments to the tribes and princes in Mongolia and Ílí, and other unusual demands, more than exceed this surplus. In 1833, the *Peking Gazette* contained an elaborate paper on the revenue, proposing various ways and means for increasing it. The author, named Na, says the income from land tax, the gabel, customs and transit duty, does not in all exceed forty millions of taels, while the expenditures should not much transcend thirty in years of peace.[1] This places the budget much lower than other authorities, but the censor perhaps includes only the imperial resources, though the estimate would then be too high. The pay and equipment of the troops is the largest item of expenditure, and it is probable that here the apparent force and pay are far too great, and that reductions are constantly made in this department by compelling the soldiers to depend more and more for support upon the plats of land belonging to them. It is considered the best evidence of good government on the part of an officer to render his account of the revenue satisfactorily, but from the injudicious system which exists of combining fiscal, legislative, and judicial functions and control in the same person, the temptations to defraud are strong, and the peculations proportionably great.

The salaries of officers, for some reasons, are placed so low as

[1] *Chinese Repository*, Vol. II., p. 431.

to prove that the legal allowances were really the nominal incomes, and the sums set against their names in the *Red Book* as *yang tien*, or anti-extortion perquisites (lit., 'nourishing frugality'), are the salaries. That of a governor-general is from 15,000 to 25,000 taels for the latter, and only 180 or 200 taels for the legal salary; a governor gets 15,000 when he is alone, and 10,000 or 12,000 when under a governor-general; a treasurer from 4,500 to 10,000; a judge from 3,000 to 8,000; a prefect from 2,000 to 4,500; district magistrates from 700 to 1,000, according to the onerousness of the post; an intendant from 3,000 to 4,500; a literary chancellor from 2,000 to 5,000; and military men from 4,000 taels down to 100 or 150 per annum. The perquisites of the highest and lowest officers are disproportionate, for the people prefer to lay their important cases before the highest courts at once, in order to avoid the expense of passing through those of a lower grade. The personal disposition of the functionary modifies the exactions he makes upon the people so much, that no guess can be made as to the amount.

The land tax is the principal resource for the revenue in rural districts, and this is well understood by all parties, so that there is less room for exactions. The land tax is from 1½ to 10 cents a *mao* (or from 10 to 66 cents an acre), according to the quality of the land, and difficulty of tillage; taking the average at 25 cents an acre, the income from this source would be upward of 150 millions of dollars. The clerks, constables, lictors, and underlings of the courts and prisons, are the "claws" of their superiors, as the Chinese aptly call them, and perform most of their extortions, and are correspondingly odious to the people. In towns and trading places, it is easier for the officers to exact in various ways from wealthy people, than in the country, where rich people often hire bodies of retainers to defy the police, and practise extortion and robbery themselves. Like other Asiatic governments, China suffers from the consequences of bribery, peculation, extortion, and poorly paid officers, but she has no powerful aristocracy to retain the money thus squeezed out of the people, and ere long it finds its way out of the hands of emperors and ministers back into the mass of the people.

The Chinese believe, however, that the Emperor annually remits such amounts as he is able to collect into Mukden, in time of extremity; but latterly he has not been able to do so at all, and probably never sent as much to that city as the popular ideas imagine. The sum applied to filling the granaries is much larger, but this popular provision in case of need is really a light draft upon the resources of the country, as it is usually managed. In Canton, there are only fourteen buildings appropriated to this purpose, few of them more than thirty feet square, and none of them full.

CHAPTER VI.

NATURAL HISTORY OF CHINA.

THE succinct account of the natural history of China given by Sir John Davis in 1836, contained nearly all the popular notices of much value then known, and need not be repeated, while summarizing the items derived from other and later sources. Malte-Brun observed long ago, "That of even the more general, and, according to the usual estimate, the more important features of that vast sovereignty, we owe whatever knowledge we have obtained to some ambassadors who have seen the courts and the great roads—to certain merchants who have inhabited a suburb of a frontier town—and to several missionaries who, generally more credulous than discriminating, have contrived to penetrate in various directions into the interior." The volumes upon China in the Edinburgh Cabinet Library contain the best digest of what was known forty years since on this subject. The botanical collections of Robert Fortune in 1844–1849, and those of Col. Champion at Hongkong, have been studied by Bentham, while the later researches of Hance, Bunge and Maximowitch have brought many new forms to notice. In geology, Pumpelly, Kingsmill, Bickmore, and Baron Richthofen have greatly enlarged and certified our knowledge by their travels and memoirs; while Père David, Col. Prejevalsky, Swinhoe, Stimpson, and Sir John Richardson have added hundreds of new species to the scientific fauna of the Empire.

Personal investigation is particularly necessary in all that relates to the geology and fossils of a country, and the knowledge possessed on these heads is, it must be conceded, still meagre, though now sufficient to convey a general idea of the formations, deposits, and contents of the mountains and mines, as well as the agencies at work in modifying the surface of this land. The descriptions and observed facts recorded in native books may furnish valuable hints when they can be compared with the places and productions, for at present the difficulty of explaining terms used, and understanding the processes described, render these treatises hard to translate. The empirical character of Chinese science compels a careful sifting of all its facts and speculations by comparisons with nature, while the amount of real information contained in medical, topographical, and itinerant works render them always worth examining. Large regions still await careful examination in every part of the Empire; and it will be well for the Chinese Government if no tempting metallic deposits are found to test its strength to protect and work them for its own benefit. But in mere science it cannot be doubted that so peculiar a part of the world as the plateau of Central Asia will, when thoroughly examined, solve many problems relating to geology, and disclose many important facts to illustrate the obscure phenomena of other parts of the world.

A few notices of geological formations furnished in the writings of travellers, have already been given in the geographical account of the provinces. The summary published by Davis is a well digested survey of the observations collected by the gentlemen attached to the embassies.[1]

The loess-beds, covering a great portion of Northern China, are among the most peculiar natural phenomena and interesting fields for geological investigation on the world's surface. Since attention was first directed to this deposit by Pumpelly, in 1864, its formation and extent have been more carefully examined by other geologists, whose hypotheses are now pretty generally discarded for that of Baron von Richthofen. The loess territory begins, at its eastern limit, with the foot hills of the great alluvial plane. From this rises a terrace of from 90 to 250 feet in height, consisting entirely of loess, and westward of it, in

[1] *The Chinese*, Vol. II., pp. 333–343.

a nearly north and south line, stretches the Tai-hang shan or dividing range between the alluvial land and the hill country of Shansí. An almost uninterrupted loess-covered country extends west of this line to the Koko-nor and head-waters of the Yellow River. On the north the formation can be traced from the vicinity of Kalgan, along the water-shed of the Mongolian steppes, and into the desert beyond the Ala shan. Toward the south its limits are less sharply defined; though covering all the country of the Wei basin (in Shensí), none is found in Sz'chuen, due south of this valley, but it appears in parts of Honan and Eastern Shantung. Excepting occasional spurs and isolated spots—as at Nanking and the Lakes Poyang and Tungting—loess may be considered as ending everywhere on the north side of the Yangtsz' valley, and, roughly speaking, to cover the parallelogram between longs. 99° and 115°, and lats. 33° and 41°. The district within China Proper represents a territory half as large again as that of the German Empire, while outside of the Provinces there is reason to believe that loess spreads far toward the east and north. In the Wu-tai shan (Shansí), Richthofen observed this deposit to a height of 7,200 feet above the sea, and supposes that it may occur at higher levels.

The term *loess*, now generally accepted, has been used to designate a tertiary deposit appearing in the Rhine valley and several isolated sections of Europe; its formation has heretofore been ascribed to glaciers, but its enormous extent and thickness in China demand some other origin. The substance is a brownish colored earth, extremely porous, and when dry easily powdered between the fingers, when it becomes an impalpable dust that may be rubbed into the pores of the skin. Its particles are somewhat angular in shape, the lumps varying from the size of a peanut to a foot in length, whose appearance warrants the peculiarly appropriate Chinese name meaning 'ginger stones.' After washing, the stuff is readily disintegrated, and spread far and wide by rivers during their freshets; Kingsmill[1] states that a number of specimens which crumbled in the moist

[1] *Journal of the Geolog. Soc.*, London, for 1871, p. 379.

air of a Shanghai summer, rearranged themselves afterward in the bottom of a drawer in which they had been placed. Every atom of loess is perforated by small tubes, usually very minute, circulating after the manner of root-fibres, and lined with a thin coating of carbonate of lime. The direction of these little canals being always from above downward, cleavage in the loess mass, irrespective of its size, is invariably vertical, while from the same cause surface water never collects in the form of rain puddles or lakes, but sinks at once to the local water level.

One of the most striking, as well as important phenomena of this formation is the perpendicular splitting of its mass into sudden and multitudinous clefts that cut up the country in every direction, and render observation, as well as travel, often exceedingly difficult. The cliffs, caused by erosion, vary from cracks measured by inches to cañons half a mile wide and hundreds of feet deep; they branch out in every direction, ramifying through the country after the manner of tree-roots in the soil—from each root a rootlet, and from these other small fibres—until the system of passages develops into a labyrinth of far-reaching and intermingling lanes. Were the loess throughout of the uniform structure seen in single clefts, such a region would indeed be absolutely impassable, the vertical banks becoming precipices of often more than a thousand feet. The fact, however, that loess exhibits all over a terrace formation, renders its surface not only habitable, but highly convenient for agricultural purposes; it has given rise, moreover, to the theory advanced by Kingsmill and some others, of its stratification, and from this a proof of its origin as a marine deposit. Richthofen argues that these apparent layers of loess are due to external conditions, as of rocks and débris sliding from surrounding hillsides upon the loess as it sifted into the basin or valley, thus interrupting the homogeneity of the gradually rising deposit. In the sides of gorges near the mountains are seen layers of coarse débris which, in going toward the valley, become finer, while the layers themselves are thinner and separated by an increasing vertical distance; along these rubble beds are numerous calcareous concretions which stand upright. These are then the terrace-forming layers which, by their resistance to the action of water, cause the broken chasms and step-like contour of the loess regions. Each bank does indeed cleave vertically, sometimes—since the erosion works from below—leaving an overhanging bank; but meeting with this horizontal layer of marl stones, the abrasion is interrupted, and a ledge is made. Falling clods upon such spaces are gradually spread over their surfaces by natural action, converting them into rich fields. When seen from a height in good seasons, these systems of terraces present an endless succession of green fields and growing crops; viewed from the deep cut of a road below, the traveller sees nothing but yellow walls of loam and dusty tiers of loess ridges. As may be readily imagined, a country of this nature exhibits many landscapes of unrivalled picturesqueness, especially when lofty crags, which some variation in the water-course has left as giant guardsmen in fertile river valleys, stand out in bold relief against the green background of neighboring hills and a fruitful alluvial bottom, or when an opening of some ascending pass allows the eye to range over leagues of sharp-cut ridges and teaming crops, the work of the careful cultivator.

The extreme ease with which loess is cut away tends at times to seriously embarrass traffic. Dust made by the cart-wheels on a highway is taken up by strong winds during the dry season and blown over the surrounding lands, much after the manner in which it was originally deposited here. This action continued over centuries, and assisted by occasional deluges of rain, which find a ready channel in the road-bed, has hollowed the country routes into depressions of often 50 or 100 feet, where the passenger may ride for miles without obtaining a glimpse of the surrounding scenery. Lieutenant Kreitner, of the Széchenyí exploring expedition, illustrates,[1] in a personal experience in Shansí, the difficulty and danger of leaving these deep cuts; after scrambling for miles along the broken loess above the road, he only regained it when a further passage was cut off by a precipice on the one side, while a jump of some 30 feet into the beaten track below awaited him on the other. Difficult as

[1] *Im fernen Osten*, p. 462.

may be such a territory for roads and the purposes of trade, the advantages to a farmer are manifold. Wherever this deposit extends, there the husbandman has an assured harvest, two and even three times in a year. It is easily worked, exceedingly fertile, and submits to constant tillage, with no other manure than a sprinkling of its own loam dug from the nearest bank.

Facade of Dwelling in Loess Cliffs, Ling-shí hien. (From Richthofen.)

But loess performs still another service to its inhabitants. Caves made at the base of its straight clefts afford homes to millions of people in the northern provinces. Choosing an escarpment where the consistency of the earth is greatest, the natives cut for themselves rooms and houses, whose partition walls, cement, bed and furniture are made from the same loess. Whole villages cluster together in a series of adjoining or superimposed chambers, some of which pierce the soil to a depth of often more than 200 feet. In more costly dwellings the terrace or succession of terraces thus perforated are faced with brick, as well as the arching of rooms within. The advantages of such habitations consist as well in imperviousness to changes of temperature without, as in their durability when constructed in properly selected places, many loess dwellings outlasting six or seven generations. The capabilities of defence in a country such as this, where an invading army must inevitably become lost in the tangle of interlacing ways, and where the defenders may always remain concealed, is very suggestive.

There remains, lastly, a peculiar property of loess which is perhaps more important than all other features when measured by its man-serving efficiency. This is the manner in which it brings forth crops without the aid of manure. From a period more than 2,000 years before Christ, to the present day, the province of Shansí has borne the name of Grainery of the Empire, while its fertile soil, *hwang-tu*, or 'yellow earth,' is the origin of the imperial color. Spite of this productiveness, which, in the fourteenth century, caused the Friar Odoric to class it as the second country in the world, its present capacity for raising crops seems to be as great as ever. In the nature of this substance lies the reason for this apparently inexhaustible fecundity. Its remarkably porous structure must indeed cause it to absorb the gases necessary to plant life to a much greater degree than other soils, but the stable production of those mineral substances needful to the yearly succession of crops is in the ground itself. The salts contained more or less in solution at the water level of the region are freed by the capillary action of the loess when rain-water sinks through the spongy mass from above. Surface moisture following the downward direction of the tiny loess tubes establishes a connection with the waters compressed below, when, owing to the law of diffusion, the ingredients, being released, mix with the moisture of the little canals, and are taken from the lowest to the topmost levels, permeating the ground and furnishing nourishment to the plant roots at the surface. It is on account of this curious action of loess that a copious rain-fall is more necessary in North

China than elsewhere, for with a dearth of rain the capillary communication from above, below, and *vice versa*, is interrupted, and vegetation loses both its manure and moisture. Drought and famine are consequently synonymous terms here.

As to the formation and origin of loess, Richthofen's theory is substantially as follows:[1] The uniform composition of this material over extended areas, coupled with the absence of stratification and of marine or fresh-water organic remains, renders impossible the hypothesis that it is a water deposit. On the other hand, it contains vast quantities of land-shells and the vestiges of animals (mammalia) at every level, both in remarkably perfect condition. Concluding, also, that from the conformation of the neighboring mountain chains and their peculiar weathering, the glacial theory is inadmissible, he advances the supposition that loess is a sub-aërial deposit, and that its fields are the drained analogues of the steppe-basins of Central Asia. They date from a geological era of great dryness, before the existence of the Yellow and other rivers of the northern provinces. As the rocks and hills of the highlands disintegrated, the sand was removed, not by water-courses seaward, but by the high winds ranging over a treeless desert landward, until the dust settled in the grass-covered districts of what is at present China Proper. New vegetation was at once nourished, while its roots were raised by the constantly arriving deposit; the decay of old roots produced the lime-lined canals which impart to this material its peculiar characteristics. Any one who has observed the terrible dust-storms of North China, when the air is filled with an impalpable yellow powder, which leaves its coating upon everything, and often extends, in a fog-like cloud, hundreds of miles to sea, will understand the power of this action during many thousand years. This deposition received the shells and bones of innumerable animals, while the dissolved solutions contained in its bulk stayed therein, or saturated the water of small lakes. By the sinking of mountain chains in the south, rain-clouds emptied themselves over this region with much greater frequency, and gradually the system became

---

[1] *China: Ergebnisse eigener Reisen.* Band I., S. 74. Berlin, 1877.

drained, the erosion working backward from the coast, slowly cutting into one basin after another. With the sinking of its salts to lower levels, unexampled richness was added to the wonderful topography of this peculiar formation.[1]

Pumpelly, while accepting this ingenious theory in place of his own (that of a fresh-water lake deposit), adds that the supply of loess might have been materially increased by the vast *mers-de-glace* of High Asia and the Tien shan, whose streams have for ages transported the products of glacial attrition into Central Asia and Northwest China. Again, he insists that Richthofen has not given importance enough to the parting planes, wrongly considered by his predecessors as planes of stratification. "These," he says, "account for the marginal layers of débris brought down from the mountains. And the continuous and more abundant growth of grasses *at one plane* would produce a modification of the soil structurally and chemically, which superincumbent accumulations could never efface. It should seem probable that we have herein, also, the explanation of the calcareous concretions which abound along these planes; for the greater amount of carbonic acid generated by the slow decay of this vegetation would, by forming a bicarbonate, give to the lime the mobility necessary to produce the concretions."

The metallic and mineral productions used in the arts comprise nearly everything found in other countries, and the common ones are furnished in such abundance, and at such rates, as conclusively prove them to be plenty and easily worked. The careful digest of observations published by Pumpelly through the Smithsonian Institution, carries out this remark, and indicates the vast field still to be explored. Coal exists in every province in China, and Pumpelly enumerates seventy-four localities which have been ascertained. Marco Polo's well-known notice of its use shows that the people had long employed it: "It is a fact that all over the country of Cathay there is a kind of black stone existing in beds in the mountains, which they dig out and burn like firewood. It is true that they have plenty of

---

[1] Compare Kingsmill, in the *Quar. Journal of the Geol. Soc. of London*, 1868, pp. 119 ff., and in the *North China Herald*, Vol. IX., 85, 86.

wood also, but they do not burn it, because those stones burn better and cost less.[1] This mineral seems to have been unknown in Europe till after the return of the Venetian to his native land, while it was employed before the Christian era in China, and probably in very ancient times, if the accessible deposits in Shensí then cropped out in its eroded gorges, as represented by Richthofen. The few fossil plants hitherto examined indicate that the mass of these deposits are of the Mesozoic age. The mode of working the coal mines is described by Pumpelly,[2] and was probably no worse two thousand five hundred years ago. Want of machinery for draining them prevents the miners from going much below the water-level, and a rain-storm will sometimes flood and ruin a shaft. An inclined plane seldom takes the workmen more than a hundred feet below the level of the mouth, and then a horizontal gallery conducts him to the end of the mine. Some water is bailed out by buckets handed from one level up to another at the top, and the coal is carried out in baskets on the miners' backs, or dragged in sleds over smooth, round sticks along passages too low for the coolies to do better than crawl as they work. Mr. Pumpelly found the gallery of one mine near Peking so low that he had to crawl the whole distance (six thousand feet) to see its construction, and when he emerged into daylight, with his knees nearly skinned, ascertained that the workmen padded theirs. The timbering is very expensive, yet, with all drawbacks, the coal sells, at the pit's mouth, for $2.00 down to 50 cents a ton. The mines, lying on the slopes of the plateau reaching from near Corea to the Yellow River, supply the plain with cheap and excellent fuel.

Blakiston gives an account of the manner in which coal is worked on the Upper Yangtsz', near the town of Süchau: "Having to be got out at a great height up in the cliff, very thick hawsers, made of plaited bamboo, are tightly stretched from the mouth, or near the mouth, of the working gallery, to a space near the water where the coal can be deposited. These

---

[1] Yule's *Marco Polo*, Vol. I., p. 395.
[2] *Across America and Asia*, pp. 291 ff.

ropes are in pairs, and large pannier-shaped baskets are made to traverse on them, a rope passing from one over a large wheel at the upper landing, and down again to the other, so that the full basket going down pulls the empty one up, the velocity being regulated by a kind of brake on the wheel at the top. At some places the height at which the coal is worked is so great that two or more of these contrivances are used, one taking to a landing half way down, and another from thence to the river. The hawsers are kept taut by a windlass for that purpose at the bottom."[1] This useful mineral appears to be abundant throughout Sz'chuen Province, and is used here much less sparingly than in the east. With such inexpensive methods of getting coal to the water-courses, foreign machinery can hardly be expected to reduce its price very materially.

The economical use of coal in the household and the arts has been carried to great perfection. Anthracite is powdered and mixed with wet clay, earth, sawdust or dung, according to the exigencies of the case, in the proportion of about seven to one; the balls thus made are dried in the sun. The brick-beds (*kang*) are effective means of warming the house, and the hand furnaces enable the poor to cook with these balls—aided by a little charcoal or kindlings—at a trifling expense. This form of consumption is common north of the Yellow River, and brings coal within reach of multitudes who otherwise would suffer and starve. Bituminous, brown, and other varieties of coal occur in the same abundance and extent as in other great areas, giving promise of adequate supplies for future ages. The coal worked on the Peh kiang, in Kwangtung, contains sulphur, and is employed in the manufacture of copperas.[2]

Crystallized gypsum is brought from the northwest of the province to Canton, and is ground to powder in mills; plaster

[1] *Five Months on the Yang-tsze*, p. 265. *Annales de la Foi*, Tome IX., p. 457.

[2] *N. C. Br. R. A. Soc. Journal*, New Series, No. III., pp. 94–106, and No. IV., pp. 243 ff. Notes by Mr. Hollingworth of a Visit to the Coal Mines in the Neighborhood of Loh-Ping. *Blue Book, China*, No. 2, 1870, p. 11. *Notes and Queries on China and Japan*, Vol. II., pp. 74–76. *North China Herald*, passim. Richthofen's *Letters*, and in *Ocean Highways*, Nov., 1873. *Chinese Repository*, Vol. XIX., pp. 385 ff.

COAL GORGE ON THE YANGTSZ'. (FROM BLAKISTON.)

of Paris and other forms of this sulphate are common all over China. It is not used as a manure, but the flour is mixed with wood-oil to form a cement for paying the seams of boats after they have been caulked. The powder is employed as a dentifrice, a cosmetic, and a medicine, and sometimes, also, is boiled to make a gruel in fevers, under the idea that it is cooling. The bakers who supplied the English troops at Amoy, in 1843, occasionally put it into the bread to make it heavier, but not, as was erroneously charged upon them, with any design of poisoning their customers, for they do not think it noxious; its employment in coloring green tea, and adulterating powdered sugar, is also explainable by other motives than a wish to injure the consumers.

Limestone is abundant at Canton, both common clouded marble and blue limestone; the last is extensively used in the artificial rockwork of gardens. Even if the Cantonese knew of the existence of lime in limestone, which they generally do not, the expense of fuel for calcining it would prevent their burning it while oyster-shells are so abundant in that region. In other provinces stone-lime is burned, by the aid of coal, in small kilns. The fine marble quarried near Peking is regarded as fit alone for imperial uses, and is seen only in such places as the Altar of Heaven and palace grounds. The marble used for floors is a fissile crystallized limestone, unsusceptible of polish; no statues or ornaments are sculptured from this mineral, but slabs are sometimes wrought out, and the surfaces curiously stained and corroded with acids, forming rude representations of animals or other figures, so as to convey the appearance of natural markings. Some of these simulated petrifactions are exceedingly well done. Slabs of argillaceous slate are also chosen with reference to their layers, and treated in the same manner. An excellent granite is used about Canton and Amoy for building, and no people exceed the Chinese in cutting it. Large slabs are split out by wooden wedges, cut for basements and foundations, and laid in a beautiful manner; pillars are also hewn from single stones of different shapes, though of no extraordinary dimensions, and their shafts embellished with inscriptions. Ornamental walls are frequently formed of large slabs set in posts, like panels, the outer faces of which are beautifully carved with figures representing a landscape or procession. Red and gray sandstone, gneiss, mica slate, and other species of rock, are also worked for pavements and walls.

Nitre is cheap and common enough in the northern provinces to obviate any fear of its being smuggled into the country from abroad; it is obtained in Chihlí by lixiviating the soil, and furnishes material for the manufacture of gunpowder. A lye is obtained from ashes, which partially serves the purposes of soap; but the people are still ignorant of the processes necessary for manufacturing it. Fourteen localities of alum are given in Pumpelly's list, but the greatest supply for the eastern provinces comes from deposits of shale, in Ping-yang hien, in Chehkiang, which produces about six thousand tons annually. It is used mostly by the dyers, also to purify turbid water, and whiten paper. Other earthy salts are known and used, as borax, sal-ammoniac (which is collected in Mongolia and Ílí from lakes and the vicinity of extinct volcanoes), and blue and white vitriol, obtained by roasting pyrites. Common salt is procured along the eastern and southern coasts by evaporating sea-water, rock-salt not having been noticed; in the western provinces and Shansí, it is obtained from artesian wells and lakes as cheaply as from the ocean; in Tsing-yen hien, in Central Sz'chuen, two hundred and thirty-seven wells are worked. At Chusan the sea-water is so turbid that the inhabitants filter it through clay, afterward evaporating the water.

The minerals heretofore found in China have, for the most part, been such as have attracted the attention of the natives, and collected by them for curiosity or sale. The skilful manner in which their lapidaries cut crystal, agate, and other quartzose minerals, is well known.[1] The corundum used for polishing and finishing these carvings occurs in China, but a good deal of emery in powder is obtained from Borneo. A composition of granular corundum and gum-lac is usually employed by workmen in order to produce the highest lustre of

---

[1] Compare Rémusat, *Histoire de Khotan*, pp. 163 ff., where there is an extended list of Chinese precious stones drawn from native sources.

which the stones are capable. The three varieties of the silicate of alumina, called jade, nephrite, and jadeite by mineralogists, are all named *yuh* by the Chinese, a word which is applied to a vast variety of stones—white marble, ruby, and cornelian all coming under it—and therefore not easy to define. Jade has long been known in Europe as a variety of jasper, its separation from that stone into a species by itself being of comparatively recent origin. Since the third edition of Boetius, in 1647, the two minerals have been regarded as entirely distinct. Its value in the eyes of the Chinese depends chiefly upon its sonorousness and color. The costliest specimens are brought from Yunnan and Khoten; a greenish-white color is the most highly prized, a plain color of any shade being of less value. A cargo of this mineral was once imported into Canton from New Holland, but the Chinese would not purchase it, owing to a fancy taken against its origin and color. The patient toil of the workers in this hard mineral is only equalled by the prodigious admiration with which it is regarded; both fairly exhibit the singular taste and skill of the Chinese. Its color is usually a greenish-white, or grayish-green and dark grass-green; internally it is scarcely glimmering. Its fracture is splintery; splinters white; mass semi-transparent and cloudy; it scratches glass strongly, and can itself generally be scratched by flint or quartz, but while not excessively hard it is remarkable for toughness. The stone when freshly broken is less hard than after a short exposure. Specific gravity from 2.9 to 3.1.[1] Fischer (pp. 314–318) gives some one hundred and fifty names as occurring in various authors—ancient and modern—for jade or nephrite.[2] An interesting testimony to the esteem

[1] Murray's *China*, Edinburgh, 1843, Vol. III., p. 276; compare also an article on this stone by M. Blondel, of Paris, published in the *Smithsonian Report* for 1876. *Mémoires concernant les Chinois*, Tome XIII., p. 389. Rémusat in the *Journal des Şavans*, Dec., 1818, pp. 748 ff. *Notes and Queries on C. and J.*, Vol. II., pp. 173, 174, and 187; Vol. III., p. 63; Vol. IV., pp. 13 and 33. *Macmillan's Magazine*, October, 1871. Yule, *Cathay and the Way Thither*, Vol. II., p. 564.

[2] *Nephrit und Jadeit, nach ihren mineralogischen Eigenschaften sowie nach ihrer urgeschichtlichen und ethnographischen Bedeutung.* Heinrich Fischer, Stuttgart, 1880. An exhaustive treatise on every phrase and variety of the mineral.

in which this stone was held in China during the middle ages comes from Benedict Goës (1602), who says: "There is no article of traffic more valuable than lumps of a certain transparent kind of marble, which we, from poverty of language, usually call jasper. . . . Out of this marble they fashion a variety of articles, such as vases, brooches for mantles and girdles, which, when artistically sculptured in flowers and foliage, certainly have an effect of no small magnificence. These marbles (with which the Empire is now overflowing) are called by the Chinese Iusce. There are two kinds of it; the first and more valuable is got out of the river at Cotan, almost in the same way in which divers fish for gems, and this is usually extracted in pieces about as big as large flints. The other and inferior kind is excavated from the mountains." The ruby, diamond, amethyst, sapphire, topaz, pink tourmaline, lapis-lazuli,[1] turquoises, beryl, garnet, opal, agate, and other stones, are known and most of them used in jewelry. A ruby brought from Peking is noticed by Bell as having been valued in Europe at $50,000. The seals of the Boards are in many instances cut on valuable stones, and private persons take great pride in quartz or jade seals, with their names carved on them; lignite and jet are likewise employed for cheaper ornaments, of which all classes are fond.

All the common metals, except platina, are found in China, and the supply would be sufficient for all the purposes of the inhabitants, if they could avail themselves of the improvements adopted in other countries in blasting, mining, etc. The importations of iron, lead, tin, and quicksilver, are gradually increasing, but they form only a small proportion of the amount used throughout the Empire, especially of the two first named; iron finds its way in because of its convenient forms more than its cheapness. The careful examination of Chinese topographical works by Pumpelly,[2] records the leading localities of iron in every province, and where copper, tin, lead, silver, and quicksilver have been observed; he also mentions fifty-two places pro-

---

[1] Obtained from Badakshan. Wood, *Journey to the Oxus*, p. 263.

[2] *Geological Researches in China*, Chap. X.

ducing gold in various forms, most of them in Sz'chuen. The rumor of gold-washings occurring not far from Chifu, in Shantung, caused much excitement in 1868, but they were soon found to be not worth the labor. Gold has never been used as coin in China, but is wrought into jewelry; most of it is consumed in gilding and exported to India as bullion, in the shape of small bars or coarse leaves.

Silver is mentioned in sixty-three localities by the same author; large amounts are brought from Yunnan, and the mines in that region must be both extensive and easily worked to afford such large quantities as have been exported. The working of both gold and silver mines has been said to be prohibited, but this interdiction is rather a government monopoly of the mines than an injunction upon working those which are known. The importation of gold into China during the two centuries the trade has been opened, does not probably equal the exportation which has taken place since the commencement of the opium trade. It is altogether improbable that the Chinese are acquainted with the properties of quicksilver in separating these two metals from their ores, though its consumption in making vermilion and looking-glasses calls for over two thousand flasks yearly at Canton. Cinnabar occurs in Kweichau and Shensí and furnishes most of the "water silver," as the Chinese call it, by a rude process of burning brushwood in the wells, and collecting the metal after condensation.

Copper is used for manufacturing coin, bells, bronze articles, domestic and cooking utensils, cannon, gongs, and brass-foil. It is found pure in some instances, and the sulphuret, the blue and green carbonates, pyrities, and other ores are worked; malachite is ground for a paint. It occurs in every province, and is specially rich in Shansí and Kweichau. The ores of zinc and copper in Yunnan and Sz'chuen furnish spelter, and the peculiar alloy known as white copper or argentan, containing in addition tin, iron, nickel, and lead. So much use indicates large deposits of the ores. Tin is rather abundant, but lead is more common; thirty-nine localities of the first are mentioned, some of which are probably zinc ores, as the Chinese confound tin and zinc under one generic name. Lead occurs with silver in many places; twenty-four mines are mentioned in Pumpelly's list, and those in Fuhkien are rich; but the extensive importations prove that its reduction is too expensive to compete with the foreign.

Realgar is quite common, this and orpiment being used as paints; statuettes and other articles are carved from the former, while arsenic is used in agriculture to quicken grain and preserve it from insects. Amber and fossilized copal are collected in several localities; the first is much employed in the making of court necklaces and hair ornaments. The *fei-tsui* or jadeite is the most prized of the semi-precious stones; it is cut into ear-rings, finger-rings, necklaces, etc. Pumpelly mentions pieces of this mineral set in relics obtained from tombs in Mexico, though no locality where it abounds has yet been found in America. Lapis-lazuli is employed in painting upon copper and porcelain ware; this mineral is obtained in Chehkiang and Kansuh; jadeite, topaz, and other fine stones are most plenty in Yunnan. A few minerals and fossils have been noticed in the vicinity and shops at Canton, but China thus far has furnished very few petrifactions in any strata. Coarse epidote occurs at Macao, and tungstate of iron has been noticed in the quartz rocks at Hongkong. Petrified crabs (*macrophthalmus*) have been brought to Canton from Hainan, which are prized by the natives for their supposed medicinal qualities. Scientists have hitherto described a score or more species of Devonian shells, and recognized fragments of the hyena, tapir, rhinoceros, and stegedon, among some other doubtful vertebratæ in the "dragon's bones" sold in medicine shops; but further examinations will doubtless increase the list. Orthoceratites and bivalve shells of various kinds are noticed in Chinese books as being found in rocks, and fossil bones of huge size in caves and river banks.

There are many hot springs and other indications of volcanic action along the southern acclivities of the table land in the provinces of Shensí and Sz'chuen; and at Jeh-ho, in Chihlí, there are thermal springs to which invalids resort. The *Ho tsing*, or Fire wells, in Sz'chuen are apertures resembling artesian springs, sunk in the rock to a depth of one thousand five hundred or one thousand eight hundred feet, whilst their breadth does not exceed five or six inches. This is a work of great difficulty, and requires in some cases the labor of two or three years. The water procured from them contains a fifth part of salt, which is very acrid, and mixed with much nitre. When a lighted torch is applied to the mouth of some of those which have no water, fire is produced with great violence and a noise like thunder, bursting out into a flame twenty or thirty feet high, and which cannot be extinguished without great danger and expense. The gas has a bituminous smell, and burns with a bluish flame and a quantity of thick, black smoke. It is conducted under boilers in bamboos, and employed in evaporating the salt-water from the other springs.[1] Besides the gaseous and aqueous springs in these provinces, there are others possessing different qualities, some sulphurous and others chalybeate, found in Shansí and along the banks of the Yellow River. Sulphur occurs, as has been noted, in great abundance in Formosa, and is purified for powder manufacturers.

The animal and vegetable productions of the extensive regions under the sway of the Emperor of China include a great variety of types of different families. On the south the islands of Hainan and Formosa, and parts of the adjacent coasts, slightly partake of a tropical character, exhibiting in the cocoanuts, plantains, and peppers, the parrots, lemurs, and monkeys, decided indications of an equatorial climate. From the eastern coast across through the country to the northwest provinces occur mountain ranges of gradually increasing elevation, interspersed with intervales and alluvial plateaus and bottoms, lakes and rivers, plains and hills, each presenting its peculiar productions, both wild and cultivated, in great variety and abundance. The southern ascent of the high land of Mongolia, the uncultivated wilds of Manchuria, the barren wastes of the desert of Gobi, with its salt lakes, glaciers, extinct volcanoes, and isolated mountain ranges; and lastly the stupendous

---

[1] Humboldt, *Fragmens Asiatiques*, Tome I., p. 196. *Annales de la Foi*, Janvr., 1829, pp. 416 ff.

chains and valleys of Tibet, Koko-nor, and Kwănlun all differ from each other in the character of their productions. In one or the other division, every variety of soil, position, and temperature occur which are known on the globe; and what has been ascertained within the past fifteen years by enterprising naturalists is an earnest of future greater discoveries.

Of the quadrumanous order of animals, there are several species. The Chinese are skilful in teaching the smaller kinds of monkeys various tricks, but M. Breton's picture of their adroitness and usefulness in picking tea in Shantung from plants growing on otherwise inaccessible acclivities, is a fair instance of one of the odd stories furnished by travellers about China, inasmuch as no tea grows in Shantung, and monkeys are taught more profitable tricks.[1] One of the most remarkable animals of this tribe is the *douc*, or Cochinchinese monkey (*Semnopithecus nemœus*). It is a large species of great rarity, and remarkable for the variety of colors with which it is adorned. Its body is about two feet long, and when standing in an upright position its height is considerably greater. The face is of an orange color, and flattened in its form. A dark band runs across the front of the forehead, and the sides of the countenance are bounded by long spreading yellowish tufts of hair. The body and upper parts of the forearms are brownish gray, the lower portions of the arms, from the elbows to the wrists, being white; its hands and thighs are black, and the legs of a bright red color, while the tail and a large triangular spot above it are pure white. Such a creature matches well, for its grotesque and variegated appearance, with the mandarin duck and gold fish, also peculiar to China.

Chinese books speak of several species of this family, and small kinds occur in all the provinces. M. David has recently added two novelties to the list from his acquisitions in Eastern Koko-nor, well fitted for that cold region by their abundant hair. The *Rhinopithecus roxellanæ* inhabits the alpine forests, nearly two miles high, where it subsists on the buds of plants and bamboo shoots laid up for winter supply; its face is green-

---

[1] Breton, *China, its Costumes, Arts*, etc., Vol. II.

ish, the nose remarkably *rétroussé*, and its strong, brawny limbs well fitted for the arboreal life it leads; the hair is thick and like a mane on the back, shaded with yellow and white tints. In this respect it is like the Gelada monkey of Abyssinia, and a few others protected in this part of the body from cold. This is no doubt the kind called *fí-fí* in native books, and once found in flocks along many portions of western China, as these authors declare. Their notices are rather tantalizing, but, now that we have found the animal, are worth quoting: "The *fí-fí* resembles a man; it is clothed with its hair, runs quick and eats men; it has a human face, long lips, black, hairy body, and turns its heels. It laughs on seeing a man and covers its eyes with its lips; it can talk and its voice resembles a bird. It occurs in Sz'chuen, where it is called *jin hiung*, or 'human bear;' its palms are good eating, and its skin is used; its habit is to turn over stones, seeking for crabs as its food. Its form is like that of the men who live in the Kwănlun Mountains."

Another large simia (*Macacus thibetanus*) comes from the same region; it lives in bands like the preceding, but lower down the mountains. A third species of great size was reported to occur in the southwestern part of Sz'chuen, and described as greenish like the *Macacus tcheliensis* from the hills northwest of Peking—the most northern species of monkey known. The former of these two may possibly be the *sing-sing* of the Chinese books, though its characteristics involve some confusion of the Macacus and baboon on the part of those writers. Two other species of Macacus, and as many of the gibbons, have been noticed in Hainan, Formosa, and elsewhere in the south.

The singular proboscis monkey (*Nasalis laivalus*), called *khi-doc* in Cochinchina and *hai-tuh* by the Chinese, exhibits a strange profile, part man and part beast, reminding one of the combinations in Da Vinci's caricatures. It is a large animal, covered with soft yellowish hair tinted with red; the long nose projects in the form of a sloping spatula. The Chinese account says: "Its nose is turned upward, and the tail very long and forked at the end, and that whenever it rains, the animal thrusts the forks into its nose. It goes in herds, and lives in friendship; when one dies, the rest accompany it to burial. Its activity is so great that it runs its head against the trees; its fur is soft and gray, and the face black."[1]

The *Chinese Herbal*, from which the preceding extract is taken, describes the bat under various names, such as 'heavenly rat,' 'fairy rat,' 'flying rat,' 'night swallow,' and 'belly wings;'

Fî-fî and Hai-tuh. (From a Chinese cut.)

it also details the various uses made of the animal in medicine, and the extraordinary longevity attained by some of the white species. The bat is in form like a mouse; its body is of an ashy black color; and it has thin fleshy wings, which join the four legs and tail into one. It appears in the summer, but becomes torpid in the winter; on which account, as it eats nothing during that season, and because it has a habit of swallowing its breath, it attains a great age. It has the character of a night

[1] Bridgman's *Chinese Chrestomathy*, p. 469.

rover, not on account of any inability to fly in the day, but it dares not go abroad at that time because it fears a kind of hawk. It subsists on mosquitoes and gnats. It flies with its head downward, because the brain is heavy.[1] This quotation is among the best Chinese descriptions of animals, and shows how little there is to depend upon in them, though not without interest in their notices of habits. Bats are common everywhere, and seem to be regarded with less aversion than in certain other countries. Twenty species belonging to nine genera are given in one list, most of them found in southern China; the wings of some of these measure two feet across; a large sort in Sz'chuen is eaten.

The brown bear is known, and its paws are regarded as a delicacy; trained animals are frequently brought into cities by showmen, who have taught them tricks. The discovery by David of a large species (*Ailuropus melanoleurus*) allied to the Himalayan panda (*Ailurus fulgens*), also found on the Sz'chuen Mountains, adds another instance of the strange markings common in Tibetan fauna. This beast feeds on flesh and vegetables; its body is white, but the ears, eyes, legs, and tip of the tail are quite black; the fur is thick and coarse. It is called *peh hiung*, or white bear, by the hunters, but is no doubt the animal called *pi* in the classics, common in early times over western China, and now rare even in Koko-nor. The Tibetan black bear occurs in Formosa, Shantung, and Hainan, showing a wide range. The badger is quite as widespread, and the two species have the same general appearance as their European congeners.

Carnivorous animals still exist, even in thickly settled districts. The lion may once have roamed over the southwestern Manji kingdom, but the name and drawings both indicate a foreign origin. It has much connection with Buddhism, and grotesque sculptures of rampant lions stand in pairs in front of temples, palaces, and graves, as a mark of honor and symbol of protection. The last instance of a live lion brought as tribute was to Hientsung in A.D. 1470, from India or Ceylon.

---

[1] *Chinese Repository*, Vol. VII., p. 90.

Many other species of *felis* are known, some of them peculiar to particular regions. The royal tiger has been killed near Amoy, and in Manchuria the panther, leopard, and tiger-cat all occur in the northern and southern provinces, making altogether a list of twelve species ranging from Formosa to Sagalien. Mr. Swinhoe's[1] account of his rencounter with a tiger near Amoy in 1858 explains how such large animals still remain in thickly settled regions where food is abundant and the people are timid and unarmed. In thinly peopled parts they become a terror to the peasants. M. David enumerates six kinds, including a lynx, in Monpin alone, one of which (*Felis scripta*) is among the most prettily marked of the whole family. Hunting-leopards and tigers were used in the days of Marco Polo by Kublai, but the manly pastime of the chase, on the magnificent scale then practised, has fallen into disuse with the present princes. A small and fierce species of wild-cat (*Felis chinensis*), two feet long, of a brownish-gray color, and handsomely marked with chestnut spots and black streaks, is still common in the southwestern portions of Fuhkien. Civet cats of two or three kinds, tree-civets (*Helictes*), and a fine species of marten (*Martes*), with yellow neck and purplish-brown body, from Formosa, are among the smaller carnivora in the southern provinces.

The domestic animals offer few peculiarities. The cat, *kia lí*, or 'household fox,' is a favorite inmate of families, and the ladies of Peking are fond of a variety of the Angora cat, having long silky hair and hanging ears. The common species is variously marked, and in the south often destitute of a tail; when reared for food it is fed on rice and vegetables, but is not much eaten. Popular superstition has clustered many omens of good and bad luck about cats; it is considered, for example, the prognostic of certain misfortune when a cat is stolen from a house—much as, in some countries of the western world, it is unlucky when a black cat crosses one's pathway.

The dog differs but little from that reared among the Esquimaux, and is perhaps the original of the species. There is

---

[1] *Zoöl. Soc. Proc.*, 1870, p. 626.

little variation in their size, which is about a foot high and two feet in length; the color is a pale yellow or black, and always uniform, with coarse bristling hair, and tails curling up high over the back, and rising so abruptly from the insertion that it has been humorously remarked they almost assist in lifting the legs from the ground. The hind legs are unusually straight, which gives them an awkward look, and perhaps prevents them running very rapidly. The black eyes are small and piercing, and the insides of the lips and mouths, and the tongue, are of the same color, or a blue black. The bitch has a dew-claw on each hind leg, but the dog has none. The ears are sharp and upright, the head peaked, and the bark a short, thick snap, very unlike the deep, sonorous baying of our mastiffs. In Nganhwui a peculiar variety has pendant ears of great length, and thin, wirey tails. One item in the Chinese description of the dog is that it 'can go on three legs'—a gait that is often exhibited by them. They are used to watch houses and flocks; the Mongolian breed is fierce and powerful. The dogs of Peking are very clannish, and each set jealously guards its own street or yard; they are fed by the butchers in the streets, and serve as scavengers there and in all large towns. They are often mangey, presenting hideous spectacles, and instances of *plica polonica* are not uncommon, but, as among the celebrated street dogs of Constantinople, hydrophobia is almost unheard of among them. Dog markets are seen in every city where this meat is sold; the animals are reared expressly for the table, but their flesh is expensive.

One writer remarks on their habits, when describing the worship offered at the tombs: "Hardly had the hillock been abandoned by the worshippers, when packs of hungry dogs came running up to devour the part of the offerings left for the dead, or to lick up the grease on the ground. Those who came first held up their heads, bristled their hair, and showed a proud and satisfied demeanor, curling and wagging their tails with selfish delight; while the late-comers, tails between their legs, held their heads and ears down. There was one of them, however, which, grudging the fare, held his nose to the wind as if sniffing for better luck; but one lean, old, and ugly beast, with a flayed back and hairless tail, was seen gradually separating himself from the band, though without seeming to hurry himself, making a thousand doublings and windings, all the while looking back to see if he was noticed. But the old sharper knew what he was about, and as soon as he thought himself at a safe distance, away he went like an arrow, the whole pack after him, to some other feast and some other tomb."[1]

Wolves, raccoon-dogs, and foxes are everywhere common, in some places proving to be real pests in the sheepfold and farmyard. In the vicinity of Peking, it is customary to draw large white rings on the plastered walls, in order to terrify the wolves, as these beasts, it is thought, will flee on observing such traps. The Chinese regard the fox as the animal into which human spirits enter in preference to any other, and are therefore afraid to destroy or displease it. The elevated steppes are the abodes of three or four kinds, which find food without difficulty. The Tibetan wolf (*Canis chanco*) has a warm, yellowish-white covering, and ranges the wilds of Tsaidam and Koko-nor in packs. The fox (*Canis cossac*) spreads over a wide range, and is famed for its sagacity in avoiding enemies.

The breed of cattle and horses is dwarfish, and nothing is done to improve them. The oxen are sometimes not larger than an ass; some of them have a small hump, showing their affinity to the zebu; the dewlap is large, and the contour neat and symmetrical. The forehead is round, the horns small and irregularly curved, and the general color dun red. The buffalo (*shui niu*), or 'water ox,' is the largest beast used in agriculture. It is very docile and unwieldy, larger than an English ox, and its hairless hide is a light black color; it seeks coolness and refuge from the gnat in muddy pools dug for its convenience, where it wallows with its nose just above the surface. Each horn is nearly semi-circular, and bends downward, while the head is turned back so as almost to bring the nose horizontal. The herd-boys usually ride it, and the metaphor of a lad astride a buffalo's back, blowing the flute, frequently enters into Chinese

[1] Borget, *La Chine Ouverte*, p. 147.

descriptions of rural life. The yak of Tibet is employed as a beast of burden, and to furnish food and raiment. It is covered with a mantle of hair reaching nearly to the ground, and the soft pelage is used for making standards among the Persians, and its tail as fly-flaps or chowries in India; the hair is woven into carpets. The wild yak (*Poephagus grunniens*) has already been described. Great herds of these huge bovines roam over the wastes of Koko-nor, where their dried droppings furnish the only fuel for the nomads crossing those barren wilds.

The domestic sheep is the broad-tailed species, and furnishes excellent mutton. The tail is sometimes ten inches long and three or four thick; and the size of this fatty member is not affected by the temperature. The sheep are reared in the north by Mohammedans, who prepare the fleeces for garments by careful tanning; the animal is white, with a black head. Goats are raised in all parts, but not in large numbers. The argali and wild sheep of the Ala shan Mountains (*Ovis Burrhel*) furnish exciting sport in chasing them over their native cliffs, which they clamber with wonderful agility. Another denizen of those dreary wilds is the *Antilope picticauda*, a small and tiny species, weighing about forty pounds, of a dusky gray color, with a narrow yellow stripe on the flanks. Its range is about the head-waters of the Yangtsz' River; its swiftness is amazing; it seems absolutely to fly. It scrapes for itself trenches in which to lie secure from the cold.

Many genera of ruminants are represented in China and the outlying regions; twenty-seven rare species are enumerated in Swinhoe's and David's lists, of which eleven are antelopes and deer. The range of some of them is limited to a narrow region, and most of them are peculiar to the country. The wealthy often keep deer in their grounds, especially the spotted deer (*Cervus pseudaxis*), from Formosa, whose coat is found to vary greatly according to sex and age; its name, *kin-tsien luh*, or 'money deer,' indicates its markings. Mouse-deer are also reared as pets in the southern provinces.

One common species is the *dzeren* or *hwang yang* (*Antilope gutturosa*), which roams over the Mongolian wilds in large herds, and furnishes excellent venison. It is heavy in comparison to the gazelle; horns thick, about nine inches long, annulated to the tips, lyrated, and their points turned inward. The goitre, which gives it its name, is a movable protuberance occasioned by the dilatation of the larnyx; in the old males it is much enlarged. The animal takes surprising bounds when running. Great numbers are killed in the autumn, and their flesh, skins, and horns are all of service for food, leather, and medicine.

Several kinds of hornless (or nearly hornless) deer, allied to the musk-deer, exist. One is the river-deer (*Hydropotes*), common near the Yangtsz' River, which resembles the pudu of Chili; it is very prolific on the bottoms and in the islands. Another sort in the northwest (*Elaphodus*) is intermediary between the muntjacs and deer, having long, trenchant, canine upper teeth, and a deep chocolate-colored fur. Three varieties of the musk-deer (*Moschus*) have been observed, differing a little in their colors, all called *shié* or *hiang chang* by the Chinese, and all eagerly hunted for their musk. This perfume was once deemed to be useful in medicine, and is cited in a Greek prescription of the sixth century; the abundance of the animal in the Himalayan regions may be inferred from Tavernier's statement that he bought 7673 bags or pods at Patna in one of his journeys over two hundred years ago. This animal roams over a vast extent of alpine territory, from Tibet and Shensí to Lake Baikal, and inhabits the loftiest cliffs and defiles, and makes its way over rugged mountains with great rapidity. It is not unlike the roe in general appearance, though the projecting teeth makes the upper lip to look broad. Its color is grayish-brown and its limbs slight; the hair is coarse and brittle, almost like spines. The musk is contained in a pouch beneath the tail on the male, and is most abundant during the rutting season. He is taken in nets or shot, and the hunters are said to allure him to destruction by secreting themselves and playing the flute, though some would say the animal showed very little taste in listening to such sounds as Chinese flutes usually produce. The musk is often adulterated with clay or mixed with other substances to moderate its powerful odor. A singular and interesting member of this family is reared in the great park south of Peking--a kind of elk with short horns. This large animal (*Elaphurus Davidianus*), of a gentle disposition, equals in size the largest deer; its native name, *sz'-puh siang*, indicates that it is neither a horse, a deer, a camel, nor an ox, but partakes in some respects of the characteristics of each of them. Its gentle croaking voice seems to be unworthy of so huge a body; the color is a uniform fawn or light gray.

The horse is not much larger than the Shetland pony; it is bony and strong, but kept with little care, and presents the worst possible appearance in its usual condition of untrimmed coat and mane, bedraggled fetlocks, and twisted tail. The Chinese language possesses a great variety of terms to designate the horse; the difference of age, sex, color, and disposition, all being denoted by particular characters. Piebald and mottled, white and bay horses are common; but the improvement of this noble animal is neglected, and he looks sorry enough compared with the coursers of India. He is principally used for carrying the post, or for military services; asses and mules being more employed for draught. He is hardy, feeds on coarse food, and admirably serves his owners. The mule is well-shaped, and those raised for the gentry are among the very best in the world for endurance and strength; dignitaries are usually drawn by sumpter mules. Donkeys are also carefully raised. Chinese books speak of a mule of a cow and horse, as well as from the ass and horse, though, of course, no such hybrid as the former ever existed.

The wild ass, or onager (under the several names by which it is known in different lands, *kyang*, *djang*, *kulan*, *djiggetai*, *ghor-khar*, and *yé-lu*), still roams free and untameable. It is abundant in Koko-nor, gathering in troops of ten to fifty, each under the lead of a stallion to defend the mares. The flesh is highly prized, and the difficulty of procuring it adds to the delicacy of the dish; the color is light chestnut, with white belly.

Elephants are kept at Peking for show, and are used to draw the state chariot when the Emperor goes to worship at the Altars of Heaven and Earth, but the sixty animals seen in the days of Kienlung, by Bell, have since dwindled to one or two. Van Braam met six going into Peking, sent thither from Yunnan. The deep forests of that province also harbor the rhinoceros and tapir. The horn of the former is sought after as medicine, and the best pieces are carved most beautifully into ornaments or into drinking cups, which are supposed to sweat whenever any poisonous liquid is put into them. The tapir is the white and brown animal found in the Malacca peninsula, and strange stories are recorded of its eating stones and copper. The wild boar grows to weigh over four hundred pounds and nearly six feet long. In cold weather its frozen carcass is brought to Peking, and sold at a high price. A new species of

The Chinese Pig.

hog has been found in Formosa, about three feet long, twenty-one inches high, and showing a dorsal row of large bristles ; a third variety occurs among the novelties discovered in Sz'chuen (*Sus moupinensis*), having short ears. Wild boars are met with even in the hills of Chehkiang, and seriously annoy the husbandmen in the lowlands by their depredations. Deep pits are dug near the base of the hills, and covered with a bait of fresh grass, and many are annually captured or drowned in them. They are fond of the bamboo shoots, and persons are stationed near the groves to frighten them away by striking pieces of wood together.

The Chinese hollow-backed pig is known for its short legs,

round body, crooked back, and abundance of fat; the flesh is the common meat of the people south of the Yangtsz' River. The black Chinese breed, as it is called in England, is considered the best pork raised in that country. The hog in the northern provinces is a gaunt animal, uniformly black, and not so well cared for as its southern rival. Piebald pigs are common in Formosa, resulting from crossing; sometimes animals of this kind are quite woolly. The Chinese in the south, well aware of the perverse disposition of the hog, find it much more expeditious to carry instead of drive him through their narrow

Mode of Carrying Pigs.

streets. For this purpose cylindrical baskets, open at both ends, are made; and in order to capture the obstinate brute, it is secured just outside the half-opened gate of the pen. The men seize him by the tail and pull it lustily; his rage is roused by the pain, and he struggles; they let go their hold, whereupon he darts out of the gate to escape, and finds himself snugly caught. He is lifted up and unresistingly carried off.

The camel is employed in the trade carried on across the desert, and throughout Mongolia, Manchuria, and northern China near the plateau; without his aid those regions would be impassible; the passes across the ranges near Koko-nor, sixteen thousand feet high, are traversed by his help, though amid suffering and danger. In the summer season it sheds all its hair, which is gathered for weaving into ropes and rugs; at this period, large herds pasture on the plateau to recuperate. The humps at this season hang down the back like empty bags, and the poor animal presents a distressed appearance during the hot weather. In its prime condition it carries about six hundred pounds weight, but is not used to ride upon as is the Arabian species. The two kinds serve man in one continuous *kafilah* from the Sea of Tartary across two continents to Timbuctoo. The Chinese have employed the camel in war, and trained it to carry small gingalls so that the riders could fire them while resting on its head, but this antique kind of cavalry has disappeared with the introduction of better weapons.

Among the various tribes of smaller animals, the Chinese Empire furnishes many interesting peculiarities, and few families are unrepresented. No marsupials have yet been met, and the order of edentata is still restricted to one instance. Several families in other orders are rare or wanting, as baboons, spider-monkeys, skunks, and ichneumons. In the weasel tribe, some new species have been added to the already long list of valuable fur-bearing animals found in the mountains—the sable ermine, marten, pole-cat, stoat, etc., whose skins still repay the hunters. The weasel is common, but not troublesome. The otter is trained in Sz'chuen to catch fish in the mountain streams with the docility of a spaniel; another species (*Lutia swinhosi*) occurs along the islands on the southern coast, while in Hainan Island appears a kind of clawless otter of a rich brown color above and white beneath; each of these is about twenty inches long. The furs of all these, and also the sea-otter, are prepared for garments, especially collars and neck-wraps.

A kind of mole exists in Sz'chuen, having a muzzle of extreme length, while the scent of another variety near Peking is so musky as to suggest its name (*Scaptochirus moschatus*). Musk-rats and shrew-mice are found both north and south; and one western species has only a rudimentary tail; while another, the

Scaptonyx, forms an intermediate species between a mole and a shrew, having a blunt muzzle, strong fore feet and a long tail; and lastly, a sort fitted for aquatic habits, with broad hind feet and flattened tail. Tiny hedgehogs are common even in the streets and by-lanes of Peking, where they find food and refuge in the alluvial earth. Two or three kinds of marmots and mole-rats are found in the north and west (*Siphucus Arctomys*), all specifically unlike their congeners elsewhere. The Chinese have a curious fancy in respect to one beast, one bird, and one fish, each of which, they say, requires that two come together to make one complete animal, viz., the jerboa, the spoonbill and sole-fish; the first (*Dipus annulatus*) occurs in the sands of northern China, the second in Formosa, and the third along the coasts.

Many kinds of rodents have been described. The alpine hare (*Lagomys ogotona*) resembles a marmot in its habits and is met with throughout the grassy parts of the steppes; its burrows riddle the earth wherever the little thing gathers, and endangers the hunters riding over it. It is about the size of a rat, and by its wonderful fecundity furnishes food to a great number of its enemies—man, beasts, and birds; it is not dormant, but gathers dry grass for food and warmth during cold weather; this winter store is, however, often consumed by cattle before it is stored away. Hares and rabbits are well known. Two species of the former are plenty on the Mongolian grass-lands, one of which has very long feet; in winter their frozen bodies are brought to market. One species is restricted to Hainan Island. Ten or twelve kinds of squirrels have been described, red, gray, striped, and buff; one with fringed ears. Their skins are prepared for the furriers, and women wear winter robes lined with them. Two genera of flying-squirrel (*Pteromys* and *Sciuropterus*) have been noticed, the latter in Formosa and the former mostly in the western provinces. Chinese writers have been puzzled to class the flying-squirrel; they place it among birds, and assure their readers that it is the only kind which suckles its young when it flies, and that "the skin held in the hand during parturition renders delivery easier, because the animal has a remarkably lively disposition." The long, dense fur of the *P. alborufous* makes beautiful dresses, the white tips of the hair contrasting prettily with the red ground.

Of the proper rats and mice, more than twenty-five species have been already described. Some of them are partially arboreal, others have remarkably long tails, and all but three are peculiar to the country. A Formosan species, called by Swinhoe the spinous county rat, had been dedicated to Koxinga, the conqueror of that island; while another common in Sz'chuen bears the name of *Mus Confucianus.* The extent to which the Chinese eat rats has been greatly exaggerated by travellers, for the flesh is too expensive for general use.

One species of porcupine (*Hystrix subcristata*) inhabits the southern provinces, wearing on its head a purplish-black crest of stout spines one to five inches long; the bristles are short, but increase in size and length to eight or nine inches toward the rump; the entire length is thirty-three inches. The popular notion that the porcupine darts its quills at its enemies as an effectual weapon is common among the Chinese.

No animal has puzzled the Chinese more than the scaly anteater or pangolin (*Manis dalmanni*), which is logically considered as a certain and useful remedy by them, simply because of its oddity. It is regarded as a fish out of water, and therefore named *ling-lí*, or 'hill carp,' also dragon carp, but the most common designation is *chuen shan kiah*, or the 'scaly hill borer.' One author says: "Its shape resembles a crocodile; it can go in dry paths as well as in the water; it has four legs. In the daytime it ascends the banks of streams, and lying down opens its scales wide, putting on the appearance of death, which induces the ants to enter between them. As soon as they are in, the animal closes its scales and returns to the water to open them; the ants float out dead, and he devours them at leisure." A more accurate observer says: "It continually protrudes its tongue to entice the ants on which it feeds;" and true to Chinese physiological deductions, *similia similibus curantur*, he recommends the scales as a cure for all antish swellings. He also remarks that the scales are not bony, and consist of the agglutinated hairs of the body. The adult specimens measure thirty-three inches. It walks on the sides of the hind feet and tips of the claws of the fore feet, and can stand upright for a minute or two. The large scales are held to the skin by a fleshy nipple-like pimple, which adheres to the base.

Among the cetaceous inhabitants of the Chinese waters, one of the most noticeable is the great white porpoise (*Delphinus chinensis*), whose uncouth tumbles attract the traveller's notice as he sails into the estuary of the Pearl River on his way to Hongkong, and again as he steams up the Yangtsz' to Hankow. The Chinese fishermen are shy of even holding it in their nets, setting it free at once, and never pursuing it; they call it *peh-kí* and deem its presence favorable to their success. A species of fin-whale (*Balænoptera*) has been described by Swinhoe, which ranges the southern coast from the shores of Formosa to Hainan. Its presence between Hongkong and Amoy induced some foreigners to attempt a fishery in those waters, but the yield of oil and bone was too small for their outlay. The native fishermen join their efforts in the winter, when it resorts to the seas near Hainan, going out in fleets of small boats from three to twenty-five tons burden each, fifty boats going together. The line is about three hundred and fifty feet long, made of native hemp, and fastened to the mast, the end leading over the bow. The harpoon has one barb, and is attached to a wooden handle; through an eye near the socket, the line is so fastened along the handle, that when the whale begins to strain upon it, the handle draws out upon the line, leaving only the barb buried in the skin. The boat is sailed directly upon the fish, and the harpooner strikes from the bow just behind the blow-hole. As soon as the fish is struck the sail is lowered, the rudder unshipped, and the boat allowed to drag stern foremost until the prey is exhausted. Other boats come up to assist, and half a dozen harpoons soon dispatch it. The species most common there yield about fifty barrels each; the oil, flesh, and bone are all used for food or in manufactures. The fish resort to the shallow waters in those seas for food, and to roll and rub on the banks and reefs, thus ridding themselves of the barnacles and insects which torment them; they are often seen leaping entirely out of water, and falling back perpendicularly against the hard bottom.[1]

The Yellow Sea affords a species of cow-fish, or round headed cachalot (*Globicephalus Rissii*), which the Japanese capture.[2] Seals have been observed on the coast of Liautung, but nothing is known of their species or habits; the skins are common and cheap in the Peking market. Native books speak of a marine animal in Koko-nor, from which a rare medicine is obtained, that probably belongs to this family.

This imperfect account of the mammalia known to exist in China has been drawn from the lists and descriptions inserted in the zoölogical periodicals of Europe, and may serve to indicate the extent and richness of the field yet to be investigated. The lists of Swinhoe and David alone contain nearly two hundred species, and within the past ten years scores more have been added, but have not exhausted the new and unexplored zoölogical regions. The emperors of the Mongol dynasty were very fond of the chase, and famous for their love of the noble amusement of falconry; Marco Polo says that Kublai employed no less than seventy thousand attendants in his hawking excursions. Falcons, kites, and other birds were taught to pursue their quarry, and the Venetian speaks of eagles trained to stoop at wolves, and of such size and strength that none could escape their talons.[3] Ranking has collected[4] a number of notices of the mode and sumptuousness of the field sports of the Mongols in China and India, but they convey little more information to the naturalist, than that the game was abundant and comprised a vast variety. Many species of accipitrine birds are described in Chinese books, but they are spoken of so vaguely that nothing definite can be learned from the notices. Few of them are now trained for sport by the Chinese, except a kind of sparrow-hawk to amuse dilettanti hunters in showing their skill in catching small birds. The fondness for sport in the wilds of Manchuria which the old emperors

[1] *Chinese Repository*, Vol. XII., p. 608.
[2] Ibid., Vol. VI., p. 411.
[3] Yule's *Marco Polo*, Vol. I., p. 353.
[4] *Wars and Sports of the Mongols and Romans.*

encouraged two centuries ago has all died out among their descendants.

Within the last fifteen years a greater advance has been made in the knowledge of the birds of China than in any other branch of its natural history, perhaps owing somewhat to their presenting themselves for capture to the careful observer. The list of described species already numbers over seven hundred, of which the careful paper of the lamented Swinhoe, in the *Proceedings of the Zoölogical Society* for May, 1871, gives the names of six hundred and seventy-five species, and M. David's list, in the *Nouvelles Archives* for 1871, gives four hundred and seventy as the number observed north of the River Yangtsz'. The present sketch must confine itself to selecting a few of the characteristic birds of the country, for this part of its fauna is as interesting and peculiar as the mammalia.

Among birds of prey are vultures, eagles, and ernes, all of them widespread and well known. One of the fishing-eagles (*Haliætus macei*) lives along the banks of the bend of the Yellow River in the Ortous country. The golden eagle is still trained for the chase by Mongols; Atkinson accompanied a party on a hunt. "We had not gone far," he says, "when several large deer rushed past, bounding over the plain about three hundred yards from us. In an instant the barkut was unhooded and his shackles removed, when he sprung from his perch and soared on high. He rose to a considerable height, and seemed to poise for a minute, gave two or three flaps with his wings, and swooped off in a straight line for the prey. I could not see his wings move, but he went at a fearful rate, and all of us after the deer; when we were about two hundred yards off, the bird struck the deer, and it gave one bound and fell. The barkut had struck one talon in his neck, the other into his back, and was tearing out his liver. The Kirghis sprung from his horse, slipped the hood over the eagle's head and the shackles on his legs, and easily took him off, remounting and getting ready for another flight."[1] Other smaller species are trained to capture or worry hares, foxes, and lesser game.

---

[1] *Oriental and Western Siberia*, p. 416.

The falcons which inhabit the gate-towers and trees in Peking form a peculiar feature of the place, from their impudence in foraging in the streets and markets, snatching things out of the hands of people, and startling one by their responsive screams. Much quarrelling goes on between them and the crows and magpies for the possession of old nests as the spring comes on. Their services as scavengers insures them a quiet residence in their eyries on the gate-towers. Six sorts of harriers (*Circus*), with various species of falcons, bustards, gledes, and sparrow-hawks, are enumerated. The family of owls is well represented, and live ones are often exposed for sale in the markets; its native name of 'cat-headed hawk' (*mao-'rh-tao ying*) suggests the likeness of the two. Out of the fifty-six species of accipitrine birds, the hawks are much the most numerous.

The great order of Passerinæ has its full share of beautiful and peculiar representatives, and over four hundred species have been catalogued. The night-hawks have only three members, but the swallows count up to fifteen species. Around Peking they gather in vast numbers, year after year, in the gate-towers, and that whole region was early known by the name of *Yen Kwoh*, or 'Land of Swallows.' The immunity granted by the natives to this twittering, bustling inmate of their houses has made it a synonym for domestic life; the phrase *yin yen* (*lit.* to 'drink swallows') means to give a feast. The family of king-fishers contains several most exquisitely colored birds, and multitudes of the handsome ones, like the turquoise king-fisher (*Halcyon smyrnensis*), are killed by the Chinese for the sake of the plumage. Beautiful feather-work ornaments are made from this at Canton. The hoopoe, bee-eater, and cuckoo are not uncommon; the first goes by the name of the *shan ho-shang*, or 'country priest,' from its color. Six species of the last have been recognized, and its peculiar habits of driving other birds from their nests has made it well known to the people, who call it *ku-ku* for the same reason as do the English. On the upper Yangtsz' the short-tailed species makes its noisy agitated flight in order to draw off attention from its nest. The Chinese say it weeps blood as it bewails its mate all night long. The *Cucutus striatus* varies so greatly in different provinces that it has much perplexed naturalists; all of them are only summer visitants.

The habit of the shrike of impaling its prey on thorns and elsewhere before devouring it has been noticed by native writers; no less than eleven species have been observed to cross the country in their migrations from Siberia to the Archipelago. Of the nuthatches, tree and wall creepers, wrens, and chats, there is a large variety, and one species of willow-wren (*Sylvia borealis*) has been detected over the entire eastern hemisphere; six sorts of redstarts (*Ruticilla*) are spread over the provinces.

Among the common song birds reared for the household, the thrush and lark take precedence; their fondness for birds and flowers is one of the pleasant features of Chinese national character. A kind of grayish-yellow thrush (*Garrulax perspicilatus*), called *hwa-mí*, or 'painted eyebrows,' is common about Canton, where a well-trained bird is worth several dollars. This genus furnishes six species, but they are not all equally musical; another kind (*Suthoria webbiana*) is kept for its fighting qualities, as it will die before it yields. These and other allied birds furnish the people with much amusement, by teaching them to catch seeds thrown into the air, jump from perches held in the hand, and perform tricks of various kinds. A party of gentlemen will often be seen on the outskirts of a town in mild weather, each one holding his pet bird, and all busily engaged in catching grasshoppers to feed them. The spectacle thrush (*Leucodioptrum*) has its eyes surrounded by a black circle bearing a fancied resemblance to a pair of spectacles; it is not a very sweet songster, but a graceful, lively fellow. The species of wagtail and lark known amount to about a score altogether, but not all of them are equally good singers. The southern Chinese prefer the lark which comes from Chihlí, and large numbers are annually carried south. The shrill notes of the field lark (*Alauda cœlivox* and *arvensis*) are heard in the shops and streets in emulous concert with other kinds—these larks becoming at times well-nigh frantic with excitement in their struggles for victory. The Chinese name of *peh-ling*, or 'hundred spirits,' given to the Mongolian lark, indicates the reputation it has earned as an active songster; and twenty-five dollars is not an uncommon price for a good one.[1]

The tits (*Parus*) and reedlings (*Emberiza*), together with kindred genera, are among the most common small birds, fifteen or twenty species of each having been noticed. In the proper season the latter are killed for market in such numbers as to excite surprise that they do not become extinct. In taking many of the warblers, orioles, and jays, for rearing or sale as fancy birds, the Chinese are very expert in the use of birdlime. In all parts of the land, the pie family are deemed so useful as scavengers that they are never molested, and in consequence become very common. The magpie is a favorite bird, as its name, *hi tsioh*, or 'joyous bird,' indicates, and occurs all over the land. Ravens, choughs, crows, and blackbirds keep down the insects and vermin and consume offal. The palace grounds and inclosures of the nobility in Peking are common resorts for these crows, where they are safe from harm in the great trees. Every morning myriads of them leave town with the dawn, returning at evening with increased cawing and clamor, at times actually darkening the sky with their flocks. A pretty sight is occasionally seen when two or three thousand young crows assemble just at sunset in mid-air to chase and play with each other. The crow is regarded as somewhat of a sacred bird, either from a service said to have been rendered by one of his race to an ancestor of the present dynasty, or because he is an emblem of filial duty, from a notion that the young assist their parents when disabled. The owl, on the other hand, has an odious name because it is stigmatized as the bird which eats its dam. One member of the pie family deserving mention is the long-tailed blue jay of Formosa (*Urocissa*), remarkable for its brilliant plumage. Another, akin to the sun birds (*Æthopyga dabryi*), comes from Sz'chuen, a recent discovery. The body is red, the head, throat, and each side of the neck a brilliant violet, belly yellow, wings black with the primaries tinted green along the edge, and the feathers long, tapering, of a black or steel blue.

---

[1] *Journal of the North China Branch of the Royal Asiatic Society*, May, 1859, p. 289.

The *Mainah*, or Indian mino (*Acridotheus*), known by its yellow carbuncles, which extend like ears from behind the eye, is reared, as are also three species of *Munia*, at Canton. Sparrows abound in every province around houses, driving away other birds, and entertaining the observer by their quarrels and activity. Robins, ouzels, and tailor-birds are not abundant. None of the humming-birds or birds of paradise occur, and only one species has hitherto been seen of the parrot group. Woodpeckers (*Picus*) are of a dozen species, and the wryneck occasionally attracts the eye of a sportsman. The canary is reared in great numbers, being known under the names of 'white swallow' and 'time sparrow;' the chattering Java sparrow and tiny avedavat are also taught little tricks by their fanciers, in compensation for their lack of song. The two or three proper parrots are natives of Formosa.

The family of pigeons (*Columbidæ*) is abundantly represented in fourteen species, and doves form a common household bird; their eggs are regarded as proper food to prevent smallpox, and sold in the markets, being also cooked in birdnest and other kinds of soups. The Chinese regard the dove as eminently stupid and lascivious, but grant it the qualities of faithfulness, impartiality, and filial duty. The cock is said to send away its mate on the approach of rain, and let her return to the nest with fine weather. They have an idea that it undergoes periodic metamorphoses, but disagree as to the form it takes, though the sparrow-hawk has the preference.[1] The bird is most famed, however, for its filial duty, arising very probably from imperfect observations of the custom of feeding its young with the macerated contents of its crop; the wood pigeon is said to feed her seven young ones in one order in the morning, and reversing it in the evening. Its note tells the husbandman when to begin his labors, and the decorum observed in the nests and cotes of all the species teach men how to govern a family and a state. The visitor to Peking is soon attracted by the æolian notes proceeding from doves which circle around their homes for a short time (forty or fifty or less in a flock), and

[1] *Journal N. C. Br. R. A. Soc.*, Vol. IV., 1867, Art. XI., by T. Watters.

then settle. These birds are called *pan-tien kiao-jin*, or 'mid-sky houris,' and their weird music is caused by ingenious wooden whistles tied on the rumps of two or three of the flock, which lead the others and delight themselves. Carrier pigeons are used to some extent, and training them is a special mystery. One of the prettiest sort is the rose pigeon, and half a dozen kinds of turtles enliven the village groves with their gentle notes and peculiar plumage.

No tribe of birds in China, however, equals the Gallinaceous for its beauty, size, and novelty, furnishing some of the most elegant and graceful birds in the world, and yet none of them have become domesticated for food. As a connecting link between this tribe and the last is the sand-grouse of the desert (*Syrrhaptis paradoxus*), whose singular combination attracted Marco Polo's eye. "This bird, the *barguerlac*, on which the falcons feed," says he, "is as big as a partridge, has feet like a parrot's, tail like a swallow's, and is strong in flight."[1] Abbé Huc speaks of the immense flocks which scour the plateau.

The gold and silver pheasants are reared without trouble in all the provinces, and have so long been identified with the ornithology of China as to be regarded as typical of its grotesque and brilliant fauna. Among other pheasants may be mentioned the Impeyan, Reeves, Argus, Medallion, Amherst, l'Huys, and Pallas, each one vieing with the other for some peculiarly graceful feature of color and shape, so that it is hard to decide which is the finest. The Amherst pheasant has the bearing, the elegance, and the details of form like the gold pheasant, but the neck, shoulders, back and wing covers are of a sparkling metallic green, and each feather ends in a belt of velvet black. A little red crest allies it to the gold pheasant, and a pretty silvery ruff with a black band, a white breast and belly, and a tail barred with brown, green, white, and red bands, complete the picturesque dress. Hidden away in these Tibetan wilds are other pheasants that dispute the palm for beauty, among which four species of the eared pheasant (*Crossoptilon*) attract notice. One is of a pure white, with a black tail curled up and spread

[1] Yule's *Marco Polo*, Vol. I., p. 237.

out like a plume, and is well called the snow pheasant. Another is the better known Pallas pheasant, nearly as large as a turkey, distinguished by ear-like appendages or wattles behind the head, and a red neck above a white body, whence its native name of *ho-kí*, or 'fire hen.' Another genus (*Lophophorus*) contains some elegant kinds, of which the l'Huys pheasant is new, and noted for a coppery-green tail bespangled with white. The longer known Reeves pheasant is sought for by the natives for the sake of its white and yellow-barred tail feathers, which are used by play actors to complete a warrior's dress; Col. Yule proves a reference to it in Marco Polo from this part of its plumage, which the Venetian states to be ten palms in length—not far beyond the truth, as they have been seen seven feet long.[1] It is a long time for a bird of so much beauty to have been unknown, from 1350 to 1808, when Mr. Thomas Beale procured a specimen in Canton, and sent others to England in 1832; Mr. Reeves took it thither, and science has recorded it in her annals. As New Guinea is the home of the birds of paradise, so do the Himalayas contain most of these superb pheasants and francolins, each tribe serving as a foil and comparison with the Creator's handiwork in the other.

The island of Formosa has furnished a second species, Swinhoe's pheasant, of the same genus as the silver pheasant (*Euplocamus*), and another smaller kind (*Phasianus formosanus*); the list is also increased by fresh acquisitions from Yunnan and Cochinchina through Dr. Anderson. This is not, however, the place where we may indulge in details respecting all of these gorgeous birds; we conclude, then, with the Medallion, or horned pheasant. It has a "beautiful membrane of resplendent colors on the neck, which is displayed or contracted according as the cock is more or less roused. The hues are chiefly purple, with bright red and green spots, which vary in intensity according to the degree of excitement."

The peacock, though not a native, is reared in all parts; it bears the name of *kung tsioh*, sometimes rendered 'Confucius'

[1] Yule's *Marco Polo*, Vol. I., p. 246—where there is an admirable wood-cut of one from Wood.

bird,' though it is more probable that the name means the great or magnificent bird. The use of the tail feathers to designate official rank, which probably causes a large consumption of them, does not date previous to the present dynasty. Poultry is reared in immense quantities, but the assortment in China does not equal in beauty, excellence, and variety the products of Japanese culture. The silken cock, the vane of whose plume is so minutely divided as to resemble curly hair, is probably the same sort with that described by some writers as having wool like sheep. The Mongols succeed very well in rearing the tall, Shanghai breed, and their uniform cold winter enables them to preserve frozen flesh without much difficulty. The smaller gallinaceous birds already described, grouse, quails, francolins, partridges, sand-snipe, etc., amount to a score or more species, ranging all over the Empire. The red partridge is sometimes tamed to keep as a house bird with the fowls. The Chinese quail (*Coturnix*) has a brown back, sprinkled with black spots and white lines, blackish throat and chestnut breast. It is reared for fighting in south China, and, like its bigger Gallic rival, is soon eaten if it allows itself to be beaten.

The widespread family of waders sends a few of its representatives from Europe to China, but most of the members are Oriental. The marshes and salt lakes of Mongolia attract enormous numbers of migratory birds in summer to rear their young in safety, in the midst of abundant food. Col. Prejevalsky watched the arrival of vast flocks early in February, and thus describes their appearance: "For days together they sped onward, always from the W.S.W., going further east in search of open water, and at last settling down among the open pools; their favorite haunts were the flat mud banks overgrown with low saline bushes. Here every day vast flocks would congregate toward evening, crowding among the ice; the noise they made on rising was like a hurricane, and at a distance they resembled a thick cloud. Flocks of one, two, three, and even five thousand, followed one another in quick succession, hardly a minute apart. Tens and hundreds of thousands, even millions of birds appeared at Lob-nor during the fortnight ending the 21st of February, when the flight was at its height. What prodigious quantities of food must be necessary for such numbers!"[1] Wading and web-footed birds all harmlessly mix in these countless hosts, but hawks, eagles, and animals gather too, to prey on them.

Among the noticeable waders of China, the white Manchurian or Montigny crane is one of the finest and largest; it is the official insigna of the highest rank of civilians. Five species of crane (*Grus*) are recognized, and seven of plovers, together with as many more allied genera, including an avocet, bustard, and oyster-catcher. Curlews abound along the flat shores of the Gulf of Pechele, and are so tame that they race up and down with the naked children at low tide, hunting for shell-fish; as the boy runs his arm into the ooze the curlew pokes his long bill up to the eyes in the same hole, each of them grasping a crab. Godwits and sandpipers enliven the coasts with their cries, and seven species of gambets (*Totanus*) give them them the largest variety of their family group, next to the snipes (*Tringa*), of which nine are recorded. Herons, egrets, ibis, and night-herons occur, and none of them are discarded for food. At Canton, a pure white egret is often exposed for sale in the market, standing on a shelf the livelong day, with its eyelids sewed together—a pitiable sight. Its slender, elegant shape is imitated by artists in making bronze candlesticks. The singular spoonbill (*Platalea*) is found in Formosa, and the jacana in southwestern China. The latter is described by Gould as "distinguished not less by the grace of its form than its adaptation to the localities which nature has allotted it. Formed for traversing the morass and lotus-covered surface of the water, it supports itself upon the floating weeds and leaves by the extraordinary span of the toes, aided by the unusual lightness of the body."[2] Gallinules, crakes, and rails add to this list, but the flamingo has not been recorded.

In the last order, sixty-five species of web-footed birds are enumerated by naturalists as occurring in China. The fenny

---

[1] *From Kulja to Lob-nor*, p. 116.

[2] John Gould, *Century of Birds*. London, 1831–32.

margins of lakes and rivers, and the seacoast marshes, afford food and shelter to flocks of water-fowl. Ten separate species of duck are known, of which four or five are peculiar. The whole coast from Hainan to Manchuria swarms with gulls, terns, and grebes, while geese, swans, and mallards resort to the inland waters and pools to rear their young. Ducks are sometimes caught by persons who first cover their heads with a gourd pierced with holes, and then wade into the water where the birds are feeding; these, previously accustomed to empty calabashes floating about on the water, allow the fowler to approach, and are pulled under without difficulty. The wild goose is a favorite bird with native poets. The reputation for conjugal fidelity has made its name and that of the mandarin duck emblems of that virtue, and a pair of one or the other usually forms part of wedding processions. The epithet *mandarin* is applied to this beautiful fowl, and also to a species of orange, simply because of their excellence over other varieties of the same genus, and not, as some writers have inferred, because they are appropriated to officers of government.

The *yuen-yang*, as the Chinese call this duck, is a native of the central provinces. It is one of the most variegated birds known, vieing with the humming-birds and parrots in the diversified tints of its plumage, if it does not equal them for brilliancy. The drake is the object of admiration, his partner being remarkably plain, but during the summer season he also loses much of his gay vesture. Mr. Bennet tells a pleasant story in proof of the conjugal fidelity of these birds, the incidents of which occurred in Mr. Beale's aviary at Macao. A drake was stolen one night, and the duck displayed the strongest marks of despair at her loss, retiring into a corner and refusing all nourishment, as if determined to starve herself to death from grief. Another drake undertook to comfort the disconsolate widow, but she declined his attentions, and was fast becoming a martyr to her attachment, when her mate was recovered and restored to her. Their reunion was celebrated by the noisiest demonstrations of joy, and the duck soon informed her lord of the gallant proposals made to her during his absence; in high dudgeon, he instantly attacked the luckless bird which would have supplanted him, and so maltreated him as to cause his death.

The aviary here mentioned was for many years, up to 1838, one of the principal attractions of Macao. Its owner, Mr. Thomas Beale, had erected a wire cage on one side of his house, having two apartments, each of them about fifty feet high, and containing several large trees; small cages and roosts were placed on the side of the house under shelter, and in one corner a pool afforded bathing conveniences to the water-fowl. The genial climate obviated the necessity of any covering, and only those species which would agree to live quietly together were allowed the free range of the two apartments. The great attraction of the collection was a living bird of paradise, which, at the period of the owner's death, in 1840, had been in his possession eighteen years, and enjoyed good health at that time. The collection during one season contained nearly thirty specimens of pheasants, and besides these splendid birds, there were upward of one hundred and fifty others, of different sorts, some in cages, some on perches, and others going loose in the aviary. In one corner a large cat had a hole, where she reared her young; her business was to guard the whole from the depredations of rats. A magnificent peacock from Damaun, a large assortment of macaws and cockatoos, a pair of magpies, another of the superb crowned pigeons (*Goura coronata*), one of whom moaned itself to death on the decease of its mate, and several Nicobar ground pigeons, were also among the attractions of this curious and valuable collection.

Four or five kinds of grebe and loon frequent the coast, of which the *Podiceps cristatus*, called *shui nu*, or 'water slave,' is common around Macao. The same region affords sustenance to the pelican, which is seen standing motionless for hours on the rocks, or sailing on easy wing over the shallows in search of food. Its plumage is nearly a pure white, except the black tips of the wings; its height is about four feet, and the expanse of the wings more than eight feet. The bill is flexible like whalebone, and the pouch susceptible of great dilatation. Gulls abound on the northeast coasts, and no one who has seen it can forget the beautiful sight on the marshes at the entrance of the Pei ho, where myriads of white gulls assemble to feed, to preen, and to quarrel or scream—the bright sun rendering their plumage like snow. The albatross, black tern, petrel, and noddy increase the list of denizens in Chinese waters, but offer nothing of particular interest.[1]

There are four fabulous animals which are so often referred to by the Chinese as to demand a notice. The *kí-lin* is one of these, and is placed at the head of all hairy animals; as the *fung-hwang* is pre-eminent among feathered races; the dragon and tortoise among the scaly and shelly tribes; and *man* among naked animals! The naked, hairy, feathered, shelly, and scaly tribes constitute the quinary system of ancient Chinese naturalists. The *kí-lin* is pictured as resembling a stag in its body and a horse in its hoofs, but possessing the tail of an ox and a parti-colored or scaly skin. A single horn having a fleshy tip proceeds out of the forehead. Besides these external marks to identify it, the *kí-lin* exhibits great benevolence of

The Kí-lin, or Unicorn.

[1] On the birds of China, see in general *Les Oiseaux de la Chine*, par M. l'Abbé Armand David, avec un Atlas de 124 Planches dessinées et lith. par M. Arnoul. Paris, 1877. R. Swinhoe, in the *Proceedings of the Scientific Meetings of the Zoölogical Soc. of London*, and in *The Ibis, a Magazine of General Ornithology*, passim. *Journ. N. C. Br. R. A. Soc.*, Nos. II., p. 225, and III., p. 287.

disposition toward other living animals, and appears only when wise and just kings, like Yau and Shun, or sages like Confucius, are born, to govern and teach mankind. The Chinese description presents many resemblances to the popular notices of the unicorn, and the independent origin of their account adds something to the probability that a single-horned equine or cervine animal has once existed.[1]

Cuvier expresses the opinion that Pliny's description of the

The Fung-hwang, or Phœnix.

Arabian phœnix was derived from the golden pheasant, though others think the Egyptian plover is the original type. From his likening it to an eagle for size, having a yellow neck with purple, a blue tail varied with red feathers, and a richly feathered tufted head, it is more probable that the Impeyan pheasant was Pliny's

[1] *Chinese Repository*, Vol. VII., p. 213. Compare Yule's note, *Marco Polo*, Vol. I., p. 232. Huc, *Travels in Tartary*, etc., Vol. II., p. 246. Bell, *Journey from St. Petersburgh in Russia to Ispahan in Persia*, Vol. I., p. 216. Also Heeren, *Asiatic Nations*, Vol. I., p. 98, where there is a *résumé* of Ctesias' account of the unicorn.

type. The Chinese *fung-hwang*, or phœnix, is probably based on the Argus pheasant. It is described as adorned with every color, and combines in its form and motions whatever is elegant and graceful, while it possesses such a benevolent disposition that it will not peck or injure living insects, nor tread on growing herbs. Like the *kí-lin*, it has not been seen since the halcyon days of Confucius, and, from the account given of it, seems to have been entirely fabulous. The etymology of the characters implies that it is the emperor of all birds. One Chinese author describes it "as resembling a wild swan before and a unicorn behind; it has the throat of a swallow, the bill of a cock, the neck of a snake, the tail of a fish, the forehead of a crane, the crown of a mandarin drake, the stripes of a dragon, and the vaulted back of a tortoise. The feathers have five colors, which are named after the five cardinal virtues, and it is five cubits in height; the tail is graduated like Pandean pipes, and its song resembles the music of that instrument, having five modulations." A beautiful ornament for a lady's head-dress is sometimes made in the shape of the *fung-hwang*, and somewhat resembles a similar ornament, imitating the vulture, worn by the ladies of ancient Egypt.

The *lung*, or dragon, is a familiar object on articles from China. It furnishes a comparison among them for everything terrible, imposing, and powerful; and being taken as the imperial coat of arms, consequently imparts these ideas to his person and state. The type of the dragon is probably the boa-constrictor or sea-serpent, or other similar monster, though the researches of geology have brought to light such a near counterpart of the *lung* in the iguanadon as to tempt one to believe that this has been the prototype. There are three dragons, the *lung* in the sky, the *lí* in the sea, and the *kiao* in the marshes. The first is the only *authentic* species, according to the Chinese; it has the head of a camel, the horns of a deer, eyes of a rabbit, ears of a cow, neck of a snake, belly of a frog, scales of a carp, claws of a hawk, and palm of a tiger. On each side of the mouth are whiskers, and its beard contains a bright pearl; the breath is sometimes changed into water and sometimes into fire, and its voice is like the jingling of copper pans. The dragon of the sea occasionally ascends to heaven in water-spouts, and is the ruler of all oceanic phenomena.[1] The dragon is worshipped and feared by Chinese fishermen, and their *lung-wang*, or 'dragon king,' answers to Neptune in western mythology; perhaps the ideas of all classes toward it is a modified relic of the widespread serpent worship of ancient times. The Chinese suppose that elfs, demons, and other supernatural beings often transform themselves into snakes; and M. Julien has translated a fairy story of this sort, called *Blanche et Bleue*. The *kwei*, or tortoise, has so few fabulous qualities attributed to it that it hardly comes into the list; it was, according to the story, an attendant on Pwanku when he chiselled out the world. A semi-classical work, the *Shan-hai King*, or 'Memoirs upon the Mountains and Seas,' contains pictures and descriptions of these and kindred monsters, from which the people now derive strange notions respecting them, the book having served to embody and fix for the whole nation what the writer anciently found floating about in the popular legends of particular localities.

A species of alligator (*A. sinensis*) has been described by Dr. A. Fauvel in the *N. C. Br. R. A. Soc. Journal*, No. XIII., 1879, in which he gives many historical and other notices of its existence. Crocodiles are recorded as having been seen in the rivers of Kwangtung and Kwangsí, but none of this family attain a large size.

Marco Polo's account of the huge serpent of Yunnan,[2] having two forelegs near the head, and one claw like that of a lion or hawk on each, and a mouth big enough to swallow a man whole, referring no doubt to the crocodile, is a good instance of the way in which truth and fable were mingled in the accounts of those times. The flesh is still eaten by the Anamese, as he says it was in his day. A gigantic salamander, analogous to the one found in Japan (the *Sieboldia*), has suggested it as the

---

[1] *Chinese Repository*, Vol. VII., p. 250. For a careful analysis of this relic of ancient lore, see the *Nouveau Journal Asiatique*, Tome XII., pp. 232–243, 1833; also Tome VIII., 3d Series, pp. 337–382, 1839, for M. Bazin's estimate of its value.

[2] Yule's *Marco Polo*, Vol. II., p. 46.

type of the dragon which figures on the Chinese national flag. Small lizards abound in the southern parts, and the variety and numbers of serpents, both land and water, found in the maritime provinces, are hardly exceeded in any country in the world; they are seldom poisonous. A species of naja is the only venomous snake yet observed at Chusan, and the hooded cobra is one of the few yet found around Canton. Another species frequents the banks, and is driven out of the drains and creeks by high water into the houses. A case is mentioned by Bennet of a Chinese who was bitten, and to whose wound the mashed head of the reptile had been applied as a poultice, a mode of treatment which probably accelerated his death by mixing more of the poison diluted in the animal's blood with the man's own blood. It is, however, rare to hear of casualties from this source. This snake is called 'black and white,' from being marked in alternate bands of those two colors. A species of acrochordon, remarkable for its abrupt, short tail, has been noticed near Macao.

It is considered felicitous by the Buddhist priests to harbor snakes around their temples; and though the natives do not play with poisonous serpents like the Hindoos, they often handle or teach them simple tricks. The common frog is taken in great numbers for food. Tortoises and turtles from fresh and salt water are plenty along the coast, while both the emys and trionyx are kept in tubs in the streets, where they grow to a large size. An enormous carnivorous tortoise inhabits the waters of Chehkiang near the ocean. The natives have strange ideas concerning the hairy turtle of Sz'chuen, and regard it as excellent medicine; it is now known that the supposed hair consists of confervæ, whose spores, lodged on the shell, have grown far beyond the animal's body.

The ichthyology of China is one of the richest in the world, though it may be so more from the greater proportion of food furnished by the waters than from any real superabundance of the finny tribes. The offal thrown from boats near cities attracts some kinds to those places, and gives food and employment to multitudes. Several large collections of fishes have been made in Canton, and Mr. Reeves deposited one of the richest in the British Museum, together with a series of drawings made by native artists from living specimens; they have been described by Sir John Richardson in the *Report of the British Association for the Advancement of Science, for* 1845. In this paper he enumerates one hundred and ninety genera and six hundred and seventy-one species, nearly all of which are marine or come out to sea at certain times. Since it was prepared great accessions to this branch have been made from the inland waters, so that probably a thousand sorts in all have been observed. The salmon and cod families are comparatively scarce, but the mackerel, goby, and herring families are very abundant. The variety of fish is so great in Macao, that if one is willing to eat all that are brought to market, as the Chinese do (including the sharks, torpedoes, gudgeons, etc.), one can have a different species every day in the year. It may with truth be said that the Chinese eat nearly every living thing found in the water, some of the hideous fishing frogs or gurnards alone excepted.

The cartilaginous fishes, sharks, rays, and saw-fish, are abundant on the sea-coast. The sturgeon is not common at the south, but in the winter it is brought from the Songari and other rivers to Peking for the imperial table, being highly prized by Chinese epicures. There is found in the Yangtsz' a singular species of sturgeon, the *yiu yü*, which lies under the banks in still water and sucks its prey into a sac-like mouth projecting like a cusp under the long snout; it has no scales, and is four feet long. Common sturgeon, weighing a thousand pounds, are caught in this river. The hammer-headed and zebra shark (*Cestracion zebra*) are seen in the markets at Macao; also huge skates, some of them measuring five feet across; the young of all these species are regarded as particularly good eating. A kind of torpedo (*Narcine lingula*) is not uncommon on the southern coast, but the natives do not seem to be aware of any electrical properties. It is said that the fishermen sometimes destroy the shark by boiling a melon and throwing it out as a bait; when swallowed, the heat kills the fish. The true cod has not been observed on the Chinese coast, but several species of serrani (as *Plectropoma susuki*, *Serranus shihpan*, *Megachir*, etc.), generally called *shih-pan* by the natives, and garoupa by foreigners, are common off Canton, and considered to be most delicate fare. Another fine fish is the *Polynemus tetradactylus*, or bynni-carp, often called salmon by foreigners; isinglass is prepared from its skin. The pomfret, or *tsang yü* (*Stromateus argenteus*), is a good pan-fish, but hardly so delicate as the sole, many fine species of which abound along the whole coast. Besides these, two or three species of mackerel, the *Sciæna lucida*, an ophicephalus, the mullet, and the 'white rice fish' occur. The shad is abundant off the Yangtsz', and is superior to the American species; Chinese epicures will sometimes pay fifty dollars for the first one of the season.

The carp family (*Cyprinidæ*) is very abundant in the rivers and lakes of China, and some species are reared in fish-pools and tubs to a monstrous size; fifty-two species are mentioned in Richardson's list. The gold-fish is the most celebrated, and has been introduced into Europe, where it was first seen toward the end of the seventeenth century. The Chinese say that its native place is Lake Tsau, in the province of Nganhwui. The effects of domestication in changing the natural form of this fish are great; specimens are often seen without any dorsal fin, and the tail and other fins tufted and lobed to such a degree as to resemble artificial appendages or wings rather than natural organs. The eyes are developed till the globe projects beyond the socket like goggles, presenting an extraordinary appearance. Some of them are so fantastic, indeed, that they would be regarded as lusus naturæ were they not so common. The usual color is a ruddy golden hue, but both sexes exhibit a silvery or blackish tint at certain stages of their growth; and one variety, called the silver-fish, retains this shade all its life. The Chinese keep it in their garden ponds, or in earthern jars, in which are placed rocks covered with moss, and overgrown with tufts of ferns, to afford them a retreat from the light. When the females spawn, the eggs must be removed to a shallow vessel, lest the males devour them, where the heat of the sun hatches them; the young are nearly black, but gradually become whitish or reddish, and at last assume a golden or silvery hue. Specimens upward of two feet long have been noticed, and those who rear them emulate each other in producing new varieties.

The rearing of fish is an important pursuit, the spawn being collected with the greatest care and placed in favorable positions for hatching. The *Bulletin Universel* for 1829 asserts that in some part of China the spawn so taken is carefully placed in an empty egg-shell and the hole closed; the egg is then replaced in the nest, and, after the hen has sat a few days upon it, reopened, and the spawn placed in vessels of water warmed by the sun, where it soon hatches.

The immense fleets of fishing boats on the Yangtsz' and its tributaries indicate the finny supplies its waters afford. A species of pipe-fish (*Fistularia immaculata*), of a red color, and the gar-pike, with green bones, are found about Canton; as are also numerous beautiful parrot-fish and sun-fish (*Chætodon*). An ingenious mode of taking its prey is practised by a sort of chætodon, or chelmon; it darts a drop of water at the flies or other insects lighting on the bank near the edge, in such a manner as to knock them off, when they are devoured. All the species of ophicephalus, or *săng yü*, so remarkable for their tenacity of life, are reared in tanks and pools, and are hawked alive through the streets.

Eels, mullets, alewives or file-fish, breams, gudgeons, and many other kinds, are seen in the markets. Few things eaten by the Chinese look more repulsive than the gobies as they lie wriggling in the slime which keeps them alive; one species (*Trypauchen vagina*), called *chu pih yü*, or 'vermilion pencil-fish,' is a cylindrical fish, six or eight inches long, of a dark red color; its eyes protrude so that it can see behind, like a giraffe. Some kinds of gobies construct little hillocks in the ooze, with a depression on the top, in which their spawn is hatched by the sun; at low tide they skip about on the banks like young frogs, and are easily captured with the hand. A delicious species of Saurus (*Leucosoma Chinensis*), called *pih fan yü*, or 'white rice fish,' and *yin yü*, or silver-fish, ranges from Hakodate to Canton. It is six or eight inches long, the body scaleless and transparent, so that the muscles, intestines, and spinal column can be seen without dissection; the bones of the head are thin, flexible, and diaphanous. Many species of file-fish, sole-fish, anchovy, and eels, are captured on the coast. Vast quantities of dried fish, like the stock fish in Sweden, are sent inland to sell in regions where fish are rare. The most common sorts are the perch, sun-fish, gurnard, and hair-tail (*Trichinrus*).

Shell-fish and mollusks, both fresh and salt, are abundant in the market. Oysters of a good quality are common along the coast, and a species of mactra, or sand-clam, is fished up near Macao. The Pearl River affords two or three kinds of fresh-water shell-fish (*Mytilus*), and snails (*Voluta*) are plenty in all pools. The crangons, prawns, shrimps, crabs, and other kinds of crustacea met with, are not less abundant than palatable; one species of craw-fish, as large as (but not taking the place of) the lobster, called *lung hai*, or 'dragon crab,' together with cuttle-fish of three or four kinds, and the king-crab (*Polyphemus*), are all eaten. The inland waters produce many species of shells, and the new genus theliderma, allied to the unio, was formed by Mr. Benson, of Calcutta, from specimens obtained of a shopkeeper at Canton. The land shells are abundant, especially various kinds of snails (*Helix*, *Lymnea*, etc.); twenty-two species of helix alone were contained in a small collection sent from Peking, in which region all this kind of food is well known. A catalogue of nearly sixty shells obtained in Canton is given in Murray's *China*,[1] but it is doubtful whether even half of them are found in the country, as the shops there are supplied in a great degree from the Archipelago. Dr. Cantor[2] mentions eighty-eight genera of shells occurring between Canton and Chusan. Pearls are found in China, and Marco Polo speaks of a salt lake, supposed now to be in Yunnan, which produced them in such quantity that the fishery in his day was farmed out and restricted lest they should become too cheap and common. In Chehkiang the natives take a large kind of clam (*Alasmodonta*) and gently attach leaden images

---

[1] Vol. III., p. 445.

[2] Conspectus of collections made by Dr. Cantor, *Chinese Repository*, Vol. X., p. 434. General features of Chusan, with remarks on the Flora and Fauna of that Island, by T. E. Cantor, *Annal. Nat. Hist.*, Vol. IX. (1842), pp. 265, 361, and 481. *Journal As. Soc. of Bengal*, Vol. XXIV., 1855.

of Buddha under the fish, after which it is thrown back into the water. Nacre is deposited over the lead, and after a few months the shells are retaken, cleaned, and then sent abroad to sell as proofs of the power and presence of Buddha. The *Quarterly Review* speaks of a mode practised by the Chinese of making pearls by dropping a string of small mother-of-pearl beads into the shell, which in a year are covered with the pearly crust. Leeches are much used by native physicians; the hammer-headed leech has been noticed at Chusan.

The insects of China are almost unknown to the naturalist. In Dr. Cantor's collection, from Chusan, there are fifty-nine genera mentioned, among which tropical forms prevail; there are also six genera of arachnidæ, and the list of spiders could easily be multiplied to hundreds; among them are many showing most splendid coloring. One large and strong species is affirmed to capture small birds on the trees. Locusts sometimes commit extensive ravages, and no part of the land is free from their presence, though their depredations do not usually reach over a great extent of country, or often for two successive years. They are, however, sufficiently troublesome to attract the notice of the government, as the edict against them, inserted in another chapter, proves. Centipedes, scorpions, and some other species in the same order are known, the former being most abundant in the central and western regions, where scorpions are rare.

The most valuable insect is the silkworm, which is reared in nearly every province, and the silk from other wild worms found on the oak and ailantus in Shantung, Sz'chuen, and elsewhere also gathered; the proper silkworm itself has been met with to some extent in northern Shansí and Mongolia. Many other insects of the same order (*Lepidopteræ*) exist, but those sent abroad have been mostly from the province of Kwangtung. Eastward of the city of Canton, on a range of hills called Lofau shan, large butterflies and night moths of immense size and brilliant coloring are captured. One of these insects (*Bombyx atlas*) measures about nine inches across; the ground color is a rich and varied orange brown, and in the centre of each wing there is a triangular transparent spot, resembling a piece of mica. Sphinxes of great beauty and size are common, and in their splendid coloring, rapid noiseless flight from flower to flower, at the close of the day, remind one of the humming-bird. Some families are more abundant than others; the coleopterous exceed the lepidopterous, and the range of particular tribes in each of these is often very limited. The humid regions of Sz'chuen furnished a great harvest of beautiful butterflies to M. David, while the lamellicorn beetles and cerambycidæ are the most common in the north and central parts.

Many tribes of coleopterous insects are abundant, but the number of species yet identified is trifling. Several water beetles, and others included under the same general designation, have been found in collections sold at Canton, but owing to the careless manner in which those boxes are filled, very few specimens are perfect, the antennæ or tarsi being broken. The mole-cricket occurs everywhere. The common cricket is caught and sold in the markets for gambling; persons of all ranks amuse themselves by irritating two of these insects in a bowl, and betting upon the prowess of their favorites. The cicada, or broad locust, is abundant, and its stridulous sound is heard from trees and groves with deafening loudness. Boys tie a straw around the abdomen of the male, so as to irritate the sounding apparatus, and carry it through the streets in this predicament, to the great annoyance of every one. This insect was well known to the Greeks; the ancient distich—

"Happy the cicadas' lives,
For they all have voiceless wives,"

hints at their knowledge of this sexual difference, as well as intimates their opinion of domestic quiet. Again it forms the subject of Meleager's invocation:

"O shrill-voiced insect! that with dew-drops meet,
Inebriate, dost in desert woodlands sing;
Perch'd on the spray top with indented feet,
Thy dusky body's echoings harp-like ring."

The lantern-fly (*Fulgora*) is less common than the cicada. It is easily recognized by its long cylindrical snout, arched in an upward direction, its greenish reticulated elytra, and orange-yellow wings with black extremities; but its appearance in the evening is far from being as luminous as are the fire-fly and glow-worm of South America. The *Peh lah shu*, or 'white wax tree' (*Fraxinus chinensis*), affords nourishment to an insect of this order called *Coccus pela*. The larvæ alone furnish the wax, the secretion being the result of disease. Sir Geo. L. Staunton first described the fly from specimens seen in Annam in 1795, where the natives collected a white powder from the bark of the tree on which it occurs. Daniel Hanbury figured the insect and tree with the deposit of crude wax on the limbs, all obtained in Chekhiang province.[1] Baron Richthofen speaks of this industry in Sz'chuen as one furnishing employment to great multitudes. The department of Kia-ting furnishes the best wax, as its climate is warmer than Chingtu. The eggs of the insect are gathered in Kien-chang and Ning-yuen, where the tree flourishes on which it deposits them, and its culture is carefully attended to. The insect lives and breeds on this evergreen, and in April the eggs are collected and carried up to Kia-ting by porters. This journey is mostly performed by night so as to avoid the risk of hatching their loads; 300 eggs weigh one tael. They are instantly placed on the same kind of tree, six or seven balls of eggs done up in palm-leaf bags and hung on the twigs. In a few days the larvæ begin to spread over the branches, but do not touch the leaves; the bark soon becomes incrusted with a white powder, and is not disturbed till August. The loaded branches are then cut off and boiled, when the wax collects on the surface of the water, is skimmed off, and melted again to be poured into pans for sale. A tael's weight of eggs will produce two or three catties of the translucent, highly crystalline wax; it sells there for five mace a tael and upward. The annual income is reckoned at Tls. 2,000,000.[2] The purposes to which this singular product are applied include all those of beeswax. Pills are ingeniously enclosed in small

---

[1] Hanbury's notes on *Chinese Materia Medica*, 1862; *Pharmaceutical Journal*, Feb., 1862.

[2] Baron Richthofen's *Letters*, No. VII., to Shanghai Chamber of Commerce, May, 1872, p. 52.

globes of it, and candles of every size made. Wax is also gathered from wild and domestic bees, but honey is not much used; a casing of wax, colored with vermilion, is used to inclose the tallow of great painted candles set before the idols and tablets.

The *Chinese Herbal* contains a singular notion, prevalent also in India, concerning the generation of the sphex, or solitary wasp. When the female lays her eggs in the clayey nidus she makes in houses, she encloses the dead body of a caterpillar in it for the subsistence of the worms when they hatch. Those who observed her entombing the caterpillar did not look for the eggs, and immediately concluded that the sphex took the worm for her progeny, and say that as she plastered up the hole of the nest, she hummed a constant song over it, saying, "*Class with me! Class with me!*"—and the transformation gradually took place, and was perfected in its silent grave by the next spring, when a winged wasp emerged to continue its posterity in the same mysterious way.[1]

White ants are troublesome in the warmer parts, and annoy the people there by eating up the coffins in the graves. They form passages under ground, and penetrate upward into the woodwork of houses, and the whole building may become infested with them almost before their existence is suspected. They will even eat their way into fruit trees, cabbages, and other plants, destroying them while in full vigor. Many of the internal arrangements of the nests of bees and ants, and their peculiar instincts, have been described by Chinese writers with considerable accuracy. The composition of the characters for the bee, ant, and mosquito, respectively, denote the *awl* insect, the *righteous* insect, and the *lettered* insect; referring thereby to the sting of the first, the orderly working and subordination of the second, and the letter-like markings on the wings of the latter. Mosquitoes are plenty, and gauze curtains are considered to be a more necessary part of bed furniture than a mattress.

The botany of China is rather better known than its zoölogy,

[1] Darwin, *Naturalist's Voyage*, p. 35, notices a similar habit of the sphex in the vicinity of Rio Janeiro. The insect partially kills the spider or caterpillar by stinging, when they are stored in a rotting state with her eggs.

though vast and unexplored fields, like that reaching from Canton to Silhet and Assam, still invite the diligent collector to gather, examine, and make known their treasures. One of the earliest authors in this branch was Père Loureiro, a Portuguese for thirty-six years missionary in Cochinchina, and professor of mathematics and physic in the royal palace. He gathered a large herbarium there and in southern Kwangtung, and published his *Flora Cochinchinensis* in 1790, in which he described one hundred and eighty-four genera and more than three hundred new species. The only other work specially devoted to Chinese botany is Bentham's *Flora Hongkongensis*, published in 1861. The materials for it were collected by Drs. Hinds, Hance and Harland, Col. Champion, and others, during the previous twenty years, and amounted in all to upward of five thousand specimens, gathered exclusively on the island. Since its publication, Dr. Hance has added to our accurate knowledge of the Chinese flora many new specimens growing in other parts of the Empire, whose descriptions are scattered through various publications. Père David, during his extensive travels in northern China, gathered thousands of specimens which have yet to be carefully described. The Russian naturalists Maximowitch, Bunge, Tatarinov, Bretschneider, Prejevalsky, and others have largely increased our knowledge of the plants of Mongolia, the Amur basin, and the region about Peking. The first named has issued a separate work on the Amur flora, but most of the papers of these scientists are to be found in periodicals. In very early days, China was celebrated for the camphor, varnish, tallow, oil, tea, cassia, dyes, etc., obtained from its plants; and the later monographs of professed botanists, issued since Linneus looked over the two hundred and sixty-four species brought by his pupil Osbeck in 1750, down to the present day, have altogether given immense assistance to a thorough understanding of their nature and value.

Mr. Bentham's observations on the range of the plants collected in the island of Hongkong represent its flora, in general character, as most like that of tropical Asia, of which it offers, in numerous instances, the northern limit. The damp, wooded ravines on the north and west furnish plants closely allied to those of Assam and Sikkim; while other species, in considerable numbers, have a much more tropical character, extending with little variation over the Archipelago, Malaysia, Ceylon, and even to tropical Africa, but not into India. Within two degrees north of the island these tropical features (so far as is known) almost entirely cease, and out of the one thousand and fifty-six species described in the *Flora Hongkongensis*, only about eighty have been found in Japan; thus indicating that very few of the plants known to range across from the Himalaya to Japan grow south of Amoy. On the twenty-nine square miles forming the area of Hongkong there exists, Mr. Bentham says, a greater number of monotypic genera than in any other flora from an equal area in the world; he gives a comparative table of the floras of Hongkong, Aden and Ischia islands, about equal in extent, showing one thousand and three species growing on the first, ninety-five on the second, and seven hundred and ninety-two on the third. The proportion of woody to herbaceous species in Hongkong is nearly one-half, while in Ischia it is one to eleven; yet Hongkong has actually fewer trees than Ischia. Out of the one thousand and three species of wild plants there, three hundred and ninety-eight also occur in the tropical Asiatic flora, while one hundred and eighty-seven others have been found as well on the mainland; one hundred and fifty-nine are peculiar to the island.

Many species of coniferæ are floated down to Canton, taken from the Mei ling, or brought from Kwangsí; the timber is used for fuel, but more for rafters and pillars in buildings. The wood of the pride of India is employed for cabinet work; there are also many kinds of fancy wood, some of which are imported, and more are indigenous. The *nan muh*, or southern wood, a magnificent species of laurus common in Sz'chuen, which resists time and insects, is peculiarly valuable, and reserved for imperial use. The cœsalpinia, rose wood, aigle wood, and the camphor, elm, willow, and aspen, are also serviceable in carpentry.

The people collect seaweed to a great extent, using it in the arts and also for food; among these the *Gigartina tenax* affords an excellent material for glues and varnishes. It is boiled, and the transparent glue obtained is brushed upon very coarse silk or mulberry paper, filling up their substance, and making a transparent covering for lanterns; it is also used as a size for stiffening silks and gauze. This and other kinds of fuci are boiled to a jelly and used for food; it is known in commerce under the name of agar-agar. The thick fronds of the laminaria are gathered on the northern coasts and imported from Japan. Among other cryptogams, the Tartarian lamb (*Aspidium barometz*), so graphically described by Darwin in his *Botanic Garden*, has long been celebrated; it is partly an artificial production of the ingenuity of Chinese gardeners taking advantage of the natural habits of the plant to form it into a shape resembling a sheep or other object.

Among remarkable grasses the zak or saxaul (*Haloxylon*) and the *sulhir* (*Agriophyllum*), which grow in the sandy parts of the desert of Gobi, should be mentioned. The first is found across the whole length of this arid region, growing on the bare sand, furnishing to the traveller a dry and ready fuel in its brittle twigs, while his camels greedily browse on its leafless but juicy and prickly branches. The Mongols pitch their tents beneath its shelter, seeking for some covert from the wintry winds, and encouraged to dig at its roots for water which has been detained by their succulent nature, a wonderful provision furnished by God in the bleakest desert. The *sulhir* is even more important, and is the "gift of the desert." It grows on bare sand, is about two feet high, a prickly saline plant, producing many seeds in September, of a nutritious, agreeable nature, food for man and beast.

The list of gramineous plants cultivated for food is large; the common sorts include rice, wheat, barley, oats, maize, sugar-cane, panic, sorghum, spiked and panicled millet, of each kind several varieties. The grass (*Phragmites*) raised along the river banks is carefully cut and dried, to be woven into floor-matting; a coarser sort, called *atap*, is made of bamboo splints for roofs of huts, awnings, and sheds. In the milder climes of the southern coasts, cheap houses are constructed of these materials. The coarse grass and shrubbery on the hills is cut in the autumn for fuel by the poor; and when the hills are well sheared of their grassy covering, the stubble is set on fire, in order to supply ashes for manuring the next crop—an operation which tends to keep the hills bare of all shrubbery and trees.

Few persons who have not seen the bamboo growing in its native climes get a full idea from pictures of its grace and beauty. A clump of this magnificent grass will gradually develop by new shoots into a grove, if care be taken to cut down the older stems as they reach full maturity, and not let them flower and go to seed; for as soon as they have perfected the seed, they die down to the root, like other grasses. The stalks usually attain the height of fifty feet, and in the Indian islands often reach seventy feet and upward, with a diameter of ten or twelve inches at the bottom. A road lined with them, with their feathery sprays meeting overhead, presents one of the most beautiful avenues possible to a warm climate.

In China the industry and skill of the people have multiplied and perpetuated a number of varieties (one author contents himself with describing sixty of them), among which are the yellow, the black, the green, the slender sort for pipes, and a slenderer one for writing-pencils, the big-leaved, etc. Its uses are so various that it is not easy to enumerate them all. The shoots come out of the ground nearly full-sized, four to six inches in diameter, and are cut like asparagus to eat as a pickle or a comfit, or by boiling or stewing. Sedentary Buddhist priests raise this lenten fare for themselves or to sell, and extract the tabasheer from the joints of the old culms, to sell as a precious medicine for almost anything which ails you. The roots are carved into fantastic and ingenious images and stands, or divided into egg-shaped divining-blocks to ascertain the will of the gods, or trimmed into lantern handles, canes, and umbrella-sticks.

The tapering culms are used for all purposes that poles can be applied to in carrying, propelling, supporting, and measuring, for which their light, elastic, tubular structure, guarded by a coating of silicious skin, and strengthened by a thick septum at each joint, most admirably fits them. The pillars and props of houses, the framework of awnings, the ribs of mat-sails, and the shafts of rakes are each furnished by these culms. So, also, are fences and all kinds of frames, coops, and cages, the wattles of abatis, and the ribs of umbrellas and fans. The leaves are sewed into rain-cloaks for farmers and sailors, and thatches for covering their huts and boats, pinned into linings for tea-boxes, plaited into immense umbrellas to screen the huckster and his stall from the sun and rain, or into coverings for theatres and sheds. Even the whole lot where a two-story house is building is usually covered in by a framework of bamboo-poles and *attap*—as this leaf covering is called, from its Malay name—all tied together by rattan, and protecting the workmen and their work from sun and rain.

The wood, cut into splints of proper sizes and forms, is woven into baskets of every shape and fancy, sewed into window-curtains and door-screens, plaited into awnings and coverings for tea-chests or sugar-cones, and twisted into cables. The shavings and curled threads aid softer things in stuffing pillows; while other parts supply the bed for sleeping, the chopsticks for eating, the pipe for smoking, and the broom for sweeping. The mattress to lie upon, the chair to sit upon, the table to eat on, the food to eat, and the fuel to cook it with, are also derivable from bamboo. The master makes his ferule from it, the carpenter his foot-measure, the farmer his water-pipes, irrigating wheels, and straw-rakes, the grocer his gill and pint cups, and the mandarin his dreaded instrument of punishment. This last use is so common that the name of the plant itself has come in our language to denote this application, and the poor wretch who is *bambooed* for his crimes is thus taught that laws cannot be violated with impunity.

The paper to write on, the book to study from, the pencil to write with, the cup to hold the pencils, and the covering of the lattice-window instead of glass are all indebted to this grass in their manufacture. The shaft of the soldier's spear, and oftentimes the spear altogether, the plectrum for playing the lute, the reed in the native organ, the skewer to fasten the hair, the undershirt to protect the body, the hat to screen the head, the bucket to draw the water, and the easy-chair to lounge on, besides cages for birds, fish, bees, grasshoppers, shrimps, and cockroaches, crab-nets, fishing-poles, sumpitans or shooting-tubes, flutes, fifes, fire-holders, etc., etc., are among the things furnished from this plant, whose beauty when growing is commensurate to its usefulness when cut down. A score or two of bamboo-poles for joists and rafters, fifty fathoms of rattan ropes, with plenty of palm-leaves and bamboo-matting for roof and sides, supply material for a common dwelling in the south of China. Its cost is about five dollars. Those houses built over creeks, or along the low banks of rivers and sea-beaches, are elevated a few feet, and their floors are neatly made of split bamboos, which allow the water to be seen through. The decks, masts, yards, and framework of the mat-sails of the small boats of the islanders in the Archipelago are all more or less made of this useful plant. Throughout the south of Asia it enters into the daily life of the people in their domestic economy more than anything else, or than any other one thing does in any part of the world. The Japanese supply us with fans neatly formed, ribs and handle, from a single branch of bamboo, and covered with paper made from mulberry bark, while their skill is shown also in the exquisite covering of fine bamboo threads woven around cups and saucers.[1]

In ancient times the date palm was cultivated in China, but is now unknown. The cocoanut flourishes in Hainan and the adjacent coasts, where its fruit, leaves, and timber are much used. A great variety of utensils are carved from the nut-case, and ropes spun from the coir, while the cultivators drink the toddy made from the juice. The fan palm (*Chamærops*) is the common palm of the country, two species being cultivated for the wiry fibres in the leaf-sheaths, and for their broad leaves. This fibre is far more useful than that from cocoanut husks, as it is longer and smoother, and is woven into ropes, mats, cloaks, and brushes. The tree is spread over the greater part of the provinces, one of their most ornamental and useful trees. Another sort (*Caryota*) also furnishes a fibre employed in the same way, but its timber is more valuable; sedan thills are made of its wood. Still another is the talipot palm (*Borassus*), from

---

[1] Compare Yule's *Marco Polo*, Vol. I., p. 271; A. R. Wallace, *The Malay Archipelago*, pp. 87-91, American Ed.

whose leaves a material for writing books upon was once produced, as is the case now in Siam.[1]

Several species of Aroideæ are cultivated, among which the *Caladium cuculatum*, *Arum esculentum*, and *Indicum* are common. The tuberous farinaceous roots of the *Sagittaria sinensis* are esteemed; the roots of these plants, and of the water-chestnut, are manufactured into a powder resembling arrow-root. The sweet-flag (*Calamus*) is used in medicine for its spicy warmth. The stems of a species of Juncus are collected and the pith carefully taken out and dried for the wicks of water-lamps, and the inner layers of the pith hats so generally worn in southern China.

The extensive group of lillies contains many splendid ornaments of the conservatory and garden, natives of China; some are articles of food. The *Agapanthus*, or blue African lily, four species of *Hemerocallis*, or day lily, and the fragrant tuberose, are all common about Canton; the latter is widely cultivated for its blossoms to scent fancy teas. Eight or ten species of Lilium (among which the speckled tiger lily and the unsullied white are conspicuous) also add their gay beauties to the gardens; while the modest Commelina, with its delicate blue blossoms, ornaments the hedges and walks. Many alliaceous plants, the onion, cives, garlic, etc., belong to this group; and the Chinese relish them for the table as much as they admire the flowers of their beauteous and fragrant congeners for bouquets. The singular red-leaved iron-wood (*Dracæna*) forms a common ornament of gardens.

The yam, or *ta-shu* (*i.e.*, 'great tuber'), is not much raised, though its wholesome qualities as an article of food are well understood. The same group (*Musalæs*) to which the yam belongs furnishes the custard-apple, one of the few fruits which have been introduced from abroad. The Amaryllidæ are represented by many pretty species of Crinum, Nerine, and Amaryllis. Their unprofitable beauty is compensated by the plain but useful plantain, said to stand before the potato and sago palm as producing the greatest amount of wholesome food, in propor-

[1] See also in *Notes and Queries on C. and J.*, Vol. III., pp. 115, 129, 139, 147, 150, 170.

tion to its size, of any cultivated plant.[1] There are many varieties of this fruit, some of them so acid as to require cooking before eating.

That pleasant stomachic, ginger, is cultivated through all the country, and exposed for sale as a green vegetable, to spice dishes, and largely made into a preserve. The Alpinia and Canna, or Indian shot, are common garden flowers. The large group of Orchideæ has nineteen genera known to be natives of China, among which the air plants (*Vanda* and *Ærides*) are great favorites. They are suspended in baskets under the trees, and continue to unfold their blossoms in gradual succession for many weeks, all the care necessary being to sprinkle them daily. The true species of Ærides are among the most beautiful productions of the vegetable world, their flowers being arrayed in long racemes of delicate colors and delicious fragrance. The beautiful Bletia, Arundina, Spathoglottis, and Cymbidium are common in damp and elevated places about the islands near Macao and Hongkong.

Many species of the pine, cypress, and yew, forming the three subdivisions of cone-bearing plants, furnish a large proportion of the timber and fuel. The larch is not rare, and the *Pinus massoniana* and *Cunninghamia* furnish most of the common pine timber. The finest member of this order in China is the white pine (*Pinus bungiana*), peculiar to Chihlí; its trunk is a clear white, and as it annually sheds the bark it always looks as if whitewashed. Some specimens near Peking are said to be a thousand years old. Two members of the genus *Sequaia*, of a moderate size, occur near Tibet. The juniper and thuja are often selected by gardeners to try their skill in forcing them to grow into rude representations of birds and animals, the price of these curiosities being proportioned to their grotesqueness and difficulty. The nuts of the maiden-hair tree (*Salisburia adiantifolia*) are eaten, and the leaves are sometimes put into books as a preservative against insects.

The willow is a favorite plant and grows to a great size, Staunton mentioning some which were fifteen feet in girth;

[1] From calculations of Humboldt it was estimated that the productiveness of this plant as compared with wheat is as 133 to 1, and as against potatoes, 44 to 1.

they shade the roads near the capital, and one of them is the true Babylonian willow; the trees are grown for timber and for burning into charcoal. Their leaves, shape, and habits afford many metaphors to poets and writers, much more use being made of the tree in this way, it might almost be said, than any other. The oak is less patronized by fine writers, but the value of its wood and bark is well understood; the country affords several species, one of which, the chestnut oak, is cultivated for the cupules, to be used in dyeing. The galls are used for dyeing and in medicine, and the acorns of some kinds are ground in mills, and the flour soaked in water and made into a farinaceous paste. Some of the missionaries speak of oaks a hundred feet high, but such giants in this family are rare. "One of the largest and most interesting of these trees, which," writes Abel, "I have called *Quercus densifolia*, resembled a laurel in its shining green foliage. It bore branches and leaves in a thick head, crowning a naked and straight stem; its fruit grew along upright spikes terminating the branches. Another species, growing to the height of fifty feet, bore them in long, pendulous spikes."

The chestnut, walnut, and hazelnut together furnish a large supply of food. The queer-shaped ovens fashioned in imitation of a raging lion, in which chestnuts are roasted in the streets of Peking, attract the eye of the visitor. The Jack-fruit (*Artocarpus*) is not unknown in Canton, but it is not much used. There are many species of the banian, but none of them produce fruit worth plucking; the Portuguese have introduced the common fig, but it does not flourish. The bastard banian is a magnificent shade tree, its branches sometimes overspreading an area a hundred or more feet across. The walls of cities and dwellings are soon covered with the *Ficus repens*, and if left unmolested its roots gradually demolish them. The paper mulberry (*Broussonetia*) is largely cultivated in the northern provinces, and serves the poor with their chief material for windows. The leaf of the common mulberry is the principal object of its culture, but the fruit is eaten and the wood burned for lampblack to make India-ink.

Hemp (*Cannabis*) is cultivated for its fibres, and the seeds furnish an oil used for household purposes and medicinal preparations; the intoxicating substance called *bang*, made in India, is unknown in China. The family Proteaceæ contains the *Eleococca cordata*, or *wu-tung*, a favorite tree of the Chinese for its beauty, the hard wood it furnishes, and the oil extracted from its seeds. The *Stillingia* belongs to the same family; this symmetrical tree is a native of all the eastern provinces, where it is raised for its tallow; it resembles the aspen in the form and color of the leaf and in its general contour. The castor-oil is cultivated as a hedge plant, and the seeds are used both in the kitchen and apothecaries' shop.

The order Hippurinæ furnishes the water caltrops (*Trapa*), the seeds of which are vended in the streets as a fruit after boiling; one native name is 'buffalo-head fruit,' which the unopened nuts strikingly resemble. Black pepper is imported, not so much as a spice as for its infusion, to be administered in fevers. The betel pepper is cultivated for its leaves, which are chewed with the betel-nut. The pitcher plant (*Nepenthes*), called pig-basket plant, is not unfrequent near Canton; the leaves, or ascidia, bear no small resemblance to the open baskets employed for carrying hogs.

Many species of the tribe *Rumicinæ* are cultivated as esculent vegetables, among which may be enumerated spinach, green basil, beet, amaranthus, cockscomb, broom-weed (*Kochia*), buckwheat, etc. Two species of Polygonum are raised for the blue dye furnished by the leaves, which is extracted, like indigo, by maceration. Buckwheat is prepared for food by boiling it like millet; one native name means 'triangular wheat.' The flour is also employed in pastry. The cockscomb is much admired by the Chinese, whose gardens furnish several splendid varieties. The rhubarb is a member of this useful tribe, and large quantities are brought from Kansuh and Koko-nor, where its habits have lately been observed by Prejevalsky. The root is dug by Chinese and Tanguts during September and October, dried in the shade, and transported by the Yellow River to the coast towns, where Europeans pay from six to ten times its rate among the mountain markets.[1] The Chinese consider the rest

[1] Compare Yule's *Marco Polo*, Vol. I., p. 197.

of the world dependent on them for tea and rhubarb, whose inhabitants are therefore forced to resort thither to procure means to relieve themselves of an otherwise irremediable costiveness. This argument was made use of by Commissioner Lin in 1840, when recommending certain restrictive regulations to be imposed upon foreign trade, because he supposed merchants from abroad would be compelled to purchase them at any price.

The order *Ilicinæ*, or holly, furnishes several genera of Rhamneæ, whose fruits are often seen on tables. The Zizyphus furnishes the so-called Chinese dates[1] in immense quantities throughout the northern provinces. The fleshy peduncles of the Hovenia are eaten; they are common in the southeastern provinces. The leaves of the *Rhamnus theezans* are among the many plants collected by the poor as a make-shift for the true tea. The fruit called the Chinese olive, obtained from the Pimela, is totally different from and is a poor substitute for the rich olive of the Mediterranean countries.[2]

The Leguminosæ hold an important place in Chinese botany, affording many esculent vegetables and valuable products. Peas and beans are probably eaten more in China than any other country, and soy is prepared chiefly from the Soja or Dolichos. One of the modes of making this condiment is to skin the beans and grind them to flour, which is mixed with water and powdered gypsum, or turmeric. It is eaten as a jelly or curd, or in cakes, and a meal is seldom spread without it in some form. One genus of this tribe affords indigo, and from the buds and leaves of a species of Colutea a kind of green dye is said to be obtained. Liquorice is esteemed in medicine; and the red seeds of the *Abrus precatorius* are gathered for ornaments. The Poinciana and Bauhinia are cultivated for their flowers, and the Erythrina and Cassia are among the most magnificent flowering trees in the south.

---

[1] The application of this name to the jujube plum by foreigners, because the kind cured in honey resembled Arabian dates in color, size, and taste when brought on the table, is a good instance of the manner in which errors arise and are perpetuated from mere carelessness.

[2] Compare Dr. H. F. Hance, in *Journal of Botany*, Vol. IX., p. 38.

The fruits are, on the whole, inferior in flavor and size to those of the same names at the west. Several varieties of pears, plums, peaches, and apricots are known; it is probable that China is the native country of each of these fruits, and some of the varieties equal those found anywhere. Erman[1] mentions an apple or haw which grows in "long bunches and is round, about the size of a cherry, of a red color, and very sweet taste," found in abundance near Kiakhta. There are numerous species of Amygdalus cultivated for their flowers; and at new year the budding stems of the flowering almond, narcissus, plum, peach, and bell-flower (*Enkianthus reticulatus*) are forced into blossom for exhibition, as indicating good luck the coming year. The apples and quinces are generally destitute of that flavor looked for in them elsewhere, but the *lu-kuh*, or *loquat*, is a pleasant acid spring fruit. The pomegranate is chiefly cultivated for its beauty as a flowering plant; but the guava and Eugenia, or rose-apple, are sold in the market or made into jellies. The rose is a favorite among the Chinese and extensively cultivated; twenty species are mentioned, together with many varieties, as natives of the country; the Banks rose is developed and trained with great skill. The Spiræa or privet, myrtle, Quisqualis, Lawsonia or henna, white, purple, and red varieties of crape-myrtle or Lagerstrœmia, Hydrangea, the passion-flower, and the house-leek are also among the ornamental plants found in gardens. Few trees in any country present a more elegant appearance, when in full flower, than the Lagerstrœmias. The Pride of India and Chinese tamarix are also beautiful flowering trees. Specimens of the Cactus and Cereus, containing fifty or more splendid flowers in full bloom, are not unusual at Macao in August.

The watermelon, cucumber, squash, tomato, brinjal or egg-plant, and other garden vegetables are abundant; the tallow-gourd (*Benincasa cerifera*) is remarkable for having its surface covered with a waxy exudation which smells like rosin. The dried bottle-gourd (*Cucurbita lagenaria*) is tied to the backs of children on the boats to assist them in floating if they should

---

[1] *Travels in Siberia*, Vol. II., p. 151.

unluckily fall overboard. The fruit and leaves of the papaw, or *muh kwa*, 'tree melon,' are eaten after being cooked; the Chinese are aware of the intenerating property of the exhalations from the leaves of this tree, and make use of them sometimes to soften the flesh of ancient hens and cocks, by hanging the newly killed birds in the tree or by feeding them upon the fruit beforehand. The carambola (*Averrhoa*) or tree gooseberry is much eaten by the Chinese, but is not relished by foreigners; the tree itself is also an ornament to any pleasure grounds.

Ginseng is found wild in the forests of Manchuria, where it is collected by detachments of soldiers detailed for this purpose; these regions are regarded as imperial preserves, and the medicine is held as a governmental monopoly. The importation of the American root does not interfere to a very serious degree with the imperial sales, as the Chinese are fully convinced that their own plant is far superior. Among numerous plants of the malvaceous and pink tribes (*Dianthaceæ*) remarkable for their beauty or use, the *Lychnis coronata*, five sorts of pink, the *Althæa Chinensis*, eight species of Hibiscus, and other malvaceous flowers may be mentioned; the cotton tree (*Salmalia*) is common at Canton; the fleshy petals are sometimes prepared as food, and the silky stamens dried to stuff cushions. The *Gossypium herbaceum* and *Pachyrrhizus* afford the materials for cotton and grasscloth; both of them are cultivated in most parts of China. The latter is a twining, leguminous plant, cultivated from remote antiquity, and still grown for its fibres, which are woven into linen. The petals of the *Hibiscus rosa-sinensis* furnish a black liquid to dye the eyebrows, and at Batavia they are employed to polish shoes. The fruits of the *Hibiscus ochra*, or okers, are prepared for the table in a variety of ways.

The *Camellia Japonica* is allied to the same great tribe as the Hibiscus, and its elegant flowers are as much admired by the people of its native country as by florists abroad; thirty or forty varieties are enumerated, many of them unknown out of China, while Chinese gardeners are likewise ignorant of a large proportion of those found in our conservatories. This flower is cultivated solely for its beauty, but other species of Camellia are raised for their seeds, the oil expressed from them being serviceable for many household and mechanical purposes. From the fibres of a species of Waltheria, a plant of the same tribe, a fine cloth is made; and the *Pentapetes Phœnicia*, or 'noon flower,' is a common ornament of gardens.

The widely diffused tribe Ranunculiaceæ has many representatives, some of them profitable for their timber, others sought after for their fruit or admired for their beauty, and a few prized for their healing properties. There are eight species of Magnolia, all of them splendid flowering plants; the bark of the *Magnolia yulan* is employed as a febrifuge. The seed vessels of the *Ilicium anisatum*, or star-aniseed, are gathered on account of their spicy warmth and fragrance. The *Artabotrys odoratissimus* and *Unona odorata* are cultivated for their perfume. Another favorite is the *mowtan*, or tree pæony, reared for its large and variegated flowers; its name of *hwa wang*, or 'king of flowers,' indicates the estimation in which it is held. The skill of native gardeners has made many varieties, and their patience is rewarded by the high prices which fine specimens command. Good imitations of full-grown plants in flower are sometimes made of pith paper. The Clematis, the foxglove, the *Berberis Chinensis*, and the magnificent lotus, all belong to this tribe; the latter, one of the most celebrated plants in Asia, is more esteemed by the Chinese for its edible roots than reverenced for its religious associations. The *Actæa aspera* is sometimes collected, as is the scouring rush, for cleaning pewter vessels, for which its hispid leaves are well fitted.

The groups which include the poppy, mustard, cabbage, cress, and many ornamental species, form an important portion of native agriculture. The poppy has become a common crop in all the provinces, driving out the useful cereals by its greater value and profit. The leaves of many cruciferous plants are eaten, whether cultivated or wild; and one kind (*Isates*) yields a fine blue dye in the eastern provinces; the variety and amount of such food consumed by the Chinese probably exceeds that of any other people. Another tribe, Rutaceæ, contains the oranges and shaddocks, and some very fragrant shrubs, as the

Murraya exotica and *paniculata*, and the *Aglaia odorata;* while the bladder-tree (*Koelreuteria*) is a great attraction when its whole surface is brilliant with golden flowers. The *whampe*, *i.e.*, yellow skin (*Cookia punctata*), is a common and superior fruit. The seeds of the Gleditschia, besides their value in cleansing, are worn as beads, "because," say the Buddhists, "all demons are afraid of the wood;" one name means 'preventive of evil.' Two native fruits, the *líchí* and *lungan*, are allied to the Sapindus in their affinities; while the *fung shu*, or Liquidambar, and many sorts of maple, with the *Pittosporum tobira*, an ornamental shrub, may be mentioned among plants used for food or sought after for timber.

These brief notices of Chinese plants may be concluded by mentioning some of the most ornamental not before spoken of; but all the beautiful sorts are soon introduced into western conservatories by enterprising florists. In the extensive tribe of Rubiacinæ are several species of honeysuckle, and a fragrant Viburnum resembling the snowball. The Serissa is cultivated around beds like the box; the *Ixora coccinea*, and other species of that genus, are among common garden shrubs. The seeds of two or three species of Artemisia are collected, dried, and reduced to a down, to be burned as an actual cautery. The dried twigs are frequently woven into a rope to slowly consume as a means of driving away mosquitoes. From the *Carthamus tinctoirus* a fine red dye is prepared. The succory, lettuce, dandelion, and other cichoraceous plants, either wild or cultivated, furnish food; while innumerable varieties of Chrysanthemums and Asters are reared for their beauty.

The Labiatæ afford many genera, some of them cultivated; and the Solanaceæ, or nightshades, contain the tomato, potato, tobacco, stramony, and several species of Capsicum, or red pepper. It has been disputed whether tobacco is native or foreign, but the philological argument and historical notices prove that both this plant and maize were introduced within half a century after the discovery of America, or about the year 1530. The Chinese dry the leaves and cut them into shreds for smoking; the snuff is coarser and less pungent than the Scotch; it is said that powdered cinnabar is sometimes mixed with it.

Among the Convolvulaceæ are many beautiful species of Ipomea, especially the cypress vine, or *quamoclit*, trained about the houses even of the poorest. The *Ipomea maritima* occurs, trailing over the sandy beaches along the coast from Hainan to Chusan and Lewchew. The *Convolvulus reptans* is planted around the edges of pools on the confines of villages and fields, for the sake of its succulent leaves. The narcotic family of Apocyneæ contains the oleander and Plumeria, prized for their fragrance; while the yellow milkweed (*Asclepias curassavica*) and the *Vinca rosea*, or red periwinkle, are less conspicuous, but not unattractive, members of the same group. The jasmine is a deserved favorite, its clusters of flowers being often wound by women in their hair, and planted in pots in their houses. The *Olea fragrans*, or *kwei hwa*, is cultivated for scenting tea.

In the eastern provinces the hills are adorned with yellow and red azaleas of gorgeous hue, especially around Ningpo and in Chusan. "Few," says Mr. Fortune, "can form any idea of the gorgeous beauty of these azalea-clad hills, where, on every side, the eye rests on masses of flowers of dazzling brightness and surpassing beauty. Nor is it the azalea alone which claims our admiration; clematises, wild roses, honeysuckles, and a hundred others, mingle their flowers with them, and make us confess that China is indeed the 'central flowery land.'"[1]

A few notices of the advance made by the Chinese themselves in the study of natural history, taken from their great work on materia medica, the *Pun tsao*, or 'Herbal,' will form an appropriate conclusion to this chapter. This work is usually bound in forty octavo volumes, divided into fifty-two chapters, and contains many observations of value mixed up with a deal of incorrect and useless matter; and as those who read the book have not sufficient knowledge to discriminate between what is true and what is partly or wholly wrong, its reputation tends greatly to perpetuate the errors. The compiler of the *Pun tsao*, Lí Shí-chin, spent thirty years in collecting all the information on these subjects extant in his time, arranged it in a methodical manner for popular use, adding his own observations, and pub-

---

[1] *Wanderings in China.*

lished it about 1590. He consulted some eight hundred preceding authors, from whom he selected one thousand five hundred and eighteen prescriptions, and added three hundred and seventy-four new ones, arranging his materials in fifty-two books in a methodical and (for his day) scientific manner. But how far behind the writings of Pliny and Dioscorides! The nucleus of Lí's production is a small work which tradition ascribes to Shinnung, the God of Agriculture, and is doubtless anterior to the Han dynasty. His composition was well received, and attracted the notice of the Emperor, who ordered several succeeding editions to be published at the expense of the state. It was, in fact, so great an advance on all previous books, that it checked future writers in that branch, and Lí is likely now to be the first and last purely native critical writer on natural science in his mother tongue.

The first two volumes contain a collection of prefaces and indices, together with many notices of the theory of anatomy and medicine, and three books of pictorial illustrations of the rudest sort. Chapters I. and II. consist of introductory observations upon the practice of medicine, and an index of the recipes contained in the work, called the *Sure Guide to a Myriad of Recipes*; the whole filling the first seven volumes. Chapters III. and IV. contain lists of medicines for the cure of all diseases, occupying three volumes and a half, and comprising the therapeutical portion of the work, except a treatise on the pulse in the last volume.

In the subsequent chapters the author carefully goes over the entire range of nature, first giving the correct name and its explanation; then comes descriptive remarks, solutions of doubts and corrections of errors being interspersed, closing with notes on the savor, taste, and application of the recipes in which it is used. Chapters V. and VI. treat of inorganic substances under water and fire, and minerals under Chapters VII. to XI., as earth, metals, gems, and stones. Water is divided into aerial and terrestrial, *i.e.*, from the clouds, and from springs, the ocean, etc. Fire is considered under eleven species, among which are the flames of coal, bamboo, moxa, etc. The chapter on earth comprises the secretions from various animals, as well as soot, ink, etc.; that on metals includes metallic substances and their common oxides; and gems are spoken of in the next division. The eleventh chapter, in true Chinese style, groups together what could not be placed in the preceding sections, including salts, minerals, etc. In looking at this arrangement one detects the similarity between it and the classification of characters in the language itself, showing the influence this has had upon it; thus *ho*, *shui*, *tu*, *kin*, *yuh*, *shih*, and *lu*, or fire, water, earth, metals, gems, stones, and salts, are the seven radicals under which the names of inorganic substances are classified in the imperial dictionary. A like similarity runs through other parts of the *Herbal*.

Chapters XII. to XXXVII., inclusive, treat of the vegetable kingdom, under five *pu*, or 'divisions,' viz.: herbs, grains, vegetables, fruits, and trees; which are again subdivided into *lui*, or 'families,' though the members of these families have no more relationship to each other than the heterogeneous family of an Egyptian slave dealer. The lowest term in the Chinese scientific scale is *chung*, which sometimes includes a genus, but quite as often corresponds to a species or even a variety, as Linneus understood those terms.

The first division of herbs contains nine families, viz.: hill plants, odoriferous, marshy, noxious, scandent or climbing, aquatic, stony, and mossy plants, and a ninth of one hundred and sixty-two miscellaneous plants not used in medicine, making six hundred and seventy-eight species in all. In this classification the habitat is the most influential principle of arrangement for the families, while the term *tsao*, or 'herb,' denotes whatever is not eaten or used in the arts, or which does not attain to the magnitude of a tree.

The second division of grains contains four families, viz.: 1, that of hemp, sesamum, buckwheat, wheat, rice, etc.; 2, the family of millet, maize, opium, etc.; 3, leguminous plants, pulse, peas, vetches, etc.; and 4, fermentable things, as bean curd, boiled rice, wine, yeast, congee, bread, etc., which, as they are used in medicine, and produced from vegetables, seem most naturally to come in this place. The first three families embrace thirty-nine species, and the last tweny-nine articles.

The third division of kitchen herbs contains five families: 1, offensive pungent plants, as leeks, mustard, ginger; 2, soft and mucilaginous plants, as dandelions, lilies, bamboo sprouts; 3, vegetables producing fruit on the ground, as tomatoes, egg-plants, melons; 4, aquatic vegetables; and 5, mushrooms and fungi. The number of species is one hundred and thirty-three, and some part of each of them is eaten.

The fourth division of fruits contains seven families: 1, the five fruits, the plum, peach, apricot, chestnut, and date (Rhamnus); 2, hill fruits, as the orange, pear, citron, persimmon; 3, foreign fruits, as the cocoanut, líchí, carambola; 4, aromatic fruits, as pepper, cubebs, tea; 5, trailing fruits, as melons, grape, sugar-cane; 6, aquatic fruits, as water caltrops, water lily, water chestnuts, etc.; and 7, fruits not used in medicine, as whampe. In all, one hundred and forty-seven species.

The fifth division of trees has six families: 1, odoriferous trees, as pine, cassia, aloes, camphor; 2, stately trees, as the willow, tamarix, elm, soapberry, palm, poplar, julibrissin or silk tree; 3, luxuriant growing trees, as mulberry, cotton, Cercis, Gardenia, Bombax, Hibiscus; 4, parasites or things attached to trees, as the mistletoe, pachyma, and amber; 5, flexible plants, as bamboo; this family has only four species; 6, includes what the other five exclude, though it might have been thought that the second and third families were sufficiently comprehensive to contain almost all miscellaneous plants. The number of species is one hundred and ninety-eight. All botanical subjects are classified in this manner under five divisions, thirty-one families, and one thousand one hundred and ninety-five species, excluding all fermentable things.

The arrangement of the botanical characters in the language does not correspond so well to this as does that of inorganic substances. The largest group in the language system is *tsao*, which comprises in general such herbaceous plants as are not used for food. The second, *muh*, includes all trees or shrubs; and the bamboo, on account of its great usefulness, stands by itself, though the characters mostly denote names of articles made of bamboo. No less than four radicals, viz., rice, wheat, millet, and grain, serve as the heads under which the esculent grasses are arranged; there are consequently many synonymes and superfluous distinctions. One family includes beans, and another legumes; one comprises cucurbitaceous plants, another the alliaceous, and a fourth the hempen; the importance of these plants as articles of food or manufacture no doubt suggested their adoption. Thus all vegetable substances are distributed in the language under eleven different heads.

The zoölogical grouping in the *Pun tsao* is as rude and unscientific as that of plants. There are five *pu*, or divisions, namely: insect, scaly, shelly, feathered, and hairy animals. The first division contains four families: 1 and 2, insects born from eggs, as bees and silkworms, butterflies and spiders; 3, insects produced by metamorphosis, as glow-worms, mole-crickets, bugs; and 4, water insects, as toads, centipedes, etc. The second division has four families: 1, the dragons, including the manis, "the only fish that has legs;" 2, snakes; 3, fishes having scales; and 4, scaleless fishes, as the eel, cuttle-fish, prawn. The third division is classified under the two heads of tortoises or turtles and mollusks, including the star-fish, echinus, hermit-crab, etc. The fourth division contains birds arranged under four families: 1, water-fowl, as herons, king-fishers, etc.; 2, heath-fowl, sparrows, and pheasants; 3, forest birds, as magpies, crows; and 4, wild birds, as eagles and hawks. Beasts form the fifth division, which likewise contains four families: 1, the nine domesticated animals and their products; 2, wild animals, as lions, deers, otters; 3, rodentia, as the squirrel, hedgehog, rat; and 4, monkeys and fairies. The number of species in these five divisions is three hundred and ninety-one, but there are only three hundred and twenty different objects described, as the roe, fat, hair, exuviæ, etc., of animals are separately noticed.

The sixteen zoölogical characters in the language are not quite so far astray from being types of classes as the eleven botanical ones. Nine of them are mammiferous, viz.: the tiger, dog, and leopard, which stand for the carnivora; the rat for rodentia; the ox, sheep, and deer for ruminants; and the horse and hog for pachydermatous. Birds are chiefly comprised under one radical *niao*, but there is a sub-family of short-tailed gallinaceous fowls, though much confusion exists in the division. Fishes form one group, and improperly include crabs, lizards, whales, and snakes, though most of the latter are placed along with insects, or else under the dragons. The tortoise, toad, and dragon are the types of three small collections, and insects are comprised in the sixteenth and last. These groups, although they contain many anomalies, as might be expected, are still sufficiently natural to teach those who write the language something of the world around them. Thus, when one sees that a new character contains the radical *dog* in composition, he will be sure that it is neither fowl, fish, nor bug, nor any animal of the pachydermatous, cervine, or ruminant tribes, although he may have never seen the animal nor heard its name. This peculiarity runs through the whole language, indeed, but in other groups, as for instance those under the radicals man, woman, and child, or heart, hand, leg, etc., the characters include mental and passionate emotions, as well as actions and names, so that the type is not sufficiently indicative to convey a definite idea of the words included under it; the names of natural objects being most easily arranged in this manner.

Between the account of plants and animals the *Herbal* has one chapter on garments and domestic utensils, for such things "are used in medicine and are made out of plants." The remaining chapters, XXXIX.–LII., treat of animals, as noticed above. The proportion of the objects spoken of are discussed in a very methodical manner, so that a student can immediately turn to a plant or mineral and ascertain its virtue. For instance, the information relative to the history and uses of the horse is contained in twenty-four sections. The first explains the character, *ma*, which was originally intended to represent the outline of the animal. The second describes the varieties of horses, the best kinds for medical use, and gives brief descriptions of them, for the guidance of the practitioner. "The pure white are the best for medicine. Those found in the south and east are small and weak. The age is known by the teeth. The eye reflects the full image of a man. If he eats rice his feet will become heavy; if rat's dung, his belly will grow long; if his teeth be rubbed with dead silkworms, or black plums, he will not eat, nor if the skin of a rat or wolf be hung in his manger. He should not be allowed to eat from a hog's trough, lest he contract disease; and if a monkey is kept in the stable he will not fall sick."

The third section goes on to speak of the flesh, which is an article of food; that of a pure white stallion is the most wholesome. One author recommends "eating almonds, and taking a rush broth, if the person feel uncomfortable after a meal of horse-flesh. It should be roasted and eaten with ginger and pork; and to eat the flesh of a black horse, and not drink wine with it, will surely produce death." The fourth describes the crown of the horse, the "fat of which is sweet, and good to make the hair grow and the face to shine." The fifth and succeeding sections to the twenty-fourth treat of the sanative properties and mode of exhibiting the milk, heart, lungs, liver, kidneys, placenta, teeth, bones, skin, mane, tail, brains, blood, perspiration, and excrements.

Some of the directions are dietetic, and others are prescriptive. "When eating horse-flesh do not eat the liver," is one of the former, given because of the absence of a gall-bladder in the liver, which imports its poisonous qualities. "The heart of a white horse, or that of a hog, cow, or hen, when dried and rasped into spirit and so taken, cures forgetfulness; if the patient hears one thing he knows ten." "Above the knees the horse has *night-eycs* (warts), which enable him to go in the night; they are useful in the toothache;" these sections partake both of the descriptive and prescriptive. Another medical one is: "If a man be restless and hysterical when he wishes to sleep, and it is requisite to put him to rest, let the ashes of a skull be mingled with water and given him, and let him have a skull for a pillow, and it will cure him." The same preservative virtues appear to be ascribed to a horse's hoof hung in a house as are supposed, by some who should know better, to belong to a horseshoe when nailed upon the door.[1] The whole of this extensive work is liberally sprinkled with such whimsies, but the practice of medicine among the Chinese is vastly

[1] *Chinese Repository*, Vol. VII., p. 393.

better than their theories; for as Rémusat justly observes, "To see well and reason falsely are not wholly incompatible, and the naturalists of China, as well as the chemists and physicians of our ancient schools, have sometimes tried to reconcile them."

Another work on botany besides the *Herbal*, issued in 1848, deserves notice for its research and the excellence of its drawings. It is the *Chih Wuh Ming-shih Tu-kao*, or *Researches into the Names and Virtues of Plants*, with plates, in sixty volumes. There are one thousand seven hundred and fifteen drawings of plants, with descriptions of each, arranged in eleven books, followed by medical and agricultural observations on the most important in four books. One of its valuable points to the foreigner is the terminology furnished by the two authors for describing the parts and uses of plants. Rémusat read a paper in 1828, 'On the State of the Natural Sciences among the Orientals,' in which he indicates the position attained by Chinese in their researches into the nature and uses of objects around them. After speaking of the adaptation the language possesses, from its construction, to impart some general notions of animated and vegetable nature, he goes on to remark upon the theorizing propensities of their writers, instead of contenting themselves with examining and recording facts. "In place of studying the organization of bodies, they undertake to determine by reasoning how it should be, an aim which has not seldom led them far from the end they proposed. One of the strangest errors among them relates to the transformation of beings into each other, which has arisen from popular stories or badly conducted observations on the metamorphoses of insects. Learned absurdities have been added to puerile prejudices; that which the vulgar have believed the philosophers have attempted to explain, and nothing can be easier, according to the oriental systems of cosmogony, in which a simple matter, infinitely diversified, shows itself in all beings. Changes affect only the apparent properties of bodies, or rather the bodies themselves have only appearances; according to these principles, they are not astonished at seeing the electric fluid or even the stars converted into stones, as happens when aerolites fall. That animated beings become inanimate is proven by fossils and petrifactions. Ice enclosed in the earth for a millennium becomes rock crystal; and it is only necessary that lead, the *father* of all metals (as Saturn, its alchemistic type, was of gods), pass through four periods of two centuries each to become successively cinnabar, tin, and silver. In spring the rat changes into a quail, and quails into rats again during the eighth month.

"The style in which these marvels is related is now and then a little equivocal; but if they believe part of them proved, they can see nothing really impossible in the others. One naturalist, less credulous than his fellows, rather smiles at another author who reported the metamorphosis of an oriole into a mole, and of rice into a carp; 'it is a ridiculous story,' says he; 'there is proof only of the change of rats into quails, which is reported in the almanac, and which I have often seen myself, for there is an unvaried progression, as well of transformations as of generations.' Animals, according to the Chinese, are viviparous as quadrupeds, or oviparous as birds; they grow by transformations, as insects, or by the effect of humidity, as snails, slugs, and centipedes. . . . . . . The success of such systems is almost always sure, not in China alone either, because it is easier to put words in place of things, to stop at nothing, and to have formulas ready for solving all questions. It is thus that they have formed a scientific jargon, which one might almost think had been borrowed from our dark ages, and which has powerfully contributed to retain knowledge in China in the swaddling-clothes we now find it. Experience teaches that when the human mind is once drawn into a false way, the lapse of ages and the help of a man of genius are necessary to draw it out. Ages have not been wanting in China, but the man whose superior enlightenment might dissipate these deceitful glimmerings, would find it very difficult to exercise this happy influence as long as their political institutions attract all their inquiring minds or vigorous intellects far away from scientific researches into the literary examinations, or put before them the honors and employments which the functions and details of magisterial appointments bring with them."[1]

---

[1] *Mélanges Orientales, Posthumes*, p. 215.

This last observation indicates the reason, to a great degree, for the fixedness of the Chinese in all departments of learned inquiry; hard labor employs the energy and time of the ignorant mass, and emulation in the strife to reach official dignities consumes and perverts the talents of the learned. Then their language itself disheartens the most enthusiastic students in this branch of study, on account of its vagueness and want of established terms. When the vivifying and strengthening truths of revelation shall be taught to the Chinese, and its principles acted upon among them, we may expect more vigor in their minds and more profit in their investigations into the wonders of nature.

CHAPTER VII.

LAWS OF CHINA, AND PLAN OF ITS GOVERNMENT.

THE consideration of the theory and practice of the Chinese government recommends itself to the attention of the intelligent student of man by several peculiar reasons, among which are its acknowledged antiquity, the multitudes of people it rules, and the comparative quiet enjoyed by its subjects. The government of a heathen nation is so greatly modified by the personal character of the executive, and the people are so liable to confound institutions with men, either from imperfect acquaintance with the nature of those institutions, or from being, through necessity or habit, easily guided and swayed by designing and powerful men, that the long continuance of the Chinese polity is a proof both of its adaptation to the habits and condition of the people, and of its general good management. The antiquity and excellence of such a government, and its orderly administration, might, however, be far greater than it is in China, without being invested with the interest which at present attaches to it in that Empire in consequence of the immense population, whose lives and property, food and well-being, depend to so great a degree upon it. What was at first rather a feeling of curiosity, gradually becomes one of awe, when the evil results of misgovernment, or the beneficent effects of equitable rule, are seen to be so momentous.

The theory of the Chinese government is undoubtedly the patriarchal; the Emperor is the sire, his officers are the responsible elders of its provinces, departments, and districts, as every father of a household is of its inmates. This may, perhaps, be the theory of other governments, but nowhere has it been systematized so thoroughly, and acted upon so consistently and for so long a period, as in China. Two causes, mutually acting upon each other, have, more than anything else, combined to give efficiency to this theory. The ancient rule of Yau and Shun [1] was strictly, so far as the details are known, a patriarchal chieftainship, conferred upon them on account of their excellent character; and their successors under Yu of the Hia dynasty were considered as deriving their power from heaven, to whom they were amenable for its good use. When Chingtang, founder of the Shang dynasty, B.C. 1766, and Wu Wang, of the Chau, B.C. 1122, took up arms against the Emperors, the excuse given was that they had not fulfilled the decrees of heaven, and had thereby forfeited their claim to the throne.

Confucius, in teaching his principles of political ethics, referred to the conduct of those ancient kings both for proof of the correctness of his instructions and for arguments to enforce them. The large number of those who followed him during his lifetime furnishes some evidence that his countrymen assented to the propriety of his teachings. This may account for their reception, illustrated as they were by the high character the sage bore; but it was not till the lapse of two or three centuries that the rulers of China perceived the great security the adoption and diffusion of these doctrines would give their sway. They therefore turned their attention toward the embodiment of these precepts into laws, and toward basing the institutions of government upon them; through all the convulsions and wars which have disturbed the country and changed the reigning families, these writings have done more than any one thing else to uphold the institutions of the Chinese and give them their character and permanence. Education being founded on them, those who as students had been taught to receive and reverence them as the oracles of political wisdom, would, when they entered upon the duties of office, endeavor to carry out, in some degree at least, their principles. Thus the precept and the practice have mutually modified, supported, and enforced each other.

---

[1] 2357 and 2255 before Christ.

But this civilization is Asiatic and not European, pagan and not Christian. The institutions of China are despotic and defective, and founded on wrong principles. They may have the element of stability, but not of improvement. The patriarchal theory does not make men honorable, truthful, or kind; it does not place woman in her right position, nor teach all classes their obligations to their Maker; the wonder is, to those who know the strength of evil passions in the human breast, that this huge mass of mankind is no worse. We must, indeed, look into its structure in order to discover the causes of this stability, inasmuch as here we have neither a standing army to enforce nor the machinery of a state religion to compel obedience toward a sovereign. A short inspection will show that the great leading principles by which the present administration preserves its power over the people, consist in a system of *strict surveillance* and *mutual responsibility* among all classes. These are aided in their efficiency by the geographical isolation of the country, a remarkable spirit of loyal pride in their own history, and a general system of political education and official examinations.

These two principles are enforced by such a minute gradation of rank and subordination of offices as to give the government more of a military character than at first appears, and the whole system is such as to make it one of the most unmixed oligarchies now existing. It is like a network extending over the whole face of society, each individual being isolated in his own mesh but responsibly connected with all around him. The man who knows that it is almost impossible, except by entire seclusion, to escape from the company of secret or acknowledged emissaries of government, will be cautious of offending the laws of the country, knowing, as he must, that though he should himself escape, yet his family, his kindred, or his neighbors will suffer for his offence; that if unable to recompense the sufferers, it will probably be dangerous for him to return home; or if he does, it will be most likely to find his property in the possession of neighbors or officials, who feel conscious of security in plundering one whose offences have forever placed him under a ban.

The effect of these two causes upon the mass of the people is to imbue them with a great fear of the government, both of its officers and its operations; each man considers that safety is best to be found in keeping aloof from both. This mutual surveillance and responsibility, though only partially extended throughout the multitude, necessarily undermines confidence and infuses universal distrust; while this object of complete isolation, though at the expense of justice, truth, honesty, and natural affection, is what the government strives to accomplish and actually does to a wonderful degree. The idea of government in the minds of the uneducated people is that of some ever-present terror, like a sword of Damocles; and so far has this undefined fear of some untoward result when connected with it counteracted the real vigor of the Chinese, that to it may be referred much of their indifference to improvement, contentment with what is already known and possessed, and submission to petty injustice and spoliation.

Men are deterred, too, as much by distrust of each other as by fear of the police, from combining in an intelligent manner to resist governmental exactions because opposed to principles of equity, or joining with their rulers to uphold good order; no such men, and no such instances, as John Hampden going to prison for refusing to subscribe to a forced loan, or Thomas Williams and his companions throwing the tea overboard in Boston harbor, ever occurred in China or any other Asiatic country. They dread illegal societies quite as much from the cruelties this same distrust induces the leaders to exercise over recreant or suspected members, as from apprehensien of arrest and punishment by the regular authorities. Thus, with a state of society at times on the verge of insurrection, this mass of people is kept in check by the threefold cord of responsibility, fear, and isolation, each of them strengthening the other, and all depending upon the character of the people for much of their efficiency. Since all the officers of government received their intellectual training when commoners under these influences, it is easy to understand why the supreme powers are so averse to improvement and to foreign intercourse—from both of which causes, in truth, the monarch has the greatest reason to dread lest the charm of his power be weakened and his sceptre pass away.

There is, however, a further explanation for the general peace which prevails to be found back of this. It is owing partly to the diffusion of a political education among the people —teaching them the principles on which all government is founded, and the reasons for those principles flowing from the patriarchal theory—and partly to their plodding, industrious character. A brief exposition of the construction and divisions of the central and provincial governments and their mutual relations, and the various duties devolving upon the departments and officers, will exhibit more of the operation of these principles.

Although the Emperor is regarded as the head of this great organization, as the fly-wheel which sets other wheels of the machine in motion, he is still considered as bound to rule according to the code of the land; and when there is a well-known law, though the source of law, he is expected to follow it in his decrees. The statutes of China form an edifice, the foundations of which were laid by Lí Kwei twenty centuries ago. Successive dynasties have been building thereon ever since, adding, altering, pulling down, and putting together as circumstances seemed to require. The people have a high regard for the code, "and all they seem to desire is its just and impartial execution, independent of caprice and uninfluenced by corruption. That the laws of China are, on the contrary, very frequently violated by those who are their administrators and constitutional guardians, there can, unfortunately, be no question; but to what extent, comparatively with the laws of other countries, must at present be very much a matter of conjecture: at the same time it may be observed, as something in favor of the Chinese system, that there are substantial grounds for believing that neither flagrant nor repeated acts of injustice do, in point of fact, often, in any rank or station, ultimately escape with impunity."[1] Sir George Staunton is well qualified to speak on this point, and his opinion has been corroborated

[1] *Penal Code*, Introduction, p. xxviii.

by most of those who have had similar opportunities of judging; while his translation of the *Code* has given all persons interested in the question the means of ascertaining the principles on which the government ostensibly acts.

This body of laws is called *Ta Tsing Liuh Lí*, *i.e.*, 'Statutes and Rescripts of the Great Pure Dynasty,' and contains all the laws of the Empire. They are arranged under seven leading heads, viz.: General, Civil, Fiscal, Ritual, Military, and Criminal laws, and those relating to Public Works; and subdivided into four hundred and thirty-six sections, called *liuh*, or 'statutes,' to which the *lí*, or modern clauses, to limit, explain or alter them, are added; these are now much more numerous than the original statutes. A new edition is published by authority every five years; in the reprint of 1830 the Emperor ordered that the Supreme Court should make but few alterations, lest wily litigants might take advantage of the discrepancies between the new and old law to suit their own purposes. This edition is in twenty-eight volumes, and is one of the most frequently seen books in the shops of any city. The clauses are attached to each statute, and have the same force. No authorized reports of cases and decisions, either of the provincial or supreme courts, are published for general use, though their record is kept in the court where they are decided; the publication of such adjudged cases, as a guide to officers, is not unknown. An extensive collection of notes, comments, and cases, illustrating the practice and theory of the laws, was appended to the edition of 1799.

A short extract from the original preface of the *Code*, published in 1647, only three years after the Manchu Emperors took the throne, will explain the principles on which it was drawn up. After remarking upon the inconveniences arising from the necessity of aggravating or mitigating the sentences of the magistrates, who, previous to the re-establishment of an authentic code of penal laws, were not in possession of any fixed rules upon which they could build a just decision, the Emperor Shunchí goes on to describe the manner of revising the code:

"A numerous body of magistrates was assembled at the capital, at our command, for the purpose of revising the penal code formerly in force under the late dynasty of Ming, and of digesting the same into a new code, by the exclusion of such parts as were exceptionable and the introduction of others which were likely to contribute to the attainment of justice and the general perfection of the work. The result of their labors having been submitted to our examination, we maturely weighed and considered the various matters it contained, and then instructed a select number of our great officers of state carefully to revise the whole, for the purpose of making such alterations and emendations as might still be found requisite. Wherefore, it being now published, let it be your great care, officers and magistrates of the interior and exterior departments of our Empire, diligently to observe the same, and to forbear in future to give any decision, or to pass any sentence, according to your private sentiments, or upon your unsupported authority. Thus shall the magistrates and people look up with awe and submission to the justice of these institutions, as they find themselves respectively concerned in them; the transgressor will not fail to suffer a strict expiation of his crimes, and will be the instrument of deterring others from similar misconduct; and finally both officers and people will be equally secured for endless generations in the enjoyment of the happy effects of the great and noble virtues of our illustrious progenitors."

Under the head of General Laws are forty-seven sections, comprising principles and definitions applicable to the whole, and containing some singular notions on equity and criminality. The description of the five ordinary punishments, definition of the ten treasonable offences, regulations for the eight privileged classes, and general directions regarding the conduct of officers of government, are the matters treated of under this head. The title of Section XLIV. is "On the decision of cases not provided for by law;" and the rule is that "such cases may then be determined by an accurate comparison with others which are already provided for, and which approach most nearly to those under investigation, in order to ascertain afterward to what extent an aggravation or mitigation of the punishment would be equitable. A provisional sentence conformable thereto shall be laid before the superior magistrates, and, after receiving their approbation, be submitted to the Emperor's final decision. Any erroneous judgment which may be pronounced, in consequence of adopting a more summary mode of proceeding in cases of a doubtful nature, shall be punished as wilful deviation from justice." This, of course, gives great latitude to the magistrate, and as he is thus allowed to decide and act before the new law can be confirmed or annulled, the chief restraints to his injustice in such cases (which, however, are not numerous) lie in the fear of an appeal and its consequences, or of summary reprisals from the suffering parties.

The six remaining divisions pertain to the six administrative boards of the government. The second contains Civil Laws, under twenty-eight sections, divided into two books, one of them referring to the system of government, and the other to the conduct of magistrates, etc. The hereditary succession of rank and titles is regulated, and punishments laid down for those who illegally assume these honors. Most of the nobility of China are Manchus, and none of the hereditary dignities existing previous to the conquest were recognized, except those attached to the family of Confucius. Improperly recommending unfit persons as deserving high honors, appointing and removing officers without the Emperor's sanction, and leaving stations without due permission, are the principal subjects regulated in the first book. The second book contains rules regarding the interference of superior magistrates with the proceedings of the lower courts, and prohibitions against cabals and treasonable combinations among officers, which are of course capital crimes; all persons in the employ of the state are required to make themselves acquainted with the laws, and even private individuals "who are found capable of explaining the nature and comprehending the objects of the laws, shall receive pardon in all offences resulting purely from accident, or imputable to them only from the guilt of others, provided it be the first offence."

The third division, of Fiscal Laws, under eighty-two sections, contains rules for enrolling the people, and of succession and inheritance; also laws for regulating marriages between various classes of society, for guarding granaries and treasuries, for preventing and punishing smuggling, for restraining usury, and for overseeing shops. Section LXXVI. orders that persons and families truly represent their profession in life, and restrains them from indulging in a change of occupation; "generation after generation they must not vary or alter it." This rule is, however, constantly violated. Section XC. exempts the buildings of literary and religious institutions from taxation. The general aim of the laws relating to holding real estate is to secure the cultivation of all the land taken up, and the regular payment of the tax. The proprietor, in some cases, can be deprived of his lands because he does not till them, and though in fact owner in fee simple, he is restricted in the disposition of them by will in many ways, and forfeits them if the taxes are not paid.

The fourth division, of Ritual Laws, under twenty-six sections, contains the regulations for state sacrifices and ceremonies, those appertaining to the worship of ancestors, and whatever belongs to heterodox and magical sects or teachers. The heavy penalties threatened in some of these sections against all illegal combinations under the guise of a new form of worship presents an interesting likeness to the restrictions issued by the English, French, and German princes during and after the Reformation. The Chinese authorities had the same dread lest the people should meet and consult how to resist them. Even processions in honor of the gods may be forbidden for good reason, and are not allowed at all at Peking; while, still more, the rites observed by the Emperor cannot be imitated by any unauthorized person; women are not allowed to congregate in the temples, nor magicians to perform any strange incantations. Few of these laws are really necessary, and those against illegal sects are in fact levelled against political associations, which usually take on a religious guise.

The fifth division, of Military Laws, in seventy-one sections, provides for the protection of the palace and government of the army, for guarding frontier passes, management of the imperial cattle, and forwarding despatches by couriers. Some of these ordinances lay down rules for the protection of the Emperor's person, and the disposition of his body-guard and troops in the palace, the capital, and over the Empire. The sections relating to the government of the army include the rules for the police of cities; and those designed to secure the protection of the frontier comprise all the enactments against foreign intercourse, some of which have already been referred to in passing. The supply of horses and cattle for the army is a matter of some importance, and is minutely regulated; one law orders all persons who possess vicious and dangerous animals to restrain them, and if through neglect any person is killed or wounded, the owner of the animal shall be obliged to redeem himself from the punishment of manslaughter by paying a fine. This provision to compel the owners of unruly beasts to exercise proper restraint over them is like that laid down by Moses in Exodus XXI., 29, 30. There is as yet no general post-office establishment, but governmental couriers often take private letters; local mails are safely carried by express companies. The required rate of travel for the official post is one hundred miles a day, but it does not ordinarily go more than half that distance. Officers of government are allowed ninety days to make the journey from Peking to Canton, a distance of twelve hundred miles, but couriers frequently travel it in twelve days.

The sixth division, on Criminal Laws, is arranged in eleven books, containing in all one hundred and seventy sections, and is the most important of the whole. The clauses under some of the sections are numerous, and show that it is not for want of proper laws or insufficient threatenings that crimes go unpunished. The books of this division relate to robbery, in which is included high treason and renunciation of allegiance; to homicide and murder; quarrelling and fighting; abusive language; indictments, disobedience to parents, and false accusations; bribery and corruption; forging and frauds; incest and adultery; arrests and escapes of criminals, their imprisonment and execution; and, lastly, miscellaneous offences.

Under Section CCCXXIX. it is ordered that any one who is guilty of addressing abusive language to his or her father or mother, or father's parents, or a wife who rails at her husband's parents or grandparents, shall be strangled; provided always that the persons so abused themselves complain to the magistrate, and had personally heard the language addressed to them. This law is the same in regard to children as that contained in Leviticus XX., 9, and the power here given the parent does not seem to be productive of evil. Section CCCLXXXI. has reference to "privately hushing up public crimes," but its penalties are for the most part a dead letter, and a full account of the various modes adopted in the courts of withdrawing cases from the cognizance of superiors, would form a singular chapter in Chinese jurisprudence. Consequently those who refuse every offer to suppress cases are highly lauded by the people. Another section (CCCLXXXVI.) ordains that whoever is guilty of improper conduct, contrary to the spirit of the laws, but not a breach of any specific article, shall be punished at least with forty blows, and with eighty when of a serious nature. Some of the provisions of this part of the code are praiseworthy, but no part of Chinese legislation is so cruel and irregular as criminal jurisprudence. The permission accorded to the judge to torture the criminal opens the door for much inhumanity.

The seventh division contains thirteen sections relating to Public Works and Ways, such as the weaving of interdicted patterns of silk, repairing dikes, and constructing edifices for government. All public residences, granaries, treasuries and manufactories, embankments and dikes of rivers and canals, forts, walls, and mausolea, must be frequently examined, and kept in repair. Poverty or peculation render many of these laws void, and many subterfuges are often practised by the superintending officer to pocket as much of the funds as he can. One officer, when ordered to repair a wall, made the workmen go over it and chip off the faces of the stones still remaining, then plastering up the holes.

Besides these laws and their numerous clauses, every high provincial officer has the right to issue edicts upon such public matters as require regulation, some of them even affecting life and death, either reviving some old law or giving it an application to the case before him, with such modifications as seem to be necessary. He must report these acts to the proper board at Peking. No such order, which for the time has the force of law, is formally repealed, but gradually falls into oblivion, until circumstances again require its reiteration. This mode of publishing statutes gives rise to a sort of common and unwritten law in villages, to which a council of elders sometimes compels individuals to submit; long usage is also another ground for enforcing them.

Still, with all the tortures and punishments allowed by the law, and all the cruelties superadded upon the criminals by irritated officers or rapacious underlings and jailors, a broad survey of Chinese legislation, judged by its results and the general appearance of society, gives the impression of an administration far superior to other Asiatic countries. A favorable comparison has been made in the *Edinburgh Review:*[1] "By far the most remarkable thing in this code is its great reasonableness, clearness, and consistency, the business-like brevity and directness of the various provisions, and the plainness and moderation in which they are expressed. There is nothing here of the monstrous *verbiage* of most other Asiatic productions, none of the superstitious deliration, the miserable incoherence, the tremendous *non-sequiturs* and eternal repetitions of those oracular performances—nothing even of the turgid adulation, accumulated epithets, and fatiguing self-praise of other Eastern despotisms—but a calm, concise, and distinct series of enactments, savoring throughout of practical judgment and European good sense, and if not always conformable to our improved notions of expediency, in general approaching to them more nearly than the codes of most other nations. When we pass, indeed, from the ravings of the Zendavesta or the Puranas to the tone of sense and business in this Chinese collection, we seem to be passing from darkness to light, from the drivellings of dotage to the exercise of an improved understanding; and redundant and absurdly minute as these laws are in many particulars, we scarcely know any European code that is at once so copious and so consistent, or that is so nearly free from intricacy, bigotry, and fiction. In everything relating to political freedom or individual independence it is indeed wofully defective; but for the repression of disorder and the gentle coer-

[1] Vol. XVI., 1810.

cion of a vast population, it appears to be equally mild and efficacious. The state of society for which it was formed appears incidentally to be a low and wretched one; but how could its framers have devised a wiser means of maintaining it in peace and tranquillity?"

This encomium is to a certain extent just, but the practice of legislation in China has probably not been materially improved by the mere possession of a reasonable code of laws, though some melioration in jurisprudence has been effected.[1] The infliction of barbarous punishments, such as blinding, cutting off noses, ears, or other parts of the body, still not uncommon in Persia and Turkey, is not allowed or practised in China; and the government, in minor crimes, contents itself with but little more than opprobrious exposure in the pillory, or castigation, which carry with them no degradation.

The defects in this remarkable body of laws arise from several sources. The degree of liberty that can safely be awarded to the subject is not defined in it, and his rights are unknown in law. The government is despotic, but having no efficient military power in their hands, the lawgivers resort to a minuteness of legislation upon the practice of social and relative virtues and duties which interferes with their observance; though it must be remembered that no pulpit or Sabbath-school exists there to expound and enforce them from a higher code, and the laws must be the chief guide in most cases. The code also exhibits a minute attention to trifles, and an effort to legislate for every possible contingency, which must perplex the judge when dealing with the infinite shades of difference occurring in human actions. There are now many vague and obsolete statutes, ready to serve as a handle to prosecute offenders for the gratification of private pique; and although usage and precedent both combine to prove their disuse, malice and bribery can easily effect their reviviscence and application to the case.

Sheer cruelty, except in cases of treason against the Emperor, cannot be charged against this code as a whole, though many of the laws seem designed to operate chiefly *in terrorem*,

---

[1] *Chinese Repository*, Vol. IV., pp. 24–29.

and the penalty is placed higher than the punishment really intended to be inflicted, to the end that the Emperor may have scope for mercy, or, as he says, "for leniency beyond the bounds of the law." The principle on which this is done is evident, and the commonness of the practice proves that such an exercise of mercy has its effect. The laws of China are not altogether unmeaning words, though the degree of efficiency in their execution is subject to endless variations; some officers are clement, others severe; the people in certain provinces are industrious and peaceable, in others turbulent and averse to quiet occupations, so that one is likely to form a juster idea of their administration by looking at the results as seen in the general aspect of society, and judging of the tree by its fruits, than by drawing inferences applicable to the whole machine of state from particular instances of oppression and insubordination, as has been so often the case with travellers and writers.

The general examination of the Chinese government here proposed may be conveniently considered under the heads of the Emperor and his court, classes of society, the different branches of the supreme administration, the provincial authorities, and the execution of the laws.

The Emperor is at the head of the whole; and if the possession of great power, and being the object of almost unbounded reverence, can impart happiness, he may safely be considered as the happiest mortal living; though to his power there are many checks, and the reverence paid him is proportioned somewhat to the fidelity with which he administers the decrees of heaven. "The Emperor is the sole head of the Chinese constitution and government; he is regarded as the vice-gerent of heaven, especially chosen to govern all nations; and is supreme in everything, holding at once the highest legislative and executive powers, without limit or control." Both he and the Pope claim to be the vice-gerent of heaven and interpreter of its decrees to the whole world, and these two rulers have emulated each other in their assumption of arrogant titles. The most common appellation employed to denote the Emperor in state papers and among the people is *hwangtí*, or 'august sovereign;' it is defined as "the appellation of one possessing complete virtues, and able to act on heavenly principles."[1] This title is further defined as meaning heaven: "Heaven speaks not, yet the four seasons follow in regular succession, and all things spring forth. So the three august ones (Fuhhí, Shinnung, and Hwangtí) descended in state, and without even uttering a word the people bowed to their sway; their virtue was inscrutable and boundless like august heaven, and therefore were they called *august* ones."

Among the numerous titles given the monarch may be mentioned *hwang shang*, the 'august lofty one;' *tien hwang*, 'celestial august one;' *shing hwang*, the 'wise and august,' *i.e.*, infinite in knowledge and complete in virtue; *tien tí*, 'celestial sovereign;' and *shing tí*, 'sacred sovereign,' because he is able to act on heavenly principles. He is also called *tien tsz'*, 'son of heaven,' because heaven is his father and earth is his mother, and *shing tien tsz'*, 'wise son of heaven,' as being born of heaven and having infinite knowledge; terms which are given him as the ruler of the world by the gift of heaven. He is even addressed, and sometimes refers to himself, under designations which pertain exclusively to heaven. *Wan sui yé*, 'sire of ten thousand years,' is a term used when speaking of him or approaching him, like the words, *O king, live forever!* addressed to the ancient kings of Persia. *Pí hia*, 'beneath the footstool,' is a sycophantic compellation used by his courtiers, as if they were only worthy of being at the edge of his footstool.

The Emperor usually designates himself by the terms *chin*, 'ourself;' *kwa jin*, the 'solitary man,' or the one man; and *kwa kiun*, the 'solitary prince.' He has been loaded with many ridiculous titles by foreign writers, as Brother of the Sun and Moon, Grandson of the Stars, King of Kings, etc., but no such epithets are known among his subjects. His palace has various appellations, such as hall of audience, golden palace, the ninth entrance, vermilion avenue, vermilion hall, rosy hall, forbidden pavilion, the crimson and forbidden palace, gemmeous steps, golden steps, meridian portal, gemmeous avenue, celestial steps,

---

[1] *Chinese Repository*, Vol. IV., p. 12; *Chinese Chrestomathy*, p. 558.

celestial court, great interior, the maple pavilion, royal house, etc. To see him is to see the dragon's face; the throne is called the "dragon's throne," and also the "divine utensil," *i.e.*, the thing given him by heaven to sit in when executing his divine mission; his person is styled the dragon's body, and a five-clawed dragon is emblazoned, like a coat of arms, on his robes, which no one can use or imitate. Thus the Old Dragon, it might be almost said, has coiled himself around the Emperor of China, one of the greatest upholders of his power in this world, and contrived to get himself worshipped, through him, by one-third of mankind.

The Emperor is the fountain of power, rank, honor, and privilege to all within his dominions, which are termed *tien hia*, meaning all under heaven, and were till recently, even by his highest officers, ignorantly supposed to comprise all mankind. As there can be but one sun in the heavens, so there can be but one *hwangti* on earth, the source and dispenser of benefits to the whole world.[1] The same absolute executive power held by him is placed in the hands of his deputies and governor-generals, to be by them exercised within the limits of their jurisdiction. He is the head of religion and the only one qualified to adore heaven; he is the source of law and dispenser of mercy; no right can be held in opposition to his pleasure, no claim maintained against him, no privilege protect from his wrath. All the forces and revenues of the Empire are his, and he has a right to claim the services of all males between sixteen and sixty. In short, the whole Empire is his property, and the only checks upon his despotism are public opinion, the want of an efficient standing army, poverty and the venality of the agents of his power.

When the Manchus found themselves in possession of Peking, they regarded this position as fully entitling them to assume all imperial rights. Their sovereign thus announced his elevation in November, 1644: "I, the Son of Heaven, of the Ta-tsing

---

[1] The attributes ascribed to a *chakrawartti* in the Buddhist mythology have many points of resemblance to the *hwangti*, and Hardy's *Manual of Buddhism* (p. 126) furnishes an instructive comparison between the two characters, one fanciful and the other real.

dynasty, humbly as a subject dare to announce to Imperial Heaven and Sovereign Earth. Though the world is vast, Shangtí looks on all without partiality. My Imperial Grandfather received the gracious decree of Heaven and founded a kingdom in the East, which became firmly established. My Imperial Father succeeding to the kingdom, extended it; and I, Heaven's servant, in my poor person became the inheritor of the dominion they transmitted. When the Ming dynasty was coming to its end, traitors and men of violence appeared in crowds, involving the people in misery. China was without a ruler. It fell to me reverentially to accept the responsibility of continuing the meritorious work of my ancestors. I saved the people, destroyed their oppressors; and now, in accordance with the desires of all, I fix the urns of Empire at Yen-king. . . . I, receiving Heaven's favor, and in accordance with their wishes, announce to Heaven that I have ascended the throne of the Empire, that the name I have chosen for it is the Great Pure, and that the style of my reign is *Shun-chi* ('Obedient Rule'). I beg reverentially Heaven and Earth to protect and assist the Empire, so that calamity and disturbance may soon come to an end, and the land enjoy universal peace. For this I humbly pray, and for the acceptance of this sacrifice."

The present Emperor is the ninth of the Tsing dynasty who has reigned in China. *Tsing* means Pure, and was taken by the Manchus as a distinctive term for their new dynasty, alluding to the purity of justice they intended to maintain in their sway. Some of the founders of the ancient dynasties derived their dynastic name from their patrimonial estates, as *Sung*, *Han*, *Chau*, etc., but the later ones have adopted names like *Yuen*, or 'Original,' *Ming*, or 'Illustrious,' etc., which indicate their vanity.

The present monarch is still a minor, and the affairs of government are nominally under the direction of the Empress-dowager, who held the same office during the minority of his predecessor, Tungchí. The surname of the reigning family is *Gioro*, or 'Golden,' derived from their ancestral chief, Aisin Gioro, whom they feign to have been the son of a divine virgin. They are the lineal descendants of the Kin, a rude race which drove out the Chinese rulers and occupied the northern provinces about 1130, making Peking their capital for many years. On the approach of the Mongols they were chased away to the east, and retained only a nominal independence; changing their name from Nüchih to Manjurs, they gradually increased in numbers, but did not assume any real importance until they became masters of China. The acknowledged founder of the reigning house was the chief Hien-tsu (1583–1615), whose actual descendants are collectively designated *Tsung-shih*, or 'Imperial Clan.' The second Emperor further limited the Clan by giving to each of his twenty-four sons a personal name of two characters, the first of which, Yun, was the same for all of them. For the succeeding generations he ordered a series of characters to be used by all the members of each, so that through all their ramifications the first name would show their position. Kanghí's own name was *Hiuen*, then followed *Yun*, *Hung*, *Yung*, *Mien*, *Yih*, and *Tsai*, the last and present sovereigns being both named *Tsai*. All who bear this name are direct descendants of Kanghí. Since the application of these seven generation names, eight more have been selected for future use by imperial scions.

In order still further to distinguish those most nearly allied in blood, as sons, nephews, etc., it is required that the second names of each family always consist of characters under the same radical. Thus Kiaking and his brothers wrote their first names *Yung*, and under the radical *gun* for the second; Taukwang and his brothers and cousins *Mien*, and under the radical *heart*. For some unexplained reason the radicals *silk* and *gold*, chosen for the second names of the next two generations, were altered to *words* and *water*. This peculiarity is easily represented in the Chinese characters; a comparison can be made in English with the supposed names of a family of sons, as Louis Edward, Louis Edwin, Louis Edwy, Louis Edgar, etc., the word *Louis* answering to *Mien*, and the syllable *Ed* to the radical *heart*.

The present Emperor's personal name is Tsai-tien, and, like those of his predecessors, is deemed to be too sacred to be spoken, or the characters to be written in the common form

The same reverence is observed for the names after death, so that twelve characters have been altered since the Manchu monarchs began to reign; Hiuen-wa, which was the personal name of Kanghí, has become permanently altered in its formation. The present sovereign was born August 15, 1871, and on January 12, 1875, succeeded his cousin Tsaishun, who died without issue—the first instance in the Gioro family for nearly three centuries. At this time there was some delay as to which of his cousins should succeed to the dragon throne, when the united council of the princes was led by the mother of the deceased Emperor to adopt her nephew, the son of Prince Chun. The little fellow was sent for at night to be immediately saluted as *hwangtí*, and ere long brought in before them, cross and sleepy as he was, to begin his reign under the style of Kwangsü, or 'Illustrious Succession.'

This title is called a *kwoh hao*, or national designation, and answers more nearly to the name that a new Pope takes with the tiara than to anything else in western lands. It is the expression of the idea which the monarch wishes to associate with his reign, and is the name by which he is known to his subjects during his life. It has been called a *period* by some writers, but while it is not strictly his name, yet period is not so correct as *reign*. Usage has made it equivalent in foreign books to the personal name, and it is plainer to say the Emperor Taukwang than the period Taukwang or the reign Taukwang, or still more than to write, as Wade has done, "the Emperor Mien-Ning, the style of whose reign was Tau Kwang;" or than Legge has done, to say, "the Emperor Pattern, of the period Yungching." In such cases it is not worth the trouble to attempt strict accuracy in a matter so entirely unlike western usages.

The use of the *kwoh hao* began with Wăn-tí, of the Han dynasty,[1] B.C. 179, and has continued ever since. Some of

[1] The remark of Heeren (*Asiatic Nations*, Vol. I., p. 57), that the names by which the early Persian monarchs, Darius, Xerxes, and others, were called, were really titles or surnames, and not their own personal names, suggests the further comparison whether those renowned names were not like the *kwoh hao* of the Chinese emperors, whose adoption of the custom was after the ex-

the early monarchs changed their *kwoh hao* many times during their reigns; Kao-tsung (A.D. 650–684), for example, had thirteen in a régime of thirty-four years, which induced historians to employ the *miao hao*, or ancestral name, as more suitable and less liable to confusion. The reason for thus investing the sovereign with a title different from his real name is not fully apparent, but arose probably out of the vanity of the monarch, who wished thus to glorify himself by a high-sounding title, and make his own name somewhat ineffable at the same time. The custom was adopted in Japan about A.D. 645, and is practised in Corea and Annam.

When a monarch ascends the throne, or as it is expressed in Chinese, "when he receives from Heaven and revolving nature the government of the world," he issues an inaugural proclamation. There is not much change in the wording of these papers, and an extract from the one issued in 1821 will exhibit the practice on such occasions:

"Our Ta Tsing dynasty has received the most substantial indication of Heaven's kind care. Our ancestors, Taitsu and Taitsung, began to lay the vast foundation [of our Empire]; and Shítsu became the sole monarch of China. Our sacred ancestor Kanghí, the Emperor Yungching, the glory of his age, and Kienlung, the eminent in honor, all abounded in virtue, were divine in martial prowess, consolidated the glory of the Empire, and moulded the whole to peaceful harmony.

"His late Majesty, who has now gone the great journey, governed all under Heaven's canopy twenty-five years, exercising the utmost caution and industry. Nor evening nor morning was he ever idle. He assiduously aimed at the best possible rule, and hence his government was excellent and illustrious the court and the country felt the deepest reverence and the stillness of profound awe. A benevolent heart and a benevolent

tinction of the Persian monarchy. Herodotus (Book VI., 98) seems to have been familiar with these names, not so much as being arbitrary and meaningless terms as epithets whose significations were associated with the kings. The new names given to the last two sons of Josiah, who became kings of Judah by their conquerors (2 Kings, 23: 34, and 24: 17), indicate even an earlier adoption of this custom.

administration were universally diffused: in China Proper, as well as beyond it, order and tranquillity prevailed, and the tens of thousands of common people were all happy. But in the midst of a hope that this glorious reign would be long protracted, and the help of Heaven would be received many days, unexpectedly, on descending to bless, by his Majesty's presence, Lwanyang, the dragon charioteer (the holy Emperor) became a guest on high.

"My sacred and indulgent Father had, in the year that he began to rule alone, silently settled that the divine utensil should devolve on my contemptible person. I, knowing the feebleness of my virtue, at first felt much afraid I should not be competent to the office; but on reflecting that the sages, my ancestors, have left to posterity their plans; that his late Majesty has laid the duty on me—and Heaven's throne should not be long vacant—I have done violence to my feelings and forced myself to intermit awhile my heartfelt grief, that I may with reverence obey the unalterable decree; and on the 27th of the 8th moon (October 3d) I purpose devoutly to announce the event to Heaven, to earth, to my ancestors, and to the gods of the land and of the grain, and shall then sit down on the imperial throne. Let the next year be the first of Taukwang.

"I look upward and hope to be able to continue former excellences. I lay my hand on my heart with feelings of respect and cautious awe.—When a new monarch addresses himself to the Empire, he ought to confer benefits on his kindred, and extensively bestow gracious favors: what is proper to be done on this occasion is stated below."

(Here follow twenty-two paragraphs, detailing the gifts to be conferred and promotions made of noblemen and officers; ordering the restoration of suspended dignitaries to their full pay and honors, and sacrifices to Confucius and the Emperors of former dynasties; pardons to be extended to criminals, and banished convicts recalled; governmental debts and arrearages to be forgiven, and donations to be bestowed upon the aged.)

"Lo! now, on succeeding to the throne, I shall exercise myself to give repose to the millions of my people. Assist me to sustain the burden laid on my shoulders! With veneration I receive charge of Heaven's great concerns.—Ye kings and statesmen, great and small, civil and military, let every one be faithful and devoted, and aid in supporting the vast affairs, that our family dominion may be preserved hundreds and tens of thousands of years in never-ending tranquillity and glory! Promulgate this to all under Heaven—cause every one to hear it!"

The programme of ceremonies to be observed when the Emperor "ascends the summit," and seats himself on the dragon's throne, was published for the Emperor Taukwang by the Board of Rites a few days after. It details a long series of prostrations and bowings, leading out and marshalling the various officers of the court and members of the imperial family. After they are all arranged in proper precedence before the throne, "at the appointed hour the president of the Board of Rites shall go and entreat his Majesty to put on his mourning, and come forth by the gate of the eastern palace, and enter at the left door of the middle palace, where his Majesty, before the altar of his deceased imperial father, will respectfully announce that he receives the decree—kneel thrice and bow nine times."

He then retires, and soon after a large deputation of palace officers "go and solicit his Majesty to put on his imperial robes and proceed to the palace of his mother, the Empress-dowager, to pay his respects. The Empress-dowager will put on her court robes and ascend her throne, before which his Majesty shall kneel thrice and bow nine times." After this filial ceremony is over the golden chariot is made ready, the officer of the Astronomical Board—whose business is to *observe times*—is stationed at the palace gate, and when he announces the arrival of the chosen and felicitous moment, his Majesty comes forth and mounts the golden chariot, and the procession advances to the Palace of Protection and Peace. Here the great officers of the Empire are marshalled according to their rank, and when the Emperor sits down in the palace they all kneel and bow nine times.

"This ceremony over, the President of the Board of Rites, stepping forward, shall kneel down and beseech his Majesty, saying, 'Ascend the imperial throne.' The Emperor shall then rise from his seat, and the procession moving on in the same order to the Palace of Peace, his Majesty shall ascend the seat of gems and sit down on the imperial throne, with his face to the south." All present come forward and again make the nine prostrations, after which the proclamation of coronation, as it would be called in Europe, is formally sealed, and then announced to the Empire with similar ceremonies. There are many other lesser rites observed on these occasions, some of them appropriate to such an occasion, and others, according to our notions, bordering on the ludicrous; the whole presenting a strange mixture of religion, splendor, and farce, though as a whole calculated to impress all with a sentiment of awe toward one who gives to heaven, and receives from man, such homage and worship.[1]

Nothing is omitted which can add to the dignity and sacredness of the Emperor's person or character. Almost everything used by him, or in his personal service, is tabued to the common people, and distinguished by some peculiar mark or color, so as to keep up the impression of awe with which he is regarded, and which is so powerful an auxiliary to his throne. The outer gate of the palace must always be passed on foot, and the paved entrance walk leading up to it can only be used by him. The vacant throne, or even a screen of yellow silk thrown over a chair, is worshipped equally with his actual presence, and an imperial dispatch is received in the provinces with incense and prostrations; the vessels on the canal bearing articles for his special use always have the right of way. His birthday is celebrated by his officers, and the account of the opening ceremony, as witnessed by Lord Macartney, shows how skilfully every act tends to maintain his assumed character as the son of heaven.

"The first day was consecrated to the purpose of rendering a solemn, sacred, and devout homage to the supreme majesty of the Emperor. The ceremony was no longer performed in a tent, nor did it partake of the nature of a banquet. The princes,

---

[1] *Chinese Repository*, Vol. X., pp. 87–98. *Indo-Chinese Gleaner*, February, 1821.

tributaries, ambassadors, and great officers of state were assembled in a vast hall; and upon particular notice were introduced into an inner building, bearing at least the semblance of a temple. It was chiefly furnished with great instruments of music, among which were sets of cylindrical bells suspended in a line from ornamental frames of wood, and gradually diminishing in size from one extremity to the other, and also triangular pieces of metal, arranged in the same order as the bells. To the sound of these instruments a slow and solemn hymn was sung by eunuchs, who had such a command over their voices as to resemble the effect of musical glasses at a distance. The performers were directed, in the gliding from one tone to the other, by the striking of a shrill and sonorous cymbal; and the judges of music among the gentlemen of the embassy were much pleased with their execution. The whole had, indeed, a grand effect. During the performance, and at particular signals, nine times repeated, all present prostrated themselves nine times, except the ambassador and his suite, who made a profound obeisance. But he whom it was meant to honor continued, as if in imitation of the Deity, invisible the whole time. The awful impression intended to be made upon the minds of men by this apparent worship of a fellow-mortal was not to be effaced by any immediate scenes of sport or gaiety, which were postponed to the following day."[1] The mass of the people are not admitted to participate in these ceremonies; they are kept at a distance, and care, in fact, very little about them. In every provincial capital there is a hall, called *Wan-shao kung*, dedicated solely to the honor of the Emperor, and where, three days before and after his birthday, all the civil and military officers and the most distinguished citizens assemble to do him the same homage as if he were present. The walls and furniture are yellow.

The right of succession is hereditary in the male line, but it is always in the power of the sovereign to nominate his successor from among his own children. The heir-apparent is not commonly known during the lifetime of the incumbent, though

[1] Staunton's *Embassy*, 8vo edition, London, 1797, Vol. III., p. 63.

there is a titular office of guardian of the heir-apparent. During the Tsing dynasty the succession has varied, but the bloody scenes enacted in Turkey, Egypt, and India to remove competitors are not known at Peking, and the people have no fear that they will be enacted. Of the eight preceding sovereigns, Shunchí was the ninth son, Kanghí the third, Yungching the fourth, Kienlung the fourth, Kiaking the fifteenth, Taukwang the second, Hienfung the fourth, and Tungchí the only son. When Kwangsü was chosen this regular line failed, and thus was terminated an unbroken succession during two hundred and fifty-nine years (1616 to 1875), when ten rulers (including two in Manchuria) occupied the throne. It can be paralleled only in Judah, where the line of David down to Jehoiachin (B.C. 1055 to 599) continued regularly in the same manner—twenty kings in four hundred and fifty-six years.

In the reign of Kienlung, one of the censors memorialized him upon the desirableness of announcing his sucsessor, in order to quiet men's minds and repress intrigue, but the suggestion cost the man his place. The Emperor said that the name of his successor, in case of his own sudden death, would be found in a designated place, and that it was highly inexpedient to mention him, lest intriguing men buzzed about him, forming factions and trying to elevate themselves. The soundness of this policy cannot be doubted, and it is not unlikely that Kienlung knew the evils of an opposite course from an acquaintance with the history of some of the princes of Central Asia or India. One good result of not indicating the heir-apparent is that not only are no intrigues formed by the crown-prince, but when he begins to reign he is seldom compelled, from fear of his own safety, to kill or imprison his brothers or uncles; for, as they possess no power or party to render them formidable, their ambition finds full scope for its exercise in peaceful ways. In 1861, when the heir was a child of five years, a palace intrigue was started to remove his custody out of the hands of his mother into those of a cabal who had held sway for some years, but the promoters were all executed.

The management of the imperial clan appertains entirely to the Emperor, and has been conducted with considerable sagacity. All its members are under the control of the *Tsung-jin fu*, a sort of clansmen's court, consisting of a presiding controller, two assistant directors, and two deputies of the family. Their duties are to regulate whatever belongs to the government of the Emperor's kindred, which is divided into two branches, the direct and collateral, or the *tsung-shih* and *Gioro*. The *Tsung-shih*, or 'Imperial House,' comprise only the lineal descendants of Tienming's father, named Hien-tsu, or 'Illustrious Sire,' who first assumed the title of Emperor A.D. 1616. The collateral branches, including the children of his uncles and brothers, are collectively called Gioro. Their united number is unknown, but a genealogical record is kept in the national archives at Peking and Mukden. The *Tsung-shih* are distinguished by a yellow girdle, and the *Gioro* by a red one; when degraded, the former take a red, the latter a carnation girdle. There are altogether twelve degrees of rank in the *Tsung-shih*, and consequently some of the distant kindred are reduced to straitened circumstances. They are shut out from useful careers, and generally exhibit the evils ensuent upon the system of education and surveillance adopted toward them, in their low, vicious pursuits, and cringing imbecility of character. The sum of $133 is allowed when they marry, and $150 to defray funeral expenses, which induces some of them to maltreat their wives to death, in order to receive the allowance and dowry as often as possible.

The titular nobility of the Empire, as a whole, is a body whose members are without power, land, wealth, office, or influence, in virtue of their honors; some of them are more or less hereditary, but the whole system has been so devised, and the designations so conferred, as to tickle the vanity of those who receive them, without granting them any real power. The titles are not derived from landed estates, but the rank is simply designated in addition to the name, and it has been a question of some difficulty how to translate them. For instance, the title *Kung tsin-wang* literally means the 'Reverent Kindred Prince,' and should be translated Prince Kung, not Prince of Kung, which conveys the impression to a foreign reader that *Kung* is an appanage instead of an epithet.

The twelve orders of nobility are conferred solely on the members of the imperial house and clan: 1. *Tsin wang*, 'kindred prince,' *i.e.*, prince of the blood, conferred usually on his Majesty's brothers or sons. 2. *Kiun wang*, or 'prince of a princedom;' the eldest sons of the princes of these two degrees take a definite rank during their father's lifetime, but the collateral branches descend in precedence as the generations are more and more remote from the direct imperial line, until at last the person is simply a member of the imperial clan. These two ranks were termed *regulus* by the Jesuit writers, and each son of an Emperor enters one or other as he becomes of age. The highest princes receive a stipend of about $13,300, some rations, and a retinue of three hundred and sixty servants, altogether making an annual tax on the state of $75,000 to $90,000. The second receive half that sum, and inferior grades in a decreasing ratio, down to the simple members, who each get four dollars a month and rations. 3 and 4. *Beile* and *Beitse*, or princes of and in collateral branches. The 5th to 8th are dukes, called Guardian and Sustaining, with two subordinate grades not entitled to enter the court on state occasions. The 9th to 12th ranks are nobles, or rather generals, in line of descent. The number of persons in the lower ranks is very great. Few of these men hold offices at the capital, and still more rarely are they placed in responsible situations in the provinces, but the government of Manchuria is chiefly in their hands.

Besides these are the five ancient orders of nobility, *kung*, *hao*, *peh*, *tsz'*, and *nan*, usually rendered duke, count, viscount, baron, and baronet, which are conferred without distinction on Manchus, Mongols, and Chinese, both civil and military, and as such are highly prized by their recipients as marks of honor. The three first take precedence of the highest untitled civilians, but an appointment to most of the high offices in the country carries with it an honorary title. The direct descendant of Confucius is called *Yen-shing kung*, 'the Ever-sacred duke,' and of Koxinga *Hai-ching kung*, or 'Sea-quelling duke;' these two are the only perpetual titles among the Chinese, but among the Manchus, the chiefs of eight families which aided in settling the crown in the Gioro line were made hereditary princes, who are collectively called princes of the iron crown. Besides the above-mentioned, there are others, which are deemed even more honorable, either from their rarity or peculiar privileges, and answer to membership of the various orders of the Garter, Golden Fleece, Bath, etc., in Europe.

The internal arrangements of the court are modelled somewhat after those of the Boards, the general supervision being under the direction of the *Nui-wu fu*, composed of a president and six assessors, under whom are seven subordinate departments. It is the duty of these officers to attend upon the Emperor and Empress at sacrifices, and conduct the ladies of the harem to and from the palace; they oversee the households of the sons of the Emperor, and direct, under his Majesty, everything belonging to the palace and whatever appertains to its supplies and the care of the imperial guard. The seven departments are arranged so as to bear no little resemblance to a miniature state: one supplies food and raiment; a second is for defence, to regulate the body-guard when the Emperor travels; the third attends to the etiquette the members of this great family must observe toward each other, and brings forward the inmates of the harem when the Emperor, seated in the inner hall of audience, receives their homage, led by the Empress herself; a fourth department selects ladies to fill the harem, and collects the revenue from crown lands; a fifth superintends all repairs necessary in the palace, and sees that the streets of the city be cleared whenever the Emperor, Empress, or any of the women or children in the palace wish to go out; a sixth department has in charge the herds and flocks of the Emperor; and the last is a court for punishing the crimes of soldiers, eunuchs, and others attached to the palace.

The Emperor ought to have three thousand eunuchs, but the actual number is rather less than two thousand, who perform the work of the household. His sons and grandsons are allowed from thirty down to four, while the iron-crown princes and imperial sons-in-law have twenty or thirty; all these nobles are constrained to employ some eunuchs in their establishments, if not able to maintain the full quota, for show. Most of this class are compelled to submit to mutilation by their parents before the age of eight (and not always from poverty), as it usually insures a livelihood. Some take to this condition from motives of laziness and the high duties falling to their share if they behave themselves. From very ancient times certain criminals have been punished by castration. There is a separate control for the due efficiency of these servants of the court, who are divided into forty-eight classes; during the present dynasty they have never caused trouble. The highest pay any of them receive is twelve taels a month.

The number of females attached to the harem is not accurately known; all of them are under the nominal direction of the Empress. Every third year his Majesty reviews the daughters of the Manchu officers over twelve years of age, and chooses such as he pleases for concubines; there are only seven legal concubines, but an unlimited number of illegal. The latter are restored to liberty when they reach the age of twenty-five, unless they have borne children to his Majesty. It is generally considered an advantage to a family to have a daughter in the harem, especially by the Manchus, who endeavor to rise by this backstairs influence.[1] To the poor women themselves it is a monotonous, weary life of intriguing unrest. As soon as one enters the palace she bids final adieu to all her male relatives, and rarely sees her female friends; the eunuchs who take care of her are her chief channels of communication with the outer world. It may be added, however, that the comforts and influence of her condition are vastly superior to those of Hindu females.

In the forty-eighth volume of the *Hwui Tien*, from which work most of the details in this chapter are obtained, is an account of the supplies furnished his Majesty and the court. There should daily be placed before the Emperor thirty pounds of meat in a basin and seven pounds boiled into soup; hog's fat and butter, of each one and one-third pound; two sheep, two fowls, and two ducks, the milk of eighty cows, and seventy-

---

[1] *Chinese Repository*, Vol. XIV., p. 521; *N. C. Br. R. As. Soc. Journal*, No. XI.

five parcels of tea. Her Majesty receives twenty-one pounds of meat in platters and thirteen pounds boiled with vegetables; one fowl, one duck, twelve pitchers of water, the milk of twenty-five cows, and ten parcels of tea. Her maids and the concubines receive their rations according to a regular fare.

The Empress-dowager is the most important subject within the palace, and his Majesty does homage at frequent intervals, by making the highest ceremony of nine prostrations before her. When the widow of Kiaking reached the age of sixty in 1836, many honors were conferred by the Emperor. An extract from the ordinance issued on this festival will exhibit the regard paid her by the sovereign:

"Our extensive dominions have enjoyed the utmost prosperity under the shelter of a glorious and enduring state of felicity. Our exalted race has become most illustrious under the protection of that honored relative to whom the whole court looks up. To her happiness, already unalloyed, the highest degree of felicity has been superadded, causing joy and gladness to every inmate of the Six Palaces. The grand ceremonies of the occasion shall exceed in splendor the utmost requirements of the ancients in regard to the human relations, calling forth the gratulation of the whole Empire. It is indispensable that the observances of the occasion should be of an exceedingly unusual nature, in order that our reverence for our august parent and care of her may both be equally and gloriously displayed. . . . . . In the first month of the present winter occurs the sixtieth anniversary of her Majesty's sacred natal day. At the opening of the happy period, the sun and moon shed their united genial influences on it. When commencing anew the revolution of the sexagenary cycle, the honor thereof adds increase to her felicity. Looking upward and beholding her glory, we repeat our gratulations, and announce the event to Heaven, to Earth, to our ancestors, and to the patron gods of the Empire. On the nineteenth day of the tenth moon in the fifteenth year of Taukwang, we will conduct the princes, the nobles, and all the high officers, both civil and military, into the presence of the great Empress, benign and dignified, universally placid, thoroughly virtuous, tranquil and self-collected, in favors unbounded; and we will then present our congratulations on the glad occasion, the anniversary of her natal day. The occasion yields a happiness equal to what is enjoyed by goddesses in heaven; and while announcing it to the gods and to our people, we will tender to her blessings unbounded."

Besides the usual tokens of favor, such as rations to soldiers, pardons, promotions, advances in official rank, etc., it was ordered in the eleventh article, "That every perfectly filial son or obedient grandson, every upright husband or chaste wife, upon proofs being brought forward, shall have a monument erected, with an inscription in his or her honor." Soldiers who had reached the age of ninety or one hundred received money to erect an honorary portal, and tombs, temples, bridges, and roads were ordered to be repaired; but how many of these "exceedingly great and special favors" were actually carried into effect cannot be stated.[1]

For the defence and escort of the Emperor and his palaces there are select bodies of troops, which are stationed within the *Hwang-ching* and the capital and at the various cantonments near the city. The Bannermen form three separate corps, each containing the hereditary troops of Manchu, Mongol, and enrolled Chinese, organized at the beginning of the dynasty under eight standards. Their flags are triangular, a plain yellow, white, red, and blue for troops in the left wing, and the same bordered with a narrow stripe of another color for troops in the right wing. All the families of these soldiers remain in the corps into which they were born.

Two special forces are selected, one named the Vanguard Division, the other the Flank Division, from the Manchu and Mongol Bannermen; these guard the Forbidden City, form his Majesty's escort when he goes out, and number respectively about one thousand five hundred and fifteen thousand men. For the preservation of the peace of the capital a force of upward of twenty thousand, called the Infantry Division, or Gendarmerie, is stationed in and around the walls, in addition to the palace forces. Besides these a cadet corps of five hundred

[1] *Chinese Repository*, Vol. IV., p. 576.

young men armed with bows and spears, two battalions with firearms, and four larger battalions of eight hundred and seventy-five men each, drilled in rifle-practice, are relied on to aid the Gendarmerie and Vanguard in case of danger. Whenever the One Man goes out of the palace gate to cross the city, the streets through which he passes are screened with matting, to keep off the crowds as well as diminish the risks of his person. The result has been that few of the citizens have ever seen their sovereign's face during the last two hundred years. The young Emperor Tungchí obtained great favor among them on one occasion of his return from the Temple of Heaven by ordering the screen of mats to be removed so that he and his people could see each other.

Under the Emperor is the whole body of the people, a great family bound implicitly to obey his will as being that of heaven, and possessing no right or property *per se;* in fact, having nothing but what has been derived from or may at any time be reclaimed by him. The greatness of this family, and the absence of an entailed aristocracy to hold its members or their lands in serfdom, have been partial safeguards against excess of oppression. Liberty is unknown among the people; there is not even a word for it in the language. No acknowledgment on the part of the sovereign of certain well-understood rights belonging to the people has ever been required, and is not likely to be demanded or given by either party until the Gospel shall teach them their respective rights and duties. Emigration abroad, and even removal from one part of the Empire to another, are prohibited or restrained by old laws, but at present no real obstacle exists to changing one's place of residence or occupation. Notwithstanding the fact that Chinese society is so homogeneous when considered as distinct from the sovereign, inequalities of many kinds are constantly met with, some growing out of birth or property, others out of occupation or merit, but most of them derived from official rank. There is no caste as in India, though the attempt to introduce the miserable system was vainly made by Wăn-tí about A.D. 590. The ancient distinctions of the Chinese into scholars, agriculturists, artisans, and traders is far superior to that of Zoroaster into priests, warriors, agriculturists, and artisans; a significant index of the different polities of eastern and western Asiatic nations is contained in this early quaternary division, and the superiority of the Chinese in its democratic element is also noticeable. There are local prejudices against associating with some portions of the community, though the people thus shut out are not remnants of old castes. The *tankia*, or boat-people, at Canton form a class in some respects beneath the other portions of the community, and have many customs peculiar to themselves. At Ningpo there is a degraded set called *to min*, amounting to nearly three thousand persons, with whom the people will not associate. The men are not allowed to enter the examinations or follow an honorable calling, but are play-actors, musicians, or sedan-bearers; the women are match-makers or female barbers and are obliged to wear a peculiar dress, and usually go abroad carrying a bundle wrapped in a checkered handkerchief. The *tankia* at Canton also wear a similar handkerchief on their head, and do not cramp their feet. The *to min* are supposed to be descendants of the Kin, who held northern China in A.D. 1100, or of native traitors who aided the Japanese, in 1555–1563, in their descent upon Chehkiang. The *tankia* came from some of the Miaotsz' tribes so early that their origin is unknown.[1]

The modern classifications of the people, recognized, however, more by law than custom, are various and comprehensive. First, natives and aliens; the latter include the unsubdued mountaineers and aboriginal tribes living in various parts, races of boat-people on the coasts, and all foreigners residing within the Empire, each of whom are subject to particular laws. Second, conquerors and conquered; having reference almost entirely to a prohibition of intermarriages between Manchus and Chinese. Third, freemen and slaves; every native is allowed to purchase slaves and retain their children in servitude, and free persons sometimes forfeit their freedom on account of their crimes, or mortgage themselves into bondage. Fourth, the

---

[1] *Missionary Chronicle*, Vol. XIV., p. 324; Hardy, *Manual of Buddhism*, p 69; Heeren, *Asiatic Nations*, Vol. I., p. 246.

honorable and the mean, who cannot intermarry without the former forfeiting their privileges; the latter comprise, besides aliens and slaves, criminals, executioners, police-runners, actors, jugglers, beggars, and all other vagrant or vile persons, who are in general required to pursue for three generations some honorable and useful employment before they are eligible to enter the literary examinations. These four divisions extend over the whole body of the people, but really affect only a small minority.

It is worthy of note how few have been the slaves in China, and how easy has been their condition in comparison with what it was in Greece and Rome. Owing chiefly to the prevalence of education in the liberal principles of the Four Books, China has been saved from this disintegrating element. The proportion of slaves to freemen cannot be stated, but the former have never attracted notice by their numbers nor excited dread by their restiveness. Girls are more readily sold than boys; at Peking a healthy girl under twelve years brings from thirty to fifty taels, rising to two hundred and fifty or three hundred for one of seventeen to eighteen years old. In times of famine orphans or needy children are exposed for sale at the price of a few cash.[1]

There are also eight privileged classes, of which the privileges of imperial blood and connections and that of nobility are the only ones really available; this privilege affects merely the punishment of offenders belonging to either of the eight classes. The privilege of imperial blood is extended to all the blood relations of the Emperor, all those of the Empress-mother and grandmother within four degrees, of the Empress within three, and of the consort of the crown prince within two. Privileged noblemen comprise all officers of the first rank, all of the second holding office, and all of the third whose office confers a command. These ranks are distinct from titles of nobility, and are much thought of by officers as honorary distinctions. There are nine, each distinguished by a different colored ball placed on the apex of the cap, by a peculiar emblazonry of a bird for

[1] M. Ed. Biot furnished a good account to the *Journal Asiatique* (3d series, Vol. III.) of the legal condition of slaves in China; see also *Chinese Repository*, Vol. XVIII., pp. 347–363, and passim; Archdeacon Gray's *China*.

civilians and a beast for military officers on the breast, and a different clasp to the girdle.

Civilians of the first rank wear a precious ruby or transparent red stone; a Manchurian crane is embroidered on the back and breast of the robe, while the girdle clasp is jade set in rubies; military men have a unicorn, their buttons and clasps being the same as civilians.

Civilians of the second rank wear a red coral button, a robe embroidered with a golden pheasant, and a girdle clasp of gold set in rubies; the lion of India is emblazoned on the military.

Civilians of the third rank carry a sapphire and one-eyed peacock's feather, a robe with a peacock worked on the breast, and a clasp of worked gold; military officers have a leopard.

Different Styles of Official Caps.

Civilians of the fourth rank are distinguished by a blue opaque stone, a wild goose on the breast, and a clasp of worked gold with a silver button; military officers carry a tiger in place of the embroidered wild goose.

Civilians of the fifth rank are denoted by a crystal button, a silver pheasant on the breast, and a clasp of plain gold with a silver button; the bear is the escutcheon of military men.

Civilians of the sixth rank wear an opaque white shell button, a blue plume, an egret worked on the breast, and a mother-of-pearl clasp; military men wear a tiger-cat.

Civilians of the seventh rank have a plain gold button, a mandarin duck on the breast, and a clasp of silver; a mottled bear designates the military, as it also does in the last rank.

The eighth rank wear a worked gold button, a quail on the breast, and a clasp of clear horn ; military men have a seal.

The ninth rank are distinguished by a worked silver button, a long-tailed jay on the breast, and a clasp of buffalo's horn ; military men are marked by a rhinoceros embroidered on the robe. All under the ninth can embroider the oriole on their breasts, and unofficial Hanlin take the egret.

The mass of people show their democratic tendencies in many ways, some of them conservative and others disorganizing. They form themselves into clans, guilds, societies, professions, and communities, all of which assist them in maintaining their rights, and give a power to public opinion it would not otherwise possess. Legally, every subject is allowed access to the magistrates, secured protection from oppression, and can appeal to the higher courts, but these privileges are of little avail if he is poor or unknown. He is too deeply imbued with fear and too ignorant of his rights to think of organized resistance; his mental independence has been destroyed, his search after truth paralyzed, his enterprise checked, and his whole efforts directed into two channels, viz., labor for bread and study for office. The people of a village, for instance, will not be quietly robbed of the fruits of their industry ; but every individual in it may suffer multiplied insults, oppressions, and cruelties, without thinking of combining with his fellows to resist. Property is held by a tolerably secure tenure, but almost every other right and privilege is shamefully trampled on.

Although there is nominally no deliberative or advisatory body in the Chinese government, and nothing really analogous to a congress, parliament, or *tiers état*, still necessity and law compel the Emperor to consult and advise with the heads of tribunals. There are two imperial councils, which are the organs of communication between the head and the body politic ; these are the Cabinet, or Imperial Chancery, and the Council of State ; both of them partake of a deliberative character, but the first has the least power. Subordinate to these two councils are the administrative parts of the supreme government, consisting of the six Boards, the Colonial Office, Censorate, Courts of Representation and Appeal, and the Imperial Academy;

making in all thirteen principal departments, each of which will require a short description. It need hardly be added that there is nothing like an elective body in any part of the system; such a feature would be almost as incongruous to a Chinese as the election of a father by his family.

1. The Nui Koh, or Cabinet, sometimes called the Grand Secretariat, consists of four *ta hioh-sz'*, or principal, and two *hiehpan ta hioh-sz'*, or 'joint assistant chancellors,' half of them Manchus and half Chinese. Their duties, according to the Imperial Statutes, are to "deliberate on the government of the Empire, proclaim abroad the imperial pleasure, regulate the canons of state, together with the whole administration of the great balance of power, thus aiding the Emperor in directing the affairs of state." Subordinate to these six chancellors are six grades of officers, amounting in all to upward of two hundred persons, of whom more than half are Manchus. Under the six chancellors are ten assistants, called *hioh-sz'*, 'learned scholars;' some of the sixteen are constantly absent in the provinces or colonies, when their places are supplied by substitutes. What in other countries is performed by one person as prime minister, is in China performed by the four chancellors, of whom the first in the list is usually considered to be the premier, though perhaps the most influential man and the real leader of government holds another station.

The most prominent daily business of the Cabinet is to receive imperial edicts and rescripts, present memorials, lay before his Majesty the affairs of the Empire, procure his instructions thereon, and forward them to the appropriate office to be copied and promulgated. In order to expedite business in court, it is the custom, after the ministers have read and formed an opinion upon each document, to fasten a slip of paper at the foot—or more than one if elective answers are to be given—and thus present the document to his Majesty, in the presence-chamber, who, with a stroke of his pencil on the answer he chooses, decides its fate. The papers, having been examined and arranged, are submitted to the sovereign at daylight on the following morning; one of the six Manchu *hioh-sz'* first reads each document and hands it over to one of the four Chinese *hioh-sz'*, who inscribes the answer dictated by the sovereign, or hands it to him to perform that duty with the vermilion pencil. By this arrangement a large amount of business can be summarily despatched; but it is also evident that much depends upon the manner in which the answer written upon the slip is drawn up, as to the reception or rejection of the paper, though care has been taken in this particular by requiring that codicils be prepared showing the reasons for each answer. The appointment, removal, and degradation of all officers throughout his vast dominions, orders respecting the apportionment or remittal of the revenue and taxes, disposition of the army, regulation of the nomadic tribes—in short, all concerns, from the highest appointments and changes down to petty police cases of crime, are in this way brought to the notice and action of the Emperor.

Besides these daily duties there are additional functions devolving upon the members of the Cabinet, who are likewise all attached to other bureaus, such as presiding on all state occasions and sacrifices, coronations, reception of embassies, etc.; these duties are fulfilled by the ten assistant *hioh-sz'*, who are all vice-presidents of the Board of Rites. They are the keepers of the twenty-five seals of government, each of which is of a different form and used for different and special purposes, according to the custom of orientals, who place so much dependence upon the seal for vouching for the authenticity of a document.[1] Attached to the Cabinet are ten subordinate offices, one of which is for translating documents into the various languages found in the Empire. The higher members of the Cabinet are familiarly called *koh lao*, *i.e.*, elders of the council-room, from which the word *colao*, often met with in old books upon China, is derived.[2]

---

[1] *Chinese Chrestomathy*, Chap. XVII., Sec. 4, p. 570.

[2] A still more common designation for officers of every rank in the employ of the Chinese government has not so good a parentage; this is the word *mandarin*, derived from the Portuguese *mandar*, to command, and indiscriminately applied by foreigners to every grade, from a premier to a tide-waiter; it is not needed in English as a general term for officers, and ought to be disused, moreover, from its tendency to convey the impression that they are in some way unlike similar officials in other lands. Compare *Notes and Queries on China and Japan*, Vol. III., p. 12.

2. The Kiun-kí Chu, Council of State or General Council, was organized about 1730, but has now become the most influential body in the government; and, though quite unlike in its construction, corresponds to the *ministry* of western nations more than does any other branch of the Chinese system. It can be composed of any grandees, as princes of the blood, chancellors, presidents and vice-presidents of the Six Boards, and chief officers of all the other metropolitan courts. They are selected at the Emperor's pleasure, and unitedly called "great ministers directing the machinery of the army"—the army being here taken to signify the nation. Its duties are "to write imperial edicts and decisions, and determine such things as are of importance to the army and nation, in order to aid the sovereign in regulating the machinery of affairs." The number of members of the General Council probably varies according to his Majesty's pleasure, for no list of them is given in the *Red Book;* but latterly their number has been four, two of each nationality, and Prince Kung as the president. This body is one of the mainsprings of the government, and its composition shows the tendency of the national councils and polity.

The members of the General Council assemble daily in the Forbidden Palace, between five and six in the morning; when summoned by his Majesty into the council-chamber they sit upon mats or low cushions, no person being permitted to sit on chairs in the real or supposed presence of the Emperor. His Majesty's commands being written down by them, are, if public, transmitted to the Inner Council to be promulgated; but on any matter requiring secrecy or expedition, a despatch is forthwith made up and sent under cover to the Board of War, to be forwarded. In all important consultations or trials this Council, either alone or in connection with the appropriate court, is called in; and in time of war it is formed into a committee of ways and means. Lists of officers entitled to promotion are kept by it, and the names of proper persons to supply vacancies furnished the Emperor. Many of the residents in the colonies are members of the Council, and communicate directly with his Majesty through it, and receive allowances and gifts with great formality from the throne—a device of statecraft designed to maintain an awe of the imperial character and name as much as possible among the mixed races under them.

The General Council fills an important station in the system, and tends greatly to consolidate the various branches of government, facilitating their harmonious action as well as supplying the deficiencies of an imbecile, or restraining the acts of a tyrannical monarch. The statutes speak of various record-books, both public and secret, kept by the members for noting down the opinions of his Majesty, and add that there are no fixed times for audiences, one or more sessions being held daily, according to the exigencies of the state. Besides these functions, its members are further charged with certain literary matters, and three subordinate offices are attached to the Council for their preparation. One is for drawing up narratives of important transactions—a few of those relating to the wars and negotiations with foreigners since 1839 would be of much interest now; a second is for translating documents; and the third, entitled "an office for observing that imperial edicts are carried into effect," must be at times rather an arduous task, though probably its responsibility ends when the despatch goes forward. An office with this title shows that the Chinese government, with all its business-like arrangements, is still an Asiatic one.[1]

The duties of these supreme councils are general, comprising matters relating to all departments of the government, and serving to connect the head of the state with the subordinate bodies, not only at the capital, but throughout the provinces, so that he can, and probably does to a very great degree, thereby maintain a general acquaintance with what is done in all parts, and sooner rectify disorders and malpractices. The rivalry between their members, and the dislike entertained by the Chinese and Manchus composing them, cause, no doubt, some trouble to the Emperor; but this has some effect in thwarting conspiracies and intrigues. It must not be supposed, however, that every high officer in the Chinese government is wholly unprincipled, venal, and intriguing; most of them desire to serve and maintain their country. The personal character and knowledge of

[1] *Chinese Repository*, Vol. IV., p. 138. *Chinese Chrestomathy*, p. 573.

the monarch has much to do with the efficiency of his government, and the guidance of its affairs demands constant oversight. If he allows his ministers to conduct their trusts without restraint, they soon engross and misuse this power for selfish ends. In natural sequence every branch feels the fatal laxity, while its functionaries lose no time in imitating their superiors. This was the case during the reign of Hienfung, but matters have much improved under the regency since 1861. In ordinary times, the daily intercourse between the Emperor of China and his ministers presents very similar features of confidence, courtesy, and esteem between them as those seen in western lands.

The *King Pao, i.e.*, '*Metropolitan Reporter*,' usually called the *Peking Gazette*, is compiled from the papers presented before the General Council, and constitutes the principal source of information available to the people for ascertaining what is going on in the Empire. Every morning ample extracts from the papers decided upon or examined by the Emperor, including his own orders and rescripts, are placarded upon boards in a court of the palace, and form the materials for the annals of government and the history of the Empire. Couriers are despatched to all parts of the land, carrying copies of these papers to the high provincial officers; certain persons are also permitted to print these documents, but always without note or change, and circulate them at their own charges to their customers. This is the *Peking Gazette*, and such the mode of its compilation. It is simply a record of official acts, promotions, decrees, and sentences, without any editorial comments or explanations; and as such of great value in understanding the policy of government. It is very generally read and discussed by educated people in cities, and tends to keep them more acquainted with the character and proceedings of their rulers than ever the Romans were of their sovereigns and Senate. In the provinces thousands of persons find employment by copying and abridging the *Gazette* for readers who cannot afford to purchase the complete edition.[1]

[1] *Fraser's Magazine*, February, 1873. *China Review*, Vol. III., p. 13. *Note on the Condition and Government of the Chinese Empire in* 1849. By T F. Wade. Hongkong, 1850. Translations of several years of the *Gazette* have appeared since 1872, reprinted from the columns of the *North China Herald*.

澳门基金会
※
北京外国语大学
中国海外汉学研究中心
※
大象出版社

合作项目

卫三畏文集
Selected Works of Samuel Wells Williams

中国总论

（卷Ⅰ）（下）

The Middle Kingdom

［美］
卫三畏 著
Samuel Wells Williams

大象出版社

The principal executive bodies under these two Councils are the *Luh Pu*, or 'Six Boards,' which were modelled on much the same plan during the ancient dynasties. At the head of each Board are two presidents, called *shang-shu*, and four vice-presidents, called *shilang*, alternately a Manchu and a Chinese; and over three of them—those of Revenue, War, and Punishment—are placed superintendents, who are frequently members of the Cabinet; sometimes the president of one Board is superintendent of another. There are three subordinate grades of officers in each Board, who may be called directors, under-secretaries, and controllers, with a great number of minor clerks, and their appropriate departments for conducting the details of the general and peculiar business coming under the cognizance of the Board, the whole being arranged and subordinated in the most business-like style. The detail of all the departments in the general and provincial governments is regulated in the same manner. For instance, each Board has a different style of envelope for its despatches, and the papers in the offices are filed away in them.

3. The Lí Pu, or Board of Civil Office, "has the government and direction of all the various officers in the civil service of the Empire, and thereby it assists the Emperor to rule all people;" these duties are further defined as including "whatever appertains to the plans of selecting rank and gradation, to the rules of determining degradation and promotion, to the ordinances of granting investitures and rewards, and the laws for fixing schedules and furloughs, that the civil service may be supplied." Civilians are presented to the Emperor, and all civil and literary officers throughout the Empire distributed by this Board. The great power apparently thus entrusted is shared by the two preceding, whose members are made advisory overseers of the highest appointments, while the provincial authorities put men in vacant posts as fast as they are needed. The danger arising from the arrangement is noticed by Biot[1] as having early attracted criticism.

This Board is subdivided into four bureaus. The first at-

[1] *Essai sur l'Instruction en Chine*, pp. 540–589.

tends to the distinctions, precedence, promotion, exchanging, etc., of officers. The second investigates their merits and worthiness to be recorded and advanced, or contrariwise; ascertains the character each officer bears and the manner in which he fulfils his duties, and prescribes his furloughs. The third regulates retirement from office on account of mourning or filial duties, and supervises the registration of official names; it is through this bureau that Hwang Ngăn-tung, the Governor of Kwangtung, was degraded in 1846 for not resigning his office on the death of his mother. The fourth regulates the distribution of titles, patents, and posthumous honors. The Chinese is the only government that ennobles ancestors for the merits of their descendants; the custom arose out of the worship paid them, in which the rites are proportionate to the rank of the deceased, not of the survivor; and if the deceased parent or grandparent were commoners, they receive proper titles in consequence of the elevation of their son or grandson. This custom is not a trick of state to get money, for commoners cannot buy these posthumous titles; they can only buy nominal titles for themselves. The usage, however, offers an unexpected illustration of the remark of Job, "His sons come to honor, and he knoweth it not."

4. The HU PU, or Board of Revenue, "directs the territorial government of the Empire, and keeps the lists of population in order to aid the Emperor in nourishing all people; whatever appertains to the regulations for levying and collecting duties and taxes, to the plans for distributing salaries and allowances, to the rates for receipts and disbursements at the granaries and treasuries, and to the rights for transporting by land and water are reported to this Board, that sufficient supplies for the country may be provided." Besides these duties, it obtains the admeasurement of all lands in the Empire, and proportions taxes and conscriptions, according to the divisions, population, etc., regulates the expenditure, and ascertains the latitude and longitude of places. One minor office prepares lists of all the Manchu girls fit to be introduced into the palace for selection as inmates of the harem, a duty which is enjoined on it because the allowances, outfits, and positions of these women

come within its control. The injudicious mode of collecting revenue common under the Persian and Syrian kings, by which the sums obtained from single cities and provinces were apportioned among the royal family and favorites, and carried directly to them, has never been practised by the Chinese.

There are fourteen subordinate departments to attend to the receipt of the revenue from each of the provinces, each of which corresponds with the treasury department in its respective province. The revenue being paid in sundry ways and articles, as money, grain, manufactures, etc., the receipt and distribution of the various articles require a large force of assistants. This Board is moreover a court of appeal on disputes respecting property, and superintends the mint in each province; one bureau is called the "great ministers of the Three Treasuries," viz., of metals, silks and dye-stuffs, and stationery.

5. The Lí Pu, or Board of Rites, "examines and directs concerning the performance of the five kinds of ritual observances, and makes proclamation thereof to the whole Empire, thus aiding the Emperor in guiding all people. Whatever appertains to the ordinances for regulating precedence and literary distinctions, to the canons for maintaining religious honor and fidelity, to the orders respecting intercourse and tribute, and to the forms of giving banquets and granting bounties, are reported to this Board in order to promote national education." The five classes of rites are defined to be those of a propitious and those of a felicitous nature, military and hospitable rites, and those of an infelicitous nature. Among the subordinate departments is that of ceremonial forms, which "has the regulation of the etiquette to be observed at court on all occasions, on congratulatory attendances, in the performance of official duties, etc.; also the regulation of dresses, caps, etc.; as to the figure, size, color, and nature of their fabrics and ornaments, of carriages and riding accoutrements, their form, etc., with the number of followers and insignia of rank. It has also the direction of the entire ceremonial of personal intercourse between the various ranks or peers, minutely defining the number of bows and degree of attention which each is to pay to the other when meeting in official capacities, according as they are

on terms of equality or otherwise. It has also to direct the forms of their written official intercourse, including those to be observed in addresses to and from foreign states. The regulation of the literary examinations, the number of the graduates, the distinction of their classes, the forms of their selection, and the privileges of successful candidates, with the establishment of governmental schools and academies, are all under this department."

Another office superintends the rites to be observed in worshipping deities and spirits of departed monarchs, sages, and worthies, and in "saving the sun and moon" when eclipsed. The third, called "host and guest office," looks after tribute and tribute-bearers, and takes the whole management of foreign embassies, supplying not only provisions, but translators, and ordering the mode of intercourse between China and other states. The fourth oversees the supplial of food for banquets and sacrifices. The details of all the multifarious ritual duties of this Board occupy fourteen volumes of the Statutes. "Truly nothing is without its ceremonies," as Confucius taught, and no nation has paid so much attention to them in the ordering of its government as the Chinese. The *Book of Rites* is the foundation of ceremonies and the infallible standard as to their meaning; the importance attached to them has elevated etiquette and ritualism into a kind of crystallizing force which has molded Chinese character in many ways.

Connected with the Board of Rites is a Board of Music, containing an indefinite number of officers whose duties "are to study the principles of harmony and melody, to compose musical pieces and form instruments proper to play them, and then suit both to the various occasions on which they are required." Nor are the graces of posture-making neglected by these ceremony-mongers; but it may with truth be said, that if no other nation ever had a Board of Music, and required so much official music as the Chinese, certainly none ever had less real melody.

6. The Ping Pu, or Board of War, "has the duty of aiding the sovereign to protect the people by the direction of all military affairs in the metropolis and the provinces, and to

regulate the hinge of the state upon the reports received from the various departments regarding deprivation of, or appointment to, office; succession to, or creation of, hereditary military rank; postal or courier arrangements; examination and selection of the deserving, and accuracy of returns." The navy is also under the control of this Board. The management of the post is confided to a special department, and the transmission of official despatches is performed with great efficiency and regularity. A minor bureau of the courier office is called "the office for the announcement of victories," which, from a recital of its duties, appears to be rather a *grande vitesse*, whose couriers should hasten as if they announced a victory.

To enable this Board of War to discharge its duties, they are apportioned under four *sz'*, or bureaus, severally attending to promotion for various reasons; to the regulation of the distribution of rewards and punishments, inspection of troops and issue of general orders, answering to an adjutant-general's department; to the supply and distribution of horses for the cavalry; and, lastly, to the examination of candidates, preparation of estimates and rosters, with all the details connected with equipments and ammunition. The conception of all government with the Manchus being military and not civil, they have developed this Board more than was the case during the last dynasty, the possessions in Central Asia having drawn greatly on their resources and prowess.

The Household troops and city Gendarmerie have already been noticed; their control is vested in the *Nui-wu Fu*, and the oversight of all the Bannermen in the Empire vests in the metropolitan office of the *Tu-tung*, or Captains-general, of whom there are twenty-four, one to every banner of each race. The Board of War has no control directly over this large portion of the Chinese army, and as the direction of the land and sea forces in each province is entrusted in a great degree to the local authorities, its duties are really more circumscribed than one would at first imagine. The singular subordination of military to civil power, which has ever distinguished the Chinese polity, makes the study of the army, as at present constituted, a very interesting feature of the national history; for while it has often proved inefficient to repress insurrection and defend the people against brigandage, it has never been used to destroy their institutions. In times of internal commotion the national soldiers have usually been loyal to their flag, though it must be confessed that discipline within the ranks is not so perfect as to prevent the soldiers from occasionally harassing and robbing those whom they are set to protect.[1]

7. The Hing Pu, or Board of Punishments, "has the government and direction of punishments throughout the Empire, for the purpose of aiding the sovereign in correcting all people. Whatever appertains to measures of applying the laws with leniency or severity, to the task of hearing evidence and giving decisions, to the rights of granting pardons, reprieves, or otherwise, and to the rate of fines and interest, are all reported to this Board, to aid in giving dignity to national manners." The *Hing Pu* partakes of the nature of both a criminal and civil court; its officers usually meet with those of the Censorate and Talí Sz', the three forming the *San Fah Sz'*, or 'Three Law Chambers,' which decide on capital cases brought before them. In the autumn these three unite with members from six other courts, forming collectively a Court of Errors, to revise the decisions of the provincial judges before reporting them to his Majesty. These precautions are taken to prevent injustice when life is involved, and the system shows an endeavor to secure a full and impartial consideration for all capital cases, which, although it may signally fail of its full effect, does the rulers high credit, when the small value set upon life generally by Asiatic governments is considered. These bodies are expected to conform their decisions to the law, nor are they permitted to cite the Emperor's own decisions as precedents, without the law on these decisions has been expressly entered as a supplementary clause in the code.

It also belongs to sub-officers in the Board of Punishments to record all his Majesty's decisions upon appeals from the provinces at the autumnal assizes, when the entire list is presented

[1] *Chinese Repository*, Vol. IV., pp. 188, 276–287; Vol. V., pp. 165–178; Vol. XX., pp. 250, 300, and 363. *Mémoires concernant les Chinois, par les Missionaires à Pekin*, Tomes VII. and VIII., passim.

for his examination and ultimate decision, and see that these sentences are transmitted to the provincial judges. Another office superintends the publication of the code, with all the changes and additions; a third oversees jails and jailers; a fourth receives the fines levied by commutation of punishments, and a fifth registers the receipts and expenditures. If the administration of the law in China at all corresponded with the equity of most of its enactments, or the caution taken to prevent collusion, malversation, and haste on the part of the judges, it would be incomparably the best governed country out of Christendom; but the painful contrast between good laws and wicked rulers is such as to show the utter impossibility of securing the due administration of justice without higher moral principles than heathenism can teach.

The *yamun* of the *Hing Pu* in the capital is the most active of all the Boards, but little is known of what goes on within its walls. Its prisoners are mostly brought from the provinces, officers of high rank arrested for malfeasance or failure, and criminals convicted or condemned there who have appealed to the highest tribunals. Few of those who enter its gates ever return through them, and their sufferings seldom end as long as they have any property left. The narrative of the horrible treatment endured by Loch and his comrades in 1860, while confined within this *yamun*, gives a vivid picture of their sufferings, but native prisoners are not usually kept bound and pinioned. In the rear wall of the establishment is an iron door, through which dead bodies are thrust to be carried away to burial.

8. The KUNG PU, or Board of Works, "has the government and direction of the public works thoughout the Empire, together with the current expenses of the same, for the purpose of aiding the Emperor to keep all people in a state of repose. Whatever appertains to plans for buildings of wood or earth, to the forms of useful instruments, to the laws for stopping up or opening channels, and to the ordinances for constructing the mausolea and temples, are reported to this Board in order to perfect national works." Its duties are of a miscellaneous nature, and are performed in other countries by no one department, though

the plan adopted by the Chinese is not without its advantages One bureau takes cognizance of the condition of all city walls, palaces, temples, altars, and other public structures; sits as a prize-office, and furnishes tents for his Majesty's journeys; supplies timber for ships, and pottery and glassware for the court. A second attends to the manufacture of military stores and utensils employed in the army; sorts the pearls from the fisheries according to their value; regulates weights and measures, furnishes "death-warrants" to governors and generals; and, lastly, takes charge of arsenals, stores, camp-equipage, and other things appertaining to the army. A third department has charge of all water-ways and dikes; it also repairs and digs canals, erects bridges, oversees the banks of rivers by means of deputies stationed at posts along their course, builds vessels of war, collects tolls, mends roads, digs the sewers in Peking and cleans out its gutters, preserves ice, makes book-cases for public records, and, lastly, looks after the silks sent as taxes. The fourth of these offices confines its attention chiefly to the condition of the imperial mausolea, the erection of the sepulchres and tablets of meritorious officers buried at public expense, and the adornment of temples and palaces, as well as superintending all workmen employed by the Board.

The mint is under the direction of two vice-presidents, and the manufacture of gunpowder is specially intrusted to two great ministers. One would think, from this recital, that the functions of the Board of Works were so diverse that it would be one of the most efficient parts of government; but if the condition of forts, ports, dikes, etc., in other parts of the country corresponds to those along the coast, there is, as the Emperor once said of the army, "the appearance of going to war, but not the reality"—most of the works being on record, and suffered to remain there, except when danger threatens, or his Majesty specially orders a public work, and, what is more important, furnishes the money.

9. The Lí Fan Yuen, or Court for the Government of Foreigners, commonly called the Colonial Office, "has the government and direction of the external foreigners, orders their emoluments and honors, appoints their visits to court, and

regulates their punishments, in order to display the majesty and goodness of the state." This is an important branch of the government, and has the superintendence of all the wandering and settled tribes in Mongolia, Cobdo, Ílí, and Koko-nor. All these are called *wai fan*, or 'external foreigners,' in distinction from the tributary tribes in Sz'chuen and Formosa, who are termed *nui fan*, or 'internal foreigners.' There are also *nui í* and *wai í*, or 'internal and external barbarians,' the former comprising the unsubdued mountaineers of Kweichau, and the latter the inhabitants of all foreign countries who do not choose to range themselves under the renovating influences of the Celestial Empire. The Colonial Office regulates the government of the nomads and restricts their wanderings, lest they trespass on each other's pasture-grounds. Its officers are all Manchus and Mongols, having over them one president and two vice-presidents, Manchus, and one Mongolian vice-president appointed for life.

Besides the usual secretaries for conducting its general business, there are six departments, whose combined powers include every branch necessary for the management of these clans. The first two have jurisdiction over the numerous tribes and corps of the Inner Mongols, who are under more complete subjection than the others, and part have been placed under the control of officers in Chihlí and Shansí. The appointment of local officers, collecting taxes, allotting land to Chinese settlers, opening roads, paying salaries, arranging the marriages, retinues, visits to courts, and presents made by the princes and the review of the troops, all appertain to these two departments. The third and fourth have a similar, but less effectual control over the princes, lamas, and tribes of Outer Mongolia. At Urga reside two high ministers, organs of communication with Russia, and general overseers of the frontier. The oversight of the lama hierarchy in Mongolia is now completely under the control of this office; and in Tibet their power has been considerably abridged. The fifth department directs the actions, restrains the powers, levies the taxes, and orders the tributary visits of the Mohammedan begs in the Tien shan Nan Lu, who are quiet pretty much as they are paid by presents and flattered by honors. The sixth department regulates the penal discipline of the tributary tribes. The salaries paid the Mongolian princes are distributed according to an economical scale. A *tsin wang* annually receives $2,600 and twenty-five pieces of silk; a *kiun wang* receives about $1,666 and fifteen pieces of silk; and so on through the ranks of Beile, Beitse, Duke, etc., the last of whom gets a stipend of only $133 and four pieces of silk. The internal organization of these tribes is probably the same now as it was at first among the Scythians and Huns, and partakes of the features of the feudal and tribal system, modified by the nomadic lives they are obliged to lead. The Chinese government is endeavoring to reduce the influence and retinues of the khans and begs and elevate the people to positions of independent owners and cultivators of the soil.

10. The TU-CHAH YUEN, or Censorate, *i.e.*, 'All-examining Court,' is entrusted with the "care of manners and customs, the investigation of all public offices within and without the capital, the discrimination between the good and bad performance of their business, and between the depravity and uprightness of the officers employed in them; taking the lead of other censors, and uttering each his sentiments and reproofs, in order to cause officers to be diligent in attention to their daily duties, and to render the government of the Empire stable." The Censorate, when joined with the Board of Punishments and Court of Appeal, forms a high court for the revision of criminal cases and hearing appeals from the provinces; and, in connection with the Six Boards and the Court of Representation and Appeal, makes one of the *Kiu King*, or 'Nine Courts,' which deliberate on important affairs of government.

The officers are two censors and four deputy censors, besides whom the governors, lieutenant-governors, and the governors of rivers and inland navigation are *ex-officio* deputy censors. A class of censors is placed over each of the Six Boards, whose duties are to supervise all their acts, to receive all public documents from the Cabinet, and after classifying them transmit them to the several courts to which they belong, and to make a semi-monthly examination of the papers entered on the archives of each court. All criminal cases in the provinces come under the oversight of the censors at the capital, and the department which superintends the affairs of the metropolis revises its municipal acts, settles the quarrels, and represses the crimes of its inhabitants. These are the duties of the Censorate, than which no part of the Chinese government has attracted more attention. The privilege of reproof given by the law to the office of censor has sometimes been exercised with remarkable candor and plainness, and many cases are recorded in history of these officers suffering for their fidelity, but such instances must be few indeed in proportion to the failures.

The celebrated Sung, who was appointed commissioner to accompany Lord Macartney, once remonstrated with the Emperor Kiaking upon his attachment to play-actors and strong drink, which degraded him in the eyes of his people and incapacitated him from performing his duties. The Emperor, highly irritated, called him to his presence, and on his confessing to the authorship of the memorial, asked him what punishment he deserved. He answered, "Quartering." He was told to select some other; "Let me be beheaded;" and on a third command, he chose to be strangled. He was then ordered to retire, and the next day the Emperor appointed him governor in Íli, thus acknowledging his rectitude, though unable to bear his censure.

History records the reply of another censor in the reign of an Emperor of the Tang dynasty, who, when his Majesty once desired to inspect the archives of the historiographer's office, in order to learn what had been recorded concerning himself, under the excuse that he must know his faults before he could well correct them, was answered: "It is true your Majesty has committed a number of errors, and it has been the painful duty of our employment to take notice of them; a duty which further obliges us to inform posterity of the conversation which your Majesty has this day, very improperly, held with us."

The censors usually attend on all state occasions by the side of his Majesty, and are frequently allowed to express their opinions openly, but in a despotic government this is little else than a fiction of state, for the fear of offending the imperial ear, and consequent disgrace, will usually prove stronger than the consciousness of right or the desires of a public fame and martyrdom for the sake of principle. The usual mode of advising is to send in a remonstrance against a proposed act, as when one of the body in 1832 remonstrated against the Emperor paying attention to anonymous accusations; or to suggest a different procedure, as the memorials of Chu Tsun against legalizing opium. The number of these papers inserted in the *Peking Gazette* for the information of the Empire, in many of which the acts of officers are severely reprehended, shows that the censors are not altogether idle. In 1833 a censor named Sü requested the Emperor to interdict official persons at court from writing private letters concerning public persons and affairs in the provinces. He stated that when candidates left the capital for their provincial stations, private letters were sent by them from their friends to the provincial authorities, "sounding the voice of influence and interest," by which means justice was perverted. The Emperor ordered the Cabinet to examine the censor and get his facts in proof of these statements, but on inquiry he either would not or could not bring forward any cases, and he himself consequently received a reprimand. "These censors are allowed," says the Emperor, "to tell me the reports they hear, to inform me concerning courtiers and governors who pervert the laws, and to speak plainly about any defect or impropriety which they may observe in the monarch himself; but they are not permitted to employ their pencils in writing memorials which are filled with vague surmises and mere probabilities or suppositions. This would only fill my mind with doubts and uncertainty, and I would not know what men to employ; were this spirit indulged, the detriment of government would be most serious. Let Sü be subjected to a court of inquiry."

The suspension or disgrace of censors for their freedom of speech is a common occurrence, and among the forty or fifty persons who have this privilege a few are to be found who do not hesitate to lift up their voice against what they deem to be wrong; and there is reason for supposing that only a small portion of their remonstrances appears in the *Gazette*. With regard to this department of government, it is to be observed that although it may tend only in a partial degree to check oppression and reform abuses, and while a close examination of its real operations and influence and the character of its members may excite more contempt than respect, still the existence of such a body, and the publication of its memorials, can hardly fail to rectify misconduct to some degree, and check maladministration before it results in widespread evil. The Censorate is, however, only one of a number of checks upon the conduct of officers, and perhaps by no means the strongest.[1]

11. The TUNG-CHING Sz', which may be called a Court of Transmission, consists of a small body of six officers, whose duty is to receive memorials from the provincial authorities and appeals from their judgment by the people and present them to the Cabinet. Attached to this Court is an office for attending at the palace-gate to await the beating of a drum, which, in conformity with an ancient custom, is placed there that applicants may by striking it obtain a hearing. It is also the channel through which the people can directly appeal to his Majesty, and cases occur of individuals, even women and girls, travelling to the capital from remote places to present their petitions for redress before the throne. The feeling of blood revenge prevails among the Chinese, and impels many of these weak and unprotected persons to undergo great hardships to obtain legal redress, when the lives of their parents have been unjustly taken by powerful and rich enemies.

12. The TA-LÍ Sz', or Court of Judicature and Revision, has the duty of adjusting all the criminal courts in the Empire, and forms the nearest approach to a Supreme Court in the government, though the cases brought before it are mostly criminal. When the crimes involve life, this and the preceding unite with the Censorate to form one court, and if the judges are not unanimous in their decisions they must report their reasons to the Emperor, who will pass judgment upon them. In a despotic government no one can expect that the executive officers of courts will exercise their functions with that caution and

---

[1] Compare an article by E. C. Taintor, in *Notes and Queries on China and Japan*. *Chinese Repository*, Vols. IV., pp. 148, 164, and 177, and XII., pp. 32 and 67.

equity required in Christian countries, but considerable care has been taken to obtain as great a degree of justice as possible.

14. The Hanlin Yuen, or Imperial Academy, is entrusted "with the duty of drawing up governmental documents, histories, and other works; its chief officers take the lead of the various classes, and excite their exertions to advance in learning in order to prepare them for employments and fit them for attending upon the sovereign." This body has, it is highly probable, some similarity to the collection of learned men to whom the King of Babylon entrusted the education of promising young men, for although the members of the Hanlin Yuen do not, to any great degree, educate persons, they are constantly referred to as the Chaldeans were by Belshazzar. Sir John Davis likens it to the Sorbonne, inasmuch as it expounds the sacred books of the Chinese. Its chief officers are two presidents or senior members, called *chwang yuen hioh-sz'*, who are usually appointed for life; they attend upon the Emperor, superintend the studies of graduates, and furnish semi-annual lists of persons to be "speakers" at the "classical feasts," where the literary essays of his Majesty are translated from and into Manchu and read before him.

Subordinate to the two senior members are four grades of officers, five in each grade, together with an unlimited number of senior graduates, each forming a sort of college, whose duties are to prepare all works published under governmental sanction; these persons are subject from time to time to fresh examination, and are liable to lose their degrees or be altogether dismissed from office if found faulty or deficient. Subordinate to the Hanlin Yuen is an office consisting of twenty-two selected members, who in rotation attend on the Emperor and make a record of his words and actions. There is also an additional office for the preparation of national histories.

The situation of a member of the Hanlin is one of considerable honor and literary ease, and scholars look forward to a station in it as one which confers dignity in a government where all officers are appointed according to their literary merit, but much more from its being the body from which the Emperor selects his most responsible officers. A graduate of this rank is most likely to be nominated to a vacant office, though the possession of the title does not of itself warrant a place.[1]

Before proceeding to consider the provincial governments, notices of some of the other departments not connected with the general machinery of the state are here in place. The municipality of Peking has already been mentioned when describing the capital; it is intimately connected with the general government and forms an integral part of the machine. Among the courts not connected with the municipal rule of the metropolis, nor forming one of the great departments of state, is *Tai-chang Sz'*, or 'Sacrificial Court,' whose officers "direct the sacrificial observances and distinguish the various instruments and the quality of the sacrifices." Their duties are of importance in connection with the state religion, and they rank high among the court dignitaries of the Empire, but as members of this, possess no power. The *Tai-puh Sz'*, or Superintendent of H. I. M.'s Stud, is an office for "rearing horses, taking account of their increase, and regulating their training;" large tracts of land beyond the Great Wall are appropriated to this purpose, and the clerks of this office, under the direction of the Board of War, oversee the herdsmen and grooms.

The *Kwangluh Sz'*, or 'Banqueting House,' has the charge of "feasting the meritorious and banqueting the deserving;" it is somewhat subordinate to the Board of Rites, and provides whatever is necessary for banquets given to literary graduates, foreign ambassadors, etc. The *Hunglu Sz'*, or 'Ceremonial Court,' regulates the forms to be observed at these banquets, which consist in little else than marshalling the guests according to their proper ranks and directing them when to make the *kotow*, called also *san kwei kiu kao*, "three kneelings and nine knockings." The *Kwoh-tsz' Kien*, or 'National College,' is a different institution from the Hanlin Yuen, and intended for teaching graduates of the lower degrees; the departments of study are the Chinese language, the classics and mathematics, each branch having its appropriate teachers, with some higher officers, both Chinese and Manchu.

---

[1] Dr. W. A. P. Martin, *The Chinese*.

The *Kin Tien Kien*, or 'Imperial Astronomical College,' as might be expected, is much more astrological than astronomical; its duties are defined to be "to direct the ascertainment of times and the movements of the heavenly bodies, in order to attain conformity with the celestial periods and to regulate the notation of time among men; all things relating to divination and the selection of days are under its charge." The preparation of the almanac, in which, among other things, lucky and unlucky days are marked for the performance of all the important acts of life, and astrological and chiromantic absurdities inserted for the amusement of fortune-tellers and others, the instruction of a few pupils, and care of the observatory, occupy most of the time of its officers. It is now of no practical use, and as the *Tung-wăn Kwan* develops into a learned and efficient college, including astronomy and medicine and their kindred branches, these native Boards will gradually pass away.

The other local courts of the capital seem to have been subdivided and multiplied to a great degree for the purpose of affording employment to a larger number of persons, especially Manchus and graduates, so that the Emperor can attach them to himself and be surer of their support in case of any insurrection on the part of the people, and also that he may have them more under his control. The number of clerks and minor offices in all the general departments of state is doubtless more numerous than it would be in a European government. In the mutual relations of the great departments of the Chinese government the principles of responsibility and surveillance among the officers are plainly exhibited, while regard has been paid to such a division and apportionment of labor as would secure great efficiency and care, if every member of the machine faithfully did his duty. Two presidents are stationed over each Board to assist and watch each other, while the two presidents oversee the four vice-presidents; the president of one Board is sometimes the vice-president of another; and by means of the Censorate and the General Council every portion is brought under the cognizance of several independent officers, whose mutual jealousy and regard for individual advancement, or a partial desire for the well-being of the state, affords the Emperor some guarantee of fidelity. The seclusion in which he lives makes it difficult for any conspirator to approach his person, but his own fears regarding the management of such an immense Empire compel him to inform himself respecting the actions of ministers, generals, and proconsular governors. The conduct and devotion of hundreds of officers, both civil and military, during the wars with Great Britain and the suppression of rebellions within the last thirty years, afford proof enough that he has attached his subordinates to his service by some other principle than fear. The total number of civilians holding office is estimated at about fourteen thousand persons, but those dependent on the government are many times this amount.

The rulers of China have contrived the system of provincial governments in an admirable manner, considering the character of the people and the materials they had to work with; no better proof of their sagacity in this respect can be required than the general degree of good order which has been maintained for nearly two centuries, and the great progress the people have made in wealth, numbers, and power. By a well-arranged plan of checks and changes in the provincial authorities, the chances of their abusing position and power and combining to overthrow the supreme government have been reduced almost to an impossibility; the influence of mutual responsibility among them does something to prevent outrageous oppression of the people, by leading one to accuse another of high crimes in order to exonerate himself or obtain his place. The sons and relatives of the Emperor being excluded from civil office in the provinces, the high-spirited and talented native Chinese do not feel inclined to cabal against the government because every avenue to emolument and power is filled and closed against them by creatures and connections of the sovereign; nor when in office are they disposed to attempt the overthrow of the reigning family, lest they lose what has cost them many years of toilsome study and the wealth and influence of friends to attain. The examination of these pashaliks is furthermore entitled to notice from the degree of power delegated to their highest officers, and the shrewd manner in which its exercise has been circumscribed and rendered amenable to its imperial source.

The highest officers in the provinces are a *tsungtuh*, lit. 'general director,' or governor-general, and the *futai* or *fuyuen*, 'soother' or governor. The former is often called a viceroy, but that term seems to be quite inapplicable when used to denote an officer within the limits of the state; governor-general, or proconsul, is more analogous to his duties. A translation of these and many other Chinese titles does not convey their exact functions, but in some cases an equivalent is more intelligible than a translation.[1] The *tsungtuh* has rule over two provinces, or else fills two high offices in one province, while the *futai* is placed over one province, either independent of or in subordination to a *tsungtuh*, as enumerated in the table on page 61.

An examination of the *Red Book* for 1852 showed that out of a total of 20,327 names in it, 16,474 were Chinese, 3,295 were Manchus and Mongols, and 558 enrolled Chinese; in the copy for 1844, out of 12,758 names, 10,463 were Chinese, 1,768 Manchus, and 527 enrolled Chinese; these figures include only civilians and the employees in Peking. The Eighteen Provinces have altogether less than two thousand persons in office above the rank of assistant district magistrate, viz.: 8 governor-generals, 15 governors, 19 treasurers, 18 judges, 17 chancellors, 15 commanders of the forces, including 2 admirals and 1,740 prefects and magistrates. All those filling the high grades in this series report themselves to the Emperor twice every month, by sending him a salutatory card upon yellow paper, enclosed in a silken envelope; stating, for instance, that 'Lin Tseh-sü, governor-general of Liang Kwang, humbly presents his duty to the throne, wishing his Majesty repose.' The Emperor replies with the vermilion pencil, *Chin ngan*, *i.e.*, 'Ourself is well.'

The duties of the governor-general consist in the collective control of all affairs, civil and military, in the region under his jurisdiction; he occupies, in his sphere, under correction, the same authority that the Emperor does over the whole Empire.

[1] Mayers' *Manual of Chinese Titles* furnishes the best compend for learning their duties and names.

The *futai* has a similar control, but in an inferior degree when there is a *tsungtuh*, in the more special supervision of the administrative part of the civil government, as distinguished from the revenue, gabel, or literary branches.

The departments of the civil government are five, viz.: administrative, literary, gabel, commissariat, and excise; the first being also divided into the territorial and financial and the judicial branches. At the head of the first branch is the *pu-ching sz'* (*i.e.*, regulating-government commissioner), who is usually called the treasurer; the *ngan-chah sz'*, or 'criminal judge,' presides over the second. These two officers often unite their deliberations in the direction of any territorial or financial business, or the trial of important cases. The literary department is placed under the direction of an officer selected from among the members of the Hanlin Academy, called a *hioh-ching*, director of learning, or literary chancellor; there are seventeen of them altogether. The gabel and commissariat are usually supervised by certain intermediate officers called *tao*, or *taotai*, sometimes termed intendants of circuit, who have other functions in addition. The excise, or commercial department, is under *kientuh*, or superintendents, but the details of these three branches vary considerably in different provinces. The officers of the excise, either in the interior or on the coast, are made amenable to their superiors in the province, but their functions are exercised in an irregular manner; for the collection of the revenue is a difficult affair, and mostly entrusted to the local magistrates.

The military government of a province includes both the land and sea forces. It is under a *títuh*, or commander-in-chief, of which rank there are in all sixteen, twelve of them commanding one arm alone, and four controlling both land and sea forces. In five provinces the *futai* is commander-in-chief, and in Kansuh there are two. Above the *títuh*, in point of rank but not of power, are placed garrisons of Manchu Bannermen under a *tsiang-kiun*, or general, whose office is conferred, and his actions directly controlled, by the captains-general in Peking; he has jurisdiction, usually, only in the city itself, the principal object of the appointment, apparently, being to check any treasonable designs of the civil authorities.

The duties and relations of these various grades with one another require some further explanation, however, to be understood. The three officers, *tsungtuh*, *futai*, and *tsiangkiun* (if there be one), form a supreme council, and unite in deliberating upon a measure, calling in the subordinate officer to whose department it particularly belongs, and to whom its execution is to be committed, the whole forming a deliberative board, though the responsibility of the act rests with the two highest officers. By this means the various members of the provincial government become better acquainted with each other's character and plans, though their intercourse is much restricted by precedence and rivalry. In the provincial courts civilians always take precedence of military officers; the governor-general and Banner commander, governor and major-general, the literary chancellor and collector of customs, rank with each other; then follow the treasurer, the judge, and other civilians. The authority of the governor-general extends to life and death, to the temporary appointment to all vacant offices in the province, to ordering the troops to any part of it, issuing such laws and taking such measures as are necessary for the security and peace of the region committed to his care, or any other steps he sees necessary. The *futai* also has the power of life and death, and attends to appeals of criminal cases; he oversees, moreover, the conduct of the lower civilians.

Next in rank to the *pu-ching sz'* and *ngan-chah sz'*, who always reside in the provincial capital, are the intendants of circuit, who are located in the circuits consisting of two or three prefectures united for this purpose. They are deputies of the two highest functionaries, and their delegated power often includes military as well as civil authority, the chief object of their appointment being to relieve and assist those high functionaries in the discharge of their extensive duties. Some of the intendants are appointed to supervise the proceedings of the prefects and district magistrates; others are stationed at important posts to protect them, and those connected with foreign trade at the open ports have no territorial jurisdiction.

Subordinate to the governors, through the intendants of circuits, are the prefects or head magistrates of departments, called *chífu*, *chíchau*, and *ting tungchí*, *i.e.*, 'knowers' of them, according as they are placed over *fu*, *chau*, or *ting* departments. It is the duty of these persons to make themselves acquainted with everything that takes place within their jurisdiction, and they are held responsible for the full execution of whatever orders are transmitted to them, all presenting their reports and receiving their orders through the intendants.

The practical efficiency of the Chinese government in promoting the welfare of the people and preserving the peace depends chiefly upon these officers. The people themselves are prone to quarrel and oppress each other; beggars, robbers, tramps, and shysters stir up disorders in various ways, and need wise and vigorous hands to repress and punish them; while all classes avoid and resist the tax-gatherer as much as is safe. The proverb, "A *chífu* can exterminate a family, a *chíhien* can confiscate a patrimony," indicates the popular fear of their power.

The subdivisional parts of departments, called *ting*, *chau*, and *hien*, have each their separate officers, who report to the *chífu* and *chíchau* above them; these are called *tungchí*, *chíchau*, and *chíhien*, and may all be denominated district magistrates. The parts of districts called *sz'* are placed under the control of *siunkien*, circuit-restrainers, or hundreders, who form the last in the regular series of descending rank—the last of the "commissioned officers," as they might not improperly be called. The prefects sometimes have deputies directly under them, as the governor has his intendants, when their jurisdiction is very large or important, who are called *kiunmin fu* and *tungchí*, *i.e.*, 'joint-knowers.' The deputies of district magistrates are termed *chautung* and *chaupwan* for the *chíchau*, and *hienching* and *chufu* for the *chíhien*; the last also have others called *tso-tang* and *yu-tang*, *i.e.*, left-tenants and right-tenants.

Besides these assistants there are others, both in the departments and districts, having the oversight of the police, collection of the taxes and management of the revenue, care of waterways, and many other subdivisions of legislative duties, which it is unnecessary to particularize. They are appointed whenever and wherever the territory is so large and the duties so onerous that one man cannot attend to all, or it is not safe to entrust him with them. They have nearly as much power as their superiors in the department entrusted to them, but none of them have judicial or legislative functions, and the routine of their offices affords them less scope for oppression. Nor is it worth while to notice the great number of clerks, registrars, and secretaries found in connection with the various ranks of dignitaries here mentioned, or the multitude of petty subordinates found in the provinces and placed over particular places or duties as necessity may require. Their number is very large, and the responsibility of their proceedings devolves upon the higher officers who receive their reports and direct their actions.

The common people suffer more from these "rats under the altar," as a Chinese proverb calls them, than from their superiors, because, unlike them, they are usually natives of the place and better acquainted with the condition of the inhabitants, and are not so often removed. The fear of getting into their clutches restrains from evil doings perhaps more than all punishments, though the people soon complain of high-handed acts in a way not to be disregarded. One saying, "Underlings see money as a fly sees blood," indicates their penchant, as another, "Cash drops into an underling's paw as a sheep falls into a tiger's jaw," does the popular notion how to please them. Each intendant, prefect, and district magistrate has special secretaries in his office for filing papers, writing and transmitting despatches, investigating cases, recording evidence, keeping accounts, and performing other functions. All above the *chi-hien* are allowed to keep private secretaries, called *sz' ye*, who are usually personal friends, and accompany the officers wherever they go for the purpose of advising them and preparing their official documents. The *ngan-chah sz'* have jailers under their control, as have also the more important prefects.

The appointment of officers being theoretically founded on literary merit, those to whom is committed the supervision of students and conferment of degrees would naturally be of a high grade. The *hioh-ching*, or literary chancellor, of the province, therefore ranks next to the governor, more, however, because he is specially appointed by his Majesty and oversees this branch of the government, than from the power committed to his hands. Under him are head-teachers of different degrees of authority, residing in the chief towns of departments and districts, the whole forming a similar series of functionaries to what exists in the civil department. These subordinates have merely a greater or less degree of supervision over the studies of students, and the colleges established for the promotion of learning in the chief towns of departments. The business of conferring the lower degrees appertains exclusively to the chancellor, who makes an annual circuit through the province for that purpose, and holds examinations in the chief town of each department, to which all students residing within its limits can come.

The gabel, or salt department, is under the control of a special officer, called a "commissioner for the transport of salt," and forming in the five maritime provinces one of the *san sz'*, or three commissioners, of which the *pu-ching sz'* and *ngan-chah sz'* are the other two. There are, above these commissioners, eight directors of the salt monopoly, stationed at the dépôts in Chihlí and Shantung, who, however, also fill other offices, and have rather a nominal responsibility over the lower commissioners. The number and rank of the officers connected with the salt monopoly show its importance, and is proof of how large a revenue is derived from an article which will bear such an expensive establishment. At present its administration costs about as much as its receipts.

The commissariat and revenue department is unusually large in China compared with other countries, for the plan of collecting any part of the revenue in kind necessarily requires numerous vehicles for transporting and buildings for storing it, which still further multiplies the number of clerks and hands employed. The transportation of grain along the Yangtsz' River is under the control of a *tsungtuh*, who also oversees the disposal and directs the collectors of it in eight of the provinces adjacent to this river. The office of *liang-chu tao*, or commissioner to collect grain, is found in twelve provinces, the *pu-ching sz'* attending to this duty in six; the supervision of the subordinate agents of this department in the several districts is in the hands of the prefects and district magistrates. That feature of the

Chinese system which makes officers mutually responsible, seems to lead the superior powers to confer such various duties upon one functionary, in order that he may thus have a general knowledge of what is going on about and under him, and report what he deems amiss. It is not, indeed, likely that such was the original arrangement, for the Chinese government has come to its present composition by slow degrees; but such is, so far as can be seen, the effect of it, and it serves in no little degree to accomplish the designs of the rulers to bind the main and lesser wheels of the huge machine to themselves and to one another.

The customs and excise are under the management of different grades of officers according to the importance of their posts. The transit duties levied at the excise stations placed in every town are collected by officers acting under the local authorities, and have nothing to do with the collection of maritime duties. This tax, called *li-kin*, or 'a cash a catty,' has lately been greatly increased, and the natural result has been to destroy the trade it preyed on, or divert it to other channels. The foreign merchants and officers have, too, protested against its imposition, seeing that their trade was checked.

Recapitulating in tabular form, we may say that outside of the Cabinet, Council, Boards, and Courts at the capital, the government (in the Eighteen Provinces) is in the hands of:

8 Governors-General (6 governing two provinces each).	64 Intendants of Circuit.
15 Governors.	182 Prefects.
19 Commissioners of Finance (2 for Kiangsu).	68 Prefects of Inferior Departments.
18 Commissioners of Justice.	18 Independent Subprefects.
4 Directors of the Salt Gabel.	180 Dependent Subprefects.
9 Collectors (independent of these).	139 Deputy Subprefects.
13 Commissioners of Grain, or Commissaries.	141 District Magistrates of the Fifth Class.
	1,232 District Magistrates of the Seventh Class.

The military section of the provincial governments is under the control of a *títuh*, or major-general, who resides at a central post, and, in conjunction with the governor-general and governor, directs the movements of the forces, while these last have also an independent control over a certain body of troops belonging to them officially. The various grades of officers in the native army, and the portion of troops under each of them, stationed in the garrisons and forts in different parts of the provinces, are all arranged in a methodical manner, which will bear examination and comparison with the army of any country in the world. The native force in each province is distinct from the Manchu troops, and is divided somewhat according to the Roman plan of legion, cohort, maniple, and century, over each of which are officers, from colonel down to sergeant. Nothing is wanting to the Chinese army to make it fully adequate to the defence of the country but discipline and confidence in itself; for lack of practice and systematic drilling have made it an army of paper warriors against a resolute enemy. Nevertheless, the recent campaigns against the rebels in the extreme western colonies indicate the fact that its regeneration is already of some weight. On the other hand, it has no doubt been for the good of the Chinese people and government—the advance of the first in wealth, numbers, and security, and the consolidation and efficiency of the latter—that they have cultivated letters rather than arms, peace more than war.

All the general officers in the army have fixed places of residence, at which the larger portion of their respective brigades remain, while detachments are stationed at various points within their command. The governor, major-general, and Banner commandant have commands independent of each other, but the *títuh*, or major-general, exercises the principal military sway. The naval officers have the same names as those in the army, and the two are interchanged and promoted from one service to the other. Admirals and vice-admirals usually reside on shore, and despatch their subordinates in squadrons or single vessels wherever occasion requires. This system must, ere long, give place to a better division of the two arms with the building of steam vessels and management of arsenals, when junks are superseded.

The system of mutually checking the provincial officers is also exhibited in their location. For example, in the city of Canton the governor-general is stationed in the New city near the collector of customs, while the lieutenant-governor and Manchu general are so located in the Old city that should circumstances require they can act against the two first. The governor has the general command of all the provincial troops, estimated to be one hundred thousand men, but the particular command of only five thousand, and they are stationed fifty miles off, at Shauking fu. The *tsiang kiun* has five thousand men under him in the Old city, which, in an extreme case, would make him master of the capital, while his own allegiance is secured by the antipathy between the Manchus and Chinese preventing him from combining with the latter. Again, the governor-general has the power of condemning certain criminals to death, but the *wang-ming*, or death-warrant, is lodged with the *futai*, and the order for execution must be countersigned by him; his despatches to court must be also countersigned by his coadjutor. The general absence of resistance to the imperial sway on the part of these high officers during the two centuries of Manchu rule, when compared with the multiplied intrigues and rebellions of the pashas in the Turkish Empire, proves how well the system is concocted.

In order to enable the superior officers to exercise greater vigilance over their inferiors, they have the privilege of sending special messengers, invested with full power, to every part of their jurisdiction. The Emperor himself never visits the provinces judicially, nor has an Emperor been south of the capital during the present century; he therefore constantly sends commissioners or legates, called *kinchai*, to all parts of the Empire, ostensibly entrusted with the management of a particular business, but required also to take a general surveillance of what is going on. The ancient Persians had a similar system of commissioners, who were called the eyes and ears of the prince, and made the circuit of the empire to oversee all that was done. There are many points of resemblance between the structure of these two ancient monarchies, the body of councillors who assisted the prince in his deliberations, the presidents over the provinces, the satraps, etc.; but the Persians had not the elements of perpetuity which the system of common schools and official examinations give to the Chinese government.[1]

---

[1] Rollin's *Ancient History*, Chap. IV. *Manners of the Assyrians.* Heeren's *Asiatic Researches*, Vol. I., Chap. II.

Governors in like manner send their deputies and agents, called *weiyuen*, over the province; and even the prefects and intendants despatch their messengers. All these functionaries, during the time of their mission, take rank with the highest officers according to the quality of their employers; but the imperial commissioners, who for one object or another are constantly passing and repassing through the Empire in every direction, exercise great influence in the government, and are powerful agents in the hands of the Emperor for keeping his proconsuls at their duty.

CHAPTER VIII.

ADMINISTRATION OF THE LAWS.

THE preceding chapter contains a general view of the plan upon which the central and provincial governments of the Empire are constructed; and if an examination of the conduct of officers in every department shows their extortion, cruelty, and venality, it will not, in the opinion of the liberal-minded reader, detract from the general excellence of the theory of the government, and the sagacity exhibited in the system of checks designed to restrain the various parts from interfering with the well-being of the whole. In addition to the division of power and the restrictions upon Chinese officers already mentioned, there are other means adopted in their location and alternation to prevent combination and resistance against the head of the state. One of them is the law forbidding a man to hold any civil office in his native province, which, besides stopping all intrigue where it would best succeed, has the further effect of congregating aspirants for office at Peking, where they come in hope of obtaining some post, or of succeeding in the examination for the highest literary degrees. The central government could not contrive a better plan for bringing all the ambitious and talented men in the country under its observation before appointing them to clerkships in the capital, or scattering them in the provinces.

Moreover, no officer is allowed to marry in the jurisdiction under his control, nor own land in it, nor have a son, brother, or near relative holding office under him; and he is seldom continued in the same station or province for more than three or four years. Manchus and Chinese are mingled together in high stations, and obligations are imposed on certain grandees to inform the Emperor of each other's acts. Members of the imperial clan are required to attend the meetings of the Boards at the capital, and observe and report what they deem amiss or of interest to the Emperor and his council; while in all the upper departments of the general and provincial governments, a system of espionage is carried out, detrimental to all principles of honorable fidelity, such as we look for in officials, but not without some good effects in a weak despotism like China. There is, besides this constant surveillance, a triennial catalogue made out of the merits and demerits of all officers in the Empire, which is submitted to imperial inspection by the Board of Civil Office. In order to collect the details for this catalogue, it is incumbent upon every provincial officer to report upon the character and qualifications of those under him, and the list, when made out, is forwarded by the governor to the capital. The points of character are arranged under six different heads, viz.: those who are not diligent, the inefficient, the superficial, the untalented, superannuated, and diseased. According to the opinion given in this report, officers are elevated or degraded so many steps in the scale of merit, like school-boys in a class, and whenever they issue an edict are required to state how many steps they have been advanced or degraded, and how many times recorded. Officers are required to accuse themselves, when guilty of crime, either in their own conduct or that of their subordinates, and request punishment. The results of this peculiar and patriarchal mode of teaching officers their duty will be best exhibited by quoting from a rescript of Taukwang's, issued in February, 1837, after one of the catalogues had been submitted to his Majesty.

"The cabinet minister Changling has strenuously exerted himself during a long lapse of years; he has reached the eightieth year of his age, yet his energies are still in full force. His colleagues Pwan Shí-ngăn and Muchangah, as well as the assistant cabinet minister Wang Ting, have invariably displayed diligence and attention, and have not failed in yielding us assistance. Tang Kin-chau, president of the Board of Office, has knowledge and attainments of a respectable and sterling character, and has shown himself public-spirited and intelligent in the performance of special duties assigned to him. Shí Chí-yen, president of the Board of Punishments, retains his usual strength and energies, and in the performance of his judicial duties has displayed perspicacity and circumspection. The assistant cabinet minister and governor of Chihlí province, Kíshen, transacts the affairs of his government with faithfulness, and the military force under his control is well disciplined. Husungé, the governor of Shensí and Kansuh provinces, is cautious and prudent, and performs his duties with careful exactness. Ílípu, governor of Yunnan and Kweichau, is well versed in the affairs of his frontier government, and has fully succeeded in preserving it free from disturbance. Linking, who is entrusted with the general charge of the rivers in Kiangnan, has not failed in his care of the embankments, and has preserved the surrounding districts from all disquietude. To show our favor unto all these, let the Board of Office determine on appropriate marks of distinction for them.

"Kweisan, subordinate minister of the Cabinet, is hasty and deficient, both in precision and capacity; he is incapable of moving and acting for himself; let him take an inferior station, and receive an appointment in the second class of the guards. Yihtsih, vice-president of the Board of Works for Mukden, possesses but ordinary talents, and is incompetent to the duties of his present office; let him also take an inferior station, and be appointed to a place in the first class of guards. Narkingé, the governor-general of Hukwang, though having under him the whole civil and military bodies of two provinces, has yet been unable, these many days, to seize a few beggarly impish vagabonds: after having in the first instance failed in prevention, he has followed up that failure by idleness and remissness, and has fully proved himself inefficient. Let him take the lower station of governor in Hunan, and within one year let him, by the apprehension of Lan Ching-tsun, show that he is aroused to greater exertions.

"Let all our other servants retain their present appointments. Among them Tau Shu, the governor of Kiangnan and Kiangsí, is bold and determined in the transaction of affairs, but has not yet attained enlarged views in regard to the salt department; Chung Tsiang, the governor of Fuhkien and Chehkiang, finds his energies failing; Tăng Ting-ching, the governor of Kwangtung and Kwangsí, possesses barely an adequate degree of talent and knowledge; and Shin Kí-hien, though faithful and earnest in the performance of his duties, has, in common with these others, been not very long in office.

"That all ministers will act with purity and devotedness of purpose, with public spirit and diligence, is our most fervent hope. A special edict."[1]

The effect of such confessions and examination of character is to restrain the commission of outrageous acts of oppression; it is still further enforced by the privilege, common alike to censors and private subjects, of complaining to the Emperor of misdeeds done to them by persons in authority. Fear for their own security has suggested this multiplicity of checks, but the Emperor and his ministry have no doubt thereby impeded the

[1] *Chinese Repository*, Vol. VI., p. 48.

efficiency of their subordinates, and compelled them to attend so much to their own standing that they care far less than they otherwise would for the prosperity of the people.

The position of an officer in the Chinese government can hardly be ascertained from the enumeration of his duties, nor can we easily appreciate, from a general account of the system, his temptations to oppress inferiors and deceive superiors. His duties, as indicated in the code, are so minute, and often so contradictory, as to make it impossible to fulfil them strictly; it is found, accordingly, that few or none have ascended the slippery heights of promotion without frequent relapses. Degradation, when to a step or two and temporary, carries with it of course no moral taint in a country where the award for bribery is graduated to the amount received, without any reference to moral violation; where the bamboo is the standard of punishment as well for error in judgment or remissness as for crime —only commuted to a fine in honor of official rank; where, as a distinction in favor of the imperial race, the bamboo is softened to the whip and banishment mitigated to the pillory.[1] The highest officers have of course the greatest opportunity to oppress, but their extortions are limited by the venality and mendacity of the agents they are compelled to employ. Inferiors also can carry on a system of exactions if they keep on the right side of those above them. The whole class form a body of men mutually jealous of each other's advance, where every incumbent endeavors to supplant his associate; they all agree in regarding the people as the source of their profits, the sponge which all must squeeze, but differ in the degree to which they should carry on the same plan with each other. Although sprung from the mass of the people, the welfare of the community has little place in their thoughts. Their life is spent in ambitious efforts to rise upon the fall of others, though they do not lose all sense of character or become reckless of the means of advance, for this would destroy their chance of success. The game they play with each other and their imperial master is, however, a harmless one compared with what was

---

[1] *Chinese Repository*, Vol. IV., p. 59.

done in old Rome or in Europe four or five centuries ago, or even lately among the pashas and viziers of the sultans and shahs in Western Asia. To the honor of the Chinese, life is seldom sacrificed for political crime or envious emulation; no officer dreads a bowstring or a poisoned cup from his lord paramount, nor is he on the watch against the dagger of an assassin hired by a vindictive competitor. Whatever heights of favor or depths of umbrage he may experience, the servant of the Emperor of China need not, in unproved cases of delinquency, fear for his life; but he not unfrequently takes it himself from conscious guilt and dread of just punishment.

The names and standing of all officers are published quarterly by permission of government in the *Red Book* (which by an usual coincidence is bound in red), called the "Complete Record of the Girdle Wearers" (*Tsin Shin Tsiuen Shu*), comprised in four volumes, 12mo, to which are added two others of the Army and Bannermen. This publication was first issued at the command of Wanlih, of the Ming dynasty, about 1580, and mentions the native province of each person, whether Chinese, Manchu, Mongol, or enrolled Chinese, describes the title of the office, its salary, and gives much general information. The publishers of the book expect that officers will inform them of the changes that take place in their standing, and sometimes omit to mention those who do not thus report themselves.

A memoir of the public life of a high officer in China would present a singular picture of ups and downs, but, on account of their notorious disregard of truth, Chinese documents are unsafe to trust entirely in drawing such a sketch. One of the most conspicuous men in late times was Duke Ho, the premier in the time of Macartney's embassy, who for many years exercised a greater control over the counsels of a Chinese sovereign than is recorded of any other man during the present dynasty. This man was originally a private person, who attracted the notice of the Emperor by his comeliness, and secured it by his zeal in discharging the offices entrusted to him. With but few interruptions he gradually mounted the ladder of promotion, and for some years before Kienlung's death, when the latter's energies had begun to fail from age, was virtual master of the country. Staunton describes him as possessing eminent abilities.; "the manners of Hokwăn were not less pleasing than his understanding was penetrating and acute. He seemed indeed to possess the qualities of a perfect statesman."[1] The favorite had gradually filled the highest posts with his friends, and his well-wishers were so numerous in the general and provincial governments that some began to apprehend a rising in his favor when the Emperor died. Kiaking, on coming to the throne, began to take those cautious measures for his removal which showed the great influence he possessed; one of these proceedings was to appoint him superintendent of the rites of mourning, in order, probably, that his official duties might bring him often to the palace. After four years the Emperor drew up sixteen articles of impeachment, most of them frivolous and vexatious, though of more consequence in the eyes of a Chinese prince than they would have been at other courts. One article alleged that he had ridden on horseback up to the palace gate; another, that he had appropriated to his own household the females educated for the imperial harem; a third, that he had detained the reports of officers in time of war from coming to the Emperor's eye, and had appointed his own retainers to office, when they were notoriously incompetent; a fourth, that he had built many apartments of *nan-muh*, a kind of laurel-wood exclusively appropriated to royalty, and imitated regal style in his grounds and establishment; a fifth, that "on the day previous to our Royal Father's announcement of our election as his successor, Hokwăn waited upon us and presented the insignia of the newly conferred rank—thereby betraying an important secret of state, in hopes of obtaining our favor." He was also accused of having pearls and jewels of larger size than those even in the Emperor's regalia. But so far as can be inferred from what was published, this Cardinal Wolsey of China was, comparatively speaking, not cruel in the exercise of his power, and the real cause of his fall was evidently his riches. In the schedule of his confiscated property it was mentioned that besides houses, lands, and other immovable property to an amazing extent, not less

[1] *Embassy to China*, Vol. III., p. 26.

than one hundred and five millions of dollars in bullion and gems were found in his treasury. A special tribunal was instituted for his trial, and he was allowed to become his own executioner, while his constant associate was beheaded. These were the only deaths, the remainder of his relatives and dependents being simply removed and degraded. His power was no doubt too great for the safety of his master if he had proved faithless; but his wealth was too vast for his own security, even had he been innocent. The Emperor, in the edict which contains the sentence, cites as a precedent for his own acts similar condemnation of premiers by three of his ancestors in the present dynasty, but nothing definite is known of their crimes or trials.[1]

Taukwang was more clement, or more fortunate than his father, and upon coming to the throne continued Tohtsin in power; this statesman had held the premiership from 1815 to 1832, with but few interruptions, when he was allowed to retire at the age of seventy-five. He had served under three emperors, having risen step by step from the situation of clerk in one of the offices. His successor, Changling, experienced a far more checkered course, but remained in favor at last, and retired from the premiership in 1836, aged about seventy-nine. He became very popular with his master from his ability in quelling the insurrection of Jehangír in Turkestan in 1827. Even a few such instances of the honor in which an upright, energetic, and wise minister is regarded by prince and people have great influence in encouraging young men to act in the same way.

Few Chinese statesmen have been oftener brought into the notice of western foreigners than Sung, one of the commissioners attached to Lord Macartney's embassy, and a favorite of all its members. His lordship speaks of him then as a young man of high quality, possessing an elevated mind; and adds that "during the whole time of our connection with him he has on all occasions conducted himself toward us in the most friendly and gentleman-like manner." This was in 1793. In 1817 he is mentioned as one of the Cabinet; but not long after, for some unknown reason, he was degraded by Kiaking to the sixth rank, and ap-

---

[1] *Chinese Repository*, Vol. III., p. 241.

pointed adjutant-general among the Tsakhar Mongols; from thence he memorialized his master respecting the ill conduct of some lamas, who had been robbing and murdering. Sung and his friends opposed the Emperor's going to Manchuria, and were involved in some trouble on this account, the reasons of which it is difficult to understand. He was promoted, however, to be captain-general of Manchuria, but again fell under censure, and on his visit to his paternal estate at Mukden the Emperor took him back to the capital and appointed him to some important office. He soon got into new trouble with the Emperor, who in a proclamation remarks that "Sung is inadequate to the duties of minister of the imperial presence; because, although he formerly officiated as such, he is now upward of seventy years of age, and rides badly on horseback;" he is therefore sent to Manchuria to fill his old office of captain-general. The next year the ex-minister and his adherents were involved in a long trial about the loss of a seal, and he was deprived of his command and directed to retire to his own Banner; the real reasons of this disgrace were probably connected with the change of parties ensuent upon the accession of Taukwang.

Soon afterward Sung was restored to favor and made adjutant at Jeh ho, after having been president of the Censorate for a month. He was allowed to remain there longer than usual, and employed his spare time in writing a book upon the newly acquired territory in Turkestan. In 1824 he was reinstated as president of the Censorate, with admonitions not to confuse and puzzle himself with a multiplicity of extraneous matters. In 1826 he was sent on a special commission to Shansí, and when he returned was honored with a dinner at court on new year's day. He then appears as travelling tutor to the crown-prince, but where his royal highness went for his education does not appear; from this post we find him made president of the Board of Rites, and appointed to inspect the victims for a state sacrifice. He is then ordered to Jeh ho, from whence, in a fit of penitence, or perhaps from fear of a dun, he memorialized the Emperor about a debt of $52,000 he had incurred nearly thirty years before, which he proposed to liquidate by foregoing his salary of $1,000 until the arrears were paid up; the Emperor was in good humor with the old man, and forgave him the whole amount, being assured, he says, of Sung's pure official character. In this memorial, when recounting his services, the aged officer says that he has been twice commander-in-chief and governor of Ílí, governor-general at Nanking, Canton, etc., but had never saved much.

Shortly after this he is recalled from Jeh ho and made *tí-tuh* of Peking, then president of the Board of War; and in a few months he is ordered to proceed across the desert to Cobdo to investigate some affair of importance—a long and toilsome journey of fifteen hundred miles for a man over seventy-five years old. He returned the next year and resumed his post as president of the Board of War, in which capacity he acted as examiner of the students in the Russian College. In 1831 he was made president of the Colonial Office, and later received an appointment as superintendent of the Three Treasuries, but was obliged to resign from ill health. A month's relaxation seems to have wonderfully restored him, for the Emperor, in reply to his petition for employment, expresses surprise that he should so soon be fit for official duties, and plainly intimates his opinion that the disease was all sham, though he accedes to his request so far as to nominate him commander of one of the eight Banners. In 1832 Sung again became involved in intrigues, and was reduced to the third degree of rank; the resignation of Tohtsin and the struggle for the vacant premiership was probably the real reason of this new reverse, though a frivolous accusation of two years' standing was trumped up against him. He was restored again, after a few months' disgrace, at the petition of a beg of a city in Turkestan, which illustrates, by the way, the influence which those princes exert. Old age now began to come upon the courtier in good earnest, and in 1833 he was ordered to retire with the rank and pay of adjutant, which he lived to enjoy only two years. Much of the success of Sung was said to be owing to his having had a daughter in the harem, but his personal character and kindness were evidently the main sources of his enduring influence among all ranks of people and officers; one account says the Manchus almost worshipped him, and beggars clung to his chair in the streets to ask alms. It is wortny of notice that in all his reverses there is no mention made of any severer punishment than degradation or banishment, and in this particular the political life of Sung is probably a fair criterion of the usual fortune of high Chinese statesmen. The leading events in the life of Changling, the successor of Tohtsin, together with a few notices of the governor of Canton in 1833, Lí Hung-pin, are given in the *Repository*.[1]

Commissioners Lin and Kíying became more famous among foreigners than their compeers in the capital, from the parts they acted in the war with England in 1840, but only a few notices of their lives are accessible. Lin Tseh-sü was born in 1785, in Fuhchau, and passed through the literary examinations, becoming a graduate of the second rank at the age of nineteen, and of the third when twenty-six. After filling an office or two in the Imperial Academy, he was sent as assistant literary examiner to Kiangsí in 1816, and during three subsequent years acted as examiner and censor in various places. In 1819 he filled the office of intendant of circuit, in Chehkiang; and after absence on account of health, he was, in 1823, appointed to the post of treasurer of Kiangsu, in the absence of the incumbent. In 1826 he was made overseer of the Yellow River, but hearing of his mother's death, resigned his office to mourn for her. After the period of mourning was finished he went to Peking and received the office of judge in Shensí; but before he had been in it a month he was made treasurer of Kiangsu, and before he could enter upon this new office he heard of his father's death, and was obliged to resign once more. In 1832 he was nominated treasurer in Hupeh, and five months later transferred to the same office in Honan, and six months after that sent to Kiangsu again. Three months after this third transfer he was reinstated overseer of the Yellow River, and within a short time elevated to be governor of Kiangsí, which he retained three years, and acted as governor-general of Liang Kiang two years more. In 1838 he was made governor-general of Hu Kwang; and shortly after

[1] *Chinese Repository*, Vol. IV., pp. 61–66.

this ordered to come to Peking to be admitted to an imperial audience, and by special favor permitted to ride on horseback within the palace.

He was at this audience appointed imperial commissioner to put down the opium trade and manage the affairs of the maritime frontier of Kwantung, receiving at the time such plenipotentiary powers to act for the Emperor as had only once before been committed to a subject since 1644, viz., when Changling was sent to Turkestan to quell the insurrection. Lin's ill success in dealing with the opium trade and its upholders in the British government reflect no discredit on his own ability, for the task was beyond the powers of the Empire; but his fame even now stands high among the Cantonese. One incident showing his kindness to the crew of the Sunda, an English vessel lost on Hainan Island, on their arrival in Canton in October, 1839, while he was fighting their consular officers, gave a good insight into the candor of the man. In December, 1839, he was appointed governor-general of Liang Kiang; but succeeded to that of Liang Kwang in February, 1840. In October of the same year the seals of office were taken away, and he was ordered to return to Peking. He remained, however, till May of the next year to advise with Kíshen in his difficult negotiations with the English. Lin left Canton in May, 1841, leading two thousand troops to defend Ningpo, but this rôle was not his forte. In July, 1842, he was banished to Ílí, but the sentence was suspended for a season by giving him a third time the oversight of the Yellow River. However, in 1844 we find him in Ílí, holding an inferior appointment and trying to bring waste lands near the Mohammedan cities under cultivation; his zeal was rewarded the next year by a pardon, and the year after that by the high post of governor-general of Shensí and Kansuh, in which region he set himself to work to reform the civil service and increase the revenue. In 1847 the cares of office wore upon him, so that he asked for a furlough and went back to Fuhchau, aged sixty-two. His ambition was not yet satisfied, for he was made governor-general in Yunnan in 1848, but his strength was not equal to its duties, and he again retired in 1849. The young Emperor Hienfung, startled at the rapid rise of the Tai-ping rebels, applied to the aged statesman to help him as he had his father. Lin responded to the call of his sovereign, but death came upon him before he reached Kwangsí, on the 22d of November, 1850, at the age of sixty-seven. More enduring than some of his official acts was the preparation and publication of the *History of Maritime Nations*, with maps, in fifty books, in which he gave his countrymen all the details he could gather of other nations.[1]

Much less is known of the official life of Kíying than of Lin, but the Manchu proved himself superior to the Chinese in trimming his course to meet the inevitable and avoid the rocks his predecessor struck. In 1835 his name is mentioned as president of the Board of Revenue and controller of the Tsung-jin fu. He was detained at the capital as commander-in-chief of the forces there until 1842, when his Majesty sent him to Canton to take the place of Yihshan. He was ordered to stop at Hangchau, however, on his way, and make a report of the condition of affairs; his memorials seem to have had great influence, for he was appointed joint commissioner with Ílípu in April of that year. At the negotiations of Nanking Kíying acted as chief commissioner, and was mainly instrumental in bringing the war to a conclusion. He proceeded to Canton in May, 1843, to succeed Ílípu, and there acted as sole commissioner in negotiating the supplementary treaty and the commercial regulations with the British, returning to tho capital in December, 1843. His prudence and vigor had great effect in calming the irritation of the people of Canton. On the arrival of the American plenipotentiary he was vested with full powers to treat with Mr. Cushing, and soon after with the French and Swedish envoys, with all of whom he signed treaties. During the progress of these negotiations Kí Kung died and Kíying succeeded him.

His administration as governor-general continued till January, 1848, when he returned to Peking to receive higher honors from the Emperor. In 1849 he went to Kiangsu to inquire

---

[1] Compare Dr. Bowring in *N. C. Br. R. A. Soc. Journal*, Part III., Art. VII. (Dec., 1852).

into the salt department, and then to Northern Shansí to settle differences with the Mongols. From this period he held various posts in the cabinet and capital, busy in all court intrigues, and rather losing his good name, till he fell into disgrace. In 1856, when the envoys of the four western Powers were at Tientsin, he entered into some underhand dealings against the policy of Kweiliang and Hwashana, and was sent there as joint commissioner. He had hardly entered upon his functions by the presentation of his commission, when he suddenly returned to Peking against the Emperor's will, and was ordered to take poison in the presence of the head of the Clan to avoid the ignominy of a public execution.[1] Few Chinese statesmen in modern times have borne a higher character for prudence, dignity, and intelligence than Kíying, and the confidence reposed in him is creditable to his imperial master. In his demeanor, says Sir Thomas Wade, "there was a combination of dignity and courtesy which more than balanced the deficiencies of a by no means attractive exterior." The portrait of him has been engraved from a native painting made at Canton, and is a good one. It was kindly furnished for this work by J. R. Peters, Jr.

The facts of this man's career are not all known, but his connection by birth with the Clan brought him into an entirely different set of influences from Lin, while his training removed him from the contact with the people which made the other so popular and influential. Both of them were good instances of Chinese statesmen, and their checkered lives as here briefly noticed resemble that of their compeers in the highest grades of official dignity. The sifting which the personnel of the Emperor's employees in all their various grades receive generally brings the cleverest and most trustworthy to the top; no one can come in contact with them in state affairs without an increase of respect for their shrewdness, loyalty, and skill. One observable feature of the Chinese political world is the great age of the high officers, and it is not easy to account for their

---

[1] *Chinese Repository*, passim. Oliphant, *Lord Elgin's Mission to China and Japan*, Chap. XVII. Minister Reed, in *U. S. Dip. Correspondence*, 1857–58.

being kept in their posts, when almost worn out, by a monarch who wished to have efficient men around him, until we learn how little real power he can arbitrarily exert over the details of the branches of his government. It is somewhat explainable on the ground that, as long as the old incumbents are alive, the Emperor, being more habituated to their company and advice, prefers to retain those whose competency has been proven by their service. The patriarch, kept near the Emperor, is moreover a kind of hostage for the loyalty of his following; and the latter, scattered throughout the provinces, can be managed and moved about through him with less opposition: he is, still further, a convenient medium through which to receive the exactions of the younger members of the service, and convey such intimations as are thought necessary. The system of clientelage which existed among the Gauls and Franks is also found in China with some modifications, and has a tendency to link officers to one another in parties of different degrees of power. The Emperor published an order in 1833 against this system of patronage, and it is evident that he would find it seriously interfering with his power were it not constantly broken up by changing the relations of the parties and sending them away in different directions. Peking is almost the only place where the "teacher and pupils," as the patron and client call each other, could combine to much purpose; and the principal safeguard the throne seems to have against intrigues and parties around it lies in the conflicting interests arising among themselves, though a long-established or unscrupulous favorite, as in the cases of Duke Ho and Suhshun in 1855–61, can sometimes manage to engross the whole power of the crown.

Notwithstanding the heavy charges of oppression, cruelty, bribery, and mendacity which are often brought against officers with more or less justice, it must not be inferred that no good qualities exist among them. Thousands of them desire to rule equitably, to clear the innocent and punish the guilty, and exert all the knowledge and power they possess to discharge their functions to the acceptance of their master and their own good name among the inhabitants. Such officers, too, generally rise, while the cruelties of others are visited with degradation. The pasquinades which the people stick up in the streets indicate their sentiments, and receive much more attention than would such vulgar expressions in other countries, because it is almost the only way in which their opinions can be safely uttered. The popularity which upright officers receive acts as an incentive to others to follow in the same steps, as well as a reward to the person himself. The governor of Kwangtung in 1833, Chu, was a very popular officer, and when he obtained leave to resign his station on account of age, the people vied with each other in showing their hearty regret at losing him. The old custom was observed of retaining his boots and presenting him with a new pair at every city he passed through, and many other testimonials of their regard were adopted. On leaving the city of Canton he circulated a few verses, "to console the people and excite them to virtue," for he heard that some of them wept on learning of his departure.

From ancient days, my fathers trod the path
Of literary fame, and placed their names
Among the wise; two generations past,
Attendant on their patrons, they have come
To this provincial city.[1] Here this day
'Tis mine to be imperial envoy;
Thus has the memory of ancestral fame
Ceased not to stimulate this feeble frame.

My father held an office at Lungchau.[2]
And deep imprinted his memorial there;
He was the sure and generous friend
Of learning unencouraged and obscure.
When now I turn my head and travel back
In thought to that domestic hall, it seems
As yesterday, those early happy scenes—
How was he pained if forced to be severe!

[1] The Chinese have a great affection for the place of their nativity, and consider a residence in any other province like being in a foreign settlement. They always wish to return thither in life, or have their remains carried and interred there after death.

[2] A district in the province of Kwangsí.

From times remote Kwangtung has been renowned
For wise and mighty men ; but none can stand
Among them, or compare with Kiuh Kiang : [1]
Three idle and inglorious years are past,
And I have raised no monument of fame,
By shedding round the rays of light and truth,
To give the people knowledge. In this heart
I feel the shame, and cannot bear the thought.

But now, in flowered pavilions, in street
Illuminations, gaudy shows, to praise
The gods and please themselves, from year to year
The modern people vie, and boast themselves,
And spend their hard-earned wealth—and all in vain:
For what shall be the end ? Henceforth let all
Maintain an active and a useful life,
The sober husband and the frugal wife.

The gracious statesman,[2] politic and wise,
Is my preceptor and my long-tried friend ;
Called now to separate, spare our farewell
The heartrending words affection so well loves.
That he may still continue to exhort
The people, and instruct them to be wise,
To practice virtue and to keep the laws
Of ancient sages, is my constant hope.

When I look backward o'er the field of fame
Where I have travelled a long fifty years,
The struggle for ambition and the sweat
For gain seem altogether vanity.
Who knoweth not that heaven's toils are close,
Infinitely close ? Few can escape.
Ah ! how few great men reach a full old age !
How few unshorn of honors end their days !

Inveterate disease has twined itself
Around me, and binds me in slavery.
The kindness of his Majesty is high [3]
And liberal, admitting no return

---

[1] Kiuh Kiang was an ancient minister of state during the Tang dynasty. His imperial master would not listen to his advice and he therefore retired. Rebellion and calamities arose. The Emperor thought of his faithful servant and sent for him ; but he was already dead.

[2] Governor Loo.

[3] In permitting Chu to retire from public life.

Unless a grateful heart; still, still my eyes
Will see the miseries of the people—
Unlimited distresses, mournful, sad,
To the mere passer-by awaking grief.

Untalented, unworthy, I withdraw,
Bidding farewell to this windy, dusty world;
Upward I look to the supremely good—
The Emperor—to choose a virtuous man
To follow me. Henceforth it will be well—
The measures and the merits passing mine;
But I shall silent stand and see his grace
Diffusing blessings like the genial spring.

Ilípu, Kí Kung, the late governor-general of Kwangtung, and Shu, the prefect of Ningpo in 1842, are other officers who have been popular in late years. When Lin passed through Macao in 1839, the Chinese had in several places erected honorary portals adorned with festoons of silk and laudatory scrolls; and when he passed the doors of their houses and shops they set out tables decorated with vases of flowers, "in order to manifest their profound gratitude for his coming to save them from a deadly vice, and for removing from them a dire calamity by the destruction and severe interdiction of opium." Alas, that his efforts and intentions should have been so fruitless!

The *Peking Gazette* frequently contains petitions from old officers describing their ailments, their fear lest they shall not be able to perform their duties, the length of their official service, and requesting leave of absence or permission to retire. It is impossible to regard all the expressions of loyalty in these papers, coming as they do from every class of officers, as heartless and made out according to a prescribed form; but we are too ready to measure them by our own standard and fashion, forgetting that it is not the defects of a system which give the best standard of its value and efficiency. Let us rather, as an honest expression of feeling, quote a few lines from a memorial of Shí, a censor in 1824: "Reflecting within myself that, notwithstanding the decay of my strength, it has still pleased the imperial goodness to employ me in a high office instead of rejecting and discarding me at once, I have been most anxious to effect a cure, in order that, a weak old horse as I am, it might be still in my power, by the exertion of my whole strength, to recompense a ten-thousandth part of the benevolence which restored me to life."[1]

Connected with the triennial schedule of official merits and demerits is the necessity the high officers of state are under of confessing their faults of government; and the two form a peculiar and somewhat stringent check upon their intrigues and malversation, making them, as Le Comte observes, "exceeding circumspect and careful, and sometimes even virtuous against their own inclinations." The confessions reported in the *Peking Gazette* are, however, by no means satisfactory as to the real extent or nature of these acts; most of the confessors are censors, and perhaps it is in virtue of their office that they thus sit in judgment upon themselves. Examples of the crimes mentioned are not wanting. The governor-general of Chihlí requested severe punishment in 1832 for not having discovered a plotting demagogue who had collected several thousand adherents in his and the next provinces; his request was granted. An admiral in the same province demands punishment for not having properly educated his son, as thereby he went mad and wounded several people. Another calls for judgment upon himself because the Empress-dowager had been kept waiting at the palace gate by the porters when she paid her Majesty a visit. One officer accused himself for not being able to control the Yellow River; and his Majesty's cook in 1830 requested punishment for being too late in presenting his bill of fare, but was graciously forgiven. The rarity of these confessions, compared with the actual sins, shows either that they are, like a partridge's doublings, made to draw off attention from the real nest of malversation, or that few officers are willing to undergo the mortification.

The Emperor, in his character of vicegerent of heaven, occasionally imposes the duty of self-confession upon himself. Kiaking issued several public confessions during his reign, but the *Gazette* has not contained many such papers within the last thirty years. These confessions are drawn from him more by

[1] *Chinese Repository*, Vol. IV., p. 71.

natural calamities, such as drought, freshets, epidemics, etc., than by political causes, though insurrections, fires, ominous portents, etc., sometimes induce them. The personal character of the monarch has much to do with their frequency and phraseology. On occasion of a drought in 1817 the Emperor Kiaking said: "The remissness and sloth of the officers of government constitute an evil which has long been accumulating. It is not the evil of a day; for several years I have given the most pressing admonitions on the subject, and have punished many cases which have been discovered, so that recently there appears a little improvement, and for several seasons the weather has been favorable. The drought this season is not perhaps entirely on their (the officers') account. I have meditated upon it, and am persuaded that the reason why the azure Heavens above manifest disapprobation by withholding rain for a few hundred miles only around the capital, is that the fifty and more rebels who escaped are secreted somewhere near Peking. Hence it is that fertile vapors are fast bound, and the felicitous harmony of the seasons interrupted." On the 14th of May, 1818, between five and six o'clock in the evening, a sudden darkness enveloped the capital, attended by a violent wind from the southeast and much rain. During its action two intervals occurred when the sky became a lurid red and the air offensive, terrible claps of thunder startling the people and frightening the monarch. His astrologers could not relieve his forebodings of evil, and he issued a manifesto to explain the matter to his subjects and discharge his own conscience. One sentence is worth quoting: "Calumnious accusations cause the ruin and death of a multitude of innocent people; they alone are capable of provoking a sign as terrible as this one just seen. The wind coming from the southeast is proof enough that some great crime has been committed in that region, which the officials, by neglecting their duties, have ignored, and thereby excited the ire of Heaven." [1]

One of the most remarkable specimens of these papers is a prayer for rain issued by Taukwang, July 24, 1832, on occasion

[1] *Annales de la Foi,* No. 6, 1823, pp. 21–24.

of a severe drought at the capital. Before publishing this paper he had endeavored to mollify the anger and heat of heaven by ordering all suspected and accused persons in the prisons of the metropolis to be tried, and their guilt or innocence established, in order that the course of justice might not be delayed, and witnesses be released from confinement. But these vicarious corrections did not avail, and the drought continuing, he was obliged, as high-priest of the Empire, to show the people that he was mindful of their sufferings, and would relieve them, if possible, by presenting the following memorial:

"Kneeling, a memorial is hereby presented, to cause affairs to be heard.

"Oh, alas! imperial Heaven, were not the world afflicted by extraordinary changes, I would not dare to present extraordinary services. But this year the drought is most unusual. Summer is past, and no rain has fallen. Not only do agriculture and human beings feel the dire calamity, but also beasts and insects, herbs and trees, almost cease to live. I, the minister of Heaven, am placed over mankind, and am responsible for keeping the world in order and tranquillizing the people. Although it is now impossible for me to sleep or eat with composure, although I am scorched with grief and tremble with anxiety, still, after all, no genial and copious showers have been obtained.

"Some days ago I fasted, and offered rich sacrifices on the altars of the gods of the land and the grain, and had to be thankful for gathering clouds and slight showers; but not enough to cause gladness. Looking up, I consider that Heaven's heart is benevolence and love. The sole cause is the daily deeper atrocity of my sins; but little sincerity and little devotion. Hence I have been unable to move Heaven's heart, and bring down abundant blessings.

"Having searched the records, I find that in the twenty-fourth year of Kienlung my exalted Ancestor, the Emperor Pure, reverently performed a 'great snow service.' I feel impelled, by ten thousand considerations, to look up and imitate the usage, and with trembling anxiety rashly assail Heaven, examine myself, and consider my errors; looking up and hoping that I may obtain pardon. I ask myself whether in sacrificial services I have been disrespectful? Whether or not pride and prodigality have had a place in my heart, springing forth there unobserved? Whether, from length of time, I have become remiss in attending to the affairs of government, and have been unable to attend to them with that serious diligence and strenuous effort which I ought? Whether I have uttered irreverent words, and have deserved reprehension? Whether perfect equity has been attained in conferring rewards or inflicting punishments? Whether in raising mausolea and laying out gardens I have distressed the people and wasted property? Whether in the appointment of officers I have failed to obtain fit persons, and thereby the acts of government have been petty and vexatious to the people? Whether punishments have been unjustly inflicted or not? Whether the oppressed have found no means of appeal? Whether in persecuting heterodox sects the innocent have not been involved? Whether or not the magistrates have insulted the people and refused to listen to their affairs? Whether, in the successive military operations on the western frontiers, there may not have been the horrors of human slaughter for the sake of imperial rewards? Whether the largesses bestowed on the afflicted southern provinces were properly applied, or the people were left to die in the ditches? Whether the efforts to exterminate or pacify the rebellious mountaineers of Hunan and Kwangtung were properly conducted; or whether they led to the inhabitants being trampled on as mire and ashes? To all these topics to which my anxieties have been directed I ought to lay the plumb-line, and strenuously endeavor to correct what is wrong; still recollecting that there may be faults which have not occurred to me in my meditations.

"Prostrate I beg imperial Heaven (*Hwang Tien*) to pardon my ignorance and stupidity, and to grant me self-renovation; for myriads of innocent people are involved by me, the One man. My sins are so numerous it is difficult to escape from them. Summer is past and autumn arrived; to wait longer will really be impossible. Knocking head, I pray imperial Heaven to hasten and confer gracious deliverance—a speedy and divinely beneficial rain, to save the people's lives and in some degree redeem my iniquities. Oh, alas! imperial Heaven, observe these things. Oh, alas! imperial Heaven, be gracious to them. I am inexpressibly grieved, alarmed, and frightened. Reverently this memorial is presented."[1]

This paper apparently intimates some acknowledgment of a ruling power above, and before a despot like the Emperor of China would place himself in such an equivocal posture before his people, he would assure himself very thoroughly of their sentiments; for its effects as a state paper would be worse than null if the least ridicule was likely to be thrown upon it. In this case heavy showers followed the same evening, and appropriate thanksgivings were ordered and oblations presented before the six altars of heaven, earth, land, and grain, and the gods of heaven, earth, and the revolving year.

The orders of the court are usually transmitted in manuscript, except when some grand event or state ceremony requires a general proclamation, in which cases the document is printed on yellow paper and published in both the Chinese and Manchu languages, encircled with a border of dragons. The governors and their subordinates, imperial commissioners, and collectors of customs are the principal officers in the provinces who pub-

[1] *Chinese Repository*, Vol. I., p. 236.

lish their orders to the people, consisting of admonitions, exhortations, regulations, laws, special ordinances, threatenings, and municipal requirements. Standing laws and local regulations are often superbly carved on tablets of black marble, and placed in the streets to be "held in everlasting remembrance," so that no one can plead ignorance; a custom which recalls the mode of publishing the Twelve Tables at Rome. Several of these monuments, beautifully ornamented, are to be seen at Canton and Macao. The usual mode of publishing the commands of government is to print the document in large characters, and post copies at the door of the offices and in the streets in public places, with the seal of the officer attached to authenticate them. The sheets on which they are printed being common bamboo paper, and having no protection from the weather, are, however, soon destroyed; the people read them as they are thus exposed, and copy them if they wish, but it is not uncommon, too, for the magistrates to print important edicts in pamphlet form for circulation. These placards are written in an official style, differing from common writing as much as that does in English, but not involved or obscure. A single specimen of an edict issued at Canton will suffice to illustrate the form of such papers, and moreover show upon what subjects a Chinese ruler sometimes legislates, and the care he is expected to take of the people.

"Sü and Hwang, by special appointment magistrates of the districts of Nanhai and Pwanyu, raised ten steps and recorded ten times, hereby distinctly publish important rules for the capture of grasshoppers, that it may be known how to guard against them in order to ward off injury and calamity. On the 7th day of the 8th month in the 13th year of Taukwang [September 20, 1833], we received a communication from the prefect of the [department of Kwangchau], transmitting a despatch from their excellencies the governor-general and governor, as follows:

"'During the fifth month of the present year flights of grasshoppers appeared in the limits of Kwangsí, in [the departments of] Liu, Tsin, Kwei, and Wu, and their vicinage, which have already, according to report, been clean destroyed and driven off. We have heard that in the department of Kauchau and its neighborhood, conterminous to Kwangsí, grasshoppers have appeared which multiply with extreme rapidity. At this time the second crop is in the blade (which if destroyed will endamage the people), and it is proper, therefore, immediately, wherever they are found, to capture and drive them off, marshalling the troops to advance and wholly exterminate them. But Kwangtung heretofore has never experienced this calamity, and we apprehend the officers and people do not understand the mode of capture; wherefore we now exhibit in order the most important rules for catching grasshoppers. Let the governor's combined forces be immediately instructed to capture them *secundum artem;* at the same time let orders be issued for the villagers and farmers at once to assemble and take them, and for the magistrate to establish storehouses for their reception and purchase, thus without fail sweeping them clean away. If you do not exert yourselves to catch the grasshoppers, your guilt will be very great; let it be done carefully, not clandestinely delaying, thus causing this misfortune to come upon yourselves, transgressing the laws, and causing us again, according to the exigencies of the case, to promulgate general orders and make thorough examination, etc., etc. Appended hereto are copies of the rules for catching grasshoppers, which from the lieutenant-governor must be sent to the treasurer, who will enjoin it upon the magistrates of the departments, and he again upon the district magistrates.'

"Having received the preceding, besides respectfully transmitting it to the colonel of the department to be straightway forwarded to all the troops under his authority, and also to all the district justices, that they all with united purpose bend their energies to observe, at the proper time, that whenever the grasshoppers become numerous they join their forces and extirpate them, thus removing calamity from the people; we also enjoin upon whomsoever receives this that the grasshoppers be caught according to these several directions, which are therefore here arranged in order as follows:

"'1. When the grasshoppers first issue forth they are to be seen on the borders of large morasses, from whence they quickly multiply and fill large tracts of land; they produce their young in little hillocks of black earth, using the tail to bore into the ground, not quite an inch in depth, which still remain as open holes, the whole somewhat resembling a bee's nest. One grasshopper drops ten or more pellets, in form like a pea, each one containing a hundred or more young. For the young grasshoppers fly and eat in swarms, and this laying of their young is done all at once and in the same spot; the place resembles a hive of bees, and therefore it is very easily sought and found.

"'2. When the grasshoppers are in the fields of wheat and tender rice and the thick grass, every day at early dawn they all alight on the leaves of the grass, and their bodies being covered with dew are heavy and they cannot fly or hop; at noon they begin to assemble for flight, and at evening they collect in one spot. Thus each day there are three periods when they can be caught, and the people and gentry will also have a short respite. The mode of catching them is to dig a trench before them, the broader and longer the better, on each side placing boards, doors, screens, and such like things, one stretched on after another, and spreading open each side. The whole multitude must then cry aloud, and, holding boards in their hands, drive them all into the trench; meanwhile those on the opposite side, provided with brooms and rakes, on seeing any leaping or crawling out, must sweep them back; then covering them with dry grass, burn them all up. Let the fire be first kindled in the trench, and then drive them into it; for if they are only buried up, then many of them will crawl out of the openings and so escape.

" '3. When the swarms of grasshoppers see a row of trees, or a close line of flags and streamers, they usually hover over and settle; and the farmers frequently suspend red and white clothes and petticoats on long poles, or make red and green paper flags, but they do not always settle with great rapidity. Moreover, they dread the noise of gongs, matchlocks, and guns, hearing which they fly away. If they come so as to obscure the heavens, you must let off the guns and clang the gongs, or fire the crackers; it will strike the front ranks with dread, and flying away, the rest will follow them and depart.

" '4. When the wings and legs of the grasshoppers are taken off, and [their bodies] dried in the sun, the taste is like dried prawns, and moreover, they can be kept a long time without spoiling. Ducks can also be reared upon the dried grasshoppers, and soon become large and fat. Moreover, the hill people catch them to feed pigs; these pigs, weighing at first only twenty catties or so, in ten days' time grow to weigh more than fifty catties; and in rearing all domestic animals they are of use. Let all farmers exert themselves and catch them alive, giving rice or money according to the number taken. In order to remove this calamity from your grain, what fear is there that you will not perform this? Let all these rules for catching the grasshoppers be diligently carried into full effect.'

"Wherefore these commands are transcribed that all you soldiers and people may be fully acquainted with them. Do you all then immediately in obedience to them, when you see the proper time has come, sound the gong; and when you see the grasshoppers and their young increasing, straightway get ready, on the one hand seizing them, and on the other announcing to the officers that they collect the troops, that with united strength you may at once catch them, without fail making an utter extermination of them; thus calamity will be removed from the people. We will also then confer rewards upon those of the farmers and people who first announce to the magistrates their approach. Let every one implicitly obey. A special command.

"Promulgated Taukwang, 13th year, 8th month, and 15th day."[1]

The concluding part of an edict affords some room for displaying the character of the promulgator. Among other endings are such as these: "Hasten! hasten! a special edict." "Tremble hereat intensely." "Lay not up for yourselves future repentance by disobedience." "I will by no means eat my words." "Earnestly observe these things." In their state papers Chinese officers are constantly referring to ultimate truths and axioms, and deducing arguments therefrom in a peculiarly national grandiloquent manner, though some of their

---

[1] *Easy Lessons in Chinese*, pp. 223–227. The effect of these instructions relating to grasshoppers does not appear to have equalled the zeal of the officers composing them; swarms of locusts, however, are in general neither numerous nor devastating in China.

conclusions are preposterous non-sequiturs. Commissioner Lin addressed a letter to the Queen of England regarding the interdiction of opium, which began with the following preamble:

"Whereas, the ways of Heaven are without partiality, and no sanction is allowed to injure others in order to benefit one's self, and that men's natural feelings are not very diverse (for where is he who does not abhor death and love life?)—therefore your honorable nation, though beyond the wide ocean at a distance of twenty thousand *li*, also acknowledges the same ways of Heaven, the same human nature, and has the like perceptions of the distinctions between life and death, benefit and injury. Our heavenly court has for its family all that is within the four seas; and as to the great Emperor's heaven-like benevolence—there is none whom it does not overshadow; even regions remote, desert, and disconnected have a part in his general care of life and well-being."

The edicts furnish almost the only exponents of the intentions of government. They present several characteristic features of the ignorant conceit and ridiculous assumptions of the Chinese, while they betray the real weakness of the authorities in the mixture of argument and command, coaxing and threatening, pervading every paragraph. According to their phraseology, there can possibly be no failure in the execution of every order; if they are once made known, the obedience of the people follows almost as a matter of course; while at the same time both the writer and the people know that most of them are not only perfunctory but nearly useless. The responsibility of the writer in a measure ceases with the promulgation of his orders, and when they reach the last in the series their efficiency has well nigh departed. Expediency is the usual guide for obedience; deceiving superiors and oppressing the people the rule of action on the part of many officials; and their orders do not more strikingly exhibit their weakness and ignorance than their mendacity and conceit. A large proportion of well-meaning officers are sensible too that all their efforts will be neutralized by the half-paid, unscrupulous retainers and clerks in the *yamuns;* and this checks their energy.

It is not easy, without citing many examples accompanied

with particular explanations, to give a just idea of the actual execution of the laws, and show how far the people are secured in life and property by their rulers; and perhaps nothing has been the source of such differing views regarding the Chinese as the predominance writers give either to the theory or the practice of legislation. Old Magaillans has hit this point pretty well when he says: "It seems as if the legislators had omitted nothing, and that they had foreseen all inconveniences that were to be feared; so that I am persuaded no kingdom in the world could be better governed or more happy, if the conduct and probity of the officers were but answerable to the institution of the government. But in regard they have no knowledge of the true God, nor of the eternal rewards and punishments of the other world, they are subject to no remorses of conscience, they place all their happiness in pleasure, in dignity and riches; and therefore, to obtain these fading advantages, they violate all the laws of God and man, trampling under foot religion, reason, justice, honesty, and all the rights of consanguinity and friendship. The inferior officers mind nothing but how to defraud their superiors, they the supreme tribunals, and all together how to cheat the king; which they know how to do with so much cunning and address, making use in their memorials of words and expressions so soft, so honest, so respectful, so humble and full of adulation, and of reasons so plausible, that the deluded prince frequently takes the greatest falsehoods for solemn truths. So that the people, finding themselves continually oppressed and overwhelmed without any reason, murmur and raise seditions and revolts, which have caused so much ruin and so many changes in the Empire. Nevertheless, there is no reason that the excellency and perfection of the laws of China should suffer for the depravity and wickedness of the magistrates."[1]

Magaillans resided in China nearly forty years, and his opinion may be considered on the whole as a fair judgment of the real condition of the people and the policy of their rulers.

---

[1] *A new History of China, containing a description of the most considerable particulars of that Empire, written by* Gabriel Magaillans, *of the Society of Jesus, Missionary Apostolick. Done out of French.* London, 1688, p. 249.

When one is living in the country itself, to hear the complaints of individuals against the extortion and cruelty of their rulers, and to read the reports of judicial murder, torture, and crime in the *Peking Gazette*, are enough to cause one to wonder how such atrocities and oppressions are endured from year to year, and why the sufferers do not rise and throw aside the tyrannous power which thus abuses them. But the people are generally conscious that their rulers are no better than themselves, and that they would really gain nothing by such a procedure, and their desire to maintain as great a degree of peace as possible leads them to submit to many evils, which in western countries would soon be remedied or cause a revolution. In order to restrain the officers in their misrule, Section CCX. of the code ordains that "If any officer of government, whose situation gives him power and control over the people, not only does not conciliate them by proper indulgence, but exercises his authority in a manner so inconsistent with the established laws and approved usages of the Empire, that the sentiments of the once loyal subjects being changed by his oppressive conduct, they assemble tumultuously and openly rebel, and drive him at length from the capital city and seat of his government; such officer shall suffer death."

By the laws of China, every officer of the nine ranks must be previously qualified for duty by a degree; in the ninth are included village magistrates, deputy treasurers, jailers, etc., but the police, local interpreters, clerks, and other attendants on the courts are not considered as having any rank, and most of them are natives of the place where they are employed. The only degradation they can feel is to turn them out of their stations, but this is hardly a palliative of the evils the people suffer from them; the new leech is more thirsty than the old. The cause of many of the extortions the people suffer from their rulers is found in the system of purchasing office, at all times practised in one shape or other, but occasionally resorted to by the government. As the counterpart of this system, that of receiving bribes must be expected therefore to prevail, and being in fact practised by all grades of dignitaries, and sometimes even upheld by them as a "necessary evil," it adds still more to the bad consequences resulting from this mode of obtaining office. Indeed, so far is the practice of "covering the eyes" carried in China, that the people seldom approach their rulers without a gift to make way for them.

One mode taken by the highest ranks to obtain money is to notify inferiors that there are certain days on which presents are expected, and custom soon increases these as much as the case will admit. Subscriptions for objects of public charity or disbursements, such as an inundation, a bad harvest, bursting of dikes, and other similar things which the government must look after, are not unfrequently made a source of revenue to the incumbents by requiring much more than is needed; those who subscribe are rewarded by an empty title, a peacock's feather, or employment in some insignificant formality. The sale of titular rank is a source of revenue, but the government never attempts to subvert or interfere with the well-known channel of attaining office by literary merit, and it seldom confers much real power for money when unconnected with some degree of fitness. The security of its own position is not to be risked for the sake of an easy means of filling its exchequer, yet it is impossible to say how far the sale of office and title is carried. The censors inveigh against it, and the Emperor almost apologizes for resorting to it, but it is nevertheless constantly practised. The government stocks of this description were opened during the late rebellions and foreign wars, as the necessities of the case were a sufficient excuse for the disreputable practice. In 1835 the sons of two of the leading hong-merchants were promoted, in consequence of their donations of $25,000 each to repair the ravages of an inundation; subscribers to the amount of $10,000 and upward were rewarded by an honorary title, whose only privilege is that it saves its possessor from a bambooing, it being the law that no one holding any office can be personally chastised.[1]

Besides the lower officers, the clerks in their employ and the police, who are often taken from the garrison soldiery, are the agents in the hands of the upper ranks to squeeze the people.

---

[1] Compare the *Chinese Repository*, Vol. XVIII., p. 207.

There are many clerks of various duties and grades about all the offices who receive small salaries, and every application and petition to their superiors, going through their hands, is attended by a bribe to pass them up. The military police and servants connected with the offices are not paid any regular salary, and their number is great. In the large districts, like those of Nanhai and Pwanyu, which compose the city of Canton and suburbs, it is said there are about a thousand unpaid police; in the middle-sized ones between three and four hundred, and in the smallest from one to two hundred. This number is increased by the domestics attending high officers as part of their suite, and by their old acquaintances, who make themselves known when there is any likelihood of being employed. Among other abuses mentioned by the censors is that of magistrates appointing their own creatures to fill vacancies until those nominated by his Majesty arrive; like a poor man oppressing the poor, such officers are a sweeping rain. A similar abuse arises when country magistrates leave their posts to go to the provincial capital to dance attendance upon their superiors, and get nominated to a higher place or taken into their service as secretaries, because they will work for nothing; the duties of their vacated offices are meantime usually left undone, and underlings take advantage of their absence to make new exactions. The governor fills vacant offices with his own friends, and recommends them to his Majesty to be confirmed; but this has little effect in consolidating a system of oppression from the constant changes going on. In fact, it is hard to say which feature of the Chinese polity is the least disastrous to good government, these constant changes which neutralize all sympathy with the people on the part of rulers, or on the other hand make it useless for seditious men to try to foment rebellion.

The retinues of high provincial officers contain many dependents and expectant supernumeraries, all subservient to them; among them are the descendants of poor officers; the sons of bankrupt merchants who once possessed influence; dissipated, well bred, unscrupulous men, who lend themselves to everything flagitious; and lastly, fortune-seekers without money, but possessing talents of good order to be used by any one who will hire them. Such persons are not peculiar to China, and their employment is guarded against in the code, but no law is more of a dead letter. Officers of government, too, conscious of their delinquencies, and afraid their posts will soon be taken from them, of course endeavor to make the most of their opportunities, and by means of such persons, who are usually well acquainted with the leading inhabitants of the district, harass and threaten such as are likely to pay well for being left in quiet. It does them little or no good, however, for if they are not removed they must fee their superiors, and if they are punished for their misdeeds they are still more certain of losing their wicked exactions.

In the misappropriation of public funds, and peculation of all kinds in materials, government stores, rations, wages, and salaries, the Chinese officials are skilled experts, and are never surprised at any disclosures.

Another common mode of plundering the people is for officers to collude with bands of thieves, and allow them to escape for a composition when arrested, or substitute other persons for the guilty party in case the real offenders are likely to be condemned. Sometimes these banditti are too strong even for an upright magistrate, and he is obliged to overlook what he cannot remedy; for, however much he may wish to arrest and bring them to justice, his policemen are too much afraid of their vengeance to venture upon attacking them. An instance of this occurred near Canton in 1839, when a boat, containing a clerk of the court and three or four police, came into the fleet of European opium-ships to hunt for some desperate opium smugglers who had taken refuge there. The fellows, hearing of the arrival of the boat, came in the night, and surrounding it took out the crew, bound their pursuers, and burned them alive with the boat in sight of the whole fleet, to whom the desperadoes looked for protection against their justly incensed countrymen.

A censor in 1819, complaining of flagrant neglect in the administration of justice in Chihlí, says: "Among the magistrates are many who, without fear or shame, connive at robbery and deceit. Formerly, horse-stealers were wont to conceal themselves in some secret place, but now they openly bring their plunder to market for sale. When they perceive a person to be weak, they are in the habit of stealing his property and returning it to him for money, while the officers, on hearing it, treat it as a trivial matter, and blame the sufferer for not being more cautious. Thieves are apprehended with warrants on them, showing that when they were sent out to arrest thieves they availed of the opportunity to steal for themselves. And at a village near the imperial residence are very many plunderers concealed, who go out by night in companies of twenty or thirty persons, carrying weapons with them; they frequently call up the inhabitants, break open the doors, and having satisfied themselves with what food and wine they can obtain, they threaten and extort money, which if they cannot procure they seize their clothes, ornaments, or cattle, and depart. They also frequently go to shops, and having broken open the shutters impudently demand money, which if they do not get they set fire to the shop with the torches in their hands. If the master of the house lay hold on a few of them and sends them to the magistrate, he merely imprisons and beats them, and before half a month allows them to run away."[1]

The unpaid retainers about the *yamuns* are very numerous, and are more dreaded than the police; one censor says they are looked upon by the people as tigers and wolves; he effected the discharge of nearly twenty-four thousand of them in the province of Chihlí alone. They are usually continued in their places by the head magistrate, who, when he arrives, being ignorant of the characters of those he must employ, re-engages such as are likely to serve. In cases of serious accusation the clerks frequently subpœna all who are likely to be implicated, and demand a fee for liberating them when their innocence is shown. These myrmidons still fear the anger of their superiors and a recoil of the people so far as to endeavor to save appearances by hushing up the matter, and liberating those

[1] *Chinese Repository*, Vol. IV., p. 218.

unjustly apprehended, with great protestations of compassion. It may be added that, as life is not lightly taken, thieves are careful not to murder or maltreat their victims dangerously, nor do the magistrates venture to take life outright by torture, though their cruelties frequently result in death by neglect or starvation. Money and goods are what both policemen and officials want, not blood and revenge. Parties at strife with each other frequently resort to legal implication to gratify their ill-will, and take a pitiful revenge by egging on the police to pillage and vex their enemy, though they themselves profit nowise thereby.

The evils resulting from a half-paid and venal magistracy are dreadful, and the prospects of their removal very slight. The governor of Chihlí, in 1829, memorialized the Emperor upon the state of the police, and pointed out a remedy for many abuses, one of which was to pay them fair salaries out of the public treasury; but it is plain that this remedy must begin with the monarch, for until an officer is released from sopping his superior he will not cease exacting from his inferiors. Experience has shown the authorities how far it can safely be carried; while many officers, seeing how useless it is to irritate the people, so far as ultimately enriching themselves is concerned, endeavor to restrain their policemen. One governor issued an edict, stating that none of his domestics were allowed to browbeat shopmen, and thus get goods or eatables below the market price, and permitted the seller to collar and bring them to him for punishment when they did so. When an officer of high rank, as a governor, treasurer, etc., takes the seals of his post, he ofttimes issues a proclamation, exhorting the subordinate ranks to do as he means to do—"to look up and embody the kindness of the high Emperor," and attend to the faithful discharge of their duties. The lower officers, in their turn, join in the cry, and a series of proclamations, by turns hortative and mandatory, are echoed from mastiff, spaniel, and poodle, until the cry ends upon the police. Thus the prefect of Canton says: "There are hard-hearted soldiers and gnawing lictors who post themselves at ferries or markets, or rove about the streets, to extort money under various pretexts; or, being intoxicated, they disturb and annoy the people in a hundred ways. Since I came into office here I have repeatedly commanded the inferior magistrates to act faithfully and seize such persons, but the depraved spirit still continues."

A censor, speaking of the police, says: "They no sooner get a warrant to bring up witnesses than they assail both plaintiff and defendant for money to pay their expenses, from the amount of ten taels to several scores. Then the clerks must have double what the runners get; if their demands be not satisfied they contrive every species of annoyance. Then, again, if there are people of property in the neighborhood, they will implicate them. They plot also with pettifogging lawyers to get up accusations against people, and threaten and frighten them out of their money." [1]

One natural consequence of such a state of society and such a perversion of justice is to render the people afraid of all contact with the officers of government and exceedingly selfish in all their intercourse, though the latter trait needs no particular training to develop it in any heathen country. It also tends to an inhuman disregard of the life of others, and chills every emotion of kindness which might otherwise arise; for by making a man responsible for the acts of his neighbors, or by involving a whole village in the crimes of an individual, all sense of justice is violated. The terror of being implicated in any evil that takes place sometimes prevents the people from quenching fires until the superior authorities be first informed, and from relieving the distressed until it is often too late. Hence, too, it not unfrequently happens that a man who has had the ill fortune to be stabbed to death in the street, or who falls down from disease and dies, remains on the spot till the putrescence obliges the neighbors, for their own safety, to remove the corpse. A dead body floating down the river and washing ashore is likely to remain on the banks until it again drifts away or the authorities get it buried, for no unofficial person would voluntarily run the risk of being seen interring it. One censor reports that when he asked the people why they did not remove the loathsome ob-

[1] Compare Doolittle, *Social Life of the Chinese*, Vol. I., p. 330.

ject, they said: "We always let the bodies be either buried in the bellies of fishes or devoured by the dogs; for if we inform the magistrates they are sure to make the owner of the ground buy a coffin, and the clerks and assistants distress us in a hundred ways." The usual end of these memorials and remonstrances is that the police are ordered to behave better, the clerks commanded to abstain from implicating innocent people and retarding the course of justice, and their masters, the magistrates, threatened with the Emperor's displeasure in case the grievance is not remedied: after which all goes on as before, and will go on as long as both rulers and ruled are what they are.

The working out of the principle of responsibility accounts for many things in Chinese society and jurisprudence that otherwise appear completely at variance with even common humanity. It makes an officer careless of his duties if he can shift the responsibility of failure upon his inferiors, who, at the same time, he knows can never execute his orders; it renders the people dead to the impulses of relationship, lest they become involved in what they cannot possibly control and hardly know at the time of its commission. Mr. Lindsay states that when he was at Tsungming in 1832 the officers were very urgent that he should go out of the river, and in order to show him the effect of his non-compliance upon others a degraded subaltern was paraded in his sight. "His cap with its gold button was borne before him, and he marched about blindfolded in procession between two executioners, with a small flag on a bamboo pierced through each ear. Before him was a placard with the inscription, 'By orders of the general of Su and Sung: for a breach of military discipline, his ears are pierced as a warning to the multitude.' His offence was having allowed our boat to pass the fort without reporting it."

During the first war with England, fear of punishment induced many of the subordinates to commit suicide when unable to execute their orders, and the same motive impelled their superiors to avoid the wrath of the Emperor in like fashion. The hong-merchants and linguists at Canton, during the old regime, were constantly liable, from the operation of this principle, to exactions and punishments for the acts of their foreign customers. One of them, Sunshing, was put in prison and ruined because Lord Napier came to Canton from Whampoa in the boat of a ship which the unhappy merchant had "secured" several weeks before, and the linguist and pilot were banished for allowing what they could not possibly have hindered even if they had known it.

Having examined in this general manner the various grades of official rank, we come to the people; and a close view will show that this great mass of human beings exhibits many equally objectionable traits, while oppression, want, clannish rivalry, and brigandage combine to keep it in a constant state of turmoil. The subdivisions into tithings and hundreds are better observed in rural districts than in cities, and the headmen of those communities, in their individual and collective character, possess great influence, from the fact that they represent the popular feeling. In all parts of the country this popular organization is found in some shape or other, though, as if everything was somehow perverted, it not unfrequently is an instrument of greater oppression than defence. The division of the people into clans is far more marked in the southern provinces than in those lying north of the Yangtsz', and has had a depressing effect upon their good government. It resembles in general the arrangement of the Scottish clans, as do the evils arising from their dissensions and feuds those which history records as excited among the Highlanders by the rivalry between Campbells and Macgregors.

The eldership of villages has no necessary connection with the clans, for the latter are unacknowledged by the government, but the clan having the majority in a village generally selects the elders from among their number. This system is of very ancient date; its elementary details are given in the *Chau-lí*, one of the oldest works extant in China; Heeren furnishes the same details for India and Raffles for Java, reaching back in their duration to remote antiquity.[1] In the vicinity of Canton the elder

[1] Heeren, *Asiatic Nations*, Vol. II., p. 259. Raffles, *Java*, Vol. II. App. Biot, *L'Instruction publique*, pp. 59, 200.

is elected by a sort of town meeting, and holds his office during good behavior, receives such a salary as his fellow villagers give him, and may be removed to make way for another whenever the principal persons in the village are displeased with his conduct. His duties are limited to the supervision of the police and general oversight of what is done in the village, and to be a sort of agent or spokesman between the villagers and higher authorities; the duties, the power, and the rank of these officers vary almost indefinitely. The preponderance of one clan prevents much strife in the selection of the elder, but the degree of power reposed in his hand is so small that there is probably little competition to obtain the dignity. A village police is maintained by the inhabitants, under the authority of the elder; the village of Whampoa, for instance, containing about eight thousand inhabitants, pays the elder $300 salary, and employs fourteen watchmen. His duties further consist in deciding upon the petty questions arising between the villagers and visiting the delinquents with chastisement, enforcing such regulations as are deemed necessary regarding festivals, markets, tanks, streets, collection of taxes, etc. The system of surveillance is, however, kept up by the superior officers, who appoint excise officers, grain agents, tide-waiters, or some other subordinate, as the case may require, to exercise a general oversight of the headmen.

The district magistrate, with the *siunkien* and their deputies over the hundred, are the officers to whom appeals are carried from the headmen; they also receive the reports of the elders respecting suspicious characters within their limits, or other matters which they deem worthy of reference or remonstrance. A similarity of interests leads the headmen of many villages to meet together at times in a public hall for secret consultation upon important matters, and their united resolutions are generally acted upon by themselves or by the magistrates, as the case may be. This system of eldership, and the influential position the headmen occupy, is an important safeguard the people possess against the extremity of oppressive extortion; while, too, it upholds the government in strengthening the loyalty of those who feel that the only security they possess against theft, and loss of all things from their seditious countrymen, is to uphold the institutions of the land, and that to suffer the evils of a bad magistracy is less dreadful than the horrors of a lawless brigandage.

The customs and laws of clanship perpetuate a sad state of society, and render districts and villages, otherwise peaceful, the scenes of unceasing turmoil and trouble. There are only about four hundred clans in the whole of China, but inasmuch as all of the same surname do not live in the same place, the separation of a clan answers the same purpose as multiplying it. Clannish feelings and feuds are very much stronger in Kwangtung and Fuhkien than in other provinces. As an instance which may be mentioned, the *Gazette* contains the petition of a man from Chauchau fu, in Kwangtung, relating to a quarrel, stating that "four years before, his kindred having refused to assist two other clans in their feuds, had during that period suffered most shocking cruelties. Ten persons had been killed, and twenty men and women, taken captives, had had their eyes dug out, their ears cut off, their feet maimed, and so rendered useless for life. Thirty houses were laid in ruins and three hundred acres of land seized, ten thousand taels plundered, ancestral temples thrown down, graves dug up, dikes destroyed, and water cut off from the fields. The governor had offered a reward of a thousand taels to any one who would apprehend these persons, but for the ten murders no one had been executed, for the police dare not seize the offenders, whose numbers have largely increased, and who set the laws at defiance." This region is notorious for the turbulence of its inhabitants; it adjoins the province of Fuhkien, and the people, known at Canton as *Hoklo*, emigrate in large numbers to the Indian Archipelago or to other provinces. The later *Gazettes* contain still more dreadful accounts of the contests of the clans, and the great loss of life and property resulting from their forays, no less than one hundred and twenty villages having been attacked, and thousands of people killed. These battles are constantly occurring, and the authorities, feeling themselves too weak to put them down, are obliged to connive at them and let the clans fight it out.

Ill will is kept up between the clans, and private revenges gratified, by every personal annoyance that malice can suggest or opportunity tempt. If an unfortunate individual of one clan is met alone by his enemy, he is sure to be robbed or beaten, or both; the boats or the houses of each party are plundered or burned, and legal redress is almost impossible. Graves are defaced and tombstones injured, and on the annual visit to the family sepulchre perhaps a putrid corpse is met, placed there by the hostile clan; this insult arouses all their ire, and they vow deadly revenge. The villagers sally out with such arms as they possess, and death and wounds are almost sure to result before they separate. In Shunteh (a district between Canton and Macao) upward of a thousand men engaged with spears and firearms on one of these occasions, and thirty-six lives were lost; the military were called in to quell the riot. In Tungkwan district, southeast of Canton, thirty-six ringleaders were apprehended, and in 1831 it was reported that four hundred persons had been killed in these raids; only twenty-seven of their kindred appealed to government for redress.

When complaint is made to the prefect or governor, and investigation becomes inevitable, the villagers have a provision to meet the exigencies of the case, which puts the burden of the charges as equally as possible upon the whole clan. A band of "devoted men" are found—persons who volunteer to assume such crimes and run their chance for life—whose names are kept on a list, and they come forward and surrender themselves to government as the guilty persons. On the trial their friends employ witnesses to prove it a justifiable homicide, and magnify the provocation, and if there are several brought on the stand at once they try to get some of them clear by proving an alibi. It not unfrequently happens that the accused are acquitted—seldom that they are executed; transportation or a fine is the usual result. The inducement for persons to run this risk of their lives is security from the clan of a maintenance for their families in case of death, and a reward, sometimes as high as $300, in land or money when they return. This sum is raised by taxing the clan or village, and the imposition falls heavily on the poorer portion of it, who can neither avoid nor easily pay it. This system of substitution pervades all parts of society, and for all misdemeanors. A person was strangled in Macao in 1838 for having been engaged in the opium trade, who had been hired by the real criminal to answer to his name. Another mode of escape, sometimes tried in such cases when the person has been condemned, is to bribe the jailers to report him dead and carry out his body in a coffin; but this device probably does not often answer the end, as the turnkeys require a larger bribe than can be raised. There can be little doubt of the prevalence of the practice, and for crimes of even minor penalty.

To increase the social evils of clanship and systematized thieving, local tyrants occasionally spring up, persons who rob and maltreat the villagers by means of their armed retainers, who are in most cases, doubtless, members of the same clan. One of these tyrants, named *Yeh*, or Leaf, became quite notorious in the district of Tungkwan in 1833, setting at defiance all the power of the local authorities, and sending out his men to plunder and ravage whoever resisted his demands, destroying their graves and grain, and particularly molesting those who would not deliver up their wives or daughters to gratify him. He was arrested through craft by the district magistrate at Canton leaving his office and inducing him, for old acquaintance sake, to return with him to the provincial city; he was there tried and executed by the governor, although it was at the time reported that the Board of Punishments endeavored to save his life because he had been in office at the capital. In order that no attempt should be made to rescue him, he was left in ignorance of his sentence until he was put into the sedan to be carried to execution.

Clannish banditti often supply themselves with firearms, and prowling the country to revenge themselves on their enemies, soon proceed to pillage every one; in disarming them the government is sometimes obliged to resort to contemptible subterfuges, which conspicuously show its weakness and encourage a repetition of the evil. Parties of tramps, called *hakka*, or 'guests,' roam over Kwangtung province, squatting on vacant places along the shores, away from the villages, and forming small clannish communities; as soon as they increase, occupying more and more of the land, they begin to commit petty depredations upon the crops of the inhabitants, and demand money for the privilege of burying upon the unoccupied ground around them. The government is generally unwilling to drive them off by force, because there is the alternative of making them robbers thereby, and they are invited to settle in other waste lands, which they can have free of taxation, and leave those they have cultivated if strictly private property. This practice shows the populousness of the country in a conspicuous manner. To these evils must be also added the large bodies of floating banditti or dakoits, who rove up and down all the watercourses "like sneaking rats" and pounce upon defenceless boats. Hardly a river or estuary in the land is free from these miscreants, and lives and property are annually destroyed by them to a very great amount, especially on the Yangtsz', the Pearl River, and other great thoroughfares.

The popular associations in cities and towns are chiefly based upon a community of interests, resulting either from a similarity of occupation, when the leading persons of the same calling form themselves into guilds, or from the municipal regulations requiring the householders living in the same street to unite to maintain a police and keep the peace of their division. Each guild has an assembly-hall, where its members meet to hold the festival of their patron saint, to collect and appropriate the subscriptions of the members and settle the rent or storage on the rooms and goods in the hall, to discuss all public matters as well as the good cheer they get on such occasions, and to confer with other guilds. The members often go to a great expense in emulating each other in their processions, and some rivalry exists regarding their rights, over which the government keeps a watchful eye, for all popular assemblies are its horror. The shopkeepers and householders in the same street are required to have a headman to superintend the police, watchmen, and beggars within his limits. The rulers are sometimes thwarted in their designs by both these forms of popular assemblies, and they no doubt tend in many ways to keep up a degree of independence and of mutual acquaintance, which compels the respect of the government. The governor of Canton in 1838 endeavored to search all the shops in a particular street, to ascertain if there was opium in them; but the shopmen came in a body at the head of the street, and told the policemen that they would on no account permit their shops to be searched. The governor deemed it best to retire. Those who will not join or agree to what the majority orders in these bodies occasionally experience petty tyranny, but in a city this must be comparatively trifling. Several of the leading men in the city are known to hold meetings for consultation in still more popular assemblies for different reasons of a public and pressing nature. There is a building at Canton called the *Ming-lun Tang*, or "Free Discussion Hall," where political matters are discussed under the knowledge of government, which rather tries to mould than put them down, for the assistance of such bodies, rightly managed, in carrying out their intentions, is considerable, while discontent would be roused if they were forcibly suppressed. In October, 1842, meetings were held in this hall, at one of which a public manifesto was issued, here quoted entire as a specimen of the public appeals of Chinese politicians and orators:

"We have been reverently consulting upon the Empire—a vast and undivided whole! How can we permit it to be severed in order to give it to others? Yet we, the rustic people, can learn to practise a rude loyalty; we too know to destroy the banditti, and thus requite his Majesty. Our Great Pure dynasty has cared for this country for more than two hundred years, during which a succession of distinguished monarchs, sage succeeding sage, has reigned; and we who eat the herb of the field, and tread the soil, have for ages drank in the dew of imperial goodness, and been imbued with its benevolence. The people in wilds far remote beyond our influence have also felt this goodness, comparable to the heavens for height, and been upheld by this bounty, like the earth for thickness. Wherefore peace being now settled in the country, ships of all lands come, distant though they be from this for many a myriad of miles; and of all the foreigners on the south and west there is not one but what enjoys the highest peace and contentment, and entertains the profoundest respect and submission.

"But there is that English nation, whose ruler is now a woman and then a man, its people at one time like birds and then like beasts, with dispositions more fierce and furious than the tiger or wolf, and hearts more greedy than the snake or hog—this people has ever stealthily devoured all the southern barbarians, and like the demon of the night they now suddenly exalt themselves. During the reigns of Kienlung and Kiaking these English barbarians humbly besought entrance and permission to make a present; they also presumptuously requested to have Chusan, but those divine personages, clearly perceiving their traitorous designs, gave them a peremptory refusal. From that time, linking themselves in with traitorous traders, they have privily dwelt at Macao, trading largely in opium and poisoning our brave people. They have ruined lives—how many millions none can tell; and wasted property—how many thousands of millions who can guess! They have dared again and again to murder Chinese, and have secreted the murderers, whom they have refused to deliver up, at which the hearts of all men grieved and their heads ached. Thus it has been that for many years past the English, by their privily watching for opportunities in the country, have gradually brought things to the present crisis.

"In 1838, our great Emperor having fully learned all the crimes of the English and the poisonous effects of opium, quickly wished to restore the good condition of the country and compassionate the people. In consequence of the memorial of Hwang Tsioh-sz', and in accordance to his request, he specially deputed the public-minded, upright, and clear-headed minister, Lin Tseh-sü, to act as his imperial commissioner with plenipotentiary powers, and go to Canton to examine and regulate. He came and took all the stored-up opium and stopped the trade, in order to cleanse the stream and cut off the fountain; kindness was mixed with his severity, and virtue was evident in his laws, yet still the English repented not of their errors, and as the climax of their contumacy called troops to their aid. The censor Hwang, by advising peace, threw down the barriers, and bands of audacious robbers willingly did all kinds of disreputable and villainous deeds. During the past three years these rebels, depending upon their stout ships and effective cannon, from Canton went to Fuhkien, thence to Chehkiang and on to Kiangsu, seizing our territory, destroying our civil and military authorities, ravishing our women, capturing our property, and bringing upon the inhabitants of these four provinces intolerable miseries. His Imperial Majesty was troubled and afflicted, and this added to his grief and anxiety. If you wish to purify their crimes, all the fuel in the Empire will not suffice, nor would the vast ocean be enough to wash out our resentment. Gods and men are alike filled with indignation, and Heaven and Earth cannot permit them to remain.

"Recently, those who have had the management of affairs in Kiangnan have been imitating those who were in Canton, and at the gates of the city they have willingly made an agreement, peeling off the fat of the people to the tune of hundreds of myriads, and all to save the precious lives of one or two useless officers; in doing which they have exactly verified what Chancellor Kin Ying-lin had before memorialized. Now these English rebels are barbarians dwelling in a petty island beyond our domains; yet their coming throws myriads of miles of country into turmoil, while their numbers do not exceed a few myriads. What can be easier than for our celestial dynasty to exert its fulness of power and exterminate these contemptible sea-going imps, just as the blast bends the pliant bamboo? But our highest officers and ministers cherish their precious lives, and civil and military men both dread a dog as they would a tiger; regardless of the enemies of their country or the griefs of the people, they have actually sundered the Empire and granted its wealth; acts more flagitious these than those of the traitors in the days of the Southern Sung dynasty, and the reasons for which are wholly beyond our comprehension. These English barbarians are at bottom without ability, and yet we have all along seen in the memorials that officers exalt and dilate upon their prowess and obstinacy; our people are courageous and enthusiastic, but the officers on the contrary say that they are dispirited and scattered: this is for no other reason than to coerce our prince to make peace, and then they will luckily avoid the penalty due for 'deceiving the prince and betraying the country.' Do you doubt? Then look at the memorial of Chancellor Kin Ying-lin, which says: 'They take the occasion of war to seek for self-aggrandizement;' every word of which directly points at such conduct as this.

"We have recently read in his Majesty's lucid mandate that 'There is no other way, and what is requested must be granted;' and that 'We have conferred extraordinary powers upon the ministers, and they have done nothing but deceive us.' Looking up we perceive his Majesty's clear discrimination and divine perception, and that he was fully aware of the imbecility of his ministers; he remembers too the loyal anger of his people. He has accordingly now temporarily settled all the present difficulties, but it is that, having matured his plans, he may hereafter manifest his indignation, and show to the Empire that it had not fathomed the divine awe-inspiring counsels.

"The dispositions of these rebellious English are like that of the dog or sheep, whose desires can never be satisfied; and therefore we need not inquire whether the peace now made be real or pretended. Remember that when they last year made disturbance at Canton they seized the Square fort, and thereupon exhibited their audacity, everywhere plundering and ravishing. If it had not been that the patriotic inhabitants dwelling in Hwaitsing and other hamlets, and those in Shingping, had not killed their leader and destroyed their devilish soldiers, they would have scrupled at nothing, taking and pillaging the city, and then firing it in order to gratify their vengeance and greediness: can we imagine that for the paltry sum of six millions of dollars they would, as they did, have raised the siege and retired? How to be regretted! That when the fish was in the frying-pan, the Kwangchau fu should come and pull away the firewood, let loose the tiger to return to the mountains, and disarm the people's indignation. Letting the enemy thus escape on one occasion has successively brought misery upon many provinces: whenever we speak of it, it wounds the heart and causes the tears to flow.

"Last year, when the treaty of peace was made, it was agreed that the English should withdraw from beyond Lankeet, that they should give back the forts near there and dwell temporarily at Hongkong, and that thenceforth all military operations were forever to cease. Who would have supposed that before the time stipulated had passed away they would have turned their backs upon this agreement, taken violent possession of the forts at the Bogue with their 'wooden dragons' [*i.e.*, ships of war]—and when they came upon the gates of the City of Rams with their powerful forces, who was there to oppose them? During these three years we have not been able to restore things as at first, and their deceptive craftiness, then confined to these regions, has rapidly extended itself to Kiangnan. But our high and mighty Emperor, preeminently intelligent and discerning [*lit.* grasping the golden mirror and holding the gemmeous balances], consents to demean himself to adopt soothing counsels of peace, and therefore submissively accords with the decrees of Heaven. Having a suspicion that these outlandish people intended to encroach upon us, he has secretly arranged all things. We have respectfully read through all his Majesty's mandates, and they are as clear-sighted as the sun and moon; but those who now manage affairs are like one who, supposing the raging fire to be under, puts himself as much at ease as swallows in a court, but who, if the calamity suddenly reappears, would be as defenceless as a grampus in a fish-market. The law adjudges the penalty of death for betraying the country, but how can even death atone for their crimes? Those persons who have been handed down to succeeding ages with honor, and those whose memories have been execrated, are but little apart on the page of righteous history; let our rulers but remember this, and we think they also must exert themselves to recover their characters. We people have had our day in times of great peace, and this age is one of abundant prosperity; scholars are devising how to recompense the kindness of the government, nor can husbandmen think of forgetting his Majesty's exertions for them. Our indignation was early excited to join battle with the enemy, and we then all urged one another to the firmest loyalty.

"We have heard the English intend to come into Pearl River and make a settlement; this will not, however, stop at Chinese and foreigners merely dwelling together, for men and beasts cannot endure each other; it will be like opening the door and bowing in the thief, or setting the gate ajar and letting the wolf in. While they were kept outside there were many traitors within; how much more, when they encroach even to our bedsides, will our troubles be augmented? We cannot help fearing it will eventuate in something strange, which words will be insufficient to express. If the rulers of other states wish to imitate the English, with what can their demands be waived? Consequently, the unreasonable demands of the English are going to bring great calamity upon the people and deep sorrow to the country. If we do not permit them to dwell with us under the same heaven, our spirits will feel no shame; but if we willingly consent to live with them, we may in truth be deemed insensate.

"We have reverently read in the imperial mandate, 'There must indeed be some persons among the people of extraordinary wisdom or bravery, who can stir them up to loyalty and patriotism or unite them in self-defence; some who can assist the government and army to recover the cities, or else defend passes of importance against the robbers; some who can attack and burn their vessels, or seize and bring the heads of their doltish leaders; or else some with divine presence and wisdom, who can disclose all their silly counsels and get to themselves a name of surpassing merit and ability and receive the highest rewards. We can confer,' etc., etc. We, the people, having received the imperial words, have united ourselves together as troops, and practise the plan of joining hamlets and villages till we have upward of a million of troops, whom we have provisioned according to the scale of estimating the produce of respective farms; and now we are fully ready and quite at ease as to the result. If nothing calls us, then each one will return to his own occupation; but if the summons come, joining our strength in force we will incite each other to effort; our brave sons and brothers are all animated to deeds of arms, and even our wives and daughters, finical and delicate as jewels, have learned to discourse of arms. At first, alas, those who guarded the passes were at ease and careless, and the robbers came unbidden and undesired; but now [if they come], we have only zealously to appoint each other to stations, and suppress the rising of the waves to the stillest calm [*i.e.*, to exterminate them]. When the golden pool is fully restored to peace, and his Majesty's anxiety for the south relieved; when the leviathan has been driven away, then will our anger, comparable to the broad ocean and high heavens, be pacified.

"Ah! We here bind ourselves to vengeance, and express these our sincere intentions in order to exhibit great principles; and also to manifest Heaven's retribution and rejoice men's hearts, we now issue this patriotic declaration. The high gods clearly behold: do not lose your first resolution."[1]

This spirited paper was subsequently answered by the party desirous of peace, but the anti-English feeling prevailed, and the committee appointed by the meeting set the English consulate on fire a few days after, to prevent it being occupied. There were many reasons at the time for this dislike; its further exhibition, however, ended with this attack, and has now pretty much died out with the rising of a new generation.

The many secret associations existing among the people are mostly of a political character, but have creeds like religious sects, and differ slightly in their tenets and objects of worship. They are traceable to the system of clans, which giving the people at once the habit and spirit for associations, are easily made use of by clever men for their own purposes of opposition to government. Similar grievances, as local oppression, hatred of the Manchus, or hope of advantage, add to their numbers and strength, and were they founded on a full acquaintance with the grounds of a just resistance to despotism, they would soon overturn the government; but as out of an adder's egg only a cockatrice can be hatched, so until the people are enlightened with regard to their just rights, no permanent melioration can be expected. It is against that leading feature in the Manchu policy, *isolation*, that these societies sin, which further prompts to systematic efforts to suppress them. The only objection

[1] *Chinese Repository*, Vol. XI., p. 630.

the supreme government seems to have against the religion of the people is that it brings them together; they may be Buddhists, Rationalists, Jews, Mohammedans, or Christians, apparently, if they will worship in secret and apart. On the other hand, the people naturally connect some religious rites with their opposition and cabals in order to more securely bind their members together.

The name of the most powerful of these associations is mentioned in Section CLXII. of the code for the purpose of interdicting it; since then it has apparently changed its designation from the *Pih-lien kiao*, or 'Water-lily sect,' to the *Tien-tí hwui* or *San-hoh hwui*, *i.e.*, 'Triad society,' though both names still exist, the former in the northern, the latter in the maritime provinces and Indian Archipelago; their ramifications take also other appellations. The object of these combinations is to overturn the reigning dynasty, and in putting this prominently forward they engage many to join them. About the beginning of the century a wide-spread rebellion broke out in the northwestern and middle provinces, which was put down after eight years' war, attended with desolation and bloodshed; since that time the Water-lily sect has not been so often spoken of. The Triad society has extended itself along the coasts, but it is not popular, owing more than anything else to its illegality, and the intimidation and oppression employed toward those who will not join it. The members have secret regulations and signs, and uphold and assist each other both in good and bad acts, but, as might be inferred from their character, screening evil doers from just punishment oftener than relieving distressed members. The original designs of the association may have been good, but what was allowable in them soon degenerated into a systematic plan for plunder and aim at power. The government of Hongkong enacted in 1845 that any Chinese living in that colony who was ascertained to belong to the Triad society should be declared guilty of felony, be imprisoned for three years, and after branding expelled the colony. These associations, if they cause the government much trouble by interfering with its operations, in no little degree, through the overbearing conduct of the leaders, uphold it by showing the people what may be expected if they should ever get the upper hand.[1]

The evils of mal-administration are to be learned chiefly from the memorials of censors, and although they may color their statements a little, very gross inaccuracies would be used to their own disadvantage, and contradicted by so many competitors, that most of their statements may be regarded as having some foundation. An unknown person in Kwangtung memorialized the Emperor in 1838 concerning the condition of that province, and drew a picture of the extortions of the lower agents of government that needs no illustrations to deepen its darkness or add force to its complaints. An extract from each of the six heads into which the memorial is divided will indicate the principal sources of popular insurrection in China, besides the exhibition they give of the tyranny of the officers.

In his preface, after the usual laudation of the beneficence and popularity of the monarch, the memorialist proceeds to express his regret that the imperial desires for the welfare of his subjects should be so grievously thwarted by the villany of his officers. After mentioning the calamities which had visited the province in the shape of freshets, insurrections, and conflagrations, he says that affairs generally had become so bad as to compel his Majesty to send commissioners to Canton repeatedly in order to regulate them. "If such as this be indeed the state of things," he inquires, "what wonder is it if habits of plunder characterize the people, or the clerks and under officers of the public courts, as well as village pettifoggers, lay themselves out on all occasions to stir up quarrels and instigate false accusations against the good?" He recommends reform in six departments, under each of which he thus specifies the evils to be remedied:

---

[1] Compare Dr. Milne, in *Transactions R. A. S. of Gr. Brit. and Irel.*, Vol. I., p. 240 (1825). *Journal of the R. A. S.*, Vol. I., p. 93, and Vol. VI., p. 120. *Chinese Repository*, Vol. XVIII., pp. 280–295. A. Wylie, in the *Shanghai Almanac for* 1854. *Notes and Queries on C. and J.*, Vol. III., p. 55. T. T. Meadows, *The Chinese and their Rebellions*, London, 1856. Gustave Schlegel, *Thian Ti Hwui, the Hung-League or Heaven-Earth-League. A Secret Society with the Chinese in China and India*, Batavia, 1866.

First.—In the department of police there is great negligence and delay in the decision of judicial cases. Cases of plunder are very common, most of which are committed by banditti under the designations of Triad societies, Heaven and Earth brotherhoods, etc. These men carry off persons to extort a ransom, falsely assume the character of policemen, and in simulated revenue cutters pass up and down the rivers, plundering the boats of travellers and forcibly carrying off the women. Husbandmen are obliged to pay these robbers an "indemnity," or else as soon as the crops are ripe they come and carry off the whole harvest. In the precincts of the metropolis, where their contiguity to the tribunals prevents their committing depredations in open day, they set fire to houses during the night, and under the pretence of saving and defending the persons and property carry off both of them; hence, of late years, calamitous fires have increased in frequency, and the bands of robbers multiplied greatly. In cases of altercations among the villagers, who can only use their local patois, it rests entirely with the clerks to interpret the evidence; and when the magistrate is lax or pressed with business, they have the evidence pre-arranged and join with bullies and strife-makers to subvert right and wrong, fattening themselves upon bribes extorted under the names of "memoranda of complaints," "purchases of replies," etc., and retarding indefinitely the decision of cases. They also instigate thieves to bring false accusations against the good, who are thereby ruined by legal expenses. While the officers of the government and the people are thus separated, how can it be otherwise than that appeals to the higher tribunals should be increased and litigation and strife prevail?

Second.—Magistrates overrate the taxes with a view to a deduction for their own benefit, and excise officers connive at non-payment. The revenue of Kwangtung is paid entirely in money, and the magistrates, instead of taking the commutation at a regular price of about five dollars for one hundred and fifty pounds of rice, have compelled the people to pay nine dollars and over, because the inundation and bad harvests had raised the price of grain. In order to avoid this extortion the police go to the villagers and demand a douceur, when they will get them off from all payment. But the imperial coffers are not filled by this means, and the people are by and by forced to pay up their arrearages, even to the loss of most of their possessions.

Third.—There is great mismanagement of the granaries, and instead of being any assistance to the people in time of scarcity, they are only a source of peculation for those who are charged with their oversight.

Fourth.—The condition of the army and navy is a disgrace; illicit traffic is not prevented, nor can insurrections be put down. The only care of the officers is to obtain good appointments, and reduce the actual number of soldiers below the register in order that they may appropriate the stores. The cruisers aim only to get fees to allow the prosecution of the contraband traffic, nor will the naval officers bestir themselves to recover the property of plundered boats, but rather become the protectors of the lawless and partakers of their booty. Robberies are so common on the rivers that the traders from the island of Hainan, and Chauchau near Fuhkien, prefer to come by sea, but the revenue cutters overhaul them under pretence of searching for contraband articles, and practise many extortions.

Fifth.—The monopoly of salt needs to be guarded more strictly, and the private manufacture of salt stopped, for thereby the revenue from this source is materially diminished.

Sixth.—The increase of smuggling is so great, and the evils flowing from it so multiplied, that strong measures must be taken to repress it. Traitorous Chinese combine with depraved foreigners to set the laws at defiance, and dispose of their opium and other commodities for the pure silver. In this manner the country is impoverished and every evil arises, the revenues of the customs are diminished by the unnecessary number of persons employed and by the fees they receive for connivance. If all these abuses can be remedied, "it will be seen that when there are men to rule well, nothing can be found beyond the reach of their government."

The chief efforts of officials are directed to put down banditti, and maintain such a degree of peace as will enable them to collect the revenue and secure the people in the quiet possession of their property; but the people are too ready to resist their rulers, and this brings into operation a constant struggle of opposing desires. One side gets into the habit of resisting even the proper requisitions of the officers, who, on their part, endeavor in every way to reimburse their outlay in bribes to their superiors; and the combined action of the two proves an insurmountable impediment to the attainment of even that degree of security a Chinese officer wishes. The general commission of robbery and dakoity, and the prevalence of bands of thieves, therefore proves the weakness of the government, not the insurrectionary disposition of the people. In one district of Hupeh the governor reported in 1828 that "very few of the inhabitants have any regular occupation, and their dispositions are exceedingly ferocious; they fight and kill each other on every provocation. In their villages they harbor thieves who flee from other districts, and sally forth again to plunder." In the northern parts of Kwangtung the people have erected high and strongly built houses to which they flee for safety from the attacks of robbers. These bands sometimes fall upon each other, and the feudal animosities of clanship adding fuel and rage to the rivalry of partisan warfare, the destruction of life and property is great. Occasionally the people zealously assist their rulers to apprehend them, though their exertions depend altogether upon the energy of the incumbent; an officer in Fuhkien is recommended for promotion because he had apprehended one hundred and seventy-three persons, part of a band of robbers which had infested the department for years, and tried and convicted one thousand one hundred and sixty criminals, most or all of whom were probably executed.

In 1821 there were four hundred robbers taken on the borders of Fuhkien; in 1827 two hundred were seized in the south of the province, and forty-one more brought to Canton from the eastward. The governor offered $1,000 reward for the capture of one leader, and $3,000 for another. The judge of the province put forth a proclamation upon the subject in the same year, in which he says there were four hundred and thirty undecided cases of robbery by brigands then on the calendar; and in 1846 there were upward of two thousand waiting his decision, for each of which there were perhaps five or six persons in prison or under constraint until the case was settled. These bands prowl in the large cities and commit great cruelties. In 1830 a party of five hundred openly plundered a rich man's house in the western suburbs of Canton; and in Shunteh, south of the city, $600 were paid for the ransom of two persons carried off by them. The ex-governor, in 1831, was attacked by them near the Mei ling pass on his departure from Canton, and plundered of about ten thousand dollars. The magistrates of Hiangshan district, south of Canton, were ordered by their superiors the same year to apprehend five hundred of the robbers. Priests sometimes harbor gangs in their temples and divide the spoils with them, and occasionally go out themselves on predatory excursions. No mercy is shown these miscreants when they are taken, but the multiplication of executions has no effect in deterring them from crime.

Cruelty to individual prisoners does not produce so much disturbance to the general peace of the community as the forcible attempts of officers to collect taxes. The people have the impression that their rulers exact more than is legal, and consequently consider opposition to the demands of the tax-gatherer as somewhat justifiable, which compels, of course, more stringent measures on the part of the authorities, whose station depends not a little on their punctuality in remitting the taxes. Bad harvests, floods, or other public calamities render the people still more disinclined to pay the assessments. In 1845 a serious disturbance arose near Ningpo on this account, which with unimportant differences could probably be paralleled in every prefecture in the land. The people of Funghwa hien having refused to pay an onerous tax, the prefect of Ningpo seized three literary men of the place, who had been deputed to collect it, and put them in prison; this procedure so irritated the gentry that the candidates at the literary examination which occurred at Funghwa soon afterward, on being assembled at the public hall before the *chihien*, rose upon him and beat him severely. They were still further incensed against him from having recently detected him in deceitful conduct regarding a petition they had made at court to have their taxes lightened; he had kept the answer and pocketed the difference. He was consequently superseded by another magistrate, and a deputy of the intendant of circuit was sent with the new incumbent to restore order. But the deputy, full of his importance, carried himself so haughtily that the excited populace treated him in the same manner, and he barely escaped with his life to Ningpo. The intendant and prefect, finding matters rising to such a pitch, sent a detachment of twelve hundred troops to keep the peace, but part of these were decoyed within the walls and attacked with such vigor that many of them were made prisoners, a colonel and a dozen privates killed, and two or three hundred wounded or beaten, and all deprived of their arms. In this plight they returned to Ningpo, and, as the distance is not great, apprehensions were entertained lest the insurgents should follow up their advantage by organizing themselves and marching upon the city to seize the prefect. The officers sent immediately to Hangchau for assistance, from whence the governor sent a strong force of ten thousand men to restore order, and soon after arrived himself. He demanded three persons to be given up who had been active in fomenting the resistance, threatening in case of non-compliance that he would destroy the town; the prefect and his deputy from the intendant's office were suspended and removed to another post. These measures restored quiet to a considerable extent.[1]

The existence of such evils in Chinese society would rapidly disorganize it were it not for the conservative influence upon society of early education and training in industry. The government takes care to avail itself of this better element in public opinion, and grounds thereon a basis of action for the establishment of good order. But this, and ten thousand similar instances, only exhibit more strongly how great a work there is to be done before high and low, people and rulers, will understand their respective duties and rights; before they will, on the one hand, pay that regard to the authority of their rulers which is necessary for the maintenance of good order, and, on the other, resist official tyranny in preserving their own liberties.

If the character of the officers, therefore, be such as has been

[1] *Missionary Chronicle*, Vol. XIV., p. 140. Smith's *China*, p. 250.

briefly shown—open to bribery, colluding with criminals, sycophantic toward superiors, and cruel to the people; and the constituents of society present so many repulsive features—opposing clans engaged in deadly feuds, bandits scouring the country to rob, policemen joining to oppress, truth universally disregarded, selfishness the main principle of action, and almost every disorganizing element but imperfectly restrained from violent outbreaks and convulsions, it will not be expected that the regular proceedings of the courts and the execution of the laws will prove on examination to be any better than the materials of which they are composed. As civil and criminal cases are all judged by one officer, one court tries nearly all the questions which arise. A single exception is provided for in the code, wherein it is ordered that " in cases of adultery, robbery, fraud, assaults, breach of laws concerning marriage, landed property or pecuniary contracts, or any other like offences committed by or against individuals in the military class—if any of the people are implicated or concerned, the military commanding officer and the civil magistrate shall have a concurrent jurisdiction." [1]

At the bottom of the judicial scale are the village elders. This incipient element of the democratic principle has also existed in India in much the same form; but while its power ended in the local eldership there, in China it is only the lowest step of the scale. The elders give character to the village, and are expected to manage its public affairs, settle disputes among its inhabitants, arrange matters with other villages, and answer to the magistrates on its behalf. The code provides that all persons having complaints and informations address themselves in the first instance to the lowest tribunal of justice in the district, from which the cognizance of the affair may be transferred to the superior tribunals. The statement of the case is made in writing, and the officer is required to act upon it immediately; if the parties are dissatisfied with the award, the judgment of the lower courts is carried up to the superior ones. No case can

[1] For cases of this sort in Cambodia, Rémusat makes mention of a variety of ordeals which curiously resemble those resorted to on the continent of Europe during the Middle Ages. *Nouveaux Mélanges*, Tome I., p. 126.

be carried directly to the Emperor; it must go through the Board of Punishments; old men and women, however, sometimes present petitions to him on his journeys, but such appeals seldom occur, owing to the difficulty of access. The captains in charge of the gates of Peking, in 1831, presented a memorial upon the subject, in which they attribute the number of appeals to the obstinacy of many persons in pressing their cases and the remissness of local officers, so that even women and girls of ten years of age take long journeys to Peking to state their cases. The memorialists recommend that an order be issued requiring the two high provincial officers to adjudicate all cases, either themselves or by a court of errors, and not send the complainants back to the district magistrates. These official porters must have been much troubled with young ladies coming to see his Majesty, or perhaps were advised to present such a paper to afford a text for the Emperor to preach from; to confer such power upon the governor and his associates would almost make them the irresponsible sovereigns of the provinces. Appeals frequently arise out of delay in obtaining justice, owing to the amount of business in the courts; for the calendar may be expected to increase when the magistrate leaves his post to curry favor with his superiors. The almost utter impossibility of learning the truth of the case brought before them, either from the principal parties or the witnesses, must be borne in mind when deciding upon the oppressive proceedings of the magistrates to elicit the truth. Mention is made of one officer promoted for deciding three hundred cases in a year; again of a district magistrate who tried upward of a thousand within the same period; while a third revised and decided more than six hundred in which the parties had appealed. What becomes of the appeals in such cases, or whose decision stands, does not appear; but if such proceedings are common, it accounts for the constant practice of sending appeals back to be revised, probably after a change in the incumbent.

Few or no civil cases are reported in the *Gazette* as being carried up to higher courts, and probably only a small proportion of them are brought before the authorities, the rest being settled by reference. Appeals to court receive attention, and it may be inferred, too, that many of them are mentioned in the *Gazette* in order that the carefulness of the supreme government in revising the unjust decrees against the people should be known through the country, and this additional check to malversation on the part of the lower courts be of some use. Many cases are reported of widows and daughters, sons and nephews, of murdered persons, to whom the revenge of kindred rightly belongs, appealing against the unjust decrees of the local magistrates, and then sent back to the place they came from; this, of course, was tantamount to a *nolle prosequi*. At other times the wicked judges have been degraded and banished. One case is reported of a man who found his way to the capital from Fuhkien to complain against the magistracy and police, who protected a clan by whom his only son had been shot, in consideration of a bribe of $2,000. His case could not be understood at Peking in consequence of his local pronunciation, which indicates that all cases are not reported in writing. One appeal is reported against the governor of a province for not carrying into execution the sentence of death passed on two convicted murderers; and another appellant requests that two persons, who were bribed to undergo the sentence of the law instead of the real murderers, might not be substituted—he, perhaps, fearing their subsequent vengeance.

All officers of government are supposed to be accessible at any time, and the door of justice to be open to all who claim a hearing; and in fact, courts are held at all hours of night and day, though the regular time is from sunrise to noonday. The style of address varies according to the rank; *tajin*, or magnate, for the highest, *ta laoyé*, or great Sir, and *laoyé*, Sir, for the lower grade, are the most common. A drum is said to be placed at the inferior tribunals, as well as before the Court of Representation in Peking, which the plaintiff strikes in order to make his presence known, though from the number of hangers-on about the doors of official residences, the necessity of employing this mode of attracting notice is rare. At the gate of the governor-general's palace are placed six tablets, having appropriate inscriptions for those who have been wronged by wicked officers; for those who have suffered from thieves; for persons falsely accused; for those who have been swindled; for such as have been grieved by other parties; and lastly, for those who have secret information to impart. The people, however, are aware how useless it would be to inscribe their appeals upon these tablets; they write them out and carry them up to his excellency, or to the proper official—seldom forgetting the indispensable present.

Magistrates are not allowed to go abroad in ordinary dress and without their official retinue, which varies for the different grades of rank. The usual attendants of the district magistrates are lictors with whips and chains—significant of the punishments they inflict; they are preceded by two gong-

Mode of Carrying High Officers in Sedan.

bearers, who every few moments strike a certain number of raps to intimate their master's rank, and by two avant-couriers, who howl out an order for all to make room for the great man. A servant bearing aloft a *lo*, or state umbrella (of which a drawing is given on the title-page), also goes before him, further to increase his display and indicate his rank.[1] A subaltern usually runs by the side of his sedan, and his secretary and messengers, seated in more ordinary chairs or following on foot, make up the cortége. The highest officers are carried by eight bearers, others by four, and the lowest by two. Lanterns are used at night and red tablets in the daytime, to indicate his rank. Officers of higher ranks are attended by a few soldiers

[1] Heeren informs us that a similar insignia was used in Persia in early days.

in addition, and in the capital are required to have mounted attendants if they ride in carts; those who bear the sedan are usually in a uniform of their master's devising. The parade and noise seen in the provinces are all hushed in Peking, where the presence of majesty subdues the glory of the officers which it has created. When in court the officer sits behind a desk upon which are placed writing materials; his secretaries, clerks, and interpreters being in waiting, and the lictors with their instruments of punishment and torture standing around. Persons who are brought before him kneel in front of the tribunal. His official seal, and cups containing tallies which are thrown down to indicate the number of blows to be given the culprits, stand upon the table, and behind his seat a *kí-lin*, or unicorn, is depicted on the wall. There are inscriptions hanging around the room, one of which exhorts him to be merciful. There is little pomp or show, either in the office or attendants, compared with our notions of what is usual in such matters among Asiatics. The former is a dirty, unswept, tawdry room, and the latter are beggarly and impertinent.

No counsel is allowed to plead, but the written accusations, pleas, or statements required must be prepared by licensed notaries, who may also read them in court, and who, no doubt, take opportunity to explain circumstances in favor of their client. These notaries buy their situations, and repay themselves by a fee upon the documents; they are the only persons who are analogous to the lawyers in western countries, and most of them have the reputation of extorting largely for their services. Of course there is no such thing as a jury, or a chief justice stating the case to associate judges to learn their opinion; nor is anything like an oath required of the witnesses.

The presiding officer can call in others to assist him in the trial to any extent he pleases. In one Canton court circular it is stated that no less than sixteen officers assisted the governor-general and governor in the trial of one criminal. The report of the trial is as summary as the recital of the bench of judges is minute: "H. E. Gov. Tăng arrived to join the futai in examining a criminal; and at 8 A.M., under a salute of guns, the doors of the great hall of audience were thrown open, and their

PRISONER CONDEMNED TO THE CANGUE, IN COURT.
(His son praying to take his place.)

excellencies took their seats, supported by all the other functionaries assembled for the occasion. The police officers of the judge were then directed to bring forward the prisoner, Yeh A-shun, a native of Tsingyuen hien; he was forthwith brought in, tried, and led out. The futai then requested the imperial death-warrant, and sent a deputation of officers to conduct the criminal to the market-place and there decapitate him. Soon after the officers returned, restored the death-warrant to its place, and reported that they had executed the criminal." The prisoner, or his friends for him, are allowed to appear in every step of the inquiry prior to laying the case before the Emperor, and punishment is threatened to all the magistrates through whose hands it passes if they neglect the appeal; but this extract shows the usage of the courts.

The general policy of officers is to quash cases and repress appeals, and probably they do so to a great degree by bringing extorted confessions of the accused party and the witnesses in proof of the verdict. Governor Lí of Canton issued a prohibition in 1834 against the practice of old men and women presenting petitions—complaining of the nuisance of having his chair stopped in order that a petition might be forced into it, and threatening to seize and punish the presumptuous intruders if they persisted in this custom. He instructs the district magistrates to examine such persons, to ascertain who pushed them forward, and to punish the instigators, observing, "if the people are impressed with a due dread of punishment, they will return to respectful habits." It seems to be the constant effort on the part of the officers to evade the importunities of the injured and shove by justice, and were it not owing to the perseverance of the people, a system of irremediable oppression would soon be induced. But the poor have little chance of being heard against the rich, and if they do appeal they are in most cases remanded to the second judgment of the very officer against whom they complain; and of course as this is equivalent to a refusal from the high grades to right them at all, commotions gradually grow out of it, which are managed according to the exigencies of the case by those who are likely to be involved in their responsibility. The want of an irresistible police to compel obedience has a restraining effect on the rulers, who know that Lynch law may perhaps be retaliated upon them if they exasperate the people too far. A prefect was killed in Chauchau fu some years ago for his cruelty, and the people excused their act by saying that it was done because the officer had failed to carry out the Emperor's good rule, and they would not endure it longer. Amid such enormities it is no wonder if the peaceably disposed part of the community prefer to submit in silence to petty extortions and robberies, rather than risk the loss of all by unavailing complaints.

The code contains many sections regulating the proceedings of courts, and provides heavy punishments for such officers as are guilty of illegalities or cruelty in their decisions, but the recorded cases prove that most of these laws are dead letters. Section CCCCXVI. ordains that "after a prisoner has been tried and convicted of any offence punishable with temporary or perpetual banishment or death, he shall, in the last place, be brought before the magistrate, together with his nearest relations and family, and informed of the offence whereof he stands convicted, and of the sentence intended to be pronounced upon him in consequence; their acknowledgment of its justice or protest against its injustice, as the case may be, shall then be taken down in writing: and in every case of their refusing to admit the justice of the sentence, their protest shall be made the ground of another and more particular investigation." All capital cases must be reviewed by the highest authorities at the metropolis and in the provinces, and a final report of the case and decision submitted to the Emperor's notice. Section CCCCXV. requires that the law be quoted when deciding. The numerous wise and merciful provisions in the code for the due administration of justice only place the conduct of its authorized executives in a less excusable light, and prove how impossible it is to procure an equitable magistracy by mere legal requirements and penalties.

The confusion of the civil and criminal laws in the code, and the union of both functions in the same person, together with the torture and imprisonment employed to elicit a confession, serve as an indication of the state of legislation and jurisprudence. The common sense of a truthful people would revolt against the infliction of torture to get out the true deposition of a witness, and their sense of honor would resist the disgraceful exposure of the cangue for not paying debts. As the want of truth among a people indicates a want of honor, the necessity of more stringent modes of procedure suggests the practice of torture; its application is allowed and restricted by several sections of the code, but in China, as elsewhere, it has always been abused. Torture is practised upon both criminals and witnesses, in court and in prison; and the universal dread among the people of coming before courts, and having anything to do with their magistrates, is owing in great measure to the illegal sufferings they too often must endure. It has also a powerful deterrent effect in preventing crime and disorder. Neither imprisonment nor torture are ranked among the five punishments, but they cause more deaths, probably, among arrested persons than all other means.

Among the modes of torture employed in court, and reported in the *Gazette*, are some revolting to humanity, but which of them are legal does not appear. The clauses under Section I. in the code describe the legal instruments of torture; they consist of three boards with proper grooves for compressing the ankles, and five round sticks for squeezing the fingers, to which may be added the bamboo; besides these no instruments of torture are legally allowed, though other ways of putting the question are so common as to give the impression that some of them at least are sanctioned. Pulling or twisting the ears with roughened fingers, and keeping them in a bent position while making the prisoner kneel on chains, or making him kneel for a long time, are among the illegal modes. Striking the lips with sticks until they are nearly jellied, putting the hands in stocks before or behind the back, wrapping the fingers in oiled cloth to burn them, suspending the body by the thumbs and fingers, tying the hands to a bar under the knees, so as to bend the body double, and chaining by the neck close to a stone, are resorted to when the prisoner is contumacious. One magistrate is accused of having fastened up two criminals to boards by nails driven through their palms; one of them tore his hands loose and was nailed up again, which caused his death; using beds of iron, boiling water, red hot spikes, and cutting the tendon Achilles are also charged against him, but the Emperor exonerated him on account of the atrocious character of the criminals. Compelling them to kneel upon pounded glass, sand, and salt mixed together, until the knees become excoriated, or simply kneeling upon chains is a lighter mode of the same infliction. Mr. Milne mentions seeing a wretch undergoing this torture, his hands tied behind his back to a stake held in its position by two policemen; if he swerved to relieve the agony of his position, a blow on his head compelled him to resume it. The agonies of the poor creature were evident from his quivering lips, his pallid and senseless countenance, and his tremulous voice imploring relief, which was refused with a cold, mocking command, "Suffer or confess."[1]

Flogging is one of the five authorized punishments, but it is used more than any other means to elicit confession; the bamboo, rattan, cudgel, and whip are all employed. When death ensues the magistrate reports that the criminal died of sickness, or hushes it up by bribing his friends, few of whom are ever allowed access within the walls of the prison to see and comfort the sufferers. From the manner in which such a result is spoken of it may be inferred that immediate death does not often take place from torture. A magistrate in Sz'chuen being abused by a man in court, who also struck the attendants, ordered him to be put into a coffin which happened to be near, when suffocation ensued; he was in consequence dismissed the service, punished one hundred blows, and transported three years. One check on outrageous torture is the fear that the report of their cruelty will come to the ears of their superiors, who are usually ready to avail of any mal-administration to get an officer removed, in order to fill the post. In this case, as in other parts of Chinese government, the dread of one evil prevents the commission of another.

The five kinds of punishment mentioned in the code are from ten to fifty blows with the lesser bamboo, from fifty to

---

[1] W. C. Milne, *Life in China*, London, 1857, p. 99.

one hundred with the greater, transportation, perpetual banishment, and death, each of them modified in various ways. The small bamboo weighs about two pounds, the larger two and two-thirds pounds. Public exposure in the *kia*, or cangue, is considered rather as a kind of censure or reprimand than a punishment, and carries no disgrace with it, nor comparatively much bodily suffering if the person be fed and screened from the sun. The frame weighs between twenty and thirty pounds, and is so made as to rest upon the shoulders without chafing the neck, but so broad as to prevent the person feeding himself. The name, residence, and offence of the delinquent are written upon it for the information of every passer-by, and a policeman is stationed over him to prevent escape. Branding is applied to deserters and banished persons. Imprisonment and fines are not regarded as legal punishments, but rather correctives; and flogging, as Le Comte says, "is never wanting, there being no condemnation in China without this previous disposition, so that it is unnecessary to mention it in their condemnation; this being always understood to be their first dish." When a man is arrested he is effectually prevented from breaking loose by putting a chain around his neck and tying his hands.

Mode of Exposure in the Cangue.

Most punishments are redeemable by the payment of money if the criminal is under fifteen or over seventy years of age, and a table is given in the code for the guidance of the magistrate in such cases. An act of grace enables a criminal condemned even to capital punishment to redeem himself, if the offence be not one of wilful malignity; but better legislation would have shown the good effects of not making the punishments so severe. It is also ordered in Section XVIII., that "any offender under sentence of death for a crime not excluded from the contingent benefit of an act of grace, who shall have infirm parents or grandparents alive over seventy years of age, and no other male child over sixteen to support them, shall be recommended to the mercy of his Majesty; and if only condemned to banishment, shall receive one hundred blows and redeem himself by a fine." Many atrocious laws may be forgiven for one such exhibition of regard for the care of decrepid parents. Few governments exhibit such opposing principles of actions as the Chinese: a strange blending of cruelty to prisoners with a maudlin consideration of their condition, and a constant effort to coax the people to obedience while exercising great severity upon individuals, are everywhere manifest. One who has lived in the country long, however, knows well that they are not to be held in check by rope-yarn laws or whimpering justices, and unless the rulers are a terror to evil-doers, the latter will soon get the upper hand. Dr. Field well considers this point in his interesting notes describing his visit to a *yamun* at Canton.[1] The general prosperity of the Empire proves in some measure the equity of its administration.

Banishment and slavery are punishments for minor official delinquencies, and few officers who live long in the Emperor's employ do not take an involuntary journey to Mongolia, Turkestan, or elsewhere, in the course of their lives. The fates and conduct of banished criminals are widely unlike; some doggedly serve out their time, others try to ingratiate themselves with their masters in order to alleviate or shorten the time of service, while hundreds contrive to escape and return to their homes, though this subjects them to increased punishment. Persons banished for treason are severely dealt with if they return without leave, and those convicted of crime in their

---

[1] Dr. H. M. Field, *From Egypt to Japan*, Chap. XXIV., passim. New York, 1877. *Chinese Repository*, Vol. IV., pp. 214, 260.

place of banishment are increasingly punished; one man was sentenced to be outlawed for an offence at his place of banishment, but seeing that his aged mother had no other support than his labor, the Emperor ordered that a small sum should be paid for her living out of the public treasury. Whipping a man through the streets as a public example to others is frequenty practised upon persons detected in robbery, assault, or some other minor offences. The man is manacled, and one policeman goes before him carrying a tablet, on which are

Publicly Whipping a Thief through the Streets.

written his name, crime, and punishment, accompanied by another holding a gong. In some cases little sticks bearing flags are thrust through his ears, and the lictor appointed to oversee the fulfilment of the sentence follows the executioner, who strikes the criminal with his whip or rattan as the rap on the gong denotes that the appointed number is not yet complete.

Decapitation and strangling are the legal modes of executing criminals, though Kí Kung having taken several incendiaries at Canton, in 1843, who were convicted of firing the city for purposes of plunder, starved them to death in the public squares of the city. The least disgraceful mode of execution is strangulation, which is performed by tying a man to a post and tightening the cord which goes round his neck by a winch; the infliction is very speedy, and apparently less painful than hanging. The least crime for which death is awarded appears to be a third and aggravated theft, and defacing the branding inflicted for former offences. Decollation is considered more disgraceful than strangling, owing to the dislike the Chinese have of dissevering the bodies which their parents gave them entire. There are two modes of decapitation, that of simple decollation being considered, again, as less disgraceful than being "cut into ten thousand pieces," as the phrase *ling chih* has been rendered. The military officer who superintends the execution is attended by a guard, to keep the populace from crowding upon the limits and prevent resistance on the part of the prisoners. The bodies are given up to the friends, except when the head is exposed as a warning in a cage where the crime was committed. If no one is present to claim the corpse it is buried in the public pit. The criminals are generally so far exhausted that they make no resistance, and submit to their fate without a groan—much more, without a dying speech to the spectators. In ordinary cases the executions are postponed until the autumnal assize, when the Emperor revises and confirms the sentences of the provincial governors; criminals guilty of extraordinary offences, as robbery attended with murder, arson, rape, breaking into fortifications, highway robbery, and piracy, may be immediately beheaded without reference to court, and as the expense of maintenance and want of prison room are both to be considered, it is the fact that criminals condemned for one or other of these crimes comprise the greater part of the unreferred executions in the provinces.

It is impossible to ascertain the number of persons executed in China, for the life of a condemned criminal is thought little of; in the court circular it is merely reported that "the execution of the criminals was completed," without mentioning their crimes, residences, or names. At the autumnal revises at Peking the number sentenced is given in the *Gazette;* 935 were sentenced in 1817, of which 133 were from the province of

Kwangtung; in 1826 there were 581; in 1828 the number was 789, and in the next year 579 names were marked off, none of whose crimes, it is inferrible, are included in the list of offences mentioned above. The condemnations are sent from the capital by express, and the executions take place immediately. Most of the persons condemned in a province are executed in its capital, and to hear of the death of a score or more of felons on a single day is no uncommon thing. The trials are more speedy than comports with our notions of justice, and the executions are performed in the most summary manner. It is reported on one occasion that the governor-general of Canton ascended his judgment-seat, examined three prisoners brought before him, and having found them guilty, condemned them, asked himself for the death-warrant (for he temporarily filled the office of governor), and, having received it, had the three men carried away in about two hours after they were first brought before him. A few days after he granted the warrant to execute a hundred bandits in prison. During the terrible rebellion in Kwangtung, in 1854–55, the prisoners taken by the Imperialists were usually transported to Canton for execution. In a space of fourteen months, up to January, 1856, about eighty-three thousand malefactors suffered death in that city alone, besides those who died in confinement; these men were arrested and delivered to execution by their countrymen, who had suffered untold miseries through their sedition and rapine.

When taken to execution the prisoners are clothed in clean clothes.[1] A military officer is present, and the criminals are brought on the ground in hod-like baskets hanging from a pole borne of two, or in cages, and are obliged to kneel toward the Emperor's residence, or toward the death-warrant, which indicates his presence, as if thanking their sovereign for his care. The list is read aloud and compared with the tickets on the prisoners; as they kneel, a lictor seizes their pinioned hands and jerks them upward so that the head is pushed down horizontally, and a single down stroke with the heavy hanger severs

[1] Persons who commit suicide also dress themselves in their best, the common notion being that in the next world they will wear the same garments in which they died.

it from the neck. In the slow and ignominious execution, or *ling chih*, the criminal is tied to a cross and hacked to pieces; the executioner is nevertheless often hired to give the coup-de-grace at the first blow. It is not uncommon for him to cut out the gall-bladder of notorious robbers and sell it, to be eaten as a specific for courage. There is an official executioner besides the real one, the latter being sometimes a criminal taken out of the prisons.

Probably the number of persons who suffer by the sword of the executioner is not one-half of those who die from the effects of torture and privations in prisons. Not much is known of the internal arrangement of the *hells*, as prisons are called; they seem to be managed with a degree of kindness and attention to the comfort of the prisoners, so far as the intentions of government are concerned, but the cruelties of the turnkeys and older prisoners to exact money from the new comers are terrible. In Canton there are jails in the city under the control of four different officers, the largest covering about an acre, and capable of holding upward of five hundred prisoners. Since it is the practice of distant magistrates to send their worst prisoners up to the capital, these jails are not large enough, and jail distempers arise from over-crowding; two hundred deaths were reported in 1826 from this and other causes, and one hundred and seventeen cases in 1831. Private jails were hired to accommodate the number, and one governor reports having found twenty-two such places in Canton where every kind of cruelty was practised. The witnesses and accusers concerned in appellate causes had, he says, also been brought up to the city and imprisoned along with the guilty party, where they were kept months without any just reason. In one case, where a defendant and plaintiff were imprisoned together, the accuser fell upon the other and murdered him. Sometimes the officer is unable from press of business to attend to a case, and confines all the principals and witnesses concerned until he can examine them, but the government takes no means to provide for them during the interval, and many of the poorer ones die. No security or bail is obtainable on the word of a witness or his friends, so that if unable to fee the jailers he is in nearly as bad a case as the criminal. Extending bail to an accused criminal is nearly unknown, but female prisoners are put in charge of their husbands or parents, who are held responsible for their appearance. The constant succession of criminals in the provincial head prison renders the posts of jailers and turnkeys very lucrative. The letters of the Roman Catholic missionaries from China during the last century, found in the *Lettres Édifiantes* and *Annales de la Foi*, contain many sad pictures of the miseries of prison life there.

The prisons are arranged somewhat on the plan of a large stable, having an open central court occupying nearly one-fourth of the area, and small cribs or stalls covered by a roof extending nearly around it, so contrived that each company of prisoners shall be separated from its neighbors on either side night and day, though more by night than by day. The prisoners cook for themselves in the court, and are secured by manacles and gyves, and a chain joining the hands to the neck; one hand is liberated in the daytime in order to allow them to take care of themselves. Heinous criminals are more heavily ironed, and those in the prisons attached to the judge's office are worse treated than the others. Each criminal should receive a daily ration of two pounds of rice, and about two cents with which to buy fuel, but the jailer starves them on half this allowance if they are unable to fee him; clothing is also scantily provided, but those who have money can procure almost every convenience. Each crib full of criminals is under the control of a turnkey, who with a few old offenders spends much time torturing newly arrived persons to force money from them, by which many lose their lives, and all suffer far more in this manner than they do from the officers of government. Well may the people call their prisons hells, and say, when a man falls into the clutches of the jailers or police, "the flesh is under the cleaver."

There are many processes for the recovery of debts and fulfilment of contracts, some legal and others customary, the latter depending upon many circumstances irrelevant to the merits of the case. The law allows that debtors be punished by bambooing according to the amount of the debt. A creditor often resorts to illegal means to recover his claim, which give rise to many excesses; sometimes he quarters himself upon the debtor's family or premises, at others seizes him or some of his family and keeps them prisoners, and, in extreme cases, sells them. Unscrupulous debtors are equally skilful and violent in eluding, cheating, and resisting their incensed creditors, according as they have the power. They are liable, when three months have expired after the stipulated time of payment, to be bambooed, and their property attached. In most cases, however, disputes of this sort are settled without recourse to government, and if the debtor is really without property, he is not imprisoned till he can procure it. The effects of absconding debtors are seized and divided by those who can get them. Long experience, moreover, of each other's characters has taught them, in contracting debts, to have some security at the outset, and therefore in settling up there is not so much loss as might be supposed considering the difficulty of collecting debts. Accusations for libel, slander, breach of marriage contract, and other civil or less criminal offences are not all brought before the authorities, but are settled by force or arbitration among the people themselves and their elders.

The nominal salaries of Chinese officers have already been stated (p. 294). It is a common opinion among the people that on an average they receive about ten times their salaries; in some cases they pay thirty, forty and more thousand dollars beforehand for the situation. One encouragement to the harassing vexations of the official secretaries and police is the dislike of the people to carry their cases before officers who they know are almost compelled to fleece and peel them; they think it cheaper and safer to bear a small exaction from an underling than run the risk of a greater from his master.

If the preventives against popular violence which the supreme government has placed around itself could be strengthened by an efficient military force, its power would be well secured indeed; but then, as in Russia, it would probably become, by degrees, an intolerable tyranny. The troops are, in fact, everywhere present, ostensibly to support the laws, protect the innocent, and punish the guilty; such of them as are employed by the authorities as guards and policemen are, on the whole, efficient and courteous, though miserably paid, while the regiments in garrison are contemptible to both friend and foe.

The efficacy of the system of checks upon the high courts and provincial officers is increased by their intrigues and conflicting ambition, and long experience has shown that the Emperor's power has little to fear from proconsular rebellion. The inefficiency of the army is a serious evil to the people in one respect, for more power in that arm would repress banditti and pirates; while the sober part of the community would coöperate in a hearty effort to quell them. The greatest difficulty the Emperor finds in upholding his authority lies in the general want of integrity in the officers he employs; good laws may be made, but he has few upright agents to execute them. This has been abundantly manifested in the laws against opium and gambling; no one could be found to carry them into execution, though everybody assented to their propriety.

The chief security on the side of the people against an unmitigated oppression such as now exists in Turkey, besides those already pointed out, lies as much as anywhere in their general intelligence of the true principles on which the government is founded and should be executed. With public opinion on its side the government is a strong one, but none is less able to execute its designs when it runs counter to that opinion, although those designs may be excellent and well intended. Elements of discord are found in the social system which would soon effect its ruin were they not counteracted by other influences, and the body politic goes on like a heavy, shackly, lumbering van, which every moment threatens a crashing, crumbling fall, yet goes on still tottering, owing to the original goodness of its construction. From the enormous population of this ancient van, it is evident that any attempt to remodel it must seriously affect one or the other of its parts, and that when once upset it may be impossible to reconstruct it in its original form. There is encouragement to hope that the general intelligence and shrewdness of the government and people of China, their language, institutions, industry, and love of peace, will all act as powerful conservative influences in working out the changes which cannot now be long delayed; and that she will maintain her unity and industry while going through a thorough reform of her political, social, and religious systems.

It is very difficult to convey to the reader a fair view of the administration of the laws in China. Notwithstanding the cruelty of officers to the criminals before them, they are not all to be considered as tyrants; because insurrections arise, attended with great loss of life, it must not be supposed that society is everywhere disorganized; the Chinese are so prone to falsify that it is difficult to ascertain the truth, yet it must not be inferred that every sentence is a lie; selfishness is a prime motive for their actions, yet charity, kindness, filial affection, and the unbought courtesies of life still exist among them. Although there is an appalling amount of evil and crime in every shape, it is mixed with some redeeming traits; and in China, as elsewhere, good and bad are intermingled. Some of the evils in the social system arise from the operation of the principles of mutual responsibility, while this very feature produces sundry good effects in restraining people who have no higher motive than the fear of injuring the innocent. We hear so much of the shocking cruelties of courts and prisons that the vast number of cases before the bench are all supposed to exhibit the same fatiguing reiteration of suffering, injustice, bribery, and cruelty. One must live in the country to see how the antagonistic principles found in Chinese society act and react upon each other, and are affected by the wicked passions of the heart. Officers and people are bad almost beyond belief to one conversant only with the courtesy, justice, purity, and sincerity of Christian governments and society; and yet we think they are not as bad as the old Greeks and Romans, and have no more injustice or torture in their courts, nor impurity or mendacity in their lives. As in our own land we are apt to forget that the recitals of crimes and outrages which the daily papers bring before our eyes furnish no index of the general condition of society, so in China, where that condition is immeasurably worse, we must be mindful that this is likewise true.

CHAPTER IX.

EDUCATION AND LITERARY EXAMINATIONS.

Among the points relating to the Chinese people which have attracted the attention of students in the history of intellectual development, their long duration and literary institutions have probably taken precedence. To estimate the causes of the first requires much knowledge of the second, and from them one is gradually led onward to an examination of the government, religion, and social life of this people in the succeeding epochs of their existence. The inquiry will reveal much that is instructive, and show us that, if they have not equalled many other nations in the arts and adornments of life, they have attained a high degree of comfort and developed much that is creditable in education, the science of rule, and security of life and property.

Although the powers of mind exhibited by the greatest writers in China are confessedly inferior to those of Greece and Rome for genius and original conceptions, the good influence exerted by them over their countrymen is far greater, even at this day, than was ever obtained by western sages, as Plato, Aristotle, or Seneca. The thoroughness of Chinese education, the purity and effectiveness of the examinations, or the accuracy and excellency of the literature must not be compared with those of modern Christian countries, for there is really no common measure between the two; they must be taken with other parts of Chinese character, and comparisons drawn, if necessary, with nations possessing similar opportunities. The importance of generally instructing the people was acknowledged even before the time of Confucius, and practised to a good degree at an age when other nations in the world had no such system; and although in his day feudal institutions prevailed, and offices and rank were not attainable in the same manner as at present, on the other hand magistrates and noblemen deemed it necessary to be well acquainted with their ancient writings. It is said in the *Book of Rites* (B.C. 1200), "that for the purposes of education among the ancients, villages had their schools, districts their academies, departments their colleges, and principalities their universities." This, so far as we know, was altogether superior to what obtained among the Jews, Persians, and Syrians of the same period.

The great stimulus to literary pursuits is the hope thereby of obtaining office and honor, and the only course of education followed is the classical and historical one prescribed by law. Owing to this undue attention to the classics, the minds of the scholars are not symmetrically trained, and they disparage other branches of literature which do not directly advance this great end. Every department of letters, except jurisprudence, history, and official statistics, is disesteemed in comparison; and the literary graduate of fourscore will be found deficient in most branches of general learning, ignorant of hundreds of common things and events in his national history, which the merest schoolboy in the western world would be ashamed not to know in his. This course of instruction does not form well-balanced minds, but it imbues the future rulers of the land with a full understanding of the principles on which they are to govern, and the policy of the supreme power in using those principles to consolidate its own authority.

Centralization and conservatism were the leading features of the teachings of Confucius which first recommended them to the rulers, and have decided the course of public examinations in selecting officers who would readily uphold these principles. The effect has been that the literary class in China holds the functions of both nobles and priests, a perpetual association, *gens æterna in qua nemo nascitur*, holding in its hands public opinion and legal power to maintain it. The geographical isolation of the people, the nature of the language, and the absence of a landed aristocracy, combine to add efficiency to this system; and when the peculiarities of Chinese character, and the nature of the class-books which do so much to mould that character, are considered, it is impossible to devise a better plan for insuring the perpetuity of the government, or the contentment of the people under that government.

It was about A.D. 600, that Taitsung, of the Tang dynasty, instituted the present plan of preparing and selecting civilians by means of study and degrees, founding his system on the facts that education had always been esteemed, and that the ancient writings were accepted by all as the best instructors of the manners and tastes of the people. According to native historians, the rulers of ancient times made ample provision for the cultivation of literature and promotion of education in all its branches. They supply some details to enable us to understand the mode and the materials of this instruction, and glorify it as they do everything ancient, but probably from the want of authentic accounts in their own hands, they do not clearly describe it. The essays of M. Édouard Biot on the *History of Public Instruction in China*, contains well-nigh all the information extant on this interesting subject, digested in a very lucid manner. Education is probably as good now as it ever was, and its ability to maintain and develop the character of the people as great as at any time; it is remarkable how much it really has done to form, elevate, and consolidate their national institutions. The Manchu monarchs were not at first favorably disposed to the system of examinations, and frowned upon the literary hierarchy who claimed all honors as their right; but the next generation saw the advantages and necessity of the *concours*, in preserving its own power.

Boys commence their studies at the age of seven with a teacher; for, even if the father be a literary man he seldom instructs his sons, and very few mothers are able to teach their offspring to read. Maternal training is supposed to consist in giving a right direction to the morals, and enforcing the obedience of the child; but as there are few mothers who do more than compel obedience by commands, or by the rod, so there are none who can teach the infantile mind to look up to its God in prayer and praise.

Among the many treatises for the guidance of teachers, the

Siao Hioh, or 'Juvenile Instructor,' is regarded as most authoritative. When establishing the elements of education, this book advises fathers to "choose from among their concubines those who are fit for nurses, seeking such as are mild, indulgent, affectionate, benevolent, cheerful, kind, dignified, respectful, and reserved and careful in their conversation, whom they will make governesses over their children. When able to talk, lads must be instructed to answer in a quick, bold tone, and girls in a slow and gentle one. At the age of seven, they should be taught to count and name the cardinal points; but at this age the sexes should not be allowed to sit on the same mat nor eat from the same table. At eight, they must be taught to wait for their superiors, and prefer others to themselves. At ten, the boys must be sent abroad to private tutors, and there remain day and night, studying writing and arithmetic, wearing plain apparel, learning to demean themselves in a manner becoming their age, and acting with sincerity of purpose. At thirteen, they must attend to music and poetry; at fifteen, they must practise archery and charioteering. At the age of twenty, they are in due form to be admitted to the rank of manhood, and learn additional rules of propriety, be fathful in the performance of filial and fraternal duties, and though they possess extensive knowledge, must not affect to teach others. At thirty, they may marry and commence the management of business. At forty, they may enter the service of the state; and if their prince maintains the reign of reason, they must serve him, but otherwise not. At fifty, they may be promoted to the rank of ministers; and at seventy, they must retire from public life."

Another injunction is, "Let children always be taught to speak the simple truth; to stand erect and in their proper places, and listen with respectful attention." The way to become a student, "is, with gentleness and self-abasement, to receive implicitly every word the master utters. The pupil, when he sees virtuous people, must follow them, when he hears good maxims, conform to them. He must cherish no wicked designs, but always act uprightly; whether at home or abroad, he must have a fixed residence, and associate with the benevolent, carefully regulating his personal deportment, and controlling the feelings of his heart. He must keep his clothes in order. Every morning he must learn something new, and rehearse the same every evening." The great end of education, therefore, among the ancient Chinese, was not so much to fill the head with knowledge, as to discipline the heart and purify the affections. One of their writers says, "Those who respect the virtuous and put away unlawful pleasures, serve their parents and prince to the utmost of their ability, and are faithful to their word; these, though they should be considered unlearned, we must pronounce to be educated men." Although such terms as purity, filial affection, learning, and truth, have higher meanings in a Christian education than are given them by Chinese masters, the inculcation of them in any degree and so decided a manner does great credit to the people, and will never need to be superseded —only raised to a higher grade.[1]

In intercourse with their relatives, children are taught to attend to the minutest points of good breeding; and are instructed in everything relating to their personal appearance, making their toilet, saluting their parents, eating, visiting, and other acts of life. Many of these directions are trivial even to puerility, but they are none too minute in the ideas of the Chinese, and still form the basis of good manners, as much as they did a score of centuries ago; and it can hardly be supposed that Confucius would have risked his influence upon the grave publication of trifles, if he had not been well acquainted with the character of his countrymen. Yet nothing is trifling which conduces to the growth of good manners among a people, though it may not have done all that was wished.[2]

Rules are laid down for students to observe in the prosecution of their studies, which reflect credit on those who set so high a standard for themselves. Dr. Morrison has given a synopsis of a treatise of this sort, called the 'Complete Collection of Family Jewels,' and containing a minute specification of

---

[1] Compare Du Halde, *Description de l'Empire de la Chine*, Tome II., pp. 365–384; A. Wylie, *Notes*, p. 68; *Chinese Repository*, Vols. V., p. 81, and VI., pp. 185, 393, and 562; *China Review*, Vol. VI., pp. 120, 195, 253, 328, etc.; *New Englander*, May, 1878.

[2] *Chinese Repository*, Vol. IV., pp. 83–87, 306–316.

duties to be performed by all who would be thorough students. The author directs the tyro to form a fixed resolution to press forward in his studies, setting his mark as high as possible, and thoroughly understanding everything as he goes along. "I have always seen that a man who covets much and devotes himself to universal knowledge, when he reads he presumes on the quickness and celerity of his genius and perceptions, and chapters and volumes pass before his eyes, and issue from his mouth as fluently as water rolls away; but when does he ever apply his mind to rub and educe the essence of a subject? In this manner, although much be read, what is the use of it? Better little and fine, than much and coarse." He also advises persons to have two or three good volumes lying on their tables, which they can take up at odd moments, and to keep common-place books in which they can jot down such things as occur to them. They should get rid of distracting thoughts if they wish to advance in their studies; as "if a man's stomach has been filled by eating greens and other vegetables, although the most precious dainties with exquisite tastes should be given him, he cannot swallow them, he must first get rid of a few portions of the greens; so in reading, the same is true of the mixed thoughts which distract the mind, which are about the dusty affairs of a vulgar world." The rules given by these writers correspond to those laid down among ourselves, in such books as Todd's *Manual for Students*, and reveal the steps which have given the Chinese their intellectual position.[1]

For all grades of scholars, there is but one mode of study; the imitative nature of the Chinese mind is strikingly exhibited in the few attempts on the part of teachers to improve upon the stereotyped practice of their predecessors, although persons of as original minds as the country affords are constantly engaged in education. When the lad commences his studies, an impressive ceremony takes place—or did formerly, for it seems to have fallen into desuetude: the father leads his son to the teacher, who kneels down before the name of some one or other of the ancient sages, and supplicates their blessing upon his

[1] Morrison's *Chinese Dictionary*, Vol. I., Part I., pp. 749–758.

pupil; after which, seating himself, he receives the homage and petition of the lad to guide him in his lessons.[1] As is the case in Moslem countries, a present is expected to accompany this initiation into literary pursuits. In all cases this event is further marked by giving the lad his *shu ming* or 'book name,' by which he is called during his future life. The furniture of the school merely consists of a desk and a stool for each pupil, and an elevated seat for the master, for maps, globes, blackboards, diagrams, etc., are yet to come in among its articles of furniture. In one corner is placed a tablet or an inscription on the wall, dedicated to Confucius and the god of Letters; the sage is styled the 'Teacher and Pattern for All Ages,' and incense is constantly burned in honor of them both.

The location of school-rooms is usually such as would be considered bad elsewhere, but by comparison with other things in China, is not so. A mat shed which barely protects from the weather, a low, hot upper attic of a shop, a back room in a temple, or rarely a house specially built for the purpose, such are the school-houses in China. The chamber is hired by the master, who regulates his expenses and furnishes his apartment according to the number and condition of his pupils; their average number is about twenty, ranging between ten and forty in day schools, and in private schools seldom exceeding ten. The most thorough course of education is probably pursued in the latter, where a well-qualified teacher is hired by four or five persons living in the same street, or mutually related by birth or marriage, to teach their children at a stipulated salary. In such cases the lads are placed in bright, well-aired apartments, superior to the common school-room. The majority of teachers have been unsuccessful candidates for literary degrees, who having spent the prime of their days in fruitless attempts to attain office, are unfit for manual labor, and unable to enter on mercantile life. In Canton, a teacher of twenty boys receives from half a dollar to a dollar per month from each pupil; in country villages, three, four or five dollars a year are given, with the addition, in most cases, of a small present of eatables

---

[1] This custom obtains also in Bokhara.

from each scholar three or four times a year. Private tutors receive from $150 to $350 or more per annum, according to particular engagement. There are no boarding-schools, nor anything answering to infant schools; nor are public or charity schools established by government, or by private benevolence for the education of the poor.

The first hours of study are from sunrise till ten A.M., when the boys go to breakfast; they reassemble in an hour or more, and continue at their books till about five P.M., when they disperse for the day. In summer, they have no lessons after dinner, but an evening session is often held in the winter, and evening schools are occasionally opened for mechanics and others who are occupied during the day. When a boy comes into school in the morning, he bows reverentially before the tablet of Confucius, salutes his teacher, and then takes his seat. The vacations during the year are few; the longest is before new year, at which time the engagement is completed, and the school closes, to be reöpened after the teacher and parents have made a new arrangement. The common festivals, of which there are a dozen or more, are regarded as holydays, and form very necessary relaxations in a country destitute of the rest of the Sabbath. The requisite qualifications of a teacher are gravity, severity, and patience, and acquaintance with the classics; he has only to teach the same series of books in the same fashion in which he learned them himself and keep a good watch over his charge.

When the lads come together at the opening of the school, their attainments are ascertained; the teacher endeavors to have his pupils nearly equal in this respect, but inasmuch as they are all put to precisely the same tasks, a difference is not material. If the boys are beginners, they are brought up in a line before the desk, holding the *San-tsz' King*, or 'Trimetrical Classic,' in their hands, and taught to read off the first lines after the teacher until they can repeat them without help. He calls off the first four lines as follows:

Jin chí tsu, sing pun shen;
Sing siang kin, sih siang yuen;

when his pupils simultaneously cry out:

Jin chí tsu, sing pun shen ;
Sing siang kin, sih siang yuen.

Mispronunciations are corrected until each can read the lesson accurately; they are then sent to their seats to commit the sounds to memory. As the sounds are all entire words (not letters, nor syllables, of which they have no idea), the boys are not perplexed, as ours are, with symbols which have no meaning. All the children study aloud, and when one is able to recite the task, he is required to *back* it—come up to the master's desk, and stand with his back toward him while rehearsing it.

The *San-tsz' King* was compiled by Wang Pih-hao of the Sung dynasty (A. D. 1050) for his private school. It contains ten hundred and sixty-eight words, and half that number of different characters, arranged in one hundred and seventy-eight double lines. It has been commented upon by several persons, one of whom calls it "a ford which the youthful inquirer may readily pass, and thereby reach the fountain-head of the higher courses of learning, or a passport into the regions of classical and historical literature." This hornbook begins with the nature of man, and the necessity and modes of education, and it is noticeable that the first sentence, the one quoted above, which a Chinese learns at school, contains one of the most disputed doctrines in the ancient heathen world:

> "Men at their birth, are by nature radically good;
> Though alike in this, in practice they widely diverge.
> If not educated, the natural character grows worse;
> A course of education is made valuable by close attention.
> Of old, Mencius' mother selected a residence,
> And when her son did not learn, cut out the [half-wove] web.
> To nurture and not educate is a father's error;
> To educate without rigor shows a teacher's indolence.
> That boys should not learn is an unjust thing;
> For if they do not learn in youth, what will they do when old?
> As gems unwrought serve no useful end,
> So men untaught will never know what right conduct is."

The importance of filial and fraternal duties are then inculcated by precept and example, to which succeeds a synopsis of the various branches of learning in an ascending series, under several heads of numbers; the three great powers, the four seasons and four cardinal points, the five elements and five constant virtues, the six kinds of grain and six domestic animals, the seven passions, the eight materials for music, nine degrees of kindred, and ten social duties. A few extracts will exhibit the mode in which these subjects are treated.

"There are three powers,—heaven, earth, and man.
There are three lights,—the sun, moon, and stars.
There are three bonds,—between prince and minister, justice;
Between father and son, affection; between man and wife, concord.

Humanity, justice, propriety, wisdom, and truth,—
These five cardinal virtues are not to be confused.
Rice, millet, pulse, wheat, sorghum, millet grass,
Are six kinds of grain on which men subsist.

Mutual affection of father and son, concord of man and wife;
The older brother's kindness, the younger one's respect;
Order between seniors and juniors, friendship among associates;
On the prince's part regard, on the minister's true loyalty;—
These ten moral duties are ever binding among men."

To this technical summary succeed rules for a course of academical studies, with a list of the books to be learned, and the order of their use, followed by a synopsis of the general history of China, in an enumeration of the successive dynasties. The work concludes with incidents and motives to learning drawn from the conduct of ancient sages and statesmen, and from considerations of interest and glory. The examples cited are curious instances of pursuit of knowledge under difficulties, and form an inviting part of the treatise.

"Formerly Confucius had young Hiang Toh for his teacher;
Even the sages of antiquity studied with diligence.
Chau, a minister of state, read the Confucian Dialogues,
And he too, though high in office, studied assiduously.
One copied lessons on reeds, another on slips of bamboo;
These, though without books, eagerly sought knowledge.
[To vanquish sleep] one tied his head [by the hair] to a beam, and another pierced his thigh with an awl;
Though destitute of instructors, these were laborious in study.
One read by the glowworm's light, another by reflection from snow;

These, though their families were poor, did not omit to study.
One carried faggots, and another tied his books to a cow's horn,
And while thus engaged in labor, studied with intensity.
Su Lau-tsiuen, when he was twenty-seven years old
Commenced close study, and applied his mind to books;
This man, when old, grieved that he commenced so late;
You who are young must early think of these things.
Behold Liang Hau, at the ripe age of eighty-two,
In the imperial hall, amongst many scholars, gains the first rank;
This he accomplished, and all regarded him a prodigy;
You, my young readers, should now resolve to be diligent.
Yung, when only eight years old, could recite the Odes;
And Pí, at the age of seven, understood the game of chess;
These displayed ability, and all deemed them to be rare men;
And you, my hopeful scholars, ought to imitate them.
Tsai Wăn-kí could play upon stringed instruments;
Sié Tau-wăn, likewise, could sing and chant;
These two, though girls, were bright and well informed;
You, then, my lads, should surely rouse to diligence.
Liu Ngan of Tang, when only seven years old,
Proving himself a noble lad, was able to correct writing:
He, though very young, was thus highly promoted.
You, young learners, strive to follow his example,
For he who does so, will acquire like honors.
"Dogs watch by night; the cock announces the morning;
If any refuse to learn, how can they be esteemed men?
The silkworm spins silk, the bee gathers honey;
If men neglect to learn, they are below the brutes.
He who learns in youth, to act wisely in mature age,
Extends his influence to the prince, benefits the people,
Makes his name renowned, renders his parents honorable;
Reflects glory on his ancestors, and enriches his posterity.
Some for their offspring, leave coffers filled with gold;
While I to teach children, leave this one little book.
Diligence has merit; play yields no profit;
Be ever on your guard! Rouse all your energies!"

These quotations illustrate the character of the *Trimetrical Classic*, and show its imperfections as a book for young minds. It is a syllabus of studies rather than a book to be learned, and ill suited to entice the boy on in his tasks by giving him mental food in an attractive form. Yet its influence has been perhaps as great as the classics during the last four dynasties, from its general use in primary schools, where myriads of lads have "backed" it who have had no leisure to study much more, and when they had crossed this ford could travel no farther. The boy commences his education by learning these maxims; and by the time he has got his degree—and long before, too—the highest truths and examples known in the land are more deeply impressed on his mind than are ever Biblical truths and examples on graduates of Yale, Oxford, Heidelberg or the Sorbonne. Well was it for them that they had learned nothing in it which they had better forget, for its deficiencies, pointed out by Bridgman in his translation, should not lead us to overlook its suggestive synopsis of principles and examples. The commentary explains them very fully, and it is often learned as thoroughly as the text. Many thousands of tracts containing Christian truths written in the same style and with the same title, have been taught with good effect in the mission schools in China.[1]

The next hornbook put into the boy's hands is the *Pih Kia Sing*, or 'Century of Surnames.' It is a list of the family or clan names commonly in use. Its acquisition also gives him familiarity with four hundred and fifty-four common words employed as names, a knowledge, too, of great importance lest mistakes be made in choosing a wrong character among the scores of homophonous characters in the language. For instance, out of eighty-three common words pronounced *kí*, six only are clan names, and it is necessary to have these very familiar in the daily intercourse of life. The nature of the work forbids its being studied, but the usefulness of its contents probably explains its position in this series.[2]

The third in the list is the *Tsien Tsz' Wăn*, or 'Millenary Classic,' unique among all books in the Chinese language, and whose like could not be produced in any other, in that it consists

---

[1] Compare Dr. Morrison in the *Horæ Sinicæ*, pp. 122–146; B. Jenkins, *The Three-Character Classic, romanized according to the Shanghai dialect*, Shanghai, 1860. The Classic has also been translated into Latin, French, German, Russian, and Portuguese. For the Trimetrical Classic of the Tai-ping régime see a version in the *North China Herald*, No. 147, May 21, 1853, by Dr. Medhurst; also a translation by Rev. S. C. Malan, of Balliol College, Oxford. London, 1856.

[2] E. C. Bridgman in the *Chinese Repository*, Vol. IV., p. 152. *Livre de Cent familles*, Perny, *Dict.*, App., No. XIV., pp. 156 ff.

of just a thousand characters, no two of which are alike in form or meaning. The author, Chau Hing-tsz', flourished about A.D. 550, and according to an account given in the history of the Liang dynasty, wrote it at the Emperor's request, who had ordered his minister Wang Hí-chí to write out a thousand characters, and give them to him, to see if he could make a connected ode with them. This he did, and presented his performance to his majesty, who rewarded him with rich presents in token of his approval. Some accounts (in order that so singular a work might not want for corresponding wonders) add that he did the task in a single night, under the fear of condign punishment if he failed, and the mental exertion was so great as to turn his hair white. It consists of two hundred and fifty lines, in which rhyme and rhythm are both carefully observed, though there is no more poetry in it than in a multiplication table. The contents of the book are similar but more discursive than those of the *Trimetrical Classic.* Up to the one hundred and second line, the productions of nature and virtues of the early monarchs, the power and capacities of man, his social duties and mode of conduct, with instructions as to the manner of living, are summarily treated. Thence to the one hundred and sixty-second line, the splendor of the palace, and its high dignitaries, with other illustrious persons and places, are referred to. The last part of the work treats of private and literary life, the pursuits of agriculture, household government, and education, interspersed with some exhortations, and a few illustrations. A few disconnected extracts from Dr. Bridgman's translation[1] will show the mode in which these subjects are handled. The opening lines are,

> "The heavens are sombre ; the earth is yellow;
> The whole universe [at the creation] was one wide waste ; "

after which it takes a survey of the world and its products, and Chinese history, in a very sententious manner, down to the thirty-seventh line, which opens a new subject.

---

[1] *Chinese Repository*, Vol. IV., p. 229.

"Now this our human body is endowed
With four great powers and five cardinal virtues:
Preserve with reverence what your parents nourished,—
How dare you destroy or injure it?
Let females guard their chastity and purity,
And let men imitate the talented and virtuous.
When you know your own errors then reform;
And when you have made acquisitions do not lose them.
Forbear to complain of the defects of other people,
And cease to brag of your own superiority.
Let your truth be such as may be verified,
Your capacities, as to be measured with difficulty.
"Observe and imitate the conduct of the virtuous,
And command your thoughts that you may be wise.
Your virtue once fixed, your reputation will be established;
Your habits once rectified, your example will be correct.
Sounds are reverberated in the deep valleys,
And the vacant hall reëchoes all it hears;
So misery is the penalty of accumulated vice,
And happiness the reward of illustrious virtue.
"A cubit of jade stone is not to be valued,
But an inch of time you ought to contend for.
"Mencius esteemed plainness and simplicity;
And Yu the historian held firmly to rectitude.
These nearly approached the golden medium,
Being laborious, humble, diligent, and moderate.
Listen to what is said, and investigate the principles explained:
Watch men's demeanor, that you may distinguish their characters.
Leave behind you none but purposes of good;
And strive to act in such a manner as to command respect.
When satirized and admonished examine yourself,
And do this more thoroughly when favors increase.
"Years fly away like arrows, one pushing on the other;
The sun shines brightly through his whole course.
The planetarium keeps on revolving where it hangs;
And the bright moon repeats her revolutions.
To support fire, add fuel; so cultivate the root of happiness,
And you will obtain eternal peace and endless felicity."

The commentary on the *Thousand Character Classic* contains many just observations and curious anecdotes to explain this book, whose text is so familiar to the people at large that its lines or characters are used as labels instead of figures, as they take up less room. If Western scholars were as familiar with the acts and sayings of King Wăn, of Su Tsin, or of Kwan Chung, as they are with those of Sesostris, Pericles, or Horace, these incidents and places would naturally enough be deemed more interesting than they now are. But where the power of genius, or the vivid pictures of a brilliant imagination, are wanting to illustrate or beautify a subject, there is comparatively little to interest Europeans in the authors and statesmen of such a distant country and remote period.[1]

The fourth in this series, called *Yiu Hioh Shi-tieh*, or 'Odes for Children,' is written in rhymed pentameters, and contains only thirty-four stanzas of four lines. A single extract will show its character, which is, in general, a brief description and praise of literary life, and allusion to the changes of the season, and the beauties of nature.

> It is of the utmost importance to educate children;
> Do not say that your families are poor,
> For those who can handle well the pencil,
> Go where they will, need never ask for favors.
>
> One at the age of seven, showed himself a divinely endowed youth,
> 'Heaven,' said he, 'gave me my intelligence:
> Men of talent appear in the courts of the holy monarch,
> Nor need they wait in attendance on lords and nobles.
>
> 'In the morning I was an humble cottager,
> In the evening I entered the court of the Son of Heaven:
> Civil and military offices are not hereditary,
> Men must, therefore, rely on their own efforts.
>
> 'A passage for the sea has been cut through mountains,
> And stones have been melted to repair the heavens;
> In all the world there is nothing that is impossible;
> It is the heart of man alone that is wanting resolution.
>
> 'Once I myself was a poor indigent scholar,
> Now I ride mounted in my four-horse chariot,
> And all my fellow-villagers exclaim with surprise.'
> Let those who have children thoroughly educate them.

The examples of intelligent youth rising to the highest offices of state are numerous in all the works designed for beginners,

[1] Compare *Das Tsiän dsü wen, oder Buch von Tausend Wörtern, aus dem Schinesischen, mit Berückschtigung der Koraischen und Japanischen Uebersetzung, ins Deutsche übertragen*, Ph. Fr. de Siebold, *Nippon*, Abh. IV., pp. 165-191; B. Jenkins, *The Thousand-Character Classic, romanized*, etc. Shanghai, 1860; *Thsien-Tseu-Wen, Le Livre des Mille Mots*, etc., par Stanislas Julien (with Chinese text), Paris, 1864; *China Review*, Vol. II., pp. 182 ff.

and stories illustrative of their precocity are sometimes given in toy-books and novels. One of the most common instances is here quoted, that of Confucius and Hiang Toh, which is as well known to every Chinese as is the story of George Washington barking the cherry-tree with his hatchet to American youth.

"The name of Confucius was Yu, and his style Chungní; he established himself as an instructor in the western part of the kingdom of Lu. One day, followed by all his disciples, riding in a carriage, he went out to ramble, and on the road, came across several children at their sports; among them was one who did not join in them. Confucius, stopping his carriage, asked him, saying, 'Why is it that you alone do not play?' The lad replied, 'All play is without any profit; one's clothes get torn, and they are not easily mended; above me, I disgrace my father and mother; below me, even to the lowest, there is fighting and altercation; so much toil and no reward, how can it be a good business? It is for these reasons that I do not play.' Then dropping his head, he began making a city out of pieces of tile.

"Confucius, reproving him, said, 'Why do you not turn out for the carriage?' The boy replied, 'From ancient times till now it has always been considered proper for a carriage to turn out for a city, and not for a city to turn out for a carriage.' Confucius then stopped his vehicle in order to discourse of reason. He got out of the carriage, and asked him, 'You are still young in years, how is it that you are so quick?' The boy replied, saying, 'A human being, at the age of three years, discriminates between his father and his mother; a hare, three days after it is born, runs over the ground and furrows of the fields; fish, three days after their birth, wander in rivers and lakes; what heaven thus produces naturally, how can it be called brisk?'

"Confucius added, 'In what village and neighborhood do you reside, what is your surname and name, and what your style?' The boy answered, 'I live in a mean village and in an insignificant land; my surname is Hiang, my name is Toh, and I have yet no style.'

"Confucius rejoined, 'I wish to have you come and ramble with me; what do you think of it?' The youth replied, 'A stern father is at home, whom I am bound to serve; an affectionate mother is there, whom it is my duty to cherish; a worthy elder brother is at home, whom it is proper for me to obey, with a tender younger brother whom I must teach; and an intelligent teacher is there from whom I am required to learn. How have I leisure to go a rambling with you?'

"Confucius said, 'I have in my carriage thirty-two chessmen; what do you say to having a game together?' The lad answered, 'If the Emperor love gaming, the Empire will not be governed; if the nobles love play, the government will be impeded; if scholars love it, learning and investigation will be lost and thrown by; if the lower classes are fond of gambling, they will utterly lose the support of their families; if servants and slaves love to game, they will get a cudgelling; if farmers love it, they miss the time for ploughing and sowing; for these reasons I shall not play with you.'

"Confucius rejoined, 'I wish to have you go with me, and fully equalize the Empire; what do you think of this?' The lad replied, 'The Empire cannot be equalized; here are high hills, there are lakes and rivers; either there are princes and nobles, or there are slaves and servants. If the high hills be levelled, the birds and beasts will have no resort; if the rivers and lakes be filled up, the fishes and the turtles will have nowhere to go; do away with kings and nobles, and the common people will have much dispute about right and wrong; obliterate slaves and servants, and who will there be to serve the prince! If the Empire be so vast and unsettled, how can it be equalized?'

"Confucius again asked, 'Can you tell, under the whole sky, what fire has no smoke, what water no fish; what hill has no stones, what tree no branches; what man has no wife, what woman no husband; what cow has no calf, what mare no colt; what cock has no hen, what hen no cock; what constitutes an excellent man, and what an inferior man; what is that which has not enough, and what which has an overplus; what city is without a market, and who is the man without a style?'

"The boy replied, 'A glowworm's fire has no smoke, and well-water no fish; a mound of earth has no stones, and a rotten tree no branches; genii have no wives, and fairies no husbands; earthen cows have no calves, nor wooden mares any colts; lonely cocks have no hens, and widowed hens no cocks; he who is worthy is an excellent man, and a fool is an inferior man; a winter's day is not long enough, and a summer's day is too long; the imperial city has no market, and little folks have no style.'

"Confucius inquiring said, 'Do you know what are the connecting bonds between heaven and earth, and what is the beginning and ending of the dual powers? What is left, and what is right; what is out, and what is in; who is father, and who is mother; who is husband, and who is wife. [Do you know] where the wind comes from, and from whence the rain? From whence the clouds issue, and the dew arises? And for how many tens of thousands of miles the sky and earth go parallel?'

"The youth answering said, 'Nine multiplied nine times make eighty-one, which is the controlling bond of heaven and earth; eight multiplied by nine makes seventy-two, the begining and end of the dual powers. Heaven is father, and earth is mother; the sun is husband, and the moon is wife; east is left, and west is right; without is out, and inside is in; the winds come from Tsang-wu, and the rains proceed from wastes and wilds; the clouds issue from the hills, and the dew rises from the ground. Sky and earth go parallel for ten thousand times ten thousand miles, and the four points of the compass have each their station.'

"Confucius asking, said, 'Which do you say is the nearest relation, father and mother, or husband and wife?' The boy responded, 'One's parents are near; husband and wife are not [so] near.'

"Confucius rejoined, 'While husband and wive are alive, they sleep under the same coverlet; when they are dead they lie in the same grave; how then can you say that they are not near?' The boy replied, 'A man without a wife is like a carriage without a wheel; if there be no wheel, another one is made, for he can doubtless get a new one; so, if one's wife die, he seeks again, for he also can obtain a new one. The daughter of a worthy family must certainly marry an honorable husband; a house having ten rooms always has a plate and a ridgepole; three windows and six lattices do not give the light of a single door; the whole host of stars with all their sparkling brilliancy do not equal the splendor of the solitary moon: the affection of a father and mother—alas, if it be once lost!'

"Confucius sighing, said, 'How clever! how worthy!' The boy asking the sage said, 'You have just been giving me questions, which I have answered one by one; I now wish to seek information; will the teacher in one sentence afford me some plain instruction? I shall be much gratified if my request be not rejected.' He then said, 'Why is it that mallards and ducks are able to swim; how is it that wild geese and cranes sing; and why are firs and pines green through the winter?' Confucius replied, 'Mallards and ducks can swim because their feet are broad; wild geese and cranes can sing because they have long necks; firs and pines remain green throughout the winter because they have strong hearts.' The youth rejoined, 'Not so; fishes and turtles can swim, is it because they all have broad feet? Frogs and toads can sing, is it because their necks are long? The green bamboo keeps fresh in winter, is it on account of its strong heart?'

"Again interrogating, he said, 'How many stars are there altogether in the sky?' Confucius replied, 'At this time inquire about the earth; how can we converse about the sky with certainty?' The boy said, 'Then how many houses in all are there on the earth?' The sage answered, 'Come now, speak about something that's before our eyes; why must you converse about heaven and earth?' The lad resumed, 'Well, speak about what's before our eyes—how many hairs are there in your eyebrows?'

"Confucius smiled, but did not answer, and turning round to his disciples called them and said, 'This boy is to be feared; for it is easy to see that the subsequent man will not be like the child.' He then got into his carriage and rode off."[1]

Next in course to this rather trifling primer comes the *Hiao King*, or 'Canons of Filial Duty,' a short tractate of only 1,903 characters, which purports to be the record of a conversation held between Confucius and his disciple Tsăng Tsan on the principles of filial piety. Its authenticity has been disputed by critics, but their doubts are not shared by their countrymen, who commit it to memory as the words of the sage. The legend is that a copy was discovered in the wall of his dwelling, and compared with another secreted by Yen Chí at the burning of the books; from the two Liu Hiang chose eighteen of the chapters contained in it as alone genuine, and in this shape it has since remained. The sixth section of the Imperial Catalogue is entirely devoted to writers on the *Hiao King*, one of whom was

[1] *Chinese Repository*, Vol. X., p. 614.

Yuentsung, an emperor of the Tang dynasty (A.D. 733). Another comment was published in 32 volumes in Kanghí's reign, discussing the whole subject in one hundred chapters. Though it does not share in critical eyes the confidence accorded to the nine classics, the brevity and subject matter of this work have commended it to teachers as one of the best books in the language to be placed in the hands of their scholars; thus its influence has been great and enduring. It has been translated by Bridgman, who regards the first six sections as the words of Confucius, while the other twelve contain his ideas. Two quotations are all that need be here given to show its character.

SECTION I.—*On the origin and nature of filial duty.*—Filial duty is the root of virtue, and the stem from which instruction in the moral principle springs. Sit down, and I will explain this to you. The first thing which filial duty requires of us is, that we carefully preserve from all injury, and in a perfect state, the bodies which we have received from our parents. And when we acquire for ourselves a station in the world, we should regulate our conduct by correct principles, so as to transmit our names to future generations, and reflect glory on our parents. This is the ultimate aim of filial duty. Thus it commences in attention to parents, is continued through a course of services rendered to the prince, and is completed by the elevation of ourselves. It is said in the *Book of Odes*,

Ever think of your ancestors;
Reproducing their virtue.

SECTION V.—*On the attention of scholars to filial duty.*—With the same love that they serve their fathers, they should serve their mothers; and with the same respect that they serve their fathers, they should serve their prince; unmixed love, then, will be the offering they make to their mothers; unfeigned respect the tribute they bring to their prince; while toward their fathers both these will be combined. Therefore they serve their prince with filial duty and are faithful to him; they serve their superiors with respect and are obedient to them. By constant obedience and faithfulness toward those who are above them, they are enabled to preserve their stations and emoluments, and to offer the sacrifices which are due to their deceased ancestors and parents. Such is the influence of filial piety when performed by scholars. It is said in the *Book of Odes*,

When the dawn is breaking, and I cannot sleep,
The thoughts in my breast are of our parents.[1]

[1] Compare Père Cibot in *Mémoires concernant les Chinois*, Tome IV., pp. 1 ff.; Dr. Legge, *The Sacred Books of China*, Part I. *The Shû-king, Religious Portions of the Shih-king, the Hsiâo-king*, Oxford, 1879; *Asiatic Journal*, Vol. XXIX., pp. 302 ff., 1839.

The highest place in the list of virtues and obligations is accorded to filial duty, not only in this, but in other writings of Confucius and those of his school. "There are," to quote from another section, "three thousand crimes to which one or the other of the five kinds of punishment is attached as a penalty; and of these no one is greater than disobedience to parents. When ministers exercise control over the monarch, then there is no supremacy; when the maxims of the sages are set aside, then the law is abrogated; and so those who disregard filial duty are as though they had no parents. These three evils prepare the way for universal rebellion."

This social virtue has been highly lauded by all Chinese writers, and its observance inculcated upon youth and children by precept and example. Stories are written to show the good effects of obedience, and the bad results of its contrary sin, which are put into their hands, and form also subjects for pictorial illustration, stanzas for poetry, and materials for conversation. The following examples are taken from a toy-book of this sort, called the *Twenty-four Filials*, one of the most popular collections on the subject.

"During the Chau dynasty there lived a lad named Tsăng Tsan (also Tsz'-yu), who served his mother very dutifully. Tsăng was in the habit of going to the hills to collect fagots; and once, while he was thus absent, many guests came to his house, toward whom his mother was at a loss how to act. She, while expecting her son, who delayed his return, began to gnaw her fingers. Tsăng suddenly felt a pain in his heart, and took up his bundle of fagots in order to return home; and when he saw his mother, he kneeled and begged to know what was the cause of her anxiety. She replied, 'there have been some guests here, who came from a great distance, and I bit my finger in order to arouse you to return to me.'

"In the Chau dynasty lived Chung Yu, named also Tsz'-lu, who, because his family was poor, usually ate herbs and coarse pulse; and he also went more than a hundred *lí* to procure rice for his parents. Afterward, when they were dead, he went south to the country of Tsu, where he was made commander of a hundred companies of chariots; there he became rich, storing up grain in myriads of measures, reclining upon cushions, and eating food served to him in numerous dishes; but sighing, he said, 'Although I should now desire to eat coarse herbs and bring rice for my parents, it cannot be!'

"In the Chau dynasty there flourished the venerable Lai, who was very obedient and reverential toward his parents, manifesting his dutifulness by exerting himself to provide them with every delicacy. Although upward of seventy years of age, he declared that he was not yet old; and usually dressed himself in parti-colored embroidered garments, and like a child would playfully stand by the side of his parents. He would also take up buckets of water, and try to carry them into the house; but feigning to slip, would fall to the ground, wailing and crying like a child: and all these things he did in order to divert his parents.

"During the Han dynasty lived Tung Yung, whose family was so very poor that when his father died he was obliged to sell himself in order to procure money to bury his remains. After this he went to another place to gain the means of redeeming himself; and on his way he met a lady who desired to become his wife, and go with him to his master's residence. She went with him, and wove three hundred pieces of silk, which being completed in two months, they returned home; on the way, having reached the shade of the cassia tree where they before met, the lady bowed and ascending, vanished from his sight.

"During the Han dynasty lived Ting Lan, whose parents both died when he was young, before he could obey and support them; and he reflected that for all the trouble and anxiety he had caused them, no recompense had yet been given. He then carved wooden images of his parents, and served them as if they had been alive. For a long time his wife would not reverence them; but one day, taking a bodkin, she in derision pricked their fingers. Blood immediately flowed from the wound; and seeing Ting coming, the images wept. He examined into the circumstances, and forthwith divorced his wife.

"In the days of the Han dynasty lived Koh Kü, who was very poor. He had one child three years old; and such was his poverty that his mother usually divided her portion of food with this little one. Koh says to his wife, 'We are so poor that our mother cannot be supported, for the child divides with her the portion of food that belongs to her. Why not bury this child? Another child may be born to us, but a mother once gone will never return.' His wife did not venture to object to the proposal; and Koh immediately dug a hole of about three cubits deep, when suddenly he lighted upon a pot of gold, and on the metal read the following inscription: 'Heaven bestows this treasure upon Koh Kü, the dutiful son; the magistrate may not seize it, nor shall the neighbors take it from him.'

"Măng Tsung, who lived in the Tsin dynasty, when young lost his father. His mother was very sick; and one winter's day she longed to taste a soup made of bamboo sprouts, but Măng could not procure any. At last he went into the grove of bamboos, clasped the trees with his hands, and wept bitterly. His filial affection moved nature, and the ground slowly opened, sending forth several shoots, which he gathered and carried home. He made a soup with them, of which his mother ate and immediately recovered from her malady

"Wu Măng, a lad eight years of age, who lived under the Tsin dynasty, was very dutiful to his parents. They were so poor that they could not afford to furnish their bed with mosquito-curtains; and every summer's night, myriads of mosquitos attacked them unrestrainedly, feasting upon their flesh and blood. Although there were so many, yet Wu would not drive them away, lest they should go to his parents, and annoy them. Such was his affection."[1]

---

[1] *Chinese Repository*, Vol. VI., p. 131.

The last book learned before entering on the classics has had almost as great an influence as any of them, and none of the works of later scholars are so well calculated to show the ideas of the Chinese in all ages upon the principles of education, intercourse of life, and rules of conduct as this; precepts are illustrated by examples, and the examples referred back to precepts for their moving cause. This is the *Siao Hioh*, or "Juvenile Instructor," and was intended by Chu Hí, its author, as a counterpart of the *Ta Hiào*, on which he had written a commentary. It has had more than fifty commentators, one of whom says, "We confide in the *Siao Hioh* as we do in the gods, and revere it as we do our parents." It is divided into two books, the "fountain of learning," and "the stream flowing from it," arranged in 20 chapters and 385 short sections. The first book has four parts and treats of the first principles of education; of the duties we owe our kindred, rulers, and fellow-men, of those we owe ourselves in regard to study, demeanor, food, and dress; and lastly gives numerous examples from ancient history, beginning with very early times down to the end of the Chau dynasty, B.C. 249, confirmatory of the maxims inculcated, and the good effects resulting from their observance. The second book contains, in its first part, a collection of wise sayings of eminent men who flourished after B.C. 200, succeeded by a series of examples of distinguished persons calculated to show the effects of good principles; both designed to establish the truth of the teachings of the first book. One or two quotations, themselves extracted from other works, will suffice to show something of its contents.

"Confucius said, 'Friends must sharply and frankly admonish each other, and brothers must be gentle toward one another.'"

"Tsz'-kung, asking about friendship, Confucius said, 'Faithfully to inform and kindly to instruct another is the duty of a friend; if he is not tractable, desist; do not disgrace yourself.'"

"Whoever enters with his guests, yields precedence to them at every door; when they reach the innermost one, he begs leave to go in and arrange the seats, and then returns to receive the guests; and after they have repeatedly declined he bows to them and enters. He passes through the right door, they through the left. He ascends the eastern, they the western steps. If a guest be of a lower grade, he must approach the steps of the host, while the latter

must repeatedly decline this attention; then the guest may return to the western steps, he ascending, both host and guest must mutually yield precedence: then the host must ascend first, and the guests follow. From step to step they must bring their feet together, gradually ascending--those on the east moving the right foot first, those on the west the left."

The great influence which these six school-books have had is owing to their formative power on youthful minds, a large proportion of whom never go beyond them (either from want of time, means, or desire), but are really here furnished with the kernel of their best literature.

The tedium of memorizing these unmeaning sounds is relieved by writing the characters on thin paper placed over copy slips. The writing and the reading lessons are the same, and both are continued for a year or two until the forms and sounds of a few thousand characters are made familiar, but no particular effort is taken to teach their meanings. It is after this that the teacher goes over the same ground, and with the help of the commentary, explains the meaning of the words and phrases one by one, until they are all understood. It is not usual for the beginner to attend much to the meaning of what he is learning to read and write, and where the labor of committing arbitrary characters is so great and irksome, experience has probably shown that it is not wise to attempt too many things at once. The boy has been familiarizing himself with their shapes as he sees them all the time around him, and he learns what they mean in a measure before he comes to school. The association of form with ideas, as he cons his lesson and writes their words, gradually strengthens, and results in that singular interdependence of the eye and ear so observable among the scholars of the far East. They trust to what is read to help in understanding what is heard much more than is the case in phonetic languages. No effort is made to facilitate the acquisition of the characters by the boys in school by arranging them according to their component parts; they are learned one by one, as boys are taught the names and appearance of minerals in a cabinet. The effects of a course of study like this, in which the powers of the tender mind are not developed by proper nourishment of truthful knowledge, can hardly be otherwise than to stunt the genius, and drill the fac ulties of the mind into a slavish adherence to venerated usage and dictation, making the intellects of Chinese students like the trees which their gardeners so toilsomely dwarf into pots and jars—plants, whose unnaturalness is congruous to the insipidity of their fruit.

The number of years spent at school depends upon the means of the parents. Tradesmen, mechanics, and country gentlemen endeavor to give their sons a competent knowledge of the usual series of books, so that they can creditably manage the common affairs of life. No other branches of study are pursued than the classics and histories, and what will illustrate them, meanwhile giving much care and practice to composition. No arithmetic or any department of mathematics, nothing of the geography of their own or other countries, of natural philosophy, natural history, or scientific arts, nor the study of other languages, are attended to. Persons in these classes of society put their sons into shops or counting-houses to learn the routine of business with a knowledge of figures and the style of letter-writing; they are not kept at school more than three or four years, unless they mean to compete at the examinations. Working men, desirous of giving their sons a smattering, try to keep them at their books a year or two, but millions must of course grow up in utter ignorance. It is, however, an excellent policy for a state to keep up this universal honor paid to education where the labor is so great and the return so doubtful, for it is really the homage paid to the principles taught.

Besides the common schools, there are grammar or high schools and colleges, but they are far less effective. In Canton, there are fourteen grammar schools and thirty colleges, some of which are quite ancient, but most of them are neglected. Three of the largest contain each about two hundred students and two or three professors. The chief object of these institutions is to instruct advanced scholars in composition and elegant writing; the tutors do a little to turn attention to general literature, but have neither the genius nor the means to make many advances. In rural districts students are encouraged to meet at stated times in the town-house, where the headman, or deputy of the *sz'* or township, examines them on themes previously proposed by him.[1] In large towns, the local officers, assisted by the gentry and graduates, hold annual examinations of students, at which premiums are given to the best essayists. At such an examination in Amoy in March, 1845, there were about a thousand candidates, forty of whom received sums varying from sixty to sixteen cents

One of the most notable, as well as the most ancient of collegiate institutions, is the *Kwoh-tsz' Kien*, or 'School for the Sons of the State,' whose extensive buildings in Peking, now empty and dilapidated, show how much easier it is to found and plan a good thing than to maintain its efficiency. This state school originated as early as the Chau dynasty, and the course of study as given in the *Ritual of Chau* was much the same three thousand years ago as at present. Its officers consisted of a rector, usually a high minister of state, aided by five councillors, two directors, two proctors, two secretaries, a librarian, two professors in each of the six halls, and latterly five others for each of the colleges for Bannermen. These halls are named Hall of the Pursuit of Wisdom, the Sincere of Heart, of True Virtue, of Noble Aspiration, of Broad Acquirements, and the Guidance of Nature. The curriculum was not intended to go beyond the classics and the six liberal arts of music, charioteering, archery, etiquette, writing, and mathematics; but as if to encourage the professors to "seek out by wisdom concerning all things that are done under heaven," as Solomon advises, they were told to take their students to the original sources of strategy, astronomy, engineering, music, law, and the like, and points out the defects and merits of each author. The *Kwoh-tsz' Kien* possesses now only the husk of its ancient goodness; and if its professors were not honored, and made eligible to be distinct magistrates after three years' term, the buildings would soon be left altogether empty. Instead of reviving and rearranging it, the Chinese Government

---

[1] *Chinese Repository*, Vol. IV., p. 414. See also Vol. VI., pp. 229–241; Vol. IV., pp. 1–10; Vol. XI., pp. 545–557; and Vol. XIII., pp. 626–641, for further notices of the modes and objects of education; Biot, *Essai sur l'Histoire de l'Instruction Publique en Chine*, and his translation of the *Chao-li*, Vol. II., p. 27, Paris, 1851. *Chinese Recorder*, September, 1871.

has wisely supplanted it by a new college with its new professors and new course of studies—the *Tung-wăn Kwan* mentioned on p. 436. Native free schools, established by benevolent persons in city or country, are not uncommon, and serve to maintain the literary spirit; some may not be very long-lived, but others take their place. In Peking, each of the Banners has its school, and so has the Imperial Clan; retired officials contribute to schools opened for boys connected with their native districts living in the capital. Such efforts to promote education are expected from those who have obtained its high prizes.

How great a proportion of the people in China can read, is a difficult question to answer, for foreigners have had no means of learning the facts in the case, and the natives never go into such inquiries. More of the men in cities can read than in the country, and more in some provinces than in others. In the district of Nanhai, which forms part of the city of Canton, an imperfect examination led to the belief that nearly all the men are able to read, except fishermen, agriculturists, coolies, boat-people, and fuelers, and that two or three in ten devote their lives to literary pursuits. In less thickly settled districts, not more than four- or five-tenths, and even less, can read. In Macao, perhaps half of the men can read. From an examination of the hospital patients at Ningpo, one of the missionaries estimated the readers to form not more than five per cent. of the men; while another missionary at the same place, who made inquiry in a higher grade of society, reckoned them at twenty per cent. The villagers about Amoy are deplorably ignorant; one lady who had lived there over twenty years, writes that she had never found a woman who could read, but these were doubtless from among the poorer classes. It appears that as one goes north, the extent and thoroughness of education diminishes. Throughout the Empire the ability to understand books is not commensurate with the ability to read the characters, and both have been somewhat exaggerated. Owing to the manner in which education is commenced—learning the forms and sounds of characters before their meanings are understood—it comes to pass that many persons can call over the names of the characters while they do not comprehend in the least the sense of what they read. They can pick out a word here and there, it may be a phrase or a sentence, but they derive no clearer meaning from the text before them than a lad, who has just learned to scan, and has proceeded half through the Latin Reader, does from reading Virgil; while in both cases an intelligent audience, unacquainted with the facts, might justly infer that the reader understood what he was reading as well as his hearers did. Moreover, in the Chinese language, different subjects demand different characters; and although a man may be well versed in the classics or in fiction, he may be easily posed by being asked to explain a simple treatise in medicine or in mathematics, in consequence of the many new or unfamiliar words on every page. This is a serious obstacle in the way of obtaining a general acquaintance with books. The mind becomes weary with the labor of study where its toil is neither rewarded by knowledge nor beguiled by wit; consequently, few Chinese are well read in their natural literature. The study of books being regarded solely as the means wherewith to attain a definite end, it follows naturally that when a cultivated man has reached his goal he should feel little disposed to turn to these implements of his profession for either instruction or pleasure.

Wealthy or official parents, who wish their sons to compete for literary honors, give them the advantages of a full course in reading and rhetoric under the best masters. Composition is the most difficult part of the training of a Chinese student, and requires unwearied application and a retentive memory. He who can most readily quote the classics, and approach the nearest to their terse, comprehensive, energetic diction and style, is, *cæteris paribus*, most likely to succeed; while the man who can most quickly throw off well rhythmed verses takes the palm from all competitors. In novels, the ability to compose elegant verses as fast as the pencil can fly is usually ascribed to the hero of the plot. How many of those who intend to compete for degrees attend at the district colleges or high schools is not known, but they are resorted to by students about the time of the examinations in order to make the acquaintance of those who are to compete with them. No public examinations take place in either day or private schools, nor do parents often visit them, but rewards for remarkable proficiency are occasionally conferred. There is little gradation of studies, nor are any diplomas conferred on students to show that they have gone through a certain course. Punishments are severe, and the rattan or bamboo hangs conspicuously near the master, and its liberal use is considered necessary: "To educate without rigor, shows the teacher's indolence," is the doctrine, and by scolding, starving, castigation, and detention, the master tries to instil habits of obedience and compel his scholars to learn their task.

Notwithstanding the high opinion in which education is held, the general diffusion of knowledge, and the respect paid to learning in comparison with mere title and wealth, the defects of the tuition here briefly described, in extent, means, purposes, and results, are very great. Such, too, must necessarily be the case until new principles and new information are infused into it. Considered in its best point of view, this system has effected all that it can in enlarging the understanding, purifying the heart, and strengthening the minds of the people; but in none of these, nor in any of the essential points at which a sound education aims (as we understand the matter), has it accomplished half that is needed. The stream never rises even as high as its source, and the teachings of Confucius and Mencius have done all that is possible to make their countrymen thinking, useful, and intelligent men.

Turn we now from this brief sketch of primary education among the Chinese, to a description of the mode of examining students and conferring the degrees which have been made the passport to office, and learn what are the real merits of the system. Persons from almost every class of society may become candidates for degrees under the certificates of securities, but none are eligible for the second diploma who have not already received the first. It therefore happens that the republican license apparently allowed to well-nigh every subject, in reality reserves the prizes for the few most talented or wealthy persons in the community. A majority of the clever, learned, ambitious, and intelligent spirits in the land look forward to these examinations as the only field worthy of their efforts, and where they are most likely to find their equals and friends. How much better for the good of society, too, is this arena than the camp or the feudal court, the tournament or the monastery!

There are four regular literary degrees, with some intermediate steps of a titular sort. The first is called *siu-tsai*, meaning 'flowering talent,' because of the promise held out of the future success of the scholar; it has often been rendered 'bachelor of arts' as its nearest equivalent. The examinations to obtain it are held under the supervision of the *chíhien* in a public building belonging to the district situated near his yamun; and the chief literary officer, called *hioh-ching*, 'corrector of learning,' or *kiao-yu*, 'teacher of the commands,' has the immediate control. When assembled at the hall of examination, the district magistrate, the deputy chancellor, and prefect, having prepared the lists of the undergraduates and selected the themes, allow only one day for writing the essays. The number of candidates depends upon the population and literary spirit of the district; in the districts of Nanhai and Pwanyu, upward of two thousand persons competed for the prize in 1832, while in Hiangshan not half so many came together. The rule for apportioning them was at first according to the annual revenue. When the essays are handed in, they are looked over by the board of examiners, and the names of the successful students entered on a roll, and pasted upon the walls of the magistrate's hall; this honor is called *hien ming*, *i.e.*, 'having a name in the village.' Out of the four thousand candidates referred to above, only thirteen in one district, and fourteen in the other, obtained a name in the village; the entire population of these two districts is not much under a million and a half. Many of the competitors at this primary tripos are unable to finish their essays in the day, others make errors in writing, and others show gross ignorance, all of which so greatly diminish their numbers, that only those who stand near the head of the list of *hien ming* do really or usually enter on the next trial before the prefect. But all have had an equal chance, and few complain that their performances were disregarded, for they can try as often as they please.

Those who pass the first examination are entered as candidates for the second, which takes place in the chief town of the department before the literary chancellor and the prefect, assisted by a literary magistrate called *kiao-shao*, 'giver of instructions;' it is more rigorous than that held before the *chíhien*, though similar to it in nature. The prefect arranges the candidates from each district by themselves according to their standing on their several lists, and it is this vantage ground which makes the first trial in one's native place so important to the ambitious scholar. The themes on which they have tested their scholarship are published for the information of friends and the other examiners. If the proportion given above of successful candidates at the district examinations hold for each district, there would not be more than two hundred students assembled at the prefect's hall, but the number is somewhat increased by persons who have purchased the privilege; still the second trial is made among a small number in proportion to the first, and yet more trifling when compared with the amount of population. The names of the successful students at the second trial are exposed on the walls of the office, which is called *fu ming*, *i.e.*, 'having a name in the department,' and these only are eligible as candidates for the third trial. In addition to their knowledge of the classics, the candidates at this trial are often required to write off the text of the *Shing Yu*, or 'Sacred Edict,' from memory, as this work consists of maxims for the guidance of officers. The literary chancellor exercises a superintendence over the previous examinations, and makes the circuit of the province to attend them in each department, twice in three years. There are various ranks among these educational officials, corresponding to the civilians in the province; transfers are occasionally made from one service to the other, and the oversight of the latter is always given at the examinations wherever they are held. Most of the literary officers, however, remain in their own line, as it is highly honorable and more permanent. At the third trial in the provincial capital, he confers the first degree of *siu-tsai* upon those who are chosen out of the whole list as the best scholars.

There are several classes of bachelors, depending somewhat on the manner in which they obtained their degree; those who get it in the manner here described take the precedence. The possession of this degree protects the person from corporeal punishment, raises him above the common people, renders him a conspicuous man in his native place, and eligible to enter the triennial examination for the second degree. Those who have more money than learning, purchase this degree for sums varying from $200 up to $1,000, and even higher; in later years, according to the necessities of the government, diplomas have been sold as low as $25 to $50, but such men seldom rise. They are called *kien-săng*, and, as might be supposed, are looked upon somewhat contemptuously by those who have passed through the regular examinations, and "won the battle with their own lance." A degree called *kung-săng* is purchased by or bestowed upon the *siu-tsai*, but is so generally recognized that it has almost become a fifth degree, which does not entitle them to the full honors of a *kü-jin*. What proportion of scholars are rewarded by degrees is not known, but it is a small number compared with the candidates. A graduate of considerable intelligence at Ningpo estimated the number of *siu-tsai* in that city at four hundred, and in the department at nearly a thousand. In Canton City, the number of *shin-kin*, or gentry, who are allowed to wear the sash of honor, and have obtained literary degrees, is not over three hundred; but in the whole province there are about twelve thousand bachelors in a population of nineteen millions. Those who have not become *siu-tsai* are still regarded as under the oversight of the *kiao-yu* and others of his class, who still receive their essays; but the body of provincial *siu-tsai* are obliged to report themselves and attend the prefectural tripos before the chancellor, under penalty of losing all the privileges and rank obtained. This law brings them before those who may take cognizance of misdeeds, for these men are often very oppressive and troublesome to their countrymen. The graduates in each district are placed under the control of a chief, whose power is almost equal to the deputy chancellor's; from them are taken the two securities required by each applicant to enter the tripos.

The candidates for *siu-tsai* are narrowly examined when they enter the hall, their pockets, shoes, wadded robes, and ink-stones, all being searched, lest precomposed essays or other aids to composition be smuggled in. When they are all seated in the hall in their proper places, the wickets, doors, windows, and other entrances are all guarded, and pasted over with strips of paper. The room is filled with anxious competitors arranged in long seats, pencil in hand, and ready to begin. The theme is given out, and every one immediately writes off his essay, carefully noting how many characters he erases in composing it, and hands it up to the board of examiners; the whole day is allotted to the task, and a signal-gun announces the hour when the doors are thrown open, and the students can disperse. A man is liable to lose his acquired honor of *siu-tsai* if at a subsequent inspection he is found to have discarded his studies, and he is therefore impelled to pursue them in order to maintain his influence, even if he does not reach the next degree.[1]

Since the first degree is sometimes procured by influence and money, it is the examination for the second, called *kü-jin,* or 'promoted men,' held triennially in the provincial capitals before two imperial commissioners, that separates the candidates into students and officers, though all the students who receive a diploma by no means become officers. This examination is held at the same time in all the eighteen provincial capitals, viz., on the 9th, 12th, and 15th days of the eighth moon, or about the middle of September; while it is going on, the city appears exceedingly animated, in consequence of the great number of relatives and friends assembled with the students. The persons who preside at the examination, besides the imperial commissioners, are ten provincial officers, with the futai at their head, who jointly form a board of examiners, and decide upon the merits of the essays. The number of candidates who entered the lists at Canton in the years 1828 and 1831 was 4,800; in 1832 there were 6,000, which is nearer the usual number. In the largest provinces it reaches as many as 7,000, 8,000, and upward.

Previous to entering the *Kung Yuen,* each candidate has given in all the necessary proofs and particulars, which entitle

---

[1] *Chinese Repository,* Vol. II., p. 249; Vol. XVI., pp. 67–72. Doolittle, *Social Life of the Chinese,* Vol. I., pp. 376–443. Dr. Martin, *The Chinese.*

INTERIOR OF KUNG YUEN, OR 'EXAMINATION HALL,' PEKING.

him to a cell, and receives the ticket which designates the one he is to occupy. He enters the night before, and is searched to see that no manuscript essay, "skinning paper," or miniature edition of the classics, is secreted on his person. If anything of the sort is discovered, he is punished with the cangue, degraded from his first degree, and forbidden again to compete at the examination; his father and tutor are likewise punished. Some of the pieces written for this purpose are marvels of penmanship, and the most finished compositions; one set contained an essay on every sentence in the Four Books, each of the sheets covered with hundreds of characters, and the paper so thin that they could be easily read through it. The practice is, however, quite common, notwithstanding the penalties, and one censor requested a law to be passed forbidding small editions to be printed, and booksellers' shops to be searched for them.

The general arrangement of the examination halls in all the provincial capitals is alike. A description of that at Canton, given on page 166, is typical of them all.

The Hall at Peking, situated on the eastern side, not far from the observatory, contains ten thousand cells, and these do not always suffice for the host which assembles. The Hall at Fuhchau is equally large; each cell is a little higher than a man's head, and is open on but one side—letting in more rain and wind during inclement days than is comfortable. Confinement in these cramped cells is so irksome as to frequently cause the death of aged students, who are unable to sustain the fatigue, but who still enter the arena in hopes of at last succeeding. Cases have occurred where father, son, and grandson, appeared at the same time to compete for the same prize. Dr. Martin[1] found that out of a list of ninety-nine successful competitors for the second degree, sixteen were over forty years of age, one sixty-two, and one eighty-three. The average age of the whole number was over thirty—while in comparison with like statistics for the third degree, a proportionate increase might be looked for. The unpleasantness of the strait cell is much increased by the smoke arising from the cooking, and by the heat of the weather. All ser-

[1] *The Chinese*, p. 50.

vants are provided by government, but each candidate takes in the rice and fuel which he needs, together with cakes, tea, candles, bedding, etc., as he can afford; no one can go in with him. The enclosure presents a bustling scene during the examination, and its interest intensifies until the names of the successful scholars are published. Should a student die in his cell, the body is pulled through a hole made in the wall of the enclosure, and left there for his friends to carry away. Whenever a candidate breaks any of the prescribed regulations of the contest, his name and offence are reported, and his name is "pasted out" by placarding it on the outer door of the hall, after which he is not allowed to enter until another examination comes around. More than a hundred persons are thus "pasted out" each season, but no heavy disgrace seems to attach to them in consequence.

On the first day after the doors have been sealed up, four themes are selected by the examiners from the Four Books, one of which subjects must be discussed in a poetical essay. The minimum length of the compositions is a hundred characters, and they must be written plainly and elegantly, and sent in without any names attached. In 1828, the acumen of four thousand eight hundred candidates was exercised during the first day on these themes: "Tsăng-tsz' said, 'To possess ability, and yet ask of those who do not; to know much, and yet inquire of those who know little; to possess, and yet appear not to possess; to be full, and yet appear empty.' "—"He took hold of things by the two extremes, and in his treatment of the people maintained the golden medium." "A man from his youth studies eight principles, and when he arrives at manhood, he wishes to reduce them to practice."—The fourth essay, to be written in pentameters, had for its subject, "The sound of the oar, and the green of the hills and water." Among the themes given out in 1843, were these: "He who is sincere will be intelligent, and the intelligent man will be faithful."—"In carrying out benevolence, there are no rules." In 1835, one was, "He acts as he ought, both to the common people and official men, receives his revenue from Heaven, and by it is protected and highly esteemed." Among other more practical texts are the following: "Fire-arms began with the use of rockets in the Chau dynasty; in what book do we first meet with the word for cannon? Is the defence of Kaifung fu its first recorded use? Kublai khan, it is said, obtained cannon of a new kind; from whom did he obtain them? When the Ming Emperors, in the reign of Yungloh, invaded Cochinchina, they obtained a kind of cannon called the weapons of the gods; can you give an account of their origin?"

The three or five themes (for the number seems to be optional) selected from the Five Classics are similar to these, but as those works are regarded as more recondite than the Four Books, so must the essayists try to take a higher style. An officer goes around to gather in the papers, which are first handed to a body of scholars in waiting, who look them over to see if the prescribed rules have all been observed, and reject those which infringe them. The rest are then copied in red ink, to prevent recognition of the handwriting, and the original manuscripts given to the governor. The copies are submitted to another class of old scholars for their criticism, each of whom marks the essays he deems best with a red circle, and these only are placed in the hands of the chancellors sent from Peking for their decision. The examining board are aided by twelve scholars of repute, to each of whom forty or fifty essays are given to read. The students are dismissed during the night of the ninth day, and reassemble before sunrise of the eleventh; all whose essays were rejected on the first review are refused entrance to their cells. At the second tripos, five themes are given out from the Five Classics, and everything proceeds as before in respect to the disposal of the manuscripts. The students are liberated early on the thirteenth as before by companies, under a salute and music as they leave the great door; their number has been much reduced by this time. On the next morning the roll is called, and those who answer to their names for the last struggle are furnished with five themes for essays, one for poetry, taken from the classics or histories, upon doubtful matters of government, or such problems as might arise in law and finance. These questions take even a more extended range, including topics relating to the laws, history, geography, and customs of the Empire in former times, doubtful points touching the classical works, and the interpretation of obscure passages, and biographical notices of statesmen. It is forbidden, however, to discuss any points relating to the policy of the present family, or the character and learning of living statesmen; but the conduct of their rulers is now and then alluded to by the candidates. Manuals of questions on such subjects as candidates are examined in, are commonly exposed for sale in shops about the time of these examinations.[1] By noon of the sixteenth day of the eighth moon, all the candidates throughout the Empire have left their halls, and the examination is over.

The manner in which subjects are handled may be readily illustrated by introducing an essay upon this theme: "When persons in high stations are sincere in the performance of relative and domestic duties, the people generally will be stimulated to the practice of virtue." It is a fair specimen of the jejune style of Chinese essayists, and the mode of reasoning in a circle which pervades their writings.

"When the upper classes are really virtuous, the common people will inevitably become so. For, though the sincere performance of relative duties by superiors does not originate in a wish to stimulate the people, yet the people do become virtuous, which is a proof of the effect of sincerity. As benevolence is the radical principle of all good government in the world, so also benevolence is the radical principle of relative duties amongst the people. Traced back to its source, benevolent feeling refers to a first progenitor; traced forward, it branches out to a hundred generations yet to come. The source of personal existence is one's parents, the relations which originate from Heaven are most intimate; and that in which natural feeling blends is felt most deeply. That which is given by Heaven and by natural feeling to all, is done without any distinction between noble or ignoble. One feeling pervades all. My thoughts now refer to him who is placed in a station of eminence, and who may be called a good man. The good man who is placed in an eminent station, ought to lead forward the practice of virtue; but the way to do so is to begin with his own relations, and perform his duties to them.

"In the middle ages of antiquity, the minds of the people were not yet dissipated—how came it that they were not humble and observant of relative duties, when they were taught the principles of the five social relations? This having been the case, makes it evident that the enlightening of the people must depend entirely on the cordial performance of immediate relative duties. The person in an eminent station who may be called a good man, is he who appears at the head of all others in illustrating by his practice the relative duties.

[1] Biot, *Essai sur l'Instruction en Chine*, p. 603.

In ages nearer to our own, the manners of the people were not far removed from the dutiful; how came it that any were disobedient to parents, and without brotherly affection, and that it was yet necessary to restrain men by inflicting the eight forms of punishment? This having been the case, shows that in the various modes of obtaining promotion in the state, there is nothing regarded of more importance than filial and fraternal duties. The person in an eminent station who may be called a good man, is he who stands forth as an example of the performance of relative duties.

"The difference between a person filling a high station and one of the common people, consists in the department assigned them, not in their relation to Heaven: it consists in a difference of rank, not in a difference of natural feeling; but the common people constantly observe the sincere performance of relative duties in people of high stations. In being at the head of a family and preserving order amongst the persons of which it is composed, there should be sincere attention to politeness and decorum. A good man placed in a high station says, 'Who of all these are not related to me, and shall I receive them with more external forms?' The elegant entertainment, the neatly arranged tables, and the exhilarating song, some men esteem mere forms, but the good man esteems that which dictates them as a divinely instilled feeling, and attends to it with a truly benevolent heart. And who of the common people does not feel a share of the delight arising from fathers, and brothers, and kindred? Is this joy resigned entirely to princes and kings?

"In favors conferred to display the benignity of a sovereign, there should be sincerity in the kindness done. The good man says, 'Are not all these persons whom I love, and shall I merely enrich them by largesses?' He gives a branch as the sceptre of authority to a delicate younger brother, and to another he gives a kingdom with his best instructions. Some men deem this as merely extraordinary good fortune, but the good man esteems it the exercise of a virtue of the first order, and the effort of inexpressible benevolence. But have the common people no regard for the spring whence the water flows, nor for the root which gives life to the tree and its branches? Have they no regard for their kindred? It is necessary both to reprehend and to urge them to exercise these feelings. The good man in a high station is sincere in the performance of relative duties, because to do so is virtuous, and not on account of the common people. But the people, without knowing whence the impulse comes, with joy and delight are influenced to act with zeal in this career of virtue; the moral distillation proceeds with rapidity, and a vast change is effected.

"The rank of men is exceedingly different; some fill the imperial throne, but every one equally wishes to do his utmost to accomplish his duty; and success depends on every individual himself. The upper classes begin and pour the wine into the rich goblet; the poor man sows his grain to maintain his parents; the men in high stations grasp the silver bowl, the poor present a pigeon; they arouse each other to unwearied cheerful efforts, and the principles implanted by Heaven are moved to action. Some things are difficult to be done, except by those who possess the glory of national rule; but the kind feeling is what I myself possess, and may increase to an unlimited degree.

The prince may write verses appropriate to his vine bower; the poor man can think of his gourd shelter; the prince may sing his classic odes on fraternal regards; the poor man can muse on his more simple allusions to the same subject, and asleep or awake indulge his recollections; for the feeling is instilled into his nature. When the people are aroused to relative virtues, they will be sincere; for where are there any of the common people that do not desire to perform relative duties? But without the upper classes performing relative duties, this virtuous desire would have no point from which to originate, and therefore it is said, 'Good men in high stations, as a general at the head of his armies, will lead forward the world to the practice of social virtues.'"

The discipline of mind and memory which these examinations draw out furnishes a grade of intellect which only needs the friction and experience of public life to make statesmen out of scholars, and goes far to account for the influence of Chinese in Asia. The books studied in preparation for such trials must be remembered with extraordinary accuracy, though we may wish they contained more truth and better science. The following are among the questions proposed in 1853, and must be taken as an average: "In the Han dynasty, there were three commentators on the *Yih King*, whose explanations, and divisions into chapters and sentences were all different: can you give an account of them?"—"Sz'ma Tsien took the classics and ancient records in arranging his history according to their facts; some have accused him of unduly exalting the Taoists and thinking too highly of wealth and power. Pan Ku is clear and comprehensive, but on Astronomy and the Five Elements, he has written more than enough. Give examples and proof of these two statements."—"Chin Shao had admirable abilities for historical writings. In his *San Kwoh Chí* he has depreciated Chu-koh Liang, and made very light of Ĭ and Ĭ, two other celebrated characters. What does he say of them?" This kind of question involves a wide range of reading within the native literature, though it of course contracts the mind to look upon that literature as containing all that is worth anything in the world.

Twenty-five days are allowed for the examining board to de cide on the essays; and few tasks can be instanced more irksome to a board of honest examiners than the perusal of between fifty and seventy-five thousand papers on a dozen subjects, through which the most monotonous uniformity must necessarily run, and out of which they have to choose the seventy or eighty best —for the number of successful candidates cannot vary far from this, according to the size of the province. The examiners, as has already been described, are aided by literary men in sifting this mass of papers, which relieves them of most of the labor, and secures a better decision. If the number of students be five thousand, and each writes thirteen essays, there will be sixty-five thousand papers, which allots two hundred and sixty essays for each of the ten examiners. With the help of the assistants who are intrusted with their examination, most of the essays obtain a reading, no doubt, by some qualified scholar. There is, therefore, no little sifting and selection, so that when at the last the commissioners choose three rolls of essays and poems from each of the sessions belonging to the same scholar, to pass their final judgment, the company of candidates likely to succeed has been reduced as small in proportion as those in Gideon's host who lapped water. One of the examining committee, in 1832, who sought to invigorate his nerves or clear his intellect for the task by a pipe of opium, fell asleep in consequence, and on awaking, found that many of the essays had caught fire and been consumed. It is generally supposed that hundreds of them are unread, but the excitement of the occasion, and the dread on the part of the examining board to irritate the body of students, act as checks against gross omissions. Very trivial errors are enough to condemn an essay, especially if the examiners have not been gained to look upon it kindly. Section LII. of the code regulates the conduct of the examiners, but the punishments are slight. One candidate, whose essay had been condemned without being read, printed it, which led to the punishment of the examiner, degradation of the graduate, and promulgation of a law forbidding this mode of appealing to the public. Another essay was rejected because the writer had abbreviated a single character.

When the names of the successful wranglers are known, they are published by a crier at midnight, on or before the tenth of the ninth moon; at Canton, he mounts the highest tower, and, after a salute, announces them to the expectant city; the next morning, lists of the lucky scholars are hawked about the streets, and rapidly sent to all parts of the province. The proclamation which contains their names is pasted upon the governor's office under a salute of three guns; his excellency comes out and bows three times towards the names of the *promoted men*, and retires under another salute. The disappointed multitude must then rejoice in the success of the few, and solace themselves with the hope of better luck next time; while the successful ones are honored and feasted in a very distinguished manner, and are the objects of flattering attention from the whole city. On an appointed day, the governors, commissioners, and high provincial officers banquet them all at the futai's palace; inferior officers attend as servants, and two lads, fantastically dressed, and holding fragrant branches of the olive (*Olea fragrans*) in their hands grace the scene with this symbol of literary attainments. The number of A.M., licentiates, or *kü-jin*, who triennially receive their degrees in the Empire, is upwards of thirteen hundred: the expense of the examinations to the government in various ways, including the presents conferred on the graduates, can hardly be less than a third of a million of taels. Besides the triennial examinations, special ones are held every ten years, and on extraordinary occasions, as a victory, a new reign, or an imperial marriage. One was granted in 1835 because the Empress-dowager had reached her sixtieth year.

The third degree of *tsin-sz'*, 'entered scholars,' or doctors, is conferred triennially at Peking upon the successful licentiates who compete for it, and only those among the *kü-jin*, who have not already taken office, are eligible as candidates. On application at the provincial treasury, they are entitled to a part of their travelling expenses to court, but it doubtless requires some interest to get the mileage granted, for many poor scholars are detained from the metropolitan examination, or must beg or borrow in order to reach it. The procedure on this trial is the same as in the provinces, but the examiners are of higher rank; the themes are taken from the same works, and the essays are but little else than repetitions of the same train of thought and argument. After the degrees are conferred upon all who are deemed worthy, which varies from one hundred and fifty to four hundred each time, the doctors are introduced to the Emperor, and do him reverence, the three highest receiving rewards from him. At this examination, candidates, instead of being promoted, are occasionally degraded from their acquired standing for incompetency, and forbidden to appear at them again. The graduates are all inscribed upon the list of candidates for promotion, by the Board of Civil Office, to be appointed on the first vacancy; most of them do in fact enter on official life in some way or other by attaching themselves to high dignitaries, or getting employment in some of the departments at the capital. One instance is recorded of a student taking all the degrees within nine months; and some become *hanlin* before entering office. Others try again and again, till gray hairs compel them to retire. There are many subordinate offices in the Academy, the Censorate, or the Boards, which seem almost to have been instituted for the employment of graduates, whose success has given them a partial claim upon the country. The Emperor sometimes selects clever graduates to prepare works for the use of government, or nominates them upon special literary commissions;[1] It can easily be understood that no small address in managing and appeasing such a crowd of disciplined active minds is required on the part of the bureaucracy, and only the long experience of many generations of the graduates could suffice to keep the system so vigorous as it is.

The fourth and highest degree of *hanlin* is rather an office than a degree, for those who attain it are enrolled as members of the Imperial Academy, and receive salaries. The triennial examination for this distinction is held in the Emperor's palace, and is conducted on much the same plan as all preceding ones, though being in the presence of the highest personages in the Empire, it exceeds them in honor.[2] Manchus and Mongols

---

[1] *Chinese Repository*, Vol. IX., p. 541; Vol. III., p. 118.

[2] See Morrison's *Chinese Dictionary*, Vol. I., Part I., pp. 759–779, for the laws and usages of the several trials. Also Doolittle's *Social Life*, Vol. I., Chaps. XV., XVI., and XVII.; Biot, *Essai sur l'Histoire de l'Instruction Publique en Chine*; W. A. P. Martin, *The Chinese*, pp. 39 ff.; *Journal Asiatique*, Tomes III., pp. 257 and 321, IV., p. 3, and VII. (3d Series, 1839), pp. 32–81; *Journal Asiatic Soc. Bengal*, Vol. XXVIII., No. 1, 1859; *Journal N. C. Br. R. As. Soc.*, New Series, Vol. VI., pp. 129 ff.; *China Review*, Vol. II., p. 309.

compete at these trials with the Chinese, but many facts show that the former are generally favored at the expense of the latter; the large proportion of men belonging to these races filling high offices indicates who are the rulers of the land. The candidates are all examined at Peking; one instance is recorded of a Chinese who passed himself off for a Manchu, but afterward confessed the dissimulation; the head of the division was tried in consequence of his oversight. It is the professed policy of the government to discourage literary pursuits among them, in order to maintain the ancient energy of the race; but where the real power is lodged in the hands of civilians, it is impossible to prevent so powerful a component of the population from competing with the others for its possession.

The present dynasty introduced examinations and gradations among the troops on the same principles as obtain in the civil service; nothing more strikingly proves the power of literary pursuits in China, than this vain attempt to harmonize the profession of arms in all its branches with them. Their enemies were, however, no better disciplined and equipped than they themselves were. Candidates for the first degree present themselves before the district magistrate, with proper testimonials and securities. On certain days they are collected on the parade-grounds, and exhibit their skill in archery (on foot and in the saddle), in wielding swords and lifting weights, graduated to test their muscle. The successful men are assembled afterward before the prefect; and again at a third trial before the literary chancellor, who at the last tripos tests them on their literary attainments, before giving them their degrees of *siu-tsai*. The number of successful military *siu-tsai* is the same as the literary. They are triennially called together by the governor at the provincial capital to undergo further examination for *kü-jin* in four successive trials of the same nature. These occasions are usually great gala days, and three or four scores of young warriors who carry off prizes at these tournaments receive honors and degrees in much the same style as their literary compeers. The trials for the highest degree are held at Peking; and the long-continued efforts in this service generally obtain for the young men posts in the body-guard of the governors or staff appointments. The forty-nine successful candidates out of several thousands at the triennial examination for *kü-jin* in Canton, November, 1832, all hit the target on foot six times successively, and on horseback six times; once with the arrow they hit a ball lying on the ground as they passed it at a gallop; and all were of the first class in wielding the iron-handled battle-axe, and lifting the stone-loaded beam. The candidates are all persons of property, who find their own horses, dresses, arms, etc., and are handsomely dressed, the horses, trimmings, and accoutrements in good order—the arrows being without barbs, to prevent accidents. One observer says, "the marks at which they fired, covered with white paper, were about the height of a man and somewhat wider, placed at intervals of fifty yards; the object was to strike these marks successively with their three arrows, the horses being kept at full speed. Although the bull's-eye was not always hit, the target was never missed: the distance did not exceed fifteen or twenty feet."[1]

Since military honors depend so entirely on personal skill, it may partly account for the inferior rank the graduates hold in comparison with civilians. No knowledge of tactics, gunnery, engineering, fortifications, or even letters in general, seems to be required of them; and this explains the inefficiency of the army, and the low estimation its officers are held in. Sir J. Davis mentions one military officer of enormous size and strength, whom he saw on the Pei ho, who had lately been promoted for his personal prowess; and speaks of another attached to the guard on one of the boats, who was such a foolish fellow that none of the civilians would associate with him.[2] All the classes eligible to civil promotion can enter the lists for military honors; the Emperor is present at the examination for the highest, and awards prizes, such as a cap decorated with a peacock's feather; but no system of prizes or examinations can supply the want of knowledge and courage. Military distinctions not being much sought by the people, and conferring but

[1] Ellis, *Embassy to China*, p. 87; *Chinese Repository*, Vol. XVI., p. 62; Vol. IV., p. 125.

[2] Davis, *Sketches*, Vol. I., pp. 99, 101.

little emolument or power, do not stand as high in public estimation as the present government wishes. The selection of officers for the naval service is made from the land force, and a man is considered quite as fit for that branch after his feats of archery, as if the trials had been in yacht-sailing or manning the yards.

Such is the outline of the system of examinations through which the civil and military services of the Chinese government are supplied, and the only part of their system not to be paralleled in one or other of the great monarchies of past or present times; though the counterpart of this may have also existed in ancient Egypt. "It is the only one of their inventions," as has been remarked, "which is perhaps worth preserving, and has not been adopted by other countries, and carried to greater perfection than they were equal to." But such a system would be unnecessary in an enlightened Christian country, where the people, pursuing study for its own sake, are able and willing to become as learned as their rulers desire without any such inducement. Nor would they submit to the trammels and trickery attendant on competition for office; the ablest politicians are by no means found among the most learned scholars. The honor and power of official position have proved to be ample stimulus and reward for years of patient study. Not one in a score of graduates ever obtains an office, not one in a hundred of competitors ever gets a degree; but they all belong to the literary class, and share in its influence, dignity, and privileges. Moreover, these books render not only those who get the prizes well acquainted with the true principles on which power should be exercised, but the whole nation—gentry and commoners—know them also. These unemployed *literati* form a powerful middle class, whose members advise the work-people, who have no time to study, and aid their rulers in the management of local affairs. Their intelligence fits them to control most of the property, while few acquire such wealth as gives them the power to oppress. They make the public opinion of the country, now controlling it, then cramping it; alternately adopting or resisting new influences, and sometimes successfully thwarting the acts of officials, when the rights of the people are in danger of encroachment; or at other times combining with the authorities to repress anarchy or relieve suffering.

This class has no badge of rank, and is open to every man's highest talent and efforts, but its complete neutralization of hereditary rights, which would have sooner or later made a privileged oligarchy and a landed or feudal aristocracy, proves its vitalizing, democratic influence. It has saved the Chinese people from a second disintegration into numerous kingdoms, by the sheer force of instruction in the political rights and duties taught in the classics and their commentaries. While this system put all on equality, human nature, as we know, has no such equality. At its inception it probably met general support from all classes, because of its fitness for the times, and soon the resistance of multitudes of hopeful students against its abrogation and their consequent disappointment in their life-work aided its continuance. As it is now, talent, wealth, learning, influence, paternal rank, and intrigue, each and all have full scope for their greatest efforts in securing the prizes. If these prizes had been held by a tenure as slippery as they are at present in the American Republic, or obtainable only by canvassing popular votes, the system would surely have failed, for "the game would not have been worth the candle." But in China the throne gives a character of permanency to the government, which opposes all disorganizing tendencies, and makes it for the interest of every one in office to strengthen the power which gave it to him. This loyalty was remarkably shown in the recent rebellion, in which, during the eighteen years of that terrible carnage and ruin, not one imperial official voluntarily joined the Tai-pings, while hundreds died resisting them.

There is no space here for further extracts from the classics which will adequately show their character. They would prove that Chinese youth, as well as those in Christian lands, are taught a higher standard of conduct than they follow. The former are, however, drilled in the very best moral books the language affords; if the Proverbs of Solomon and the New Testament were studied as thoroughly in our schools as the

Four Books are in China, our young men would be better fitted to act their part as good and useful citizens.

In this way literary pursuits have taken precedence of warlike, and no unscrupulous Cæsar or Napoleon has been able to use the army for his own aggrandizement. The army of China is contemptible, certainly, if compared with those of Western nations, and its use is rather like a police, whose powers of protection or oppression are exhibited according to the tempers of those who employ them. But in China the army has not been employed, as it was by those great captains, to destroy the institutions on which it rests; though its weakness and want of discipline often make it a greater evil than good to the people. But had the military waxed strong and efficient, it would certainly have become a terror in the hands of ambitious monarchs, a drain on the resources of the land, perhaps a menace to other nations, or finally a destroyer of its own. The officials were taught, when young, what to honor in their rulers; and, now that they hold those stations, they learn that discreet, upright magistrates do receive reward and promotion, and experience has shown them that peace and thrift are the ends and evidence of good government, and the best tests of their own fitness for office.

Another observable result of this republican method of getting the best-educated men into office is the absence of any class of slaves or serfs among the population. Slavery exists in a modified form of corporeal mortgage for debt, and thousands remain in this serfdom for life through one reason or another. But the destruction of a feudal baronage involved the extinction of its correlative, a villein class, and the oppression of poor debtors, as was the case in Rome under the consuls. Only freemen are eligible to enter the *concours*, but the percentage of slaves is too small to influence the total. To this cause, too, may, perhaps, to a large degree, be ascribed the absence of anything like caste, which has had such bad effects in India.

The system could not be transplanted; it is fitted for the genius of the Chinese, and they have become well satisfied with its workings. Its purification would do great good, doubtless, if the mass of the people are to be left in their present state of ignorance, but their elevation in knowledge would, ere long, revolutionize the whole. There can be no doubt as to the important and beneficial results it has accomplished, with all its defects, in perpetuating and strengthening the system of government, and securing to the people a more equitable and vigorous body of magistrates than they could get in any other way. It offers an honorable career to the most ambitious, talented, or turbulent spirits in the country, which demands all their powers; and by the time they enter upon office, those aspirations and powers have been drilled and molded into useful service, and are ever after devoted to the maintenance of the system they might otherwise have wrecked. Most of the real benefits of Chinese education and this system of examinations are reached before the conferment of the degree of *kü-jin.* These consist in diffusing a general respect and taste for letters among the people; in calling out the true talent of the country to the notice of the rulers in an honorable path of effort; in making all persons so thoroughly acquainted with the best moral books in the language that they cannot fail to exercise some salutary restraint; in elevating the general standard of education so much that every man is almost compelled to give his son a little learning in order that he may get along in life; and finally, through all these influences, powerfully contributing to uphold the existing institutions of the Empire.

From the intimate knowledge thus obtained of the writings of their best minds, Chinese youth learn the principles of democratic rule as opposed to personal authority; and from this instruction it has resulted that no monarch has ever been able to use a standing army to enslave the people, or seize the proceeds of their industry for his own selfish ends. Nothing in Chinese politics is more worthy of notice than the unbounded reverence for the Emperor, while each man resists unjust taxation, and joins in killing or driving away oppressive officials. Educated men form the only aristocracy in the land; and the attainment of the first degree, by introducing its owner into the class of *gentry*, is considered ample compensation for all the expense and study spent in getting it. On the whole, it may safely be asserted that these examinations have done more to maintain the stability, and explain the continuance, of the Chinese government than any other single cause.

The principal defects and malversations in the system can soon be shown. Some are inherent, but others rather prove the badness of the material than of the system and its harmonious workings. One great difficulty in the way of the graduated students attaining office according to their merits is the favor shown to those who can buy nominal and real honors. Two censors, in 1822, laid a document before his Majesty, in which the evils attendant on selling office are shown; viz., elevating priests, highwaymen, merchants, and other unworthy or uneducated men, to responsible stations, and placing insurmountable difficulties in the way of hard-working, worthy students reaching the reward of their toil. They state that the plan of selling offices commenced during the Han dynasty, but speak of the greater disgrace attendant upon the plan at the present time, because the avails all go into the privy purse instead of being applied to the public service; they recommend, therefore, a reduction in the disbursements of the imperial establishment. Among the items mentioned by these oriental Joseph Humes, which they consider extravagant, are a lac of taels (100,000) for flowers and rouge in the seraglio, and 120,000 in salaries to waiting-boys; two lacs were expended on the gardens of Yuenming, and almost half a million of taels upon the parks at Jeh ho, while the salaries to officers and presents to women at Yuenming were over four lacs. "If these few items of expense were abolished," they add, "there would be a saving of more than a million of taels of useless expenditure; talent might be brought forward to the service of the country, and the people's wealth be secured."

In consequence of the extensive sale of offices, they state that more than five thousand *tsin-sz'* doctors, and more than twenty-seven thousand *kü-jin* licentiates, are waiting for employment; and those first on the list obtained their degrees thirty years ago, so that the probability is that when at last employed, they will be too old for service, and be declared superannuated in the first examination of official merits and demerits. The rules to be observed at the regular examinations are strict, but no questions are asked the buyers of office; and they enter, too, on their duties as soon as the money is paid. The censors quote three sales, whose united proceeds amounted to a quarter of a million of taels, and state that the whole income from this source for twenty years was only a few lacs. Examples of the flagitious conduct of these purse-proud magistrates are quoted in proof of the bad results of the plan. "Thus the priest Siang Yang, prohibited from holding office, bought his way to one; the intendant at Ningpo, from being a mounted highwayman, bought his way to office; besides others of the vilest parentage. But the covetousness and cruelty of these men are denominated purity and intelligence; they inflict severe punishments, which make the people terrified, and their superiors point them out as possessing decision: these are our able officers!"

After animadverting on the general practice "of all officers, from governor-generals down to village magistrates, combining to gain their purposes by hiding the truth from the sovereign," and specifying the malversations of Tohtsin, the premier, in particular, they close their paper with a protestation of their integrity. "If your Majesty deems what we have now stated to be right, and will act thereon in the government, you will realize the designs of the souls of your sacred ancestors; and the army, the nation, and the poor people, will have cause for gladness of heart. Should we be subjected to the operation of the hatchet, or suffer death in the boiling caldron, we will not decline it."

These censors place the proceeds of "button scrip" far too low, for in 1826, the sale produced about six millions of taels, and was continued at intervals during the three following years. In 1831, one of the sons of Howqua was created a *kü-jin* by patent for having subscribed nearly fifty thousand dollars to repair the dikes near Canton; and upon another was conferred the rank and title of "director of the salt monopoly" for a lac of taels toward the war in Turkestan. Neither of these persons ever held any office of power, nor probably did they expect it; and such may be the case with many of those who are satisfied with the titles and buttons, feathers and robes, which their money procures. The sale of office is rather accepted as a State necessity which does not necessarily bring tyrants upon the bench; but when, as was the case in 1863, Peiching, head of the Examining Board at Peking, fraudulently issued two or three diplomas, his execution vindicated the law, and deterred similar tampering with the life-springs of the system. During the present dynasty, military men have been frequently appointed to magistracies, and the detail of their offices intrusted to needy scholars, which has tended, still further, to disgust and dishearten the latter from resorting to the literary arena.

The language itself of the Chinese, which has for centuries aided in preserving their institutions and strengthening national homogeneity amid so many local varieties of speech, is now rather in the way of their progress, and may be pointed to as another unfortunate feature which infects this system of education and examination; for it is impossible for a native to write a treatise on grammar about another language in his own tongue, through which another Chinese can, unaided, learn to speak that language. This people have, therefore, no ready means of learning the best thoughts of foreign minds. Such being the case, the ignorance of their first scholars as regards other races, ages, and lands has been their misfortune far more than their fault, and they have suffered the evils of their isolation. One has been an utter ignorance of what would have conferred lasting benefit resulting from the study of outside conceptions of morals, science, and politics. Inasmuch as neither geography, natural history, mathematics, nor the history or languages of other lands forms part of the curriculum, these men, trained alone in the classics, have naturally grown up with distorted views of their own country. The officials are imbued with conceit, ignorance, and arrogance as to its power, resources, and comparative influence, and are helpless when met by greater skill or strength. However, these disadvantages, great as they are and have been, have mostly resulted naturally from their secluded position, and are rapidly yielding to the new influences which are acting upon government and people. To one contemplating this startling metamorphosis, the foremost wish, indeed, must be that these causes do not disintegrate their ancient economies too fast for the recuperation and preservation of whatever is good therein.

Another evil is the bribery practised to attain the degrees. By certain signs placed on the essays, the examiner can easily pick out those he is to approve; $8,000 was said to be the price of a bachelor's degree in Canton, but this sum is within the reach of few out of the six thousand candidates. The poor scholars sell their services to the rich, and for a certain price will enter the hall of examination, and personate their employer, running the risk and penalties of a disgraceful exposure if detected; for a less sum they will drill them before examination, or write the essays entirely, which the rich booby must commit to memory. The purchase of forged diplomas is another mode of obtaining a graduate's honors, which, from some discoveries made at Peking, is so extensively practised, that when this and other corruptions are considered, it is surprising that any person can be so eager in his studies, or confident of his abilities, as ever to think he can get into office by them alone. In 1830, the *Gazette* contained some documents showing that an inferior officer, aided by some of the clerks in the Board of Revenue, during the successive superintendence of twenty presidents of the Board had sold twenty thousand four hundred and nineteen forged diplomas; and in the province of Nganhwui, the writers in the office attached to the Board of Revenue had carried on the same practice for four years, and forty-six persons in that province were convicted of possessing them. All the principal criminals convicted at this time were sentenced to decapitation, but these cases are enough to show that the real talent of the country does not often find its way into the magistrate's seat without the aid of money; nor is it likely that the tales of such delinquencies often appear in the *Gazette*. Literary chancellors also sell bachelors' degrees to the exclusion of deserving poor scholars; the office of the *hiohching* of Kiangsí was searched in 1828 by a special commission, and four lacs of taels found in it; he hung himself to avoid further punishment, as did also the same dignitary in Canton in 1833, as was supposed, for a similar cause. It is in this way, no doubt, that the ill-gotten gains of most officers return to the general cir culation.

Notwithstanding these startling corruptions, which seem to involve the principle on which the harmony and efficiency of the whole machinery of state stand, it cannot be denied, judging from the results, that the highest officers of the Chinese government do possess a very respectable rank of talent and knowledge, and carry on the unwieldy machine with a degree of integrity, patriotism, industry, and good order which shows that the leading minds in it are well chosen. The person who has originally obtained his rank by a forged diploma, or by direct purchase, cannot hope to rise or to maintain even his first standing, without some knowledge and parts. One of the three commissioners whom Kíying associated with himself in his negotiations with the American minister in 1844, was a supernumerary *chíhien* of forbidding appearance, who could hardly write a common document, but it was easy to see the low estimation the ignoramus was held in. It may therefore be fairly inferred that enough large prizes are drawn to incite successive generations of scholars to compete for them, and thus to maintain the literary spirit of the people. At these examinations the superior minds of the country are brought together in large bodies, and thus they learn each others views, and are able to check official oppressions with something like a public opinion. In Peking the concourse of several thousands, from the remotest provinces, to compete at or assist in the triennial examinations, exerts a great and healthy influence upon their rulers and themselves. Nothing like it ever has been seen in any other metropolis.

The enjoyment of no small degree of power and influence in their native village, is also to be considered in estimating the rewards of studious toil, whether the student get a diploma or not; and this local consideration is the most common reward attending the life of a scholar. In those villages where no governmental officer is specially appointed, such men are almost sure to become the headmen and most influential persons in the very spot where a Chinese loves to be distinguished. Graduates are likewise allowed to erect flag-staffs, or put up a red sign over the door of their houses showing the degree they have obtained, which is both a harmless and gratifying reward of study; like the additions of *Cantab.* or *Oxon.*, D.D. or LL.D., to their owner's names in other lands.

The fortune attending the unsuccessful candidates is various. Thousands of them get employment as school-teachers, pettifogging notaries, and clerks in the public offices, and others who are rich return to their families. Some are reduced by degrees to beggary, and resort to medicine, fortune-telling, letter-writing, and other such shifts to eke out a living. Many turn their attention to learning the modes of drawing up deeds and forms used in dealings regarding property; others look to aiding military men in their duties, and a few turn authors, and thus in one way or another contrive to turn their learning to account.

During the period of the examinations, when the students are assembled in the capital, the officers of government are careful not to irritate them by punishment, or offend their *esprit de corps*, but rather, by admonitions and warnings, induce them to set a good example. The personal reputation of the officer himself has much to do with the influence he exerts over the students, and whether they will heed his *caveats*. One of the examiners in Chehkiang, irritated by the impertinence of a bachelor, who presumed upon his immunity from corporeal chastisement, twisted his ears to teach him better manners; soon after, the student and two others of equal degree were accused before the same magistrate for a libel, and one of them beaten forty strokes upon his palms. At the ensuing examination, ten of the *siu-tsai*, indignant at this unauthorized treatment, refused to appear, and all the candidates, when they saw who was to preside, dispersed immediately. In his memorial upon the matter, the governor-general recommends both this officer, and another one who talked much about the affair and produced a great effect upon the public mind, to be degraded, and the bachelors to be stripped of their honors. A magistrate of Honan, having punished a student with twenty blows, the assembled body of students rose and threw their caps on the ground, and walked off, leaving him alone. The prefect of Canton, in 1842, having become obnoxious to the citizens from the part he took in ransoming the city when surrounded by the British forces, the students refused to receive him as their examiner, and when he appeared in the hall to take his seat, drove him out of the room by throwing their ink-stones at him; he soon after resigned his station. Perhaps the *siu-tsai* are more impatient than the *kü-jin* from being better acquainted with each other, and being examined by local officers, while the *kü-jin* are overawed by the rank of the commissioners, and, coming from distant parts of a large province, have little mutual sympathy or acquaintance. The examining boards, however, take pains to avoid displeasing any gathering of graduates.

We have seen, then, in what has been of necessity a somewhat cursory *resumé*, the management and extent of an institution which has opened the avenues of rank to all, by teaching candidates how to maintain the principles of liberty and equality they had learned from their oft-quoted 'ancients.' All that these institutions need, to secure and promote the highest welfare of the people—as they themselves, indeed, aver—is their faithful execution in every department of government; as we find them, no higher evidence of their remarkable wisdom can be adduced, than the general order and peace of the land. When one sees the injustice and oppressions in law courts, the feuds and deadly fights among clans, the prevalence of lying, ignorance, and pollution among commoners, and the unscrupulous struggle for a living going on in every rank of life, he wonders that universal anarchy does not destroy the whole machine. But 'the powers that be are ordained of God.' The Chinese seem to have attained the great ends of human government to as high a degree as it is possible for man to go without the knowledge of divine revelation. That, in its great truths, its rewards, its hopes, and its stimulus to good acts has yet to be received among them. The course and results of the struggle between the new and the old in the land of Sinim will form a remarkable chapter in the history of man.

With regard to female education, it is a singular anomaly among Chinese writers, that while they lay great stress upon maternal instruction in forming the infant mind, and leading it on to excellence, no more of them should have turned their attention to the preparation of books for girls, and the establishment of female schools. There are some reasons for the absence of the latter to be found in the state of society, notable among which must stand, of course, the low position of woman in every oriental community, and a general contempt for the capacity of the female mind. It is, moreover, impossible to procure many qualified schoolmistresses, and to this we must add the hazard of sending girls out into the streets alone, where they would run some risk of being stolen. The principal stimulus for boys to study—the hope and prospect of office—is taken away from girls, and Chinese literature offers little to repay them for the labor of learning it in addition to all the domestic duties which devolve upon them. Nevertheless, education is not entirely confined to the stronger sex; seminaries for young women are not at all uncommon in South China, and it is not unusual to find private tutors giving instruction to young ladies at their houses.[1] Though this must be regarded as a comparative statement, and holding much more for the southern than for the northern provinces, on the other hand, it may be asserted that literary attainments are considered creditable to a woman, more than is the case in India or Siam; the names of authoresses mentioned in Chinese annals would make a long list. Yuen Yuen, the governor-general of Canton, in 1820, while in office, published a volume of his deceased's daughter's poetical effusions; and literary men are usually desirous of having their daughters accomplished in music and poetry, as well as in composition and classical lore. Such an education is considered befitting their station, and reflecting credit on the family.

One of the most celebrated female writers in China is Pan Hwui-pan, also known as Pan Chao, a sister of the historian Pan Ku, who wrote the history of the former Han dynasty. She was appointed historiographer after his death, and completed his unfinished annals; she died at the age of seventy, and was honored by the Emperor Ho with a public burial, and

---

[1] Archdeacon Gray, *China*, Vol. I., p. 167.

the title of the Great Lady Tsao. About A.D. 80, she was made preceptress of the Empress, and wrote the first work in any language on female education; it was called *Nü Kiai* or *Female Precepts*, and has formed the basis of many succeeding books on female education. The aim of her writings was to elevate female character, and make it virtuous. She says, "The virtue of a female does not consist altogether in extraordinary abilities or intelligence, but in being modestly grave and inviolably chaste, observing the requirements of virtuous widowhood, and in being tidy in her person and everything about her; in whatever she does to be unassuming, and whenever she moves or sits to be decorous. This is female virtue." Instruction in morals and the various branches of domestic economy are more insisted upon in the writings of this and other authoresses, than a knowledge of the classics or histories of the country.

One of the most distinguished Chinese essayists of modern times, Luhchau, published a work for the benefit of the sex, called the *Female Instructor;* an extract from his preface will show what ideas are generally entertained on female education by Chinese moralists.

"The basis of the government of the Empire lies in the habits of the people, and the surety that their usages will be correct is in the orderly management of families, which last depends chiefly upon the females. In the good old times of Chau, the virtuous women set such an excellent example that it influenced the customs of the Empire—an influence that descended even to the times of the Ching and Wei states. If the curtain of the inner apartment gets thin, or is hung awry [*i.e.*, if the sexes are not kept apart], disorder will enter the family, and ultimately pervade the Empire. Females are doubtless the sources of good manners; from ancient times to the present this has been the case. The inclination to virtue and vice in women differs exceedingly; their dispositions incline contrary ways, and if it is wished to form them alike, there is nothing like education. In ancient times, youth of both sexes were instructed. According to the *Ritual of Chau*, 'the imperial wives regulated the law for educating females, in order to instruct the ladies of the palace in morals, conversation, manners, and work; and each led out her respective classes, at proper times, and arranged them for examination in the imperial presence.' But these treatises have not reached us, and it cannot be distinctly ascertained what was their plan of arrangement. . . . .

"The education of a woman and that of a man are very dissimilar. Thus, a man can study during his whole life; whether he is abroad or at home, he can always look into the classics and history, and become thoroughly acquainted with the whole range of authors. But a woman does not study more than ten years, when she takes upon her the management of a family, where a multiplicity of cares distract her attention, and having no leisure for undisturbed study, she cannot easily understand learned authors; not having obtained a thorough acquaintance with letters, she does not fully comprehend their principles; and like water that has flowed from its fountain, she cannot regulate her conduct by their guidance. How can it be said that a standard work on female education is not wanted! Every profession and trade has its appropriate master; and ought not those also who possess such an influence over manners [as females] to be taught their duties and their proper limits? It is a matter of regret, that in these books no extracts have been made from the works of Confucius in order to make them introductory to the writings on polite literature; and it is also to be regretted that selections have not been made from the commentaries of Ching, Chu, and other scholars, who have explained his writings clearly, as also from the whole range of writers, gathering from them all that which was appropriate, and omitting the rest. These are circulated among mankind, together with such books as the *Juvenile Instructor*; yet if they are put into the hands of females, they cause them to become like a blind man without a guide, wandering hither and thither without knowing where he is going. There has been this great deficiency from very remote times until now.

"Woman's influence is according to her moral character, therefore that point is largely explained. First, concerning her obedience to her husband and to his parents; then in regard to her complaisance to his brothers and sisters, and kindness to her sisters-in-law. If unmarried, she has duties toward her parents, and to the wives of her elder brothers; if a principal wife, a woman must have no jealous feelings; if in straitened circumstances, she must be contented with her lot; if rich and honorable, she must avoid extravagance and haughtiness. Then teach her, in times of trouble and in days of ease, how to maintain her purity, how to give importance to right principles, how to observe widowhood, and how to avenge the murder of a relative. Is she a mother, let her teach her children; is she a step-mother, let her love and cherish her husband's children; is her rank in life high, let her be condescending to her inferiors; let her wholly discard all sorcerers, superstitious nuns, and witches; in a word let her adhere to propriety and avoid vice.

"In conversation, a female should not be froward and garrulous, but observe strictly what is correct, whether in suggesting advice to her husband, in remonstrating with him, or teaching her children, in maintaining etiquette, humbly imparting her experience, or in averting misfortune. The deportment of females should be strictly grave and sober, and yet adapted to the occasion; whether in waiting on her parents, receiving or reverencing her husband, rising up or sitting down, when pregnant, in times of mourning, or when fleeing in war, she should be perfectly decorous. Rearing the silkworm and working cloth are the most important of the employments of a female; preparing and serving up the food for the household, and setting in order the

sacrifices, follow next, each of which must be attended to; after them, study and learning can fill up the time."[1]

The work thus prefaced, is similar to Sprague's *Letters to a Daughter*, rather than to a text-book, or a manual intended to be read and obeyed rather than recited by young ladies. Happy would it be for the country, however, if the instructions given by this moralist were followed; it is a credit to a pagan, to write such sentiments as the following: "During infancy, a child ardently loves its mother, who knows all its traits of goodness: while the father, perhaps, cannot know about it, there is nothing which the mother does not see. Wherefore the mother teaches more effectually, and only by her unwise fondness does her son become more and more proud (as musk by age becomes sourer and stronger), and is thereby nearly ruined."—"Heavenly order is to bless the good and curse the vile; he who sins against it will certainly receive his punishment sooner or later: from lucid instruction springs the happiness of the world. If females are unlearned, they will be like one looking at a wall, they will know nothing: if they are taught, they will know, and knowing they will imitate their examples."

It is vain to expect, however, that any change in the standing of females, or extent of their education, will take place until influences from abroad are brought to bear upon them—until the same work that is elswhere elevating them to their proper place in society by teaching them the principles on which that elevation is founded, and how they can themselves maintain it, is begun. The Chinese do not, by any means, make slaves of their females, and if a comparison be made between their condition in China and other modern unevangelized countries, or even with ancient kingdoms or Moslem races, it will in many points acquit them of much of the obloquy they have received on this behalf.

There are some things which tend to show that more of the sex read and write sufficiently for the ordinary purposes of life, than a slight examination would at first indicate. Among these may be mentioned the letter-writers compiled for their use, in which instructions are given for every variety of note and epis-

[1] *Chinese Repository*, Vol. IX., p. 542.

tle, except, perhaps, love letters. The works just mentioned, intended for their improvement, form an additional fact. A Manchu official of rank, named Sin-kwăn, who rose to be governor of Kiangsí in Kiaking's reign, wrote a primer in 1838, for girls, called the *Nü-rh Yü*, or '*Words for Women and Girls.*' It is in lines of four characters, and consists of aphorisms and short precepts on household management, behavior, care of children, neatness, etc., so written as to be easily memorized. It shows one of the ways in which literary men interest themselves, in educating youth, and further that there is a demand for such books. A few lines from this primer will exhibit its tenor

Vile looks should never meet your eye,
Nor filthy words defile your ear ;
Ne'er look on men of utterance gross,
Nor tread the ground which they pollute.
Keep back the heart from thoughts impure,
Nor let your hands grow fond of sloth ;
Then no o'ersight or call deferred
Will, when you're pressed, demand your time

In all your care of tender babes,
Mind lest they're fed or warmed too much ;
The childish liberty first granted
Must soon be checked by rule and rein ;
Guard them from water, fire, and fools ;
Mind lest they're hurt or maimed by falls.
All flesh and fruits when ill with colds
Are noxious drugs to tender bairns—
Who need a careful oversight,
Yet want some license in their play.
Be strict in all you bid them do,
For this will guard from ill and woe.

The pride taken by girls in showing their knowledge of letters is evidence that it is not common, while the general respect in which literary ladies are held proves them not to be so very rare ; though for all practical good, it may be said that half of the Chinese people know nothing of books. The fact that female education is so favorably regarded is encouraging to those philanthropic persons and ladies who are endeavoring to establish female schools at the mission stations, since they have not prejudice to contend with in addition to ignorance.

CHAPTER X.

STRUCTURE OF THE CHINESE LANGUAGE.

It might reasonably be inferred, judging from the attention paid to learning, and the honors conferred upon its successful votaries, that the literature of the Chinese would contain much to repay investigation. Such is not the case, however, to one already acquainted with the treasures of Western science, and, in fairness, such a comparison is not quite just. Yet it has claims to the regard of the general student, from its being the literature of so vast a portion of the human species, and the result of the labors of its wisest and worthiest minds during many successive ages. The fact that it has been developed under a peculiar civilization, and breathes a spirit so totally different from the writings of Western sages and philosophers, perhaps increases the curiosity to learn what are its excellences and defects, and obtain some criteria by which to compare it with the literature of other Asiatic or even European nations. The language in which it is written—one peculiarly mystical and diverse from all other media of thought—has also added to its singular reputation, for it has been surmised that what is "wrapped up" in such complex characters must be pre-eminently valuable for matter or elegant for manner, and not less curious than profound. Although a candid examination of this literature will disclose its real mediocrity in points of research, learning, and genius, there yet remains enough to render it worthy the attention of the oriental or general student.

Some of its peculiarities are owing to the nature of the language, and the mode of instruction, both of which have affected the style and thoughts of writers: for, having, when young, been taught to form their sentences upon the models of antiquity, their efforts to do so have moulded their thoughts in the same channel. Imitation, from being a duty, soon became a necessity. The Chinese scholar, forsaking the leadings of his own genius, soon learned to regard his models as not only being all truth themselves, but as containing the sum total of all things valuable. The intractable nature of the language, making it impossible to study other tongues through the medium of his own, moreover tended to repress all desire in the scholar to become acquainted with foreign books; and as he knew nothing of them or their authors, it was easy to conclude that there was nothing worth knowing in them, nothing to repay the toil of study, or make amends for the condescension of ascertaining. The neighbors of the Chinese have unquestionably been their inferiors in civilization, good government, learning, and wealth; and this fact has nourished their conceit, and repressed the wish to travel, and ascertain what there was in remoter regions. In judging of the character of Chinese literature, therefore, these circumstances among others under which it has risen to its present bulk, must not be overlooked; we shall conclude that the uniformity running through it is perhaps owing as much to the isolation of the people and servile imitation of their models, as to their genius: each has, in fact, mutually acted upon and influenced the other.

The "homoglot" character of the Chinese people has arisen more from the high standard of their literature, and the political institutions growing out of its canonical books (which have impelled and rewarded the efforts of students to master the language), than from any one other cause. This feature offers a great contrast to the polyglot character which the Romans possessed even to the last, and suggests the cause and results as interesting topics of inquiry. The Egyptian, Jewish, Syriac, Greek, and Latin languages had each its own national literature, and its power was enough to retain these several nations attached to their own mother tongue, while the Gauls, Iberians, and other subject peoples, having no books, took the language and literature of their rulers and conquerors. Thus the kingdom, "part iron and part clay," fell apart as soon as the grasp of Rome was weakened; while the tendency in China always has been to reunite and homologate.

In this short account of the Chinese tongue, it will be sufficient to give such notices of the origin and construction of the characters, and of the idioms and sounds of the written and spoken language, as shall convey a general notion of all its parts, and to show the distinction between the spoken and written media, and their mutual action. They are both archaic, because the symbols prevented all inflexion and agglutination in the sounds, and all signs to indicate what part of speech each belonged to. They are like the ten digits, containing no vocable and imparting their meaning more to the eye than the ear.

Chinese writers, unable to trace the gradual formation of their characters (for, of course, there could be no intelligible historical data until long after their formation), have ascribed them to Hwangtí, one of their primeval monarchs, or even earlier, to Fuh-hí, some thirty centuries before Christ; as if they deemed writing to be as needful to man as clothes or marriage, all of which came from Fuh-hí. A mythical personage, Tsangkieh, who flourished about B.C. 2700, is credited with the invention of symbols to represent ideas, from noticing the marking on tortoise-shell, and thence imitating common objects in nature.

The Japanese have tried to attach their *kana* to the Chinese characters to indicate the case or tense, but the combination looks incongruous to an educated Chinese. We might express, though somewhat crudely, analogous combinations in English by endeavoring to write 1-*ty*, 1-*ness*, 1-*ted*, for *unity*, *oneness*, *united*, or 3-1 *God* for *triune God*.

At this crisis, when a medium for conveying and giving permanency to ideas was formed, Chinese historians say: "The heavens, the earth, and the gods, were all agitated. The inhabitants of hades wept at night; and the heavens, as an expression of joy, rained down ripe grain. From the invention of writing, the machinations of the human heart began to operate; stories false and erroneous daily increased, litigations and imprisonments sprang up; hence, also, specious and artful language, which causes so much confusion in the world. It was for these reasons that the shades of the departed wept at night. But from the invention of writing, polite intercourse and music proceeded; reason and justice were made manifest; the relations of social life were illustrated, and laws became fixed. Governors had laws to which they might refer; scholars had authorities to venerate; and hence, the heavens, delighted, rained down ripe grain. The classical scholar, the historian, the mathematician, and the astronomer can none of them do without writing; were there no written language to afford proof of passing events, the shades might weep at noonday, and the heavens rain down blood."[1] This singular myth may, perhaps, cover a genuine fact worthy of more than passing notice—indicating a consentaneous effort of the early settlers on the Yellow River to substitute for the purpose of recording laws and events something more intelligible than the knotted cords previously in use. Its form presents a curious contrast to the personality of the fable of Cadmus and his invention of the Greek letters.

The date of the origin of this language, like that of the letters of Western alphabets, is lost in the earliest periods of postdiluvian history, but there can be no doubt that it is the most ancient language now spoken, and along with the Egyptian and cuneiform, among the oldest written languages used by man. The Ethiopic and Coptic, the Sanscrit and Pali, the Syriac, Aramaic, and Pehlvic, have all become dead languages; and the Greek, Latin, and Persian, now spoken, differ so much

---

[1] Professor H. A. Sayce, of Oxford, in reference to a suggested possible connection between the Chinese and primitive Accadian population of Chaldea, says in a letter to the London *Times*: "I would mention one fact which may certainly be considered to favor it. The cuneiform characters of Babylonia and Assyria are, as is well known, degenerated hieroglyphics, like the modern Chinese characters. The original hieroglyphics were invented by the Accadians before they descended into Babylonia from the mountains of Elam, and I have long been convinced that they were originally written in vertical columns. In no other way can I explain the fact that most of the pictures to which the cuneiform characters can be traced back stand upon their sides. There is evidence to show that the inventors of the hieroglyphics used papyrus, or some similar vegetable substance, for writing purposes before the alluvial plain of Babylonia furnished them with clay, and the use of such a writing material will easily account for the vertical direction in which the characters were made to run."

from the ancient style, as to require special study to understand the books in them: while during successive eras, the written and spoken language of the Chinese has undergone few alterations, and done much to deepen the broad line of demarkation between them and other branches of the human race. The fact, then, that this is the only living language which has survived the lapse of ages is, doubtless, owing to its ideographic character and its entire absence of sound as an integral factor of any symbol. Their form and meaning were, therefore, only the more strongly united because each reader was at liberty to sound them as he pleased or had been taught by local instructors. He was not hindered, on account of his local *brogue*, from communicating ideas with those who employed the same signs in writing. Upon the subsequent rise of a great and valuable literature, the maintenance of the written language was the chief element of national life and integrity among those peoples who read and admired the books. Nor has this language, like those of the Hebrews, the Assyrians, and others already mentioned, ever fallen into disuse and been supplanted by the sudden rise and physical or intellectual vigor of some neighboring community speaking a *patois*. For we find that alphabetic languages, whose words represent at once meaning and sound, are as dependent upon local dialects as is the Chinese tongue upon its symbols; consequently, when in the former case the sounds had so altered that the meanings were obscured, the mode of writing was likely to be changed. The extent of its literature and uses made of it were then the only safeguard of the written forms; while as men learned to read books they became more and more prone to associate sense and form, regarding the sound as traditionary. We have, in illustration of this, to look no further than to our own language, whose cumbersome spelling is in a great measure resulting from a dislike of changing old associations of sense and form which would be involved in the adoption of a phonetic system.

The Chinese have had no inducement, at any stage of their existence, to alter the forms of their symbols, inasmuch as no nation in Asia contiguous to their own has ever achieved a literature which could rival theirs; no conqueror came to impose his tongue upon them; their language completely isolated them from intellectual intercourse with others. This isolation, fraught with many disadvantages in the contracted nature of their literature, and the reflux, narrowing influence on their minds, has not been without its compensations. A national life of a unique sort has resulted, and to this self-nurtured language may be traced the origin of much of the peace, industry, population, and healthy pride of the Chinese people.

The Chinese have paid great and praiseworthy attention to their language, and furnished us with all needed books to its study. Premising that the original symbols were ideographic, the necessities of the case compelled their contraction as much as possible, and soon resulted in arbitrary signs for all common uses. Their symbols varied, indeed, at different times and in different States; it was not until a genuine literature appeared and its readers multiplied that the varients were dropped and uniformity sought. The original characters of this language are derived from natural or artificial objects, of which they were at first the rude outlines. Most of the forms are preserved in the treatises of native philologists, where the changes they have gradually undergone are shown. The number of objects chosen at first was not great; among them were symbols for the sun, moon, hills, animals, parts of the body, etc.; and in drawing them the limners seem to have proposed nothing further than an outline sketch, which, by the aid of a little explanation, would be intelligible. Thus the picture  would probably be recognized by all who saw it as representing the *moon*; that of  as a *fish*; and so of others. It is apparent that the number of pictures which could be made in this manner would bear no proportion to the wants and uses of a language, and therefore recourse must soon be had to more complicated symbols, to combining those already understood, or to the adoption of arbitrary or phonetic signs. All these modes have been more or less employed.

Chinese philologists arrange all the characters in their language into six classes, called *luh shu*, or 'six writings.' The first, called *siang hing*, morphographs, or 'imitative symbols,' are those in which a plain resemblance can be traced between the original form and the object represented; they are among the first characters invented, although the six hundred and eight placed in this class do not include all the original symbols. These pristine forms have since been modified so much that the resemblance has disappeared in most of them, caused chiefly by the use of paper, ink, and pencils, instead of the iron style and bamboo tablets formerly in use for writing; circular strokes being more distinctly made with an iron point upon the hard wood than with a hair pencil upon thin paper; angular strokes and square forms, therefore, gradually took the place of round or curved ones, and contracted characters came into use in place of the original imitative symbols. In this class such characters as the following are given:

tortoise, chariot, child, elephant, deer, vase, hill, eye.

altered to

龜 車 子 象 鹿 壺 山 目

kwei, chí, tsz', siang, luh, hu, shan, muh

The second class, only one hundred and seven in number, is called *chí sz'*, *i.e.*, 'symbols indicating thought.' They differ from the preceding chiefly in that the characters are formed by combining previously formed symbols in such a way as to indicate some idea easily deducible from their position or combination, and pointing out some property or relative circumstance belonging to them. Chinese philologists consider these two classes as comprising all the symbols in the language, which depict objects either in whole or in part, and whose meaning is apparent from the resemblance to the object, or from the position of the parts. Among those placed in this class are,

moon half appearing, signifies evening; now written 夕
sun above the horizon, denotes morning; now written 旦
something in the mouth, meaning sweet; now written 甘

The third class, amounting to seven hundred and forty characters, is called *hwui í*, *i.e.*, 'combined ideas,' or ideographs, and comprises characters made up of two or three symbols to form a single idea, whose meanings are deducible either from their position, or supposed relative influence upon each other. Thus the union of the sun and moon, 明 *ming*, expresses brightness; 閑 *kien*, a piece of wood in a doorway, denotes obstruction; two trees stand for a forest, as 林 *lin;* and three for a thicket, as 森 *săn;* two men upon the ground conveys the idea of sitting; a *mouth* in a *door* signifies to ask; *man* and *words* means truth and to believe; *heart* and *death* imports forgetfulness; *dog* and *mouth* means to bark; *woman* and *broom* denotes a wife, referring to her household duties; *pencil* and *to speak* is a book, or to write. But in none of these compounded characters is there anything like that perfection of picture writing stated by some writers to belong to the language, which will enable one unacquainted with the meaning of the separate symbols to decide upon the signification of the combined group. On the contrary it is in most cases certain that the third idea made by combining two already known symbols, usually required more or less explanation to fix its precise meaning, and remove the doubt which would otherwise arise. For instance, the combination of the sun and moon might as readily mean a solar or lunar eclipse, or denote the idea of time, as brightness. A piece of wood in a doorway would almost as naturally suggest a *threshold* as an *obstruction;* and so of others. A straight line in a doorway would more readily suggest a closed or bolted door, which is the signification of 閂 *shan*, anciently written 閂; but the idea intended to be conveyed by these combinations would need prior explanation as much as the primitive symbol, though it would thenceforth readily recur to mind when noticing the construction.

It is somewhat singular that the opinion should have obtained so much credence, that their meanings were easily deducible from their shape and construction. It might almost be said, that not a single character can be accurately defined from a mere inspection of its parts; and the meanings now given of some of those which come under this class are so arbitrary and far-fetched, as to show that Chinese characters have not been formed by rule and plummet more than words in other languages. The mistake which Du Ponceau so learnedly combats arose, probably, from confounding *sound* with *construction*, and inferring that, because persons of different nations, who used this as their written language, could understand it when written, though mutually unintelligible when speaking, that it addressed itself so entirely to the eye, as to need no previous explanation.

The fourth class, called *chuen chu*, 'inverted significations,' includes three hundred and seventy-two characters, being such as by some inversion, contraction, or alteration of their parts, acquire different meanings. This class is not large, but these and other modifications of the original symbols to express abstract and new ideas show that those who used the language either saw at once how cumbrous it would become if they went on forming imitative signs, or else that their invention failed, and they resorted to changes more or less arbitrary in characters already known to furnish distinctive signs for different ideas. Thus *yu* 又 the *hand*, turning toward the right means the right; inclined in the other direction, as *tso* 𠂇 it means the left. The *heart* placed beneath *slave*, 怒 signifies anger; *threads obstructed*, as 𢇍, means to sunder; but turned the other way, as 㡭, signifies continuous.

The fifth class, called *kiai shing*, *i.e.*, 'uniting sound symbols,' or phonogram, contains twenty-one thousand eight hundred and ten characters, or nearly all in the language. They are formed of an imitative symbol united to one which merely imparts its sound to the compound; the former usually partakes more or less of the new idea, while the latter loses its own meaning, and gives only its name. In this respect, Chinese characters are superior to the Arabic numerals, inasmuch as combinations like 25, 101, etc., although conveying the same meaning to all nations using them, can *never* indicate sound. This plan of forming new combinations by the union of symbols expressing idea and sound, enables the Chinese to increase the number of characters without multiplying the original symbols; but these compounds, or *lexigraphs*, as Du Ponceau calls them, do not increase very rapidly. In Annam they have become so numerous in the course of years that the Chinese books made in that country are hard to read. The probable mode in which this arose can best be explained by a case which occurred at Canton in 1832. Immature locusts were to be described in a proclamation, but the word *nan*, by which they were called, was not contained in any dictionary. It would be sufficient to designate this insect to all persons living where it was found by selecting a well-understood character, like 南 *south*, having the exact sound *nan*, by which the insect itself was called, and joining it to the determinative symbol *chung* 虫 insect. It would then signify, to every one who knew the sound and meaning of the component parts, the *insect nan;* and be read *nan*, 蝻 meaning this very insect to the people in Kwangtung. If this new combination was carried to a distant part of the country, where the insect itself was unknown, it would convey no more information to the Chinese who *saw* the united symbol, than the sounds *insect nan* would to an Englishman who *heard* them; to both persons a meaning must be given by describing the insect. If, however, the people living in this distant region called the phonetic part of the new character by another sound, as *nam*, *nem*, or *lam*, they would attach another name to the new compound, but the people on the spot would, perhaps, not understand them when they spoke it by that name. If they wrote it, however, both would give it the same signification, but a different sound.

In this way, the thousands of characters under this class have probably originated. But this rule of sounding them according to the phonetic part is not in all cases certain; for in the lapse of time, the sounds of many characters have changed, while those of the parts themselves have not altered; in other cases, the parts have altered, and the sounds remained; so that now only a great degree of probability as to the correct sound can be obtained by inspecting the component parts. The similarity in sound between most of the characters having the same phonetic part is a great assistance in reading Chinese, though very little in understanding it, and has had much influence in keeping the sounds unchanged.

There are a few instances of an almost inadvertent arrival at a true syllabic system, by which the initial consonant of one part, when joined to the final vowel of the other, gives the sound of the character; as *ma* and *fí*, in the character 靡, when united in this way, make *mí*. The meanings of the components are *hemp* and *not*, that of the compound is *extravagant*, *wasteful*, etc., showing no relation to the primary signification. The number of such characters is very small, and the syllabic composition here noticed is probably fortuitous, and not intentional.

The sixth class, called *kia tsié*, *i.e.*, 'borrowed uses,' includes metaphoric symbols and combinations, in which the meaning is deduced by a somewhat fanciful accommodation; their number is five hundred and ninety-eight. They differ but little from the second class of indicative symbols. For instance, the symbol 字 or 字, meaning a written character, is composed of a *child* under a *shelter*—characters being considered as the well-nurtured offspring of hieroglyphics. The character for *hall* means also *mother*, because she constantly abides there. The word for *mind* or *heart* is *sin* 心, originally intended to represent that organ, but now used chiefly in a metaphorical sense. Chinese grammarians find abundant scope for the display of their fancy in explaining the etymology and origin of the characters, but the aid which their researches give toward understanding the language as at present used is small. This classification under six heads is modern, and was devised as a means of arranging what existed already, for they confess that their characters were not formed according to fixed rules, and have gradually undergone many changes.

The total number in the six classes is twenty-four thousand two hundred and thirty-five, being many less than are found in Kanghí's Dictionary, which amount to forty-four thousand four hundred and forty-nine; but in the larger sum are included the obsolete and synonymous characters, which, if deducted, would reduce it to nearly the same number. It is probable that the total of really different characters in the language sanctioned by good usage, does not vary greatly from twenty-five thousand, though authors have stated them at from fifty-four thousand four hundred and nine, as Magaillans does, up to two hundred and sixty thousand eight hundred and ninety-nine, as Montucci. The Chinese editor of the large lexicon on which Dr. Morrison founded his Dictionary, gives it as his opinion that there are fifty thousand characters, including synonyms and different forms; and taking in every variety of tones given to the words, and sounds for which no characters exist, that there are five thousand different words. But even the sum of twenty-five thousand different characters contains thousands of unusual ones which are seldom met with, and which, as is the case with old words in English, are not often learned.

The burden of remembering so many complicated symbols, whose form, sound, and meanings are all necessary to enable the student to read and write intelligibly, is so great that the result has been to diminish those in common use, and increase their meanings. This course of procedure really occurs in most languages, and in the Chinese greatly reduces the labor of acquiring it. It may be safely said, that a good knowledge of ten thousand characters will enable one to read any work in Chinese, and write intelligibly on any subject; and Prémare says a good knowledge of four or five thousand characters is sufficient for all common purposes, while two-thirds of that number might in fact suffice. The troublesome ones are either proper names or technics peculiar to a particular science. The nine canonical works contain altogether only four thousand six hundred and one *different* characters, while in the Five Classics alone there are over two hundred thousand words. The entire number of different characters in the code of laws translated by Staunton is under two thousand.

The invention of printing and the compilation of dictionaries have given to the form of modern characters a greater degree of certainty than they had in ancient times. The variants of some of the most common ones were exceediugly numerous before this period; Callery gives forty-two different modes of writing *pao*, 'precious;' and forty-one for writing *tsun*, 'honorable;' showing the absence of an acknowledged standard, and the slight intercourse between learned men. The best mode of arranging the characters so as to find them easily, has been a subject of considerable trouble to Chinese lexicographers, and the various methods they have adopted renders it difficult to consult their dictionaries without considerable previous knowledge of the language. In some, those having the same sound are grouped together, so that it is necessary to know what a character is called before it can be found; and this arrangement has been followed in vocabularies designed principally for the use of the common people. One well-known vocabulary used at Canton, called the *Făn Yun*, or 'Divider of Sounds,' is arranged on this plan, the words being placed under thirty-three orders, according to their terminations. Each order is subdivided into three or four classes according to the tones, and all the characters having the same tone and termination are placed together, as *kam*, *lam*, *tam*, *nam*, etc. As might be supposed, it requires considerable time to find a character whose tone is not exactly known; and even with the tone once mastered, the uncertainty is equally troublesome if the termination is not familiar: for singular as it may seem to those who are acquainted only with phonetic languages, a Chinese can, if anything, more readily distinguish between two words ♯*ming* and ♭*ming*, whose tones are unlike, than he can between ♯*ming* and ♯*meng*, ♯*ming* or ♯*bing*, where the initial or final differs a little, and the tones are the same.

An improvement on this plan of arrangement was made by adopting a mode of expressing the sounds of Chinese characters introduced by the Buddhists, in the *Yuh Pien*, published A.D. 543, and ever since used in all dictionaries. This takes the initial of the sound of one character and the final of another, and combines them to indicate the sound of the given character; as from *li*-en and y-*ing* to form *ling*. There are thirty-six characters chosen for the initial consonants, and thirty-eight for the final sounds, but the student is perplexed by the different characters chosen in different works to represent them.[1] The inhabitants of Amoy use a small lexicon called the *Shih-wu Yin*, or 'Fifteen Sounds,' in which the characters are classified

[1] Biot has a brief note upon the methods employed by native scholars for studying pronunciation. *Essai sur l'instruction en Chine*, p. 597.

on this principle, by first arranging them all under fifty finals, and then placing all those having the same termination in a regular series under fifteen initials. Supposing a new character, *chien*, is seen, whose sound is given, or the word is heard in conversation and its meanings are wanted, the person turns to the part of the book containing the final *ien*, which is designated perhaps by the character *kien*, and looks along the initials until he comes to *ch*, which is indicated by the character *chang*. In this column, all the words in the book read or spoken *chien*, os whatever tone they may be, are placed together according to their tones; and a little practice readily enables a person speaking the dialect to use this manual. It is, however, of little or no avail to persons speaking other dialects, or to those whose vernacular differs much from that of the compiler, whose own ear was his only guide. Complete dictionaries have been published on the phonetic plan, the largest of which, the *Wu Ché Yun Fu*, is arranged with so much minuteness of intonation as to puzzle even the best educated natives, and consequently abridge its usefulness as an expounder of words.

The unfitness of either of these modes of arrangement to find an unknown character, led to another classification according to their composition, by selecting the most prominent parts of each character as its key, or radical, and grouping those together in which the same key occurred. This plan was adopted subsequently to that of arranging the characters according to the sounds, about A.D. 543, when their number was put at five hundred and forty-two; they were afterward reduced to three hundred and sixty, and toward the close of the Ming dynasty finally fixed at two hundred and fourteen in the *Tsz' Lui*. It is now in general use from the adoption of the abridged dictionary, the *Kanghí Tsz' Tien*; though this number could have been advantageously reduced, as has been shown by Gonçalves, its universal adoption, more than anything else, renders it the best system. All characters found under the same radical are placed consecutively, according to the number of strokes necessary to write them, but no regularity is observed in placing those having the same number of strokes. The term *primitive* has been technically applied to the remaining part of the character, which, though perhaps no older than the radical, is conveniently denoted by this word. The characters selected for the radicals are all common ones, and among the most ancient in the language; they are here grouped according to their meanings in order to show something of the leading ideas followed in combination.

Corporal.—Body, corpse, head, hair, down, whiskers, face, eye, ear, nose, mouth, teeth, tusk, tongue, hand, heart, foot, hide, leather, skin, wings, feathers, blood, flesh, talons, horn, bones.

Biological.—Man, woman, child; horse, sheep, tiger, dog, ox, hog, hog's head, deer; tortoise, dragon, reptile, mouse, toad; bird, gallinaceous fowls; fish; insect.

Botanical.—Herb, grain, rice, wheat, millet, hemp, leeks, melon, pulse, bamboo, sacrificial herb; wood, branch, sprout, petal.

Mineral.—Metal, stone, gems, salt, earth.

Meteorological.—Rain, wind, fire, water, icicle, vapor, sound; sun, moon, evening; time.

Utensils.—A chest, a measure, a mortar, spoon, knife, bench, couch, crockery, clothes, tiles, dishes, napkin, net, plough, vase, tripod, boat, carriage, pencil; bow, halberd, arrow, dart, ax, musical reed, drum, seal.

Descriptives.—Black, white, yellow, azure, carnation, sombre; color; high, long, sweet, square, large, small, strong, lame, slender, old, fragrant, acrid, perverse, base, opposed.

Actions.—To enter, to follow, to walk slowly, to arrive at, to stride, to walk, to run, to reach to, to touch, to stop, to fly, to overspread, to envelop, to encircle, to establish, to overshadow, to adjust, to distinguish, to divine, to see, to eat, to speak, to kill, to fight, to oppose, to stop, to embroider, to owe, to compare, to imitate, to bring forth, to use, to promulge.

Miscellaneous.—A desert, cave, field, den, mound, hill, valley, rivulet, cliff, retreat. A city; roof, gate, door, portico. One, two, eight, ten. Demon; an inch, mile; without, not, false; a scholar, statesman, letters; art, wealth; motion; self, myself, father; a point; again; wine; silk; joined hands; a long journey; print of a bear's foot; a surname; classifier of cloth.

The number of characters found under each of these radicals in Kanghí's Dictionary varies from five up to one thousand three hundred and fifty-four. The radical is not uniformly placed, but its usual position is on the left of the primitive. Some occur on the top, others on the bottom; some inclose the primitive, and many have no fixed place, making it evident that no uniform plan was adopted in the original construction. They must be thoroughly learned before the dictionary can be readily used.

and some practice had before a character can be quickly found.[1] The groups occurring under a majority of the radicals are more or less natural in their general meaning, a feature of the language which has already been noticed (page 375). Some of the radicals are interchanged, and characters having the same meaning sometimes occur under two or three different ones—variations which seem to have arisen from the little importance of a choice out of two or three similar radicals. Thus the same word *tsien*, 'a small cup,' is written under the three radicals *gem*, *porcelain*, and *horn*, originally, no doubt, referring to the material for making it. This interchange of radicals adds greatly to the number of duplicate forms, which are still further increased by a similar interchange of primitives having the same sound. These two changes very seldom occur in the same character, but there are numerous instances of synonymous forms under almost every radical, arising from an interchange of primitives, and also under analogous radicals caused by their reciprocal use. Thus, from both these causes, there are, under the radical *ma*, 'a horse,' one hundred and eighteen duplicate forms, leaving two hundred and ninety-three different words; of the two hundred and four characters under *niu*, 'an ox,' thirty-nine are synonymous forms; and so under other radicals. These characters do not differ in meaning more than *favor* and *favour*, or *lady* and *ladye*; they are mere variations in the form of writing, and though apparently adding greatly to the number of characters, do not seriously increase the difficulty of learning the language.

Variants of other descriptions frequently occur in books, which needlessly add to the labor of learning the language. Ancient forms are sometimes adopted by pedantic writers to show their learning, while ignorant and careless writers use abridged or vulgar forms, because they either do not know the correct form, or are heedless in using it. When such is the case, and the character cannot be found in the dictionary, the reader is entirely at fault, especially if he be a foreigner, though in China itself he would not experience much difficulty

---

[1] *Easy Lessons in Chinese*, pp. 3–29; *Chinese Repository*, Vol. III., pp. 1–37.

where the natives were at hand to refer to. Vulgar forms are very common in cheap books and letters, which are as unsanctioned by the dictionaries and good usage, as cockney phrases or miner's slang are in pure English. They arise, either from a desire on the part of the writer to save time by making a contracted form of few strokes instead of the correct character of many strokes; or he uses common words to express an energetic vulgar phrase, for which there are no authorized characters, but which will be easily understood phonetically by his readers. These characters would perchance not be understood at all outside of the range of the author's dialect, because the phrase itself was new; their individual meaning, indeed, has nothing to do with the interpretation of the sentence, for in this case they are merely signs of sound, like words in other languages, and lose their lexigraphic character. For instance, the words *kia-fi* for coffee, *kap-tan* for captain, *mí-sz'* for *Mr*, etc., however they were written, would be intelligible to a native of Canton if they expressed those sounds, because he was familiar with the words themselves; but a native of Shensí would not understood them, because, not knowing the things intended, he would naturally refer to the characters themselves for the meaning of the phrase, and thus be wholly misled. In such cases, the characters become mere syllables of a phonetic word. Foreign names are often transliterated by writers on geography or history, and their recognition is no easy task to their readers.[1]

In addition to the variations in the forms of characters, there are six different styles of writing them, which correspond to black-letter, script, italic, roman, etc., in English. The first is called *Chuen shu* (from the name of the person who invented it), which foreigners have styled the *seal character*, from its use in seals and ornamental inscriptions. It is next to the picture hieroglyphics, the most ancient fashion of writing, and has undergone many changes in the course of ages. It is studied by those who cut seals or inscriptions, but no books are ever printed in it.

---

[1] One may gain some idea of this difficulty by referring to the geographical names contained in the Russo-Chinese Treaty, quoted on page 215.

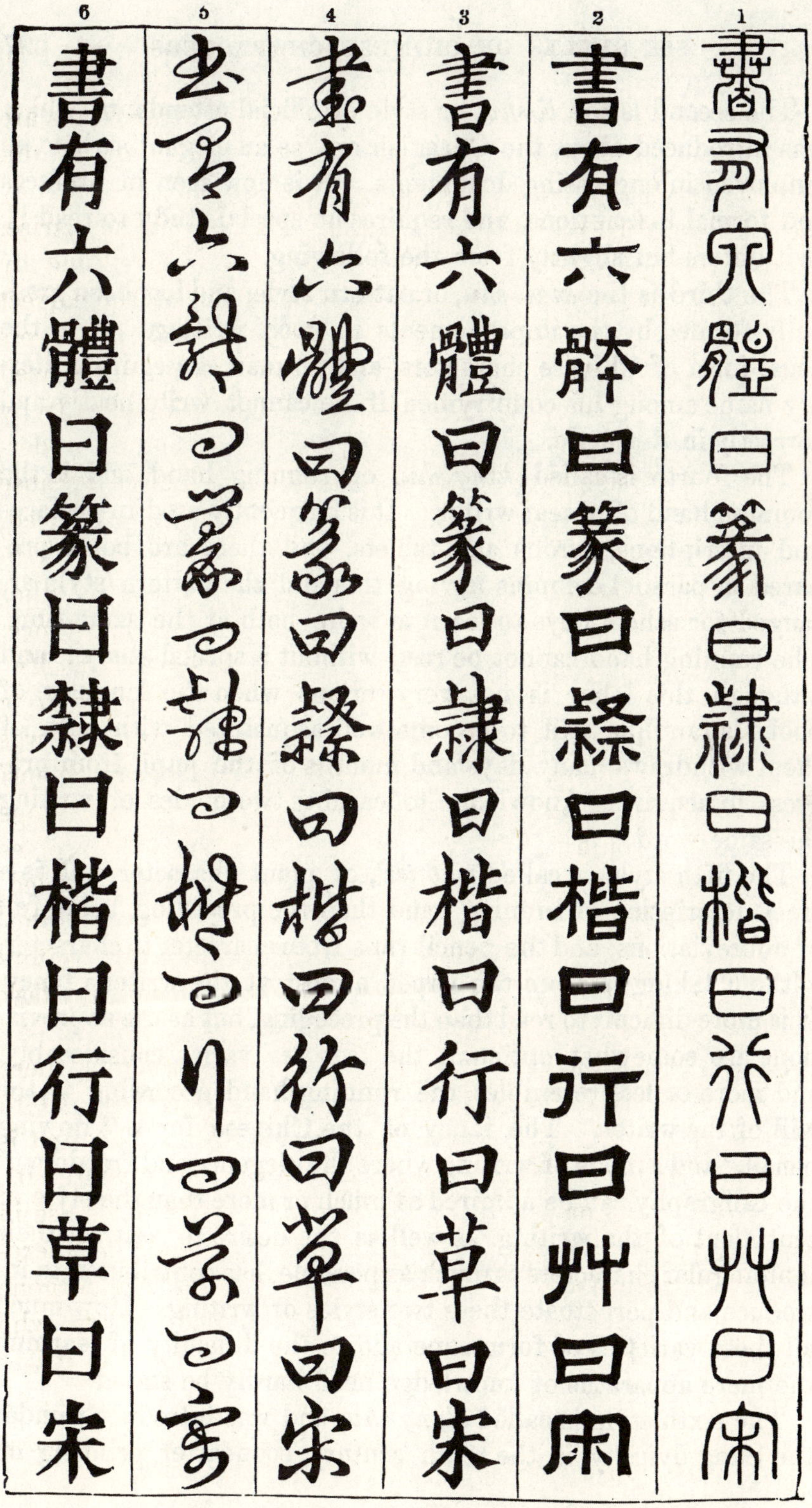
1 書有六體曰篆曰隸曰楷曰行曰草曰宋
2 書有六體曰篆曰隸曰楷曰行曰草曰宋
3 書有六體曰篆曰隸曰楷曰行曰草曰宋
4 書有六體曰篆曰隸曰楷曰行曰草曰宋
5 書有六體曰篆曰隸曰楷曰行曰草曰宋
6 書有六體曰篆曰隸曰楷曰行曰草曰宋

The second is the *li shu*, or style of official attendants, which was introduced about the Christian era, as an elegant style to be employed in engrossing documents. It is now seen in prefaces and formal inscriptions, and requires no special study to read it, as it differs but slightly from the following.

The third is the *kiai shu*, or pattern style, and has been gradually formed by the improvements in good writing. It is the usual form of Chinese characters, and no man can claim a literary name among his countrymen if he cannot write neatly and correctly in this style.

The fourth is called *hing shu*, or running hand, and is the common hand of a neat writer. It is frequently used in prefaces and inscriptions, scrolls and tablets, and there are books prepared in parallel columns having this and the pattern style arranged for school-boys to learn to write both at the same time. The running hand cannot be read without a special study; and although this labor is not very serious when the language of books is familiar, still to become well acquainted with both of them withdraws many days and months of the pupil from progress in acquiring knowledge to learning two modes of writing the same word.

The fifth style is called *tsao tsz'*, or plant character, and is a freer description of running hand than the preceding, being full of abbreviations, and the pencil runs from character to character, without taking it from the paper, almost at the writer's fancy. It is more difficult to read than the preceding, but as the abbreviations are somewhat optional, the *tsao tsz'* varies considerably, and more or less resembles the running hand according to the will of the writer. The fancy of the Chinese for a "flowing pencil," and a mode of writing where the elegance and freedom of the caligraphy can be admired as much or more than the style or sentiment of the writing, as well as the desire to contract their multangular characters as much as possible, has contributed to introduce and perpetuate these two styles of writing. How much all these varieties of form superadd to the difficulty of learning the mere apparatus of knowledge need hardly be stated.

The sixth style is called *Sung shu*, and was introduced under the Sung dynasty in the tenth century, soon after printing on wooden blocks was invented. It differs from the third style, merely in a certain squareness and angularity of stroke, which transcribers for the press only are obliged to learn. Of these six forms of writing, the pattern style and running hand are the only two which the people learn to any great extent, although many acquire the knowledge of some words in the seal character, and the running hand of every person, especially those engaged in business, approaches more or less to the plant character. But foreigners will seldom find time or inclination to learn to write more than one form, to be able to read and communicate on all occasions.

Besides these styles, there are fanciful ones, called 'tadpole characters,' in imitation of various objects;[1] the Emperor Kienlung brought together thirty-two of them in an edition of his poem, the *Elegy upon the City of Mukden*.[2]

All the strokes in the characters are reduced to eight elementary ones, which are contained in the single character 永 *yung*, 'eternal.'

A dot, a line, a perpendicular, a hook, a spike, a sweep, a stroke, a dash-line.

Each of these is subdivided into many forms in copy-books, having particular names, with directions how to write them, and numerous examples introduced under each stroke.[3]

---

[1] The writer has an edition of the *Thousand Character Classic*, containing each couplet of eight words in a different form of character, making one hundred and twenty-five styles of type—too grotesque to be imitated, and probably never actually in use.

[2] See page 193. In order that the Manchu portion of this famous poem might not appear inferior to the Chinese, the Emperor ordered thirty-two varieties of Manchu characters to be *invented* and published in like manner with the others. Rémusat, *Mélanges*, Tome II., p. 59. Père Amiot, *Éloge de la Ville de Moukden*. *Trad. en françois*. Paris, 1770.

[3] *Chinese Chrestomathy*, Chap. I., Secs. 5 and 6, where the rules for writing Chinese are given in full with numerous examples; *Easy Lessons in Chinese*, p. 59; *Chinese Repository*, Vol. III., p. 37.

The Chinese regard their characters as highly elegant, and take unwearied pains to learn to write them in a beautiful, uniform, well-proportioned manner. Students are provided with a painted board upon which to practise with a brush dipped in blackened water. The articles used in writing, collectively called *wan fang sz' pao*, or 'four precious things of the library,' are the pencil, ink, paper, and ink-stone. The best pencils are made of the bristly hair of the sable and fox, and cheaper ones from the deer, cat, wolf and rabbit; camel's hair is not used. A combination of softness and elasticity is required, and those who are skilled in their use discern a difference and an excellence altogether imperceptible to a novice. The hairs are laid in a regular manner, and when tied up are brought to a delicate tip; the handle is made of the twigs of a bamboo cultivated for the purpose. The ink, usually known as India ink, is made from the soot of burning oil, pine, fir, and other substances, mixed with glue or isinglass, and scented. It is formed into oblong cakes or cylinders, inscribed with the maker's name, the best kinds being put up in a very tasteful manner. A singular error formerly obtained credence regarding this ink, that it was inspissated from the fluid found in the cuttle-fish. When used, the ink is rubbed with water upon argillite, marble, or other stones, some of which are cut and ground in a beautiful manner. Chinese paper is made from bamboo, by triturating the woody fibre to a pulp in mortars after the pieces have been soaked in ooze, and then taking it up in moulds; the pulp is sometimes mixed with a little cotton fibre. Inferior sorts are made entirely from cotton refuse; and in the North, where the bamboo does not grow, the bark of the *Broussonetia*, or paper mulberry, furnishes material for a tough paper used for windows, wrappings, and account books, etc. Bamboo paper has no sizing in it, and is a frail material for preserving valuable writings, as it is easily destroyed by insects, mildew, or handling.[1]

In the days of Confucius, pieces of bamboo pared thin, palm

---

[1] *Journal Asiatic Soc. Bengal*, Vol. III. (Sept., 1834), p. 477. S. Julien in the *Revue de l'Orient et de l'Algerie*, XX., p. 74, 1856.

leaves, and reeds, were all used for writing upon with a sharp stick or stile. About the third century before Christ, silk and cloth were employed, and hair pencils made for writing. Paper was invented about the first century, and cotton-paper may have been brought from India, where it was in use more than a hundred years before. India ink was manufactured by the seventh century; and the present mode of printing upon blocks was adopted from the discovery of Fungtau in the tenth century, of taking impressions from engraved stones. In the style of their notes and letters, the Chinese show both neatness and elegance; narrow slips of tinted paper are employed, on which various emblematic designs are stamped in water lines, and enclosed in fanciful envelopes. It is common to affix a cipher instead of the name, or to close with a periphrasis or sentence well understood by the parties, and thereby avoid any signature; this, which originated, no doubt, in a fear of interception and unpleasant consequences, has gradually become a common mode of subscribing friendly epistles.

The mode of printing is so well fitted for the language that few improvements have been made in its manipulations, while the cheapness of books brings them within reach of the poorest. Cutting the blocks, and writing the characters, form two distinct branches of the business; printing the sheets, binding the volumes, and publishing the books, also furnish employment to other craftsmen. The first step is to write the characters upon thin paper, properly ruled with lines, two pages being cut upon one block, and a heavy double line surrounding them. The title of the work, chapter, and paging are all cut in a central column, and when the leaf is printed it is folded through this column so as to bring the characters on the edge and partly on both pages. Marginal notes are placed on the top of the page; comments, when greatly extended, occupy the upper part, separated from the text by a heavy line, or when mere scholia, are interlined in the same column in characters of half the size. Sometimes two works are printed together, one running through the volume on the upper half of the leaves, and separated from that occupying the lower half by a heavy line. Illustrations usually occupy separate pages at the commencement of the book, but there are a few works with woodcuts of a wretched description, inserted in the body of the page. In books printed by government, each page is sometimes surrounded with dragons, or the title page is adorned in red by this emblem of imperial authority.

When the leaf has been written out as it is to be printed, it is turned over and pasted upon the block, face downward. The wood usually used by blockcutters is pear or plum; the boards are half or three-fourths of an inch thick, and planed for cutting on both sides. The paper, when dried upon the board, is carefully rubbed off with the wetted finger, leaving every character and stroke plainly delineated. The cutter then, with his chisels, cuts away all the blank spots in and around the characters, to the depth of a line or more, after which the block is ready for the printer, whose machinery is very simple. Seated before a bench, he lays the block on a bed of paper so that it will not move nor chafe. The pile of paper lies on one side, the pot of ink before him, and the pressing brush on the other. Taking the ink brush, he slightly rubs it across the block twice in such a way as to lay the ink equably over the surface; he then places a sheet of paper upon it, and over that another, which serves as a tympanum. The impression is taken with the fibrous bark of the gomuti palm; one or two sweeps across the block complete the impression, for only one side of the paper is printed. Another and cheaper method in common use for publishing slips of news, court circulars, etc., consists in cutting the characters in blocks of hard wax, from which as many as two hundred impressions can often be taken before they become entirely illegible. The ink is manufactured from lampblack mixed with vegetable oil; the printers grind it for themselves.

The sheets are taken by the binder, who folds them through the middle by the line around the pages, so that the columns shall register with each other, he then collates them into volumes, placing the leaves evenly by their folded edge, when the whole are arranged, and the covers pasted on each side. Two pieces of paper stitch it through the back, the book is trimmed, and sent to the bookseller. If required, it is stitched firmly with thread, but this part, as well as writing the title on the bottom edges of the volume, and making the pasteboard wrapper, are usually deferred till the taste of a purchaser is ascertained. Books made of such materials are not as durable as European volumes, and those who can afford the expense frequently have valuable works inclosed in wooden boxes. They are printed of all sizes between small *sleeve* editions (as the Chinese call 24 and 32 mos) up to quartos, twelve or fourteen inches square, larger than which it is difficult to get blocks.

The price varies from one cent—for a brochure of twenty-five or thirty pages—to a dollar and a half a volume. It is seldom higher save for illustrated works. A volume rarely contains more than a hundred leaves, and in fine books their thickness is increased by inserting an extra sheet inside of each leaf. At Canton or Fuhchau, the *History of the Three States*, bound in twenty-one volumes 12mo, printed on white paper, is usually sold for seventy-five cents or a dollar per set. Kanghí's Dictionary, in twenty-one volumes 8vo, on yellow paper, sells for four dollars; and all the nine classics can be purchased for less than two. Books are hawked about the streets, circulating libraries are carried from house to house upon movable stands, and booksellers' shops are frequent in large towns. No censorship, other than a prohibition to write about the present dynasty, is exercised upon the press; nor are authors protected by a copyright law. Men of wealth sometimes show their literary taste by defraying the expense of getting the blocks of extensive works cut, and publishing them. Pwan Sz'-ching, a wealthy merchant at Canton, published, in 1846, an edition of the *Pei Wăn Yun Fu*, in one hundred and thirty thick octavo volumes, the blocks for which must have cost him more than ten thousand dollars. The number of good impressions which can be obtained from a set of blocks is about sixteen thousand, and by retouching the characters, ten thousand more can be struck off.

The disadvantages of this mode of printing are that other languages cannot easily be introduced into the page with the Chinese characters; the blocks occupy much room, are easily spoiled or lost; and are incapable of correction without much expense. It possesses some compensatory advantages peculiar to the Chinese and its cognate languages, Manchu, Corean, Japanese, etc., all of which are written with a brush and have few or no circular strokes. Its convenience and cheapness, coupled with the low rate of wages, will no doubt make it the common mode of printing Chinese among the people for a long time.

The honor of being the first inventor of movable types undoubtedly belongs to a Chinese blacksmith named Pí Shing, who lived about A.D. 1000, and printed books with them nearly five hundred years before Gutenberg cut his matrices at Mainz. They were made of plastic clay, hardened by fire after the characters had been cut on the soft surface of a plate of clay in which they were moulded. The porcelain types were then set up in a frame of iron partitioned off by strips, and inserted in a cement of wax, resin, and lime to fasten them down. The printing was done by rubbing, and when completed the types were loosened by melting the cement, and made clean for another impression.

This invention seems never to have been developed to any practical application in superseding block-printing. The Emperor Kanghí ordered about two hundred and fifty thousand copper types to be engraved for printing publications of the government, and these works are now highly prized for their beauty. The cupidity of his successors led to melting these types into cash, but his grandson Kienlung directed the casting of a large font of lead types for government use.

The attention of foreigners was early called to the preparation of Chinese movable types, especially for the rapid manufacture of religious books, in connection with missionary work. The first fonts were made by P. P. Thoms, for the E. I. Company's office at Macao in 1815, for the purpose of printing Morrison's Dictionary. The characters were cut with chisels on blocks of type metal or tin, and though it was slow work to cut a full font, they gradually grew in numbers and variety till they served to print over twenty dictionaries and other works, designed to aid in learning Chinese, before they were destroyed by fire in 1856. A small font had been cast at Serampore in 1815, and in 1838, the Royal Printing Office at Paris had obtained a set of blocks engraved in China, from which thick castings were made and the separate types obtained by sawing the plates. M. Le Grand, a type-founder in Paris, about the year 1836, prepared an extensive font of type with comparatively few matrices, by casting the radical and primitive on separate bodies; and the plan has been found, within certain limits, to save so much expense and room that it has been adopted in other fonts.

These experiments in Europe showed the feasibility of making and using Chinese type to any extent, but their results as to elegance and accuracy of form were not satisfactory, and proved that native workmen alone could meet the native taste. Rev. Samuel Dyer of the London Mission at Singapore began in 1838, under serious disadvantages, for he was not a practical printer, to cut the matrices for two complete fonts. He continued at his self-appointed task until his death in 1844, having completed only one thousand eight hundred and forty-five punches. His work was continued by R. Cole, of the American Presbyterian Missions, a skilful mechanic in his line, and in 1851 he was able to furnish fonts of two sizes with four thousand seven hundred characters each. Their form and style met every requirement of the most fastidious taste, and they are now in constant use.

While Mr. Dyer's fonts were suspended by his death, an attempt was made by a benevolent printer, Herr Beyerhaus of Berlin, to make one of an intermediate size on the Le Grand principle of divisible types; his proposal was taken up by the Presbyterian Board of Missions in New York, and after many delays a beautiful font was completed and in use about 1859. At this time, Mr. W. Gamble of that Mission in Shanghai, carried out his plan of making matrices by the electrotype process, and completed a large font of small pica type in about as many months as Dyer and Beyerhaus had taken years. By means of these various fonts books are now printed in many parts of China, in almost any style, and type foundries cast in whatever quantities are needed. The government has opened an extensive printing office in Peking, and its example will encourage native booksellers to unite typography with xylographic printing. More than this as conducing to the diffusion of knowledge among the people is the stimulus these cheap fonts of type have given to the circulation of newspapers in all the ports; but for their convenient and economical use Chinese newspapers could not have been printed at all. It will be quite within the reach of native workmen, who are skilled in electrotyping, stereotyping, and casting type, to make types of all sizes and styles for their own books, as the growing intelligence of the people creates a demand for illustrated and scientific publications, as well as cheap ones.'

Nothing has conduced more to a misapprehension of the nature of the Chinese language than the way in which its phonetic character has been spoken of by different authors. Some, describing the primitive symbols, and the modifications they have undergone, have conveyed the impression that the whole language consisted of hieroglyphic or ideographic signs, which depicted ideas, and conveyed their meaning entirely to the eye, irrespective of the sound. For instance, Rémusat says, "The character is not the delineation of the sound, nor the sound the expression of the character;" forgetting to ask himself how or when a character in any language ever delineated a sound. Yet every Chinese character is sounded as much as the words in alphabetic languages, and some have more than one to express their different meanings; so that, although the character could not delineate the sound of the thing it denoted, the sound is the expression of the character. Others, as Mr. Lay,[2] have dissected the characters, and endeavored to trace back some analogy in the meanings of all those in which the same primitive is found, and by a sort of analysis, to find out how much of the signification of the radical was infused into the primitive to form the present meaning. His plan, in general terms, is to take all the characters containing a certain primitive, and find out how much of the meaning of that primitive is contained in each one; then he reconstructs the series by defining the primitive, incidentally showing the intention of the framers of the characters in choos-

[1] *Chinese Repository*, Vol. III., pp. 246–252, 528; Vol. XIV., p. 124; *Missionary Recorder*, January, 1875.

[2] *Chinese as They Are*, Chap. XXXIV.

ing that particular one, and apportioning so much of its aggregate meaning to each character as is needed, and adding the meaning of the radical to form its whole signification. If we understand his plan, he wishes to construct a formula for each group containing the same primitive, in which the signification of the primitive is a certain function in that of all the characters containing it; to add up the total of their meanings, and divide the amount among the characters, allotting a quotient to each one. Languages are not so formed, however, and the Chinese is no exception. Some of Mr. Lay's statements are correct, but his theory is fanciful. It is impossible to decide what proportion was made by combining a radical and a primitive with any reference to their meanings, according to Mr. Lay's theory, and how many of them were simply phonetic combinations; probably nine-tenths of the compound characters have been constructed on the latter principle.

The fifth class of syllabic symbols were formed by combining the symbolic and syllabic systems, so as to represent sound chiefly, but bearing in the construction of each one some reference to its general signification. The original hieroglyphics contained no sound, *i.e.*, were not formed of phonetic constituents; the object depicted had a name, but there was no clue to it. It was impossible to do both--depict the object, and give its name in the same character. At first, the number of people using these ideographic symbols being probably small, every one called them by the same name, as soon as he knew what they represented, and began to read them. But when the ideas attempted to be written far exceeded in number the symbols, or, what is more likely, the invention of the limmers, recourse was had to the combination of the symbols already understood to express the new idea. This was done in several modes, as noticed above, but the syllabic system needs further explanation, from the extent to which it has been carried. The character 蝻 *nan*, to denote the young of the locust, has been adduced. The same principle would be applied in *reading* every new character, of which the phonetic primitive merely was recognized, although its meaning might not be known. Probably all the characters in the fifth class were sounded in strict accordance with their phonetic primitives when constructed, but usage has changed some of their sounds, and many characters belonging to other classes, apparently containing the same primitive, are sounded quite differently; this tends to mislead those who infer the sound from the primitive. This mode of constructing and naming the characters also explains the reason why there are so few sounds compared with the number of characters; the phonetic primitive perpetuated its name in all its progeny.

More than seven-eighths of the characters have been formed from less than two thousand symbols, and it is difficult to imagine how it could have been used so long and widely without some such method to relieve the memory of the burden of retaining thousands of arbitrary marks. But, until the names and meanings of the original symbols are learned, neither the sound nor sense of the compound characters will be more apparent to a Chinese than they are to any one else; until those are known, their combinations cannot be understood, nor even then the meaning wholly deduced; each character must be learned by itself, just as words in other languages. The sounds given the original symbols doubtless began to vary early after coming into use. Intercommunication between different parts of the country was not so frequent as to prevent local dialects from arising; but however strong the tendency of the spoken monosyllables to coalesce into polysyllables, the intractable symbols kept them apart. It is surprising, too, what a tendency the mind has to trust to the eye rather than to the ear, in getting and retaining the sense of a book; it is shown in many ways, and arises from habit more than any real difficulty in catching the idea *vivâ voce*. If the characters could have coalesced, their names would soon have run together, and been modified as they are in other languages. The classics, dictionaries, and unlimited uses of a written language, maintained the same meaning; but as their sounds must be learned traditionally, endless variations and patois arose. Moreover, as new circumstances and increasing knowledge give rise to new words in all countries, so in China, new scenes and expressions arise requiring to be incorporated into the written language. Originally they were unwritten though well understood sounds; and when first written must be explained, as is the case with foreign words like *tabu*, *ukase*, *vizier*, etc., *ad infin.*, when introduced into English. Different writers might, however, employ different primitives to express the sound, not aware that it had already been written, and hence would arise synonyms; they might use dissimilar radicals, and this as well would increase the modes of writing the sound. But the inconvenience of thus multiplying characters would be soon perceived in the obscurity of the sentence, for if the new character was not in the dictionary, its sound and composition were not enough to explain the meaning. When the language had attained a certain copiousness, the mode of education and the style of literary works compelled scholars to employ such characters only as were sanctioned by good use, or else run the risk of not being understood.

The unwritten sounds, however, could not wait for this slow mode of adoption, but the risk of being misunderstood by using characters phonetically led to descriptive terms, conveying the idea and not the sound. Where alphabetic languages adopt a technic for a new thing, the Chinese make a new phrase. This is illustrated by the terms *Hung-mao jin*, or 'Red Bristled men,' for Englishmen; *Hwa-kí*, or 'Flowery Flag,' for Americans; *Si-yang*, or 'Western Ocean,' for Portuguese, etc., used at Canton, instead of the proper names of those countries. Cause and effect act reciprocally upon each other in this instance; the effect of using unsanctioned characters to express unwritten sounds, is to render a composition obscure, while the restriction to a set of characters compels their meaning to be sufficiently comprehensive to include all occasions. Local, unwritten phrases, and unauthorized characters, are so common, however, owing to the partial communication between distant parts of so great a country and mass of people, that it is evident, if this bond of union were removed by the substitution of an alphabetical language, the Chinese would soon be split into many small nations. However desirable, therefore, might be the introduction of a written language less difficult of acquisition, and more flexible, there are some reasons for wishing it to be delayed until more intelligence is diffused and juster principles of government obtain. When the people themselves feel the need of it, they will contrive some better medium for the promotion of knowledge.

The monosyllabic sound of the primitive once imparted to the ideophonous compound, explains the existence of so many characters having the same sound. When these various characters were presented to the eye of the scholar, no trouble was felt in recognizing their sense and sound, but confusion was experienced in speaking. This has been obviated in two ways. One is by repeating a word, or joining two of similar meanings but of different sounds, to convey a single idea; or else by adding a classifying word to express its nature. Both these modes do in fact form a real dissyllable, and it would appear so in an alphabetical language. The first sort of these *hien-hioh sz'*, or 'clam-shell words,' as they are called, are not unfrequent in books, far more common in conversation and render the spoken more diffuse than the written language—more so, perhaps, than is the case in other tongues. Similar combinations of three, four, and more characters occur, especially where a foreign article or term is translated, but the genius of the language is against the use of polysyllables. Such combinations in English as *household*, *house-warming*, *housewife*, *house-room*, *houseleeks*, *hot-house*, *wood-house*, *household-stuff*, etc., illustrate these dissyllables in Chinese; but they are not so easily understood. Such terms as *understand*, *courtship*, *withdraw*, *upright*, etc., present better analogies to the Chinese compounds. In some the real meaning is totally unlike either of the terms, as *tungkia* (lit. 'east house'), for master; *tungsí* (lit. 'east west'), for thing; *kungchu* (lit. 'lord ruler'), for princess, etc. The classifiers partake of the nature of adjectives, and serve not only to sort different words, but the same word when used in different senses. They correspond to such words in English as *herd*, *fleet*, *troop*, etc. To say a fleet of cows, a troop of ships, or a herd of soldiers, would be ridiculous only in English, but a similar misapplication would confuse the sense in Chinese.

The other way of avoiding the confusion of homophonous monosyllables, which, notwithstanding the "clam-shell words," and the extensive use of classifiers, are still liable to misapprehension, is by accurately marking its right *shing* or tone, but as nothing analogous to them is found in European languages, it is rather difficult to describe them. At Canton there are eight arranged in an upper and lower series of four each; at Peking there are only four, at Nanking five, and at Swatow seven. The Chinese printers sometimes mark the *shing* on certain ambiguous characters, by a semicircle put on one corner: but this is rarely done, as every one who can read is supposed to know how to speak, and consequently to be familiar with the right tone. These four tones are called *ping*, *shang*, *kü*, and *jih*, meaning, respectively, the *even*, *ascending*, *departing*, and *entering* tone. They are applied to every word, and have nothing to do either with accent or emphasis; in asking or answering, entreating or refusing, railing or flattering, soothing or recriminating, they remain ever the same. The unlettered natives, even children and females, who know almost nothing of the distinctions into four, five, seven, or eight *shing*, observe them closely in their speech, and detect a mispronunciation as soon as the learned man. A single illustration of them will suffice. The *even* tone is the natural expression of the voice, and native writers consider it the most important. In the sentence,

"When I asked him, 'Will you let me see it?' he said, 'No, I'll do no such thing,'"

the different cadence of the question and reply illustrate the upper and lower even tone. The *ascending* tone is heard in exclamatory words as *ah! indeed!* It is a little like the crescendo in music, while the *departing tone* corresponds in the same degree to the diminuendo. The drawling tone of repressed discontent, grumbling and eking out a reply, is not unlike the departing tone. The entering tone is nearly eliminated in the northern provinces, but gives a marked feature to speech in the southern; it is an abrupt ending, in the same modulation that the even tone is, but as if broken off; a man about to say *lock*, and taken with a hiccup in the middle so that he leaves off the last two letters, or the final consonant, pronounces the *juh shing*. A few characters have two tones, which give them different meanings; the *ping shing* often denotes the substantive, and the *kü shing*, the verb, but there is no regularity in this respect.

The tones are observed by natives of all ranks, speaking all patois and dialects, and on all occasions. They present a serious difficulty to the adult foreigner of preaching or speaking acceptably to the natives, for although by a proper use of classifiers, observance of idioms, and multiplication of synonyms, he may be understood, his speech will be rude and his words distasteful, if he does not learn the tones accurately. In Amoy and Fuhchau, he will also run a risk of being misunderstood. If the reader, in perusing the following sentence, will accent the italicized syllables, he will have an imperfect illustration of the confusion a wrong intonation produces: "The pre*sent* of that ob*ject* occasioned such a trans*port* as to *ab*stract my mind from all around." In Chinese, however, it is not *accent* upon one of two syllables which must be learned, but the integral tone of a single sound, as much as in the musical octave.

It is unnecessary here to enter into any detailed description or enumeration of the words in the Chinese language. One remarkable feature is the frequency of the termination *ng* preceded by all the vowels, which imparts a peculiar singing character to Chinese speech, as *Kwangtung*, *Yangtsz' kiang*, etc. In a list of sounds in the court dialect, about one-sixth of the syllables have this termination, but a larger proportion of characters are found under those syllables, than the mere list indicates. In Morrison's Dictionary the number of separate words in the court dialect is 411, but if the aspirated syllables be distinguished, there are 533. In the author's *Syllabic Dictionary* the number is 532; Wade reduces the Peking dialect to 397 syllables in one list, and increases it to 420 in another. In the Cantonese there are 707; in the dialect of Swatow, 674; at Amoy, about 900; at Fuhchau, 928; and 660 at Shanghai. All these lists distinguish between aspirated and unaspirated words, as *ting* and *t'ing*, *pa* and *p'a*, which to an English ear are nearly identical. The largest part of the sounds are common to the dialects, but the distinctions are such as to render it easy to detect each when spoken; the court dialect is the most mellifluous of the whole and easiest to acquire. All the consonants in English are found in one or another of the dialects, besides many not occurring in that language, as *bw*, *chw*, *gw*, *jw*, *lw*, *mw*, *nw*, etc. There are also several imperfect vowel sounds not known in any European language, as *hm* or *'m*, *hn* or *'n*, ^{ng} (a high nasal sound), *sz'*, *'rh*, *ch'*, etc. The phrase *'m 'ng tăk* in the Canton dialect, meaning *cannot be pushed*, or *chain*^{n} *mai*^{n} *lang*, 'a blind man,' in the Amoy, cannot be so accurately expressed by these or any other letters that one can learn the sound from them. If it is difficult for us to express their sounds by Roman letters, it is still stranger for the Chinese to write English words. For instance, *baptize* in the Canton dialect becomes *pa-pí-tai-sz'*; *flannel* becomes *fat-lan-yin*; *stairs* becomes *sz'-ta-sz'*; *impregnable* becomes *ím-pí-luk-na-pu-lí*; etc. Such words as *Washington*, *midshipman*, *tongue*, etc., can be written nearer their true sound, but the indivisible Chinese monosyllables offer a serious obstacle in the way of introducing foreign words and knowledge into the language.

The preceding observations explain how the numerous local variations from the general language found in all parts of China have arisen. Difficult as the spoken language is for a foreigner to acquire, from the brevity of the words and nicety of their tones, the variety of the local pronunciations given to the same character adds not a little to the labor, especially if he be situated where he is likely to come in contact with persons from different places. Amid such a diversity of pronunciation, and where one sound is really as correct as another, it is not easy to define what should constitute a dialect, a patois, or a corruption. A dialect in other languages is usually described as a local variation in pronunciation, or the use of peculiar words and expressions, not affecting the idiom or grammar of the tongue; but in the Chinese, where the written character unites the mass of people in one language, a dialect has been usually regarded by those who have written on the subject, as extending to variations in the idiom, and not restricted to differences in pronunciation and local expressions. According to this definition, there are only four or five dialects (which would in fact be as many languages if they were not united by the written character), but an endless variety of patois or local pronunciations. The Chinese have published books to illustrate the court, Changchau or Amoy, the Canton and Fuhchau dialects. The differences in the idioms and pronunciation are such as to render persons speaking them mutually unintelligible, but do not affect the style of writing, whose idioms are founded upon the usage of the best writers, and remain unchanged.

The court language, the *kwan hwa*, or mandarin dialect, is rather the proper language of the country—*the Chinese language*—than a dialect. It is studied and spoken by all educated men, and no one can make any pretence to learning or accomplishments who cannot converse in it in whatever part of the Empire he may be born. It is the common language throughout the northeastern provinces, especially Honan, Shantung, and Nganhwui, though presenting more or less variations even in them from the standard of the court and capital. This speech is characterized by its soft and mellifluous tones, the absence of all harsh, consonantal endings, and the prevalence of liquids and labials. In parts of the provinces where it is spoken, as the eastern portions of Chehkiang and Kiangsu, gutturals are common, and the initials softened or changed.

This tongue is the most ancient speech now spoken, for stanzas of poetry written twenty-five centuries ago, in the times previous to Confucius, are now read with the same rhymes as when penned. The expressions of the *kwan hwa*, although resembling the written language more than the other dialects, are still unlike it, being more diffuse, and containing many synonyms and particles not required to make the sense clear when it is addressed to the eye. The difference is such in this respect that two well-educated Chinese speaking in the terse style of books would hardly understand each other, and be obliged to use more words to convey their meaning when speaking than they would consider elegant or necessary in an essay. This is, to be sure, more or less the case in all languages, but from the small variety of sounds and their monosyllabic brevity, it is unavoidable in Chinese, though it must not be inferred that the language cannot be written so as to be understood when read off; it can be written as diffusely as it is spoken, but such a style is not considered very elegant. There are books written in the colloquial, however, from which it is not difficult to learn the style of conversation, and such books are among the best to put into the hands of a foreigner when beginning the study.

The local patois of a place is called *tu tan*, or *hiang tán*, *i.e.*, local or village brogue, and there is an interpreter of it attached to almost every officer's court for the purpose of translating the peculiar phrases of witnesses and others brought before him. The term *dialect* cannot, strictly, in its previous definition, be applied to the *tu tan*, though it is usually so called; it is a patois or brogue. The Canton dialect is called by its citizens *pak wa*, 'the plain speech,' because it is more intelligible than the court dialect. It is comparatively easy of acquisition, and differs less from the *kwan hwa*, in its pronunciation and idioms, than that of Amoy and its vicinity; but the diversity is still enough to render it unintelligible to people from the north. A very few books have been written in it, but none which can afford assistance in learning it. A native scholar would consider his character for literary attainments almost degraded if he should write books in the provincial dialects, and forsake the style of the immortal classics. The principal feature in the pronunciation of the Canton dialect which distinguishes it from the general language, is the change of the abrupt vowel terminations, as *loh*, *kiah*, *pih*, into the well-defined consonants *k*, *p*, and *t*, as *lok*, *kap*, *pít*, a change that considerably facilitates the discrimination of the syllables. The idioms of the two cannot well be illustrated without the help of the written character, but the differences between the sounds of two or three sentences may be exhibited: The phrase, *I do not understand what he says*, is in the

Court dialect: *Wo min puh tụng teh ta kiang shim mo.*

Canton dialect: *Ngo 'm hiu kü kong măt yé.*

The rice contains sand in it.

Court dialect: *Na ko mí yu sha tsz'.*

Canton dialect: *Ko tik mai yau sha tsoi noi.*

None of the provincial patois differ so much from the *kwan hwa*, and afford so many peculiarities, as those spoken in the province of Fuhkien and eastern portions of Kwangtung. All of them are nasal, and, compared with those spoken elsewhere, harsh and rough. They have a large number of unwritten sounds, and so supply the lack; the same character often has one sound when read and another when spoken; all of them are in common use. This curious feature obliges the foreigner to learn two parallel languages when studying this dialect, so intimate and yet so distinct are the two. The difference between them will be more apparent by quoting a sentence: "He first performed that which was difficult, and afterward imitated what was easier." The corresponding words of the colloquial are placed underneath the reading sounds.

Sien k'i su chí sé lan, jí ho k'i hau chí sé tek.
Tai seng chó i é su é sé oh, jí tui au k'w^{n}a i é hau giern é sé tit tióh.

The changes from one into the other are exceedingly various both in sound and idiom. Thus, *bien chien*, 'before one's face,' becomes *bin chan* when spoken; while in the phrase *cheng jit*, 'a former day,' the same word *chien* becomes *cheng* and not *chan*; *bòé chu*, 'pupil of the eye,' becomes *ang a*; *sit hwan*, 'to eat rice,' becomes *chiah pui^{n}*. Their dialect, not less than their trafficking spirit, point out the Amoy people wherever they are met, and as they are usually found along the whole coast and in the Archipelago, and are not understood except by their provincial compatriots, they everywhere clan together and form separate communities. Dr. Medhurst published a dictionary of the Changchau dialect, in which the sounds of the characters are given as they are read. Dr. C. Douglas has gathered a great vocabulary of words and phrases used in the Amoy colloquial, in which he has attempted to reduce everything to the Romanized system of writing, and omitted all the characters.

The dialects of Fuhchau, Swatow, and Canton have been similarly investigated by Protestant missionaries. Messrs. Maclay and Baldwin have taken the former in hand, and their work leaves very little to be desired for the elucidation of that speech. Goddard's vocabulary of the Swatow has no examples; and Williams' *Tonic Dictionary* of the Canton dialect gave no characters with the examples. This deficiency was made up in Lobscheid's rearrangement of it under the radicals.

The extent to which the dialects are used has not been ascertained, nor the degree of modification each undergoes in those parts where it is spoken; for villagers within a few miles, although able to understand each other perfectly, still give different sounds to a few characters, and have a few local phrases, enough to distinguish their several inhabitants, while towns one or two hundred miles apart are still more unlike. For instance, the citizen of Canton always says *shui* for water, and *tsz'* for child, but the native of Macao says *sui* and *chí* for these two words; and if his life depended upon his uttering them as they are spoken in Canton, they would prove a shibboleth which he could not possibly enunciate. Strong peculiarities of speech also exist in the villages between Canton and Macao which are found in neither of those places. Yet whatever sound they give to a character it has the same tone, and a Chinese would be much less surprised to hear water called ‡*chwui*, than he would to hear it called ♭*shui* in the lower even tone, instead of its proper ascending tone. The tones really approach vowels in their nature more than mere musical inflections; and it is by their nice discrimination, that the people are able to understand each other with less difficulty than we might suppose amidst such a jargon of vocables.

This accurate discrimination in the vowel sounds, and comparative indifference to consonants, which characterize the Chinese spoken languages, has arisen, no doubt, from the monosyllabic nature, and the constant though slight variations the names of characters undergo from the traditionary mode in which they must be learned. There being no integral sound in any character, each and all of them are, of course, equally correct, *per se*; but the various general and local dictionaries have each tended somewhat to fix the pronunciation, just as books and education have fixed the spelling of English words. Nor do the Chinese more than other people learn to pronounce their mother tongue from dictionaries, and the variations are consequently but partially restrained by them. It may truly be said, that no two Chinese speak all words alike, while yet, through means of the universally understood character, the greatest mass of human beings ever collected under one government are enabled to express themselves without difficulty, and carry on all the business and concerns of life.

The grammar of the Chinese language is unique, but those writers who say it has no grammar at all must have overlooked the prime signification of the word. There are in all languages words which denote things, and others which signify qualities; words which express actions done by one or many, already done, doing or to be done; actions absolute, conditional, or ordered. The circumstances of the doer and the subject of the action, make prepositions necessary, as well as other connecting words. Thus the principles of grammar exist in all intelligible speech, though each may require different rules. These rules the Chinese language possesses, and their right application, the proper collocation of words, and use of particles, which supply the place of inflection, constitute a difficult part in its acquisition. It has no etymology, properly speaking, for neither the characters nor their names undergo any change; whether used as verbs or nouns, adjectives or particles, they remain the same. The same word may be a noun, a verb, an adverb, or any part of speech, nor can its character be certainly known till it is placed in a sentence, when its meaning becomes definite. Its grammar, therefore, is confined chiefly to its syntax and prosody. This feature of the Chinese language is paralleled in English by such words as *light*, used as a noun, adjective, and verb; *like*, used as a verb, adjective, and adverb; *sheep* and *deer*, used both in the singular and plural; *read*, used in the past, present, and future tenses; and in all cases without undergoing any change. But what is occasional and the exception in that tongue, becomes the rule in Chinese; nor is there any more confusion in the last than in the first.

A good summary of the principles of Chinese grammar is given by Rémusat, who says that generally,

"In every Chinese sentence, in which nothing is understood, the elements of which it is composed are arranged in the following order: the subject, the verb, the complement direct, and the complement indirect.

"Modifying expressions precede those to which they belong: thus, the adjective is placed before the substantive, subject, or complement; the substantive governed before the verb that governs it; the adverb before the verb, the proposition incidental, circumstantial, or hypothetical, before the principal proposition, to which it attaches itself by a conjunction expressed or understood.

"The relative position of words and phrases thus determined, supplies the place often of every other mark intended to denote their mutual dependence, their character whether adjective or adverbial, positive, conditional, or circumstantial.

"If the subject be understood, it is because it is a personal pronoun, or that it is expressed above, and that the same substantive that is omitted is found in the preceding sentence, and in the same quality of subject, and not in any other.

"If the verb be wanting, it is because it is the substantive verb, or some other easily supplied, or one which has already found place in the preceding sentences, with a subject or complement not the same.

"If several substantives follow each other, either they are in construction with each other, or they form an enumeration, or they are synonyms which explain and determine each other.

"If several verbs succeed each other, which are not synonyms and are not employed as auxiliaries, the first ones should be taken as adverbs or verbal nouns, the subjects of those which follow; or these latter as verbal nouns, the complements of those which precede."

Chinese grammarians divide all words into *shih tsz'* and *'hü tsz'*, *i.e.*, essential words and particles. The former are subdivided into *sz' tsz'* and *hwoh tsz'*, *i.e.*, nouns and verbs; the latter into initials or introductory words, conjunctions, exclamations, finals, transitive particles, etc. They furnish examples under each, and assist the student, with model books, in which the principles of the language and all rhetorical terms are explained. The number and variety of grammatical and philological works prove that they have not neglected the elucidation and arrangement of their mother tongue. The rules above cited are applicable to the written language, and these treatises refer entirely to that; the changes in the phraseology of the colloquial do not affect its grammar, however, which is formed upon the same rules.

Although the characters are, when isolated, somewhat indefinite, there are many ways of limiting their meaning in sentences. Nouns are often made by suffixing formative particles, as *nu kí*, 'angry spirit,' merely means *anger; í kí*, 'righteous spirit,' is *rectitude; chin 'rh*, 'needle child,' is a needle, etc.; the suffix, in these cases, simply materializing the word. Gender is formed by distinctive particles, prefixed or suffixed by appropriate words for each gender, or by denoting one gender always by a dissyllabic compound; as *male*-being, for the masculine; horse-*sire*, or horse-*mother*, for stallion or dam; *hero*, *heroine*, *emperor*, *empress*, etc.; and lastly as *wang-hau*, *i.e.*, king-*queen*, for *queen*, while *wang* alone means *king*. Number is formed by prefixing a numeral, as *Yung*, *Tsin*, *two* men; by suffixing a formative, *mun*, *tăng*, and others, as *jin-tăng*, man-*sort*, or men; *ta-mun*, he-*s* or they; by repeating the word, as *jin-jin*, man-man or *men; chu-chu*, place-place, or places, *i.e.*, everywhere; and lastly, by the scope of the passage. The nominative, accusative, and vocative cases are commonly known by their position; the genitive, dative, and ablative are formed by appropriate prepositions, expressed or understood. The vocative is common in light reading and historical studies.

Adjectives precede nouns, by which position they are usually determined. Comparisons are made in many ways. *Hau* is *good*, *kăng hau* is *better*, and *chí hau* is *best; shih făn hau hau* is *very good; hau hau tih* is *pretty good*, etc. The position of an adjective determines its comparison, as *chang yih chih* means *longer by one cubit; yih chih chang* is a *cubit long*. The comparison of ideas is made by placing the two sentences parallel to each other; for instance, "Entering the hills and seizing a tiger is easy, opening the mouth and getting men to lean to is difficult," is the way of expressing the comparison, "It is easier to seize a tiger in the hills, than to obtain the good offices of men." The proper use of antithesis and parallelism is considered one of the highest attainments in composition. The numerals are thirteen in number, with the addition of the character 零 *ling* to denote a cipher. All amounts are written just as they are to be read, as *yih peh sz' shih san*, 一百四十三 *i.e.*, 'one hundred four tens three.' They are here introduced, with their pronunciation in three dialects.

	1	2	3	4	5	6	7	8	9	10	100	1,000	10,000
	一	二	三	四	五	六	七	八	九	十	百	千	萬
Court Dialect.	*yih*	*'rh*	*san*	*sz'*	*wu*	*luh*	*tsih*	*pah*	*kiu*	*shih*	*peh*	*tsien*	*wan.*
Canton Dialect.	*yat*	*í*	*sam*	*sz'*	*'ng*	*luk*	*tsat*	*pat*	*kau*	*shap*	*pak*	*tsín*	*man.*
Fuhkien Dialect.	*it*	*jí*	*sam*	*su*	*ngou*	*liok*	*chit*	*pat*	*kiu*	*sip*	*pek*	*chien*	*ban.*

The Chinese, like the ancient Greeks, enumerate only up to a myriad, expressing sums higher than that by stating how many myriads there are; the notation of 362,447,180 is three myriads, six thousand, two hundred and forty-four myriads, seven thousand, one hundred, and eighty. Pronouns are few in number, and their use is avoided whenever the sense is clear without them. The personal pronouns are three, *wo*, *ní*, and *ta*, but other pronouns can all be readily expressed by adjectives, by collocation, and by participial phrases. The classifiers sometimes partake of the nature of adjective pronouns, but usually are mere distributive or numerical adjectives.

Verbs, or "living characters," constitute the most important part of speech in the estimation of Chinese grammarians, and the *shun tuh*, or easy flow of expression, in their use, is carefully studied. The dissyllabic compounds, called *clam-shell words*, are usually verbs, and are made in many ways; by uniting two similar words, as *kwei-kien* (lit. peep-look), 'to spy;' by doubling the verb, as *kien-kien*, meaning to look earnestly; by prefixing a formative denoting action, as *ta shwui* (lit. strike sleep), 'to sleep;' by suffixing a modifying word, as *grasp-halt*, to grasp firmly; *think-arise*, to cogitate, etc. No part of the study requires more attention than the right selection of these formatives in both nouns and verbs; perfection in the *shun tuh* and use of antitheses is the result only of years of study.

The various accidents of voice, mood, tense, number, and person, can all be expressed by corresponding particles, but the genius of the language disfavors their frequent use. The passive voice is formed by prefixing particles indicative of agency before the active verb, as "The villain *received* my sword's *cutting*," for "The villain was wounded by my sword." The imperative, potential, and subjunctive moods are formed by particles or adjuncts, but the indicative and infinitive are not designated, nor are the number and person of verbs usually distinguished. The number of auxiliaries, particles, adjuncts, and suffixes of various kinds, employed to express what in other languages is denoted by inflections, is really very moderate; and a nice discrimination exhibited in their use indicates the finished scholar.[1]

---

[1] *Chinese Repository*, Vol. VIII., p. 347.

The greatest defect in the Chinese language is the indistinct manner in which time is expressed; not that there is any want of terms to denote its varieties, but the terseness of expression admired by Chinese writers leads them to discard every unessential word, and especially those relating to time. This defect is more noticed by the foreigner than the native, who has no knowledge of the precision of time expressed by inflection in other languages. Adverbs, prepositions, conjunctions, and interjections are not distinguished by native grammarians; the former are classed with adjectives, and the others are collectively called *hü tsz'*—'empty words.'

No distinction is made between proper and common names, and as every word can be employed as a name it becomes a source of confusion to the translator; in some books a single line drawn on the side of characters denotes the names of persons, and a double line the names of places; important words are denoted by commencing a new line with them, raised one or two characters above the other columns, which answers to capitalizing them. In most books an entire absence of all marks of punctuation, and divisions into sentences and paragraphs, causes needless doubt in the mind of the reader. The great convenience experienced in European languages from the use of capital letters, marks of punctuation, separation into sentences and paragraphs, and the distinction of time, is more plainly seen when a translation is to be made from languages like the Chinese and Japanese, in which they are disregarded. A false taste prevents them from using them; they admire a page of plain characters so much that a student who should punctuate his essay would run a risk of being ridiculed.

It is not easy yet to decide on the best way to adapt the technical words in western science to the genius of this language. The vast terminology in natural history, with the still greater array of scientific names, need not be introduced into it, but can remain in their original Latin and Greek, where Chinese scientists can consult them. New compounds have already been proposed for gases, metals, earths, acids, and other elementary substances, in which the radical and primitive are chosen with reference to their meanings, the latter being more complicated than usual for this purpose. These will gradually get into use as the sciences are studied, and their number will not be troublesomely large.

There are several distinct styles of composition recognized. The *ku wăn*, or the terse antithetic style of the ancient classics, is considered as inimitable and unimprovable, and really possesses the qualities of energy, vivacity, and brevity in a superior degree; the *wăn chang*, or style of elevated composition, adopted in essays, histories, and grave works; and the *siao shwoh*, or colloquial style, used in stories.

If there are serious defects, this language also possesses some striking beauties. The expressive nature of the characters, after their component parts have become familiar, causes much of the meaning of a sentence to pass instantly before the eye, while the energy arising from the brevity attainable by the absence of all inflections and partial use of particles, add a vigor to the style that is hardly reached by any alphabetic language. Dr. Morrison observes that "Chinese fine writing darts upon the mind with a vivid flash, a force and a beauty, of which alphabetic language is incapable." It is also better fitted than any other for becoming a universal medium of communication, and has actually become so to a much greater extent than any other; but the history of its diffusion, and the modifications it has undergone among the five nations who use it, though presenting a curious topic for philological inquiry, is one far too extensive to be discussed here. So general a use of one written language, however, affords some peculiar facilities for the diffusion of knowledge by means of books as introductory to the general elevation of the people using it, and their preparation for substituting an alphabetic language for so laborious and unwieldy a vehicle of thought, which it seems impossible to avoid as Christian civilization and knowledge extend.

It is often asked, is the Chinese language hard to learn? The preceding account of it shows that to become familiar with its numerous characters, to be able to speak the delicately marked tones of its short monosyllables, and to compose in it with perspicuity and elegance, is the labor of years of close application. To do so in Greek, Latin, English, or any settled tongue, is also a toilsome task, and excepting the barren labor of remembering so many different characters, it is not more so in Chinese than in others. But knowledge sufficient to talk intelligibly, to write perspicuously, and read with considerable ease, is not so herculean a task as some suppose, though this degree is not to be attained without much hard study. Moreover, dictionaries, manuals, and translations are now available which materially diminish the labor, and their number is constantly increasing.

The rules for studying it cannot be laid down so that they will answer equally well for all persons. Some readily catch the most delicate inflections of the voice, and imitate and remember the words they hear; such persons soon learn to speak, and can make themselves understood on common subjects with merely the help of a vocabulary. Others prefer to sit down with a teacher and learn to read, and for most persons this is the best way to begin. At first, the principal labor should be directed to the characters, reading them over with a teacher and learning their form. Commence with the two hundred and fourteen radicals, and commit them to memory, so that they can be repeated and written in their order; then learn the primitives, or at least become familiar with the names and meaning of all the common ones. The aid this preliminary study gives in remembering the formation of characters is worth all the time it takes. Students make a mistake if they begin with the Testament or a tract; they can learn more characters in the same period, and lay a better foundation for acquiring others, by commencing with the radicals and primitives. Meanwhile, they will also be learning sounds and becoming familiar with the tones, which should be carefully attended to as a particular study from the living voice.

When these characters are learned, short sentences or reading lessons selected from good *Chinese* authors, with a translation attached, should be taken up and committed to memory. Phrases may also be learned at the same time, for use in conversation; an excellent way is to memorize one or two hundred common words, and then practise putting them together in sentences. The study of reading lessons and phrases, with practice in speaking and writing them, will prepare the way for commencing the study of the classics or other native authors. By the time the student has reached this point he needs no further directions; the path he wishes thenceforth to pursue can easily be marked out by himself. It is not amiss here to remark that many persons ardently desirous of fitting themselves soon for preaching or talking to the people, weary their minds and hinder their ultimate progress by too hard study at first upon the dry characters; others come to look upon the written language as less important so long as they can talk rapidly and well, but in the end find that in this, as in every other living tongue, there is no royal road which does not lead them through the grammar and literature.[1]

This sketch of the Chinese language would be incomplete without a notice of the singular jargon which has grown up between the natives and foreigners along the coast, called *pigeon-English.* It has been so long in use as the medium of traffic and household talk that it now bids fair to become an unwritten patois, of which neither the Chinese nor the English will own the parentage. The term *pigeon*, a corruption from *business*, shows, in its transformation, some of the influences which our words must undergo as they pass through the Chinese characters. The foreigners who first settled at Canton had no time nor facilities for learning the dialect, and the traders with whom they bargained soon picked up more foreign words than the former did native. The shopmen ere long formed vocabularies of foreign words obtained from their customers, and wrote the sounds as nearly as possible; these were committed to memory and formed into sentences according to the idioms of their own language, and disregarding all our inflections, in which they had no instruction. Thus the two parties gradually came to understand each other enough for all practical ends; the foreigners were rather pleased to talk

[1] Many aids in learning the general language and all the leading dialects have been prepared in English, French, German, and Portuguese, but several of the early ones, as Morrison, Gonçalves, Medhurst, and Bridgman, are already out of print. The names of all of these may be found most easily in the first volume of M. Cordier's exhaustive *Dictionnaire Bibliographique des ouvrages relatifs à l'Empire chinois*, pp. 725–804. Paris, 1881.

"broken China," as it was not inaptly called, and habit soon made it natural to a new-comer to talk it to the natives, and it obviated all necessity for studying Chinese. The body of the jargon is English, the few Chinese, Portuguese, and Malay words therein imparting a raciness which, with the novelty of the expressions, has of late attracted much attention to this new language. Though apparently without any rules, the natives are very liable to misapprehend what is said to them by their masters or customers, because these rules are not followed, and constant difficulty arises from mutual misunderstanding of this sort. The widening study of Chinese is not likely to do away with this droll lingo at the trade ports, and several attempts have been made to render English pieces into it. On the other hand, in California and elsewhere, the Chinese generally succeed in learning the languages of their adopted countries better than in talking *pigeon-English*, or the similar mongrel vernacular spoken at Macao by the native-born Chinese.

A knowledge of the Chinese language is a passport to the confidence of the people, and when foreigners generally learn it the natives will begin to divest themselves of their prejudices and contempt. As an inducement to study, the scholar and the philanthropist have the prospect of benefiting and informing through it vast numbers of their fellow-men, of imparting to them what will elevate their minds, purify their hearts, instruct their understandings, and strengthen their desire for more knowledge; they have an opportunity of doing much to counteract the tremendous evils of the opium trade by teaching the Chinese the only sure grounds on which they can be restrained, and at the same time of making them acquainted with the discoveries in science, medicine, and arts among western nations.

CHAPTER XI.

CLASSICAL LITERATURE OF THE CHINESE.

THE literature contained in the language now briefly described is very ample and discursive, but wanting in accuracy and unenlivened by much variety or humor. The books of the Chinese have formed and confirmed their national taste, which consequently exhibits a tedious uniformity. The unbounded admiration felt for the classics and their immaculate authors, fostered by the examinations, has further tended to this result, and caused these writings to become still more famous from the unequalled influence they have exerted. It may be very readily seen, then, with what especial interest the student of Chinese sociology turns to an investigation of their letters, the immense accumulation of forty centuries. Were its amount and prominence the only features of their literature, these would suffice to make necessary some study thereof; but in addition, continued research may reveal some further qualities of "eloquence and poetry, enriched by the beauty of a picturesque language, preserving to imagination all its colors," which will substantiate the hearty expressions used by Rémusat when first he entered upon a critical examination of its treasures.

In taking a survey of this literature, the *Sz' Ku Tsiuen Shu Tsung-muh*, or 'Catalogue of all Books in the Four Libraries,' will be the best guide, since it embraces the whole range of letters, and affords a complete and succinct synopsis of the contents of the best books in the language. It is comprised in one hundred and twelve octavo volumes, and is of itself a valuable work, especially to the foreigner. The books are arranged into four divisions, viz., Classical, Historical, and Professional writings, and Belles-lettres. This Catalogue contains about 3,440 separate titles, comprising upward of 78,000 books; besides these, 6,764 other works, numbering 93,242 books, have been described in other catalogues of the imperial collections. These lists comprise the bulk of Chinese literature, except novels, Buddhist translations, and recent publications.

The works in the first division are ranged under nine sections; one is devoted to each of the five Classics (with a subsidiary section upon these as a whole), one to the memoir on Filial Duty, one to the Four Books, one to musical works, and the ninth to treatises on education, dictionaries, etc.

At the head of the 'Five Classics' (*Wu King*) is placed the *Yih King*, or 'Book of Changes,' a work which if not—as it has been repeatedly called—*Antiquissimus Sinarum liber*, can be traced with tolerable accuracy to an origin three thousand years ago. It ranks, according to Dr. Legge, third in antiquity among the Chinese classics, or after the *Shu* and portions of the *Shí King*; but if an unbounded veneration for enigmatical wisdom supposed to lie concealed under mystic lines be any just claim for importance, to this wondrous monument of literature may easily be conceded the first place in the estimation of Chinese scholars.

While following Dr. Legge in his recent exposition of this classic,[1] a clearer idea of its subject-matter can hardly be given than by quoting his words stating that "the text may be briefly represented as consisting of sixty-four short essays, enigmatically and symbolically expressed, on important themes, mostly of a moral, social, and political character, and based on the same number of lineal figures, each made up of six lines, some of which are whole and the others divided." The evolution of the eight diagrams from two original principles is ascribed to Fuh-hí (B.C. 3322), who is regarded as the founder of the nation, though his history is, naturally enough, largely fabulous. From the *Liang Í*, or 'Two Principles' (—) (– –), were fashioned the *Sz' Siang*, or 'Four Figures,' by placing these over themselves and each of them over the other, thus:

[1] *The Sacred Books of China. The Texts of Confucianism.* Translated by James Legge. Part II. *The Yî King.* Oxford, 1882.

The same pairs placed in succession under the original lines formed eight trigrams called the

PAH KWA of FUH-HÍ.

☰	☱	☲	☳	☴	☵	☶	☷
kien	*tui*	*lí*	*chin*	*siuen*	*kan*	*kăn*	*kwăn*
Heaven, the Sky.	Water collected, as in a marsh or lake.	Fire, as in lightning; the Sun.	Thunder.	The Wind; Wood.	Water, as in rain, clouds, springs, streams, and defiles. The Moon.	Hills or Mountains.	The Earth.
S.	S.E.	E.	N.E.	S.W.	W.	N.W.	N.
Untiring strength; power.	Pleasure; complacent satisfaction.	Brightness; elegance.	Moving, exciting power.	Flexibility; penetration.	Peril; difficulty.	Resting the act of arresting.	Capaciousness; submission.

The table furnishes us with the natural objects that these figures are said to represent, the attributes which should seem to be suggested by them, and which, with the application of the eight points of the compass, together form the material for a cabalistic logomancy peculiarly pleasing to Chinese habits of thought. The trigrams furnish, moreover, the state and position, at any given place or time, of the twofold division of the one primordial *kí*, or 'Air,' called *Yang* and *Yin*, and have thus become the source from whence the system of *Fung-shui* is derived and on whose changes it is founded. This substance *kí* answers sufficiently closely to the animated air of the Grecian philosopher Anaximenes; its divisions are a subtle and a coarse principle which, acting and reacting upon each other, produce four *siang*, or 'forms,' and these again combine into eight *kwa*, or trigrams. Fuh-hí is thus said to have arranged the first four of the *Pah Kwa* under the *Yang* (strong or hard) principle, and the last four under the *Yin* (weak or soft) principle; the former indicate vigor or authority, and it is their part to command, while of the latter, representing feebleness or submission, it is the part to obey.

It was probably Wăn Wang, King Wăn, chief of the principality of Chau in 1185 B.C., who when thrown into prison by his jealous suzerain Shau, the tyrant of Shang, arranged and multiplied the trigrams—long before his time used for purposes of divination—into the sixty-four hexagrams as they now occur in the *Yih King*. His was a wholly different disposition, both of names, attributes, and the compass points, from the original trigrams of Fuh-hí; again, he added to them certain social relations of father, mother, three sons, and three daughters, which has ever since been found a convenient addition to the conjuring apparatus of the work. "I like to think," says Dr. Legge, "of the lord of Chau, when incarcerated in Yu-lí, with the sixty-four figures arranged before him. Each hexagram assumed a mystic meaning and glowed with a deep significance. He made it to tell him of the qualities of various objects of nature, or of the principles of human society, or of the condition, actual and possible, of the kingdom. He named the figures each by a term descriptive of the idea with which he had connected it in his mind, and then he proceeded to set that idea forth, now with a note of exhortation, now with a note of warning. It was an attempt to restrict the follies of divination within the bounds of reason. . . . But all the work of King Wăn in the *Yih* thus amounts to no more than sixty-four short paragraphs. We do not know what led his son Tan to enter into his work and complete it as he did. Tan was a patriot, a hero, a legislator, and a philosopher. Perhaps he took the lineal figures in hand as a tribute of filial duty. What had been done for the whole hexagram he would do for each line, and make it clear that all the six lines 'bent one way their precious influence,' and blended their rays in the globe of light which his father had made each figure give forth. But his method strikes us as singular. Each line seemed to become living, and suggested some phenomenon in nature, or some case of human experience, from which the wisdom or folly, the luckiness or unluckiness, indicated by it could be inferred. It cannot be said that the duke carried out his plan in a way likely to interest any one but a *hien shăng* who is a votary of divination and admires the style of its oracles. According to our notions, a framer of emblems should be a good deal of a poet; but those of the *Yih* only make us think of a dryasdust. Out of more than three hundred and fifty, the greater number are only grotesque. We do not recover from the feeling of disappointment till we remember that both father and son had to write 'according to the trick,' after the manner of diviners, as if this lineal augury had been their profession."

Such is the text of the *Yih*. The words of King Wăn and his son are followed by commentaries called the *Shih Yih*, or 'Ten Wings.' These are of a much later period than the text, and are commonly ascribed to Confucius, though it is extremely doubtful if the sage was author of more than the sentences introduced by the oft-repeated formula, "The Master said," occurring in or concluding many chapters of the 'Wings.' Without lingering over the varied contents of these appendices, more than to point out that the fifth and sixth Wings ('Appended Sentences'), known as the 'Great Treatise,' contains for the first time the character *Yih*, or 'Change,' it will be necessary, before leaving this classic, to illustrate its curious nature by means of a single quotation.

XXXI.—THE *HIEN* HEXAGRAM.

Hien indicates that [on the fulfilment of the conditions implied in it] there will be free course and success. Its advantageousness will depend on the being firm and correct, [as] in marrying a young lady. There will be good fortune.

1. The first line, divided, shows one moving his great toes.

2. The second line, divided, shows one moving the calves of his leg. There will be evil. If he abide [quiet in his place] there will be good fortune.

3. The third line, undivided, shows one moving his thighs, and keeping close hold of those whom he follows. Going forward [in this way] will cause regret.

4. The fourth line, undivided, shows that firm correctness which will lead to good fortune and prevent all occasion for repentance. If its subject be unsettled in his movements, [only] his friends will follow his purpose.

5. The fifth line, undivided, shows one moving the flesh along the spine above the heart. There will be no occasion for repentance.

6. The sixth line, divided, shows one moving his jaws and tongue.

An idea of the several commentaries, or 'Wings,' upon such a passage may be gained from the following excerpts. First comes the 'Treatise on the Twan,' or King Wăn's paragraphs; then the 'Treatise on the Symbols,' consisting of observations on Duke Chau's exposition.

From the *Second Wing.*—1. *Hien* is here used in the sense of *Kan*, meaning [mutually] influencing.

2. The weak [trigram] above, and the strong one below; their two influences moving and responding to each other, and thereby forming a union; the repression [of the one] and the satisfaction [of the other]; [with their relative position] where the male is placed below the female—all these things convey the notion of 'a free and successful course [on the fulfilment of the conditions], while the advantage will depend on being firm and correct, as in marrying a young lady, and there will be good fortune.' . . . etc., etc.

Fourth Wing.—[The trigram representing] a mountain and above it that for [the waters of] a marsh form *Hien.* The superior man, in accordance with this, keeps his mind free from preoccupation, and open to receive [the influences of] others.

1. 'He moves his great toe'—his mind is set on what is beyond [himself].

2. Though 'there would be evil, yet if he abide [quiet] in his place there will be good fortune'—through compliance [with the circumstances of his condition and place] there will be no injury.

3. 'He moves his thighs'—he still does not [want to] rest in his place. His will is set on 'following others;' what he holds in his grasp is low.

4. 'Firm correctness will lead to good fortune, and prevent all occasion for repentance'—there has not yet been any harm from [a selfish wish to] influence. 'He is unsettled in his movements'—[his power to influence] is not yet either brilliant or great.

5. 'He [tries to] move the flesh along the spine above the heart'—his aim is trivial.

6. 'He moves his jaws and tongue'—he [only] talks with loquacious mouth.

Sixth Wing ('Appended Sentences').—Chapter I.—1. The eight trigrams having been completed in their proper order, there were in each the [three] emblematic lines. They were then multiplied by a process of addition till the [six] component lines appeared.

2. The strong line and the weak push themselves each into the place of the other, and hence the changes [of the diagrams] take place. The appended explanations attach to every form of them its character [of good or ill], and hence the movements [suggested by divination] are determined accordingly.

3. Good fortune and ill, occasion for repentance or regret, all arise from these movements . . . etc., etc.

The hundreds of fortune-tellers seen in the streets of Chinese towns, whose answers to their perplexed customers are more or less founded on these cabala, indicate their influence among the illiterate; while among scholars, who have long since conceded all divination to be vain, it is surprising to remark the profound estimation in which these inane lines are held as the consummation of all wisdom—the germ, even, of all the truths which western science has brought to light! Each hexagram is supposed to represent, at any given time, six different phases of the primordial *ki*. "As all the good and evil in the world," observes McClatchie, "is attributed by the Chinese philosophers to the purity or impurity of the animated air from which the two-fold soul in man is formed, a certain moral value attaches to each stroke, and the diviner prognosticates accordingly that good or evil luck, as the case may be, will result to the consulter of the oracle with regard to the matter on which he seeks it. Nine is the number of Heaven, or the undivided stroke, and six is the number of Earth, or the divided stroke, and hence each stroke has a double designation. The first stroke, if undivided, is designated 'First-Nine,' but if divided it is designated 'First-Six,' and so on. The second and fifth strokes in each diagram are important, being the centre or medium strokes of their respective lesser diagrams. The fifth stroke, however, is the most important in divination, as it represents that portion of the air which is the especial throne of the imperial power, and is the 'undeflected due medium.' Nothing but good luck can follow if the person divining with the straws obtains this stroke. Tao, or the Divine Reason, which is the supreme soul of the whole Kosmos, animates the air, pervading its six phases, and thus giving power to the diagrams to make known future events to mankind."

Of course anything and everything could be deduced from such a fanciful groundwork, but the Chinese have taken up the discussion in the most serious manner, and endeavored to find the hidden meaning and evolutions of the universe from this curious system. The diagrams have, moreover, supplied the basis for many species of divination by shells, letters, etc., by which means the mass of the people are deluded into the belief of penetrating futurity, and still more wedded to their superstitions. The continued influence of such a work as the *Yih* illustrates the national *penchant* for laws and method, while equally indicating the general indifference to empirical research and the facts deduced from study of natural history. If, from a philosophical standpoint, we consider the barrenness of its results, there is little, indeed, to say for the *Yih King*, save concurrence in Dr. Gustave Schlegel's epithet, "a mechanical play of idle abstractions;" nevertheless, this classic contains in its whimsical dress of inscrutable strokes much of practical wisdom, giving heed to which it is not hard to agree with Dr. Legge in concluding that "the inculcation of such lessons cannot have been without good effect in China during the long course of its history."[1]

The second section of the Imperial Catalogue contains treatises upon the *Shu King*, or 'Book of Records.' This classic,

[1] Some fourteen hundred and fifty treatises on the *Yih*—consisting of memoirs, digests, expositions, etc. —are enumerated in the Catalogue. The foreign literature upon it has heretofore been scant. The only other translations of the classic *in extenso*, besides Dr. Legge's, already quoted, are the *Y-King; Antiquissimus Sinarum liber quem ex latina interpretatione;* P. Regis, *aliorumque ex Soc. Jesu P.P.*, *edidit* Julius Mohl, 2 vols., Stuttgart, 1834–39; and *A Translation of the Confucian Yih King, or the Classic of Change*, by the Rev. Canon McClatchie, Shanghai, 1876 (with Chinese text). Compare further *Notice du livre chinois nommé Y-king, avec des notes, par* M Claude Visdelou, contained in Père Gaubil's *Chou king*, Paris, 1843; *Die verbogenen Alterthümer der Chineser aus dem uralten Buche Yeking untersuchet, von* M. Joh. Heinrich Schuhmacher, Wolfenbüttel, 1763; Joseph Haas, in *Notes and Queries on China and Japan*, Vol. III., 1869; *China Review*, Vols. I., p. 151; IV., p. 257; and V., p. 132.

first in importance as it is in age among the five *King*, consists of a series of documents relating to the history of China from the times of Yao down to King Hiang, of the Chau dynasty (B.C. 2357–627). Its earlier chapters were composed at periods following the events of which they relate, but after the twenty-second century B.C. the *Shu* comes to us, though in a mutilated condition, as the contemporary chronicle of proclamations, addresses, and principles of the early sovereigns. Internal evidence leads to the conclusion that Confucius acted chiefly as editor of documents existing in his day; he probably wrote the preface, but what alterations it received at his hand cannot now be ascertained. When it left his care it contained eighty-one documents in one hundred books, arranged under the five dynasties of Yao, Shun, Hia, Shang, and Chau, the last one coming down to within two hundred and twenty-one years of his own birth. Most of these are lost, and others are doubted by Chinese critics, so that now only forty-eight documents remain, thirty of them belonging to the Chau, with the preface ascribed to Confucius. He showed his estimate of their value by calling the whole *Shang Shu*, or the 'Highest Book,' and we may class their loss with that of other ancient works in Hebrew or Greek literature. The *Shu King* now contains six different kinds of state papers, viz., imperial ordinances, plans drawn up by statesmen as guides for their sovereign, instructions prepared for the guidance of the prince, imperial proclamations and charges to the people, vows taken before Shangti by the monarch when going out to battle, and, lastly, mandates, announcements, speeches, and canons issued to the ministers of state.[1]

The morality of the *Shu King*, for a pagan work, is extremely good; the principles of administration laid down in it, founded on a regard to the welfare of the people, would, if carried out, insure universal prosperity. The answer of Kaoyao to the

[1] Several translations have been made by missionaries. One by P. Gaubil was edited by De Guignes in 1770; a second by Rev. W. H. Medhurst, in 1846; but the most complete by J. Legge, D.D., in 1865, with its notes and text, has brought this *Record* better than ever before to the knowledge of western scholars.

monarch Yu is expressive of a mild spirit: "Your virtue, O Emperor, is faultless. You condescend to your ministers with a liberal ease; you rule the multitude with a generous forbearance. Your punishments do not extend to the criminal's heirs, but your rewards reach to after-generations. You pardon inadvertent faults, however great, and punish deliberate crime, however small. In cases of doubtful crimes you deal with them lightly; of doubtful merit, you prefer the highest estimate. Rather than put to death the guiltless, you will run the risk of irregularity and laxity. This life-loving virtue has penetrated the minds of the people, and this is why they do not render themselves liable to be punished by your officers." [1]

In the counsels of Yu to Shun are many of the best maxims of good government, both for rulers and ruled, which antiquity has handed down in any country. The following are among them: "Yih said, Alas! Be cautious. Admonish yourself to caution when there seems to be no reason for anxiety. Do not fail in due attention to laws and ordinances. Do not find enjoyment in indulgent ease. Do not go to excess in pleasure. Employ men of worth without intermediaries. Put away evil advisers, nor try to carry out doubtful plans. Study that all your purposes may be according to reason. Do not seek the people's praises by going against reason, nor oppose the people to follow your own desires. Be neither idle nor wayward, and even foreign tribes will come under your sway."

The *Shu King* contains the seeds of all things that are valuable in the estimation of the Chinese; it is at once the foundation of their political system, their history, and their religious rites, the basis of their tactics, music, and astronomy. Some have thought that the knowledge of the true God under the appellation of Shangti is not obscurely intimated in it, and the precepts for governing a country, scattered through its dialogues and proclamations, do their writers credit, however little they may have been followed in practice. Its astronomy has attracted much investigation, but whether the remarks of the commentators are to be ascribed to the times in which they

---

[1] Legge, *The Chinese Classics*, Vol. III. *Shoo King*, p. 59.

themselves flourished, or to the knowledge they had of the ancient state of the science, is doubtful. The careful and candid discussions by Legge in the introduction to his translation furnish most satisfactory conclusions as to the origin, value, and condition of this venerable relic of ancient China. For his scholarly edition of the *Classics* he has already earned the hearty thanks of every student of Chinese literature.[1]

The third of the classics, the *Shí King*, or 'Book of Odes,' is ranked together with the two preceding, while its influence upon the national mind has been equally great; a list of commentators upon this work fills the third section of the Catalogue. These poetical relics are arranged into four parts: The *Kwoh Fung*, or 'National Airs,' numbering one hundred and fifty-nine, from fifteen feudal States; the *Siao Ya*, or 'Lesser Eulogiums,' numbering eighty, and arranged under eight decades; the *Ta Ya*, or 'Greater Eulogiums,' numbering thirty-one, under three decades (both of these were designed to be sung on solemn occasions at the royal court); and the *Sung*, or 'Sacrificial Odes,' numbering forty-one chants connected with the ancestral worship of the rulers of Chau, Lu, and Shang. Out of a total number of three hundred and eleven now extant, six have only their titles preserved, while to a major part of the others native scholars give many various readings.

In the preface to his careful translation Dr. Legge has collected all the important information concerning the age, origin, and purpose of these odes, as furnished by native commentators, whose theory is that "it was the duty of the kings to make themselves acquainted with all the odes and songs current in

---

[1] *Chinese Repository*, Vol. VIII., p. 385; Vol. IX., p. 573. *Le Chou-king, un des Livres Sacrés des Chinois, qui renferme les Fondements de leur ancienne Histoire*, etc. Traduit par Feu le P. Gaubil. Paris, 1770, in-4. *La Morale du Chou-king ou le Livre Sacré de la Chine.* (The same), Paris, 1851. *Ancient China. The Shoo King, or the Historical Classic: being the most ancient authentic Record of the Annals of the Chinese Empire*, translated by W. H. Medhurst, Sen., Shanghae, 1846. *Nouveau Journal Asiatique*, Tomes V. (1830), p. 401; VI., p. 401, and XIV. (1842), p. 152. *China Review*, Vol. IV., p. 13. Dr. Legge's translation has recently (1879) appeared, without the Chinese text, in Max Müller's series of *Sacred Books of the East*, Vol. III. Richthofen, *China*, Bd. I., pp. 277–365, an exhaustive treatise on the early geography of China, with valuable historical maps.

the different States, and to judge from them of the character of the rule exercised by their several princes, so that they might minister praise or blame, reward or punishment accordingly." These odes and songs seem to have been gathered by Wăn Wang and Duke Chau at the beginning of the Chau dynasty (B.C. 1120), some of them at the capital, others from the feudal rulers in the course of royal progresses through the land, the royal music-master getting copies from the music-masters of the princes. The whole were then arranged, set to music, too, it may be, and deposited for use and reference in the national archives, as well as distributed among the feudatories. Their ages are uncertain, but probably do not antedate B.C. 1719 nor come after 585, or about thirty years before Confucius. Their number was not improbably at first fully up to the three thousand mentioned by the biographers of Confucius, but long before the sage appeared disasters of one kind and another had reduced them to nearly their present condition. What we have is, therefore, but a fragment of various collections made in the early reigns of the Chau sovereigns, which received, perhaps, larger subsequent additions than were preserved to the time of Confucius. He probably took them as they existed in his day, and feeling, possibly, like George Herbert, that

> " A verse may finde him, who a sermon flies,
> And turn delight into a sacrifice,"

did everything he could to extend their adoption among his countrymen. It is difficult to estimate the power they have exerted over the subsequent generations of Chinese scholars—nor has their influence ever tended to debase their morals, if it has not exalted their imagination. They have escaped the looseness of Moschus, Ovid, or Juvenal, if they have not attained the grandeur of Homer or the sweetness of Virgil and Pindar. There is nothing of an epic character in them—nor even a lengthened narrative—and little of human passions in their strong development. The metaphors and illustrations are often quaint, sometimes puerile, and occasionally ridiculous. Their acknowledged antiquity; their religious character, and their illustration of early Chinese customs and feelings form their principal claims to our notice and appreciative study. M. Ed. Biot, of Paris, was the first European scholar who studied them carefully in this aspect, and his articles in the *Journal Asiatique* for 1843 are models of analytic criticism and synthetic compilation, enabling one, as he says, "to contemplate at his ease the spectacle of the primitive manners of society in the early age of China, so different from what was then found in Europe and Western Asia."

An ode referred to the time of Wăn Wang (a contemporary of Saul) contains a sentiment reminding us of Morris' lines beginning "Woodman, spare that tree." It is in Part I., Book II., and is called *Kan-tang*, or the 'Sweet pear-tree.'

1. O fell not that sweet pear-tree!
   See how its branches spread.
Spoil not its shade,
For Shao's chief laid
   Beneath it his weary head.

2. O clip not that sweet pear-tree!
   Each twig and leaflet spare—
'Tis sacred now,
Since the lord of Shao,
   When weary, rested him there.

3. O touch not that sweet pear-tree!
   Bend not a twig of it now;
There long ago,
As the stories show,
   Oft halted the chief of Shao.[1]

The eighth ode in Book III., called *Hiung Chí*, or 'Cock Pheasant,' contains a wife's lament on her husband's absence.

1. Away the startled pheasant flies,
   With lazy movement of his wings;
Borne was my heart's lord from my eyes—
   What pain the separation brings!

2. The pheasant, though no more in view,
   His cry below, above, forth sends.
Alas! my princely lord, 'tis you,—
   Your absence, that my bosom rends.

---

[1] Dr. Legge, *The She King, translated into English verse*, p. 70. London, 1876.

3. At sun and moon I sit and gaze,
   In converse with my troubled heart.
Far, far from me my husband stays!
   When will he come to heal its smart?

4. Ye princely men, who with him mate,
   Say, mark ye not his virtuous way?
His rule is, covet nought, none hate:
   How can his steps from goodness stray?[1]

From the same book we translate somewhat freely an example (No. 17) of love-song, or serenade, not uncommon among these odes.

Maiden fair, so sweet, retiring,
   At the tryst I wait for thee;
Still I pause in doubt, inquiring
   Why thou triflest thus with me.

Ah! the maid so coy, so handsome,
   Pledged she with a rosy reed;
Than the reed is she more winsome.
   Love with beauty hard must plead!

In the meadows sought we flowers,
   These she gave me—beauteous, rare:
Far above the gift there towers
   The dear giver—lovelier, fair!

Among the 'Lesser Eulogiums' (Book IV., Ode 5) is one more ambitious in its scope, relating to the completion of a palace of King Siuen, about B.C. 800.

1. On yonder banks a palace, lo! upshoots,
   The tender blue of southern hill behind,
Time-founded, like the bamboo's clasping roots;
   Its roof, made pine-like, to a point defined.
Fraternal love here bears its precious fruits,
   And unfraternal schemes be ne'er designed!

2. Ancestral sway is his. The walls they rear
   Five thousand cubits long, and south and west
The doors are placed. Here will the king appear,
   Here laugh, here talk, here sit him down and rest.

[1] *Ib.*, p. 83.

3. To mould the walls, the frames they firmly tie;
   The toiling builders beat the earth and lime;
The walls shall vermin, storm, and bird defy—
   Fit dwelling is it for his lordly prime.

4. Grand is the hall the noble lord ascends;
   In height, like human form, most reverent, grand;
And straight, as flies the shaft when bow unbends;
   Its tints like hues when pheasant's wings expand.

5. High pillars rise the level court around;
   The pleasant light the open chamber steeps,
And deep recesses, wide alcoves are found,
   Where our good king in perfect quiet sleeps.

6. Laid is the bamboo mat on rush mat square;
   Here shall he sleep; and waking say, "Divine
What dreams are good? For bear and piebald bear,
   And snakes and cobras haunt this couch of mine."

7. Then shall the chief diviner glad reply,
   "The bears foreshow their signs of promised sons.
The snakes and cobras daughters prophesy:
   These auguries are all auspicious ones."

8. Sons shall be his—on couches lulled to rest;
   The little ones enrobed, with sceptres play;
Their infant cries are loud as stern behest,
   Their knees the vermeil covers shall display.
As king hereafter one shall be addressed;
   The rest, our princes, all the States shall sway.

9. And daughters also to him shall be born.
   They shall be placed upon the ground to sleep;
Their playthings tiles, their dress the simplest worn;
   Their part alike from good and ill to keep,
And ne'er their parents' hearts to cause to mourn;
   To cook the food, and spirit-malt to steep.[1]

The last two stanzas indicate the comparative estimate, in ancient days, of boys and girls born into a family; and this estimate, still maintained, has been in a great degree upheld by this authority. Another ode in the 'Greater Eulogies' (Book III., Ode 10) deplores the misery that prevailed about B.C. 780, owing to the interference of women and eunuchs in the govern-

[1] *Id.*, *The She King*, p. 222.

ment. Two stanzas only are quoted, which are supposed to have been specially directed against Pao Sz', a mischief-maker in the court of King Yu, like Agrippina and Pulcheria in Roman and Byzantine annals.

3. A wise man builds the city wall,
   But a wise woman throws it down.
Wise is she ? Good you may her call;
   She is an owl we should disown!
To woman's tongue let scope be given
   And step by step to harm it leads.
Disorder does not come from Heaven;
   'Tis woman's tongue disorder breeds.
Women and eunuchs! Never came
   Lesson or warning words from them!

4. Hurtful and false, their spite they wreak;
   And when exposed their falsehood lies—
The wrong they do not own, but sneak
   And say, "No harm did we devise."
"Thrice cent. per cent.!" Why, that is trade!
   Yet 'twould the princely man disgrace.
So public things to wife and maid
   Must not silkworms and looms displace.[1]

There are, however, numerous stanzas among the odes in the 'National Airs' which show their fairer side and go far to neutralize these, giving the same contrasts in female character which were portrayed by King Solomon during the same age.

The versification in a monosyllabic language appears very tame to those who are only familiar with the lively and varied rhythms of western tongues; but the Chinese express more vivacity and cadence in their ballads and ditties when sung than one would infer from these ancient relics when transliterated in our letters. As the young lad has usually committed all the three hundred and five odes to memory before he enters the Examination Hall, their influence on the matter and manner of his own future poetical attempts can hardly be exaggerated. It is shown throughout the thousands of volumes enumerated in the fourth division of the Imperial Catalogue. Most of the

---

[1] *Id.*, *The She King*, p. 347.

Shí King is written in tetrametres, and nothing can be more simple. They have been most unfortunately likened to the Hebrew Psalms by some of the early missionaries, but neither in manner nor matter is the comparison a happy one. One point of verbal resemblance is noticed by Dr. Legge between the first ode in Part III. and the one hundred and twenty-first psalm, where the last line of a stanza is generally repeated in the first line of the next, a feature something like the repetitions in *Hiawatha.* The rhymes and tones both form an essential part of Chinese poetry, one which can only be imperfectly represented in our language. The following furnishes an example of the general style, to which a literal rendering is subjoined:

1. *Nan yin kiao muh,*	South has stately trees,
Puh k'o hiu sih ;	Not can shelter indeed ;
Han yin yin nü,	Han has rambling women,
Puh k'o kiu sz'.	Not can solicit indeed.
Han chí kwang i,	Han's breadth be sure,
Puh k'o yung sz';	Not can be dived indeed ;
Kiang chí yung i	Kiang's length be sure,
Puh k'o fang sz'.	Not can be rafted indeed.
2. *Kiao kiao tso sin,*	Many many mixed faggots,
Yen i kí chu ;	Willingly I cut the brambles ;
Chí tsz' yü kwei	Those girls going home,
Yen moh kí ma ;	Willingly I would feed their horses ;
Han chí kwang i, etc.	Han's breadth be sure, etc.
3. *Kiao kiao tso sin,*	Many many mixed faggots,
Yen i kí lao ;	Willingly I cut the artemisia ;
Chí tsz' yü kwei	Those girls going home,
Yen moh kí kü.	Willingly I would feed their colts ;
Han chí kwang i, etc.	Han's breadth be sure, etc.

The highest range of thought in the odes is contained in Part IV., but the whole collection is worthy of perusal, and through the labors of Dr. Legge has been made more accessible than it was ever before. The amount of native literature extant, illustrative, critical, and philological, referring to the *Book of Odes*[1] is not so large as that on the *Yih King ;* but the

[1] A recent German translation of these odes has combined, with much accuracy and a smooth versification, the peculiar adaptability of that tongue to the

fifty-five works quoted in his preface [1] contain enough to indicate their industry and acumen. These works will elevate the character of Chinese scholarship in the opinion of those foreigners who remember the disadvantages of its isolation from the literature of other lands, and the difficulties of a language which rendered that literature inaccessible.[2]

The fourth section in the Catalogue contains the Rituals and a list of their editions and commentators, but only one of the three is numbered among the *King* and used as a text-book at the public examinations. This is the *Lí Kí*, or 'Book of Rites,' the *Memorial des Rites*, as M. Callery calls it in his translation,[3] and one of the works which has done so much to mold and maintain Chinese character and institutions. It is not superior in any respect to the *Chau Lí* and the *Í Lí*, but owes its influence to its position. They were all the particular objects of Tsin Chí Hwangti's ire in his efforts to destroy every ancient literary production in his kingdom; the present texts were recovered from their hiding-places about B.C. 135. The *Chau Lí*, or 'Ritual of Chau,' is regarded as the work of Duke Chau (B.C. 1130), who gives the detail of the various offices established under the new dynasty, in which he bore so prominent a part. The sections containing the divisions of the administrative part of the Chinese government of that day have furnished the types for the six boards of the present day and their subdivisions. So far as we now know, no nation then existing could show so methodical and effective a system of national polity.

---

reproduction (in some degree) of sounds so foreign to the language as Chinese. *Shi King. Das kanonische Liederbuch der Chinesen. Uebersetzt von* Victor von Strauss. Heidelberg, 1880.

[1] *The Chinese Classics*, Vol. IV., pp. 172–180. Hongkong, 1871.

[2] Compare *Confucii Chi-king sive Liber Carminum, ex latina* P. Lacharme *interpretatione edidit* J. Mohl, Stuttgart, 1830; *Essai sur le Chi-king, et sur l'ancienne poésie chinoise, par* M. Brosset jeune, Paris, 1828; *Bibliothèque orientale*, Vol.II., p. 247 (1872). *Chi-king, ou Livre des Vers*, Traduction de M. G. Pauthier; *China Review*, Vol. VI., pp. 1 ff. and 166 ff. *Journal N. C. Br. R. As. Soc.*, Vol. XII., pp. 97 ff.

[3] *Li-ki ou Mémorial des Rites, traduit pour la première fois du chinois, et accompagné de notes, de commentaires et du texte original, par* J. M. Callery. Turin et Paris, 1853.

The *I Lí* is a smaller work, treating of family affairs, and as its name, 'Decorum Ritual,' indicates, contains directions for domestic life, as the other does for state matters. That is in forty-four sections and this is in seven, and both are now accepted as among the most ancient works extant. The former was translated by Ed. Biot,[1] and remains a monument of his scholarship and research.

The *Lí Kí* owes its position among the classics to the belief that Confucius here gives his views on government and manners, although these chapters are not regarded as the same in their integrity as those said to have been found in the walls of his house, and brought to light in the second century B.C. by Kao Tang of Lu, under the name of *Sz' Lí*, or the 'Scholar's Ritual.' In the next century Tai Teh collected all the existing documents relating to the ancient rituals in two hundred and fourteen sections, only a portion of which were then held to have emanated from the sage and recorded by his pupils. His work, in eighty-five sections, is called *Ta Tai Lí*, or the 'Senior Tai's Ritual,' to distinguish it from the *Siao Tai Lí*, or the 'Junior Tai's Ritual,' a work in forty-nine sections, by his nephew, Tai Shing. This is the work now known as the *Lí Kí*, M. Callery's translation of which contains the authorized text of Kanghí according to Fan Tsz'-tăng, in thirty-six sections, with many notes. His translation is wearisome reading from the multitude of parentheses interjected into the text, distracting the attention and weakening its continuity.

Those who have read Abbé Huc's entertaining remarks on the Rites in China will find in these three works the reason and application of their details. In explanation of their importance, M. Callery shows in a few words what a wide field they cover: "Ceremony epitomizes the entire Chinese mind; and, in my opinion, the *Lí Kí* is *per se* the most exact and complete monograph that China has been able to give of itself to other nations. Its affections, if it has any, are satisfied by cere-

---

[1] *Le Tcheou-Li ou Rites des Tcheou, traduit pour la première fois du chinois, par* Feu Édouard Biot. 2 Tomes. Paris, 1851.

mony; its duties are fulfilled by ceremony; its virtues and vices are referred to ceremony; the natural relations of created beings essentially link themselves in ceremonial—in a word, to that people ceremonial is man as a moral, political, and religious being in his multiplied relations with family, country, society, morality, and religion." This explanation shows, too, how meagre a rendering *ceremony* is for the Chinese idea of *lí*, for it includes not only the external conduct, but involves the right principles from which all true etiquette and politeness spring. The state religion, the government of a family, and the rules of society are all founded on the true *lí*, or relations of things. Reference has already been made to this profoundly esteemed work (p. 520), and one or two more extracts will suffice to exhibit its spirit and style, singular in its object and scope among all the bequests of antiquity.

Affection between father and son.

In the Domestic Rules it is said, "Men in serving their parents, at the first cock-crowing, must all wash their hands; rinse their mouth; comb their hair; bind it together with a net; fasten it with a bodkin, forming it into a tuft; brush off the dust; put on the hat, tying the strings, ornamented with tassels; also the waistcoat, frock, and girdle, with the note-sticks placed in it, and the indispensables attached on the right and left; bind on the greaves; and put on the shoes, tying up the strings. Wives must serve their husband's father and mother as their own; at the first cock-crowing, they must wash their hands; rinse their mouth; comb their hair; bind it together with a net; fasten it with a bodkin, forming it into a tuft; put on their frocks and girdles, with the indispensables attached on the right and left; fasten on their bags of perfumery; put on and tie up their shoes. Then go to the chamber of their father and mother, and father-in-law and mother-in-law, and having entered, in a low and placid tone they must inquire whether their dress is too warm or too cool; if the parents have pain or itching, themselves must respectfully press or rub [the part affected]; and if they enter or leave the room, themselves either going before or following, must respectfully support them. In bringing the apparatus for washing, the younger must present the bowl; the elder the water, begging them to pour it and wash; and after they have washed, hand them the towel. In asking and respectfully presenting what they wish to eat, they must cheer them by their mild manner; and must wait till their father and mother, and father-in-law and mother-in-law have eaten, and then retire. Boys and girls, who have not arrived at the age of manhood and womanhood, at the first cock-crowing must wash their hands; rinse their mouth; comb their hair; bind it together with a net; and form it into a tuft;

brush off the dust; tie on their bags, having them well supplied with perfumery; then hasten at early dawn to see their parents, and inquire if they have eaten and drunk; if they have, they must immediately retire; but if not, they must assist their superiors in seeing that everything is duly made ready."

Of reproving parents.

"When his parents are in error, the son with a humble spirit, pleasing countenance, and gentle tone, must point it out to them. If they do not receive his reproof, he must strive more and more to be dutiful and respectful toward them till they are pleased, and then he must again point out their error. But if he does not succeed in pleasing them, it is better that he should continue to reiterate reproof, than permit them to do injury to the whole department, district, village, or neighborhood. And if the parents, irritated and displeased, chastise their son till the blood flows from him, even then he must not dare to harbor the least resentment; but, on the contrary, should treat them with increased respect and dutifulness."

Respect to be paid parents in one's conduct.

"Although your father and mother are dead, if you propose to yourself any good work, only reflect how it will make their names illustrious, and your purpose will be fixed. So if you propose to do what is not good, only consider how it will disgrace the names of your father and mother, and you will desist from your purpose."[1]

These extracts show something of the molding principles which operate on Chinese youth from earliest years, and the scope given in his education to filial piety. From conning such precepts the lad is imbued with a respect for his parents that finally becomes intensified into a religious sentiment, and forms, as he increases in age, his only creed—the worship of ancestors. His seniors, on the other hand, have but to point to the textbooks before him as authority for all things they exact, and as being the only possible source of those virtues that conduct to happiness. The position of females, too, has remained, under these dogmas, much the same for hundreds of years. Nor is it difficult to account for the influence which they have had. Those who were most aware of their excellence, and had had some experience in the tortuous dealings of the human heart, as husbands, fathers, mothers, officers, and seniors, were those who had the power to enforce obedience upon wives, children,

[1] *Chinese Repository*, Vol. V., pp. 306-312.

daughters, subjects, and juniors, as well as teach it to them. These must wait till increasing years brought about their turn to fill the upper rank in the social system, by which time habit would lead them to exercise their sway over the rising generation in the same manner. Thus it would be perpetuated, for the man could not depart from the way his childhood was trained; had the results been more disastrous, it would have been easy for us to explain why, amid the ignorance, craft, ambition, and discontent found in a populous, uneducated, pagan country, such formal rules had failed of benefiting society to any lasting extent. We must look higher for this result, and acknowledge the degree of wholesome restraint upon the passions of the Chinese which the Author of whatever is good in these tenets has seen fit to confer upon them in order to the preservation of society.

The fifth section contains the *Chun Tsiu*, or 'Spring and Autumn Record,' and its literature. This is the only one of the *King* attributed to Confucius, though whether we have in the *Record*, as it now exists, a genuine compilation of the sage, does not appear to be beyond doubt. His object being to construct a narrative of events in continuation of the *Shu King*, he, with assistance from his pupils, drew up a history of his own country, extending from the reign of Ping Wang to about the period of his birth (B.C. 722 to 480). Inasmuch as the author of this chronicle confined himself to the relation of such facts as he deemed worthy to be recorded, and was not above altering or concealing such details as in his private judgment appeared unworthy of the princes of his dynasty, this history cannot be regarded as exactly in conformity with modern notions of what is desirable in works of this class. That Confucius wished to leave behind him a lasting monument to his own name, as well as a narration of events, we gather from more than one of his utterances: "The superior man is distressed lest his name should not be honorably mentioned after death. My principles do not make way in the world; how shall I make myself known to future ages?" In order, therefore, to insure the preservation of his *chef d'œuvre* to all time, he combines with the annals certain censures and righteous decisions which should render it at once a history and a text-book of moral lessons; and in giving the book to his disciples, "It is by the *Chun Tsiu*," he said, "that after-ages will know me, and also by it that they will condemn me."

The title, "Spring and Autumn," is understood by many Chinese scholars to be a term for chronological annals; in this case the name being explained "because their commendations are life-giving like spring, and their censures life-withering like autumn," or, as we find in the *Trimetrical Classic*, "which by praise and blame separates the good and bad."[1] A closer inspection of the *Chun Tsiu* is sure to prove disappointing; spite of the glowing accounts of Mencius and its great reputation, this history is simply a bald record of incidents whose entire contents afford barely an hour's reading. "Instead of a history of events," writes Dr. Legge, "woven artistically together, we find a congeries of the briefest possible intimations of matters in which the court and State of Lu were more or less concerned, extending over two hundred and forty-two years, without the slightest tincture of literary ability in the composition, or the slightest indication of judicial opinion on the part of the writer. The paragraphs are always brief. Each one is designed to commemorate a fact; but whether that fact be a display of virtue calculated to command our admiration, or a deed of atrocity fitted to awaken our disgust, it can hardly be said that there is anything in the language to convey to us the shadow of an idea of the author's feelings about it. The notices—for we cannot call them narratives—are absolutely unimpassioned. A base murder and a shining act of heroism are chronicled just as the eclipses of the sun are chronicled. So and so took

[1] This somewhat fanciful explanation of the title is from the Han commentators. Dr. Legge (*Classics*, Vol. V., Prolegomena, p. 7) observes that "not even in the work do we find such 'censures' and 'commendations;' and much less are they trumpeted in the title of it." His interpretation that Spring and Autumn are put by synechdoche for all four seasons, *i.e.*, the entire record of the year, appears to be a more natural account. The same writer declares that "the whole book is a collection of riddles, to which there are as many answers as there are guessers." The interesting chapters of his *prolegomena* to this translation, and his judicious criticisms on these early records, should tempt all sinologues to read them throughout.

place; that is all. No details are given; no judgment is expressed."

So imperturbable a recital could hardly have been saved from extinction even by the great reputation of the sage, had it not been for the amplification of Tso, a younger contemporary or follower of Confucius, who filled up the meagre sentences and added both flesh and life to the skeleton. It is possible that the enthusiastic praises of Mencius are due to the fact that he associated the text and commentary as one work. The Chuen of Tso has indeed always been regarded as foremost among the secondary classics; nor is it too much, considering his terse yet vivid and pictorial style, to call its author, as does Dr. Legge, "the Froissart of China."[1] In addition to his purpose of explaining the text of the *Chun Tsiu*, Tso's secondary object was to give a general view of the history of China during the period embraced by that record; unless he had put his living tableaux into the framework of his master, there is grave reason to fear that many most important details relating to the sixth and seventh centuries B.C. would have been forever lost. Two other early commentaries, those of Kung Yang and Kuh Liang, dating from about the second century B.C., occupy a high position in the estimation of Chinese scholars as illustrative of the original chronicle. They do not compare with the *Tso Chuen* either in interest or in authority, though it may be said that a study of the *Chun Tsiu* can hardly be made unless attended with a careful perusal of their contents. It will not be without interest to give an example of the *Record*, followed with elucidations of the text by these three annotators. The second year of Duke Hí of Lu (B.C. 657) runs as follows:

1. In the [duke's] second year, in spring, in the king's first month, we [aided in the] walling of Tsu-kin.
2. In summer, in the fifth month, on Sin-sz', we buried our duchess, Gai Kiang.
3. An army of Yu and an army of Tsin extinguished Hia-yang.

---

[1] The same writer adds, in summing up the merits of the *Tso Chuen*: "It is, in my opinion, the most precious literary treasure which has come down to posterity from the Chow dynasty."—*Classics*, Vol. V., Proleg., p. 35.

4. In autumn, in the ninth month, the Marquis of Tsz', the Duke of Sung an officer of Kiang, and an officer of Hwang, made a covenant in Kwan.
5. In winter, in the tenth month, there was no rain.
6. A body of men from Tsu made an incursion into Ching.

Upon the third entry for this year the *Tso Chuen* enlarges:

Seun Seih, of Tsin, requested leave from the marquis to take his team of Kiuh horses and his *peih* of Chui-keih jade, and with them borrow a way from Yu to march through it and attack Kwoh. "They are the things I hold most precious," said the marquis. Seih replied, "But if you get a way through Yu, it is but like placing them in a treasury outside the State for a time." "There is Kung Che-kí in Yu," objected the duke. "Kung Che-kí," returned the other, "is a weak man, and incapable of remonstrating vigorously. And, moreover, from his youth up he has always been with the Duke of Yu. who is so familiar with him that though he should remonstrate the duke will not listen to him." The marquis accordingly sent Seun Seih to borrow a way through Yu with this message: "Formerly Kí, against right and reason, entered your State from Tien-ling, and attacked the three gates of Ming. It suffered for so doing, all through your grace. Now Kwoh, against right and reason, has been keeping guards about the travellers' lodges, to make incursions from them into my southern borders, and I venture to beg a right of way from you to ask an account of its offence." The Duke of Yu granted the request, and even asked to take the lead in invading Kwoh. Kung Che-kí remonstrated with him, but in vain; and he raised his army for the enterprise. In summer, Lí Kih and Seun Seih brought on the army of Tsin, made a junction with that of Yu, and invaded Kwoh, when they extinguished Hia-yang. The army of Yu is mentioned first, because of the bribes which the duke accepted.

The commentary of Kung Yang says on the same paragraph:

Yu was a small State; why is it that it is here made to take precedence of a great one? To make Yu take the lead in the wickedness.

Why is Yu made to take the lead in the wickedness? Yu received the bribes with which those [who were going to] extinguish the State [of Kwoh] borrowed a way through it, and thus brought on its own ruin.

How did it receive [those] bribes? Duke Hien [of Tsin] gave audience to his great officers, and asked them why it was that he had lain all night without sleeping. One of them advanced and said, "Was it because you did not feel at ease [in your mind]? or was it because your [proper] bedfellow was not by your side?" The duke gave no answer, and then Seun Seih came forward and said, "Was it because Yu and Kwoh were appearing to you?" The duke motioned to him to come [more] forward, and then went with him into an inner apartment to take counsel. "I wish," said he, "to attack Kwoh, but Yu will go to its relief, and if I attack Yu Kwoh will succor it; what is to be done? I wish to consider the case with you." Seun Seih replied, "If you will use my counsel, you shall take Kwoh to-day and Yu to-morrow; why should your lordship be troubled?" "How is this to be accomplished?" asked the duke. "Please let [me go to] Yu," said the other, "with your team of Kiuh horses and your white *peih* of Chui-keih, and you are sure to get [what you want]. It will only be taking your valuable [*peih*] from your inner treasury and depositing it in an outer one; your lordship will lose nothing by it." The duke said, "Yes; but Kung Che-kí is there. What are we to do with him?" Seun Seih replied, "Kung Che-kí is indeed knowing; but the Duke of Yu is covetous, and fond of valuable curios; he is sure not to follow his minister's advice. I beg you, considering everything, to let me go." . . . etc., etc.

The following, as a brief sample of the Kuh Liang commentary, takes up the narrative where we have broken off. There is so much that is similar in these two latter exegeses as to lead to the belief that they were composed with reference to each other.

On this Duke Hien sought [in the way proposed] for a passage [through Yu] to invade Kwoh. Kung Che-kí remonstrated, saying, "The words of the envoy of Tsin are humble, but his offerings are great; the matter is sure not to be advantageous to Yu." The Duke of Yu, however, would not listen to him, but received the offerings and granted the passage through the State. Kung Che-kí remonstrated [again], suggesting that the case was like that in the saying about the lips being gone and the teeth becoming cold; after which he fled with his wife and children to Tsao.

Duke Hien then destroyed Kwoh, and in the fifth year [of our Duke Hí] he dealt in the same way with Yu. Seun Seih then had the horses led forward, while he carried the *peih* in his hand, and said: "The *peih* is just as it was, but the horses' teeth are grown longer!"[1]

Meagre as are the items of the text, they show, together with its copious commentaries, the methodical care of the early Chinese in preserving their ancient records. The hints which these and other books give of their intellectual activity during the eight centuries before Christ, naturally compel a higher estimate of their culture than we have hitherto allowed them.[2]

The sixth section of the Catalogue has already been noticed as comprising the literature of the *Hiao King*.

---

[1] To this the Kung Yang commentator adds: "This he said in joke."

[2] Compare *Tchun Tsieou, Le Printemps & l'Automne, ou Annales de la Principauté de Lou, depuis* 722 *jusqu' en* 481, etc. *Traduites en françois, par* Le Roux Deshauterayes. 1750. Dr. E. Bretschneider, in the *Chinese Recorder*, Vol. IV., pp. 51–52, 1871.

The seventh section contains a list of works written to elucidate the Five Classics as a whole, and if their character for originality of thought, variety of research, extent of illustration, and explanation of obscurities was comparable to their size and numbers, no books in any language could boast of the aids possessed by the *Wu King* for their right comprehension. Of these commentators, Chu Hí of Kiangsí, who lived during the Sung dynasty, has so greatly exceeded all others in illustrating and expounding them, that his explanations are now considered of almost equal authority with the text, and are always given to the beginner to assist him in ascertaining its true meaning.

The eighth section of the Catalogue comprises memoirs and comments upon the *Sz' Shu*, or 'Four Books,' which have been nearly as influential in forming Chinese mind as the *Wu King*. They are by different authors, and since their publication have perhaps undergone a few alterations and interpolations, but the changes either in these or the Five Classics cannot be very numerous or great, since the large body of disciples who followed Confucius, and had copies of his writings, would carefully preserve uncorrupt those which he edited, and hand down unimpaired those which contained his sayings. None of the Four Books were actually written by Confucius himself, but three of them are considered to be a digest of his sentiments; they were arranged in their present form by the brothers Ching, who flourished about eight centuries ago.

The first of the Four Books is the *Ta Hioh*, *i.e.*, 'Superior' or 'Great Learning,' which originally formed one chapter of the *Book of Rites*. It is now divided into eleven chapters, only the first of which is ascribed to the sage, the remainder forming the comment upon them; the whole does not contain two thousand words. The argument of the *Ta Hioh* is briefly summed up in four heads, "the improvement of one's self, the regulation of a family, the government of a state, and the rule of an empire." In the first chapter this idea is thus developed in a circle peculiarly Chinese:

The ancients, who wished to illustrate renovating virtue throughout the Empire, first ordered well their own states. Wishing to order well their states, they first regulated their families. Wishing to regulate their families, they first cultivated their persons. Wishing to cultivate their persons, they first rectified their hearts. Wishing to rectify their hearts, they first sought to be sincere in their thoughts. Wishing to be sincere in their thoughts, they first extended their knowledge to the utmost. Such extension of knowledge lay in the investigation of things. Things being investigated, knowledge became complete: knowledge being complete, their thoughts were sincere: their thoughts being sincere, their hearts were then rectified: their hearts being rectified, their persons were cultivated: their persons being cultivated, their families were regulated: families being regulated, states were rightly governed; and states being rightly governed, the Empire was made tranquil.

From the Son of Heaven to the man of the people, all must consider the cultivation of the person to be the foundation.

The subsequent chapters mainly consist of the terse sayings of ancient kings and authors gathered and arranged by Tsăng and afterward by Chu Hí, designed to illustrate and enforce the teachings of Confucius contained in the first. One quotation only can be given from Chapter X.

In the Declaration of [the Duke of] Tsin, it is said: "Let me have but one minister plain and sincere, not pretending to other abilities, but with a simple upright mind; and possessed of generosity, regarding the talents of others as though he possessed them himself, and where he finds accomplished and perspicacious men, loving them in his heart more than his mouth expresses, and really showing himself able to avail himself of them; such a minister will be able to preserve my descendants and the Black-haired people, and benefits to the kingdom might well be looked for. But if it be, when he finds men of ability, he is jealous and hateful to them; and when he meets accomplished and perspicacious men, he opposes them and will not allow their advancement, showing that he is really not able to avail himself of them; such a minister will not be able to protect my descendants and the Black-haired people. May he not even be pronounced dangerous?"

It will be willingly allowed, when reading these extracts, that, destitute as they were of the high sanctions and animating hopes and promises of the Word of God, these Chinese moralists began at the right place in their endeavors to reform and benefit their countrymen, and that they did not fully succeed was owing to causes beyond their reforming power.

The second of the Four Books is called *Chung Yung*, or the 'Just Medium,' and is, in some respects, the most elaborate treatise in the series. It was composed by Kung Kih, the grandson of Confucius (better known by his style Tsz'-sz'), about ninety years after the sage's death. It once also formed part of the *Lí Kí*, from which it, as well as the *Ta Hioh*, were taken out by Chu Hí to make two of the *Sz' Shu*. It has thirty-three chapters, and has been the subject of numerous comments. The great purpose of the author is to illustrate the nature of human virtue, and to exhibit its conduct in the actions of an ideal *kiun tsz'*, or 'princely man' of immaculate propriety, who always demeans himself correctly, without going to extremes. He carries out the advice of Hesiod:

> "Let every action prove a mean confess'd;
> A moderation is, in all, the best."

True virtue consists in never going to extremes, though it does not appear that by this the sage meant to repress active benevolence on the one hand, or encourage selfish stolidity on the other. *Ching*, or uprightness, is said to be the basis of all things; and *ho*, harmony, the all-pervading principle of the universe; "extend uprightness and harmony to the utmost, and heaven and earth will be at rest, and all things be produced and nourished according to their nature." The general character of the work is monotonous, but relieved with some animated passages, among which the description of the *kiun tsz'*, or princely man, is one. "The princely man, in dealing with others, does not descend to anything low or improper. How unbending his valor! He stands in the middle, and leans not to either side. The princely man enters into no situation where he is not himself. If he holds a high situation, he does not treat with contempt those below him; if he occupies an inferior station, he uses no mean arts to gain the favor of his superiors. He corrects himself and blames not others; he feels no dissatisfaction. On the one hand, he murmurs not at Heaven; nor, on the other, does he feel resentment toward man. Hence, the superior man dwells at ease, entirely waiting the will of Heaven."[1]

Chinese moralists divide mankind into three classes, on these principles: "Men of the highest order, as sages, worthies, philanthropists, and heroes, are good without instruction; men of

---

[1] Collie's *Four Books*, pp. 6–10.

the middling classes are so after instruction, such as husbandmen, physicians, astrologers, soldiers, etc., while those of the lowest are bad in spite of instruction, as play-actors, pettifoggers, slaves, swindlers, etc." The first are *shing*, or sages; the second are *hien*, or worthies; the last are *yu*, or worthless. Sir John Davis notices the similarity of this triplicate classification with that of Hesiod. The *Just Medium* thus describes the first character:

It is only the sage who is possessed of that clear discrimination and profound intelligence which fit him for filling a high station; who possesses that enlarged liberality and mild benignity which fit him for bearing with others; who manifests that firmness and magnanimity that enable him to hold fast good principles; who is actuated by that benevolence, justice, propriety, and knowledge which command reverence; and who is so deeply learned in polite learning and good principles as to qualify him rightly to discriminate. Vast and extensive are the effects of his virtue; it is like the deep and living stream which flows unceasingly; it is substantial and extensive as Heaven, and profound as the great abyss. Wherever ships sail or chariots run; wherever the heavens overshadow and the earth sustains; wherever the sun and moon shine, or frosts and dews fall, among all who have blood and breath, there is not one who does not honor and love him.[1]

Sincerity or conscientiousness holds a high place among the attributes of the superior or princely man; but in translating the Chinese terms into English, it is sometimes puzzling enough to find those which will exhibit the exact idea of the original. For instance, sincerity is described as "the origin or consummation of all things; without it, there would be nothing. It is benevolence by which a man's self is perfected, and knowledge by which he perfects others." In another place we read that "one sincere wish would move heaven and earth." The *kiun tsz'* is supposed to possess these qualities. The standard of excellence is placed so high as to be absolutely unattainable by unaided human nature; and though Kih probably intended to elevate the character of his grandfather to this height, and thus hand him down to future ages as a *shing jin*, or 'perfect and holy man,' he has, in the providence of God, done his countrymen great service in setting before them such a character as is

---

[1] *Ib.*, p. 28.

here given in the *Chung Yung*. By being made a text-book in the schools it has been constantly studied and memorized by generations of students, to their great benefit.

The third of the Four Books, called the *Lun Yu*, or 'Analects of Confucius,' is divided into twenty chapters, in which the collective body of his disciples recorded his words and actions, much in the same way that Boswell did those of Johnson. It has not, however, the merit of chronological arrangement, and parts of it are so sententious as to be obscure, if not almost unintelligible. This work discloses the sage's shrewd insight into the character of his countrymen, and knowledge of the manner in which they could best be approached and influenced. Upon the commencement of his career as reformer and teacher, he contented himself with reviving the doctrines of the "Ancients;" but finding his influence increasing as he continued these instructions, he then—yet always as under their authority—engrafted original ideas and tenets upon the minds of his generation. Had even his loftiest sentiments been propounded as his own, they would hardly have been received in his day, and, perhaps, through the contempt felt for him by his contemporaries, have been lost entirely.

Among the most remarkable passages of the Four Books are the following: Replying to the question of Tsz'-kung, "Is there one word which may serve as a rule of practice for all of one's life?" Confucius said: "Is not *shu* ('reciprocity') such a word? What you do not want done to yourself, do not do to others." In a previous place Tsz'-kung had said: "What I do not wish men to do to me, I also wish not to do to men." Confucius replied: "Tsz', you have not attained to that." The same principle is repeated in the *Chung Yung*, where it is said that the man who does so is not far from the path. Another is quoted in the Imperial Dictionary, under the word *Fuh:* "The people of the west have sages," or "There is a sage (or holy man) among the people of the west," where the object is to show that he did not mean Buddha. As Confucius was contemporary with Ezra, it is not impossible that he had heard something of the history of the Israelites scattered throughout the one hundred and twenty-seven provinces of the Persian monarchy, or of the writings of their prophets, though there is not the least historical evidence that he knew anything of the countries in Western Asia, or of the books extant in their languages.

Some idea of the character of the *Lun Yu* may be gathered from a few detached sentences, selected from Marshman's translation.[1]

Grieve not that men know you not, but be grieved that you are ignorant of men.

Governing with equity resembles the north star, which is fixed, and all the stars surround it.

Have no friends unlike yourself.

Learning without reflection will profit nothing; reflection without learning will leave the mind uneasy and miserable.

Knowledge produces pleasure clear as water; complete virtue brings happiness solid as a mountain; knowledge pervades all things; virtue is tranquil and happy; knowledge is delight; virtue is long life.

Without virtue, both riches and honor seem to me like the passing cloud.

The sage's conduct is affection and benevolence in operation.

The man who possesses complete virtue wishes to fix his own mind therein, and also to fix the minds of others; he wishes to be wise himself, and would fain render others equally wise.

Those who, searching for virtue, refuse to stay among the virtuous, how can they obtain knowledge?

The rich and honorable are those with whom men desire to associate; not obtaining their company in the paths of virtue, however, do not remain in it.

In your appearance, to fall below decency would be to resemble a savage rustic, to exceed it would be to resemble a fop; let your appearance be decent and moderate, then you will resemble the honorable man.

When I first began with men, I heard words and gave credit for conduct; now I hear words and observe conduct.

I have found no man who esteems virtue as men esteem pleasure.

The perfect man loves all men; he is not governed by private affection or interest, but only regards the public good or right reason. The wicked man, on the contrary, loves if you give, and likes if you commend him.

The perfect man is never satisfied with himself. He that is satisfied with himself is not perfect.

He that is sedulous and desires to improve in his studies is not ashamed to stoop to ask of others.

Sin in a virtuous man is like an eclipse of the sun and moon; all men gaze at it, and it passes away; the virtuous man mends, and the world stands in admiration of his fall.

Patience is the most necessary thing to have in this world.

---

[1] *The Works of Confucius; containing the original text, with a Translation*, by J. Marshman. Vol. I. Serampore, 1807.

A few facts respecting the life, and observations on the character, of the great sage of Chinese letters, may here be added, though the extracts already made from his writings are sufficient to show his style. Confucius was born B.C. 551, in the twentieth year of the Emperor Ling (about the date at which Cyrus became king of Persia), in the kingdom of Lu, now included in Yenchau, in the south of Shantung. His father was a district magistrate, and dying when he was only three years old, left his care and education to his mother, who, although not so celebrated as the mother of Mencius, seems to have nurtured in him a respect for morality, and directed his studies. During his youth he was remarkable for a grave demeanor and knowledge of ancient learning, which gained him the respect and admiration of his townsmen, so that at the age of twenty, the year after his marriage, he was entrusted with the duties of a subordinate office in the revenue department, and afterward appointed a supervisor of fields and herds. In his twenty-fourth year his mother deceased, and in conformity with the ancient usage, which had then fallen into disuse, he immediately resigned all his employments to mourn for her three years, during which time he devoted himself to study. This practice has continued to the present day.

His examination of the ancient writings led him to resolve upon instructing his countrymen in them, and to revive the usages of former kings, especially in whatever related to the rites. His position gave him an entry to court in Lu, where he met educated and influential men, and by the time he was thirty he was already in repute among them as a teacher. His own king, Siang, gave him the means of visiting the imperial court at Lohyang. Here, together with his disciples, he examined everything, past and present, with close scrutiny, and returned home with renewed regard for the ancient founders of the House of Chau. His scholars and admirers increased in numbers, and a corresponding extension of fame followed, so that ere long he had an invitation to the court of the prince of Tsí, but on arrival there was mortified to learn that curiosity had been the prevailing cause of the invitation, and not a desire to adopt his principles. He accordingly left him and went home, where the struggles between three rival families carried disorder and misery throughout the kingdom; it was with the greatest difficulty that he remained neutral between these factions. His disciples were from all parts of the land, and public opinion began to be influenced by his example. At length an opportunity offered to put his tenets into practice. The civil strife had resulted in the flight of the rebels, and Lu was settling down into better government, when in B.C. 500 Confucius was made the magistrate of the town of Chung-tu by his sovereign, Duke Ting. He was now fifty years old, and began to carry out the best rule he could in his position as minister of crime. For three years he administered the affairs of State with such a mixture of zeal, prudence, severity, and regard for the rights and wants of all classes, that Lu soon became the envy and dread of all other States. He even succeeded in destroying two or three baronial castles whose chiefs had set all lawful authority at defiance. His precepts had been fairly put in practice, and, like Solomon, his influence in after-ages was increased by the fact of acknowledged success.

It was but little more than an experiment, however; for Duke King of Tsí, becoming envious of the growing power of his neighbor, sent Ting a tempting present, consisting of thirty horses beautifully caparisoned, and a number of curious rarities, with a score of the most accomplished courtesans he could procure in his territories. This scheme of gaining the favor of the youthful monarch, and driving the obnoxious cynic from his councils, succeeded, and Confucius soon after retired by compulsion into private life. He moved into the dominions of the prince of Wei, accompanied by such of his disciples as chose to follow him, where he employed himself in extending his doctrines and travelling into the adjoining States.

He was at times applauded and patronized, but quite as often the object of persecution and contumely; more than once his life was endangered. He compared himself to a dog driven from his home: "I have the fidelity of that animal, and I am treated like it. But what matters the ingratitude of men? They cannot hinder me from doing all the good that has been appointed me. If my precepts are disregarded, I have the consolation of knowing in my own breast that I have faithfully performed my duty." He sometimes spoke in a manner that showed his own impression to be that heaven had conferred on him a special commission to instruct the world. On one or two occasions, when he was in jeopardy, he said: "If Heaven means not to obliterate this doctrine from the earth, the men of Kwang can do nothing to me." And "as Heaven has produced whatever virtue is in me, what can Hwan Tui do to me?"

In his instructions he improved passing events to afford useful lessons, and some of those recorded are at least ingenious. Observing a fowler one day sorting his birds into different cages, he said, "I do not see any old birds here; where have you put them?" "The old birds," replied the fowler, "are too wary to be caught; they are on the lookout, and if they see a net or cage, far from falling into the snare they escape and never return. Those young ones which are in company with them likewise escape, but only such as separate into a flock by themselves and rashly approach are the birds I take. If perchance I catch an old bird it is because he follows the young ones." "You have heard him," observed the sage, turning to his disciples; "the words of this fowler afford us matter for instruction. The young birds escape the snare only when they keep with the old ones, the old ones are taken when they follow the young; it is thus with mankind. Presumption, hardihood, want of forethought, and inattention are the principal reasons why young people are led astray. Inflated with their small attainments they have scarcely made a commencement in learning before they think they know everything; they have scarcely performed a few common virtuous acts, and straight they fancy themselves at the height of wisdom. Under this false impression they doubt nothing, hesitate at nothing, pay attention to nothing; they rashly undertake acts without consulting the aged and experienced, and thus securely following their own notions, they are misled and fall into the first snare laid for them. If you see an old man of sober years so badly advised as to be taken with the sprightliness of a youth, attached to him, and thinking and acting with him, he is led astray by him and soon taken in the same snare. Do not forget the answer of the fowler."

Once, when looking at a stream, he compared its ceaseless current to the transmission of good doctrine through succeeding generations, and as one race had received it they should hand it down to others. "Do not imitate those isolated men [the Rationalists] who are wise only for themselves; to communicate the modicum of knowledge and virtue we possess to others will never impoverish ourselves." He seems to have entertained only faint hopes of the general reception of his doctrine, though toward the latter end of his life he had as much encouragement in the respect paid him personally and the increase of his scholars as he could reasonably have wished.

Confucius returned to his native country at the age of sixty-eight, and devoted his time to completing his edition of the classics and in teaching his now large band of disciples. He was consulted by his sovereign, who had invited him to return, and one of his last acts was to go to court to urge an attack on Tsí and punish the murder of its duke. Many legends have gathered around him, so that he now stands before his countrymen as a sage and a demigod; yet there is a remarkable absence of the prophetic and the miraculous in every event connected with these later writings. One story is that when he had finished his writings he collected his friends around him and made a solemn dedication of his literary labors to heaven as the concluding act of his life. "He assembled all his disciples and led them out of the town to one of the hills where sacrifices had usually been offered for many years. Here he erected a table or altar, upon which he placed the books; and then turning his face to the north, adored Heaven, and returned thanks upon his knees in a humble manner for having had life and strength granted him to enable him to accomplish this laborious undertaking; he implored Heaven to grant that the benefit to his countrymen from so arduous a labor might not be small. He had prepared himself for this ceremony by privacy, fasting, and prayer. Chinese pictures represent the sage in the attitude of supplication, and a beam of light or a rainbow descending from the sky upon the books, while his scholars stand around in admiring wonder."[1]

A few days before his death he tottered about the house, sighing,

Tai shan, kí tui hu!—Liang muh, kí hwai hu!—Chí jin, kí wei hu!

The great mountain is broken!
The strong beam is thrown down!
The wise man withers like a plant!

He died soon after, B.C. 478, aged seventy-three, leaving a single descendant, his grandson Tsz'-sz, through whom the succession has been transmitted to the present day. During his life the return of the Jews from Babylon, the invasion of Greece by Xerxes, and conquest of Egypt by the Persians took place. Posthumous honors in great variety, amounting to idolatrous worship, have been conferred upon him. His title is the 'Most Holy Ancient Teacher' Kung tsz', and the 'Holy Duke.' In the reign of Kanghí, two thousand one hundred and fifty years after his death, there were eleven thousand males alive bearing his name, and most of them of the seventy-fourth generation, being undoubtedly one of the oldest families in the world. In the *Sacrificial Ritual* a short account of his life is given, which closes with the following pæan:

Confucius! Confucius! How great is Confucius!
Before Confucius there never was a Confucius!
Since Confucius there never has been a Confucius!
Confucius! Confucius! How great is Confucius!

The leading features of the philosophy of Confucius are subordination to superiors and kind, upright dealing with our fellow-men; destitute of all reference to an unseen Power to whom all men are accountable, they look only to this world for their sanctions, and make the monarch himself only partially amenable to a higher tribunal. It would indeed be hard to overestimate the influence of Confucius in his ideal *princely scholar*, and the power for good over his race this conception ever since has exerted. It might be compared to the glorious work of the

[1] *Chinese Repository*, Vol. XI., p. 421. Pauthier, *La Chine*, Paris, 1839, pp. 121–184.

sculptor on the Acropolis of Athens—that matchless statue more than seventy feet in height, whose casque and spear of burnished brass glittered above all the temples and high places of the city, and engaged the constant gaze of the mariner on the near Ægean; guiding his onward course, it was still ever beyond his reach. Like the Athena Promachos to the ancient Attic voyager, so stands the *kiun-tsz'* of Confucius among the ideal men of pagan moralists. The immeasurable influence in after-ages of the character thus portrayed proves how lofty was his own standard, and the national conscience has ever since assented to the justice of the portrait.

From the duty, honor, and obedience owed by a child to his parents, he proceeds to inculcate the obligations of wives to their husbands, subjects to their prince, and ministers to their king, together with all the obligations arising from the various social relations. Political morality must be founded on private rectitude, and the beginning of all real advance was, in his opinion, comprised in *nosce teipsum.* It cannot be denied that among much that is commendable there are a few exceptionable dogmas among his tenets, and Dr. Legge, as has already been seen, reflects severely on his disregard of truth in the *Chun Tsiu* and in his lifetime. Yet compared with the precepts of Grecian and Roman sages, the general tendency of his writings is good, while in adaptation to the society in which he lived, and their eminently practical character, they exceed those of western philosophers. He did not deal much in sublime and unattainable descriptions of virtue, but rather taught how the common intercourse of life was to be maintained—how children should conduct themselves toward their parents, when a man should enter on office, when to marry, etc., etc., which, although they may seem somewhat trifling to us, were probably well calculated for the times and people among whom he lived.[1]

---

[1] Compare Dr. Legge's *Religions of China;* Prof. R. K. Douglas, *Confucianism and Taouism*, London, 1879; S. Johnson, *Oriental Religions: China*, Boston, 1877; *A Systematical Digest of the Doctrines of Confucius, according to the Analects, Great Learning, and Doctrine of the Mean*, etc., by Ernst Faber. Translated from the German by Möllendorff, Hongkong, 1875; *Histoire de Confucius*, par J. Sénamaud, Bordeaux et Paris, 1878.

Had Confucius transmitted to posterity such works as the Iliad, the De Officiis, or the Dialogues of Plato, he would no doubt have taken a higher rank among the commanding intellects of the world, but it may be well doubted whether his influence among his own countrymen would have been as good or as lasting. The variety and minuteness of his instructions for the nurture and education of children, the stress he lays upon filial duty, the detail of etiquette and conduct he gives for the intercourse of all classes and ranks in society, characterize his writings from those of all philosophers in other countries, who, comparatively speaking, gave small thought to the education of the young. The Four Books and the Five Classics would not, so far as regards their intrinsic character in comparison with other productions, be considered as anything more than curiosities in literature for their antiquity and language, were it not for the incomparable influence they have exerted over so many millions of minds; in this view they are invested with an interest which no book, besides the Bible, can claim. The source and explanation of this influence is to be found in their use as text-books in the schools and competitive examinations, and well would it be for Christian lands if their youth had the same knowledge of the writings of Solomon and the Evangelists. Their freedom from descriptions of impurity and licentiousness, and allusions to whatever debases and vitiates the heart, is a redeeming quality of the Chinese classics which should not be overlooked. Chinese literature contains enough, indeed, to pollute even the mind of a heathen, but its scum has become the sediment; and little or nothing can be found in the writings that are most highly prized which will not bear perusal by any person in any country. Every one acquainted with the writings of Hindu, Greek, and Roman poets knows the glowing descriptions of the amours of gods and goddesses which fill their pages, and the purity of the Chinese canonical books in this respect must be considered as remarkable.

For the most part the Chinese, in worshipping Confucius, content themselves with erecting a simple tablet in his honor; to carve images for the cult of the sage is uncommon. The incident represented in the adjoining wood-cut illustrates, however,

Worship of Confucius and his Disciples.

an exception to the prevailing severity of this worship. A certain Wei Kí, a scholar living in the Tang dynasty (A.D. 657), not content, it is said, with giving instruction in the classics, set up the life-size statues of Confucius and his seventy-two disciples in order to incite the enthusiasm of his own pupils. Into this sanctuary of the divinities of learning were wont to come the *savant* Wei and his scholars—among whom were numbered both his grandfather and several of his grandchildren—to prostrate themselves before the ancient worthies. "But of his descendants," concludes the chronicler, "there were many who arose to positions of eminence in the State."

The last of the Four Books is nearly as large as the other three united, and consists entirely of the writings of Mencius, Măng tsz', or Măng fu-tsz', as he is called by the Chinese.[1] This sage flourished upward of a century after the death of his master, and although, in estimating his character, it must not be forgotten that he had the advantages of his example and stimulus of his fame and teachings, in most respects he displayed an originality of thought, inflexibility of purpose, and extensive views superior to Confucius, and must be regarded as one of the greatest men Asiatic nations have ever produced.

Mencius was born B.C. 371,[2] in the city of Tsau, now in the province of Shantung, not far from his master's native district. He was twenty-three years old when Plato died, and many other great men of Greece were his contemporaries. His father died early, and left the guardianship of the boy to his widow, Changshí. "The care of this prudent and attentive mother," to quote from Rémusat, "has been cited as a model for all virtuous parents. The house she occupied was near that

---

[1] It may here be remarked that the terms *tsz'* or *fu-tsz'* do not properly form a part of the name, but are titles, meaning *rabbi* or *eminent teacher*, and are added to the surnames of some of the most distinguished writers, by way of peculiar distinction; and in the words Mencius and Confucius have been Latinized with Măng and Kung, names of the persons themselves, into one word. The names of other distinguished scholars, as Chu fu-tsz', Ching fu-tsz', etc., have not undergone this change into Chufucius, Chingfucius; but usage has now brought the compellation for these two men into universal use as a distinctive title, somewhat like the term *venerable* applied to Bede.

[2] Rémusat, *Nouveaux Mélanges*, Tome II., pp. 115–129.

of a butcher; she observed that at the first cry of the animals that were being slaughtered the little Măng ran to be present at the sight, and that on his return he sought to imitate what he had seen. Fearful that his heart might become hardened, and be accustomed to the sight of blood, she removed to another house which was in the neighborhood of a cemetery. The relations of those who were buried there came often to weep upon their graves and make the customary libations; the lad soon took pleasure in their ceremonies, and amused himself in imitating them. This was a new subject of uneasiness to Changshí; she feared her son might come to consider as a jest what is of all things the most serious, and that he would acquire a habit of performing with levity, and as a matter of routine merely, ceremonies which demand the most exact attention and respect. Again, therefore, she anxiously changed her dwelling, and went to live in the city, opposite to a school, where her son found examples the most worthy of imitation, and soon began to profit by them. I should not have spoken of this trifling anecdote but for the allusion which the Chinese constantly make to it in the common proverb, 'Formerly the mother of Mencius chose out a neighborhood.'" On another occasion her son, seeing persons slaughtering pigs, asked her why they did it. "To feed you," she replied; but reflecting that this was teaching her son to lightly regard the truth, went and bought some pork and gave him.

Mencius devoted himself early to the classics, and probably attended the instructions of noted teachers of the school of Confucius and his grandson Kih. After his studies were completed, at the age of forty, he came forth as a public teacher, and offered his services to the feudal princes of the country. Among others, he was received by Hwui, king of Wei, but, though much respected by this ruler, his instructions were not regarded; and he soon perceived that among the numerous petty rulers and intriguing statesmen of the day there was no prospect of restoring tranquillity to the Empire, and that discourses upon the mild government and peaceful virtues of Yao and Shun, King Wăn and Chingtang, offered little to interest persons whose minds were engrossed with schemes of conquest or pleasure. He thereupon accepted an invitation to go to Tsí, the adjoining State, and spent most of his public life there; the records show that he was often called on for his advice by statesmen of many governments. As he went from one State to another his influence extended as his experience showed him the difficulties of good government amidst the general disregard of justice, mercy, and frugality. His own unyielding character and stern regard for etiquette and probity chilled the loose, unscrupulous men of those lawless times. At length he retired to his home to spend the last twenty years of his life in the society of his disciples, there completing the work which bears his name and has made him such a power among his countrymen. He has always been an incentive and guide to popular efforts to assert the rights of the subject against the injustice of rulers, and an encourager to rulers who have governed with justice. His assertion of the proper duties and prerogatives belonging to both parties in the State was prior to that of any western writer; some of his principles of liberal government were taught before their enunciation in Holy Writ. He died when eighty-four years old (B.C. 288), shortly before the death of Ptolemy Soter at the same age.

After his demise Mencius was honored, by public act, with the title of 'Holy Prince of the country of Tsau,' and in the temple of the sages he receives the same honors as Confucius; his descendants bear the title of 'Masters of the Traditions concerning the Classics,' and he himself is called *A-shing*, or the 'Secondary Sage,' Confucius being regarded as the first. His writings are in the form of dialogues held with the great personages of his time, and abound with irony and ridicule directed against vice and oppression, which only make his praises of virtue and integrity more weighty. After the manner of Socrates, he contests nothing with his adversaries, but, while granting their premises, he seeks to draw from them consequences the most absurd, which cover his opponents with confusion.

The king of Wei, one of the turbulent princes of the time, was complaining to Mencius how ill he succeeded in his endeavors to make his people happy and his kingdom flourishing.

"Prince," said the philosopher, "you love war; permit me to draw a comparison from thence: two armies are in presence; the charge is sounded, the battle begins, one of the parties is conquered; half its soldiers have fled a hundred paces, the other half has stopped at fifty. Will the last have any right to mock at those who have fled further than themselves?"

"No," said the king; "they have equally taken flight, and the same disgrace must attend them both."

"Prince," says Mencius quickly, "cease then to boast of your efforts as greater than your neighbors'. You have all deserved the same reproach, and not one has a right to take credit to himself over another." Pursuing then his bitter interrogations, he asked, "Is there a difference, O king! between killing a man with a club or with a sword?" "No," said the prince. "Between him who kills with the sword, or destroys by an inhuman tyranny?" "No," again replied the prince.

"Well," said Mencius, "your kitchens are encumbered with food, your sheds are full of horses, while your subjects, with emaciated countenances, are worn down with misery, or found dead of hunger in the middle of the fields or the deserts. What is this but to breed animals to prey on men? And what is the difference between destroying them by the sword or by unfeeling conduct? If we detest those savage animals which mutually tear and devour each other, how much more should we abhor a prince who, instead of being a father to his people, does not hesitate to rear animals to destroy them. What kind of father to his people is he who treats his children so unfeelingly, and has less care of them than of the wild beasts he provides for?"

On one occasion, addressing the prince of Tsí, Mencius remarked: "It is not the ancient forests of a country which do it honor, but its families devoted for many generations to the duties of the magistracy. Oh, king! in all your service there are none such; those whom you yesterday raised to honor, what are they to-day?"

"In what way," replied the king, "can I know beforehand that they are without virtue, and remove them?"

"In raising a sage to the highest dignities of the State," replied the philosopher, "a king acts only as he is of necessity bound to do. But to put a man of obscure condition over the nobles of his kingdom, or one of his remote kindred over princes more nearly connected with him, demands most careful deliberation. Do his courtiers unite in speaking of a man as wise, let him distrust them. If all the magistrates of his kingdom concur in the same assurance, let him not rest satisfied with their testimony, but if his subjects confirm the story, then let him convince himself; and if he finds that the individual is indeed a sage, let him raise him to office and honor. So, also, if all his courtiers would oppose his placing confidence in a minister, let him not give heed to them; and if all the magistrates are of this opinion, let him be deaf to their solicitations; but if the people unite in the same request, then let him examine the object of their ill-will, and, if guilty, remove him. In short, if all the courtiers think that a minister should suffer death, the prince must not content himself with their opinion merely. If all the high officers entertain the same sentiment, still he must not yield to their convictions; but if the people declare that such a man is unfit to live, then the prince, inquiring himself and being satisfied that the charge is true, must condemn the guilty to death; in such a case, we may say that the people are his judges. In acting thus a prince becomes the parent of his subjects."

The will of the people is always referred to as the supreme power in the State, and Mencius warns princes that they must both please and benefit their people, observing that "if the country is not subdued in heart there will be no such thing as governing it;" and also, "He who gains the hearts of the people secures the throne, and he who loses the people's hearts loses the throne." A prince should "give and take what is pleasing to them, and not do that which they hate." "Good laws," he further remarks, "are not equal to winning the people by good instruction." Being consulted by a sovereign, whether he ought to attempt the conquest of a neighboring territory, he answered: "If the people of Yen are delighted, then take it; but if otherwise, not." He also countenances the dethroning of a king who does not rule his people with a regard to their happiness, and adduces the example of the founders of the Shang and Chau dynasties in proof of its propriety. "When the prince is guilty of great errors," is his doctrine, "the minister should reprove him; if, after doing so again and again, he does not listen, he ought to dethrone him and put another in his place."

His estimate of human nature, like many of the Chinese sages, is high, believing it to be originally good, and that "all men are naturally virtuous, as all water flows downward. All men have compassionate hearts, all feel ashamed of vice." But he says also, "Shame is of great moment to men; it is only the designing and artful that find no use for shame." Yet human nature must be tried by suffering, and to form an energetic and virtuous character a man must endure much; "when Heaven was about to place Shun and others in important trusts, it first generally tried their minds, inured them to abstinence, exposed them to poverty and adversity; thus it moved their hearts and taught them patience." His own character presents traits widely differing from the servility and baseness usually ascribed to Asiatics, and especially to the Chinese; and he seems to have been ready to sacrifice everything to his principles. "I love life, and I love justice," he observes, "but if I cannot preserve both, I would give up life and hold fast justice. Although I love life, there is that which I love more than life; although I hate death, there is that which I hate more than death." And as if referring to his own integrity, he elsewhere says: "The nature of the superior man is such that, although in a high and prosperous situation, it adds nothing to his virtue; and although in low and distressed circumstances, it impairs it in nothing." In many points, especially in the importance he gives to filial duty, his reverence for the ancient books and princes, and his adherence to old usages, Mencius imitated and upheld Confucius; in native vigor and carelessness of the reproaches of his compatriots he exceeded him. Many translations of his work have appeared in European languages, but Legge's [1] is in most respects the best for its comments, and the notices of Men-

---

[1] *Chinese Classics*, Vol II. Hongkong, 1862.

cius' life and times, and a fair estimate of his character and influence.

Returning to the Imperial Catalogue, its ninth section contains a list of musical works, and a few on dancing or posture-making; they hold this distinguished place in the list from the importance attached to music as employed in the State worship and domestic ceremonies.

The tenth section gives the names of philological treatises and lexicons, most of them confined to the Chinese language, though a few are in Manchu. The Chinese government has excelled in the attention it has given to the compilation of lexicons and encyclopædias. The number of works of this sort here catalogued is two hundred and eighteen, the major part issued during this dynasty, and including only works on the general language, none on the dialects. For their extent of quotation, the variety of separate disquisitions upon the form, origin, and composition of characters, and treatises upon subjects connected with the language, they indicate the careful labor native scholars have bestowed upon the elucidation of their own tongue.

One of them, the *Pei Wăn Yun Fu*, or 'Treasury of compared Characters and Sounds,' is so extensive and profound as to deserve a short notice, which cannot be better made than by an extract from the preface of M. Callery to his prospectus to its translation, of which he only issued one livraison. He says the Emperor Kanghí, who planned its preparation, "assembled in his palace the most distinguished literati of the Empire, and laying before them all the works that could be got, whether ancient or modern, commanded them carefully to collect all the words, allusions, forms and figures of speech of every style, of which examples might be found in the Chinese language; to class the principal articles according to the pronunciation of the words; to devote a distinct paragraph to each expression; and to give in support of every paragraph several quotations from the original works. Stimulated by the munificence, as well as the example, of the Emperor, who reviewed the performances of every day, seventy-six literati assembled at Peking, labored with such assiduity, and kept up such an active correspondence with the learned in all parts of the Empire, that at the end of eight years the work was completed (1711), and printed at the public expense, in one hundred and thirty thick volumes." The peculiar nature of the Chinese language, in the formation of many dissyllabic compounds of two or more characters to express a third and new idea, renders such a work as this thesaurus more necessary and useful, perhaps, than it would be in any other language. Under some of the common characters as many as three hundred, four hundred, and even six hundred combinations are noticed, all of which modify its sense more or less, and form a complete monograph of the character, of the highest utility to the scholar in composing idiomatic Chinese. This magnificent monument of literary labor reflects great credit on the monarch who took so much interest in its compilation (as he remarks in his preface), as to devote the leisure hours of every day, notwithstanding his manifold occupations, for eight years, to overlooking the labors of the scholars engaged upon it.

CHAPTER XII.

POLITE LITERATURE OF THE CHINESE.

THE three remaining divisions of the Imperial Catalogue comprise lists of Historical, Professional, and Poetical works. The estimate made of their value will depend somewhat on the peculiar line of research of the student, and to give him the means of doing this would require copious extracts from poetical, religious, topographical or moral writings. Those who have studied them the longest, as Rémusat, Julien, Staunton, Pauthier, the two Morrisons, Legge, etc., speak of them with the most respect, whether it arose from a higher appreciation of their worth as they learned more, or that the zealousness of their studies imparted a tinge of enthusiasm to their descriptions. A writer in the *Quarterly Review* gives good reasons for placing the polite literature of the Chinese first for the insight it is likely to give Europeans into their habits of thought. "The Chinese stand eminently distinguished from other Asiatics by their early possession and extensive use of the important art of printing—of printing, too, in that particular shape, the stereotype, which is best calculated, by multiplying the copies and cheapening the price, to promote the circulation of every species of their literature. Hence they are, as might be expected, a reading people; a certain degree of education is common among even the lower classes, and among the higher it is superfluous to insist on the great estimation in which letters must be held under a system where learning forms the very threshold of the gate that conducts to fame, honors, and civil employment. Amid the vast mass of printed books which is the natural offspring of such a state of things, we make no scruple to avow that the circle of their *belles-lettres*, comprised under the heads of drama, poetry, and novels, has always possessed the highest place in our esteem; and we must say that there appears no readier or more agreeable mode of becoming intimately acquainted with a people from whom Europe can have so little to learn on the score of either moral or physical science than by drawing largely on the inexhaustible stores of their ornamental literature."

The second division in the Catalogue, *Sz' Pu*, or 'Historical Writings,' is subdivided into fifteen sections. These writings are very extensive; even their mere list conveys a high idea of the vast amount of labor expended upon them; and it is impossible to withhold respect, at least, to the industry displayed in compilations like the *Seventeen Histories*, in two hundred and seventeen volumes, and its continuation, the *Twenty-two Histories*, a still larger work. Though the entertaining episodes and sketches of character found in Herodotus and other ancient European historians are wanting, there is plenty of incident in court, camp, and social life, as well as public acts and royal biography. The dynastic records became the duty of special officers, and the headings adopted from the Sui, A.D. 590, have since been followed in arranging the historic materials under twelve heads. From the mass of materials digested by careful scholars have been compiled the records now known; they form, with all their imperfections, the best continuous history of any Asiatic people. Popular abridgments are common, among which the *Tung Kien Kang-muh*, or 'General Mirror of History,' and a compiled abridgment of it, the *Kang Kien Í Chí*, or 'History made Easy,' are the most useful.

The earliest historian among the Chinese is Sz'ma Tsien,[1] who flourished about B.C. 104, in which year he commenced the *Sz' Kí*, or 'Historical Memoirs,' in one hundred and thirty chapters. In this great work, which, like the Muses of Herodotus in Greek, forms the commencement of credible modern history with the Chinese, the author relates the actions of the Emperors

---

[1] Compare Rémusat, *Nouveaux Mélanges*, Tome II., pp. 130 ff., where there are excellent biographical notices of Sz'ma Tsien and other native historians.

in regular succession and the principal events which happened during their reigns, together with details and essays respecting music, astronomy, religious ceremonies, weights, public works, etc., and the changes they had undergone during the twenty-two centuries embraced in his Memoirs. It is stated by Rémusat that there are in the whole work five hundred and twenty-six thousand five hundred characters, for the Chinese, like the ancient Hebrews, number the words in their standard authors. The *Sz' Kí* is in five parts, and its arrangement has served as a model for subsequent historians, few of whom have equalled its author in the vivacity of their style or carefulness of their research.

The *General Mirror to Aid in Governing*, by Sz'ma Kwang, of the Sung dynasty, in two hundred and ninety-four chapters, is one of the best digested and most lucid annals that Chinese scholars have produced, embracing the period between the end of the Tsin to the beginning of the Sung dynasty (A.D. 313 to 960). Both the historians Sz'ma Tsien and Sz'ma Kwang filled high offices in the State, were both alternately disgraced and honored, and were mixed up with all the political movements of the day. Rémusat speaks in terms of deserved commendation of their writings, and to a notice of their works adds some account of their lives. One or two incidents in the career of Sz'ma Kwang exhibit a readiness of action and freedom in expressing his sentiments which are more common among the Chinese than is usually supposed. In his youth he was standing with some companions near a large vase used to rear gold fish, when one of them fell in. Too terrified themselves to do anything, all but young Kwang ran to seek succor; he looked around for a stone with which to break the vase and let the water flow out, and thus saved the life of his companion. In subsequent life the same common sense was joined with a boldness which led him to declare his sentiments on all occasions. Some southern people once sent a present to the Emperor of a strange quadruped, which his flatterers said was the mythological *kí-lin* of happy omen. Sz'ma Kwang, being consulted on the matter, replied: "I have never seen the *kí-lin*, therefore I cannot tell whether this be one or not. What I do know is that the real *kí-lin* could never be brought hither by foreigners; he appears of himself when the State is well governed." [1] An extension of this great work by Lí Tao, of the Sung dynasty, in five hundred and twenty books, gave their countrymen a fair account of the thirty-six centuries of their national fortunes; and the digest under Chu Hí's direction has made them still more accessible and famous to succeeding ages.

Few works in Chinese literature are more popular than a historical novel by Chin Shau, about A.D. 350, called the *San Kwoh Chí*, or 'History of the Three States;' its scenes are laid in the northern parts of China, and include the period between A.D. 170 and 317, when several ambitious chieftains conspired against the imbecile princes of the once famous Han dynasty, and, after that was overthrown, fought among themselves until the Empire was again reconsolidated under the Tsin dynasty. This performance, from its double character and the long period over which it extends, necessarily lacks that unity which a novel should have. Its charms, to a Chinese, consist in the animated descriptions of plots and counterplots, in the relations of battles, sieges, and retreats, and the admirable manner in which the characters are delineated and their acts intermixed with entertaining episodes. The work opens with describing the distracted state of the Empire under the misrule of Ling tí and Hwan tí, the last two monarchs of the House of Han (147 to 184), who were entirely swayed by eunuchs, and left the administration of government to reckless oppressors, until ambitious men, taking advantage of the general discontent, raised the standard of rebellion. The leaders ordered their partisans to wear yellow head-dresses, whence the rebellion was called that of the Yellow Caps, and was suppressed only after several years of hard struggle by a few distinguished generals who upheld the throne. Among these was Tung Choh, who, gradually drawing to himself all the power in the State, thereby arrayed against himself others equally ambitious and unscrupulous. Disorganization had not yet proceeded so far that all hope of supporting the rightful throne had left the minds of its adher-

---

[1] *Chinese Repository*, Vol. IX., pp. 210, 274.

ents, among whom was Wang Yun, a chancellor of the Empire, who, seeing the danger of the State, devised a scheme to inveigle Tung Choh to his ruin, which is thus narrated:

One day Tung Choh gave a great entertainment to the officers of government. When the wine had circulated several times, Lü Pu (his adopted son) whispered something in his ear, whereupon he ordered the attendants to take Chang Wăn from the table into the hall below, and presently one of them returned, handing up his head in a charger. The spirits of all present left their bodies, but Tung, laughing, said, "Pray, sirs, do not be alarmed. Chang Wăn has been leaguing with Yuen Shuh how to destroy me; a messenger just now brought a letter for him, and inadvertently gave it to my son; for which he has lost his life. You, gentlemen, have no cause for dread." All the officers replied, "Yes! Yes!" and immediately separated.

Chancellor Wang Yun returned home in deep thought: "The proceedings of this day's feast are enough to make my seat an uneasy one;" and taking his cane late at night he walked out in the moonlight into his rear garden, when standing near a rose arbor and weeping as he looked up, he heard a person sighing and groaning within the peony pavillion. Carefully stepping and watching, he saw it was Tiau Chen, a singing-girl belonging to the house, who had been taken into his family in early youth and taught to sing and dance; she was now sixteen, and both beautiful and accomplished, and Wang treated her as if she had been his own daughter.

Listening some time, he spoke out, "What underhand plot are you at now, insignificant menial?" Tiau Chen, much alarmed, kneeling, said, "What treachery can your slave dare to devise?" "If you have nothing secret, why then are you here late at night sighing in this manner?" Tiau replied, "Permit your handmaid to declare her inmost thoughts. I am very grateful for your excellency's kind nurture, for teaching me singing and dancing, and for the treatment I have received. If my body should be crushed to powder [in your service], I could not requite a myriad to one [for these favors]. But lately I have seen your eyebrows anxiously knit, doubtless from some State affairs, though I presumed not to ask; this evening, too, I saw you restless in your seat. On this account I sighed, not imagining your honor was overlooking me. If I can be of the least use, I would not decline the sacrifice of a thousand lives." Wang, striking his cane on the ground, exclaimed, "Who would have thought the rule of Han was lodged in your hands! Come with me into the picture-gallery." Tiau Chen following in, he ordered his females all to retire, and placing her in a seat, turned himself around and did her obeisance. She, much surprised, prostrated herself before him, and asked the reason of such conduct, to which he replied, "You are able to compassionate all the people in the dominions of Han." His words ended, the tears gushed like a fountain. She added, "I just now said, if I can be of any service I will not decline, though I should lose my life."

Wang, kneeling, rejoined, "The people are in most imminent danger, and the nobility in a hazard like that of eggs piled up; neither can be rescued without your assistance. The traitor Tung Choh wishes soon to seize the throne, and none of the civil or military officers have any practicable means of defence. He has an adopted son, Lü Pu, a remarkably daring and brave man, who, like himself, is the slave of lust. Now I wish to contrive a scheme to inveigle them both, by first promising to wed you to Lü, and then offering you to Tung, while you must seize the opportunity to raise suspicions in them, and slander one to the other so as to sever them, and cause Lü to kill Tung, whereby the present great evils will be terminated, the throne upheld, and the government re-established. All this is in your power, but I do not know how the plan strikes you." Tiau answered, "I have promised your excellency my utmost service, and you may trust me that I will devise some good scheme when I am offered to them."

"You must be aware that if this design leaks out, we shall all be utterly exterminated." "Your excellency need not be anxious, and if I do not aid in accomplishing your patriotic designs, let me die a thousand deaths."

Wang, bowing, thanked her. The next day, taking several of the brilliant pearls preserved in the family, he ordered a skilful workman to inlay them into a golden coronet, which he secretly sent as a present to Lü Pu. Highly gratified, Lü himself went to Wang's house to thank him, where a well-prepared feast of viands and wine awaited his arrival. Wang went out to meet him, and waiting upon him into the rear hall, invited him to sit at the top of the table, but Lü objected: "I am only a general in the prime minister's department, while your excellency is a high minister in his Majesty's court—why this mistaken respect?"

Wang rejoined, "There is no hero in the country now besides you; I do not pay this honor to your office, but to your talents." Lü was excessively pleased. Wang ceased not in engaging him to drink, the while speaking of Tung Choh's high qualities, and praising his guest's virtues, who, on his side, wildly laughed for joy. Most of the attendants were ordered to retire, a few waiting-maids stopping to serve out wine, when, being half drunk, he ordered them to tell the young child to come in. Shortly after, two pages led in Tiau Chen, gorgeously dressed, and Lü, much astonished, asked, "Who is this?"

"It is my little daughter, Tiau Chen, whom I have ordered to come in and see you, for I am very grateful for your honor's misapplied kindness to me, which has been like that to near relatives." He then bade her present a goblet of wine to him, and, as she did so, their eyes glanced to and from each other.

Wang, feigning to be drunk, said: "The child strongly requests your honor to drink many cups; my house entirely depends upon your excellency." Lü requested her to be seated, but she acting as if about to retire, Wang remarked, "The general is my intimate friend; be seated, my child; what are you afraid of?" She then sat down at his side, while Lü's eyes never strayed from their gaze upon her, drinking and looking.

Wang, pointing to Tiau, said to Lü, "I wish to give this girl to you as a concubine, but know not whether you will receive her?" Lü, leaving the table to thank him, said, "If I could obtain such a girl as this, I would emulate the requital dogs and horses give for the care taken of them."

Wang rejoined, "I will immediately select a lucky day, and send her to your house" Lü was delighted beyond measure, and never took his eyes off her, while Tiau herself, with ogling glances, intimated her passion. The feast shortly after broke up, and Lü departed.

The scheme here devised was successful, and Tung Choh was assassinated by his son when he was on his way to depose the monarch. His death, however, brought no peace to the country, and three chieftains, Tsau Tsau, Liu Pí, and Sun Kiuen, soon distinguished themselves in their struggles for power, and afterward divided the Empire into the three States of Wu, Shuh, and Wei, from which the work derives its name. Many of the personages who figure in this work have since been deified, among whom are Liu Pí's sworn brother Kwan Yü, who is now the Mars (*Kwan ti*), and Hwa To, the Esculapius, of Chinese mythology. Its scenes and characters have all been fruitful subjects for the pencil and the pen of artists and poetasters. One commentator has gone so far as to incorporate his reflections in the body of the text itself, in the shape of such expressions as "Wonderful speech! What rhodomontade! This man was a fool before, and shows himself one now!" Davis likens this work to the Iliad for its general arrangement and blustering character of the heroes; it was composed when the scenes described and their leading actors existed chiefly in personal recollection, and the remembrances of both were fading away in the twilight of popular legends.

Among the numerous historians of China, only a few would repay the labor of an entire translation, but many would furnish good materials for extended epitomes. Among these are the *Tso Chuen*, already noticed; the *Anterior Han Dynasty*, by Pan Ku and his sister; the *Wei Shu*, by Wei Shau (A.D. 386–556); and the works of Sz'ma Kwang. In addition to the dynastic histories, numerous similar works classified under the heads of annals and complete records in two sections of this division would furnish much authentic material for the foreign archæologist. The most valuable relic after the *Chun Tsiu*, of a historic character, is the "Bamboo Books," reported to have been found in a tomb in Honan, A.D. 279; it gives a chronological list down to B.C. 299, with incidents interspersed, and bears many internal evidences of genuineness. Legge and Biot have each translated it.[1]

Biographies of distinguished men and women are numerous, and their preparation forms a favorite branch of literary labor. It is noticeable to observe the consideration paid to literary women in these memoirs, and the praises bestowed upon discreet mothers whose talented children are considered to be the criteria of their careful training. One work of this class is in one hundred and twenty volumes, called *Sing Pu*, but it does not possess the incident and animation which are found in some less formal biographical dictionaries. The *Lieh Nü Chuen*, or 'Memoirs of Distinguished Ladies' of ancient times, by Liu Hiang, B.C. 125, is often cited by writers on female education who wish to show how women were anciently trained to the practice of every virtue and accomplishment. If a Chinese author cannot quote a case to illustrate his position at least eight or ten centuries old, he thinks half its force abated by its youth. Biographical works are almost as numerous as statistical, and afford one of the best sources for studying the national character; some of them, like the lives of Washington or Cromwell in our own literature, combine both history and biography.

Some of the statistical and geographical works mentioned in this division are noticed on p. 49. Among those on the Constitution is the 'Complete Antiquarian Researches' of Ma Twan-lin (A.D. 1275), in three hundred and forty-eight chapters. It forms a most extensive and profound work, containing researches upon every matter relating to government, and extending through a series of dynasties which held the throne nearly forty centuries. Rémusat goes so far as to say: "This excellent work is a library by itself, and if Chinese literature possessed no other, the language would be worth learning for the sake of reading this alone." No book has been more drawn upon by Europeans for information concerning matters relating to Eastern Asia than this; Visdelou and De Guignes took from

---

[1] Legge's *Chinese Classics*, Vol. III.; *Prolegomena*, Chap. IV. E. Biot in the *Journal Asiatique*, 2e Series, Tomes XII., p. 537, and XIII., pp. 203, 381.

it much of their information relating to the Tartars and Huns; and Pingsé extracted his account of the comets and ærolites from its pages, besides some geographical and ethnographical papers. Rémusat often made use of its stores, and remarks that many parts merit an entire translation, which can be said, indeed, of few Chinese authors. A supplement prepared and published in 1586 by Wang Kí brings it down to that date. A further revision was issued under imperial patronage in 1772, and a final one not long afterward, continuing the narrative to the reign of Kanghí.[1] It elevates our opinion of a nation whose literature can boast of a work like this, exhibiting such patient investigation and candid comparison of authorities, such varied research and just discrimination of what is truly important, and so extensive a mass of facts and opinions upon every subject of historic interest. Although there be no quotations in it from Roman or Greek classic authors, and the ignorance of the compiler of what was known upon the same subjects in other countries disqualified him from giving his remarks the completeness they would otherwise have had, yet when the stores of knowledge from western lands are made known to a people whose scholars can produce such works as this, the *Memoirs* of Sz'ma Tsien, and others equally good, it may reasonably be expected that they will not lack in industry or ability to carry on their researches.

The third division of *Tsz' Pu*, 'Scholastic' or 'Professional Writings,' is arranged under fourteen sections, viz.: Philosophical, Military, Legal, Agricultural, Medical, Mathematical, and Magical writings, works on the Liberal Arts, Collections, Miscellanies, Encyclopædias, Novels, and treatises on the tenets of the Buddhists and Rationalists. The first section is called *Jü Kia Lui*, meaning the 'Works of the Literary Family,' under which name is included those who maintain, discuss, and teach the tenets of the sages, although they may not accept all that Confucius taught. This class of books is worthy of far more examination than foreigners have hitherto given to it, and they

---

[1] Compare Rémusat, *Mélanges Asiatiques*, Tome II., p. 166; *Chinese Repository*, Vol. IX., p. 143; Wylie's *Notes*, p. 55; Mayer's *Chinese Reader's Manual*, p. 149.

will find that Chinese philosophers have discussed morals, government, cosmogony, and like subjects, with a freedom and acuteness that has not been credited to them.

It was during the Sung dynasty, when Europe was utterly lethargic and unprogressive, that China showed a marvellous mental activity, and received from Ching, Chu, Chau, and their disciples a molding and conservative influence which has remained to this day. An extract from a discussion by Chu Hí will show the way in which he reasons on the *primum mobile.*

Under the whole heaven there is no primary matter (*li*) without the immaterial principle (*kí*), and no immaterial principle apart from the primary matter. Subsequent to the existence of the immaterial principle is produced primary matter, which is deducible from the axiom that the one male and the one female principle of nature may be dominated *tao* or *logos* (the active principle from which all things emanate); thus nature is spontaneously possessed of benevolence and righteousness (which are included in the idea of *tao*).

First of all existed *tien li* (the celestial principle or soul of the universe), and then came primary matter; primary matter accumulated constituted *chih* (body, substance, or the accidents and qualities of matter), and nature was arranged.

Should any ask whether the immaterial principle or primary matter existed first, I should say that the immaterial principle on assuming a figure ascended, and primary matter on assuming form descended; when we come to speak of assuming form and ascending or descending, how can we divest ourselves of the idea of priority and subsequence? When the immaterial principle does not assume a form, primary matter then becomes coarse, and forms a sediment.

Originally, however, no priority or subsequence can be predicated of the immaterial principle and primary matter, and yet if you insist on carrying out the reasoning to the question of their origin, then you must say that the immaterial principle has the priority; but it is not a separate and distinct thing; it is just contained in the centre of the primary matter, so that were there no primary matter, then this immaterial principle would have no place of attachment. Primary matter consists, in fact, of the four elements of metal, wood, water, and fire, while the immaterial principle is no other than the four cardinal virtues of benevolence, righteousness, propriety, and wisdom. . . .

Should any one ask for an explanation of the assertion that the immaterial principle has first existence, and after that comes primary matter, I say, it is not necessary to speak thus: but when we know that they are combined, is it that the immaterial principle holds the precedence, and the primary matter the subsequence, or is it that the immaterial principle is subsequent to the primary matter? We cannot thus carry our reasoning; but should we endeavor to form some idea of it, then we may suppose that the primary matter relies on the immaterial principle to come into action, and wherever the primary matter is coagulated, there the immaterial principle is present. For the primary matter can concrete and coagulate, act and do, but the immaterial principle has neither will nor wish, plan nor operation: but only where the primary matter is collected and coagulated, then the immaterial principle is in the midst of it. Just as in nature, men and things, grass and trees, birds and beasts, in their propagation invariably require seed, and certainly cannot without seed from nothingness produce anything; all this, then, is the primary matter, but the immaterial principle is merely a pure, empty, wide-stretched void, without form or footstep, and incapable of action or creation; but the primary matter can ferment and coagulate, collect and produce things. . . .

Should any one ask, with regard to those expressions, "The Supreme Ruler confers the due medium on the people, and when Heaven is about to send down a great trust upon men, out of regard to the people it sets up princes over them;" and, "Heaven in producing things treats them according to their attainments: on those who do good, it sends down a hundred blessings, and on those who do evil, a hundred calamities;" and, "When Heaven is about to send down some uncommon calamity upon a generation, it first produces some uncommon genius to determine it;" do these and such like expressions imply that above the azure sky there is a Lord and Ruler who acts thus, or is it still true that Heaven has no mind, and men only carry out their reasonings in this style? I reply, these three things are but one idea; it is that the immaterial principle of order is thus. The primary matter in its evolutions hitherto, after one season of fulness has experienced one of decay; and after a period of decline it again flourishes; just as if things were going on in a circle. There never was a decay without a revival.

When men blow out their breath their bellies puff out, and when they inhale their bellies sink in, while we should have thought that at each expiration the stomach would fall in, and swell up at each inspiration; but the reason of it is that when men expire, though the mouthful of breath goes out, the second mouthful is again produced, therefore the belly is puffed up; and when men inspire, the breath which is introduced from within drives the other out, so that the belly sinks in. Lau-tsz' said nature is like an open pipe or bag; it moves, and yet is not compelled to stop, it is empty, and still more comes out; just like a fan-case open at both ends. . . .

The great extreme (*tai kih*) is merely the immaterial principle. It is not an independent separate existence; it is found in the male and female principles of nature, in the five elements, in all things; it is merely an immaterial principle, and because of its extending to the extreme limit, is therefore called the *great extreme*. If it were not for it, heaven and earth would not have been set afloat. . . . From the time when the great extreme came into operation, all things were produced by transformation. This one doctrine includes the whole; it was not because this was first in existence and then that, but altogether there is only one great origin, which from the substance extends to the use, and from the subtle reaches to that which is manifest. Should one ask, because all things partake of it, is the great extreme split up and divided? I should reply, that originally there is only one great extreme (*anima mundi*), of which all things partake, so that each one is provided with a great extreme;

just as the moon in the heavens is only one, and yet is dispersed over the hills and lakes, being seen from every place in succession; still you cannot say that the moon is divided.

The great extreme has neither residence, nor form, nor place which you can assign to it. If you speak of it before its development, then previous to that emanation it was perfect stillness; motion and rest, with the male and female principles of nature, are only the embodiment and descent of this principle. Motion is the motion of the great extreme, and rest is its rest, but these same motion and rest are not to be considered the great extreme itself. . . . Should any one ask, what is the great extreme? I should say, it is simply the principle of extreme goodness and extreme perfection. Every man has a great extreme, everything has one; that which Chao-tsz' called the great extreme is the exemplified virtue of everything that is extremely good and perfect in heaven and earth, men and things.

The great extreme is simply the extreme point, beyond which one cannot go; that which is most elevated, most mysterious, most subtle, and most divine, beyond which there is no passing. Lienkí was afraid lest people should think that the great extreme possessed form, and therefore called it the boundless extreme, a principle centred in nothing, and having an infinite extent. . . . It is the immaterial principle of the two powers, the four forms, and the eight changes of nature; we cannot say that it does not exist, and yet no form or corporeity can be ascribed to it. From this point is produced the one male and the one female principle of nature, which are called the dual powers; the four forms and eight changes also proceed from this, all according to a certain natural order, irrespective of human strength in its arrangement. But from the time of Confucius no one has been able to get hold of this idea.[1]

And, it might be added, no one ever will be able to "get hold" thereof. Such discussions as this have occupied the minds and pens of Chinese metaphysicians for centuries, and in their endeavors to explain the half-digested notions of the *Book of Changes*, they have wandered far away from the road which would have led them in the path of true knowledge, namely, the observation and record of the works and operations of nature around them; and one after another they have continued to roll this stone of Sisyphus until fatigue and bewilderment have come over them all. Some works on female education are found in this section, which seems designed as much to include whatever philosophers wrote as all they wrote on philosophy.

The second and third sections, on military and legal subjects,

---

[1] Translated by Rev. W. H. Medhurst, in the *Chinese Repository*, Vol. XIII., pp. 552, 609 et seq.

contain no writings of any eminence. The isolation of the Chinese prevented them from studying the various forms of government and jurisprudence observed in other countries and ages; it is this feature of originality which renders their legislation so interesting to western students. Among the fourth, on agricultural treatises, is the *Kăng Chih Tu Shí*, or 'Plates and Odes on Tillage and Weaving,' a thin quarto, which was written A.D. 1210, and has been widely circulated by the present government in order "to evince its regard for the people's support." The first half contains twenty-three plates on the various processes to be followed in raising rice, the last of which represents the husbandmen and their families returning thanks to the gods of the land for a good harvest, and offering a portion of the fruits of the earth; the last plate in the second part of the work also represents a similar scene of returning thanks for a good crop of silk, and presenting an offering to the gods. The drawings in this work are among the best for perspective and general composition which Chinese art has produced; probably their merit was the chief inducement to publish the work at governmental expense, for the odes are too brief to contain much information, and too difficult to be generally understood. The *Encyclopedia of Agriculture*, by Sü Kwang-kí, a high officer in 1600, better known as Paul Sü, gives a most elaborate detail of farming operations and utensils existing in the Ming. Other treatises on special topics and crops have been written, but it is the untiring industry of the people which secures to them the best returns from the soil, for they owe very little to science or machinery.

Among the numerous writings published for the improvement and instruction of the people by their rulers, none have been more influential than the *Shing Yu*, or 'Sacred Commands,' a politico-moral treatise, which has been made known to English readers by the translation of Dr. Milne.[1] The groundwork

[1] *The Sacred Edict*, London, 1817; a second edition of this translation appeared in Shanghai in 1870, and another in 1878. Compare Wylie's *Notes*, p. 71; Sir G. T. Staunton's *Miscellaneous Notices*, etc., pp. 1–56 (1812); *Le Saint Edit, Étude de Littérature chinoise*, préparée par A. Théophile Piry, Shanghai, 1879.

consists of sixteen apothegms, written by the Emperor Kanghí, containing general rules for the peace, prosperity, and wealth of all classes of his subjects. In order that none should plead ignorance in excuse for not knowing the Sacred Commands, it is by law required that they be proclaimed throughout the Empire by the local officers on the first and fifteenth day of every month, in a public hall set apart for the purpose, where the people are not only permitted, but requested and encouraged, to attend. In point of fact, however, this *political preaching*, as it has been called, is neglected except in large towns, though the design is not the less commendable. It is highly praiseworthy to monarchs, secure in their thrones as Kanghí and Yungching were, to take upon themselves the teaching of morality to their subjects, and institute a special service every fortnight to have their precepts communicated to them. If, too, it should soon be seen that their designs had utterly failed of all real good results from the mendacity of their officers and the ignorance or opposition of the people, still the merit due them is not diminished. The sixteen apothegms, each consisting of seven characters, are as follows:

1. Pay just regard to filial and fraternal duties, in order to give due importance to the relations of life.
2. Respect kindred in order to display the excellence of harmony.
3. Let concord abound among those who dwell in the same neighborhood, thereby preventing litigations.
4. Give the chief place to husbandry and the culture of the mulberry, that adequate supplies of food and raiment be secured
5. Esteem economy, that money be not lavishly wasted.
6. Magnify academical learning, in order to direct the scholar's progress.
7. Degrade strange religions, in order to exalt the orthodox doctrines.
8. Explain the laws, in order to warn the ignorant and obstinate.
9. Illustrate the principles of a polite and yielding carriage, in order to improve manners.
10. Attend to the essential employments, in order to give unvarying determination to the will of the people.
11. Instruct the youth, in order to restrain them from evil.
12. Suppress all false accusing, in order to secure protection to the innocent.
13. Warn those who hide deserters, that they may not be involved in their downfall.
14. Complete the payment of taxes, in order to prevent frequent urging.
15. Unite the *pao* and *kia*, in order to extirpate robbery and theft.
16. Settle animosities, that lives may be duly valued.

The amplifications of these maxims by Yungching contain much information respecting the theory of his government, and the position of the writer entitles him to speak from knowledge; his amplification of the fourteenth maxim shows their character.

From of old the country was divided into districts, and a tribute paid proportioned to the produce of the land. From hence arose revenues, upon which the expense of the five *li* and the whole charges of government depended. These expenses a prince must receive from the people, and they are what inferiors should offer to superiors. Both in ancient and modern times this principle has been the same and cannot be changed. Again, the expenses of the salaries of magistrates that they may rule our people; of pay to the army that they may protect them; of preparing for years of scarcity that they may be fed; as all these are collected from the Empire, so they are all employed for its use. How then can it be supposed that the granaries and treasury of the sovereign are intended to injure the people that he may nourish himself? Since the establishment of our dynasty till now, the proportions of the revenue have been fixed by an universally approved statute, and all unjust items completely cancelled; not a thread or hair too much has been demanded from the people. In the days of our sacred Father, the Emperor Pious, his abounding benevolence and liberal favor fed this people upward of sixty years. Daily desirous to promote their abundance and happiness, he greatly diminished the revenue, not limiting the reduction to hundreds, thousands, myriads, or lacs of taels. The mean and the remote have experienced his favor; even now it enters the muscles, and penetrates to the marrow. To exact with moderation, diminish the revenue, and confer favors on the multitude, are the virtues of a prince: to serve superiors, and to give the first place to public service and second to their own, are the duties of a people. Soldiers and people should all understand this. Become not lazy and trifling, nor prodigally throw away your property. Linger not to pay in the revenue, looking and hoping for some unusual occurrence to avoid it, nor entrust your imposts to others, lest bad men appropriate them to their own use.

Pay in at the terms, and wait not to be urged. Then with the overplus you can nourish your parents, complete the marriages of your children, satisfy your daily wants, and provide for the annual feasts and sacrifices. District officers may then sleep at ease in their public halls, and villagers will no longer be vexed in the night by calls from the tax-gatherers; on neither hand will any be involved. Your wives and children will be easy and at rest, than which you have no greater joy. If unaware of the importance of the revenue to government, and that the laws must be enforced, perhaps you will positively refuse or deliberately put off the payment, when the magistrates, obliged to balance their accounts, and give in their reports at stated times, must be rigorously severe. The assessors, suffering the pain of the whip, cannot help indulging their rapacious demands on you; knocking and pecking at your doors like hungry hawks, they will devise numerous methods of getting their wants supplied. These nameless ways of spending will probably amount to more than the sum which ought to have been paid, and that sum, after all, cannot be dispensed with.

We know not what benefit can accrue from this. Rather than give presents to satisfy the rapacity of policemen, how much better to clear off the just assessments! Rather than prove an obstinate race and refuse the payment of the revenue, would it not be better to keep the law? Every one, even the most stupid, knows this. Furthermore, when superiors display benevolence, inferiors should manifest justice; this belongs to the idea of their being one body. Reflect that the constant labors and cares of the palace are all to serve the people. When freshes occur, dikes must be raised to restrain them; if the demon of drought appear, prayer must be offered for rain: when the locusts come, they must be destroyed. If the calamities be averted, you reap the advantage; but if they overwhelm you, your taxes are forborne, and alms liberally expended for you. If it be thus, and the people still can suffer themselves to evade the payment of taxes and hinder the supply of government, how, I ask, can you be easy? Such conduct is like that of an undutiful son. We use these repeated admonitions, only wishing you, soldiers and people, to think of the army and nation, and also of your persons and families. Then abroad you will have the fame of faithfulness, and at home peacefully enjoy its fruits. Officers will not trouble you, nor their clerks vex you—what joy equal to this! O soldiers and people, meditate on these things in the silent night, and let all accord with our wishes.[1]

Wang Yu-pí, a high officer under Yungching, paraphrased the amplifications in a colloquial manner. His remarks on the doctrines of the Buddhists and Rationalists will serve as an illustration; the quotation here given is found under the seventh maxim.

You simple people know not how to discriminate; for even according to what the books of Buddha say, he was the first-born son of the king Fan; but, retiring from the world, he fled away alone to the top of the Snowy Mountains, in order to cultivate virtue. If he regarded not his own father, mother, wife, and children, are you such fools as to suppose that he regards the multitude of the living, or would deliver his laws and doctrines to you? The imperial residence, the queen's palace, the dragon's chamber, and halls of state—if he rejected these, is it not marvellous to suppose that he should delight in the nunneries, monasteries, temples, and religious houses which you can build for him? As to the Gemmeous Emperor, the most honorable in heaven, if there be indeed such a god, it is strange to think he should not enjoy himself at his own ease in the high heavens, but must have you to give him a body of molten gold, and build him a house to dwell in!

All these nonsensical tales about keeping fasts, collecting assemblies, building temples, and fashioning images, are feigned by those sauntering,

---

[1] *Sacred Edict*, pp. 254–259.

worthless priests and monks to deceive you. Still you believe them, and not only go yourselves to worship and burn incense in the temples, but also suffer your wives and daughters to go. With their hair oiled and faces painted, dressed in scarlet and trimmed with green, they go to burn incense in the temples, associating with the priests of Buddha, doctors of Reason and bare-stick attorneys, touching shoulders, rubbing arms, and pressed in the moving crowd. I see not where the good they talk of doing is; on the contrary, they do many shameful things that create vexation, and give people occasion for laughter and ridicule.

Further, there are some persons who, fearing that their good boys and girls may not attain to maturity, take and give them to the temples to become priests and priestesses of Buddha and Reason, supposing that after having removed them from their own houses and placed them at the foot of grandfather Fuh (Buddha), they are then sure of prolonging life! Now, I would ask you if those who in this age are priests of these sects, all reach the age of seventy or eighty, and if there is not a short-lived person among them?

Again, there is another very stupid class of persons who, because their parents are sick, pledge their own persons by a vow before the gods that if their parents be restored to health, they will worship and burn incense on the hills, prostrating themselves at every step till they arrive at the summit, whence they will dash themselves down! If they do not lose their lives, they are sure to break a leg or an arm. They say to themselves, "To give up our own lives to save our parents is the highest display of filial duty." Bystanders also praise them as dutiful children, but they do not consider that to slight the bodies received from their parents in this manner discovers an extreme want of filial duty.

Moreover, you say that serving Fuh is a profitable service; that if you burn paper money, present offerings, and keep fasts before the face of your god Fuh, he will dissipate calamities, blot out your sins, increase your happiness, and prolong your age! Now reflect: from of old it has been said, "The gods are intelligent and just." Were Buddha a god of this description, how could he avariciously desire your gilt paper, and your offerings to engage him to afford you protection? If you do not burn gilt paper to him, and spread offerings on his altar, the god Fuh will be displeased with you, and send down judgments on you! Then your god Fuh is a scoundrel! Take, for example, the district magistrate. Should you never go to compliment and flatter him, yet, if you are good people and attend to your duty, he will pay marked attention to you. But transgress the law, commit violence, or usurp the rights of others, and though you should use a thousand ways and means to flatter him, he will still be displeased with you, and will, without fail, remove such pests from society.

You say that worshipping Fuh atones for your sins. Suppose you have violated the law, and are hauled to the judgment-seat to be punished; if you should bawl out several thousand times, "O your excellency! O your excellency!" do you think the magistrate would spare you? You will, however, at all risks, invite several Buddhist and Rationalist priests to your houses to recite their canonical books and make confession, supposing that to chant their

mummery drives away misery, secures peace, and prolongs happiness and life. But suppose you rest satisfied with merely reading over the sections of these Sacred Commands several thousands or myriads of times without acting conformably thereto; would it not be vain to suppose that his Imperial Majesty should delight in you, reward you with money, and promote you to office?[1]

This ridicule of the popular superstitions has, no doubt, had some effect, repeated as it is in all parts of the country; but since the literati merely tear down and build up nothing, giving the people no substitute for what they take away, but rather, in their times of trouble, doing the things they decry, such homilies do not destroy the general respect for such ceremonies. The *Shing Yu* has also been versified for the benefit of children, and colloquial explanations added, which has further tended to enforce and inculcate its admonitions. The praise bestowed on this work by Johnson, in his *Oriental Religions*, has a good degree of actual usefulness among the people to confirm his observations; yet they are quite used to hearing the highest moral platitudes from their rulers, to whom they would not lend a dollar on their word.

In the fifth section, on medical writings, separate works are mentioned on the treatment of all domestic animals; among them is one on veterinary surgery, whose writers have versified most of their observations and prescriptions. The *Herbal* of Lí Shí-chin, noticed on p. 370, and monographs on special diseases, all show the industry of Chinese physicians to much better advantage than their science. Works on medicine and surgery are numerous, in which the surface of the body is minutely represented in pictures, together with drawings of the mode of performing various operations. Works on judicial astrology, chiromancy, and other modes of divination, on the rules for finding lucky spots for houses, graves, and temples, are exceedingly numerous, a large number of them written by Rationalists.

The eighth section, on art, contains writings on painting, music, engraving, writing, posturing, and archery, and they will doubtless furnish many new points to western artists on the

---

[1] *Sacred Edict*, p. 146.

principles and attainments of the Chinese in these branches when the works have been made better known.

The ninth section, entitled 'Collections' or 'Repertories,' is divided into memoirs on antiques, swords, coins, and bronzes, and presents a field of interesting research to a foreign archæologist likely to reward him. Another division, containing the monographs on tea, bamboo, floriculture, etc., is not so promising.

The tenth section, on philosophical writings, having a tinge of heterodoxy, is a very large one, and offers a rare opportunity of research to those curious to know what China can contribute to moral science. The writings of Roman Catholics and Moslems are included in this long catalogue.

Under the head of encyclopædias, a list of summaries, compends, and treasuries of knowledge is given, which for extent and bulkiness cannot be equalled in any language. Among them is the *Tai Tien*, or 'Great Record' of the Emperor Yungloh (A.D. 1403), in twenty-two thousand eight hundred and seventy-seven chapters, and containing the substance of all classical, historical, philosophical, and scientific writings in the language. Parts of this compilation were lost, and on the accession of the Manchus one-tenth of it was missing; but by means of the unequalled interest on the part of Yungloh in his national literature, three hundred and eighty-five ancient and rare works were rescued from destruction. The *San Tsai Tu*, or 'Plates [Illustrative of the] Three Powers' (*i.e.*, heaven, earth, and man, by which is meant the entire universe), in one hundred and thirty volumes, is one of the most valuable compilations, by reason of the great number of plates it contains, which exhibit the ideas of the compilers much better than their descriptions.

The twelfth section, containing novels and tales, called *Siao Shwoh*, or 'Trifling Talk,' gives the titles of but few of the thousands of productions of this class in the language. Works of fiction are among the most popular and exceptionable books the Chinese have, and those which are not demoralizing are, with some notable exceptions, like the *Ten Talented Authors*, generally slighted. The books sold in the streets are chiefly of this class of writings, consisting of tales and stories generally destitute of all intricacy of plot, fertility of illustration, or elevation of sentiment. They form the common mental aliment of the lower classes, being read by those who are able, and talked about by all; their influence is consequently immense. Many of them are written in the purest style, among which a collection called *Liao Chai*, or 'Pastimes of the Study,' in sixteen volumes, is pre-eminent for its variety and force of expression, and its perusal can be recommended to every one who wishes to study the copiousness of the Chinese language. The preface is dated in 1679; most of the tales are short, and few have any ostensible moral to them, while those which are objectionable for their immorality, or ridiculous from their magic whimsies, form a large proportion. A quotation or two will illustrate the author's invention:

A villager was once selling plums in the market, which were rather delicious and fragrant, and high in price; and there was a Tao priest, clad in ragged garments of coarse cotton, begging before his wagon. The villager scolded him, but he would not go off; whereupon, becoming angry, he reviled and hooted at him. The priest said, "The wagon contains many hundred plums, and I have only begged one of them, which, for you, respected sir, would certainly be no great loss; why then are you so angry?" The spectators advised to give him a poor plum and send him away, but the villager would not consent. The workmen in the market disliking the noise and clamor, furnished a few coppers and bought a plum, which they gave the priest. He bowing thanked them, and turning to the crowd said, "I do not wish to be stingy, and request you, my friends, to partake with me of this delicious plum." One of them replied, "Now you have it, why do you not eat it yourself?" "I want only the stone to plant," said he, eating it up at a munch. When eaten, he held the stone in his hand, and taking a spade off his shoulder, dug a hole in the ground several inches deep, into which he put it and covered it with earth. Then turning to the market people, he procured some broth with which he watered and fertilized it; and others, wishing to see what would turn up, brought him boiling dregs from shops near by, which he poured upon the hole just dug. Every one's eyes being fixed upon the spot, they saw a crooked shoot issuing forth, which gradually increased till it became a tree, having branches and leaves; flowers and then fruit succeeded, large and very fragrant, which covered the tree. The priest then approached the tree, plucked the fruit and gave the beholders; and when all were consumed, he felled the tree with a colter—chopping, chopping for a good while, until at last, having cut it off, he shouldered the foliage in an easy manner, and leisurely walked away.

When first the priest began to perform his magic arts, the villager was also among the crowd, with outstretched neck and gazing eyes, and completely forgot his own business. When the priest had gone, he began to look int his wagon, and lo! it was empty of plums; and for the first time he perceived that what had just been distributed were all his own goods. Moreover, looking narrowly about his wagon, he saw that the dashboard was gone, having just been cut off with a chisel. Much excited and incensed he ran after him, and as he turned the corner of the wall, he saw the board thrown down beneath the hedge, it being that with which the plum-tree was felled. Nobody knew where the priest had gone, and all the market folks laughed heartily.

The Rationalists are considered as the chief magicians among the Chinese, and they figure in most of the tales in this work, whose object probably was to exalt their craft, and add to their reputation. Like the foregoing against hardheartedness, the following contains a little sidewise admonition against theft:

On the west of the city in the hamlet of the White family lived a rustic who stole his neighbor's duck and cooked it. At night he felt his skin itch, and on looking at it in the morning saw a thick growth of duck's feathers, which, when irritated, pained him. He was much alarmed, for he had no remedy to cure it; but, in a dream of the night, a man informed him, "Your disease is a judgment from heaven; you must get the loser to reprimand you, and the feathers will fall off." Now this gentleman, his neighbor, was always liberal and courteous, nor during his whole life, whenever he lost anything, had he even manifested any displeasure in his countenance. The thief craftily told him, "The fellow who stole your duck is exceedingly afraid of a reprimand; but reprove him, and he will no doubt then fear in future." He, laughing, replied, "Who has the time or disposition to scold wicked men?" and altogther refused to do so; so the man, being hardly bestead, was obliged to tell the truth, upon which the gentleman gave him a scolding, and his disorder was removed.

Rémusat compares the construction of Chinese novels to those of Richardson, in which the "authors render their characters interesting and natural by reiterated strokes of the pencil, which finally produce a high degree of illusion. The interest in their pages arose precisely in proportion to the stage of my progress; and in approaching to the termination, I found myself about to part with some agreeable people, just as I had duly learned to relish their society." He briefly describes the defects in Chinese romances as principally consisting in long descriptions of trifling particulars and delineations of localities, and the characters and circumstances of the interlocutors, while the thread of the narrative is carried on mostly in a conversational way, which, from its minuteness, soon becomes tedious. The length of their poetic descriptions and prolix display of the wonders of art or the beauties of nature, thrown in at the least hint in the narrative, or moral reflections introduced in the most serious manner in the midst of diverting incidents, like a long-metre psalm in a comedy, tend to confuse the main story and dislocate the unity requisite to produce an effect.

Chinese novels, however, generally depend on something of a plot, and the characters are sometimes well sustained. "Visits and the formalities of polished statesmen; assemblies, and above all, the conversations which make them agreeable; repasts, and the social amusements which prolong them; walks of the admirers of beautiful nature; journeys; the manœuvres of adventurers; lawsuits; the literary examinations; and, in the sequel, marriage, form their most frequent episodes and ordinary conclusions." The hero of these plots is usually a young academician, endowed with an amiable disposition and devotedly attached to the study of classic authors, who meets with every kind of obstacle and ill luck in the way of attaining the literary honors he has set his heart on. The heroine is also well acquainted with letters; her own inclinations and her father's desires are that she may find a man of suitable accomplishments, but after having heard of one, every sort of difficulty is thrown in the way of getting him; which, of course, on the part of both are at last happily surmounted.

The adventures which distinguished persons meet in wandering over the country incognito, and the happy dénouement of their interviews with some whom they have been able to elevate when their real characters have been let out, form the plan of other tales. There is little or nothing of high wrought description of passion, nor acts of atrocious vengeance introduced to remove a troublesome person, but everything is kept within the bounds of probability; and at the end the vicious are punished by seeing their bad designs fail of their end in the rewards and success given those who have done well. In most of the stories whose length and style are such as to entitle them to the name of novel, and which have attained any reputation, the story is not disgraced by anything offensive; it is rather in the shorter tales that decency is violated. Among them the *Hung Lao Mung*, or 'Dreams of the Red Chamber,' is one of the most popular stories, and open not a little to this objection.

The historical novels, of which there are many, would, if translated, prove more interesting to foreign readers than those merely describing manners, because they interweave much information in the story. The *Shui Hu Chuen*, or 'Narrative of the Water Marshes,' and 'The Annals of the Contending States,' are two of the best written; the latter is more credible as a history than any other work in this class.

The fourth division of the Catalogue is called *Tsih Pu*, or 'Miscellanies,' and the works mentioned in it are chiefly poems or collections of songs, occupying nearly one-third of the whole collection. They are arranged in five sections, namely: Poetry of Tsu, Complete Works of Individuals, and General Collections, On the Art of Poetry, and Odes and Songs. The most ancient poet in the language is Yuh Yuen, a talented Minister of State who flourished previous to the time of Mencius, and wrote the *Lí Sao*, or 'Dissipation of Sorrows.' It has been translated into German and French. His name and misfortunes are still commemorated by the Festival of Dragon-boats on the fifth day of the fifth moon. More celebrated in Chinese estimation are the poets Li Tai-peh and Tu Fu of the Tang dynasty, and Su Tung-po of the Sung, who combined the three leading traits of a bard, being lovers of flowers, wine, and song, and attaining distinction in the service of government.[1] The incidents in the life of the former of these bards were so varied, and his reckless love of drink brought him into so many scrapes, that he is no less famed for his adventures than for his sonnets. The following story is told of him in the 'Remarkable Facts of all Times,' which is here abridged from the translation of T. Pavié:

Lí, called *Tai-peh*, or 'Great-white,' from the planet Venus, was endowed with a beautiful countenance and a well-made person, exhibiting in all his

[1] The second of these, Tu Fu, is a poet of some distinction noticed by Rémusat (*Nouveaux Mélanges*, Tome II., p. 174). He lived in the eighth century A.D., dying of hunger in the year 768. His writings are usually edited with those of Lí Tai-peh.

movements a gentle nobility which indicated a man destined to rise above his age. When only ten years old, he could read the classics and histories, and his conversation showed the brilliancy of his thoughts, as well as the purity of his diction. He was, in consequence of his precocity, called the Exiled Immortal, but named himself the Retired Scholar of the Blue Lotus. Some one having extolled the quality of the wine of Niauching, he straightway went there, although more than three hundred miles distant, and abandoned himself to his appetite for liquor. While singing and carousing in a tavern, a military commandant passed, who, hearing his song, sent in to inquire who it was, and carried the poet off to his own house. On departing, he urged Lí to go to the capital and compete for literary honors, which, he doubted not, could be easily attained, and at last induced him to bend his steps to the capital. On his arrival there, he luckily met the academician Ho near the palace, who invited him to an alehouse, and laying aside his robes, drank wine with him till night, and then carried him home. The two were soon well acquainted, and discussed the merits of poetry and wine till they were much charmed with each other.

As the day of examination approached, Ho gave the poet some advice. "The examiners for this spring are Yang and Kao, one a brother of the Empress, the other commander of his Majesty's body-guard; both of them love those who make them presents, and if you have no means to buy their favor, the road of promotion will be shut to you. I know them both very well, and will write a note to each of them, which may, perhaps, obtain you some favor." In spite of his merit and high reputation, Lí found himself in such circumstances as to make it desirable to avail of the good-will of his friend Ho; but on perusing the notes he brought, the examiners disdainfully exclaimed, "After having fingered his *protégé's* money, the academician contents himself with sending us a billet which merely rings its sound, and bespeaks our attention and favors toward an upstart without degree or title. On the day of decision we will remember the name of Lí, and any composition signed by him shall be thrown aside without further notice." The day of examination came, and the distinguished scholars of the Empire assembled, eager to hand in their compositions. Lí, fully capable to go through the trial, wrote off his essay on a sheet without effort, and handed it in first. As soon as he saw the name of Lí, the examiner Yang did not even give himself time to glance over the page, but with long strokes of his pencil erased the composition, saying, "Such a scrawler as this is good for nothing but to grind my ink!" "To grind your ink!" interrupted the other examiner Kao; "say rather he is only fit to put on my stockings, and lace up my buskins."

With these pleasantries, the essay of Lí was rejected: but he, transported with anger at such a contemptuous refusal at the public examination, returned home and exclaimed, "I swear that if ever my wishes for promotion are accomplished, I will order Yang to grind my ink, and Kao to put on my stockings and lace up my buskins; then my vows will be accomplished." Ho endeavored to calm the indignation of the poet: "Stay here with me till a new examination is ordered in three years, and live in plenty; the examiners will not be the same then, and you will surely succeed." They therefore continued to live as they had done, drinking and making verses.

After many months had elapsed, some foreign ambassadors came to the capital charged with a letter from their sovereign, whom he was ordered to receive and entertain in the hall of ambassadors. The next day the officers handed in their letter to his Majesty's council, who ordered the doctors to open and read it, but they could none of them decipher a single word, humbly declaring it contained nothing but fly-tracks; "your subjects," they added, "have only a limited knowledge, a shallow acquaintance with things; they are unable to read a word." On hearing this, the Emperor turned to the examiner Yang and ordered him to read the letter, but his eyes wandered over the characters as if he had been blind, and he knew nothing of them. In vain did his Majesty address himself to the civil and military officers who filled the court; not one among them could say whether the letter contained words of good or evil import. Highly incensed, he broke out in reproaches against the grandees of his palace: "What! among so many magistrates, so many scholars and warriors, cannot there be found a single one who knows enough to relieve us of the vexation of this affair? If this letter cannot be read, how can it be answered? If the ambassadors are dismissed in this style, we shall be the ridicule of the barbarians, and foreign kings will mock the court of Nanking, and doubtless follow it up by seizing their lance and buckler and join to invade our frontiers. What then? If in three days no one is able to decipher this letter, every one of your appointments shall be suspended; if in six days you do not tell me what it means, your offices shall every one be taken away; and death shall execute justice on such ignorant men if I wait nine days in vain for its explanation, and others of our subjects shall be elevated to power whose virtue and talents will render some service to their country."

Terrified by these words, the grandees kept a mournful silence, and no one ventured a single reply which only irritated the monarch the more. On his return home, Ho related to his friend Lí everything that had transpired at court, who, hearing him with a mournful smile, replied, "How to be regretted, how unlucky it is that I could not obtain a degree at the examination last year, which would have given me a magistracy; for now, alas! it is impossible for me to relieve his Majesty of the chagrin which troubles him." "But truly," said Ho, suddenly, "I think you are versed in more than one science, and will be able to read this unlucky letter. I shall go to his Majesty and propose you on my own responsibility." The next day he went to the palace, and passing through the crowd of courtiers, approached the throne, saying, "Your subject presumes to announce to your Majesty that there is a scholar of great merit called Lí, at his house, who is profoundly acquainted with more than one science; command him to read this letter, for there is nothing of which he is not capable."

This advice pleased the Emperor, who presently sent a messenger to the house of the academician, ordering him to present himself at court. But Lí offered some objections: "I am a man still without degree or title; I have neither talents nor information, while the court abounds in civil and military officers, all equally famous for their profound learning. How then can you have recourse to such a contemptible and useless man as I? If I presume to accept this behest, I fear that I shall deeply offend the nobles of the palace"—referring especially to the premier Yang and the general Kao. When his reply was announced to the Emperor, he demanded of Ho why his guest did not come when ordered. Ho replied, "I can assure your Majesty that Lí is a man of parts beyond all those of the age, one whose compositions astonish all who read them. At the trial of last year, his essay was marked out and thrown aside by the examiners, and he himself shamefully put out of the hall. Your Majesty now calling him to court, and he having neither title nor rank, his self-love is touched; but if your Majesty would hear your minister's prayer, and shed your favors upon his friend, and send a high officer to him, I am sure he will hasten to obey the imperial will." "Let it be so," rejoined the Emperor; "at the instance of our academician, we confer on Lí Peh the title of doctor of the first rank, with the purple robe, yellow girdle, and silken bonnet; and herewith also issue an order for him to present himself at court. Our academician Ho will charge himself with carrying this order, and bring Lí Peh to our presence without fail."

Ho returned home to Lí, and begged him to go to court to read the letter, adding how his Majesty depended on his help to relieve him from his present embarrassment. As soon as he had put on his new robes, which were those of a high examiner, he made his obeisance toward the palace, and hastened to mount his horse and enter it, following after the academician. Seated on his throne, Hwantsung impatiently awaited the arrival of the poet, who, prostrating himself before its steps, went through the ceremony of salutation and acknowledgment for the favors he had received, and then stood in his place. The Emperor, as soon as he saw Lí, rejoiced as poor men do on finding a treasure, or starvelings on sitting at a loaded table; his heart was like dark clouds suddenly illuminated, or parched and arid soil on the approach of rain. "Some foreign ambassadors have brought us a letter which no one can read, and we have sent for you, doctor, to relieve our anxiety." "Your minister's knowledge is very limited," politely replied Lí, with a bow, "for his essay was rejected by the judges at the examination, and lord Kao turned him out of doors. Now that he is called upon to read this letter from a foreign prince, how is it that the examiners are not charged with the answer, since, too, the ambassadors have already been kept so long waiting? Since I, a student turned off from the trial, could not satisfy the wishes of the examiners, how can I hope to meet the expectation of your Majesty?" "We know what you are good for," said the Emperor; "a truce to your excuses," putting the letter into his hands. Running his eyes over it, he disdainfully smiled, and standing before the throne, read off in Chinese the mysterious letter, as follows:

"Letter from the mighty Ko To of the kingdom of Po Hai to the prince of the dynasty of Tang: Since your usurpation of Corea, and carrying your conquests to the frontiers of our States, your soldiers have violated our territory in frequent raids. We trust you can fully explain to us this matter, and as we cannot patiently bear such a state of things, we have sent our ambassadors to announce to you that you must give up the hundred and sixty-six towns of Corea into our hands. We have some precious things to offer you in compensation, namely, the medicinal plants from the mountains of Tai Peh, and the byssus from the southern sea, gongs of Tsíching, stags from Fuyu, and horses from Sopin, silk of Wuchau, black fish from the river Meito, prunes from

Kiutu, and building materials from Loyu; some of all these articles shall be sent you. If you do not accept these propositions, we shall raise troops and carry war and destruction into your borders, and then see on whose side victory will remain."

After its perusal, to which they had given an attentive ear, the grandees were stupefied and looked at each other, knowing how improbable it was that the Emperor would accept the propositions of Ko To. Nor was the mind of his Majesty by any means satisfied, and after remaining silent for some time, he turned himself to the civil and military officers about him, and asked what means were available to repulse the attacks of the barbarians in case their forces invaded Corea. Scholars and generals remained mute as idols of clay or statues of wood; no one said a word, until Ho ventured to observe, "Your venerable grandfather Taitsung, in three expeditions against Corea, lost an untold number of soldiers, without succeeding in his enterprise, and impoverished his treasury. Thanks to Heaven Kai-su-wăn died, and profiting by the dissensions between the usurper's sons, the glorious Emperor Taitsung confided the direction of a million of veterans to the old generals Lí Sié and Pí Jinkwei, who, after a hundred engagements, more or less important, finally conquered the kingdom. But now having been at peace for a long time, we have neither generals nor soldiers; if we seize the buckler and lance, it will not be easy to resist, and our defeat will be certain. I await the wise determination of your Majesty."

"Since such is the case, what answer shall we make to the ambassadors?" said Hwantsung. "Deign to ask Lí," said the doctor; "he will speak to the purpose." On being interrogated by his sovereign, Lí replied, "Let not this matter trouble your clear mind. Give orders for an audience to the ambassadors, and I will speak to them face to face in their own language. The terms of the answer will make the barbarians blush, and their Ko To will be obliged to make his respects at the foot of your throne." "And who is this Ko To?" demanded Hwantsung. "It is the name the people of Po Hai give to their king after the usage of their country; just as the Hwui Hwui call theirs Kokan; the Tibetans, Tsangpo; the Lochau, Chau; the Holing, Sí-mo-wei: each one according to the custom of his nation."

At this rapid flood of explanations, the mind of the wise Hwantsung experienced a lively joy, and the same day he honored Lí with the title of an academician; a lodging was prepared for him in the palace of the Golden Bell; musicians made the place re-echo with their harmony; women poured out the wine, and young girls handed him the goblets, and celebrated the glory of Lí with the same voices that lauded the Emperor. What a delicious, ravishing banquet! He could hardly keep within the limits of propriety, but ate and drank until he was unconscious of anything, when the Emperor ordered the attendants to carry him into the palace and lay him on a bed.

The next morning, when the gong announced the fifth watch, the Emperor repaired to the hall of audience; but Lí's faculties, on awaking, were not very clear, though the officers hastened to bring him. When all had gone through their prostrations, Hwantsung called the poet near him, but perceiving that the visage of the new-made doctor still bore the marks of his debauch and discovering the discomposure of his mind, he sent into the kitchen for a little wine and some well-spiced fish broth, to arouse the sleepy bard. The servants presently sent it up on a golden tray, and the Emperor seeing the cup was fuming, condescended to stir and cool the broth a long time with the ivory chopsticks, and served it out himself to Lí, who, receiving it on his knees, ate and drank, while a pleasing joy illumined his countenance. While this was going on, some among the courtiers were much provoked and displeased at the strange familiarity, while others rejoiced to see how well the Emperor knew to conciliate the good will of men. The two examiners, Yang and Kao, betrayed in their features the dislike they felt.

At the command of the Emperor, the ambassadors were introduced, and saluted his Majesty by acclamation, whilst Lí Tai-peh, clad in a purple robe and silken bonnet, easy and gracious as an immortal, stood in the historiographer's place before the left of the throne, holding the letter in his hand, and read it off in a clear tone, without mistaking a word. Then turning toward the frightened envoys, he said, "Your little province has failed in its etiquette, but our wise ruler, whose power is comparable to the heavens for vastness, disdains to take advantage of it. This is the answer which he grants you: hear and be silent." The terrified ambassadors fell trembling at the foot of the throne. The Emperor had already prepared near him an ornamented cushion, and taking a jade stone with which to rub the ink, a pencil of leveret's hair bound in an ivory tube, a cake of perfumed ink, and a sheet of flowery paper, gave them to Lí, and seated him on the cushion ready to draw up the answer.

"May it please your Majesty," objected Lí, "my boots are not at all suitable, for they were soiled at the banquet last evening, and I trust your Majesty in your generosity will grant me some new buskins and stockings fit for ascending the platform." The Emperor acceded to his request, and ordered a servant to procure them; when Lí resumed, "Your minister has still a word to add, and begs beforehand that his untoward conduct may be excused; then he will prefer his request." "Your notions are misplaced and useless, but I will not be offended at them: go on, speak," said Hwantsung; to which Lí, nothing daunted, said, "At the last examination, your minister was turned off by Yang, and put out of doors by Kao. The sight of these persons here to-day at the head of the courtiers casts a certain discomposure over his spirits; let your voice deign to command Yang to rub my ink, whilst Kao puts on my stockings and laces up my buskins; then will my mind and wits begin to recover their energies, and my pencil can trace your answer in the language of the foreigners. In transmitting the reply in the name of the Son of Heaven, he will then not disappoint the confidence with which he is honored." Afraid to displease Lí when he had need of him, the Emperor gave the strange order; and while Yang rubbed the ink and Kao put on the buskins of the poet, they could not help reflecting, that this student, so badly received and treated by them, only fit at the best to render such services to them, availed himself now of the sudden favors of the Emperor to take their own words pronounced against him as a text, and revenge himself upon them for past injuries. But what could they do? They could not oppose the sovereign will, and if they did feel chagrined, they did not dare at least to express it. The proverb hath it true:

"Do not draw upon you a person's enmity, for enmity is never appeased; injury returns upon him who injures, and sharp words recoil against him who says them."

The poet triumphed, and his oath was accomplished. Buskined as he desired, he mounted the platform on the carpet and seated himself on the cushion, while Yang stood at his side and rubbed the ink. Of a truth, the disparity was great between an ink-grinder and the magnate who counselled the Emperor. But why did the poet sit while the premier stood like a servant at his side? It was because Lí was the organ of the monarch's words, while Yang, reduced to act the part of an ink-rubber, could not request permission to sit. With one hand Lí stroked his beard, and seizing his pencil in the other, applied it to the paper, which was soon covered with strange characters, well turned and even without a fault or rasure, and then laid it upon the dragon's table. The Emperor gazed at it in amaze, for it was identical with that of the barbarians; not a character in it resembled the Chinese; and as he handed it about among the nobles, their surprise was great. When requested to read it, Lí, placed before the throne, read in a clear loud tone the answer to the strangers:

"The mighty Emperor of the Tang dynasty, whose reign is called Kiayuen, sends his instructions to Ko To of the Po Hai.

"From ancient times the rock and the egg have not hit each other, nor the serpent and dragon made war. Our dynasty, favored by fate, extends its power, and reigns even to the four seas; it has under its orders brave generals and tried soldiers, solid bucklers and glittering swords. Your neighbor, King Hiehlí, who refused our alliance, was taken prisoner; but the people of Putsau, after offering a present of a metal bird, took an oath of obedience.

"The Sinlo, at the southern end of Corea, have sent us praises written on the finest tissues of silk; Persia, serpents which can catch rats; India, birds that can speak; and Rome, dogs which lead horses, holding a lantern in their mouth; the white parrot is a present from the kingdom of Koling, the carbuncle which illumines the night comes from Cambodia, and famous horses are sent by the tribe of Kolí, while precious vases are brought from Níal: in short, there is not a nation which does not respect our imposing power, and does not testify their regard for the virtue which distinguishes us. Corea alone resisted the will of Heaven, but the divine vengeance has fallen heavily upon it, and a kingdom which reckoned nine centuries of duration was overthrown as in a morning. Why, then, do you not profit by the terrible prognostics Heaven vouchsafes you as examples? Would it not evince your sagacity?

"Moreover, your little country, situated beyond the peninsula, is little more than as a province of Corea, or as a principality to the Celestial Empire; your resources in men and horses are not a millionth part those of China. You are like a chafed locust trying to stop a chariot, like a stiff-necked goose which will not submit. Under the arms of our warriors your blood will run a thousand *li*. You, prince, resemble that audacious one who refused our alliance, and whose kingdom became annexed to Corea. The designs of our sage Emperor are vast as the ocean, and he now bears with your culpable and unreasonable conduct; but hasten to prevent misfortune by repentance, and cheerfully pay the tribute of each year, and you will prevent the shame and opprobrium which will cover you and expose you to the ridicule of your neighbors. Reflect thrice on these instructions."

The reading of this answer filled the Emperor with joy, who ordered Li to make known its contents to the ambassadors; he then sealed it with the imperial seal. The poet called Kao to put on the boots which he had taken off, and he then returned to the palace of Golden Bells to inform the envoys concerning his sovereign's orders, reading the letter to them in a loud tone, while they heard tremblingly. The academician Ho reconducted them to the gates of the capital, and there the ambassadors asked who it was who had read the imperial instructions. "He is called Lí, and has the title of Doctor of the Hanlin." "But among so many dignitaries, why did the first Minister of State rub his ink, and the general of the guards lace up his buskins?" "Hear," added Ho; "those two personages are indeed intimate ministers of his Majesty, but they are only noble courtiers who do not transcend common humanity, while Doctor Lí, on the contrary, is an immortal descended from heaven on the earth to aid the sovereign of the Celestial Empire. How can any one equal him?" The ambassadors bowed the head and departed, and on their return rendered an account of their mission to their sovereign. On reading the answer of Lí, the Ko To was terrified, and deliberated with his counsellors: "The Celestial Empire is upheld by an immortal descended from the skies! Is it possible to attack it?" He thereupon wrote a letter of submission, testifying his desire to send tribute each year, which was thenceforth allowed.

Lí Tai-peh afterward drowned himself from fear of the machinations of his enemies, exclaiming, as he leaped into the water, "I'm going to catch the moon in the midst of the sea!"

The poetry of the Chinese has been investigated by Sir John Davis, and the republication of his first paper in an enlarged form in 1870, with the versification of Legge's translations of the *Shí King* by his nephew, and two volumes of various pieces by Stent, have altogether given a good variety.[1] Davis explains the principles of Chinese rhythm, touches upon the tones, notices the parallelisms, and distinguishes the various kinds of verse, all in a scholarly manner. The whole subject, however, still awaits more thorough treatment. Artificial poetry, where

---

[1] Davis, *Poetry of the Chinese*, London, 1870; G. C. Stent, *The Jade Chaplet*, London, 1874; *Entombed Alive, and other Verses*, 1878; Le Marquis D'Hervey-Saint-Denys, *Poésies de l'Epoque des Thang*, Paris, 1862. A number of extracts of classical and modern literature will be found in *Confucius and the Chinese Classics*, compiled by Rev. A. W. Loomis, San Francisco, 1867. *China Review*, Vols. I., p. 248, IV., p. 46, and passim.

the sound and jingle is regarded more than the sense, is not uncommon; the great number of characters having the same sound enables versifiers to do this with greater facility than is possible in other languages, and to the serious degradation of all high sentiment. The absence of inflections in the words cripples the easy flow of sounds to which our ears are familiar, but renders such lines as the following more spirited to the eye which sees the characters than to the ear which hears them:

Liang kiang, siang niang, yang hiang tsiang,
Kí ní, pí chí, lí hí mi, etc.

Lines consisting of characters all containing the same radical are also constructed in this manner, in which the sounds are subservient to the meaning. This bizarre fashion of writing is, however, considered fit only for pedants.

The Augustan age of poetry and letters was in the ninth and tenth centuries, during the Tang dynasty, when the brightest day of Chinese civilization was the darkest one of European. No complete collection of poems has yet been translated into any European language, and perhaps none would bear an entire version. The poems of Lí Tai-peh form thirty volumes, and those of Su Tung-po are contained in one hundred and fifteen volumes, while the collected poems of the times of the Tang dynasty have been published by imperial authority in nine hundred volumes. The proportion of descriptive poetry in it is small compared with the sentimental. The longest poem yet turned into English is the *Hwa Tsien Kí*, or 'The Flower's Petal,' by P. P. Thoms, under the title of *Chinese Courtship;* it is in heptameter, and his version is quite prosaic. Another of much greater repute among native scholars, called *Lí Sao*, or 'Dissipation of Sorrows,' dating from about B.C. 314, has been rendered into French by D'Hervey-Saint-Denys.[1]

It is a common pastime for literary gentlemen to try their

[1] *Chinese Courtship. In Verse. To which is added an Appendix treating of the Revenue of China*, etc., etc., by Peter Perring Thoms, London, 1824. Compare the *Quarterly Review* for 1827, pp. 496 ff. *Le Li-Sao, Poème du IIIe Siècle avant notre ère. Traduit du Chinois*, par le Marquis d'Hervey de Saint-Denys, Paris, 1870.

skill in versification; epigrams and pasquinades are usually put into metre, and at the examinations every candidate must hand in his poetical exercise. Consequently, much more attention is paid by such rhymesters to the jingle of the words and artificial structure of the lines than to the elevation of sentiment or copiousness of illustrations; it is as easy for them to write a sonnet on shipping a cargo of tea as to indite a love-epistle to their mistress. Extemporaneous verses are made on every subject, and to illustrate occurrences that are elsewhere regarded as too prosaic to disturb the muse.

Still, human emotions have been the stimulus to their expression in verse among the Chinese as well as other people; and all classes have found an utterance to them. Ribald and impure ditties are sung by street-singers to their own low classes, but such subjects do not characterize the best poets, as they did in old Rome. A piece called 'Chang Liang's Flute' is a fair instance of the better style of songs:

'Twas night—the tired soldiers were peacefully sleeping,
The low hum of voices was hushed in repose;
The sentries, in silence, a strict watch were keeping
'Gainst surprise or a sudden attack of their foes;

When a low mellow note on the night air came stealing,
So soothingly over the senses it fell—
So touchingly sweet—so soft and appealing,
Like the musical tones of an aërial bell.

Now rising, now falling—now fuller and clearer—
Now liquidly soft—now a low wailing cry;
Now the cadences seem floating nearer and nearer—
Now dying away in a whispering sigh.

Then a burst of sweet music, so plaintively thrilling,
Was caught up by the echoes which sang the refrains
In their many-toned voices—the atmosphere filling
With a chorus of dulcet mysterious strains.

The sleepers arouse, and with beating hearts listen;
In their dreams they had heard that weird music before;
It touches each heart—with tears their eyes glisten,
For it tells them of those they may never see more.

In fancy those notes to their childhood's days brought them,
To those far-away scenes they had not seen for years;
To those who had loved them, had reared them, and taught them,
And the eyes of those stern men were wetted with tears.

Bright visions of home through their mem'ries came thronging,
Panorama-like passing in front of their view;
They were *home-sick*—no power could withstand that strange yearning;
The longer they listened the more home-sick they grew.

Whence came those sweet sounds?—who the unseen musician
That breathes out his soul, which floats on the night breeze
In melodious sighs—in strains so elysian
As to soften the hearts of rude soldiers like these?

Each looked at the other, but no word was spoken,
The music insensibly tempting them on:
They must return home. Ere the daylight had broken
The enemy looked, and behold! they were gone.

There's a magic in music—a witchery in it,
Indescribable either with tongue or with pen;
The flute of Chang Liang, in one little minute,
Had stolen the courage of eight thousand men![1]

The following verses were presented to Dr. Parker at Canton by a Chinese gentleman of some literary attainments, upon the occasion of a successful operation for cataract. The original may be considered as a very creditable example of extempore sonnet:

A fluid, darksome and opaque, long time had dimmed my sight,
For seven revolving, weary years one eye was lost to light;
The other, darkened by a film, during three years saw no day,
High heaven's bright and gladd'ning light could not pierce it with its ray.

Long, long I sought the hoped relief, but still I sought in vain,
My treasures lavished in the search, brought no relief from pain;
Till, at length, I thought my garments I must either pawn or sell,
And plenty in my house, I feared, was never more to dwell.

Then loudly did I ask, for what cause such pain I bore—
For transgressions in a former life unatoned for before?
But again came the reflection how, of yore, oft men of worth,
For slight errors, had borne suff'ring great as drew my sorrow forth.

---

[1] Stent's *Jade Chaplet*.

"And shall not one," said I then, "whose worth is but as naught,
Bear patiently, as heaven's gift, what it ordains ?" The thought
Was scarce completely formed, when of a friend the footstep fell
On my threshold, and I breathed a hope he had words of joy to tell.

"I've heard," the friend who enter'd said, "there's come to us of late
A native of the 'Flowery Flag's' far-off and foreign State;
O'er tens of thousand miles of sea to the Inner Land he's come—
His hope and aim to heal men's pain, he leaves his native home."

I quick went forth, this man I sought, this gen'rous doctor found;
He gained my heart, he's kind and good; for, high up from the ground,
He gave a room, to which he came, at morn, at eve, at night—
Words were but vain were I to try his kindness to recite.

With needle argentine he pierced the cradle of the tear.
What fears I felt! Su Tung-po's words rung threat'ning in my ear:
"Glass hung in mist," the poet says, "take heed you do not shake;"
(The words of fear rung in my ear), "how if it chance to break!"

The fragile lens his needle pierced: the dread, the sting, the pain,
I thought on these, and that the cup of sorrow I must drain;
But then my mem'ry faithful showed the work of fell disease,
How long the orbs of sight were dark, and I deprived of ease.

And thus I thought: "If now, indeed, I were to find relief,
'Twere not too much to bear the pain, to bear the present grief."
Then the words of kindness which I heard sunk deep into my soul,
And free from fear I gave myself to the foreigner's control.

His silver needle sought the lens, and quickly from it drew
The opaque and darksome fluid, whose effect so well I knew;
His golden probe soon clear'd the lens, and then my eyes he bound,
And laved with water sweet as is the dew to thirsty ground.

Three days thus lay I, prostrate, still; no food then could I eat;
My limbs relax'd were stretched as though th' approach of death to meet
With thoughts astray—mind ill at ease—away from home and wife,
I often thought that by a thread was hung my precious life.

Three days I lay, no food had I, and nothing did I feel;
Nor hunger, sorrow, pain, nor hope, nor thought of woe or weal;
My vigor fled, my life seemed gone, when, sudden, in my pain,
There came one ray—one glimm'ring ray,—I see,—I live again!

As starts from visions of the night he who dreams a fearful dream,
As from the tomb uprushing comes one restored to day's bright beam,
Thus I, with gladness and surprise, with joy, with keen delight,
See friends and kindred crowd around; I hail the blessed light.

With grateful heart, with heaving breast, with feelings flowing o'er,
I cried, "O lead me quick to him who can the sight restore!"
To kneel I tried, but he forbade; and, forcing me to rise,
"To mortal man bend not the knee;" then pointing to the skies:—

"I'm but," said he, "the workman's tool; another's is the hand;
Before *his* might, and in *his* sight, men, feeble, helpless, stand:
Go, virtue learn to cultivate, and never thou forget
That for some work of future good thy life is spared thee yet!"

The off'ring, token of my thanks, he refused; nor would he take
Silver or gold—they seemed as dust; 'tis but for virtue's sake
His works are done. His skill divine I ever must adore,
Nor lose remembrance of his name till life's last day is o'er.

Thus have I told, in these brief words, this learned doctor's praise:
Well does his worth deserve that I should tablets to him raise.

In this facility of versification lies one of the reasons for the mediocrity of common Chinese poetry, but that does not prevent its power over the popular mind being very great. Men and women of all classes take great delight in recitation and singing, hearing street musicians or strolling play-actors; and these results, whatever we may judge by our standards, prove its power and suitableness to influence them. One or two additional specimens on different subjects may be quoted, inasmuch as they also illustrate some of the better shades of feeling and sentiment. A more finished piece of poetry is one written about A.D. 370, by Su-Hwui, whose husband was banished. Its talented authoress is said to have written more than five thousand lines, and among them a curious anagram of about eight hundred characters, which was so disposed that it would make sense equally well when read up or down, crosswise, backward, or forward.[1] Nothing from her pen remains

[1] A translation is given in the *Chinese Repository* (Vol. IX., p. 508) of a supposed complaint made by a cow of her sad lot in being obliged to work hard and fare poorly during life, and then be cut up and eaten when dead; the ballad is arranged in the form of the animal herself, and a herdboy leading her, who in his own form praises the happiness of a rural life. This ballad is a Buddhist tractate, and that fraternity print many such on broad-sheets; one common collection of prayers is arranged like a pagoda, with images of Buddha sitting in the windows of each story.

except this ode, interesting for its antiquity as well as sentiment.

ODE OF SU-HWUI.

When thou receiv'dst the king's command to quiet the frontier,
Together to the bridge we went, striving our hearts to cheer—
Hiding our grief. These words I gasped upon that mournful day:
"Forget not, love, my fond embrace, nor tarry long away!"
Ah! Is it true that since that time no message glads my sight?
Think you that *now* your lone wife's heart even in bright spring delights?
Our pearly stairs and pleasant yard the foul weeds have o'ergrown;
Our nuptial room—and couch—and walls—are now with dust o'erstrown.
Whene'er I think of our farewell, my soul with fear grows cold;
My mind resolves what shape I'd take to see thee as of old.
Now as I watch the deep-sea moon, I long her form to be;
Again, the mountain cloud has filled my dull heart with envy.
For deep-sea moon shines year by year upon the land abroad;
And ye, O mountain clouds, may meet the form of my adored!
Aye, flying here and flying there, seek my beloved's place,
And at ten thousand thousand miles--speed!—gaze on his fair face.
Alas! for *me* the road is long, steep mountain peaks now sever
Our loving souls. I can but weep—O! may't not be forever!
The long reed's leaves had yellow grown when we our farewell said;
Who then had thought the plum-tree's bough so oft would turn to red?
The fairy flowers spreading their leaves have met the early spring—
Ah, genial months, what time for love!—But who can ease *my* sting?
The pendant willows strew the court, for thee I pull them down;
The falling flowers enrich the earth, none pick these from the ground
And scatter vernal growth, as once, before the ancestral tomb!
Taking the lute of Tsun I strive to chase away the gloom
By thrumming, as I muse of thee, songs of departed friends.
Sending my inmost thoughts away, they reach the northern ends—
Those northern bounds!—how far they seem, o'erpassed the hills and streams.
No news, no word from those confines to lighten e'en my dreams!
My dress, my pillow, once so white, are deeply stained with tears;
My broidered coat with gilded flowers, all spotted now appears.
The very geese and storks to me, when in their passage north,
Seemed by their cries, my distant love, to tear my heartstrings forth.
No more my lute—though thou wert strong, with passion was I wrung;
My grief was its utmost bent—my song was still unsung.
Ah! husband, lord, thy love I feel is stable as the hills;
'Tis joy to think each hour of this—a balm for countless ills!

I had but woven half my task—I gave it to his Grace:
O grant my husband quick release, I pine for his embrace!

Among the best of Chinese ballads, if regard be had to the character of the sentiment and metaphors, is one on Picking Tea, which the girls and women sing as they collect the leaves.

BALLAD OF THE TEA-PICKER.

I.

Where thousand hills the vale enclose, our little hut is there,
And on the sloping sides around the tea grows everywhere;
And I must rise at early dawn, as busy as can be,
To get my daily labor done, and pluck the leafy tea.

II.

At early dawn I seize my crate, and sighing, Oh, for rest!
Thro' the thick mist I pass the door, with sloven hair half drest;
The dames and maidens call to me, as hand in hand they go,
"What steep do you, miss, climb to-day—what steep of high Sungio?"[a]

III.

Dark is the sky, the twilight dim still on the hills is set;
The dewy leaves and cloudy buds may not be gathered yet:
Oh, who are they, the thirsty ones, for whom this work we do,
For whom we spend our daily toil in bands of two and two?

IV.

Like fellows we each other aid, and to each other say,
As down we pull the yielding twigs, "Sweet sister, don't delay;
E'en now the buds are growing old, all on the boughs atop,
And then to-morrow—who can tell?—the drizzling rain may drop."

V.

We've picked enow; the topmost bough is bare of leaves; and so
We lift our brimming loads, and by the homeward path we go;
In merry laughter by the pool, the lotus pool, we hie,
When hark! uprise a mallard pair, and hence affrighted fly.

VI.

Limpid and clear the pool, and there how rich the lotus grows,
And only half its opening leaves, round as the coins, it shows—
I bend me o'er the jutting brink, and to myself I say,
"I marvel in the glassy stream, how looks my face to-day?"

VII.

My face is dirty; out of trim my hair is, and awry;
Oh, tell me, where's the little girl so ugly now as I?
'Tis all because whole weary hours I'm forced to pick the tea,
And driving winds and soaking showers have made me what you see!

VIII.

With morn again come wind and rain, and though so fierce and strong,
With basket big, and little hat, I wend my way along;
At home again, when all is picked, and everybody sees
How muddy all our dresses are, and drabbled to the knees.

IX.

I saw this morning through the door a pleasant day set in;
Be sure I quickly dressed my hair and neatly fixed my pin,
And fleetly sped I down the path to gain the wonted spot,
But, never thinking of the mire, my working shoes forgot!

X.

The garden reached, my bow-shaped shoes are soaking through and through;
The sky is changed—the thunder rolls—and I don't know what to do;
I'll call my comrades on the hill to pass the word with speed
And fetch my green umbrella-hat to help me in my need.

XI.

But my little hat does little good; my plight is very sad!
I stand with clothes all dripping wet, like some poor fisher-lad;
Like him I have a basket, too, of meshes woven fine—
A fisher-lad, if I only had his fishing-rod and line.

XII.

The rain is o'er; the outer leaves their branching fibres show;
Shake down the branch, the fragrant scent about us 'gins to blow;
Gather the yellow golden threads that high and low are found—
Oh, what a precious odor now is wafted all around!

XIII.

No sweeter perfume does the wild and fair Aglaia shed,
Throughout Wu-yuen's bounds my tea the choicest will be sald;
When all are picked we'll leave the shoots to bud again in spring,
But for this morning we have done the third, last gathering.

XIV.

Oh, weary is our picking, yet do I my toil withhold?
My maiden locks are all askew, my pearly fingers cold;
I only wish our tea to be superior over all,
O'er this one's "sparrow-tongue," and o'er the other's "dragon-ball."

XV.

Oh, for a month I weary strive to find a leisure day;
I go to pick at early dawn, and until dusk I stay;
Till midnight at the firing-pan I hold my irksome place:
But will not labor hard as this impair my pretty face?

XVI.

But if my face be somewhat lank, more firm shall be my mind;
I'll fire my tea that all else shall be my golden buds behind;
But yet the thought arises who the pretty maid shall be
To put the leaves in jewelled cup, from thence to sip my tea.

XVII.

Her griefs all flee as she makes her tea, and she is glad; but oh,
Where shall she learn the toils of us who labor for her so?
And shall she know of the winds that blow, and the rains that pour their wrath,
And drench and soak us thro' and thro', as plunged into a bath?

XVIII.

In driving rains and howling winds the birds forsake the nest,
Yet many a loving pair are seen still on the boughs to rest:
Oh, wherefore, loved one, with light look, didst thou send me away?
I cannot, grieving as I grieve, go through my work to-day.

XIX.

But though my bosom rise and fall, like bucket in a well,
Patient and toiling as I am, 'gainst work I'll ne'er rebel;
My care shall be to have my tea fired to a tender brown,
And let the *flag* and *awl*, well rolled, display their whitish down.[1]

XX.

Ho! for my toil! Ho! for my steps! Aweary though I be,
In our poor house, for working folk, there's lots ot work, I see;
When the firing and the drying's done, off at the call I go,
And once again, this very morn, I climb the high Sunglo.

XXI.

My wicker basket slung on arm, and hair entwined with flowers,
To the slopes I go of high Sunglo, and pick the tea for hours;
How laugh we, sisters, on the road; what a merry turn we've got;
I giggle and say, as I point down the way, There, look, there lies our cot!

XXII.

Your handmaid 'neath the sweet green shade in sheltered cot abides,
Where the pendant willow's sweeping bough the thatchy dwelling hides;
To-morrow, if you wish it so, my guests I pray you'll be!
The door you'll know by the fragrant scent, the scent of the firing tea.

---

[1] The *ki*, or 'flag,' is the term by which the leaflets are called when they just begin to unroll; the *tsiang*, or 'awl,' designates those leaves which are still wrapped up and which are somewhat sharp.

XXIII.

Awhile 'tis cold, and then 'tis warm, when I want to fire my tea,
The sky is sure to shift and change—and all to worry me;
When the sun goes down on the western hills, on the eastern there is rain!
And however fair he promises, he promises in vain.

XXIV.

To-day the tint of the western hills is looking bright and fair,
And I bear my crate to the stile,[1] and wait my fellow toiler there;
A little tender lass is she—she leans upon the rail
And sleeps, and though I hail her she answers not my hail.

XXV.

And when at length to my loudest call she murmurs a reply,
'Tis as if hard to conquer sleep, and with half-opened eye;
Up starts she, and with straggling steps along the path she's gone;
She brings her basket, but forgets to put the cover on!

XXVI.

Together trudge we, and we pass the lodge of the southern bowers,
Where the beautiful sea-pomegranate waves all its yellow flowers;
Fain would we stop and pluck a few to deck our tresses gay,
But the tree is high, and 'tis vain to try and reach the tempting spray.

XXVII.

The pretty birds upon the boughs sing songs so sweet to hear,
And the sky is so delicious now, half cloudy and half clear;
While bending o'er her work, each maid will prattle of her woe,
And we talk till our hearts are sorely hurt, and tears unstinted flow.

XXVIII.

Our time is up, and yet not full our baskets to the mouth—
The twigs anorth are fully searched, let's seek them in the south;
Just then by chance I snapped a twig whose leaves were all apair;
See, with my taper fingers now I fix it in my hair.

XXIX.

Of all the various kinds of tea, the bitter beats the sweet,
But for whomever either seeks, for him I'll find a treat;
Though who it is shall drink them, as bitter or sweet they be,
I know not, my friend—but the pearly end of my finger only see!

---

[1] The *ting* is not exactly a stile, being a kind of shed, or four posts supporting a roof, which is often erected by villagers for the convenience of wayfarers, who can stop there and rest. It sometimes contains a bench or seat, and is usually over or near a spring of water.

XXX.

Ye twittering swallows, rise and fall in your flight around the hill,
But when next I go to the high Sunglo, I'll change my gown—I will;
And I'll roll up the cuff and show arm enough, for my arm is fair to see:
Oh, if ever there were a fair round arm, that arm belongs to me!

In the department of plays and dramas, Chinese literature shows a long list of names, few or none of which have ever been heard of away from their native soil. Some of their pieces have been translated by Julien, Bazin, Davis, and others, most of which were selected from the *Hundred Plays of Yuen*. The origin of the present Chinese drama does not date back, according to M. Bazin, beyond the Tang dynasty, though many performances designed to be played and sung in pantomime had been written before that epoch. He cites the names of eighty-one persons, besides mentioning other plays of unknown authors, whose combined writings amount to five hundred and sixty-four separate plays; all of whom flourished during the Mongol dynasty. The plays that have been translated from this collection give a tolerably good idea of Chinese talent in this difficult department; and, generally speaking, whatever strictures may be made upon the management of the plot, exhibition of character, unity of action, or illustration of manners, the tendency of the play is on the side of justice and morality. Père Prémare first translated a play in 1731, under the title of the *Orphan of Chau*,[1] which was taken by Voltaire as the groundwork of one of his plays. *The Heir in Old Age* and the *Sorrows of Han* are the names of two translated by Sir J. F. Davis. The *Circle of Chalk* was translated and published in 1832 by Julien, and a volume of Bazin, ainé, containing the *Intrigues of an Abigail*, the *Compared Tunic*, the *Songstress*, and *Resentment of Tau Ngo*, appeared in 1838, at Paris. None of these pieces exhibit much intricacy of plot, nor would the simple arrangements of Chinese theatres allow much increase to the *dramatis personæ* without confusion. M. Bazin, moreover, translated the *Pí-pa Ki*, or *History of a Lute*,

[1] *Tchao-chi-cou-eulh, ou l'Orphelin de la Maison de Tchao, tragédie chinoise, traduite* par le R. P. de Prémare, Miss. de la Chine, 1755. Julien published a translation of the same, Paris, 1834.

a drama in twenty-four acts, of more pretensions, partaking of the novel as well as the drama; the play is said to have been represented at Peking in 1404, under the Ming dynasty.[1]

Besides plays in the higher walks of the drama, which form the principal part of the performances at theatres, there are by-plays or farces, which, being confined to two or three interlocutors, depend for their attractiveness upon the droll gesticulations, impromptu allusions to passing occurrences, and excellent pantomimic action of the performers. They are usually brought on at the conclusion of the bill, and from the freedom given in them to an exhibition of the humor or wit of the players, are much liked by the people. A single illustration will exhibit the simple range and character of these burlettas.

THE MENDER OF CRACKED CHINAWARE.

DRAMATIS PERSONÆ. { *Niu Chau*........ A wandering tinker.
Wang Niang...... A young girl.

Scene—A Street.

NIU CHAU *enters—across his shoulder is a bamboo, to each end of which are suspended boxes containing the various tools and implements of his trade, and a small stool. He is dressed meanly; his face and head are painted and decorated in a fantastic manner.*

(*Sings*) Seeking a livelihood by the work of my hands,
Daily do I traverse the streets of the city.
(*Speaks*) Well, here I am, a mender of broken jars,
An unfortunate victim of ever changing plans.
To repair old fractured jars
Is my sole occupation and support.
'Tis even so. I have no other employment.
(*Takes his boxes from his shoulder, places them on the ground, sits beside them, and drawing out his fan, continues speaking*)—
A disconsolate old man—I am a slave to inconveniences.
For several days past I have been unable to go abroad,

[1] Since the appearance of M. Bazin's *Théâtre Chinois* (Paris, 1838) and Davis' *Sorrows of Han* (London, 1829), there has been astonishingly little done in the study of Chinese plays. Compare, for the rest, an article on this subject by J. J. Ampère, in the *Revue des Deux Mondes*, September, 1838; *The Far East*, Vol. I. (1876), pp. 57 and 90; *Chinese Repository*, Vol. VI., p. 575; *China Review*, Vol. I., p. 26; also Lay's *Chinese as They Are*, and Dr. Gray's *China*, passim. Lieut. Kreitner gives an interesting picture of the Chinese theatre in a country town, together with a few pages upon the drama, of which his party were spectators. *Im fernen Osten*, pp. 595–599.

But, observing this morning a clear sky and fine air,
I was induced to recommence my street wanderings.

(*Sings*) At dawn I left my home,
But as yet have had no job.
Hither and yon, and on all sides,
From the east gate to the west,
From the south gate to the north,
And all over within the walls,
Have I been, but no one has called
For the mender of cracked jars. Unfortunate man!
But this being my first visit to the city of Nanking,
Some extra exertion is necessary;
Time is lost sitting idle here, and so to roam again I go.

(*Shoulders his boxes and stool, and walks about, crying*)—
Plates mended! Bowls mended!
Jars and pots neatly repair'd!

Lady Wang (*heard within*). Did I not hear the cry of the mender of cracked jars?
I'll open the door and look. (*She enters, looking around.*)
Yes, there comes the repairer of jars.

Niu Chau. Pray, have you a jar to mend?
I have long been seeking a job.
Did you not call?

Lady W. What is your charge for a large jar—
And how much for a small one?

Niu Chau. For large jars, one mace five.

Lady W. And for small ones?

Niu Chau. Fifty pair of cash.

Lady W. To one mace five, and fifty pair of cash,
Add nine candareens, and a new jar may be had.

Niu Chau. What, then, will you give?

Lady W. I will give one candareen for either size.

Niu Chau. Well, lady, how many cash can I get for this candareen?

Lady W. Why, if the price be high, you will get eight cash.

Niu Chau. And if low?

Lady W. You will get but seven cash and a half.

Niu Chau. Oh, you wicked, tantalizing thing!

(*Sings*) Since leaving home this morning,
I have met but with a trifler,
Who, in the shape of an old wife,
Tortures and gives me no job;
I'll shoulder again my boxes, and continue my walk,
And never again will I return to the house of Wang.

(*He moves off slowly.*)

Lady W. Jar-mender! return, quickly return; with a loud voice, I entreat you; for I have something on which I wish to consult with you.

Niu Chau. What is it on which you wish to consult me?
Lady W. I will give you a hundred cash to mend a large jar.
Niu Chau. And for mending a small one?
Lady W. And for mending a small one, thirty pair of cash.
Niu Chau. One hundred, and thirty pair!—truly, lady, this is worth consulting about.
Lady Wang, where shall I mend them?
Lady W. Follow me. (*They move toward the door of the house.*)
(*Sings*) Before walks the Lady Wang.
Niu Chau. And behind comes the *pu-kang* (or jar-mender).
Lady W. Here, then, is the place.
Niu Chau. Lady Wang, permit me to pay my respects.
(*Bows repeatedly in a ridiculous manner.*)
We can exchange civilities.
I congratulate you; may you prosper—before and behind.
Lady W. Here is the jar; now go to work and mend it.
(*Takes the jar in his hand and tosses it about, examining it.*)
Niu Chau. This jar has certainly a very appalling fracture.
Lady W. Therefore, it requires the more care in mending.
Niu Chau. That is self-evident.
Lady W. Now, Lady Wang will retire again to her dressing room,
And, after closing the door, will resume her toilet.
Her appearance she will beautify;
On the left, her hair she will comb into a dragon's head tuft,
On the right, she will arrange it tastefully with flowers;
Her lips she will color with blood-red vermilion,
And a gem of chrysoprase will she place in the dragon's head tuft.
Then, having completed her toilet, she will return to the door,
And sit down to look at the jar-mender. (*Exit.*)

(*Niu Chau sits down, straps the jar on his knee, and arranges his tools before him, and as he drills holes for the clamps, sings*)—

Every hole drilled requires a pin,
And every two holes drilled require pins a pair.
As I raise my head and look around,
(*At this moment Lady Wang re-enters, beautifully dressed, and sits down by the door.*)
There sits, I see, a delicate young lady;
Before she had the appearance of an old wife,
Now she is transformed into a handsome young girl.
On the left, her hair is comb'd into a dragon's head tuft;
On the right it is adorn'd tastefully with flowers.
Her lips are like plums, her mouth is all smiles,
Her eyes are as brilliant as the phœnix's; and
She stands on golden lilies, but two inches long.
I look again, another look,—down drops the jar.
(*The jar at this moment falls, and is broken to pieces.*)

(*Speaks*)	Heigh-ya! Here then is a dreadful smash!
Lady W.	You have but to replace it with another, and do so quickly.
Niu Chau.	For one that was broken, a good one must be given. Had two been broken, then were a pair to be supplied; An old one being smashed, a new one must replace it.
Lady W.	You have destroyed the jar, and return me nothing but words. Give me a new one, then you may return home,—not before.
Niu Chau.	Here upon my knees upon the hard ground, I beg Lady Wang, while she sits above, to listen to a few words. Let me receive pardon for the accident her beauty has occasioned, and I will at once make her my wife.
Lady W.	Impudent old man! How presume to think That I ever can become your wife!
Niu Chau.	Yes, it is true, I am somewhat older than Lady Wang, Yet would I make her my wife.
Lady W.	No matter then for the accident, but leave me now at once.
Niu Chau.	Since you have forgiven me, I again shoulder my boxes, And I will go elsewhere in search of a wife. And here, before high heaven, I swear never again to come near the house of Wang. You a great lady! You are but a vile ragged girl, And will yet be glad to take up with a much worse companion. (*Going away, he suddenly throws off his upper dress, and appears as a handsome young man.*)
Lady W.	Henceforth, give up your wandering profession, And marrying me, quit the trade of a jar-mender. With the Lady Wang pass happily the remainder of your life. (*They embrace, and exeunt.*)

Such is the general range and survey of Chinese literature, according to the Catalogue of the Imperial Libraries. It is, take it in a mass, a stupendous monument of human toil, fitly compared, so far as it is calculated to instruct its readers in useful knowledge, to their Great Wall, which can neither protect from its enemies, nor be of any real use to its makers. Its deficiencies are glaring. No treatises on the geography of foreign countries nor truthful narratives of travels abroad are contained in it, nor any account of the languages of their inhabitants, their history, or their governments. Philological works in other languages than those spoken within the Empire are unknown, and must, owing to the nature of the language, remain so until foreigners prepare them. Works on natural history, medicine, and physiology are few and useless, while those on mathematics and the exact sciences are much less popular and useful than they might be; and in the great range of theology, founded on the true basis of the Bible, there is almost nothing. The character of the people has been mostly formed by their ancient books, and this correlate influence has tended to repress independent investigation in the pursuit of truth, though not to destroy it. A new infusion of science, religion, and descriptive geography and history will lead to comparison with other countries, and bring out whatever in it is good.

A survey of this body of literature shows the effect of governmental patronage, in maintaining its character for what appears to us to be a wearisome uniformity. New ideas, facts, and motives must now come from the outer world, which will gradually elevate the minds of the people above the same unvarying channel. If the scholar knows that the goal he strives for is to be attained by proficiency in the single channel of classical knowledge, he cannot be expected to attend to other studies until he has secured the prize. A knowledge of medicine, mathematics, geography, or foreign languages, might, indeed, do the candidate much more good than all he gets out of the classics, but knowledge is not his object; and where all run the same race, all must study the same works. But let there be a different programme of themes and essays, and a wider range of subjects required of the students, and the present system of governmental examinations in China, with all its imperfections, can be made of great benefit to the people, if it is not put to a strain too great for the end in view.

The Chinese are fond of proverbs and aphorisms. They employ them in their writings and conversation as much as any people, and adorn their houses by copying them upon elegant scrolls, carving them upon pillars, and embroidering them upon banners. A complete collection of the proverbs of the Chinese has never been made, even among the people themselves any more than among those of other lands. Davis published, in 1828, a volume called *Moral Maxims*, containing two hundred aphorisms; P. Perny issued an assortment of four hundred and forty-one in 1869; and J. Doolittle collected several hundred proverbs, signs, couplets, and scrolls in his *Vocabulary.* Besides these, a collection of two thousand seven hundred and twenty proverbs was published in 1875 by W. Scarborough, furnished with a good index, and, like the others noted here, with the original text. Davis mentions the *Ming Sin Pao Kien*, or 'Jewelled Mirror for Illumining the Mind,' as containing a large number of proverbs. The *Ku Sz' Kiung Lin*, or 'Coral Forest of Ancient Matters,' is a similar collection; but if that be compared to a dictionary of quotations, this is better likened to a classical dictionary, the notes which follow the sentences leaving the reader in no doubt as to their meaning.

Manuscript lists of sentences suitable for hanging upon doors or in parlors are collected by persons who write them at New Year's, and whose success depends upon their facility in quoting elegant couplets. The following selection will exhibit to some extent this branch of Chinese wisdom and wit:

Not to distinguish properly between the beautiful and ugly, is like attaching a dog's tail to a squirrel's body.

An avaricious man, who can never have enough, is as a serpent wishing to swallow an elephant.

While one misfortune is going, to have another coming, is like driving a tiger out of the front door, while a wolf is entering the back.

The tiger's cub cannot be caught without going into his den.

To paint a snake and add legs. (Exaggeration.)

To sketch a tiger and make it a dog, is to imitate a work of genius and spoil it.

To ride a fierce dog to catch a lame rabbit. (Useless power over a contemptible enemy.)

To attack a thousand tigers with ten men. (To attempt a difficulty with incommensurate means.)

To cut off a hen's head with a battle-axe. (Unnecessary valor.)

To cherish a bad man is like nourishing a tiger; if not well fed he will devour you: or like rearing a hawk; if hungry he will stay by you, but fly away when fed.

To instigate a villain to do wrong is like teaching a monkey to climb trees.

To catch a fish and throw away the net;—not to requite benefits.

To take a locust's shank for the shaft of a carriage;—an inefficient person doing important work.

A pigeon sneering at a roc;—a mean man despising a prince.

To climb a tree to catch a fish, is to talk much and get nothing.

To test one good horse by judging the portrait of another.

A fish sports in the kettle, but his life will not be long.

Like a swallow building her nest on a hut is an anxious statesman.

Like a crane among hens is a man of parts among fools.

Like a sheep dressed in a tiger's skin is a superficial scholar.

Like a cuckoo in a magpie's nest is one who enjoy's another's labor.

To hang on the tail of a beautiful horse. (To seek promotion.)

Do not pull up your stockings in a melon field, or arrange your hat under a peach tree, lest people think you are stealing.

An old man marrying a young wife is like a withered willow sprouting.

Let us get drunk to-day while we have wine; the sorrows of to-morrow may be borne to-morrow.

If the blind lead the blind, they will both go to the pit.

Good iron is not used for nails, nor are soldiers made of good men.

A fair wind raises no storm.

A little impatience subverts great undertakings.

Vast chasms can be filled, but the heart of man is never satisfied.

The body may be healed, but the mind is incurable.

When the tree falls the monkeys flee.

Trouble neglected becomes still more troublesome.

Wood is not sold in the forest, nor fish at the pool.

He who looks at the sun is dazzled, he who hears the thunder is deafened. (Do not come too near the powerful.)

He desires to hide his tracks, and walks on the snow.

He seeks the ass, and lo! he sits upon him.

Speak not of others, but convict yourself.

A man is not always known by his looks, nor the sea measured by a bushel.

Ivory does not come from a rat's mouth.

If a chattering bird be not placed in the mouth, vexation will not sit between the eyebrows.

Prevention is better than cure.

For the Emperor to break the laws is one with the people's doing so.

Doubt and distraction are on earth, the brightness of truth in heaven.

Punishment can oppose a barrier to open crime, laws cannot reach to secret offences.

Wine and good dinners make abundance of friends, but in time of adversity not one is to be found.

Let every man sweep the snow from before his own doors, and not trouble himself about the hoarfrost on his neighbor's tiles.

Better be upright with poverty than depraved with abundance. He whose virtue exceeds his talents is the good man; he whose talents exceed his virtues is the fool.

Though a man may be utterly stupid, he is very perspicuous when reprehending the bad actions of others; though he may be very intelligent, he is dull enough when excusing his own faults: do you only correct yourselves on the same principle that you correct others, and excuse others on the same principles you excuse yourselves.[1]

If I do not debauch other men's wives, my own will not be polluted.

Better not be than be nothing.

The egg fights with the rock—hopeless resistance.

One thread does not make a rope; one swallow does not make a summer.

To be fully fed and warmly clothed, and dwell at ease without learning, is little better than a bestial state.

A woman in one house cannot eat the rice of two. (A wise woman does not marry again.)

Though the sword be sharp, it will not wound the innocent.

Sensuality is the chief of sins, filial duty the best of acts.

Prosperity is a blessing to the good, but to the evil it is a curse.

Instruction pervades the heart of the wise, but cannot penetrate the ears of a fool.

The straightest trees are first felled; the cleanest wells first drunk up.

The yielding tongue endures; the stubborn teeth perish.

The life of the aged is like a candle placed between two doors—easily blown out.

The blind have the best ears, and the deaf the sharpest eyes.

The horse's back is not so safe as the buffalo's. (The politician is not so secure as the husbandman.)

A wife should excel in four things: virtue, speech, deportment, and needle-work.

He who is willing to inquire will excel, but the self-sufficient man will fail.

Anger is like a little fire, which if not timely checked may burn down a lofty pile.

Every day cannot be a feast of lanterns.

Too much lenity multiplies crime.

If you love your son, give him plenty of the cudgel; if you hate him, cram him with dainties.

When the mirror is highly polished, the dust will not defile it; when the heart is enlightened with wisdom, impure thoughts will not arise in it.

A stubborn wife and stiffnecked son no laws can govern.

He is my teacher who tells me my faults, my enemy who speaks my virtues.

He has little courage who knows the right and does it not.

To sue a flea, and catch a bite—the results of litigation.

Would you understand the character of a prince, look at his ministers; or the disposition of a man, observe his companions; or that of a father, first mark his son.

The fame of good deeds does not leave a man's door, but his evil acts are known a thousand miles off.

---

[1] The commendation by Lord Brougham of this "admirable precept," as he called it, is cited by Sir J. Davis.

A virtuous woman is a source of honor to her husband, a vicious one disgraces him.

The original tendency of man's heart is to do right, and if well ordered will not of itself be mistaken.

They who respect themselves will be honored, but disesteeming ourselves we shall be despised.

The load a beggar cannot carry he himself begged.

The happy-hearted man carries joy for all the household.

The more mouths to eat so much the more meat.

The higher the rat creeps up the cow's horn the narrower he finds it.

CHAPTER XIII.

ARCHITECTURE, DRESS, AND DIET OF THE CHINESE.

It is a sensible remark of De Guignes,[1] that "the habit we fall into of conceiving things according to the words which express them, often leads us into error when reading the relations of travellers. Such writers have seen objects altogether new, but they are compelled, when describing them, to employ equivalent terms in their own language in order to be understood; while these same terms tend to deceive the reader, who imagines that he sees such palaces, colonnades, peristyles, etc., under these designations as he has been used to, when, in fact, they are quite another thing." The same observation is true of other things than architecture, and of other nations than the Chinese, and this confusion of terms and meanings proves a fruitful source of error in regard to an accurate knowledge of foreign nations, and a just perception of their condition. For instance, the terms *a court of justice*, *a common school*, *politeness*, *learning*, *navy*, *houses*, etc., as well as the names of things, like *razor*, *shoe*, *cap*, *bed*, *pencil*, *paper*, etc., are inapplicable to the same things in England and China; while it is plainly impossible to coin a new word in English to describe the Chinese article, and equally inexpedient to introduce the native term. If, for example, the utensil used by the Chinese to shave with were picked up in Portsmouth by some English navvy who had never seen or heard of it, he would be more likely to call it an oyster-knife, or a wedge, than a razor; while the use to which it is

[1] *Voyage à Péking*, Vol. II., p. 173.

applied must of course give it that name, and would, if it were still more unlike the western article. So with other things. The ideas a Chinese gives to the terms *hwangtí*, *kwanfu*, *pao*, *pih*, and *shu*, are very different from those conveyed to an American by the words *emperor*, *magistrate*, *cannon*, *pencil*, and *book*. Since a person can only judge of what he hears or reads by what he knows, it is desirable that when he meets with western names applied to their equivalents in eastern countries, the function of a different civilization, habits, and notions should not be overlooked in the opinion he forms. These remarks are peculiarly applicable to the domestic life of the Chinese, to their houses, diet, dress, and social customs; although careful descriptions may go a good way in conveying just ideas, it cannot be hoped that they will do what the most cursory examination of the object or trait would instantly accomplish.

The notions entertained abroad on these particulars are, it need hardly be remarked, rather more accurate than those the Chinese have of distant countries, and it is scarcely possible that they can lose their conceit in their own civilization and position among the nations so long as such ideas are entertained as the following extract exhibits. Tien Kí-shih, a popular essayist of the last century, thus congratulates himself and his readers: "I felicitate myself that I was born in China, and constantly think how very different it would have been with me if I had been born beyond the seas in some remote part of the earth, where the people, far removed from the converting maxims of the ancient kings, and ignorant of the domestic relations, are clothed with the leaves of plants, eat wood, dwell in the wilderness, and live in the holes of the earth; though born in the world, in such a condition I should not have been different from the beasts of the field. But now, happily, I have been born in the Middle Kingdom. I have a house to live in; have food and drink, and elegant furniture; have clothing and caps, and infinite blessings: truly, the highest felicity is mine." This extract well indicates the isolation of the writer and his race from their fellow-men; among the neighboring nations even the Japanese would have shown him his erroneous view. The seclusion which had been forced upon both these peoples, who closed their doors as the surest possible defence against aggression from foreign traders and sought in this fashion to remove all cause of quarrel, brought with it in time the almost equal dangers of ignorance and inability to understand their true position among the nations of the world.

The architecture of the Chinese suggests, in its general outline and the peculiar concave roof, a canvas tent as its primary *motive*, though there is no further proof than this likeness of its origin. From the palace to the hovel, in temples and in private dwellings, this type everywhere stands confessed,[1] and almost nothing like a dome or cupola, a spire or a turret, is anywhere

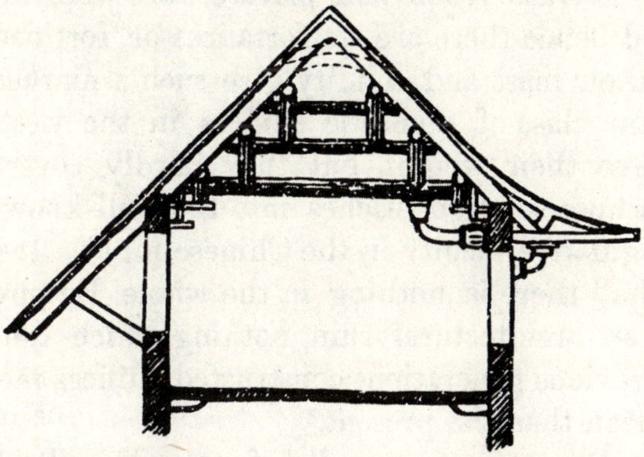

Diagram of Chinese Roof Construction. (From Fergusson.)

found. Few instances occur of an attempt to develop even this simple model into a grand or imposing building. While the Mogul princes in India reared costly mausolea and palaces to perpetuate their memory and the splendor of their reigns, the monarchs of China, with equal or greater resources at command, seldom indulged in this princely pastime, or even attempted the erection of any enduring monument to commemorate their taste or their splendor. Whether it was owing to the absence of the beautiful and majestic models seen in western countries,

[1] It is said that when Ghengis in his invasion of China took a city, his soldiers immediately set about pulling down the four walls of the houses, leaving the overhanging roofs supported by the wooden columns—by which process they converted them into excellent tents for themselves and their horses.—*Encyclopædia Britannica:* Art. CHINA.

or to ignorance of the mechanical principles of the art, the fact is not the less observable, and the inference as to the advance made by them in knowledge and taste not less just.

Fergusson has no doubt assigned one good reason for this fact, in that "the Chinese never had either a dominant priesthood or a hereditary nobility. The absence of the former class is important, because it is to sacred art that architecture has owed its highest inspiration, and sacred art is never so strongly developed as under the influence of a powerful and splendid hierachy. In the same manner the want of a hereditary nobility is equally unfavorable to domestic architecture of a durable description. Private feuds and private wars were till lately unknown, and hence there are no fortalices or fortified mansions, which by their mass and solidity give such a marked character to a certain class of domestic edifices in the west."[1] These reasons have their weight, but they hardly cover the whole question, whose solution reaches into the well-known inertness of the imaginative faculty in the Chinese mind. It is nevertheless true that there is nothing in the whole Empire worthy to be called an architectural ruin, nothing which can inform us whether previous generations constructed edifices more splendid or more mean than the present.[2]

Dwelling-houses are generally of one story, having neither cellars nor basements, and lighted by lattices opening into a court; they must not equal adjacent temples in height, nor possess the ornaments appropriated to palaces and religious establishments. The common building materials are bricks, adobie or matting for the walls, stone for the foundation, brick tiling for the roof, and wood only for the inner work; stone and wooden houses are not unknown, but are so rare as to attract

---

[1] James Fergusson, *History of Indian and Eastern Architecture*, p. 687; compare also *Mémoires Concernant les Chinois*, where Chinese architecture is treated of in almost every volume.

[2] The foreign literature upon this subject is as yet scant and unimportant. Compare the rare and costly *Designs of Chinese Buildings, Furniture, Dresses, etc., from Originals drawn in China by* Mr. Chambers, London, 1757, folio; J. M. Callery, *De l'Architecture Chinoise*, in the *Revue d'Architecture;* Wm. Simpson, in *Transactions of the Royal Institute of British Architects*, 1873–74, p. 33; *Notes and Queries on China and Japan.*

attention. The high prices of timber and the very partial use of window-glass have both tended to modify and restrict the construction of dwellings. The *ní chuen*, or sifted earth, is a compound of decomposed granite or gravel and lime mixed with water, and sometimes a little oil, of which durable walls are made by pounding it into a solid mass between planks secured at the sides and elevated as the wall rises, or by beating it into large blocks; when stuccoed and protected from the rain this material gradually hardens into stone. In houses of the better sort the stone work of the foundation rises three or four feet above the ground, and sometimes the finished surfaces, great size of the stones and the regularity of their arrangement make one regret that the same skill had not been expended on large edifices. In towns their fronts present no opening except the door, and when the outer walls of several houses join those of gardens and enclosures, the street presents an uninteresting sameness, unrelieved by steps, windows, balconies, porticoes, or front yards. The walls are twenty-five or thirty feet high, usually hollow, or too thin to safely support the roof unaided. In the common buildings a framework of wood is erected on the foundation, which has large stones so arranged as to receive the posts, and on these rests the entire weight of the roof. The brick nogging fills up the intervals, but supports nothing; it is sometimes solid, more frequently merely a face-work, and if the roof becomes leaky or broken a heavy rain will destroy the wall, as it soaks through the courses and washes out the mud within. In the central provinces common walls are often made of small bricks four inches square and one thick, which are laid on their edges in a series of hollows; between the courses a plank sometimes adds greater strength to the wall. These cellular constructions are more durable than would be imagined provided the stucco remains uninjured.

The bricks are the same size as our own, and usually burned to a grayish slate color; they are made by hand, and sell at a price varying from three dollars to eight dollars a thousand. In the sea-coast districts lime is cheaply obtained from shells, but in the interior from limestone calcined by anthracite coal; the people use it pure, only occasionally mixing sand with it for either mortar or stucco. The walls are often stuccoed, and when not thus covered the bricks are occasionally rubbed smooth and pointed with fine cement. In place of a broad cornice the top is frequently relieved by a pretty ornament of moulded work of painted clay figures in *alto relievo*, representing a battle scene, a landscape, clusters of flowers, or some other design, defended from the weather by the projecting eaves. A black painted band, relieved by corners and designs of flowers and scrolls, is a cheap substitute for the carved figures.

The roofs are hipped in some provinces, but rarely in the north. They are steep, and if kept tight will last several years; the grass which is apt to spring up on them is a source of injury, and its growth or removal alike endangers the soundness of the construction. The yellow and green glazed tiles of public buildings add to their beauty, as do the dragon's heads and globes on their ridge-poles; these features, together with the earthen dogs at the corners of temples or official houses, make the structures exceedingly picturesque. In Peking the framework under the wide eaves of palaces is tastefully painted in green and gold, and protected by a netting of copper wire. Roofs are made of earthen tiles laid on coarse clapboarding that rests on the purlines in alternate ridges and furrows. The under layer consists of square thin pieces, laid side by side in ascending rows with the lower edges overlapping; the sides are covered by the semi-cylindrical tiles, which are further protected by a covering of mortar. In the northern provinces the tiles are laid in a course of mud resting on straw over the clapboarding. The workmen begin the tiling at the ridge-pole and finish as they come down to the eaves, so as not to walk over the tiles and crack them; but such roofs easily leak in driving storms. No chimneys are seen; the slope is steep, for quick discharge of rain and snow. Terraces are erected on shops, but balustrades or flat roofs are seldom seen. Occasionally the gable walls rise above the roof in degrees, imparting a singular, bow-like aspect to the edifice. The purlines and ridge-pole extend from wall to wall, and the rafters are slender strips. In all roofs the principal weight rests on the two rows of pillars at the sides, that uphold the plates, and the antefixæ which support the broad eaves far beyond the wall. A series of beams and posts above the plates and tie-beams make the roof very heavy but also secure; curb and mansard roofs are unknown.

The pillars of stone or timber in Chinese temples are often noticeable, owing to their size or length as single pieces. They are, however, unadorned with either capital or carved base, though the shaft may be finely carved and painted, the color decoration being often upon a thick coating of *papier-maché*, laid on to protect the wood. In two-story houses the sleepers of the floor are supported on tie-beams attached to the main posts if they do not rest on the wall. Posts form an element of all Chinese buildings, either to support the roof or the veranda. The entrance is on the sides, and the wall is set back from the outer line of the eaves so as to afford a shelter or porch. Hipped roofs enable the architect to encompass the entire building with a veranda, this being a common arrangement in the southern provinces. A slight ceiling usually conceals the tiling, but the apartment appears lofty owing to the cavity of the roof.

The pavilion is a prominent feature of Chinese architecture, and its ornamentation calls out the best talent of the builder in making his edifice acceptable. One charming specimen of this style at the Emperor's summer palace of Yuen-ming Yuen is already famous, its material being of pure copper; it is about fourteen feet square and twenty high.

Another beautiful structure which well exhibits the pavilion is shown in the adjoining cut. It is the *Pih-yung Kung*, or 'Classic Hall,' built by Kienlung adjacent to the Confucian Temple at Peking (page 74), and devoted to expounding the classics. This lofty building, which may be here seen through an ornamental arch across the court, is perfectly square, covered with a four-sided double roof, whose bright yellow tiles and gilded ball at the apex produce a most brilliant effect in the sunlight. The deep veranda, completely encircling the structure and supported by a score of colored wooden pillars, very ably relieves the dead mass and heavy upper roof of the pavilion

PIH-YUNG KUNG, OR 'CLASSIC HALL,' PEKING.

proper. Around flow the waters of a circular tank, edged with marble balustrades and spanned by four bridges which form the approaches to each of the sides.

The general disposition of a Chinese dwelling of the better sort is that of a series of rooms separated and lighted by intervening courts, and accessible along a covered corridor communicating with each, or by side passages leading through the courts. In cities, where the houses are cramped and the lots irregular in shape, there is more diversity in the arrangement and size of rooms; and in the country establishments of wealthy families, where the gradual increase of the members calls for additional space, the succession of courts and buildings, interspersed with gardens and pools, sometimes renders the whole not a little complicated. The great expense of timber for floors, posts, and sleepers has been the chief reason for retaining the single story, rather than the awkwardness caused by cramping women's feet. No contrivance for warming the rooms by means of chimneys or flues exists, except that found in the *kang*, or brick bed, on which the inmates lie and sit.

The entrance into large mansions in the country is by a triple gate leading through a lawn or garden up to the hall; in towns, a single door, usually elevated a step or two above the street, introduces the visitor into a porch or court. A wall or movable screen is placed inside of the doorway, and the intervening space is occupied by the porter; upon the wall on the left is often seen a shrine dedicated to the gods of the threshold. In the houses of officials, upon this wall is inscribed a list of dignities and offices which the master has held during his life. The door is solidly constructed, and moves upon pivots turning in sockets. Under the projecting eaves hang paper lanterns informing the passer-by of the name and title of the householder, and when lighted at night serving to illumine the street and designate his habitation; for door-plates and numbers are unknown. The roughness of the gate is somewhat concealed by the names or grotesque representations of two tutelar gods, Shintu and Yuhlui, to whom the guardianship of the house is entrusted; while the sides and lintel are embellished with felicitous quotations written upon red paper, or with sign-boards of official rank. The doorkeeper and other servants lodge in small rooms within the gateway, and above the porch is an attic containing one or two apartments, to be reached by a rude stairway.

On passing behind the screen a court, occasionally adorned with flowers or a fancy fish-pool, is crossed before reaching the principal hall. The upper end of the hall is furnished with a high table, on which incense vases, idolatrous utensils, and offerings are placed in honor of the divinities and lares worshipped there, whose tablets and names are on the wall. Sometimes the table merely contains flowers in jars, fancy pieces of white quartz, limestone or jade, or ornaments of various kinds. Before the table is a large couch, with a low stand in its centre, and a pillow for reclining upon. In front of it the chairs are arranged down the room in two rows facing each other, each pair having a small table between them. The floors are made of thick, large tiles of brick or marble, or of hard cement. Even in a bright day the room is dim, and the absence of carpets and fireplaces, and of windows to afford a prospect abroad, renders it cheerless to a foreigner accustomed to his own glazed and loftier houses.

A rear door near the side wall opens either into a kitchen or court, across which are the female apartments, or directly into the latter and the rooms for domestics. Instead of being always rectangular the doors are sometimes made round, leaf-shaped, or semi-circular, and it is thought desirable that they should not open opposite each other, lest evil spirits find their way in from the street. The rear rooms are lighted by skylights when other modes are unavailable, and along the southern sea-coasts the thin laminæ of a species of oyster (*Placuna*) cut into small squares supply the place of window-glass. Commerce is gradually bringing this material into greater use all over the land, though the fear of thieves still limits it. Corean paper is the chief substitute for glass in the north. The kitchen is a small affair, for the universal use of portable furnaces enables the inmates to cook wherever the smoke will be least troublesome. Warming the house, even as far north as Ningpo, is not frequent, as the inmates rely on their quilted and fur garments foı protection. The flue of the tiled-brick divan, or *kang*, is connected with a pit lined with brick dug in the floor in front; when the pot of coal is well lighted and placed near the opening, the draft carries the heat into the passages running under the surface, and soon warms the room without much smoke. The pot of burning coal furnishes all the cooking-fire the poor have, and at night the inmates sleep on the warm bricks.

The country establishments of wealthy men furnish the best expression of Chinese ideas of elegance and comfort. In these enclosures the hall of ancestors, library, school-room, and summer-houses are detached and erected upon low plinths, surrounded by a veranda, and frequently decorated with tracery and ornamental carving. Near the rear court are the female apartments and offices, many of the former and the sleeping apartments being in attics. Considerable space is occupied by the quadrangles, which are paved and embellished by fish-pools, flowering shrubs, and other plants. Mr. Fortune describes[1] the house and garden of a gentleman at Ningpo as being connected by rude-looking caverns of rock-work, "and what at first sight appears to be a subterranean passage leading from room to room, through which the visitor passes to the garden. The small courts, of which a glimpse is caught in passing along, are fitted up with rock-work; dwarf trees are planted here and there in various places, and graceful creepers hang down into the pools in front. These being passed, another cavernous passage leads into the garden, with its dwarf trees, vases, ornamented lattices, and beautiful shrubs suddenly opening to the view. By windings and glimpses along the rocky passages into other courts, and hiding the real boundary by masses of shrubs and trees, the grounds are made to appear much larger than they really are."

The houses of the poor are dark, dirty, low, and narrow tenements, where the floor is of earth covered with mats or tiled, and the doorway the only opening, on which a swinging mat conceals the interior. The whole family often sleep, eat, and live in a single room. Pigs, dogs, and hens dispute the space

[1] *Wanderings in China*, p. 98.

with children and furniture—if a table and a few trestles and stools, pots and plates, deserve that name. The filthy street without is a counterpart to the gloomy, smoky abode within, and a single walk through the streets and lanes of such a neighborhood is sufficient to reconcile a person to any ordinary condition of life. On the outskirts of the town a still poorer class take up with huts made of mats and thatch upon the ground, through which the rain and wind find free course. It is surprising that people can live and enjoy health, and even be cheerful, as the Chinese are, in such circumstances. Between these hovels and the abodes of the rich is a class of middle houses, consisting of three or four small rooms surrounding a court, each one lodging a family, which uses its portion of the quadrangle.

The best furniture is made of a heavy wood stained to resemble ebony; camphor, elm, pine, aspen, and melia woods furnish cheaper material. Ornamental articles, porcelain vases, copper tripods or pots, stone screens, book-shelves, flowers in pots, etc., show the national taste. Ink sketches of landscapes, gay scrolls inscribed with sentences suspended from the walls, and pretty lanterns relieve the baldness of the room; their combined effect is not destitute of variety and elegance, though there is a lack of *comfort*. Partitions are sometimes fancifully made of lattice-work, with openings neatly arranged for the reception of boxes containing books. The bedrooms are small, poorly ventilated, and seldom visited except at night. A massive bedstead of costly woods, elaborately carved, and supporting a tester for the silk curtains and mosquito-bars, is often shown as the family pride and heirloom; a scroll of fine writing adorns its fringe or valance. Mattresses or feather beds are not used, and the pillow is a hollow square frame of rattan or bamboo. The bed, wardrobe, and toilet usually complete the furniture of the sleeping apartments of the Chinese; but if this is also the sitting room, the bed is rolled up so as often to furnish seats on its boards.

The grounds of the rich are laid out in good style, and were not the tasteful arrangements and diversified shrubbery which would render them charming resorts almost always spoiled by general bad keeping—neglect and ruin, if not nastiness and offals, being often visible—they would please the most fastidious. The necessity of having a place for the women and children to recreate themselves is one reason for having an open enclosure, even if it be only a plat of flowers or a bed of vegetables. In the imperial gardens the attempt to make an epitome of nature has been highly successful. De Guignes describes their art of gardening as "imitating the beauties and producing the inequalities of nature. Instead of alleys planted symmetrically or uniform grounds, there are winding footpaths, trees here and there as if by chance, woody or sterile hillocks, and deep gulleys with narrow passages, whose sides are steep or rough with rocks, and presenting only a few miserable shrubs. They like to bring together in gardening, in the same view, cultivated grounds and arid plains; to make the field uneven and cover it with artificial rock-work; to dig caverns in mountains, on whose tops are arbors half overthrown, and around which tortuous footpaths run and return into themselves, prolonging, as it were, the extent of the grounds and increasing the pleasure of the walk."

A fish-pond, supplied by a rivulet running wildly through the grounds, forms a pretty feature of such gardens, in which, if there be room, a summer-house is erected on a rocky islet, or on piles over the water, accessible by a rugged causey of rock-work. The nelumbium lily, with its plate-like leaves and magnificent flowers, is a general favorite in such places; carp and other fish are reared in their waters, and gold-fish in small tanks. Whenever it is possible a gallery runs along the sides of the pond for the pleasure and use of the females in the household. A tasteful device in some gardens, which beguiles the visitor's ramble, is a rude kind of shell or pebble mosaic inlaid in the gravelly paths, representing birds, animals, or other figures; the time required to decipher them prolongs the walk, and apparently increases the size of the grounds. The pieces of rock-work are cemented and bound with wire; and in fish-pools, grottos, or causeways this unique ornament has a charming effect, the moss and plants which grow upon it adding rather to its appropriateness.

The wood and mason work is unsubstantial, requiring constant repairs; when new they present a pretty appearance, but both gardens and houses, when neglected, soon fall into a ruinous condition. Some of the principal merchants at Canton, in the former days of the hong monopoly, had cultivated grounds of greater or less extent attached to their establishments. One of them, by way of variety, constructed a summer-house entirely of glass, this wonderful structure being made so that it could be closed and protected with shutters.

The arrangement of shops and warehouses is modified by the uses to which they are applied, but they still resemble dwelling-houses more than is the case with stores in western cities. The rear room of the shop is a small apartment, used for a dormitory, store-room, or workshop, and sometimes for all these purposes together; it is in most cases on an upper floor. Small ones are lighted from the street, but the largest by a skylight, in which cases there is a latticed screen reaching across the room, to secure the inside from the street. The whole shop-front is thrown open by day and closed at night by shutters running in grooves, and secured by heavy cross-bars to a row of posts which fit in sockets in the threshold and lintel. The doorway recedes a foot or two, and the projecting roof serves to protect customers, and such goods as are exposed, from the rain and sun. In small shops there are two counters, a long one running back from the door, and another at right angles to it, reaching partly across the front. The shopman sits within the angle formed by these, and as they are low he can easily serve a customer in the street as well as in the shop. At night the smaller one often forms a lodging place for homeless beggars. The facing of the outer counter is of granite, and in Canton a niche containing a tablet inscribed to the god of wealth is cut in the end, where incense is burned. Another shrine is placed on high within the apartment, dedicated to the deity of the place, whoever he may be.

The loft is much contracted; and that it may not intercept the skylight, it is usually a small chamber reached by a gallery, and lighted in front. Chinese tradesmen do not make much display in exhibiting their goods, and the partial use of glass renders it somewhat unsafe for them to do so. The want of a yard compels them to cook and wash either behind or on top of the building; clerks and workmen usually eat and sleep under the shop roof. In the densest parts of Canton the roofs are covered with a loose framework, on which firewood is piled, clothes washed and dried, and meals cooked; it also affords a sleeping place in summer. In case of fire, however, these lumbered roofs become like so many tinder-boxes, and aid not a little to spread the flames.

The narrowness of the streets in Chinese cities is a source of many inconveniences; few exceed ten or twelve feet in width, and most of those in Canton are less than eight. No large squares having fountains and shrubbery, nor any open spaces except the areas in front of temples relieve the closeness of these lanes. The absence of horses and carriages in southern cities, and a custom of huddling together, a desire to screen the thoroughfare from the sun, and ignorance of the advantages of another mode, are among the leading reasons for making them so contracted; while the difficulty of collecting a mob in them should be mentioned as one point in their favor. In case of fire it is difficult to get access to the burning buildings, and dangerous for the inmates to move or save their property. At all times porters carrying burdens are impeded by the crowd of passengers, who likewise must pass Indian file lest they tilt against the porters. Ventilation is imperfect where the buildings are packed so closely, and the public necessaries and their offal carried through the streets by the scavengers pollute the air. Drainage is very superficial and incomplete; the sewers easily choke up or get broken and exude their contents over the pathway. The ammoniacal and other gases which are generated aggravate the ophthalmic diseases so prevalent; and it is a matter of surprise that the cholera, plague, or yellow fever does not visit the inhabitants of such confined abodes, who breathe so tainted an atmosphere. The peculiar government of cities by means of wards and neighborhoods, each responsible to the officials, combined with the ignorance among all ranks of the principles of hygiene, will account for the evils so patent to one accustomed to the energetic sway of a mayor and board of health in most European cities, who can bring knowledge and power to coöperate for the well-being of all.

The streets are usually paved with slabs of stone laid crosswise, and except near markets and wells are comparatively clean. They are not laid out straight, and some present a singularly irregular appearance from the slight angle which each house makes with its neighbors; it being considered rather unlucky to have them exactly even. The names of the streets are written on the gateways crossing them, whenever they are marked at all; occasionally, as at Canton, each division makes a separate neighborhood and has its own name; a single long street will thus have five, six, or more names. The general arrangement of a Chinese city presents a labyrinth of streets, alleys, and byways very perplexing to a stranger who has neither plan nor directory to guide him, nor numbers upon the houses and shops to direct him. The sign-boards are hung each side of the door, or securely inserted in stone sockets; some of them are ten or fifteen feet high, and being gaily painted and gilded on both sides with picturesque characters, a succession of them as seen down a street produces a gay effect. The inscriptions simply mention the kind of goods sold, and without half the puffing seen in western cities; accounts sometimes given of the inscriptions on sign-boards in Chinese cities, as "No cheating here," and others, describe the exception and not the rule. The edicts of government, handbills of medicines and the famous doctors who make them, notices offering rewards for children who are lost or slaves escaped, new shops opened, houses to let, or other events, cover blank walls in great variety, printed on red, black, white, or yellow paper; the absence of newspapers leads shopmen to depend more for patronage upon a circle of customers and the distribution of cards than to spend much money in handbills. The shrines of the street gods occur in southern cities, located in niches in the wall, with altars before them.

The temples and assembly-halls are the only public buildings in Chinese cities belonging to the people. Their courts and cloisters, with such gardens, tea-houses, and pools as may be accessible, attract constant crowds, and furnish the only places of common resort. The priests derive no small portion of their income from travellers, and their establishments are consequently made more commodious and extensive than the number of priests or the throng of worshippers require.

The assembly-halls or club-houses form a peculiar feature of Chinese society. There are more than a hundred in Canton and many hundreds in Peking. They are built sometimes by a particular craft as its guildhall, or more commonly erected by persons resorting to the place for trade, study, or amusement, who subscribe to fit up a commodious establishment to accommodate persons coming from the same town. In this way their convenience, assistance, oversight, and general safety are all increased.[1] All buildings pay a ground rent to the government, but no data are available for comparing this tax with that levied in western cities. The government furnishes the owner of the ground with a *hung kí*, or 'red deed,' in testimony of his right to occupancy, which puts him in possession as long as he pays the taxes. There is a record office in the local magistracy of such documents.

Houses are rented on short leases, and the rent collected quarterly in advance; the annual income from real estate is between nine and twelve per cent. The yearly rent of the best shops in Canton is from $150 to $400; there is no system of insuring against fire, which, with the municipal taxes and the difficulty of collecting bad rents, enhances their price. Such kind of property in China is liable to many risks.

The taverns are numerous and adapted for every calling. Though they will not bear comparison with western hotels, they are far in advance of the cheerless khans and caravansaries found in Western Asia. The traveller brings his own bedding, sometimes also his own provision, and when night comes spreads his mat upon the floor or divan and lies down in his clothes. The better sort of travellers order a room for themselves, but officials or rich men go to temples, or hire a boat in which to travel and sleep; this usage takes off the best class of customers. One considerable source of income to innkeepers is the prepa-

[1] Compare pp. 76 and 167.

ration of dinners for parties of men, who either come to the house or send to it for so many covers; for when a gentleman invites his friends to an entertainment it is common to serve it up at his warehouse, or at an inn. In towns and cities thousands of men eat in the streets; the number of eating and cooking-stalls produces a most lively impression upon a stranger. This custom has had a good effect in promoting the general courtesy so conspicuous among the people, and is increased by great numbers of street story-tellers. The noisy hilarity of the customers, as they ply their "nimble lads," or chopsticks, and the vociferous cries of the cooks recommending their cakes and dishes, with the steaming savor from the frying-pan and kettles, form only one of the many objects to attract the notice of the foreign observer. Their appearance and the variety of bustling scenes and picturesque novelties presented to him afford constant instruction and entertainment. Those at Canton have been thus described by an eye-witness.

The number of itinerant workmen of one kind or another which line the sides of the streets or occupy the areas before public buildings in Chinese towns is a remarkable feature. Fruiterers, pastrymen, cooks, venders of gimcracks, and wayside shopmen are found in other countries as well as China; but to see a travelling blacksmith or tinker, an itinerant glass-mender, a peripatetic repairer of umbrellas, a locomotive seal-cutter, an ambulatory barber, a migratory banker, a peregrinatory apothecary or druggist, or a walking shoemaker and cobbler, one must travel hitherward. These movable establishments, together with fortune-tellers, herb and booksellers, chiromancers, etc., pretty well fill up the space, so that one often sees both sides of the streets literally lined with the stalls, wares, or tools of persons selling or making something to eat or to wear. The money-changer sits behind a small table, on which his strings of cash are chained, and where he weighs the silver he is to change; his neighbor, the seal-cutter, sits next him near a like fashioned table. The barber has his chest of drawers made to serve for a seat, and if he has not a furnace of his own he heats his water at the cook's or the blacksmith's fire near by, perhaps shaving his friend gratis by way of recompense.

The herbseller chooses an open place where he will not be trampled on, and there displays his simples and his plasters, while the dentist, with a ghastly string of fangs and grinders around his neck, testimonials of his skill, sits over against him, each with his infallible remedy. The book-peddler and chooser of lucky days, and he who searches for stolen goods by divination, arrange themselves on either side, with their tables and stalls, and array of sticks, pencils, signs, and pictures, all trying to "catch a little pigeon." The spectacle-mender and razor-grinder, the cutler and seller of bangles and bracelets, and the maker of clay puppets or mender of old shoes, are not far off, all plying their callings as busily as if they were in their own shops. Then, besides the hundreds of stalls for selling articles of food, dress, or ornament, there are innumerable hucksters going up and down with baskets and trays slung on their shoulders, each bawling or making his own peculiar note, which, with coolies transporting burdens, chair-bearers carrying sedans, and passengers following one another like a stream, with here and there a woman among them, so fill up the streets that it is no easy matter to navigate one's way. Notwithstanding all these obstructions, it is worthy of note and highly praiseworthy to see these crowds pass and repass with the greatest rapidity in the narrow streets without altercation or disturbance, and seldom with accident.[1]

Streets at the north present a somewhat different, and on the whole a less inviting because less entertaining and picturesque aspect. Their greater width allows carts to pass, and it also offers more room for the garbage, the rubbish, and the noisome sights that are most disgusting, all of which are made worse in rainy weather by the mud through which one flounders. Barrow thus delineates those in Peking: "The multitude of movable workshops of tinkers and barbers, cobblers and blacksmiths, the tents and booths where tea and fruit, rice and other eatables were exposed for sale, with the wares and merchandise arrayed before the doors, had contracted this spacious street to a narrow road in the middle, just wide enough for two little vehicles to pass each other. The processions of men in office attended by their numerous retinues, bearing umbrellas and flags, painted lanterns and a variety of strange insignia of their rank and station, different trains that were accompanying, with lamentable cries, corpses to their graves, and with squalling music, brides to their husbands; the troops of dromedaries laden with coals from Tartary; the wheel-barrows and hand-carts stuffed with vegetables, occupied nearly the whole of this middle space in one continued line. All was in motion. The sides of the streets were filled with an immense concourse of people, buying and selling and bartering their different commodities. The buzz and confused noises of this mixed multitude, proceeding from the loud bawling of those who were crying their wares, the wrangling of others, with every now and then a strange twanging sound like the jarring of a cracked jewsharp (the barber's

[1] *Chinese Repository*, Vol. X., p. 473.

signal), the mirth and laughter that prevailed in every group, could scarcely be exceeded. Peddlers with their packs, jugglers and conjurers, fortune-tellers, mountebanks and quack doctors, comedians and musicians, left no space unoccupied."[1]

Shops are closed at nightfall, and persons going abroad carry a lantern or torch. Over the thoroughfares slender towers are erected, where notice of a fire is given and the watches of the night announced by striking a gong. Few persons are met in the streets at night, and the private watch kept by all who are able greatly assists the regular police in preserving order and apprehending thieves. These watchers go up and down their wards beating large bamboos, to let "thieves know they are on the lookout." Considering all things, large Chinese cities are remarkably quiet at night. Beggars find their lodgings in the porches and squares of temples, or sides of the streets, and nestle together for mutual warmth. This class is under the care of a headman, who, in order to collect the poor-tax allowed by law, apportions them in the neighborhoods with the advice of the elders and constables. During the day they go from one door to another and receive their allotted stipend, which cannot be less than one cash to each person. They sit in the doorway and sing a ditty or beat their clap-dishes and sticks to attract attention, and if the shopkeeper has no customers he lets them keep up their cries, for he knows that the longer they are detained so much the more time will elapse before they come again to his shop. Many are blind and all present a sickly appearance, their countenances begrimed with dirt and furrowed by sorrow and suffering. The very difficult question how to assist, restrain, and employ the poor has been usually left to the mercy and wisdom of the municipal officers in the cities; and the results are not on the whole discreditable to their humanity and benevolence. Many persons give the headman a dollar or more per month to purchase exemption from the daily importunity of the beggars, and families about to have a house-warming, marriage, or funeral, as also newly arrived junks, are obliged to fee him to get rid of the clamorous and loathsome crowd.

---

[1] *Travels in China*, p. 96.

When fires occur the officers of government are held responsible; the law being that if ten houses are burned *within the walls*, the highest officer in it shall be fined nine months' pay; if more than thirty, a year's salary; and if three hundred are consumed, he shall be degraded one degree. The governor and other high officers, attended by a few troops, are frequently seen at fires in Canton, as much to prevent thievery as to direct in extinguishing the flames. The engines are hurried through the narrow streets at a fearful rate; those who carry away property are armed with swords to defend it, and usually add to the crash of the burning houses by loud cries. The police do not hesitate to pull down houses if the fire can thereby be sooner extinguished, but there is no organized body of firemen, nor any well-arranged system of operations in such cases, though conflagrations are ordinarily soon under control. Cruel men often take the opportunity at such times to steal and carry off defenceless persons, especially young girls.

At Canton the usage is general of levying a bonus on the owners of the houses adjacent to the burnt district, whose dwellings were saved by the exertions of the firemen, the appraisement decreasing as the distance increases; the sum is divided among the firemen. The householders thus saved also employ priests to erect an altar near by, whereon to perform a service, and "return thanks for Heaven's mercy." On the whole, the fire control in China is superior to that in Turkey, where the firemen pay themselves for their efforts by extortions practised upon house-owners.

The pagoda is a building considered as so peculiar to the Chinese that a landscape or painting relating to China without a pagoda perched on a hill—like one of Egyptian scenery destitute of a pyramid—would be considered deficient. The term *pagoda* is used in its proper sense by most of the French and Portuguese writers to denote a temple for idols, but in English books it has always been appropriated to the polygonal towers seen throughout the country. Some confusion has arisen in consequence of applying the account of an immense temple full of idols to these towers. The English use is the most definite in China, although its misapplication is indefensible if we regard its derivation.

The form of the Chinese *tah* is probably derived from the spire on the top of the Hindu dagoba, as its name is doubtless taken from the first syllable; but their purpose has so long been identified with the geomantic influences which determine the luck of a place that the people do not associate them with Buddhism. Mr. Milne explains this in his remark that "the presence of such an edifice not only secures to the site the protection of heaven, if it already bears evidence of enjoying it, but represses any evil influences that may be native to the spot, and imparts to it the most salutary and felicitous omens."[1] Those in the southern and central provinces seldom contain idols of any pretensions. They are ascended by stairways built in the thick walls on alternate sides of the stories. In the north there is another kind, designed to contain a *shé-lí*, or relic of Buddha, having a large room near the base for worshipping the idol placed in it, but otherwise entirely solid and nearly uniform in size to the top; the stories are merely numerous narrow projections, like eaves or string courses, on which hundreds of small images are sometimes placed. These structures more nearly resemble the Indian *dagobä* than the other kind, and are always connected with a monastery, while those are not uniformly so placed, though under a priestly oversight.

No town is considered complete without a pagoda, and many large cities have several; there must be nearly two thousand in the Empire, some of which are quite celebrated. It is rare to see a new one, and the ruinous condition of most of them indicates the weakness of the faith which erected them. They vary in height from five to thirteen stories, and are mostly built in so solid a manner that they are likely to remain for centuries. One at Hangchau is octagonal, each face twenty-eight feet wide and the wall at the base eighteen feet thick; the top is reached by a spiral stairway between the walls; a covered gallery on the outside of each story affords resting-places and ever-changing views to the visitor; it is one hundred and seventy feet high, and was built during the Sung dynasty, in the twelfth century. The prospect from its summit is superb; the pic-

[1] *Life in China*, p. 453.

turesque combination of sea and shore, land and water, city and country, wilderness, gardens, and hills, with many historical and religious associations interesting to a native, make it one of the most charming landscapes in China.

Sir John Davis visited one near Lintsing chau in Shantung, in very good repair, inhabited by Buddhist priests, and containing two idols; each of its nine stories was inscribed with *Ometo Fuh*, in large characters. It was erected since the completion of the Grand Canal. A winding stairway of near two hundred steps conducted to the top, about one hundred and fifty feet from the ground, from whence an extensive view was obtained of the surrounding country. The basement was excellently built of granite, and all the rest of glazed brick, beautifully joined and cemented.

The objects in building these structures being of a mixed nature, sometimes geomantic and sometimes religious, their materials, size, and structure vary considerably. There are two inside of Canton, and three near the Pearl River, below the city; fifteen others occur in the prefecture. Suchau has two, Ningpo one, Fuhchau two, and Peking six in and out of the walls. One of those at Canton was built by the Moslems about a thousand years ago, a plain brick tower nearly two hundred feet high, from which the faithful were probably called to prayers in the adjacent mosque. Fergusson's remarks upon Chinese architecture would probably have been modified had the writer enjoyed a wider range of observation and a fuller knowledge of the designs of native builders. They are, however, the conclusions of a competent observer, and the position he gives to the pagoda among the tower-like buildings of the world, arising from its peculiar form, its divisions, and its apparent uselessness, will be generally accepted as just.

Mr. Milne, in his interesting work, has a good account of pagodas; he shows that while their model is of Hindu origin, and has been carefully followed since the first one was erected (about A.D. 250) at Nanking, the popular geomantic ideas connected with their octagonal form and great height have gradually increased and influenced their location. The Buddhists seem themselves to have lost their ancient confidence in the protection of the *shé-lí* (or *saina*) supposed to be built in them. The number of Indian words transliterated in Chinese accounts of these edifices further proves their foreign origin. For convenience and accuracy in describing them, it would be best to restrict the term *pagoda* to the hollow octagonal towers, the word *dagoba* to the solid ones covering the relics, and *tope* to the erections over priests when buried.

Pagodas are sometimes made of cast iron; those hitherto observed are in the central provinces. One exists in Chehkiang province, nearly fifty feet high and of nine stories. The octagonal pieces forming the walls are each single castings, as are also the plates forming the roof. The whole structure, including the base and spire, was made of twenty pieces of iron. Its interior is filled with brick, probably with the design to strengthen it against storms. The ignorance of the Chinese of later days of the Hindu origin of pagodas has led to their regarding those now in existence as of native design, and appropriated by the Buddhists for their own ends. Most of them are falling to ruins; and the assurances held out by the geomancers that the pagoda will act like an electric tractor to draw down every felicitous omen from above, so that fire, water, wood, earth, and metal will be at the service of the people, the soil productive, trade prosperous, and the natives submissive and happy, all fail to call out funds for repairing them.[1]

The dull appearance of a Chinese city when seen from a distance is unlike that of European cities, in which spires, domes, and towers of churches and cathedrals, halls, palaces, and other public buildings relieve the uniformity of rows of dwellings. In China, temples, houses, and palaces are nearly of one height; their sameness being only partially relieved by trees mingled with pairs of tall flag-staffs with frames near their tops, which at a distance rather suggest the idea of dismantled gallows. Nature, however, charms and delights, and few countries present more beautiful landscapes; even the tameness of the works of man serves as a foil for the diversified beauties of the cultivated landscape.

---

[1] *Voyages à Peking*, Tome II., p. 79; Davis' *Sketches*, Vol. I., p. 213; Fergusson, *Indian and Eastern Architecture*, 1876, p. 695; Milne's *Life in China*, p. 429 seq.; *Chinese Repository*, Vol. XIX., pp. 535–540.

A Chinese usually prefers to travel by water, and in the southeastern provinces it may be said that vehicles solely designed for carrying travellers or goods do not exist, for the carts and wheelbarrows which are met with are few and miserably made. But north of the Yangtsz' River, all over the Great Plain carts and wheelbarrows form the chief means of travel and transportation. The high cost of timber and the bad roads compel the people to make these vehicles very rude and strong, having axles and wheels able to bear the strains or upsets which befall them. Carts for goods are drawn by three or four horses

Wheelbarrows Used for Travelling.

usually driven tandem, and fastened by long traces to the axletree, one remaining within the thills. The common carts, drawn by one or two mules, are oblong boxes fastened to an axle, covered with cotton cloth, and cushioned to alleviate the jolting; the passengers get in and out at the front, where the driver sits close to the horse. In Peking the members of the imperial clan and family are allowed to use carts having the wheel behind the body; their ranks are further indicated by a red or yellow covering, and a greater or less number of outriders to escort them. The wheelbarrow is in great use for short distances throughout the same region. The position of the wheel in the centre enables the man to propel a heavy load readily. When on a good road, and aided by a donkey, the larger varieties of barrow carry easily a burden of a ton's weight; two men are necessary to maintain the balance and guide the rather top-heavy vehicle.

Where travelling by water is impossible, sedan chairs are used to carry passengers, and coolies with poles and slings transport their luggage and goods. There are two kinds of sedan, neither of them designed for reclining like the Indian *palky*. The light one is made of bamboo, and so narrow that the sitter is obliged to lean forward as he is carried; the large one, called *kiao*, is, whether viewed in regard to lightness, comfort, or any other quality associated with such a mode of carriage, one of the most convenient articles found in any country. Its use is subject to sumptuary laws, and forbidden to the common people unless possessing some kind of rank. In Peking only the highest officials ride in them, with four bearers. In other cities two chairmen manage easily enough to maintain a gait of four miles an hour with a sedan upon their shoulders. Goods are carried upon poles, and however large or heavy the package may be, the porters contrive to subdivide its weight between them by means of their sticks and slings. The number of persons who thus gain a livelihood is great, and in cities they are employed by headmen, who contract for work just as carmen do elsewhere; when unengaged by overseers, parties station themselves at corners and other public places, ready to start at a beck, after the manner of *Dienstmänner* in German cities. In the streets of Canton groups of brawny fellows are often seen idling away their time in smoking, gambling, sleeping, or jeering at the wayfarers; and, like the husbandmen mentioned in the parable, if one ask them why they stand there all the day idle? the answer will be, " Because no man hath hired us."

The chair-bearers form a distinct guild in cities, and the establishments where sedans and their bearers are to be hired suggest a comparison with the livery stables of western cities; the men, in fact, are nicknamed at Canton *mo mí ma*, 'tailless horses.' A vehicle used sometimes by the Emperor and high officers consists of an open chair set upon poles, so made that the incumbent can be seen as well as see around him. It undergoes many changes in different parts of the country, as it is both cheap and light and well fitted for traversing mountainous regions.

In the construction and management of their river craft the Chinese excel. As boats are intended to be the residences of those who navigate them, regard is had to this in their arrangement. Only a part of the fleets of boats seen on the river at Canton are intended for transportation, a large number being designed for fixed residences, and perhaps half of them are permanently moored. They are not obliged to remain where they station themselves, but the boats and their inmates are both under the supervision of a water police, who register them and point out the position they may occupy. Barges for families, those in which oil, salt, fuel, or other articles are sold, lighters, passage-boats, flower-boats, and other kinds, are by this means grouped together, and more easily found. It was once ascertained that there were eighty-four thousand boats registered as belonging to the city of Canton, but whether all remained near the city and did not go to other parts of the district, or whether old ones were erased from the register when broken up, was not determined. It is not likely, however, that at one time this number of boats ever lay opposite the city. No one who has been at Canton can forget the noisy, animating sight the river offers, nor failed to have noticed the good-humored carefulness with which boats of every size pass each other without collision.

It is difficult to describe the many kinds of craft found on Chinese waters without the assistance of drawings. They are furnished with stern sculls moving upon a pivot, and easily propelling the boat. Large boats are furnished with two or three of these, which, when not in use, are conveniently hauled in upon the side. They are provided with oars, the loom and blade of which are fastened by withs, and work through a band attached to a stake; the rower stands up and pushes his oar with the same motion as that employed by the Venetian gondolier. Occasionally an oarsman is seen rowing with his feet. The mast in some large cargo boats consists of two sticks, resting on the gunwales, joined at top, and so arranged as to be hoisted from the bow; in those designed for residences no provision is made for a mast. Fishing boats, lighters, and sea-going craft have one or two permanent masts. In all, except the smallest, a wale or frame projects from the side, on which the boatmen walk when poling the vessel. The sails in the south are woven of strips of matting, sewed into a single sheet, and provided with yards at the top and bottom; the bamboo ribs crossing it serve to retain the hoops that run on the mast, and enable the boatmen to haul them close on the wind. A driver is sometimes placed on the taffrail, and a small foresail near the bow, but the mainsail is the chief dependence. No Chinese boat has a bowsprit, and very few are coppered, or have two decks, further than an orlop in the stern quarter in which to stow provisions; no dead-lights give even a glimmer to these recesses, which are necessarily small.

The internal arrangement of dwelling-boats is simple. The better sort are from sixty to eighty feet long, and about fifteen wide, divided into three rooms; the stem is sharp, and upholds a platform on which, when they are moored alongside, it is easy to pass from one boat to another. Each one is secured by ropes to large hawsers which run along the whole line at the bow and stern. The room nearest the bow serves for a lobby to the principal apartment, which occupies about half the body of the boat; the two are separated by trellis bulkheads, but the sternmost room, or sleeping apartment, is carefully screened. Cooking and washing are performed on a high stern framework, which is admirably contrived, by means of furnaces and other conveniences above and hatches and partitions below deck, to serve all these purposes, contain all the fuel and water necessary, and answer for a sleeping place as well. By means of awnings and frameworks the top of the boat also subserves many objects of work or pleasure. The window-shutters are movable, fitted for all kinds of weather and for flexibility of arrangement, meeting all the demands of a family and the particular service of a vessel; nothing can be more ingenious.

The handsomest of these craft are called *hwa ting*, or flower-boats, and are let to parties for pleasure excursions on the river;

a large proportion of them are also the abodes of public women. The smaller sorts at Canton are generally known as *tankia* boats; they are about twenty-five feet long, contain only one room, and are fitted with moveable mats to cover the whole vessel; they are usually rowed by women. In these "egg-houses" whole families are reared, live, and die; the room which serves for passengers by day is a bedroom by night; a kitchen at one time, a washroom at another, aud a nursery always.

As to this custom of living upon the water, we have an interesting testimony of its practice so far back as the fourteenth century, from the letter of a Dominican Friar in 1330. "The realm of Cathay," writes the missionary, "is peopled passing well. . . . . And there be many great rivers and great sheets of water throughout the Empire; insomuch that a good half of the realm and its territory is under water. And on these waters dwell great multitudes of people because of the vast population that there is in the said realm. They build wooden houses upon boats, and so their houses go up and down upon the waters; and the people go trafficking in their houses from one province to another, whilst they dwell in these houses with all their families, with their wives and children, and all their household utensils and necessaries. And so they live upon the waters all the days of their life. And there the women be brought to bed, and do everything else just as people do who dwell upon dry land."[1]

It is unnecessary to particularize the various sorts of lighters or *chop-boats* found along the southern coast, the passenger boats plying from town to town along the hundreds of streams, and the smacks, revenue cutters, and fishing craft to be seen in all waters, except to call attention to their remarkable adaptation for the ends in view. The best sorts are made in the southern provinces; those seen at Tientsin or Niuchwang suffer by comparison for cleanliness, safety, and speed, owing partly to the high price of wood and the less use made of them for dwellings. On the head waters of the River Kan the boats are of a peculiarly light construction, with upper works entirely of

[1] Yule, *Cathay and the Way Thither*, Vol. I., p. 243.

matting, and the hull like a crescent, well fitted to encounter the rapids and rocks which beset their course.

Besides these various kinds the revenue service employs a narrow, sharp-built boat, propelled by forty or fifty rowers, armed with swivels, spears, boarding-hooks, and pikes, and lined on the sides with a menacing array of rattan shields painted with tigers' heads. Smugglers have similarly made boats, and now and then imitate the government boats in their appearance, which, on their part, often compete with them in smuggling. In 1863 the imperial government was induced to adopt a national flag for all its own vessels, which will no doubt gradually extend to merchant craft. It is triangular in shape, and has a dragon with the head looking upward. It is usual for naval officers to exhibit long yellow flags with their official titles at full length; the vessels under them are distinguished by various pennons. Junks carry a great assortment of flags, triangular and square, of white, red, and other colors, most of them bearing inscriptions. The number of governmental boats and war junks, and those used for transporting the revenue and salt, is proportionately very small; but if all the craft found on the rivers and coasts of China be included, their united tonnage perhaps equals that of all other nations put together. The dwellers on the water near Canton are not, as has been sometimes said, debarred from living ashore. A boat can be built cheaper than a brick house, and is equally comfortable; it is kept clean easier, pays no ground-rent, and is not so obnoxious to fire and thieves. Most of them are constructed of fir or pine and smeared with wood oil; the seams are caulked with rattan shavings and paid over with a cement of oil and gypsum. The sailing craft are usually flat-bottomed, sharp forward, and guided by an enormous rudder which can be hoisted through the open stern sheets when in shallow waters. The teak-wood anchors have iron-bound flukes, held by coir or bamboo hawsers—now often replaced by iron chain and grapnel.[1]

---

[1] Compare an article by W. F. Mayers in *Notes and Queries on C. and J.*, Vol. I., pp. 170–173 (with illustrations); Mrs. Gray, *Fourteen Months in Canton*, passim; Dr. Edkins in *Journal N. C. Br. R. A. Soc.*, Vol. XI., p. 123; Doolittle, *Vocabulary*, Part III., No. LXVIII; Engineer J. W. King in *The United Service*, Vol. II., p. 382 (Phila., 1880).

The old picturesque junk, with its bulging hull, high stern, and great eyes on the bow, is rapidly disappearing before steamers. Its original model is said to be a huge sea monster; the teeth at the cutwater and top of the bow define its mouth, the long boards on each side of the bow form the armature of the head, the eyes being painted on them, the masts and sails are the fins, and the high stern is the tail frisking aloft. The cabins look more like niches in a sepulchre than the accommodations for a live passenger. The crew live upon deck most of the time, and are usually interested in the trade of the vessel or an adventure of their own. The hold is divided into water-tight compartments, a contrivance that has its advantages when the vessel strikes a rock, but prevents her carrying a cargo comparable to her size. The great number of passengers which have been stowed in these vessels entailed a frightful loss of life when they were wrecked. In February, 1822, Capt. Pearl, of the English ship Indiana, coming through Gaspar Straits, fell in with the cargo and crew of a wrecked junk, and saved one hundred and ninety-eight persons (out of one thousand six hundred with whom she had left Amoy), whom he landed at Pontianak; this humane act cost him $55,000.[1]

Among secondary architectural works deserving notice are bridges and honorary portals. There is good reason for supposing that the Chinese have been acquainted with the arch from very early times, though they make comparatively little use of it. Certain bridges have pointed arches, others have semicircular, and others approach the form of a horse-shoe, the transverse section of an ellipse, or even like the Greek Ω, the space being widest at the top. In some the arch is high for the accommodation of boats passing beneath; and where no heavy wains or carriages cross and jar the fabric, it can safely be made light. A graceful specimen of this class is the structure seen in the illustration on page 754. This bridge, though serving no practical purpose, is one of the greatest ornaments about the Emperor's summer palace of Yuen-ming Yuen. The material is marble; its summit is reached by forty steps rising abruptly

---

[1] *Chinese Repository*, Vol. VI., p. 149.

from the causeway, and impracticable, of course, for any but pedestrians.

The balustrades and paving of the long marble bridges near Peking and Hangchau, some of them adorned with statues of elephants, lions, and other animals, present a pleasing effect, while their solidity and endurance of freshes running over the top at times attest the skill of the architects. Wooden bridges furnish means for crossing small streams in all parts of the land; when the river is powerful, or the rise and fall of the tide great,

Bridge in Wan-shao Shan Gardens, near Peking.

it is crossed on boats fastened together, with contrivances for drawing out two or three in the centre when the passing craft demand a passage. At Tientsin, Ningpo, and other cities, this means of crossing entails little delay in comparison to its cheapness. Some of the bridges in and about Peking are beautiful structures; their erection, however, presented no difficult problem, while that at Fuhchau was a greater feat of engineering. It is about four hundred yards long and five wide, consisting of nearly forty solid buttresses of hewn stone placed at unequal distances and joined by slabs of granite; some of these slabs are three feet square and forty-five feet long. They support a granite pavement. The bridge was formerly lined with shops, which the increased traffic has caused to be removed. Another similar bridge lies seven miles north of it on the River Min, and a third of equal importance at the city of Chinchew, north of Amoy. Some of the mountain streams and passes in the west and north are crossed by rope bridges of ingenious construction, and by chain suspension bridges.

Mr. Lowrie describes a bridge at Changchau, near Amoy, and these structures are more numerous in the eastern provinces than elsewhere. "It is built on twenty-five piles of stone about thirty feet apart, and perhaps twenty feet each in height. Large round beams are laid from pile to pile, and smaller ones across in the simplest and rudest manner; earth is then placed above these and the top paved with brick and stone. One would suppose that the work had been assigned to a number of different persons, and that each one had executed his part in such manner as best suited his own fancy, there being no regularity whatever in the paving. Bricks and stone were intermingled in the most confused manner, and the railing was here wood and there stone. We were particularly struck with the length of some of the granite stones used in paving the bridge; one was eight, another eleven, and three others eighteen paces, or about forty-five feet long, and two broad. The bridge averaged eight or ten feet in width, and about half its length on both sides was occupied by shops."[1]

A causeway of ninety arches crosses a feeder of the Grand Canal near Hangchau. The stones for the arch in one bridge noticed by Barrow were cut so as to form a segment of the arch, and at each end were mortised into transverse blocks of stone stretching across the bridge; they decreased in length from ten feet at the spring of the arch to three at the vertex, and the summit stone was mortised, like the rest, into two transverse blocks lying next to it.[2] The tenons were short, and the dis-

[1] *Chinese Repository*, Vol. XII., p. 528; Medhurst's *Hohkeën Dictionary*, Introduction pp. XXII, XXIII.

[2] Barrow's *Travels*, p. 338.

position of the principal pieces such that a bridge built in this way would not support great weights or endure many ages. The mode of placing the pieces can be seen in the cut. In other instances the stones are laid in the same manner as in Europe; many small bridges over creeks and canals have cambered or straight arches. When one of these structures falls into ruins or becomes dangerous, the people seldom bestir themselves to repair the damage, preferring to wait for the government; they thereby lose the benefit of self-dependence and action.

Bridge showing the mode of Mortising the Arch.

It is singular how the term *triumphal arch* came to be applied to the *pai-fang* and *pai-lau*, or honorary portals or tablets, of the Chinese; for a triumph was perhaps never heard of in that country, and these structures are never arched. They consist merely of a broad gateway flanked with two smaller ones, and suggest a turnpike gate with side-ways for foot passengers rather than a triumphal monument. They are scattered in great numbers over the provinces, and are erected in honor of distinguished persons, or by officers to commemorate their parents, by special favor from the Emperor. Some are put up in honor of women who have distinguished themselves for their chastity and filial duty, or to widows who have refused a second marriage. Permission to erect them is considered a high honor, and perhaps the term *triumphal* was given them from this circumstance. The economical and peaceful nature of such honors conferred upon distinguished men in China is most characteristic; a man is allowed to build a stone gateway to himself or his parents, and the Emperor furnishes the inscription, or perhaps sends with it a patent of nobility. Their general arrangement is exhibited in the title-page of this work; the two characters, *shing chí*, at the top, meaning 'sacred will,' intimate that it was erected by his Majesty's permission.

Some of the *pai-lau* are elaborately ornamented with carved work and inscriptions; and as a protection to the frieze a ponderous covering of tiles projects over the top, which, however, exposes the structure to injury from tempests. They are placed in conspicuous places in the outskirts of towns, and in the streets before temples or near government edifices. Travellers looking for what they had read about have sometimes strangely mistaken the gateways at the heads of streets or the entrance to temples for the honorary portals.[1] Those built of stone are fastened by mortises and tenons in the same manner as the wooden ones; they seldom exceed twenty or twenty-five feet in height. The skill and taste displayed in the symmetry and carving upon some of them are creditable; but as the man in whose honor it is erected is, generally speaking, "the architect of his own fame," he prudently considers the worth of that commodity, and makes an inferior structure to what would have been done if his fellow-subjects, "deeply sensible of the honor," had come together to appoint a committee and open a subscription list for the purpose. Among the numerous *pai-lau* in and near Peking, two or three deserve mention for their beauty. One lies in the Confucian Temple in front of the *Pih-yung Kung*, and is designed to enhance the splendor of its approach by presenting, as it were, a frame before its façade. It is built of stone and overlaid with square encaustic tiles of many hues.

---

[1] *Encyclopædia Americana*, Art. CANTON.

The arrangement of the colors, the carving on the marble, and the fine proportions of the structure render it altogether one of the most artistic objects in China. Another like it is built in the Imperial Park, but the position is not so advantageous. Fergusson points out the similarity between these *pai-lau* and certain Hindu gateways, and claims that India furnished the model. The question of priority is hardly susceptible of proof; but his fancy that a large *pai-lau* in a street of Amoy presented a simulated coffin on it above the principal cornice, leads us to suspect that he was looking for what was never in the builder's mind.

The construction of forts and towers presents little worthy of observation, since there is no other evidence of science than what the erection of lines of massive stone wall displays. The port-holes are too large for protection and the parapet too slight to resist modern missiles. The Chinese idea of a fortification is a wall along the water's edge, with embrasures and battlements, and a plain wall landward without port-holes or parapets, enclosing an area in which a few houses accommodate the garrison and ammunition. Some erected at the junction of streams are pierced on all sides; others are so unscientifically planned that the walls can be scaled at angles where not a single gun can be brought to bear. The towers are rectangular edifices of brick on a stone foundation, forty feet square and fifty or sixty high, to be entered by ladders through a door half way up the side.

The forts in the neighborhood of Canton, probably among the best in the Empire, are all constructed without fosse, bastion, glacis, or counter-defence of any kind. Both arrangement and placement are alike faulty: some are square and approachable without danger; others circular on the outer face but with flank or rear exposed; others again built on a hillside like a pound, so that the garrison, if dislodged from the battlements, are forced to fly up the slope in full range of their enemy's fire. The gate is on the side, unprotected by ditch, drawbridge, or portcullis, and poorly defended by guns upon the walls or in the area behind. In general the points chosen for their forts display a misapprehension of the true principles of defence, though some may be noted as occupying commanding positions.

In recent times mud defences and batteries of sand-bags have proved a much safer defence than such buildings against ships and artillery, and show the aptitude of the people to adopt practical things. Though not particularly resolute on the field, the Chinese soldier stands well to his guns when behind a fortification of whose strength he is assured. The forts which have recently been constructed under supervision of European engineers are rapidly taking the place of native works in all parts of the country.

Dress, like other things, undergoes its changes in China, and fashions alter there as well as elsewhere, but they are not as rapid or as striking as among European nations. The full costume of both sexes is, in general terms, commodious and graceful, combining all the purposes of warmth, beauty, and ease which could be desired, excepting always the shaven crown and braided queue of the men and the crippled feet of the women, in both of which fashions they have not less outraged nature than deformed themselves. On this point different tastes exist, and some prefer the close-fitting dress of Europeans to the loose robes of Asiatics; but when one has become in a measure habituated to the latter, one is willing to allow the force of the criticism that the European male costume is "a mysterious combination of the inconvenient and the unpicturesque: hot in summer and cold in winter, useless for either keeping off rain or sun, stiff but not plain, bare without being simple, not durable, not becoming, and not cheap." The Chinese dress has remained, in its general style, the same for centuries; and garments of fur or silk are handed down from parent to child without fear of attracting attention by their antique shapes. The fabrics most worn are silk, cotton, and grass-cloth for summer, with the addition of furs and skins in winter; woollen is used sparingly, and almost wholly of foreign manufacture.

The principal articles of dress are inner and outer tunics of various lengths made of cotton or silk, reaching below the loins or to the feet; the lapel on the right side folds over the breast and fits close about the neck, which is left uncovered. The sleeves are much wider and longer than the arms, have no cuffs or facings, and in common cases serve for pockets. A Chinese, instead of saying "he pocketed the book," would say "he sleeved it." In robes of ceremony the end of the sleeve resembles a horse's hoof, and good breeding requires the hand to be kept in a position to exhibit the cuff when sitting. In warm weather one upper garment is deemed sufficient; in winter a dozen can be put on without discommodity, and this number is sometimes

Barber's Establishment, showing also the Dress of the Common People.

actually seen upon persons engaged in sedentary employments, or on those who sit in the air. Latterly, underwear of flannel has become common among the better dressed, who like the knitted fabric so close-fitting and warm. The lower limbs are comparatively slightly protected; a pair of loose trousers, covered to the knee by cloth stockings, is the usual summer garment; tight leggings are pulled over both in winter and attached to the girdle by loops; and as the trousers are rather voluminous and the tunic short, the excess shows behind from under these leggings in a rather unpleasant manner. Gentlemen and officers always wear a robe with the skirt opened at the sides, which conceals this intermission of the under apparel. The colors preferred for outer garments are various hues of buff, purple, or blue.

The shoes are made of silk or cotton, usually embroidered for women's wear in red and other colors. The soles are of felt, sometimes of paper inside a rim of felt, and defended on the bottom by hide. These shoes keep the feet dry and unchilled on the tiles or ground, so that a Chinese may be said really to carry the floor of his house under his feet instead of laying it on the ground. The thick soles render it necessary for ease in walking to round up their ends, which constrains the toes into an elevated position so irksome that all go slipshod who conveniently can do so. The cost of a cotton suit need not exceed five dollars, and a complete silken one, of the gayest colors and best materials, can easily be procured for twenty-five or thirty. Quilted cotton garments are exceedingly common, and are so made as to protect the whole person from the cold and obviate the need of fires. In the north dressed sheepskin robes furnish bedding as well as garments, and their durability will long make them more desirable than woven fabrics.

The ancient Chinese wore the hair long, bound upon the top of the head, somewhat after the style of the Lewchewans; and taking pride in its glossy black, called themselves the *black-haired race*. But in 1627 the Manchus, then in possession of only Liautung, issued an order that all Chinese under them should adopt their coiffure as a sign of allegiance, on penalty of death; the fashion thus begun by compulsion is now followed from choice. The fore part of the head is shaved to the crown and the hair braided in a single plait behind. Laborers often wind it about the head or knot it into a ball out of the way when barebacked or at work. The size of the queue can be enlarged by permitting an additional line of hair to grow; the appearance it gives the wearer is thus described by Mr. Downing, and the quotation is not an unfair specimen of the remarks of travellers upon China: "At the hotel one of the waiters was dressed in a peculiar manner about the head. Instead of the hair being shaved in front, he had it cut round the top of the forehead about an inch and a half in length. All the other part was turned as usual and plaited down the back. This thin semi-circular ridge of hair was then made to stand bolt upright, and as each hair was separate and stiff as a bristle, the whole looked like a very fine-toothed comb turned upward. This I imagined to be the usual way of dressing the head by single unengaged youths, and of course must be very attractive." Thus what the wearer regarded as ill-looking, and intended to braid in as soon

Tricks Played with the Queue.

as it was long enough, is here taken as a device for beautifying himself in the eyes of those he never saw or cared to see.

The people are vain of a long thick queue, and now and then play each other tricks with it, as well as use it as a ready means for correction; but nothing irritates them more than to cut it off. Men and women oftener go bareheaded than covered, warding off the sun by means of a fan; in winter felt or silk skull-caps, hoods, and fur protect them from cold. Laborers shelter themselves from rain under an umbrella hat and a grotesque thatch-work of leaves neatly sewn upon a coarse network—very effectual for the purpose. In illustration of the remark at the beginning of this chapter, it might be added that if they were not worn on the head such hats would be called trays, so unlike are they to the English article of that name. The formal head-dress is the conical straw or felt hat so peculiar to this nation, usually covered with a red fringe of silk or hair.

The various forms, fabrics, colors, and ornaments of the dresses worn by grades of officers are regulated by sumptuary laws. Citron-yellow distinguishes the imperial family, but his Majesty's apparel is less showy than many of his courtiers, and in all that belongs to his own personal use there is an appearance of disregard of ornament. The five-clawed dragon is figured upon the dress and whatever pertains to the Emperor, and in certain things to members of his family. The monarchs of China formerly wore a sort of flat-topped crown, shaped somewhat like a Cantab's cap, and having a row of jewels pendent from each side. The summer bonnet of officers is made of finely woven straw covered with a red fringe; in winter it is trimmed with fur. A string of beads hanging over an embroidered robe, a round knob on the cap, thick-soled satin boots, two or three pouches for fans or chopsticks, and occasionally a watch or two hanging from the girdle, constitute the principal points of difference between the official and plebeian costume. No company of men can appear more splendid than a large party of officers in their winter robes made of fine, lustrous crapes, trimmed with rich furs and brilliant with gay embroidery. In winter a silk or fur spencer is worn over the robe, and forms a handsome and warm garment. Lambskins are much used, and the downy coats of unyeaned lambs, which, with the finer furs and the skins of hares, wild cats, rabbits, foxes, wolves, otter, squirrels, etc., are worn by all ranks. Some years ago a lad used to parade the streets of Canton, who presented an odd appearance in a long spencer made of a tiger's skin. The Chinese like strong contrasts in the colors of their garments, sometimes wearing yellow leggings underneath a light blue robe, itself set off by a purple spencer.

The dress of women is likewise liable to few fluctuations, and all ranks can be sure that the fashion will last as long as the gown. The garments of both sexes among the common people resemble each other more than in Western Asia. The tunic or short gown is open in front, buttoning around the neck and under the arm, reaching to the knee, like a smock-frock in its general shape. The trousers among the lower orders are usually worn over the stockings, both being covered, on ceremonial occasions, by a petticoat reaching to the feet. Laboring women, whose feet are left their natural size, go barefoot or slipshod in the warm latitudes, but cover their feet carefully farther north. Both sexes have a paucity of linen in their habiliments—if not a shiftless, the Chinese certainly are a shirtless race, and such undergarments as they have are not too often washed.

The head-dress of married females is becoming and even elegant. The copious black hair is bound upon the head in an oval-formed knot, which is secured in its place and shape by a broad pin placed lengthwise on it, and fastened by a shorter one thrust across and under the bow. The hair is drawn back from the forehead into the knot, and elevated a little in front by combing it over the finger; in order to make it lie smooth the locks are drawn through resinous shavings moistened in warm water, which also adds an extra gloss, at the cost, however, of injury to the hair. In front of the knot a tube is often inserted, in which flowers can be placed. The custom of wearing them is nearly universal, fresh blossoms being preferred when obtainable, and artificial at other times. Having no covering on the head there is more opportunity than in the west to display pretty devices in arranging the hair. A widow is known by her white flowers, a maiden by one or two plaits instead of a knot, and so on; in their endless variety of form and ornament, Chinese women's head-dresses furnish a source of constant study. Mr. Stevens tells us that the animated appearance of the dense crowd which assembled on the bridge and banks of the river at Fuhchau when he passed in 1835, was still more enlivened by the flowers worn by the women.

Matrons wear an embroidered fillet on the forehead, an inch or more wide, pointed between the eyebrows, and covering the front of the hair though not concealing the baldness which often comes on early from the resinous bandoline used. This fillet is embroidered, or adorned with pearls, a favorite ornament with

PROCESSION OF LADIES TO AN ANCESTRAL TEMPLE.

Chinese ladies. The women along the Yangtsz' River wear a band of fur around the head, which relieves their colorless complexions. A substitute for bonnets is common in summer, consisting of a flat piece of straw trimmed with a fringe of blue cloth. The hair of children is unbound, but girls more advanced allow the side locks to reach to the waist and plait a tress down the neck; their coarse hair does not curl, and the beautiful luxuriance of curls and ringlets seen in Europe is entirely unknown. False hair is made use of by both sexes, the men being particularly fond of eking out their queues to the fullest length. Gloves are not worn, the long sleeves being adequate for warmth; in the north the ears are protected from freezing by ear-tabs lined with fur, and often furnished with a tiny looking-glass on the outside.

The dress of gentlewomen, like that of their husbands, is regulated by sumptuary laws, but none of these prevent their costumes from being as splendid as rich silks, gay colors, and beautiful embroidery can make them. The neck of the robe is protected by a stiff band, and the sleeves are large and long, just the contrary of the common style, which being short allows the free use and display of a well-turned arm. The official embroidery allowed to the husband is changed to another kind on his wife's robe indicative of the same rank. No belt or girdle is seen, nor do stays compress the waist to its lasting injury. One of the prettiest parts of a lady's dress is the petticoat, which appears about a foot below the upper robe covering the feet. Each side of the skirt is plaited about six times, and in front and rear are two pieces of buckram to which they are attached; the plaits and front pieces are stiffened with wire and lining. Embroidery is worked upon these two pieces and the plaits in such a way that as the wearer steps the action of the feet alternately opens and shuts them on each side, disclosing a part or the whole of two different colored figures, as may be seen in the illustration. The plaits are so contrived that they are the same when seen in front or from behind, and the effect is more elegant when the colors are well contrasted. In order to produce this the plaits close around the feet, unlike the wider skirt of western ladies.

Ornaments are less worn by the Chinese than other Asiatic nations. The men suspend a string of fragrant beads together with the tobacco-pouch from the jacket lapel, or occasionally wear seal-rings, finger-rings, and armlets of strass, stone, or glass. They are by law prohibited from carrying weapons of any sort. The women wear bangles, bracelets, and ear-rings of glass, stone, and metal; most of these appendages are regarded more as amulets to ward off evil influences than mere ornaments. Felicitous charms, such as aromatic bags, old coins, and rings, are attached to the persons of children, and few adults venture to go through life without some preservative of this kind; no sacred thread or daub of clay, as in India, is known, however, nor any image of a saint or other figurine, as in Romish countries. The queer custom of wearing long nails is practised by comparatively few; and although a man or woman with these appendages would not be deemed singular, it is not regarded as in good taste by well-bred persons. Pedantic scholars wear them more than other professions, in order to show that they are above manual labor; but the longest set the writer ever saw was, oddly enough, on a carpenter's fingers, who thereby showed that he was not obliged to use his tools. Fine ladies protect theirs with silver sheaths.

The practice of compressing the feet, so far as investigation has gone, is more an inconvenient than a dangerous custom, for among the many thousands of patients who have received aid in the missionary hospitals, few have presented themselves with ailments chargeable to this source. A difference of opinion exists respecting its origin. Some accounts state that it arose from a desire thereby to remove the reproach of the club feet of a popular empress, others that it gradually came into use from the great admiration of and attempt to imitate delicate feet, and others that it was imposed by husbands to keep their wives from gadding.[1] Its adoption was gradual, however it may have commenced, and not without resistance. It is practised

[1] It is recorded that Hau-Chu, of the Chin dynasty, in the year A.D. 583 ordered Lady Yao to bind her feet so as to make them look like the new moon; and that the evil fashion has since prevailed against all subsequent prohibitions.—*Notes and Queries on China and Japan*, Vol. II., pp. 27 and 43.

by all classes of society except the Manchus and Tartars, poor as well as rich (for none are so poor as not to wish to be fashionable); and so habituated does one become to it after a residence in the country, that a well-dressed lady with large feet seems to be denationalized. There is no certain age at which the operation must be commenced, but in families of easy circumstances the bandages are put on before five; otherwise not until betrothment, or till seven or eight years old. The whole operation is performed, and the shape maintained, by bandages, which are never permanently removed or covered by stockings; iron or wooden shoes are not used, the object being rather to prevent the feet growing than to make them smaller.

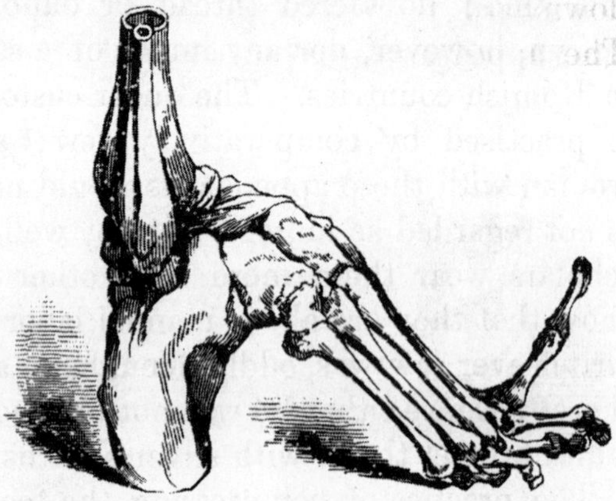

Appearance of the Bones of a Foot when Compressed.

A good account of the effects of this practice is given in a paper contained in the *Transactions of the Royal Society of London*, written by Dr. Cooper, detailing the appearances presented on dissection. The foot belonged to a person in low life; it was five and one-fourth inches long, which is full eighteen lines over the most fashionable size. The big toe was bent upward and backward on the foot, and the second twisted under it and across, so that the extremity reached the inner edge of the foot. The third toe somewhat overlapped the second, but lying less obliquely, and reaching to the first joint of the great toe. The ball of the great toe, much flattened, separated these two from the fourth and fifth toes. The fourth toe stretched obliquely inward under the foot, but less so than the little toe, which passed under and nearly across the foot, and had been bound down so strongly as to bend the tarsal bone. The dorsum of the foot was much curved, and a deep fissure crossed the sole and separated the heel and little toe, as if the two ends of the foot had been forced together; this was filled for three inches with a very condensed cellular tissue; the instep was three and one-half inches high. The heel-bone, which naturally forms a considerable angle with the ankle, was in a direct line with the leg-bones; and the heel itself was large and flat, covered with a peculiarly dense integument, and forming, with the end of the metatarsal bone of the great toe and the two smallest toes bent under the sole, the three points of taction in walking. When the operation is begun earlier, and the bones are more flexible, four of the toes are bent under the foot and only the big toe laid upon the top. The development of the muscles of the calf being checked, the leg tapers from the knee downward, though there is no particular weakness in the limb. The appearance of the deformed member when uncovered is shocking, crushed out of all proportion and beauty, and covered with a wrinkled and lifeless skin like that of a washerwoman's hand. It is surprising how the circulation is kept up in the member without any pain or wasting away; the natural supposition would be that if any nutriment was conveyed to it, there would be a disposition to grow until maturity was attained, and consequently constant pain ensue, or else that it would be destroyed or mortify for want of nourishment.

Feet of Chinese Ladies.

The gait of these victims of fashion can be imitated by a person walking on the heels. Women walking alone swing their arms and step quick and short, elderly women availing themselves, when practicable, of an umbrella, or leaning upon the shoulder of a lad or maid for support—literally making a walking-stick of them. The pain is said to be severe at first, and a recurrence now and then is felt in the sole; but the evident freedom from distress exhibited in the little girls who are seen walking or playing in the streets, proves that the amount of suffering and injurious effects upon life and health are perhaps not so great as has been imagined. The case is different when the girl is not victimized until ten or more years old. The toes are then bent under and the foot forced into the smallest compass; the agony arising from the constrained muscles and excoriated flesh is dreadful, while, too, the shape of the member is, even in Chinese eyes, a burlesque upon the beautiful littleness so much desired.

The opinion prevails abroad that only the daughters of the rich or learned pay this price to Dame Fashion. A greater proportion is indeed found among the well-to-do classes, and in the southern provinces near the rivers the unfashionables form perhaps half of the whole; for those who dwell in boats, and all who in early life may have lived on the water or among the farmsteads, and slave girls sold in infancy for domestics, are usually left in the happy though low-life freedom of nature. Close observation in the northern provinces show general adoption of the usage among the poor, whose feet are not, however, usually so small as in the south. Foreigners, on their arrival at Canton or Fuhchau, seeing so many women with natural feet on the boats and about the streets, wonder where the "little-footed Celestials" they had heard of were, the only specimens they see being a few crones by the wayside mending clothes. Across the Mei ling range the proportion increases. All the women who came to the hospital at Chusan in 1841, to the number of eight hundred or one thousand, had their feet more or less cramped; and some of them walked several miles to the hospital and home again the same day. Although the operation may be less painful than has been represented, the people are so much accustomed to it that most men would refuse to wed a woman whose feet were of the natural size; and a man who should find out that his bride had large feet when he expected small ones would be exonerated if he instantly sent her back to her parents. The *kin lien*, or 'golden lilies,' are desired as the mark of gentility; the hope of rising to be one of the upper ten, and escaping the roughness and hard work attached to the lower class, goes far

Shape of a Lady's Shoe.

to strengthen even children to endure the pain and loss of freedom consequent on the practice. The secret of the prevalence of the cruel custom is the love of ease and praise; and not till the principles of Christianity extend will it cease. In Peking, where the Manchus have shown the advantages nature has over fashion, the example of their women for two hundred and fifty years, aided by the earnest efforts of the great Emperor Kanghi, has not had the least effect in inducing Chinese ladies to give it up. The shoes are made of red silk and prettily embroidered; but no one acquainted with Chinese society would say that "if a lady ever breaks through the prohibition against displaying her person, she presents her feet as the surest darts with which a lover's heart can be assailed!"[1]

Cosmetics are used by females to the serious injury of the skin. On grand occasions the face is entirely bedaubed with white paint, and rouge is added to the lips and cheeks, giving a singular starched appearance to the physiognomy. A girl thus beautified has no need of a fan to hide her blushes, for they cannot be seen through the paint, her eye being the only index of emotion. The eyebrows are blackened with charred sticks, and arched or narrowed to resemble a nascent willow leaf, or the moon when first seen—as in the ballad translated by Mr. Stent, which pictures the beauty as possessing

> Eyebrows shaped like leaves of willows
> Drooping over "autumn billows;"
> Almond shaped, of liquid brightness,
> Were the eyes of Yang-kuei-fei.[2]

A belle is described as having cheeks like the almond flower, lips like a peach's bloom, waist as the willow leaf, eyes bright as dancing ripples in the sun, and footsteps like the lotus flower. Much time and care is bestowed, or said to be, by females upon their toilet, but if those in the upper classes have anything like

[1] Murray's *China*, Vol. II., p. 266. Compare the *Chinese Repository*, Vol. III., p. 537; *Rec. de Mém. de Médecine milit.* (Paris), 1862–63–64 passim; *Chinese Recorder*, Vols. I., II., and III. passim (mostly a series of articles on this subject by Dr. Dudgeon); *The Far East*, February, 1877, p 27.

[2] *The Jade Chaplet*, p. 121.

the variety of domestic duties which their sisters in common life perform, they have little leisure left for superfluous adorning. If dramas give an index of Chinese manners and occupations, they do not convey the idea that most of the time of well-bred ladies is spent in idleness or dressing.

At his toilet a Chinese uses a basin of tepid water and a cloth, and it has been aptly remarked that he never appears so dirty as when trying to clean himself. Shaving is done by the barber, for no man can shave the top of his head. Whiskers are never worn, even by the very few who have them, and mustaches are not considered proper for a man under forty. Snuff bottles and tobacco pipes are carried and used by both sexes, but the practice of chewing betel-nut is confined to the men, who, however, take much pains to keep their teeth white. Among ornamental articles of dress, in none do they go to so much expense and style as in the snuff bottle, which is often carved from stone, amber, agate, and other rare minerals with most exquisite taste. Snuff is put on the thumb-nail with a spoon fastened to the stopper—a more cleanly way than the European mode of "pinching."[1]

The articles of food which the Chinese eat, and the mode and ceremonies attending their feasts, have aided much in giving them the odd character they bear abroad, though uncouth or unsavory viands form an infinitesimal portion of their food, and ceremonious feasts not one in a thousand of their repasts. Travellers have so often spoken of birdsnest soup, canine hams, and grimalkin fricassees, rats, snakes, worms, and other culinary novelties, served up in equally strange ways, that their readers get the idea that these articles form as large a proportion of the food as their description does of the narrative. In general, the diet of the Chinese is sufficient in variety, wholesome, and

---

[1] On Chinese costume, see Wm. Alexander, *The Costume of China*, illustrated, London, 1805; *Mœurs et Coutumes des Chinois et leurs costumes en couleur*, par J. G. Grohmann, Leipzig; Breton, *China: Its Costume, Arts, etc.*, 4 vols., translated from the French, London, 1812; another translation is from Auguste Borget, *Sketches of China and the Chinese*, London, 1842; *Illustrations of China and its People. A series of two hundred photographs, with letterpress descriptive of the places and people represented*, by J. Thompson, London, 1874, 4 vols. quarto.

well cooked, though many of the dishes are unpalatable to a European from the vegetable oils used in their preparation, and the alliaceous plants introduced to savor them. In the assortment of dishes, Barrow has truly said that "there is a wider difference, perhaps, between the rich and the poor of China than in any other country. That wealth, which if permitted would be expended in flattering the vanity of its possessors, is now applied to the purchase of dainties to pamper the appetite."

The proportion of animal food is probably smaller among the Chinese than other nations on the same latitude, one platter of fish or flesh, and sometimes both, being the usual allowance on the tables of the poor. Rice, maize, Italian millet, and wheat furnish most of the cereal food; the first is emphatically the staff of life, and considered indispensable all over the land. Its long use is indicated in the number of terms employed to describe it and the variety of allusions to it in common expressions. To *take a meal* is *chih fan*, 'eat rice;' and the salutation equivalent to *how d'ye?* is *chih kwo fan?* 'have you eaten rice?' The grain is deprived of its skin by wooden pestles worked in a mortar by levers, either by a water-wheel or more commonly by oxen or men. It is cleaned by rubbing it in an earthen dish scored on the inside, and steamed in a shallow iron boiler partly filled with water, over which a basket or sieve containing the rice is supported on a framework; a wooden dish fits over the whole and confines the steam. By this process the kernels are thoroughly cooked without forming a pasty mass, as is too often the result when boiled by cooks in Christian countries. Bread, vegetables, and other articles are cooked in a similar manner; four or five sieves, each of them full and nicely fitting into each other, are placed upon the boiler and covered with a cowl; in the water beneath, which supplies the steam, meats or other things are boiled at the same time. Wheat flour is boiled into cakes, dumplings, and other articles, but not baked into bread. Maize, buckwheat, oats, and barley are not ground, but the grain is cooked in various ways, alone or mixed with other dishes. Italian millet, or canary-seed (*Setaria*), furnishes a large amount of nutritious cereal food in the north; the flour is yellow and sweet, and boiled or baked for eating, often seasoned with jujube plums in the cakes. Its cultivation is easy, and its prolific crop makes up in a measure for the small seeds; ten thousand kernels have been counted on one spike in a good season.

The Chinese have a long list of culinary vegetables, and much of their agriculture consists in rearing them. Leguminous and cruciferous plants occupy the largest part of the kitchen garden; more than twenty sorts of peas and beans are cultivated, some for camels and horses, but mostly for men. *Soy* is made by boiling the beans and mixing water, salt, and wheat, and producing fermentation by yeast; its quality is inferior to the foreign. Another more common condiment, called bean curd or bean jam, is prepared by boiling and grinding black beans and mixing the flour with water, gypsum, and turmeric. The consumption of cabbage, broccoli, kale, cauliflower, cress, colewort, and other cruciferous plants is enormous; a great variety of modes are adopted for cooking, preserving, and improving them. The leaves and stems of many plants besides these are included in the variety of greens, and a complete enumeration of them would form a curious list. Lettuce, sow thistle (*Sonchus*), spinach, celery, dandelion, succory, sweet basil, ginger, mustard, radishes, artemisia, amaranthus, tacca, pig weed (*Chenopodium*), burslane, shepherd's purse, clover, ailantus, and others having no English names, all furnish green leaves for Chinese tables. Garlics, leeks, scallions, onions, and chives are eaten by all classes, detected upon all persons, and smelt in all rooms where they are eating or cooking. Carrots, gourds, squashes, cucumbers, watermelons, tomatoes, turnips, radishes, brinjals, pumpkins, okers, etc., are among the list of garden vegetables; the variety of cucurbitaceous plants extends to nearly twenty. Most of these vegetables are inferior to the same articles in the markets of western cities, where science has improved their size or flavor. Several aquatic plants increase the list, among which the nelumbium covers extensive marshes in the eastern and northern provinces, otherwise unsightly and barren. The root is two or three feet long, and pierced longitudinally with several holes; when boiled it is of a yellowish color and sweetish taste, not unlike a turnip. Taro is used less than the nelumbium, and so are the water-caltrops (*Trapa*) and water-chestnuts. The taste of water-caltrops when boiled resembles that of new cheese; water-chestnuts are the round roots of a kind of sedge, and resemble that fruit in color more than in taste, which is mealy and crisp. The sweet potato is the most common tuber; although the Irish potato has been cultivated for scores of years it has not become a common vegetable among the people, except on the borders of Mongolia.

The catalogue of fruits comprises most of those occurring elsewhere in the tropic and temperate zones, and China is probably the earliest home of the peach, plum, and pear. The pears are large and juicy, sometimes weighing eight or ten pounds; the white and strawberry pear are equal to any western variety. The apples are rather dry and insipid. The peaches, plums, quinces, and apricots are better, and offer many good varieties. Cherries are almost unknown. The orange is the common fruit at the south, and the baskets, stalls, and piles of this golden fruit, mixed with and heightened by contrast with other sorts and with vegetables, which line the streets of Canton and Amoy in winter, present a beautiful sight. Many distinct species of Citrus, as the lemon, kumquot, pumelo, citron, and orange, are extensively cultivated. The most delicious is the *chu-sha kih*, or 'mandarin orange;' the skin, when ripe, is of a cinnabar red color, and adheres to the pulp by a few loose fibres. The citron is more prized for its fragrance than taste, and the thick rind is now and then made more abundant by cutting it into strips when growing, each of which becomes a roundish end like a finger, whence the name of *Fuh shao*, or 'Buddha's hand,' given it. It will remain uncorrupt for two or three months, diffusing an agreeable perfume.

Chapter VI. contains brief notices of other fruits. The banana and persimmon are common, and several varieties are enumerated of each; the plantain is eaten raw and cooked, and forms a large item in the subsistence of the poor. The pomegranate, carambola or tree gooseberry, mango, custard-apple, pine-apple, rose-apple, bread-fruit, fig, guava, and olive, some of them as good and others inferior to what are found in other countries, increase the list. The *whampe*, *lichi*, *lungan*, or 'dragon's eyes,' and *loquat*, are the native names of four indigenous fruits at Canton. The whampe (*Cookia*) resembles a grape in size and a gooseberry in taste; the loquat or *pebo* (*Eriobotrya*) is a kind of medlar. The líchí looks like a strawberry in size and shape; the tough, rough red skin encloses a sweet watery pulp of a whitish color surrounding a hard seed. Grapes are plenty and cheap; in the northern cities they are preserved during the winter, and even till May, by constant care in regulating the temperature.

Chestnuts, walnuts, ground-nuts, filberts (*Torreya*), almonds, and the seeds of the salisburia and nelumbium, are the most common nuts. The Chinese date (*Rhamnus*) has a sweetish, acidulous flesh; the olive is salted or pickled; the names of both these fruits are given them because of a resemblance to the western sorts, for neither the proper date nor olive grows in China. A pleasant sweetmeat, like cranberry, is made from the seeds of the arbutus (*Myrica*), and another still more acid from a sort of haw, both of them put up for exportation.

Preserved fruits are common, and the list of sweetmeats and delicacies is increased by the addition of many roots, some of which are preserved in syrup and others as comfits. Ginger, nelumbium roots, bamboo shoots, the common potato, and other vegetables are thus prepared for export as well as domestic consumption. The natives consume enormous quantities of pickles of an inferior quality, especially cabbages and onions, but foreigners consider them detestable. The Chinese eat but few spices; black pepper is used medicinally as a tea, and cayenne pepper when the pod is green.

Oils and fats are in universal use for cooking; crude lard or pork fat, castor oil, sesamum oil, and that expressed from two species of Camellia and the ground-nut, are all employed for domestic and culinary purposes. The Chinese use little or no milk, butter, or cheese; the comparatively small number of cattle raised and the consequent dearness of these articles may have caused them to fall into disuse, for they are all common among the Manchus and Mongols. A Chinese table seems ill furnished to a foreigner when he sees neither bread, butter, nor milk upon it, and if he express his disrelish of the oily dishes or alliaceous stews before him, the Chinese thinks that he delivers a sufficient retort to his want of taste when he answers, "You eat cheese, and sometimes when it can almost walk." Milk is used a little, and no one who has lived in Canton can forget the prolonged mournful cry of *ngao nai!* of the men hawking it about the streets late at night. Women's milk is sold for the sustenance of infants and superannuated people, the idea being prevalent that it is peculiarly nourishing to aged persons.[1]

Sugar is grown only in Formosa and the three southern provinces, which supply the others; neither molasses nor rum are manufactured from it. No sugar is expressed from sorghum stalks, nor do the Chinese know that it contains syrup. The tobacco is milder than the American plant; it is smoked and not chewed or made into cigars, though these are being imported from Manila in steadily increasing quantities, and find favor among many of the wealthier Chinese; snuff is largely used. The betel-nut is a common masticatory, made up of a slice of the nut and the fresh leaf of the betel-pepper with a little lime rubbed on it. The common beverages are tea and arrack, both of which are taken warm; cold water is not often drunk, cold liquids of any kind being considered unwholesome. The constant practice of boiling water before drinking, in preparing tea, doubtless tends to make it less noxious, when the people are not particular as to its sources. Coffee, chocolate, and cocoa are unknown, as are also beer, cider, porter, wine, and brandy.

The meats consumed by the Chinese comprise, perhaps, a greater variety than are used in other countries; while, at the same time, very little land is appropriated to rearing animals for food. Beef is not a common meat, chiefly from a Buddhistic prejudice against killing so useful an animal. Mutton in the southern provinces is poor and dear compared with its ex-

---

[1] Dr. Hobson mentions a case at Shanghai where he was called upon to examine a child well-nigh dead with spurious hydrocephalus. Upon investigation he found that the nurse, "a young healthy-looking woman, with breasts full of milk to overflowing," had "been in the habit of selling her milk in small cupfuls to old persons, under the idea of its highly nutritive properties, and was actually poisoning the child dependent on it." The nurse being promptly changed, the infant recovered almost immediately.—*Journal N. C. Br. R. A. Soc.* New Series, Vol. I., p. 51.

cellence and cheapness north of the Yangtsz' River, where the greater numbers of Mohammedans cause a larger demand for it. The beef of the buffalo and the mutton of the goat are still less used; pork is consumed more than all other kinds, and no meat can be raised so economically. Hardly a family so poor that it cannot possess a pig; the animals are kept even on the boats and rafts, to consume and fatten upon what others leave. Fresh pork probably constitutes more than half of the meat eaten by the Chinese; hams are tolerably plenty, and a dish called "golden hams," from the amber appearance of the joint, makes a conspicuous object in feasts. Horseflesh, venison, wild boar, and antelope are now and then seen, but in passing through the markets mutton, pork, fowls, and fish are the viands which everywhere meet the eye.

A few kittens and puppies are sold alive in cages, mewing and yelping as if in anticipation of their fate, or from pain caused by the pinching and handling they receive at the hands of dissatisfied customers. Those intended for the table are usually fed upon rice, so that if the nature of their food be considered, their flesh is far more cleanly than that of the omnivorous hog; few articles of food have, however, been so identified abroad with the tastes of the people as kittens, puppies, and rats have with the Chinese. American school geographies often contain pictures of a market-man carrying baskets holding these unfortunate victims of a perverse taste (as we think), or else a string of rats and mice hanging by their tails to a stick across his shoulders, which almost necessarily convey the idea that such things form the usual food of the people. Travellers hear beforehand that the Chinese devour everything, and when they arrive in the country straightway inquire if these animals are eaten, and hearing that such is the case, perpetuate the idea that they form the common articles of food. However commonly live kittens and puppies or dressed dogs may be exposed for sale, one may live in a city like Canton or Fuhchau for many years and never see rats offered for food, unless he hunts up the people who sell them for medicine or aphrodisiacs; in fact, they are not so easily caught as to be either common or cheap. A peculiar prejudice in favor of black dogs and cats exists among natives of the south; these animals invariably command a higher price than others, and are eaten at midsummer in the belief that the meat ensures health and strength during the ensuing year.

Rats and mice are, no doubt, eaten now and then, and so are many other undesirable things, by those whom want compels to take what they can get; but to put these and other strange eatables in the front of the list gives a distorted idea of the everyday food of the people. There are perhaps half a dozen restaurants in Canton city where dog's-meat appears upon the *menu*; it is, however, by no means an inexpensive delicacy.[1] The flesh of rats is eaten by old women as a hair restorative.

The blood of ducks, pigs, and sheep is used as food, or prepared for medicine and as a paste; it forms an ingredient in priming and some kind of varnish. It is coagulated into cakes for sale, and in cooking is mixed with the meats and sauces. The blood of all animals is eaten without repugnance so far as concerns religious scruples, except in the case of Buddhist priests.

Frogs are caught in a curious manner by tying a young jumper lately emerged from tadpole life to a line and bobbing him up and down in the grass and grain of a rice field, where the old croakers are wont to harbor. As soon as one of them sees the young frog sprawling and squirming he makes a plunge at him and swallows him whole, whereupon he is immediately conveyed to the frog-fisher's basket, losing his life, liberty, and lunch together, for the bait is rescued from his maw and used again as long as life lasts.

Poultry, including chickens, geese, and ducks, are everywhere raised; of the three the geese are the best flavored, but all of them are reared cheaply and supply a large portion of the poor with the principal meat they eat. The eggs of fowls and ducks are hatched artificially, and every visitor to Canton remembers the duck-boats in which those birds are hatched and reared and carried up and down the river seeking for pasture along its muddy banks. Sheds are erected for hatching, in which are

[1] Archdeacon Gray, *China*, Vol. II., p. 76.

a number of high baskets well lined to retain the heat. Each one is placed over a fireplace, so that the heat shall be conveyed to the eggs through the tile in its bottom and retained in the basket by a close cover. When the eggs are brought a layer is put into the bottom of each basket, and a fire kept in the room at a uniform heat of about 80° F. After four or five days they are examined in a strong light, to separate the addled ones; the others are put back in the baskets and the heat kept up for ten days longer, when they are all placed upon shelves in the centre of the shed and covered with cotton and felt for fourteen days. At the end of the twenty-eighth day the shells are broken to release the inmates, which are sold to those who rear them. Pigeons are raised to a great extent; their eggs form an ingredient in soups. Wild and water fowl are caught in nets or shot; the wild duck, teal, grebe, wild goose, plover, snipe, heron, egret, partridge, pheasant, and ortolan or rice bird are all procurable at Canton, and the list could be increased elsewhere.

If the Chinese eat many things which are rejected by other peoples, they are perfectly omnivorous with respect to aquatic productions; here nothing comes amiss; all waters are vexed with their fisheries. Their nets and other contrivances for capturing fish display great ingenuity, and most of them are admirably adapted to the purpose. Rivers, creeks, and stagnant pools, the great ocean and the little tank, mountain lakes and garden ponds, tubs and rice fields, all furnish their quota to the sustenance of man, and tend to explain, in a great degree, the dense population. The right to fish in running streams and natural waters is open to all, while artificial reservoirs, as ponds, pools, tanks, tubs, etc., are brought into available use; near tide-water the rice grounds are turned into fish-ponds in winter if they will thereby afford a more profitable return. The inhabitants of the water are killed with the spear, caught with the hook, scraped up by the dredge, ensnared by traps, and captured by nets; they are decoyed to jump into boats by painted boards, and frightened into nets by noisy ones, taken out of the water by lifting nets and dived for by birds—for the cormorant seizes what his owner could not easily reach. In short, every possible way of catching or rearing fish is practised in one part of the country or another. Tanks are placed in the streets, with water running through them, where carp or perch are reared until they become so large they can hardly turn round in their pens; eels and water-snakes of every color and size are fed in tubs and jars until customers carry them off.

King-crabs, cuttle-fish, sharks, sting-rays, gobies, tortoises, turtles, crabs, prawns, crawfish, and shrimps add to the variety. The best fish in the Canton market are the garoupa or rock cod, pomfret, sole, mackerel, bynni carp or mango fish, and the polynemus, erroneously called salmon. Carp and tench of many kinds, herring, shad, perch, mullet, and bream, with others less common at the west, are found in great abundance. They are usually eaten fresh, or merely opened and dried in the sun, as stock-fish. Both salt and fresh-water shell-fish are abundant. The oysters are not so well flavored as those on the Atlantic coast of America; the crabs and prawns are excellent, but the clams, mussels, and other fresh-water species are less palatable. Insect food is confined to locusts and grasshoppers, grubs and silk-worms; the latter are fried to a crisp when cooked. These and water-snakes are decidedly the most repulsive things the Chinese eat.

Many articles of food are sought after by this sensual people for their supposed aphrodisiac qualities, and most of the singular productions brought from abroad for food are of this nature. The famous birdsnest soup is prepared from the nest of a swallow (*Collocalia esculenta*) found in caves and damp places in some islands of the Indian Archipelago; the bird macerates the material of the nest from seaweed (*Gelidium* chiefly) in the crop, and constructs it by drawing the food out in fibres, which are attached to the damp stone with the bill. The nest has the same shape as those which chimney swallows build, and holds the young against the cliffs; they rarely exceed three or four inches in the longest diameter. The operation of cleaning is performed by picking away each morsel of dirt or feathers from the nest, and involves considerable labor. After they come forth perfectly free from impurities they are stewed with pigeons' eggs, spicery, and other ingredients into a soup; when cooked they resemble isinglass, and the dish depends upon sauces and seasoning for most of its taste. The biche-de-mer, tripang, or sea-slug, is a marine substance procured from the Polynesian Islands; it is sought after under the same idea of its invigorating qualities, and being cheaper than the birdsnest is a more common dish; when cooked it resembles pork-rind in appearance and taste. Sharks' fins and fish-maws are imported and boiled into gelatinous soups that are nourishing and palatable; and the sinews, tongues, palates, udders, and other parts of different animals are sought after as delicacies. A large proportion of the numerous made dishes seen at great feasts consists of such odd articles, most of which are supposed to possess some peculiar strengthening quality.

The art of cooking has not reached any high degree of perfection. Like the French, it is very economical, and consists of stews and fried dishes more than of baked or roasted. Salt is proportionately dear from its preparation being a government monopoly, and this has led to a large use of onions for seasoning. The articles of kitchen furniture are few and simple; an iron boiler, shaped like the segment of a sphere, for stewing or frying, a portable earthen furnace, and two or three different shaped earthenware pots for boiling water or vegetables constitute the whole establishment of thousands of families. A few other utensils, as tongs, ladles, forks, sieves, mills, etc., are used to a greater or less extent, though the variety is quite commensurate with the simple cookery. Both meats and vegetables, previously hashed into mouthfuls, are stewed or fried in oil or fat; they are not cooked in large joints or steaks for the table of a household. Hogs are baked whole for sacrifices and for sale in cookshops, but before being eaten are hashed and fried again. Cutting the food into small pieces secures its thorough cooking with less fuel than it would otherwise require, and is moreover indispensable for eating with chopsticks. Two or three vegetables are boiled together, but meat soups are seldom seen; and the immense variety of puddings, pastry, cakes, pies, custards, ragouts, creams, etc., made in western lands is almost unknown in China.[1]

---

[1] *Mémoires conc. les Chinois*, Tome XI., pp. 78 ff. C. C. Coffin in the *Atlantic Monthly*, 1869, p. 747. Doolittle's *Vocabulary*, Part III., No. XVIII. M. Henri Cordier in the *Journal des Débats*, Nov. 19, 1879. *Notes and Queries on C. and J.*, Vol. II., pp. 11 and 26.

CHAPTER XIV.

SOCIAL LIFE AMONG THE CHINESE.

THE preceding chapter, in a measure, exhibits the attainments the Chinese have reached in the comforts and elegances of living. These terms, as tests of civilization, however, are so comparative that it is rather difficult to define them; for the notions which an Englishman, an Egyptian, and a Chinese severally might have of comfort and elegance in the furniture and arrangement of their houses are almost as unlike as their languages. If Fisher's *Views of China* be taken as a guide, one can easily believe that the Chinese need little from abroad to better their condition in these particulars; while if one listen to the descriptions of some persons who have resided among them, it will be concluded that they possess neither comfort in their houses, civility in their manners, nor cleanliness in their persons. In passing to an account of their social life, this variety of tastes should not be overlooked; and if some points appear objectionable when taken alone, a little further examination will, perhaps, show that they form part of a system which requires complete reconstruction before it could be happily and safely altered.

The observations of a foreigner upon Chinese society are likely to be modified by his own feelings, and the way in which he has been treated by natives there; but their behavior to him might be very unlike what would be deemed good breeding among themselves. If a Chinese feared or expected something from a foreigner, he would act toward him more politely than if the contrary were the case; on the one hand better, on the other worse, than he would toward one of his own countrymen in like circumstances. In doing so, it may be remarked with regret that he would only imitate the conduct of a host of foreigners who visit China, and whose coarse remarks, rude actions, and general supercilious conduct toward the natives ill comport with their superior civilization and assumed advantages. One who looked at the matter reasonably would not expect much true politeness among a people whose conceit and ignorance, selfishness and hauteur, were nearly equal; nor be surprised to find the intercourse between the extremes of society present a strange mixture of brutality and commiseration, formality and disdain. The separation of the sexes modifies and debases the amusements, even of the most moral, leads the men to spend their time in gambling, devote it to the pleasures of the table, or dawdle it away when the demands of business, study, or labor do not arouse them. Political parties, which exert so powerful an influence upon the conduct of men in Christian countries, leading them to unite and communicate with each other for the purpose of watching or resisting the acts of government, do not exist; and where there is a general want of confidence, such institutions as insurance companies, savings or deposit banks, corporate bodies to build a railroad or factory, and associations of any kind in which persons unite their funds and efforts to accomplish an object, are not to be expected; they do not exist in China, nor did they in Rome or ancient Europe. Nor will any one expect to hear that literary societies or voluntary philanthropic associations are common. These, as they are now found in the west, are the products of Christianity alone, and we must wait for the planting of the tree before looking for its fruit. The legal profession, as distinct from the possession of office, is not an occupation in which learned men can obtain an honorable livelihood; the priesthood is confined to monasteries and temples, and its members do not enter into society; while the practice of medicine is so entirely empirical and strange that the few experienced practitioners are not enough to redeem the class. These three professions, which elsewhere do so much to elevate society and guide public opinion, being wanting, educated men have no stimulus to draw them out into independent action. The competition for literary degrees and official rank, the eager pursuit of trade, or the dull routine of mechanical and agricultural labor, form the leading avocations of the Chinese people. Unacquainted with the intellectual enjoyments found in books and the conversation of learned men, and having no educated taste, as we understand that term (while, too, he cannot find such a thing as virtuous female society), the Chinese resorts to the dice-box, the opium-pipe, or the brothel for his pleasures, though even there with a loss of character among his peers.

The separation of the sexes has many bad results, only partially compensated by some conservative ones. Woman owes her present elevation at the west to Christianity, not only in the degree of respect, support, freedom from servile labor, and education which she receives, but also in the reflex influences she exerts of a purifying, harmonizing, and elevating character. Where the requirements of the Gospel exert no force, her rights are more or less disregarded, and if she become as debased as the men, she can exert little good influence even upon her own family, still less upon the community. General mixed society can never be maintained with pleasure unless the better parts of human nature have the acknowledged preëminence, and where she, who imparts to it all its gracefulness and purity, is herself uneducated, unpolished, and immodest, the common sense of mankind sees its impropriety. By advocating the partition of the sexes, legislators and moralists in China have acted as they best could in the circumstances of the case, and by preventing the evils beyond their remedy, provided the best safeguards they could against general corruption. In her own domestic circle a Chinese female, in the character and duties of daughter, wife, or mother, finds as much employment, and probably as many enjoyments, as the nature of her training has fitted her for. She does not hold her proper place in society simply because she has never been taught its duties or exercised its privileges.

In ordinary cases the male and female branches of a household are strictly kept apart; not only the servants, but even brothers and sisters do not freely associate after the boys commence their studies. At this period of life, or even earlier, an anxious task devolves upon parents, which is to find suitable partners for their children. Betrothment is entirely in their hands, and is conducted through the medium of a class of persons called *mei-jin*, or go-betweens, who are expected to be well acquainted with the character and circumstances of the parties. Mothers sometimes contract their unborn progeny on the sole contingency of a difference of sex, but the usual age of forming these engagements is ten, twelve, or older, experience having shown that the casualties attending it render an earlier period undesirable.

There are six ceremonies which constitute a regular marriage, though their details vary much in different parts of the Empire: 1. The father and elder brother of the young man send a go-between to the father and brother of the girl, to inquire her name and the moment of her birth, that the horoscope of the two may be examined, in order to ascertain whether the proposed alliance will be a happy one. 2. If the eight characters[1] seem to augur aright, the boy's friends send the *mei-jin* back to make an offer of marriage. 3. If that be accepted, the second party is again requested to return an assent in writing. 4. Presents are then sent to the girl's parents according to the means of the parties. 5. The go-between requests them to choose a lucky day for the wedding. 6. The preliminaries are concluded by the bridegroom going or sending a party of friends with music to bring his bride to his own house. The match-makers contrive to multiply their visits and prolong the negotiations, when the parties are rich, to serve their own ends.

In Fuhkien parents often send pledges to each other when their children are mere infants, and registers containing their names and particulars of nativity are exchanged in testimony of the contract. After this has been done it is impossible to retract the engagement, unless one of the parties becomes a leper or is disabled. When the children are espoused older, the boy sometimes accompanies the go-between and the party carrying the presents to the house of his future mother-in-law, and receives from her some trifling articles, as melon-seeds, fruits, etc., which

[1] Compare p. 628.

he distributes to those around. Among the presents sent to the girl are fruits, money, vermicelli, and a ham, of which she gives a morsel to each one of the party, and sends its foot back. These articles are neatly arranged, and the party bringing them is received with a salute of fire-crackers.

From the time of engagement until marriage a young lady is required to maintain the strictest seclusion. Whenever friends call upon her parents she is expected to retire to the inner apartments, and in all her actions and words guard her conduct with careful solicitude. She must use a close sedan whenever she visits her relations, and in her intercourse with her brothers and the domestics in the household maintain great reserve. Instead of having any opportunity to form those friendships and acquaintances with her own sex which among ourselves become a source of so much pleasure at the time and advantage in after life, the Chinese maiden is confined to the circle of her relations and her immediate neighbors. She has few of the pleasing remembrances and associations that are usually connected with school-day life, nor has she often the ability or opportunity to correspond by letter with girls of her own age. Seclusion at this time of life, and the custom of crippling the feet, combine to confine women in the house almost as much as the strictest laws against their appearing abroad; for in girlhood, as they know only a few persons except relatives, and can make very few acquaintances after marriage, their circle of friends contracts rather than enlarges as life goes on. This privacy impels girls to learn as much of the world as they can, and among the rich their curiosity is gratified through maid-servants, match-makers, pedlers, visitors, and others. Curiosity also stimulates young ladies to learn something of the character and appearance of their intended husbands, but the rules of society are too strict for young persons to endeavor to form a personal attachment, though it is not impossible for them to *see* each other if they wish, and there are, no doubt, many contracts suggested to parents by their children.

The office of match-maker is considered honorable, and both men and women are employed to conduct nuptial negotiations. Great confidence is reposed in their judgment and veracity, and as their employment depends somewhat upon their tact and character, they have every inducement to act with strict propriety in their intercourse with families. The father of the girl employs their services in collecting the sum agreed upon in the contract, which, in ordinary circumstances, varies from twenty-five to forty dollars, increasing to a hundred and over according to the condition of the bridegroom; until that is paid the marriage does not take place. The presents sent at betrothment are sometimes costly, consisting of silks, rice, cloths, fruits, etc.; the bride brings no dower, but both parents frequently go to expenses they can ill afford when celebrating the nuptials of their children, as the pride of family stimulates each party to make undue display.

The principal formalities of a marriage are everywhere the same, but local customs are observed in some regions which are quite unknown and appear singular elsewhere. In Fuhkien, when the lucky day for the wedding comes, the guests assemble in the bridegroom's house to celebrate it, where also sedans, a band of music, and porters are in readiness. The courier, who acts as guide to the chair-bearers, takes the lead, and in order to prevent the onset of malicious demons lurking by the road, a baked hog or large piece of pork is carried in front, that the procession may safely pass while these hungry souls are devouring the meat. Meanwhile the bride arrays herself in her best dress and richest jewels. Her girlish tresses have already been bound up, and her hair arranged by a matron, with due formality; an ornamental and complicated head-dress made of rich materials, not unlike a helmet or corona, often forms part of her coiffure. Her person is nearly covered by a large mantle, over which is an enormous hat like an umbrella, that descends to the shoulders and shades the whole figure. Thus attired she takes her seat in the red gilt marriage sedan, called *hwa kiao*, borne by four men, in which she is completely concealed. This is locked by her mother or some other relative, and the key given to one of the bridemen, who hands it to the bridegroom or his representative on reaching his house.

The procession is now rearranged, with the addition of as many red boxes and trays to contain the wardrobe, kitchen utensils, and the feast, as the means of the family or the extent of her paraphernalia require. As the procession approaches the bridegroom's house the courier hastens forward to announce its coming, whereupon the music strikes up, and fire-crackers salute her until she enters the gate. As she approaches the door the bridegroom conceals himself, but the go-between brings forward a young child to salute her, while going to seek the closeted bridegroom. He approaches with becoming gravity and opens the sedan to hand out his bride, she still retaining the hat and mantle; they approach the ancestral tablet, which they reverence with three bows, and then seat themselves at a table upon which are two cups of spirits. The go-between serves them, though the bride can only make the motions of drinking, as the large hat completely covers her face. They soon retire into a chamber, where the husband takes the hat and mantle from his wife, and sees her, perhaps, for the first time in his life. After he has considered her for some time, the guests and friends enter the room to survey her, when each one is allowed to express an opinion; the criticisms of the women are severest, perhaps because they remember the time they stood in her unpleasant position. This cruel examination being over, she is introduced to her husband's parents, and then salutes her own. Such are some of the customs among the Fuhkienese. Other usages followed in marriages and betrothals have been carefully described by Doolittle, with particular reference to the same people, and by Archdeacon John H. Gray, alluding to other parts of the Empire.[1]

The bridegroom, previous to the wedding, receives a new name or "style," and is formally capped by his father in presence of his friends, as an introduction to manhood. He invites the guests, sending two red cakes with each invitation, and to him each guest, a few days before the marriage, returns a present or a sum of money worth about ten or fifteen cents, nominally equal to the expenses he will be considered as occasioning. Another invitation is sent the day after to a feast, and the bride also calls on the ladies who attended her wedding,

[1] *Social Life of the Chinese*, Chapters II. and III.; *China*, Chap. VII.; also *Fourteen Months in Canton*, by Mrs Gray.

from whom she receives a ring or some other article of small value. The gentlemen also make the bridegroom a present of a pair of lanterns to hang at his gateway. On the night of the wedding they sometimes endeavor to get into the house when the pair is supposed to be asleep, in order to carry off some article, which the bridegroom must ransom at their price.

Among the poor the expenses of a wedding are much lessened by purchasing a young girl, whom the parents bring up as a daughter until she is marriageable, and in this way secure her services in the household. A girl already affianced is for a like reason sometimes sent to the boy's parents, that they may support her. In small villages the people call upon a newly married couple near the next full moon, when they are received standing near the bedside. The men enter first and pay their respects to the bride, while her husband calls the attention of his visitors to her charms, praises her little feet, her beautiful hands, and other features, and then accompanies them into the hall, where they are regaled with refreshments. After the men have retired the women enter and make their remarks upon the lady, whose future character depends a good deal upon the manner in which she conducts herself. If she shows good temper, her reputation is made. Many a prudent woman on this occasion says not a word, but suffers herself to be examined in silence in order that she may run no risk of offending.[1] Far different is this introduction to married life from the bridal tour and cordial greetings of friends which ladies receive in western lands during the honeymoon!

The bridal procession is a peculiar feature of Chinese social life. It varies in its style, nature of the ornaments, and the whole get-up in all parts of the land, but is always as showy as the means of the parties will allow. It is composed of bearers of lanterns and official tablets, musicians, relatives of the bride and groom and their personal friends, framed stands with roofs carried on thills to hold the bride's effects, all centering around her sedan. In Peking such a procession will sometimes be stretched out half a mile, and the sedan borne by a dozen or

[1] *Chinese Repository*, Vols. IV., p. 568, and X., pp. 65–70; *Annales de la Foi*, No. XL., 1835.

more bearers. The coolies are dressed in red, and they and their burdens are usually provided by special shopmen, who purvey on such occasions. The tablets of literary rank held by members of the family, wooden dragons' heads, titular lanterns, and other official insignia are borne in state, an evidence of its high standing. In some places an old man, elegantly dressed, heads the procession, bearing a large umbrella to hold over the bride when she enters and leaves her sedan; behind him come bearers with lanterns, one of which carries the inscription, "The phœnixes sing harmoniously." To these succeed the music and the honorary tablets, titular flags, state umbrella, etc., and two stout men as executioners dressed in a fantastic manner, wearing long feathers in their caps, and lictors, chain-bearers, and other emblems of office. Parties of young lads, prettily dressed and playing on drums, gongs, and flutes, or carrying lanterns and banners, occasionally form a pleasing variety in the train, which is continued by the trays and covered tables containing the bride's trousseau, and ended with the sedan containing herself.

The ceremonies attending her reception at her husband's house are not uniform. In some parts she is lifted out of the sedan, over a pan of charcoal placed in the court, and carried into the bed-chamber; in other places she enters and leaves her sedan on rugs spread for her use, and walks into the chamber. After a brief interval she returns into the hall, bearing a tray of betel-nut for the guests, and then worships a pair of geese brought in the train with her husband, this bird being an emblem of conjugal affection. On returning to her chamber the bridegroom follows her and takes off the red veil, after which they pledge each other in wine, the cups being joined by a thread. While there a matron who has borne several children to one husband comes in to pronounce a blessing upon them and make up the nuptial bed. The assembled guests then sit down to the feast and ply the *sin lang*, 'new man' or bridegroom, pretty well with liquor; the Chinese on such occasions do not, however, often overpass the rules of sobriety. The *sin fujin*, 'new lady' or bride, and her mother-in-law also attend to those of her own sex who are present in other apartments, but among the poor a pleasanter sight is now and then seen in all the guests sitting at one table.

In the morning the pair worship the ancestral tablets and salute all the members of the family; among the poor this important ceremony occurs very soon after the pair have exchanged their wine-cups. The pledging of the bride and groom in a cup of wine, and their worship of the ancestral tablets and of heaven and earth, are the important ceremonies of a wedding after the procession has reached the house. Marriages are celebrated at all hours, though twilight and evening are preferred; the spring season, or the last month in the year, are regarded as the most felicitous nuptial periods. From the way in which the whole matter is conducted there is some room for deception by sending another person in the sedan than the one betrothed, or the man may mistake the name of the girl he wishes to marry. Mr. Smith mentions one of his acquaintances, who, having been captivated with a girl he saw in the street, sent a go-between with proposals to her parents, which were accepted; but he was deeply mortified on receiving his bride to find that he had mistaken the number of his charmer, and had received the fifth daughter instead of the fourth.

The Chinese do not marry another woman with these observances while the first one is living, but they may bring home concubines with no other formality than a contract with her parents, though it is considered somewhat discreditable for a man to take another bedfellow if his wife have borne him sons, unless he can afford each of them a separate establishment. It is not unfrequent for a man to secure a maid-servant in the family with the consent of his wife by purchasing her for a concubine, especially if his occupation frequently call him away from home, in which case he takes her as his travelling companion and leaves his wife in charge of the household. The fact that the sons of a concubine are considered as legally belonging to the wife induces parents to betroth their daughters early, and thus prevent their entering a man's family in this inferior capacity. The Chinese are sensible of the evils of a divided household, and the laws place its control in the hands of the wife. If she have no sons of her own, she looks out for a likely boy among her clansmen to adopt, knowing that otherwise her husband will probably bring a concubine into the family. It is difficult even to guess at the extent of polygamy, for no statistics have been or can be easily taken. Among the laboring classes it is rare to find more than one woman to one man, but tradesmen, official persons, landholders, and those in easy circumstances frequently take one or more concubines; perhaps two-fifths of such families have them. Show and fashion lead some to increase the number of their women, though aware of the discord likely to arise, for they fully believe their own proverb, that "nine women out of ten are jealous." Yet it is probably true that polygamy finds its greatest support from the women themselves. The wife seeks to increase her own position by getting more women into the house to relieve her own work and humor her fancies. The Chinese illustrate the relation by comparing the wife to the moon and the concubines to the stars, both of which in their appropriate spheres wait upon and revolve around the sun.

If regard be had to the civilization of the Chinese and their opportunities for moral training, the legal provisions of the code to protect females in their acknowledged rights and punish crimes against the peace and purity of the family relation reflect credit upon their legislators. In these laws the obligation of children to fulfil the contract made by their parents is enforced, even to the annulling of an agreement made by a son himself in ignorance of the arrangements of his parents. The position of the *tsí*, or wife taken by the prescribed formalities, and that of the *tsieh*, or women purchased as concubines, are accurately defined, and the degradation of the former or elevation of the latter so as to interchange their places, or the taking of a second *tsí*, are all illegal and void. The relation between the two is more like that which existed between Sarah and Hagar in Abraham's household, or Zilpah and Bilhah and their mistresses in Jacob's, than that indicated by our terms first and second wife, of which idea the Chinese words contain no trace. The degrees of unlawful marriages are comprehensive, extending even to the prohibition of persons having the same *sing*, or family name, and to two brothers marrying sisters. The laws forbid the marriage of a brother's widow, of a father's or grandfather's wife, or a father's sister, under the penalty of death; and the like punishment is inflicted upon whoever seizes the wife or daughter of a freeman and carries them away to marry them.

These regulations not only put honor upon marriage, but render it more common among the Chinese than almost any other people, thereby preventing a vast train of evils. The tendency of unrestrained desire to throw down the barriers to the gratification of lust must not be lost sight of; and as no laws on this subject can be effectual unless the common sense of a people approve of them, the Chinese, by separating the sexes in general society, have removed a principal provocation to sin, and by compelling young men to fulfil the marriage contracts of their parents have also provided a safeguard against debauchery at the age when youth is most tempted to indulge, and when indulgence would most strongly disincline them to marry at all. They have, moreover, provided for the undoubted succession of the inheritance by disallowing more than one *wife*, and yet have granted men the liberty they would otherwise take, and which immemorial usage in Asiatic countries has sanctioned. They have done as well as they could in regulating a difficult matter, and better, on the whole, perhaps, than in most other unchristianized countries. If any one supposes, however, that because these laws exist sins against the seventh commandment are uncommon in China, he will be as mistaken as those who infer that because the Chinese are pagans nothing like modesty, purity, or affection exists between the sexes.

When a girl "spills the tea"—that is, loses her betrothed by death—public opinion honors her if she refuse a second engagement; and instances are cited of young ladies committing suicide rather than contract a second marriage. They sometimes leave their father's house and live with the parents of their affianced husband as if they had been really widows. It is considered derogatory for widows to marry; though it may be that the instances quoted in books with so much praise only indicate how rare the practice is in reality. The widow is occasionally sold for a concubine by her father-in-law, and the grief and contumely of her degradation is enhanced by separation from her children, whom she can no longer retain. Such cases are, however, not common, for the impulses of maternal affection are too strong to be thus trifled with, and widows usually look to their friends for support, or to their own exertions if their children be still young; they are assisted, too, by their relatives in this laudable industry and care. It is a lasting stigma to a son to neglect the comfort and support of his widowed mother. A widower is not restrained by any laws, and weds one of his concubines or whomsoever he chooses; nor is he expected to defer the nuptials for any period of mourning for his first wife.

The seven legal reasons for divorce, viz., barrenness, lasciviousness, jealousy, talkativeness, thievery, disobedience to her husband's parents, or leprosy, are almost nullified by the single provision that a woman cannot be put away whose parents are not living to receive her back again. Parties can separate on mutual disagreement, but the code does not regulate the alimony; and a husband is liable to punishment if he retain a wife convicted of adultery. If a wife merely elopes she can be sold by her husband, but if she marry while absent she is to be strangled; if the husband be absent three years a woman must state her case to the magistrates before presuming to remarry.

In regard to the general condition of females in China the remark of De Guignes is applicable, that "though their lot is less happy than that of their sisters in Europe, their ignorance of a better state renders their present or prospective one more supportable; happiness does not always consist in absolute enjoyment, but in the idea which we have formed of it."[1] She does not feel that any injustice is done her by depriving her of the right of assent as to whom her partner shall be; her wishes and her knowledge go no farther than her domestic circle, and where she has been trained in her mother's apartments to the various duties and accomplishments of her sex, her removal to a husband's house brings to her no great change.

This, however, is not always the case, and the power accorded to the husband over his wife and family is often used with great tyranny. The young wife finds in her new home little of the

---

[1] *Voyages à Peking*, Tome II., p. 283.

sympathy and love her sisters in Christian lands receive. Her mother-in-law is not unfrequently the source of her greatest trials, and demands from her both the submission of a child and the labor of a slave, which is not seldom returned by disobedience and bitter revilings. If the husband interfere she has less likelihood of escaping his exactions; though in the lower walks of life his cruelty is restrained by fear of losing her and her services, and in the upper diverted by indifference as to what she does, in the pursuit of other objects. If the wife behave well till she herself becomes a mother and a mother-in-law, then the tables are turned; from being a menial she becomes almost a goddess. Luhchau, a writer on female culture, mentions the following indirect mode of reproving a mother-in-law: "Loh Yang travelled seven years to improve himself, during which time his wife diligently served her mother-in-law and supported her son at school. The poultry from a neighbor's house once wandered into her garden, and her mother-in-law stole and killed them for eating. When she sat down to table and saw the fowls she would not dine, but burst into tears, at which the old lady was much surprised and asked the reason. 'I am much distressed that I am so poor and cannot afford to supply you with all I wish I could, and that I should have caused you to eat flesh belonging to another.' Her parent was affected by this, and threw away the dish."

The evils attending early betrothment induce many parents to defer engaging their daughters until they are grown, and a husband of similar tastes can be found; for even if the condition of the families in the interval of betrothment and marriage unsuitably change, or the lad grows up to be a dissipated, worthless, or cruel man, totally unworthy of the girl, still the contract must be fulfilled, and the worst party generally is most anxious for it. The unhappy bride in such cases often escapes from her present sufferings and dismal prospects by suicide. A case occured in Canton in 1833 where a young wife, visiting her parents shortly after marriage, so feelingly described her sufferings at the hands of a cruel husband to her sisters and friends that she and three of her auditors joined their hands together and drowned themselves in a pond, she to escape present misery and they to avoid its future possibility. Another young lady, having heard of the worthless character of her intended, carried a bag of money with her in the sedan, and when they retired after the ceremonies were over thus addressed him: "Touch me not; I am resolved to abandon the world and become a nun. I shall this night cut off my hair. I have saved $200, which I give you; with the half you can purchase a concubine, and with the rest enter on some trade. Be not lazy and thriftless. Hereafter, remember me." Saying this, she cut off her hair, and her husband and his kindred, fearing suicide if they opposed her, acquiesced, and she returned to her father's house.[1] Such cases are common enough to show the dark side of family life, and young ladies implore their parents to rescue them in this or some other way from the sad fate which awaits them. Sometimes girls become skilled in female accomplishments to recommend themselves to their husbands, and their disappointment is the greater when they find him to be a brutal, depraved tyrant. A melancholy instance of this occurred in Canton in 1840, which ended in the wife committing suicide. Her brother had been a scholar of one of the American missionaries, and took a commendable pride in showing specimens of his sister's exquisite embroidery, and not a few of her attainments in writing, which indicated their reciprocal attachment. The contrary happens too, sometimes, where the husband finds himself compelled to wed a woman totally unable to appreciate or share his pursuits, but he has means of alleviating or avoiding such misalliances which the weaker vessel has not. On the whole, as we have said, one must admit that woman holds a fairly high position in China. If she suffers from the brutality of her husband, the tyranny of her mother-in-law, or the overwork of household, field, or loom, she is as often herself blameworthy for indolence, shiftlessness, gadding, and bad temper. The instances which are given by Gray[2] in his account of marital atrocities prove the length to which a man will wreak his rage on the helpless; but they are the exception to the general testi-

---

[1] *Chinese Repository*, Vol. I., p. 293. [2] *China*, Chap. VII.

mony of the people themselves. So far as general purity of society goes, one may well doubt whether such abominable conduct as is legalized among Mormons in Utah is any improvement on the hardships of woman among the Chinese.

Pursuing this brief account of the social life of the Chinese, the right of parents in managing their children comes into notice. It is great, though not unlimited, and in allowing them very extensive power, legislators have supposed that natural affection of the parents, a desire to continue the honorable succession of the family, together with the influence of proper education, were as good securities against paternal cruelty and neglect as any laws which could be made. Fathers give their sons the *ju ming*, or 'milk name,' about a month after birth. The mother, on the day appointed for this ceremony, worships and thanks the goddess of Mercy, and the boy, dressed and having his head shaved, is brought into the circle of assembled friends, where the father confers the name and celebrates the occasion by a feast. The milk name is kept until the lad enters school, at which time the *shu ming*, or 'school name,' is conferred upon him, as already mentioned. The *shu ming* generally consists of two characters, selected with reference to the boy's condition, prospects, studies, or some other event connected with him ; sometimes the milk name is continued, as the family have become accustomed to it. Such names as *Ink-grinder*, *Promising-study*, *Opening-olive*, *Entering-virtue*, *Rising-advancement*, etc., are given to young students at this time. Though endearing or fanciful names are often conferred, it is quite as common to vilify very young children by calling them *dog*, *hog*, *puppy*, *flea*, etc., under the idea that such epithets will ward off the evil eye. Girls have only their milk and marriage names; the former may be *a flower*, *a sister*, *a gem*, or such like; the latter are terms like *Emulating the Moon*, *Orchis Flower*, *the Jasmine*, *Delicate Perfume*, etc. A mere number at Canton, as *A-yat*, *A-sam*, *A-luk* (No. 1, No. 3, No. 6), often designates the boys till they get their book names.[1]

[1] Doolittle's *Handbook*, Vol. III., p. 660, gives a list of names collected at Fuhchau, which are applicable to other provinces.

The personal names of the Chinese are written contrariwise to our own, the *sing*, or surname, coming first, then the *ming*, or given name, and then the complimentary title; as Liang Wăn-tai siensăng, where *Liang*, or 'Millet,' is the family name, *Wăn-tai*, or 'Terrace of Letters,' the given name, and *siensăng*, Mr. (*i.e.*, Master), or 'Teacher.' A few of the surnames are double, as *Sz'ma Tsien*, where Sz'ma is the family name and Tsien the official title. A curious idea prevails among the people of Canton, that foreigners have no surname, which, as Pliny thought of the inhabitants of Mt. Atlas, they regard as one of the proofs of their barbarism; perhaps this notion came by inference from the fact that the Manchus write only their given name, as Kíshen, Kíying, Ílípu, etc. When writing Chinese names in translations and elsewhere, some attention should be paid to these particulars; the names of Chinese persons and places are constantly appearing in print under forms as singular as would be *Williamhenryharrison*, *Rich-Ard-Ox-Ford*, or *Phila Delphia-city* in English. The name being in a different language, and its true nature unknown to most of those who write it, accounts for the misarrangement.

In Canton and its vicinity the names of people are abbreviated in conversation to one character, and an *A* prefixed to it;—as *Tsinteh*, called *A-teh* or *A-tsin*. In Amoy the *A* is placed after, as *Chin-a;* in the northern provinces no such usage is known. Some families, perhaps in imitation of the imperial precedent, distinguish their members from others in the clan by adopting a constant character for the first one in the *ming*, or given name; thus a family of brothers will be named Lin Tung-pei, Lin Tung-fung, Lin Tung-peh, where the word *Tung* distinguishes this sept of the clan Lin from all others. There are no characters exclusively appropriated to proper names or different sexes, as George, Agnes, etc., all being chosen out of the language with reference to their meanings. Consequently, a name is sometimes felt to be incongruous, as Naomi, when saluted on her return to Bethlehem, felt its inappropriateness to her altered condition, and suggested a change to Mara. Puns on names and sobriquets are common, from the constant contrast of the sounds of the characters with circumstances suggesting a comparison or a play upon their meanings; sly jokes are also played when writing the names of foreigners, by choosing such characters as will make a ridiculous meaning when read according to their sense and not their sound.

When a man marries he adopts a third name, called *tsz'*, or 'style,' by which he is usually known through life; this is either entirely new or combined from previous names. When a girl is married her family name becomes her given name, and the given name is disused, her husband's name becoming her family name. Thus *Wa Salah* married to *Wei San-wei* drops the *Salah*, and is called *Wei Wa shí*, *i.e.*, Mrs. Wei [born of the clan] Wa, though her husband or near relatives sometimes retain it as a trivial address. A man is frequently known by another compellation, called *pieh tsz'*, or 'second style,' which the public do not presume to employ. When a young man is successful in attaining a degree, or enters an office, he takes a title called *kwan ming*, or 'official name,' by which he is known to government. The members or heads of licensed mercantile companies each have an official name, which is entered in their permit, from whence it is called among foreigners their *chop name*. Each of the heads of the co-hong formerly licensed to trade with foreigners at Canton had such an official name. Besides these various names, old men of fifty, shopkeepers, and others take a *hao*, or 'designation;' tradesmen use it on their signboards as the name of their shop, and not unfrequently receive it as their personal appellation. Of this nature are the appellations of the tradesmen who deal with foreigners, as *Cutshing*, *Chanlung*, *Linchong*, etc., which are none of them the names of the shopmen, but the designation of the shop. It is the usual way in Canton for foreigners to go into a shop and ask "Is Mr. Wanglik in?" which would be almost like one in New York inquiring if Mr. Alhambra or Mr. Atlantic-House was at home, though it does not sound quite so ridiculous to a Chinese. The names taken by shopkeepers allude to trade or its prospects, such as *Mutual Advantage*, *Obedient Profit*, *Extensive Harmony*, *Rising Goodness*, *Great Completeness*, etc.; the names of the partners as such are not employed to form the firm. Besides this use of the *hao*, it is also employed as a brand upon goods; the terms *Hoyuen*, *Kinghing*, *Yuenkí*, meaning 'Harmonious Springs,' 'Cheering Prospects,' 'Fountain's Memorial,' etc., are applied to particular parcels of tea, silk, or other goods, just as brands are placed on lots of wine, flour, or pork. This is called *tsz'-hao*, or 'mark-designation,' but foreigners call both it and the goods it denotes a *chop*.

When a man dies he receives another and last, though not necessarily a new name in the hall of ancestors; upon emperors and empresses are bestowed new ones, as *Benevolent*, *Pious*, *Discreet*, etc., by which they are worshipped and referred to in history, as *that* designation which is most likely to be permanent.

In their common intercourse the Chinese are not more formal than is considered to be well-bred in Europe; it is on extraordinary or official occasions that they observe the precise etiquette for which they are famous. The proper mode of behavior toward all classes is perhaps more carefully inculcated upon youth than it is in the west, and habit renders easy what custom demands. The ceremonial obeisance of a court or a levee, or the salutations proper for a festival, are not carried into the everyday intercourse of life; for as one chief end of the formalities prescribed for such times is to teach due subordination among persons of different rank, they are in a measure laid aside with the robes which suggested them. True politeness, exhibited in an unaffected regard for the feelings of others, cannot, we know, be taught by rules; but a great degree of urbanity and kindness is everywhere shown, whether owing to the naturally placable disposition of the people or to the effects of their early instruction in the forms of politeness. Whether in the crowded and narrow thoroughfares, the village green, the market, the jostling ferry, or the thronged procession—wherever the people are assembled promiscuously, good humor and courtesy are observable; and when altercations do arise wounds or serious injuries seldom ensue, although from the furious clamor one would imagine that half the crowd were in danger of their lives.

Chinese ceremonial requires superiors to be honored according to their station and age, and equals to depreciate themselves while lauding those they address. The Emperor, considering himself as the representative of divine power, exacts the same prostration which is paid the gods; and the ceremonies which are performed in his presence partake, therefore, of a religious character, and are not merely particular forms of etiquette, which may be altered according to circumstances. There are eight gradations of obeisance, commencing with "the lowest form of respect, called *kung shao*, which is merely joining the hands and raising them before the breast. The next is *tso yih*, bowing low with the hands thus joined. The third is *ta tsien*, bending the knee as if about to kneel; and *kwei*, an actual kneeling, is the fourth. The fifth is *ko tao* (*kotow*), kneeling and striking the head on the ground, which when thrice repeated makes the sixth, called *san kao*, or 'thrice knocking.' The seventh is the *luh kao*, or kneeling and knocking the head thrice upon the ground, then standing upright and again kneeling and knocking the head three times more. The climax is closed by the *san kwei kiu kao*, or thrice kneeling and nine times knocking the head. Some of the gods of China are entitled to the *san kao*, others to the *luh kao*, while the Emperor and Heaven are worshipped by the last. The family now on the throne consider this last form as expressing in the strongest manner the submission and homage of one state to another."[1] The extreme submission which the Emperor demands is partaken by and transferred to his officers of every grade in a greater or less degree; the observance of these forms is deemed, therefore, of great importance, and a refusal to render them is considered to be nearly equivalent to a rejection of their authority.

Minute regulations for the times and modes of official intercourse are made and promulgated by the Board of Rites, and to learn and practise them is one indispensable part of official duty. In court the master of ceremonies stands in a conspicuous place, and with a loud voice commands the courtiers to rise and kneel, stand or march, just as an orderly sergeant directs the drill of

[1] *Memoir of Dr. Morrison*, Vol. II., p. 142.

recruits. The same attention to the ritual is observed in their mutual intercourse, for however much an inferior may desire to dispense with the ceremony, his superior will not fail to exact it. In the salutations of entrée and exit among officers these forms are particularly conspicuous, but when well acquainted with each other, and in moments of conviviality, they are in a great measure laid aside; but the juxtaposition of art and nature among them, at one moment laughing and joking, and the next bowing and kneeling to each other as if they had never met, sometimes produces amusing scenes to a foreigner. The entire ignorance and disregard of these forms by foreigners unacquainted with the code leaves a worse impression upon the natives at times, who ascribe such rudeness to hauteur and contempt.

Without particularizing the tedious forms of official etiquette, it will be sufficient to describe what is generally required in good society. Military men pay visits on horseback; civilians and others go in sedans or carts; to walk is not common. Visiting cards are made of vermilioned paper cut into slips about eight inches long and three wide, and are single or folded four, six, eight, or more times, according to the position of the visitor. If he is in recent mourning, the paper is white and the name written in blue ink, but after a stated time this is indicated by an additional character. The simple name is stamped on the upper right corner, or if written on the lower corner, with an addition thus, "Your humble servant (*lit.*, 'stupid younger brother') Pí Chí-wăn bows his head in salutation." On approaching the house his attendant hands a card to the doorkeeper, and if he cannot be received, instead of saying "not at home," the host sends out to "stay the gentleman's approach," and the card is left. If contrariwise the sedan is carried through the doorway into the court, where he comes forth to receive his guest; as the latter steps out each one advances just so far, bowing just so many times, and going through the ceremonies which they mutually understand and expect, until both have taken their seats at the head of the hall, the guest sitting on the left of the host, and his companions, if he have any, in the chairs on each side. The inquiries made after the mutual welfare of friends and each other are couched in a form of studied laudation and depreciation, which when literally translated seem somewhat affected, but to them convey no more than similar civilities do among ourselves—in truth, perhaps not so much of sincere good-will. For instance, to the remark, "It is a long time since we have met, sir," the host replies (literally), "How presume to receive the trouble of your honorable footsteps; is the person in the chariot well?"—which is simply equivalent to, "I am much obliged for your visit, and hope you enjoy good health."

Tea and pipes are always presented, together with betel-nut or sweetmeats on some occasions, but it is not, as among the Turks, considered disrespectful to refuse them, though it would be looked upon as singular. If the guest inquire after the health of relatives he should commence with the oldest living, and then ask how many sons the host has; but it is not considered good breeding for a formal acquaintance to make any remarks respecting the mistress of the house. If the sons of the host are at home they are generally sent for, and make their obeisance to their father's friend by coming up before him and performing the *kotow* as rapidly as possible, each one making haste, as if he did not wish to delay him. The guest raises them with a slight bow, and the lads stand facing him at a respectful distance. He will then remark, perhaps, if one of them happen to be at his studies, that "the boy will perpetuate the literary reputation of his family" (*lit.*, 'he will fully carry on the fragrance of the books'); to which his father rejoins, "The reputation of our family is not great (*lit.*, 'hills and fields' happiness is thin'); high expectations are not to be entertained of him; if he can only gain a livelihood it will be enough." After a few such compliments the boys say *shao pei*, 'slightly waiting on you,' *i.e.*, pray excuse us, and retire. Girls are seldom brought in, and young ladies never.

The periphrases employed to denote persons and thus avoid speaking their names in a measure indicate the estimation in which they are held. For instance, "Does the honorable great man enjoy happiness?" means "Is your father well?" "Distinguished and aged one what honorable age?" is the mode of asking how old he is; for among the Chinese, as it seems to have been among the Egyptians, it is polite to ask the names and ages of all ranks and sexes. "The old man of the house," "excellent honorable one," and "venerable great prince," are terms used by a visitor to designate the father of his host. A child terms his father "family's majesty," "old man of the family," "prince of the family," or "venerable father." When dead a father is called "former prince," and a mother "venerable great one in repose;" and there are particular characters to distinguish deceased parents from living. The request, "Make my respects to your mother"—for no Chinese gentleman ever asks to *see* the ladies—is literally, "Excellent-longevity hall place in my behalf wish repose," the first two words denoting she who remains there. Care should be taken not to use the same expressions when speaking of the relatives of the guest and one's own; thus, in asking, "How many worthy young gentlemen [sons] have you?" the host replies, "I am unfortunate in having had but one boy," literally, "My fate is niggardly; I have only one little bug." This runs through their whole Chesterfieldian code. A man calls his wife *tsien nui*, *i.e.*, 'the mean one of the inner apartments,' or 'the foolish one of the family;' while another speaking of her calls her "the honorable lady," "worthy lady," "your favored one," etc.

Something of this is found in all oriental languages; to become familiar with the right application of these terms in Chinese, as elsewhere in the east, is no easy lesson for a foreigner. In their salutations of ceremony they do not, however, quite equal the Arabs, with their kissing, bowing, touching foreheads, stroking beards, and repeated motions of obeisance. The Chinese seldom embrace or touch each other, except on unusual occasions of joy or among family friends; in fact, they have hardly a common word for a kiss. When the visitor rises to depart he remarks, "Another day I will come to receive your instructions;" to which his friend replies, "You do me too much honor; I rather ought to wait on you to-morrow." The common form of salutation among equals is for each to clasp his own hands before his breast and make a slight bow, saying, *Tsing! Tsing!* *i.e.*, 'Hail! Hail!' This is repeated by both at the same time, on meeting as well as separating.[1] The formalities of leave-taking correspond to those of receiving, but if the parties are equal, or nearly so, the host sees his friend quite to the door and into his sedan.

Officers avoid meeting each other, especially in public, except when etiquette requires them. An officer of low rank is obliged to stop his chair or horse, and on his feet to salute his superior, who receives and returns the civility without moving. Those of equal grades leave their places and go through a mock struggle of deference to get each first to return to it. The common people never presume to salute an officer in the streets, nor even to look at him very carefully. In his presence, they speak to him on their knees, but an old man, or one of consideration, is usually requested to rise when speaking, and even criminals with gray hairs are treated with respect. Officers do not allow their inferiors to sit in their presence, and have always been unwilling to concede this to foreigners; those of the lowest rank consider themselves far above the best of such visitors, but this affectation of rank is already passing away. The converse, of not paying them proper respect, is more common among a certain class of foreigners.

Children are early taught the forms of politeness toward all ranks. The duties owed by younger to elder brothers are peculiar, the firstborn having a sort of birthright in the ancestral worship, in the division of property, and in the direction of the family after the father's decease. The degree of formality in the domestic circle inculcated in the ancient *Book of Rites* is never observed to its full extent, and would perhaps chill the affection which should exist among its members, did not habit render it easy and proper; and the extent to which it is actually carried depends a good deal upon the education of the family. In forwarding presents it is customary to send a list with the note, and if the person deems it proper to decline some of them, he marks on the list those he takes and returns the rest; a douceur is always expected by the bearer, and needy fellows some-

---

[1] *Chinese Chrestomathy*, Chap. V., Sec. 12, p. 182. This phrase is the origin of the word *chinchin*, so often heard among the Chinese.

times pretend to have been sent with some insignificant present from a grandee in hopes of receiving more than its equivalent as a cumshaw from the person thus honored. De Guignes mentioned one donor who waited until the list came back, and then sent out and purchased the articles which had been marked and sent them to his friend.

Travellers have so often described the Chinese formal dinners, that they have almost become one of their national traits in the view of foreigners; so many of these banquets, however, were given by or in the name of the sovereign, that they are hardly a fair criterion of usual private feasts. The Chinese are both a social and a sensual people, and the pleasures of the table form a principal item in the list of their enjoyments; nor are the higher delights of mental recreation altogether wanting, though this part of the entertainment is according to their taste and not ours. Private meals and public feasts among the higher classes are both dull and long to us, because ladies do not participate; but perhaps we judge more what our own tables would be without their cheerful presence, while in China each sex is of the opinion that the meal is more enjoyable without interference from the other.

An invitation to dinner is written on a slip of red paper like a visiting-card, and sent some days before. It reads, "On the — day a trifling entertainment will await the light of your countenance. Tsau San-woi's compliments." Another card is sent on the day itself, stating the hour of dinner, or a servant comes to call the guests. The host, dressed in his cap and robes, awaits their arrival, and after they are all assembled, requests them to follow his example and lay aside their dresses of ceremony. The usual way of arranging guests is by twos on each side of small uncovered tables, placed in lines; an arrangement as convenient for serving the numerous courses which compose the feast, and removing the dishes, as was the Roman fashion of reclining around a hollow table; it also allows a fair view of the musical or theatrical performances. On some occasions, in the sunny south, however, a single long or round table is laid out in a tasteful manner, having pyramids of cakes alternating with piles of fruits and dishes of preserves, all covered more or less with flowers, while the table itself is partly hidden from view by nosegays and leaves. If the party be large, ten minutes or more are consumed by the host and guests going through a tedious repetition of requests and refusals to take the highest seats, for not a man will sit down until he sees the host occupying his chair.

On commencing, the host, standing up, salutes his guests, in a cup, apologizing for the frugal board before them, his only desire being to show his respects to them. At a certain period in the entertainment, they reply by simultaneously rising and drinking his health. The Western custom of giving a sentiment is not known; and politeness requires a person when drinking healths to turn the bottom of the tiny wine-cup upward to show that it is drained. Glass dishes are gradually becoming cheap and common among the middle class, but the table furniture still mainly consists of porcelain cups, bowls, and saucers of various sizes and quality, porcelain spoons shaped like a child's pap-boat, and two smooth sticks made of bamboo, ivory, or wood, of the size of quills, well known as the *chop-sticks*, from the native name *kwai tsz'*, *i.e.*, 'nimble lads.' Grasping these implements on each side of the forefinger, the eater pinches up from the dishes meat, fish, or vegetables, already cut into mouthfuls, and conveys one to his mouth. The bowl of rice or millet is brought to the lips, and the contents shovelled into the mouth in an expeditious manner, quite suitable to the name of the tools employed. Less convenient than forks, chopsticks are a great improvement on fingers, as every one will acknowledge who has seen the Hindus throw the balls of curried rice into their mouths.

The succession of dishes is not uniform; soups, meats, stews, fruits, and preserves are introduced somewhat at the discretion of the major-domo, but the end is announced by a bowl of plain rice and a cup of tea. The fruit is often brought in after a recess, during which the guests rise and refresh themselves by walking and chatting, for three or four hours are not unfrequently required even to taste all the dishes. It is not deemed impolite for a guest to express his satisfaction with the good fare before him, and exhibit evidences of having stuffed himself to repletion; nor is it a breach of manners to retire before the dinner is ended. The guests relieve its tedium by playing the game of *chai mei*, or morra (the *micare digitis* of the old Romans), which consists in showing the fingers to each other across the table, and mentioning a number at the same moment; as, if one opens out two fingers and mentions the number four, the other instantly shows six fingers, and repeats that number. If he mistake in giving the complement of ten, he pays a forfeit by drinking a cup. This convivial game is common among all ranks, and the boisterous merriment of workmen or friends at their meals is frequently heard as one passes through the streets in the afternoon.[1] The Chinese generally have but two meals a day, breakfast at nine and dinner at four, or thereabouts.

The Chinese are comparatively a temperate people. This is owing principally to the universal use of tea, but also to taking their arrack very warm and at their meals, rather than to any notions of sobriety or dislike of spirits. A little of it flushes their faces, mounts into their heads, and induces them when flustered to remain in the house to conceal the suffusion, although they may not be really drunk. This liquor is known as toddy, arrack, saki, tsiu, and other names in Eastern Asia, and is distilled from the yeasty liquor in which boiled rice has fermented under pressure many days. Only one distillation is made for common liquor, but when more strength is wanted, it is distilled two or three times, and it is this strong spirit alone which is rightly called *samshu*, a word meaning 'thrice fired.' Chinese moralists have always inveighed against the use of spirits, and the name of Í-tih, the reputed inventor of the deleterious drink, more than two thousand years before Christ, has been handed down with opprobrium, as he was himself banished by the great Yu for his discovery.

The *Shu King* contains a discourse by the Duke of Chau on the abuse of spirits. His speech to his brother Fung, B.C. 1120, is the oldest temperance address on record, even earlier than the words of Solomon in the Proverbs. "When your reverend

---

[1] Compare the *China Review*, Vol. IV., p. 400.

father, King Wăn, founded our kingdom in the western region, he delivered announcements and cautions to the princes of the various states, their officers, assistants, and managers of affairs, morning and evening, saying, 'For sacrifices spirits should be employed. When Heaven was sending down its [favoring] commands and laying the foundations of our people's sway, spirits were used only in the great sacrifices. [But] when Heaven has sent down its terrors, and our people have thereby been greatly disorganized, and lost their [sense of] virtue, this too can be ascribed to nothing else than their unlimited use of spirits; yea, further, the ruin of the feudal states, small and great, may be traced to this one sin, the free use of spirits.' King Wăn admonished and instructed the young and those in office managing public affairs, that they should not habitually drink spirits. In all the states he enjoined that their use be confined to times of sacrifices; and even then with such limitations that virtue should prevent drunkenness."[1]

The general and local festivals of the Chinese are numerous, among which the first three days of the year, one or two about the middle of April to worship at the tombs, the two solstices, and the festival of dragon-boats, are common days of relaxation and merry-making, only on the first, however, are the shops shut and business suspended. Some persons have expressed their surprise that the unceasing round of toil which the Chinese laborer pursues has not rendered him more degraded. It is usually said that a weekly rest is necessary for the continuance of the powers of body and mind in man in their full activity, and that decrepitude and insanity would oftener result were it not for this relaxation. The arguments in favor of this observation seem to be deduced from undoubted facts in countries where the obligations of the Sabbath are acknowledged, though where the vast majority cease from business and labor, it is not easy for a few to work all the time even if they wish, owing to the various ways in which their occupations are involved with those of others; yet, in China, people who appa-

[1] *Chinese Repository*, Vol. XV., p. 433. *Book of Records*, Part V., Book X., Legge's translation; also Medhurst's and Gaubil's translations.

rently tax themselves uninterruptedly to the utmost stretch of body and mind, live in health to old age. A few facts of this sort incline one to suppose that the Sabbath was designed by its Lord as a day of rest for man from a constant routine of relaxation and mental and physical labor, in order that he might have leisure for attending to the paramount duties of religion, and not alone as a day of relaxation and rest, without which they could not live out all their days. Nothing like a seventh day of rest, or religious respect to that interval of time, is known among the Chinese, but they do not, as a people, exercise their minds to the intensity, or upon the high subjects common among Western nations, and this perhaps is one reason why their yearly toil produces no disastrous effects. The countless blessings which flow from an observance of the fourth commandment can be better appreciated by witnessing the wearied condition of the society where it is not acknowledged, and whoever sees such a society can hardly fail to wish for its introduction.

Converts to Christianity in China, who are instructed in its strict observance, soon learn to prize it as a high privilege; and its general neglect among the native Roman Catholics has removed the only apparent difference between them and the pagans. The former prime minister of China once remarked that among the few really valuable things which foreigners had brought to China, the rest of the Sabbath day was one of the most desirable; he often longed for a quiet day.[1]

The return of the year is an occasion of unbounded festivity and hilarity, as if the whole population threw off the old year with a shout, and clothed themselves in the new with their change of garments. The evidences of the approach of this chief festival appear some weeks previous. The principal streets are lined with tables, upon which articles of dress, furniture, and fancy are disposed for sale in the most attractive manner. Necessity compels many to dispose of certain of their treasures or superfluous things at this season, and sometimes exceedingly curious bits of bric-a-brac, long laid up in families, can be pro-

[1] Nevius, *China and the Chinese*, pp. 399–408.

cured at a cheap rate. It is customary for superiors to give their dependents and employees a present, and for shopmen to send an acknowledgment of favors to their customers; one of the most common gifts among the lower classes is a pair of new shoes. Among the tables spread in the streets are many provided with pencils and red paper of various sizes, on which persons write sentences appropriate to the season in various styles, to be pasted upon the doorposts and lintels of dwellings and shops,[1] or suspended from their walls. The shops also put on a most brilliant appearance, arrayed in these papers interspersed among the *kin hwa*, or 'golden flowers,' which are sprigs of artificial leaves and flowers made in the southern cities of brass tinsel and fastened upon wires; the latter are designed for an annual offering in temples, or to place before the household tablet. Small strips of red and gilt paper, some bearing the word *fuh*, or 'happiness,' large and small vermilion candles, gaily painted, and other things used in idolatry, are likewise sold in great quantities, and with the increased throng impart an unusually lively appearance to the streets. Another evident sign of the approaching change is the use of water upon the doors, shutters, and other woodwork of houses and shops, washing chairs, utensils, clothes, etc., as if cleanliness had not a little to do with joy, and a well-washed person and tenement were indispensable to the proper celebration of the festival. Throughout the southern rivers all small craft, tankia-boats, and lighters are beached and turned inside out for a scrubbing.

A still more praiseworthy custom attending this season is that of settling accounts and paying debts; shopkeepers are kept busy waiting upon their customers, and creditors urge their debtors to arrange these important matters. No debt is allowed to overpass new year without a settlement or satisfactory arrangement, if it can be avoided; and those whose liabilities altogether exceed their means are generally at this season obliged to wind up their concerns and give all their available property into the hands of their creditors. The consequences of this general pay-

---

[1] A like custom existed among the Hebrews, now continued in the modern *mezuzaw*. Deut. vi. 9. Jahn's *Archæology*, p. 38.

day are a high rate of money, great resort to the pawnbrokers, and a general fall in the price of most kinds of produce and commodities. Many good results flow from the practice, and the conscious sense of the difficulty and expense of resorting to legal proceedings to recover debts induces all to observe and maintain it, so that the dishonest, the unsuccessful, and the wild speculator may be sifted out from amongst the honest traders.

De Guignes mentions one expedient to oblige a man to pay his debts at this season, which is to carry off the door of his shop or house, for then his premises and person will be exposed to the entrance and anger of all hungry and malicious demons prowling around the streets, and happiness no more revisit his abode; to avoid this he is fain to arrange his accounts. It is a common practice among devout persons to settle with the gods, and during a few days before the new year, the temples are unusually thronged by devotees, both male and female, rich and poor. Some persons fast and engage the priests to intercede for them that their sins may be pardoned, while they prostrate themselves before the images amidst the din of gongs, drums, and bells, and thus clear off the old score. On new year's eve the streets are full of people hurrying to and fro to conclude the many matters which press upon them. At Canton, some are busy pasting the five slips upon their lintels, signifying their desire that the five blessings which constitute the sum of all human felicity (namely, longevity, riches, health, love of virtue, and a natural death) may be their favored portion. Such sentences as "May the five blessings visit this door," "May heaven send down happiness," "May rich customers ever enter this door," are placed above them; and the doorposts are adorned with others on plain or gold sprinkled red paper, making the entrance quite picturesque. In the hall are suspended scrolls more or less costly, containing antithetical sentences carefully chosen. A literary man would have, for instance, a distich like the following:

May I be so learned as to secrete in my mind three myriads of volumes:
May I know the affairs of the world for six thousand years.

A shopkeeper adorns his door with those relating to trade:

May profits be like the morning sun rising on the clouds.
May wealth increase like the morning tide which brings the rain.
Manage your occupation according to truth and loyalty.
Hold on to benevolence and rectitude in all your trading.

The influence of these mottoes, and countless others like them which are constantly seen in the streets, shops, and dwellings throughout the land, is inestimable. Generally it is for good, and as a large proportion are in the form of petition or wish, they show the moral feeling of the people.

Boat-people in Kwangtung and Fuhkien provinces are peculiarly liberal of their paper prayers, pasting them on every board and oar in the boat, and suspending them from the stern in scores, making the vessel flutter with gaiety. Farmers stick theirs upon barns, trees, wattles, baskets, and implements, as if nothing was too insignificant to receive a blessing. The house is arranged in the most orderly and cleanly manner, and purified with religious ceremonies and lustrations, firing of crackers, etc., and as the necessary preparations occupy a considerable portion of the night, the streets are not quiet till dawn. In addition to the bustle arising from business and religious observances, which marks this passage of time, the constant explosion of firecrackers, and the clamor of gongs, make it still more noisy. Strings of these crackling fireworks are burned at the doorposts, before the outgoing and incoming of the year, designed to expel and deter evil spirits from the house. The consumption is so great as to cover the streets with the fragments, and farmers come the week after into Canton city and sweep up hundreds of bushels for manure.

The first day of the year is also regarded as the birthday of the entire population, for the practice among the Hebrews of dating the age from the beginning of the year, prevails also in China; so that a child born only a week before new year, is considered as entering its second year on the first day of the first month. This does not, however, entirely supersede the observance of the real anniversary, and parents frequently make a solemnity of their son's birthday. A missionary thus describes the celebration of a son's sixth birthday at Ningpo. "The little fellow was dressed in his best clothes, and his father had brought gilt paper, printed prayers, and a large number of bowls of meats, rice, vegetables, spirits, nuts, etc., as an offering to be spread out before the idols. The ceremonies were performed in the apartment of the *Tao Mu*, or 'Bushel Mother,' who has special charge of infants before and after birth. The old abbot was dressed in a scarlet robe, with a gilt image of a serpent fastened in his hair; one of the monks wore a purple, another a gray robe. A multitude of prayers, seemingly a round of repetitions, were read by the abbot, occasionally chanting a little, when the attendants joined in the chorus, and a deafening clamor of bells, cymbals, and wooden blocks, added force to their cry; genuflexions and prostrations were repeatedly made. One part of the ceremony was to pass a live cock through a barrel, which the assistants performed many times, shouting some strange words at each repetition; this act symbolized the dangers through which the child was to pass in his future life, and the priests had prayed that he might as safely come out of them all, as the cock had passed through the barrel. In conclusion, some of the prayers were burned and a libation poured out, and a grand symphony of bell, gong, drum, and block, closed the scene."[1]

A great diversity of local usages are observed at this period in different parts of the country. In Amoy, the custom of "surrounding the furnace" is generally practised. The members of the family sit down to a substantial supper on new year's eve, with a pan of charcoal under the table, as a supposed preservative against fires. After the supper is ended, the wooden lamp-stands are brought out and spread upon the pavement with a heap of gold and silver paper, and set on fire after all demons have been warned off by a volley of fire-crackers. The embers are then divided into twelve heaps, and their manner of going out carefully watched as a prognostic of the kind of weather to be expected the ensuing year. Many persons wash their bodies in warm water, made aromatic by the infusion of leaves, as a

---

[1] *Presbyterian Missionary Chronicle*, 1846.

security against disease; this ceremony, and ornamenting the ancestral shrine, and garnishing the whole house with inscriptions, pictures, flowers, and fruit, in the gayest manner the means of the family will allow, occupy most of the night.

The stillness of the streets and the gay inscriptions on the closed shops on new year's morning present a wonderful contrast to the usual bustle and crowd, resembling the Christian Sabbath. The red papers of the doors are here and there interspersed with the blue ones, announcing that during the past year death has come among the inmates of the house; a silent but expressive intimation to passers that some who saw the last new year have passed away. In certain places, white, yellow, and carnation colored papers are employed, as well as blue, to distinguish the degree of the deceased kindred. Etiquette requires that those who mourn remain at home at this period. By noontide the streets begin to be filled with well-dressed persons, hastening in sedans or afoot to make their calls; those who cannot afford to buy a new suit hire one for this purpose, so that a man hardly knows his own domestics in their finery and robes. The meeting of friends in the streets, both bound on the same errand, is attended with particular demonstrations of respect, each politely struggling who shall be most affectedly humble. On this day parents receive the prostrations of their children, teachers expect the salutations of their pupils, magistrates look for the calls of their inferiors, and ancestors of every generation, and gods of various powers are presented with the offerings of devotees in the family hall or public temple. Much of the visiting is done by cards, on which is stamped an emblematic device representing the three happy wishes—of children, rank, and longevity; a common card suffices for distant acquaintances and customers. It might be a subject of speculation whether the custom of visiting and renewing one's acquaintances on new year's day, so generally practised among the Dutch and in America, was not originally imitated from the Chinese; but as in many other things, so in this, the westerns have improved upon the easterns, in calling upon the ladies. Persons, as they meet, salute each other with

Kung-hi! Kung-hi! 'I respectfully wish you joy!'—or *Sin-hi! Sin-hi!* 'May the new joy be yours,' either of which, from its use at this season, is quite like the *Happy New Year!* of Englishmen.

Toward evening, the merry sounds proceeding from the closed doors announce that the sacrifice provided for presentation before the shrines of departed parents is cheering the worshippers; while the great numbers who resort to gambling-shops show full well that the routine of ceremony soon becomes tiresome, and a more exciting stimulus is needed. The extent to which play is now carried is almost indescribable. Jugglers, mountebanks, and actors also endeavor to collect a few coppers by amusing the crowds. Generally speaking, however, the three days devoted to this festival pass by without turmoil, and business and work then gradually resume their usual course for another twelvemonth.

The festival of the dragon-boats, on the fifth day of the fifth month, presents a very different scene wherever there is a serviceable stream for its celebration. At Canton, long, narrow boats, holding sixty or more rowers, race up and down the river in pairs with huge clamor, as if searching for some one who had been drowned. This festival was instituted in memory of the statesman Küh Yuen, about 450 B.C., who drowned himself in the river Mih-lo, an affluent of Tungting Lake, after having been falsely accused by one of the petty princes of the state. The people, who loved the unfortunate courtier for his fidelity and virtues, sent out boats in search of the body, but to no purpose. They then made a peculiar sort of rice-cake called *tsung*, and setting out across the river in boats with flags and gongs, each strove to be first on the spot of the tragedy and sacrifice to the spirit of Küh Yuen. This mode of commemorating the event has been since continued as an annual holiday. The bow of the boat is ornamented or carved into the head of a dragon, and men beating gongs and drums, and waving flags, inspirit the rowers to renewed exertions. The exhilarating exercise of racing leads the people to prolong the festival two or three days, and generally with commendable good humor, but their eagerness to beat often breaks the boats, or leads them into so much danger that the magistrates sometimes forbid the races in order to save the people from drowning.[1]

The first full moon of the year is the feast of lanterns, a childish and dull festival compared with the two preceding. Its origin is not certainly known, but it was observed as early as A.D. 700. Its celebration consists in suspending lanterns of different forms and materials before each door, and illuminating those in the hall, but their united brilliancy is dimness itself compared with the light of the moon. At Peking, an exhibition of transparencies and pictures in the Board of War on this evening attracts great crowds of both sexes if the weather be good. Magaillans describes a firework he saw, which was an arbor covered with a vine, the woodwork of which seemed to burn, while the trunk, leaves, and clusters of the plant gradually consumed, yet so that the redness of the grapes, the greenness of the leaves, and natural brown of the stem were all maintained until the whole was burned. The feast of lanterns coming so soon after new year, and being somewhat expensive, is not so enthusiastically observed in the southern cities. At the capital this leisure time, when public offices are closed, is availed of by the jewellers, bric-a-brac dealers, and others to hold a fair in the courts of a temple in the Wai Ching, where they exhibit as beautiful a collection of carvings in stone and gems, bronzes, toys, etc., as is to be seen anywhere in Asia. The respect with which the crowds of women and children are treated on these occasions reflects much credit on the people.

In the manufacture of lanterns the Chinese surely excel all other people; the variety of their forms, their elegant carving, gilding, and coloring, and the laborious ingenuity and taste displayed in their construction, render them among the prettiest ornaments of their dwellings. They are made of paper, silk, cloth, glass, horn, basket-work, and bamboo, exhibiting an infinite variety of shapes and decorations, varying in size from a small hand-light, costing two or three cents, up to a magnificent chandelier, or a complicated lantern fifteen feet in diameter, contain-

[1] Compare Morrison's Dictionary under *Tsung;* Doolittle, *Social Life*, Vol. II., pp. 55–60; *Notes and Queries on China and Japan*, Vol. II., p. 157.

ing several lamps within it, and worth three or four hundred dollars. The uses to which they are applied are not less various than the pains and skill bestowed upon their construction are remarkable. One curious kind is called the *tsao-ma-tăng*, or 'horse-racing lantern,' which consists of one, two, or more wire frames, one within the other, and arranged on the same principle as the smoke-jack, by which the current of air caused by the flame sets them revolving. The wire framework is covered with paper figures of men and animals placed in the midst of appropriate scenery, and represented in various attitudes; or, as Magaillans describes them, "You shall see horses run, draw chariots and till the earth; vessels sailing, kings and princes go in and out with large trains, and great numbers of people, both afoot and a horseback, armies marching, comedies, dances, and a thousand other divertissements and motions represented."

One of the prettiest shows of lanterns is seen in a festival observed in the spring or autumn by fisherman on the southern coasts to propitiate the gods of the waters. An indispensable part of the procession is a dragon fifty feet or more long, made of light bamboo frames of the size and shape of a barrel, connected and covered with strips of colored cotton or silk; the extremities represent the gaping head and frisking tail. This monster symbolizes the ruler of the watery deep, and is carried through the streets by men holding the head and each joint upon poles, to which are suspended lanterns; as they follow each other their steps give the body a wriggling, waving motion. Huge models of fish, similarly lighted, precede the dragon, while music and fireworks—the never-failing warning to lurking demons to keep out of the way—accompany the procession, which presents a very brilliant sight as it winds in its course through the dark streets. These sports and processions give idolatry its hold upon a people; and although none of them are required or patronized by government in China as in other heathen countries, most of the scenes and games which please the people are recommended by connecting with them the observances or hopes of religion and the merrymaking of the festive board.

In the middle of the sixth moon lanterns are hung from the

top of a pole placed on the highest part of the house. A single small lantern is deemed sufficient, but if the night be calm, a greater display is made by some householders, and especially in boats, by exhibiting colored glass lamps arranged in various ways. The illumination of a city like Canton when seen from a high spot is made still more brilliant by the moving boats on the river. On one of these festivals at Canton, an almost total eclipse of the moon called out the entire population, each one carrying something with which to make a noise, kettles, pans, sticks, drums, gongs, guns, crackers, and what not to frighten away the dragon of the sky from his hideous feast. The advancing shadow gradually caused the myriads of lanterns to show more and more distinctly and started a still increasing clamor, till the darkness and the noise were both at their climax; silence gradually resumed its sway as the moon recovered her fulness.

The Chinese are fond of processions, and if marriages and funerals be included, have them more frequently than any other people. Livery establishments are opened in every city and town where processions are arranged and supplied with everything necessary for bridal and funeral occasions as well as religious festivals. Not only are sedans, bands of music, biers, framed and gilded stands for carrying idols, shrines, and sacrificial feasts, red boxes for holding the bride's trousseau, etc., supplied, but also banners, tables, stands, curiosities, and uniforms in great variety. The men and boys required to carry them and perform the various parts of the ceremony are hired, a uniform hiding their ragged garments and dirty limbs. Guilds often go to a heavy expense in getting up a procession in honor of their patron saint, whose image is carried through the streets attended by the members of the corporation dressed in holiday robes and boots. The variety and participators of these shows are exceedingly curious and characteristic of the people's taste. Here are seen splendid silken banners worked with rich embroidery, alternating with young girls bedizened with paint and flowers, and perched on high seats under an artificial tree or apparently almost in the air, resting upon frames on men's shoulders; bands of music; sacrificial meats and fruits adorned with flowers; shrines, images, and curious rarities laid out upon red pavilions;

boys gaily dressed in official robes and riding upon ponies, or harnessed up in a covered framework to represent horses, all so contrived and painted that the spectator can hardly believe they are not riding Lilliputian ponies no bigger than dogs. A child standing in a car and carrying a branch on its shoulder, on one twig of which stands another child on one foot or a girl holding a plate of cakes in her hand, on the top of which stands another miss on tiptoe, the whole borne by coolies, sometimes add to the diversion of the spectacle and illustrate the mechanical skill of the exhibitors. Small companies dressed in a great variety of military uniforms, carrying spears, shields, halberds, etc., now and then volunteer for the occasion, and give it a more martial appearance. The carpenters at Canton are famous for their splendid processions in honor of their hero, Lu Pan, in which also other craftsmen join; for this demi-god corresponds to the Tubal-cain of Chinese legends, and is now regarded as the patron of all workmen, though he flourished no longer ago than the time of Confucius. Besides these festivities and processions, there are several more strictly religious, such as the annual mass of the Buddhists, the supplicatory sacrifice of farmers for a good crop, and others of more or less importance, which add to the number of days of recreation.

Theatrical representations constitute a common amusement, and are generally connected with the religious celebration of the festival of the god before whose temple they are exhibited. They are got up by the priests, who send their neophytes around with a subscription paper, and then engage as large and skilful a band of performers as the funds will allow. There are few permanent buildings erected for theatres, for the Thespian band still retains its original strolling character, and stands ready to pack up its trappings at the first call. The erection of sheds for playing constitutes a separate branch of the carpenter's trade; one large enough to accommodate two thousand persons can be put up in the southern cities in a day, and almost the only part of the materials which is wasted is the rattan which binds the posts and mats together. One large shed contains the stage, and three smaller ones before it enclose an area, and are furnished with rude seats for the paying spectators. The subscribers' bounty is acknowledged by pasting red sheets containing their names and amounts upon the walls of the temple. The purlieus are let as stands for the sale of refreshments, for gambling tables, or for worse purposes, and by all these means the priests generally contrive to make gain of their devotion.[1]

Parties of actors and acrobats can be hired cheaply, and their performances form part of the festivities of rich families in their houses to entertain the women and relatives who cannot go abroad to see them. They are constituted into separate corporations or guilds, and each takes a distinguishing name, as the 'Happy and Blessed company,' the 'Glorious Appearing company,' etc.

The performances usually extend through three entire days, with brief recesses for sleeping and eating, and in villages where they are comparatively rare, the people act as if they were bewitched, neglecting everything to attend them. The female parts are performed by lads, who not only paint and dress like women, but even squeeze their toes into the "golden lilies," and imitate, upon the stage, a mincing, wriggling gait. These fellows personate the voice, tones, and motions of the sex with wonderful exactness, taking every opportunity, indeed, that the play will allow to relieve their feet by sitting when on the boards, or retiring into the green-room when out of the acts. The acting is chiefly pantomine, and its fidelity shows the excellent training of the players. This development of their imitative faculties is probably still more encouraged by the difficulty the audience find to understand what is said; for owing to the differences in the dialects, the open construction of the theatre, the high falsetto or recitative key in which many of the parts are spoken, and the din of the orchestra intervening between every few sentences, not one quarter of the people hear or understand a word.

The scenery is very simple, consisting merely of rudely painted mats arranged on the back and sides of the stage, a few tables, chairs, or beds, which successively serve for many

---

[1] Gray's *China* (Vol. II., p. 273) contains a cut of a mat theatre from a native drawing. See also Doolittle, *Social Life*, Vol. II., pp. 292–299.

uses, and are brought in and out from the robing-room. The orchestra sits on the side of the stage, and not only fill up the intervals with their interludes, but strike a crashing noise by way of emphasis, or to add energy to the rush of opposing warriors. No falling curtain divides the acts or scenes, and the play is carried to its conclusion without intermission. The dresses are made of gorgeous silks, and present the best specimens of ancient Chinese costume of former dynasties now to be seen. The imperfections of the scenery require much to be suggested by the spectator's imagination, though the actors themselves supply the defect in a measure by each man stating what part he performs, and what the person he represents has been doing while absent. If a courier is to be sent to a distant city, away he strides across the boards, or perhaps gets a whip and cocks up his leg as if mounting a horse, and on reaching the end of the stage cries out that he has arrived, and there delivers his message. Passing a bridge or crossing a river are indicated by stepping up and then down, or by the rolling motion of a boat. If a city is to be impersonated, two or three men lie down upon each other, when warriors rush on them furiously, overthrow the wall which they formed, and take the place by assault. Ghosts or supernatural beings are introduced through a wide trap-door in the stage, and, if he thinks it necessary, the impersonator cries out from underneath that he is ready, or for assistance to help him up through the hole.

Mr. Lay describes a play he saw, in which a medley of celestial and terrestrial personages were introduced. "The first scene was intended to represent the happiness and splendor of beings who inhabit the upper regions, with the sun and moon and the elements curiously personified playing around them. The man who personated the sun held a round image of the sun's disk, while the female who acted the part of the moon had a crescent in her hand. The actors took care to move so as to mimic the conjunction and opposition of these heavenly bodies as they revolve round in their apparent orbs. The Thunderer wielded an axe, and leaped and dashed about in a variety of extraordinary somersaults. After a few turns the monarch, who had been so highly honored as to find a place, through the partiality of a mountain nymph, in the abodes of the happy, begins to feel that no height of good fortune can secure a mortal against the common calamities of this frail life. A wicked courtier disguises himself in a tiger's skin, and in this garb imitates the animal itself. He rushes into the retired apartments of the ladies, frightens them out of their wits, and throws the heir-apparent into a moat. The sisters hurry into the royal presence, and casting themselves on the ground divulge the sad intelligence that a tiger has borne off the young prince, who it appears was the son of the mountain nymph aforesaid. The loss the bereaved monarch takes so much to heart, that he renounces the world and deliberates about the nomination of a successor. By the influence of a crafty woman he selects a young man who has just sense enough to know that he is a fool. The settlement of the crown is scarcely finished when the unhappy king dies, and the blockhead is presently invested with the crown, but instead of excelling in his new preferment the lout bemoans his lot in the most awkward strains of lamentation, and cries, 'O dear! what shall I do?' with such piteous action, and yet withal so truly ludicrous, that the spectator is at a loss to know whether to laugh or to weep. The courtier who had taken off the heir and broken the father's heart finds the new king an easy tool for prosecuting his traitorous purposes, and the state is plunged into the depths of civil discord at home and dangerous wars abroad.

"In the sequel a scene occurred in which the reconciliation of this court and some foreign prince depends upon the surrender of a certain obnoxious person. The son-in-law of the victim is charged with the letter containing this proposal, and returns to his house and disguises himself for the sake of concealment. When he reaches the court of the foreign prince he discovers that he has dropped the letter in changing his clothes, and narrowly escapes being taken for a spy without his credentials. He hurries back, calls for his garments, and shakes them one by one in an agony of self-reproach, but no letter appears. He sits down, throwing himself with great violence upon the chair, with a countenance inexpressibly full of torture and despair: reality could have added nothing to the imitation. But while every eye was riveted upon him, he called the servant-maid and inquired if she knew anything about the letter; she replied she overheard her mistress reading a letter whose contents were so and so. The mistress had taken her seat at a distance from him and was nursing her baby; and the instant he ascertained the letter was in her possession, he looked toward her with such a smile upon his cheek, and with a flood of light in his eye, that the whole assembly heaved a loud sigh of admiration; for the Chinese do not applaud by clapping and stamping, but express their feelings by an ejaculation that is between a sigh and a groan. The aim of the husband was to wheedle his wife out of the letter, and this smile and look of affection were merely the prelude; for he takes his chair, places it beside her, lays one hand softly on her shoulder, and fondles the child with the other in a style so exquisitely natural and so completely English, that in this dramatic picture it was seen that nature fashioneth men's hearts alike. His addresses were, however, ineffectual, and her father's life was not sacrificed."[1]

The morals of the Chinese stage, so far as the sentiments of the pieces are concerned, are better than the acting, which sometimes panders to depraved tastes, but no indecent exposure, as of the persons of dancers, is ever seen in China. The audience stand in the area fronting the stage, or sit in the sheds around it; the women present are usually seated in the galleries. The police are at hand to maintain order, but the crowd, although in an irksome position, and sometimes exposed to a fierce sun, is remarkably peaceable. Accidents seldom occur on these occasions, but whenever the people are alarmed by a crash, or the stage takes fire, loss of life or limb generally ensues. A dreadful destruction took place at Canton in May, 1845, by the conflagration of a stage during the performances, by which more than two thousand lives were sacrificed; the survivors had occasion to remember that fifty persons had been killed many years before in the same place, and while a play was going on, by the falling of a wall.[2]

Active, manly plays are not popular in the south, and instead

---

[1] *Chinese as They Are*, p. 114. [2] *Chinese Repository*, Vol. XIV., p. 335.

of engaging in a ball-game or regatta, going to a bowling alley or fives' court, to exhibit their strength and skill, young men lift beams headed with heavy stones, like huge dumb-bells, to prove their muscle, or kick up their heels in a game of shuttlecock. The out-door amusements of gentlemen consist in flying kites, carrying birds on perches and throwing seeds high in the air for them to catch, sauntering through the fields, or lazily boating on the water. Pitching coppers, fighting crickets or quails, tossing up several balls at once, kicking large leaden balls against each other, snapping sticks, chucking stones, or guessing the number of seeds in an orange, are plays for lads.

Gambling is universal. Hucksters at the roadside are provided with a cup and saucer, and the clicking of their dice is heard at every corner. A boy with but two cash prefers to risk their loss on the throw of a die to simply buying a cake without trying the chance of getting it for nothing. Gaming-houses are opened by scores, their keepers paying a bribe to the local officers, who can hardly be expected to be very severe against what they were brought up in and daily practise; and women, in the privacy of their apartments, while away their time at cards and dominoes. Porters play by the wayside when waiting for employment, and hardly have the retinue of an officer seen their superiors enter the house, than they pull out their cards or dice and squat down to a game. The most common game of luck played at Canton is called *fan tan*, or 'quadrating cash.' The keeper of the table is provided with a pile of bright large cash, of which he takes a double handful, and lays them on the table, covering the pile with a bowl. The persons standing outside the rail guess the remainder there will be left after the pile has been divided by four, whether one, two, three, or nothing, the guess and stake of each person being first recorded by a clerk; the keeper then carefully picks out the coins four by four, all narrowly watching his movements. Cheating is almost impossible in this game, and twenty people can play at it as easily as two. Chinese cards are smaller and more numerous than our own; but the dominoes are the same.

Combats between crickets are oftenest seen in the south,

where the small field sort is common. Two well-chosen combatants are put into a basin and irritated with a straw until they rush upon each other with the utmost fury, chirruping as they make the onset, and the battle seldom ends without a tragical result in loss of life or limb. Quails are also trained to mortal combat; two are placed on a railed table, on which a handful of millet has been strewn, and as soon as one picks up a kernel the other flies at him with beak, claws, and wings, and the struggle is kept up till one retreats by hopping into the

Boys Gambling with Crickets.

hand of his disappointed owner. Hundreds of dollars are occasionally betted upon these cricket or quail fights, which, if not as sublime or exciting, are certainly less inhuman than the pugilistic fights and bull-baits of Christian countries, while both show the same brutal love of sport at the expense of life.

A favorite amusement is the flying of kites. They are made of paper and silk, in imitation of birds, butterflies, lizards, spectacles, fish, men, and other objects; but the skill shown in flying them is more remarkable than the ingenuity displayed in their construction. The ninth day of the ninth moon is a festival devoted to this amusement all over the land. Doolittle describes them as sometimes resembling a great bird, or a serpent thirty feet long; at other times the spectator sees a group of hawks hovering around a centre, all being suspended by one strong cord, and each hawk-kite controlled and moved by a separate line. On this day he estimates that as many as thirty thousand people assemble on the hills around Fuhchau to join

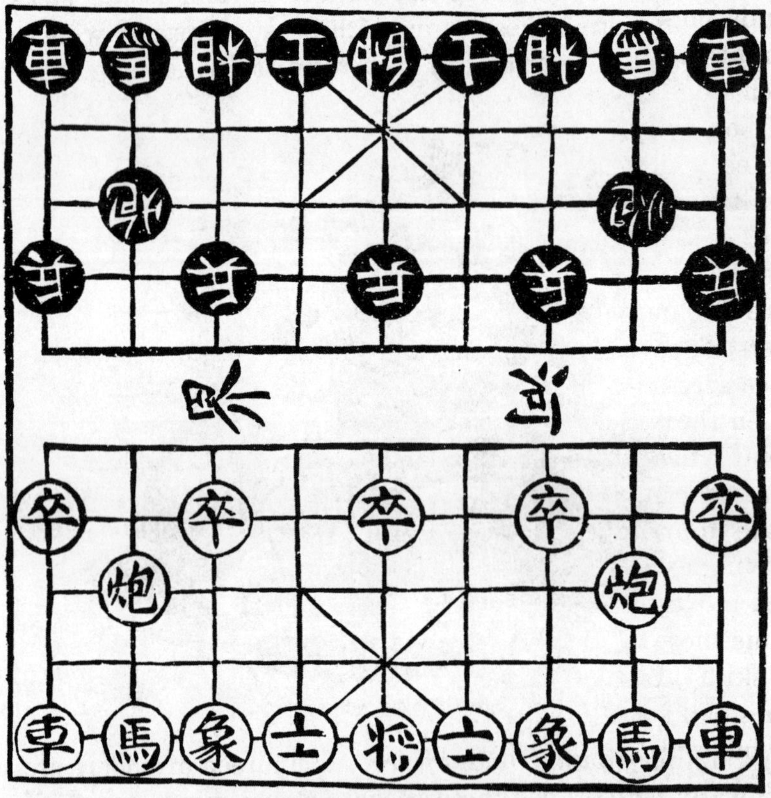

Chinese Chess-board.

in this amusement if the weather be propitious. Many of the kites are cut adrift under the belief that, as they float off, they carry away with them all impending disasters.

The Chinese game of chess is very ancient, for Wu Wang (B.C. 1120) is the reputed inventor, and its rules of playing are so unlike the Indian game as to suggest an independent origin, which is confirmed by the peculiar feature of the *kiai ho*, or river, running across the board. There are seventy-two squares, of which eight are run together to form the river, leaving thirty-two on each side; but as the men stand on the intersection of the lines, there are ninety positions for the sixteen pieces used by each player, or twenty-six more than in the European game. The pieces are arranged for playing as in the diagram above.

The pieces are like chequer-men in shape, each of the seven kinds on each side having its name cut on the top, and distinguished by its red or black colors. The four squares near each edge form the headquarters of the *tsiang*, or 'general,' out of which he and his two *sz'*, or 'secretaries,' cannot move. On each side of the headquarters are two elephants, two horses, and two chariots, whose powers are less than our bishop, knight, and castle, though similar; the chariot is the most powerful piece. In front of the horses stand two cannoniers, which capture like our knight but move like our castle. Five *pao*, soldiers or pawns, guard the river banks, but cannot return when once across it in pursuit of the enemy, and get no higher value when they reach the last row. Each piece is put down in the point where it captured its man, except the cannoniers; as the general cannot be taken, the object of each player is to checkmate him in his headquarters, therefore, by preventing his moving except into check. The want of a queen and the limited moves of the men restrict the combinations in the Chinese game more than in western chess, but it has its own elements of skill. Literary men and women play it much, and usually for small stakes. There is another game played less frequently but one of the most ancient in the Empire. It is called *wei-kí*, which may be rendered 'blockade chess,' and was common in the days of the sages, perhaps even earlier than chess. The board contains three hundred and twenty-four squares, eighteen each way, and the number of pieces is three hundred, though both the number of points and of pieces may be less than this size of the full game. The pieces are black and white and stand on the crossings of the lines, three hundred and sixty-one in number. The object of the opponents is to surround each other's men and take up the crossings they occupy, or neutralize their power over those near them.

Each player puts down a piece anywhere on the board, and continues to do so alternately, capturing his adversary's positions until all the crossings are occupied and the game is ended.[1]

If this sketch of the customs and amusements of the Chinese in their social intercourse and public entertainments is necessarily brief, it is perhaps enough to exhibit their character. Dr. Johnson has well remarked that no man is a hypocrite in his amusements. The absence of some of the violent and gladiatorial sports of other countries, and of the adjudication of doubtful questions by ordeals or duels; the general dislike of a resort to force, their inability to cope with enemies of vastly less resources and numbers, and the comparative disesteem of warlike achievements, all indicate the peaceful traits of Chinese character. Duels are unknown, assassinations are infrequent, betting on horse-races is still to begin, and running amuck à la Malay is unheard of. When two persons fall out upon a matter, after a vast variety of gesture and huge vociferation of opprobrium, they will blow off their wrath and separate almost without touching each other. Some contrarieties in their ideas and customs from those practised among ourselves have frequently been noticed by travellers, a few of which are grouped in the following sketch:

On asking the boatman in which direction the harbor lay, I was answered west-north, and the wind, he said, was west-south; he still further perplexed my ideas as to our course by getting out his compass and showing me that the needle pointed south. It was really a needle as to size, weight, and length, about an inch and a half long, the south end of it painted red, and all the time quivering on the pivot. His boat differed from our vessels, too, in many ways: the cooking was done in the stern and the passengers were all accommodated in the bow, while the sailors slept on deck and had their kits stowed in lockers amidships.

On landing, the first object that attracted my attention was a military officer wearing an embroidered petticoat, who had a string of beads around his neck and a fan in his hand. His insignia of rank was a peacock's feather pointing downward instead of a plume turning upward; he had a round knob or button on the apex of his sugar-loaf cap, instead of a star on his breast or epaulettes on his shoulders; and it was with some dismay that I saw him mount his horse on the right side. Several scabbards hung from his belt, which

[1] *Temple Bar*, Vol. XLIX., p. 45.

I naturally supposed must be dress swords or dirks; but on venturing near through the crowd I was undeceived by seeing a pair of chopsticks and a knife-handle sticking out of one, and soon his fan was folded up and put in the other. I therefore concluded that he was going to a dinner instead of a review. The natives around me shaved the hair from the front half of their heads and let it grow long behind: many of them did not shave their faces, and others employed their leisure in diligently pulling the straggling hairs down over their mouths. We arrange our toilets differently, thought I; but could easily see the happy device of chopsticks, which enabled these gentlemen to put their food into the mouth endwise under this natural fringe. A group of hungry fellows, around the stall of a travelling cook, further exhibited the utility of these *kwai-tsz'*, or 'nimble lads' (as I afterward learned chopsticks were called), for each had put his bowl of rice to his lips, and was shovelling in the contents till the mouth would hold no more. "We keep our bowls on the table," said I, "do our cooking in the house, and wait for customers to come there instead of travelling around after them;" but these chopsticks serve for knife, fork, and spoon in one.

On my way to the hotel I saw a group of old people and graybeards. A few were chirruping and chuckling to larks or thrushes, which they carried perched on a stick or in cages; others were catching flies or hunting for crickets to feed them, while the remainder of the party seemed to be delightfully employed in flying fantastic paper kites. A group of boys were gravely looking on and regarding these innocent occupations of their seniors with the most serious and gratified attention. A few of the most sprightly were kicking a shuttlecock back and forth with great energy, instead of playing rounders with bat and ball as boys would do.

As I had come to the country to reside for some time, I made inquiries respecting a teacher, and happily found one who understood English. On entering he stood at the door, and instead of coming forward and shaking my hands, he politely bowed and shook his own, clasping them before his breast. I looked upon this mode as an improvement on our custom, especially when the condition of the hands might be doubtful, and requested him to be seated. I knew that I was to study a language without an alphabet, but was not prepared to see him begin at what I had always considered to be the end of the book. He read the date of its publication, "the fifth year, tenth month, and first day." "We arrange our dates differently," I observed, and begged him to read—which he did, from top to bottom, and proceeding from right to left. "You have an odd book here," remarked I, taking it up; "what is the price?" "A dollar and eight-thirds," said he, upon which I counted out three dollars and two-thirds and went on looking at it. The paper was printed only on one side; the running title was on the edge of the leaves instead of the top of the page, the paging was near the bottom, the number and contents of the chapters were at their ends, the marginal notes on the top, where the blank was double the size at the foot, and a broad black line across the middle of each page, like that seen in some French newspapers, separated the two works composing the volume, instead of one being printed after the other. The back was open and the sewing outside, and the name neatly written on the bottom edge. "You have given me too much," said he, as he handed me back two dollars and one-third, and then explained that eight-thirds meant eight divided by three, or only three-eighths. A small native vocabulary which he carried with him had the characters arranged according to the termination of their sounds, *ming*, *sing*, *king*, being all in a row, and the first word in it being *seen*. "Ah! my friend," said I, "English won't help me to find a word in that book; please give me your address." He accordingly took out a red card, big as a sheet of paper, on which was written Ying San-yuen in large characters, and pointed out the place of his residence, written on the other side. "I thought your name was Mr. Ying; why do you write your name wrong end first?" "It is you who are in the wrong," replied he; "look in your yearly directory, where alone you write names as they should be written, putting the honored family name first."

I could only say, "Customs differ;" and begged him to speak of ceremony, as I gave him back the book. He commenced, "When you receive a distinguished guest, do not fail to place him on your left, for that is the seat of honor; and be careful not to uncover the head, as that would be an unbecoming act of familiarity." This was a little opposed to my established notions; but when he reopened the volume and read, "The most learned men are decidedly of the opinion that the seat of the human understanding is in the belly," I cried out, "Better say it is in the feet!" and straightway shut up the book, dismissing him for another day; for this shocked all my principles of correct philosophy, even if King Solomon was against me.

On going abroad I met so many things contrary to my early notions of propriety that I readily assented to a friend's observation, that the Chinese were our antipodes in many things besides geographical position. "Indeed," said I, "they are so; I shall expect shortly to see a man walking on his head. Look! there's a woman in trousers and a party of gentlemen in petticoats; she is smoking and they are fanning themselves." However, on passing them I saw that the latter had on tight leggings. We soon met the steward of the house dressed in white, and I asked him what merry-making he was invited to; with a look of concern he told me he was returning from his father's funeral. Instead of having crape on his head he wore white shoes, and his dress was slovenly and neglected. My companion informed me that in the north of China it was common for rich people at funerals to put a white harness on the mules and shroud the carts in coarse cotton; while the chief mourners walked next to the bier, making loud cryings and showing their grief by leaning on the attendants. The friends rode behind and the musicians preceded the coffin—all being unlike our sable plumes and black crapes.

We next went through a retired street, where we heard sobbing and crying inside a court, and I inquired who was dead or ill. The man, suppressing a smile, said, "It is a girl about to be married, who is lamenting with her relatives and fellows as she bids adieu to the family penates and lares and her paternal home. She has enough to cry about, though, in the prospect of going to her mother-in-law's house."

I thought, after these unlucky essays, I would ask no more questions, but use my eyes instead. Looking into a shop, I saw a stout fellow sewing lace on a bonnet for a foreign lady; and going on to the landing-place, behold, all the ferry-boats were rowed by women, and from a passage-boat at the wharf I saw all the women get out of the bow to go ashore. "What are we coming to next?" said I; and just then saw a carpenter take his foot-rule out of his stocking to measure some timber which an apprentice was cutting with a saw whose blade was set nearly at right angles with the frame. Before the door sat a man busily engaged in whitening the thick soles of a pair of cloth shoes. "That's a shoewhite, I suppose," said I; "and he answers to the shoeblacks in New York, who cry 'Shine! shine!'" "Just so," said my friend; "and beyond him see the poor wretch in *chokey*, with a board or cangue around his neck for a shirt-collar; an article of his toilet which answers to the cuns with which the lads in the Tombs there are garnished instead of bracelets. In the prisons in this land, instead of cropping the hair of a criminal, as with us, no man is allowed to have his head shaved."

In the alleys called streets, few of them ten feet wide, the signs stood on their ends or hung from the eaves; the counters of the shops were next the street, the fronts were all open, and I saw the holes for the upright bars which secured the shop at night. Everything was done or sold in the streets or markets, which presented a strange medley. The hogs were transported in hampers on the shoulders of coolies, to the evident satisfaction of the inmates, and small pigs were put into baskets carried in slings, while the fish were frisking and jumping in shallow tubs as they were hawked from door to door.

A loud din led us to look in at an open door to see what was going on, and there a dozen boys were learning their tasks, all crying like auctioneers; one lad reciting his lesson out of Conufcius turned his back to the master instead of looking him in the face, and another who was learning to write put the copy-slip under the paper to imitate it, instead of looking at it as our boys would do.

We next passed a fashionable lady stepping out of her sedan chair. Her head was adorned with flowers instead of a bonnet, her hands gloveless, and her neck quite bare. Her feet were encased in red silk pictured shoes not quite four inches long; her plaited, embroidered petticoat was a foot longer than her gown, and her waist was not to be seen. As she entered the court-yard, leaning on the shoulder of her maid to help her walk on those cramped feet, my friend observed, "There you see a good example of a live walking-stick."

A little after we met one of his acquaintances accompanying a prettily carved coffin, and he asked who was dead.

"No man hab catchee die," replied the Celestial; "this one piecy coffin I just now gib my olo fader. He likee too much counta my numba one ploper; s'pose he someteem catchee die, can usee he."

"So fashion, eh?" rejoined my friend; "how muchee plice can catchee one alla same same for that?"

"I tinky can get one alla same so fashion one tousan dollar, so; this hab first chop hansom, lo."

"Do you call that gibberish English or Chinese?" I asked; for the language sounded no less strange than the custom of presenting a coffin to a living father differed from my preconceived notions of filial duty.

"That's the purest pigeon-English," replied he; "and you must be the Jack Downing of Canton to immortalize it."

"Come, rather let us go home, for soon I shall hardly be able to tell where or who I am in this strange land."[1]

In summing up the moral traits of Chinese character—a far more difficult task than the enumeration of its oddities—we must necessarily compare them with that perfect standard given us from above. While their contrarieties indicate a different external civilization, a slight acquaintance with their morals proves their similarity to their fellow-men in the lineaments of a fallen and depraved nature. Some of the better traits of their character have been marvellously developed. They have attained, by the observance of peace and good order, to a high degree of security for life and property; the various classes of society are linked together in a remarkably homogeneous manner by the diffusion of education in the most moral books in their language and a general regard for the legal rights of property. Equality of competition for office removes the main incentive to violence in order to obtain posts of power and dignity, and industry receives its just reward of food, raiment, and shelter with a uniformity which encourages its constant exertion. If any one asks how they have reached this point, we would primarily ascribe it to the blessing of the Governor of the nations, who has for His own purposes continued one people down to the present time from remote antiquity. The roots of society among them have never been broken up by emigration or the overflowing conquest of a superior race, but have been fully settled in a great regard for the family compact and deep reverence for parents and superiors. Education has strengthened and disseminated the morality they had, and God has blessed their filial piety by fulfilling the first commandment with promise and making their days long in the land which He has given them. Davis lays rather too much stress upon geographical and climatic causes in accounting for their advancement in these particulars, though their isolation has no doubt had much to do with their security and progress.

When, however, these traits have been mentioned, the Chinese are still more left without excuse for their wickedness, since

[1] *Chinese Repository*, Vol. X., p. 106; *New York Christian Weekly*, 1878.

being without law, they are a law unto themselves; they have always known better than they have done. With a general regard for outward decency, they are vile and polluted in a shocking degree; their conversation is full of filthy expressions and their lives of impure acts. They are somewhat restrained in the latter by the fences put around the family circle, so that seduction and adultery are comparatively infrequent, the former may even be said to be rare; but brothels and their inmates occur everywhere on land and on water. One danger attending young girls going abroad alone is that they will be stolen for incarceration in these gates of hell. By pictures, songs, and aphrodisiacs they excite their sensuality, and, as the Apostle says, "receive in themselves that recompense of their error which is meet."

More uneradicable than the sins of the flesh is the falsity of the Chinese, and its attendant sin of base ingratitude; their disregard of truth has perhaps done more to lower their character than any other fault. They feel no shame at being detected in a lie (though they have not gone quite so far as not to know when they do lie), nor do they fear any punishment from their gods for it. On the other hand, the necessity of the case compels them, in their daily intercourse with each other, to pay some regard to truth, and each man, from his own consciousness, knows just about how much to expect. Ambassadors and merchants have not been in the best position to ascertain their real character in this respect; for on the one side the courtiers of Peking thought themselves called upon by the mere presence of an embassy to put on some fictitious appearances, and on the other, the integrity and fair dealing of the hong merchants and great traders at Canton is in advance of the usual mercantile honesty of their countrymen. A Chinese requires but little motive to falsify, and he is constantly sharpening his wits to cozen his customer—wheedle him by promises and cheat him in goods or work. There is nothing which tries one so much when living among them as their disregard of truth, and renders him so indifferent as to what calamities may befall so mendacious a race; an abiding impression of suspicion toward everybody rests upon the mind, which chills the warmest wishes for their welfare and thwarts many a plan to benefit them. Their better traits diminish in the distance, and patience is exhausted in its daily proximity and friction with this ancestor of all sins. Mr. Abeel mentions a case of deceit which may serve as a specimen.

Soon after we arrived at Kulang su, a man came to us who professed to be the near relation and guardian of the owners of the house in which we live, and presented a little boy as the joint proprietor with his widowed mother. From the appearance of the house and the testimony of others we could easily credit his story that the family were now in reduced circumstances, having not only lost the house when the English attacked the place, but a thousand dollars besides by native robbers; we therefore allowed him a small rent, and gave the dollars to the man, who put them into the hands of the child. The next month he made his appearance, but our servant, whom we had taken to be peculiarly honest for a heathen, suggested the propriety of inquiring whether the money was ever given to those for whom it was professedly received; and soon returned with the information that the mother had heard nothing of the money, the man who received it not living in the family, but had now sent a lad to us who would receive it for her, and who our servants assured us would give it to the proper person. A day or two afterward our cook whispered to me that our *honest* servant, who had taken so much pains to prevent all fraud in the matter, had made the lad give him one-half of the money for his disinterestedness in preventing it from falling into improper hands; and further examination showed us that this very cook had himself received a good share to keep silent.

Thieving is exceedingly common, and the illegal exactions of the rulers, as has already been sufficiently pointed out, are most burdensome. This vice, too, is somewhat restrained by the punishments inflicted on criminals, though the root of the evil is not touched. While the licentiousness of the Chinese may be in part ascribed to their ignorance of pure intellectual pleasures and the want of virtuous female society, so may their lying be attributed partly to their truckling fear of officers, and their thievery to the want of sufficient food or work. Hospitality is not a trait of their character; on the contrary, the number and wretched condition of the beggars show that public and private charity is almost extinct; yet here too the sweeping charge must be modified when we remember the efforts they make to sustain their relatives and families in so densely peopled a country. Their avarice is not so distinguishing a feature as their love of money, but the industry which this desire induces or presupposes is the source of most of their superiority to their neighbors. The politeness which they exhibit seldom has its motive in good-will, and consequently, when the varnish is off, the rudeness, brutality, and coarseness of the material is seen; still, among themselves this exterior polish is not without some good results in preventing quarrels, where both parties, fully understanding each other, are careful not to overpass the bounds of etiquette.

On the whole, the Chinese present a singular mixture: if there is something to commend, there is more to blame; if they have some glaring vices, they have more virtues than most pagan nations. Ostentatious kindness and inbred suspicion, ceremonious civility and real rudeness, partial invention and servile imitation, industry and waste, sycophancy and self-dependence, are, with other dark and bright qualities, strangely blended. In trying to remedy the faults of their character by the restraints of law and the diffusion of education, they have no doubt hit upon the right mode; and their shortcomings show how ineffectual both must be until the Gospel comes to the aid of ruler and subject in elevating the moral sense of the whole nation. Female infanticide in some parts openly confessed, and divested of all disgrace and penalties everywhere; the dreadful prevalence of all the vices charged by the Apostle Paul upon the ancient heathen world; the alarming extent of the use of opium (furnished, too, under the patronage, and supplied in purity by the power and skill of Great Britain from India), destroying the productions and natural resources of the people; the universal practice of lying and dishonest dealings; the unblushing lewdness of old and young; harsh cruelty toward prisoners by officers, and tyranny over slaves by masters—all form a full unchecked torrent of human depravity, and prove the existence of a kind and degree of moral degradation of which an excessive statement can scarcely be made, or an adequate conception hardly be formed.

END OF VOLUME I.

澳门基金会
※
北京外国语大学
中国海外汉学研究中心
※
大象出版社

合作项目

卫三畏文集
Selected Works of
Samuel Wells Williams

中国总论

（卷II）（下）

The Middle Kingdom

［美］
卫三畏 著
Samuel Wells Williams

大象出版社

Mats of rattan for table furniture, and of grass for floors, are all made by hand. The latter is manufactured of two or three sorts of grass in different widths and patterns, and though the amount annually sent to the United States and elsewhere exceeds five million yards, it forms a very small proportion to the home consumption. Floor matting is put up in rolls containing twenty mats, or forty yards. *Musk*, though still in demand, is often and much adulterated, or its quality impaired by disease. It comes in bags about as large as a walnut; when good, it is of a dark purplish color, dry and light, and generally in concrete, smooth, and unctuous grains; its taste is bitter and smell strong; when rubbed on paper the trace is of a bright yellow color, and the feel free from grittiness. A brown unctuous earth is sometimes mixed with it, and the bags are frequently artificial; the price is about forty-five dollars a pound for the best quality.

Nankeen is a foreign name given to a kind of reddish cotton cloth manufactured near Nanking and Tsungming Island; it was once largely exported, but the product has now nearly ceased. It is the most durable kind of cotton cloth known, and its excellence always repays the cultivator. The opening of the country to foreigners, and the disorders ensuent on the Tai-ping rebellion, altered the character of the *silk* trade. The loss of capital and dispersion of workmen in the vicinity of Canton nearly destroyed the export of raw silk and piece-goods formerly made at Fatshan, and the pongees once woven there are seldom seen. The elegant crape shawls and scarfs, gauzes and checked lustrings, satins and lining silks, which were sent abroad from Canton, have all dwindled away. Raw silk makes the bulk of the export, amounting to over a hundred thousand bales, of which nearly two-thirds goes to Great Britain. The annual average for the six years ending 1860 was seventy-eight thousand five hundred bales; in 1836 it was twenty-one thousand; the price of the best sorts was about five hundred and fifty dollars a pecul. Silk goods are exported to the annual value of about two million taels; they consist chiefly of gauzes, pongees, handkerchiefs, scarfs, sarsnet, senshaws, levantines, and satins; ribbons, sewing-thread, and organzine, or thrown silk, are not much shipped. The silk trade is more likely to increase than any other branch of the commerce, after tea, and the Chinese can furnish almost any amount of raw and manufactured silks, according to the demand for them. *Soy* is a name derived from the Japanese *sho-ya;* it is made by boiling the beans of the *Dolichos soja*, adding an equal quantity of wheat or barley, and leaving the mass to ferment; a layer of salt and three times as much water as beans are afterward put in, and the whole compound stirred daily for two months, when the liquid is pressed and strained. Another method of making the condiment has already been mentioned in Volume I., p. 365.

Besides the articles above-mentioned, there are many others which singly form very trifling items in the trade, but their total exportation annually amounts to many lacs of dollars. Among them fire-crackers, and straw braid woven in Shantung from a variety of wheat, are both sent to the United States. Among other sundries, vermilion, gold leaf, amber, sea-shells, preserved insects, fans, ginger, sweetmeats and jellies, rhubarb, gamboge, camphor, grass-cloth, artificial flowers, insect wax, fishing-lines, joss-sticks, spangles, window-blinds, vegetable tallow, and pictures are the most deserving of mention. Some of them may perhaps become important articles of commerce, and all of them, except vermilion, gamboge, and rattans, are the produce of the country.

The imports make a much longer list than the exports, for almost everything that should or might sell there is from time to time offered in the market; and if the Chinese at Canton had had any inclination or curiosity to obtain the productions or manufactures of other lands, they have had no want of specimens. It will only be necessary to mention articles of import whose names are not of themselves a sufficient description. Opium, rice, raw cotton, longcloths, domestics and sheetings among manufactured cottons, ginseng, tin, lead, bar, rod, and hoop iron, and woollen goods, constitute the great bulk of the import trade. Rice is brought from southern islands, and a bounty used to be paid on its importation into Canton by taking off the tonnage dues on ships laden with this alone—a bonus of about three thousand dollars on a large vessel.

The importations from the Indian Archipelago comprise a

large variety of articles, though their total amount and value are not very great. *Agar-agar*, or *agal-agal*, is the Malay name for the *Plocaria tenax*, *Gracillaria*, and other sorts of seaweed; it is boiled and clarified to make a vegetable glue which is largely employed in lantern and silk manufacture instead of isinglass; it is also made into a jelly, but the *seaweed* (*Laiminaria*) from Japan has supplanted it. *Betel-nut* is the fruit of the areca palm, and is called *betel-nut* because it is chewed with the leaf of the betel pepper (*Chavica*) as a masticatory. The nut is the only part brought to China, the leaf being raised along the southern coast; it resembles a nutmeg in shape and color, is a little larger, and the whole of the nut is chewed. They are boiled or eaten raw, the former being cut into slices and boiled with a small quantity of cutch and then dried. Those brought to China are simply deprived of the husk and dried. When chewed, a slice of the nut is wrapped in the fresh leaf smeared with a mixture of gambier or shell-lime colored red, and the whole masticated to a pulp before spitting it out. The teeth become dark red from using it, but the Chinese are careful to remove this stain. The taste of the fresh pepper leaf is herbaceous and aromatic with a little pungency, and those who chew have it seldom out of their mouths; the habit is not general where the fresh leaf cannot be obtained.

Biche-de-mer, *i.e.*, slug of the sea, or tripang, is a marine gasteropod (*Holothuria*) resembling, when alive, a crawling sausage more than anything else; it is sometimes over a foot long and two or three inches through; it inhabits the shallow waters around the islands of the Pacific and Indian Archipelago, and is obtained by diving or spearing, and prepared by cleansing and smoking it. In the market it appears hard and rigid, of a dirty brown color; when soaked in water it resembles pork-rind, and when stewed is not unlike it in taste. The Chinese distinguish nearly thirty sorts of *hai săng*—'sea ginseng;' in commerce, however, all are known as white or black, the prices ranging from two dollars up to eighty dollars a pecul.

Birds' nests, *sharks' fins*, and *fish-maws* are three other articles of food prized by Chinese epicures for their supposed stimulating quality, and they readily fetch high prices. The first is the nest of a species of swallow (*Collocalia*), which makes the gelatinous fibres from its own crop out of the seaweed (*Gelidium*) it feeds on. These nests resemble those of the chimney swallow in shape, and are collected in most dangerous places along the cliffs and caves in the Indian Islands. The article varies from thirty dollars to three dollars a pound, and its total import is hardly five hundred peculs a year. The taste of the Chinese for the gelatinous fins and stomachs of the shark aids in clearing the seas of that ferocious fish even as far as the Persian Gulf. The soup made from the fins resembles that from isinglass, and is worthy of acceptance on other tables.

Amber is found on various eastern shores, along the Mozambique coast, in the Indian Islands, and localities in Annam and Yunnan. The consumption for court beads and other ornaments is great, and shows that the supply is permanent, for none is brought from Prussia. The Chinese use the powder of amber in their high-priced medicines. Their artists have also learned to imitate it admirably in a variety of articles made of copal, shell-lac, and colophony.

The *bezoars*, or biliary calculi from ruminating and other animals, always find a ready market in China for drugs; that from the cow is most prized, and is often imitated with pipeclay and ox-gall mixed with hair, or adulterated by the camel bezoar. The Mongols prize these substances very highly; the pure goat and cow bezoars are ground for paints by the Cantonese.

Cutch, or terra japonica, is a gummy resin, obtained from a species of areca palm and the *Acacia catechu*, and was for a long time supposed to be a sort of earth found in Japan; it is called *cutch* from the Runn of Cutch, near which the tree grows. The best is friable between the fingers, is of a reddish-brown color, and used in China as a dye. There are two kinds, *black* and *pale;* the former is made by boiling the heartwood of the acacia and putting the resin into small cakes; it is now brought in small quantities, as gambier has supplanted it.

Rose-maloes, corrupted from *rasamala*, the Javanese name of the *Altingia excelsa*, is a liquid storax obtained from the *Styrax;* it is a scented gummous oil of the consistency of tar, and is brought from Bombay to China for medicine. *Gum benzoin*, or *benjamin*, is one of the gum-resins brought from abroad, and highly prized by Chinese doctors; its Chinese name indicates that it came from Parthia; but it is collected from the *Styrax benzoin* in Sumatra and Borneo by making incisions in the bark in much the same manner as opium, until the plant withers and dies. It comes to market in cakes, which in some parts of those islands formerly served as standards of value. Good benzoin is full of clear light-colored spots, marbled on the broken surface, and giving off an agreeable odor when heated or rubbed; it is the frankincense of the far East, and has been employed by many nations in their religious ceremonies; for what was so acceptable to the worshippers was soon inferred to be equally grateful to the gods, and sought after by all devotees as a delightful perfume. The quantity of benzoin imported is, however, small, and the Arabian frankincense, or *olibanum*, is more commonly seen in the market, and is employed for the same purposes. This gum-resin exudes from the *Boswellia thurifera* cultivated in Coromandel; the drops have a pale reddish color, a strong and somewhat unpleasant smell, a pungent and bitterish taste, and when chewed give the saliva a milky color; it burns with a pleasant fragrance and slight residuum. *Dragon's blood* is probably an equivalent of the Chinese name *lung-yen hiang*, given to this resin from its coming to market in lumps formed from the agglutinated tears. It is the gummy covering of the seeds of a rattan palm (*Dæmonorops draco*) common in Sumatra, which is separated by shaking them in a basket or bag; an inferior sort is made by boiling the nuts. It is used in varnishing, painting, and medical preparations.

Cloves are consumed but little by the Chinese, and mostly in expressing an oil which forms an ingredient in condiments and medicines, like the oil of peppermint made by themselves. *Pepper* is much more used than cloves, the tea being considered beneficial in fevers; the good effects as a febrifuge seem to be doubted lately, for the importation is only twenty thousand peculs, not one-half what it was fifty years ago. *Baroos camphor* is still imported from Borneo, the people supposing that the drops and lumps found in the fissures of the tree (*Dryobalanops*) in that island are more powerful than their own gum; the proportion between the two, both in price and quantity, is about eighteen to one.

Gambier is obtained from the gambier vine (*Uncaria*) by boiling the leaves and inspissating the decoction; a soapy substance of a brownish-yellow color remains, which is both chewed with betel-nut and forms a good and cheap material for tanning and dyeing. *Putchuck* is the root of a kind of thistle (*Aucklandia*) cultivated in Cashmere; it comes in dry, brown, broken pieces, resembling rhubarb in color and smell, and affording an agreeable perfume when burned; the powder is employed in making incense-sticks and the thin shavings mixed in medicines.

Cornelians, agates, and other stones of greater or less value are purchased by the Chinese for manufacturing into official insignia, rings, beads, and other articles of ornament; they are brought chiefly from India or Central Asia. *Seed pearls*, to the amount of three hundred thousand dollars, are annually brought from Bombay to Canton, where they are run on strings to be worn in ladies' head-dresses; *coral* is also a part of cargoes from the Archipelago. *Mother-o'-pearl* shells and *tortoise-shell* are brought from the same region and the Pacific islands, Muscat, and Bombay, a large part of which is re-exported in the shape of buttons, combs, and other productions of Chinese skill.

Ivory still comes from Africa *via* Bombay, and Malaysia, mostly from Bangkok; the fossil ivory of Siberia has furnished the material for the inlaid tables of Ningpo; but the cost of fine ivory has prevented the manufacture of many articles once common at Canton. *Rhinoceros' horns* are all brought to China to be carved into ornaments, or served in remedies and tonics.[1] But the principal use of these horns is in medicine and for amulets, for only one good cup can be carved from the end of each horn; the parings and fragments are carefully preserved to serve for the other purposes. The teeth of the sperm whale, walrus, lamantine, and other phocine animals, form an article of import in limited quantities under the designation

[1] The elegant plumage of the turquois kingfisher and some other birds is also worked into ornaments and head-dresses.

of "sea-horse teeth;" these tusks weigh from sixteen to forty ounces, their ivory being nearly as compact though not so white as that of the elephant.

Several kinds of *wood* are brought for cabinet and inlaid work, medical preparations, and dyeing. Among these are *ebony* and *camagon* (*mao tsz'*), both obtained from species of *Diospyros* growing in India and Luzon; they are often very cleverly imitated by covering teak and other hard woods with a black stain. *Gahru wood*—also called eagle or agila wood (*Aquilaria*)—furnishes the calambak timber, highly prized for its perfume; the diseased heart-wood of this tree is the precious aloes wood, the lign aloes of the Bible.[1] Among dye-stuffs the *laka* wood (*Tanarius*) from Sumatra, mangrove bark, sapan wood (*Cæsalpinia*), and red wood are important articles; the imports of sandal wood for incense, rosewood, satin wood, amboyna or knot wood, camphor and *kranjee* are employed in various ways for junks, buildings, and furniture.

The greater facilities of trade with foreign countries since 1860 have vastly enlarged the list of imports and exports, and brought many new and useful articles within reach of the natives living far from the ports. In their fear and ignorance the Chinese associated everything dreadful with the name and coming of those whom they called devils and barbarians, and knew chiefly in connection with war and opium. By degrees, however, they are learning the benefits of a wider commercial as well as intellectual intercourse. One of the most notable among the imports, which carries with it something of this broadening influence, is kerosene; the traveller in China, as well as in Algeria, Greece, and Egypt, can hardly fail to note with interest the multitude of benefits arising from the introduction of a cheap and brilliant lamp into a house whose only light before has been a water-lamp or tallow candle. Electric lighting is now employed in certain of the foreign settlements, and will doubtless become as popular in the far East as among Western nations. It is needless, however, to enumerate the novelties in which the Chinese are constantly urged and tempted to invest.

The mode of conducting the trade is described in the author's

[1] *Chinese Commercial Guide*, Fifth Edition, p. 106.

Chinese Commercial Guide (fifth edition, Hongkong, 1863), which contains the treaties, tariffs, regulations, etc., of other nations as well as of China. A peculiar feature of this trade is the fact that the natives have always conducted it in English,—that is, they do business in the jargon called *pigeon-English*, whose curious formation has already received some attention in a previous chapter. The Chinaman using it deems no sentence complete until it contains the same number of words and in the same idiom as its equivalent phrase in his own language. A sample of this hybrid lingo, with its *mélange* of Chinese, Portuguese, and Malay words and grammatical constructions, may not be out of place here. We will suppose a shopkeeper is soliciting custom from a foreigner: "My chin-chin you," he says, "one good fleen [friend], take care for my [patronize me]; 'spose you wanchee any first chop ting, my can catchee for you [obtain]. I secure sell 'em plum cash [prime cost], alla same cumsha [present]; can do?" The foreigner, with great gravity, replies: "Just now my no wanchee anyting; any teem [time] 'spose you got vely number one good ting, p'rhaps I come you shop look see." After hearing for a few days such sentences, the foreigner begins to imitate them, soon learning to adapt his speech to his interlocutor's, and thus perpetuating the jargon. Other nationalities are also obliged to learn it, and the whole trade is conducted in this meagre gibberish, which the natives suppose, however, to be correct English, but which hardly enables the two parties to exchange ideas upon even household subjects. Much of the misunderstanding and trouble experienced in daily intercourse with the Chinese is doubtless owing to this imperfect medium.[1]

The trade at the five ports opened by the treaty of Nanking in 1842 was conducted by native custom-house officers, as it had been previously at Canton, but under regulations which insured more honesty and efficiency. In 1853, however, the capture of Shanghai by insurgents threw the whole trade into such confusion that the collector, who had been formerly

[1] Mr. Schuyler mentions hearing some Chinese residents at Vierny speaking a mongrel with the Russian officers of the post, which might be called "pigeon-Russian." *Turkistan*, Vol. II., p. 147.

a hong merchant at Canton, called in the aid of foreigners to carry on his duties. A trio of inspectors was nominated for this purpose by the British, American, and French ministers from their nationalities; and so well did it work in honestly collecting the revenue for the imperial coffers, that when the city was recaptured the system was made permanent for that port. In the negotiations growing out of the treaties of Tientsin in 1858, the Chinese government felt so much confidence in the feasibility of the plan, that it was extended to all the ports and placed under the entire control of an inspector-general. By thus utilizing the experience and integrity of foreign employés in carrying on this important branch of its administration, the rulers broke through their long seclusion and isolation, and opened the way for removing the impediments to their own progress in every branch of polity.

The following tables, compiled or abridged from the so-called "Yellow Books," or Trade Reports, issued by the Imperial Maritime Customs, will furnish a general idea of the foreign trade with China and some statistics concerning its domestic commerce. It is hardly necessary to add, however, that concerning the latter when unconnected with foreigners, there are almost no figures of value attainable. The *Haikwan tael*, it may be well to repeat, is valued at \$1.36½, or 5*s.* 6½*d.* The *pecul* weighs 133½ pounds.

ANNUAL VALUE OF THE FOREIGN TRADE OF CHINA, 1871 TO 1881.

YEAR.	Net Imports.[1]	Exports.	Total.
	Hk. Tls.	*Hk. Tls.*	*Hk. Tls.*
1871	70,103,077	66,853,161	136,956,238
1872	67,317,049	75,288,125	142,605,174
1873	66,637,209	69,451,277	136,088,486
1874	64,360,864	66,712,868	137,073,732
1875	67,803,247	68,912,929	136,716,176
1876	70,269,574	80,850,512	151,120,086
1877	73,233,896	67,445,022	140,678,918
1878	70,804,027	67,172,179	137,976,206
1879	82,227,424	72,281,262	154,508,686
1880	79,293,452	77,883,587	157,177,039
1881	91,910,877	71,452,974	163,363,851

[1] Meaning the value of foreign goods imported direct from foreign countries, less the value of the foreign goods re-exported to foreign countries during the year.

CUSTOMS REVENUE, 1871 TO 1881.

YEAR.	DUTIES ON NATIVE PRODUCE EXPORTED TO—		TOTAL REVENUE FROM—		
	Foreign Countries.	Chinese Ports.	Foreign Trade.	Home Trade.	Total.
	Hk. Tls.	*Hk. Tls.*	*Hk. Tls.*	*Hk. Tls.*	*Hk. Tls.*
1871........	5,246,467	1,138,116	9,508,972	1,707,174	11,216,146
1872........	5,840,261	1,099,724	10,029,050	1,649,586	11,678,636
1873........	4,978,179	1,158,933	9,228,675	1,738,407	10,977,082
1874........	5,535,041	1,147,686	9,775,743	1,721,529	11,497,272
1875........	5,640,062	1,291,922	10,030,226	1,937,883	11,968,109
1876........	5,772,709	1,222,860	10,318,631	1,834,290	12,152,921
1877........	5,703,321	1,140,442	10,356,415	1,710,663	12,067,078
1878........	5,803,485	1,306,118	10,524,811	1,956,177	12,483,988
1879........	5,958,176	1,426,894	11,391,329	2,140,341	13,531,670
1880........	6,696,290	1,572,392	11,899,995	2,358,588	14,258,583
1881........	6,869,436	1,460,182	12,494,889	2,190,273	14,685,162

EXPORT OF TEA FROM CHINA DURING TEN YEARS.

YEAR.	Black.	Green.	Leaf.	Dust.	Brick.	Total.
	Peculs.	*Peculs.*	*Peculs.*	*Peculs.*	*Peculs.*	*Peculs.*
1872........	1,420,170	256,464	85	950	96,994	1,774,663
1873........	1,274,232	235,413	372	416	107,330	1,617,763
1874........	1,444,249	212,834	....	3,504	74,792	1,735,379
1875........	1,438,611	210,282	....	2,594	166,900	1,818,387
1876........	1,415,349	189,714	74	3,799	153,951	1,762,887
1877........	1,552,174	197,522	36	12,158	147,810	1,909,700
1878........	1,517,617	172,826	....	14,236	194,277	1,898,956
1879........	1,523,419	183,234	....	5,270	275,540	1,987,463
1880........	1,661,325	188,623	....	14,201	232,969	2,097,118
1881........	1,636,724	238,064	....	15,186	247,498	2,137,472

EXPORT OF NATIVE CHINESE GOODS TO FOREIGN COUNTRIES, 1880 AND 1881.

Description of Goods.	Classifier of Quantity.	1880. Quantity	1880. Value.	1881. Quantity.	1881. Value.
			Hk. Tls.		*Hk. Tls.*
Silk, all kinds................	Peculs.	114,821	29,831,444	106,632	26,868,200
Tea, all kinds....	"	2,097,119	35,728,169	2,137,473	32,890,268
Bags, all kinds.....	Pieces.	749,383	20,555	860,558	31,002
Bamboo, all kinds	Value.	....	74,597	....	86,167
Beans and beancake	Peculs.	154,645	159,996	112,628	139,066
Cassia lignea	"	38,785	225,692	57,456	300,303
Camphor	"	12,327	100,679	9,317	79,625
Chinaware and pottery.......	"	75,142	379,574	78,503	387,066
Coal..........................	"	161	34	1,478	308
Clothing, boots, and shoes....	Value.	....	327,548	....	358,301
Cotton, raw and waste.......	Peculs.	20,315	182,918	23,139	228,391
Curios....	Value.	....	44,948	....	43,364
Dyes, colors, and paints..	Peculs.	676	3,196	20	183
Fans, all kinds..............	Pieces.	6,287,989	38,881	2,017,157	27,710
Fish, provisions, and vegetables	Peculs.	68,940	165,922	66,008	146,262
Fire-crackers....	"	27,051	260,010	34,380	322,522
Flour, grain, and pulse........	"	149,394	139,653	39,911	49,361
Fruits, all kinds............	"	73,720	92,913	87,140	106,756
Grasscloth......	"	1,185	104,719	1,589	148,985
Hemp	"	19,548	160,602	20,771	158,143
Hides and boops..............	"	20,786	253,548	38,526	473,555
Indigo......	"	2,847	13,768	1,764	7,168
Lung-ngans...	"	8,080	34,669	7,592	30,753
Mats and matting....	Pieces.	384,680	533,027	360,827	358,537
Medicines....	Peculs.	28,676	194,451	31,916	194,090
Metals, manufactured.......	"	14,284	147,405	14,804	185,778
Metals, unmanufactured..	"	217	875	2	4
Nankeens and wool...........	"	6,511	122,815	8,750	172,205
Nutgalls and preserves........	"	47,690	432,774	44,260	402,017
Oil, all kinds................	"	3,692	70,295	9,442	159,516
Paper, books, tin, and brass foil	"	43,581	512,720	53,438	597,496
Rattans and rattanware......	"	2,085	8,975	2,757	11,901
Rhubarb.....	"	6,153	212,527	6,814	245,957
Skins, all kinds..............	Pieces.	244,193	152,486	330,922	262,780
Straw braid	Peculs.	48,970	1,227,670	50,502	1,363,984
Sugar, white, brown, candy...	"	1,138,196	3,263,889	957,564	2,584,000
Tobacco.....................	"	19,077	167,931	7,250	73,386
Vermicelli and macaroni......	"	26,991	125,422	40,122	154,159
Sundries, unenumerated......	Value.	....	2,366,290	....	1,853,865
Total value....	....	....	77,883,587	....	71,452,974

CHAPTER XXI.

FOREIGN INTERCOURSE WITH CHINA.

THE most important notices which the research of authors had collected respecting the intercourse between China and the West, and the principal facts of interest of a political and commercial nature down to the year 1834, are carefully arranged in the first three chapters of Sir John Davis' work.[1] In truth, the terms *intercourse* and *ambassies*, so often used with reference to the nations of Eastern Asia, indicate a peculiar state of relations with them; for while other courts send and receive resident ministers, those of China, Japan, Corea, and Cochinchina have until very recently kept themselves aloof from this national interchange of civilities, neither understanding its principles nor appreciating its advantages. Embassies have been sent by most European nations to the two first, which have tended rather to strengthen their assumptions of supremacy than to enlighten them as to the real objects and wishes of the courts proposing such courtesies. The commercial intercourse has, like the political, either been forced upon or begged of these governments, constantly subject to those vexatious restrictions and interruptions which might be expected from such ill-defined arrangements; and though mutually advantageous, has never been conducted on those principles of reciprocity and equality which characterize commerce at the West. As yet, the rulers and merchants of oriental nations are hardly well enough acquainted with their own and others' rights to be able or willing

---

[1] *The Chinese*, 2 Vols., Harper's Family Library, 1837. See also Murray's *China*, Vol. I., 1843. Montgomery Martin's *China*, passim, 1847. *Mémoires conc. les Chinois*, Tome V., pp. 1–23. T. W. Kingsmill in *N. C. Br. R. A. Soc. Journal*, N. S., No. XIV., 1879.

to enter into close relations with European powers. Both magistrates and people are ignorant and afraid of the resources, power, and designs of Christian nations, and consequently disinclined to admit them or their subjects to unrestrained intercourse. When western adventurers, as Pinto, Andrade, Weddell, and others came to the shores of China and Japan in the sixteenth and seventeenth centuries, they found the governments disposed to traffic, but the conquests subsequently made by Europeans in the neighboring regions of Luçonia, Java, and India, and their cruel treatment of the natives, led these two powers to apprehend like results for themselves if they did not soon take precautionary measures of exclusion and restriction. Nor can there be much doubt that this policy was the safest measure, in order to preserve their independence and maintain their authority over even their own subjects. Might made right more generally among nations then than it does now, and the belief entertained by most Europeans at that period, that all pagan lands belonged justly to the Pope, only wanted men and means to be everywhere carried into effect. Had the Chinese and Japanese governments allowed Portuguese, Spanish, French, and English colonists to settle and increase within their borders, they would, probably, long since have crumbled to pieces and their territories have been possessed by others.

The data brought together by Davis in 1838 on this subject has since been enlarged and illustrated by Col. Yule in his admirable "Preliminary Essay" of 1866, prefixed to *Cathay and the Way Thither*, and by Richthofen, the latter half of whose first volume on China is devoted to an exhaustive treatise upon the "Development of the Knowledge of China."[1] A digest of these elaborate works would be too long for our purpose here,

---

[1] *China, Ergebnisse eigener Reisen und darauf gegründeter Studien*, Berlin, 1877. This author's arrangement of the subject into "Periods" is as follows: I.—Legendary notices of intercourse before the year 1122 B.C. II.—From the accession of the Chaus to the building of the Great Wall (1122–212 B.C.). III.—From the building of the Great Wall to the accession of the Tangs (212 B.C.–619 A.D.). IV.—From the Tangs to the Mongols (619–1205). V.—From the rise of the Mongol power to the arrival of the Portuguese in China (1205–1517). VI.—From the arrival of the Portuguese to the present time.

where only the most interesting points can be noticed. The first recorded knowledge of China among the nations of the West does not date further back than the geographer Ptolemy, A.D. 150, who seems himself to have been indebted to the Tyrian author Marinus. The Periplus of the Erythræan Sea, however, refers to the same land under the name *Θὶν*, or *Thin*, at perhaps an earlier date. Previous to this time, moreover, accounts of the existence of the land of Confucius, and an appreciation and demand for the splendid silks made there, had reached Persia, judging from the legends found in its writers alluding to ancient wars and embassies with China, in which the country, the government, people, and fabrics are invested with a halo of power and wealth which has not yet entirely vanished. These legends strengthen the conclusion that the Prophet Isaiah has the first mention now extant of the Flowery Land under the name *Sinim*. The interchange of the initial in *China*, *Thina* or *Tina*, and *Sina* ought to give no trouble in identifying the land, for such changes in pronunciation are still common in it; *e.g.*, *Chau-chau fu* into *Tiè-chiu hu*.

The Periplus of Arrian places the city of Thina perhaps as far east as Si-ngan, but too vaguely to be relied on; that great city must certainly have then been known, however, among the traders of Central Asia, who probably were better acquainted with its geography than the authors who have survived them. Under the term *Seres* the Chinese are more clearly referred to at even an earlier date than *Sina*, and among the Latin writers it was about the only term used, its association with the silks brought thence keeping it before them. The two names were used for different regions,[1] the Seres being understood as lying to the north. Mela places them between the Indians and Scythians; Ptolemy calls the country *Serice* and the capital *Sera*, but regarded them as distinct from the *Sinæ*, precisely as a Chinese geographer might confuse Britain and England. He says there

[1] The different appellations seem to have been employed according as it was regarded as the terminus of a southern sea route or a journey across the continent. In the former aspect the name has nearly always been some form of *Sin*, *Chin*, Sinæ, China; in the latter, to the ancients as the land of the *Seres*, to the middle ages as the Empire of *Cathay*.—Yule.

was a long and dangerous land route leading to Sera through Persia to Bactria, over mountain defiles and perilous paths, which occupied the largest part of a year. Besides Ptolemy, there are notices by Pliny of the Seres, and these two authors furnished their successors with most of their knowledge down to the reign of Justinian. Col. Yule concisely summarizes the knowledge of China down to that date among the Romans: "The region of the Seres is a vast and populous country, touching on the east the ocean and the limits of the habitable world; and extending west nearly to Imaus and the confines of Bactria. The people are civilized men, of mild, just, and frugal temper; eschewing collisions with their neighbors, and even shy of close intercourse, but not averse to dispose of their own products, of which raw silk is the staple, but which include also silk stuffs, furs, and iron of remarkable quality." He further explains how authors writing at Rome and Constantinople were quite unable to traverse and rectify what was said of the marts and nations spoken of in the farthest East, and place them with any precision. They were, in truth, in the same difficulty in coming to an accurate conclusion that the Chinese geographer Seu Kí-yu was when writing at Fuhchau in 1847; he could not explain the discrepancies he found between Rhodes and its colossus and Rhode Island in the United States.

Among the marts mentioned in the various authors, Greek, Roman, and Persian, only a few can be identified with even fair probability. The "Stone Tower" of Ptolemy seems to have denoted *Tashkend*, a name of the same meaning, and a town still resorted to for trade. His port of Cattigara may have been a mart at the mouth of the Meinam, the Meikon, the Chu Kiang, or some other large stream in that region, where seafaring people could exchange their wares with the natives, then quite independent of the Chinese in Shensí, who were known to him as Seres. Cattigara is more probably to be looked for near Canton, for its annals state that in the reign of Hwan tí (A.D. 147–168) "Tienchuh (India), Ta-tsin (Rome, Egypt or Arabia), and other nations came by the southern sea with tribute, and from this time trade was carried on at Canton with foreigners." During the same dynasty (the Eastern Han), foreigners came from Cantoo, Lu-hwang-chí, and other nations in the south. The nearest was about ten days' journey, and the farthest about five months'.'[1]

On the land frontier, the Chinese annals of the Han dynasty record the efforts of Wu tí (B.C. 140–86) to open a communication with the Yuehchí, or Getæ, who had driven out the Greek rulers in Bactria and settled themselves north of the River Oxus, in order to get their help against his enemies the Huns. He sent an envoy, Chang Kiang, in 135, who was captured by the Huns and kept prisoner for ten years, when he escaped with some of his attendants and got to *Ta-wan*, or Ferghana, and thence reached the Yuehchí further south. He was unsuccessful in his mission, and attempted to return home through Tibet, but was re-taken by the Huns, and did not succeed in reporting himself at Chang-an till thirteen years had elapsed. The introduction of the vine into China is rather doubtfully ascribed to this brave envoy.

De Guignes concludes that this notice about trade at Canton refers to the embassy sent in A.D. 166 by the Emperor Marcus Aurelius (whom the Chinese call *An-tun*), which entered China by the south at Tongking, or Canton. The Latin author Florus, who lived in Trajan's reign, about fifty years before, has a passage showing, as proof of the universal awe and veneration in which the power of Rome was held under Augustus, that ambassadors from the remotest nations, the Seres and the Indians, came with presents of elephants, gems, and pearls—a rhetorical exaggeration quite on a par with the Chinese account of the tribute sent from An-tun, and not so well authenticated. Whether, indeed, the *Ta-tsin kwoh* mentioned by Chinese writers meant Judea, Rome, or Persia, cannot now be exactly ascertained, though Yule concludes that this name almost certainly means the Roman Empire, otherwise called the Kingdom of the Western Sea. The title was given to these regions because of the analogy of its people to those of the Middle King-

---

[1] *Chinese Repository*, I., p. 365. Heeren, *Asiatic Researches*, II., pp. 285–295. Murray's *China*, I., p. 141. Yule's *Cathay*, Vol. I., pp. xli–xlv. Smith, *Classical Dictionary*, Art. SERES.

dom.[1] The envoys sent to that country reported that "beyond the territory of the Tau-shí (perhaps the Persians) there was a great sea, by which, sailing due west, one might arrive at the country where the sun sets." Like most attempts of the kind in subsequent days, the mission of Antoninus appears to have been a failure, and to have returned without accomplishing any practical benefit to intercourse or trade between the two greatest empires in the world. It was received, no doubt, at Lohyang, then the capital, with ostentatious show and patronizing kindness, and its occurrence inscribed in the national records as another evidence of the glory and fame of the Son of Heaven. That a direct trade between Rome and China did not result at this period may have been largely due to the jealousy of the Parthian merchants, who reaped great profits as middle-men in the traffic, and disposed of their own woven and colored stuffs to the Romans, all of which gain they knew would have passed over their heads had the extreme East and West come into more intimate relations.

It is worthy of observation how, even from the earliest times, the traffic in the rich natural and artificial productions of India and China has been the great stimulus to urge adventurers to come from Europe, who on their part offered little in exchange besides precious metals. The *Serica vestis*, whether it was a silken or cotton fabric, and other rarities found in those regions, bore such a high price at Rome as to tempt the merchants to undertake the longest journeys and undergo the greatest hardships to procure them; and such was the case likewise during the long period before the discovery of the Cape of Good Hope. The existence of this trade early enabled the Nestorian missionaries to penetrate into those remote regions, and keep up a communication with their patrons at home; the more extended

---

[1] *Cathay and the Way Thither*, p. lvi. Klaproth, *Tableaux Historiques de l'Asie* (Paris, 1826), p. 68. So Richthofen (*China*, Bd. I., p. 470), who adds: "It is accepted now, by almost all those who have written on the subject, that the Chinese by *Ta-tsin* meant to denote 'Great-China,' and through this, on the other hand, we have a proof that the Chinese called their own country *Tsin*. It will hardly do, however, to suppose that so prejudiced a people as they would recognize another folk as greater. The appellation *Ta* (great) is given to every nation whose power the Chinese feel to be considerable."

voyages of modern commerce likewise assist benevolent persons in reaching the remotest tribes; and carrying on their labors, through their patrons on the other side of the world, probably with less danger and delay than a mission at Cadiz could have been directed from Jerusalem in the days of the apostles.

The notices in Cosmas (a Greek monk who had been a merchant, and wrote his "Universal Christian Topography" between 530 and 550 A.D.) of China and its products refer to the maritime trade under the Byzantine emperors. This country he locates very correctly as occupying the extreme east of Asia, and calls *Tzinista*, a name probably picked up from the Persians or old Hindus, and nearly similar to the *Tzinisthan* of the tablet at Si-ngan. Another Greek, Theophylact, in the next century describes the internal intercourse in Central Asia, and a great Turkish people, the *Taugas*, whom he was unaware were the Chinese. It may be that he miswrote *Tang* in a grecized form for the dynasty just about that time settling its power. The indirect commerce between China and the Greek Empire increased by sea and land until the rise of the Moslem power. The same indifference on the part of the Chinese respecting the power, resources, and position of other lands is seen through all their notices of those western kingdoms. The products carried west were silk in various forms, but the demand for this article diminished after the worms had been successfully taken to Greece about A.D. 550. Cotton fabrics, medicines, and spices went westward as well as silk, but it is impossible to distinguish the trade with China from that with India. The leaf called *malabathrum* in the Periplus was not a Chinese plant, but the *tamalapatra*, a kind of cassia (*Cinnamomum nitidum*, whose leaves were purchased in Rome for three hundred denarii per pound), and now called Malabar leaf; it was probably mixed or confounded with the Indian *nard* and with camphor. The people called *Sesatæ* in the Periplus are probably to be looked for in Assam or Sikkim, where wild cassia grows, and where the real tea plant is native; but neither tea nor betel-leaf can be regarded as the ancient malabathrum.[1]

---

[1] Heeren's *Asiatic Researches*, II., p. 294; Yule's *Cathay*, pp. xlvi, cxliv.

Within the last few years the translations of the travels of Buddhist pilgrims between China and India have furnished more satisfactory details of the peoples inhabiting the central and western parts of Asia than all the Greek and Latin authors. Those of Fahian (399–414), of Hiuen-tsang (628–645), and of Hwui-sing (518), are the most extensive. Further researches into conventual libraries in China and Tibet are encouraged by what has been found on their shelves, and from them enough has already been gained to reward the labor. Of greater worth than these, perhaps, are the official histories of the Han, Tsin, and Tang dynasties, reaching from B.C. 200 to A.D. 900, only portions of which have yet been made accessible in full. Their trivialties are so numerous that their entire translation into English would hardly repay the printing, as the experiment by Mailla, in 1785, of the *Tang Kien Kang-muh*, in thirteen volumes quarto, shows. These histories, on the whole, supply more accurate information about Syria, Persia, Greece, and Parthia, than the writers of those countries give about China;—for example, the notices of *Fulin*, or Constantinople, are more minute than any account of Chang-an in western writers. But as Yule well remarks, there is much analogy between the fragmentary views each party had, the same uncertainty as to exact position, and the same application of facts belonging to the nearer skirts of a half-seen empire to the whole land. It can well be paralleled by reading some of our own travellers who applied all that they saw and heard at Canton to the Eighteen Provinces. Only a few embassies from *Ta-tsin* and *Fulin* are enumerated by Pauthier in his *Chine* as coming down to the year 1091; but the tractate by Dr. E. Bretschneider, of the Russian Legation at Peking,[1] shows how constant were the visits of the Arabs down to the Sung (A.D. 1086), and especially during the Tang dynasty. During the Tsin and Wei dynasties the visits of envoys from Ceylon were frequent, all of them an outgrowth of Buddhism, but repaid in more ways than one by the trade and its results—as shown by Sir E. Tennent in his *History of Ceylon*. In 1266 the King of Ceylon had Chinese soldiers in

[1] *On the Knowledge of the Arabs and Arabian Colonies possessed by the Ancient Chinese*, London, 1871.

his service, and envoys came to him to buy Buddha's sacred alms-dish. In 1405 the Emperor Yungloh of the Ming dynasty, taking umbrage at the indignities offered to his representative by Wijayabahu IV., despatched Ching Ho with a fleet of sixty-two ships and a land force to cruise along the coasts of Cambodia, Siam, and other places, demanding tribute and conferring gifts as the successor of the throne held by the great Kublai. Going again the next year as far as Ceylon, Ching Ho evaded a snare set by the king, and captured him and his whole family and officials, carrying them all to Peking. In 1411 the latter were set free, but a new king was appointed to the vacant throne, who reigned fifty years and sent tribute till 1459; this was only thirty-eight years before Gama arrived at Calicut. It was the last attempt of the Chinese to assert their sway beyond the limits of the Middle Kingdom seaward.[1]

One intimation of a continuance of the intercourse with China from the time of Justinian to that of the Arab travellers Wahab and Abu Zaid, is the Nestorian inscription (page 277). The narratives of the Arabs (A.D. 850 and 877) are trustworthy in their general statements as to the course pursued in the voyage, the port to which they sailed in China, the customs of the people there, and the nature and mode of conducting the trade; they form, in fact, the first authentic accounts we have of the Chinese from western writers, and make us doubt a little whether others like them have not been lost, rather than suppose that such were never written. These interesting relics were translated by Reinaud in 1845, with the text and notes.[2] The second traveller speaks of the sack of the city of Canfu, then the port of all the Arabian merchants, in which one hundred and twenty thousand Mohammedans, Jews, Christians, and Magians, or Parsees, engaged in traffic, were destroyed. This shows the extent and value of the trade. Canfu was Kanpu, a fine port near the modern town of the same name, twenty-five miles from Hangchau, and near Chapu on the Bay of Hangchau; the

---

[1] Tennent's *Ceylon*, I., pp. 607–626. Yule's *Cathay*, pp. lxvi–lxxvi.

[2] *Relation des Voyages faits par les Arabes et les Persans dans l'Inde et à la Chine dans le IXme Siècle de l'ère Chrètienne*, 2 Vols., Paris, 1845.

Gates of China were probably in the Chusan Archipelago and its numerous channels. Much of the statement made by Abu Zaid respecting the wealth, extent, and splendor of Canfu really refers to the city of Hangchau. The bore in the Tsientang River makes it impossible for ships to lie off that place, and this had its effect in developing Kanpu. The destruction of the capital in 877 contributed to direct part of the trade to Canton, which even then and long after was comparatively a small place, and the people of that part of the country but little removed from gross barbarism. In Marco Polo's time Ganpu was frequented by all the ships that bring merchandise from India.[1]

Prior to the date when he reached the confines of the Pacific, the ravages of the Mongols, under Genghis and his successors, in the regions between the Mediterranean and Caspian, and their great victory near Lignitz, April 12, 1241, had aroused the fears of the Pope and other potentates for their own safety. After the sudden recall of the hosts of Okkodai, in the same year, at his death, and their retreat from Bohemia and Poland to the Dneiper, the Pope determined to send two missions to the Tartars to urge them to greater humanity. One was a Franciscan monk, John of Piano Carpini, who carried the following letter to Batu khan on the Wolga:

INNOCENT, BISHOP, SERVANT OF THE SERVANTS OF GOD, TO THE KING AND PEOPLE OF THE TARTARS.

Since not only men, but also irrational animals, and even the mechanical mundane elements, are united by some kind of alliance, after the example of superior spirits, whose hosts the Author of the universe has established in a perpetual and peaceful order, we are compelled to wonder, not without reason, how you, as we have heard, having entered many lands of Christians and others, have wasted them with horrible desolation, and still, with continued fury, not ceasing to extend further your destroying hands, dissolving every natural tie, neither sparing sex nor age, direct indifferently against all the fury of the sword. We therefore, after the example of the Prince of Peace, desiring to unite all mankind in unity and the fear of God, warn, beseech, and exhort you henceforth to desist wholly from such outragos, and especially from

[1] *Chinese Repository*, Vol. I., pp. 6, 42, 252; Vol. III., p. 115. Yule's *Marco Polo*, Vol. II., pp. 149, 156. *Cathay*, p. cxciii.

the persecution of Christians ; and since, by so many and so great offences, you have doubtless grievously provoked the wrath of the Divine majesty, that you make satisfaction to him by suitable penitence ; and that you be not so daring as to carry your rage further, because the omnipotent God has hitherto permitted the nations to be laid prostrate before your face. He sometimes thus passes by the proud men of the age ; but if they do not humble themselves, he will not fail to inflict the severest temporal punishment on their guilt. And now, behold, we send our beloved brother John, and his companions, bearers of these presents, men conspicuous for religion and honesty, and endued with a knowledge of sacred Scripture, whom we hope you will kindly receive and honorably treat as if they were ourselves, placing confidence in what they may say from us, and specially treat with them on what relates to peace, and fully intimate what has moved you to this extermination of other nations, and what you further intend, providing them in going and returning with a safe conductor, and other things needful for returning to our presence. We have chosen to send to you the said friars, on account of their exemplary conduct and knowledge of the sacred Scriptures, and because they would be more useful to you as imitating the humility of our Saviour, and if we had thought they would be more grateful and useful to you, we would have sent other prelates or powerful men.[1]

M. D'Avezac's essay contains a full account of the travels and proceedings of Carpini and his companion, Benedict, in their hazardous journey of a hundred days from Kiev, across the plains of Russia and Bokhara, to the court of Kuyuk, who had succeeded Okkodai. They were first sent forward by the commanding officers of the several posts to Batu's camp, where the Pope's letter was translated ; from hence they were again despatched at the most rapid rate, on horseback, to Kara-korum, where they arrived July 22, 1246, almost exhausted. After they had been there a few days the election was decided, and all ambassadors were introduced to an audience to the khan. when the Pope's envoys alone were without a present. The letter was read, and an answer returned in a few weeks in the same style. These two potentates, so singularly introduced to each other in their mutual ignorance by the letters carried by John, had much more in common in their pretensions to universal dominion by the command of God than they suspected. The khan's letter was as follows :

---

[1] Murray's *Marco Polo*, p. 49. Yule's *Cathay*, p. cxxiii ff. D'Avezac's essay in the *Recueil de Voyages*, IV., p. 399.

LETTER OF THE KING OF THE TARTARS TO THE LORD POPE.

The strength of God, Kuyuk khan, the ruler of all men, to the great Pope. You and all the Christian people who dwell in the West have sent by your messengers sure and certain letters for the purpose of making peace with us. This we have heard from them, and it is contained in your letter. Therefore, if you desire to have peace with us, you Pope, emperors, all kings, all men powerful in cities, by no means delay to come to us for the purpose of concluding peace, and you will hear our answer and our will. The series of your letters contained that we ought to be baptized and to become Christians; we briefly reply, that we do not understand why we ought to do so. As to what is mentioned in your letters, that you wonder at the slaughter of men, and chiefly of Christians, especially Hungarians, Poles, and Moravians, we shortly answer, that this too we do not understand. Nevertheless, lest we should seem to pass it over in silence, we think proper to reply as follows: It is because they have not obeyed the precept of God and of Genghis khan, and, holding bad counsel, have slain our messengers;[1] wherefore God has ordered them to be destroyed, and delivered them into our hands. But if God had not done it, what could man have done to man? But you, inhabitants of the West, believe that you only are Christians, and despise others; but how do you know on whom he may choose to bestow his favor? We adore God, and, in his strength, will overwhelm the whole earth from the east to the west. But if we men were not strengthened by God, what could we do?[2]

The khan took the precaution, which the Pope did not, of putting his reply into an intelligible language, and when it was written in Tartar he had it carefully explained to the friars, who translated it into Latin, and were soon after dismissed. They left the court on November 13, 1246, and "travelled all winter through a wide open country, being commonly obliged to sleep on the ground after clearing away the snow, with which in the morning they often found themselves covered." They reached Kiev the next June, and Carpini was rewarded for his hardships by being appointed Archbishop of Antivari in Dalmatia. As Yule remarks, "they were the first to bring to western Europe the revived knowledge of a great and civilized nation lying in the extreme East upon the shores of the ocean."

Louis XI. of France having heard that Sartach, the son of Batu, then commanding on the western frontier, was a Chris-

---

[1] Allusion is here made to Tartar ambassadors, whom the Russians murdered before the battle of Kalka.

[2] Murray's *Marco Polo*, p. 59.

tian, sent a mission to him, consisting of the friar William Rubruquis[1] and three companions. They left Constantinople May 7, 1253, and proceeded to the Crimea, from whence they set out with a present of wines, fruits, and biscuits intended for the khan. In three days they met the Tartars, who conducted them first to Scacatai, a chieftain by whom, after considerable delay and vexation, they were furnished with everything necessary for a journey across the plains of southern Russia to the Wolga and the camp of Sartach. The monks attempted to convert the rude nomads, but ignorance of the language and suspicions of their intentions interposed great obstacles on both sides. On arriving at the end of their journey, they were disappointed at finding the ruler of these warriors a besotted infidel, who expected all persons admitted into his presence to bring him costly presents. A Nestorian named Cojat, whom Rubruquis regarded as no better than a heretic, was high in authority, and the only medium of communication with the khan. He told the friar to bring his books and vestments and make himself ready to appear before the khan on the morrow; their elegance was such that at the close of the audience Cojat seized most of them under an idle pretext that it was improper to appear in them a second time before Batu khan, to whom Rubruquis and his companions were to be sent.

Their journey was soon after prosecuted by following up the Wolga some distance, and when they arrived at the encampment of Batu khan, he made many inquiries about the resources and power of the French king and the war he was waging with the Saracens. On his introduction, "the friar bent one knee, but finding this unsatisfactory did not choose to contend, and dropped on both. Misled by his position, instead of answering questions he began a prayer for the conversion of the khan, with warning of the dreadful consequences of unbelief. The prince merely smiled; but the derision which was loudly expressed by the surrounding chiefs threw him into a good deal of confusion." The interview was followed by an order to proceed to the court

[1] Or, more correctly, Rubruk, as D'Avezac has pointed out (*Bull. de la Soc. de Géogr.*, 1868), and in whose conclusions Yule joins (*Marco Polo*, second edition, p. 536).

of Mangu, who had succeeded Kuyuk as Grand khan. This long journey occupied four months, through the high land of Central Asia (farther eastward than where Carpini found Kuyuk's court), and subjected them to severe hardships. Mangu received the mission hardly with civility, but having been examined by some Nestorian priests, they were admitted to an audience. The same ceremonies were required as at Batu's court, and inquiries made as to the possessions of the French king, especially the number of rams, horses, and oxen he owned, which, the friar was amazed to learn, were soon to be attacked by the Tartars. No permission to remain could be obtained, but he was furnished with a house and allowed to tarry till the cold mitigated. In this remote region he found a European architect, William Bourchier, and his wife, from Mentz, besides many Armenians, Saracens, and Nestorians, all of whom the khan received. He accompanied the court to Kara-korum, where he nearly became involved in dangerous religious disputes, and on the approach of milder weather was compelled to return to Batu khan, by whom he was sent on, in a south-westerly direction, until he entered Armenia, and thence found his way to Iconium, having been absent nearly two years.

These ambassadors had not the aid of printing to diffuse their narratives, and it was perhaps chiefly owing to the high standing of those who sent them that their relations have been preserved. In the case of many travellers of humbler origin or pretensions, there was no inducement to write what they had seen; these therefore only told their stories, which were lost with the narrators. Even the travels of Marco Polo would perhaps never have been given to the world if the leisure of captivity had not induced him to adopt this method of relieving its tedium. Every examination of his record has added to its reputation for accuracy, both in the position of the cities he mentions or visited and in the events he details; and when it is considered that he dictated it several years after his return to a fellow-prisoner, Rusticiano of Pisa, who wrote it in French, his accuracy is wonderful. The edition by Marsden in 1818 remained for fifty years the chief authority, but the recent editions by Pauthier and Yule, with their full notes, have made the traveller's record vastly better understood, while adding much to our knowledge of mediæval Asia.

Ser Marco Polo, the Venetian, was the son of Nicolo Polo, who with his brother Matteo, nobles and merchants of Venice, first left that city about 1254, and Constantinople in 1260, on a mercantile voyage to the Crimea, from which point a series of events led them eastward as far as China, then lately conquered by Kublai, the Grand Khan and successor of Mangu khan, whom Rubruquis visited. They were favorably received, and when they left Kublai it was under a promise to return, which they did about December, 1274, bearing letters from Gregory X., and accompanied by young Marco, then about sixteen years old. He soon became a favorite with the Emperor, and was able to travel to many parts of the country, spending in all about twenty-one years in the East; the three Polos reached Venice again in 1295. Marco was prefect at Yangchau on the Grand Canal for three years, and this involves a knowledge of Mongolian and Chinese speech and writing, without which he could hardly have administered its official duties. His possession of these accomplishments was nearly indispensable to the post, though Col. Yule infers, from an easily explained mistake in Chapter LXXV., that he did not have them. On reaching Venice, by way of India and Persia, the long-lost travellers appeared so completely altered that their friends and countrymen did not recognize them. Their wealth and entertaining recitals, however, soon restored them to the highest ranks of society. The industry of recent editors has probably brought together all that can be learned of their subsequent history, which is now so well known as to require no further words here.

In the year 1254, Hethum, or Hayton, king of Little Armenia, undertook a journey to Mangu khan, to petition for an abatement of the tribute which he had been obliged to pay the Mongols. Having first sent forth his brother, Sempad, or Sinibald (in 1246), to Kuyuk khan, Hayton himself set out upon the accession to the throne of his successor. Passing through Kars and Armenia Proper to the Wolga, he was there received by Batu and forwarded by a route to the north of that traversed by Carpini to Kara-korum and the Grand khan. At the end of a six weeks' sojourn with the court, during which time he appears to have been kindly received, Hayton commenced his homeward journey via Bishbalig and Songaria to Samarkand, Bokhara, Khorasan, and thence to Tabriz. The accounts of these two embassies, wherein are described many wonderful things concerning the heathens of the East and barbarians upon the route, made up, doubtless, a large part of the "History" (written in 1307) by the king's relative, Hayton of Gorigos.[1] The different positions held by these men and the Polos naturally led each of them to look upon the same people and events with vastly different feelings. The efforts of John of Montecorvino to propagate Christianity in China were undertaken just as the Polos returned, but no detailed accounts of his labors (beyond what Col. Yule has gathered in his *Cathay*) have been preserved.

Among the most important mediæval travellers in Asia was the Moor, Ibn Batuta, who at the age of twenty-one set out (in 1325) upon his journeys, from which he did not return until thirty years later.[2] Abu-Abdullah Mahomed (nicknamed Ibn Batuta, "The Traveller") commenced his wanderings, which were contemporaneous with those of the more doubtful Englishman, Sir John Mandeville, by a series of pilgrimages to the sacred places of his religion; among other excursions, he found time at one period to continue three years in Mecca. Going from one city to another, along the shores of the Mediterranean, and in the countries between it and the Caspian, he at length reached Delhi, where he resided eight years, enjoying—until the latter end of his stay—high favor from the Sultan Mahomed. The versatile Moor occupied the position of judge, though there is good reason to doubt his serious attention to any business while at this magnificent court, other than that of spending his master's money. In the spring of 1342, having recovered

[1] The chapter concerning Cathay appears in Yule's *Cathay*, p. cxcv. A translation of the elder Hayton's narrative is given by Klaproth in the *Journal Asiatique*, IIe Séries, Tome XII., pp. 273 ff.

[2] His work has been very ably edited and translated into French by M. Defrémery and Dr. Sanguinetti (four volumes, Paris, 1858–59), under the patronage of the Asiatic Society of Paris. Several partial translations of the journal have appeared from time to time within the present century.

from a temporary disgrace, he was despatched on an ambassy to China by the Sultan. It seems that a Chinese envoy had arrived at Delhi to request permission for the natives to rebuild a temple in Butan, as they were poor and dependent upon the inhabitants of the plain, and had besought the Chinese government to intercede for them. Ibn Batuta was sent with lavish presents to the Emperor, but a refusal to assist in the building project unless that sovereign would go through the form of paying a poll-tax to the Sultan. This embassy was attacked by a body of Hindus when scarcely out of Delhi, and obliged to return. Again it was sent out, going to Calicut on the Malabar coast, where were found fifteen Chinese vessels or galleys at anchor, whose crews and guard amounted to a thousand men each. The envoy embarked his attendants on one of these ships, but while he remained on shore to pray for a prosperous voyage, a storm sunk the vessel and all on board. After this second mishap the luckless Moor was afraid to return to his master, and went to Sumatra, from whence he found his way to China, landing at Zayton, the present Chinchew, in Fuhkien.

Though it is doubtful if Ibn Batuta, notwithstanding his description of the place, ever reached Peking, his spirited accounts of Zayton, Sinkalan (Canton), Khansa (Hangchau), Kanjanfu, and other centres of trade in the south, are both entertaining and important. Spite of exaggerations, confusion of names and dates, and certain cases of positive fiction, one can hardly fail to put faith in the generality of his statements and conclude in favor of his veracity and genuine character. He mentions that the circulation of paper money, which Marco Polo thought so excellent a device for a king to raise funds, had entirely driven out the use of metallic currency. In every large town he found Mohammedans, ruled by officers of their own persuasion.

The journal of Friar Odoric (1286–1331) contains much of interest in connection with China of the middle ages. This worthy priest landed at "Censcalan" (Canton), after a long and tedious trip from Bagdad round by Sumatra and thence northeast by land to Zayton. Here, says he, "we friars minor have two houses, and there I deposited the bones of our friars who suffered martyrdom for the faith of Jesus Christ." He had brought these relics from Tana, near Bombay. Thence he journeyed to Fuhchau, Hangchau, and Nanking, going on northward to Peking, where the aged archbishop, Corvino, was still living, and remained there three years. His return journey as far as H'lassa was not very different from that of Huc and Gabet in 1843; from the Tibetan capital he probably continued on a westerly course to Cabul and Tabriz, reaching Venice in 1330, after an absence of thirteen years. His itinerary was taken down the following year by William of Solagna, a brother of the order, at Padua.

In this narrative there is mention of a number of characteristics of the Chinese, well known to all the world of to-day, but left wholly unnoticed by other travellers of his age. "His notices of the custom of fishing with cormorants, of the habits of letting the finger-nails grow long, and of compressing the women's feet, as well as of the divisions of the khan's Empire into twelve provinces, with four chief vizirs, are peculiar to him, I believe, among all the European travellers of the age. Polo mentions none of them. The names which he assigns to the Chinese post-stations, and to the provincial Boards of Administration, the technical Turki term which he uses for a sack of rice, etc., are all tokens of the reality of his experience."[1] On the other hand, the influence of superstition upon their own minds rendered most of the religious travellers into Central Asia—Odoric as well as the others—less trustworthy and observant than they would perhaps have been either centuries before or after that period. Everything of a religious sort they regarded as done under the direct agency of the powers of darkness, into whose dominions they were venturing. Too fearful, moreover, to examine candidly or record accurately what they beheld, these pious adventurers were constantly misled by endeavors to explain any uncommon experience by referring the same to their own imperfect or erroneous conceptions. This is true as well of the Romish priests connected with the Peking mission, a few of whose letters have been preserved and re-

[1] Yule, *Cathay and the Way Thither*, p. 21.

cently made known to the public by Col. Yule; among these are Friar Jordanus, Bishop Andrew of Zayton, Pascal of Vittoria, together with the Archbishop of Soltania, author of the "Book of the Estate and Governance of the Great Caan of Cathay."[1]

But much fairer than these missionaries, in his reputation for veracity, was the Jesuit Benedict Goës, who in the century preceding what may be termed the modern period of our knowledge of China, undertook a journey across the desert, to die on the threshold of the Empire. Born in one of the islands of the Azore group, Goës spent his youth in the profession of a soldier on board of the Portuguese fleet. Becoming suddenly converted, he entered the service of the Jesuits as a lay brother—which humble rank he resolutely held during the rest of his career—and was sent to the court of Akbar. His residence in India gained him a high reputation for courage, judgment, and skill in the Persian tongue, the *lingua franca* of Asia at that date. He was selected, therefore, to undertake a journey to the Cathay of Marco Polo, in the capital of which Jerome Xavier thought he had hopes of finding the Christian ruler and descendant of Prester John. Goës set out from Agra in 1602, joined a company of merchants, and with them took a route passing through Cabul, the Hindu kush, along the River Oxus to its head-waters on the Pamir table-land, and so to Yangi Hissar, Yarkand, Aksu, and Suh-chau, where he was detained seventeen months, and finally died, shortly after assistance had been sent him from the mission at Peking.

His journey was full of terrible hardships, and it was to these as well as to the careless treatment he suffered in Suh-chau that he owed his untimely end. Could we have Goës' own narrative of his experience, the information concerning the unknown regions of Central Asia over which he toiled would be of priceless worth. His journals, however, were either lost or destroyed during his miserable detention at the frontier town, and nothing remained save a few meagre notes

[1] About 1330. See ibid., pp. 238–250.

and his faithful Armenian servant Isaac, whose language no one at Peking could understand. Such as it was, an account was compiled from these sources by Ricci himself, and published soon after that missionary's death in the work of Trigautius, *De Christiana Expeditione apud Sinas.*[1] To Benedict Goës we may give the credit of the discovery that *Cathay* and *China* (*Sina*) were in reality one and the same land. It is a curious illustration of the condition of intercommunication between distant parts of the world in those days, that this fact must have been known to the earliest Jesuit missionaries in Peking, though the friars of the same order stationed in India held to a belief in Cambaluc and its Christian prince until far into the seventeenth century.

In many particulars the practical descriptions of Abu Zaid, Masudi,[2] Ibn Wahab, and Marco Polo stand in decided contrast to the details noted down by such as Rubruquis and Odoric. The accounts of all these writers convey the impression that China was in their time free to all travellers. Ibn Wahab, speaking of the regulations practised under the Tang dynasty, observes:

> If a man would travel from one province to another, he must take two passes with him, one from the governor, the other from the eunuch [or lieutenant]. The governor's pass permits him to set out on his journey and contains the names of the traveller and those also of his company, also the ages of the one and the other and the clan to which he belongs. For every traveller in China, whether a native or an Arab, or other foreigner, cannot avoid carrying a paper with him containing everything by which he can be verified. The eunuch's pass specifies the quantities of money or goods which the traveller and those with him take along; this is done for the information of officers at the frontier places where these two passes are examined. Whenever a traveller arrives at any of them, it is registered that "Such a one, son of such a one, of such a calling, passed here on such a day, month, and year, having

[1] A translation of this notice appears in Col. Yule's oft-quoted *Cathay and the Way Thither*, pp. 529–591. Trigautius' work appeared in 1615, and was subsequently translated into all the continental languages. Compare Purchas, *His Pilgrimes*, Vol. III., pp. 380, ff.—*A Discourse of the Kingdome of China, taken out of Riccivs and Trigavtivs, contayning the Countrey, People, Gouernment*, etc., etc.

[2] Reinaud, *Relation des Voyages*, etc. MM. Barbier de Meynard and Pavet de Courteille, *Les Praries d'Or*, Paris, 1861–66.

such things with him." The government resorts to this means to prevent danger to travellers in their money or goods; for should one suffer loss or die, everything about him is immediately known and he himself or his heirs after his death receive whatever is his.[1]

The same writer speaks of the Mabed, a nation dwelling in Yunnan, on the south-west, who sent ambassadors every year with presents to the Emperor; and in return he sent presents annually to them. These embassies, indeed, were simply trading companies in disguise, who came from the Persians, Arabs, and other nations, with every protestation of respect and humility, bearing presents to the Son of Heaven. The dignity of the Emperor demanded that these should be returned with gifts three or four times the value of this "tribute," and that the ambassadors should be royally entertained during their sojourn at the capital. It is needless to add that such missions were repeated by the merchants as often as circumstances would permit. Entrance into the country overland otherwise than by some such ruse seems to have been withheld after the fall of the Mongol dynasty.

It was, however, not until the subjugation of the Empire by the Manchus that foreign trade was limited to Canton, the jealous conduct of the present rulers being to a certain extent actuated by a fear of similar reprisals from some quarter, which the Mongols experienced. The outrageous behavior of foreign traders themselves must, moreover, be regarded as a chief cause of the watchful seclusion with which they were treated. "Their early conduct," says Sir John Davis, referring to the Portuguese, "was not calculated to impress the Chinese with any favorable idea of Europeans; and when in course of time they came to be competitors with the Dutch and the English, the contests of mercantile avarice tended to place them all in a still worse point of view. To this day the character of the Europeans is represented as that of a race of men intent alone on the gains of commercial traffic, and regardless altogether of the means of attainment. Struck by the perpetual hostilities which existed among these foreign adventurers, as-

---

[2] Reinaud, *Relation*, Tome I., p. 41.

similated in other respects by a close resemblance in their costumes and manners, the government of the country became disposed to treat them with a degree of jealousy and exclusion which it had not deemed necessary to be exercised toward the more peaceable and well ordered Arabs, their predecessors." [1]

These characteristics of avarice, lawlessness, and power have been the leading traits in the Chinese estimate of foreigners from their first acquaintance with them, and the latter have done little to effectually disabuse orientals upon these points. The following record of their first arrival, taken from a Chinese work, is still good authority in the general opinion of the natives:

> During the reign of Chingtih [1506], foreigners from the West, called Fah-lan-kí [Franks], who said that they had tribute, abruptly entered the Bogue, and by their tremendously loud guns, shook the place far and near. This was reported at court, and an order returned to drive them away immediately and stop their trade. At about this time also the Hollanders, who in ancient times inhabited a wild territory and had no intercourse with China, came to Macao in two or three large ships. Their clothes and their hair were red; their bodies tall; they had blue eyes, sunk deep in their heads. Their feet were one cubit and two-tenths long; and they frightened the people by their strange appearance. [2]

The Portuguese Rafael Perestrello sailed in a junk for China in 1516, five years after the conquest of Malacca, and was the first person who ever conducted a vessel to China under a European flag. Ferdinand Andrade came in the next year, in four Portuguese and four Malay ships, and gave great satisfaction to the authorities at Canton by his fair dealings; his galleons were allowed to anchor at Shangchuen, or St. John's Island. His brother Simon came the following year, and by his atrocious conduct entirely reversed the good opinion formed of his countrymen; the Chinese besieged him in port and drove him away in 1521. Others of his countrymen followed him, and one of the earliest ships accompanied some Chinese junks along the coast, and succeeded in establishing a factory

---

[1] *The Chinese*, Vol. I., p. 20.

[2] The term *Hung-mâo*, or 'red-haired,' then applied to the Dutch, has since been transferred to the English.

at Ningpo; trade was also conducted at Amoy. In 1537 there were three Portuguese settlements near Canton, one at St. John's, one at a smaller island called Lampaçao (Lang-peh-kau), lying north-west of the Grand Ladrones, and the third just begun on Macao.[1] In 1542 traders had left St. John's for Lampaçao, and ten years afterward, at the time of Xavier's death, trade was concentrated at the latter, where five or six hundred Portuguese constantly resided in 1560. Macao was commenced under the pretext of erecting sheds for drying goods introduced under the appellation of tribute, and alleged to have been damaged in a storm. In 1573 the Chinese government erected a barrier wall across the isthmus joining Macao to the island of Hiangshan, and in 1587 established a civil magistracy to rule the Chinese. By their ill conduct at Ningpo the Portuguese drew upon them the vengeance of the people, who rose upon them and "destroyed twelve thousand Christians, including eight hundred Portuguese, and burned thirty-five ships and two junks." One of their provocative acts is stated to have been going out in large parties into the neighboring villages and seizing the women and virgins, by which they justly lost their privileges in one of the provinces and ports best adapted to European trade. Four years later, in 1549, they were also driven from their newly formed settlement at Chinchew.

The Portuguese have sent four embassies to the Emperor of China. The first envoy, Thomé Pires, was appointed by the Governor at Goa, and accompanied Ferdinand Andrade to Canton, in 1517, where he was received and treated in the usual style of foreign ambassadors. When his mission was reported at Peking the Emperor Chingtih was influenced against it by a subject of the Sultan of Malacca, and detained Pires at Canton three years; the flagitious conduct of Andrade's brother

---

[1] There stood originally on the site of this town an idol known as *Ama. Amau-gau*, or *Ama-kau*, then, meant the 'Harbor of Ama,' which in Portuguese was written *Amacao*, and afterward shortened to *Macao*. Comp. Trigautius, *De Christiana Expeditione apud Sinas*, 1615. Nieuwhof, *Nauwkeurige Beschryvinge vau't Gesandschap*, etc., Amsterdam, 1664. Sir A. Ljungstedt, *Historical Sketch of the Portuguese Settlements in China*, Boston, 1836. *Chinese Commercial Guide*, fifth edition, p. 229.

and the character of the Portuguese induced the Emperor to appoint a court to examine whether the embassy was legitimate or spurious, and Pires and his companions were adjudged to be spies and sent back to Canton to be detained till Malacca was restored. This not being done, he and others suffered death in September, 1523; other accounts lead to the inference that he died in prison. Thus the innocent were made to suffer for the guilty. The next embassy was undertaken in 1552, at the suggestion of Xavier, by the Viceroy of Goa, but the mission proceeded no farther than Malacca, the governor of that town refusing to allow it to leave the place—a significant intimation of the degree of subordination and order maintained by the Portuguese in the administration of their new colonies. The third was also sent from Goa in 1667, in the name of Alfonso VI., on occasion of the suspension of the trade of Macao by Kanghí; the expense was defrayed by that colony (about forty thousand dollars), and "the result of it so little answered their expectations that the Senate solicited his Majesty not to intercede in behalf of his vassals at Macao with the government of China, were it not in an imperious and cogent case."

A good opportunity and necessity for this, it was thought, presented itself in 1723, when Magaillans returned to China carrying the answer of the Pope to Kanghí, to send an envoy, Alexander Metello, along with him to Peking. He arrived at court in May, 1727, and had his audience of leave in July, receiving in exchange for the thirty chests of presents which he offered, and which Yungching received with pleasure "as evidences of the affection of the King of Portugal," as many for his master, besides a cup of wine and some porcelain dishes, sent from the Emperor's table, and other presents for himself and his retinue, which were "valuable solely because they were the gifts of a monarch." No more advantage resulted from this than the embassy sent a century previous, though it cost the inhabitants of Macao a like heavy sum. Another and last Portuguese embassy reached Peking in 1753, conducted and ending in much the same manner as its predecessors; all of them exhibiting, in a greater or less degree, the spectacle of humiliating submission of independent nations through their envoys to a court which took pleasure in arrogantly exalting itself on the homage it received, and studiously avoided all reference to the real business of the embassy, that it might neither give nor deny anything. But in estimating its conduct in these respects, it must not be overlooked that the imperial court never associated commercial equality and regulations with embassies and tribute.

The influence and wealth of the Portuguese in China for the last century and a half have gradual decreased. A. Swedish knight, Sir Andrew Ljungstedt, published a historical sketch of their doings down to 1833, including an account of the colony, which is still the fullest book on the subject. In 1820 the opium trade was removed to Lintin, and that being the principal source of income, the commerce of the place for many years was at a low ebb. The imperial commissioner Kíying granted some additional privileges to the settlement in 1844, among others, permitting the inhabitants to build and repair new houses, churches, and ships without a license, and to trade at the five ports open to foreign commerce on the same terms as other nations; it was just three centuries before this that the Portuguese were driven away from Ningpo. The anchorage of the Typa was included in the jurisdiction of Macao, but the application of the Portuguese commissioner to surcease payment of the annual ground-rent of five hundred taels to the Chinese met with a decided refusal. Its advantages as a summer resort and its accessibility to a densely peopled region west invite visitors and traders to some extent, but the proximity and wealth of Hongkong make it secondary to that. Its short-lived prosperity in 1839–50, during the opium war and early days of Hongkong, was followed by the enlargement of the coolie trade, which for twenty-five years was the only real business. The Chinese have never ceded the peninsula to the Portuguese crown, although they were powerless to prevent the export of coolies; the relations now between the two countries are not distinctly defined. In 1862 a treaty was negotiated at Peking by Governor Guimaraēs, in which the supremacy of the Portuguese authority over the territory within the Barrier was implied rather than declared in Article IX., wherein the equal appointment of consular officers was mutually agreed to. The Chinese found out, however, that this virtually acknowledged the independence of the colony, and refused to ratify the treaty without an express stipulation asserting their right of domain to the peninsula. It has never been ratified, therefore, but trade is unfettered, and the Chinese inhabitants continue to increase; no rental has been paid for the ground-tax since 1849. The cessation of the coolie trade in 1873 has reduced Macao lower than ever, and it now hardly pays its own officials; all the thrifty or wealthy foreign citizens have removed elsewhere.

The trade between the Spaniards and Chinese has been smaller, and their relations less important than most other European nations. The Spanish admiral Legaspi conquered the Philippines in 1543, and Chinese merchants soon began to trade with Manila; but the first attempt of the Spaniards to enter China was not made until 1575, when two Augustine friars accompanied a Chinese naval officer on his return home from the pursuit of a famous pirate named Li-ma-hon, whom the Spaniards had driven away from their new colony. The missionaries landed at Tansuso, a place on the coast of Kwangtung, and went up to Canton, where they were courteously received. The prefect sent them to the governor at Shauking, by whom they were examined; they stated that their chief object was to form a close alliance between the two nations for their mutual benefit, adding at the same time what their countrymen had done against Li-ma-hon; a second object was their wish to learn the language of China and teach its inhabitants their religion. The governor kept them in a sort of honorable bondage several weeks, and at last sent them back to Manila, doubtless by orders from court, though he alleged as a reason that the pirate Li-ma-hon was still at large. After the return of this mission the governor of the Philippines deemed it advisable to let the trade take its own course, and therefore refused the proposal of a body of Franciscans to enter the country. They, however, made the attempt in a small native vessel, and passed up the river to Tsiuenchau, where they were seized and examined as to their designs. Not being acquainted with the language, they were both themselves deluded and misrepresented to the prefect by a professed native friend who understood Portuguese; after many months' delay they were mortified to learn that no permission to remain would be given, and in 1580 they returned to Manila, not at all disposed to renew the enterprise.

Philip II., however, having received the suggestion made by the Chinese admiral that he should send an embassy to Peking, had already ordered the governor to undertake such an enterprise. He fitted out a mission, therefore, in 1580, at the head of which was Martin Ignatius. It gives one a low idea of the skill of navigators at that day to learn that in this short trip, the vessel being carried up the coast northward of Canton, the party thought it better to land than to try to beat back to their destination. The envoy and all with him were brought before the Chinese officers, who, probably entirely misunderstanding their object, imprisoned them; after considerable delay they were brought before a higher officer and sent on to Canton, where they were again imprisoned; the Portuguese governor of Macao subsequently obtained their liberation. This unlucky attempt, if Mendoza is right in calling it an embassy, was the only one ever made by the Spanish government to communicate with the court of Peking until the mission of Don Sinibaldo de Mas in 1847 and his treaty of 1864. The pecular feature of that treaty was the privilege, first granted to Spanish merchants, of engaging coolies as contract laborers for Cuba. The harsh treatment they received there led the Chinese to send a commission of inquiry in 1873, and to suspend the validity of this article until the truth could be ascertained. This procedure has resulted in a cessation of imported Chinese laborers at Havana.

The Chinese have carried on a valuable trade at Manila, but the Spaniards have treated them with peculiar severity. They are burdened with special taxes, and their immigration is rather restrained than encouraged. The harsh treatment of Chinese settlers there excited the attention and indignation of one of their countrymen many years ago, and on his return to Canton he exercised all his influence with officers of his own government, making what he had seen the model and the motive to induce them to treat all foreigners at Canton in the same way. It ended in perfecting the principal features of the system of espionage and restriction of the co-hong which existed for nearly a century, until the treaty of 1842;—another instance of the treatment requited upon foreigners for their own acts.

The Dutch commerce with the East commenced after their successful struggle against the Spanish yoke, and soon after completing their independence they turned their arms against the oriental possessions of their enemies, capturing Malacca, the Spice Islands, and other places. They appeared before Macao in 1622 with a squadron of seventeen vessels, but being repulsed with the loss of their admiral and about three hundred men, they retired and established themselves on the Pescadores in 1624. Their occupation of this position was a source of great annoyance both to the Spaniards and to the Chinese authorities in Fuhkien. According to the custom of those days, they began to build a fort, and forced the native Chinese to do their work, treating them with great severity. Many of the laborers were prisoners, whom the Dutch had taken in their attacks. Alternate hostilities and parleys succeeded, the Chinese declaring that the Dutch must send an envoy to the authorities on the mainland; they accordingly despatched Von Mildert to Amoy, and the sub-prefect forwarded him to Fuhchau to the governor. He decided to send a messenger to the Dutch to state to them that trade would be allowed if they would remove to Formosa, but this proposition was refused. However, after a series of attacks and negotiations, the Chinese constantly increasing their forces and the Dutch diminishing in their supplies, the latter acceded to the proposition, and removed to Formosa, where they erected Fort Zealandia in 1624. It is recorded that the Chinese landed five thousand troops on one of the Pescadore Islands; and their determined efforts in repelling the aggressions or occupation of their soil by the Dutch probably raised their reputation for courage, and prevented the repetition of similar acts by others. It was doubtless a good stroke of policy on their part to propose the occupation of Formosa to the Dutch in exchange for the Pescadores, for they had not the least title to it themselves, and hardly knew its exact size or the character of the inhabitants. The Dutch endeavored to extend their power over it, but with only partial success; in the villages around Fort Zealandia they introduced new laws among the inhabitants, and instead of their councils of elders, constituted one of their chief men supervisor in every village, to administer justice and report his acts to the governor of the island.

The moral interests of the natives were not neglected, and in 1626 George Candidius, a Protestant minister, was appointed to labor among them, and took great pains to introduce Christianity. The natives were ignorant of letters, their superstitions resting only on traditions or customs which were of recent origin; the prospects, therefore, of teaching them a better religion were favorable. In sixteen months he had instructed over a hundred in the leading truths of Christianity. The work was progressing favorably, churches and schools were multiplying, the intermarriages of the colonists and natives were bringing them into closer relationship with each other, and many thousands of the islanders had been baptized, when the Dutch governors in India, fearful of offending the Japanese, who were then persecuting the Christians in Japan—in which the Dutch helped them, to their lasting disgrace—restricted these benevolent labors, and discouraged the further conversion of the islanders. Thus, as often elsewhere in Asia, the interests of true religion were sacrificed upon the altar of mammon, and the trade thus bought died from inanition.

During the struggles ensuent upon the overthrow of the Ming dynasty, many thousands of families emigrated to Formosa, some of whom settled under the Dutch, while others planted separate colonies; their industry soon changed the desolate island into a cultivated country, and increased the produce of rice and sugar for exportation. The immigration went on so rapidly as to alarm the Dutch, who, instead of taking wise measures to conciliate and instruct the colonists, tried to prevent their landing, and thereby did much to irritate them and lead them to join in any likely attempt to expel the foreigners.

Meanwhile, their trade with China itself was trifling compared with that of their rivals, the Portuguese, and when the undoubted ascendancy of the Manchus was evident, the government of Batavia resolved to despatch a deputation to Canton to petition for trade. In January, 1653, Schedel was sent in a richly freighted ship, but the Portuguese succeeded in preventing any further traffic, even after the envoy had spent considerable sums in presents to the authorities, and obtained the governor's promise to allow his countrymen to build a factory. Schedel was informed, however, that his masters would do well to send an embassy to Peking, a suggestion favorably entertained by the Company, which, in 1655, appointed Goyer and Keyzer as its envoys. The narrative of this embassy by Nieuwhof, the steward of the mission, made Europeans better acquainted with the country than they had before been—almost the only practical benefit it produced, for as a mercantile speculation it proved nearly a total loss. Their presents were received and others given in return; they prostrated themselves not only before the Emperor in person, but made the *kotow* to his name, his letters, and his throne, doing everything in the way of humiliation and homage likely to please the new rulers. The only privilege their subserviency obtained was permission to send an embassy once in eight years, at which time they might come in four ships to trade.

This mission left China in 1657, and very soon after, the Chinese chieftain, Ching Ching-kung (Koshinga, or Koxinga as his name is written by the Portuguese), began to prepare an attack upon Formosa. The Dutch had foreseen the probability of this onset, and had been strengthening the garrison of Zealandia since 1650 while they were negotiating for trade; Koxinga, too, had confined himself to sending emissaries among his countrymen in Formosa, to inform them of his designs. He set about preparing an armament at Amoy, ostensibly to strengthen himself against the Manchus, meanwhile carrying on his ordinary traffic with the colony to lull all apprehensions until the council had sent away the admiral and force despatched from Java to protect them, when in June, 1661, he landed a force of twenty-five thousand troops, and took up a strong position. The communication between the forts being cut off, the governor sent two hundred and forty men to dislodge the enemy, only half of whom returned alive; one of the four ships in the harbor was burned by the Chinese, and another hastened to Batavia for reinforcements. Koxinga followed up these successes by cutting off all communication between the garrison and the surrounding country, and compelling the surrender of the garrison and cannon in the small fort. Fort Zealandia was now closely invested, but finding himself severely galled, he turned the siege into a blockade, and vented his rage against the Dutch living in the surrounding country, and such Chinese as abetted them. Some of the ministers and schoolmasters were seized and crucified, under the pretext that they encouraged their parishioners to resist; others were used as agents to treat concerning the surrender of the fort. Valentyn has given a clear history of the occupation of Formosa by his countrymen in his great work, and especially of their defeat at Zealandia. He narrates an incident of Rev. A. Hambroek, as does also Nieuwhof, from whose travels it is quoted.

Among the Dutch prisoners taken in the country, was one Mr. Hambroek, a minister. This man was sent by Koxinga to the governor, to propose terms for surrendering the fort; and that in case of refusal, vengeance would be taken on the Dutch prisoners. Mr. Hambroek came into the castle, being forced to leave his wife and children behind him as hostages, which sufficiently proved that if he failed in his negotiation, they had nothing but death to expect from the chieftain. Yet was he so far from persuading the garrison to surrender, that he encouraged them to a brave defence by hopes of relief, assuring them that Koxinga had lost many of his best ships and soldiers, and began to be weary of the siege. When he had ended, the council of war left it to his choice to stay with them or return to the camp, where he could expect nothing but present death; every one entreated him to stay. He had two daughters within the castle, who hung upon his neck, overwhelmed with grief and tears to see their father ready to go where they knew he must be sacrificed by the merciless enemy. But he represented to them that having left his wife and two other children as hostages, nothing but death could attend them if he returned not: so unlocking himself from his daughters' arms, and exhorting everybody to a resolute defence, he returned to the camp, telling them at parting that he hoped he might prove serviceable to his poor fellow-prisoners. Koxinga received his answer sternly; then causing it to be rumored that the prisoners excited the Formosans to rebel, he ordered all the Dutch male prisoners to be slain; some being beheaded, others killed in a more barbarous manner, to the number of five hundred, their bodies stripped quite naked and buried; nor were the women and children spared, many of them likewise being slain, though some of the best were preserved for the use of the commanders, and the rest sold to the common soldiers. Among the slain were Messrs. Hambroek, Mus, Winsam, Ampzingius, and Campius, clergymen, and many schoolmasters.

A force of ten ships and seven hundred men arriving from Batavia, the besieged began to act on the offensive, but were unable to drive Koxinga from the town, though they checked his operations and brought down the garrisons from Kílung and Tamsui to their aid. A letter from the governor of Fuhkien to Coyet, the Dutch governor, came soon after, suggesting a junction of their forces to drive Koxinga away from the coast, after which both could easily conquer him in Formosa. This proposal was followed, but no sooner had the five vessels gone than Koxinga made his advances so vigorously that the garrison was forced to surrender, after a siege of nine months and the loss of one thousand six hundred men. Thus ended the Dutch rule in Formosa, after twenty-eight years' duration.[1]

This loss induced the council at Batavia to prosecute their former enterprise against Amoy, where Koxinga still had a garrison. Twelve vessels were fitted out under Bort, who arrived, in 1662, at the mouth of the River Min, where he was visited by deputies from the governor, and induced to send two of his officers to arrange with him concerning operations. The governor was in the country, and the two officers, on reaching his camp, soon saw that thoro could be no cordiality between their leaders; this proposal of a foreign power to assist them against the Chinese was too much like that of Wu San-kwei to their chieftains in 1644 for the Manchus to entertain it. Bort, desirous of doing something, commenced a series of attacks on the fleet and garrisons of Koxinga, burning and destroying them

[1] *Chinese Repository*, Vols. I., p. 414, and XX., p. 543. *Journal N. C. Br. R. As. Soc.*, Vol. XI. (1876), Art. I. Moreau de St.-Mêry, *Voyage de l'Ambassade de la Compagnie des Indes orientales Hollandaises vers l'Empereur de la Chine, tiré du journal d'André Everard van Braam Houckgeest*, translated and published in London, 2 Vols., 1798. J. Nieuwhof, *Nauwkeurige Beschryvinge van't Gesandschap der Nederlandtsche Oost-Indische Compagnie van Batavia nar Peking in Sina, door de Heeren Pieter de Goyer en Jacob de Keyser*, Amsterdam, 1664.

in a piratical manner, that was not less ineffectual toward regaining Formosa and obtaining privilege of trade at Canton than harassing to the Chinese on the coast. He returned to Batavia in 1663, and was despatched to Fuhkien in a few months with a stronger force, and ordered to make reprisals on both Manchus and Chinese, if necessary, in order to get satisfaction for the loss of Formosa. The governor received him favorably, and after a number of skirmishes against the rebellious Chinese, Amoy was taken and its troops destroyed, which completed the subjugation of the province to the Manchus. As a reward for this assistance, the real value of which cannot, however, be easily ascertained, the governor lent *two junks* to the Dutch to retake Formosa, but Koxinga laughed at the pitiful force sent against him, and Bort sailed for Batavia.

These results so chagrined the council that they fitted out no more expeditions, preferring to despatch an embassy, under Van Hoorn, to Peking, to petition for trade and permission to erect factories. He landed at Fuhchau in 1664, where he was received in a polite manner. The imperial sanction had been already received, but he unwisely delayed his journey to the capital until his cargo was sold. While discussing this matter the Dutch seized a Chinese vessel bringing bullion from Java contrary to their colonial regulations, and the governor very properly intimated that until restitution was made no amicable arrangement could be completed; consequently Van Hoorn, in order to save his dignity and not contravene the orders of his own government, was obliged to allow the bullion to be carried off, as if by force, by a police officer.

These preliminary disputes were not settled till nearly a year had elapsed, when Van Hoorn and his suite left Fuhchau, and after a tedious journey up the River Min and across the mountains to Hangchau, they reached the canal and Peking, having been six months on the way, "during which they saw thirty-seven cities and three hundred and thirty-five villages." The same succession of prostrations before an empty throne, followed by state banquets, and accompanied by the presentation and conferring of presents, characterized the reception of this embassy as it had all its predecessors. It ended with a similar farce, alike pleasing to the haughty court which received it, and unworthy the Christian nation which gave it; and the "only result of this grand expedition was a sealed letter, of the contents of which they were wholly ignorant, but which did not, in fact, grant any of the privileges they so anxiously solicited." They had, by their performance of the act of prostration, caused their nation to be enrolled among the tributaries of the Grand khan, and then were dismissed as loyal subjects should be, at the will of their liege lord, with what he chose to give them. It was a fitting end to a career begun in rapine and aggression toward the Chinese, who had never provoked them.

The Dutch sent no more embassies to Peking for one hundred and thirty years, but carried on trade at Canton on the same footing as other nations. The ill success of Macartney's embassy in 1793 induced Van Braam, the consular agent at Canton, to propose a mission of salutation and respect from the government of Batavia, on the occasion of Kienlung reaching the sixtieth year of his reign. He hoped, by conforming to Chinese ceremonies, to obtain some privileges which would place Dutch trade on a better footing, but one would have supposed that the miscarriage of former attempts might have convinced him that nothing was to be gained by new humiliations before a court which had just dismissed a well-appointed embassy. The Company appointed Isaac Titsingh, late from Japan, as chief commissioner, giving Van Braam the second place, and making up their cortege with a number of clerks and interpreters, one of whom, De Guignes, wrote the results of his researches during a long residence in Canton, and his travels with the embassy to Peking, under the title of *Voyages à Peking*. It is needless to detail the annoyances, humiliations, and contemptuous treatment experienced by the embassy on its overland journey in midwinter, and the degrading manner in which the Emperor received the envoys: his hauteur was a befitting foil to their servility, at once exhibiting both his pride and their ignorance of their true position and rights. They were brought to the capital like malefactors, treated when there like beggars, and then sent back to Canton like mountebanks to perform the three-times-three prostration at all times and before everything their conductors saw fit; who on their part stood by and laughed at their embarrassment in making these evolutions in their tight clothes. They were not allowed a single opportunity to speak about business, which the Chinese never associate with an embassy, but were entertained with banquets and theatrical shows, and performed many skilful evolutions themselves upon their skates, greatly to the Emperor's gratification, and received, moreover, a present of broken victuals from him, which had not only been honored by coming from his Majesty's own table, but bore marks of his teeth and good appetite; "they were upon a dirty plate, and appeared rather destined to feed a dog than form the repast of a human creature." Van Braam's account of this embassy is one of the most humiliating records of ill-requited obsequiousness before insolent government lackeys which any European was ever called upon to pen. The mission returned to Canton in April, 1796, having attained no more noble end than that of saluting the Emperor, and this, indeed, was all the Chinese meant should be done when themselves suggesting the entire performance; for in order to understand much of their conduct toward their guests, the feelings they entertained toward them must not be lost sight of.

In 1843 the governor-general at Batavia sent T. Modderman to Canton to make inquiries respecting trade at the newly opened ports and establish consulates. The council there had, in 1839, forbidden Chinese to settle in any of their Indian colonies, owing to their skill in engrossing the native trade; but when this prohibition was removed about 1875, the Chinese showed no disposition to emigrate to Java. In 1863 a treaty was negotiated by M. Van der Hoeven at Tientsin, which placed the trade on the same footing as other nations.

The French Government has never sent a formal mission to the capital to petition for trade and make obeisance, though through their missionaries that nation has made Europeans better acquainted with China and given the Chinese more knowledge of western countries than all other Christian nations together. In the year 1289 Philip the Fair received a letter from Argun khan in Persia, and in 1305 another from Oljaitu, both of them proposing joint action against their enemies the Saracens. The originals are still to be seen in Paris. In 1688 Louis XIV. addressed a letter to Kanghí, whom he called "Most high, most excellent, most puissant, and most magnanimous prince, dearly beloved good friend;" and signed himself "Your most dear and good friend, Louis." In 1844 diplomatic relations were resumed by the appointment of a large mission, at the head of which was M. Lagrené, by whom a treaty was formed between France and China.[1]

The Russians have sent several embassies to Peking, and compelled the Chinese to treat them as equals. The first recorded visit of Russian agents at Peking is that of two Cossacks, Petroff and Yallysheff, in 1567, who, however, did not see the Emperor Lungking, who succeeded to the throne that year, because they had brought no presents. In 1619 Evashko Pettlin reached that city, having come across the desert from Tomsk; but he and his companion, having no presents, could not see the "dragon's face," and were dismissed with a letter, which all the learning at Tobolsk and Moscow could not decipher. Thirty-four years after, the Czar Alexis (1653) sent his envoy Baikoff, who refused to prostrate himself before the Emperor Shunchí, and was promptly dismissed. This repulse did not interfere with trade, for in the years 1658, 1672, and 1677 three several trading embassies reached Peking. During all this time Russian and Chinese subjects and soldiers frequently quarrelled, especially along the banks of the Amur, and the necessity of settling these disturbances and pretexts for trouble by fixing the boundary line being evident to both nations, commissioners were appointed and met at Nipchu, where, on August 27, 1689, they signed the first treaty ever agreed upon by the court of Peking. The principal points in it were the retirement of the Russians from Albazin and Manchuria, where they had held their own for thirty-eight years, the freedom of trade, and defining the frontier along the Daourian Mountains. The missionary Gerbillon was mainly instrumental

[1] *Chinese Repository*, Vol. XIX., pp. 526–535. Yule's *Cathay*, p. cxxx. Rémusat in *Mém. de l'Acad. Ins.*, Vol. VII., pp. 367, 391 ff.

in settling these disputes, and neither party would probably have lowered its arrogant claims if it had not been through his influence; the Chinese were far the most difficult to please.[1]

Peter sent Ysbrandt Ides in 1692 as his envoy to Peking to exchange the ratifications. His journey across the wilds and wastes of Central Asia took up more time than a voyage by sea, for it was not till a year and eight months that "he could return thanks to the great God, who had conducted them all safe and well to their desired place." Ides' own account of his mission contains very slight notices regarding its object or how he was received; but it is now credibly believed that he performed the *kotow* before the Emperor. About twenty years after his departure, Kanghí sent a Manchu envoy, Tulishen, through Russia to confer with the khan of the Tourgouth Tartars about their return to China, which a portion of them accomplished some years after. Tulishen executed his mission so well that he was sent again as envoy to the Czar about 1730, and reached Petersburg in the reign of Peter II. In 1719 Peter the Great despatched another embassy, under Ismailoff, to arrange the trade then conducted on a precarious footing--an account of which was drawn up by John Bell in 1763. Ismailoff refused to prostrate himself until it was agreed that a Chinese minister, whenever sent to Petersburg, should conform to the usages of the Russians; a safe stipulation, certainly, to a court which never demeans itself to send missions. The evident desirableness of keeping on good terms with the Russians led the Chinese to treat their envoys with unusual respect and attend to the business they came to settle. One of the most instructive books on the kind of intercourse carried on during this period is the *Journal* of Lange, who went first in 1716, and thrice afterward, and has left an account of his residence at Kanghí's capital.[2]

---

[1] *Chinese Repository*, Vol. VIII., pp. 417, 506. Du Halde, *Description géographique, historique, chronologique, politique et physique de l'Empire de la Chine et de la Tartarie chinoise*, 4 vols., Paris, 1735. G. Timkowski, *Travels of the Russian Mission through Mongolia to China*, etc., 2 vols., London, 1827. Klaproth, *Mémoires sur l'Asie*, Tome I., pp. 1–81.

[2] Published in one volume with Bell: *Journey from St. Petersburgh in Russia to Ispahan in Persia*, etc., London, 1715.

In 1727 a fifth mission was sent by the Empress Catherine under Count Vladislavitch, which succeeded in establishing the intercourse on a still better basis, viz., that a mission, consisting of six ecclesiastical and four lay members, should remain at Peking to study the Chinese and Manchu languages, so that interpreters could be prepared and communications carried on satisfactorily; the members were to be changed decennially. The caravans, which had been the vehicles of trade, were regulated about 1730 by the establishment, at Kiakhta and Maimaichin, of two marts on the frontier, where it could be brought under regulations; the last reached Peking in 1755. This embassy was the most successful of all, and partly owing to the Emperor Yungching's desire to counterbalance Jesuit intrigues by raising up other interpreters. This treaty, signed August 27, 1727, remained in force till June, 1858—the longest lived treaty on record. The narrative of George Timkowski, who conducted the relief sent in 1821, gives an account of his trip from Kiakhta across the desert, together with considerable information relating to the Kalkas and other Mongol tribes subject to China. The archimandrite, Hyacinth Batchourin, has given a description of Peking, but such works as the members of the Russian college have written are for the most part still in that language. Up to the present date there have been sixteen archimandrites (1736 to 1880) and many monks attached to the ecclesiastical mission in Peking.[1]

The intercourse of the English with China, though it commenced later than other maritime nations of Europe, has been far more important in its consequences, and their trade greater in amount than all other foreign nations combined. This intercourse has not been such as was calculated to impress the Chinese with a just idea of the character of the British nation as a leading Christian people; for the East India Company, which had the monopoly of the trade between the two countries for nearly two centuries, systematically opposed every effort to diffuse Christian doctrine and general knowledge among them down to the end of their control in 1834.

[1] Dudgeon's monograph on *Russian Intercourse with China* contains notices of all events of any importance between the two nations, digested with great care, pp. 80, Peking, 1872. Also, Martin's *China*, Vol. I., p. 386.

The first English vessels anchored off Macao in July, 1635, under the command of Weddell, who was sent to China in accordance with a "truce and free trade" which had been entered into between the English merchants and the viceroy of Goa, who gave letters to the governor of Macao. The fleet was coldly received and Weddell deluded with vain promises until the Portuguese fleet had sailed for Japan, when he was denied permission to trade. Two or three of his officers having visited Canton, he was very desirous to participate in the traffic, and proceeded with his whole fleet up to the Bogue forts, where this desire was made known to the commanders of the forts, who promised to return an answer in a week. Meanwhile the Portuguese so misrepresented them to the Chinese that the commander of the forts concluded to end the matter by driving them away. Having made every preparation during the period the fleet was waiting, an attack was first made upon a watering-boat by firing shot at it when passing near the forts.

"Herewith the whole fleet, being instantly incensed, did, on the sudden, display their bloody ensigns; and, weighing their anchors, fell up with the flood, and berthed themselves before the castle, from whence came many shot, yet not any that touched so much as hull or rope; whereupon, not being able to endure their bravadoes any longer, each ship began to play furiously upon them with their broadsides; and after two or three hours, perceiving their cowardly fainting, the boats were landed with about one hundred men: which sight occasioned them, with great distractions, instantly to abandon the castle and fly; the boats' crews, in the meantime, without let, entering the same and displaying his Majesty's colors of Great Britain upon the walls, having the same night put aboard all their ordnance, fired the council-house and demolished what they could. The boats of the fleet also seized a junk laden with boards and timber, and another with salt. Another vessel of small moment was surprised, by whose boat a letter was sent to the chief mandarins at Canton, expostulating their breach of truce, excusing the assailing of the castle, and withal in fair terms requiring the liberty of trade." [1] This letter was shortly answered,

[1] Staunton's *Embassy*, Vol. I., pp. 5–12.

and after a little explanatory negotiation, hastened to a favorable conclusion on the part of the Chinese by what they had seen, trade was allowed after the captured guns and vessels were restored and the ships supplied with cargoes.

No other attempt to open a trade was made till 1664, and during the change of dynasty which took place in the interim, the trade of all nations with China suffered. The East India Company had a factory at Bantam in Java, and one at Madras, but their trade with the East was seriously incommoded by the war with the Dutch; when it was renewed in 1664, only one ship was sent to Macao, but such were the exactions imposed upon the trade by the Chinese, and the effect of the misrepresentations of the Portuguese, that the ship returned without effecting sale. This did not discourage the Company, however, who ordered their agents at Bantam to make inquiries respecting the most favorable port and what commodities were most in demand. They mentioned "Fuhchau as a place of great resort, affording all China commodities, as raw and wrought silk, tutenague, gold, china-root, tea, etc." A trade had been opened with Koxinga's son in Formosa and at Amoy, but this rude chieftain had little other idea of traffic than a means of helping himself to every curious commodity the ships brought, and levying heavy imposts upon their cargoes. A treaty was indeed entered into with him, in which the supercargoes, as was the case subsequently in 1842, stipulated for far greater privileges and lighter duties than Chinese goods and vessels would have had in English ports. Besides freedom to go where they pleased without any one attending them, access at all times to the king, liberty to choose their own clerks and trade with whom they pleased, it was also agreed "that what goods the king buys shall pay no custom; that rice imported pay no custom; that all goods imported pay three per cent. *after sale*, and all goods exported be custom free." The trade at Amoy was more successful than at Zealandia, and a small vessel was sent there in 1677, which brought back a favorable report. In 1678 the investments for these two places were $30,000 in bullion and $20,000 in goods; the returns were chiefly in silk goods, tutenague, rhubarb, etc.;

the trade was continued for several years, apparently with considerable profit, though the Manchus continually increased the restrictions under which it labored. In 1681 the Company ordered their factories at Amoy and Formosa to be withdrawn, and one established at Canton or Fuhchau, but in 1685 the trade was renewed at Amoy.

The Portuguese managed to prevent the English obtaining a footing at Canton until about 1684; and, as Davis remarks, the stupid pertinacity with which they endeavored to exclude them from this port and trade is one of the most striking circumstances connected with these trials and rivalries. It is the more inexplicable in the case of the Portuguese, for they could carry nothing to England, nor could they force the English to trade with them at second hand; theirs was truly the "dog in the manger" policy, and they have subsequently starved upon it. In 1689 a duty of five shillings per pound was laid upon tea imported into England; and the principal articles of export are stated to have been wrought silks of every kind, porcelain, lacquered-ware, a good quantity of fine tea, some fans and screens. Ten years after, the court of directors sent out a consul's commission to the chief supercargo, Mr. Catchpoole, which constituted him king's minister or consul for the whole Empire of China and the adjacent islands. In 1701 an attempt was made by him to open a trade, and he obtained permission to send ships to Chusan or Ningpo; an investment in three vessels, worth £101,300, was accordingly made, but he found the exactions of the government so grievous, and the monopoly of the merchants so oppressive, that the adventure proved a great loss, and the traders were compelled to withdraw. The Company's hopes of trade at that port must, however, have been great, for their investment to Amoy that year was only £34,400, and to Canton £40,800. In 1702 Catchpoole also established a factory at Pulo Condore, an island near the coast of Cochinchina which had been taken by the English. The whole concern, however, experienced a tragical end in 1705, when the Malays rose upon the English, murdered them all, and burned the factory. The Cochinchinese are said to have instigated this treacherous attack to regain the island, which was claimed by them.

The extortions and grievances suffered by the traders at Canton were increased in 1702 by the appointment of an individual who alone had the right of trading with them and of farming it out to those who had the means of doing so. The trade seems hardly, even at this time, to have taken a regular form, but by 1720 the number and value of the annual commodities had so much increased that the Chinese established a uniform duty of four per cent. on all goods, and appointed a body of native merchants, who, for the privilege of trading with foreigners, became security for their payment of duties and good behavior. The duty on imports was also increased to about sixteen per cent. and an enormous fee demanded of purveyors before they could supply ships with provisions, besides a heavy measurement duty and cumshaw to the collector of customs. These exactions seemed likely to increase unless a stand was taken against them. This was done by a united appeal to the governor in person in 1728; yet the relief was only temporary, for the plan was so effectual and convenient for the government that the co-hong was ere long re-established as the only medium through which the foreign trade could be conducted. An additional duty of ten per cent. was laid upon all exports, which no efforts were effectual in removing until the accession of Kienlung in 1736. This apparently suicidal practice of levying export duties is, in China, really a continuation of the internal excise or transit duties paid upon goods exported in native vessels as well as foreign.

The Emperor, in taking off the newly imposed duty of ten per cent., required that the merchants should hear the act of grace read upon their knees; but the foreigners all met in a body, and each one agreed on his honor not to submit to this slavish posture, nor make any concession or proposal of accommodation without acquainting the rest. The Emperor also required the delivery of all the arms on board ship, a demand afterward waived on the payment of about ten thousand dollars. The hong merchants shortly became the only medium of communication with the government, themselves being the exactors of the duties and contrivers of the grievances, and when complaints were made, the judges of the equity of their own acts.

In 1734 only one English ship came to Canton, and one was sent to Amoy, but the extortions there were greater than at the other port, whereupon the latter vessel withdrew. In 1736 the number of ships at Canton was four English, two French, two Dutch, one Danish, and one Swedish vessel; the Portuguese ships had been restricted to Macao before this date.

Commodore Anson arrived at Macao in 1742, and as the Centurion was the first British man-of-war which had visited China, his decided conduct in refusing to leave the river until provisions were furnished, and his determination in seeking an interview with the governor, no doubt had a good effect. A mixture of decision and kindness, such as that exhibited by Anson when demanding only what was in itself right, and backed by an array of force not lightly to be trifled with or incensed, has always proved the most successful way of dealing with the Chinese, who on their part need instruction as well as intimidation. The constant presence of a ship of war on the coast of China would perhaps have saved foreigners much of the personal vexations, and prevented many of the imposts upon trade which the history of foreign intercourse exhibits, making it in fact little better than a recital of annoyances on the part of a government too ignorant and proud to understand its own true interests, and recriminations on the part of traders unable to do more than protest against them.

In consequence of the exactions of the government and the success of the co-hong in preventing all direct intercourse with the local authorities, the attempt was again made to trade at Amoy and Ningpo. The Hardwicke was sent to Amoy in 1744, and obliged to return without a cargo. Messrs. Flint and Harrison were despatched to Ningpo in 1755, and were well received; but when the Holderness subsequently came to trade, it was with difficulty that she procured a cargo, and an imperial edict was promulgated soon after restricting all foreign ships to Canton. In 1759 the factory at Ningpo was demolished, so that Mr. Flint, who repaired there that year, was unable to do anything toward restoring the trade. This gentleman was a person of uncommon perseverance and talents, and had mastered the difficulties of the Chinese language so as to act as interpreter at Canton twelve years before he was sent on his mission. "The ungrateful return which his energy and exertions in their service met with from his employers," justly observes Sir John Davis, "was such as tended in all probability, more than any other cause, to discourage his successors from undertaking so laborious, unprofitable, and even hazardous a work of supererogation."

On his arrival at Ningpo, Mr. Flint, finding it useless to attempt anything there, proceeded in a native vessel to Tientsin, from whence he succeeded in making his case known to the Emperor Kienlung. A commissioner was deputed to accompany him overland to Canton; Mr. Flint proceeded to the English factory soon after his arrival, and the foreigners of all nations assembled before the commissioner, who informed them that the hoppo had been superseded, and all duties remitted over six per cent. on goods and the cumshaw and tonnage dues on ships. The sequel of Mr. Flint's enterprise was unfortunate, and the mode the Chinese took to bring it about thoroughly characteristic.

It proved, however, that these fair appearances were destined only to be the prelude to a storm. Some days afterward the governor desired to see Mr. Flint for the purpose of communicating the Emperor's orders, and was accompanied by the council of his countrymen. When the party had reached the palace, the hong merchants proposed their going in one at a time, but they insisted on proceeding together; and on Mr. Flint being called for, they were received at the first gate and ushered through two courts with seeming complaisance by the officers in waiting; but on arriving at the gate of the inner court they were hurried, and even forced into the governor's presence, where a struggle ensued with their brutal conductors to force them to do homage after the Chinese fashion until they were overpowered and thrown down. Seeing their determination not to submit to these base humiliations, the governor ordered the people to desist; and then telling Mr. Flint to advance, he pointed to an order, which he called the Emperor's edict, for his banishment to Macao, and subsequent departure for England, on account of his endeavoring to open a trade at Ningpo contrary to orders from Peking. He added that the native who had written the petition in Chinese was to be beheaded that day for traitorously encouraging foreigners, which was performed on a man quite innocent of what these officers were pleased to call a crime. Mr. Flint was soon after conveyed to Tsienshan, a place near Macao, called Casa Branca by the Portuguese, where he was imprisoned two years and a half and then sent to England.[1]

[1] Davis, *Chinese*, Vol. I., p. 58.

Mr. Flint stated to the Company that a fee of one thousand two hundred and fifty dollars to the governor would set him at liberty, but they contented themselves with a petition. The punishment he received from the Chinese for this attempt to break their laws would not have been considered as unmerited or unjust in any other country, but the neglect of the Company to procure the liberation of one who had suffered so much to serve them reflects the greatest reproach upon that body.

The whole history of the foreign trade, as related by Auber in his chronological narrative, during the one hundred and fifty years up to 1842 is a melancholy and curious chapter in national intercourse. The grievances complained of were delay in loading ships and plunder of goods on their transit to Canton; the injurious proclamations annually put up by the government accusing foreigners of horrible crimes; the extortions of the underlings of office; and the difficulty of access to the high authorities. The hong merchants, from their position as traders and interpreters between the two parties, were able to delude both to a considerable extent, though their responsibility for the acts and payments of foreigners, over whom they could exercise no real restraint, rendered their situation by no means pleasant. The rule on which the Chinese government proceeded in its dealings with foreigners was this: "The barbarians are like beasts, and not to be ruled on the same principles as citizens. Were any one to attempt controlling them by the great maxims of reason, it would tend to nothing but confusion. The ancient kings well understood this, and accordingly ruled barbarians by misrule; therefore, to rule barbarians by misrule is the true and best way of ruling them." The same rule in regard to foreign traders was virtually acted on in England during the reign of Henry VII., and the ideas among the Chinese of their power over those who visit their shores are not unlike those which prevailed in Europe before the Reformation.

The entire ignorance of foreign traders of the spoken and written language of China brought them into contempt with all classes, and where all intercourse was carried on in a jargon which each party despised, the results were often misunderstanding, dislike, and hatred. Another fruitful source of difficulty was the turbulent conduct of sailors. The French and English seamen at Whampoa, in 1754, carried their national hatred to such a degree that they could not pursue their trade without quarrelling; and a Frenchman having killed an English sailor, the Chinese stopped the trade of the former nation until the guilty person was given up, though he was subsequently liberated. The Chinese allotted two different islands in the river at Whampoa for the recreation of the seamen of each nation, in order that such troubles might be avoided in future. A similar case occurred at Canton in 1780, when a Frenchman killed a Portuguese sailor at night in one of the merchants' houses and fled to the consul's for refuge. The Chinese demanded the criminal, and after some days he was given up to them and publicly strangled; this punishment he no doubt merited, although it was the first case in which they had interfered where the matter was altogether among foreigners. In 1784 a native was killed by a ball left in a gun when firing a salute, and the Chinese, on the principle of requiring life for life, demanded the man who had fired the gun. Knowing that the English were not likely to give him up, the police seized Mr. Smith, the supercargo of the vessel, and carried him a prisoner into the city. On the seizure of this gentleman the ships' boats were ordered up from Whampoa with armed crews to defend the factories. A messenger from the Chinese, however, declared that their purpose in seizing Smith was simply to examine him on the affair, to which statement the captive himself added a request that the gunner should be sent up to the authorities and submit to their questions. Trusting too much to their promises, the man was allowed to go alone before the officials within the city walls, when Mr. Smith was immediately liberated and the unhappy gunner strangled, after some six weeks' confinement, by direct orders of the Emperor. The man, probably, underwent no form of trial intelligible to himself, and his condemnation was the more unjust, as by Section CCXCII. of the Chinese code he was allowed to ransom himself by a fine of about twenty dollars. As a counterpart of this tragedy, the Chinese stated (and there was reason for believing them) that a native who had accidentally killed a British seaman about the same time was executed for the casualty.

The Chinese mode of operations, when it was impracticable to get possession of the guilty or accused party, was well exhibited in the case of a homicide occurring in 1807. A party of sailors had been drinking at Canton, when a scuffle ensued, and the sailors put the populace to flight, killing one of the natives in the onset. The trade was promptly stopped, and the hong merchant who had *secured* the ship held responsible for the delivery of the offender. Eleven men were arrested and a court instituted in the Company's hall before Chinese judges, Captain Rolles, of H. B. M. ship Lion, being present with the committee. The actual homicide could not be found, but one Edward Sheen was detained in custody, which satisfied the Chinese while he remained in Canton; but when the committee wished to take him to Macao with them they resisted, until Captain Rolles declared that otherwise he should take the prisoner on board his own ship, which he did. Being now beyond their reach, the authorities were fain to account for the affair to the supreme tribunal at the capital by inventing a tale, stating that the prisoner had caused the death of a native by raising an upper window and accidentally dropping a stick upon his head as he was passing in the street below. This statement was reported to his Majesty as having been concurred in by the English after a full examination of witnesses who attested to the circumstances; the imperial rescript affirmed the sentence of the Board of Punishments, which ordered that the prisoner should be set at liberty after paying the usual fine of twenty dollars provided by law to defray the funeral expenses. The trade was thereupon resumed.[1]

Another case of homicide occurred at Whampoa in 1820, when the authorities reported that the butcher of another ship, who had committed suicide the day of the inquest, was the guilty person. The court of directors very properly blamed their agents at Canton for their complicity in this subterfuge, and spoke of "the paramount advantages which must invari-

[1] Sir G. T. Staunton, *Penal Code of China*, p. 516.

ably be derived from a strict and inflexible adherence to truth as the foundation of all moral obligations."[1]

Other cases of murder and homicide have since occurred between foreigners and natives. In the instance of the British frigate Topaze at Lintin Island in 1822, whose crew had been attacked on shore, her captain successfully resisted the surrender of a British subject for the death of two natives in the affray. The dignified and united action of the British authorities on this occasion was a striking contrast to the weakness of the Americans the year before in the case of Terranova. It proved the beneficial results of a stand for the right, for no foreigner has since been executed by the Chinese. It also proved the necessity and advantages of competent interpreters and translators, inasmuch as the case owed much of its success to Dr. Morrison's aid, which had been rejected by the hong merchants the previous year.[2]

These cases are brought together to illustrate the anomalous position which foreigners once held in China. They constituted a community by themselves, subject chiefly to their own sense of honor in their mutual dealings, but their relations with the Chinese were like what lawyers call a "state of nature." The change of a governor-general, of a collector of customs, or senior hong merchant, involved a new course of policy according to the personal character of these functionaries. The committee of the East India Company had considerable power over British subjects, especially those living in Canton, and could deport them if they pleased; but the consuls of other nations had little or no authority over their countrymen. Trade was left at the same loose ends that politics were, and the want of an acknowledged tariff encouraged smuggling and kept up a constant spirit of resistance and dissatisfaction between the native and foreign merchants, each party endeavoring to get along as advantageously to itself as practicable. Nor was there any acknowledged medium of communication between them, for the

---

[1] Auber, *China: An Outline of its Government, Laws, Policy*, etc., p. 286, London, 1834.

[2] *Chinese Repository*, Vol. II., pp. 513–515. Morrison's *Memoirs*, Vol. II., App., p. 10. Auber, *China, its Government*, etc., pp. 288–309.

consuls, not being credited by the Chinese Government, came and went, hoisted or lowered their flags, without the slightest notice from the authorities. Trade could proceed, perhaps, without involving the nations in war, since if it was unprofitable it would cease; but while it continued on such a precarious footing national character suffered, and the misrepresentations produced thereby rendered explanations difficult, inasmuch as neither party understood or believed the other.

The death of the unfortunate gunner in 1784, and the large debts owed to the English by the hong merchants, which there seemed no probability of recovering, induced the British Government to turn its attention to the situation of the king's subjects in China with the purpose of placing their relations on a better footing. The flagitious conduct of a Captain M'Clary, who seized a Dutch vessel at Whampoa in 1781, which Davis narrates,[1] and the inability of the Company to restrain such proceedings, also had its weight in deciding the crown to send an embassy to Peking. Colonel Cathcart was appointed envoy in 1788, but his death in the Straits of Sunda temporarily deferred the mission, which was resumed on a larger scale in 1792, when the Earl of Macartney was sent as ambassador, with a large suite of able men, to place the relations between the two nations, if possible, on a well-understood and secure footing. Two ships were appointed as tenders to accompany his Majesty's ship Lion (64), and nothing was omitted, either in the composition of the mission or the presents to the Emperor, to insure its success. Little is known regarding its real impression upon the Chinese; they treated it with great consideration while it remained in the country, although at an estimated cost of $850,000, and probably dismissed it with the feeling that it was one of the most splendid testimonials of respect that a tributary nation had ever paid their court. The English were henceforth registered among the nations who had sent tribute-bearers, and were consequently only the more bound to obey the injunctions of their master.[2]

---

[1] *The Chinese*, Vol. I., p. 63.

[2] Sir G. L. Staunton, *Authentic Account of an Embassy from the King of Great Britain to the Emperor of China*, 3 vols., London, 1798.

To the European world, as well as to the British nation, however, this expedition may be said to have opened China, so great was the interest taken in it and so well calculated were the narratives of Staunton and Barrow to convey better ideas of that remote country. "Much of the lasting impression which the relations of Lord Macartney's embassy leave on the mind of his reader," to quote from a review of it, "must be ascribed, exclusive of the natural effect of clear, elegant, and able composition, to the number of persons engaged in that business, the variety of their characters, the reputation they already enjoyed or afterward acquired; the bustle and stir of a sea voyage; the placidity and success which finally characterized the intercourse of the English with the Chinese; the splendor of the reception the latter gave to their European guests; the walks in the magnificent gardens of the 'Son of Heaven;' the picturesque and almost romantic navigation upon the imperial canal; and perhaps, not less for the interest we feel for every grand enterprise, skilfully prepared, and which proves successful, partly in consequence of the happy choice of the persons and the means by which it was to be carried into effect." This impression of the grandeur and extent of the Chinese Empire has ever since more or less remained upon the minds of all readers of Staunton's narrative; but truer views were imparted than had before been entertained concerning its real civilization and its low rank among the nations.

That the embassy produced some good effect is undeniable, though it failed in most of the principal points. It also afforded the Chinese an opportunity of making arrangements concerning that future intercourse which they could not avoid, even if they would not negotiate, and of acquiring information concerning foreign nations which would have proved of great advantage to them. Their contemptuous rejection, ignorant though they decided to remain of the real character of these courtesies, of peaceful missions like those of Macartney, Titsingh, and others, takes away much of our sympathy for the calamities which subsequently came upon them. With characteristic shortsightedness they looked upon the very means taken to arrange existing ill-understood relations as a reason for considering those relations as settled to their liking, and a motive to still further exactions.

For many years subsequent to this embassy the trade went on without interruption, though the demands and duties were rather increased than diminished, and the personal liberty of foreigners more and more restricted. The government generally, down to the lowest underling, systematically endeavored to degrade and insult foreigners in the eyes of the populace and citizens of Canton, in order, in case of any disturbance, to have their co-operation and sympathy against the "barbarian devils." The dissolute and violent conduct of many foreigners toward the Chinese gave them, alas, too many arguments for their aspersions and exactions, and both parties too frequently considered the other fair subjects for imposition.

In 1802 the English troops occupied Macao by order of the governor-general of India, lest it should be attacked by the French, but the news of the treaty of peace arriving soon after, they re-embarked almost as soon as the Chinese remonstrated. The discussion was revived, however, in 1808, when the French again threatened the settlement; and the English, under Admiral Drury, landed a detachment to assist the Portuguese in defending it. The Chinese, who had previously asserted their complete jurisdiction over this territory, and which a little examination would have plainly shown, now protested against the armed occupation of their soil, and immediately stopped the trade and denied provisions to the ships. The English traders were ordered by the Committee to go aboard ship, and the governor refused to have the least communication with the admiral until the troops were withdrawn. He attempted to proceed to Canton in armed boats, but was repulsed, and finally, in order not to implicate the trade any further (a step not at all apprehended in protecting the Portuguese), he wisely withdrew his troops and sailed for India. The success of the native authorities greatly rejoiced them; a temple was built on the river's bank to commemorate their victory, and a fort, called "Howqua's Folly" by foreigners (since washed away), erected to guard the river at that point.

The Chinese, ignorant of the principles on which international intercourse is regulated among western powers, regarded every hostile demonstration between them in their waters as directed toward themselves, and demanding their interference. Though often powerless to defend themselves against their own piratical subjects, as has been manifested again and again—for example, in 1810, and also in 1660, when Koxinga ravaged the coast—they still assume that they are able to protect all foreigners who "range themselves under their sway." This was exhibited in 1814, when the British frigate Doris, against all the acknowledged rights of a nation over its own waters, and simply because it could be done with impunity, cruised off the port of Canton to seize American vessels. The provincial authorities ordered the Committee to send her away, saying that if the English and Americans had any petty squabbles they must settle them between themselves and not bring them to China. The Committee stated their inability to control the proceedings of men-of-war, whereupon the Chinese began a series of annoyances against the merchants and shipping, prohibiting the employment of native servants, entering their houses to seize natives, molesting and stopping ships' boats proceeding up and down the river on business, hindering the loading of the ships, and other like harassing acts so characteristic of Asiatic governments when they feel themselves powerless to cope with the real object of their fear or anger. These measures proceeded at last to such a length that the Committee determined to stop the British trade until the governor would allow it to go on, as before, without molestation, and they had actually left Canton for Whampoa, and proceeded down the river some distance, before he showed a sincere wish to arrange matters amicably. A deputation from each party accordingly met in Canton, and the principal points in dispute were at last gained. In this affair the Chinese would be adjudged to have been altogether in the right according to international law. At this time the governor-general conceded three important points to the Committee, viz., the right of corresponding with the government, under seal, in the Chinese language, the unmolested employment of native servants, and the assurance that the houses of foreigners should not be entered without permission; nor were these stipulations ever retracted or violated.

The proceedings in this affair were conducted with no little apprehension on both sides, for the value of the traffic was of such importance that neither party could really think of stopping it. Besides the revenue accruing to government from duties and presents, the preparation and shipment of the articles in demand for foreign countries give employment to millions of natives in different parts of the Empire, and had caused Canton to become one of the greatest marts in the world. The governor and his colleagues were responsible for the revenue and peaceful continuance of the trade; but through their ignorance of the true principles of a prosperous commerce, their fear of the consequences resulting from any innovation or change, or the least extension of privileges to the few half-imprisoned foreigners, they thought their security lay rather in restriction than in freedom, in a haughty bearing to intimidate, and not in conciliation to please their customers. On the other hand, the existence of the East India Company's charter depended in a good degree upon keeping a regular supply of tea in England, and therefore the success of the Committee's bold measure of stopping the trade depended not a little upon the ignorance of the Chinese of the great power a passive course of action would give them.

The government at home, on learning these proceedings, resolved to despatch another ambassy to Peking in order to state the facts of the case at court, and if possible agree upon some understood mode of conducting trade and communicating with the heads of government. Lord Amherst, who like Lord Macartney had been governor-general of India, was appointed ambassador to Peking, and Henry Ellis and Sir George T. Staunton associated with him as second and third commissioners. A large suite of able men, with Dr. Morrison as principal interpreter, accompanied the ambassy, and the usual quantity and variety of presents.[1] The mission reached the capital August 28, 1816, but was summarily dismissed without an audience, because the ambassador would not perform the kotow

---

[1] Ellis, *Embassy to China*, London, 1840. Sir J. F. Davis, *Sketches of China*, 2 Vols., London, 1841. Clarke Abel, *Narrative of a Journey in the Interior of China and a Voyage to and from that Country in* 1816 *and* 1817, London, 1818. R. Morrison, *A View of China*, etc., Macao, 1817.

or appear before his Majesty as soon as he arrived; the intrigues of the authorities at Canton with the high officers about the Emperor to defeat the ambassy by deceiving their master have also been adduced as reasons for its failure. Its real failure, as we can now see, was owing to the utter misconception of their true position by the Emperor and his officials, arising from their ignorance, pride, isolation, and mendacity, all combining to keep them so until resistless force should open them to meliorating influences. It was the last attempt of the kind, and three alternatives only remained: the resort to force to compel them to enter into some equitable arrangement, entire submission to whatever they ordered, or the withdrawal of all trade until they proposed its resumption. The course of events continued the second until the first was resorted to, and eventuated in laying open the whole coast to the enterprise of western nations.

At the close of the East India Company's exclusive rights in China, the prospect for the continuance of a peaceful trade was rather dubious. The enterprising Mr. Marjoribanks despatched a vessel to ascertain how far trade could be carried on along the coast, which resulted in satisfactorily proving that the authorities were able and determined to stop all traffic, however desirous the people might be for it. The contraband trade in opium was conducted in a manner that threatened ere long to involve the two nations, but the Company nominally kept itself aloof from it by bringing none in its ships: the same Company, however, did everything in India to encourage the growth and sale of the drug, and received from it at the time of its dissolution an annual revenue of nearly two millions sterling. During its whole existence in China the East India Company stood forward as the defenders of the rights of foreigners and humanity, in a manner which no community of isolated merchants could have done, and to some extent compelled the Chinese to treat all more civilly. As a body it did little for the encouragement of Chinese literature or the diffusion of Christian truth or of science among the Chinese, except the printing of Morrison's Dictionary and an annual grant to the Anglo-Chinese College; and although Dr. Morrison was their official translator for twenty-five years, the directors never gave him the empty compliment of enrolling him in the list of their servants, nor contributed one penny for carrying on his great work of translating and printing the Bible in Chinese. They set themselves against all such efforts, and during a long existence the natives of that country had no means put into their hands, by their agency, of learning that there was any great difference in the religion, science, or civilization of European nations and their own.

The trade of the Americans to China commenced in 1784, the first vessel having left New York February 22d of that year, and returned May 11, 1785; it was commanded by Captain Green, and the supercargo, Samuel Shaw, on his return, gave a lucid narrative of his voyage to Chief Justice Jay. His journal, published in 1847, contains the only record of this voyage, and furnishes many curious facts about the political and social relations existing between foreigners then in China. Our trade with China steadily increased after this date, and has been the second in amount for many years. The only political event in the American intercourse up to 1842 was the suspension of trade in October, 1821, in consequence of the homicide of a Chinese by a sailor at Whampoa. The American merchants were really helpless to carry the trial of Terranova to a just conclusion against the Chinese law, which peremptorily required life for life wherever foreigners were concerned, and gave him up on the assurance that his life was in no danger. They are stated, in a narrative published in the *North American Review*, to have told Howqua at the trial on board the Emily at Whampoa, "We are bound to submit to your laws while we are in your waters; be they ever so unjust, we will not resist them." The poor man was taken out of the ship by force, while all the Americans present protested against the unfair trial he had had; he was then promptly carried to Canton and strangled at the public execution ground (October 25); his body was given up next day, and the trade reopened.[1]

[1] Shaw's *Journal*, Boston, 1847. *North American Review*, January, 1835. *Chinese Repository*, September, 1836. Sir Geo. T. Staunton's *Notices of China*, second edition, pp. 409–432, 1850.

The American Government neither took notice of this affair nor made remonstrance against its injustice, but still left the commerce, lives, and property of its citizens wholly unprotected, and at the mercy of Chinese laws and rulers. The consuls at Canton were merely merchants, having no salary from their government, no funds to employ interpreters when necessary, or any power over their countrymen, and came and went without the least notice or acknowledgment from the Chinese.

The trade and intercourse of the Swedes, Danes, Prussians, Italians, Austrians, Peruvians, Mexicans, or Chilians, at Canton, have been attended with no peculiarities or events of any moment. None of these nations ever sent "tribute" to the court of the Son of Heaven, and their ships traded at Canton on the same footing with the English. The voyage of Peter Osbeck, chaplain to a Swedish East Indiaman, in 1753, contains considerable information relating to the mode of conducting the trade and the position of foreigners, who then enjoyed more liberty and suffered fewer extortions than in later years.[1]

The term *fan-kwei*, by which they were all alike called by the Cantonese, indicated the popular estimation, and this epithet of '*foreign devil*' did much, in the course of years, to increase the contempt and ill will which it expressed, not only there but throughout the Empire, for they were thereby maligned before they were known. Another term, *í*, has been raised into notice by its condemnation in the British Treaty as an epithet for British subjects or countries. This word, there rendered '*barbarian*,' conveys to a native but little more than the idea that the people thus called do not understand the Chinese language and usages, and are consequently less civilized. This epithet *barbarian* meant to the Greeks those who could not speak Greek, as it did to Shakspeare those who were not English; likewise among the Chinese, under *í* were included great masses of their own subjects. By translating *wai í* as '*outside barbarians*,' foreigners have been misrepresented in the status they

[1] *A Voyage to China and the East Indies, translated from the German by* John R. Forster, 2 vols., London, 1771.

held among educated natives, which was not that of savages but of the illiteracy growing out of their ignorance of the language and writings of Confucius.

The ancient Chinese books speak of four wild nations on the four sides of the country, viz., the *fan*, *í*, *tih*, *man*; the first two seem to have been applied to traders from the south and west, and grew into more distinct expressions because these traders often acted so outrageously. Other terms, as "western ocean men," "far-travelled strangers," and "men from afar," have occasionally been substituted when *í* was objected to. When used as a general term, without an opprobrious addition, *í* is as well adapted as any to denote all foreigners; but the most recent usage gives prominence to the terms *wai kwoh* and *yang jăn* ('outside country' and 'ocean man'). Among educated natives the national names are becoming more and more common, as *Ying kwoh*, *Fah kwoh*, *Mei kwoh*, *Teh kwoh*, for England, France, America, Germany, etc.

CHAPTER XXII.

ORIGIN OF THE FIRST WAR WITH ENGLAND.

THE East India Company's commercial privileges ceased in 1834, and it is worthy of note that an association should have been continued in the providence of God as the principal representative of Christendom among the Chinese, which by its character, its pecuniary interests, and general inclination was bound in a manner to maintain peaceful relations with them, while every other important Asiatic kingdom and island, from Arabia to Japan, was at one time or another during that period the scene of collision, war, or conquest between the nations and their visitors. Its monopoly ceased when western nations no longer looked upon these regions as objects of desire, nor went to Rome to get a privilege to seize or claim such pagan lands as they might discover, and when, too, Christians began to learn and act upon their duty to evangelize these ignorant races. China and Japan were once open to such agencies as well as trade, but no effective measures were taken to translate or distribute the pure word of God in them.

Believing that the affairs of the kingdoms of this world are ordered by their Almighty Governor with regard to the fulfilment of his promises and the promulgation of his truth, the first war between England and China is not only one of great historical interest, but one whose future consequences cannot fail to exercise increasing influence upon many millions of mankind. This war was extraordinary in its origin as growing chiefly out of a commercial misunderstanding; remarkable in its course as being waged between strength and weakness, conscious superiority and ignorant pride; melancholy in its end as forcing the weaker to pay for the opium within its borders against all its laws, thus paralyzing the little moral power its feeble government could exert to protect its subjects; and momentous in its results as introducing, on a basis of acknowledged obligations, one-half of the world to the other, without any arrogant demands from the victors or humiliating concessions from the vanquished. It was a turning-point in the national life of the Chinese race, but the compulsory payment of six million dollars for the opium destroyed has left a stigma upon the English name:

In 1834 the select Committee of the East India Company repeated its notice given in 1831 to the authorities at Canton, that its ships would no longer come to China, and that a king's officer would be sent out as chief to manage the affairs of the British trade. The only "chief" whom the Chinese expected to receive was a commercial headman, qualified to communicate with their officers by petition, through the usual and legal medium of the hong merchants. The English Government justly deemed the change one of considerable importance, and concluded that the oversight of their subjects and the great trade they conducted required a commission of experienced men. The Rt. Hon. Lord Napier was consequently appointed as chief superintendent of British trade, and arrived at Macao July 15, 1834, where were associated with him in the commission John F. Davis and Sir G. B. Robinson, formerly servants of the Company, and a number of secretaries, surgeons, chaplains, interpreters, etc., whose united salaries amounted to $91,000. On arriving at Canton the tide-waiters officially reported that three "foreign devils" had landed. As soon as Governor Lu had learned that Lord Napier had reached Macao, he ordered the hong merchants to go down and intimate to him that he must remain there until he obtained legal permission to come to Canton; for, having received no orders from court as to the manner in which he should treat the English superintendent, he thought it the safest plan to adhere to the old regulations.

Lord Napier had been ordered to report himself to the governor at Canton *by letter*. A short extract from his instructions will show the intentions of the English Government in constituting the commission, and the entirely wrong views it had of the notions of the Chinese respecting foreign intercourse, and the character they gave to the English authorities. Lord Palmerston says:

In addition to the duty of protecting and fostering the trade of his Majesty's subjects with the port of Canton, it will be one of your principal objects to ascertain whether it may not be practicable to extend that trade to other parts of the Chinese dominions. . . . It is obvious that, with a view to the attainment of this object, the establishment of direct communications with the port of Peking would be desirable; and you will accordingly direct your attention to discover the best means of preparing the way for such communications, bearing constantly in mind, however, that peculiar caution and circumspection will be indispensable on this point, lest you should awaken the fears or offend the prejudices of the Chinese Government, and thus put to hazard even the existing opportunities of intercourse by a precipitate attempt to extend them. In conformity with this caution you will abstain from entering into any new relations or negotiations with the Chinese authorities, except under very urgent and unforeseen circumstances. But if any opportunity for such negotiations should appear to you to present itself, you will lose no time in reporting the circumstance to his Majesty's government, and in asking for instructions; but previously to the receipt of such instructions you will adopt no proceedings but such as may have a general tendency to convince the Chinese authorities of the sincere desire of the king to cultivate the most friendly relations with the Emperor of China, and to join with him in any measures likely to promote the happiness and prosperity of their respective subjects.

Governor Lu's messengers arrived too late to detain the British superintendent at Macao, and a military officer despatched to intercept him passed him on the way; so that the first intimation the latter received of the governor's disposition was in an edict addressed to the hong merchants, from which two paragraphs are extracted:

On this occasion the barbarian *eye*, Lord Napier, has come to Canton without having at all resided at Macao to wait for orders; nor has he requested or received a permit from the superintendent of customs, but has hastily come up to Canton—a great infringement of the established laws! The custom-house waiters and others who presumed to admit him to enter are sent with a communication requiring their trial. But in tender consideration for the said barbarian *eye* being a new-comer, and unacquainted with the statutes and laws of the Celestial Empire, I will not strictly investigate. . . . As to his object in coming to Canton, it is for commercial business. The Celestial Empire appoints officers, civil ones to rule the people, military ones to intimidate the wicked. The petty affairs of commerce are to be directed by the merchants themselves: the officers have nothing to hear on the subject. . . . If any affair is to be newly commenced, it is necessary to wait till a respectful memorial be made, clearly reporting it to the great Emperor, and his mandate be received; the great ministers of the Celestial Empire are not permitted to have intercourse by letters with outside barbarians. If the said barbarian eye *throws in* private letters, I, the governor, will not at all receive or look at them. With regard to the foreign factory of the Company without the walls of the city, it is a place of temporary residence for foreigners coming to Canton to trade; they are permitted only to eat, sleep, buy and sell in the factories; they are not allowed to go out to ramble about.[1]

How unlike were these two documents and the expectations of their writers! The governor felt that it was safest to wait for an imperial mandate before commencing a new affair, and refused to receive *a letter* from a foreign officer. Had he done so he would have laid himself open to reprimand and perhaps punishment from his superiors; and in saying that the superintendent should report himself and apply for a permit before coming to Canton, he only required what the members of the Company had always done when they returned from their summer vacation at Macao. Lord Napier thought he had the same liberty to come to Canton without announcing himself that other and private foreigners exercised; but an officer of his rank would have pleased the Chinese authorities better by observing their regulations. He had thought of this contingency before leaving England, and had requested "that in case of necessity he might have authority to treat with the government at Peking;" this request being denied, he desired that his appointment to Canton might be announced at the capital; this not being granted, he wished that a communication from the home authorities might be addressed to the governor of Canton; but this was deemed inexpedient, and he was directed to "go to Canton and report himself by letter." These reasonable requests involved no loss of dignity, but the court of St. James chose to send out a superintendent of trade, an officer partaking of both ministerial and consular powers, and ordered him to act in a certain manner, involving a violation of the regulations of the country where he was going, without providing for the alternative of his rejection.

---

[1] *Correspondence relating to China* (Blue Book), p. 4. *Chinese Repository*. Vol. III., p. 188; Vol. XI., p. 188.

To Canton, therefore, he came, and the next day reported himself by letter to the governor, sending it to the city gates. His lordship was directed to have nothing to do with the hong merchants; and therefore when they waited upon him the morning of his arrival, with the edict they had been sent down to Macao to "enjoin upon him," he courteously dismissed them, with an intimation that "he would communicate immediately with the viceroy in the manner befitting his Majesty's commission and the honor of the British nation." The account of the reception of his communication is taken from his correspondence:

On the arrival of the party at the city gates, the soldier on guard was despatched to report the circumstance to his superior. In less than a quarter of an hour an officer of inferior rank appeared, whereupon Mr. Astell offered my letter for transmission to the viceroy, which duty this officer declined, adding that his superior was on his way to the spot. In the course of an hour several officers of nearly equal rank arrived in succession, each refusing to deliver the letter on the plea that higher officers would shortly attend. After an hour's delay, during which time the party were treated with much indignity, not unusual on such occasions, the linguists and hong merchants arrived, who entreated to become the bearers of the letter to the viceroy. About this time an officer of rank higher than any of those who had preceded him joined the party, to whom the letter was in due form offered, and as formally refused. The officer having seen the superscription on the letter, argued, that "as it came from the superintendent of trade, the hong merchants were the proper channels of communication:" but this obstacle appeared of minor importance in their eyes, upon ascertaining that the document was styled a *letter*, and not a *petition*. The linguists requested to be allowed a copy of the address, which was of course refused.

About this time the *kwang-hieh*, a military officer of the rank of colonel, accompanied by an officer a little inferior to himself, arrived on the spot, to whom the letter was offered three several times and as often refused. The senior hong merchant, Howqua, after a private conversation with the colonel, requested to be allowed to carry the letter in company with him and ascertain whether it would be received. This being considered as an insidious attempt to circumvent the directions of the superintendents, a negative was made to this and other overtures of a similar tendency. Suddenly all the officers took their departure for the purpose, as it was afterward ascertained, of consulting with the viceroy. Nearly three hours having been thus lost within the city, Mr. Astell determined to wait a reasonable time for the return of the officers, who shortly afterward reassembled; whereupon Mr. Astell respectfully offered the letter in question three separate times to the colonel and afterward to the other officers, all of whom distinctly refused even to touch it; upon which the party returned to the factory.[1]

---

[1] *Chinese Repository*, Vol. XI., p. 27.

The governor reported this occurrence at court in a memorial, in which, after stating that his predecessor had instructed the Company's supercargoes to make arrangements that "a *taipan* [or supercargo, the word being applied to all foreign consuls] acquainted with affairs should still be appointed to come to Canton to control and direct the trade," he states what had occurred, and adds:

> The said barbarian eye would not receive the hong merchants, but afterward repaired to the outside of the city to present a letter to me, your Majesty's minister, Lu. On the face of the envelope the forms and style of equality were used, and there were absurdly written the characters *Ta Ying kwoh* ['Great English nation']. Now it is plain on the least reflection, that in keeping the central and outside [people] apart, it is of the highest importance to maintain dignity and sovereignty. Whether the said barbarian eye has or has not official rank there are no means of thoroughly ascertaining. But though he be really an officer of the said nation, he yet cannot write letters on equality with the frontier officers of the Celestial Empire. As the thing concerned the national dignity, it was inexpedient in the least to allow a tendency to any approach or advance by which lightness of esteem might be occasioned. Accordingly orders were given to Han Shau-king, the colonel in command of the military forces of this department, to tell him authoritatively that, by the statutes and enactments of the Celestial Empire, there has never been intercourse by letters with outside barbarians; that, respecting commercial matters, petitions must be made through the medium of the hong merchants, and that it is not permitted to offer or present letters. . . . On humble examination it appears that the commerce of the English barbarians has hitherto been managed by the hong merchants and *taipans;* there has never been a barbarian eye to form a precedent. Now it is suddenly desired to appoint an officer, a superintendent, which is not in accordance with old regulations. Besides, if the said nation has formed this decision, it still should have stated in a petition the affairs which, and the way how, such superintendent is to manage, so that a memorial might be presented requesting your Majesty's mandate and pleasure as to what should be refused, in order that obedience might be paid to it and the same be acted on accordingly. But the said barbarian eye, Lord Napier, without having made any plain report, suddenly came to the barbarian factories outside the city to reside, and presumed to desire intercourse to and fro by official documents and letters with the officers of the Central Flowery Land; this was, indeed, far out of the bounds of reason.[1]

The governor here intimates that the intention of his government in requesting a *taipan* to come to Canton was only to have a responsible officer with whom to communicate. In refusing

---

[1] *Chinese Repository,* Vol. III., p. 327.

to receive an 'eye,' or superintendent, therefore, he did not, in his own view of the case, suppose that he was refusing, nor did he or the court of Peking intend to refuse, the residence of a supercargo, for they were desirous to have responsible heads appointed over the commerce and subjects of every nation trading at Canton. These occurrences were discussed by the Hon. John Quincy Adams in his lecture upon the war with China, delivered in 1841, in which he alleged that the rejection of Lord Napier's letter and mission was a sufficient reason for the subsequent contest. He showed the impolicy of allowing the Chinese ideas of supremacy over other nations, and exhibited their natural results in the degraded position of foreigners. He had, however, only an imperfect conception of the strength of this assumption, but it was not debated in this contest between Governor Lu and Lord Napier. The former was not blameworthy for endeavoring to carry the laws of his own country into execution, while the latter was doing his best to obey the instructions of his own sovereign. The question of the propriety of those laws, involving as they did the supremacy of the Emperor over the English, or the feasibility of those instructions, could only be discussed and settled by their principals. Whether this assumption was a proper ground of hostilities is altogether another question. When Lord Napier's letter was rejected he would probably have referred home to his government for further instructions if it had intended to settle the question of supremacy, but he did not do so, nor did the ministry refer to it or remonstrate against the unhandsome treatment their representative received.

The refusal of Lord Napier to confer with the hong merchants, and of the governor to receive any communication except a petition, placed the two parties in an awkward position. In his letter the former stated the object of his coming to Canton, and requested that his excellency would accord him an interview in order that their future intercourse might be arranged; and considering the desirableness of giving him accurate views, the party at the gate would have acted wisely in permitting the hong merchants to take it to him. The governor was irritated and alarmed, and vented his anger upon the unfortunate hong merchants. These had two or three interviews with Lord Napier after the rejection of the letter, but as they now said it would not be received unless superscribed *pin*, or 'petition,' they were dismissed. Having heard that there was a party among the British residents in Canton who disapproved of the proceedings of the superintendent, they vainly endeavored to call a meeting of the disaffected on the 10th of August, while his lordship assembled all of his countrymen next day, and found that they generally approved of his conduct. On the 14th he reviews his position in consequence of the rejection of his letter and the subsequent conduct of the governor. After recommending the renewal of the effort to open better understood relations with the court of Peking by a demand upon the Emperor to allow the same privileges to all foreigners residing in China which Chinese received in foreign countries, he goes on to say:

My present position is, in one point of view, a delicate one, because the trade is put in jeopardy on account of the difference existing between the viceroy and myself. I am ordered by his Majesty to "go to Canton and there report myself by letter to the viceroy." I use my best endeavors to do so; but the viceroy is a presumptuous savage, and will not grant the same privileges to me that have been exercised constantly by the chiefs of the committee. He rakes up obsolete orders, or perhaps makes them for the occasion; but the fact is, the chiefs used formerly to wait on the viceroy on their return from Macao, and continued to do it until the viceroy gave them an order to wait upon him, whereupon they gave the practice up. Had I even degraded the king's commission so far as to petition through the hong merchants for an interview, it is quite clear by the tenor of the edicts that it would have been refused. Were he to send an armed force and order me to the boat, I could then retreat with honor, and he would implicate himself; but they are afraid to attempt such a measure. What then remains but the stoppage of the trade or my retirement? If the trade is stopped for any length of time the consequences to the merchants are most serious, as they are also to the unoffending Chinese. But the viceroy cares no more for commerce, or for the comfort and happiness of the people as long as he receives his pay and plunder, than if he did not live among them. My situation is different; I cannot hazard millions of property for any length of time on the mere score of etiquette. If the trade shall be stopped, which is probable enough in the absence of the frigate, it is possible I may be obliged to retire to Macao to let it loose again. Then has the viceroy gained his point and the commission is degraded. Now, my lord, I argue that whether the commission retires by force of arms or by the injustice practised on the merchants, the viceroy has committed an outrage on the British crown which should be equally chastised. The whole system of government here is that of subterfuge and shifting the blame from the shoulders of the one to the other. . . . I shall not go, however, without publishing in Chinese and disseminating far and wide the base conduct of the viceroy in oppressing the merchants, native as well as foreign, and of my having taken the step out of pure compassion to them. I can only once more implore your lordship to force them to acknowledge my authority and the king's commission, and if you can do that you will have no difficulty in opening the ports at the same time.[1]

Such were the sentiments and desires which filled the mind of the English superintendent. He is in error in saying that the governor would not grant him the same privileges as had been accorded to the chiefs of the Company. The present question was not about having an interview, but regarding the superscription of his letter; for the chiefs of the Company sent their sealed communications through the hong merchants as petitions. The governor stopped the English trade on the 16th, and two days after issued an explanatory paper in reply to the report that his orders on that subject had been carried into effect. This document sets forth his determination to uphold the old regulations, and a few sentences from it are here introduced as a contrast with the preceding despatch. The conviction of the governor in the supremacy of his Emperor over all foreign nations which had sent embassies to his court, and his own official position making him responsible for successfully maintaining the laws over foreigners, must be borne in mind:

To refer to England: should an official personage from a foreign country proceed to the said nation for the arrangement of any business, how could he neglect to have the object of his coming announced in a memorial to the said nation's king, or how could he act contrary to the requirements of the said nation's dignity, doing his own will and pleasure? Since the said barbarian eye states that he is an official personage, he ought to be more thoroughly acquainted with these principles. Before, when he offered a letter, I, the governor, saw it inexpedient to receive it, because the established laws of the Celestial Empire do not permit ministers and those under authority to have private intercourse by letter with outside barbarians, but have, hitherto, in commercial affairs, held the merchants responsible; and if perchance any barbarian merchant should have any petition to make requesting the investigation of any affair, [the laws require] that by the said *taipan* a duly prepared petition should be in form presented, and an answer by proclamation awaited. There has never been such a thing as outside barbarians sending in a letter.

---

[1] *Chinese Repository*, Vol. XV., p. 68.

He then says that there had never been any official correspondence to and fro between the native officers and the barbarian merchants; by this he means a correspondence of equality, which the Chinese Government had indeed never yielded. The idea of supremacy never leaves him—witness, for example, the following strain, peculiarly Chinese:

The hong merchants, because the said barbarian eye will not adhere to the old regulations, have requested that a stop should be put to the said nation's commerce. This manifests a profound knowledge of the great principles of dignity. It is most highly praiseworthy. Lord Napier's perverse opposition necessarily demands such a mode of procedure, and it would be most right immediately to put a stop to buying and selling. But considering that the said nation's king has hitherto been in the highest degree reverently obedient, he cannot in sending Lord Napier at this time have desired him thus obstinately to resist. The some hundreds of thousands of commercial duties yearly coming from the said country concern not the Celestial Empire the extent of a hair or a feather's down. The possession or absence of them is utterly unworthy of one careful thought. Their broadcloths and camlets are still more unimportant, and of no regard. But the tea, the rhubarb, the raw silk of the Inner Land, are the sources by which the said nation's people live and maintain life. For the fault of one man, Lord Napier, must the livelihood of the whole nation be precipitately cut off? I, the governor, looking up and embodying the great Emperor's most sacred, most divine wish, to nurse and tenderly cherish as one all that are without, feel that I cannot bring my mind to bear it! Besides, all the merchants of the said nation dare dangers, crossing the seas myriads of miles to come from far. Their hopes rest wholly in the attainment of gain by buying and selling. That they did not attend when summoned by the hong merchants to a meeting for consultation, was because they were under the direction of Lord Napier; it assuredly did not proceed from the several merchants' own free will. Should the trade be wholly cut off in one morning, it would cause great distress to many persons, who, having travelled hither by land and sea, would by one man, Lord Napier, be ruined. They cannot in such case but be utterly depressed with grief. . . . I hear the said eye is a man of very solid and expansive mind and placid speech. If he consider, he can himself doubtless distinguish right and wrong: let him on no account permit himself to be deluded by men around him. . . . Hereafter, when the said nation's king hears respecting these repeated orders and official replies, [he will know] that the whole wrong lies on the barbarian eye; it is in nowise owing to any want on the part of the Celestial Empire of extreme consideration for the virtue of reverential obedience exercised by the said nation's king.[1]

He consequently sent a deputation of officials to Lord Napier to inquire why he had come to Canton, what business he

---

[1] *Chinese Repository*, Vol. III., p. 235.

was appointed to perform, and when he would retire to Macao. The letter was again handed them, but the superscription still remained, and they refused to touch it. They, however, learned enough to be able to inform their master what he wished to know: the real point of dispute between the two could only be settled between their sovereigns. The governor by this deputation showed a desire to make some arrangement, and the trade would probably have been shortly reopened had not Lord Napier carried out his idea, two days after, of appealing to the people in order to explain the reasons why the governor had stopped the trade and brought distress on them. The paper simply detailed the principal events which had occurred since his arrival, laying the blame upon the "ignorance and obstinacy" of the governor in refusing to receive his letter, and closing with—"The merchants of Great Britain wish to trade with all China on principles of mutual benefit; they will never relax in their exertions till they gain a point of equal importance to both countries; and the viceroy will find it as easy to stop the current of the Canton River as to carry into effect the insane determination of the hong."

In many of the former proceedings between the Chinese and foreigners, based as they were upon incorrect ideas, the rules of diplomacy elsewhere observed formed no guide; but the publication of this statement was unwise and dangerous. Not only did it jeopardize the lives and property of British subjects, but of all other foreigners residing at Canton, to whose safety and interests, as involved with his own dispute, Lord Napier makes no reference in his despatches. Happily, Governor Lu did not appease his irritation by letting loose the populace of Canton, which was highly excited, but by imprisoning members of the co-hong for allowing the superintendent to come to the city.

The governor and his colleagues stopped the English trade on September 2d, in a proclamation containing many inaccurate statements and absurd reasonings, in which he forbade either natives or foreigners to give aid or comfort to Lord Napier. Communication with the shipping at Whampoa was also interdicted, so that, in reality, the entire foreign trade was interrupted. A guard of Chinese troops was placed near the Company's factory, but no personal distress was felt on account of the interdict. H. B. M. frigates Andromache and Imogene were ordered up to protect the shipping and persons of British subjects, and the two vessels anchored at Whampoa on the 11th. In their passage through the Bogue they returned the fire from the forts, with little damage to either; and on anchoring, a lieutenant and boat's crew were despatched to Canton to protect the English factory. These decisive proceedings troubled the native authorities not a little, who, on their part, prepared for stronger measures by blocking up the river and stationing troops about Whampoa, but were relieved when they found that the ships remained at their anchorage.

Lord Napier sent a protest against the proceedings of the governor in stopping the trade, through the Chamber of Commerce and hong merchants; but at this juncture his health gave way so rapidly that three days after the frigates had anchored he decided to return to Macao and wait for instructions. The Chinese detained him on his passage down until the ships were out of the river; but he sank and died October 11th, a fortnight after reaching that city. As soon as he left Canton the trade was reopened. On hearing that the ships had reached Whampoa, the Emperor degraded or suspended all the officials who had been in any way responsible; but when he learned that "Lord Napier had been driven out, and the two ships of war dragged over the shallows and expelled," he restored most of those whom he had thus punished. The governor also vented his indignation upon ten of his subordinates, by subjecting them to torture in order to "ascertain if they were guilty of illicit connection with foreigners." The drama was closed on the part of the Chinese by an imperial mandate: "The English barbarians have an open market in the Inner Land, but there has hitherto been no interchange of official communications. Yet it is absolutely requisite that there should be a person possessing general control, to have the special direction of affairs; wherefore let the governor immediately order the hong merchants to command the said separate merchants, that they send a letter back to their country calling for the appointment of another person as *taipan*, to come for the control and direction of commercial affairs, in accordance with the old regulations."

The principles on which the Chinese acted in this affair are plainly seen. To have granted official intercourse by letter would have been to give up the whole question, to consider the king of England as no longer a tributary, and so release him and his subjects from their allegiance. To do so would not only permit them to come into their borders as equals, subject to no laws or customs, but would further open the door for resistance to their authority, armed opposition to their control, and ultimate in possession of their territory. The governor hints at this when speaking of the necessity of restraining the barbarian eye: "With regard to territory, it would also have its consequences." These would be the probable results of allowing such a mode of address from the Kalkas, or Tibetans, and the Emperor felt the importance of its concession in a way that Lord Napier himself could not appreciate. Nevertheless, with the inconsistency of children, the Son of Heaven and his courtiers, in the mandate just quoted, yield their obligations to justly govern the far-travelled strangers, by requiring them to get a countryman "to exercise general control" and live among them —thus establishing the principle of ex-territoriality within their borders which they now find so irksome.

It is pitiable, and natural too, that the Chinese should have had notions so incorrect and dangerous, for it led them to misinterpret every act of foreigners. Their entire intercourse with Europeans, since the Portuguese first came to their shores, had conspired to strengthen the opinion that all traders were crafty, domineering, avaricious, and contumacious, and must be kept down in every possible way to insure safety to the Chinese natives. The indignation of the Emperor on hearing of the entrance of the ships of war was mixed with great apprehension, "lest there were yet other ships staying at a distance ready to bring in aid to him" [Lord Napier]. Ignorant as he was of the true character of the embassies which had been received at Peking, he was still more likely to take alarm at any attempt to open an equal intercourse, and disposed to resist it as he would a forcible occupation of his territory, of which it was, in his view, only the precursor.

That these were the feelings of the rulers at Peking cannot be doubted; and we must know what views and fears actuated them in order to understand their proceedings. If the position of England in the eyes of the Chinese had been fully known in London, the unequal contest imposed upon Lord Napier would either have been avoided or directed against the imperial government. The offer of an amicable intercourse was given to the Chinese, but through the inapplicable instructions which his lordship received this offer was not made to the weaker and ignorant party in such a way as not to excite its fears, while it fully explained the real position and intentions of England, and through her all Christendom, in seeking intercourse with China. Yet so long as the court of Peking, in virtue of the Emperor's vicegerency over mankind, claimed supremacy over other nations, the struggle to maintain that assumption was sure to come. This false notion did, however, really continue among them for about forty years, till five foreign ministers had their first audience with the Emperor Tungchí, June, 1873, and stood before his throne as they presented their credentials.

The British residents at Canton saw the point of difficulty clearly, and in a petition to the king in council, dated December 4, 1834, recommended that a commissioner be sent to one of the northern ports with a small fleet to arrange the matter of future intercourse. In this petition they "trace the disabilities and restrictions under which British commerce now labors to a long acquiescence in the arrogant assumption of supremacy over the monarchs and people of other countries claimed by the Emperor of China for himself and his subjects," and conclude that "no essentially beneficial result can be expected to arise out of negotiations in which such pretensions are not decidedly repelled." The recommendations of the petitioners were disregarded in England. The cabinet disapproved of the spirit of Lord Napier's despatches, and intimated to him that it was "not by force and violence that his Majesty intended to establish a commercial intercourse between his subjects and China, but by conciliatory measures." After the events of 1834 if a commissioner, backed by a small fleet, had been immediately appointed to Peking to arrange the terms of future intercourse, the subsequent war might have been averted, though it is more likely that the imperial court would have rejected all overtures until compelled to treat by force.

As things were situated at Canton, it was really impossible for the Chinese Government to carry on a line of policy with respect to foreign intercourse which would at once maintain its assumptions, avoid the risk of a rupture, squeeze all the money possible out of the trade, and repress the complaints of the British merchants. The cessation of the Company's monopoly, as well as its control over all British subjects, had weakened the leverage of the local authorities to manage them, to a greater degree than they were aware.

The trade was conducted during the next season to the satisfaction of all parties. That of other nations had been practically stopped with that of the English, but the suspension was at a dull season of the year. Their consuls took no official part in the dispute, though they had some ground for complaint in the suspension of their trade and the imprisonment of their countrymen. The Chinese shopkeepers known as "outside merchants" having been interdicted trading at all with foreigners, went to the governor's palace in a large body and soon obtained a removal of the restriction. The hong merchants themselves instigated this decree, for these shopkeepers, while deriving large profits from their business, were almost free from the extortions which the monopolists suffered. All the extraordinary expenses incurred by the provincial exchequer in the late affair were required of these unfortunate men; and they *must* get it out of the trade in the best way they could. Amelioration could not be expected from such a system; for as soon as the foreigners began to complain, the hong merchants were impelled by every motive to misrepresent their complaints to the governor and quash every effort to obtain redress. The situation of foreigners there was aptly likened by a writer on the subject to the inmates of the Zoölogical Garden in Regent's Park: "They [the animals] have been free to play what pranks they pleased, so that they made no uproar nor escaped from confinement. The keepers looked sharply after them and tried to keep them quiet, because annoyed by the noise they made and responsible for the mischief they might commit if they got at liberty. They might do what was right in their own eyes with each other. The authorities of China do not expect from wild and restless barbarians the decorum and conduct exemplified in their own great family."

The peculiar position of the relations with the Chinese and the value of the trade, present and prospective, was so great that these events called out many pamphleteers both in England and the East. The servants of the Company naturally recommended a continuance of the peaceable system, urging that foreigners should obey the laws of the Empire where they lived and not interfere with the restrictions put upon them. Others counselled the occupation of an island on the coast, to which Chinese traders would immediately resort, and which was to be held only so long as the Emperor refused to open his ports and allow a fair traffic with his people. Others deprecated resort to force until a commissioner to Peking had explained the designs and wishes of his government, demanded the same privileges for foreigners in China that the Chinese enjoyed abroad, and then, in the event of a refusal, compel acquiescence. Some advised letting things take their own course and conducting trade as it could be at Canton until circumstances compelled the Chinese to act. "That which we now require is not to lose the enjoyment of what we have got," said the Duke of Wellington, and his advice was followed in most respects. A few thought it would be the wiser way to disseminate juster ideas of the position, power, and wishes of England and all foreign nations among the Chinese in their own language. They argued very properly that ignorance on these points would neutralize every attempt to bring about a better state of things; that although the Chinese were to blame for their uncompromising arrogance, it was also their great misfortune that they really had had little opportunity to learn the truth respecting their visitors. All these suggestions looked forward to no long continuance of the present undefined, anomalous relations, and all of them contained much pertinent advice and many valuable items of information; but it was a question not more difficult than important what course of procedure was the best. While the point of supremacy seemed to be settled in favor of the Son of Heaven, the virus of the contraband opium trade was working out its evil effects among his subjects and hastening on a new era.

The British superintendents now lived in Macao pending the action of their government, merely keeping a clerk at Canton to sign manifests. The foreign residents established the Society for the Diffusion of Useful Knowledge, and other benevolent projects mentioned in a previous chapter; they also sent two or three vessels along the coast to see what openings existed for entering the country, preaching the gospel, or living on shore. The results of the voyages fully proved the impossibility of entering the country in an open manner without the permission of the rulers, and the limited intercourse with the people also showed that the character of foreigners was generally associated with the opium trade. The dwellers immediately on the coast were eager for an extension of the traffic, because it brought them large gains, and the officers at the principal ports were desirous of participating in the emoluments of their fellows at Canton; but those who had the good of the country at heart (and there are many such in China) thought that the extension of foreign trade would bring with it unmitigated evil from the increased use of opium.

Sir G. B. Robinson, the superintendent, remained at Lintin on board a cutter among opium ships anchored there during the season of 1835–36, and was so well satisfied with his position that he recommended his government to purchase a small ship for the permanent accommodation of the commission there beyond the reach of the Chinese officers, and to vest its powers in a single individual. He also expressed his conviction that there was little hope of establishing a proper understanding with the Chinese Government, except by a resort to force and the occupation of an island off the mouth of the river:

I see no grounds to apprehend the occurrence of any fearful events on the north-east coast, nor can I learn what new danger exists. I am assured from the best authority that the scuffles between different parties of smugglers and mandarins, alike engaged and competing in the traffic, are not more serious or frequent than in this province. In no case have Europeans been engaged in any kind of conflict or affray : and while this increasing and lucrative trade is in the hands of the parties whose vital interests are so totally dependent on its safety and continuance, and by whose prudence and integrity it has been brought into its present increasing and flourishing condition, I think little apprehension may be entertained of dangers emanating from imprudence on their part. Should any unfortunate catastrophe take place, what would our position at Canton entail upon us but responsibility and jeopardy, from which we are now free ? On the question of smuggling opium I will not enter in this place, though, indeed, smuggling carried on actively in the government boats can hardly be termed such. Whenever his Majesty's government directs us to prevent British vessels engaging in the traffic, we can enforce any order to that effect, but a more certain method would be to prohibit the growth of the poppy and the manufacture of opium in British India ; and if British ships are in the habit of committing irregularities and crimes, it seems doubly necessary to exercise a salutary control over them by the presence of an authority at Lintin.

Taking all things into consideration, this is a remarkable despatch to be sent by the representative of a Christian government writing from the midst of a fleet of smugglers on the shores of a pagan country. "The scuffles caused by the introduction of opium are," he remarks, "*not more* serious or frequent on the coast than about Canton ;" though even there, probably, not one-half which did occur were known ; but Europeans never personally engaged in any of them. They only brought the cause and object of these collisions where the people could get it, and then quietly looked on to see them fight about it. The "prudence and integrity" of the merchants were engaged in cherishing it to a high degree of prosperity, and they were not likely to act imprudently. The orders of the supreme government for its officers on the coast to stop the traffic were utterly powerless, through the cupidity and venality of those officers and their underlings ; yet their almost complete failure to execute them does not impugn the sincerity of the court in issuing them. There is not the least evidence to show that the court of Peking was not sincere in its desire to suppress the trade, from the first edict in 1800 till the war broke out in 1840. The excuse that the government smuggled because its revenue cruisers engaged in it and the helpless provincial authorities winked at it, is no more satisfactory than to make the successful bribery of custom-house officers in England or elsewhere a proof of the corruption of the treasury department. The temptation of an "increasing and lucrative" trade was as strong to the unenlightened pagan Chinese smuggler as it was to the Christian merchants and monopolists who placed the poisonous drug constantly within his reach. It would have been far more frank on the part of the British superintendent to have openly defended a traffic affording a revenue of more than two millions sterling to his own government, and suggested that such an "increasing and lucrative" business should not be impeded, than to say that he could stop British ships engaging in it as soon as he received orders to that effect.

The existence of the commission at the outer anchorages was fully known to the authorities at Canton, but no movement toward reopening the intercourse was made by either party. Lord Palmerston instructed the superintendent not to communicate with the governor-general through the hong merchants, nor to give his written communications the name of petitions. Captain Elliot succeeded Sir George in 1836, and immediately set about reopening the communication with the Chinese officers in the same way that the supercargoes of the Company had conducted it. He defended this course upon the grounds that he had no right to direct official communication with the governor, and that the remarkable movements of the Chinese and the state of uncertainty in respect to the whole foreign trade rendered it desirable to be at Canton. The successor of Lu, Tăng Ting-ching, willingly responded to this proposition by sending a deputation of three officers to Macao with the hong merchants to make some inquiries before memorializing the Emperor. In his report the governor avoided all reference to Lord Napier, and requested his Majesty's sanction to the present request as being in accordance with the orders that the English merchants should send home to have a supercargo come out to manage them. It was of course granted; and the British commission, having received a "red permit" from the collector of customs, returned to Canton April 12, 1837, after an absence of about thirty months. In his note to the governor upon receiving the imperial sanction, Captain Elliot says: "The undersigned respectfully assures his excellency that it is at once his duty and his anxious desire to conform in all things to the imperial pleasure; and he will therefore heedfully attend to the points adverted to in the papers now before him." This language was decided, and his excellency afterward called upon the superintendent to do as he had promised.

The remarkable movements of the supreme government here referred to grew out of a memorial from Hü Nai-tsí, formerly salt commissioner and judge at Canton, proposing the legalization of the opium trade. In this paper he acknowledges that it is impossible to stop the traffic or use of the drug; if the foreign vessels be driven from the coast, they will go to some island near by, where the native craft will go off to them; and if the laws be made too severe upon those who smoke the drug they will be disregarded. By legalizing it, he says, the drain of specie will be stopped, the regular trade rendered more profitable and manageable, and the consumption of the drug regulated. He proposes instant dismissal from office as the penalty for all functionaries convicted of smoking, while their present ineffectual attempts to suppress the trade, which resulted in general contempt for all law, would cease, and consequently the dignity of government be better maintained. The trade on the coast would be concentrated at Canton, and the fleet at Lintin broken up, thereby bringing all foreigners more completely under control.

This unexpected movement at the capital caused no little stir at Canton, and the hong merchants presently advertised the foreigners that soon there would no longer be any use for the receiving-ships at Lintin. Captain Elliot wrote that he thought legalization had come too late to stop the trade on the coast, and, with a prescient eye, adds that the "feeling of independence created among British subjects from the peculiar mode of conducting this branch of the trade," would ere long lead to graver difficulties and acts of violence requiring the armed interference of his government. The impression was general at Canton that the trade would be legalized, and increased preparations were accordingly made in India to extend the cultivation. The governor and his colleagues recommended its legalization on the grounds that "the tens of millions of precious money which now annually ooze out of the Empire will be saved," the duties be increased, the evil practices of transporting contraband goods by deceit and violence suppressed, numberless quarrels and litigations arising therefrom and the crimes of worthless vagrants diminished. They also deluded themselves with the idea that if the officers were dismissed as soon as convicted, the intelligent part of society would not indulge their depraved appetites, but let the "victims of their own self-sacrificing folly," the poor opium-smokers, be found only among the lower classes. In connection with this report, the hong merchants replied to various inquiries respecting the best mode of carrying on the opium trade in case it should be legalized, and their mode of conducting commerce generally; adding that it was beyond their power to control the smuggling traffic or restrain the exportation of sycee, and showed that the balance of trade would naturally leave the country in bullion. These papers are fairly drawn up, and their perusal cannot fail to elevate the character of the Chinese for consideration, carefulness, and business-like procedure.[1]

There were other statesmen, however, who regarded Hü Naitsí's memorial as a dangerous step in the downward path, and sounded the alarm. Among these the foremost was Chu Tsun, a cabinet minister, who sent in a counter-memorial couched in the strongest terms. He advised that the laws be more strictly maintained, and cited instances to show that when the provincial authorities earnestly set about it they could put the trade down; that the people would soon learn to despise all laws if those against opium-smoking were suspended; and that recreant officers should be superseded and punished. His indignation warms as he goes on: "It has been represented that advantage is taken of the laws against opium by extortionate underlings and worthless vagrants, to benefit themselves. Is it not known, then, that when government enacts a law, there is necessarily an infraction of that law? And though the law should sometimes be relaxed and become ineffectual, yet surely it should not on that account be abolished; any more than we

[1] *Chinese Repository*, Vol. V., pp. 139, 259, 385 ff.

should altogether cease to eat because of stoppage of the throat. The laws which forbid the people to do wrong may be likened to the dikes which prevent the overflowing of water. If any one urging, then, that the dikes are very old and therefore useless, we should have them thrown down, what words could express the consequences of the impetuous rush and all-destroying overflow! Yet the provincials, when discussing the subject of opium, being perplexed and bewildered by it, think that a prohibition which does not *utterly* prohibit is better than one which does not effectually prevent the importation of the drug. . . . If we can but prevent the importation of opium, the exportation of dollars will then cease of itself, and the two offences will both at once be stopped. Moreover, is it not better, by continuing the old enactments, to find even a partial remedy for the evil, than by a change of the laws to increase the importation still further?"

He then proceeds to show that the native article could not compete with the foreign, for it would not be as well manufactured, and moreover "all men prize what is strange and undervalue whatever is in ordinary use." Its cultivation would occupy rich and fertile land now used for nutritive grains: "To draw off in this way the waters of the great fountain requisite for the production of food and raiment, and to lavish them upon the root whence calamity and disaster spring forth, is an error like that of the physician who, when treating a mere external disease, drives it inward to the heart and centre of the body. Shall the fine fields of Kwangtung, which produce their three crops every year, be given up for the cultivation of this noxious weed?" He says the question does not concern property and duties, but the welfare and vigor of the people; and quotes from the *History of Formosa* a passage showing the way in which the natives there were enervated by using it, and adds that the purpose of the English in introducing opium into the country has been to weaken and enfeeble it. Kanghí long ago (1717) remarked, he observes, "There is cause for apprehension, lest in the centuries or millenniums to come China may be endangered by collisions with the various nations of the West who come hither from beyond the seas." And now, in less than two centuries, "we see the commencement of that danger which he apprehended."

The suggestion of Hü Nai-tsí, to allow it to the people and interdict the officers, is called bad casuistry, "like shutting a woman's ears before you steal her earrings." He shows that this distinction will be vain, for it will be impossible to say who is of the people and who are officers, for all the latter are taken from the body of the former. The permission will induce people to use it who now refrain from fear of the laws; for even the proposal has caused "thieves and villains on all hands to raise their heads and open their eyes, gazing about and pointing the finger under the notion that when once these prohibitions are repealed, thenceforth and forever they may regard themselves far from every restraint and cause of fear." He asserts that nothing but strong laws rigidly carried into effect will restrain them from their evil ways, and concludes by recommending increased stringency in their execution as the only hope of reformation.

This spirited paper was supported by another from a sub-censor, Hü Kiu, on the necessity of checking the exportation of silver, and recommending that a determined officer be sent to punish severely the native traitors, which would add dignity to the laws; and then the barbarians would be awed and consequently reform and be entirely defeated in their designs of conquering the country. He cites several instances of their outrageous violation of the laws, such as levelling graves in Macao for the purpose of making a road over them, landing goods there for entering them at Canton in order to evade the duties and port charges, and even riding in sedans with four bearers, like Chinese officers. Force needed only to be put forth a little and they would again be humbled to subjection; but if they still brought the pernicious drug, then inflict capital punishment upon them as well as upon natives. The sub-censor agrees with Chu Tsun regarding the designs of foreigners in doing so, that they wished first to debilitate and impoverish the land as a preparatory measure, for they never smoked the drug in their own country, but brought it all to China. This prevailing impression was derived mainly from the abstinence of foreign merchants and seamen.

Both these papers were transmitted to Canton for deliberation, although the local officers had already sent a memorial to the cabinet approving the suggestions of Hü Nai-tsí. At this time, however, it was properly remarked that "there had been a diversity of opinion in regard to it, some requesting a change in the policy hitherto adopted, and others recommending the continuance of the severe prohibitions. It is highly important to consider the subject carefully in all its bearings, surveying at once the whole field of action so that such measures may be adopted as shall continue forever in force, free from all failure." This subject, the most important, it cannot be doubted, which had ever been deliberated upon by the Emperor of China and his council, was now fairly brought before the whole nation; and if all the circumstances be taken into consideration, it was one of the most remarkable consultations of any age or country. A long experience of the baneful effects of opium-smoking upon the health, minds, and property of those who used it, had produced a deep conviction in the minds of well-wishers of their country of the necessity of some legal restraint over the people; while the annual drainage of specie at the rate of three or four million sterling for what brought misery and poverty in its train, alarmed those who cared only for the stability and prosperity of the country. The settlement or management of the question was one of equal difficulty and importance, and the result proved that it was quite beyond the reach of both their power and wisdom. Fully conscious of the weak moral principle in themselves and in their countrymen, they considered it right to restrain and deter the people by legislative enactments and severe penalties. Ignorant of the nature of commercial dealings, they thought it both practicable and necessary to limit the exportation of specie; for not having any substitute for coin or any system of national credit, there was serious hazard, otherwise, that the government would ultimately be bankrupted. It is unjust to the Chinese to say, as was argued by those who had never felt these sufferings, that all parties were insincere in their efforts to put down this trade, that it was a mere affectation of morality, and that no one would be more chagrined to see it stop than those apparently so strenuous against it. This assertion was made by Lord Palmerston in Parliament and re-echoed by the Indian officials; but those who have candidly examined the proceedings of the Chinese, or have lived among the people in a way to learn their real feelings, need not be told how incorrect is the remark. The highest statesman and the debilitated, victimized smoker alike agreed in their opinion of its bad effects, and both were pretty much in the position of a miserable lamb in the coil of a hungry anaconda.

The debate among the Chinese excited a discussion among foreigners, most of whom were engaged in the traffic. Here the gist of the question turned upon the points whether opium was really a noxious stimulant *per se*, and whether the Chinese government was sincere in its prohibitions in the face of the notorious connivance of the officers along the coast from Hainan to Tientsin. One writer conclusively proved its baneful effects upon the system when taken constantly, and that its habitual use in the smallest degree almost certainly led to intemperate or uncontrollable use; he then charges the crime of murder upon those who traffic in it, and asserts that "the perpetuating and encouraging and engaging in a trade which promotes disease, misery, crime, madness, despair, and death, is to be an accomplice with the guilty principals in that tremendous pursuit." He exposes the fallacy, hypocrisy, and guilt of the question whether it be less criminal for a man to engage in a pursuit which he knows to be injurious to his fellow-men, because if he does not do so some one else will. The Court of Directors, even, whom all the world knows to be chief managers of the cultivation, manufacture, and sale of the drug, says in one of its despatches that "so repugnant are their feelings to the opium trade, they would gladly, in compassion to mankind, put a total end to the consumption of opium if they could. But they cannot do this, and as opium will be grown somewhere or other, and will be largely consumed in spite of all their benevolent wishes, they can only do as they do"!

Another Englishman engaged in the traffic defended it on the ground that what is bad now was always bad; and the Emperor and his ministers had doubtless other grounds for their sudden opposition. He asserts that opium is "a useful soother, a harmless luxury, and a precious medicine, except to those who abuse it," and that while a few destroy themselves, the prudent many enjoy a pleasing solace, to get which tends to produce the persevering economy and the never-ceasing industry of the Chinese. He estimates that at a daily allowance of one and one-third ounce not more than one person in three hundred and twenty-six touches the pipe, and that there were not *more* than nine hundred and twelve thousand victimized smokers in the Empire. He also remarked that the present mode of conducting the trade by large capitalists kept it respectable, and that if their characters were held up to odium and infamy it would get into the hands of desperadoes, pirates, and marauders. He looked upon the efforts to put it down as utterly futile as the proclamations of Elizabeth were to put down hops, or the Counterblaste of James to stop tobacco.

This rejoinder was responded to by two writers, who clearly exhibited its unsoundness and ridiculed the plea that the trade should be kept in the hands of gentlemen and under the direction of a monopoly. The smuggler brought his vessel on the coast, and there waited till the people came off for his merchandise, disposing of it without the least risk to himself, "coolly commenting on the injustice of the Chinese government in refusing the practice of international law and reciprocity to countries whose subjects it only knows as engaged in constant and gross infraction of laws, the breaking of which affects the basis of all good government, the morals of the country." The true character of the smuggling trade is well set forth:

Reverse the picture. Suppose, by any chance, that Chinese junks were to import into England, as a foreign and fashionable luxury, so harmless a thing as arsenic or corrosive sublimate; that after a few years it became a rage; that thousands, yea, hundreds of thousands used it, and that its use was, in consequence of its bad effects, prohibited. Suppose that, in opposition to the prohibition, junks were stationed in St. George's Channel with a constant supply, taking occasional trips to the Isle of Wight and the mouth of the Thames when the officers were sufficiently attentive to their duty at the former station to prevent its introduction there. Suppose the consumption to increase annually, and to arouse the attention of the government and of those sound-thinking men who foresaw misery and destruction from the rapid spread of an insidious, unprofitable, and dangerous habit. Suppose, in fact, that, *mutato nomine*, all which has been achieved here had been practised there. Suppose some conservators of the public morals to be aroused at last, and to remonstrate against its use and increase; and that among the nation sending forth this destroyer to prey on private happiness and public virtue, one or two pious and well-meaning *bonzes* were to remonstrato with their countrymen on the enormity of their conduct:—how wonderfully consolatory to one party, and unanswerable to the other, must be the remark of the well-dressed and well-educated Chinese merchant: "Hai ya! my friend, do not you see my silk dress and the crystal knob on my cap; don't you know that I have read and can quote Confucius, Mencius, and all the Five Books; do you not see that the barbarians are passionately fond of arsenic, that they will have it, and even go so far as to pay for it; and can you, for one moment, doubt that it would not be much worse for them if, instead of my bringing it, it were left to the chance, needy, and uncertain supply which low men of no capital could afford to bring?"[1]

The writer shows that instead of only one person in every three hundred and twenty-six using the pipe, it was far more probable that at least one out of every one hundred and fifty (or about two million five hundred thousand in all) of the population was a victimized smoker. The assertion of its being a harmless luxury to the many, like wine or beer, is disputed, and the sophisticated argument of its use as a means of hospitality exploded. "What would a benevolent and sober-minded Chinese think," he asks, "were the sophistry of the defenders of this trade translated for him? Where would he find the high-principled and high-minded inhabitants of the far-off country? How could he be made to comprehend that the believers in and practisers of Christian morality advocated a trade so ruinous to his country? That the government of India compelled the growth of it by unwilling ryots; and that, instead of its being brought to China by 'desperadoes, pirates, and marauders,' it was purveyed by a body of capitalists, not participating certainly in what they carry, but supplying the Indian revenue safely and peaceably; that the British government and others encouraged it; and that the agents in the traffic were constantly residing at Canton, protected by the government whose laws they outraged, but monstrously indignant, and appealing to their governments, if No. 2 longcloths are classed as No. 1 through the desperate villany of some paltry custom-house servant?"

The other writer exposes the sinful fallacy of the argument

---

[1] *Chinese Repository*, Vol V., p. 409.

of expediency, and then proceeds to show how great an obstacle it is in the way of diffusing the gospel among the Chinese. We must refer to their own remarks[1] for the fuller development of the arguments, but this one showed the earnestness of his convictions by offering a premium of £100 for the best essay "showing the effects of the opium trade on the commercial, political, and moral interests of the nations and individuals connected therewith, and pointing out the course they ought to pursue in regard to it." There was, however, so little interest in the subject that this premium was never awarded, though the proposal was extensively advertised both in China and England.

The governor of Canton and his colleagues soon learned that the feeling at court was rather against legalizing the drug, though they were directed to report concerning the amount of duty proper to be levied on it; and to show their zeal, arrested several brokers and dealers. A-ming, one of the linguists, was severely tortured and exposed in the cangue for exporting sycee; others escaped similar treatment by absconding. The chief superintendent naïvely expressed his opinion that "the legalization of the trade in opium would afford his Majesty's government great satisfaction," but suggested that the gradual diversion of British capital into other channels would be attended with advantageous consequences. To one situated between his own government, which promoted the preparation and importation of opium, and the Chinese government, which was now making extraordinary efforts to regulate it, and deeply sensible of the injury resulting from its use to the people around him, and to the reputation of his own and all foreign nations from the constant infraction of the laws, the proposed step of legalization offered a timely relief. No one was more desirous of putting a stop to this destructive traffic than Captain Elliot, but knowing the impossibility of checking it by laws, he naturally wished to see the multitude of political and commercial evils growing out of smuggling done away with. There were, indeed, many things to urge in favor of this

---

[1] *Chinese Repository*, Vol. V., pp. 407, 413, and passim.

course; but the fact ought never to be lost sight of, and be mentioned to the lasting credit of the Emperor Taukwang and his advisers, in the midst of their perplexity and weakness, that he would not admit opium because it was detrimental to his people.

The conflict was now fairly begun; its issue between the parties, so unequally matched—one having almost nothing but the right on its side, the other assisted by every material and physical advantage—could easily be foreseen. Captain Elliot, as the recognized head of the British trade, received an order through the hong merchants from the provincial authorities to drive away the receiving-ships from Lintin, and send the Emperor's commands to his king, that henceforth they be prohibited coming. He replied that he could not transmit any orders to his own sovereign which did not come to him direct from the government, and quoted the recent instance of the governor-general of Fuhkien communicating directly with the captain of a British ship of war. The governor was therefore forced to send his orders to the prefect and colonel of the department to be enjoined on Captain Elliot. He replied by promising to send it to his country, and adds, in true diplomatic style, unworthy of himself and his nation: "He has already signified to your excellency, with truth and plainness, that his commission extends only to the regular trade with this Empire; and further, that the existence of any other than this trade has never yet been submitted to the knowledge of his own gracious sovereign." Captain Elliot transmitted with these "orders" a minute account of the condition of the opium trade, and a memorandum respecting the desirableness of opening communication with the court. Lord Palmerston, in reply, intimates that "her Majesty's government do not see their way in such a measure with sufficient clearness to justify them in adopting it at the present moment." He adds that no protection can be afforded to "enable British subjects to violate the laws of the country to which they trade. Any loss, therefore, which such persons may suffer in consequence of the more effectual execution of the Chinese laws on this subject, must be borne by the parties who have brought that loss on themselves by their own acts." A most paradoxical but convenient position for this "honorable" officer of the English government to assume, and worthy to be recorded in contrast to the utterances from Peking.

Near the close of 1837 the British flag was again hauled down at Canton, and the superintendent returned to Macao because he refused to superscribe the word *pin*, or 'petition,' upon his communications, according to his instructions, and the governor declined to receive them without it. In July, 1838, Sir Frederick Maitland arrived in the Wellesley (74), and was brought into correspondence with the Chinese Admiral Kwan, in consequence of the forts firing upon an English schooner passing the Bogue and stopping her to inquire whether he or any of his crew or women were on board. The Wellesley and her two consorts were anchored near the forts, and the Chinese admiral made a full apology for the mistake; his conduct in the affair was very creditable both to his judgment and temper. As soon as Sir Frederick arrived, Captain Elliot vainly endeavored to reopen correspondence with the governor by sending an open letter to the city gates, which was received and taken to him, but returned in the evening because it had not the required superscription.

Having now fully taken the sense of the Empire in the replies received from all its highest officials, the Emperor Taukwang increased his efforts to suppress the trade. In April, 1838, a native named Kwoh Sí-ping was publicly strangled at Macao by express command of the Emperor, as a warning to others not to engage in exporting sycee or introducing opium. The execution was conducted by the district magistrate and subprefect with dignity and order in the presence of a crowd of natives and foreigners. More than fifty small craft under the English or American flag were constantly plying off the port of Canton, most of them engaged in smuggling. Sometimes the government exerted its power; boats were destroyed, smugglers seized and tortured, and the sales checked; then it went on again as briskly as ever. These boats were easily caught, for the government could exercise entire control over its own subjects; but when the foreign schooners, heavily armed and manned, sailed up and down the river delivering the drug, the revenue cruisers were afraid to attack them. The hong merchants addressed a note to all foreign residents concerning them, the close of which vividly exhibits their unlucky position as the "responsible advisers" of the barbarians: "Lately we have repeatedly received edicts from the governor and hoppo severely reprimanding us; and we have also written to you, gentlemen of the different nations, several times, giving you full information of the orders and regulations, that you might perfectly obey them and manage accordingly; but you, gentlemen, continue wholly regardless."

Collisions became more and more frequent between the Chinese and their rulers, in consequence of the increased stringency of the orders from court. In September, in an affray near Whampoa between the military and villagers, several persons were killed and scores arrested. The retailers at Canton were imprisoned, and those found in other places brought there in chains. In Hupeh it was reported that the officers had punished arrested smokers by cutting out a portion of the upper lip to incapacitate them from using the pipe. Still, such was the venality of the officers that even at this time the son of Governor Tăng himself was engaged in the traffic, and many of the underlings only seized the drug from the smuggling-boats to retail it themselves. The memorial of Hwang Tsioh-tsz', advising the penalty of death, was promulgated in Canton; and the Emperor's rescript urged to stronger measures. In a rapid survey of the ill effects from the use of the drug, Hwang acknowledges that it had extended to Manchuria, and pervaded all ranks of official and humble life. The efflux of silver "into the insatiate depths of transmarine regions" had caused the rate of exchange for cash to rise until it was difficult to carry on the business of government. He then reviews the different plans proposed for checking the cause of all this evil, such as guarding the ports, stopping the entire foreign trade, arresting the smugglers, shutting up the shops, and, lastly, encouraging the home growth. He confesses that the bribes paid the coast-guard service and the maritime officers are so great as entirely to prevent their vigilance; and that the home-prepared drug does not yield the same stimulus as the foreign article. As a last resort, he proposes to increase the penalties upon the consumers, laying all the blame upon them, and advises death to be awarded all who smoke opium after a year's warning has been given them. The well-known subdivision of responsibility was to be made doubly strong by requiring bonds of every tithing and hundred that there were no smokers within their limits. Officers found guilty were not only to be executed, but their children deprived of the privilege of competing at the public examination. One cannot withhold a degree of sympathy for the helpless condition of the officers and statesmen of a great Empire sincerely desirous of doing their country service, and yet so sadly ignorant of their false position by their assumption of supremacy over the very nation whom they could not restrain, and whose officials they rejected for a formality. They might as well have tried to concert a measure to stop the Yangtsz' River in its impetuous flow, as to check the opium trade by laws and penalties.

On December 3, 1838, about two peculs of opium were seized while landing at the factories, and the coolies carried into the city. They declared that they had been sent to Whampoa by Mr. Innes, a British merchant, to obtain the opium from an American ship consigned to Mr. Talbot. The governor ordered the hong merchants to expel these two gentlemen and the ship within three days, on the garbled testimony of the two coolies. Mr. Talbot sent in a communication, stating that neither the ship nor himself had anything to do with the opium, and obtained a reversal of the order to leave. The hong merchants were justly irritated, and informed the Chamber of Commerce that they would not rent their houses to any who would not give a bond to abstain from such proceedings, and refusing to open the trade until such bonds were given; they furthermore declared their intention to pull Mr. Innes' house down if he refused to depart. The Chamber protested that "the inviolability of their personal dwellings was a point imperatively necessary" for their security; the hong merchants then resorted to entreaty, stating their difficult position between their own rulers on one side, who held them responsible for executing their orders, and the foreigners on the other, over whom they had little or no power. The Chamber could only express its regret at the unjust punishment inflicted on a hong merchant, Punhoyqua, for this, and reassert its inability to control the acts of any foreigner.

The governor had put himself in this helpless condition by refusing Captain Elliot's letters; and it is remarkable that he hesitated to arrest Mr. Innes, when one word would have set the populace on the factories and their tenants, and destroyed them all. As an alternative, he now resolved to show foreigners what consequences befel natives who dealt in opium; and while Mr. Innes still remained in Canton, he sent an officer with fifteen soldiers to execute Ho Lau-kin, a convicted dealer, in front of the factories. The officer was proceeding to carry his orders into effect near the American flag-staff, when the foreigners sallied out, pushed down the tent he was raising, and told him in loud tones not to execute the man there. Quite unprepared for this opposition, he hastily gathered up his implements and went into a neighboring street, where the man was strangled. Meanwhile a crowd collected to see these extraordinary proceedings, whom the foreigners endeavored to drive away, supposing that a little determination would soon scatter them. Blows, however, were returned, the foreigners driven into their factories, and the gates shut; the crowd had now become a mob, and under the impression that two natives had been seized, they began to batter the fronts and break the windows with stones and brickbats. They had had possession of the square about three hours, and the danger was becoming imminent, when the Pwanyu hien, or 'district magistrate,' came up, with three or four other officers, attended by a small body of police. Stepping out of his sedan he waved his hand over the crowd, the lictors pouncing upon three or four of the most active, whom they began to chastise upon the spot, and the storm was quelled. About twenty soldiers, armed with swords and spears, took their stand in a conspicuous quarter; the magistrate and his retinue seated themselves, leaving the hong merchants and the police to disperse the crowd. The foreigners were also assured that all should be kept quiet during the night, but not a word was said to them regarding their conduct in interfering with the execution or their folly in bringing this danger upon themselves. This occurrence tended to impress both the government and people with contempt and hatred for foreigners and their characters, fear of their designs, and the necessity of restraining them. The majority of them were engaged in the opium trade, and all stood before the Empire as violators of the laws, while the people themselves suffered the dreadful penalty.

There is no room for the details and correspondence connected with this remarkable incident.[1] Captain Elliot now reappeared in Canton, and at a general meeting expressed his conviction of the cause of these untoward events in the smuggling traffic on the river, declaring his intention of ordering all the British-owned vessels to leave it within three days; he moreover expressed the hope that the further step of opening communication with the provincial authorities to obtain their co-operation to drive them out would be prevented by their speedy departure. Injunctions and entreaties to his countrymen were, however, alike unavailing, and he accordingly addressed the governor, stating his wish to co-operate in driving them out. In a public notice he remarked that "this course of traffic was rapidly staining the British character with deep disgrace" and exposing the regular commerce to imminent jeopardy, and that he meant to shrink from no responsibility in drawing it to a conclusion. The governor, as was expected, praised the superintendent for his offer, but left him to do the whole work; remarking, in that peculiar strain of Chinese conceit which so effectually forestalls our sympathy for their difficulties, that "it may well be conceived that these boats trouble me not one iota:"—as if all he had to do was to arise in his majesty, and they were gone. The boats, however, gradually left the river. Mr. Innes retired, and the regular trade was resumed in January.

No British consular officer has been placed in a more difficult and humiliating dilemma, and Captain Elliot did himself honor in his efforts. The English newspapers ridiculed him as a tide-waiter of the Chinese custom-house, a man who aided the

[1] *Chinese Repository*, Vol. VII., pp. 437–456.

cowardly authorities to carry their orders into effect, thereby staining the honor of her Majesty's commission. Although he did not intend to draw a line between the heinousness of the opium trade inside of the Bogue and its harmlessness beyond that limit, still there were good reasons, under his peculiar position, for some action to show the Chinese government that British power would not protect British subjects in violating the laws of China.

At this period the Peking government had taken its course of action. Reports had been received from the provincial authorities almost unanimously recommending increased stringency to abolish the traffic. History, so far as we know, does not record a similar example of an arbitrary, despotic, pagan government taking the public sentiment of its own people before adopting a doubtful line of conduct. It was a far more momentous and difficult question than even the cabinet deemed it to be, while their conceit and ignorance incapacitated them from dealing with it prudently or successfully. There can be no reasonable doubt that the best part of his people and the moral power of the nation were with their sovereign in this attempt. Hü Nai-tsí was dismissed for proposing legalization, and three princes of the blood degraded for smoking opium; arrests, fines, tortures, imprisonments, and executions were frequent in the provinces on the same grounds, all showing the determination to eradicate it. The governor of Hukwang, Lin Tseh-sü, was ordered to proceed to Canton, with unlimited powers to stop the traffic. The trade there was at this time almost suspended, the deliveries being small and at losing prices. Many underlings were convicted and summarily punished, and on February 26th Fung A-ngan was strangled in front of the factories for his connection with opium and participation in the affray at Whampoa. The foreign flags, English, American, Dutch, and French, were all hauled down in consequence. The entire stoppage of all trade was threatened, and the governor urged foreigners to send all opium ships from Chinese waters.

Commissioner Lin arrived in Canton March 10th. The Emperor sent him to inquire and act so as thoroughly to remove the source of the evil, for, says he, "if the source of the evil be not clearly ascertained, how can we hope that the stream of pernicious consequences shall be stayed? It is our full hope that the long-indulged habit will be forever laid aside, and every root and germ of it entirely eradicated; we would fain think that our ministers will be enabled to substantiate our wishes, and so remove from China the dire calamity." It was reported in Canton that the monarch, when recounting the evils which had long afflicted his people by means of opium, paused and wept, and turning to Lin, said: "How, alas! can I die and go to the shades of my imperial father and ancestors, until these direful evils are removed!" Such was the chief purpose of this movement on the part of the Chinese government, and Lin was invested with the fullest powers ever conferred on a subject. Although long experience of the ineffectiveness of Chinese edicts generally lead those residing in the country to regard them as mere verbiage, still, to say that they are all insincere and formal because they are ineffectual, is to misjudge and pervert the emotions of common humanity. Lin appears to have been well fitted for the mission; and if he had been half as enlightened as he was sincere, he would perhaps have averted the war which followed, and been convinced that legalization was the most judicious step he could recommend.

The commissioner spent a week making inquiries, during which time nothing was publicly heard from him; while natives and foreigners alike anxiously speculated as to his plans. It was not until March 18th that his first proclamations were issued to the hong merchants and foreigners; that to the latter required them to deliver up all the opium in the storeships, and to give bonds that they would bring no more, on penalty of death. The poor hong merchants were, as usual, instructed regarding their responsibility to admonish the foreigners, and strictly charged to procure these bonds, or they would be made examples of. Three days were allowed for compliance with these demands. The hoppo had already issued orders detaining all foreigners in Canton—in fact, making them prisoners in their own houses; communication with the shipping was suspended, troops were assembled about the factories, and armed cruisers stationed on the river. The Chamber of Commerce wrote to the hong merchants on the 20th, through their chairman, W. S. Wetmore, an American, stating that they would send a definite reply in four days, and adding that "there is an almost unanimous feeling in the community of the absolute necessity of the foreign residents of Canton having no connection with the opium traffic."

This paper was taken to the commissioner, and about ten o'clock P.M. the hong merchants again met the Chamber, and told them that if *some* opium was not given up two of their number would be beheaded in the morning. The merchants present, including British, Parsees, Americans, and others, acting as individuals, then subscribed one thousand and thirty-seven chests, to be tendered to the commissioner; but the hong merchants reported next morning that this amount was insufficient. In the afternoon Lin sent an invitation to Mr. Dent, a leading English merchant, to meet him at the city gates, who expressed his willingness to go if the commissioner would give him a safe-warrant guaranteeing his return within a day. The hong merchants returned without him; and the next morning two of them, Howqua and Mowqua, came again to his house with chains upon their necks, having been sent with an express order for him to appear. They repaired to the Chamber of Commerce then assembled, but all soon returned to Mr. Dent's house, where an animated debate took place, which resulted in the unanimous decision on the part of the foreign residents that he should not go into the city without the safe-warrant. This unexpected demand caused much discussion among foreigners, as it was doubtless a contrivance to secure a hostage; and the refusal of the former to give a written safe-warrant would probably have ended in seizing Mr. Dent and imprisoning him, if Howqua, the senior hong merchant, had not allowed everything to wait over one day till Monday. Mr. Dent's partner had that day seen the *an-chah sz'*, or 'provincial judge,' in the city to explain why he hesitated to go to Lin.

On the 22d Captain Elliot sent a note to the governor expressing his readiness to meet the Chinese officers, and use "his sincere efforts to fulfil the pleasure of the great Emperor as soon as it was made known to him." The Chinese could hardly draw any other conclusion from this admission than that he had the power, as well as the inclination to put down the opium trade, which he certainly could not do; it tended therefore to deceive them. This note was followed by a letter to Captain Blake, of the Larne, requesting his assistance in defending British property and life, and by a circular ordering all British ships, opium and others, to proceed to Hongkong and prepare themselves to resist every act of aggression. A second circular to British subjects detailed the reasons which compelled him to withdraw all confidence in the "justice and moderation of the provincial government," and demand passports for all his countrymen who wished to leave Canton, while counselling every one to make preparations to remove on board ship. Elliot now proceeded to Canton, which he safely reached about sunset Sunday evening, dressed in naval uniform and closely attended by cruisers watching his movements. The British flag was then hoisted, and Captain Elliot, conducting Mr. Dent to the consulate in the most conspicuous manner, summoned a public meeting, read his notice of the previous day, and told the hong merchants to inform the commissioner that he was willing to let Mr. Dent go into the city if he could accompany him.

His coming up the river had excited the apprehensions of the Chinese that he meant to force his way out again, and orders were issued to close every pass around the factories. By nine o'clock that evening the foreigners, about two hundred and seventy-five in number, were the only inmates of their houses. Patrols, sentinels, and officers, hastening hither and thither, with the blowing of trumpets and beating of gongs, added confusion to the darkness of the night.

On the 25th most of the foreign merchants of all nations signed a paper pledging themselves "not to deal in opium, nor to attempt to introduce it into the Chinese Empire:" how many of the individuals subsequently broke this pledge on the ground that it was forced from them cannot be stated, but part of the firms which signed it afterward actively engaged in the trade. Captain Elliot applied for passports for himself and countrymen, and requested the return of the servants, avoiding all reference to his promise of three days before, or mention of the cause of these stringent proceedings. His requests were refused; no native was allowed to bring food or water to the factories; letters could not be sent to Whampoa or Macao, except at imminent risk; the confinement was complete, and had been effected without the least personal harm. The heavy punishment which had fallen on Kwoh Sí-ping, Ho Lau-kin, and Fung A-ngan had now come near to the foreign agents of the traffic; but not an individual had been touched.

The commissioner next issued an exhortation to all foreigners, urging them to deliver the drug on four grounds, viz., because they were men and had reason; because the laws forbade its use, under severe penalties; because they should have feelings for those who suffered from using it; and because of their present duress, from which they would then be released. This paper, as were all those issued by Lin, was characterized by an unusual vigor of expression and cogency of reasoning, but betrayed the same arrogance and ignorance which had misled his predecessors. One extract will suffice. Under the first reason why the opium should be delivered up, he says that otherwise the retribution of heaven will follow them, and cites some cases to prove this:

> Now, our great Emperor, being actuated by the exalted virtue of heaven itself, wishes to cut off this deluge of opium, which is the plainest proof that such is the intention of high heaven! It is then a traffic on which heaven looks with disgust, and who is he that may oppose its will? Thus in the instance of the English chief Robarts, who violated our laws; he endeavored to get possession of Macao by force, and at Macao he died! Again, in 1834, Lord Napier bolted through the Bocca Tigris, but being overwhelmed with grief and fear he almost immediately died; and Morrison, who had been darkly deceiving him, died that very year also! Besides these, every one of those who have not observed our laws have either been overtaken with the judgments of heaven on returning to their country, or silently cut off ere they could return thither. Thus then it is manifest that the heavenly dynasty may not be opposed!

Two communications to Captain Elliot, from Lin through the prefect and district magistrates, accompanied this exhortation, stating his view of the superintendent's conduct in contumaciously resisting his commands and requiring him to give up the opium. For once in the history of foreign intercourse with China, these commands were obeyed, and after intimating his readiness to comply, Captain Elliot issued a circular on March 27th, which from its important results is quoted entire:

I, Charles Elliot, chief superintendent of the trade of British subjects in China, presently forcibly detained by the provincial government, together with all the merchants of my own and the other foreign nations settled here, without supplies of food, deprived of our servants, and cut off from all intercourse with our respective countries (notwithstanding my own official demand to be set at liberty that I might act without restraint), have now received the commands of the high commissioner, issued directly to me under the seals of the honorable officers, to deliver into his hand all the opium held by the people of my own country. Now I, the said chief superintendent, thus constrained by paramount motives affecting the safety of the lives and liberty of all the foreigners here present in Canton, and by other very weighty causes, do hereby, in the name and on the behalf of her Britannic Majesty's government, enjoin and require all her Majesty's subjects now present in Canton, forthwith to make a surrender to me for the service of her said Majesty's government, to be delivered over to the government of China, of all the opium under their respective control: and to hold the British ships and vessels engaged in the opium trade subject to my immediate direction: and to forward me without delay a sealed list of all the British-owned opium in their respective possession. And I, the said chief superintendent, do now, in the most full and unreserved manner, hold myself responsible for, and on the behalf of her Britannic Majesty's government, to all and each of her Majesty's subjects surrendering the said British-owned opium into my hands, to be delivered over to the Chinese government. And I, the said chief superintendent, do further especially caution all her Majesty's subjects here present in Canton, owners of or charged with the management of opium the property of British subjects, that failing the surrender of the said opium into my hands at or before six o'clock this day, I, the said superintendent, hereby declare her Majesty's government wholly free of all manner of responsibility in respect of the said British-owned opium. And it is specially to be understood that proof of British property and value of all British-owned opium surrendered to me agreeable to this notice, shall be determined upon principles, and in a manner hereafter to be defined by her Majesty's government.[1]

The guarantee offered in this notice was deemed sufficient by the merchants, though Captain Elliot had no authority to take such a responsibility, and exceeded his powers in giving it; being the authorized agent of the crown, however, his government was responsible for his acts, though the notice did not, nor could it, set any price upon the surrendered property.

At the time it was given it could not be honestly said that

[1] *Chinese Repository*, Vol. VII., p. 633.

the lives of foreigners were in jeopardy, and Lin had promised to reopen the trade as soon as the opium was delivered and the bonds given. What the other "very weighty causes" were must be guessed; but the requisition was promptly answered, and before night twenty thousand two hundred and eighty-three chests of opium had been surrendered, which Captain Elliot the next day tendered to the commissioner. Their market value at the time was not far from nine millions of dollars, and the cost price nearly eleven millions. Directions were sent to twenty-two vessels to anchor near the Bogue, to await orders for its delivery, the commissioner and the governor themselves going down forty miles to superintend the transfer. On April 2d the arrangements for delivering the opium were completed, and on May 21st it was all housed near the Bogue.

When the guard was placed about the factories, no native came near them for three days, but on the 29th a supply of sheep, pigs, poultry, and other provisions was "graciously bestowed" upon their inmates, most of whom refused them as gifts, which impressed Lin with the belief that they were not actually suffering for food. On May 5th the guards and boats were removed, and communication resumed with the shipping. Sixteen persons, English, Americans, and Parsees, named as principal agents in the opium trade, were ordered to leave the country and never return. On the 24th Captain Elliot left Canton, accompanied by the ten British subjects mentioned among the sixteen outlawed persons. In order still further to involve her Majesty's ministers in his acts, he forbade British ships entering the port, or any British subject living in Canton, on the ground that both life and property were insecure; there were, however, no serious apprehensions felt by other foreigners remaining there; and the propriety of the order was questioned by those who were serious sufferers from its action.

This success in getting the opium encouraged Lin to demand the bond, but although the captains of most of the ships signed it when the port was first opened, it was not required long after. The British merchants at Canton prepared a memorial to the foreign secretary of their government, recapitulating the aggressive acts of the Chinese government in stopping the legal trade, detaining all foreigners in Canton until the opium was surrendered, and requiring them to sign a bond not to bring it again, which involved their responsibility over those whom they could not control ; but nothing was said in it of their own unlawful acts, no reference to their promises of a few months before, no allusion to the causes of these acts of aggression. Its burden was, however, to urge the government to issue a notice of its intentions respecting the pledge given them by the superintendent in his demand for the opium.

Lin referred to Peking for orders concerning the disposal of the opium, and his Majesty commanded the whole to be destroyed by him and his colleagues in the presence of the civil and military officers, the inhabitants of the coast, and the foreigners, "that they may know and tremble thereat." Captain Elliot, on the other hand, before it had all been delivered, wrote to his government, April 22d, his belief that the Chinese intended to sell it at a high price, remunerating the owners and pocketing the difference, preparatory to legalizing the traffic, and making some arrangements to limit the annual importation to a certain number of chests; consequently he recommended an "immediate and strong declaration to exact complete indemnity for all manner of loss" from the Chinese. He calls Lin "false and perfidious," though it is difficult to see why he applies these epithets to one who seems to have sincerely endeavored to carry out instructions, while his own communications certainly tended to mislead him. The sense of the responsibility he had assumed, and the irritating confinement under which it was written, account, in a measure, for this despatch, so different in its tenor from his previous declarations.

The opium was destroyed in the most thorough manner, by mixing it in parcels of two hundred chests, in trenches, with lime and salt water, and then drawing off the contents into the adjacent creek at low tide. Overseers were stationed to prevent the workmen or villagers from purloining the opium, and one man was summarily executed for attempting to carry away a small quantity. No doubt remained in the minds of persons who visited the place and examined the operation, that the entire quantity of twenty thousand two hundred and ninety-one chests received from the English (eight more having been sent from Macao) was completely destroyed:—a solitary instance in the history of the world of a pagan monarch preferring to destroy what would injure his subjects, rather than to fill his own pockets with its sale. The whole transaction will ever remain one of the most remarkable incidents in human history for its contrasts, and the great changes it introduced into China.[1]

The course of events during the remainder of the year 1839 presents a strange mixture of traffic and hostility. The British merchants were obliged to send their goods to Canton in ships sailing under other flags, which led the commissioner to issue placards exhorting British captains to bring their ships into port. This procedure brought out a rejoinder from Captain Elliot, giving the reasons why he had forbidden them to do so, and complaining of his own unjust imprisonment as unbecoming treatment to the "officer of a friendly nation, recognized by the Emperor, who had always performed his duty peacefully and irreproachably." Captain Elliot's own correspondence shows, however, that this is an unfair statement of the political relations between them.

While this matter of trade was pending, a drunken affray occurred at Hongkong with some English sailors, in which an inoffensive native named Lin Wei-hí lost his life. The commissioner ordered an inquest to be held, and demanded the murderer, according to Chinese law. The superintendent empanelled a regular court of criminal and admiralty jurisdiction at Hongkong, to try the seamen who had been arrested. He also offered

---

[1] Sir Robert Peel declared that this property was obtained by her Majesty's agent without any authority; but when the six millions of dollars were received from the Chinese as indemnity, the British government made its subjects receive their money in London, charged them with all expenses instead of paying it in China, and priced the opium at scarcely half what the East India Company had received from it, by taking the market rates when the trade at Canton was nominal. The merchants lost, with accruing interest, about two millions sterling, and "Sir R. Peel transferred a million sterling from their pockets to the public treasury."—*Chinese Repository*, Vol. XIII., p. 54 (from London paper).

a reward of $200 for such evidence as would lead to the conviction of the offenders; and advanced in all $2,000 to the friends of the deceased as some compensation for their heavy loss, and to the villagers for injuries done to them in the riot. Having formed the court, he politely invited the provincial officers to attend the trial; and when it was over, informed them that he had been unable to ascertain the perpetrator of the deed. Five sailors were convicted and punished for riotous conduct by fine and imprisonment, and sent to England under arrest, but to everybody's surprise were all liberated on their arrival. The proceedings in this matter were perfectly fair, and the commissioner should have been satisfied; but his subsequent violent conduct really placed the dispute on an entirely new ground, though he regarded his action as simply exercising the same prerogative of control over foreigners in both cases. Finding his demand for the murderer disregarded, he took measures against the English then in Macao which were calculated to bring serious loss upon the Portuguese population. His course was prompted by anger at losing the trade, and only injured his own cause. In order to relieve the unoffending and helpless people in Macao, Captain Elliot and all British subjects who could do so left the settlement August 26th, and went on board ship for a time. During this interval Lin and Governor Tăng visited Macao under an escort of Portuguese troops, but retired the same day. This move placed the English beyond his reach, but did not advance his efforts to drive the opium ships from the coast, or induce the regular traders to enter the port. The sales of opium had begun again even before the destruction of the drug, and rapidly increased when it was known that that immense quantity had really been destroyed. Lin now began to see that his plan of proceedings might not ultimately prove so successful as he had anticipated, for he was bound to remain at Canton until he could report the complete suppression of the contraband and safe continuance of the legal trade.

Finding that the British fleet at Hongkong was too strong to drive away, he forbade the inhabitants supplying the ships with provisions. This led to a collision between the British and three junks near Kowlung, which resulted, however, in no serious damage. On September 11th, Captain Elliot, having ordered all British vessels engaged in the opium trade to leave the harbor and coast, they mostly proceeded to Namoh. The Chinese burned the next day a Spanish vessel, the Bilbaino, in Macao waters, under the impression that she was English.

In unison with all the strange features of this struggle, while hostilities were going on, negotiations for continuing trade were entered into in October, when the commissioner signed the agreement, and Captain Elliot furnished security for its being conducted fairly. But the unauthorized entrance of the English ship Thomas Coutts, whose captain signed the bond, led to a rupture and the renewed demand for the murderer of Lin Wei-hí. Captain Elliot ordered all British ships to reassemble at Tungku under the protection of the ships of war Volage and Hyacinth. He also proceeded to the Bogue to request a withdrawal of the threats against the British until the two governments could arrange the difficulties, when an engagement ensued between Admiral Kwan, with a fleet of sixteen junks, and the two ships of war; three junks were sunk, one blown up, and the rest scattered. The commissioner had been foiled in all his efforts to destroy the opium trade and continue the legal commerce. As a last effort against the British, he declared their trade at an end after December 6, 1839, and issued an edict like that of Napoleon at Berlin, November 19, 1806, forbidding their goods to be imported in any vessels. An enormous amount of property now lay at Canton and on board ship waiting to be exchanged in the course of regular trade, but only the opium traffic flourished.

The close of the year 1839 saw the two nations involved in serious difficulties, and as the events here briefly recounted were the cause of the war, it will be proper to compare the opinions of the two parties, in order to arrive at a better judgment upon the character of that contest. The degree of authority to be exercised over persons who visit their shores is acknowledged by Christian nations among themselves to be nearly the same as that over their own subjects; but none of these nations have conceded this authority to unchristian powers, as Turkey, Persia, or China, mainly because of the little security and justice to be expected. The Chinese have looked upon foreigners resorting to their ports as doing so by sufferance; they entered into no treaty to settle the conditions of authority on either side, for the latter considered themselves as sojourners and aliens, and the natives were unaware of their rights in the matter. Their right to prohibit the introduction of any particular articles was acknowledged, and the propriety of making regulations as to duties allowed. But traders from western nations often set light by the fiscal regulations of such countries as China, Siam, etc., if they can do so without personal detriment or loss of character; and where there is a want of power in the government, joined to a lack of moral sense in the people, all laws are imperfectly executed. No one acquainted with these countries is surprised at frequent and flagrant violations of law, order, justice or courtesy, both among rulers and ruled; yet the obligation of foreigners to obey just laws made known to them surely is not to be measured solely by the degree of obedience paid by a portion of the people themselves.

The Chinese government discussed the measure of legalizing a trade it could not suppress, but before constructing a law to that effect, it determined to make a final and more vigorous effort to stamp it out. Might makes right, or at least enforces it; had the Chinese possessed the power to destroy every ship found violating their laws, although the loss of life would have been dreadful, no voice would have been raised against the proceeding. "Her Majesty's government," said Lord Palmerston, "cannot interfere for the purpose of enabling British subjects to violate the laws of the country to which they trade." But in that case this power would not have been dared; the known weakness of the government emboldened both sellers and buyers, until Captain Elliot told the Foreign Secretary that "it was a confusion of terms to call the opium trade a smuggling trade."

Lin probably wished to get Mr. Dent as a hostage for the delivery of the opium in the hands of his countrymen, not to punish him for disobedience to previous orders; expecting no opposition to this demand, he seems to have been unwilling to seize him immediately, preferring to try persuasion and command longer, and detain him and other foreigners until he was obeyed; Captain Elliot he viewed as a mere head merchant. When, therefore, the attempt was made, as he supposed, to take Mr. Dent out of his hands, he was apprehensive of a struggle, and instantly took the strongest precautionary measures to prevent the prey escaping. Considerate allowance should be granted for the serious mistake he made of imprisoning the innocent with the guilty; but when Captain Elliot took Mr. Dent thus under his protection, the commissioner felt that his purpose would be defeated, and no opium obtained, if he began to draw a distinction. Besides, conscious that he possessed unlimited power over a few defenceless foreigners, nearly all of whom were in his eyes guilty, he cared very little where his acts fell. There is no good evidence to show that *he* seriously meditated anything which would hazard their lives. When he had received this vast amount of property, success evidently made him careless as to his conduct, and judging the probity and good faith of foreigners by his own standard, he deemed it safest to detain them until the opium was actually in his possession. Concluding that Captain Elliot did attempt to abscond with Mr. Dent, it is less surprising, therefore, that he should have looked upon his offers to "carry out the will of the great Emperor," when set at liberty, as a lure rather than a sincere proposition. In imprisoning him he had no more idea he was imprisoning, insulting, threatening, and coercing the representative of a power like Great Britain, or violating rules western powers call *jus gentium*, than if he had been the envoy from Siam or Lewchew. Whether he should not have known this is another question, and had he candidly set himself, on his arrival at Canton, to ascertain the power, position, and commerce of western countries, he would have found Captain Elliot sincerely desirous of meeting him in his endeavors to fulfil his high commission. Let us deal fairly by the Chinese rulers in their desire to restrain a traffic of which they knew and felt vastly more of its evil than we have ever done, and give Lin his due, though his endeavors failed so signally.

The opium was now obtained; no lives had been lost, nor any

one endangered; but the British government felt bound to pay its own subjects for their chests. The only source Captain Elliot suggested was to make the Chinese refund. The Emperor ordered it to be destroyed, and the commissioner, after executing that order, next endeavored to separate the legal from the contraband trade by demanding bonds; they had been taken in vain from the hong merchants, but there was more hope if taken directly from foreigners. The bonds were not made a pretext for war by the English ministry; that, on the part of England, according to Lord John Russell, was "set afoot to obtain reparation for insults and injuries offered her Majesty's superintendent and subjects; to obtain indemnification for the losses the merchants had sustained under threats of violence; and, lastly, to get security that persons and property trading with China should in future be protected from insult and injury, and trade maintained upon a proper footing." Looking at the war, therefore, as growing out of this trade, and waged to recover the losses sustained by the surrendry to the British superintendent, it was an *unjust* one. It was, moreover, an *immoral* contest, when the standing of the two nations was examined, and the fact could not be concealed that Great Britain, the first Christian power, really waged this war against the pagan monarch who had vainly endeavored to put down a vice hurtful to his people. The war was looked upon in this light by the Chinese; it will always be so looked upon by the candid historian, and known as the Opium War.

On the other hand, the war was felt by every well-wisher to China to involve far higher principles than the mere recovery of the opium; and had it been really held to be so by the English ministry, they would have done well to have alluded to them. Lin's reiterated demands for the murderer of Lin Wei-hí, though told that he could not be found, was only one form of the supremacy the Chinese arrogantly assumed over other nations. In all their intercourse with their fellow-men they maintained a patronizing, unfair, and contemptuous position, which left no alternative but withdrawal from their shores or a humiliating submission that no one feeling the least independence could endure. Not unjustly proud of their country in comparison with those near it, her Emperor, her rulers, and her people all believed her to be impregnably strong, portentously awful, and immensely rich in learning, power, wealth, and territory. None of them imagined that aught could be learned or gained from other nations; for the "outside barbarians" were dependent for their health and food upon the rhubarb, tea, and silks of the Inner Land. They had seen, indeed, bad specimens of western power and people, but there were equal opportunities for them to have learned the truth on these points. The reception of the religion of the Bible, the varied useful branches of science, and the many mechanical arts known in western lands, with the free passage of their own people abroad, were all forbidden to the millions of China by their supercilious rulers; they thereby preferred to remain the slaves of debasing superstitions, ignorant of common science, and deprived of everything which Christian benevolence, philanthropy, and knowledge could and wished to impart to them. This assumption of supremacy, and a real impression of its propriety, was a higher wall around them than the long pile of stones north of Peking. Force seemed to be the only effectual destroyer of such a barrier, and in this view the war may be said to have been necessary to compel the Chinese government to receive western powers as its equals, or at least make it treat their subjects as well as it did its own people. There was little hope of an adjustment of difficulties until the Chinese were compelled to abandon this erroneous assumption; the conviction that it was unjust, unfounded, and foolish in itself could safely be left to the gradual influences of true religion, profitable commerce, and sound knowledge.

The report of the debate in the British Parliament on this momentous question hardly contains a single reference to this feature of the Chinese government. It turned almost wholly upon the opium trade, and whether the hostilities had not proceeded from the want of foresight and precaution on the part of her Majesty's ministers. The speeches all showed ignorance of both principles and facts: Sir James Graham asserted that the governors of Canton had sanctioned the trade; Sir George Staunton that it would not be safe for British power in India if these insults were not checked, and that the Chinese had far exceeded in their recent efforts the previous acknowledged laws of the land! Dr. Lushington maintained that the connivance of the local rulers acquitted the smugglers; Sir John Hobhouse truly stated that the reason why the government had done nothing to stop the opium trade was that it was profitable; and Lord Melbourne, with still more fairness, said: "We possess immense territories peculiarly fitted for raising opium, and though I would wish that the government were not so directly concerned in the traffic, I am not prepared to pledge myself to relinquish it." The Duke of Wellington thought the Chinese government was insincere in its efforts, and therefore deserved little sympathy; while Lord Ellenborough spoke of the million and a half sterling revenue "derived from foreigners," which, if the opium monopoly was given up and its cultivation abandoned, they must seek elsewhere. No one advocated war on the ground that the opium had been seized, but the majority were in favor of letting it go on because it was begun. This debate was, in fact, a remarkable instance of the way in which a moral question is blinked even by conscientious persons whenever politics or interest came athwart its course. No declaration of war was ever published by Queen Victoria, further than an order in council to the admiralty, in which it was recited that "satisfaction and reparation for the late injurious proceedings of certain officers of the Emperor of China against certain of our officers and subjects shall be demanded from the Chinese government;" the object of this order was, chiefly, to direct concerning the disposal of such ships, vessels, and cargoes belonging to the Chinese as might be seized. Perhaps the formality of a declaration of war against a nation which knew nothing of the law of nations was not necessary, but if a minister plenipotentiary from Peking had been present at the debate in Parliament in April, 1840, he would have declared the motives and proceedings of his government strangely misrepresented. It was time that better ideas of one another should find place in their councils, and that means should be afforded the rulers of each nation to learn the truth.

The Chinese apparently foresaw the coming struggle, and

began to collect troops and repair their forts; Lin, now governor-general of Kwangtung, purchased the Chesapeake, a large ship, and appointed an intendant of circuit near Macao, to guard the coasts. The English carried on their trade under neutral flags, and Lin made no further efforts to annoy them. He, however, wrote two official letters to Queen Victoria, desiring her assistance in putting down the opium trade, in which the peculiar ideas of his countrymen respecting their own importance and their position among the nations of the earth were singularly exhibited.[1] Notwithstanding the causes of complaint he had against the English, he behaved kindly to the surviving crew of the Sunda, an English vessel wrecked on Hainan, and sent them, on their arrival at Canton, to their countrymen.

---

[1] *Chinese Repository*, Vol. VIII., pp. 9–12, 497–503; Vol. IX., pp. 241–257.

CHAPTER XXIII.

PROGRESS AND RESULTS OF THE FIRST WAR BETWEEN ENGLAND AND CHINA.

On June 22, 1840, before the advance part of the British force reached China, Sir Gordon Bremer published a notice of the blockade of the port of Canton. The Americans living there had requested Lin to let all their ships arriving before it was laid on come directly up the river. He granted the application, but declared it "to be an egregious mistake, analogous to an audacious falsehood, that the English contemplated putting on a blockade." Captain Elliot also issued a manifesto to the people, which was widely dispersed, setting forth the grievances which had been suffered by the English at the hands of Lin, and assuring them that no harm would come while they pursued their peaceful occupations—for the quarrel was entirely between the two governments, and the Queen had deputed high officers to make known the truth to the Emperor.

Sir Gordon Bremer's force of five ships of war, three steamers, and twenty-one transports reached Tinghai harbor July 4th. In reply to a summons to surrender, the Chinese officers declared their determination to resist as far as their means allowed; but complained of the hardship of being made answerable for wrongs done at Canton, upon which place the blow should properly fall. The attack was made on Sunday, July 5th, when the Wellesley (74) opened her guns on the town, which were answered by the junks and batteries. A few minutes sufficed to silence the latter, and three thousand men landed and menaced Tinghai, whose walls were lined with soldiers. The town was evacuated during the night, most of the respectable inhabitants going to Ningpo; many of the Chinese high officials were killed, which, with the experience of the terrible foreign force brought against them, disheartened their troops beyond measure.

Two days after this attack the joint plenipotentiaries, Admiral G. Elliot and Captain Elliot, arrived in the Melville (74) at Chusan. To the authorities at Amoy and Ningpo they sent copies of Lord Palmerston's letter to the Emperor, with a request to forward them to Peking; the officials declined, however, undertaking any such responsibility.

The prefect of Ningpo took measures to prevent the people of Chusan from "aiding and comforting" their conquerors by sending police-runners to mark those who supplied them; a purveyor from Canton was seized and brought back. An idea that the Chinese people wished to throw off the Manchu yoke, and a desire to conciliate the islanders, led the British to take less decided measures for supplying themselves with provisions than they otherwise would. A small party was sent to recapture the purveyor, but its unsuccessful trip over the island showed the unwillingness of the people to have anything to do with their invaders, while their dread was increased by the arrest of several village elders. Mr. Gutzlaff was stationed at Chusan, doing his best to reassure the people; and as he went around exhorting them to act peaceably, some of them asked him, "If you are so desirous of peace, why did you come here at all?"

After arranging the government of the island, the stations of the troops, and blockading of Amoy, Ningpo, and the mouths of the Min and Yangtsz' Rivers, the two plenipotentiaries left Tinghai and anchored off the Pei ho August 11th. Captain Elliot went ashore, and finding that Kíshen, the governor-general of Chihlí, was at Taku, delivered the letter to his messenger, who returned with a request for ten days' delay in which to lay it before the Emperor. During this interval the ships visited the coast of Liautung to procure provisions, which they obtained with some difficulty. No message coming off, a strong boat-force was sent ashore on the 28th, with a menacing letter to Kíshen, when it was ascertained that the reply had in reality been awaiting the return of the ships during several days. Arrangements were now made for a personal interview at Taku between Kíshen and Captain Elliot, on Sunday, August 30th, in a large tent. Kíshen argued his side of the question with great tact and ability, sincerely urging the argument that his master had the most unquestionable right to treat the English as he had done, for they were and had enrolled themselves his tributary subjects. He could not treat definitely on all the points in dispute, and obtained a further delay of six days in order to refer again to Peking. The conclusion was the reasonable arrangement that Kíshen should meet the English plenipotentiaries at Canton, where the truth could be better ascertained; and on September 15th the squadron returned to Chusan.

While these things were taking place at Taku, there had occurred a few skirmishes elsewhere. A shipwrecked crew had fallen into Chinese hands and been carried to Ningpo, and some foraging parties were roughly handled. Lin tried to inspirit his troops by offering large rewards for British ships and subjects, and a force of about one thousand two hundred men was stationed in and around the Barrier at Macao. Captain Smith, however, moved two sloops and a steamer near their position, and soon drove the soldiers away, destroying their guns and barracks.

Lin was busy enlisting volunteers and preparing the defences of Canton, but in the summer he was ordered to return "with the speed of flames" to Peking. His Majesty was unnecessarily severe upon his servant: "You have not only proved yourself unable to cut off their trade," he says, "but you have also proved yourself unable to seize perverse natives. You have but dissembled with empty words, and so far from having been any help in the affair, you have caused the waves of confusion to arise, and a thousand interminable disorders are sprouting; in fact, you have been as if your arms were tied, without knowing what to do: it appears, then, you are no better than a wooden image. When I meditate on all these things, I am filled with anger and melancholy." Trade was carried on notwithstanding the blockade, by sending tea and goods through Macao; and many ships loaded for England and the United States.

Admiral Elliot entered into a truce with Ílípu, governor-general of Chehkiang, by which each party agreed to observe certain boundaries. Sickness and death had made sad inroads into the health and numbers of the troops at Tinghai, owing to their bad location, malaria, and improper food; more than four hundred out of the four thousand landed in July having died, and three times that number being in the hospitals. The people dared not reopen their shops until after the truce; the visits paid to various parts of the island better informed the inhabitants of the personal character of their temporary rulers, and a profitable trade in provisions encouraged them to farther acquaintance.

The two plenipotentiaries returned November 20th, and immediately sent a steamer bearing a despatch from Ílípu to Kishen; the vessel was fired upon by an officer unacquainted with the meaning of a white flag—the intent and privileges of which were after this understood; Kíshen made an ample apology for this mishap. Negotiations were resumed during the month of December, but the determination of the Chinese to resist rather than grant full indemnity for the opium was more and more apparent. Kíshen probably found more zeal among the people for a fight than he had supposed, but his own desires were to settle the matter "more soon, more better." What demands were made as a last alternative are not known, but one of them, the cession of the island of Hongkong, he refused to grant, and broko off the discussion. Commodore Bremer thereupon attacked and took the forts at Chuenpí and Taikok-tau on January 7th, when the further progress of his forces was stayed by Kíshen, who was present and saw enough to convince him of the folly of resistance.

On January 20th the suspended negotiations had proceeded so far that Captain Elliot announced the conclusion of preliminary arrangements upon four points, viz., the cession of the island and harbor of Hongkong to the British crown, an indemnity of six millions of dollars in annual instalments, direct official intercourse upon an equal footing, and the immediate resumption of English trade at Canton. By these arrangements Chusan and Chuenpí were to be immediately restored to the Chinese, the prisoners at Ningpo released, and the English allowed to occupy Hongkong. One evidence of Kíshen's "scrupulous good faith," mentioned in Captain Elliot's notice, is the edict he put up on Hongkong, telling the inhabitants they were now under English authority. Two interviews took place after this, at the last of which it was plain that two of the four stipulations, viz., the first instalment of a million of dollars, and opening of trade by February 1st, would not be fulfilled. The intimations of the designs of the court were so evident that the treaty was probably never even presented to the Emperor for ratification.

Kíshen carried his negotiations thus far, with the hope perhaps that an adjustment of the difficulties on such terms would be accepted by his imperial master. On the other hand, Lin and his colleagues memorialized him as soon as Kíshen came to Canton against peaceful measures, and their recommendations as to the necessity of resistance were strongly backed by the mortifying loss of Chusan. The approach of a large force to the Pei ho alarmed his Majesty, and conciliatory measures were taken, and a reference to Canton proposed before settling the dispute; when the men-of-war left, he was inclined for peace, and issued orders not to attack the ships while the discussions were going on. But the memorials had already changed his mind, and war was determined on at the date of signing the treaty. It is probable if, instead of seizing Chusan, which had given no cause of provocation, the English had gone up the Yangtsz' kiang and Pei ho, and stationed themselves there until their demands were granted, peace would have been soon made. But, in that case, would the vain notion of their supremacy have left the Chinese?

Looking back forty years, one can recognize the benefit to both parties which resulted from the failure of this treaty. The great desire of Christian people, who believed that China was finally to receive the gospel, was that it might be opened to their benevolent efforts, but this treaty left the country as closed as ever to all good influences, commercial, political, social, and religious, while the evils of smuggling, law-breaking, and opium-smoking remained unmolested. The crisis which had brought out this expedition was not likely soon to recur, and if this failed to break down its seclusiveness, no other nation would attempt the task. Every well-wisher of China cherished the hope that, since this unfortunate conflict must needs be, its outcome would leave the entire land fully accessible to the regenerating, as well as shielded from the evil influences of Christian nations.

Captain Elliot appreciated the dilemma into which the Emperor had been brought by the acts of Lin, and knew that ignorance was much more the misfortune than the fault of both; he acted humanely, therefore, in pursuing a mild course at first, until the points at issue had been fairly brought before the people as well as the cabinet. However justly some parts of his conduct may have merited criticism, this praiseworthy feature of his policy by no means earned the torrent of abuse he received for consistently pursuing such a course. His countrymen would have had him burn, kill, and destroy, as soon as the expedition reached the coast, before even stating his demands at court; and during his negotiations with Kíshen, and when Chusan was restored, a smile of contempt at his supposed gullibility was everywhere seen. The treaty of the Bogue, though formed in good faith by both commissioners, was rejected by both sovereigns, though for opposite reasons; by Victoria, because it did not grant enough, by Taukwang, because it granted too much.

The Emperor issued orders to resume the war, collect troops from the provinces upon Canton and Tinghai, in order to "destroy and wipe clean away, to exterminate and root out the rebellious barbarians," and urged the people to regard them with the same bitterness they did their personal enemies. His mandate is couched in strong terms, saying that his enemies have been rebellious against heaven, opposing reason, one in spirit with the brute beasts, "beings that the overshadowing vault and all-containing earth can hardly suffer to live," obnoxious to angels and men, and that he must discharge his heaven-conferred trust by sweeping them from the face of the earth. This decree exhibited the true principles of action of this proud government, which deliberately rejected the offer of peace, and determined to uphold its fancied supremacy to the utmost. China must now win or break.

Hostile intentions had become so evident that Captain Elliot announced that Commodore Bremer would return to the Bogue with the force; the boats of the Nemesis were fired upon while sounding, and the battery near Anunghoy was attacked the same day that Chusan was evacuated. Rewards of $50,000 were offered for Elliot, Bremer, Morrison, and other ringleaders, and all the defences put in the best condition. On February 26th the Bogue forts were all taken, Admiral Kwan falling at his post. The British had nine ships, assisted by less than five hundred troops, and two steamers. The Chinese force was probably over three thousand, but it made no resistance after the batteries were taken; the total loss was supposed to be not far from a thousand. The forts were built so solidly that few were killed by the broadsides of the ships, and their magazines so well protected that no explosions took place; the powder found in them was used to demolish the walls. There were in all eight large forts on the sides of the river and Wangtong Island, forming altogether a line of batteries which would have been impregnable in the hands of European troops, and was not without reason deemed to be so by the Chinese themselves.

The next day the small ships moved up to the First Bar, where a long fortification on the river bank, and an intrenched camp of two thousand troops, defended by upward of a hundred cannon, with a strong raft thrown across the river, showed a resolution to make a stand. The ships and steamers opened a hot fire upon the batteries and camp, which returned it as well as they could, but the loss of life was greatest when the English landed. Many instances of personal bravery showed that the Chinese were not all destitute of courage, but without discipline and better weapons it was of no avail. Nearly one-fourth were killed, their camp burned, the Chesapeake and all her stores blown up, and most of the crew killed. The raft was easily removed by the steamers, to the mortification of the Chinese, who had trusted that this might prove a permanent barrier to the approach of ships to the city. From this point the way was open to within five miles of Canton, and when the forts at that place were taken, the prefect met Captain Elliot on March 3d with a flag of truce proposing a suspension of hostilities for three days.

Kishen had already been ordered to return to Peking to await his trial; his memorial[1] on hearing of his degradation does him credit. Íliang was left in command of the province until four general officers, leading large bodies of troops, should arrive. The highest of these was Yihshan, a nephew of the Emperor, assisted by Yang Fang, Lungwăn, and Tsíshin. On the part of the English, Major-General Sir Hugh Gough arrived from India to take command of the land forces, and Sir Gordon Bremer sailed for Calcutta to procure recruits. Bodies of troops were gathering in and around Canton to the amount of five or six thousand, most of whom had come from the North-West Provinces, and were not less strange and formidable to the citizens than were their foreign enemies.

After the truce had expired the English moved toward Canton by both the channels leading to the city, the iron steamer Nemesis proceeding up the Inner Passage, subduing all obstacles in her way until every fort, raft, battery, camp, and stockade between the ocean and Canton had been taken or destroyed, and the city lay at their mercy. The factories had been kept safely, and were occupied by British troops just two years after Lin had imprisoned the foreigners there. A second truce was agreed upon March 20th, by which trade was allowed to proceed on the old mode; merchant ships accordingly advanced up the river, and for about six weeks trade went on uninterruptedly—one party getting their tea and the other their duties. The new governor, Kí Kung, together with the "rebel-quelling general" Yihshan, then arrived, and the people, thinking that a slight cause would disturb the truce, took advantage of it to remove their effects, well aware how much they would suffer from their own army in case of trouble.

Toward the middle of May the hostile intentions of the Chinese were manifest, though cloaked under professions of amity; and on the 21st Captain Elliot notified all foreigners to go

---

[1] *Chinese Repository,* Vol. X., p. 235.

aboard ship. The secret preparations for attack were very extensive. Large fire-boats and rafts were prepared, masked batteries erected along the river, troops quartered in the temples, and large cannon placed in the streets. The day before the notice of Captain Elliot was issued, the prefect had the impudence to publish a proclamation assuring all classes of the peaceful intentions of the commissioners. Finding their prey gone, a night attack was made by land and water on the ships, but none were seriously injured. As daylight advanced the Nemesis went in pursuit of the fire-boats and junks, and burned upward of sixty, while three men-of-war silenced the batteries along shore. Meantime the Chinese troops searched the factory buildings for arms and pillaged three of the hongs, to the consternation of the prefect, who told the commissioner that he would be forced to pay for losses thus sustained. On the 24th the land and naval forces under Sir Hugh Gough and Sir Fleming Senhouse arrived from Hongkong and prepared to invest the city. Most of the troops debarked above it, at Neishing, under the personal directions of Sir Fleming, who had provided many boats in which the force of two thousand six hundred men, besides followers, guns, and stores, were towed about twelve miles. A detachment landed and took possession of the factories. Sir Hugh Gough remained near the place of debarkation till the next morning, when the whole body moved onward to attack the forts and camps behind the city. As the English advanced the Chinese found that their shot did not reach them, so that after an hour's firing they began to collect outside of the forts, preparatory to retiring. The advance pushed on, and sent them scampering down the hills toward the city; the intrenched camp was carried with considerable loss to its defenders, who everywhere ran as soon as the fight came to close quarters; but in the forts there were many furious struggles.

On the 26th a driving rain stopped all operations; and a parley was also requested from the now deserted city walls by two officers, who agreed to send a deputation to make arrangements for surrender. Night came on before any heralds appeared, so that it was not till morning that the troops were in

WALL OF CANTON CITY. (FROM FISHER.)

position, the guns loaded and primed, port-fires lighted, and everything in readiness to open fire, when a messenger arrived from Captain Elliot, desiring further operations to be delayed until he had concluded his negotiations. The terms were: that the forces should remain in position until a ransom of $6,000,000 was paid; that the three imperial commissioners and all their troops should march sixty miles from the city; that compensation for the loss of property in the factories and burning the Spanish brig Bilbaino should be at once handed over or secured; and that the Chinese troops, nearly fifty thousand in number, should evacuate the city. Captain Elliot ought indeed to have demanded a personal apology from Yihshan and his colleagues for their infamous treachery before letting them go. His acceptance of this ransom and sparing the city from capture were sharply criticised at the time, and the contemptuous bearing of the citizens during the sixteen ensuing years of their possession proved that it was an ill-timed mercy. How much influence the orders from home to be careful of the tea-trade had in this course cannot be learned.

While the English forces were occupying the heights the lawless soldiers from Kweichau and Kwangsí began to plunder the citizens, who retaliated till blood was shed and more than a thousand persons were killed in the streets; a patriot mob of villagers, numbering about fifteen thousand, attacked the few British troops left on the hills north of the city, but a prompt advance on the part of Sir Hugh drove this rabble a rout of some three miles. Upon their reappearance next day, the prefect was told that if they were not instantly dispersed the city would be bombarded; the threats and persuasions of the commissioners, aided by a British officer, finally induced the mob to retire. The superiority of discipline over mere numbers was probably never more remarkably exhibited; though the Chinese outnumbered the English more than forty to one, not a single foreigner was killed.

On the 31st the prefect furnished five hundred coolies to assist in transporting the guns and stores to the river side, and ten days after Captain Elliot's first notice everything was restored to the Chinese. The casualties among the British forces were fourteen killed and one hundred and twelve wounded, but about three hundred died from sickness. The losses of the Chinese from first to last could hardly have been much under five thousand men, besides thousands of cannon, ginjals, and matchlocks. In posting their forces, placing their masked batteries, and equipping their troops and forts, the Chinese showed considerable strategy and skill, but lack of discipline and confidence rendered every defence unavailing. Yihshan and his associates memorialized the Emperor, detailing their reasons for ransoming the city and requesting an inquiry into their conduct.[1]

The sickness of the troops compelled the British force to remain at Hongkong to recruit and wait for reinforcements. Commodore Bremer returned as joint plenipotentiary, bringing additional forces from Calcutta, and the expedition was on the point of sailing northward when both he and Captain Elliot were wrecked in a tyfoon, and this detained the ships a few days longer. Before they sailed Sir Henry Pottinger and Admiral Sir William Parker arrived direct from England to supersede them both. Sir Henry announced his appointment and duties, and also sent a communication to the governor of Canton, assuring him that the existing truce would be observed as long as the Chinese did not arm their forts, impede the regular trade, which had been lately reopened to British ships by imperial command, or trouble the merchants residing in the factories. The trade went on at Canton, after this, without any serious interruption during the war, the usual duties and charges being paid as if no hostilities existed.

The expedition moved northward, August 21st, under the joint command of Sir Hugh Gough and Admiral Parker, consisting of two seventy-fours and seven other ships of war, four steamers, twenty-three transports, and a surveying vessel, carrying in all about three thousand five hundred troops. Six ships and four or five hundred Indian troops remained off Canton and at Hongkong, to compel the observance of the truce. The force reached Amoy, and after a hasty reconnoissance attacked

[1] *Chinese Repository*, Vol. X. (p. 402), in which, and in Vols. VIII., IX., and XI., most of the official papers issued from the Chinese and English authorities during the war are contained.

all its defences, which were carried without much loss of life on either side. The city was taken on the 27th, and all the arms and public stores, wall-pieces, ginjals, matchlocks, shields, uniforms, bows, arrows, spears, and quantities of powder were destroyed; five hundred cannon were found in the forts. When H. M. S. Blonde came into this harbor, fourteen months previous, to deliver the letter for Peking, the fortifications consisted only of two or three forts near the city, but every island and protecting headland overlooking the harbor had since been occupied and armed, while a line of stone wall more than a mile long, with embrasures roofed by large slabs covered with earth to protect the guns, had been built, and batteries and bastions erected at well-chosen points. The broadsides of the ships had little effect here, and it was not until the troops landed and drove out the garrisons, who "stood right manfully to their guns," that the fire slackened, and the Chinese retreated. The city was completely pillaged by native robbers, who ran riot during several weeks until the craven authorities came back and resumed their functions. The island of Kulang su was garrisoned by a detachment of five hundred and fifty troops, and three ships left to protect them. The British found one two-decker among the war junks, built on a foreign model, launched and ready for sea, carrying twenty guns; all were burned.

The English fleet again entered the harbor of Tinghai, September 29th, and found the beach much altered since February. Stone walls and fortifications extended two miles in front of the suburbs, besides sand-bags and redoubts thrown up on well-selected positions. They were taken after a defence marked with unusual courage; the general commanding the battery and all his suite were killed at their posts, and many hand-to-hand conflicts took place. But bravery and numbers were alike unavailing, and in two hours their defences were cleared, the walls of the town escaladed, the whole force scattered, and the island subdued, with the estimated loss to the Chinese of a thousand men. Great quantities of ordnance, among which were forty brass guns made in imitation of foreign howitzers, with military stores and provisions in abundance, were seized. A detachment was sent throughout the island to drive off the enemy's troops, and announce to the inhabitants that they were now under English authority. They evinced none of the alarm they had done the year before; provisions came in, shops were opened, and confidence in these proclamations generally exhibited. A military government was appointed, and a garrison of four hundred men left to protect the island.

The military operations in Chehkiang were conducted by Yukien and Yu Pu-yun; both these men had urged war, and had done all they could to fortify Tinghai and Chinhai, whose batteries and magazines showed the vigor of their operations. The English fleet proceeded to Chinhai October 9th, and a force of about two thousand two hundred men, with twelve field pieces and mortars, landed next morning to attack the citadel and intrenched camp. There were nearly five thousand men in this position, who formed in good order as the English advanced, opening a well-directed fire upon the front column, but quite neglecting two detachments on their flanks; as the three opened upon them nearly simultaneously, their force was completely bewildered, and all soon broke and fled. Knowing nothing of the mode of asking for quarter, while some fled into the country, the greater part retreated toward the water, pursued by the three columns, hundreds being shot and hundreds drowned. Sir Hugh Gough sent out a flag with Chinese written upon it, to inform them that their lives would be spared if they yielded, but not more than five hundred either could or would throw down their arms. The water was soon covered with bodies, and fully fifteen hundred soldiers lost their lives. The town and its defences were bombarded, and the troops driven out. Yukien endeavored to drown himself on seeing the day was lost, but being prevented he retreated to Yüyau, where he committed suicide, as was said, by swallowing gold leaf. He was a Manchu, and could not brook his master's displeasure; but his atrocious cruelty to two Englishmen who fell into his hands, one of whom was flayed and then burnt to death, had aroused general detestation against him. About one hundred and fifty pieces of brass ordnance, with great quantities of gunpowder and other military stores, were destroyed. The guns and carriages in the fort and batteries were so well made and placed that in some cases the victors on entering turned them against the flying Chinese. The frame of a wheel vessel, intended to be moved by human power, was found near Chinhai, showing, as did the brass guns, traversing carriages, and frigate at Amoy, that the Chinese were already imitating the machinery of war from their foes.

Ningpo was taken without resistance on the 13th. Many of the people left the city, and those who remained shut themselves in their houses, writing *shun min*, 'submissive people,' on the doors. Captain Anstruther took possession of his old prison—where he found the identical cage he had been carried in—and released all the inmates to make way for his detachment of artillery. About $100,000 in sycee were found in this building, upward of $70,000 in the treasury, many tons of copper cash in the mint, and rice, silk, and porcelain in the public stores, forming altogether the most valuable prizes yet secured. Sir Henry Pottinger intended at first to burn the city, but, happily for his reputation, he decided to occupy it as winter quarters. Leaving a garrison at Chinhai, he returned to Hongkong in February, 1842, Sir Hugh and the admiral remaining at the north.

The fall of Amoy, Tinghai, Chinhai, and Ningpo, instead of disheartening the Emperor, served rather to inspirit him. His commissioners, generals, and high officers generally did the best their knowledge and means enabled them to do, and when defeated, endeavored to palliate the discomfiture they could not entirely conceal by misrepresenting the force brought against them, and laying the blame upon the common people, the elements, the native traitors who aided the British, or the inefficiency of the naval armaments. The troops sent home with tokens of victory from Canton stimulated the war spirit in the western provinces. After they had gone Yihshan concocted measures of defence, one of which was to enlist two or three thousand volunteers, or "village braves," near the city, and place them under their own officers. The people having been taught to despise foreigners were easily incensed against them, and several cases of insult and wantonness were repeated and magnified in order to stir up a spirit of revenge. These patriots supposed, moreover, that if the great Emperor had called on *them*, instead of entrusting the conduct of the quarrel to truckling traitorous poltroons like Kíshen and the prefect, they could have avenged him of his enemies.

Consequently the truce was soon broken in an underhand manner by sinking hundreds of tons of stones in the river. H. M. S. Royalist levelled the fortifications at the Bogue, and Captain Nias destroyed a number of boats at Whampoa. After the destruction of these forts and his retirement from the river, Yihshan directed his attention to erecting forts near the city, casting guns, and drilling the volunteers, who numbered nearly thirty thousand at the new year. He also gave a public dinner to the rich men of the city, in order to learn their willingness to contribute to the expenses of these measures. However, since no serious obstacles were placed in the way of shipping teas by the provincial officers, from the duties on which they chiefly derived the funds for these undertakings, the British officers deemed it advisable to let them alone.

The case was different at other points. The imperial government had supposed that Amoy would be attacked, because the visit of the Blonde showed that the barbarians, "sneaking in and out like rats," knew of its existence; but the people of that province, except near Amoy, took no particular interest in the dispute, and probably knew far less of it than was known in most parts of England and the United States; no newspapers, with "own correspondents" to write the "latest accounts from the seat of war," narrated the progress of this struggle, which to them was like the silent reflection of distant lightning in their own quiet firmament. The sack of Amoy was a heavy blow to its citizens, but the plunderers were mostly their countrymen; and when Captain Smith of the Druid had been there a short time in command, and his character became known, they returned to their houses and shops, supplied the garrison with provisions, and even brought back a deserter, and assisted in chasing some pirates. Rumors of attack were always brought to him, and his declarations allayed their fears, so that after the sub-prefect resumed his authority no disturbance occurred. The explanations of the missionaries on Kulang su, in diffusing a better understanding of the object in occupying that island, also contributed to this result.

The loss of Chinhai and Ningpo threw the eastern parts of Chehkiang open to the invaders, and alarmed the court far more than the destruction of Canton would have done. The Emperor appointed his nephew, Yihking, to be "majesty-bearing generalissimo," and with him Tih-í-shun and Wănwei, all Manchus, to command the grand army and arouse the dwellers on the sea-coast to arm and defend themselves. "Ministers and people! Inhabitants of our dominions! Ye are all the children of our dynasty! For two centuries ye have trod our earth and eaten our food. Whoever among you has heavenly goodness must needs detest these rebellious and disorderly barbarians even as ye do your personal foes. On no account allow yourselves to be deceived by their wiles, and act or live abroad with them." Such was the closing exhortation of an imperial proclamation issued to encourage them. In order to raise funds for its operations, the government resorted to the sale of office and titles of nobility, and levied benevolences from rich individuals and contributions from the people; which, when large in amount, were noticed and rewarded. Kíshen, who had been tried at Peking and sentenced to lose his life, was for some reason reprieved to be associated with Yihking as an adviser, but never proceeded beyond Chihlí. Lin was also recalled from Ílí, if indeed he ever went beyond the Great Wall, and Ílípu, whose treatment and release of the prisoners at Ningpo had gained him the good-will of the English, was also sentenced to banishment, but neither did he go beyond the Desert.

Defences were thrown up at Tientsin and Taku to guard the passage to the capital, but the bar at the mouth of the Pei ho was its sufficient protection. Fearing that the English would advance upon the city of Hangchau, the troops of the province and all its available means were put into requisition. Sir Hugh Gough could only approach it by a land march from Ningpo, and deemed it advisable to wait for reinforcements, his available force being reduced to six hundred men on entering that city. The rewards given to the families of those who had fallen in battle, and the posthumous honors conferred by the Emperor, stimulated others to deeds of valor and a determination to accomplish their master's vengeance. Yukien, "who gave his life for his country, casting himself into the water," received high titular honors in the hall of worthies, and his brother was permitted to bring his corpse within the city of Peking. The names of humbler servants were not forgotten in the imperial rescripts, and a place was granted them among those whom the "king delighteth to honor." Thus did the Chinese endeavor to reassert their supremacy, though their counsels and efforts to chastise the rebellious barbarians were not unlike the deliberations of the rats upon "how to bell the cat."

The occupation of Ningpo was an eyesore to the Chinese generals, but the citizens had learned their best interests and generally kept quiet. They showed their genius in various contrivances to carry off plunder, such as putting valuable articles in coffins and ash-baskets, wrapping them around corpses, packing them under vegetables or rubbish. One party overtook two persons near Ningpo running off with a basket between them; on overtaking and recovering it, a well-dressed lady was found coiled up, who, however, did not scream when detected. Another was found in a locker on board a junk, and as the captain was desirous of examining the mode of bandaging her feet, he told his men to lift the body out of the closet, when a scream explained the trick; she was dismissed, and the money she had endeavored to hide put into her hands. Opium was found in most of the official residences; its sale received no serious check from the war, and no reference was made to it by either party.

Toward the end of the year 1841, information was received of the collection of a large force at Yüyau. Two iron steamers soon landed seven hundred men, who took up a position for the night, intending to escalade the walls in the morning; but their defenders evacuated the place. The marines and seamen took the circuit of the walls, and found the troops, about a thousand strong, drawn up in array; and the two, after exchanging their fire, started on the run. The public stores were destroyed, and the town left to the care of its citizens, without much loss of life on either side. On his return the general visited Tsz'kí, but the troops and the authorities had decamped. The rice found in the granaries was distributed to the townsmen, and the detachment returned to Ningpo December 31st. On a similar visit to Funghwa it was found that the authorities and troops had fled, so that to destroy the government stores and distribute the rice to the people was all that remained to be done. These two expeditions so terrified the "majesty-bearing generalissimo," Yihking, and his colleagues, that they fled to Suchau, in Kiangsu. With such leaders it is not strange that the villagers near Ningpo wished to enrol themselves under British rule; and the effect of the moderation of the English troops was seen in the people giving them little or no molestation after the first alarm was over, and supplying their wants as far as possible.

The force had fairly settled in its quarters at Ningpo, when the Chinese opened the campaign, March 10th, by a well-concerted night attack on the city. During the preceding day, many troops entered the city in citizen's clothes, and stationed themselves near the gates; and about three o'clock in the morning the western and southern gates were attacked and driven in. Colonel Morris ordered a party to retake the south gate, which was done, with considerable loss to the enemy; as usually happened, the moment the Chinese were opposed their main object was forgotten, and every man sought his own safety, thereby exposing himself more fully to destruction. On the approach of daylight the garrison assembled at the western gate, and dragging two or three howitzers through it, came upon the main force of the enemy drawn up in compact form, headed by an officer on horseback. The volleys poured into this dense mass mowed them down so that the street was choked with dead bodies, and the horse of the leader actually covered with corpses, from which he was seen vainly endeavoring to release himself. Those who escaped the fire in front were attacked in rear; at last about six hundred were killed, and the whole force of five thousand scattered by less than two hundred Europeans, with the loss of one man killed and six wounded.

The British then prepared to attack an intrenched camp of eight thousand troops near Tsz'ki, and about twelve hundred were embarked in the steamers. The Chinese had chosen their ground well, on the acclivity of two hills behind the town, and in order to confound and disperse their enemy completely, the attacking force was divided so as to fall upon them on three sides simultaneously, which was done with great slaughter. The Chinese did not run until they began to close in with their opponents, when they soon found that their intimidating gesticulations and cheers, their tiger-faced shields and two-edged swords, were of no avail in terrifying the barbarians or resisting their pistols, bayonets, and furious onset. In these cases, emulation among the different parties of English troops to distinguish themselves occasionally degenerated into unmanly slaughter of their flying enemy, who were looked upon rather as good game than fellow-men, and pursued in some instances several miles. Most of the Chinese troops in this engagement and in the attack on Ningpo were from the western provinces, and superior in size and bodily strength to those hitherto met. They had been encouraged to attack Ningpo by a bounty to each man of four or five dollars, and pieces of sycee were found on their bodies. The Chinese lost a thousand slain on the field, many by their own act; the English casualties were six killed and thirty-seven wounded.

The conquerors set fire to the Chinese camp in the morning, consuming all the houses used as arsenals, with arms and ammunition of every kind. The force then proceeded to the Changkí pass, a defile in the mountains, but the imperialists had abandoned their camp, leaving only "a considerable quantity of good bread." In his despatch Sir Hugh speaks of the forbearance shown by his men toward the inhabitants; and efforts were taken by the English, throughout the war, to spare the people and respect their property. The English thus dispersed that part of the Grand Army which had been called out by the Emperor and his "majesty-bearing generalissimo" to annihilate the rebels. The fugitives spread such dismay among their comrades near Hangchau that the troops began to desert and exhibit symptoms of disbanding altogether; the spirit of dissatisfaction was, moreover, increased by the people, who very naturally grumbled at being obliged to support their unsuccessful defenders, as well as submit to their tyrannous exactions.

The Chinese near Ningpo and Chinhai had so much confidence in the English, and were so greatly profited by their presence, that no disturbances took place. The rewards offered by the Chinese generals for prisoners induced the people to lay in wait for stragglers. One, Sergeant Campbell, was seized near Tinghai, put into a bag to be carried to the coast, where he was shipped in a junk and landed at Chapu, before being relieved of his hood. One of his ears was cut off with a pair of scissors, but after reaching Hangchau he was well treated. During his captivity there he was often questioned by the Chinese officers as to the movements, forces, and arms of his countrymen, and received a high idea of their intelligence from the character of their inquiries.

The entire strength with Sir Hugh Gough, in May, consisted of parts of four English regiments, a naval brigade of two hundred and fifty, and a few Indian troops, in all about two thousand five hundred men; the fleet comprised seven ships of war and four steamers. On the 17th the whole anchored in the harbor of Chapu, about forty miles above Chinhai. About six thousand three hundred Chinese troops and one thousand seven hundred Manchus were posted here in forts and intrenched camps. The English landed in three columns, as usual without opposition, and promptly turned the orderly arranged army and garrisons of their opponents into a mass of fugitives, each man throwing away his arms and uniform and flying *à pas de géant*. A body of three hundred Manchus, seeing their retreat cut off, retired into an enclosed temple, whose entrance was both narrow and dark. Every one who attempted to enter it was either killed or wounded, one of whom was Lieutenant-Colonel Tomlinson. At length a part of the wall was blown in, which exposed the inmates to the rifles of their foes, and a rocket or two set the building on fire, by which the inmates were driven from their position to the rooms below; when resistance ceased only fifty were taken prisoners, the others having been burned to death or suffocated. The total loss of the invaders was thirteen killed and fifty-two wounded.

The defences of Chapu being carried, with a loss to the enemy of about one thousand five hundred, the English moved on the city. This was the first time the Manchus had really come in contact with the English; and either fearing that indiscriminate slaughter would ensue on defeat, as it would have done had *they* been the victors, or else unable to brook their disgrace, they destroyed themselves in great numbers, first immolating their wives and children, and then cutting their own throats. Scores of bodies were found in their quarters, some not entirely dead; others were prevented from self-destruction, and in many instances, young children were found attending upon their aged or infirm parents, awaiting in dread suspense the visit of the conquerors, from whom they expected little less than instant destruction. The English surgeons endeavored to bind up the wounds of such Chinese as fell in their way, and these attentions had a good effect upon the high Chinese officers, Ilípu himself sending a letter in which he thanked the general and admiral for their kindness in giving the hungry rice to eat and caring for the wounded. The old man endeavored to requite it by making the condition of his prisoners as easy as he could, and paid them money on their release. When the English generals, having destroyed all the government stores, re-embarked, the prisoners were released with a small present, and on their return to Hangchau loudly proclaimed their praises of the foreigners.

The expedition proceeded northward to the mouth of the Yangtsz' kiang, and reached the embouchure of the Wusung, where the ships took their allotted positions, June 10th, before the well-built stone batteries, extending full three miles along the western banks of the river. One of these works enclosed the town of Paushan and mounted one hundred and thirty-four guns; the others counted altogether one hundred and seventy-five guns, forty-two of which were brass. These defences were manned by a well-selected force, under the command of Chin Hwa-ching. The ships had scarcely taken their stations when the batteries opened, and both sides kept up a cannonading for about two hours, the Chinese working their guns with much skill and effect. When the marines landed and entered, they bravely measured weapons with them, and died at their posts. Among the war junks were several new wheel-boats, having two wooden paddle-wheels turned by a capstan, which interlocked its cogs into those upon the shaft, and was worked by men on the gun-deck. These were paddling out of danger, when the steamers overtook and silenced them. The number of Chinese killed was about one hundred, out of not less than five thousand men composing the garrison and army. The governor-general, Niu Kien, who was present, in reporting the loss of the forts and dispersion of the troops, says he braved the hottest of the fight, "where cannon-balls innumerable, flying in awful confusion through the expanse of heaven, fell before, behind, and on either side of him; while in the distance he saw the ships of the rebels standing erect, lofty as the mountains. The fierce daring of the rebels was inconceivable; officers and men fell at their posts. Every effort to resist and check the onset was in vain, and a retreat became inevitable."

Among the killed was General Chin, who had taken unwearied pains to drill his troops, appoint them to their places, and inspirit them with his own courageous self-devotion. In a memoir of him, it is said that on the morning of the attack "he arrayed himself in his robes of state, and having prayed to heaven and earth, ordered all his officers and soldiers to get their arms and ammunition ready." Niu Kien's conduct was not such as to cheer them on, and most of the officers "came forward and begged to retire" when they saw the dilapidated state of the batteries. Chin's second suggested a retreat when the marines entered the battery, but he drew his sword upon him, saying, "My confidence in you has been misplaced." He again inspirited his men, himself loading and firing the ginjals, and fell pierced with wounds on the walls of the fort, bowing his head as he died in the direction of the Emperor's palace. His Majesty paid him high honors, by erecting shrines to him in his native village and at the place where he fell; in the *Ching-hwang miao* at Shanghai there is a sitting image of him in his robes of state, before which incense is burned. A reward of a thousand taels was given his family, and his son was made a *kü-jin* by special patent. In this notice it is stated as a current rumor in Shanghai, that about a fortnight after his death Chin sent down the news through the divining altar at Sung-kiang, that he had been promoted by the Supreme Ruler of

Heaven to the rank of second general-in-chief of the Board of Thunder, so that although he could not, while alive, repay the imperial favor by exterminating the rebels, he could still afford some aid to his country.

The stores of every kind were destroyed, except the brass pieces, among which were one Spanish gun of old date, and a Chinese piece more than three centuries old, both of them of singular shape, the latter being like a small-mouthed jar. The British landed on the 19th, two thousand in all, and proceeded to Shanghai by land. After the capture of Wusung, Mr. Gutzlaff, who accompanied the admiral as interpreter, succeeded in reassuring the people and inducing them to stay in their dwellings; he was also employed in procuring provisions. The ships silenced two small batteries near the city with a single broadside, and the troops entered it without resistance. The good effects of previous kindness shown the people in respecting their property were here seen. Captain Loch says that on the march along the banks he passed through two villages where the shops were open, with their owners in them, and that groups of people were assembled on the right and left to see them pass. The troops occupied the arsenals, the pawnbrokers' shops, and the temples, destroying all the government stores and distributing the rice in the granaries among the people. The total number of cannon taken was three hundred and eighty-eight, of which seventy-six were of brass; some of the latter were named "tamer and subduer of the barbarians;" others, "the robbers' judgment," and one piece twelve feet long was called the "Barbarian." The citizens voluntarily came forward to supply provisions, and stated that there had been a serious affray in the city a few days before between them and their officers, who wished to levy a subsidy for the defence of the city, which even then they were on the point of abandoning. The boats before the walls were crowded with inhabitants flying with their property, many of whom returned in a few days.

The troops retired from Shanghai June 23d, leaving it less injured than any city yet taken, owing chiefly to the efforts made by the people themselves to protect their property. The eight hundred junks and upward lying off the town were unharmed, but their owners no doubt were made to contribute toward the $300,000 exacted as a ransom. Sir Henry Pottinger now rejoined the expedition, accompanied by Lord Saltoun, with large reinforcements for both arms, and immediate preparations were made for proceeding up the Yangtsz', to interrupt the communication by the Grand Canal across that river. The Chinese officers, unable to read any European language, learned the designs of their enemy chiefly by rumors, which natives in the employ of the English brought them, and consequently not unfrequently misled his Majesty—unwittingly, in mentioning the wrong places likely to be attacked, but wilfully as to their numbers and conduct in the hour of victory. The fall of Shanghai and the probable march upon Sungkiang and Suchau greatly alarmed him, and he now began to think that the rebels really intended to proceed up to Nanking and the Grand Canal, which he had been assured was not their purpose.

He accordingly concentrated his troops at Chinkiang, Nanking, Suchau, and Tientsin, four places which he feared were in danger, and associated Kíying and Ilípu as commissioners with the governor-general, Niu Kien, to superintend civil affairs; military matters were still left under the management of the imbecile Yihking. Only a few places on the Yangtsz' kiang offered eligible positions for forts, and Niu Kien wisely declined to stake the Great River at Chinkiang, lest it should alarm the inhabitants. Fire-rafts and boats were, however, ordered for the defence of that city, and reinforcements of troops collected there and at Nanking, some of whom were encamped without the city, and part incorporated with the garrison. The tone of the documents which fell into the hands of the English showed the anxiety felt at court regarding the result of this movement up the river.

The British plenipotentiary published and circulated a manifesto at this date for "the information of the people of the country." In this paper he enumerated, in much the same manner as Captain Elliot had done, the grievances the English had suffered at Canton from the spoliations, insults, and imprisonment inflicted upon them by Lin in order to extort opium, which was given up by the English superintendent to rescue himself and his countrymen from death. The duplicity of the Chinese government in sending down Kíshen as a commissioner to Canton to arrange matters, and then, while he was negotiating, to break off the treaty and treacherously resort to war, was another "grand instance of offence against England." The bad treatment of kidnapped prisoners, the mendacious reports of victories gained over the English, which misled the Emperor and retarded the settlement of the war, was another cause of offence. The restriction of the trade to Canton, establishment of the monopoly of the hong merchants, the oppressive and unjust exactions imposed upon it through their scheming, and many other minor grievances which need not be enumerated, formed the last count in this indictment. Three things must be granted before peace could be made, viz., the cession of an island for commerce and the residence of merchants; compensation for losses and expenses; and allowing a friendly and becoming intercourse between the officers of the two countries on terms of equality. This proclamation, however, made no mention of the real cause of the war, the opium trade, and in that respect was far from being an ingenuous, fair statement of the question. It was much more like one of Napoleon's bulletins in the *Moniteur*, and considering the moral and intellectual condition of Great Britain and China, failed to uphold the high standing of the former.

While Sir Henry Pottinger knew that the use of this drug was one of the greatest evils which afflicted the people, he should have, in a document of this nature, left no room for the supposition, on the part of either ruler or subject, that the war was undertaken to uphold and countenance the opium trade. He could not have been ignorant that the Emperor and his ministers supposed the unequal contest they were waging was caused by their unsuccessful efforts to suppress the traffic; and that if they were defeated the opium trade must go on unchecked. The question of supremacy was set at rest in this proclamation; it must be given up; but no encouragement was held out to reassure the Chinese government in their lawful desire to restrain the tremendous scourge. Why should he? If he encouraged any action against the trade, he could expect little promotion or reward from his superiors in India or England, who looked to it for all the revenue it could be made to bring; or consideration from the merchants, who would not thank him for telling the Chinese they might attack the opium clippers wherever they found them, and seize all the opium they could, and English power would not interfere.

The Emperor issued a proclamation about the same time, recapitulating his conduct and efforts to put a stop to the war, stating what he had done to ward off calamity and repress the rebels. The opium trade, and his efforts for a long time to repress it, and especially the measures of Lin, are in this paper regarded as the causes of the war, which concludes by expressing his regrets for the sufferings and losses occasioned his subjects by the attacks of the English at Amoy, Chusan, Ningpo, and elsewhere, and exhorting them to renewed efforts. It is a matter of lasting regret that the impression has been left upon the minds of the Chinese people that the war was an opium war, and waged chiefly to uphold it. But nations, like individuals, must usually trust to might more than right to maintain their standing; and when conscious weakness leads them to adopt underhand measures to regain their rights, the temptation which led to these acts is rarely thought of in the day of retribution. The money demands of England were not deemed at the time to be exacting, but she should, and could at this time in an effectual manner, through her plenipotentiary, have cleared herself from all sanction of this traffic. If Lord Melbourne could wish it were a less objectionable traffic, Sir Henry Pottinger might surely have intimated, in as public a manner, his regret at its existence. He probably did not deem the use of opium very deleterious.

The number of ships, steamers, transports, and all in the expedition, when it left Wusung, July 6th, was seventy-two, most of them large vessels. They were arranged in five divisions, with an advance squadron of five small steamers and tenders to survey the river, each division having a frigate or seventy-four at its head. The world has seldom seen a more conspicuous instance of the superiority of a small body possessing science, skill, and discipline, over immense multitudes of undisciplined, ignorant, and distrustful soldiers, than was exhibited in this bold manœuvre. Not to speak alone of the great disparity in numbers, the distant quarters of the globe whence the ships were collected, the many languages and tribes found in the invading force, the magnitude of their ships, abundance of their supplies, and superiority of their weapons of war, the moral energy and confidence of power in this small troop over its ineffective adversary was not less conspicuous. The sight of such a fleet sailing up their Great River struck the inhabitants with mingled astonishment and dread.

Chinkiang lies half a mile from the southern bank of the Yangtsz', surrounded by a high wall four miles in circuit, and having hills of considerable elevation in its rear. The canal comes in from the south, close to the walls on its western side, and along the shores of both river and canal are extensive suburbs—at this time completely under the command of the guns of the ships, which could also bombard the city itself from some positions. A bluff hill on the north partly concealed the town from the ships, and it was not till this hill-top had been gained that the three Chinese encampments behind the city could be seen. The general divided his small force of seven thousand men into three brigades, under the command of Major-Generals Lord Saltoun, Schoedde, and Bartley, besides an artillery brigade of five hundred and seventy rank and file, under Lieutenant-Colonel Montgomerie. The Chinese encampments contained more than three thousand men, most of them soldiers from Hupeh and Chehkiang provinces. The Manchu garrison within the city consisted of one thousand two hundred regular troops and eight hundred Mongols from Koko-nor, together with eight hundred and thirty-five Chinese troops, making altogether from two thousand six hundred to two thousand eight hundred fighting men; the entire force was under the command of Hailing, who had made such a disposition of his troops and strengthened his means of defence as well as the time allowed. He closes his last communication to the Emperor with the assurance that "he cannot do otherwise than exert his whole heart and strength in endeavors to repay a small fraction of the favors he has enjoyed from his government."

The right brigade, under Lord Saltoun, soon drove the imperialists out of their camp, who did not wait for his near approach, but broke and dispersed after firing three or four distant volleys. Captain Loch says that while the party of volunteers were approaching the camp, they passed through a small hamlet on the hills; "the village had not been deserted; some of the houses were closed, while the inhabitants of others were standing in the streets staring at us in stupid wonder; and although they were viewing a contest between foreigners and their fellow-countrymen, and in danger themselves of being shot, were coolly eating their meals."

The centre brigade, under Major-General Schoedde, landed on the northern corner of the city, to escalade the walls on that side and prevent the troops from the camp entering the gates. He was received by a well-sustained fire, his men placing their ladders and mounting in the face of a determined resistance; as soon as they gained the parapet they drove the Tartars before them, though their passage was bravely disputed. While they were mounting the walls a fire was kept up on the city on the northern and eastern sides, under cover of which, after clearing the ramparts, they proceeded to the western gate, conquering all opposition in the northern part of the city, and driving the Tartars to the southern quarter.

The left brigade, under Major-General Bartley, did not reach the western side as soon as was expected, being delayed by the canal, here between seventy and eighty feet broad, which formed a deep ditch on this side. The western gate was blown in, the blast carrying before it a high pile of sand-bags heaped against the inside to strengthen the bars. While this work was going on, seven boats carrying artillerymen entered the canal to proceed up to the gate; but when nearly opposite they were repulsed by a severe fire from the walls, and the men compelled to abandon the three leading boats and take refuge in the houses along the banks; the others halted under cover of some houses until their comrades rejoined them, when all returned to the ships. Two hundred marines now landed, and with three hundred sepoys soon recovered the boats and carried back the wounded men. The party then planted their ladders in the face of a spirited fire from the walls, and succeeded in carrying them against all opposition.

All resistance at the three gateways having been overcome, it was supposed that the city was nearly subdued. Sir Hugh consequently ordered a halt for his men on account of the heat, and despatched a small force to proceed along the western ramparts to occupy the southern gate. This squad had proceeded about half a mile when it met a body of eight hundred or one thousand Tartars regularly drawn up in an open space. They fired with steadiness and regularity, but their bravery was of no avail, for the party, giving them one volley, charged down the bank and scattered them immediately, though not without some resistance. The dispersed Tartars, however, kept up a scattering fire along the streets and from the houses, which served chiefly to irritate their enemies and increase their own loss.

The heat of the day having passed, the commander-in-chief, guided by Mr. Gutzlaff and some Chinese, marched with two regiments into the southern quarter of the city. The scenes of desolation and woe which he met seem to have sickened the gray-haired warrior, for he says in his despatches, "finding dead bodies of Tartars in every house we entered, principally women and children, thrown into wells or otherwise murdered by their own people, I was glad to withdraw the troops from this frightful scene of destruction, and place them in the northern quarter." It was indeed a terrific scene. Captain Loch, who accompanied Sir Hugh, says they went to a large building thought to be the prefect's house, which was forced open and found entirely deserted, though completely furnished and of great extent; "we set fire to it and marched on." What the object or advantage of this barbarous act was he does not say. Leaving the general, he turned down a street and burst open the door of a large mansion; the objects which met his view were shocking.

After we had forced our way over piles of furniture placed to barricade the door, we entered an open court strewed with rich stuffs and covered with clotted blood; and upon the steps leading to the hall of ancestors there were two bodies of youthful Tartars, cold and stiff, who seemed to be brothers. Having gained the threshold of their abode, they had died where they had fallen from loss of blood. Stepping over these bodies we entered the hall, and met face to face three women seated, a mother and two daughters, and at their feet lay two bodies of elderly men, with their throats cut from ear to ear, their senseless heads resting upon the feet of their relations. To the right were two young girls, beautiful and delicate, crouching over and endeavoring to conceal a living soldier. In the heat of action, when the blood is up and the struggle is for life between man and man, the anguish of the wounded and the sight of misery and pain is unheeded; humanity is partially obscured by danger; but when excitement subsides with victory, a heart would be hardly human that could feel unaffected by the retrospection. And the hardest heart of the oldest man who ever lived a life of rapine and slaughter could not have gazed on this scene of woe unmoved. I stopped, horror-stricken at what I saw. The expression of cold, unutterable despair depicted on the mother's face changed to the violent workings of scorn and hate, which at last burst forth in a paroxysm of invective, afterward in floods of tears, which apparently, if anything could, relieved her. She came close to me and seized me by the arm, and with clenched teeth and deadly frown pointed to the bodies, to her daughters, to her yet splendid house, and to herself; then stepped back a pace, and with firmly closed hands and in a husky voice, I could see by her gestures, spoke of her misery, her hate, and, I doubt not, her revenge. I attempted by signs to explain, offered her my services, but was spurned. I endeavored to make her comprehend that, however great her present misery, it might be in her unprotected state a hundredfold increased; that if she would place herself under my guidance, I would pass her through the city gates in safety into the open country; but the poor woman would not listen to me, and the whole family was by this time in loud lamentation. All that remained for me to do was to prevent the soldiers bayoneting the man, who, since our entrance, had attempted to escape.[1]

The destruction of life was appalling. Some of the Manchus shut the doors of their houses, while through the crevices persons could be seen deliberately cutting the throats of their women, and destroying their children by throwing them into wells. In one house a man was shot while sawing his wife's throat as he held her over a well into which he had already thrown his children; her wound was sewed up and the lives of the children saved. In another house no less than fourteen dead bodies, principally women, were discovered; while such was their terror and hatred of the invaders, that every Manchu preferred resistance, death, suicide, or flight, to surrender. Out of a Manchu population of four thousand, it was estimated that not more than five hundred survived, the greater part having perished by their own hands.

---

[1] Capt. G. G. Loch, *Narrative of Events in China*, p. 109.

The public offices were ransacked and all arms and stores destroyed; only $60,000 in sycee were found in the treasury. The populace began to pillage, and in one instance, fearing a stop might be put to their rapacity, they set fire to the buildings at each end of a street in order to plunder a pawnbroker's shop without interference. The streets and lanes were strewed with silken, fur, and other rich dresses which the robbers had thrown away when they saw something more valuable, and the sepoys and camp-followers took what they could find. Parties were accordingly stationed at the gates to take everything from the natives as they went out, or which they threw over the walls, and in this way the thieves were in their turn stripped. Within twenty-four hours after the troops landed, the city and suburbs of Chinkiang were a mass of ruin and destruction; part of the eastern wall was subsequently blown in and all the gates dismantled to prevent any treachery. The total loss of the English was thirty-seven killed and one hundred and thirty-one wounded.

A curious contrast to the terrible scenes going on at Chinkiang was seen at Íching hien, on the northern side of the river. Four days before, the approach of the steamer Nemesis had caused no little consternation, and in the evening a Chinese gentleman came off to her with a few presents to learn if there was any intention of attacking the town. He was told that if he would send supplies of meat and provisions no harm would be done, and all he brought should be paid for. In the morning provisions were furnished, and he remained on board to see the steamer chase and bring junks to; being much amazed at these novel operations, which gave him a new idea of the energy of the invaders. In the evening commands were given him to bring provisions in larger quantities, and three boats went up to the town to procure them. The people showed no hostility, and through his assistance the English opened a market in the courtyard of a temple, at which supplies were purchased, put aboard small junks, and conveyed to the fleet. On the 21st the same person came, according to agreement, to accompany a large party of English from the ships to his house, where he had prepared an entertainment for them. Through the medium of a Chinese boy communication was easily carried on, and the alarms of the townspeople quieted; a proclamation was also issued stating that every peaceable person would be unharmed. This gentleman had invited a large company of his relatives and friends, and served up a collation for his guests; all this time the firing was heard from Chinkiang, where the countrymen of those so agreeably occupied were engaged in hostile encounter. On returning to their boats an additional mark of respect was shown by placing a well-dressed man each side of every officer to fan him as he walked. At the market-temple another entertainment was also served up. No injury was done by either side, and the forbearance of the English was not without good effect. Such queer contrasts as this have frequently characterized the contests between the Chinese and British.

Some of the large ships were towed up to Nanking, and the whole fleet reached it August 9th, at which time preparation had been made for the assault; but desirous of avoiding a repetition of the sad scenes of Chinkiang, the British leaders had also sent a communication to Niu Kien, offering to ransom the city for $3,000,000.

This celebrated city lies about three miles south of the river, but the north-east corner of an outer wall reaches within seven hundred paces of the water; the western face runs along the base of wooded hills for part of its distance, and is then continued through flat grounds around the southern side, both being defended by a deep ditch. The suburbs are on this low ground, where Sir Hugh Gough intended to bombard the place and make an entrance on the eastern side, while diversions at other points perplexed the garrison. His force consisted of only four thousand five hundred effective men; there were, as nearly as could be learned, six thousand Manchu and nine thousand Chinese troops within the city. On the 11th Lord Saltoun's brigade landed at a village from whence a paved road led to one of the eastern gates, and other detachments were stationed in the neighborhood. Everything was in readiness for the assault by daylight of August 15th, and the governor-general was told that it would assuredly be made unless the commissioners produced their authority for treating.

In the interval between the downfall of Chinkiang and investment of Nanking, several communications were received from the Chinese officers, and one from Kiying, couched in conciliatory language, and evincing a desire for peace. Sir Henry Pottinger replied in the same strain, deploring the war and calamities caused by its continuance, but stating that he could have no interview with any individual, however exalted, who was not properly commissioned to treat for peace. It is probable that the Emperor did not receive any suggestion from his ministers in regard to making peace until after the fall of Chinkiang, and it was a matter of some importance, therefore, for Ílípu and his colleague to delay the attack on Nanking until an answer could be received from the capital. The usual doubts in the minds of the English as to their sincerity led them to look upon the whole as a scheme to perfect the defences, and gain time for the people to retire; consequently the preparations for taking the city went on, in order to deepen the conviction that if one party was practising any deception, the other certainly was in earnest.

On the night of the 14th, scarcely three hours before the artillery was to open, Ílípu, Kiying, and Niu Kien addressed a joint letter to Sir Henry Pottinger requesting an interview in the morning, when they would produce their credentials and arrange for further proceedings. This request was granted with some reluctance, for the day before the *puching sz'* and Tartar commandant had behaved very unsatisfactorily, refusing to exhibit the credentials or discuss the terms of peace or ransom. The distress ensuent upon the blockade was becoming greater and greater; more than seven hundred vessels coming from the south had been stopped at Chinkiang, and a large fleet lay in the northern branch of the canal, so that some possibility existed of the whole province falling into anarchy if the pressure were not removed. The authorities of the city of Yangchau, on the canal, had already sent half a million dollars as the ransom of that place, while Niu Kien would only offer a third of a million to ransom the capital.

The Emperor's authority to treat with the English was, however, exhibited at this meeting, and in return Sir Henry's was fully explained to them. The delegates on the part of the commissioners were Hwang Ngăn-tung, secretary to Kíying, and Chin, the Manchu commandant, while Major Malcom, secretary of legation, and Mr. J. R. Morrison acted on the part of the plenipotentiary. Captain Loch, who was present, humorously describes the solemn manner in which the Emperor's commission was brought out from the box in which it was deposited, and the dismay of the lower attendants at seeing the foreigners irreverently handle it and examine its authenticity with so little awe. The skeleton of the treaty was immediately drafted for Hwang to take to his superiors. General Chin laughingly remarked that though the conditions were hard, they were no more so than the Chinese would have demanded if they had been the victors. The bearing of these officers was courteous, and Hwang especially found favor with all who were thrown into his company.

The utmost care being requisite in drawing up the articles, most of the work falling upon Mr. Morrison, it was not till late at night on the 17th that the final draft was sent to the Chinese. The plenipotentiary, on the 18th, desired the general and admiral to suspend hostilities, at which time arrangements were also made for an interview the next day between the representatives on both sides. The English officers meantime explored the vicinity of the city, and the demand for provisions to supply the force caused a brisk trade highly beneficial to the Chinese, and well calculated to please them.

On the 19th Kíying, Ílípu, and Niu Kien, accompanied by a large suite, paid their first visit to the English. The steamer Medusa brought them alongside the Cornwallis, and Sir Henry Pottinger, supported by the admiral and general, received them on the quarter-deck. The ship was decked with flags, and the crowd of gayly dressed officers in blue and scarlet contrasted well with the bright crapes and robes of the Chinese. This visit was one of ceremony, and after partaking of refreshments and examining the ship the commissioners retired, expressing their gratification at what they saw. They conducted themselves with decorum in their novel position, and Kíying and Ílípu, though both brought up in the full persuasion of the supremacy of their sovereign over the rulers of all other nations, and particularly over the English, manifested no ill-concealed chagrin. They had previously sent up a report of the progress of the expedition after the capture of Chinkiang, requesting in it that the demands of the invaders might be conceded; the inefficiency of their troops is acknowledged, and a candid statement of the impossibility of effectual resistance laid before his Majesty, with cogent reasons for acceding to the demands of the English as the wisest course of procedure. The further disasters which will ensue if the war is not brought to a close are hinted at, and the concession of the points at issue considered in a manner least humbling to imperial vanity. The sum of $21,000,000 to be paid is regarded by them as a present to the soldiers and sailors before sending them home; partly as the liquidation of just debts due from the hong merchants, whose insolvency made them chargeable to the government, and partly as indemnification for the opium. Trade at the five ports was to be allowed, because four of them had already been seized, and this was the only way to induce the invaders to withdraw, while Hongkong could be ceded inasmuch as they had already built houses there. The memorial is a curious effort to render the bitter pill somewhat palatable to themselves and their master.

The English plenipotentiary, accompanied by a large concourse of officers, returned the visit on shore in a few days, and were met at the entrance of a temple by the commissioners, who led them through a guard of newly uniformed and unarmed soldiers into the building, the bands of both nations striking up their music at the same time. This visit continued the good understanding which prevailed; the room had been carpeted and ornamented with lanterns and scrolls for the occasion, while the adjacent grounds accommodated a crowd of natives. On the 26th Sir Henry Pottinger and his suite, consisting of his secretary, Major Malcom, Messrs. Morrison, Thom, and Gutzlaff, the three interpreters, and three other gentlemen, proceeded about four miles to the landing-place on the canal, where they were met by a brigadier and two colonels; the banks of the canal were lined with troops. The party then took their horses, and, preceded by a mounted escort, were received at the city gate by the secretaries of Ílípu; the procession advanced to the place of meeting, guarded by a detachment of Manchu cavalry, whose shaggy ponies and flowing dresses presented a singular contrast to the envoy's escort and their beautiful Arabs. He himself was conducted through the outer gate, up the court and through the second gateway, ascending the steps into the third entrance, where he dismounted and entered the building with the commissioners and governor-general. The room had been elegantly fitted up, and a crowd of official attendants dressed in their ceremonial robes stood around. Sir Henry occupied the chief seat between Kíying and Ílípu, their respective attendants being seated in proper order, with small tables between every two persons, while dinner was served up in usual Chinese style.

These formalities being over, the thirteen articles of this most important treaty were discussed:

I.—Lasting peace between the two nations.

II.—The ports of Canton, Amoy, Fuhchau, Ningpo, and Shanghai to be opened to British trade and residence, and trade conducted according to a well-understood tariff.

III.—"It being obviously necessary and desirable that British subjects should have some port whereat they may careen and refit their ships when required," the island of Hongkong to be ceded to her Majesty.

IV.—Six millions of dollars to be paid as the value of the opium which was delivered up "as a ransom for the lives of H. B. M. Superintendent and subjects," in March, 1839.

V.—Three millions of dollars to be paid for the debts due to British merchants.

VI.—Twelve millions to be paid for the expenses incurred in the expedition sent out "to obtain redress for the violent and unjust proceedings of the Chinese high authorities."

VII.—The entire amount of $21,000,000 to be paid before December 31, 1845.

VIII.—All prisoners of war to be immediately released by the Chinese.

IX.—The Emperor to grant full and entire amnesty to those of his subjects who had aided the British.

X.—A regular and fair tariff of export and import customs and other dues to be established at the open ports, and a transit duty to be levied in addition which will give goods a free conveyance to all places in China.

XI.—Official correspondence to be hereafter conducted on terms of equality according to the standing of the parties.

XII.—Conditions for restoring the places held by British troops to be according to the payments of money.

XIII.—Time of exchanging ratifications and carrying the treaty into effect.

The official English and Chinese texts of this compact and a literal translation of the Chinese text are given in the *Chinese Repository*, Vols. XIII. and XIV.; in that serial is also to be found a full account of the struggle which was thus brought to a close. Looked at in any point of view, political, commercial, moral, or intellectual, it will always be considered as one of the turning points in the history of mankind, involving the welfare of all nations in its wide-reaching consequences.

When matters connected with the treaty had been arranged, Sir Henry proposed to say a few words upon "the great cause that produced the disturbances which led to the war, viz., the trade in opium." But upon hearing this (Captain Loch says) they unanimously declined entering upon the subject, until they were assured that he had introduced it merely as a topic for private conversation.

They then evinced much interest, and eagerly requested to know why we would not act fairly toward them by prohibiting the growth of the poppy in our dominions, and thus effectually stop a traffic so pernicious to the human race. This, he said, in consistency with our constitutional laws could not be done; and he added that even if England chose to exercise so arbitrary a power over her tillers of the soil, it would not check the evil, so far as the Chinese were concerned, while the cancer remained uneradicated among themselves, but that it would merely throw the market into other hands. It, in fact, he said, rests entirely with yourselves. If your people are virtuous, they will desist from the evil practice; and if your officers are incorruptible and obey your orders, no opium can enter your country. The discouragement of the growth of the poppy in our territories rests principally with you, for nearly the entire produce cultivated in India travels east to China; if, however, the habit has become a confirmed vice, and you feel that your power is at present inadequate to stay its indulgence, you may rest assured your people will procure the drug in spite of every enactment. Would it not, therefore, be better at once to legalize its importation, and by thus securing the co-operation of the rich and of your authorities, from whom it would thus be no longer debarred, thereby greatly limit the facilities which now exist for smuggling? They owned the plausibility of the argument, but expressed themselves persuaded that their imperial master would never listen to a word upon the subject.

To convince them that what he said was not introduced from any sinister wish to gain an end more advantageous for ourselves, he drew a rapid sketch of England's rise and progress from a barbarous state to a degree of wealth and civilization unparalleled in the history of the world; which rapid rise was principally attributable to benign and liberal laws, aided by commerce, which conferred power and consequence. He then casually mentioned instances of governments having failed to attain their ends by endeavoring to exclude any particular objects of popular desire; tobacco was one of those he alluded to, and now that it was legalized, not only did it produce a large revenue to the crown, but it was more moderately indulged in in Britain than elsewhere.[1]

To the well-wisher of his fellow-men this narrative suggests many melancholy reflections. On the one hand were four or five high Chinese officers, who, although pagans and unacquainted with the principles of true virtue, had evidently sympathized with and upheld their sovereign in his fruitless, misdirected endeavors to save his people from a vicious habit. "Why will you not act fairly toward us by prohibiting the growth of the poppy?" is their anxious inquiry; for they knew that there was no moral principle among themselves strong enough to resist the opium pipe. "Your people must become virtuous and your officers incorruptible, and then you can stop the opium coming into your borders," is the reply; precisely the words that the callous rumseller gives the broken-hearted wife of the besotted drunkard when she beseeches him not to sell liquor to her enslaved husband. "Other people will bring it to you if we should stop the cultivation of the poppy; if England chose to exercise so arbitrary a power over her tillers of the soil, it would not check the evil," adds the envoy; "you cannot do better than legalize it." Although nations are somewhat different from individuals in respect to their power of resisting and suppressing a vice,

---

[1] Loch's *Events in China*, p. 173, London, 1843. This same point is slightly referred to by Lieutenant Ouchterlony, on page 448 of his *Chinese War*, where he states that Sir Henry had prepared a paper for the information of the Chinese officials, proposing to them to permit the traffic in opium to be by barter

and Sir Henry did right to speak of the legal difficulty in the way of restraining labor, yet how heartless was the excuse, "if we do not bring it to you others will." No suggestion was made to them as to the most judicious mode of restraining what they were told they could not prohibit; no hint of the farming system, which would have held out to them a medium path between absolute freedom and prohibition, and probably been seriously considered by the court; no frank explanation as to the real position the English government itself held in respect to the forced growth of this pernicious article in its Indian territories. How much nobler would that government have stood in the eyes of mankind if its head and ministers had instructed their plenipotentiary, that when their other demands were all paid and conceded no indemnity should have been asked for smuggled opium entirely destroyed by those who had seized it within their borders under threats of worse consequences. That government and ministry which had paid a hundred millions for the emancipation of slaves could surely afford to release a pagan nation from such an imposed obligation, instead of sending their armies to exact a few millions which the revenue of one year, derived from this very article alone, would amply discharge to their own subjects. For this pitiful sum must the great moral lesson to the Emperor of China and his subjects, which could have been taught them at this time, be lost.

Sir Henry inquired if an envoy would be received at Peking, should one be sent from England, which Kíying assured him would no doubt be a gratification to his master, though what ideas the latter connected with such a suggestion can only be inferred. The conference lasted three or four hours, and when the procession returned to the barges, through an immense crowd of people, nothing was heard from them to indicate dislike or dread; all other thoughts were merged in overpowering curiosity. It was remarkable that this was the anniversary of the day when English subjects, among whom were the three interpreters here present, left Macao in 1839, by order of Lin: on August 26, 1840, the plenipotentiaries entered the Pei ho to seek an interview with Kíshen; that day, the next year, Amoy and its extensive batteries fell; and now the three years' game is won and China is obliged to bend, her magnates come down from their eminences, and her wall of supremacy, isolation, and conceit is shattered beyond the possibility of restoration. Her rulers apparently submitted with good grace to the hard lesson, which seemed to be the only effectual means of compelling them to abandon their ridiculous pretensions; though it cannot be too often repeated that the effect of kindness, honorable dealing, and peaceful missions had not been fairly tried.

Arrangements were made on the 29th to sign the treaty on board the Cornwallis. After it was signed all sat down to table, and the admiral, as the host in his flagship, gave the healths of their Majesties, the Queen of England and the Emperor of China, which was announced to the fleet and army by a salute of twenty-one guns and hoisting the Union Jack and a yellow flag at the main and mizzen. The treaty was forwarded to Peking that evening. The embargo on the rivers and ports was at once taken off, the troops re-embarked, and preparations made to return to Wusung. The six millions were paid without much delay, and on September 15th the Emperor's ratification was received. The secretary of legation, Major Malcom, immediately left to obtain the Queen's ratification, going by steam the entire distance (except eighty miles in Egypt) from Nanking to London—an extraordinary feat in those days.

The imperial assent was also published in a rescript addressed to Kíying, in reply to his account of the settlement of affairs, in which he gives directions for disbanding the troops, rebuilding such forts as had been destroyed, and cultivating peace as well as providing for the fulfilment of the articles. It is, on the whole, a dignified approval of the treaty, and breathes nothing of a spirit of revenge or intention to prepare for future resistance.

The fleet of ships and transports returned down the river and reassembled at Tinghai, at the end of October, not a vessel having been lost. Even before leaving Nanking, and in the passage down the river, the troops and sailors, especially the Indian regiments, were reduced by cholera, fever, and other diseases, some of the transports being nearly disabled; the deaths amounted to more than a thousand before reaching Hongkong.

On arriving at Amoy the plenipotentiary was highly incensed on hearing of the melancholy fate of the captive crews of the Nerbudda and Ann, wrecked on Formosa. The first, a transport, contained two hundred and seventy-four souls, and when she went ashore all the Europeans abandoned two hundred and forty Hindus to their fate, most of whom fell into the hands of the Chinese. The Ann was an opium vessel, and her crew of fifty-seven souls were taken prisoners and carried to Taiwan fu. The prisoners were divided into small parties and had little communication with each other during their captivity, which was aggravated by want of food and clothing, filthy lodgings, and other hardships of a Chinese jail, so that many of the Indians died. The survivors, on August 13th, with the exception of ten persons, were carried out to a plain near the city, one of whom, Mr. Newman, a seacunnie on board the Ann and the last in the procession, gave the following account:

> On being taken out of his sedan, to have his hands shackled behind his back, he saw two of the prisoners with their irons off and refusing to have them put on. They had both been drinking and were making a great noise, crying out to him that they were all to have their heads cut off. He advised them to submit quietly, but they still refusing, he first wrenched off his own and then put them into theirs, to the great pleasure of the soldiers, but when the soldiers wished to replace his he declined. As they were on the point of securing him he accidentally saw the chief officer seated close to him. Going before him he threw himself on his head and commenced singing a few Chinese words which he had frequently heard repeated in a temple. The officer was so pleased with this procedure that he turned round to the soldiers and ordered them to carry him back to the city. All the rest, one hundred and ninety-seven in number, were placed at small distances from each other on their knees, their feet in irons and hands manacled behind their backs, thus waiting for the executioners, who went round and with a kind of two-handed sword cut off their heads without being laid on a block. Afterward their bodies were thrown into one grave and their heads stuck up in cages on the seashore.[1]

A journal was kept by Mr. Gully to within three days of his death, and another by Captain Denham of the Ann, one of the prisoners saved to send to Peking.[2] Both contain full accounts

---

[1] *Chinese Repository*, Vol. XII., p. 248.

[2] *Journals of Mr. Gully and Captain Denham during a Captivity in China in* 1842. London: Chapman & Hall, 1844.

of the treatment of the unhappy captives, and diminish the sympathy felt for the defeat of the government which allowed such slaughter. It was said to have been done by orders from court, grounded on a lying report sent up by the Manchu commandant, Tahungah. When their sad fate was learned Sir Henry Pottinger published two proclamations in Chinese, in which the principal facts were detailed, so that all might know the truth of the matter; a demand made for the degradation and punishment of the lying officers who had superintended it, and the confiscation of their property for the use of the families of the sufferers. Iliang, the governor-general, expressed his sincere regret to the English envoy at what had taken place, and examined into the facts himself, which led to the degradation and banishment of the commandant and intendant. While the prisoners were still at Taiwan fu, H. M. S. Serpent was sent over from Amoy to reclaim them, by which expedition the truth of the barbarous execution was first learned; this vessel afterward went there to receive the shipwrecked crew of the Herculaneum transport.

The citizens of Amoy, Ningpo, and Shanghai hailed the cessation of the war and the opening of their ports to foreign trade; but not so at Canton. The discharged volunteers still remained about the city, notwithstanding orders to return home and resume their usual employments, most of whom probably had neither. Scheming demagogues took advantage of a rumor that the English army intended to form a settlement opposite the city, and issued a paper in the name of the gentry, calling upon all to combine and resist the aggression. The enthusiasm it caused was worked up to a higher pitch by an inflammatory manifesto, in which desperate measures were plainly intimated; but the district magistrates took no steps against them. An invitation was circulated for the citizens and gentlemen from other provinces to meet at the public assembly hall to consult upon public affairs. A counter but less spirited manifesto was pasted up in the hall, which had the effect of inducing about half the people to disperse. The writers of this paper dissuaded their countrymen from hasty measures, by telling them that no land could be taken or dwellings occupied without permission from the provincial authorities, and urged upon them to live at peace with the English, in accordance with the injunctions of their wise sovereign.

A brawl occurred in Hog Lane on December 6th, between some hucksters and lascars, who were pursued into the Square, where the mob rapidly increased, and about two o'clock began pulling down a brick wall around the Company's garden and forcing open one of the factories, which was speedily pillaged, the inmates escaping through the back doors. The British flag-staff was fired by a party which kept guard around it, and the flames communicating to the verandah, other parts soon caught, and by midnight the three hongs east of Hog Lane were burning furiously. The ringleaders, satisfied with firing the British consulate, endeavored to prevent thieves carrying away the plunder; but they were forced to escape about midnight. These wretches soon began to quarrel among themselves for the dollars found in the ruins, and it was not till noon that the police and soldiers ventured to attack the knotted groups of struggling desperadoes and arrest the most conspicuous, and with the aid of boats' crews from the shipping recapture some of the specie. Full compensation was subsequently made to the foreigners for the losses sustained, amounting to $67,397, and some of the ringleaders were executed.

A large part of the officers in the army and navy engaged in the war received promotion or honorary titles. Sir Hugh was made a baronet, and, after more service in India, elevated to the peerage, with the title of Lord Gough, Baron of Chinkiang fu; the plenipotentiary and the admiral obtained Grand Crosses of the Bath. The three interpreters, Messrs. Morrison, Thom, and Gutzlaff, whose services had been arduous and important, received no distinctive reward from their government. The amount of prize money distributed among the soldiers and sailors was small. The losses of the English from shipwreck, sickness, and casualties during the war amounted to more than three thousand; the mortality was greatest among the Indian regiments and the European recruits, especially after the operations behind Canton and the capture of Chinkiang.

While the English government rewarded its officers, the Emperor expressed his displeasure at the conduct of the major part of his surviving generals, but distributed posthumous honors to those who had died at their posts. Hailing, with his wife and grandson, were honored with a fane, and his sons promoted. Kíying was appointed governor-general at Nanking. Though many civil and military officers were condemned to death, none actually lost their lives, except Yu Pu-yun, the governor of Chehkiang, who fled from Ningpo in October, 1841.

The settlement of the duties and regulations for carrying on foreign commerce immediately engaged the attention of the plenipotentiary. He called on the British merchants for information, but so utterly desultory was the manner in which the duties had been formerly levied, that they could give him little or no reliable information as to what was really done with the money. The whole matter was placed by both parties in the hands of Mr. Thom, who had been engaged in business at Canton, and Hwang Ngăn-tung, secretary to Kíying. To settle these multifarious affairs and restore quiet, Ílípu was sent to Canton as commissioner. On his arrival, he set about allaying the popular discontent at the treaty, and his edict[1] is a good instance of the mixture of flattery and instruction, coaxing and commanding, which Chinese officers frequently adopt when they are not sure of gaining their end by power alone, and do not wish to irritate. In this instance it did much to remove misapprehension and allay excitement, but its author had not long been engaged in these arduous duties before he "made a vacancy," aged seventy-two, having been more than half his life engaged in high employments in his country's service; his conduct and foresight in the last two years did credit to himself and elevated his nation. His associate, Kíying, took his place and exchanged the ratifications of the treaty of Nanking at Hongkong with Sir Henry Pottinger, ten months after it had been signed by the same persons. The island was then taken possession of on behalf of the Queen by proclamation, and the warrant read ap-

[1] *Chinese Repository*, Vol. XII., p. 106.

pointing Sir Henry governor of the colony. Its influence on the well-being of China since that period has been less than was anticipated by those who looked to the higher welfare and progress of a British colony so near to it as likely to be an example for good. A free port has encouraged smuggling to a degree that constantly irritates and baffles the native authorities on the mainland, and leads to armed resistance to their efforts toward collecting lawful revenue, especially on opium; while the influx of Chinese traders, attracted by its greater security, is gradually converting the island into a Chinese settlement protected by British rule. The peninsula of Kowlung, on the north side of the harbor, was added in 1860, to furnish ground for the commissary departments of the forces. The influence of a well-ordered Christian government exercising a beneficent rule over a less civilized race under its sway, is soon neutralized by licensing the opium farms and gambling saloons and lending its moral sanction to smuggling.

The tariff and commercial regulations were published July 22d. In this tariff, all emoluments and illegal exactions superimposed upon the imperial duties were prohibited, and a fixed duty put on each article, which seldom exceeded five per cent. on the cost; all kinds of breadstuffs were free. Commercial dealings were placed on a well-understood basis, instead of the former loose way of conducting business; the monopoly of the hong merchants was ended, the fees exacted on ships were abolished, and a tonnage duty of five mace per ton substituted; the charge for pilotage was reduced so much that the pilots were nearly stripped of all they received after paying the usual fees to the tidewaiters along the river. Disputes between English and Chinese were to be settled by the consuls, and in serious cases by a mixed court, when, upon conviction, each party was to punish its own criminals.

The proclamation giving effect to these regulations was one of the most important documents ever issued by the Chinese government; as an initiation of the new order of things, it was creditable to the people whose rulers were of themselves and could utter such words to them. After referring to the war and treaty of peace, Kíying goes on to say, respecting the tariff, that as soon as replies shall be received from the Board of Revenue, "it will then take effect with reference to the commerce with China of all countries, as well as of England. Henceforth, then, the weapons of war shall forever be laid aside, and joy and profit shall be the perpetual lot of all; neither slight nor few will be the advantages reaped by the merchants alike of China and of foreign countries. From this time forward, all must free themselves from prejudice and suspicions, pursuing each his proper avocation, and careful always to retain no inimical feelings from the recollection of the hostilities that have before taken place. For such feelings and recollections can have no other effect than to hinder the growth of a good understanding between the two peoples." It should be moreover added, as due praise to the imperial government, that none of the many hundreds who served the English on ship and shore against their country were afterward molested in any way for so doing. Many were apprehended, but the commissioner says he "has obtained from the good favor of his august sovereign, vast and boundless as that of heaven itself, the remission of their punishment for all past deeds; . . . they need entertain no apprehension of being hereafter dragged forward, nor yield in consequence to any fears or suspicions."[1]

These new arrangements pleased the leading Chinese merchants better than they did the hoppo and others who had lined their pockets and fed their friends with illegal exactions. The never-failing sponge of the co-hong could no longer be sucked, but for a last squeeze the authorities called upon the merchants for five millions of dollars, which they refused to pay, and withdrew from business with so much determination and union that the hoppo and his friends were foiled; they finally contributed among themselves about one million seven hundred thousand dollars, which was nearly or quite their last benevolence to their rulers. Howqua, the leading member of the body during thirty years, died about this time, aged seventy-five; he was, altogether, the most remarkable native known to foreigners, and while he filled the difficult station of senior merchant, exhibited

[1] *Chinese Repository*, Vol. XII., p. 443.

great shrewdness and ability in managing the delicate and difficult affairs constantly thrown upon him. He came from Amoy when a young man, and his property, probably over-estimated at four millions sterling, passed quietly into the hands of his children.[1]

The foreign community also suffered a great loss at this time in the death of John Robert Morrison, at the age of twenty-nine. He was born in China, and had identified himself with the best interests of her people and their advancement in knowledge and Christianity. At the age of twenty, on his father's decease, he was appointed Chinese secretary to the British superintendents, and filled that responsible situation with credit and efficiency during all the disputes with the provincial authorities and commissioner Lin, and of the war, until peace was declared. His intimate acquaintance with the policy of the Chinese government and the habits of thought of its officers eminently fitted him for successfully treating with them, and enlightening them upon the intentions and wishes of foreign powers; while his unaffected kindness to all natives assured them of the sincerity of his professions. The successful conduct of the negotiations at Nanking depended very much upon him, and the manner in which he performed the many translations to and from Chinese, connected with that event, was such as to secure the confidence of the imperial commissioners, in their ignorance of all foreign languages, that they were fairly dealt with.

He was eminently a Christian man, and whenever opportunity allowed, failed not to speak of the doctrines of the Bible to his native friends. The projected revision of the Chinese version of the Scriptures by the Protestant missionaries engaged his attention, and it was expected would receive his assistance. With his influence, his pen, his property, and his prayers, he contributed to the welfare of the people, and the confidence felt in him by natives who knew him was often strikingly exhibited

[1] Compare *The Fan Kwae at Canton before Treaty Days, by an Old Resident* (Mr. W. C. Hunter), London, 1882; a little volume which, besides many personal reminiscences of the characters mentioned in this narrative, furnishes an interesting picture of life in Canton a half century ago.

at Canton during the commotions of 1841 and the negotiations of 1843. He died at Macao August 29th, a year after the treaty of Nanking was signed, and was buried by the side of his parents in the Protestant burying-ground. Sir Henry Pottinger announced his death as a "positive national calamity," and it was so received by the government at home. He also justly added that "Mr. Morrison was so well known to every one, and so beloved, respected, and esteemed by all who had the pleasure and happiness of his acquaintance or friendship, that to attempt to pass any panegyric upon his private character would be a mere waste of words;" while his own sorrow was but a type of the universal feeling in which his memory and merit are embalmed. As a testimony of their sense of his worth, the foreign community, learning that he had died poor, leaving a maiden sister who had been dependent upon him, and that his official accounts were in some confusion, immediately came forward and contributed nearly fourteen thousand dollars to relieve his estate and relatives from all embarrassment.

The negotiations were concluded by the English and Chinese plenipotentiaries signing a supplementary treaty on October 8th (the day was a lucky one in the Chinese calendar), at the Bogue. This treaty provided, among other things, for the admission of all foreigners to the five open ports on the same terms as English subjects; it was inserted at the request of Kíying, that all might appreciate the intentions of his government; for neither he nor his master knew anything of that favorite phrase, "the most favored nation," and expected and wished to avoid all controversy by putting every ship and flag on the same footing.

It might have been expected that the Chinese government would have now taken some action upon the opium trade, which was still going on unchecked and unlicensed. Opium schooners were passing in and out of Hongkong harbor, though the drug sold by the Indian government at Calcutta was not allowed by the colonial British government at Hongkong to be stored on shore. Yet no edicts were issued, few or no seizures made, no notice taken of it; no proposition to repress, legalize, or manage it came from the imperial commissioner. The old laws denouncing its use, purchase, or sale under the penalty of death still remained on the statute book, but no one feared or cared for them. This conduct is fully explained by the supposition that, having undergone so much, the Emperor and his ministers thought safety from future trouble with the British lay in enduring what was past curing; they had already suffered greatly in attempting to suppress it, and another war might be caused by meddling with the dangerous subject, since too it was now guarded by well-armed British vessels. Public opinion was still too strong against it, or else consistency obliged the monarch to forbid legalization.[1]

Sir Henry Pottinger, hearing that persons were about sending opium to Canton under the pretense that unenumerated articles were admissible by the new tariff at a duty of five per cent., issued a proclamation in English and Chinese, to the intent that such proceedings were illegal. He also forbade British vessels going beyond lat. 32° N., and intimated to the Chinese that they might seize all persons and confiscate all vessels found above that line, or anywhere else on the coast besides the five ports; and, moreover, published an order in council which restricted, under penalty of $500 for each offence, all British vessels violating the stipulations of the treaty in this respect. All this was done chiefly to throw dust in their eyes, and put the onus of the contraband traffic on the Chinese government and the violation of law on those who came off to the smuggling vessels, and these proclamations and orders, like their edicts, were to be put "on record." This was shown when Captain Hope, of H.M.S. Thalia, for stopping two or three of the opium vessels proceeding above Shanghai, was recalled from his station and ordered to India, where he could not "interfere in such a manner with the undertakings of British subjects"—to quote Lord Palmerston's despatch to Captain Elliot. This effectually deterred other British officers from meddling with it.

Yet the commercial bearings of this trade were clearly seen in England, and a memorial to Sir Robert Peel, signed by two hundred and thirty-five merchants and manufacturers, was drawn

[1] Montgomery Martin, *China; Political, Commercial, and Social*, Vol. II., Chap. IV. (London, 1847)—a chapter containing some most suggestive reflections on this subject by a member of her Majesty's government at Hongkong.

up, in which they proved that the "commerce with China cannot be conducted on a permanently safe and satisfactory basis so long as the contraband trade in opium is permitted. Even if legalized, the trade would inevitably undermine the commerce of Great Britain with China, and prevent its being, as it otherwise might be, an advantageous market for our manufactures. It would operate for evil in a double way: first, by enervating and impoverishing the consumers of the drug, it would disable them from becoming purchasers of our productions; and second, as the Chinese would then be paid for their produce chiefly as now in opium, the quantity of that article imported by them having of late years exceeded in value the tea and silk we receive from them, our own manufactures would consequently be to a great extent precluded." The memorial shows that between 1803–08 the annual demand for woollens alone was nearly $750,000 more than it was for *all* products of British industry between 1834–39; while in that interval the opium trade had risen from three thousand to thirty thousand chests annually. Nothing in the annals of commerce ever showed more conclusively how heartless a thing trade is when it comes in contact with morality or humanity, than the discussions respecting the opium traffic. These memorialists plead for their manufactures, but the East India Company would have been sorry to have had their market spoiled: what could Sir Robert Peel, or even Wilberforce, if he had been premier, do against them in this matter? The question was which party of manufacturers should be patronized. But none of these "merchants and manufacturers of the highest standing and respectability" refer to the destruction of life, distress of families, waste of mind, body, and property, and the many other evils connected with the growth and use of opium, except as connected with the sale of their goods. One paper, in order to compound the matter, recommended the manufacture of morphine to tempt the Chinese, in order that, if they would smoke it, they might have a delicate preparation for fashionable smokers.

The conduct of the ministry in remunerating the merchants who had surrendered their property to Captain Elliot was appropriate to the character of the trade. The $6,000,000, instead of being divided in China among those who were to receive it —as could have been done without expense—was carried to England to be coined, which, with the freight, reduced it considerably. Then by the manner of ascertaining the market value at the time it was given up, and the holders of the opium script got their pay, they received scarcely one-half of what was originally paid to the East India Company, either directly or indirectly, thereby reducing it nearly a million sterling. Furthermore, by the form of payment they lost nearly one-fifth even of the promised sum, or about one million two hundred thousand dollars. Then they lost four years' interest on their whole capital, or about four million dollars more. What the merchants lost, the government profited. The Company gained during these four years at least a million sterling by the increased price of the drug, while Sir Robert Peel also transferred that amount from the pockets of the merchants to the public treasury. It was an undignified and pitiful haggling with the merchants and owners of the opium, whom that ministry had encouraged for many years in their trade along the Chinese coast, and then forced to take what was doled out.

Public opinion will ever characterize the contest thus brought to an end as an *opium war*, entered into and carried on to obtain indemnity for opium seized, and—setting aside the niceties of western international law, which the Chinese government knew nothing of—most justly seized. Tho British and American merchants who voluntarily subscribed one thousand and thirty-seven chests to Commissioner Lin, acknowledged themselves to be transgressors by this very act. Yet war seemed to be the only way to break down the intolerable assumptions of the court of Peking; that a war would do it was quite plain to every one acquainted with the character of that court and the genius of the people, and the result has shown the expectation to have been well based. Members of Parliament expressed their gratification at being at last out of a bad business; their desire, frequently uttered, that the light of the gospel and the blessings of Christian civilization might now be introduced among the millions of China, was a cheap peace-offering of good wishes, somewhat in the manner of the old Hebrews sacrificing a kid when they had committed a trespass. The short but pithy digest of the whole war by Justin McCarthy, in Chapter X. of the *History of Our Own Times*, brings out its leading features in a fairly candid manner.

The announcement of the treaty of Nanking caused considerable sensation in Europe and America, chiefly in commercial circles. M. Auguste Moxhet, the Belgian consul at Singapore, was sent on to China to make such inquiries for transmission to his government as would direct it in its efforts to open a trade. The Netherlands government sent orders to the authorities at Batavia, who despatched M. Tonco Modderman for the same purpose. The king of Prussia appointed M. Grube to proceed to China to prosecute researches as to the prospect of finding a market for German manufactures. The Spanish ministry, through the authorities at Manila, designated Don Sinibaldo de Mas in this new sphere. The governor of Macao, M. Pinto, before returning home, was appointed commissioner on behalf of H. M. F. Majesty, to treat respecting the rights and privileges of Macao under the new order of things, and succeeded in obtaining some stipulations favorable to the trade of the place, but could not get the Chinese to cede it to Portugal. These gentlemen arrived in China during the latter part of 1843, and most of them had interviews or communication with Kíying before he returned to court in December.

The governments of the United States and France early appointed ministers extraordinary to the court of Peking. Caleb Cushing, commissioner on behalf of the United States, brought a letter from the President to the Emperor, which is inserted in full as an instance of the singular mixture of patronizing and deprecatory address then deemed suitable for the Grand Khan by western nations :

LETTER TO THE EMPEROR OF CHINA FROM THE PRESIDENT OF THE UNITED STATES OF AMERICA.

I, John Tyler, President of the United States of America—which States are: Maine, New Hampshire, Massachusetts, Rhode Island, Connecticut, Vermont, New York, New Jersey, Pennsylvania, Delaware, Maryland, Virginia, North Carolina, South Carolina, Georgia, Kentucky, Tennessee, Ohio, Louisiana, Indiana, Mississippi, Illinois, Alabama, Missouri, Arkansas, and

Michigan—send you this letter of peace and friendship, signed by my own hand.

I hope your health is good. China is a great Empire, extending over a great part of the world. The Chinese are numerous. You have millions and millions of subjects. The twenty-six United States are as large as China, though our people are not so numerous. The rising sun looks upon the great mountains and great rivers of China. When he sets, he looks upon rivers and mountains equally large in the United States. Our territories extend from one great ocean to the other; and on the west we are divided from your dominions only by the sea. Leaving the mouth of one of our great rivers, and going constantly toward the setting sun, we sail to Japan and to the Yellow Sea.

Now, my words are that the governments of two such great countries should be at peace. It is proper, and according to the will of heaven, that they should respect each other, and act wisely. I therefore send to your court Caleb Cushing, one of the wise and learned men of this country. On his first arrival in China, he will inquire for your health. He has strict orders to go to your great city of Peking, and there to deliver this letter. He will have with him secretaries and interpreters.

The Chinese love to trade with our people, and to sell them tea and silk, for which our people pay silver, and sometimes other articles. But if the Chinese and the Americans will trade, there shall be rules, so that they shall not break your laws or our laws. Our minister, Caleb Cushing, is authorized to make a treaty to regulate trade. Let it be just. Let there be no unfair advantage on either side. Let the people trade not only at Canton, but also at Amoy, Ningpo, Shanghai, Fuhchau, and all such other places as may offer profitable exchanges both to China and the United States, provided they do not break your laws nor our laws. We shall not take the part of evil-doers. We shall not uphold them that break your laws. Therefore, we doubt not that you will be pleased that our messenger of peace, with this letter in his hand, shall come to Peking, and there deliver it; and that your great officers will, by your order, make a treaty with him to regulate affairs of trade—so that nothing may happen to disturb the peace between China and America. Let the treaty be signed by your own imperial hand. It shall be signed by mine, by the authority of our great council, the Senate.

And so may your health be good, and may peace reign.

Written at Washington, this twelfth day of July, in the year of our Lord one thousand eight hundred and forty-three. Your good friend.

Mr. Cushing arrived in China in the frigate Brandywine, Commodore Parker, February 24, 1844. The announcement of the general objects of his mission, and the directions he had to proceed to Peking, was made to Governor Ching, who instantly informed the court of his arrival; and with a promptitude indicative of the desire of the Emperor to give no cause of offence, Kíying was reappointed commissioner, with higher powers than before. The frigate had brought out a flagstaff and vane for the consulate at Canton; the vane was in the form of an arrow, and as it turned its barb to the four points of the compass, the superstitious people thought it conveyed destructive influences around, transfixing all the benign operations of heaven and earth, and thereby causing disease and calamity among them. An unusual degree of sickness prevailed at this time in the city and its environs, which the geomancers and doctors declared would not cease until the deadly arrow was removed. The people accordingly waited on the consul, Mr. Forbes, to request the removal of the arrow, which he acceded to, and substituted a vane of another shape. The gentry issued a placard the next day, commending its removal, and requesting the people to harbor no ill-will toward the Americans as the cause of the sickness.

Kíying having announced his appointment and powers to the people, proceeded to the Bogue to meet Sir Henry Pottinger, and be introduced to Governor Davis, from whence he went to Macao and took up his residence in the village of Wanghia, in the suburbs of that city. He had associated three assistants with himself, viz., Hwang Ngăn-tung, Pwan Sz'-shing, one of the late hong merchants, and Chau Chang-ling, a prefect. H. E. Hon. Caleb Cushing was sole commissioner and envoy extraordinary; Fletcher Webster, Esq., was secretary; Rev. E. C. Bridgman, D.D., and Rev. Peter Parker, M.D., were joint Chinese secretaries, and Dr. Bridgman, chaplain; Messrs. J. H. O'Donnell, R. McIntosh, S. Hernisz, T. R. West, and John R. Peters, Jr., were attached to the legation.

Mr. Cushing had already prepared the general outline of the treaty, which greatly abridged the negotiations, and the few disputed or doubtful points in the draft having been modified and settled, it was signed at Wanghia on July 3, 1844, by the two plenipotentiaries, Commodore Parker, and a few other Americans, a large company of Chinese being present. Its fulness of details and clear exhibition of the rights conceded by the Chinese government to foreigners dwelling within its borders, made it the leading authority in settling disputes among them until 1860.

Soon after Kíying left Canton the populace began to show signs of disturbance. A party of gentlemen were walking in the Company's garden, when the gate was burst open by a mob and they were obliged to escape by boats. On the next evening the mob again collected, with the intention of getting possession of the large garden, but were driven out of the passage without much opposition. Two or three Americans, in escorting one of their countrymen to his house, were attacked by missiles on their return; whereupon one of them fired low to drive the people back, but unhappily killed a native, named Sü A-mun. The case was investigated by the district magistrate, and a report made by the governor to Kíying; but Ching took no pains to send a sufficient force to repress the populace. In a communication to the American consul he says, after ordering him to deliver up the murderer: "It has been ascertained that the man who was killed was from the district of Tsingyuen, having no relatives in Canton. But if he had been a citizen, it would have become at the moment an occasion for attack, for it would have been told to the populace, and they would have revenged it by again setting fire to the factories and plundering their contents, or something of that sort. The people are highly irritated against the offender, and it is impossible but that they have constant debates among themselves until they are revenged."

A party of marines from the corvette St. Louis came up to Canton the next day, and quiet was restored. Kíying brought the case before Mr. Cushing, stating it to be his conviction that "the murderer ought to forfeit his life," and begging him to give orders for a speedy examination of the case. In his reply Mr. Cushing expressed his regret at what had occurred, his willingness to institute an inquiry, and added a few remarks upon the necessity of better protecting foreigners at Canton, in order to prevent the recurrence of such scenes, and embroiling the two countries. Kíying replied in a considerate manner, still upholding the authority of his government and laws: "It seems from this that, regarding our nations and their subjects, the people of our land may be peaceful, and the citizens of the United States may be peaceful, and yet, after their governments have become amicable, that then their people may become inimical; and albeit the authorities of the two governments may day after day deliberate upon friendship, it is all nothing but empty words. Thus, while we are deliberating and settling a treaty of peace, all at once the people of our two countries are at odds and taking lives." He also speaks of the overbearing and violent character of the people of Canton:

Since the period when the English brought in soldiers, these ladrones have been banding together and forming societies; and while some, taking advantage of their strength, have plundered and robbed, others have called upon the able-bodied and valiant to get their living. Therefore, employing troops, which is the endangering of the authorities and [peaceable] people, is the profit of these miscreants; peace and good order which traders, both native and foreign, desire, is what these bad men do not at all wish. . . . I have heard that usually the citizens of Canton have respected and liked the officers and people of the United States, as they were peaceable and reasonable; that they would, even when there was a cause of difference, endeavor to settle it, which is very unlike the English. But unexpectedly, on the 16th instant, a cause for animosity was given in the shooting of Sü A-mun. I have heard different accounts of this affair; I judge reasonably in thinking that the merchants of your country causelessly and rashly took life. But the populace are determined to seek a quarrel, and I very much fear lest they will avail of this to raise commotion, perhaps under the pretence of avenging his death, but doubtless with other ideas too.

The American minister referred in a subsequent communication to the death of the boy Sherry, in May, 1841, when the boat's crew from the ship Morrison was captured. This affair had been already brought to the notice of the Chinese government by Commodore Kearny, and a sum of $7,800 paid for losses and damages sustained; but the present was a fitting opportunity for reviving it, since it and the case of Sü A-mun furnished a mutual commentary upon the necessity of securing better protection for foreigners. Kíying made an investigation of the case, and reported the successive actions of his predecessor, Kí Kung; so thoroughly indeed was his reply divested of all the rhodomontade usually seen in Chinese state papers, that one could hardly believe it was written by a governor-general of Canton. The exciting circumstances of the first casualty did indeed go far to extenuate it; though now both Kíying and his superiors could not but see that the time for demanding life for life had passed away. The commissioner was, however, in a dilemma. He could only appease the populace by stating in his proclamations that he was making every effort to ascertain who was the murderer and bring him to justice, and they must leave the management of the case in the hands of the regular authorities. On the other hand, the arguments of Mr. Cushing and the stipulations in the English treaty, both convinced him that foreign nations would not give up their treaty right of judging their own countrymen. He finally escaped the trouble by deferring the petitioners and relatives of the deceased awhile, and then appeasing them by a small donation.

In conducting these negotiations, and settling this treaty "between the youngest and oldest empires in the world," Mr. Cushing exhibited both ability and knowledge of his subject. In his instructions he was directed to deliver the President's letter to the Emperor in person, or to an officer of rank in his presence; and, therefore, on his arrival he informed the governor that he had been sent to the imperial court, and being under the necessity of remaining a few weeks at Macao, he improved the first opportunity to inquire after the health of his Majesty. Whether he regarded the mere going to court as important cannot be inferred from his correspondence, but if so, he should have gone directly to the mouth of the Pei ho and waited there for a commissioner to be sent to meet him. Yet the real advantages of such a proceeding at this time would have been trifling, and its risks and contingencies very serious, as the Emperor was not disposed to forego that homage required of all who appeared before him, however willing he might be to grant commercial privileges, it was undesirable to excite discussions on this point. Moreover, the appointment of Kíying with such unusual powers indicated a favorable disposition toward the Americans. It was fortunate that the two plenipotentiaries were at hand when the riot and homicide occurred, while the discussion which grew out of those events was no small benefit to the local government. The secret of much of the power of the Emperor of China consists in the acknowledgment by his subjects of his sacred character as the Son of Heaven; and although that lofty assumption must come down before the advance of western civilization, and will ere long crumble of itself, to have asked for an audience when this formality was known to be inadmissible would have irritated him, and put the foreign minister in an indefensible position. The subsequent discussions proved how deeply rooted in the Chinese mind was this attribute; the peaceful settlement of the question in 1873 could not have been anticipated in 1844.

The French ambassador, H. E. Th. de Lagrené, arrived in China August 14th. In addition to the two secretaries, MM. le Marquis de Ferrière le Voyer and le Comte d'Harcourt, five other gentlemen were sent out to make investigations into the commerce, arts, and industrial resources of the Chinese. M. de Lagrené took possession of the lodgings prepared for him at Macao, in the same building which Mr. Cushing had occupied. Kíying immediately made arrangements for opening the negotiations by sending his three associates to congratulate the French minister on his arrival; he himself reached Macao September 29th. The gratification of the Chinese statesmen at finding that the missions from the American and French governments were not sent, like the English expedition, to demand indemnity and the cession of an island, was great. Their arrival had been foreshadowed among the people of Canton, the number of ships of war had been exaggerated, and the design of the ambassadors strangely misrepresented as including the seizure of an island. These reports could hardly fail to reach and have some effect upon the highest officers in the land. The time, therefore, was favorable, not merely to obtain the same political and commercial advantages which had been granted to England, but further to explain to the Chinese officers something of the relations their nation should enter into with the other powers of the earth. The first interviews between Kíying and M. de Lagrené were held in October, and the treaty of Wanghia taken as the basis of agreement. The negotiations were amicably settled by the signing of the treaty at Whampoa on October 23d. This act may be said to have concluded the opening of China, so far as its government was prepared for the extension of this intercourse.

The instalments due according to the treaty of Nanking were

not yet all paid, but the Chinese had shown their desire to fulfil their engagements, and the $21,000,000 were received by the English within a short period of the specified time. This was a minor consideration, however, in comparison with the great advantages gained by England for herself and all Christendom over the seclusive and exclusive system of former days, which had now received such a shock that it could not only never recover from it, but was not likely even to maintain itself where the treaties had defined it. The intercourse begun by these treaties went on as fast as the two parties found it for their benefit. The war, though eminently unjust in its cause as an opium war—and even English officers and authors do not try to disguise that the seizure of the opium was the real reason for an appeal to arms, though the imprisonment of Captain Elliot and other acts was the pretext—was still, so far as human sagacity can perceive, a wholesome infliction upon a government which haughtily refused all equal intercourse with other nations, or explanations regarding its conduct, and forbade its subjects having free dealings with their fellow-men.

If in entering upon the conflict England had published to the world her declaration of the reasons for engaging in it, the merits of the case would have been better understood. If she had said at the outset that she commenced the struggle with the Emperor because he would not treat her subjects resorting to his shores by his permission with common humanity, allowing them no intercourse with his subjects, nor access to his officers; because he contemptuously discarded her ambassadors and consular agents, sent with friendly design; because he made foolish regulations (which his own subjects did not observe) an occasion of offence against others when it suited him, and had despoiled them of their property by strange and arbitrary proceedings, weakening all confidence in his equity; lastly, because he kept himself aloof from other sovereigns, and shut out his people from that intercourse with their fellow-men which was their privilege and right; her character in this war would have appeared far better. But it is the prerogative of the Governor of nations to educe good out of evil, and make the wrath, the avarice, and the ambition of men to serve his purposes and advance his own designs, although their intentions may be far otherwise.

The external and internal relations of the Chinese Empire at the close of the year 1844 were in a far better state than one would have supposed they could have become in so short a time after such a convulsion. The cities and provinces where the storm of war had beat most violently were reviving, the authority of the officers was becoming re-established, the bands of lawless desperadoes were gradually dispersing, and the people resuming their peaceful pursuits. No ill-will was manifested in Amoy on account of the losses its citizens had sustained, nor at Ningpo or Shanghai for their occupation by English troops. The English consuls at the five ports had all been received, and trade was commencing under favorable auspices. The opium trade—for this dark feature everywhere forces itself into the prospect—was also extending, and opium schooners plying up and down the coast, and anchoring on the outside limits of every port to deliver the drug.

The citizens of Canton, however, maintained their hereditary ill-will toward foreigners, and proceeded to such lengths that the local government became powerless to carry the stipulation of the British treaty, to enter its city gates, into effect. Governor Davis proceeded to Canton in May, 1847, with several vessels of war, capturing all the guns at the Bogue in his progress up the river, and compelled the authorities to grant a larger space for residences and warehouses on the south side of the Pearl River, to be occupied as soon as arrangements could be made. It was also agreed that the gates should be unconditionally opened within two years, so that foreigners might have the same access to this city as to the other four ports. When the time came for this to be carried out, the Emperor ordered Governor-General Sü to mind the voice of the people and disregard this engagement, which had probably never received his sanction. A careful examination of the Chinese text of all the treaties showed that an explicit permission to enter the citadel (*ching*), or walled portion of the marts opened to foreign commerce, was not given. In consequence of this vagueness the Hongkong authorities, acting under instructions from London, did not press the point, and the gates of Canton remained inviolate till January, 1858.[1]

[1] *Chinese Repository*, Vols. XVIII., pp. 216, 275; XV., p. 46 ff. Davis, *China during the War and since the Peace*, 1852, Vol. II., Chaps. V. and VI., *passim.* Among other authorities on the war may be mentioned Lord Jocelyin, *Six Months with the Chinese Expedition*, London, 1841; K. Stewart Mackenzie, *Narrative of the Second Campaign in China*, London, 1842; Col. Arthur Cunynghame, *Recollections of Service in China*, 1853; Lieut. John Ouchterlony, *The Chinese War*, 1844; *The Last Year in China to the Peace of Nanking*, by a Field Officer, London and Philadelphia, 1843; Auguste Haussmann, *La Chine, résumé historique*, etc., Paris, 1858; Ad. Barrot in the *Revue des Deux Mondes* for February 15, March 1, June 1, and July 1, 1842.

CHAPTER XXIV.

THE TAI-PING REBELLION.

THE war, which was brought to an end by the treaty of Nanking, left the imperial government astonished and crippled, but not paralyzed or dejected. It had, moreover, the effect of arousing it from the old notions of absolutism and security; and though the actual heads of bureaus at Peking were unable, from their secluded position and imperfect education, to ascertain and appreciate the real nature of the contest, the maritime officials could see that its results were likely to be lasting and serious. A few thoughtful men among them, as Ílípu, Seu Kíyu, Kíying and his colleagues, understood better than their superiors at the capital that the advent of the 'Western Ocean people' at the five open ports introduced a permanent influence upon the Black-haired race. They could not, of course, estimate what this influence would become, but a sense of its power and vitality had the effect of preventing them from petty opposition in carrying out the treaty stipulations. With the major part of the officials, on the other hand, life-long prejudice, joined to utter ignorance as to the numbers, position, and resources of foreign nations, led them to withdraw from even such a measure of intercourse with consular and diplomatic officials as they could easily have held. The tone of official society was opposed to having any personal relations with their foreign colleagues, and after the old Emperor Taukwang had passed off the stage in 1850, his son showed—even eight years after the peace—that promotion was incompatible with cultivating a closer acquaintance with them.

It is not surprising that this reaction took on the form of doing as little as possible, and that its stringency was increased in reality by the device of making the governor-general at Canton the only channel of correspondence with foreign ministers. This magnate was surrounded in that city by subordinates whose training had been inimical to extending intercourse with foreigners, because they had reaped the advantages of the old system in their monopoly of the trade. The intendants at the other open ports were directed to refer difficult questions relating to foreigners to this high functionary, but as they were more disposed to let such disputes settle themselves, if possible, few cases were ever sent to him. The animus of the whole governing class gradually assumed a settled determination to keep aloof from those who had humbled them in the eyes of their subjects, and yet give no handle to these potent outsiders to repeat their descent on the coast. It was a poor policy in every point of view, only serving to hasten the evils they dreaded.

Sir John Davis was appointed governor of Hongkong in 1844, and during four years' service so soon after the war saw much of this proud and foolish spirit. His two volumes, published in 1852 (*China during the War and since the Peace*), contain a digest of the official records and acts of the Chinese government which is highly instructive. It is remarkable that he should show so much surprise at the mendacity, ill-will, and weakness of the officers in these reports to their master, or at the Emperor's persistency in wreaking his wrath on those whose poltroonery had done him so much harm. A residence of nearly thirty years in the country should have developed, in his case, an intimate acquaintance with native ideas of honor and mercy, and shown him how little of either are practised in time of war. If he blames the Chinese leaders for their ignorance and silly mistakes in its conduct, one can readily see that they never had an opportunity to learn the truth about their enemies. Their struggle against the impossible was not altogether in vain, therefore, if it prepared them for accepting the inevitable. Had Sir John manifested a little sympathy for their plight in such an unequal contest, and shown more humanity for their sufferings under the evils which afflicted them, his opinion of the best remedies would have carried much weight. As an instance of the result of his own training in the East India Company's school, he remarks respecting the imperial edicts against opium, that they fell into disuse, and that the subject had never been revived since the war; adding, "But at no time was the traffic deserving the full load of infamy with which many were disposed to heap it, for at most it only supplied the poison, which the Chinese were not obliged to take. The worst effect, perhaps, was the piracy it engendered, for this has told against the honest trade."[1] In his first interview with Kiying, in May, 1844, he proposed that the Chinese government should legalize the opium trade, for "such a wise and salutary measure would remove all chances of unpleasant occurrences between the two governments; it might provide an ample revenue for the Emperor, and check to the same extent the consumption of a commodity which was at present absolutely untaxed."[2] He, however, brought it more directly to his notice the next year in consequence of the revival of smuggling at Whampoa to as great a degree as in 1839, and the opium vessels all left the Reach.

Kíying was entirely indisposed to move, or even aid, in this matter, which he knew would be distasteful to the Emperor, other than by a truly Chinese device—that the officials of both nations should let it go on by mutual connivance. Sir John naïvely remarks on this: "The only thing wanting was that the Emperor should publicly sanction what he had once publicly condemned. . . . The trade, however, was practically tolerated, and to us this made a great difference. The Chinese government was not sufficiently honest to make a public avowal of this change in its system, but the position in which Great Britain stood became materially altered. China had distinctly declined a conventional arrangement for the remedy of the evil, and expressed a desire that we should not bring the existing abuse to its notice."[3] With two such men in command, of course nothing was ever done by either side to restrain the evils growing out of this contraband and demoralizing trade, until another war and new treaties changed the national relations.

---

[1] *China during the War*, etc., Vol. I., p. 19.
[2] *Ibid.*, Vol. II., p. 44.
[3] *Ibid.*, Vol. II., p. 203.

At Canton the long-cherished dislike to foreigners was fomented by demagogues and idlers. These worked upon the fears of the people by telling them that their lands were to be taken to build warehouses upon; and this rumor was so far believed that it soon became unsafe for foreigners to venture far into the suburbs. In December, 1847, not long after the arrangement with Sir John Davis respecting an entrance into Canton city was made, six Englishmen were attacked by a mob at Hwang-chuh-kí while on a ramble, and all killed, some of them with refined cruelty. Kíying took immediate measures—extremely creditable to his sense of what he owed to justice and maintenance of peace—to punish these villagers. A number of men whom their fellows indicated as leaders in the outrage were arrested; the prisoners were tried at Canton by the regular courts. Four were presently decapitated in the sight of a military deputation sent from Hongkong, and two others by orders from Peking. This well-timed justice secured the safety of foreigners peaceably going about the city and environs; but it was credibly stated afterward that there were numerous placards already posted in that region informing the people that foreigners would perhaps be coming thither to select sites for themselves. These unfortunate Englishmen, indeed, would perhaps have been allowed to return home, if they had been able to speak to the villagers and explain their object.

This incident makes it proper to notice a common misapprehension abroad in respect to the influence of the treaties which had been signed with China upon the people themselves. It was inferred that as soon as the three treaties with England, France, and America had been ratified, the great body of educated Chinese at least would inquire and learn what were their provisions, and a natural curiosity would be manifested to know something about the peoples of those lands. Nothing could be more likely—nothing was farther from the reality. No efforts were ever made by the imperial officers at the capital or in the provinces to promulgate these national compacts, whose original and ratified copies were never even transmitted to Peking. Consequently, the existence and nature of these *hwo yoh*, or 'peace contracts,' had to be continually taught to the natives, who on their part did not usually feel themselves under much obligation to obey them. In China, as elsewhere, just laws never execute themselves, and it is hardly surprising that not an officer of the Emperor should go out of his way to enforce their distasteful stipulations.

It was therefore uphill work to see that the treaties did not become a dead letter, and all the hardest part of this labor fell to the lot of the British consuls. They alone stood forth among foreign officials as invested with some power of their own; and being generally able to use the Chinese language, they came into personal relations with the local officers, and thus began the only effectual mode through which the treaties could become agencies for breaking down the hoary wall of prejudice, ignorance, and contempt which had so long kept China out of the pale of progress. In doing this, no fixed course could be laid down; though the constant tendency of the consuls was to encroach on the power of the mandarins, these latter were generally able to recur to the treaties, and thus learn the necessity and benefits of adherence to them. Their education was a colossal undertaking, and considering the enormous difficulties, its progress has been as rapid as was consistent with the welfare of themselves or their subjects. In this progress they bear the greatest share of the burden; its responsibilities and costs, its risks and results, almost wholly come upon them, while foreign nations, with the immense undefined rights of exterritoriality on their side, are interested on-lookers, ready to take advantage of every *faux pas* to compel them to conform to their interpretation of the treaties. Very little consideration is given to their ignorance of international law, to their full belief in the power of China, or to their consequent disinclination to accept the new order of things so suddenly forced on them. On the other hand, no one who knows all the features of this period will withhold the praise due to the British authorities in China for their conduct in relations with its functionaries; it might fairly be added that the improved state of international intercourse is mostly due to them.

The condition of the Empire at the close of the war was most discouraging to its rulers, who had not dreamed of receiving so crushing a defeat. It is creditable to them that they honorably paid up the $21,000,000 exacted of them by the British, who of course restored Chusan at the stipulated time. The name of R. Montgomery Martin, then treasurer of Hongkong colony, must be awarded due mention as being the only Queen's official who endeavored to resist its surrender, on the plea of its great benefit to her eastern empire and influence. Sir John Davis speaks of the "political and military considerations" which gave importance to it; but the proposal of Mr. Martin was promptly rejected by his superiors, and the whole archipelago has since been neglected. At the four northern ports opened by treaty, with the exception of Fuhchau, trade began without difficulty. This city having entirely escaped the ravages of the war, its proud gentry influenced the citizens against foreigners and their trade; the first European residents there met with some ill-usage, but this bitter feeling gradually wore off as the parties became better known.

At Canton the case was aggravated by the prejudices of race and the turbulence of the unemployed braves who had flocked into it on the invitation and inducements of Commissioner Lin to enlist against the English. They had been disbanded by Kiying, but had not returned to their homes; their lawlessness increased till it threatened the supremacy of the provincial government, and required the strongest measures of repression. The disorders spread rather than diminished under an impoverished treasury and ill-paid soldiery, and prepared the way for the rebellion which during the next twenty years tasked the utmost resources of the nation. The ignorance of one part of its people of what was taking place in another province—which during the foreign war so greatly crippled the Emperor's efforts to interest his subjects in this struggle—here did much to preserve them from uniting against him to his overthrow. It was plain to every candid observer that however weak, unprincipled, and tyrannical the Manchu rulers might be, they were as efficient sovereigns as the people could produce, and no substituted sway could possibly elevate and purify them until higher principles of social and political life had been adopted by the nation at large.

The protracted convulsion, known abroad as the Tai-ping

Rebellion, owed much of its duration as well to the exposure of the government's internal rottenness as to its weakness against foreign nations; but many other causes were at work. The body of the Chinese people are well aware that their rulers are no better than themselves in morals, honesty, or patriotism; but they are all ready to ascribe the evils they suffer from robbers, taxation, exactions, and unjust sentences to those in authority. The rulers are conscious that their countrymen consider it honorable to evade taxes, defy the police when they can safely do so, and oppose rather than aid in the maintenance of law and order. There is no basis of what in Christian lands is regarded as the foundation of social order and just government—the power of conscience and amenableness to law; nevertheless, from the habits of obedience taught in the family and in the schoolroom, the people have attained a good degree of security for themselves and show much regard to just rulers. The most serious evils and sufferings in Chinese society are caused by its disorderly members, not its rapacious rulers; and both can only be removed and reformed by the reception of a higher code which raises the standard of action from expediency to obligation.

In giving an account of the rise and overthrow of the Tai-ping Rebellion, it will be necessary to limit the narrative to the most important religious, political, and military events connected with it up to its suppression in 1867. The phrase "Tai-ping Rebellion" is wholly of foreign manufacture; at Peking and everywhere among those loyal to the government the insurgents were styled *Chang-mao tseh*, or 'Long-haired rebels,' while on their side, by a whimsical resemblance to English slang, the imperialists were dubbed *imps*. When the chiefs assumed to be aiming at independence in 1850, in order to identify their followers with their cause they took the term *Ping Chao*, or 'Peace Dynasty,' as the style of their sway, to distinguish it from the *Tsing Chao*, or 'Pure Dynasty,' of the Manchus. Each of them prefixed the adjective *Ta* (or *Tai*, in Cantonese), 'Great,' as is the Chinese custom with regard to dynasties and nations; thus the name *Tai-ping* became known to foreigners. The leader took the style *Tien-teh*, or 'Heavenly Virtue,' for his reign, thereby indicating his aim in seeking the throne. His own personal name, Hung Siu-tsuen, was regarded as too sacred to be used by his followers. The banners and edicts used at Nanking and in his army bore the inscription, *Tien-fu*, *Tien-hiung*, *Tien-wang Tai-ping Tien-kwoh*, or 'Heavenly Father, Heavenly Elder Brother, Heavenly King of the Great Peace [Dynasty] of the Heavenly Kingdom' (*i.e.*, China).

The incidents of this man's early life and education were ascertained in 1854, from his relative Hung Jin, by the Rev. Theodore Hamberg, whose narrative[1] bears the marks of a trustworthy recital. Hung Siu-tsuen was the youngest son of Hung Jang, a well-to-do farmer living in Hwa hien, a district situated on the North River, about thirty miles from Canton city, in a small village of which he was the headman. The family was from Kiaying prefecture, on the borders of Kiangsi, and the whole village was regarded as belonging to the Hakkas, or Squatters, and had little intercourse with the Pun-tis, or Indigenes, on that account. Siu-tsuen was born in 1813, and at the usual age of seven entered school, where he showed remarkable aptitude for study. His family being too poor to spare his services long, he had to struggle and deny himself, as many a poor aspirant for fame in all lands has done, in order to fit himself to enter the regular examinations. In 1826 his name appeared on the list of candidates in Hwa hien, but Hung Jin says: "Though his name was always among the first upon the board at the district examinations, yet he never succeeded in attaining the degree of Siu-tsai." In 1833 he was at Canton at the triennial examination, when he met with the native evangelist Liang A-fah, who was distributing and selling a number of his own writings near the Kung yuen to the candidates as they went in and out of the hall. Attracted by the venerable aspect of this man, he accepted a set of his tracts called *Kiuen Shí Liang Yen*, or 'Good Words to Exhort the Age.' He took them home with him, but threw them aside when he found that they advocated Christianity, then a proscribed doctrine.

In 1837 he was again in the provincial tripos, where his re-

---

[1] *Visions of Hung Siu-tshuen and Origin of the Kwang-sí Insurrection*, Hongkong, 1854. Mr. W. Sargent in the *North American Review* for July, 1854, Vol. LXXIX., p. 158.

peated disappointment and discontent aggravated an illness that seized him. On reaching his home he took to his bed and prepared for death, having had several visions foretokening his decease. He called his parents to his bedside and thus addressed them: "My days are counted and my life will soon be closed. O my parents! how badly have I returned the favor of your love to me; I shall never attain a name that shall reflect lustre on you." After uttering these words he shut his eyes and lost all strength and command over his body, and became unconscious of what was going on around him. His outward senses were inactive, his body appeared as dead, but his soul was acted upon by a peculiar energy, seeing and remembering things of a very extraordinary nature.

At first, when his eyes were closed he saw a dragon, a tiger, and a cock enter the room; a great number of men playing upon instruments then approached, bearing a beautiful sedan-chair in which they invited him to be seated. Not knowing what to make of this honor, he was carried away to a luminous and beautiful place wherein a multitude of fine men and women saluted him on arrival with expressions of joy. On leaving the sedan an old woman took him down to a river, saying: "Thou dirty man, why hast thou kept company with yonder people and defiled thyself? I must now wash thee clean." After the washing was over he entered a large building in company with a crowd of old and virtuous men, some of whom were the ancient sages. Here they opened his body, took out the heart and other organs, and replaced them by new ones of a red color; this done, the wound closed without leaving a scar. The whole assembly then went on to another larger hall, whose splendor was beyond description, in which an aged man, with a golden beard and dressed in black robes, sat on the highest place. Seeing Siu-tsuen, he began to shed tears and said: "All human beings in the world are produced and sustained by me; they eat my food and wear my clothing, but not one among them has a heart to remember and venerate me; what is worse, they take my gifts and therewith worship demons; they purposely rebel against me and arouse my anger. Do thou not imitate them." Hereupon he gave him a sword to destroy the demons, a seal to overcome the evil spirits, and a sweet yellow fruit to eat. Siu-tsuen received them, and straightway began to exhort his venerable companions to perform their duties to their master. After doing so even to tears, the high personage led him to a spot whence he could behold the world below, and discern the horrible depravity and vice of its inhabitants. The sight was too awful to be endured, and words were inadequate to describe it. So he awoke from his trance, and had vigor enough to rise and dress himself and go to his father. Making a bow, Siu-tsuen said: "The venerable old man above has commanded that all men shall turn to me, and that all treasures shall flow to me." This sickness continued about forty days, and the visions were multiplied. He often met with a man in them whom he called his elder brother, who instructed him how to act and assisted him in going after and killing evil spirits. He became more and more possessed with the idea, as his health returned, that he had been commissioned to be Emperor of China; and one day his father found a slip on which was written "The Heavenly King of Great Reason, the Sovereign King Tsuen." As time wore on, this lofty idea seems to have more and more developed his mind to a soberness and purity which overawed and attracted him. Nothing is said about his utterances while the war with England was progressing, but he must have known its progress and results. His cataleptic fits and visions seem not to have returned, and he pursued his avocation as a school-teacher until about 1843, having meanwhile failed in another trial to obtain his degree at Canton. In that year his wife's brother asked to take away the nine tracts of Liang A-fah to see what they contained; when he returned them to Siu-tsuen he urged him to read them too.

They consisted of sixty-eight short chapters upon common topics, selected from the Bible, and not exactly fitted to give him, in his excited state and total ignorance of western books and religion, a fair notion of Christianity. As he read them he saw, as he thought, the true meaning of his visions. The venerable old man was no other than God the Father, and his guide was Jesus Christ, who had assisted him in slaying the demons. "These books are certainly sent purposely by heaven to me to confirm the truth of my former experience. If I had received them without having gone through the sickness, I should not have dared to believe in them, and by myself to oppose the customs of the whole world. If I had merely been sick, but not also received the books, I should have had no further evidence as to the truth of my visions, which might also have been considered as mere products of a diseased imagination."

This sounds reasonable, and commends itself as wholly unlike the ravings of a madman. Nevertheless, while it would be unwise for us to closely criticise this narrative in its details, and assert that Siu-tsuen's pretensions were all hypocritical, we must bear in mind the fact that he had certainly, neither at this time nor ever afterward, a clear conception of the true nature of Christianity, judging from his writings and edicts. The nature of sin, and the dominion of God's law upon the sinner; the need of atonement from the stain and effects of sin; Christ's mediatorial sacrifice; were subjects on which he could not possibly have received full instruction from these fragmentary essays. In after days his conviction of his own divine calling to rule over China, seems to have blinded his understanding to the spiritual nature of the Christian church. His individual penchant was insufficient to resist or mould the subordinates who accepted his mission for their own ends. But he was not a tool in their hands at any time, and his personal influence permeated the ignorant mass of reckless men around him to an extraordinary degree, while his skill in turning some of the doctrines and requirements of the Bible as the ground and proofs of his own authority indicated original genius, since the results were far beyond the reach of a cunning impostor. From first to last, beginning with poverty, obscurity, and weakness in Hwa, continuing with distinction, power, and royalty at Nanking and throughout its five adjacent provinces, and ending with defeat, desertion, and death in his own palace, Hung never wavered or abated one jot of his claim to supreme rule on earth. When his end was reported at Peking in August, 1864, thirty-one years after his receiving Liang A-fah's tracts, the imperial rescript sadly said: "Words cannot convey any idea of the misery and desolation he caused; the measure of his iniquity was full, and the wrath of both gods and men was roused against him."

A career so full of exceptional interest and notable incidents cannot, of course, be minutely described in this sketch. After Hung's examination of the tracts which had lain unnoticed in his hands for ten years, followed by his conviction of the real meaning of his visions in 1837, he began to proclaim his mission and exhort those around him to accept Christianity. Hung Jin (who furnished Mr. Hamberg with his statements) and a fellow-student, Fung Yun-shan, were his first converts; they agreed to put away all idols and the Confucian tablet out of their schools, and then baptized or washed themselves in a brook near by, as a sign of their purification and faith in Jesus. As they had no portion of the Sacred Scriptures to guide them, they were at a loss to understand many things spoken of by Liang A-fah, but his expositions of the events and doctrines occurring in them were deeply pondered and accepted. The Mosaic account of creation and the flood, destruction of Sodom, sermon on the Mount, and nature of the final judgment, were given in them, as well as a full relation of Christ's life and death; and these prepared the neophytes to receive the Bible when they got it. But the same desire to find proof of his own calling led Siu-tsuen to fix on fanciful renderings of certain texts, and, after the manner of commentators in other lands, to extract meanings never intended. A favorite conceit, among others, was to assume that wherever the character *tsuen*, 全, meaning 'whole,' 'altogether,' occurred in a verse, it meant himself, and as it forms a part of the Chinese phrase for *almighty*, he thus had strong reasons (as he thought) for his course. The phrase *Tien kwoh*, denoting the 'Kingdom of Heaven' in Christ's preaching, they applied to China. With such preconceived views it is not wonderful that the brethren were all able to fortify themselves in their opinions by the strongest arguments. All those discourses in the series relating to repentance, faith, and man's depravity were apparently entirely overlooked by them.

The strange notions, unaffected earnestness, moral conduct, and new ideas about God and happiness of these men soon began to attract people to them, some to dispute and cavil, others to accept and worship with them. Their scholars, one and all, deserted them as soon as the Confucian tablet was removed from the schoolroom, and they were left penniless and unemployed, sometimes subjected to beatings and obloquy for embracing an outlandish religion, and other times ridiculed for forsaking their ancestral halls. The number of their adherents was too few to detain them at home, and in May, 1844, Siu-tsuen, Yun-shan, and two associates resolved to visit a distant relative who lived near the Miaotsz' in Kwangsí, and get their living along the road by peddling ink-stones and pencils. They reached the adjoining district, Tsingyuen, where they preached two months and baptized several persons; some time after Hung Jin took a school there, and remained several years, baptizing over fifty converts. Siu-tsuen and Yun-shan came to the confines of the Miaotsz' in Sinchau fu in three months, preaching the existence of the true God and of redemption by his Son, and after many vicissitudes reached their relative's house in Kwei hien among the mountains. Here they tarried all summer, and their earnest zeal in spreading the doctrines which they evidently had found so cheering to their own hearts, arrested the attention of these rude mountaineers, and many of them professed their faith in Christ. Siu-tsuen returned home in the winter, and was disappointed in not finding his colleague Yun-shan there as well as the other two, nor could he give any account of his course. It appeared afterward that Yun-shan had met some acquaintances on his road, and became so much interested in preaching to them at Thistle-mount that he remained there two years, teaching school and gathering churches.

Siu-tsuen continued to teach and preach the truth as he had learned it from the books in his hands. In 1846 he heard of I. J. Roberts, the American missionary, living at Canton, and the next spring received an invitation to come there and study. He and Hung Jin did so; the former remained with Mr. Roberts about two months, giving him a narrative of his own visions, conversion, and preaching, at the same time learning the nature and extent of foreign mission work in that city. He made a visit home with two native Christians, who had been sent to Hwa to learn more about him. They seem to have obtained good reports of his character; but others in Mr. Roberts' employ were afraid of his influence if he should enter their church, and therefore intrigued to have him refused admission just then. Mr. Roberts appears to have acted discreetly according to the light he had respecting the applicant's integrity, and would no doubt have baptized him had not the latter soon after left Canton, where he had no means of support. At this time the political disturbances in Kwangtung seem to have greatly influenced Siu-tsuen's course, and when he reached home he made a second visit to his relative, and thence went to Thistlemount to rejoin Fung Yun-shan. Hung Jin states that before this date he had expressed disloyal sentiments against the Manchus, but these are so common among the Cantonese that they attracted no notice. On seeing Yun-shan and meeting the two thousand converts he had gathered, it is pretty certain that hopes of a successful resistance must have revived in his breast. A woman among them also began to relate some visions she had seen ten years before, foretelling the advent of a man who should teach them how to worship God. The number of converts rapidly increased in three prefectures adjacent to the River Yuh in the eastern part of Kwangsí, and no serious hindrance was met with from the officials, though there were not wanting enemies, by one of whom Yun-shan was accused and then thrown into prison. However, the prefect and district magistrate to whom the case was referred, finding no sufficient cause for punishment, liberated him; though the new sectaries had made themselves somewhat obnoxious to the idolaters by their iconoclasm—so hard is it to learn patience and toleration in any country. In very many villages in that region the *Shangtí hwui*, or 'Associations for worshipping God,' began to be recognized, but they do not seem to have quoted the toleration edict obtained in 1844 in favor of Christianity, as that only spoke of the *Tien-chu kiao*, or Catholics. The worship of Shangtí is a peculiar function of the Emperor, as has been already explained; and it is not surprising to be told by Hung Jin that the new sect was regarded as treasonable.

In 1848 Siu-tsuen's father died trusting in the new faith and directing that no Buddhist services be held at his funeral; the whole family had by this time become its followers, and when the son and Yun-shan met them soon after, they began to discuss their future. The believers in Kwangsí were left to take care of themselves during the whole winter, and appear to have gone on with their usual meetings without hindrance. In June, 1849, the two leaders left Hwa for Kwangsí, assisted by the faithful, and found much to encourage them in their secret plans in the general unity which pervaded the association. Some members had been favored with visions, others had become exhorters, denouncing those who behaved contrary to the doctrines; others essayed to cure diseases. Siu-tsuen was immediately acknowledged by all as their leader; he set himself to introduce and maintain a rigid discipline, forbade the use of opium and spirits, introduced the observance of the Sabbath, and regulated the worship of God. No hint of calling in the aid of a foreign teacher to direct them in their new services appears to have been suggested by any member, nor even of sending to Canton to engage the services of a native convert, though Liang A-fah was still living then. The whole year was thus passed at Thistle-mount, and the nucleus of the future force thoroughly imbued with the ideas of their leader, who had, by June, 1850, gathered around him his own relatives and chosen his lieutenants.[1]

The existence of such a large body of people, acting together under the orders of one man, whose aspirations and teachings had gradually filled their minds with new ideas, could not remain unnoticed by the authorities. The governor-general lived at Canton, and received his information through local magistrates and prefects, whose policy was rather to understate the truth. But Sü Kwang-tsin felt that he was not fitted for the coming struggle. His place was therefore filled by the appoint-

[1] The insurgents cut off the tail, allowed their hair to grow, and decided that all who joined the insurrectional movement should leave off the *chang* and the Tartar tunic, and should wear the robe open in the front, which their ancestors had worn in the time of the Mings.—Callery and Yvan, *History of the Insurrection in China*, translated by John Oxenford, p. 61. London, 1853.

ment of Lin, then living in Fuhchau, who started to fulfil his new charge, but died in October, as he entered the province. Governor Sü was obliged to leave Canton on duty, but he never met the enemy nor returned to his post. The populace of the city made themselves merry over his violent conduct toward a poor paper-image maker near the landing, who had just set out to dry some effigies dressed in high official costume, each one lacking a head. Sü chose to regard this proceeding as an intentional insult, as the artisan must have known that he was to pass by that way, and ordered him to be bambooed and his effigies destroyed to neutralize the bad omen. The Peking government had just sent three Manchus to superintend operations in Kwangsí; their predecessors, Lí and Chau, with the provincial governor, Ching, were all degraded, but these new imperial officials did no better, nor did those on the spot expect that they would succeed. Tahungah was the ruffian who had executed one hundred and eighty British prisoners in Formosa nine years before; and Saishangah was the prime minister of the young Emperor Hienfung, as worthless as he was depraved. Uruntai, who had long been in command of the Manchu garrison at Canton, was also sent, in May, 1851, to check the growing power of the insurgents. They were well posted in Wusiuen hien, near the junction of two rivers, and this chieftain naïvely expresses his surprise in his report to the Emperor that the rebels should occupy an important post which he had just decided to fortify. However, his official report[1] explains the reasons for the imperial reverses better than anything which had hitherto appeared. Corruption, venality, idleness, opium-smoking, and peculation had made the whole army a mass of rottenness; no one can wonder that the Tai-pings marched without danger through the land to their goal at Nanking.

A year previous to this date, however, the conflict had been begun by the followers of Siu-tsuen. In their zeal against idolatry they had destroyed temples and irritated the people, which ere long aroused a spirit of distrust and enmity; this was further increased by the long-standing feud and mutual hatred

---

[1] *Chinese Repository*, Vol. XX., p. 493.

between the *pun-tis* and *hakkas* (natives and squatters) which ran through society. Siu-tsuen and his chiefs were mostly of the latter class, and whenever villages were attacked and the hakkas worsted, they moved over to Thistle-mount and professed to worship Shangtí with Siu-tsuen. In this way the whole population had become more or less split up into parties. When a body of imperial soldiers sent to arrest him and Yun-shan were driven off, they availed themselves of the enthusiasm of their followers to gather them and occupy Lienchu, a large market-town in Kwei hien. This proceeding attracted to their banner all the needy and discontented spirits in that region, but their own partisans were now able to regulate and employ all who came, requiring a close adherence to their religious tenets and worship. This town of Lienchu was soon fortified, and the order of a camp began to appear among its possessors, who, however, spared the townspeople. The drilling of the force, now increased to many thousands, commenced; its vitality was soon tested when it was deemed best to cross the river and advance on Taitsun in order to obtain more room. The imperialists were hoodwinked by a simple device, and when they found their enemy had marched off, their attack on the rear was repulsed with much loss. Like all their class, they turned their wrath on the peaceful inhabitants of Lienchu, killing and burning till almost nothing was left. This needless cruelty recoiled on themselves, and all the members of the *Shangtí hwui*, loyal and disaffected alike, felt that their very name carried sedition in it, and they must join Siu-tsuen's standard or give up their faith. He had induced some recent comers belonging to the Triad Society to put their money into the military chest and to submit to his rules. One of his religious teachers had been detected embezzling the funds while on their way to the commissariat, but the public trial and execution of the man had served both as a warning and an encouragement to the different classes who witnessed the affair. Most of the Triad chiefs, however, were afraid of such discipline, and drew off to the imperialists with the greater number of their followers. The defection furnished Siu-tsuen an opportunity to make known his settled opposition to this fraternity, and that every man joining his party must leave it. At this time the discipline and good order exhibited in the encampment at Taitsun must have struck the people around it with surprise and admiration, if the meagre accounts we have received are at all trustworthy.

About one year elapsed between the conflict near Lienchu and the capture of Yung-ngan chau, a city on the River Mei in Pingloh prefecture. During this period Siu-tsuen had become more and more possessed with the idea of his divine mission from the *Tien-fu*, or 'Heavenly Father,' as God was now commonly called, and the *Tien-hiung*, or 'Heavenly Elder Brother,' as he termed Jesus Christ. He began to seclude himself from the gaze of his followers, and deliver to them such revelations as he received for the management of the force committed to him to clear the land of all idolatry and oppression, and cheer the hearts of those pledged to the glorious cause. This course was destructive of all those peculiar tenets which Christianity teaches, and, so far as can be learned, neither he nor Yun-shan any longer prominently set forth the doctrines of salvation by repentance and faith in Christ, as they had done in their first journey among the Miaotsz', but held their followers together by fanaticism and the hope of final triumph. In its main features, his course was copied from that of Moses and Aaron when they withdrew into the tabernacle, and it was easy to impress upon his uninstructed followers the repetition in his person of the same mode of making known the will of Heaven. An adequate reason can also be found in this scheme why he never called in the aid of foreign missionaries to teach his followers the truth as it is in Christ Jesus, knowing full well that none of them would lend any countenance to such delusion. As early as April, 1849, when still in Kwei hien, he began to promulge his decrees in the form of revelations received from the Heavenly Father and Elder Brother, when one or the other came down into the world to tell him what course he should pursue. In March, 1853, just before capturing Nanking, he issued a book of "Celestial Decrees," containing a series of these revelations, from which the real nature of his character can be learned. Two extracts will be sufficient to quote:

The Heavenly Father addressed the multitude, saying, O my children! Do you know your Heavenly Father and your Celestial Elder Brother? To which they all replied, We know our Heavenly Father and Celestial Elder Brother. The Heavenly Father then said, Do you know your Lord, and truly? To which they all replied, We know our Lord right well. The Heavenly Father said, I have sent your Lord down into the world to become the Celestial King (*Tien-wang*); every word he utters is a celestial command; you must be obedient; you must truly assist your Lord and regard your King; you must not dare to act disorderly, nor to be disrespectful. If you do not regard your Lord and King, every one of you will be involved in difficulty.[1]

It is only from these official documents that we can learn the real political and religious tenets of the revolutionists now intrenched at Yung-ngan, and soon to burst forth in fury upon their country. It was in vain to expect gospel figs from such a bramble bush.

Another extract exhibits their jugglery still more clearly. It is dated December 9, 1851, and contains the proceedings and sentence in the case of Chau Sih-nang, who had been detected holding intercourse with General Saishangah at Taitsun. Four of the kings were that day consulting upon some weighty matters, when suddenly the Heavenly Father came down among them and secretly told them to instantly arrest Chau and two others and bring them to Yang, the Eastern King, while he returned to heaven. They did so, and reported the matter to the Tien-wang, but none of them had any evidence to proceed upon. "Happily, however, the Heavenly Father gave himself the trouble to appear once more," and ordered two of the royal cousins to go and inform the several princes of his presence. They all attended at court and entreated the Heavenly King to accompany them. Hereupon, his Majesty, guarded by the princes and body-guards, together with a host of officials, advanced into the presence of the Heavenly Father. They all kneeled down and asked, "Is the Heavenly Father come down?" He replied, addressing the Tien-wang, "Siu-tsuen, I am going to take this matter in hand to-day; a mere mortal would find it a hard task. One Chau has been holding collusive commu-

[1] This decree bears the date April 19, 1851, at Tung-hiang, a village near Wusiuen.

nication with the enemy yesterday, and has returned to court, intending to carry into effect a very serious revolt. Go and bring him here." The culprit soon came, and the examination is reported in full. In answer to the question, "Who is it that is now speaking to you?" he replied, "The Heavenly Father, the Supreme Lord and Great God (Shangti) is addressing me." He said soon after, "I am aware that the Heavenly Father is omnipotent, omniscient, and omnipresent." By a series of questions his guilt was proved, and he and his accomplices, with his wife and son, were all put to death as a warning to traitors, in presence of a large concourse, to whom they confessed the justice of their fate.

When in possession of Nanking, Hung Siu-tsuen was formally proclaimed by his army to be Emperor of China, and assumed the style and insignia of royalty. Five leading chiefs were appointed to their several corps as South, East, West, North, and Assistant Kings; Fung Yun-shan was the Southern King. Who among them were the efficient disciplinarians and leading minds in carrying on their plan cannot be now ascertained, so complete was the secrecy which enveloped the whole movement from first to last as to the *personnel* of the force. Dr. Medhurst's translations of their orders, tenets, laws, revelations, and text-books furnish the most authentic sources for estimating its character, but they fail to describe its living agents. In so large an army, composed of the most hotorogoncous elements, it cannot be expected that there would be at any time much knowledge of the sacred Scriptures, on which its leaders based their assumed powers derived from the 'Heavenly Father and Elder Brother;' but there certainly was a remarkable degree of sobriety and discipline among them during the first few years of their existence. A most perplexing question, which increased in its urgency and difficulty as soon as opposition drove the rebel general to intrench himself at Lienchu, was temporarily arranged by forming a separate encampment for the women, and placing over them officers of their own sex to see that discipline was maintained. In doing this he allowed the married people as great facilities for the care of their children as was possible under the conditions of army life; but during their progress through the land in 1852 and 1853, much suffering must have been endured.

In 1852 the state and size of the army in Yung-ngan fully authorized the leaders of the revolt to march northward. Several engagements had given their men confidence in each other as they saw the imperialists put to flight; defeats had furthermore shown that their persevering enemy entertained no idea of sparing even one of them if captured. The want of provisions during their five months' siege within its walls further trained them to a certain degree of patient endurance; when, therefore, they broke through the besieging force in three divisions on the night of April 7, 1852, they were animated by success and hope to possess themselves of the Empire. Marching north they now attacked Kweilin, the provincial capital, May 15th, but having no cannon fit to besiege a walled city of that size, crossed the border and captured Tau in Hunan, which gave them access to the River Siang and means of transportation. Their course was thenceforth an easy conquest of the towns along its valley. Kweiyang chau, Chin chau, Tunghing, Nganjin, and others were taken and evacuated, one after the other, until they reached the capital of this province, September 18th. Changsha and Siangtan together form one immense city, and its defenders fully understood their peril, and the probability of entire destruction if they allowed it to be captured. For eighty days the Tai-pings exerted themselves in vain to obtain possession, losing, however, very few men, and doing no great harm to their enemy, who kept beyond reach. December 1st they raised the siege, and by the 13th reached Yohchau on the Yangtsz', which was taken without a struggle. Ten days after, replenished and encouraged by the spoil found in Yohchau, they occupied Hanyang and Wuchang, the capital of Hupeh province, lying on the other side of the river. Its garrison was unable to escape, and many soldiers were destroyed. Hwangchau and Kiukiang, two prefect cities lower down, were captured January 12th and February 18th, while Nganking, the capital of Nganhwui, fell a week later. Nothing seemed able to resist the advance of the insurgents, and on March 8th they encamped before Nanking. It was garrisoned by

Manchus and Chinese, who, however, made no better defence than their comrades in other cities; in ten days its walls were breached, and all the defenders found inside put to death, including Luh, the governor-general of the province. Chinkiang and Yangchau soon were dragged to the same fate, thus depriving the imperialists of their control of the Grand Canal.

This rapid progress through the land since leaving Yung-ngan eleven months previously had spread consternation among the demoralized officers and soldiers of the Emperor, who, on his part, was as weak and ignorant as any of his subordinates. The march of the insurgents showed the utter hollowness of the imperial troops, the incapacity of their most trusted leaders, and the little interest taken by the great body of the nation in the conflict. Many causes which might adequately explain this extraordinary success cannot now be ascertained, but a national dislike of the Manchus on the part of the Chinese lay at the bottom of their coldness. They felt, too, that a government which could not protect them against a few thousand foreign troops might as well give place to a native one. The insurgents had perhaps not more than ten thousand adherents, including women and children, when they left Yung-ngan;[1] but these went forth in the full conviction of the heavenly commission of their leader to destroy idolatry, set up the worship of the true God, and inaugurate the kingdom of heaven in the person of the "Heavenly King." The term *Shangti* was known by every schoolboy to be the name of the God worshipped at Peking by the Emperor in his right as Son of Heaven, and the successor of the ancient sovereigns mentioned in the *Shu King;* accordingly, when the insurgents set up the worship of the true God as they had been able to learn it from Gutzlaff's revised version of the Bible, their countrymen immediately recognized the challenge. It was an attack on the religious as well as political position of Taukwang; whoever maintained his side in the gage of battle, with him were undoubtedly the powers above. The progress of the new banner

[1] Though one of their officers told Mr. Meadows, at Nanking, that the force was about three thousand.

from Yung-ngan to Nanking was like that of a fiery cross, and the sufferings of the people, except in a few large cities, were really more owing to the savage imperialists than to the Tai-pings. The latter grew in strength as they advanced, owing to indiscriminate slaughter on the part of their enemies of unoffending natives, and at last reached their goal with not much less than eighty thousand men.

Their position was now accessible to foreigners—who had been watching their rise and progress under great disadvantages in arriving at the truth—and they were soon visited by them in steamers. The first to do so was Governor Bonham in H. M. S. Hermes, accompanied by T. T. Meadows, one of the most competent linguists in China, who published the result of his inquiries. The visitors were at first received with incredulity, but this soon gave way to eager curiosity to learn the real nature of their religious views and practices. The insurgents themselves were even more ignorant of foreigners than were these of the rebels, so that the interest could not fail to be reciprocal, nor could either party desire to come into collision with the other.

About two months after the cities of Nanking, Chinkiang, and Yangchau had been taken, garrisoned, and put in a state of defence by their inhabitants, working under the direction of Tai-ping officers, the leaders felt so much confidence in their cause, their troops, and their ability, that they despatched a division to capture Peking. No particulars of its size or composition are given, but its course and achievements are recorded in the *Peking Gazette*. The force landed not far from Kwachau, where it defeated a body of Manchus, and then proceeded to Liuho and Fungyang fu without finding serious opposition. Crossing the province of Nganhwui, they entered that of Honan, and in one month from landing the troops laid siege to Kaifung, the provincial capital, June 19th. Three days later they were repulsed, and their leaders crossed the Yellow River to Hwaiking fu, about a hundred miles west of Kaifung. For two months they were baffled by an unusual resistance on the part of the imperialists, and were compelled to leave it and go west into Shansí, where they took Pingyang fu and flanked the enemy by turning east and north-east till they crossed the Liu-ming pass and got into Chihlí. It was their design to have gone down the River Wei to Lintsing chau on the Grand Canal, but they were compelled to make a detour of some hundreds of miles to reach this last place. In doing so they ascended the steep defiles leading from the basin of the Yellow River to the plateau in South Shansí. This march was accomplished in the month of September, and on October 9th the prefect city of Shinchau in Chihlí, only two hundred miles from Peking, was taken. Their army remained at Shinchau for a fortnight, when they marched across the plain north-easterly to Tsinghai hien, on the Grand Canal. Here they intrenched themselves on October 28th, but twenty miles south of Tientsin. A detachment sent to attack that city was repulsed, and the whole body were blockaded on November 3d by the Manchu force, which had followed it from Hwaiking, and other corps ordered from the north to intercept its progress toward the capital. In six months this insurgent force had traversed four provinces, taken twenty-six cities, subsisted themselves on the enemy, and defeated every body of imperialists sent against them. The men who performed this remarkable march of fully one thousand five hundred miles in the face of such odds, would have accomplished even greater deeds under better training. Considering all things, it is quite equal to General Sherman's march to the sea in 1864; yet so little is known of the details of this feat, that we are not even certain of its leader's name—whether Lin Fung-tsiang, spoken of by the *Gazette* as a 'Pretended Minister,' or some other general, was in command.

It is rather hard to understand why the Tai-pings intrenched themselves so near to Tientsin, but the officials of that city, in 1858, ascribed it to the fact that water covered the plain, preventing all operations against the town. Perhaps their want of siege guns, and the cavalry now brought from Mongolia, decided the leaders to intrench themselves at Tsinghai and send to Nanking for reinforcements. The Tai-ping Wang immediately despatched an auxiliary force, which also crossed Nganhwui to Funghien on the north bank of the Yellow River; this place was captured March 17, 1854, "after taking city after city," as the Emperor Hienfung expressed it. The ice was gone when the army reached Lintsing chau, April 12th, and that city was taken by a fierce assault against the combined resistance of its garrison and the imperialists outside, after the insurgent auxiliary was attacked in force. The other body had left Tsinghai in February, starved out rather than driven away, and gone to the district town of Hien, which they left March 10th for Fauching, and probably rejoined their comrades somewhere between that and Lintsing. They were about a hundred miles apart, and the intervening region was no doubt forcibly drained of its supplies. This joint army remained in possession of their depots as long as they saw fit, and treated the inhabitants reasonably well, among whom there were no Manchus. The inability to understand each other's speech kept the people of this district from mixing with the southerners, and, combined with the impossibility of keeping open the road to Nanking, decided the Tai-pings to return. This they did in March, 1855, by re-entering Nganhwui and rejoining the main body whereever ordered; but no details are known of their movements for nearly a year before that date. Peking and the Great Pure dynasty were saved, however; while the failure of Hung Siutsuen to risk all on such an enterprise proved his ignorance of the real point of this contest. He never was able to undertake a second campaign, and his followers soon degenerated into banditti.

The possession of Nanking, Chinkiang, and Kwachau, with the large flotilla along the Yangtsz' River west to Íchang in Hupeh, a distance of over six hundred miles, had entirely sundered the Emperor's authority over the seven south-eastern provinces. The country on each side for fifty or one hundred and fifty miles was visited by the insurgents' troops merely for supplies. Their boats penetrated to Nanchang in Kiangsí, went up the River Siang even beyond Changsha in Hunan, ravaged one town after another in quest of provisions and reinforcements, which were either taken to Nanking or used to support the crews; but nowhere did the leaders set up anything like a government, nowhere did they secure those who submitted or pursued their avocations quietly any protection against imperialist or other foes. As a revolution involving a reorganization of the Chinese nation on Christian principles, and a well-defined assertion of the rights and duties of rulers and subjects, it had failed entirely within a year after the possession of Nanking. There was no hope that any of the leaders in the movement would develop the ability to initiate the establishment of a consistent and suitable control, since not one of them was endowed either with the experience necessary to introduce provisional government over conquered communities, or with that tact calculated to impress their inhabitants with enduring confidence in them. All their prisoners were compelled to work or fight in their service, and were willing to earn their food and clothes; while in obeying such orders, and going through such religious ceremonies as were told them, they of course had not much to complain of; but this conduct did not imply hatred of the mandarins or an abjuration of Buddhism.

During the three years after Nanking had been occupied, the people in the Yangtsz' valley had suffered much from the conflict. Both armies lived on the land, and the danger of resisting the demands for food, clothes, and animals was nearly equalled by that of joining the contending forces; in either case beggary or loss of life was sure to be the end. As an instance of by no means unexampled suffering, the populous mart of Hankow and its environs was taken by assault six different times during the thirty months ending in May, 1855, and finally was left literally a heap of ruins. In country places the imperialists were, of the two parties, perhaps the more terrible scourge, but as the region became impoverished each side vied with the other in exhausting the people. The Tai-pings were gradually circumscribed to the region around Nanking and Nganking by the slow approaches of the government troops, and in 1860 seemed to be near their end. The interest which had been aroused at Shanghai in 1853, upon hearing of their Christian tenets and organization, had been satisfied in the various visits of foreign functionaries to Nanking, the intercourse with the leaders and men, perusal of their books, and observation of their policy.

One inherent defect in the enterprise, when viewed in its political bearing, ere long showed itself. Nothing could induce Hung Siu-tsuen to lead his men to the north and risk all in an attack on Peking. His own conviction of his divine mission had been most cordially received by his generals and the entire body of followers which left Yung-ngan in 1852; but their faith was not accepted by the enormous additions made to the Tai-pings as they advanced to Nanking, and gradually the original force became so diluted that it was inadequate to restrain and inspirit their auxiliaries. Moreover, the Tien-wang had never seriously worked out any conception of the radical changes in his system of government, which it would be absolutely necessary to inaugurate under a Christian code of laws. Having had no knowledge of any western kingdom, he probably regarded them all as conformed to the rules and examples given in the Bible; perhaps, too, he trusted that the "Heavenly Father and Elder Brother" would reveal the proper course of action when the time came. The great body of literati would naturally be indisposed to even examine the claims of a western religion which placed Shangtí above all other gods, and allowed no images in worship, no ritual in temples, and no adoration to ancestors, to Confucius, or to the heavenly bodies. But if this patriotic call to throw off the Manchu yoke had been fortified by a well-devised system of public examinations for office—modified to suit the new order of things by introducing more practical subjects than those found in the classics—and had been put into practice, it is hard to suppose that the intellectual classes would not gradually have ranged themselves on the side of this rising power. The unnecessary cruelty and slaughter practised toward the Manchu garrisons and troops carried more dread into the hearts of the population than stimulus to co-operate with such ruthless revolutionists. The latter had weakened their prospects by destroying confidence in their moderation, justice, and ability to carry out their aim to establish a new sway. There was a large foundation of national aspirations and real dislike to the present dynasty, on which the Tien-wang could have safely reckoned for help and sympathy. But he was far from equal to the exigency of his opportunity. The doubts of his countrymen as to his competency were proved by the satisfaction and relief felt when his movement collapsed.

When the remnants of the two corps which returned from the north in 1855 were incorporated into the forces holding the Grand Canal and the Liang Kiang province, their outposts hardly extended along the Great River beyond Chinkiang on the east and Nganking on the west. In that year dissensions sprung up among the leaders themselves inside of Nanking, which ended in the execution of Yang, the Eastern King, the next year; a fierce struggle maintained by Wei, the Northern King, on behalf of the Tien-wang, upheld his supremacy, but at a loss of his best general. Another man of note, Shih Ta-kai, the Assistant King, losing faith in the whole undertaking, managed to withdraw with a large following westward, and reached Sz'chuen. The early friend of Hung Siu-tsuen, Fung Yun-shan, known as the Southern King, disappeared about the same time. Rumors of these conflicts reached Shanghai in such a contradictory form that it was impossible to learn all their causes.

One source of strife arose by Yang assuming to be the Holy Ghost. Receiving communications from the Heavenly Father and Elder Brother, he thus placed himself above the Tien-wang, and, it is said by Wilson,[1] "required him to humble himself and receive forty lashes" for some misdemeanors complained of by the Comforter. The notices of this man which have reached us show that he early took a prominent part in the movement, and perhaps manipulated "descents of the Heavenly Father," like the one referred to above as mentioned in the "Book of Declarations" in the case of Chau Sih-nang.[2] Many proclamations were issued in his name on the progress to Nanking, which set forth the principles under which the Heavenly Dynasty were trying to conquer. Incentives addressed to the patriotic feelings of the Chinese were mixed up with their obligations to worship Shangtí, now made known to them as the Great God, our Heavenly Father, and security promised to all who submitted.

[1] *The "Ever-Victorious Army," Lt.-Col. Gordon's Chinese Campaign*, p. 43.

[2] J. Milton Mackie, *Life of Tai-ping-Wang, Chief of the Chinese Insurrection*, Chap. XXXIV., New York, 1857.

In one sent forth by him when nearing Nanking, he thus summarizes the rules which guided the Tai-pings:

I, the General, in obedience to the royal commands, have put in motion the troops for the punishment of the oppressor, and in every place to which I have come the enemy, at the first report, have dispersed like scattered rubbish. As soon as a city has been captured, I have put to death the rapacious mandarins and corrupt magistrates therein, but have not injured a single individual of the people, so that all of you may take care of your families and attend to your business without alarm and trepidation. I have heard, however, that numbers of lawless vagabonds are in the villages, who previous to the arrival of our troops take advantage of the disturbed state of the country to defile mens' wives and daughters, and burn or plunder the property of honest people. . . . I have therefore especially sent a great officer, named Yuen, with some hundreds of soldiers, to go through the villages, and as soon as he finds these vagabonds he is commissioned forthwith to decapitate them; while if the honest inhabitants stick up the word *shun* ['obedient'] over their doors, they will have nothing to fear.[1]

Such manifestoes could not reassure the timid population of the valley of the Yangtsz', and the carnage of the unresisting Manchus in Nanking, Chinkiang, and elsewhere indicated a ruthless license among the followers of the Tien-wang, which made them feel that their success carried with it no promise of melioration. In addition, as the vast spoil obtained from these cities and towns up to 1856 was consumed, the outlook of the rebels was most discouraging. Among their forces, the disheartened, the sick, and the wounded, with the captived and desperate, soon died, deserted, or skulked, and their places were filled by forced levies. Under these circumstances the dissensions within the court at Nanking imperilled the whole cause, and showed the incapacity of its leaders in face of their great aim. Yang had sunk into a sensual, unscrupulous faction leader who could no longer be endured; by October, 1856, he and all his adherents, to the number of twenty thousand, were utterly cut off by Wei. But this latter king speedily met with a like fate. Shih, the Assistant King, was at this time in the province of Kiangsí. It had become a life struggle with Siu-tsuen, and his removal of the four kings resulted in leaving him without any real military chief on whose loyalty he could depend. The rumors which

[1] Lindley, *Tai-ping Tien-kwoh*, Vol. I., p. 94.

reached Shanghai in 1856 of the fierce conflict in the city were probably exaggerated by the desire prevalent in that region that the parties would go on, like the Midianites in Gideon's time, beating down each other till they ended the matter.

The success of the Tai-pings had encouraged discontented leaders in other parts of China to set up their standards of revolt. The progress of Shih Ta-kai in Sz'chuen and Kweichau engaged the utmost efforts of the provincial rulers to restore peace. In Kwangtung a powerful band invested the city, but the operations of Governor Yeh, after the departure of Sü Kwang-tsun in 1854, were well supported by the gentry. By the middle of 1855 the rising was quenched in blood. The destruction of Fatshan, Shauking, and other large towns, had shown that the sole object of the rebels was plunder, though it was thought at first that they were Tai-pings. The executions in Canton during fourteen months up to August, 1856, were nearly a hundred thousand men; but the loss of life on both sides must be reckoned by millions. A band of Cantonese desperadoes seized the city of Shanghai in September, 1853, killing the district magistrate and some other officials. They retained possession till the Chinese New Year, January 27, 1854, leaving the city amid flames and carnage, when many of the leaders escaped in foreign vessels.[1] None of these men were affiliated with the Tai-pings.

In Formosa and Hainan, as well as in Yunnan and Kansuh, the provincial authorities had hard work with their local contingents to maintain the Emperor's authority. This wretched prince was himself fast bound under the sway of Suhshun and his miserable coterie, devising means to replenish his coffers by issuing iron and paper money, and proposing counters cut out of jade stone to take the place of bullion. The national history, however, had many notices of precisely such disastrous epochs in former times, and the nation's faith in itself was not really weakened.

By 1857 the imperialists had begun to draw close lines about

---

[1] No foreigners here or elsewhere in China were injured designedly during all this insurrection.

the rebels, when they were nearly restricted to the river banks between Nganking and Nanking, both of which cities were blockaded. Two years later the insurgent capital was beleaguered, but in its siege the loyalists trusted almost wholly to the effects of want and disease, which at last reached such an extreme degree (up to 1860) that it was said human flesh was sold on the butchers' stalls of Nanking. Their ammunition was nearly expended, their numbers were reduced, and their men apparently desirous to disperse; but the indomitable spirit of the leader never quailed. He had appointed eleven other *wang*, or generals, called *Chung Wang* ('Loyal King'), *Ying Wang* ('Heroic King'), *Kan Wang* ('Shield King'), *Ting Wang* ('Listening King'), etc., whose abilities were quite equal to the old ones. As the siege progressed events assumed daily a more threatening aspect. Chang Kwo-liang and Ho Chun, two imperialist generals, invested the city more and more closely, driving the insurgents to extremity in every direction. The efforts of these men were, however, not aggressive in consequence of the war then waging with the British and French on the Pei ho. This encouraged the beleaguered garrison to a desperate effort to free themselves, and on May 6, 1860, a well-concerted attack on the armies which had for years been intrenched behind outworks about the city scattered them in utter disorder. A small body of Tai-pings managed to get out toward the north of Kiangsu, near the Yellow River. Another body had already (in March) carried Hangchau by assault by springing a mine; as many as seventy thousand inhabitants, including the Manchu garrison, perished here during the week the city remained in possession of the rebels. On their return to Nanking the joint force carried all before it, and the needed guns and ammunition fell into their hands. The loyalist soldiers also turned against their old officers, but the larger part had been killed or dispersed. Chinkiang and Changchau were captured, and Ho Kwei-tsing, the governor-general, fled in the most dastardly manner to Suchau, without an effort to retrieve his overthrow. Some resistance was made at Wusih on the Grand Canal, but Ho Chun was so paralyzed by the onslaught that he killed himself, and Suchau fell into the hands of Chung Wang with no resistance whatever.

It was, nevertheless, burned and pillaged by the cowardly imperialists before they left it, Ho Kwei-tsing setting the large suburbs on fire to uncover the solid walls. This destruction was so unnecessary that the citizens welcomed the Tai-pings, for they would at least leave them their houses. With Suchau and Hangchau in their hands, the Kan Wang and Chung Wang had control of the great watercourses in the two provinces, and their desire now was to obtain foreign steamers to use in regaining mastery of the Yangtsz' River. The loss of their first leaders was by this time admirably supplied to the insurgents by these two men, who had had a wider experience than the Tien-wang himself, while their extraordinary success in dispersing their enemies had been to them all an assurance of divine protection and approval.

The populous and fertile region of Kiangnan and Chehkiang was wholly in their hands by June, 1860, so far as any organized Manchu force could resist them. The destruction of life, property, and industry within the three months since their sally from Nanking had been unparaleled probably since the Conquest, more than two centuries before, and revived the stories told of the ruthless acts of Attila and Tamerlane. Shanghai was threatened in August by a force of less than twenty thousand men led by the Chung Wang, and it would have been captured if it had not been protected by British and French troops. Many villages in the district were destroyed, but the flotilla approaching from Sungkiang recoiled from a collision with foreigners, and the insurgents all retired before September. They, however, could now be supplied with munitions of war, and even began to enlist foreigners to help them drill and fight. It was an anomalous condition of things, possible only in China, that while the allied force was marching upon Peking to extort a treaty, the same force was encircling the walls of Shanghai, burning its suburbs to destroy all cover, and aiding its rulers to preserve it to Hienfung—all in order to conquer a trade. It was then the moment for the Tai-pings to have moved rapidly upon Chihlí and tried the gage of battle before the metropolis, as soon as possible after Lord Elgin had withdrawn. But they had now very few left to them of the kind of troops which threatened the capital in 1853–54, and could not depend on recruits from Kiangnan in the hour of adversity.

At this juncture the imperialists began to look toward foreigners for aid in restoring their prestige and power by employing skill and weapons not to be found among themselves. An American adventurer, Frederick G. Ward, of Salem, Mass., proposed to the Intendant Wu to recapture Sungkiang from the Tai-pings; he was repulsed on his first attempt at the head of about a hundred foreigners, but succeeded on the second, and the imperialists straightway occupied the city. This success, added to the high pay, stimulated many others to join him, and General Ward ere long was able to organize a larger body of soldiers, to which the name of *Chang-shing kiun*, or 'Ever-victorious force,' was given by the Chinese; it ultimately proved to be well applied. Its composition was heterogeneous, but the energy, tact, and discipline of the leader, under the impulse of an actual struggle with a powerful foe, soon moulded it into something like a manageable corps, able to serve as a nucleus for training a native army. Foreigners generally looked down upon the undertaking, and many of the allied naval and military officers regarded it with doubt and dislike. It had to prove its character by works, but the successive defeats of the insurgents during the year 1862 in Kiangsu and Chehkiang, clearly demonstrated the might of its trained men over ten times their number of undisciplined braves.

But we must retrace our steps somewhat. In 1860 the possession of the best parts of Kiangsu and Chehkiang led the Tien Wang to plan the relief of Nganking by advancing on Hankow with four separate corps. They were under the leadership of the Chung Wang, and, so far as the details can be gathered, manifested a practical generalship hardly to be expected. The Ying Wang was to move through Nganhwui from Luchau westerly to Hwangchau; the Attendant King (Shih) was to leave Kiangsí and co-operate with the Chung Wang by reaching the Yangtsz' as near Hankow as possible, and a smaller force under the Tu Wang was to recover Hukau at the mouth of Poyang Lake and ascend the Great River in boats. The area through which this campaign was to be carried on may be understood when we learn that the Chung Wang's march of five hundred miles was over the two ranges of mountains on the frontiers of Kiangsí, and that of the Ying Wang two hundred miles through the plains of Nganhwui. This last king did act ually take his force of about eighty thousand men two hundred miles to Hwangchau (fifty miles below Hankow) in eleven days, but none of his colleagues came to his aid. The experience of eight years had quite changed the elements of the contest.

The people now generally realized that neither life, property, nor government was secured under the Tai-pings; the imperialists had learned how to obtain the co-operation of the patriotic gentry, and the rank and file of the Tai-pings were by this date mostly conquered natives of the same region, as no recruits had ever come from Kwangsí. Moreover, the region was impoverished, and this involved greater privations to all parties. Yet the Chung Wang went from Wuhu south-west to Kwangsin, crossed the water-shed into Kiangsí, defeated a force at Kienchang, crossed the River Kan near Linkiang, and marched north-west to Wuning hien on the River Siu. Here be heard of the defeat of Tu Wang, and the non-arrival of Shih's force; and, lest he should be hemmed in himself, as the failure of the campaign was evident, he led his army back across the province to Kwangsin by September, 1861. The particulars of this last great exploit of the Tai-pings are so imperfectly known, that it is impossible to judge of it as a military movement accomplished under enormous difficulties; but the Loyal King must have been a strategist of no mean rank.

In November, 1861, Nganking succumbed to the imperialists. Its defenders and the citizens endured untold sufferings at the last, while its victors had an empty shell; but the river was theirs down to Nanking. On his return east, Chung Wang moved into Chehkiang and overran all the northern half of that province, his men inflicting untold horrors upon the inhabitants, whom they killed, burned, and robbed as they listed. Ningpo was taken December 9th and held till May 10th, when it was recaptured by the allies; foreign trade had not been interrupted during this period, and the city suffered less than many others. In September the Tai-pings were driven out of the valley of the Yung River, but the death of General Ward at Tsz'kí deprived the imperialists of an able leader. The career of this man had been a strange one, but his success in training his men was endorsed by honorable dealing with the mandarins, who had reported well of him at Peking. He was buried at Sungkiang, where a shrine was erected to his memory, and incense is burned before him to this day.

It was difficult to find a successor, but the command rather devolved on his second, an American named Burgevine, who was confirmed by the Chinese, but proved to be incapable. He was superseded by Holland and Cooke, Englishmen, and in April, 1863, the entire command was placed under Colonel Peter Gordon, of the British army. During the interval between May, 1860, when Ward took Sungkiang, and April 6, 1863, when Gordon took Fushan, the best manner of combining native and foreign troops was gradually developed as they became more and more acquainted with each other and learned to respect discipline as an earnest of success. Such a motley force has seldom if ever been seen, and the enormous preponderance of Chinese troops would have perhaps been an element of danger had they been left idle for a long time.

The bravery of the Ever-victorious force in the presence of the enemy had gradually won the confidence of the allies, as well as the Chinese officials, in whose pay it was; and when it operated in connection with the French and British contingent in driving the Tai-pings out of Ningpo prefecture, the real worth of Ward's drill was made manifest. The recapture of that city by Captain Dew's skilful and brave attack in reply to their unprovoked firing at H. M. S. Encounter, brought out the bravery of all nationalities, as well as restored the safety of the port. An extract from Captain Dew's report will exhibit the dreadful results to the common people of this civil war:

I had known Ningpo in its palmy days, when it boasted itself one of the first commercial cities of the Empire; but now, on this 11th of May, one might have fancied that an angel of destruction had been at work in the city as in the suburbs. All the latter, with their wealthy hongs and thousands of houses, lay levelled; while in the city itself, once the home of half a million of people, no trace or vestige of an inhabitant could be seen. Truly it was a city of the dead. The rich and beautiful furniture of the houses had become firewood, or was removed to the walls for the use of soldiers. The canals were filled with dead bodies and stagnant filth. The stonework of bridges and pavements had been uplifted to strengthen walls and form barricades in the streets; and in temples once the pride of their Buddhist priests, the chaotic remains of gorgeous idols and war gods lay strewn about—their lopped limbs showing that they had become the sport of those Christian Tai-pings whose chief, the Tien-wang. eight years before at Nanking, had asked Sir George Bonham if the Virgin Mary had a pretty sister for him, the King of Heaven, to marry! It has been my good fortune since to assist at the wresting of many cities from these Tai-pings, and in them all I found, as at Ningpo, that the same devilish hands had been at work—the people expelled from their houses and their cities ruined.[1]

Yet so speedy was the revival from the ruins, that we are told that in one month houses had been refurnished and shops opened; their owners had mostly fled across the river into the foreign settlement. A larger force was now organized—MM. Le Brethon and Giquel being in charge of a Franco-Chinese regiment—and an advance made on Yüyau, which was retaken, and one thousand drilled Chinese left to defend it. Tsz'kí, Funghwa, and Shangyü were also cleared of rebels, and during the month of March they evacuated the prefect city of Shauhing, never again to return to this fertile valley. Their inroad had been an unmitigated scourge, for they had now given up all pretense of Christianity, and had not the least idea of instituting a regular government; to plunder, kill, and destroy was their only business. Their sense of danger from the hatred of the people whom they had so grievously maltreated led them at this time to defend the walled cities with a reckless bravery that made their capture more difficult and dangerous. This was shown in the siege of Shauhing fu, within whose walls about forty thousand Tai-pings were well led by the Shí Wang. The possession of cannon enabled them to reply to the balls thrown by Captain Dew's artillery, while despair lent energy to their resistance; so that the attack turned into a regular siege of a month's duration, when, food and ammunition being exhausted, they retreated *en masse* to Hangchau.

While this success relieved the greater part of Chehkiang from the scourge, the failure of the Ever-victorious force to

---

[1] A. Wilson, *The "Ever-Victorious Army,"* p. 102, London, 1868.

retake Taitsang and Fushan, under Holland and Brennan, had discouraged Governor Lí, who had now come into power. He applied to General Stavely, who, with a full appreciation of the exigencies of the case, and concurrence of Sir Frederick Bruce, aided in reorganizing Ward's force and placing Colonel Gordon over it with adequate powers. There were five or six infantry regiments of about five hundred men each, and a battery of artillery; at times it numbered five thousand men. The commissioned officers were all foreigners, and their national rivalries were sometimes a source of trouble; the non-commissioned officers were Chinese, many of them repentant rebels or seafaring men from Canton and Fuhkien, promoted for good conduct. The uniform was a mixture of native and foreign dress, which at first led to the men being ridiculed as 'Imitation Foreign Devils;' after victory, however, had elevated their *esprit du corps*, they became quite proud of the costume. In respect to camp equipage, arms, commissariat and ordnance departments, and means of transport, the natives soon made themselves familiar with all details; while necessity helped their foreign officers rapidly to pick up their language. It is recorded, to the credit of this motley force, that "there was very little crime and consequently very little punishment; . . . as drunkenness was unknown, the services of the provost-marshal rarely came into use, except after a capture, when the desire for loot was a temptation to absence from the ranks."[1]

In addition, the force had a flotilla of four small steamers, aided by a variety of native boats to the number of fifty to seventy-five. The plain is so intersected by canals that the troops could be easier moved by water than land, and these boats enabled it to carry out surprises which disconcerted the rebels. Wilson well remarks concerning Gordon's force: "Its success was owing to its compactness, its completeness, the quickness of its movements, its possession of steamers and good artillery, the bravery of its officers, the confidence of its men, the inability of the rebels to move large bodies of troops with

---

[1] Wilson, *ibid.*, p. 132.

rapidity, the nature of the country, the almost intuitive perception of the leader in adapting his operations to the nature of the country, and his untiring energy in carrying them out."[1]

The details of this singular troop are worth telling with more minuteness than space here allows, for its management will no doubt form a precedent in the future; but the good its remarkable chief effected in restoring peace to Kiangsu calls for that recognition which skill, tact, and high moral purpose ever deserve. Being formally put in command on March 24, 1863, he promptly reinstated the foreign officers belonging to the force, paid their dues, and within a few days was in readiness to march upon Fushan, a town on the Yangtsz' above Paushan. The fall of this place on April 6th led to the capture of Chanzu, when preparations were made for besieging Taitsang fu, where an army of ten thousand rebels, aided by foreign adventurers, presented a formidable undertaking for his force of two thousand eight hundred men, although supported by a large body of imperialists. In its capture (May 2d) the killed and wounded numbered one hundred and sixty-two officers and men; the booty obtained was so large that Colonel Gordon led his men back to Sungkiang, in order to reorganize them after this experience of their conduct. Finding that their former license in appropriating the loot thus obtained tended to demoralize them all, he accepted the resignations of some of the discontented officers, and adopted stringent measures to bring the others to render military obedience. Consequently, when he started for Kunshan with about three thousand men, he had his force in a much better condition. This city occupied an important position between Shanghai, Chanzu, Taitsang, and other large towns on the east, and Suchau on the west. The rebels had set up a cannon foundry within its walls, and from it obtained supplies for the last-named city, with which it was connected by a causeway. By means of the armed steamer Hyson, Colonel Gordon was able to bring up through one of the canals a company of three hundred and fifty men and field artillery, cutting the causeway and pursuing its defenders, some

[1] *Ibid.*, p. 138.

into the town and some toward Suchau, almost to its very gates. On the return of the steamer in the night, the commander found the imperialists engaged with the garrison in a sharp contest, in which the foreigners then aided, and completely routed the rebel body of nearly eight thousand men. Fully four thousand of them were killed outright, and others were drowned or cut off by the exasperated peasantry before the day was over. This was on May 30th. The captured town was made headquarters by its victors, as a more eligible location than Sungkiang, though against the wishes of the native officers, who desired to go back there with their booty. The loss of men, material, and position to the rebels was very great, and Colonel Gordon could now safely turn his whole thoughts to the capture of Suchau.

This city is like Venice in its approaches by canals; owing to its location it was deemed best, before attempting its capture, to reduce certain towns in the vicinity, from which it derived supplies, so that the Chung Wang should not be able to co-operate with its garrison. The district towns of Wukiang and Kahpu were both taken in July with comparatively little loss. This rapid reduction of many strong stockades, stone forts, and walled towns, with the panic exhibited by the men, proved how useless to the rebels the foreigners in their service had been in rendering them really formidable enemies, and how incapable the wangs had been to appreciate the nature and need of discipline. After these places had been occupied, Colonel Gordon found his position beset with so many unexpected annoyances, both from his rather turbulent and incongruous troops as well as from the Chinese authorities, that he went to Shanghai on August 8th for the purpose of resigning the command. Arriving here, however, he ascertained that Burgevine had just gone over to the Tai-pings with about three hundred foreigners, and was then in Suchau. The power of moral principle, which guided the career of the one, was then seen in luminous contrast to its lack as shown in the other of these soldiers of fortune. To his lasting credit Colonel Gordon decided to return at once to Kiunshan, and, in face of the ingratitude of the Chinese and jealousy of his officers, to stand by the imperialist cause. He gradually restored his influence over officers and men, ascertained that Burgevine's position in the Tai-ping army did not allow him freedom enough to render his presence dangerous to their foes, and began to act aggressively against Suchau by taking Patachiau on its southern side in September.

Emissaries from the foreigners in the city now reported considerable dissatisfaction with their position, and Colonel Gordon was able to arrange in a short time their withdrawal without much danger to themselves. It is said that Burgevine even then proposed to him to join their forces, seize Suchau, and as soon as possible march on Peking with a large army, and do to the Manchus what the Manchus had done, two hundred and twenty years before, to the Mings. Colonel Gordon's own loyalty was somewhat suspected by the imperialist leaders, but his integrity carried him safely through all these temptations to swerve from his duty.

As soon as these mercenaries among the rebels were out of the way, operations against Suchau were prosecuted with vigor, so that by November 19th the entire city was invested and carefully cut off from communication with the north. The city being now hard pushed, the besieging force prepared for a night attack upon a breach previously made in the stockade near the north-east gate. It was well planned, but the Muh Wang, *facile princeps* among the Tai-ping chiefs in courage and devotion, having been informed of it, opened such a destructive fire that the Ever-victorious force was defeated with a loss of about two hundred officers and men killed and wounded. On the next morning, however (November 28th), it was reported that the cowardly leaders in the city were plotting against the Muh Wang—the only loyal one among their number—and were talking of capitulating, using the British chief as their intermediary.

This rumor proved, indeed, to be so far true, that after some further successful operations on the part of Gordon's division, the Wangs made overtures to General Ching, himself a former rebel commander, but long since returned to the imperial cause and now the chief over its forces in Kiangsu. The Muh Wang was publicly assassinated on December 2d by his comrades, and on the 5th the negotiations had proceeded so far that interviews were held. Colonel Gordon had withdrawn his troops a short distance to save the city from pillage, but did not succeed in obtaining a donation of two months' pay for their late bravery from the parsimonious Lí. He therefore proposed to lay down his command at three o'clock P.M., and meanwhile went into the city to interview the Na Wang, who told him that everything was proceeding in a satisfactory manner. Upon learning this he repaired to the house of the murdered Muh Wang in order to get his corpse decently buried, but failed, as no one in the place would lend him the smallest assistance. While he was thus occupied, the rebel wangs and officers had settled as to the terms they would accept; and on reaching his own force, Gordon found General Ching there with a donation of one month's pay, which his men refused.

The next morning he returned into the city and was told by Ching that the rebel leaders had all been pardoned, and would deliver up the city at noon; they were preparing then to go out. Colonel Gordon shortly after started to return to his own camp and met the imperialists coming into the east gate in a tumultuous manner, prepared for slaughter and pillage. He therefore went back to the Na Wang's house to guard it, but found the establishment already quite gutted; he, however, met the Wang's uncle and went with him to protect the females of the family at the latter's residence. Here he was detained by several hundred armed rebels, who would neither let him go nor send a message by his interpreter till the next morning (December 7th), when they permitted him to leave for his boat, then waiting at the south gate; narrowly escaping, on his way thither, an attack from the imperialists, he reached his bodyguard at daybreak, and with them was able to prevent any more soldiers entering the city. His preservation amid such conflicting forces was providential, but his indignation was great when he learned that Governor Li had beheaded the eight rebel leaders the day before. It seems that they had demanded conditions quite inadmissible in respect to the control of the thirty thousand men under their orders, and were cut off for their insolent contumacy. Another account, published at

Shanghai in 1871, states that nearly twenty chiefs were executed, and about two thousand privates.

As Colonel Gordon felt that his good name was compromised by this cruelty, he threw up his command until he could confer with his superiors. On the 29th a reply came to Lí Hung-chang from Prince Kung, highly praising all who had been engaged in taking Suchau, and ordering him to send the leader of the Ever-victorious force a medal and ten thousand taels—both of which he declined. The posture of affairs soon became embarrassing to all parties. The rebellion was not suppressed; the cities in rebel hands would soon gather the desperate men escaped from Suchau; Colonel Gordon alone could lead his troops to victory; and all his past bravery and skill might be lost. He therefore resumed his command, and presently recommenced operations by leading his men against Íhing hien, west of Suchau.

Concerning this wretched business of the Suchau slaughter, much was said both in the foreign communities in China and later in England. Mr. Wilson, in his book compiled largely from Colonel Gordon's notes on this campaign, discusses the question with as great fairness as precision, and concludes—as must every well-wisher of China with him—that it was in every way fortunate, both for his reputation and the cause to which he had lent himself, that this heroic man returned to his thankless task. Summing up the arguments of the Chinese and the various attendant circumstances that brought about this execution, Mr. Wilson points to Lí's not unnatural desire after revenge for his brother's murder by the rebels before Taitsang; to the army still under control of the wangs; to the almost absolute certainty of massacre of those imperialists who had already entered the city should he refuse compliance with their demands; as also to the impossibility of arresting these chiefs without an alarm of treachery spreading among their troops within the walls, and thus giving them time to close the gates, cutting off the imperial soldiers inside the city from those who were without. "Lí was in a very difficult and critical position," he says, "which imperatively demanded sudden, unpremeditated action; and though, no doubt, it would have been more honorable for him to have made the wangs prisoners, he cannot in the circumstances be with justice severely censured for having ordered the Tai-ping chiefs who were in his power, but who defied his authority, to be immediately killed. It is also certain that Colonel Gordon need not have been in a hurry to consider himself as at all responsible for this almost necessary act, because in a letter to him (among his correspondence relating to these affairs) from the Futai [Li], dated November 2, 1863, I find the following noteworthy passage, which shows that the governor did not wish Gordon to interfere at all in regard to the capitulation of the Suchau chiefs: 'With respect to Moh Wang and other rebel leaders' proposal, I am quite satisfied that you have determined in no way to interfere. Let Ching look after their treacherous and cunning management.' "[1]

On reaching Ihing, the dreadful effects of the struggle going on around Gordon's force were seen, and more than reconciled him to do all he could to bring it to an end. Utter destitution prevailed in and out of the town; people were feeding on dead bodies, and ready to perish from exposure while waiting for a comrade to die. The town of Liyang was surrendered on his approach, and its inhabitants, twenty thousand in number, supplied with a little food. From this place to Kintan proved to be a slow and irksome march, owing to the shallow water in the canal and the bad weather. On March 21st an attack was made on this strong post by breaching the walls; but it resulted in a defeat, the loss of more than a hundred officers and men, and a severe wound which Colonel Gordon received in his leg—oddly enough the only injury he sustained, though frequently compelled to lead his men in person to a charge. Next day he retired, in order, to Liyang, but hearing that the son of the Chung Wang had retaken Fushan he started with a thousand men and some artillery for Wusih, which the rebels had left. The operations in this region during the next few weeks conclusively proved the desperate condition of the rebels, but a hopeless cause seemed often but to increase their bravery in defending what strongholds were left them. At the same time a

---

[1] Wilson, *The "Ever-Victorious Army,"* p. 204.

body of Franco-Chinese was operating, in connection with General Ching on the south of Suchau, against Kiahing fu, a large city on the Grand Canal, held by the Ting Wang. This position was taken and its defenders put to the sword on March 20th, but with the very serious loss of General Ching, one of the ablest generals in the Chinese army. Hangchau, the capital of Chehkiang, capitulated the next day, and this was soon followed by the reduction of the entire province and dispersion of the rebels among the hills.

Colonel Gordon had recovered from his wound so as to lead an attack on Waisu April 6th, which town fell on the 11th, when most of its defenders were killed by the peasantry as they attempted to escape. His force was also much weakened, and needed to be recruited. With about three thousand in all, he now went to aid Governor Lí in reducing Changchau fu, and invested it on the 25th. The entire besieging force numbered over ten thousand; and as the rebels were twice as many, on the whole well provided, and knew that no mercy would be shown, their resistance was stubborn. Several attacks were repulsed with no small loss to Gordon's force, so that slower methods of approach were resorted to till a general assault was planned on May 11th, when it succumbed. Only fifteen hundred rebels were slain, and the greater part of the prisoners were allowed to go home, the Kwangsí men alone being executed. With this capture ended the operations of the Ever-victorious force and its brave leader. Nanking was now the only strong place held by the Tai-pings, and there was nothing for that army to do there, as Tsăng Kwoh-fan, the generalissimo of the imperial armies, had ample means for its capture. Colonel Gordon, therefore, in conjunction with Governor Lí, dissolved this notable division; the latter rewarded its officers and men with liberal gratuities, and sent the natives home. During its existence of about four years down to June 1, 1864, nearly fifty places had been taken (twenty-three of them by Gordon), and its higher discipline had served to elevate the *morale* of the imperialists who operated with them. It perhaps owed its greatest triumph to the high-toned uprightness of its Christian chief, which impressed all who served with him. The

Emperor conferred on him the highest military rank of *tí-tuh*, or 'Captain-General,' and a yellow jacket (*ma-kwa*) and other uniforms, to indicate the sense of his achievements. Sir Frederick Bruce admirably summed up his character in a letter to Earl Russell when sending the imperial rescript:

HONGKONG, July 12, 1864.

MY LORD,

I enclose a translation of a despatch from Prince Kung containing the decree published by the Emperor, acknowledging the services of Lieutenant-Colonel Gordon, R. E., and requesting that her Majesty's government be pleased to recognize them. This step has been spontaneously taken. Lieutenant-Colonel Gordon well deserves her Majesty's favor; for, independently of the skill and courage he has shown, his disinterestedness has elevated our national character in the eyes of the Chinese. Not only has he refused any pecuniary reward, but he has spent more than his pay in contributing to the comfort of the officers who served under him, and in assuaging the distress of the starving population whom he relieved from the yoke of their oppressors. Indeed, the feeling that impelled him to resume operations after the fall of Suchow was one of the purest humanity. He sought to save the people of the districts that had been recovered from a repetition of the misery entailed upon them by this cruel civil war.

I have, etc.,

F. W. A. BRUCE.

The foreign merchants at Shanghai expressed their sense of his conduct in a letter dated November 24th, written on the eve of his return to England, in which they truly remark: "In a position of unequalled difficulty, and surrounded by complications of every possible nature, you have succeeded in offering to the eyes of the Chinese nation, no less by your loyal and disinterested line of action than by your conspicuous gallantry and talent for organization and command, the example of a foreign officer serving the government of this country with honorable fidelity and undeviating self-respect."[1]

Such men are not only the choice jewels of their own nation (and England may justly be proud to reckon this son among

---

[1] "The rapidity with which the long-descended hostility of the Chinese government became exchanged for relations of at least outward friendship, must be ascribed altogether to the existence of the Tai-ping Rebellion, without whose pressure as an auxiliary we might have crushed, but never conciliated the distrustful statesmen at Peking."—*Fraser's Magazine*, Vol. LXXI., p. 145, February, 1865.

her worthies), but leave behind them an example, as in the case of Colonel Gordon, which elevates Christianity itself in the eyes of the Chinese, and will remain a legacy for good to them through coming years.[1]

After the dissolution of the Ever-victorious force, its leader visited Nganking and Nanking to see the governor-general, Tsăng Kwoh-fan, and his brother, who were directing operations against the rebels, in order to propose some improvements in their future employment of foreign soldiers and military appliances. They listened with respect, and took notes of important suggestions—knowing at the same time that their subordinates were unable to comprehend or adopt many such innovations. The work before Nanking indicated the industry of its besiegers in the miles of walls connecting one hundred and forty mud forts in their circumvallations, and in various mines leading under the city walls. The Tai-pings at that date seldom appeared on the walls, and had recently sent out three thousand women and children to be fed by their enemies, proof enough of their distressed condition. The only general capable of relieving the Tien Wang was the Chung Wang, whose army remained on the southern districts of Kiangsu, while he himself was in the city with the Kan Wang (Hung Jin), now the trusted agent of his half-brother. All egress from the doomed city was stopped by June 1st, when the explosion of mines and bursting of shells forewarnod its deluded defenders of their fate. Of the last days of their leader no authentic account has been given, and the declaration of the Chung Wang in his autobiography, that he poisoned himself on June 30th, "owing to his anxiety and trouble of mind," is probably true. His body was buried behind his palace by one of his wives, and afterward dug up by the imperialists.

On July 19, 1864, the wall was breached by the explosion of forty thousand pounds of powder in a mine, and the Chung Wang, faithful to the last, defended until midnight the Tien Wang's family from the imperialists. He and the Kan Wang

---

[1] Compare further Col. C. C. Chesney's *Essays on Modern Military Biography* (from the *Edinburgh Review*), pp. 163–213, London, 1874.

then escorted Hung Fu-tien—a lad of sixteen, who had succeeded to the throne of Great Peace three weeks before—with a thousand followers, a short distance beyond the city. The three leaders now became separated, but all were ultimately captured and executed. The Chung Wang, during his captivity before death, wrote an account of his own life, which fully maintains the high estimate previously formed of his character from his public acts.[1] He was the solitary ornament of the whole movement during the fourteen years of its independent existence, and his enemies would have done well to have spared him. More than seven thousand Tai-pings were put to death in Nanking, the total number found there being hardly over twenty thousand, of whom probably very few were southern Chinese—this element having gradually disappeared.

After the recapture of Nanking, two small bodies of rebels remained in Chehkiang. The largest of them, under the Tow Wang, held Huchau fu, and made a desperate resistance until a large force, provided with artillery, compelled them to evacuate. During this siege the sanguinary conduct of the Tai-pings showed the natural result of their reckless course since their last escape from Nanking; the narrative of an escaped Irishman, who had been compelled to serve them in Huchau for some months, is terrible enough: "All offences received one punishment—death. I saw one hundred and sixty men beheaded, as I understood, for absence from parade; two boys were beheaded for smoking; all prisoners of war were executed; spies, or people accused as such, were tied with their hands behind their backs to a stake, brushwood put around them, and they burned to death." The rebel force numbered nearly a hundred thousand men, and their vigorous defence was continued for a fortnight, till on August 14th their last stockade was carried by the imperialists, and about half their number made good their escape to the neighboring hills, leaving the usual scene of desolation behind them. This body undertook to march south through the hilly regions between Kiangsi and

---

[1] *The Autobiography of the Chung-Wang, translated from the Chinese by* W. T. Lay, Shanghai, 1865.

Chehkiang. The best disciplined portion was led by the Shí Wang, who had joined it with his men from the former province, and arranged an attack on Kwangsin, near which they were defeated. The remainder managed to march across the intervening districts south-westerly to the city of Changchau, near Amoy, where they intrenched themselves till the next spring, subsisting on the supplies found in it and the neighborhood. The Shí Wang and Kan Wang then left it April 16th, in two bodies, unable to resist the disciplined force of eight thousand men brought from the north. Feeling that their days were numbered, they seem to have scrupled at nothing to show their savagery—as, for example, when they slaughtered sixteen hundred imperialists who had surrendered on a promise of safe-conduct. No mercy was therefore shown them by the inhabitants; at Chănping in Kwangtung they even cut down their growing rice in order to prevent the rebels using it. The last straggling relics of the Tai-ping Heavenly King's adherents were thus gradually destroyed, and his ill-advised enterprise brought to an end.

Fifteen years had elapsed since he had set up his standard of revolt in Kwangsí, and now there was nothing to show as a return for the awful carnage and misery that had ensued from his efforts. No new ideas concerning God or his redemption for mankind had been set forth or illustrated by the teachings or practices of the Tai-ping leader or any of his followers, nor did they ever take any practical measures to call in foreign aid to assist in developing even the Christianity they professed. True the Kan Wang called Mr. Roberts to Nanking, but instead of consulting with him as to the establishment of schools, opening chapels, preparing books, or organizing any kind of religious or benevolent work to further the welfare of his adherents, the Tien Wang did not even grant an interview to the missionary, who, on his part, was glad to escape with his life to Shanghai.

If this rebellion practically exhibited no religious truth to the educated mind of China, it was not for lack of publications setting forth the beliefs its leaders had drawn from the Bible, or for laws sanctioned by severe penalties, both of which were scattered through the land. Dr. Medhurst's careful translations of these tracts has preserved them, so that the entire disregard manifested by the new sect of their plainest injunctions may be at once seen.[1] The strong expectations of the friends of China for its regeneration through the success of Hung Siu-tsuen, would not have been indulged if they had better known the inner workings of his own mind and the flagitious conduct of his lieutenants.

In his political aspirations the Tien Wang entertained no new principle of government, for he knew nothing of other lands, their jurisprudence or their polity, and wisely enough held his followers to such legislation as they were familiar with. They all probably expected to alter affairs to their liking when they had settled in Peking. But if this mysterious iconoclast had really any ideas above those of an enthusiast like Thomas Münzer and the Anabaptists in the early days of the Reformation—whose course and end offers many parallels to his own—he must have lamented his folly as he reviewed its results to his country. The once peaceful and populous parts of the nine great provinces through which his hordes passed have hardly yet begun to be restored to their previous condition. Ruined cities, desolated towns, and heaps of rubbish still mark their course from Kwangsí to Tientsin, a distance of two thousand miles, the efforts at restoration only making the contrast more apparent. Their presence was an unmitigated scourge, attended by nothing but disaster from beginning to end, without the least effort on their part to rebuild what had been destroyed, to protect what was left, or to repay what had been stolen. Wild beasts roamed at large over the land after their departure, and made their dens in the deserted towns; the pheasant's whirr resounded where the hum of busy populations had ceased, and weeds or jungle covered the ground once tilled with patient industry. Besides millions upon millions of taels irrecoverably lost and destroyed, and the misery, sickness, and starvation

---

[1] *Pamphlets issued by the Chinese Insurgents at Nan-King; to which is added a history of the Kwangsí Rebellion*, etc., etc., compiled by W. H. Medhurst, Senr., Shanghai, 1853. Compare R. J. Forrest in *Journal N. C. Br. R. A. Soc.*, No. IV., December, 1867, pp. 187 ff. *The China Mail* for February 2, 1854.

which were endured by the survivors, it has been estimated by foreigners living at Shanghai that, during the whole period from 1851 to 1865, fully twenty millions of human beings were destroyed in connection with the Tai-ping Rebellion.[1]

---

[1] The most complete authorities on this conflict are files of the *North China Herald* (Shanghai) and the *China Mail* (Hongkong) during the years from 1853 to 1869; a careful summary of these has been made by M. Cordier in his *Bibliotheca Sinica*, pp. 273–281, which will be useful alone to those who can gain access to these newspapers. The number of articles on various phases of the rebellion contained in English and American magazines is exceedingly numerous, and can be readily found by reference to Poole's *Index*. Among these compare especially the *London Quarterly*, Vol. 112, for October, 1862; *Fraser's Magazine*, Vol. 71, February, 1865; *Blackwood's*, Vol. 100, pp. 604 and 683; W. Sargent in the *North American Review*, Vol. 79, July, 1854, p. 158. See also the various *Blue Books* relating to China; Capt. Fishbourne, *Impressions of China and the Present Revolution*, London, 1855; Callery and Yvan, *L'Insurrection en Chine*, Paris, 1853—translated into English, London, 1853; Charles Macfarlane, *The Chinese Revolution*, London, 1853; T. T. Meadows, *The Chinese and their Rebellions*, London, 1856; J. M. Mackie, *Life of Tai-ping Wang*, N. Y., 1857; Commander Lindesay Brine, *Narrative of the Rise and Progress of the Taeping Rebellion in China*, London, 1862; "Lin-le," *Ti-Ping Tien-kwoh, the History of the Ti-Ping Revolution*, London, 1866—a rather untrustworthy record; Sir T. F. Wade in the *Shanghai Miscellany*, No. I.; Richthofen, *Letter on the Province of Shensi*.

CHAPTER XXV.

THE SECOND WAR BETWEEN GREAT BRITAIN AND CHINA.

THE particulars given in the last chapter respecting the Taiping Rebellion did not include those details connected with foreign intercourse during the same period which have had such important results on the Chinese people and government. It is a notable index of the vigor and self-poise of both, that during those thirteen terrible years, the mass of inhabitants in the ten eastern provinces never lost confidence in their own government or its ability to subdue the rebels; while the leading officers at Peking and in all those provinces at no time expressed doubt as to the loyalty of their countrymen when left free to act. The narrative of foreign intercourse is now resumed from the year 1849, when the British authorities waived the right of insisting upon their admission into the city of Canton according to the terms of the convention with Kíying in 1847. The conduct of the Cantonese, in view of the forcible entrance of English troops into their city, is an interesting exhibition of their manner of arousing enthusiasm and raising funds and volunteers to cope with an emergency. The series of papers found in Vol. XVIII. of the *Chinese Repository* well illustrates the curious mixture of a sense of wrong and deep concern in public affairs, combined with profound ignorance and inaptitude as to the best means for attaining their object.

A candid examination of the real meaning of the Chinese texts of the four earlier treaties makes clear the fact that there were some grounds for their refusal; but more attractive than this appears the study of an address from the gentry of Canton, sent upon the same occasion, to Governor Bonham at Hongkong, dissuading him from attempting the entry. Their con duct was naturally regarded by the British as seditious, and of these many urged their authorities to vindicate the national honor and force a way over the walls into the city. The practice of an unwonted approach toward self-government which this popular movement in defence of their metropolis gave the citizens, was of real service to them in the year 1855, when it was beleaguered by the rebels, since they had learned how to use their powers and resources. One result of their fancied victory over the British at this time was the erection of six stone *pai-lau*, or honorary portals, in various parts of the city and suburbs, on each of which was engraved the sentence, "Reverently to commemorate glory conferred," together with a copy of the edict ordering their establishment, and a list of the wards and villages which furnished soldiers during their time of need.[1]

The outcome of the working of treaty provisions between foreigners and natives at the five opened ports during the ten years up to 1853, had been as satisfactory to both sides as could have been reasonably expected. The influx of foreigners had more than doubled their numbers; and as almost none of them could talk the Chinese language, it happened that natives of Canton became their brokers and compradores—rather more by reason of speaking *pigeon-English* than by their wealth or capacity. The vicious plan of marking off a separate plat of land for the residence of foreigners at each port was adopted, and their development tended to build up *concessions*, or settlements, which were to be governed by the various nationalities. In doing this the local authorities vacated their rights over their own territory, and these settlements have since become the germs of foreign cities, if not colonies. The British and French consuls at Shanghai claimed territorial jurisdiction over all who settled within the limits of their allotted districts, and carried this assumption so far as to exercise authority over the natives against their own rulers. The British ere long gave up this pernicious system, which had no legal basis by treaty or conquest, and yielded the entire internal management

[1] The one placed near the southern gate became a target for the British gunners in October, 1856, its demolition, most unfortunately, involving the destruction and burning of millions of Chinese books in the shops on that street.

of all consular communities to those foreigners which composed them. There were not enough residents elsewhere to raise this question of local government to any importance, but the progress of the Tai-pings and the rapid growth of Shanghai as a centre of trade for the Yangtsz' basin, compelled the preparation and adoption of a set of land regulations in order to institute some means of governing the thousands of foreigners who had flocked thither. George Balfour, the first British consul in that port, had sanctioned a series of rules in 1845, which purported to be drawn up by the *tautai*, or intendant of circuit, and which worked well enough in peaceful times.

In the year 1853, however, the civil war altered the conditions, when certain Cantonese rebels captured Shanghai and killed some of its magistrates, driving others into the British settlement, to which ground the custom-house was shortly afterward removed. The collector of the port, Wu Kien-chang, had formerly been a hong merchant at Canton, and he willingly entered into an arrangement for putting the collection of foreign duties into the hands of a commission until order was restored. The presence there of the British, American, and French ministers facilitated this arrangement. Their respective consuls, R. Alcock, R. C. Murphy, and B. Edan, accordingly met Wu on June 29, 1854, and agreed to a set of custom-house rules which in reality transferred the collection of duties into the hands of foreigners. The first rule contains the reason for this remarkable step in advance of all former positions, and has served to perpetuate the employment of foreigners at all the open ports, and maintain the foreign inspectorate:

RULE I.—The chief difficulty experienced by the superintendent of customs having consisted in the impossibility of obtaining custom-house officials with the necessary qualifications as to probity, vigilance, and knowledge of foreign languages, required for the enforcement of a close observance of treaty and custom-house regulations, the only adequate remedy appears to be in the introduction of a foreign element into the custom-house establishment, in the persons of foreigners carefully selected and appointed by the *tautai*, who shall supply the deficiency complained of, and give him efficient and trustworthy instruments wherewith to work.[1]

[1] *McLane's Correspondence*, 1858. *Senate Ex. Doc.*, No. 28, p. 154.

In carrying out the new arrangement, each consul nominated one man to the intendant, viz., T. F. Wade for the British, L. Carr for the American, and Arthur Smith for the French member of the board of inspectors, who together were to take charge of the new department. The chief responsibility for its organization fell on Mr. Wade, inasmuch as he alone of this number was familiar with the Chinese language, and possessed other qualifications fitting him for the post. He, however, resigned within a year, and the intendant appointed H. N. Lay, a clerk in the British consulate, who completed the service organization. This proceeding shows the readiness with which the Chinese will shirk their own duties and functions in government employ, and illustrates as well many peculiar traits in their character.

The city of Shanghai had been in possession of a Cantonese chief, Liu Tsz'-tsai, and his rabble since September 7, 1853, and the position of foreigners at that port in the presence of such a body of outlaws developed new points of international law. If the foreigners had all been of one nationality the consul would probably have assumed temporary control of the city and port to assure their safety ; but in this case a naval force under each flag lying in the river guaranteed ample protection of life and property. As soon as the city was occupied the difficulty of restraining the disorderly elements, as well among foreigners as natives, became painfully apparent to their rulers. Foreign rowdies eagerly purchased the plunder brought to them and supplied arms and other things in return—a line of conduct very naturally irritating to the officials in charge of the siege and inclining them at once toward coercive measures.

The fact that the French settlement adjoined the moat on the north side of the city made its authorities desirous to dislodge the brigands, which they essayed to do January 6, 1855, by joining the imperialists in breaking the walls ; they were repulsed, however, with a loss of fifteen men killed and thirty-seven wounded, out of a rank and file numbering two hundred and fifty. Another joint attack, undertaken a month later, was likewise unsuccessful, though the attempt seems to have frightened the force within the walls, since on the night of February

16th they retired, leaving the place in ruins. A like cordiality was nevertheless not always maintained between native and foreign soldiers, for in the previous year (April 4, 1854) occurred a collision with the imperialists, in consequence of their near approach to the foreign quarter, in which over three hundred Chinese soldiers were killed by the foreigners who landed to resist them. This untoward rencontre did not, however, interrupt amicable relations with the intendant, and was followed by consular notifications that whoever entered the service of the combatants in or out of the city would forfeit all protection. These notices were nevertheless soon disregarded as the struggle went on, for the temptation to enjoy a lawless life was too strong for hundreds of sailors then found in that port. It was an anomalous state of affairs, and the exigency led to some acts of violence by consuls in control of men-of-war.

The city of Amoy had been captured by insurgents on May 18, 1852, but no contravention occurred; the number of foreigners residing at this port was small, while the opposite island of Kulang su afforded a refuge beyond the range of missiles. The city was regained by the imperialists before a year had passed. The districts north of Canton, whence Hung Siu-tsuen and many of his adherents originated, began the same year to send forth their bands of robbers to pillage the province. These gangs had really no affinity with the Tai-pings, either in doctrine or plans, and none of them succeeded in gaining even a temporary success. When the booty was expended they usually quarrelled, and the imperialists destroyed them in detail. Every part of the province was at one time or another the scene of savage conflict between these contestants, and it was soon shown that no regenerating principle was involved on either side. The confidence of the educated and wealthy classes in the just cause and final success of their rulers was shown in raising men and money for the public service and organizing bodies of local police; but the want of a sagacious leader to plan and execute, so that all this material and action should not be frittered away, was painfully apparent.

In the capture of Nanking by Tai-pings, the restless leaders of sedition in Kwangtung saw their opportunity, and gathered their bands of freebooters in the southern prefectures. In June, 1854, the district town of Tungkwan near the Bogue was taken, the rich manufacturing mart of Fuhshan (or Fat-shan) near Canton fell a month later, followed by that of Shunteh, San-shui, and other lesser places, throwing the southern part of the province into a state of anarchy. The theory of the Chinese government, that if the capital is preserved the whole province is loyal, and its officers can use its revenue, enabled Governor-General Yeh to concert measures to repress these disorders. The City of Rams was environed during August by large bodies of insurgents, whose wants were supplied from Fuhshan. In this crisis about one thousand five hundred houses abutting outside the city walls were destroyed, and the ward police strengthened for the better protection of their neighborhoods against incendiaries. In all these proceedings the foreigners at Canton were never consulted or referred to by the officials, but their merchant steamers kept the Pearl River open to the sea, while their men-of-war lying off the factories proved a safeguard to the crowded city. The rebels had occupied a post near Whampoa, and their gunboats prowled through every creek in the delta, burning, destroying, capturing, and murdering without restraint. They would be followed by a band of imperialists, whose excesses were sometimes even more dreadful than those of their enemies. So terrible was the plight of the wretched countrymen that the headmen of ninety-six villages near Fuhshan formed a league and armed their people to keep soldiers from either side from entering their precincts.

In September, at a general meeting of the gentry of Canton, a proposal to save the city by asking foreign aid was approved by Yeh, but happily the project failed of fulfilment and only resulted in showing them how much better was a reliance upon their own resources. The news of this discussion led Chin Hien-liang, the rebel leader near Whampoa, to circulate proposals among the foreigners asking them to help him in capturing the city and promising as reward a portion of the island of Honan. The condition of the people at this time was sad and desperate indeed, and their only remedy was to arm in self-defence, in doing which they found out how small a proportion of the inhabitants was disloyal. No quarter was given on either side, and the carnage was appalling whenever victory remained with the imperialists. During this year the emigration to California and Australia became larger than ever before, while the coolie trade waxed flourishing, owing to the multitudes thrown out of employment who were eager in accepting the offers of the brokers to depart from the country and escape the evils they saw everywhere about them. The terrors of famine, fighting, and plundering paralyzed all industry and trade, and enabled one to better understand similar scenes described by ancient historians as occurring in Western Asia.

The exhaustion and desperation consequent on these events had almost demoralized society in and around Canton, which was overcrowded with refugees, raising food to famine prices. It was creditable to these poor and sickly people that their influx produced no other fear than that of a higher rate of living—none of pestilence or plunder, even in the extremity of their sufferings. In Fuhshan, fifteen miles away, no one was safe. The rebels had depleted its resources, killed its gentry, and oppressed the townsfolk until a quarrel broke out in their camp, and they departed about the season of Christmas, leaving the whole a smoking ruin. One of the insurgent practices consisted in driving great numbers of people into squares and there shooting them down by cannon placed in the approaching streets, while the houses around them were burning. The flames could be seen for two or three days from Canton, and it was estimated that during this conflict fully two hundred thousand human beings perished. The town was the manufacturing centre for the foreign trade, where silks, satins, shawls, paper, fire-crackers, pottery, and other staples were made, and their workmen resided. After this dreadful act the insurgents grew more and more desperate, feeling that they could not hold out much longer for want of booty and supplies to keep their men together. By March the force of fifteen thousand men inside the city was ready, and on the 6th it went quietly down to attack the fort below Whampoa. The onset and resistance were most determined ; before the position succumbed, some twenty-five thousand men must have perished by battle or flood ; the rebel leader escaped toward Hiangshan. The insurrection was, however, scotched, and its victors celebrated their triumph three days later in the city to a grateful and applauding concourse. When the city of Shauking, west of Canton, was retaken in May, its victors boasted that thirty thousand rebels were drowned or beheaded.

Notwithstanding these reverses the insurgents did not yet disappear, but maintained themselves along the watercourses in large flotillas during many months. The Portuguese and British also fitted out expeditions to pursue the pirates, as the same men were now called, destroying them and their haunts at Kulan Lantao, and elsewhere. In rooting out these land and sea brigands, the merciless character of the people was made manifest; every one convicted of rebellion was straightway executed by the authorities. At Canton, where prisoners were received from all such districts, the executions were on a terribly huge scale, as many as seven or eight hundred persons being beheaded in a single day. A count taken at the city gate whence they all issued on their way to the field of blood near the river, revealed the fact that fully eighty thousand were thus executed in the year 1855. This did not include thousands who committed suicide in places provided for them near their homes, from which their relatives could take their bodies to the family tomb. As might be expected, other thousands left the province for the north, or escaped into distant lands as coolies and emigrants.

Public attention abroad was at this time so engrossed with the greater rebellion going on along the Yangtsz' River that the horrors of that in Kwangtung were overlooked. There were many foreigners at Whampoa and Hongkong who sided with the leading brigands, reported their successes in the newspapers, and supplied them with munitions of war. The inefficiency of a foreign consul to restrain his countrymen thus flagrantly violating all their treaty obligations toward China, showed most conclusively how easy it is for the stronger party in such cases to demand their rights, and shirk their duties if it suits their convenience.

During the year 1856 affairs between the Chinese government and foreign powers became more and more hampered, while all attempts to arrange difficulties as they arose were defeated by the obstinate refusal of Yeh Ming-chin, the governor-general at Canton, to meet any foreign minister. He intrenched himself behind the city gates, and would do nothing. Sir John Bowring, the British plenipotentiary and governor of Hongkong, had most reason to be dissatisfied with this conduct, inasmuch as there were many questions which could have been easily arranged in a personal interview. It was ascertained from some documents[1] afterward found in Yeh's office that this seclusion was a part of the system devised at Peking to maintain a complete isolation and keep the dreaded foreigners at a distance. No course could be more likely to bring upon the government the evils it feared, and at the same time show more conclusively the ignorant and inapt character of those who carried it on. This state of things could not long continue when such powerful agencies were at work along the coast to disorganize legal trade and thwart the utmost efforts of all officials to restrain the reckless conduct of their subjects. The ten years now elapsed since the opening of the five ports had involved the Chinese in more complications, miseries, and disasters than had been known since the Manchu conquest; nevertheless, neither rebellion nor foreign complications seem to have impressed their lessons upon the proud bureaucracy in Peking, which was as unwilling to remedy as unable to appreciate the real nature of the difficulties that beset the country.

In the struggle between nations, as between individuals, the agony and weakness of one side becomes the opportunity of the other; and these conditions were now open to the British, who speedily found their excuse for further demands. In order to develop the trade of the free port of Hongkong, its laws encouraged all classes of shipping to resort thither, by removing all charges on vessels and granting licenses, with but few and unimportant restrictions, to Chinese craft to carry on trade under the British flag. This freedom had developed an enormous smuggling trade, especially in opium, which the Chinese revenue service was unable to restrain or unwilling to legalize.

---

[1] *Blue Book*, 1857.

These boats cruised wherever they might find a trade to invite or reward them, wholly indifferent to their own government, which could exercise no adequate control over them, and kept from the last excesses only on account of the risk of losing their cargoes. To the evils of smuggling were added the worse acts and dangers of kidnapping natives to supply baracoons at Macao. The Portuguese had many of these lorchas to carry on their commerce, and gradually a set of desperate men had so far engrossed them in acts of daring and pillage that honest native trade about any part of the coast south of Shanghai became almost impossible except under their convoy. The two free ports of Macao and Hongkong naturally became their resorts, where they all took on the aspect of legitimate traders, which, indeed, most of them were—save under great temptations.

It was not surprising that Chinese rulers should confound these two classes of vessels, nor, from the traders' side, was it a wonder that their crews should use the flag which gave them the greatest protection when beyond foreign inspection and jurisdiction. Few nations have ever been subjected to such continuous and prolonged irritation in respect to its commercial regulations as was the Canton government from those two alien communities during the ten years ending with 1856; few nations, on the other hand, have acted more unwisely in exertions toward peace and the removal of such difficulties than did the unspeakable Governor-General Yeh. That the inevitable collision between the Chinese and British was now at hand, follows almost as a matter of course, when to our knowledge of the commissioner's character we add Mr. Justin McCarthy's very appropriate estimate of the two Englishmen in whose hands well-nigh all British affairs in China were vested: "Mr. Consul Parkes," says he, "was fussy. Sir John Bowring was a man of considerable ability, but . . . full of self-conceit, and without any very clear idea of political principles on the large scale."[1]

Early in the morning of October 8th, two boat-loads of

[1] *A History of Our Own Times*, Chap. XXX.

Chinese sailors, with their officers, put off from a large war-junk, boarded the lorcha Arrow lying at anchor in the river before Canton, pinioned and carried away twelve of the fourteen natives who composed her crew, and added to this unexpected "act of violence," as Mr. Parkes stated it, "the significant insult of hauling down the British ensign." One Kennedy, a young Irishman who is described as a very respectable man of his class, was master of the lorcha, but chanced at the time to be on another boat lying in the immediate neighborhood of his own, and could in consequence offer no resistance. It is probable, judging from testimony given at the British consulate, that the hauling down of the flag was a mere bit of wantonness on the part of the junk's officer upon his finding that no foreigner was on board, and the offence might readily have been followed by an apology had the command of negotiations been in any other hands than those of Yeh. The Arrow was owned by a Chinese, Fong A-ming, her nominal master being engaged by Mr. Block, the Danish consul at Hongkong; his vessel was not, however, entitled to protection, inasmuch as her British register had expired by its own limitation eleven days before the episode in Canton River, and the lorcha was already forfeited to the crown.[1] Her papers were then at the consulate, and it was contended by Mr. Parkes that under Clause X. of the ordinance she retained a right to protection; a mere quibble, since the cause refers to the vessel when upon a voyage, and the Arrow had confessedly remained about the ports of Macao and Canton during a month.

Consul Parkes, after ascertaining the facts connected with this high-handed outrage, pushed off to the war-junk—which remained the while quietly at anchor—to claim the captured sailors and "explain to the officers, if it were possible that they had acted in error, the gross insult and violation of national

---

[1] Sir John Bowring indeed conceded that "the Arrow had no right to hoist the British flag," but alleged that the Chinese had no knowledge of the expiry of the license, and that this ignorance deprived them of the legal value of the truth. He quoted, moreover, Article IX. of the Supplementary Treaty, requiring that "all Chinese malfaisants in British ships shall be claimed through the British authorities."

rights which they had committed."[1] This was in vain. Among the men was a notorious pirate, he was told, and their orders were that the suspected crew should be sent to the governor for examination. Yeh stoutly upheld the act of his subordinate, and affirmed that the lorcha had no right to fly the British flag, disclaiming, however, any intention of molesting lawful traders under the emblem. Naturally enough, he would not yield the right of jurisdiction over his own subjects, and in doing this was asserting precisely what Great Britain and every other nation on the globe knew to be the first privilege of an independent government. The case was not unlike that much-discussed affair of the American Commodore Wilkes, who boarded the Trent in 1863 and captured Mason and Slidell—performing a right-enough action, but in a wrong and hasty fashion.

In his reply to Mr. Parkes, Yeh declares that he has held an examination of the sailors and finds that three of them were implicated in a piracy of the preceding month on St. John's Island, that the officers had good reasons for seizing these men, that the remaining nine shall be sent back to their vessel; which he straightway does, but they are as promptly returned by the consul because the entire crew is not given up. Sir John Bowring now demands, through his representative at Canton (1), "an apology for what has taken place, and an assurance that the British flag shall in future be respected;" (2) "that all proceedings against Chinese offenders on board British vessels must take place according to the conditions of the treaty;"[2] in case of refusal the consul is to concert with the naval authorities the measures necessary for enforcing redress. This threat extracted from the governor-general a promise that "hereafter Chinese officers will on no account, without reason, seize and take into custody the people belonging to foreign lorchas;" adding very properly, "but when Chinese subjects build for themselves vessels, foreigners should not sell registers to them, for if this be done, it will occasion confusion between native and foreign ships, and render it difficult to distinguish

[1] *Blue Book: Papers relating to the Proceedings of her Majesty's Naval Forces at Canton*, p. 1.

[2] *Blue Book, Ibid.*, p. 12.

between them."[1] Twelve days afterward (October 22d) the entire crew were returned, but once more refused by Mr. Parkes, ostensibly because the apology was not sent with them —and this the commissioner could not offer either in justice to his government or to the cause of truth.

Ensconced behind the walls of Canton city, Yeh resolved to stand firm on his rights as he understood them, even should the doing so involve the lives and property of thousands of his countrymen. To all foreigners in China this affair was intimately connected with most important possibilities and consequences: the inviolability of national flags, protection to every one whom they covered, personal intercourse with Chinese officers, maintenance of treaty rights. In upholding these the British drew to their side the good wishes of all intelligent observers for their success in arms, however unhappy their excuse for a resort to such means might be. One more word from Mr. McCarthy before leaving the initial episode of this war. "The truth is," he sums up, "that there has seldom been so flagrant and so inexcusable an example of high-handed lawlessness in the dealings of a strong with a weak nation,"[2] but like many another conflict where strength and justice have been ranged on opposite sides, the latter was speedily pushed to the wall. The incident of the Arrow appeared a trifling one; nevertheless on so slight a hinge turned the future welfare and progress of the Chinese people in their intercourse with other nations, a hinge which, opening outward, unclosed the door for all parties to learn the truth respecting the countries of each, and, in the end, agree upon the only grounds on which a beneficial and intelligent intercourse could be maintained.

It is hardly necessary to recount in detail the steps by which Governor Bowring and Admiral Seymour vainly attempted to bring Yeh to their terms. "Acknowledge that you are in the wrong," was their ultimatum, "by merely sending the three

---

[1] *Ibid.*, p. 15.

[2] *History of Our Own Times*, Vol. III., Chap. XXX. Lord Elgin in his journal refers frankly enough to "that wretched question of the Arrow, which is a scandal to us, and is so considered, I have reason to know, by all except the few who are personally compromised."—*Letters and Journals of Lord Elgin*, edited by T. Walrond, p. 209.

suspects to the consulate, and ask that they be returned on charge of piracy." The long-continued national policy of exclusion could not, however, be so easily overthrown; its reduction must be by force. The seizure of a military junk was the first act of the British, then the capture of the Barrier forts, followed by that of all others on the south of Canton, and lastly breaching the city wall opposite Yeh's yamun. This was entered by Admiral Seymour with a small party of marines.

Sir John Bowring had already made the demand that the city gates should be opened to them in accordance with the agreement entered into ten years before between Governor Davis and Kíying, and expresses his gratification to the consul that now one great object of hostile action had been satisfactorily accomplished—an object which Mr. Parkes declares was clearly based on treaty rights. However, they did not see Yeh, who resorted to all manner of petty annoyances, the evils of which mostly fell on his own people, without in the least advancing his cause.

On November 15th, to the complications with the English was added a quarrel with the Americans, whose boats had been twice fired into and one man killed by the Chinese officers in command of the Barrier forts. Commodore J. Armstrong had under his command the San Jacinto, Portsmouth, and Levant, then lying at Whampoa. He ordered the two latter to go as near to these forts as possible, and directed Captain A. H. Foote of the Portsmouth to destroy them all. Foote accordingly organized a large force and attacked them on the 16th, 20th, and 21st, till they were reduced and occupied. The resistance of the Chinese on this occasion was unusually brave and prolonged, the admirable position of the forts enabling each of them to lend assistance to the others. On the part of the Americans, seven were killed and twenty-two wounded; perhaps three hundred Chinese were put *hors de combat;* the guns in the forts (one hundred and seventy-six in all) were destroyed, and the sea-walls demolished with powder found in the magazines.[1] This skirmish is the only passage of arms ever

---

[1] One brass gun of eight-inch calibre was twenty-two feet five inches long; the entire armament of these forts was superior in equipment to anything before seen in China.

engaged in by American and Chinese forces—one which Yeh seemed to regard as of slight moment, and for which he cared neither to apologize nor sympathize. His unexampled indifference in referring to the affair less than two days after the demolishment of his forts[1] was met by an equal frankness on the part of Dr. Parker, who at once resumed correspondence with the commissioner, and, content with the practical lesson just administered, said no more about "apologies and guarantees." This episode is interesting chiefly as an example of the American course regarding an insult to the national flag, as contrasted with the English dealing with an injury not very different either in nature or degree.

Relations between Great Britain and China continued in this constrained position until the opening of another year, the conflict now being almost wholly restricted to unimportant collisions with village braves on land and voluminous discussions with the governor-general on paper. In November the French minister withdrew his legation from Canton, there being by that time neither French citizens nor interests to watch over. Principal among the events during this interval was the burning of the foreign factories by order of Yeh, December 14th. They were fired in the night and were entirely consumed with all their contents, as well, too, as the contiguous portion of the suburbs. The offer of thirty taels head-money for every Englishman killed or captured resulted in a few endeavors on the part of natives, whereby they kidnapped or slew two or three seamen when separated from their ships. These attempts at guerilla warfare were so promptly met and rewarded on the part of the English, by wholesale punishment of offending villages, as to cause little annoyance after the lesson of certain retribution had been taken to heart by the Chinese. More important than all these was a dastardly attempt, on January 11,

[1] "There is no matter of strife between our respective nations. Henceforth let the fashion of the flag which American ships employ be clearly defined, and inform me what it is beforehand. This will be the verification of the friendly relations which exist between the two countries."—Hoppin, *Life of Admiral Foote*, pp. 110–140. *Correspondence of McLane and Parker*, *Senate Document* No. 22, December 20, 1858, pp. 1019 ff. *Blue Book*, p. 137.

1857, to poison the foreigners at Hongkong, by putting arsenic in the bread supplied from a Chinese baker. This, it was afterward ascertained, was at the instigation of certain officials on the mainland, but fortunately even here their villany was foiled, owing to the overdose contained in the dough. It ought to be stated, in passing, that such acts are not common in China, and, in this case, that the baker's employers were proven entirely innocent.

During much of this time Canton had been reminded of the presence of the British force by intermittent bombarding of the city from guns in Dutch Folly Fort. Sir John Bowring had demanded an interview with Yeh in November, but received a prompt refusal, followed by a still more vigorous carrying on of the war in his peculiar fashion, and by raising the price on English heads. Admiral Seymour had now less reason for remaining within the Bogue, as all trade was at an end. Hundreds of foreigners had already been thrown out of employment, their property destroyed, their plans broken up, and in a few instances their lives lost in consequence of this quarrel. After holding an intrenched position around the church and barracks of the factories for the space of a month, the uselessness of this effort when sustained by so paltry a force seems to have moved the admiral (January 14, 1857) to retire from Canton, falling back upon Macao Fort until reinforcements should arrive from India. Before leaving the site of the factories, however, he burned down the warehouses of those native merchants in the vicinity, their inmates having previously been warned to leave them. These buildings and their contents were private property, and the intrenched position in the factory garden was not endangered by their remaining. The leaders of the British operations had hitherto professed to spare private property; and even if the performance was meant as a parting menace to the governor-general—"to show him," as Mr. Parkes remarked, "that we can burn too"—it was one of the few acts, on their side, which has left a stigma upon the English name in China. The hostile proceedings of the Chinese authorities had been both petty and useless, but as Admiral Seymour's force was inadequate to take and hold Canton, a more serious cannonading of the imperial quarters might have been a more honorable method of taking retribution for outrages, and better calculated than this counter-incendiarism to increase respect for British arms and civilization.

The news of these operations in China excited great interest and speculation in Europe, inasmuch as all its nations were more or less interested in the China trade. Parliament was the scene of animated argument as to the policy of Sir John Bowring and his colleagues; the moral, commercial, and political features of British intercourse with China were discussed most thoroughly in all their bearings, the arguments of both parties in the debate being drawn from the same despatches. One remarkable series of papers was presented to the House of Lords in February, 1857, entitled *Correspondence respecting Insults in China*, "containing the particulars of twenty-eight outrages committed by the Chinese upon British and other foreigners between the years 1842 and 1856." This publication was intended apparently to show how impracticable the Chinese authorities were in all their intercourse with foreigners, and its contents became to members of the House so many arguments for placing this intercourse on a better basis at the imperial court. To those who had watched since 1842 the results of treaty stipulations upon the people of China and their rulers, it was plain that no satisfactory political intercourse could be hoped for so long as the governor-general at Canton had the power of concealing and misrepresenting to his government everything that happened between foreign representatives and himself. Nevertheless such a series of papers was but one side of the insults endured. As long as the British government upheld the opium trade, and did nothing to restrain smuggling and the awful atrocities of the coolie traffic at Macao, which were filling the ears of all the world with their shocking tales, these few "outrages" seem very petty if put forward as a defence of Lord Palmerston's going to war on account of the lorcha Arrow.

In the vote upon the question of employing force in China, the better sense of Parliament protested against the policy which had directed recent events; but the Premier knew his countrymen, and in forty days from the dissolution (March 21st) England returned him a House of Commons strongly in his favor. He now decided to complete what had been wanting in the treaty of Nanking, and obtain a residence for a British minister at Peking. The governments of France, Russia, and the United States were invited to co-operate with England so far as they deemed proper, and their united interests were those of Christendom. No well-wisher to China could patiently look forward to a continuation of the past tantalizing semblance of official intercourse at Canton, and the varied experience of twelve years at other ports proved that the Chinese people did not sympathize in this policy. The French Emperor had a special grievance against H. I. M. Hienfung, on account of the judicial murder of Père Chapdelaine, a missionary in Kwangsí province, who had been tortured and beheaded at Sí-lin hien on February 29, 1856, by order of the district magistrate. This outrage was in direct violation of the rescript of 1844, and some atonement and apology were justly demanded. How totally unconscious of all these discussions and plans were Hienfung and his counsellors at Peking, may be guessed from their blind fright during subsequent events, while their inability to devise a course of action corresponded to their childish ignorance of their position and duties.

A powerful though unspoken reflection among these rulers must not here be overlooked as a secret motive in deciding many of their short-sighted counsels. Remembering the way in which their ancestors had captured the Empire over two centuries before, they felt that great risk was run in admitting the barbarians to the capital now, since the same game would probably be played over again. The visits of foreign ministers to the insurgents at Nanking, and their readiness at Canton to quarrel about so trifling a point as pulling down a flag and carrying off a few natives under its protection, all indicated, in their opinion, nothing short of conquest and spoliation. With such tremendous power arrayed against so weak an adversary, they knew well enough what would ensue. Their miserable policy of isolation had left them more helpless in their ignorance than diminished in their resources, and they had to pay dearly for their instruction.

The appointments of Lord Elgin and Baron Gros as plenipotentiaries for Great Britain and France were most fortunate as a selection of eminent diplomatists and clear-headed men. The two ambassadors entered into most cordial relations as soon as the land and sea forces placed at their disposal arrived on the Chinese coast. Lord Elgin reached Hongkong in July, but learning the state of affairs in that region, and that no advances had been made from Peking to settle the dispute, concluded to take the Shannon to Calcutta, to the assistance of Lord Canning against the mutineers; from this place he proposed to proceed in the cold weather, when the force detailed for China would all be ready. Returning to Hongkong by September 20th, he was obliged to tarry yet another month before the last of his reinforcements, or those of the French, had joined him. By the end of November the American minister, W. B. Reed, in the frigate Minnesota, and the Russian admiral, Count Poutiatine, in the gunboat Amerika, had likewise come.

Early in December, after a refusal on the part of Yeh of their ultimatum, the allied forces advanced up the Canton River. An extract from one of Lord Elgin's private letters illustrates admirably the spirit in which he entered upon the work he had been chosen to do. "December 22d.—On the afternoon of the 20th I got into a gunboat with Commodore Elliot, and went a short way up toward the Barrier forts, which were last winter destroyed by the Americans. When we reached this point, all was so quiet that we determined to go on, and we actually steamed past the city of Canton, along the whole front, within pistol-shot of the town. A line of English men-of-war are now anchored there in front of the town. I never felt so ashamed of myself in my life, and Elliot remarked that the trip seemed to have made me sad. There we were, accumulating the means of destruction under the very eyes and within the reach of a population of about one million people, against whom these means of destruction were to be employed! 'Yes,' I said to Elliot, 'I am sad, because, when I look at that town, I feel that I am earning for myself a place in the Litany, immediately after "plague, pestilence, and famine." I believe, however, that, as far as I am concerned, it was impossible for me to do otherwise than as I have done. . . . When we steamed up to Canton and saw the rich alluvial banks covered with the luxurious evidences of unrivalled industry and natural fertility combined—beyond them barren uplands sprinkled with a soil of reddish tint which gave them the appearance of heather slopes in the Highlands, and beyond these again the White Cloud mountain range standing out bold and blue in the clear sunshine—I thought bitterly of those who, for the most selfish objects, are trampling under foot this ancient civilization."[1]

On the 27th the British and French, about six thousand in all, landed on the east bank a short distance below the walls. During the whole of the following day a furious bombardment was opened upon the city from the ships, driving thousands of the frightened natives into the western suburbs and destroying considerable portions of the town. By three o'clock of the 29th the city was in the hands of the foreigners—almost exactly the two hundred and seventh anniversary of its capture and entire reduction by the Manchus (November, 1650). The victory was not a brilliant one, since scarcely any one could be found with whom to fight; three or four forts to be entered, the wall scaled, a loss of one hundred and ten in killed and wounded to the victors, perhaps five times as many to the vanquished—this was all. Immediately upon their entry within the hitherto forbidden city the chiefs were forced to turn their energy upon their own troops and prevent them from bullying and looting the helpless Chinese.

Governor-General Yeh was, after some little search, found and captured while attempting an escape from his yamun,[2] and within twenty-four hours the lieutenant-governor, Tartar general, and all others in high authority came into possession of the invaders. Yeh was carried forthwith on board H. B. M. S. Inflexible, a wise step which deprived him of further power of

---

[1] *Letters and Journals*, p. 212.

[2] Some very curious documents were found among his archives illustrating the character both of the man and his government. See Oliphant, *Elgin's Mission to China*, Vol. I., Chap. VIII. Reed's *Correspondence*, 1858, pp. 443–488.

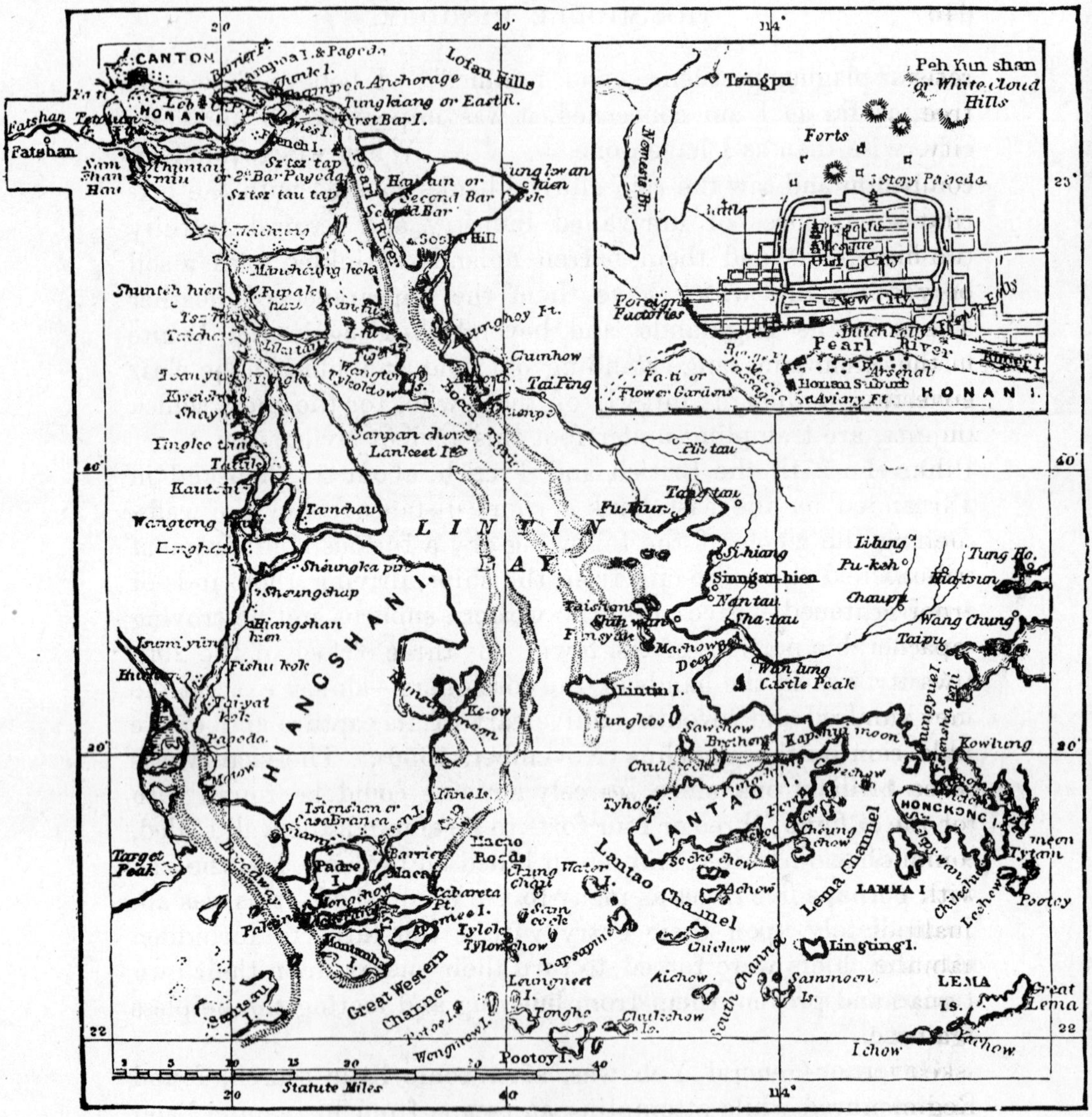

THE CITY OF CANTON AND ADJACENT ISLANDS.

resistance and misrepresentation, and left the plenipotentiaries free to arrange some method of temporary government for the city. This was a difficult problem, chiefly owing to the lack of competent interpreters, but rendered more so by the natural irritation of the conquered people at the losses they had sustained, the flight of the local officers, and the alarming extent of robbery by natives, somewhat countenanced by foreign soldiers. The skill and tact of Lord Elgin were never better shown than in the construction out of such incongruous materials of a mixed government whose subsequent easy working abundantly proved the master mind of the builder.[1] The two Manchus, Governor Pihkwei and the commandant of the garrison—called also the Tartar general—were now brought forward to assist in saving their capital from destruction and to form with the allies a joint tribunal. Pihkwei became legally (by Yeh's capture) the governor-general of the Liang Kwang, and his functions in that capacity were not interfered with; those of his colleague had always been restricted within the city walls. On January 9th they were installed by Lord Elgin and Baron Gros with all possible ceremony as rulers of the city, under the surveillance of three foreigners, Colonel Holloway and Consul Harry Parkes for the British, and Captain Martineau for the French. This commission had its headquarters in the same extensive yamun with Pihkwei, in whom happily were combined some estimable qualities for managing the difficult post he filled. The orderly habits of the literati and traders in and around Canton afforded a guaranty that no seditious proceedings would be countenanced against this joint authority if it gave them the security they had asked from the allies. A force of marines and the Fifty-ninth Regiment were quartered on Pagoda Hill, on the north side of the city, and ere long the commandant's yamun was cleared of its rubbish and put in order for the commission, leaving the other for Pihkwei. The allied chiefs deemed it wisest to attempt to govern as little in detail as possible, and their commissioners found enough to do in adjusting complaints brought by

[1] "You may imagine," he writes, "what it is to undertake to govern some millions of people when we have *in all* two or three people who understand the language! I never had so difficult a matter to arrange."

the Chinese against their own men. The Cantonese did not fail to contrast the considerate treatment they received from their foreign captors with the carnage and utter ruin which would have followed the occupation of the city by the Tai-pings or other insurgents, and during the whole period quietly submitted. The greater part of the responsible labor came upon Mr. Parkes, because of his ability to talk Chinese, but before many months he had taught many natives how to assist in carrying out the necessary details. He showed much skill in circumventing the designs of the discontented officials at Fuhshan, giving Pihkwei all the native criminals to judge, restraining the thievery or cruelty of the foreign police, and sending out proclamations for the guidance and admonition of the people.[1]

The kindness shown by Lord Elgin after the capture of Canton infused itself into the minds of those working with and under him, and the newly installed governor soon recovered his composure as he found himself in possession of his own dignities and power. The local and provincial officers under him kept themselves at Fuhshan, now recovering from its destruction of three years before. By the end of January affairs were put in order, the blockade was taken off the port, foreign merchants returned and settled in the warehouses still unharmed on Honam, while the native dealers reopened their shops in the vicinity.[2] Sixteen months had elapsed since the affair of the Arrow, and every one felt that a new day had begun to dawn on the relations of China with other lands.[3] Among the papers

---

[1] *Blue Book: Lord Elgin's Correspondence*, July 15, 1859, Despatches Nos. 88, 94, 108, and 128. Oliphant, *Elgin's Mission to China*, Vol. I., p. 170.

[2] Oddly enough, among the most earnest appeals for the restoration of commerce came one from Pihkwei himself, who wrote to Lord Elgin: "The eagerness with which merchants will devote themselves to gain, if the trade be now thrown well open, will increase manifold the good understanding between our nations, and the step will thus, at the same time, enhance your excellency's reputation."—*Blue Book*, January 24, 1858.

[3] The letters of G. W. Cooke, the *Times'* correspondent (London, Routledge, 1858), contain a fairly complete account of the proceedings of the allies at Canton; his conversations with Governor-General Yeh on the way to Calcutta are less valuable. Compare an article in the *Revue des Deux Mondes* (1e juillet, 1859), by C. Lavallée, *Un Historiographe de la Presse anglaise dans la guerre de Chine.*

taken in Yeh's yamun were the ratified copies of the treaties between China and Great Britain, France, and the United States, carefully preserved there, it was said, by directions from Peking, in order to serve for reference in case of dispute as to the text. It was, however, one of the indexes proving the desire of the Emperor to keep himself aloof from personal contact with foreigners.

The allied chiefs, early in the month of February, proposed to their American and Russian coadjutors to join them in laying their demands before the Peking Court, and affording it one more opportunity to amicably settle the pending difficulties by sending an officer to Shanghai with full powers for that end. Both Russians and Americans were cordially in unison with the allies, and their several despatches addressed to Yü, the first member of the *Nui Koh*, or 'Inner Council,' at Peking, were taken up to Shanghai and thence to Suchau, where Ho Kwei-tsing received and forwarded them before the end of February. These four letters simultaneously sent to the secluded court at Peking contained nothing which could alarm its members; but such was the ignorance of the highest officers there, that they knew not what to do—ostrich-like, hiding their heads from the approaching danger, simply declining to answer any unpleasant communication, hoping thereby to put far off the evil day. Their isolation would remain if left to themselves, and to have sent Kiying again to the south would only have cherished their stupid pride and worked their subjects ultimate injury. Their old-time policy of absolute non-intercourse lay like some great frigate sunk athwart the mouth of a river; the obstacle once removed, nothing remained to prevent the vast and populous regions beyond the barrier from an active and profitable communion with the whole world. They could no longer be left *in statu quo*, and few can find fault with the plan proposed to solve their difficulties—a plan which brought the four most powerful nations of Christendom in joint consent to set themselves on a fair and advantageous footing with the most ancient and populous nation of Asia. To those who admit the direct government of the Almighty Ruler in ordering the policy of nations in accord with His wise plans, this simultaneous approach to Peking will always be deemed as one of the waymarks of human progress.

The letters presented to the Emperor[1] form in their topics and tone a pleasant contrast to the communications in past years. That of the Russian minister was peculiar in bringing forward the desirableness of allowing the profession of Christianity to all natives desirous of embracing it; but this point was made the subject of an address by the British missionaries at Ningpo and Shanghai to Lord Elgin, whose reply was a happy exposition of the dangers and difficulties connected with the toleration of Christianity by a government ignorant of its precepts. The imperial replies to these advances were, as every one expected, in the strain of *non possumus.* Lord Elgin returned his copy to Ho Kwei-tsing at Suchau, and enclosed therewith another despatch to Yü, in which he announced his intention to proceed to Taku, where he would await the arrival of a commissioner qualified to treat upon the points in dispute.

The force designed to accompany the allied chiefs was gathering at Shanghai, and by the middle of April most of the ships and transports had anchored off the Pei ho, together with the American frigates Minnesota and Mississippi and the Russian gunboat Amerika, having the legations of those nations on board. Nothing could be more dreary than the aspect of the rendezvous at this season. The ships were obliged to anchor about eight miles from shore, which was level, and would have been invisible if it had not been for the forts at the entrance of the river. The dim, hazy horizon was lurid with the rays of the sun shining through the dust that came in clouds from the plains of Mongolia and Chihlí. The turbid waters were often lashed into foam by the conflicting forces of tides and winds which acted on it from every quarter, and kept the gulf in a turmoil. No native boats ventured out to traffic, as would have been the case in the south, and the only signs of life were the gunboats and launches running in and out of the river, or the barges passing from ship to ship. Added to other discommodi-

---

[1] These are all given in the correspondence of Mr. Reed, printed by the Senate—Despatch No. 9, *Ex. Document* No. 30, March 13, 1860, pp. 122–183.

ties, were occasional blasts of hot air which swept over the water, charged with fine dust that settled on the decks and rigging, and insinuated itself into the dress and faces in an uncomfortable manner.

As usual the Chinese had done nothing. The increasing number and size of the ships which were anchored off the Pei ho had, however, been duly reported at Peking, and the Russian admiral had received a reply to his announcement of arrival. On April 23d communications were addressed by the four ministers to Yu-ching at Peking, and on the 26th replies came from Tan Ting-siang, governor-general of Chihlí, informing them that he, with Tsunglun and Wu, had been deputed to "receive their complaints and investigate and manage." The governor-general was not empowered to settle upon the terms of a treaty, but he desired to have a personal conference to learn what was demanded. Upon the day appointed the Russian and American ministers met Tan at the Taku forts (April 30th) at separate hours, when they learned that he had not been invested with "full powers," like those granted to Kíying and Ílipu in 1842, but had authority to discuss all matters preparatory to signing a treaty. The truth was that they were quite ignorant of the important questions raised at Canton; but while willing to discuss them, they were equally set on keeping the foreigners away from the capital. Here the allied chiefs and their two colleagues took issue. The former held out for commissioners to be sent with full powers; but the latter deeming that the governor-general had adequate authority, accordingly presented him with the main points of their demands and afterward with the drafts of their treaties. The negotiations were delayed by the difficulties of the entrance, but they afforded a needed instruction to these conceited and ignorant men, who were thus enabled at their leisure to prepare for the struggle. Not only were the officers themselves brought face to face with their dreaded visitors, and made to perceive the folly of resisting the armaments at their command, but with the democratic habits usual in Chinese courts, the hundreds of attendants present at the conferences heard all that passed.

Ere the non-belligerent powers had completed their negotiations, the allies turned over theirs into the hands of the two admirals, MM. Seymour and Rigault de Genouilly. These advanced up the river on May 20th, forcing the slight boom across the stream, and capturing all the forts on both banks, with all their stores. Comparatively few Chinese were killed, and their defence of the forts was creditable to their courage and skill. All the troops fled or were driven from their intrenched camps as far as Taku town, and the other defences, stockades, and fire-rafts having been destroyed, the gunboats proceeded to Tientsin. The losses by shot on the part of the Allies were unhappily doubled by the explosion of a powder magazine in a fort as a party of Frenchmen entered. The news that the foreigners had forced the defences at the mouth of the Pei ho was soon spread through the towns along its banks, and myriads of unarmed people flocked to the shore to see the gun-boats, whose smoke and masts towering above the low land indicated their presence to the amazed inhabitants.

A house having been prepared at Tientsin for the allied chiefs, Lord Elgin and Baron Gros reached the city at daylight on May 30th, followed by the other two ministers, all of them having come up during the night without mishap or opposition. The inhabitants of the city were highly excited at the presence of the vessels and those of whom they had heard such dreadful stories, but their curiosity and fear kept them quiet and civil, and they were content with lining the shores in dense crowds, to gaze and talk. The general ignorance of each other's language did not prevent a constant intercourse with the citizens, all the more agreeable after the confinement on board ship. One old man was found managing a ferry-boat, who remembered Lord Amherst's visit in 1816. After his inquiries as to the meaning of the flags on board the ships had been answered, he exclaimed, "How easily you and we could get along if you but understood our language"—to which the crowd around reëchoed their hearty assent.

Two higher commissioners now appeared on the scene of action, Kweiliang and Hwashana, who superseded the discomfited Tan, Tsunglun, and Wu, and presented their cards as having been invested with full powers to treat. Negotiations were opened with them, and thus, after months of delay, the plan which Yeh had so foolishly adhered to at Canton in October, to refuse all personal discussion, was accomplished at Tientsin under far more promising circumstances. The Chinese were obliged to accept almost any terms offered them, for negotiations carried on under such conditions were hardly those of free agents. The high commissioners were ignorant beyond conception of the gravity of their position and the results which were to flow from these treaties, whose provisions, linked into one compact by the favored nation clause, were, in fact, to form the future magna charta between almost the two halves of the human race. It was true that the Chinese commissioners were not altogether their own masters in making them, but owing to their perverse seclusion, they had foolishly shut themselves out from the opportunity of learning their rights. They had, of course, no desire to learn what they knew nothing about, and there was no alternative other than the display of force to break down the barriers which pride alone made strong. They had some grounds for fear, from their recent occupation of Canton, that the British wished for more territory than Hongkong; and the frequent visits of the national vessels of Great Britain, the United States, and France to the insurgents at Nanking indicated serious results in the future, for the latter owed all their religious fanaticism to foreign inspiration. To the persistent smuggling of opium along the whole coast since the treaties negotiated by Kíying sixteen years before, and the many social and financial evils entailed thereby, were now added the atrocities of the coolie trade in Kwangtung province. Yet the reserve of the officials upon these and other topics on which they might be expected to have expressed their views or remonstrances, was only equalled by the politeness and freedom with which they met their enemies in consultation. Never again in the history of nations can functionaries to whom were confided the settlement of questions of so great moment, be brought together in such honest ignorance of the other's intentions, fears, and wishes. It was high time for each of the five powers, now face to face, to have the way opened for the removal of this ignorance and a better understanding substituted.

The despatches of Lord Elgin and Mr. Reed contain translations of many reports and memorials which were found in Yeh's yamun at Canton, and give one a good idea of the sort of information furnished to the Emperor by his highest officers. It is a wrong view of these papers to regard their extraordinary misstatements as altogether designed to deceive the court and screen the ill-success of the writers, for they had had no more facilities to investigate the real condition of foreign lands and the policy of their rulers than had the poor boy Caspar Hauser to learn about his neighbors.

One untoward event occurred during the negotiations. This was the sudden arrival of Kíying (June 8th) and his effort to force himself into the company of the plenipotentiaries. Since his departure from Canton in 1847 he had filled the premiership before the death of the late Emperor Taukwang, after which he had been deprived of all power and most of his honors. He seemed to have tried to recover them by making large promises at court respecting his influence over the *barbarians*; but when he reached Tientsin he was without credentials enabling him to participate, and acted as if his misfortunes had in a measure unsettled his reason. The British minister was suspicious of his designs, and sent his two secretaries, on the 9th, to learn what they could of or from him. These gentlemen plainly pointed out to the old man the difficulties in the way of settling the present troubles in any other manner than by acceding to the demands of Lord Elgin. Kíying had, however, put himself in a serious dilemma. Finding very soon that he was powerless to change the course of events and get the steamers away from Tientsin (as he no doubt had promised to do, and thus prove his influence), he returned to Peking on the 12th, though he had announced the reception of his full powers only the day before. His colleagues were not sorry to have him depart, but nothing definite was learned of his fate until at the end of three weeks, when the Emperor's rescript ordering him to commit suicide was received. His case was deemed of sufficient importance to call for a summation of the principal features in order to prove the righteousness of his sentence, and manifest the Emperor's extreme desire to be at once just and gracious in his decree. Kíying's case is rather an unusual one among Chinese officials, but the real reasons for his fall are probably not all stated; his prominence abroad, arising from his connection with the Nanking treaty, was no criterion of his influence at home or of the loss to the government by his death.[1]

Soon after his departure the impertinence of a native crowd to a party of British officers while walking through the city, lent some strength to the belief that Kíying's counsel had been warlike, and that a *coup*, similar to the one made at Canton in 1841 by Yihshan, had been suggested, and the destruction of all the foreigners in Tientsin was hoped for as its result. Their relations with the citizens thus far had been amicable on the whole, and the interruption in this desirable state of things was very brief. Negotiations continued, therefore, but with an undercurrent of doubt as to details on some important points among the foreign envoys. Lord Elgin had the greatest responsibility, indeed, and the task before him was difficult and delicate, but he failed in drawing to himself his colleagues and learning their views. They hardly knew what to do, for none of them wished to thwart his desires for complete and honorable intercourse with the central government, though the manner of reaching this end might admit of discussion. This he never invited. The position of the American and Russian envoys, pledged to their instructions not to fight, and having the feeling that their nations were to obtain the advantages resulting from the hostilities of the allies, was not a pleasant one; but it could have been made so, and he himself relieved of his main anxiety as to the result, by an interview. In contrast

[1] Oliphant's *Mission of Lord Elgin to China and Japan*, pp. 238–253 (American edition), N. Y., 1860. It is interesting to note, before leaving this episode, a Frenchman's opinion of the character of this statesman: "Kíying a été de 1842 à 1844 le grand négociateur de la Chine. Les ministres étrangers ont vanté son habileté, sa finesse, ses façons aimables et courtoises. . . . Son nom symbolisait une politique nouvelle, bienveillante pour les étrangers, tolérante, libérale; il représentait une sorte de jeune Chine."—M. C. Lavallée in the *Revue des Deux Mondes*, 15 Déc. 1859, p. 602. The same article contains an interesting account of the first expedition up the Pei ho and its results.

KÍYING.

IMPERIAL COMMISSIONER.

with Lord Elgin's general bearing toward those around him, as detailed in his correspondence, his biographer gives an extract from a private letter written the day after signing his treaty, which describes his perplexities:

June 29th.—I have not written for some days, but they have been busy ones. We went on fighting and bullying, and getting the poor commissioners to concede one point after another, till Friday the 25th, when we had reason to believe that all was settled, and that the signature was to take place the following day. On Friday afternoon, however, Baron Gros came to me with a message from the Russian and American ministers to induce me to recede from two of my demands—1, a resident minister at Peking, and, 2, permission to our people to trade in the interior of China; because, as they said, the Chinese plenipotentiaries had told them that they had received a decree from the Emperor stating that they should infallibly lose their heads if they gave way on these points.

The resident minister at Peking I consider far the most important matter gained by the treaty; the power to trade in the interior hardly less so. I had at stake not only these important points in my treaty, for which I had fought so hard, but I know not what behind. For the Chinese are such fools that it was impossible to tell, if we gave way on one point, whether they would not raise difficulties on every other. I sent for the admiral; gave him a hint that there was a great opportunity for England; that all the powers were deserting me on a point which they had *all*, in their original applications to Peking, demanded, and which they all intended to claim if I got it; that, therefore, we had it in our power to claim our place of priority in the East by obtaining this when others would not insist on it. Would he back me? This was the forenoon of Saturday, 26th, and the treaty was to be signed in the evening.

I may mention, as a proof of the state of people's minds, that Admiral Seymour told me that the French admiral had urged him to dine with him, assuring him that no treaty would be signed that day! I sent Frederick to the imperial commissioners to tell them that I was indignant beyond all expression at their having attempted to communicate with me through third parties; that I was ready to sign at once the treaty as it stood; but that if they delayed or retreated, I should consider negotiations at an end, go to Peking and demand a great deal more, etc. Frederick executed this most difficult task admirably, and at six P.M. I signed the treaty of Tientsin. I am now anxiously awaiting some communication from Peking. Till the Emperor accepts the treaty I shall hardly feel safe. Please God he may ratify without delay! I am sure that I express the wish just as much in the interest of China as in our own. Though I have been forced to act almost brutally, I am China's friend in all this.[1]

The importance of these two provisos was not exaggerated in his mind, but he might have seen that the difficulties with his colleagues were increased by his own reticence.

---

[1] Walrond's *Life and Letters of Lord Elgin*, p. 252.

However much a different course might have harmonized these discordant views, the pressure on the city of Tientsin was too near and severe upon the Chinese, and they yielded from fear of worse consequences when no other arguments could have induced them. It was not Lord Elgin alone who felt very sensibly, on that occasion, "the painfulness of the position of a negotiator who has to treat with persons who yield nothing to reason and everything to fear, and who are at the same time profoundly ignorant of the subjects under discussion and of their own real interests." Looked at in any point of view, this period of negotiation at Tientsin in 1858 was a remarkable epoch. The sole great power of paganism was being bound by the obligations of a treaty extorted from its monarch by a handful of men in possession of the entrance to its capital. As one of the British officers pithily stated it, two powers had China by the throat, while the other two stood by to egg them on, so that all could share the spoil. Yet the past sixteen years had proven most conclusively that, unless this pressure was exerted, the imperial government would make no advance, admit no opening for learning its real position among the nations of the world, but mulishly cherish its ignorance, its isolation, its conceit, and its folly, until these causes had worked out the ruin so fondly hoped to be avoided. Even the necessity of coming into personal official relations with the foreign consuls to promote the maintenance of good order between their subjects had been hampered or neutralized by the Chinese authorities at all the ports; and there was no hope of introducing a better state of things until foreign ministers were received at Peking. Happily, Lord Elgin then saw the question in all its bearings, and no one ever proved to be a truer friend to China than did he in forcing it upon her. He had little idea, probably, of one motive for their resistance, namely, the fear of the Manchu rulers, already referred to, that in admitting the enemy to the capital they would be as summarily ejected as had been their predecessors in 1644.

However, by the first week in July the four treaties had been signed and ratified by Hienfung, and all the vessels had left the Pei ho, which itself was no doubt the greatest proof to his Majesty that they were valid compacts; for if the tables had been turned he would not have let them off so easily, and perhaps wondered that Tientsin had not been ransomed at the same rate that Elliot had spared Canton in 1841. It is difficult to fully appreciate the crass ignorance and singular perversity of the men in whose hands the sway of the Chinese people were now lodged. He who is unwilling to acknowledge the overruling hand of God in this remarkable meeting of nations, would find it very difficult to acknowledge it anywhere in human history.

The revision of the tariff had been deferred for a future discussion among those qualified for the work. Five Chinese commissioners reached Shanghai early in October for this and other purposes, of whom Kweiliang and Hwashana were two. In this part of the negotiations the controlling power was properly left in the hands of the British, for their trade was worth more than all others combined. They used this power most selfishly, and fastened on the weak and distracted Empire a veritable remora, which has gone on sucking its resources without compunction or cessation. By making the tariff an integral part of the treaty, they theoretically made every infraction a *casus belli*, and as no provision was left for revision, it was virtually rendered impossible, since the original four powers could not again be brought to unite on its readjustment with a view to the rights of China. While particular provision was made in it for preventing the importation of salt and the implements and munitions of war, the trade in opium was legalized at a lower rate than was paid on tea and silk entering England, and the brand of immorality and smuggling was removed from its diffusion throughout China. The weakness and ignorance of the Chinese were such as laid them open to the power and craft of other nations, but the inherent wrong of the principle of ex-territoriality was never more unjustly applied than in breaking down the moral sense of a people by forcing them to legalize this drug. The evils of smuggling it were insufferable, but a heavy duty was desirable as a check and stigma upon the traffic. The solution to a statesman in Lord Elgin's position was exceedingly difficult in relation to this point, and he perhaps took the safest course under the existing circumstances, but it has proved to be fraught with evils to the Chinese. One who now reads his biography and learns his nice sense of right and equity in national affairs, will not be surprised to see his doubts as to the best course to take where all were so many moves in the dark.

The war which arose about the Arrow was now virtually closed, but many things remained to be enforced in carrying out the treaty stipulations or restraining the irritation they produced. The vastness of the Empire sundered its inhabitants so widely that each felt the troubles it endured only when they came near; but to all of them the obligations of treaty were of the most shadowy nature. It would require years of patient instruction to educate the mass of natives up to the idea that these obligations affected them as individuals. One means of this instruction, which subsequent years have shown to be both practical and profitable, was the extension and reorganization of the administration of the customs under foreign supervision. Its short service at Shanghai had proved it to be easy and safe of operation, and the increased fidelity everywhere in collecting the duties gratified the central and provincial governments exceedingly. It was a startling proof of the degrading effects of the opium and smuggling trade upon the honor of the foreign merchants that they generally resisted the transfer of collecting duties from native to foreign hands, and endeavored in a thousand ways to thwart and ridicule the altered system. This feeling, however, disappeared with the incoming of a new set of merchants, and the Chinese government has, since the first, found no difficulty in utilizing the skill, knowledge, and power of their employés, not only in fiscal departments, but wherever they felt the need of such qualifications. Beginning at Shanghai, when the local officers were helpless against their own subjects, mandarins and people alike desired the advantages of an honestly collected tariff to be extended to every port opened for foreign trade.

The changes formulated in the treaties of Tientsin could receive their accomplishment only after patient efforts on the part of ministers, consuls, and collectors to carry them into effect with due regard to the position of the native rulers. In order to open the way into the country, Lord Elgin visited Hankow in four ships in November, after he had signed the tariff. The rebels in possession of Nanking and other towns, being unapprised of his character, fired at him from some of their forts, for which "they were pounded pretty severely in return." But a few words afterward proved more effectual than many shots, and no further altercation occurred. The voyage to and return from Hankow occupied seven weeks, and inaugurated a commerce and intercourse which has resulted in much good to the natives by making them rapidly acquainted with foreigners. The right of China to the exclusive navigation of her internal waters was summarily set aside by making Hankow a seaport; on the other hand, the government derived many advantages in the moral assistance given her at the time against the rebels by having them restrained, and, up to the present day, in the stimulus given to internal trade and rapid intercourse between the peoples of remote districts.

The year 1858 was fraught with great events, involving the welfare of the people of China and Japan and their future position and progress. Much against their will they had been forced into political relations with Europe and America, and in a measure deprived of their independence under the guise of treaties which erected an *imperium in imperio* in their borders. Their rulers, ignorant of the real meaning of these principles of ex-territoriality, were tied down to observe them, and found themselves within a few years humbled before those of their own subjects who had begun to look to foreigners for protection. The perplexity of the Chinese commissioners at Shanghai in this new position was exhibited in a despatch addressed on November 1, 1858, to the three envoys. In it they discuss the right of foreigners who have no treaties to go into the interior, and insist upon the absolute necessity of restraining them, which their own mercantile consuls could not and would not do.

"Being unacquainted," they wrote, "with the usages of foreign nations in this respect, and unwilling of ourselves to lay down preventive regulations respecting issuing passports, we desire first to receive the result of your deliberations before we act in the premises." They then proceed to show how necessary it will be for the future peace between conflicting interests and nationalities that consuls should not be merchants, for "some of those of your respective nations have formerly and often acted in a manner calculated to impede and mar the harmony that existed between their nations and our own; wilfully disregarding everything but their own opinions, they have carried out their own high-handed measures to the ruin of all cordial feeling." The writers had no idea how this despatch was an argument and a proof of the need of strong measures to drag them out of their stupid ignorance and childish desires for isolation, and compel them to understand their duties. The education then begun was the only means through which to raise the Chinese rulers and people to a higher plane of civilization and liberty. One document like this carries in itself enough to show how ignorant were its writers and their colleagues of their own duties, and how hopeless was the prospect of their emerging voluntarily from their seclusion. The treaties bound them down to keep the peace, while they opened the channels through which the people could learn whatever was true and useful, without fear of punishment or reproach. The toleration of Christianity, the residence of foreign ministers at Peking, and the freedom to travel through the land were three avenues heretofore closed against the welfare and progress of China which the treaties opened, and through which she has already made more real advances than ever before in her history.[1]

---

[1] For full details on these important negotiations, see the Blue Book presented to Parliament July 15, 1859, containing Lord Elgin's correspondence; *U. S. Senate Executive Document* No. 30, read March 13, 1860, containing correspondence of Messrs. Reed, Williams, and Ward, from June, 1857, to September 17, 1859; Oliphant's *Mission of Lord Elgin to China and Japan*, London and New York, 1860; Lieutenant-Colonel Fisher, *Personal Narrative of Three Years' Service in China*, London, 1863; le Marquis de Moges, *Baron Gros's Embassy to China and Japan*, 1860; Walrond's *Letters and Journals of James, Earl of Elgin*, London, 1872; Lieut. J. D. Johnston, *China and Japan*, Philadelphia, 1860; *North American Review*, Vol. XC., p. 125; *Blackwood's Magazine*, Vols. LXXXVI., p. 647, LXXXVII., pp. 430, 535, and LXXXIX., p. 373.

By the end of December, 1858, the four envoys had left China, as well as most of the small force under their control. None of them had reached Peking, so that the Emperor was relieved of his fear that he would be carried off as was his commissioner, Yeh, from Canton; he had, moreover, another year of grace to learn what he ought to do to carry out the treaties. He was also relieved by the refusal of the allies to join their quarrel with the efforts of the Tai-pings and march together to the conquest of the Empire. In Canton the presence of the allies had been an irritation chiefly to the provincial officers, who busied themselves in stimulating large bodies of braves in its vicinity to assassinate and rob individual foreigners near or in the city, keeping up in this manner a lasting feeling of discontent. Several skirmishes took place, and a large district within the city near the British quarters on Kwanyin Shan was burned over to insure protection against sudden attacks. The new governor-general, Hwang, had formed a league of the gentry and braves, which chiefly exhibited their power in harassing their own countrymen. He was removed in disgrace at Lord Elgin's request, and all these puny and useless attacks brought to an end.

An incident which occurred near Canton about fifteen months after the city had been captured, strikingly shows the character of the people: "February 11th.—On the 8th a body of troops about one thousand strong started on an expedition which was to take three days. I accompanied, or rather preceded them on the first day's march, about twelve miles from Canton. We rode through a very pretty country, passing by the village of Shek-tsing, where there was a fight a fortnight ago. The people were very respectful, and apparently not alarmed by our visit. At the place where the troops were to encamp for the night a cattle fair was in progress, and our arrival did not seem to interrupt the proceedings. February 13th.—The military expedition was entirely successful. The troops were everywhere received as friends. Considering what has been of yore the state of feeling in this province toward us, I think this almost the most remarkable thing which has happened since I came here. Would it have happened if I had given way to those who wished me to carry fire and sword through all the country villages?"[1]

These same villages furnished thousands of volunteers in May, 1841, to attack Sir Hugh Gough's army, and had been engaged in a desperate struggle with their countrymen only three years before, so that this change was owing neither to cowardice nor sulkiness. It had been brought about chiefly through considerate treatment of the people by the British garrison in Canton, by honest payment for supplies, and by regard for the traffic and local government of the city; the citizens consequently had no complaint to make or revenge to satisfy. Those who from infancy had been brought up to call every foreigner a *fan-kwei*, or 'foreign devil,' now slowly appreciated the fact that they had been mistaken—nor were the misconceptions all on their side. During the three years the city was occupied, public opinion there underwent an entire change; and the Cantonese are now as courteous as they before were ill-mannered.

At this season of rebellion and foreign war under which China was now suffering, the province of Kwangtung had a special cause for just irritation against all foreigners in the coolie trade. The headquarters of this trade were at Macao, and by 1860 it had become nearly the only business carried on there. The population of the colony is perhaps seventy-odd thousand, of whom less than five thousand wear a foreign dress. Traffic and industry are mostly carried on by Chinese, who do all the work. When the trade of hiring Chinese as contract laborers to go to Cuba, Peru, and elsewhere began, there was no difficulty in obtaining men willing to try their fortunes abroad. As rumors of gold diggings open to their labors in California were spread abroad and confirmed by returning miners, the coolie ships were readily filled by men whose ignorance of outer lands made them easily believe that they were bound to El Dorado, whatever country they shipped for. The inducement for hiring them was the low rate of wages ($4 a month) at which they were willing to sell their labor, and the profits derived from introducing them into western tropical regions. The temptations

---

[1] Walrond's *Letters and Journals of Lord Elgin*, p. 308.

of this business became so great that within ten years the demand had far exceeded the supply. Seldom has the unscrupulous character of trade, where its operations are left free from the restraints either of competent authority or of morality, been more sadly exhibited than in the conduct of the agents who filled these coolie ships. The details of the manner in which natives of all classes, scholars, travellers, laborers, peddlers, and artisans, were kidnapped in town and country and sent to Macao, were seldom known, because the victims were unable to make themselves heard. When the rebels at Fuhshan were defeated in 1855, thousands of their followers were glad to save their lives by shipping as coolies, but this lasted only a short time.

The allied commissioners in charge of Canton took cognizance of these outrages, and upon the representations of Governor-General Lao took vigorous measures for breaking up the trade at Whampoa.[1] The United States minister, Hon. J. E. Ward, lent his aid in February, 1860, by allowing the Chinese authorities to take three hundred and seventeen men out of the American ship Messenger in order to ascertain whether any of them were detained on board against their will. Every one of them declined to go back to the ship, but it was not proved how many had been beguiled away on false pretences—the usual mode of kidnapping. The report of the commission sent to Cuba a dozen years later asserts, as the result of careful inquiries, that the majority of the coolies in Cuba "were decoyed abroad, not legitimately induced to emigrate."

The Portuguese rulers of Macao were unwilling to make thorough investigation into the facts about this business until after the return of the commission sent to Cuba in 1873, whose report disclosed the inevitable evils and wrongs inherent in the traffic. Urged by the British government, they finally (in 1875) closed the barracoons, and thus put an end to it. During the twenty-five years of its existence about five hundred thousand coolies were taken away.

---

[1] Compare Lieutenant-Colonel Fisher, *Personal Narrative of Three Years' Service in China*, pp. 260–342, where the matter is pretty thoroughly discussed and Lao's proclamations given in detail.

To return to the war: throughout the winter no event of note occurred in any part of China, but the imperial government was busily employed in fortifying the mouth of the Pei ho to prevent the entrance of the allies. They demolished the old forts to rebuild new ones of materials gathered on the spot, and constructed somewhat after the manner laid down in foreign authorities on fortification. These books had been translated for them by natives trained in mission schools. Notwithstanding all that Kweiliang and Hwashana may have assured them to the contrary, the Emperor and his officers could not divest themselves of their fears of serious reprisals, if not of conquest, should they permit the allied gunboats to anchor a second time at Tientsin and their embassies to enter the capital. The two commissioners awaited at Shanghai the arrival of the British, French, and American plenipotentiaries, for the purpose of urging them to exchange the ratifications in that city. Nevertheless, since Peking was expressly appointed in the first two treaties as the place for signing them, Mr. Bruce and M. Bourboulon, the English and French ministers, determined to insist upon this detail. The poor commissioners, on the other hand, knowing more than they dared to tell of the hostile preparations going on, steadily declined the offer of a passage to Taku. Mr. Ward was not tied down to any place or time for exchanging the American treaty, but decided to do so at the same place with his colleagues. The three ministers remained in the south to exchange views and allow the British gunboats to collect off Taku before their arrival, when they all joined them on June 20th. The appearance of the forts was entirely different from last year, and confirmed the reports of the great efforts making to prevent foreigners reaching the capital in large numbers. The river was found to be barred by an elaborate boom of timber and chains; but though no soldiers were in sight on the battlements, it was evident that a collision was intended. The reconnoissance had been carefully made from the 17th to the 24th, and the Chinese general, Săng-ko-lin-sin, felt confident of his ability to hold his own against the ships inside of the bar. All official intercourse was refused with Admiral Hope, though he had stated his purpose clearly, because, as was alleged, these forts and men were merely gathered by the common people to defend themselves against pirates.

In order to discover the real state of feeling toward a neutral, Commodore Tatnall took Mr. Ward, in the United States chartered steamer Toeywan, into the river on the 24th, and proceeded toward a jetty near the fort. The steamer ran aground when about half a mile short of it; the minister then sent his interpreters to the jetty, where they were met by a dozen or more miserably dressed fellows who had come from the fort for that purpose. On learning the errand of the foreigners, one or two of the men spoke up in a way which showed that they were officers—probably disguised as coolies—telling the deputation that the passage to Tientsin by the Pei ho had been barred, but that the governor-general, Hăngfuh, was then at Pehtang, a place about ten miles up the coast, where he was ready to receive the American minister. They added that they had no authority to take any letter or card for him; that they knew very well the nationality of the Toeywan, which would not be harmed if she did not attempt to break through the boom laid just above the jetty; and, lastly, that they were not at all empowered to aid or advise the Americans in getting up to Pehtang. The whole episode was a ridiculous ruse on the part of the Chinese to hide their design of forcibly preventing the ministers from ascending the river; but by so undignified a behavior the general commanding the works forfeited whatever moral advantage might otherwise have remained on his side. After Admiral Hope had commenced his operations against the barriers, Hăngfuh did indeed send a letter to the British minister—then lying nine miles off the shore—informing him of the arrangements made at Pehtang to take the allied envoys from thence to the capital. These arrangements certainly violated no article of the treaties, nor any promise made to the foreigners, though they neutralized entirely the journey to Peking upon which the British government had determined to send its plenipotentiary.

One may learn from the letters of Mr. Bruce to Lord Malmesbury (of July 5th and 13th) many details of the impertinent reception accorded to Admiral Hope's messengers by the rabble and soldiers near the Taku forts, all proving plainly enough their hostile intentions. But the minister overlooks what we, in retracing the history of these years, cannot too attentively keep in mind, namely, the ever-present fear of trickery and foul play with their unknown engines of war which the Emperor's counsellors momentarily dreaded from their foreign adversaries. On the other hand, what could be done with a government which would never condescend to appreciate its own weakness, would never speak or act the truth, would never treat any other nation as an equal? These and other despatches from the Blue Book afford a key to the policies of both parties in this remarkable contest, and convince the impartial student of the necessity of personal contact and acquaintance before it was possible to reach a lasting understanding between the holders of so widely separated views.

During the night of the 23d, after the Toeywan had floated at high water, the British advanced and blew up the first boom, leaving, however, the second and stronger obstruction untouched. The attempt to ascend the river in force was commenced by the allies in the following afternoon, when the forts opened fire upon them and by evening had sunk or silenced almost every vessel. In this fleet thirteen small gunboats were engaged, one of the largest among them, a French craft, carrying six hundred men; besides these were some six hundred marines and engineers designed to serve as an escort upon the journey to the capital. This guard was now landed in the mud before the forts and an attempt made to carry the works by escalade, but the effort failed, and by daylight the men were all once more afloat. From the gunboats twenty-five men were killed and ninety-three wounded; the loss among the marines was naturally heavier—sixty-four killed and two hundred and fifty-two wounded, while of the boats four were sunk.[1]

Throughout this action the American vessel Toeywan remained inside of the bar, being a non-combatant. The gallant energy of Commodore Tatnall, who in the thick of the fight passed through the fleet to visit the British admiral lying

---

[1] One of these afterward floated of itself and was preserved.

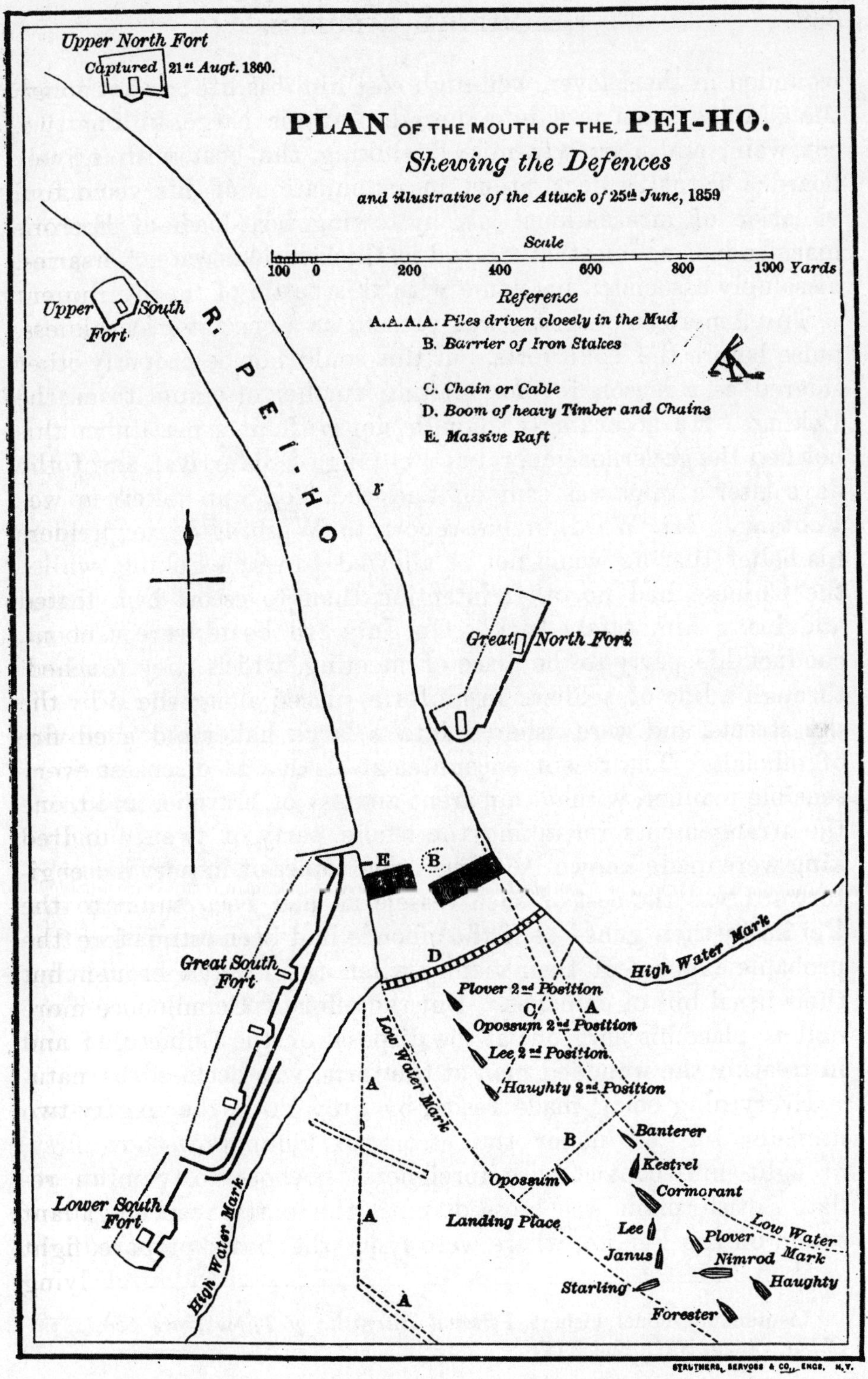
PLAN OF THE MOUTH OF THE PEI-HO.
Shewing the Defences
and Illustrative of the Attack of 25th June, 1859
Scale
100 0 200 400 600 800 1000 Yards
Reference
A.A.A.A. Piles driven closely in the Mud
B. Barrier of Iron Stakes
C. Chain or Cable
D. Boom of heavy Timber and Chains
E. Massive Raft
Upper North Fort
Captured 21st Augt. 1860.
Upper South Fort
R. PEI-HO
Great North Fort
Great South Fort
Lower South Fort
High Water Mark
Low Water Mark
Plover 2nd Position
Opossum 2nd Position
Lee 2nd Position
Haughty 2nd Position
Banterer
Kestrel
Cormorant
Opossum
Landing Place
Lee
Plover
Janus
Nimrod
Haughty
Starling
Forester
STRUTHERS, SERVOSS & CO., ENGS. N.Y.

wounded in the Plover, well-nigh cost him his life; a shot from the Chinese guns tore into the stern of his barge, killing the coxswain, and narrowly missed sinking the boat with all on board. Tatnall's declaration, in extenuation of his technical violation of international law by towing boat-loads of British marines into action, that "blood is thicker than water," has indissolubly associated his name with this battle of the Pei ho.[1]

The American minister was present as a spectator at this repulse before the Taku forts, but this could not be properly considered as a reason for not making further attempts to reach Peking. He accordingly, though not without some difficulty, notified the governor-general at Pehtang of his arrival, and four days later a pilot was sent off and the Toeywan taken up to Pehtang. Mr. Ward, in his report to Washington, expresses his belief that he would not be allowed to reach Peking, while the Chinese had no other intention than to escort him there and bring him safely back. On July 8th boats were sent to conduct his party to the place of meeting, which they reached through a line of soldiers in uniform placed along the sides of the streets, and were ushered into a large hall amid a crowd of officials. The recent encounter at Taku was discussed in a sensible manner, without apparent anxiety or bravado, and then the arrangements for taking the whole party of twenty to Peking were made known. Among other topics of inquiry brought forward was the cost of such vessels as had been sunk in the Pei ho by their guns—as if the officials had been estimating the probable expense of their victory when the English brought in their usual bill of damages. But the offer of Commodore Tatnall to place his surgeons at the disposal of the Chinese, to aid in treating the wounded men at the forts, was declined.

Everything being made ready by July 20th, the American minister set out under the escort of Chunghow, now first brought into contact with foreigners. About forty miles of flat, saltish plain was crossed, until the party reached Pehtsang, on the Pei ho, where were lying the boats prepared for

---

[1] Lieutenant-Colonel Fisher's *Personal Narrative of Three Years' Service in China*, Chaps. XIII. and XIV.

their reception. As they proceeded up the river the inhabitants flocked to the banks to behold the dreaded foreigners, but no expressions of vaunting or hostility were heard among the myriads who now gazed for the first time upon them. The vast crowd at Tungchau, when the twenty Americans landed, comprised apparently the whole population of that city; clad in white summer garments, and preserving a most remarkable stillness and decorum as they lined the river banks and highway, this silent, gazing multitude produced upon the strangers an effect incomparably weird. The day was oppressively hot, and many preferred the carts to the mules provided for the trip to Peking, where they all arrived on the 27th. A ridiculous rumor, illustrated by appropriate pictures, respecting this journey was circulated in Paris about a fortnight afterward, stating that Mr. Ward and his party were conducted from the coast in an immense "box or travelling chamber, drawn overland by oxen," and then put "on a raft to be towed up the river and Imperial Canal as far as the gate of the capital. They were well treated, and were taken back to the coast in the same manner." This *jeux d'esprit* probably expressed the popular sentiment in France of what was expected from the Chinese, and has ever since been associated with it.

On announcing his arrival, a meeting was arranged for the 30th between Mr. Ward and Kweiliang and Hwashana, at which all the time was occupied in discussing the question of the manner of audience. The minister had the advantage in this interesting colloquy, for he had come up at the invitation of the governor-general, had no directions from the President upon the matter, was quite indifferent as to the result of the conference, and had no presents to be rejected as Lord Amherst's were in 1816. The nature of the *kotow* and the reasons for requiring it of all who had audience of the Emperor were fully discussed at several interviews in the most amicable and courteous manner. The Chinese were anxious to bring about an audience, and went so far as to waive the *kotow*, or knocking head, from the first, and proposed instead that the envoy should bend one knee as he approached the sovereign. This was even less of an obeisance than English courtiers paid their Queen, and might have been accepted without difficulty—if any compromise were possible—had not one of the party previously declared the religious nature of the ceremony by saying, "If we do not kneel before the Emperor, we do not show him any respect; it is that or nothing, and is the same reverence which we pay the gods." Kweiliang further said that he himself would willingly burn incense before the President of the United States if asked to do so.[1]

During their whole national history the Chinese rulers and people had accepted this ceremony as the inseparable prerogative of the Son of Heaven; and as this discussion in their capital was in the hearing of a great crowd of officials, who, doubtless, were prompt enough in circulating among the populace a report of the disagreement, one may appreciate the feelings of the latter when the American embassy was allowed quietly to leave the city without entering into the "Great Interior" to behold the Dragon's Face. Foreigners have been so ready in China to ridicule or depreciate whatever partakes of resistance to their notions (unless it be backed up by force to make it respected), that this remarkable discussion on a vital point in Chinese etiquette and theology was generally regarded as silly verbiage on their part or ascribed to the effect of fear on the part of the Americans. As the time and place for exchanging ratifications were not mentioned in the treaty, there was no insuperable difficulty in adjourning the ceremony to another place; yet it seemed a grotesque ending to the four days' discussion for Kweiliang to seriously ask the minister for what purpose he had come to Peking, he himself being quite at a loss to understand the reason. Mr. Ward replied that it was to deliver the letter from the President, and to exchange the ratifications. It would have been better if he had held him to the promise made by the governor-general at Pehtang to do so in Peking. However, the return trip was concluded by the exchange of ratifications on August 15th at Pehtang, and the departure of the frigate for Shanghai soon after.

---

[1] See Ward's despatches, pp. 594–617, *U. S. Senate Executive Document* No. 30, read March 13, 1860; *American Eclectic Magazine*, New York, Vol. 51, April and May, 1861; *North China Br. R. A. Society*, Vol. I., No. 3, 1859.

The mortification of having been repulsed at Taku was not concealed by the British public or press, when they ascribed it to the too hasty landing at sunset on a mud flat over which there was no pathway or footing. There certainly was no treachery on the part of the Chinese, as Mr. Swinhoe declares in his *North China Campaign*, for they plainly told what they would do if the passage were attempted.[1] Yet it was a grievous disappointment to find that the exchange of ratifications had been interrupted from any cause; and though it will probably always be a debatable point whether it was right for the allied envoys to refuse the offered means of reaching Peking by way of Pehtang, there was no debate now as to the necessity of hastening to the capital at once.

The British and French governments moved immediately in the matter, and wisely decided to place the settlement of the question in the same hands that had carried it thus far. In April, 1860, Earl Russell wrote to Lord Elgin that "Her Majesty resolved to employ every means calculated to establish peace with the Emperor of China, and had determined to call upon him again to give his valuable services to promote this important object." The indispensable conditions were three, viz., an apology for the attack on the allied forces at the Pei ho; the ratification and execution of the treaty; and payment for the expenses incurred by the allies. Lord Elgin's colleague was Baron Gros, and the two were ready to leave Europe in April. They were supported in making their demands by an army of about ten thousand British troops of all arms, gathered from England, Cape Colony, and India, and nearly seven thousand French sent from France. Their respective naval forces were not largely added to, but the requisite transports increased the fleets to more than two hundred vessels in all, of which thirty-three

---

[1] Though they told many lies as well. These charges against the Chinese were reiterated until they were believed by all the world; but in the effort to find a good reason for proceeding to Peking in order to exchange the ratifications, it was not needful to say that the forts fired upon the British ships without notice. Mr. Bruce's despatches to Lord Malmesbury (of July 13th), together with the enclosures and translations of native documents, discuss this question with much good sense.

were French. The latter had small iron gunboats, fitted to carry one gun, brought from home in fifteen pieces each; when screwed together each boat had three compartments, made water-tight with layers of vulcanized rubber at the joinings. The British forces gathered at Talien-wan Bay on the south-eastern side of Prince Regent's Sword, and the French at Chifu on the coast of Shantung. The plenipotentiaries had arrived in July of this year and found the imperial government maintaining its old attitude of conciliation and undue assumption. On March 8th the foreigners' terms had been made known by Mr. Bruce, and a reply shortly afterward transmitted to him through Ho Kwei-tsing at Shanghai. In it the lurking fear of reprisals, so largely actuating its conduct, appears from the conclusion, when the council says: "If Mr. Bruce will come north without vessels of war and with but a moderate retinue, and will wait at Pehtang to exchange the treaties, China will not take him to task for what has gone by. But if he be resolved to bring up a number of war-vessels, and if he persist in proceeding by way of Taku, this will show that his true purpose is not the exchange of treaties."[1] After such a declaration there was but one way left by which to prove to the Emperor how thoroughly in earnest were the allies in their intention of exchanging the treaties. The last bulwark of Chinese seclusion was now to be broken down—never more, we may hope, to be erected against the advancing influences of a more enlightened civilization.

After the usual delays incident to moving large bodies of troops with their various equipages, the combined forces left their anchorages on July 26th, presenting with their long lines of ships a grand sight as they went up the smooth waters of the Gulf of Pechele toward the mouth of the Pehtang River. This assemblage was many times larger than the armaments sent to the same region in the two previous years, and the experiences of those years had prepared both parties to regard this third attempt to reach the Court of Cambaluc as decisive of their future relations. The forces found much inconvenience in ef-

---

[1] Wolseley's *Narrative*, p. 14. Fisher's *China*, Chap. XXIII.

fecting a landing at Pehtang, where the beach at low tide extends over miles of ooze and sticky mud, but met no forcible opposition. The towns in this region are among the most repulsive-looking on the whole Chinese coast. In consequence of the saline soil no trees or grass are to be seen on the wide plain; the only green things being a few fruit trees near the houses, or scattering patches of salsola and similar plants. The houses are built of mud and chopped straw; their walls rest on layers of sorghum stalks spread on the foundation to intercept the saline influences, while the thatched roofs also contain much mud. These soon present a scanty covering of grass, which, speedily withering in the hot sun, imparts to the dwelling a still more forlorn aspect. Cheerless enough on a bright day, the appearance of one of these hamlets in wet weather—with mud streaming from the roofs, the streets reeking with noisome filth, through which loaded carts and half-naked men wend dolefully their way—is certainly melancholy beyond any description.

The allies were on shore by the evening of August 2d, and in a most pitiable plight in their own eyes. The men had been obliged to wade through the mud left by the retiring tide to reach solid ground, and then cross a moat that received the drainings of the town, a reeking mass much worse, of course, than the other. No fresh water was to be had, and the time which elapsed before the men could be supplied from the boats was spent in putting themselves up for the night, wet, dirty, and hungry as they were. In the morning it was found that the few forts which they were to attack were merely for show, and soon the town was occupied by the troops, their generals taking the temples for quarters. In less than three days every house in it had been pillaged, and whatever was worthless for plunder was destroyed as useless, "the few natives that still lingered by their unusurped domiciles," adds Mr. Swinhoe, "quietly watching with the eye of despair the destruction of all the property they possessed in the world, and the ruin of their hopes perhaps forever." Even the poor wretches who were trying to carry off their goods in packs were stopped and stripped by the prowling soldiers.

In less than a fortnight the entire force had been brought ashore without accident or opposition. There were men, tents, guns, horses, provisions, animals, stores, ammunition, baggage, —everything, in short, which an army now needs and which steam easily brings to it. Besides these, two thousand five hundred Cantonese coolies, each of whom is estimated by Colonel Wolseley, with supreme candor, to have been of more general value than any three baggage animals. They were working constantly for ten days, carrying water, landing stores, and performing the toil devolving on camp followers, for which this author magnanimously praises them by saying: "They were easily fed, and when properly treated most manageable."

On August 12th the forces were ready to move on the Taku forts lying about five miles distant across the plain, now rendered miry by the constant rains. A single causeway three miles long, flanked by deep ditches, traversed it, and along this progress, especially for the heavy artillery, was exceedingly slow. Upon their passage of this road the Chinese general, Săngkolinsin, yielded the only vantage-ground where he could have encountered his enemy with hope of success. This ignorant blunder on the part of so energetic a commander seems all the more unaccountable, since a week previously the Chinese cavalry had been much emboldened by some slight successes over a reconnoitring party of the allies, and "approached our outposts with wonderful courage, a few even advancing to within a few hundred yards, brandishing the swords and making grotesque gesticulations."

At last the allies were ready to advance to the attack of the Chinese. The Mongol horsemen commenced the engagement by rushing fearlessly forward in several irregular lines of skirmishers, and bravely received the shot from the Armstrong guns, until they charged with a loud, wild yell the Sikh cavalry, with whom they engaged in close conflict. But "in less than a minute the Tartars had turned and were flying for their lives before our well-armed irregulars supported by two squadrons of the finest dragoons in the British army; the pursuit lasted for five miles, and was then only ended by our horses being pumped out. Had they been in good working order the results would have been far more satisfactory, and the worthy tax-payers at home would have had the pleasure of gloating over the account of an immense list of slain enemies."[1]

The allied infantry had already reached the intrenched camp, near the village of Sinho, and the "beautifully precise practice" of the Armstrongs, together with the accurate rifled guns of the French, were brilliantly successful in knocking over the Chinese who served their gingalls at the ranges of fourteen hundred or a thousand yards.

The reader cannot desire further particulars of this unequal contest as described by Colonel (now Lord) Garnet Wolseley. The various forces of the Chinese were entirely routed by the allies; the plain was speckled for miles by native corpses, while the care of wounded men called out the sympathies and skill of their conquerors. The village of Sinho was plundered, and its inhabitants fled, glad to escape with their lives.[2] The next morning an advance was made by the entire force upon the five forts and intrenched camps at Tangku, three miles off, from which the imperialists were dislodged with considerable loss on their part, the rest retreating across the Pei ho toward Taku. Tangku town was occupied by the foreigners, who took under their care everybody left in it, and relieved the wounded and starving while preparing for the intended attack on the forts. This kindness, and the consequent increased acquaintance arising between the contending parties in obtaining supplies, did much to remove their ignorance and contempt of each other—a result far more desirable and useful than the capture of forts and prisoners.

The French having already encamped on the further bank of the Pei ho, each army commenced the building of a bridge[3] across the stream, completing the structure so speedily that by the morning of August 21st the whole attacking force was in position. The twenty-three pieces of artillery now began to fire upon the north fort, from which the Chinese replied with

[1] Wolseley, *Narrative*, p. 103.

[2] A great collection of official documents disclosing the views of the court upon the struggle was found in the *yamun*.

Lieutenant-Colonel Fisher, *Personal Narrative*, pp. 404–409.

all the alacrity they could, although taken thus in rear. About six o'clock, when the fire waxed hotter and hotter, and the troops were anxiously looking for the signal to advance, "a tall black pillar, as if by magic, shot up from the midst of the nearest fort, and then bursting like a rocket after it had obtained a great height, was soon lost in the vast shower of earth and wood into which it resolved itself--a loud, bursting, booming sound marking the moment of its short existence." But the fire from the fort only ceased for a minute or two, and the gunners served their pieces most manfully, though sometimes unprotected in any way from the crushing shell fire opposed to them. The attack began about seven o'clock, nearly four thousand men all told forming the advance. A gallant defence was made to a still braver onset, but the victory naturally fell to the disciplined forces of the allies, who had possessed themselves of all the defences before noon. A few guns taken from the ships destroyed June 25, 1859, were now recovered by the British, but otherwise the fort contained nothing of value. The loss of life on both sides was comparatively slight. The British had seventeen killed and one hundred and eighty-three wounded; the French, one hundred and thirty casualties in all; the Chinese lay dead in heaps in the fort, and their total loss probably exceeded two thousand. The interior testified in every part the noble manner in which it had been defended, even after the disastrous explosion had crippled the resources and discouraged the enthusiasm of its garrison. From this position the allies moved on the other northern fort with their artillery, under a continual fire from its walls; but before the guns could open upon it, many white flags appeared on the parapets; messengers were ere long seen to leave the great southern fort. They were all given up before sunset, and the famous Taku forts, which had last year witnessed the discomfiture of the allies, now saw them enter as conquerors[1]—"the tarnished honor of our arms was gloriously vindicated."

---

[1] When the allied generals came to carefully examine the construction of the walls, casemates, and internal arrangements, with the preparation made outside to hinder the enemy, they declared them to be absolutely impregnable from seaward if defended as well as the north fort had been.

Lord Elgin was quietly resting in Tangku, and refused to receive their surrender, or even to hold intercourse with Hangfuh, the governor-general of Chihlí, then in command, but turned him over to the commander of the forces. The path being now open for the troops to march upon Tientsin, the gunboats were sent forward to see that the river was clear. On the 25th the two plenipotentiaries were again housed at Tientsin, accompanied by naval and land forces amply strong to take them to Peking. No opposition was, however, experienced in reaching that city, while the pleasing contrast in the surface of this country with that of the dreary flats near Pehtang and Taku refreshed the men as much as the abundant supplies and peacefulness of the people aided them. Such remarkable contrasts in China illustrate the inert character of this extraordinary people; and further, also lead one to inquire what is the reason for their loyalty to a government which fails so completely in protecting them from their enemies. Mr. Swinhoe records[1] a conversation held with a well-to-do Chinese, in which this inquiry receives a partial answer in the peaceful education of a race which has no alternative.

His intrenchments at Sinho and Tangku being demolished, his vaunted defences upon the river razed, his enemies' ships in possession of Tientsin, nothing now remained for Săngkolinsin save to move his entire army nearer Peking, and there again meeting the invaders, endeavor to preserve the capital from capture. He would not there be able to shift the odium of defeat on the difficulties of the river defences, while the moral effect would be incomparably greater if he were vanquished near the palace.

The aged Kweiliang, the father-in-law of Prince Kung, was again directed to repair to Tientsin, where he arrived about August 28th. He and two others (all of them Manchus) endeavored to negotiate a peace so as to prevent the allies from advancing on Peking with their armies. Finding that they were trifling, Lord Elgin stopped the palaver, and started for Tungchau on September 8th, the British taking the left bank and

---

[1] *North China Campaign*, pp. 158–161.

the French keeping the southern. Near Yangtsun a new commission of higher rank reported itself, but it was rejected, and the army continued on its way. Further on, at Hosí-wu and Matau, signs of serious strife began to appear, but the commissioners assured their negotiators, Messrs. Wade and Parkes, that everything was or would be ready at Tungchau to conclude the convention. Affairs were becoming critical in the matter of supplies and transport, for Săngkolinsin's army prevented the people from safely bringing animals and making sales. The commissariat, therefore, was obliged to seize what could be found to feed the advancing force, and this involved ransacking most of the towns and hamlets lying near the river between Hosí-wu and Tungchau. The progress of the force was, therefore, much slower than below Tientsin, though the possession of sixty or eighty small boats helped to bring on the ammunition and other supplies.

On September 14th the interpreters, Messrs. Wade and Parkes, reached Tungchau, in order to meet Prince Ĭ and his colleague to discuss the terms for stopping the army and exchanging the ratifications. This interview was marked with apparent sincerity, and resulted in an order for the army to move forward to a place designated near the town of Changkia-wan, about three leagues from Tungchau, where the troops were to encamp. The camp broke up from Hosí-wu early on the 17th to carry this arrangement into effect. Mr. Parkes was again sent forward to Tungchau (twenty-five miles), accompanied by an escort of twenty-six Sikh and other soldiers, to inform the imperial commissioners, and finally arrange terms. The ground pointed out was reached, and seemed to be well suited for the purpose. At Changkia-wan the party met an officer at the head of some cavalry, who challenged them, but allowed all to go on to Tungchau. Mr. Parkes soon met another high official in charge of a guard, who treated them with marked courtesy, informing them that he had been the general at Sinho, and let them proceed. They were received at Tungchau and conducted through the town to a temple by a messenger sent from the prince. At one o'clock the discussions began, but instead of entering into the details of carrying out the agreement, difficulties were made about Lord Elgin's delivering his letter of credence to the Emperor. The whole afternoon was consumed in this debate, which probably was grounded not a little on the recent decision of Hienfung to leave the capital for his summer palace at Jeh-ho while the way was yet clear. At eventide the commissioners waived the settlement of the audience, and soon agreed to all the other points relating to the encampment near Changkia-wan. In the morning Mr. Parkes, Colonel Walker, and eleven others, leaving the rest of their party in the temple to await the arrival of the plenipotentiaries the next day, departed to view the designated encampment. Their journey was somewhat eventful. As they reached Changkia-wan they met bodies of Chinese infantry going south, but no notice was taken of them, and the foreigners rode on to reach the appointed spot. In doing so they came across a body of a thousand dismounted horsemen concealed in a dry watercourse, or *nullah*, evidently placed there in ambush; while riding along in front no interruption was made to their progress. Further on, in a small village, they detected a large force hidden behind the houses and in gardens, but still no hindrance to their advance was interposed by these men. A short distance ahead they came upon a masked battery of twelve guns just placed in position, from which they were driven away. It was now plain that Săngkolinsin was preparing an ambushment for the allied forces to enter, feeling confident, no doubt, of his success.

Mr. Loch, who accompained Mr. Parkes thus far, was now designated to force his way through the Chinese troops, so as to meet the allied generals and tell them the state of things. Sir Hope Grant had already noticed some bodies of men on his flanks, and was preparing for them when he learned the truth; but in order to give Mr. Parkes and the others a chance to escape from Tungchau, he agreed to delay two hours before opening upon the enemy. Mr. Loch accordingly started, in company with Captain Brabazon and two horsemen, to return to Tungchau. They reached it in a few hours and found their friends, unconscious of the danger, wandering through the town. Mr. Parkes had learned something of it, and called on Prince Í at his quarters to claim protection; this dignitary was in a state of much excitement, and said that " until the question of delivering the letter of credence was settled there could be no peace; there must be war." On returning to their temple the foreigners immediately started off in a body, but some of their horses were jaded, and the country was filled with moving bodies of troops.

When about five miles were gone over they came on a brigade of matchlock men, and ere long an officer of rank stopped them from going further, but offered to accompany two of them to obtain from the general a pass allowing the whole party to ride around the Chinese army on their way back. Mr. Parkes and Mr. Loch and a Sikh accordingly went with him, and he bravely looked after their safety. Meanwhile the battle had already begun, as the booming cannon intimated. They had advanced only a few rods when the trio found themselves in the midst of a large body of infantry, some of whom seized their bridles, but their guide rushed in, striking right and left, and thus cleared the way. Ten rods in the rear they met the Chinese general, to whom Mr. Parkes addressed himself, pointing to the flag of truce and asking for a pass for the whole party to return to the British army. Săngkolinsin " gave a derisive laugh, and broke out into a torrent of abuse. He accused Parkes of being the cause of all the troubles and difficulties that had arisen. Not content with attempting to impose conditions which would have been derogatory to the dignity of the Emperor to accept, he had now brought the allied armies down to attack the imperial forces." This is only a part of his excited conversation with Mr. Parkes, as reported by Mr. Loch. They were now imprisoned, and ordered to be taken in an open cart with two French prisoners to Tungchau, and delivered over to Prince Í. The others, twenty-three in all, had also been made prisoners where they were waiting, and ere long conducted to Tungchau in charge of a guard.

The five in the cart reached Tungchau after Prince Í had left his temple, and were therefore hurried on to Peking after him, but on the way were turned off near Pa-lí-kiau (*i.e.*, ' Eight *Lí* Bridge ') and taken to the quarters of Jinlin, a general then in command of the Peking gendarmerie. He questioned Mr. Parkes upon the strength of the allied forces, until the latter ended this catechising under the torture of kneeling with the arms twisted behind him, by pretending to faint. In the afternoon, while again undergoing examination by some officials formerly with Prince I, they were suddenly interrupted by a commotion, and everybody ran off, leaving them alone. Soon a number of soldiers rushed in and bound their arms, while they were led away to be beheaded in an outer court. But just as they crossed the yard a mandarin hurried forward, and seizing hold of the soldier, then waving his sword over Mr. Loch, rescued them both and hurried them into a cart, where the other three prisoners lay, upon which they immediately started for Peking by the great stone road. The torture and jolting of this ride over the rough causeway were increased by their weariness, hunger, and cramped position, and when they got out of the cart at the *Hing Pu*, in Peking, they were utterly prostrated. Nevertheless, their misery during the ride of ten miles was transient and light compared with what awaited them inside of the Board of Punishments. They were there separated, heavily pinioned, and put with the native prisoners. Mr. Loch justly commends these wretched men for their sympathy, and mentions many little acts of kindness to him in dividing their cakes and giving him a special bench to sit on during the ten days he was quartered with them. He was then taken to the room with Mr. Parkes, and they were soon driven away to a temple in the northern part of the city, where rooms had been fitted up for them. As to the party of twenty-three English and thirteen Frenchmen left by Parkes at his capture, they had been taken to Yuen-ming Yuen under a strong guard.

Meanwhile the allied army had come up to the Chinese forces. These, about twenty thousand men in all, had been posted with considerable skill between Changkia-wan and the Pei ho, showing a front of nearly four miles, much of which was intrenched and presenting a succession of batteries. The battle on the 18th died away as the allies reached that town, having driven Săngkolinsin's troops toward Peking, captured eighty guns, and burned all his camps. The loss of life was much less among his men than at the Taku fort, for here none of them were chained to their guns, and were able to escape when their position was untenable. Changkia-wan was thoroughly pillaged that night by those who could get at it, especially the poor natives who followed the army.

On the 21st the Chinese forces made another stand near the Eight Lí Bridge over the Canal, from which the French dislodged them without much difficulty. The British came up on their flanks and drove them in upon their centre, which of course soon resulted in a general dispersion. The artillery opened up at long range; the cavalry riding in upon the Chinese horsemen, easily scattered them, often burning the separate camps before returning. The contest at the bridge was the most serious, and their loss here was estimated at three hundred; on the whole field it probably did not exceed five hundred, for neither their cavalry nor infantry often presented a solid front. The entire losses of the allies were less than fifty killed and wounded. Nothing interposed now between them and Peking, but they delayed to move until October 3d, when their entire force had come up, siege guns and commissary stores included. Full knowledge had been obtained of the environs of Peking, and negotiations had been going on respecting the return of the prisoners as a preliminary to the close of hostilities. These were now conducted with Prince Kung, the next younger brother of the Emperor, who was himself by this time safe at Jeh-ho.

On October 6th Lord Elgin and the generals were settled in the spacious quarters of the Hwang sz', a lamasary near the northwest gate of Peking, and their army occupied much of the open spaces between it and the city. On that day, the outposts of the French army and some of the British cavalry reached the great cantonment of Hai-tien (where the Manchu garrison of Peking was quartered) and the palace of Yuen-ming Yuen near by. This was soon pillaged under circumstances and in a barbarously wasteful manner which will reflect lasting obloquy upon General Montaubon, who, more than any other person, could have interposed to save the immense and precious collection of objects illustrating Chinese art, architecture, and literature. Lord Elgin's journal gives his view of this act in a few words:

October 7th, 5 o'clock P.M.—I have just returned from the Summer Palace. It is really a fine thing, like an English park—numberless buildings with handsome rooms, filled with Chinese *curios*, handsome clocks, bronzes, etc. But alas! such a scene of desolation. The French general came up, full of protestations. He had prevented looting in order that all the plunder might be divided between the armies, etc. There was not a room that I saw in which half the things had not been taken away or broken to pieces. I tried to get a regiment of ours sent to guard the place, and then sell the things by auction; but it is difficult to get things done by system in such a case, so some of the officers are left [there], who are to fill two or three carts with treasures, which are to be sold. Plundering and devastating a place like this is bad enough, but the waste and breakage are much worse. Out of a million pounds' worth of property, I daresay fifty thousand pounds will not be realized. French soldiers were destroying in every way the most beautiful silks, breaking the jade ornaments and porcelain, etc. War is a hateful business. The more one sees of it the more one detests it.[1]

Mr. Swinhoe's account of one room in this palace has now a historical interest—but his description must be condensed:

Facing the gate (he says) stood the grand reception hall, well adorned outside, and netted with copper wire under the fretted eaves to keep off the birds. Entering it we found ourselves on a marble floor in front of the Emperor's ebony throne; this was adorned with carved dragons in various attitudes; its floor was covered with light red cloth, and three low series of steps led up to it, on the central and widest of which his subjects made the kotow. The left side of the hall was adorned with a picture representing the grounds of the palace, and the side tables contained books in yellow binding and ornaments. There was somehow an air of reverence throughout this simple but neat hall. On an audience day the Emperor here seated himself attired in a yellow robe wrought with dragons in gold thread, his head surmounted with a spherical crown of gold and precious stones with pearl drops suspended around by light gold chains. Eunuchs and ministers in court costume kneel on each side in long lines, and the guard and musicians are arranged in the outer court. The name of the person to be introduced is called out, and as he approaches the band strikes up. He draws near the "Dragon's Seat" and kneels before the central step, removes his hat, placing it on the throne floor with the peacock's feather toward the imperial donor. His Majesty moves his hand and down goes the head, striking on the step three times three. The head is then raised, but with downcast eyes the man hears the behests of his great master. When

---

[1] *Elgin's Letters*, p. 361.

the voice ceases, again the head makes the nine knocks, thus acknowledging the sovereign right, and the man withdraws. How different the scene now, adds Mr. Swinhoe. The hall filled with crowds of a foreign soldiery, and the throne floor covered with the Celestial Emperor's choicest curios, destined as gifts for two far more worthy monarchs. "See here," said General Montaubon, pointing to them, "I have had a few of the most brilliant things selected to be divided between the Queen of Great Britain and the Emperor of the French." [1]

On the following day—October 8th—the commanders were greatly relieved by the return of Parkes, Loch, d'Escayrac de Lauture, and five soldiers; the first two of these gentlemen had been comparatively well treated after their terrible experiences within the Hing Pu. A few days later both armies were horrified by the appearance in camp of eleven wretched men—all who had survived from the party of French and English made prisoners near Tungchau; Anderson, Bowlby, de Norman, and others had succumbed to the dreadful tortures caused by the cords which bound them. The coffined bodies were all brought to camp within a few days, hardly recognizable from the effects of lime thrown upon them. On the 16th occurred the impressive ceremony of their interment in the Russian cemetery near Peking, Lord Elgin, Sir Hope Grant, Parkes, and Loch being chief mourners, while a deputation from every regiment in the allied armies followed in the train.

Two days after this Lord Elgin ordered the destruction of the palace of Yuen-ming Yuen; a sudden though deliberate act. Feeling probably that such a decision would be closely criticised by those who were far removed in time and place from the exciting scenes around him, he took occasion to review his position in a long despatch. It was impossible in his situation to learn whether the responsibility for the capture and savage treatment of these men rested with the same Chinese officials.[2] This

[1] Swinhoe, *North China Campaign*, pp. 294 ff.—the most detailed and interesting account of this palace and its destruction. Compare M. C. Lavallée in the *Revue des Deux Mondes* for August 1, 1865. Other French writers on this war are Lieutenant de vaisseau Pallu, *Relation de l'expédition de Chine*, Paris, 1863; le Comte d'Escayrac de Lauture, *Mémoires sur la Chine*, Paris, 1864; Sinnebaldo de Mas, *La Chine et les puissances chrétiennes*, 1861.

[2] Probably not. The prisoners were in the hands of lictors whose habit it was to torture in the hope of extorting money on their own account. The

much, nevertheless, was plain—that the Chinese were fully aware of the obligations of a flag of truce, inasmuch as they had already often availed themselves of its privileges. Lord Elgin makes the Emperor personally responsible for the crimes which had been committed, but specifies Săngkolinsin as the real culprit. He then says:

I had reason to believe that it was an act which was calculated to produce a greater effect in China and on the Emperor than persons who look on from a distance may suppose. It was the Emperor's favorite residence, and its destruction could not fail to be a blow to his pride as well as to his feelings. To this place he brought our hapless countrymen, in order that they might undergo their severest tortures within its precincts. Here have been found the horses and accoutrements of the troopers seized, the decorations torn from the breast of a gallant French officer, and other effects belonging to the prisoners. As almost all the valuables had already been taken from the palace, the army would go there, not to pillage, but to mark, by a solemn act of retribution, the horror and indignation with which we were inspired by the perpetration of a great crime. The punishment was one which would fall, not on the people, who may be comparatively innocent, but exclusively on the Emperor, whose direct personal responsibility for the crime committed is established, not only by the treatment of the prisoners at Yuen-ming Yuen, but also by the edict in which he offered a pecuniary reward for the heads of the foreigners.[1]

The work of destruction left hardly a trace of the palace of the "Round-bright Garden;" indeed, the provocation for this act was great. The despatch refers only to the palace where Hienfung spent most of his time, and it is probable that Lord Elgin intended to burn that alone. He gave no orders for the destruction of the buildings on Wan-shao shan, Yuh-tsien shan, the Imperial Park near Pih-yun sz', and other places five to ten miles distant. All of these residences or villas had been erected or enlarged by former Emperors of the present dynasty; none have since been rebuilt. It is, nevertheless, easy to gather from Colonel Wolseley's record that his lordship's satisfaction in this

---

candid spirit of Loch's narrative is wanting in the more colored accounts of Wolseley and Swinhoe, written in the flush of victory. The charges they make against Prince Í of treachery toward Mr. Parkes are not borne out; the deaths of Captain Brabazon and the Abbé de Luc seem to have been by order of Pao, and not from Săngkolinsin. Compare an article in the *Revue des Deux Mondes* (15 juillet, 1865) by C. Lavallée, *L'Expedition anglo-française en Chine*

[1] *Elgin's Letters and Journals*, p. 366.

"retribution" was not greatly impaired by its over-zealous performance on the part of the troops. In addition to the loss of the palaces, the Chinese had to pay £100,000 as indemnity to be given to the prisoners and their families, before the victors would consent to sign the convocation.

On the 13th the ultimatum had been accepted by Prince Kung, who about two hours before noon opened the An-ting or northeast gate of Peking, which commanded the whole city. Arrangements were gradually completed for the grand entry of the plenipotentiaries into Peking. The *Lí Pu*, or Board of Rites, was selected as the place for exchanging the ratifications of the treaty of Tientsin and signing the convention, while the *fu*, or palace of Prince Í, had been chosen for Lord Elgin's residence in the city. On October 24th the latter was escorted to both these places by many officers, together with a body of four hundred infantry and one hundred cavalry, while in all the streets leading to them were guards placed. The whole city was out to witness the unusual parade. The procession passed slowly through the wide avenues, the music of the band heralding its approach to the dignitaries anxiously awaiting the arrival. The utmost care had been taken that no excuse should be ever after brought forward that the Emperor had not assented to the two documents signed that day; but much besides was done to show Prince Kung and his officers that they were in the presence of their conquerors.[1]

The following day Baron Gros signed his convention and exchanged the ratifications of the French treaty under similar formalities. The principal points in the British convention of nine articles were—the payment of eight million taels; the permission given by imperial sanction for the emigration at will of Chinese subjects as contract laborers or otherwise; the cession of Kowlung to the crown as part of the colony of Hongkong.

Without delaying for additional comment, the insertion here of a portion of Lord John Russell's despatch to Lord Elgin will

---

[1] The frontispiece of this volume is intended to represent this ceremony. Its interest lies chiefly in the fact that it is from the work of one of the ablest painters in the capital, and represents from a native's stand-point one of the most remarkable and important events in the history of modern China.

not be uninteresting in connection with these treaties. His lordship's document reads like the balance-sheet of a London merchant at the termination of some successful adventure: "The Convention is entirely satisfactory to Her Majesty's Government. It records the reparation made by the Emperor of China for his disregard in the previous year of his treaty engagements; it sets Her Majesty's government free from an implied engagement not to insist in all particulars on the fulfilment of those engagements; it imposes upon China a fine in the shape of an augmented rate of indemnity; it affords an additional opening for British trade; it places on a recognized footing the emigration of Chinese coolies, whose services are so important to Her Majesty's colonial possessions; it relieves Her Majesty's colony of Hongkong from a source of previous annoyance."[1]

The French convention of ten articles contained like demands and rewards, but instead of a slice of territory, the sixth provided that Roman Catholic Christians should be indemnified for "all such churches, schools, cemeteries, lands, and buildings as were owned on former occasions by persecuted Christians, and the money handed to the French representative at Peking for transmission to the Christians in the localities concerned." The fulfilment of this article required over ten years; and as the injuries had been done in some cases as far back as the reign of Louis XIII., great irritation was aroused in the minds of the natives who had for generations been quietly in possession of lands which they had purchased.[2]

---

[1] "The practical result was not very great," concludes Mr. McCarthy. "Perhaps the most important gain to Europe was the knowledge that Peking was by no means so large a city as we had all imagined it to be. . . . There is some comfort in knowing that so much blood was not spilt wholly in vain." —*A History of Our Own Times*, Chap. XLII., Vol. III.

[2] An instance is mentioned in No. IV. of the *Journal of the N. C. Br. R. A. Soc.*, 1867, pp. 21–33, where a Roman Catholic church at Hangchau, which had been confiscated by the Emperor Yungching (about 1730), was changed into a temple dedicated to *Tien Hao*, the Queen of Heaven, "to serve the double purpose of extirpating a religion of false gossip and obduracy, and of making an offering to a spirit who really has a beneficial influence over human destinies."

The great objects of the expedition were now attained, and foreign nations could congratulate themselves upon having settled their representatives in the Chinese capital on terms of equality. Two *fu*, or palaces, were immediately occupied by those from Great Britain and France. Subsequently, the ministers from other countries have grouped themselves around these, and a foreign quarter has gradually grown up in the south-eastern part of the city. The chief agents in this important opening, Lord Elgin and Baron Gros, were well fitted by their urbanity, philanthropy, and moderation for the delicate task assigned them. The terrified officials and citizens in Peking had expected the worst consequences on the capture of their city, but besides the destruction of Yuen-ming Yuen, their capital and national unity escaped uninjured.

It was probably a great aid to the policy adopted by Prince Kung and his colleagues that the Emperor and his court had fled to Jeh-ho, for their influence, as the sequel proved, would have opposed any pacification. It was still more important for all future co-operation that he never came back at all, and thus the real guidance of affairs fell into better hands.

The 24th day of October saw the ending of the seclusion of the Chinese from their fellow-men; the contest honestly enough begun in 1839 by Lin, to rescue his country from the curse of opium, was in a manner completed on that day by the admission of those regenerating influences which could alone effectually remove that evil. The intermediate twenty years had done much to prepare the Chinese for this concluding act; and the honorable manner in which they fulfilled their promises and payments will stand as a lasting monument to their national credit.

The retirement of the allies from Peking was accomplished without impediment from the Chinese army under Săngkolinsin; the money disbursed for boats, carts, supplies, fuel, etc., as the troops went down the river, compensating many natives for their losses. By the end of November all had embarked except the garrisons left at Tientsin and Taku, which latter were removed as soon as the portion of the indemnity involving their occupation was paid up. The effectual and salutary working of the treaty stipulations for the mutual welfare of all parties depended on the diplomatic and consular officers left in the capital and open ports. The British government alone was adequately supplied in this respect, and their consulates became the expositors to the local rulers of the manner in which the treaties were to be interpreted and enforced. The great mass of natives knew almost nothing of their provisions, and looked upon the struggle chiefly as one between their sovereign and the foreigners. The defeat of the latter was in remoter districts declared proven by their retirement from Peking; but along the coasts and up the Yangtsz' the actual sight of steamers and contact with foreigners who could talk with them and explain the new state of things, really did more than anything else to show them that these strangers were by no means overcome. What was thus achieved to enlighten the people near the trading marts only required time and contact to spread into distant regions of the interior. As for the citizens of Peking, they met only those foreigners who could talk with them, for that city was not open to trade; and thus one prolific source of misunderstanding was removed. The death of the Emperor Hienfung (August 17, 1861) relieved them, too, from any attempt he might have made, in his irritation on returning to the Forbidden City and seeing his ruined palaces, to vent his wrath on the few foreigners then living near him. Christian missionaries also began their work in 1861, and thus thousands, who had had only vague ideas about the "barbarians," could easily learn the truth concerning them. Most fortunately, then, circumstances were from the first favorable for forming an intelligent public opinion in the capital.

CHAPTER XXVI.

NARRATIVES OF RECENT EVENTS IN CHINA.

TWELVE months elapsed before the political atmosphere of China was disturbed by any break or change in its condition—a period of quiet which the government sorely needed for an appreciation of its relations with the foreigners who had forced their way into the capital. His Majesty Hienfung having ascended the Dragon Throne on high, left the Empire in the hands of his only son, a child six years old; whether through incapacity or disease, the debauched sovereign had long before his death allowed his courtiers to engross the reins of government, and these now formed a coterie which at Jeh-ho was all-powerful. At his death the administration rested in the hands of a council of eight, whose nominal head was Tsai-yuen, Prince I, a member of the imperial family belonging to the same generation with the infant Emperor. The design of this cabal was to at once assume the absolute power of a regency, to retain possession of the young Emperor's person at Jeh-ho, to make way in secret with his mother and the Empress-dowager, and lastly to arrest and destroy his father's three brothers; these initiatory steps to sovereignty being accomplished, nothing would interrupt their complete mastery of the government.

But in Prince Kung,[1] the Emperor's oldest surviving brother.

---

[1] Kung Tsin-wang, 'Prince Respect'—called by the people Wu-ako, 'Fifth Elder Brother'—is the sixth son of Taukwang, and was born about 1831. Three older brothers died young; Hienfung, the fourth, succeeded his father, while the fifth, being adopted into a branch of the Emperor Kiaking's family, was dropped out of Taukwang's household, leaving Prince Kung in 1861 to be the first prince during the minority of Tungchí. His personal name, Yih-hü, is never employed by those outside his immediate family. He has a commendable record for an Asiatic statesman trained in habits of autocratic command. The background in the portrait on the opposite page is a bit of rou. work in the Foreign Office at Peking.

PRINCE KUNG

the conspirators found an opponent of no ordinary ability, to whose astuteness in outwitting their machinations (as may be safely affirmed in view of events which followed) is doubtless owing the continuance of the present reigning family. The prince was in concealment during the autumn of 1860, when his brother fled to Jeh-ho, but appearing when the capital was surrendered to the allies, he bore the brunt of that unpleasant task, signing the treaties, and undertook almost alone the management of affairs with foreigners while the government was recovering from its paralysis of defeat. It was a happy augury for the continuance of peace and friendly intercourse that to a man so well fitted by temperament for his difficult position should be joined the able and experienced statesman Kweiliang; though too old to take an active part in the settlement of the succession, this skilful diplomatist lent the greatest aid to his son-in-law by giving advice and a much needed support to the Empresses-dowager at this critical period.

Hastily quitting Jeh-ho with the boy—who had been proclaimed Emperor under the reign-name of Kí-tsiang, 'Lucky Omen'—the two Empresses availed themselves of their right to join the first prince, and repaired to Peking. Once settled in the Forbidden City they were able to impart to Prince Kung the magnitude of the plot against them, and concert measures with leading members of the imperial clan for the general safety. The arrest and trial of the traitors was promptly carried out; by a decree of December 2, 1861, Prince Í and his principal coadjutor, Prince Chin, were allowed to commit suicide, while their powerful and clever colleague, Suhshun, was executed in the market-place, to the unfeigned delight of the populace. This conspirator in his machinations and gross assumptions had acted like a veritable Tigellinus, and earned for himself a hatred and contempt which even members of the war party could not conceal. Others of this unsuccessful clique were disgraced or banished, but the punishments were not numerous or barbarous. The reign-name was now changed from Kí-tsiang to *Tung-chi*, or 'Union Rule,' to mark the successful demolition of this conspiracy, while Prince Kung (now but thirty years old), the shrewd perpetrator of the *coup d'état*, was proclaimed *I-ching-wang*, or 'Regent Prince,' and with the Empresses constituted the regency during the minority.[1]

Considering all the circumstances of this palace intrigue, the rank of its leading members, and its successful suppression by the operation of legal methods alone, it may well deserve the attention of those interested in the political and historical development of China as an admirable instance of both the strength and weakness of her paternal government. To the ordinary outlays of the Empire were superadded the immense burdens of a foreign invasion just concluded and a terrible struggle with domestic enemies; yet neither the Regent nor his colleagues appear during this period of stress to have lost a particle of their confidence in the loyalty of the people; through loss and gain, failure of material or resource, treachery in palace or camp, abuse or assistance from foreigners, this faith in one another failed not. The face of China in 1865 was perhaps as wretched as that of Central Europe after the peace of Westphalia; indeed a more general desolation could hardly be imagined. Nevertheless the rapidity with which its inhabitants not only resumed their occupations as best they could but rebuilt dwellings and reorganized trade, startled even their habitual disparagers into praise and testified to the marvellous recuperative powers of this much-despised civilization.

Pleased with the excellent results of the introduction of western drill and arms into their military service, as against the Tai-pings, certain of the mandarins at the south proposed utilizing foreign war-vessels to the same end. To this scheme as at first suggested there was not, perhaps, much to say either in its behalf or otherwise. Their purpose was to purchase three or four gun and despatch boats, man them with as many scores of native seamen, and impart to these the necessary instruction by placing them under foreign officers. Mr. Horatio N. Lay had in 1856 proposed the use of armed revenue vessels in the customs service, a very similar suggestion. But innocent as were these conceptions, they assumed the gravest proportions

[1] *Journal N. C. Br. R. A. S.*, December, 1864, pp. 110–114. Dr. Rennie, *Peking and the Pekingese*, Vol. II., passim—an interesting contemporary record of this event.

when in 1861 Mr. Lay was allowed to visit England and there contract for the construction of a steam fleet and secure a number of British naval officers for three years' service.[1] The Peking authorities were still laboring under the disadvantages of their ignorance, and nothing can illustrate better than this remarkable enterprise the good influence which Sir Frederick Bruce had acquired in their counsels, and their willingness to follow his suggestions. Their secluded life in Peking had prevented them from learning many things in respect to the conduct of affairs in their new relations, but they could hardly have had a better counsellor than he. The instructions from Prince Kung sent to Mr. Lay in England described the kind of officers and hands which the vessels were to carry; they were to be men able and willing to teach ignorant sailors the practice of navigation, the management of machinery, and the use of guns of every kind. Instead of these he contracted for eight gunboats of different sizes, one or two of them powerful vessels, able to carry two hundred and more men; they arrived in China early in 1863 under the command of Capt. Sherard Osborne, R. N. Mr. Lay's disappointment was great and undisguised when, on reaching Peking in June, he found that Prince Kung and his advisers were totally unprepared for such a fleet, and unwilling to endorse the engagements he had entered into with the Queen's officers; nor were the funds for their current expenses provided. His ideas of his own position were soon modified, for he found that the vessels must necessarily be placed under the direction of the provincial authorities in operations against the rebels. One of the articles in the agreement with Captain Osborne stipulated that he should receive all his orders on those matters from the Foreign Office through Mr. Lay, and would follow his own choice in obeying others. Mr. Lay says himself that he was "ambitious of obtaining the position of middle-man between China and the foreign powers, because I thought I saw a way of solving the problem of placing pacific relations with China upon a sure footing. . . . My position was that of a foreigner engaged by the Chinese government to perform certain work *for*

---

[1] *Blue Book*, China, No. 2 (1864), p. 7.

them, not *under* them. I need scarcely observe, in passing, that the notion of a gentleman acting *under* an Asiatic barbarian is preposterous."[1] Ideas like these quite unfitted him for working with the Chinese, either *under* or *for* them. He could not understand that the former days of coercion and bullying had passed away, and that time must be allowed for them to gradually learn in their own way how to rise in the scale of nations, and adopt such improvements as they pleased.

In his perplexity and chagrin, he began to blame the British minister for lukewarmness in supporting his schemes, and to weary the members of the Tsung-lí Yamun by his demands. The controversy continued to grow warmer after Captain Osborne's arrival at Peking in September, where he first learned its real nature. Finally, in October, Prince Kung refused to ratify Mr. Lay's agreement made in England, very properly remarking upon the obnoxious article which required the commander of the flotilla to act only under orders from Peking. Happily for China, the dissolution of the force was decided on. The ships were to be sent back, for it was impossible to prevent the native officials from selling them after they had full control, and persons were already looking at them for their own lawless designs. At this juncture Sir F. Bruce came to the relief of the Chinese, and took the ships off their hands on account of the British government, paying back from the indemnity fund due to England all claims for wages, salary, and other expenses to officers and men till their arrival in London. This settlement involved an outlay of about $525,000, but the total cost of the vessels, crews, and outfit from first to last was not much less than a million sterling. The Peking government had, therefore, by this arrangement escaped a serious imbroglio with the provincial governors and generals—one which would have soon neutralized all responsibility, and perchance, even at that late date, entailed the success of the Tai-pings.

Mr. Lay, blinded by his own egotism and ambition, ascribes his failure to the negligence, treachery, ignorance, and ill-will

---

[1] *Our Interests in China: A Letter to Earl Russell*, p. 19.

of Sir F. Bruce, whose performances in these lines are fully detailed in his *Letter to Earl Russell*[1] of November 26, 1864. This statement of what occurred in relation to the Lay-Osborne flotilla exhibits the difficulties in the progress of Asiatic nations in the path of what we call *civilization*, and the ideas which such men have as to the way in which they are to be forced into this desirable condition. This extraordinary paper is an instructive exhibition of British interference in the administration of Asiatic countries, and how totally alien "the spirit of trade and progress" is to the independence and elevation of a pagan people when it alone is the chief agency depended on. In no case, nor under the best control, could Mr. Lay's plan have worked real benefit to China; but carried out under the domineering leadership of such a man, the scheme would have not only been humiliating in the last degree to those whom it was designed to assist, but would have inevitably resulted in the restoration of the conservative party to power and another profitless struggle with the foreigners.

Upon the dismissal of Mr. Lay the management of the Imperial Maritime Customs was placed in the hands of Robert Hart, Esq., who for a period of two years had given proof of his discretion in this position, and (in the words of Mr. Burlingame) had "by his tact and ability won the regard of every one." Already the imperial officers began to appreciate the immense material advantages of a regular income from the open ports, especially in the practical help it furnished toward the expenses of the dying rebellion. The contact of native and foreign rule in the same territory necessarily involved much assumption of power and friction of authority growing out of the undefined limits of the laws of ex-territoriality; but the legitimate working of treaty provisions—the prompt reference of grievances from complainant to consul, from the consul to his minister at Peking—served to enlighten court and country as to the gen-

---

[1] *Our Interests in China*, by H. N. Lay, C.B., London, 1864, pp. 66. See also correspondence in *Blue Book*, and letter of Sir F. Bruce, of November 19, 1863. *U. S. Diplomatic Correspondence* for 1864, Part III., pp. 348–378; and for 1865, Part I., p. 670. A. Wilson, *The "Ever-Victorious Army,"* pp. 260-266. *Fraser's Magazine*, February, 1865, p. 147.

eral honesty of their quondam enemies, in a fashion which neither preaching nor fighting could ever have accomplished.[1] In the year 1866 the arsenals at Fuhchau, Nanking, and Shanghai were reorganized and made to include schools for naval and military instruction as well as engine and gun works; the value of such works was promptly understood by the Chinese, and has been already the source of a creditable navy.[2]

The retirement of the Hon. Anson Burlingame from the position of United States minister in November, 1867, furnished to the Chinese government both an admirable agent and opportunity for an initial step in establishing diplomatic intercourse with the treaty powers. Into the hands of this gentleman was placed the charge of a general mission to those governments, there being added two co-ordinate Chinese ministers, an English and French secretary, and six students from the Tung-wăn Kwan at Peking. The three ministers were appointed Imperial Envoys and furnished with a letter of credence to eleven governments. The party left Shanghai February 25, 1868, for San Francisco, which port they reached about a month later. Few persons can now appreciate the excitement and discussion in China and elsewhere caused by this first diplomatic effort of the imperial government to take its place among the family of nations. Mr. Burlingame, naturally hopeful and enthusiastic, described his mission as an earnest of future peaceful relations with the Middle Kingdom. Wherever he went he elevated the estimate held of that ancient land by his hearers, and urged the European courts to but wait in patience until its backward people might be prepared for the changes it wished to adopt. Those changes and improvements were only to be

---

[1] The trial and condemnation of an American, who was hung at Shanghai in 1864 for the murder of two Chinese, tended to repress lawlessness on the part of foreigners and assure the native rulers of their earnest co-operation in bringing the guilty to punishment. The enlightened and friendly action of Prince Kung in issuing a proclamation, at request of Mr. Burlingame, against allowing any American Confederate cruisers to enter Chinese waters, was warmly appreciated by this and the other treaty powers as an interesting testimonial of the genuine friendship which was already disarming fear.

[2] Compare Captain Bridge, *The Warlike Power of China*, in *Fraser's Magazine*, Vol. 99, pp. 778 ff.

adopted when China had become convinced of their need and practicability; but many of Mr. Burlingame's hearers were both more eager and more ambitious than he, regarding the introduction of railroads, telegraphs, and steamers as opening an enormous field for their own immediate activity and gain. The consequent indignation among foreign merchants in China and at home upon learning the extent of his exaggeration was universal; the British merchants especially representing in strong terms the evil consequences of such "baseless expectations." The different points of view of the two parties will account for their opposite opinions. On the one side, the merchants were vexed that their hopes of a general trade arising all over China, as a result of the treaties of Tientsin, were likely to be disappointed, owing to the increasing attention of native traders in their own internal and external commerce to the exclusion of foreigners; while on the other, Mr. Burlingame laid great stress on those things which the Chinese government desired and intended to do as they became more and more qualified to act for themselves, through the agencies and institutions which they were inaugurating. The merchants seemed to think that nothing had as yet been accomplished in the direction of "progress," inasmuch as their personal expectations of an instant and lucrative trade were not realized; in reply to Mr. Burlingame's "enthusiastic fictions," they called for "tangible evidence of the existence of this spirit which he celebrates so loudly—some tittle of proof to support his sweeping theory."[1]

Without dwelling further upon these discussions, it pertains to the present narrative to briefly point out the two salient features of China's initial attempt to knock at the doors of

[1] See the letters to the *Daily News* of J. Barr Robertson, of Shanghai, which have been taken as a fairly characteristic specimen of the mercantile and political view. An article by the same gentleman in the *Westminster Review* for January, 1870, is rather calmer in language. Other data and opinions may be gathered from a work filling 890 pages, by the late J. von Gumpach, entitled *The Burlingame Mission: A Political Disclosure*, etc., 1872. Compare also the English newspapers issued in Shanghai and Hongkong in 1867–70; *British Parliamentay Papers; U. S. Ex. Doc., Foreign Relations*, 1868–71; *Harper's Monthly Magazine*, Vol. XXXVII., p. 592; *The Galaxy*, Vol. VI., p. 613.

other nations. Of these the first may be described as wholly sentimental; but it was the healthy sentiment of justice and good feeling toward a distant and unknown community, which Mr. Burlingame's tact and ability called forth in behalf of his clients' cause from their recent conquerors. During the years 1868 and 1869 he spoke for the right and privilege of the Chinese to manage their own affairs, and in America, England, France, Prussia, and other countries had already created a more healthy feeling of forbearance toward them, when his sudden death at St. Petersburg (February, 1870) cut short the complete achievement of his mission.[1]

In the United States the passage of this embassy might have made but a transient impression had it not negotiated a treaty of eight articles (July 28, 1868), regarded as an integral part of the Reed treaty of ten years previous. This, the second feature of the mission, has been attended with consequences whose influence does not yet appear to have ceased. Owing to the surprise of the Chinese government, which had given no express instructions as to treaty-making, the Foreign Office was somewhat tardy in ratifying this compact. This was, however, done in the following year. Its fifth article provides that the contracting powers "cordially recognize the inherent and inalienable right of man to change his home and allegiance, and also the mutual advantage of the free migration and emigration of their citizens and subjects respectively from the one country to the other for the purposes of curiosity, or trade, or as permanent residents. The high contracting parties therefore join in reprobating any other than an entirely voluntary emigration for these purposes." At this time the British and French ministers had recently agreed to a convention with Prince Kung respecting the conduct of the coolie trade in accordance with the stipulations made at Peking in October, 1860. The draft of those regulations had been submitted to the American as well as all other foreign legations, but only the Spanish treaty contained

[1] His colleagues, Chí-kang and Sun Kia-kü, afterward visited Italy, Spain, and other countries, returning to China within the same year. Neither of them was, however, brought forward at the capital as an adviser in relation to foreign affairs.

an article allowing the engagement of Chinese laborers in their own country for service abroad. This traffic had become so infamous from the cruelties and wrongs perpetrated on the coolies, both in China before they embarked and in Cuba and Peru after they had landed, that the American Congress had already passed laws against it; and this article was drawn up almost wholly with reference to that trade, and to show the abhorrence with which it was regarded. Chinese immigrants had come to San Francisco to the number of fifty-three thousand since 1855, and had been harshly treated by the miners and others in their common struggle for gold; the Burlingame treaty simply acknowledged their right to immigrate like other foreigners.[1]

Meantime at Peking the foreign ambassadors were in the way of learning that in their relations with the government to which they were accredited they had to deal with men of acute minds, whose prejudices and conservatism only needed enlightening to bring them quite upon a level with any other body of intelligent diplomatists. It was indeed a crucial period with Prince Kung and his coadjutors of the Tsung-lí Yamun—Wănsiang, Tung Siun, Tan Ting-siang, Hăng-kí—who were placed between the two great pressures of a warped and bigoted multitude of literati wedded to the old régime and the ministers of the outside powers, themselves dwelling complacently in the imperial city and representing armies and navies which had been found invincible. The pride of the "Celestial" was necessarily brought low, but the situation was accepted, on the whole, both wisely and cautiously; the good fortune of having men of the kindness and honor of Bruce, Vlangali, Berthémy, and Burlingame as heads of the four chief legations, can hardly be exaggerated in its encouraging and healthful effects upon the impression taking root in the minds of Chinese officers.

At this juncture occurred the massacre at Tientsin of twenty

---

[1] But notwithstanding its acceptance of their "inalienable right" to freely change their residence, the clamor against this admission was afterward so great among the people on the Pacific coast that a special embassy of three commissioners was sent to Peking in 1880, which relegated the right of admitting Chinese as immigrants into American territory entirely to Congress.

French and Russians and destruction of the French consulate, cathedral, and orphanage, by a mob on June 21, 1870, attended by circumstances of great atrocity. The event was a severe blow as well to the anxious mandarins at the capital as to every honest friend of the new order of things throughout the Empire. The Peking authorities were slow at first in opening an investigation, but testified to their earnestness and righteous indignation at the enormity in disposing troops about the capital and summarily examining the criminals, so that by the end of a month every fear of a general *émeute* had vanished.

The causes which led to this outbreak appear to have been almost wholly local, taking their rise in the year 1861, when the French occupied as their consulate a temple in Tientsin, where in former times the citizens used to promenade; this and other unpopular acts kept the natives at enmity with them. A more especial account of the most important of these is contained in Mr. Low's despatch of June 27th: "At many of the principal places in China open to foreign residence, the Sisters of Charity have established institutions, each of which appears to combine in itself a foundling hospital and orphan asylum. Finding that the Chinese were averse to placing children in their charge, the managers of these institutions offered a certain sum per head for all the children placed under their control given to them, it being understood that a child once in their asylum no parent, relative, or guardian could claim or exercise any control over it. It has been for some time asserted by the Chinese, and believed by most of the non-Catholic foreigners residing here, that the system of paying bounties induced the kidnapping of children for these institutions for the sake of the reward. It is also asserted that the priests or Sisters, or both, have been in the habit of holding out inducements to have children brought to them in the last stages of illness, for the purpose of being baptized *in articulo mortis*. In this way many children have been taken to these establishments in the last stages of disease, baptized there, and soon after taken away dead. All these acts, together with the secrecy and seclusion which appear to be a part and parcel of the regulations which govern institutions of this character everywhere, have created suspicions in the minds of the Chinese, and these suspicions have engendered an intense hatred against the Sisters on the part of all the common people who live anywhere near a mission; and any rumor concerning the Sisters or their acts, however improbable or absurd, found thousands of willing and honest believers among the ignorant and superstitious people. Some time about the end of May or beginning of June an epidemic prevailed at the Sisters' institution at Tientsin, and a considerable number of the children died. In some way the report got abroad that the Sisters were killing the children to get their eyes and hearts for the purpose of manufacturing some sort of a medical specific much sought after in Europe and commanding a fabulous price. This report spread from one to another, and soon the belief became general. Crowds of people assembled from time to time near the mission buildings, demanding the liberation of the children, and on one occasion they became so noisy that the Sisters, fearing violence from the mob, consented that an examination should be made by a committee of five. The consul, hearing of the disturbance, made his appearance about this time, and although the committee had been selected and were then in the building, he stopped the whole proceeding and drove away the committee with angry words. Subsequently the district magistrate took a man who had been industriously spreading the reports, who said he could point out the persons who were guilty of acts of sorcery and other crimes, to question him in the presence of the Sisters, and when confronted by them admitted that all his stories were without foundation and false. The day prior to the outbreak the district magistrate (*chihien*) called upon the French consul, and stated that unless permission be given for a thorough examination of the Sisters' establishment, it was difficult to foretell the result. The consul, construing the language into a threat, replied that the magistrate being inferior in rank to the consul, no negotiation could take place between them for the purpose indicated or any other."[1]

[1] *Foreign Relations of the United States*, 1870, p. 355. A private letter quoted in the *Westminster Review* for April, 1871, says: "Even then (on the 19th) I think the riot could have been prevented if the consul had earnestly joined

This very unwise answer turned the popular rage against the French consulate as well as the cathedral and orphanage, and the 21st saw a surging multitude assembled in their vicinity ready for any violence. M. Fontanier, the French consul, now thoroughly alarmed, hurried off to the yamun of Chunghow (the superintendent of customs), while stones flew about the building he was quitting. For the rest, this poor man's fate is involved in uncertainty. Reaching Chunghow's office in a "state of excitement bordering upon insanity," he failed, either by persuasion or menace, in getting that dignitary to promise the impossible—to quell at once the angry mob. The officials, indeed, by this time were as helpless as he, and could only urge his remaining in the compound until the streets were clear. But the Frenchman and his clerk heeded nothing; how they were cut down in the way, after firing into the angry mob, how the rampant populace now attacked and pillaged the three or four French buildings, how the defenceless Sisters were butchered in their orphanage after suffering nameless barbarities, and how the frenzied host left the burning ruins to glut their passions upon the neighboring houses, has come to the world solely on Chinese authority, and must remain always in the obscurity resulting from greatly conflicting testimony. The children of the orphanage, however, were taken off, and though attempts upon some of the Protestant buildings were made, nothing serious resulted. Among the saddest casualties of this bloody day was the death of a Russian, his young bride, and a friend, who in escaping toward the foreign settlement of Tsz'-chuh-lin, two miles away, were mistaken for Frenchmen and promptly hacked to pieces on the road. The total number of victims in the massacre amounted to twenty foreigners and as many more Chinese servants, acolytes, and others.

To the joint note of the seven foreign ministers in Peking, calling for immediate and vigorous measures in the face of this terrible news, Prince Kung replied (on the 25th) that in vindication of the honor and justice of the imperial government toward

---

with the local authorities in making a full inquiry, with a number of the gentry, inside of the infirmary and church, to show them again that the rumors of foul deeds therein were groundless."

foreigners, Tsăng Kwoh-fan (governor-general of the province) and Chunghow had already been directed to do everything in their power to suppress the spirit of riot and arrest lawless men. An imperial edict was issued for the apprehension of Chau, Chang, and Lin, the intendant, prefect, and magistrate of Tientsin, for their remissness and complicity in the riot. The fact that no foreign armed vessel was there on the 21st doubtless had its weight with these officials in carrying out their plans at the moment. They now saw that they had pursued their ill-will too far, and that retribution was sure to follow for their atrocities. Exaggerated reports of their doings had rapidly gone over the world, and as the extent and strength of the disaffection in other provinces could not be ascertained, the inference was made that all foreigners in China were in imminent jeopardy, and that the people had at last risen in their strength to aid their sovereign to drive them out of the land. When the storm had passed over, and those in authority had examined the criminals and given such justice as they could, the opinions of the best informed observers as to the immediate causes were found to be sustained.

In a few weeks the naval forces of the leading powers had assembled at Tientsin. The French chargé d'affairs, Count Rochechouart, took the lead and demanded the execution of the prefect and magistrate for having instigated the riot. The Chinese refused to do this until a trial had proved their guilt—having, perhaps, in some measure recovered their composure upon learning of the commencement of hostilities between France and Germany. The imperial government was unable itself to coerce the turbulent populace of Tientsin, for it had no troops who could be depended on to punish the rioters, with whom the soldiers sympathized. The extravagant statements and demands continually put forth in the Shanghai and Hongkong newspapers tended to irritate and disconcert those high officials, who were already at their wits' end and were anxious to prevent a worse disaster. The foreigners seemed to think that they could utter hard charges indiscriminately against the Chinese rulers and people, who on their part were not to say a word. Minister Low, in his despatch of August 24th, when speaking of the thousands of fans sold at Tientsin containing pictures of the riot and murdering of foreigners, says: "These fans are made to suit the taste of the people, and the fact that such engravings will cause a better sale for the fans is a conclusive argument that there is no sentiment of regret or sorrow among the people over the result of the riot. There is, undoubtedly, greater unanimity of opinion in Tientsin in favor of the rioters than in Ireland among the peasantry in favor of one of their number who shoots his landlord. If this feeling in Ireland is strong enough to baffle all attempts of the English government to bring to justice by the ordinary forms of law a peasant accused of injuring the person or property of his landlord, is it surprising that this feeble central government should find it difficult to ascertain and punish the rioters in a city of four hundred thousand inhabitants, all of whom either aided in the massacre or sympathized with the rioters?"[1]

The judicial investigations in Tientsin were conducted in a dilatory manner, but the above indicates some of the difficulties in the way of the presiding judges. However, on October 5th and 10th H. I. Majesty's decrees were made known to the foreign ministers, stating that the prefect and magistrate had been banished to Manchuria, twenty criminals who had killed the foreigners sentenced to death, and twenty-one others actively aiding in the riot banished. On the morning of October 18th sixteen were decapitated in the presence of the foreign consuls and others assembled as witnesses. This closing act of the tragedy, as a condign punishment of guilt, was, however, unfortunate; it was made rather an occasion of showing to the people that the sufferers had the sympathy of their rulers, while many foreigners looked upon the execution as a ghastly farce—"a cold-blooded murder." Many believed that the sixteen men were purchased victims; the proofs were ample, however, of the complicity of all; indeed, some of them gloried in what they had done, and were escorted by admiring friends to the block.[2]

---

[1] *Foreign Relations of the United States—China*, 1871, p. 380.

[2] As an instance of some of the bitter sentiment rampant upon this occasion, may be quoted the open proposition of a British missionary, who insisted that one-half of the city of Tientsin be razed by a detachment of foreign troops of

It is a palpable exaggeration of the power or desires of a Chinese official to affirm that he is capable of buying up candidates for immediate execution.

As to the remaining four condemned culprits, M. Vlangali, the Russian minister, judiciously refused to accept their deaths as a proper satisfaction for the murder of the three Russians until satisfied personally of their direct complicity in the deed. A careful examination of their case having been made before the consul-general of the Czar at Tientsin, revealed the fact that only two were guilty of the actual crime; the minister consented then that the punishment of the other two should be commuted to banishment. The sum of Tls. 400,000 was paid to the French for loss of life and property; in addition to this the loss done to Protestant mission premises was also made good. Chunghow was appointed imperial commissioner to proceed to France and present to that government a formal apology for the affair. This mission left Peking early in 1871 and returned the following year. The American missionaries who had in August been frightened away from their post in Tăngchau[1] by the warnings and threats of certain evil disposed persons, were taken back from their asylum in Chifu two months later in the U. S. S. Benicia, and publicly received by the prefect. This was the only instance throughout the Empire, connected with the riot of June, in which foreigners were interfered with, and here grave doubts exist as to the reality of danger and need of flight from Tăngchau.

In estimating the conduct of the Chinese in dealing with this eruption, the foreign press habitually spoke of them as if they were unwilling to grant any redress or take any measures for the future safety of those living among their subjects. Little consideration was made for the enormous difficulties of their position. They had been reared in ignorance of the multiplied questions and responsibilities involved in the recent treaties with other nations; and though the foreign ministers were

---

various nationalities, and that a pillar be erected upon the open space thus made, with a suitable inscription as to the occasion and authors of the monument.

[1] On the promontory of Shantung.

really acting most kindly toward them in forcing them to carry out every plain treaty obligation, the fair-minded observer can find small excuse for the harsh criticism, not to add abuse, which was hurled at everything said or done by Prince Kung and his colleagues in their peril and perplexity. The writers in newspapers seemed to look upon China as an appanage of Europe—one Englishman even going so far as to urge the most reckless employment of force to compel her rulers to give up the three odious officials to be dealt with and publicly executed. Another says that the execution of the sixteen criminals could "hardly be viewed as other than cold-blooded murder while those men are shielded from the demands of justice." Yet these writers forgot that all the treaties required that "Chinese subjects guilty of criminal acts toward foreigners shall be arrested and punished by the Chinese authorities according to the laws of China;" and each nation obliged itself to try and punish its own criminals. Chunghow was the object of much abuse because he had not prevented or put down the mob, though he was merely a revenue officer and had neither territorial nor military jurisdiction at Tientsin. Even the members of the Tsung-lí Yamun were freely charged with complicity in the tragedy, if not knowledge or approval. In short, the whole history of the riot—its causes, growth, culmination, results, and repression—combine as many of the serious obstacles in the way of harmonizing Chinese and European civilizations as anything which ever occurred.[1]

As a natural sequence to the judicial proceedings which ter-

---

[1] The records of this event are widely scattered in the local papers published in China and in diplomatic correspondence. See the *Missionary Recorder*, November, 1870, and January, 1871: *Journal of N. C. Branch of R. A. Soc.*, No. VI., pp. 186–196; *Edinburgh Review*, January, 1871; *Westminster Review*, April, 1871, Art. VI.; *The Tientsin Massacre*, &c., by Geo. Thin, M.D., Edinburgh, 1870; *Foreign Relations of the United States* for 1870 and 1871; *Legation to China; Parliamentary Blue Book*, 1871; H. Blerzy, *Les affaires de Chine en* 1871, *Revue des Deux Mondes*, 1 juillet, 1871; *North China Daily News* and *North China Herald* for 1870. One of the most carefully prepared and interesting accounts of the massacre is contained in Baron Hübner's *Ramble Round the World*, translated by Lady Herbert, New York, 1875, pp. 526–573.

minated the Tientsin tragedy, came the inquiry of the imperial counsel into what was briefly summed up as the "missionary question." More than ten years had now elapsed since the general repeal of all pre-existing edicts against Christianity in the Empire, and the officials were already concerned as to the movements and rumors respecting the new sect which had come to their ears since that time. Accordingly in February, 1871, after an earnest study of the matter from their stand-point, the Foreign Office sent to the various legations the following note and memorandum:

TUNGCHÍ, 9th year, 12th moon, 24th day.

SIR: In relation to the missionary question, the members of the Foreign Office are apprehensive lest in their efforts to manage the various points connected with it they shall interrupt the good relations existing between this and other governments, and have therefore drawn up several rules upon the subject. These are now enclosed, with an explanatory minute, for your examination, and we hope that you will take them into careful consideration.

With compliments, cards of WĂNSIANG.
SHĂN KWEI-FĂN.

The rules proposed (1) that only the children of native Christians be received into Romish asylums; (2) that "in order to exhibit the reserve and strict propriety of Christianity," no Chinese females should enter the chapels nor foreign women propagate the doctrines; (3) that missionaries should confine themselves to their proper calling, and that they "ought not to be permitted to set up an independent style and authority;" (4) that they should not interfere in trials of their native converts when brought into criminal courts; (5) that passports given to missionaries should not be transferred, but returned to the Chinese authorities when no longer required, "nor should they avail themselves of the passport to secretly go elsewhere," as the French ofttimes did; (6) that the missionaries should never receive men of bad character into the church, nor retain those of notoriously evil characters; moreover that quarterly reports of the converts be handed in to the provincial officers, as did the Buddhist and Taoist houses; (7) that missionaries should not use official seals, nor write official despatches to the local authorities, nor otherwise act as if they were officials instead of commoners. The last rule complained of the unreasonable demands of the Romish missionaries for lands and houses to be restored to them in accordance with the Peking convention; it proposed that no more be restored, and that lands bought for erecting churches be held in the name of the native church members.

This state paper was remarkable as being the first in which the Chinese government had expressed its desire for a satisfactory discussion and decision of the difficult questions involved in Christian missions, and the quasi independence allowed their foreign agents by the treaties. The public sentiment among foreigners in China was that these good people had a right to do everything not expressly prohibited by treaty until their own consular officers notified them to the contrary. The unauthorized conduct of Romish missionaries in two western provinces had already given rise to riots, in which Frenchmen had been killed. In such judicial proceedings as that described by Abbé Huc in his interesting travels are seen the high-handed perversion of justice denounced in the seventh section of this paper.[1] The writers of these rules were hardly aware of the serious import of the questions they had grappled, still less of the ignorance they exhibited in their handling of them. All the strictures referred exclusively to the Roman Catholics, for Protestant missionaries were hardly known to the Chinese magistrates, no complaints having been entered against them.

Most of the foreign ministers long delayed their answers to this minute, so that no personal discussion ever took place between the parties most interested. The straightforward and earnest reply of Mr. Low, the United States envoy (dated March 20th), carefully went over all the main points, and gave Wănsiang and Shăn Kwei-făn a clear idea of what they might expect from other ministers, together with many good suggestions as to their own duties. Nothing practical ever came of the paper, but the discussions it caused throughout the country showed the interest felt in the whole matter.[2] A few Protestant missionaries themselves indulged in harsh strictures on the native officials,

---

[1] *Travels in the Chinese Empire*, Vol. I., Chap. VI.

[2] *Foreign Relations of the United States*, 1871, pp. 99–111; also for 1872, pp. 118–130 and 137–138. *Missionary Recorder*, Vols. III. and IV. passim.

one going the length of saying that he "looked upon the document rather as an excuse offered beforehand for premeditated outrages than as an indication of measures being taken to prevent them." However, no evil results ever came to the converts or their teachers from the discussion of the minute, and its diffusion gave many readers their first information on the whole subject. Differences of opinion led to a comparison of facts, and the small number of grievances reported upheld the conclusion that the Chinese officials and literati had been, on the whole, extremely moderate, considering their limited opportunities to examine the question and the irritation aroused by the demands and hauteur of the Romish missionaries. The unjust manner in which they possessed themselves of the ground within the city of Canton on which the governor-general's yamun once stood had made a deep impression on the citizens; and when their cathedral, towering above all the temples and offices of the metropolis, was located upon this site, their indignation knew no bounds.

The year 1873 saw the conclusion of the Mohammedan insurrection in the north-western provinces, the exact extent of which has never been perfectly made known. The capture of Suhchau (near the Kiayü Pass in Kansuh) by the imperial troops under General Tso Tsung-tang brought to an end all organized rebellion in China Proper.[1] As is customary, the central government threw the responsibility of promoting the peace of the provinces upon their governors, and the well-disposed among the people were usually sure of protection. The foreign administration of the import customs turned a large and certain revenue into the hands of the Peking officials, and their development of the defences of the coast in building forts, launching war steamers, and making war material at the new arsenals, indicated their fears of foreign reprisals and their unwisdom in deeming such outlays effectual. The same money spent in making good wagon roads, working iron, coal, and other mines, deepening navigable watercourses, and intro-

---

[1] *Foreign Relations of the United States*, 1874, p. 250. *Peking Gazette*, December 28, 1873.

ducing small steamers on them, would have brought more substantial returns. But these were achievements which the future alone could accomplish, and the people must be somewhat taught and prepared for them before any permanent advances would ensue.[1]

On October 16, 1872, occurred the marriage of the Emperor Tungchí to Aluteh, a Manchu lady. The ceremonies attending her selection, betrothal, and espousal were elaborate and complete in every particular. Such an event had only once before taken place during the Manchu dynasty—when Kanghí was a minor, in 1674—all the other emperors having been married during their fathers' reigns. The occasion, therefore, excited great attention, while the attendant expenses were enormous; but all passed off without the least disturbance and apparently to general satisfaction. The two Empresses-dowager controlled the details, the most important of which were announced to the Empire in a series of edicts prepared by members of the *Lí Pu*, or Board of Rites, containing directions for every motion of the two principal actors, as well as for those who joined the ceremonies during the occasion till the 21st of the month.[2]

The young Emperor entered into the spirit of the preparations with great interest, and on the day before sending the bride her phœnix robes and diadem he ordered three princes to offer sacrifice and burn incense on the altar to heaven, "these informing heaven that he was about to marry Aluteh, the wise, virtuous, and accomplished daughter of Chung, duke and member of the Hanlin." Another prince informed mother earth, and a third announced it to the imperial ancestors, in their special temple. During the weeks preceding and following the happy day, all courts throughout the land were closed and a general jail delivery promulgated.

Many of the ceremonies and processions in Peking were not

---

[1] Compare a rather enthusiastic article by Captain A. G. Bridge, *The Revival of the Warlike Power of China*, *Fraser's Magazine* for June, 1879, p. 778.

[2] A translation of these papers was made at Shanghai, not long after, by Miss L. M. Fay, an American lady, and furnishes an interesting and authentic account of the whole wedding.

public, for considerations of state and security demanded great care.[1] On the 19th the wedding was thus announced to the foreign ministers by H. I. Majesty, through Prince Kung: "We having with pious veneration succeeded to the vast dominion founded by Our ancestors, and enjoying in its fulness the glorious lot to which We have been destined, have chosen one virtuous and modest to be the mistress of Our imperial home. Upon October 15th, We, by patent, installed Aluteh, daughter of Chung Chí, a *shí-tsiang* in the Hanlin College, as Empress. This from the Emperor." The court had not as yet outgrown its exclusiveness further than this step of announcing the marriage and its completion; and to those best acquainted with the etiquette observed for centuries, even this seemed to be a good deal in advance of former times. The great counsellors of state soon arranged for closing the regency which had existed since 1861. The Emperor Tungchí, though born on April 27, 1856, was called seventeen at his marriage. The Empresses-dowager accordingly announced on October 22d that he would attain his majority at the next Chinese new year, and be inaugurated with all the usual ceremonies. One of his special imperial functions, that of offering sacrifices to heaven at the winter solstice, would be performed by him in person—a ceremony which had been intermitted since December, 1859. Accordingly, on February 23, 1873, he issued a decree through the Board of Rites, as follows: "We are the humble recipient of a decree from their Majesties the two Empresses, declaring it to be their pleasure that We, being now of full age, should in person assume the superintendence of business, and in concert with Our officers in the capital and in the provinces, attend to the work of good government. In respectful obedience to the commands of their Majesties, We do in person enter upon the

---

[1] For a report of what could be watched of this ceremony, see William Simpson, *Meeting the Sun*, Chap. XV. The bridal procession came off during the night, when a bright moonlight enabled him to see it pass, without molestation, from the shop where he was hidden. This chiaroscuro sort of panorama rather suited the ideas of the people, and was submitted to by the Pekingese crowd without a murmur. Compare K. Bismark in the *Galaxy*, Vol. XIX., p. 182; *Cornhill Magazine*, Vol. XXVII., p. 82.

important duty assigned to Us on the 26th day of the 1st moon of the 12th year of the reign Tungchí."

This announcement was on the same day communicated to the ministers of Russia, Germany, the United States, Great Britain, and France. They returned a collective note the following morning, and asked Prince Kung to "take his Imperial Majesty's orders with reference to their reception." This intimation could not have been unexpected to him and his colleagues, but with their usual habit of putting off the inevitable, they began to make excuses. After deferring the consultation with the envoys a fortnight on the plea of Wănsiang's illness, they met at the Russian legation on March 11th. The question of the *kotow* was the crucial point, as it had been in 1859 between Kweiliang and Mr. Ward. Then the court was willing to accept a sort of curtsey instead of a prostration when the American minister approached the throne. Now the court had put the strongest argument into the hands of foreign ministers by sending the Burlingame mission to their courts, and the rights of independent nations could not be waived or implicated by the least sign of inferiority. The conference was amicable and the matter fully ventilated. The demands upon the Chinese were summarized by the ministers: That a personal audience with the Emperor was proper and needful; that it should not be unnecessarily delayed; and that they would not kneel before him, nor perform any other ceromony derogatory to their own dignity or that of their nationalities. These points were maintained as their united decision in the weary series of conferences, correspondence, and delays which ensued during the next four months in Peking. The prince and his colleagues, by their discussion of the point, had aroused the resistance of the great body of literati and conservative officials in the Empire, who had grown up in the belief that its unity and prosperity were involved in the performance of the kotow. The discussion in July, 1859, when the Emperor Hienfung could safely decline to admit Mr. Ward to an audience without it, had exhausted their arguments; but his son had come to the throne under the new influences, which were rapidly breaking down all those old ideas and safeguards. The prince had, moreover, learned that the foreign ministers were not very strongly supported by their own governments, none of whom intended to make the audience question a *casus belli*, or even a reason for withdrawing their legations from Peking. Perhaps the Yamun thought that the departure of the Russian and German ministers would leave the other three less inclined to persist in their demand, if serious consequences were likely to result.

The American minister clearly states the pith of the matter in his despatch of March 24th in his closing words: "I attach importance to the proper settlement of the audience question at the earliest time possible. To demand it, and urge compliance with the demand, is a duty every western nation owes to its own dignity and to the welfare of its citizens and subjects residing here; it is also a kindness to this government to try through this means to improve relations, and thus prevent, or at least postpone, what are now likely at any time to occur—hostile collisions, with their dreadful consequences."[1] This alternative was not a fanciful one, and this cause of chronic dispute and irritation between China and other nations during many centuries was removed chiefly through the patient persistance of Mr. Low in this discussion. His despatches contain every fact and argument of importance in perhaps the most serious controversy ever brought before China. One cannot but sympathize with Prince Kung and his colleagues in their dilemma, and to this embarrassment Mr. Low gives due weight.

The Chinese officials took a month to discuss the points among themselves, and signs of yielding were apparent both in the note of Prince Kung of April 16th and the memorandum of the 29th brought forward at an interview with the legations. Much of the same ground was gone over again; a vacation ensued, then another protocol on May 15th appeared, followed by notes on the 20th and 29th from both sides, all tending to the desired conclusion. At last the audience question was settled on June 29th by the Emperor first

[1] *Foreign Relations of the United States*, 1873, p. 169. See also the despatches of that year, and compare Pauthier's *Histoire des Relations Politique de la Chine*, Paris, 1858. Narrative of the American Embassy's visit to Peking, *N. C. Br. R. As. So.*, Vol. I, 1859.

receiving Soyeshima, the ambassador from Japan, by himself; and immediately afterward the five ministers of Russia, the United States, Great Britain, France, and Holland, accompanied only by Mr. Carl Bismarck, the German secretary, who interpreted for them.[1] Mr. Low's despatch of July 10th, giving the details of the ceremonies and the previous discussion in settling them, with the difficulty the prince and others had in swallowing the bitter pill, is very valuable as a description of the finale of this last struggle of Chinese seclusion to resist the incoming wave of western power. The wall of their separation was at last broken down. They were really stronger and wiser than ever, and every nation interested felt a relief that the days of proud assumption were ended. The young Emperor held only three more audiences during his short reign of nineteen months; and in all these discussions he seems to have taken no active part, nor did he oppose the conclusion. His ignorance of the whole question made his opinion a matter of small moment.

Among other advantages resulting to all parties by the settlement of this question was the right adjustment of the Chinese government in its relations with other courts. This acknowledgment of their equality as independent nations did not in anywise interfere with the obeisance of native officials when approaching their sovereign; but it smoothed the way for future diplomatic relations. No western power could maintain an envoy near the *Hwangti* at Peking with the least self-respect if he were not allowed to see this potentate unless by prostrating himself. While none of the great nations would deem a mere matter of ceremony a sufficient pretext for resorting to war—since war itself often fails to convince—a long continuance of this state of affairs must inevitably have led to complications the more unpleasant to diplomatists because sure to be oft-recurring. It was probably owing to the personal influence of Prince Kung and Wănsiang, the two most enlightened statesmen of this period, that a further insistance upon the kotow was not made, and preparations thus arranged for reciprocal courtesies when Chinese ambassadors appeared at foreign courts.

---

[1] Compare the *Illustrated London News* for June 23, 1873.

WĂNSIANG.

But against what tremendous odds of superstition and national prejudice these two officials were pitted in this curious contest those who have never lived in the Empire can hardly appreciate.[1]

The years 1873 and 1874 were marked by the abolition of the coolie trade at Macao, which since its rise in 1848 had been attended with many atrocities on land and sea. During these twenty-five years attempts had been made to conduct the trade with some regard for the rights of the laborers, but experience had shown that to do this was practically impossible if the business were to be made remunerative. Driven from Hongkong and Whampoa, the agents of this traffic had long found shelter in the Portuguese harbor of Macao, from which semi-independent port they could despatch Chinese crimps on kidnapping excursions for their nefarious trade. When at last the governor closed this haven to its continuance, the Spaniards and Peruvians were the only nationalities whom the action affected; but Spain, falling back on her treaty of 1864, insisted that the coolie trade be allowed. The Yamun was advised not to admit this privilege until the harsh treatment of the laborers in Cuba had been inquired into. This was done in 1873, by means of a commission composed of three foreigners and two Chinese, who made as thorough an inquiry as the Cuban authorities would permit and reported the results in 1874. Since the dreadful disclosures which transpired in their report the trade has never revived. Peru, indeed, sent M. Garcia as its envoy to Peking to negotiate a treaty and obtain the right of engaging laborers,

[1] Of Wănsiang's personal history little is known. He was a Manchu, and a man of uncommonly prepossessing manner, being perhaps most highly esteemed of all the officials who came in contact with the foreign legations. At the termination of hostilities and the organization of the Tsung-lí Yamun in 1861, he came prominently forward as a most efficient and sagacious adviser of the government. We have already in this narrative had occasion to note the influence of his name in the settlement of the Lay-Osborne flotilla and in the missionary question, the satisfactory conclusion of which was a meet tribute to his talents and judgment. He died at an advanced age in 1875, at the head of the administration. In his death the Chinese government lost an unselfish patriot and a keen observer of those things which were for the best interests of his country.

but this gentleman met with no success whatever. The Chinese negotiations on this occasion showed the good results of their freer intercourse with foreigners in the improved character of their arguments for maintaining their rights.[1] The lamentable condition of Chinese laborers in Peru was fully enough proved, inasmuch as their appeal for relief to their home government had been before the Yamun since 1868, but it could do nothing effectual to help them.

The Japanese government undertook in this year to try the issue of war with the Chinese in order to settle its demand of redress for the murder, in 1871, of some fifty-four Lewchewan sailors by savages on the eastern coast of Formosa. Japan had recently deposed the native authorities in Shudi, and being hard pressed for some employment of the feudal retainers of the retired daimios, undertook to redress Lewchewan grievances by occupying the southern part of Formosa, asserting that it did not belong to China because she either would not or could not govern its savage inhabitants. This view of the divided ownership of the island was promptly rejected by the foreign ministers resident at Tokio, but the officials were persuaded that all they had to do was to occupy the whole southern district, and the Chinese could not drive them out when once their intrenchments were completed.

The Mikado accordingly gathered his forces in Kiusiu during the years 1873–74, placing them under the command of General Saigo, and engaging qualified foreign military men to assist. The expedition was called a High Commission, accompanied by a force sufficient for its protection, sent to aboriginal Formosa to inquire into the murder of fifty-four Japanese subjects, and take steps to prevent the recurrence of such atrocities. A proclamation was issued April 17, 1874, and another May 19th, stating that General Saigo was directed to call to an account the persons guilty of outrages on Japanese subjects. As he knew that China was not prepared to resist his landing at Liang-kiao, his chief business was to provide means to house

---

[1] *Foreign Relations of the United States*, 1874, pp. 198–232. *Westminster Review*, Vol. 100, p. 75. *Customs Report on Cuban Coolie Trade*, 1876.

and feed the soldiers under his command. The Japanese authorities do not appear very creditably in this affair. No sooner did they discover the wild and barren nature of this unknown region than they seemed fain to beat an incontinent and hasty retreat, nor did the troops landed there stand upon the order of their going. They had in some measure been misled by the fallacious arguments of Gen. Charles Le Gendre, formerly United States consul at Amoy, who had travelled through these districts in 1865; the enormous cost which they had already incurred made them hesitate about proceeding further, though they had announced their intention of retaining possession of the territory. The aborigines having fled south after the first rencontre, the Japanese leader employed his men as best he could in opening roads through the jungle and erecting houses.

Meanwhile the Peking authorities were making preparations for the coming struggle, and though they moved slowly they were much in earnest to protect their territory. General Shin Pao-chin having been invested with full powers to direct operations against the Japanese forces, began at once to draw together men and vessels in Fuhchau and Amoy. The Japanese consuls at Amoy and Shanghai were allowed to remain at their posts; and during the year two envoys arrived at Peking to treat with the Court. Their discussions soon narrowed down to a demand on the Japanese ministers, Yanagiwara and Okubo, to withdraw from Formosa before treating with them upon the outrages there; which was met by a refusal on the ground that the Emperor had voided his sovereignty by having for three years taken no steps to punish his subjects, notwithstanding the repeated requests made to this end. The Chinese proved that the Japanese had violated their treaty, and acted in an underhand manner in certain negotiations with their envoy, Soyeshima, the preceding year; but this continued sparring was mere child's play. The probabilities were strong against any settlement, when the parties were induced to arrange their quarrel by the intervention and wise counsel of Sir T. F. Wade, the British minister. The Japanese accepted five hundred thousand taels for their outlays in Formosa for roads, houses, and defences; agreeing thereupon to retire and leave the further punishment of the aborigines to the Chinese authorities. The two envoys left Peking, and this attempt at war was happily frustrated.[1]

The history of this affair was exceedingly instructive to those who saw the risks to their best interests which both these nations were running in an unnecessary appeal to force. Never, perhaps, has the resort to arbitration been more happy, when to the difficulty of keeping out of a quarrel which so many fortune-seekers were ready to encourage was added the fact that both nations had been eagerly developing their land and marine forces by adopting foreign arms, drill, ships, and defences; every friend felt the uselessness of a disastrous conflict at this time and willingly strove to prevent any such result. The civilization of all parts of Formosa has since rapidly advanced by the extension of tea and sugar culture, the establishment of Christian missions, and the better treatment of the native tribes. A single incident at this time illustrated the undefined position of the parties in this dispute. This was the arrival in Peking, after Okubo's departure, of a large embassy of Lewchewans to make their homage to the Emperor Tungchí. The Japanese chargé d'affaires was denied admittance to the Lewchewan hotel, and the Yamun refused to dismiss the embassy, but gave it an audience, as was the usage in former days—probably the last in their history. The experience acquired by these three nations in their quarrel concerning Formosa has not prevented considerable bitterness about their rights to Lewchew.

No sooner had the Chinese government escaped from the Japanese imbroglio by the payment of half a million taels than it found itself involved in another and more troublesome question with the British. This arose from the persistent attempts of the latter to open a trade through Burmah, along the Irrawadi River, with Yunnan and other south-western parts of China. The Indian government had sent or encouraged explorers to go through the little known regions lying between

---

[1] *Is Aboriginal Formosa a part of the Chinese Empire?* with eight maps, folio, Shanghai, 1874, pp. 20. *Foreign Relations of the United States* for 1873 and 1874—China and Japan, passim. *The Japan Herald* and *North China Herald* for those years record all the leading events.

the Brahmaputra and Lantsang rivers, but no trade could be developed in so wild and thinly settled a region. During the Tai-ping Rebellion the Emperor's authority in Yunnan had been practically in abeyance, and over the western half of the province it had been superseded by a revolt of the Panthays, a Mohammedan tribe long settled in that region. These sectaries date their origin from the Tang dynasty, and had been generally unmolested by the Chinese so long as they obeyed the laws. During the Mongol sway their numbers increased so that they began to participate in the government, while ever since they have enjoyed more or less the control of affairs.[1] The differences in faith and practice, however, aided in keeping them distinct; and in Yunnan their numbers were recruited by settlers from Kansuh and Koko-nor, so that they were led to throw off the Chinese rule altogether.

They began about the year 1855 to defend themselves against the imperialists, captured Talí in 1857, pushing their arms as far eastward as the provincial capital Yunnan fu, which was seized and held for a brief period; but in 1867 they proclaimed Tu Win-siu as their Imam, and located their capital in Talí. With affairs in this condition law and order speedily vanished, life and property were sacrificed, and general misrule furnished the lawless with an opportunity to burn, kill, and destroy until the land became a desert. The Panthays, as the Burmese called the insurrectionists, turned their hopes westward for succor, and to this end endeavored to keep open the trade with Burmah and India, but under the circumstances it could not flourish. The British in those countries were, however, quite ready to countenance, if not aid, the new ruler at Talí, as soon as his power was sufficiently consolidated to keep open the roads and protect traders.

In 1868 a party was ordered to proceed to this city and "discover the cause of the cessation of trade formerly existing by these routes, the exact position held by the Kakhyens, Shans, and Panthays with reference to that traffic, and their disposition or

[1] Compare Dr. Anderson, *From Mandalay to Momien*, p. 223. Du Halde, *Histoire*, Tome I., p. 199. Grosier, *China*, Vol. IV., p. 270. Garnier, *Voyaye d'Exploration*, Tome I. Cooper, *Travels of a Pioneer of Commerce.*

otherwise to resuscitate it." This party, numbering a hundred in all, was in charge of Major Sladen, assisted by five qualified men, and guarded by an escort of fifty armed police; its object embraced diplomacy, engineering, natural science, and commerce. Their steamer reached Bhamo January 22, 1868, and the party began their travels early in March, arriving after much delay at Momein (or Tăng-yueh chau), a town on the Taping River, one hundred and thirty-five miles from Bhamo and about five thousand feet above the sea. Another forced delay of nearly two months convinced them of the impossibility of their getting to Talí (nearly as far again); in face of the determined opposition, therefore, both of the hill tribes and Chinese traders, Major Sladen was fain to retire in safety to Bhamo. The retreat of this anomalous expedition could be officially ascribed to the weakness of the Panthay rulers, the wild region traversed, and its yet wilder inhabitants. But to what principles of justice or equity can we attribute the action of the British in retaining their minister at the capital of an Empire while sending a peaceful mission to a rebel in arms at its boundaries? This impertinence seems thinly veiled by dubbing the expedition one of inquiry concerning trade; no trade did or could exist with an ill-assorted rabble of wild mountaineers; when these had been duly subjected an expedition for purposes of science would meet with as ready assistance from the authorities as did that of the Frenchman, Lieutenant Garnier, then exploring eastern Yunnan. This disregard of the courtesies and rights of independent nations reflects as little credit upon the powerful nation which used her strength thus unfairly as does her similar attempt of negotiating with another rebel, Yakub Beg in Ílí.

Major Sladen's mission, owing to the admirable qualities of its leader, made so fair an impression upon the natives along his route that upon his return in 1873 his progress was materially assisted, instead of retarded, by them as far as Momein. In the years intervening the Imam at Talí, with about forty thousand of his followers, had been hemmed in by the Chinese forces under the leadership of Lí Sieh-tai, or Brigadier Lí. The Mohammedans felt their weakness against such odds, and the so-called Sultan Suleiman sent his son Hassan to London to implore recognition and aid from the British government; but before he returned his father had killed himself and the victorious Chinese had massacred most of their opponents and regained possession of the whole province in 1873. Its western half had been virtually independent since 1855, during which period the wretchedness of the inhabitants had greatly reduced their numbers and resources.

Trade soon revived. The British appointed an agent to reside at Bhamo and learn its amount and character. In 1874 an expedition—this time provided with Chinese passports—was planned to make the trip across China from Burmah to Hankow, as Lieutenant Garnier had done from Saigon. The Chinese traders in Burmah set themselves to circumvent it, for its success boded disaster to them, as they better knew the resources of their competitors. The British plan was to send an accredited agent across the country from Hankow to Bhamo, there to meet a party under charge of Col. Horace Browne, which was to "thoroughly examine the capabilities of the country beyond Momein." As only six years had passed since Sladen's party had reached that town on its way to the Panthays at Talí, there had perhaps been hardly time to remove all suspicion among the local officials about the objects of this new move. One of the consular clerks, Augustus R. Margary, was furnished with necessary passports and instructions from her Majesty's legation to go to Bhamo and act as Colonel Browne's guide and interpreter. His journals testify that no better choice could have been made, and all who knew him were hopeful of the success of this young man.[1] He left Hankow September 2d and reached Bhamo January 17th without molestation or accident, having been received with respect by all Chinese officials, whom the governor-general of Yunnan had required thus to act. While the party in Bhamo prepared the equipment for its journey, Dr. Anderson observes that the Chinese "watched its movements with a secret feeling that the objects contemplated were somewhat beyond the peaceful pursuits of commerce and scientific inquiry."[2]

---

[1] *Journals of A. R. Margary*, edited by Sir R. Alcock, London, 1877.

[2] The report was also circulated that the party was going to lay down a railroad.

Mr. Margary intimated that he thought there were intrigues going on at Manwyne adverse to the advance of the mission ; but Brigadier Lí, who treated him there with great honor, did every thing to promote his journey to Bhamo.

The arrangements as to routes and escorts were at last completed so far as to allow the party finally to leave Bhamo February 3, 1875 ; it numbered nearly fifty persons in all, together with a Burmese guard of one hundred and fifty. The rivalries and deceptions of the Kakhyen tribes proved to be worse than in 1868, and progress was slower from the difficulty of providing animals for transport. By the 18th it had crossed the frontier, and the next morning Mr. Margary left, with five Chinese, for Manwyne, to arrange there for its reception by Brigadier Lí. Increased dissensions among the tribes as to escort, transport, and pay led Colonel Browne to push on after him with a guard so as to reach that town and find some competent authority to aid his expedition. Many signs of serious opposition had by this time manifested themselves ; and when he was preparing to start from Seray on the 23d, large bodies of armed men were seen on the opposite hills coming to attack the British. A Burmese messenger also arrived from Manwyne with letters giving an account of the horrid murder of Mr. Margary and his attendants by the treacherous officials there on the 20th. The Chinese soldiers or robbers were in a manner repulsed by the bravery of Browne's escort and by firing the jungle, but the expedition was in face of too powerful an opposition to contemplate advancing after such disasters. The return to Bhamo was soon made, and the earnest efforts of the Burmese officers there to recover everything belonging to the British proved their honesty.

The disappointment at this rebuff was exceeded by the general indignation at the treachery which marked the murder. It was soon known that Lí Sieh-tai was not at Manwyne at the time, though the real actors in the tragedy belonged to his army, and must have made him cognizant of the deed.[1]

[1] *Mandalay to Momien : A Narrative of Two Expeditions to Western China*, by Dr John Anderson, contains a most satisfactory narrative of these attempts ; the writer's opinion is of the highest value.

When news of this disaster reached London and Peking, the British minister was directed to demand an investigation of the facts connected with the outrage in presence of a British officer in Yunnan, the issue by the Yamun of fresh passports for a new mission, and an indemnity. After months of delay and correspondence with the Yamun Sir Thomas Wade, the British minister, was able to make up his commission and despatch it from Hankow, November 5th, for Yunnan fu. It consisted of the Hon. T. G. Grosvenor, second secretary of the legation, and Messrs. Davenport and Baber of the consular service, all of them well fitted by previous training for attaining the objects of their expedition. The journey was performed in company with a Chinese escort, without danger or interference, the city of Yunnan being reached in March. The gentlemen found the provinces through which they travelled perfectly at peace, and the Emperor's authority everywhere acknowledged—a fact extremely creditable to the Chinese after more than twenty years of civil war.

The Chinese appointed to conduct the inquiry into the murder, in connection with Mr. Grosvenor, was Lí Han-chang, governor-general at Wuchang and brother of Lí Hung-chang. He was long in making the journey, but the two began their proceedings, having Sieh Hwan, an old member of the Yamun in 1864, as aid. Those who had any experience or acquaintance with similar joint commissions in China anticipated but one result from it—an entire failure in proving or punishing the guilty parties; while those who wish to see their character should read Mr. Grosvenor's various reports[1] to learn how slow are the advances of the Chinese in truth-telling. Nevertheless, such an investigation had some prospective benefit in that the trouble which the British made on account of the taking of one life warned the officials to exercise the greatest caution in future. In this preventive aspect, the mission doubtless accomplished more than can be estimated. Mr. Baber is sure that Margary was killed (and his opinion is entitled to great respect) by the discontented Chinese train bands then around Manwyne—

[1] *Blue Book—China*, No. 1 (1876) and No. 3 (1877).

a lawless set, who were afterward hunted to death.[1] The weight of evidence obtained at Yunnan fu went to prove that the repulse of the British party was countenanced, if not planned, by the governor-general, and carried into effect with the cognizance of Brigadier Lí. Amid so much irreconcilable evidence, the inference that the officers, chiefly by so doing, intended to prevent the extension of trade by the British, offers the most adequate explanation. When the impoverished condition of Southwestern China is remembered, the question arises, Why should the Indian government strive to open a trade where industry and population have been so destroyed? But the expectation that thereby a greater market would be found for its opium in all Western China is a sufficient reason, perhaps, for undertaking so costly an experiment.

No sooner had Sir Thomas Wade learned of Margary's death than he impressed upon the Chinese government the necessity for unremitting and vigorous measures toward the arrest and punishment of the guilty. In addition to what has been already stated concerning this reparation, he brought forward some other matters affecting the intercourse between the two countries. They were long and painfully debated, and those agreed on were embodied in a convention which was signed by himself and Lí Hung-chang, on the part of Great Britain and China, September 13, 1876. The correspondence relating to this convention is given, with its text, in the Parliamentary Blue Books,[2] and is worth perusal by all who wish to learn the workings of the Chinese government.

The Yunnan case was settled by immediate payment of two hundred thousand taels ($280,000), which included all claims of British merchants on the Chinese government; by posting an imperial proclamation in the cities and towns throughout the Empire; by sending an envoy bearing a letter of regret to Queen Victoria for what had occurred in Yunnan; and by

---

[1] *Blue Book—China*, No. 3, 1878. *Report of Mr. Baber on the route followed by Mr. Grosvenor's mission between Tali fu and Momein.* Reprinted, with his other interesting travels and researches in Western China, in *Supplementary Papers*, Vol. I., Part 1, 1882, of *Roy. Geog. Soc.*, London.

[2] *Blue Book—China*, No. 1 (1876) and No. 3 (1877).

stationing British officers at Talí or elsewhere in that province to "observe the conditions of trade." The proclamation[1] was posted very widely (three thousand copies in Kiangsu province alone), and through it the people learned that the safety of all foreigners travelling through their country was guaranteed by the Emperor. Other matters agreed upon in this convention were the manner of official intercourse between native and foreign officers at Peking and the ports, so that perfect equality might be shown; the better administration of justice in criminal cases between their respective subjects, every such case being tried by the official of the defendant's nationality, while the plaintiff's official could always be present to watch proceedings; the extension of trade by opening four new ports as consular stations, and six on the Yangtsz' River for landing goods, with other regulations as to opium, transit, and *li-kin* taxes on goods; and lastly, the appointment of a joint commission to establish some system that should enable the Chinese government to protect its revenue without prejudice to the junk trade of Hongkong.

This final article might well have been omitted. The concessions and advantages in it accrued to the British, and through them also measurably to other nationalities. But while the Chinese under the circumstances had no right to complain of paying heavily for Margary's life, it was manifestly unfair to cripple their commerce by sheltering Hongkong smugglers under promise of a commission which could never honestly agree. In order to better understand the British minister's views regarding the political and commercial bearing of his convention, the reader is referred to his labored minute of July 14, 1877,[2] in which the fruits of thirty-five years of official experience in China impart much value to his opinions. The singular mixture of advice, patronizing decisions, and varied knowledge running through the whole render the paper extremely interesting. The Chinese historian of the next century will read with wonder the implied responsibility of the British minister for the conduct of the Empire in its foreign manage-

---

[1] *Blue Book—China*, No. 3 (1877). [2] *Ibid*, pp. 111–147.

ment, and the enormous development of the principle of ex-territoriality so as to cover almost every action of every British subject. He may also be instructed by this proof of the ignorance and fears of the former rulers, as well as their conceit and hesitation in view of their wants and backwardness to cope with the advancing age. He must acknowledge, too, that the sharp and prolonged discussion of eighteen months between Sir Thomas and the Yamun was one of the most profitable exercises in political science the high officers of Peking ever had allowed them.

Since the convention of Chifu the progress of China at home and abroad has been the best evidence of an improved administration. The reign of Hienfung ended in 1861, with the prestige, resources, and peace of the realm he had so miserably governed reduced to their lowest ebb. During the twelve years of his son's nominal régime, the face of affairs had quite changed for the better. Peace and regular government had been for the most part resumed throughout the Eighteen Provinces, and even to the extreme western frontier of Kashgar and Kuldja. The people were returning to their desolated villages, while their rulers did what they could to promote agriculture and trade. The young Emperor gave small promise of becoming a wise or efficient ruler; and when he died (January 12, 1875) it was felt that an effigy only had passed away, and no change would ensue in the administration. In the question of selecting his inheritor were involved some curious features of Chinese customs. It is a rule that the succession to the *Lung-wei*, or 'Dragon's Seat,' cannot pass to the preceding generation, since this would involve the worship of a lower or younger generation by an older one. The line of Hienfung died out in his childless son; the eldest of his brothers had, as we have seen, been made posthumous heir of an uncle in 1854, consequently his son, Pu-lun, was ineligible. The elevation of Prince Kung's son Tsai-ching to be Emperor was in the highest degree inexpedient, as this would necessitate the retirement of his father from active participation in the government, arising from their relationship of father and son. The next eligible candidate, Tsai-tien, a child of Prince Chun—the seventh son of Taukwang—born August 15,

1871, was unanimously chosen by the Empresses dowager and assembled princes of the Manchu Imperial Clan. His parents were brother and sister of those of his predecessors, while the same regency had been reappointed, so that his tender age involved neither difficulty nor alteration during the minority. He took the reign-name of *Kwang-sü*, or 'Illustrious Succession,' having reference to the disturbance in the regular descent. By this arrangement the same general set of officials was continued on the government, and the risk to its peaceful working from the freaks of Tungchí avoided.[1]

A most notable event during the last decade has been the recovery of the vast regions of the Tarim Valley to the imperial sway. Their loss took place during the early part of the Tai-ping Rebellion, beginning in Kansuh, where the discontented Moslem population, aided by the reckless and seditious of all clans, arose and drove out the governmental minions even to the eastern side of Shensí. Of this extended revolt little is known in the west save the name of its figure-head and leading character under whose mastery it culminated and succumbed.

The famous Yakub Beg, whom the jealous attentions of both England and Russia had united in raising to the rank of a hero, commenced his military career as lieutenant of Buzurg khan, a son of the notable Jehangír, kojeh of Kokand. By the year 1866 the energetic lieutenant had made way with his licentious and cowardly chief, and possessed himself of a large part of Western Kashgaria; then, turning his attention to the rebellious Dunganis north of him, a series of vigorous campaigns ended in leaving him undisputed ruler of all Tien-Shan Nan Lu. These conquests over, hordes of neighboring rebels must now be recognized as fatal errors in the policy of Yakub. The Atalik Ghazi, or 'Champion Father' as he was now called, had not only attracted the distrust of Russia—manifested in their taking of Kuldja from the Dunganis before his approach was possible—but in annihilating other Moslem insurrectionists,

[1] The Eastern Empress-dowager, the legal widow of Hienfung, whose only child, a daughter, died early in 1875, followed her to the grave in 1881, leaving the regency with her coadjutor, the Empress An, aided by Prince Kung.

had constituted himself an avenger of Chinese wrongs, and prepared the way of his own enemies whenever the terrible day of reckoning should come.

The attempt on the part of China to restore its prestige in a territory where every hand was turned against her seemed indeed hopeless. Her exhausted resources, her constant fear of the foreigners within her gates, her suspicions of Russia, the immense distances to be traversed, seemed to unite every factor against her success. Nevertheless, by 1871 symptoms of disorganization began already to appear among the rebels, while in the wishes of the common people for a strong power to insure order and encourage trade Tso Tsung-tang, the Chinese general, found both assistance and men.

A moment's attention to the relations between the Chinese and Mohammedans of this region will throw much light on their contest. Since their conquest by Kienlung, the inhabitants of Eastern Turkestan had enjoyed an unexampled period of tranquillity and prosperous trade. The Chinese, known as Kitai, settled in their cities and brought a degree of wealth and civilization far ahead of anything previously known, while the rulers, or ambans, joined to their duties as administrators of justice a fostering care of trade routes and methods for developing the country. They have at all times been celebrated for irrigating their provinces, and now reproduced their wonderful canals (says Boulger) "even in this outlying dependency. Eastern Turkestan is one of the worst-watered regions in the world. In fact there is only a belt of fertile country around the Yarkand River, stretching away eastward along the slopes of the Tien Shan as far as Hami. The few small rivers which are traced here and there across the map are during many months of the year dried up, and even the Yarkand then becomes an insignificant stream. To remedy this, and to husband the supply as much as possible, the Chinese sunk dikes in all directions. By this means the cultivated country was slowly but surely spread over a great extent of territory, and the vicinity of the three cities of Kashgar, Yangi Hissar, and Yarkand became known as the garden of Asia. Corn and fruit grew in abundance, and from Yarkand to the south of the Tien

Shan the traveller could pass through one endless orchard. On all sides he saw nothing but plenty and content, peaceful hamlets and smiling inhabitants. These were the outcome of a Chinese domination."[1]

In addition to the fields and rivers, mines were worked, mountain passes cut and kept in repair, and the internal government of tribes placed on an equable basis. As to the precise manner in which discontent and rebellion crept into this apparently happy territory, it must always remain a matter of conjecture. The customs of its inhabitants have for ages been based on the tribal principle to such an extent that they found it impossible to assimilate with the Chinese and their methodical government, even though for their advantage to do so. The repeated failures of the United States to introduce a certaindegree of civilization among the Indians present an analogous case. Uneasiness among the natives caused by agents from Kokand and Tashkend was speedily followed by larger demands from turbulent Mussulmans, who saw in Chinese moderation an evidence of weakness and decline. Jehangír's rebellion not unjustly incensed a government which had devoted more than half a century to the building up of a shattered State, and was punished with merciless rigor. Oppression from the Chinese met by resistance, equitable rule alternating with weakness and injustice, trade impeded by illegal imports, ambitious Usbeck chiefs exciting their tribes to rise against their conquerors—these and similar causes had been at work to prevent all permanent progress in Turkestan.

During the lowest ebb of Manchu authority in the Empire, when foreigners and Tai-pings were straining the utmost resources of the government in the East, a small village of Kansuh was the scene of a sudden riot. When after two days couriers brought word that the disturbance was quelled with some loss of life, the authorities began to suppose that the affair had already been forgotten; but it proved to be the fuse that lighted an outbreak scarcely smaller than the other civil war

---

[1] *Life of Yakoob Beg*, London, 1878, p. 59. See also R. B. Shaw, *Visits to High Tartary, Yarkand, and Kashgar*, London, 1871, Chaps. II. and III.

within the provinces.[1] The Dunganis had arisen and spread the infection of revolt wherever they existed—over large districts of Shensí, but principally toward the west, to Turfan, Kuche, and Aksu—continuing the weary story of surprise, slaughter, and barbarity even to the city of Kuldja.[2] Allying with themselves the Tarantchi, a sort of fellah class which the Chinese had imported into the regions from Kashgar, the victorious rebels established one of those ephemeral governments over the Tien Shan and its adjoining valleys that have so frequently arisen in the history of Central Asia. Under their rule travel beyond the Kiayü Pass was of course impossible, while trade diminished throughout the country, and Russia, as we have seen, wrested Kuldja from Abul Oghlan in order to secure her own borders. The first serious check received by this confederation was its virtual overthrow, when Yakub advanced upon Aksu and from thence cleared the great road eastward to Turfan.

Tso's first labor, then, was to clear Shensí and Kansuh of the rebels, in which his progress was marked by admirable foresight and energy in disposition of men, arrangement of courier service, and use of modern arms. Establishing himself by 1876 in Barkul and Hami as headquarters, by the following spring he was prepared for a concerted movement from the north (Gutchen and Urumtsi) and east (Pidshan) upon Yakub Beg at Turfan. The redoubtable chieftain was finally caught by the tardy but certain power which he had long despised with impunity, and driven backward through the towns of Toksun and Harashar to Korla, where he died or was murdered, May, 1877. During this and the following years the governor-general succeeded in reinstating the authority which had been in abeyance nearly a score of years. His army under two able generals advanced along the parallel roads north and south of the Tien Shan, punishing the rebels without mercy, while "the Moham-

[1] "It is impossible not to connect this event in some degree with that unaccountable revival among Mohammedans, which has produced so many important events during the last thirty years, and of which we are now witnessing some of the most striking results."—Boulger. *Life of Yakoob Beg*, p. 95.

[2] Which fell in January, 1866, after the Chinese governor had destroyed himself and his citadel by gunpowder.

medans who submitted themselves were permitted to revert to their peaceful avocations."[1] When upon the desert the troops were provisioned from Russian territory, but during the early years of the campaign it appears that the soldiers were made to till the ground as well as construct fortifications. The history of the advance of this "agricultural army" would, if thoroughly known, constitute one of the most remarkable military achievements in the annals of any modern country.[2]

With the fall of Kashgar (December 17, 1877) the reconquest was practically completed, though Yarkand and the neighboring towns held out some months longer, at the end of which the chiefs of the Moslem movement had either fled to Ferghana or succumbed in the fight. The Chinese now turned their attention to the occupation of Kuldja, and sent Chunghow in December, 1878, to St. Petersburg upon a mission relating to its restoration. The envoy needed, indeed, but to remind the Czar of Russian promises made in Peking in 1871 concerning the prompt retrocession of the occupied territory when China should have reasserted her authority in those regions; but neither European nor Oriental diplomats seemed to regard the city "held in trust for China by the Russian government" as in the least likely to return to the dominion of the Hwangtí, while many were persuaded that Russia would resort to arms before surrendering one of the most prosperous of her possessions in order to keep a rash promise.[3]

Chunghow—whose capacity had been in some degree tested in the Tientsin riot—was hardly the best choice for envoy even among the still ignorant officers at Peking, inasmuch as to the seemingly apparent defect of an unusually Bœotian temperament was added a profound ignorance of any European language, of modern methods of diplomacy, and of the topography of the territory in question. It is almost needless to add that

---

[1] *Peking Gazette.*

[2] *The Spectator*, April 13, 1878, *Pall Mall Gazette*, June, 1878, and *London Times*, November, 1878. Boulger, *Life of Yakoob Beg*, Chaps. XII.-XIV.

[3] For an excellent illustration of the prevailing sentiment on this question, even after Chunghow's embassy, see Mr. D. C. Boulger in *Fraser's Magazine* for August, 1880, p. 164.

such an embassy was ill-prepared to cope with the astute diplomatists of an eager court, or that it speedily fell a prey to the designs upon it. A treaty of eighteen articles was signed at Livadia yielding a portion of the Kuldja district to China, Russia retaining, however, the fruitful valley of the Tekes River, all the more important strategic strongholds and passes in the Tien Shan, and the city of Yarkand; China, moreover, to pay as indemnity five million rubles for the cost of occupying Kuldja. Other important concessions, such as a trade route from Hankow through Suhchau to Kuldja and Siberia, the opening to Russian caravans of thirty-six frontier stations, the modification of the Kashgarian frontier, the arming of Muscovite merchants, and the navigation of the Songari River, were apparently added to this compact according as the Russians increased their experience of the "gullability" of these remarkable ambassadors.

Even officers of the Czar's army, in referring afterward to this treaty, were prone to add to their remarks some measure of apology. When in January, 1880, Chunghow returned home with the unwise and humiliating document in his possession, he could not have felt wholly certain of a triumphant reception. Nevertheless it is not likely that the luckless ambassador contemplated being at once deprived by imperial edict of all his offices and turned over to a board for trial and punishment. Statesmen of both parties joined in denouncing him, Lí Hungchang and Tso alike presenting memorials to the same effect, while a flood of petitions more or less fierce poured upon the government from mandarins of all ranks. On the 28th the returned envoy was cashiered for having signed away territory and promised indemnity without special authorization, and in punishment was sentenced to decapitation. The actors in this movement, which upon the manifestation of such prompt and furious measures assumed the phase of an intrigue of the war party, were Tso and Prince Chung, who seized upon the popular wrath as an opportune moment for a master stroke against Prince Kung.

With the appearance of danger such as this the party in power recoiled at once from its angry position, depreciated the highly bellicose tone of court officials, and accepted the good offices of the foreign ministers who joined in protesting against the unworthy treatment of Chunghow and the monstrous barbarity of his sentence. Possibly the temperance of Russia's attitude in demanding the unconditional pardon of Chunghow before consenting to receive a second ambassador—the Marquis Tsăng, minister to England, already appointed--materially aided in quieting the storm. Fortunately, too, amid the rumors of a resort to arms and manifest preparations of the palace discontents to force an issue, Colonel Gordon visited the capital, and in a communication to Governor Lí pointed out the folly of attempting a foreign conflict and the peculiar dangers in overwhelming, by courting a certain defeat, the great benefits which must come to the Chinese army by its gradual reorganization upon modern methods. "Potentially," said this unpalatable but honest critic, "you are perhaps invincible, but the outcome of this premature war will show you to be vulnerable at a thousand points." Counsels such as these carried unusual weight as coming from a man whom all parties in China respected and admired; there can be little doubt that it sensibly decreased the war feeling, and possibly prevented the country from rushing to certain disaster.

Chunghow was accordingly reprieved, and in June of this year set free. The intelligence and experience of Tsăng[1] proved an acceptable contrast to his predecessor's unguarded conduct, and resulted in an agreement (May 15th) on the part of the Czar's negotiators to recede nearly the whole of the contested district, excepting a narrow strip upon its western edge for purposes of colonization or retreat for those inhabitants of Ílí who preferred to remain under Russian control.[2] In return

[1] Upon his return to China the marquis published his diary, some portions of which have found their way into the *China Review* (Vol. XI., p. 135) and are extremely interesting as the outspoken opinion of an appreciative and enlightened Chinese gentleman.

[2] Precisely the extent of this strip depends upon the exact definition of the boundary here under Taukwang. The present line is laid down in that portion of the new treaty quoted in Volume I., p. 218; the territory forms approximately a wedge whose apex is in the Ala Tau Mountains, and whose base, about three degrees south of this point, lies against the crest of the Tien Shan. It meets the old boundary at the Muzart (or Muz-daban) Pass. Since the treaty

"for military expenses incurred by Russia in holding and protecting Ílí on behalf of China since the year 1871, and in satisfaction of all claims by Russian merchants for losses previously suffered by pillage within Chinese territory, and by Russians who have suffered outrage," the Chinese agreed to pay nine million roubles. This appears to have been less repugnant to oriental diplomacy than five millions in acknowledgment of getting back their borrowed property. As for the other points, the treaty does not seem to have been greatly altered, save in the Songari River and other more vexatious clauses. This treaty was ratified August 19, 1881.

From domestic wars and political complications, the influences of which have hardly as yet disappeared from our morning newspapers, our attention must be turned to the yet sadder spectacle of famine and pestilence. The occasional notices of a great scarcity of food in Northwestern China which drifted into the news items of western countries may still remain within the memory of many; those, however, who live under the ascendancy of occidental institutions can with difficulty appreciate, from any mere description of this scourge, its immense influence as a factor in removing somewhat the suspicions of the ignorant and apathetic Chinese against their fellow-men in other lands. The sympathies and charities of the Christian world, as called forth by this terrible visitation, were more effectual in making acceptable the distasteful presence of foreigners within their cities than had been the united influence of two wars and a half-century of trade, diplomacy, and social intercourse.

The Great Famine of 1878 was in some measure foretold over Shansí and Shensí by the decreasing rainfall of the four previous years. The peculiar nature of this loess-covered region, and its absolute dependence for fertility upon a sufficient supply of moisture, has been pointed out in another chapter of this work. Here, then, and in Shantung the missionaries of all denominations were called upon to organize methods

strenuous efforts have been made by the officers of both nationalities stationed there to entice the Usbeck, Kirghis, and Dunganis of the region to settle permanently on their side of the boundary.

of relief as early as the summer of 1877. By the opening of the following spring a central committee in Shanghai and their agents in Chifu and Tientsin—all Protestant and Roman Catholic missionaries—had put forth so great energy in their well-directed efforts as to gain the zealous co-operation of Lí Hung-chang, governor-general of Chihlí, and active countenance of the rulers and gentry in other provinces. "At the beginning of their labors," writes the secretary of the committee, "the distributors were received with a degree of prejudice and suspicion which utterly frustrated any attempt to prosecute the work. They were supposed to have sinister objects in view, and not only was their charity refused, but they were even in imminent danger of their lives. It required the utmost carefulness on their part to carry on their operations with any degree of success. They were urged to act in a way that contemplated the speedy exhaustion of their funds and their evacuation of the place. So far as we can ascertain, however, the distributors conducted themselves in a most commendable manner, and after a time at least bore down the ill-will and aspersions of all classes, changing their sentiments and feelings of doubt and distrust into those of the deepest gratitude and respect, so that they are now regarded as the very saviours of the people."[1]

After the experience of some weeks in the destitute regions, it was found that only the strictest adherence to a business system of distribution could be attended with any mitigation of the evil. Tickets representing certain amounts of money were given to the houses of each community which appeared on the catalogues of needy families furnished by village elders. Food being plenty in the south, the means of transportation and storage during distribution constituted the chief labor of those concerned in this work. When brought to the starving settlements, grain was promptly doled out in exchange for the tickets, and to the lasting credit of the Chinese character it must here be noticed that not a single raid upon the provisions or resort to force in any way has been recorded of these famished multitudes.

---

[1] Rev. W. Muirhead, in *Report of the China Famine Relief Fund*, Shanghai, 1879, p. 4.

That good-will, affection, and gratitude should take the place of the old mistrust under these conditions was most natural.[1] Nevertheless the terrors of their experiences in this awful time were hardly lightened by this cheering aspect of the curse. Misery and desolation such as this overwhelmed every other sentiment save that of compassion. The visitor was often met by the solitary remnant of a large household, to hear from him a harrowing recital of suffering and death, fitted to shock the most callous of humanity. Again, he would come upon the corpse of one recently fallen in the vain effort to walk to a neighboring town, and about it a lazy pack of wolves squatting —gorged and stupid from the fulness of many ghastly meals. At other times a silent dwelling might be found giving shelter only to the cadaverous bodies of its former inmates; or anon a ruined house would tell where the timbers had been plucked out and sold for a little bread. Of the last extreme of famine, cannibalism, which cropped out here and there, but which in most cases met with instant punishment when discovered, it is hardly necessary to add notice or description. The remarkable patience under suffering exhibited by the people made their relief comparatively easy, though the despair which had rendered them insensible to excitement or violence often prevented their recuperation from the fever and plague which laid hold upon their weakened bodies even after plenty had returned to the land.

In their report the committee at Shanghai acknowledge Tls. 204,560 as having passed through their hands, while about as much more may safely be said to have been otherwise expended by foreigners for the relief of the sufferers[2] The Chinese government furnished food and supplies amounting to

---

[1] A notable exception to this universal sentiment of kindliness was exhibited among the officials and gentry of Kaifung, the capital of Honan, in which city foreigners were to the last forbidden to remain, or even to carry on their work in the environs.

[2] About $22,670 were subscribed in the United States—which does not include, however, the donation from the Pacific slope. An effort was made to induce Congress to return on this occasion the surplus of the Chinese indemnity fund, amounting to nearly $600,000, but upon this the Committee on Foreign Affairs reported adversely, alleging among other reasons that all the starving people would be dead before the machinery of both nations would admit of this money being exchanged for food!

more than Tls. 2,000,000, while rich natives contributed very largely in their own districts. Sixty-nine foreigners were personally engaged upon the work of distribution in the four afflicted provinces, of whom Messrs. Hall, Hodge, Barradale, and Whiting died in consequence of exposure and overwork.[1] Upon the mortality connected with this frightful visitation there exist but the vaguest figures. "The destruction as a whole is stated to be from nine and a half to thirteen millions," observes the *Report*[2] already quoted, and its proofs in support of this statement are as trustworthy as any that can be compiled. No famine is recorded in the history of any land which equalled this in death-rate. The area at the base of the Tibetan and Mongolian highlands will always be subject to great vicissitudes of heat and moisture,[3] and the future, like the past, cannot but suffer from these frightful droughts unless a careful attention to the climatic influence of trees and irrigation mitigate in some degree the dreadful comings of these plagues.

The Chinese plenipotentiary in London, Kwoh Sung-tao, gave utterance to the sincere sentiments of his government in saying:

> The noble philanthropy which heard, in a far-distant country, the cry of suffering and hastened to its assistance, is too signal a recognition of the common brotherhood of humanity ever to be forgotten, and is all the more worthy to be remembered because it is not a passing response to a generous emotion, but a continued effort, persevered in until, in sending the welcome rain, Heaven gave the assuring promise of returning plenty, and the sign that the brotherly succor was no longer required. Coming from Englishmen residing in all parts of the world, this spontaneous act of generosity made a deep impression on the government and people of China, which cannot but have the effect of more closely cementing the friendly relations which now so happily exist between China and Great Britain. But the hands that gave also assumed the arduous duty of administering the relief; and here I would not forget to offer my grateful thanks and condolence to the families of those, and they are not a few, who nobly fell in distributing the fund.[4]

---

[1] Mr. Whiting was honored by the governor of Shansi with a public funeral in Taiyuen, the provincial capital.

[2] P. 7.

[3] Mr. A. Hosie in the *N. C. Br. R. A. S. Journal*, Vol. XIII., 1878, has translated the native lists of more than eight hundred famines and droughts occurring in the Yangtsz' basin and northward on the Plateau during a thousand years ending A.D. 1643.

[4] Letter of October 14, 1878, to Lord Salisbury.

One who has been acquainted with Chinese affairs for the last fifty years can better than younger persons appreciate from this letter the vast stride which has been made by China since the withdrawal of the East India Company's factory in 1834. The Empire had then been closed for more than a century, and its inhabitants had been taught to believe that all mankind outside of its boundaries were little better than ignorant savages. Their rulers had maintained that "barbarians could only be ruled by misrule," and in their honest efforts to keep them from entering the gates of the Celestial Empire in order that the people might not become contaminated, had faithfully though ineffectually endeavored to fulfil the first duty of every government. We have seen how small was their success when dealing with the iniquitous opium traffic; no amount of moral or ethical principle in the cause which he represented could make up to Commissioner Lin for his ignorance and stiff-neckedness in pushing his injudicious methods of reforming this abuse. Had he succeeded as he and his imperial master had planned, they would have sealed their country against the only possible remedies for those evils they were striving to remove—free intercourse, commercial, intellectual, and political, with their fellow-men.

The story of China's rapid progress from semi-barbarism toward her appropriate position among nations is now fully known to any whose interests have directed their attention thither. It cannot be denied that the advance has been hampered by the mass of superstitions, assumptions, and weaknesses through which every such stride to reformation must push forward; nor is it strange that interested foreigners from their vantage-ground of a more perfect civilization should at times bemoan the wearisome course and manifold errors of this regeneration. Nevertheless, hopeful signs abound on every side; against a few errors may be balanced a multitude of genuine successes, and the fact that these latter have come about deliberately assures us that they are permanent. In the hands of statesmen as far-sighted and patriotic as those who now control the government, there is little cause to apprehend retrograde steps or a return to the exclusive policy of Commissioners Lin and Yeh. As for the conservative spirit which yet characterizes the present régime, in this will be found the safeguard against extravagant and premature adoption of western machines, institutions, methods, dress, and the thousand adjuncts of modern European life which, if too rapidly applied to an effete and backward civilization, push it rather into bankruptcy and overthrow than out into a new existence.

Before closing these volumes, and as an illustration of these observations, it remains to notice the so-called Chinese Education Commission—a highly lauded project which is still fresh in the minds of many Americans. Soon after the Tientsin riot and Chunghow's mission of apology, Yung Wing, a Chinese graduate of Yale College, proposed to Lí Hung-chang and others in authority a plan of utilizing certain surplus moneys remaining from the fund for military stores, to defray the expenses of educating a number of Chinese boys in the United States. The scheme found such favor with the governor-general and members of the Foreign Office, that early in the year 1872 thirty boys were selected by competitive examination at Shanghai, and took passage for San Francisco July 12th, Yung Wing having preceded them to make the necessary arrangements. This gentleman's acquaintance with the social life and educational methods in New England was so complete as to enable him readily to place the students--usually in pairs—in comfortable households, where they might learn English and become initiated into the manner of life among western peoples as agreeably as possible.

The commission established its headquarters in Hartford and easily disposed their boys in adjoining towns of Connecticut and Massachusetts, where numbers of families welcomed them with open arms. Prince Kung's satisfaction upon learning of this friendly reception was expressed in a personal note of thanks to Mr. Low at Peking, while the fair prospects of the scheme now tended to hasten other parties of students to these shores until their number was swelled to one hundred and twenty.[1] These lads proved themselves almost without excep-

[1] The original plan included the sending of one hundred and fifty boys, but the fund laid aside for the purpose was found to be insufficient to cover the cost of the full number.

tion capable and active in the studies set before them, and as their hold upon the language increased, began to outrank all but the brightest of their American classmates. As they advanced into the higher scientific schools or colleges, greater liberty was allowed them, each boy pursuing his inclination as to a special course or institution. With the appointment of Yung Wing to the Chinese legation at Washington and the arrival of one Wu Tsz'-tăng (who knew no English) as commissioner in his place at Hartford, the complexion of this enterprise seems to have changed. In the spring of 1881 a formal memorial, endorsed by Chin Lan-pin, the minister at Washington, was addressed to the home government, complaining of the course of study pursued by these youths as including Latin and Greek and other unnecessary subjects; of the disrespectful behavior of the boys when brought before their chiefs; of their deplorable lack of patriotism; of their forgetting their mother tongue, and other sins of omission and commission. The memorial seems to have fallen in with the desires of those momentarily in power at Peking; the commission and students were all recalled by the return mail, and arrived at Shanghai in the fall of the same year.

Although this action may have been in some degree prompted by a spirit of conservatism and distrust, the leading motive of the Chinese government cannot be far to seek. Had these boys of a dozen years each received his fifteen years' instruction in our common-school, classical, and professional courses, it is impossible to believe that they would not at the end of this time have been more American than Chinese. Their speedy recall was a matter of regret to the many friends these interesting lads had made in New England, but from a truly Chinese stand-point this foreign popularity would become as the flesh-pots of Egypt to them after their return to the arid intellectual life in China—and the event in one or two instances appears to have proved the shrewdness of this surmise. However, this experiment can in no wise be considered a failure, even if we consider only the knowledge of English and elements of a western education obtained by each student; how considerable has been its success will be seen when the young men—now engaged by their government in telegraph posts, arsenals, schools, etc.—shall have achieved sufficient distinction in their various professions to prove their fitness for the pains bestowed upon them. The organization of schools for other than Chinese methods of education is already begun in China—as, for example, the Tung-wăn Kwan, under charge of Dr. Martin, at Peking—and from these a much more rational advance to their proper position in scientific knowledge may be expected, than by hazardous schemes of foreign tuition.

The pages of this brief compendium of our present knowledge of the Chinese Empire were not written in the first place, nor have they been revised, with any intent to laud that people beyond their just deserts. What there is of weakness, vice, narrowness, bigotry, in the national character has been pointed out with great frankness, while their blindness and folly after the lessons of two warlike visitations from foreign nations have not passed unnoticed. The experiences of the last three decades will probably prove more momentous for the Chinese than those of any previous century in their history, and these have not come about without much bitterness and the surly traces of misunderstanding and misrepresentation. But the great fact must have become apparent, even to the cursory reader, that in the Chinese character are elements which in due time must lift her out of the terribly backward position into which she had fallen and raise her to a rank among the foremost of nations. There is a basis of encouragement when we keep in mind the literary institutions of the country and their early attention to obtaining a corps of scientific men of their own nationality, as in the effort just mentioned.[1]

[1] The reserved force in the Chinese character was very strikingly brought out in a new-year's call at Peking, which the writer remembers, in 1870. The topic came up as to how to diminish the expense of getting coal from the mines to the city (which up to that time was carried on camels and mules), so as to put it within the reach of the poor people. I suggested a tram road as the best plan for the fifty miles distance from the mines, and involving trifling expense. After listening to the plan, Tan Ting-siang, one of the members of the Board of Revenue, and Prince Kung, together exclaimed, "*Tieh-lu lai liao! Tieh-lu lai liao!*" ('Railroads are coming in time'). The ex-

Another ground of hope—and these words are as pertinent to-day as when written thirty-five years ago—lies in the matter-of-fact habits of the Chinese, their want of enthusiasm and dislike of change, which are rather favorable than otherwise to their development as a great community. The presentation and reception of the highest truths and motives the human mind can realize always excites thought and action ; the chiefest fear must be that of going too fast in schemes of reform and correction, and demolishing the fabric before its elements are ready for reconstruction. The non-existence of caste, the weakness of a priesthood which cannot nerve its persecuting arm with the power of the State, the scanty influence religion has over the popular mind, the simplicity of ancestral worship, the absence of the allurements of gorgeous temples, splendid ritual, seductive music, gay processions, and above all, sanctified licentiousness, to uphold and render it enticing to depraved human nature, the popular origin of all government holidays, and lastly, the degree of industry, loyalty, and respect for life and property—these are characteristics which furnish some grounds for trusting that the regeneration of China will be accomplished, like the operation of leaven in meal, without shivering the vessel.

---

istence of the treaty principle of ex-territoriality and its consequences is constantly before the Chinese high officers, though they appreciate as well the fact that their country is preparing and will be the better for such improvements.

INDEX.